SPINNING AROUND: A HISTORY OF THE SOUL LP

VOLUME 1 : A - K

John Lias

First published in Great Britain by John Lias, 2 The Green, Blackboys, East Sussex TN22 5LP

Copyright John Lias © 2016

ISBN : 978-1-5262-0072-3

Printed in the E.U.

The author hereby asserts his moral rights to be identified as the author of this work.

All rights reserved. No part of this book may be reproduced or transmitted in any form or by any means, electronic or mechanical, including photocopying, recording or any information storage and retrieval system, without permission in writing from the publisher.

This book is sold subject to the condition that it shall not, by way of trade or otherwise, be lent, resold, hired out or otherwise circulated without the publisher's prior consent in any form of binding or cover other than that in which it is published and without a similar condition being imposed on the subsequent purchaser.

This book is dedicated to the three ladies in my life - Debbie, Katie and Sarah - my father, Anthony Lias, and all the wonderful soul singers, producers, arrangers, writers and musicians who created this music.

> "I hold my peace, sir? no;
> No, I will speak as liberal as the north;
> Let heaven and men and devils, let them all,
> All, all, cry shame against me, yet I'll speak."
>
> - William Shakespeare, *Othello*

Acknowledgements and Thanks

I set out on the task of writing this book just over three years ago, in November 2012, with a plan of doing absolutely everything myself. It didn't take me long to realise that this was a false conceit, although certain things – including any factual errors, omissions or lapses of judgement – remain mine alone. So I would like to say thank you to a number of people who have helped me in different ways. Firstly for their time and encouragement I wish to note Graham Betts, Adrian Corbin, Rob Cox and Bob Smith.

But five people in particular have gone way beyond the call of duty and without their assistance, the finished result would probably have been a sorry thing: my wife Debbie for the photographs and technical assistance; David Cole, editor of the excellent *In The Basement* magazine, who showed me how to get up and running; John Ridley for the loan of records and his unparalleled taste; Shaun Tobin for solving my storage and distribution challenges and last but not least Greg Burgess for his astounding detective work in seeking out information about even the most obscure of singers. If anyone ever needs to track something or someone down, Greg's your man.

PREFACE

For years I have wanted to read a book like this. It recently struck me that I therefore needed to write it. To the best of my knowledge no-one else has addressed the topic of soul LPs in quite the same way as I am doing here. The closest anyone has got was firstly when *The Blackwell Guide To Soul Recordings* was issued in 1993 and second ten years later when the *All Music Guide To Soul* appeared. Both books took soul albums as their subject matter, but neither had the scope of what I originally wanted to attempt here: to try and document virtually every soul LP ever issued by American soul artists. *The Blackwell Guide* took a geographical approach, highlighting what it felt were the most important or representative albums issued out of, for example, Chicago or Detroit, whereas the *All Music Guide* was closer in style to my book, but missed out hundreds of acts, as well as taking a more random approach to records released by the artists it did feature. Also, and crucially, neither book baulked at including reviews of CDs or recordings by non - American performers. In both cases, I do.

Because I wanted this book to have a reasonably logical, if somewhat narrow, frame of reference, I am only writing about records released as 33⅓ rpm vinyl, and also am restricting myself to discussing American soul artists - even if the records were issued on non-American labels. The reasons for this are simple: a) I don't want the book to sprawl out of control and b) I don't know enough about, say, British, Dutch or Canadian soul singers to feel anywhere near confident enough about not missing out a number of talented artists. So apologies to anyone hoping to read about the excellent Hot House or George Banton in this tome because you won't find them. Someone else will need to write that book.

But, as Ben E. King asked, what IS soul ? Who is in and who is out on musical approach alone? It is the key question I have struggled with over the last three years or so and one that caused me to change my mind a number of times.

A friend suggested that I should simply cover all the acts who posted LPs onto the U.S. soul charts. But when one considers that this includes The Beatles, Shirley Bassey and The Rolling Stones there immediately becomes a need for some culling. And if we rule all these out on the grounds they aren't American we are still faced with Herb Alpert, Blood, Sweat and Tears, Nat 'King' Cole, Johnny Mathis, The Osmonds, Bruce Willis and The Steve Miller Band. So, I'm sure we can see and agree, choices HAVE to be made.

One may say, "well it's obvious those aren't soul artists, exclude them." Indeed it is, but what about Rick James? Nancy Wilson? The Supremes? Brook Benton? The Crusaders? I guarantee that if you asked a hundred people about the soul credentials of those five acts you would not find unanimity. And, as another example, someone even expressed surprise that I have included James Brown (he believes him to be a 'funk' artist rather than a 'soul' one). This was finally the point at which I realised consensus would be out of the question.

So my rules of the game are as follows:

- The *majority* of the artists' work has to have been in a recognised soul style. Thus Esther Phillips is in (even though she recorded in a bluesy manner before her sixties breakthrough) whereas George Benson, Donald Byrd and Dobie Gray are not (more 'jazz' than 'soul' in the case of the first two and more 'country' as regards Gray.)

- There has to be a couple of 'cut-off points' otherwise I would still be writing this in 2022 (and I still have another whole volume to go) and the book would be too big. As will become apparent, I think the eighties was a turning point for soul. Songs and singers became less important, and computerised backing began to replace more traditional instrumentation. From a purely personal point of view this meant that there were now scores of artists who released records under the banner of 'soul music' which I did not enjoy one little bit. Writing about them would be a) no fun for me and b) disrespectful to the artists. I therefore have posited two rules:

    1. If an act or singer did NOT release at least one record before the end of 1982 they will be deemed to be out of scope. I chose this date as 1983 was the year in which the CD became commercially available.

    2. If an act or artist went out 'solo' after having been part of a group who cut records earlier, then he or she had to have been recording with the group before December 31st 1976.

    I realise, of course, that these are entirely arbitrary and subjective rules which some may find disappointing or even ludicrous. But they have been done for a reason, as I said above. I do not wish to write about Freddie Jackson, James Ingram, Whitney Houston, Guy or New Edition. This isn't because I do not believe they are talented artists; it's just that their music does not, and never did, speak to me. (The downside to this approach is that I will be excluding a few artists who I certainly did and do enjoy such as Billy 'Soul' Bonds and Janice Edwards.)

- The skin colour of a performer is irrelevant. Singing in a recognised soul style is key. Therefore I have no hesitation whatsoever including Eddie Hinton, Bobby Hatfield, Billy Harner and Dan Penn.

- Disco. If a group or singer recorded purely in the disco mode such as, to name a couple, The Ritchie Family or the Salsoul Orchestra, they will be omitted.

- Gospel and "Boogaloo" are generally out of scope unless an artist had an audience that also favoured soul. Thus, for example, Rance Allen and Joe Bataan will be featured.

- I have included a number of promotional only copies and other LPs that would have been next to impossible to buy, but I have not featured anything I know to be a 'bootleg'.

- Records by High School ensembles such as The Kashmere Stage Band. I just don't know enough about this sub-genre and don't wish to embarrass myself.

- Compilation albums by various artists. Simply because there are lots and lots of them and by excluding them I also stop the book from becoming too big. This also includes retrospective LPs which only feature a couple of acts such as with a number of Japanese compilations (Warren Lee & Willie West, Bobby Boseman & Joe Medwick etc. etc.) However, just to confuse matters, I HAVE included albums such as the one shared by Steve Mancha and J.J. Barnes as it came out at a time - 1969 - when it was more or less a new release for those artists.

- The LP was pretty much dead by 1994. CDs had completely taken over. Other the last few years there has been somewhat of a vinyl revival but I have also ruled out covering any records that have appeared for the first time as a long player in the last few years as, while many are excellent, they are clearly not part of the original vinyl era of the previous decades which underpins the book. Thus no Sharon Jones & Dap-Kings, Coalitions or Emperors.

- And finally there is the pure subjectivity of determining inclusion and everyone (as I said above re Rick James and co.) will have different thoughts here. So to give some examples, there will be no Chic, Chiffons, Roy Hamilton. Len Barry or Prince. You may think they - or at least some of them - should have been in and I understand that, but some-one has to have final editorial say.....

There are also a number of things that this book resolutely is not designed to be. Namely:

- A price guide. My motivation is entirely what a record sounds like, as opposed to what it costs. To me, there are few more depressing questions than "how much is it worth?" As will become apparent, I tend to believe that the best records are often the most successful, and the ones that didn't sell - thus becoming rare and valuable - are all too often devoid of any artistic merit and their failure was thus entirely understandable. There will be many exceptions to these rules, and I will highlight a record's rarity if it helps people to understand how difficult it may be to track down, but the price of a record has led to many wrong-headed opinions as to how good it sounds and anyone wishing to use the book as a buying or selling guide has probably come to the wrong place.

- A discography. I will not be listing all the tracks of an LP, the musicians who played on it, or all of the labels on which the album came out. If an LP came out on five separate occasions - as some of these did - I will only list the original issue. There are many excellent discographies out there, which are of great interest and merit, but they won't tell you what the records actually sound like, or provide much context or many clues as to their origin. I am more concerned in hopefully being able to convince readers why they may want to invest time in listening to Paul Kelly's *Don't Burn Me* and *Norman Feels* or to save people the trouble of trying to track down things that might sound intriguing, but which are actually pretty dreadful.

- A place to find out all about your favourite artists. I am not planning to provide more than cursory details of any singer or group as this information is generally available fairly easily in a number of books or websites if you want or need it.

A last word on the approach I have taken. I have tried to be absolutely vigilant in listing ALL albums recorded as albums, so to speak, by the artists in the book. Where I have allowed myself some slack is around retrospective or "after the event" compilations. By which I mean, and take James Brown as an obvious example: I have listed his "Greatest Hits" or 'Best Ofs' IF they landed on the *Billboard* charts as they were then a legitimate part of the tale as regards sales patterns. What I have NOT done is listed every Brown compilation that exists on LP, as there are dozens of them. I wanted (and started) to include *everything* when I was first drafting the book, but this had ever diminishing returns as so many of the records were more or less exactly the same and as it was therefore clearly going to substantially add to the pages, weight (and thus cost) it struck me as of little benefit. Many other well-known artists fall into the same category. Where I HAVE tried to include all known compilations is when the act in question is much less-well known and/or represented on vinyl in the first place as I feel in these instances all publicity is worthwhile. (It will also become clear in my introduction why I am more cavalier about and less interested in "Greatest Hits" collections.)

Therefore, my initial plan of documenting virtually every soul album ever released has had to be abandoned given all my exceptions noted above. I have, though, tried hard to make sure that I haven't missed anything that in my own mind should be here. However, I'm well aware that I AM going to miss records that I would have wanted to include. No-one knows every soul LP that ever existed, and even after forty plus years of buying them I still came across quite a few in the course of writing this book that I had never heard of before. So, despite my striving, if someone wants to spend time trying to catch me out, then, doubtless, they will succeed.

I seem to have spent a fair bit of time in telling readers what the book is not and who is missing. But let me reassure anyone who still wishes to buy it that I will still be covering thousands of albums in this volume and the next; despite all of my disclaimers, the number of recognisably 'soul' LPs that have been released is still dauntingly large.

INTRODUCTION

I have been listening to, buying and collecting soul LPs for about forty five years. Unlike virtually all veteran soul fans, I do not own any singles. It is hard to remember, after four decades, exactly why I favoured the long playing version over the short one, but suffice it to say I always did. Clearly, LPs have a number of undeniable advantages over 45s: they tend to have pictures of the performers, are more informative, involve less hassle in having to keep changing them on a record player and, by and large are better value for money if you apply a simple ratio of cost to song. I also wonder if there wasn't a subconscious text at play as well: it was more likely (however remote in reality) that I COULD one day own every soul LP ever made, whereas a similar ambition for singles was absolutely out of the question. Another significant factor would have been a desire to hear as many cuts by my favourite artists as possible and while there are plenty of examples of songs on 45 by those artists not making it onto an LP, there are demonstrably many more cases of songs on albums not making it onto singles. Obviously I could, and once briefly did, buy both, but given that collecting soul records is now an expensive proposition and I wanted to do other things with my money apart from spending it all on vinyl, singles (and generally they tend to be more expensive, anyway) have had to go.

So if we accept that I find LPs to be the most satisfying means of expression in recorded soul music, why have I felt compelled to write this book ? One reason, as stated in my first paragraph of the preface was that I've got fed up with waiting for someone else to do it, but, primarily it is because I feel soul LPs have been unjustly neglected over the years, and have suffered in critical comparison with rock LPs, a state of affairs that owes much to ignorance, laziness and prejudice.

I first felt the sting of injustice back in 1974 when the *New Musical Express* published a list of "The Top 100 Albums of All Time". There were precisely seven soul records included: Stevie Wonder *"Talking Book "* and *"Music Of My Mind"* (Numbers 45 and 94 respectively) Smokey Robinson and Miracles *"Anthology"* (Number 46), Otis Redding *"Otis Blue"* (Number 49) Impressions *"Big 16"* (Number 51) Aretha Franklin *"Greatest Hits"* (Number 65) and Sly Family Stone *"There's A Riot Going On"* (Number 79). The irritation was compounded by the fact that three of these seven are compilations of the singer/groups' work, not LPs in their own right, a trait that has been perpetuated ever since. You will never find *"The Beatles Greatest Hits"* or *"The Best of Bob Dylan"* on such lists, as these are artists, you know, seemingly (and preposterously) much more capable than soul singers of creating LP masterpieces. I wrote *NME* an "outraged of Tunbridge Wells" type letter, which they did at least print, but my quixotic treatise did nothing in the short term to arrest the snobbish bias against soul. One must be fair though, and soul has become much more hip and respected over the years (helped by books like Peter Guralnick's *Sweet Soul Music*) and when *NME* re-did the exercise in 1985 Marvin Gaye's *"What's Going On"* was at number 1! It was also nice to see both Jackie Wilson and Al Green included that time around, and the number of soul LPs had swelled slightly to 16, but the majority were still *"Greatest Hits"* packages.

It is easy to dismiss such lists, but I feel the critical "establishment", such as it is, has always been dominated by white middle-class men (as am I, by the way, in case anyone is thinking of accusing me of harbouring a chip on my shoulder), who have all too often had a pre-disposition towards rock and pop rather than to soul, and history will always be shaped by those wielding the pens. I therefore want to produce a book that will go some small way to redress the prevailing wisdom that soul albums are somehow not worthy of the same level of attention that has been lavished on rock LPs for decades.

Having said the above, one should not assume that *Spinning Around* will adopt a hagiographic approach as it does not. I am perfectly willing to accept - and to state - that there have been hundreds of LPs by soul artists which are, by pretty much any standard, shoddy, ill - judged or just plain dull.

The earliest LP listed in this book dates from 1958, and it wasn't until the latter part of the sixties that record companies saw the profit opportunities in soul albums, and started to market them more diligently. Until that time, they were often somewhat hastily put together, with a hit record or two surrounded by inept cover versions or other generally accepted "filler". If great records appeared - and many did - it was because they were delivered by artists with almost invariable high standards or they were entirely serendipitous. By the time we reached the seventies the rules had changed and we saw a host of soul "concept" albums (and gatefold sleeves) starting to emerge - hitherto almost exclusively the province of pop or rock artists. Companies were no longer content - as evidenced by the Stax/Volt approach to LPs in the sixties with a series of rather amateurish (yet somehow charming) covers (drawn by Ronnie Stoots) - to focus on singles rather than on albums and the world started to see soul LPs going gold and platinum. Marvin Gaye posted no LPs in the pop Hot 30 in the sixties - between 1971 and 1976 he had six such successes. Similarly, by 1970 Isaac Hayes was selling LPs in numbers that Otis Redding could only dream about when he was alive.

To illustrate further: The July 31st 1965 edition of *Billboard* featured only two soul albums in the *Billboard* Top 50 (The Miracles *"Greatest Hits From The Beginning"* and The Supremes *"Where Did Our Love Go"*). Move forward nearly a year, to July 9th 1966, and there were still only three LPs in that Top 50 chart (*"Lou Rawls Live"*, Ray Charles *"Crying Time"* and The Supremes *"I Hear A Symphony"*). By November 21st 1970, however, the number had increased to nine (including James Brown's *"Sex Machine"* and Aretha's *"Spirit In The Dark"*) and in August 5th 1972 it had further risen to eleven with the Chi-Lites, Donny Hathaway and Stevie Wonder all represented. (That August issue of *Billboard* also featured a full page advert for the new ZZ Hill LP, *"The Best Thing That's Happened To Me"*; it was almost unthinkable that a record company would have taken out a full page *Billboard* advert for one of Hill's LPs in the sixties.) Or, to return to Stax/Volt: they released more than twice the amount of albums in the seventies (and in a shorter time period given they went bust in 1975) than they did in the sixties.

There is also the question of who got to record LPs in the first place. Many artists, despite long careers, were never recorded at 33⅓ rpm, whereas others only received recognition at this speed retrospectively. The causes are manifold: lack of record company commitment, lack of funds, labels going bust at the worst possible moment, simply being with the wrong company at the wrong time, or the inability to contest the rigid rules of mortality before recording sessions were completed. For some or all of these reasons the following artists will not feature in this book: Donald Height, Shirley Wahls, Bobby Harris, Jeanne & The Darlings, Mabel John, The Soul Brothers Six, Grover Mitchell, Billy Young, Obrey Wilson, Margie Hendrix, Danny White, Eddie & Ernie and Jimmy Robins despite the fact that they all released lots of singles and all recorded for big and important labels. (Contrast this, for example, with artists lucky enough to be contracted to Sylvia and Joe Robinson's All Platinum/Stang/Turbo labels where it was almost mandatory to cut an album, regardless of your obscurity or extreme unlikelihood of actually selling any records.)

Other singers and groups, and included among them would be Bill Coday, The Knight Brothers and Harold Burrage, were not afforded the opportunity to record LPs when they had extant careers but were well served by companies specialising in reissues when an audience for such releases became apparent at the end of the seventies and early eighties.

A few labels, such as Carnival, Hep Me or Duke, always played somewhat half-heartedly in the world of LPs, each cutting a handful, but preferred to expend their energies on singles, doubtless because they thought they would provide a better return or because they couldn't muster up the funding for the greater effort of cutting an album.

In addition to the above, there were many other reasons why LPs were recorded and which would vary from label to label: tax write offs, strict contractual commitments, cashing in when a previously signed artist has made it big elsewhere and even, in the case of a handful of record owners, uxoriousness.

Soul LPs changed noticeably over time in the way in which they were presented and packaged. Take, entirely at random, early LPs such as Carla Thomas' *"Gee Whiz"* (from 1961) and Marvin Gaye's *That Stubborn Kinda Fella"* (from 1962) and contrast these with relatively unknown sets such as Solar Heats' self-titled album from 1979 or Tommy Smiley's *"We've Got Love"* from two years earlier. The Thomas and Gaye LPs are almost completely bereft of hard information - apart from who produced, engineered and (in the case of the Thomas LP) photographed the album cover. There are no details of recording musicians, back-up singers or even the year of release of the LPs themselves. Now look at the two later LPs, and let's note, recorded by artists significantly less well-known than Thomas or Gaye: we are given details of all musicians, recording locations, second engineers, arrangers and even who modelled alongside Smiley on the cover of the LP. Now all of this is a good thing and as it should be but it took a long time for such data to become commonplace.

One aspect of information, however, was to remain bafflingly inconsistent for almost the entire period in which vinyl soul albums existed: the strange reluctance of record labels to tell us the names of the singers in vocal group LPs. We may be told who made the tea, who drove the bus and which legal firm was representing the company but one would often search in vain for who actually undertook the singing on the record. Now, I am well aware that there are many instances when it is alleged that NONE of the group other than the lead singer carried out any of the vocals contained within, but I still feel it was an undeniable dereliction of duty to omit the names of the group members and I have done everything I can to track them down and display them in the book.

In terms of how to read the main body of the book I have kept it very simple. Firstly, I will list the name of the singer or group who cut the records. If it is the latter, I will provide the names of the members on the LP - but NOT everyone who was ever in the group. Next, I will furnish the title of the LP followed by the year of release, catalogue number, the record producer(s) and lastly, the highest position the record attained in the *Billboard* pop and soul charts (assuming it reached either or both). If I am unsure about any of these pieces of information I will make it clear by means of a ?. Any time I state that a record did reach a chart it can be assumed that I am referring to the *Billboard* version unless I make it clear it was *Cashbox*.

As for those charts themselves, please note that *Billboard* did not start to provide a separate listing for 'Soul' albums until January 30th 1965. It was referred to as, and remained so for years afterwards (1969 in fact), the *"R&B"*, rather than *"Soul"* chart. In itself, this change can be seen as one of the earlier attempts to recognise soul albums as taking on additional importance.

Before March 12th 1966 the chart was restricted to only 10 albums, and on that date increased to 20, being further enhanced to 30 on April 15th 1967 and 50 on April 6th 1968. It moved via 60 and then 75 arriving at the final tally of 100 on September 3rd 1988. It is important to bear this in mind because it indicates that a record could be a big seller in 1965, but unless it was one of the ten biggest, it could be erroneously retrospectively construed as a sales failure.

I also make reference to a couple of other things in the body of the book worth explaining. Firstly, I sometimes talk about The Hot 100. This is the official name of the *Billboard* pop - as opposed to soul - chart. Secondly, I use the term 'popular music' now and again. Although I think soul at its best is a distinctive and separate musical genre, it still has to be considered as a 20th century invention, one that comes under the same umbrella as pop, rock, jazz and blues, as opposed to classical.

The vast majority of these records were first released to sell as many copies as possible or to support a tour. (There are exceptions: Marvin Gaye's *Here My Dear*, for example, or the tax write-off labels.) No-one was thinking about 'art' or longevity and I think the case for soul music - any popular music, in fact - as 'art' is rather flimsy. If soul ever could be described in such exalted terms it would probably be in the "deep soul" category, as these tend to be recordings where pain and regret are on naked display, and this can lead to the exposure of universal human truths; but it doesn't happen very often.

The fact that so many of these records sound so good so many years later is a happy accident, really, but one we can be deeply thankful for.

Aalon

Aalon Butler; Ron Hammond; Luther Rabb; Louis Cabaza

Cream City 1977 Arista AB 4127 Producer: Jerry Goldstein (Billboard soul charts: 45)

The few people who have heard Aalon Butler's "Please Give Me A Chance" single on the PKC label would find no stylistic link at all between that record and his one and only LP. 'Cream City' is the nickname of Milwaukee, and one would search in vain to find another soul record to pay homage to that rather forbidding place (the 23rd most dangerous city in America according to a 2015 survey.) It's an album of reasonably meagre delights but at least the good cuts, of which there are four, outweigh the three awful ones. The title track, which I like a lot, made it one place higher on the soul singles charts than the LP, but neither had any pop success. The other best known song on here is "Rock 'N' Roll Gangster" whose sweet charms have been appreciated on the California "Lowrider" scene, while "Summer Love" and "Magic Night" have the dreamy associations at which their titles hint. The rest of the songs are rather ham-fisted attempts at rock which leave me completely cold. I must also commend the acknowledgments on the inner sleeve which has to be one of the longest ever such lists. We will probably never know exactly how Gino Washington, Jimmy Witherspoon, JB Bingham and Ike White contributed to *Cream City* but it seems they certainly did.

Buddy Ace

Root Doctor 1990 Evejim EJ2018 Producer: Leon Haywood

Buddy Ace (real name James Land) had been releasing fine records - mainly on Duke - for over thirty years before his one and only 33⅓ was issued, thanks for which need to go to Leon Haywood whose Evejim label put out a number of excellent releases at the turn of the nineties. Because this record was recorded years after Buddy's peak - such as it was, he only ever placed two singles on the soul charts, and those back in 1966 and 1967 - it cannot really be classed as the best representation of his music and is, understandably, slicker than his sixties work (which was often downright fierce) but it should still comfortably appeal to a long standing Buddy Ace fan. A blues flavour is apparent on a number of tracks, and we also find highly appealing versions of soul staples such as "The Choking Kind" and "Pouring Water On A Drowning Man" as well as a rather obscure Isley Brothers song, "She Ain't Givin' Up No Love" (which also pointed up how seldom their material was covered.) The horns are terrific, arranged by Haywood and John Stephens, and really bring things to life although plaudits should be given to all of the sadly uncredited band.

Buddy Ace recorded a couple of decent CDs before passing away in 1994 while performing on stage, surely not a bad way for a singer to go.

Ace Spectrum

Elliot Isaac; Aubrey Johnson; Rudy Gay; Ed Zant; Lawrence Coley; Frederick Duff.

Inner Spectrum 1974 Atlantic SD 7299 Producers: Tony Silvester & Ed Zant (Billboard soul charts: 28 ; Billboard pop charts: 209)

Low Rent Rendezvous 1975 Atlantic SD 18143 Producers: Tony Silvester & Ed Zant (Billboard soul charts: 35 ; Billboard pop charts: 138)

Just Like In The Movies 1976 Atlantic SD 18185 Producers: Tony Silvester & Ed Zant

It is difficult to pin down Ace Spectrum and say that they had a distinctive sound: there were too many different singers, songwriters (28 across the three records) and arrangers involved, even if the producers and recording studio remained constant over the LPs. What I would say is that the music did incrementally change, however, and that was almost certainly due to the influence of Patrick Adams, and his penchant for more "disco–oriented music". Whereas the tempo on *Inner Spectrum* (no Adams involvement) was pretty relaxed, it accelerated on *Low Rent Rendezvous* (four Adams arranged cuts) increasing to a more or less out and out gallop on *Just Like In The Movies*, all of which he arranged. But, and it is a big but, he was also responsible for the stand-out tracks, both slow and gorgeous, on the last two records: "Trust Me" (from *Rendezvous*) and the title track from the third set, a glorious neo-Philly sound that has strong echoes of Blue Magic (Bloodstone and Caress also recorded this.)

The debut set contained their one and only hit, "Don't Send Nobody Else", an excellent Nick Ashford and Valerie Simpson song recorded by others, but it was Ace Spectrum who deservedly made it a hit: #20 on the soul charts (and #57 pop) in the second half of 1974. I should also highlight the excellent arrangements by Bert De Coteaux which were seldom uninteresting, and the fact that the group covered two songs from The Isley Brothers' *3+3* LP, "Don't Let Me Be Lonely Tonight" and "If You Were There", both splendid, as was "I Don't Want To Play Around" a marvellous slice of "sweet soul". In fact, no ifs or buts, *Ace Spectrum* is a most accomplished album.

Low Rent Rendezvous was a second exceedingly strong outing but two singles, the aforementioned "Trust Me" and "Keep Holding on", one slow, one fast, surprisingly failed to do any business as they both sounded as if they had everything it took to capture large sales. De Coteaux also arranged a number of cuts on the LP including the full on classical intro to the wonderful "Without You" and a fine reading of "Laughter In The Rain" and it's a shame he wasn't involved in *Just Like In The Movies.*

This third set was not quite so compelling as the previous two and I put this down to the exclusion of De Coteaux and the inclusion of weaker material like "Sooner Or Later" and, particularly, "Sweet Sugar Daddy". "Live And Learn" is a spirited and memorable dance side, issued as a 45, but once again, failed to sell in quantity. Despite the reservations expressed here, it's still one worth owning.

What about the group themselves? Zant and Isaac were the only two to feature on all three records with Coley and Duff on board for *Movies* only. (These last two gentlemen were to re-appear with Tony Silvester and his "New Ingredient" ensemble in 1976 on the *Magic Touch* LP (a song which also appears on *Movies*.) I believe Zant took most vocals on the debut record but things appeared to be more liberally spread on the second and third LPs and it is difficult to say who was singing what, exactly.

After *Just Like In The Movies* they recorded nothing else in their own right but were heard to good effect as backing singers on four tracks from Bruce Fisher's *Red Hot* LP in 1977. Ace Spectrum will remain as somewhat of a footnote in the overall history of soul, but they had talent and good musical support and deserved to be given their opportunity to cut a handful of records.

Johnny Acey

My Home 1968 Turbo TU-7010 Producer: Joe Richardson

This is an absurdly rare record with maybe only literally a handful of copies existing anywhere in the world and so it certainly didn't do Acey (John Acey Goodelock from South Carolina) any good. He had recorded a number of singles, always in New York, in the late fifties and early sixties (including a tough and impeccable version of "Don't Deceive Me") which never charted so it was surprising to see that he had an LP issued at all but the Sylvia and Joe Robinson All Platinum/Turbo/Stang empire was almost certainly the right place for him to be as they would release LPs like most other companies would release singles. Most of the album consists of outdated blues but two tracks do classify as soul: "You", which is worth hearing, and "Nobody's Woman But My Own", which is not. He passed away in 2009.

Barbara Acklin

Love Makes A Woman 1968 Brunswick BL 754137 Producers: Carl Davis & Eugene Record (Billboard soul charts: 4 ; Billboard pop charts: 146)

Seven Days Of Night 1969 Brunswick BL 754148 Producers: Carl Davis & Eugene Record

Someone Else's Arms 1970 Brunswick BL 754156 Producers: Carl Davis & Eugene Record

I Did It 1970 Brunswick BL 754166 Producer: Eugene Record

I Call It Trouble 1972 Brunswick BL 754187 Producer: Eugene Record

Groovy Ideas 1987 Kent 072 (UK)

Like Martha Reeves and many others, Chicago's Barbara Acklin toiled as a secretary in a record company before it became apparent that she had the talent to do more. Much more, in fact, and she released one of my favourite three or four sides of all time, "Am I The Same Girl", so it can be assumed that I would be very partial to her work, and I am, but one does have to say that 33⅓ rpm wasn't really her best speed. Most of her finest recordings came out as singles and there are only a few "LP only" tracks that really bear repeated listening. Her songwriting - possibly her real strength - was always showcased on her LPs but it seems to me to be interesting that throughout her career her best records were written by others (most notably the prolific Eugene Record), and her finest songs (such as "Have You Seen Her", "Stoned Out Of My Mind" and "Whispers (Gettin' Louder)") went to the likes of Jackie Wilson and the Chi-Lites (who usually provided delightful harmonies on her albums), rather than be cut by herself.

As regards her own releases she put out an early single on the Special Agent label and a couple on Brunswick that didn't do much before she teamed up with Gene Chandler on "Show Me The Way To Go" to score her first ever soul chart entry (#30 in the spring of 1968) but it doesn't feature on any of her LPs.

Love Makes A Woman - easily her best seller - had sleevenotes that made clear her admiration for Dionne Warwick and it was thus no surprise that the opening two tracks had been cut by the Scepter recording star. "To Sir With Love" was also covered, but the remaining eight tracks were all songs from Chicago writers, including three Acklin-Record collaborations. The title track was an absolute delight and a huge hit, #3 soul and #15 pop, the only time a single of hers reached such dizzy heights. It overshadowed the rest of the set, but "Come And See Me Baby" and "Be By My Side" were nice enough.

Seven Days Of Night was where the utterly magnificent "Am I The Same Girl" is to be found but it only managed to attain #33 on the soul charts for the simple reason that Young-Holt Unlimited's "Soulful Strut", which employed the same backing track, had become a massive hit three months earlier. This always rankled with Acklin but she could take some comfort in the fact that the superb "Just Ain't No Love" had reached #23 on the soul charts in early 1969. These two singles were by some distance the finest sides on a disappointing album, which included three further run of the mill Bacharach-David covers.

Someone Else's Arms certainly had its moments including the delicious title track which somehow failed as a 45, her driving and dark version of "You've Been In Love Too Long" (her best ever "LP only" track) and excellent takes on "What's It Gonna Be" and "More Today Than Yesterday" but there were also a couple of grim covers. "After You" made it to #30 on the soul charts but possibly didn't deserve to as it was just *too* similar to "Love Makes A Woman". A significant plus point was the backing vocals of The Chi-lites throughout which were life-affirmingly brilliant.

Acklin had the misfortune to record for Brunswick, a label notorious for recycling tracks across different releases. This practice reached its nadir on the *I Did It* LP on which only four tracks out of ten were exclusive to that record. One was the title track which became her seventh charting single at #28 at the end of 1970.

Barbara closed out her Brunswick career with *I Call It Trouble,* which again suffered from the Brunswick laziness: four of the ten tracks can be found on the earlier sets. The highly catchy "Lady, Lady, Lady" and the title song both charted as singles; "I'll Bake Me A Man", on the other hand, did not and although it is undoubtedly a saccharine performance I have always loved it.

The *Groovy Ideas* LP is a superb, typically generous 16 track UK only compilation of many of her best loved Brunswick sides.

A Place In The Sun 1975 Capitol ST11377 Producer: Willie Henderson

Acklin's only non-Brunswick LP came out in 1975 on the back of her biggest single for years, "Raindrops" (#14 soul), which, while certainly enjoyable, bore more than a passing resemblance to many of her earlier sides. Unfortunately, the cover failed to list it, although it is featured as the last track on side 2. This error must have cost some sales. Next best track was Sam Dees' "How Can You Lose The Love You Never Had", good if aping the Hi sound a little, but would have been even better suited to a tougher singer. Overall, the format was much the same as before, all Chicago recorded, but the sound was more lush and a little over produced. This didn't stop "Special Loving" and "Give Me Some Of Your Sweet Love" from both charting - albeit in minor fashion, and neither were vintage Acklin - as singles, her last to do so as she more or less quit the industry at this point, re-surfacing in 1978 to perform backing vocals on an obscure single by one Joe Martin, and again in 1990 or so with a single of her own in "You're The One".

Barbara Acklin died of pneumonia, aged only 55, in 1998 but should be remembered as one of the best of all Chicago soul artists. Her light soprano voice was not well suited to the more fervent approach of many soul singers and she probably expressed joy better than sorrow but it would be wrong to think that her emotional range was narrow as poignant songs such as "Have You Seen Her" and "I'm Living With A Memory" would attest.

Act 1 (see also Special Delivery)

George Parker; Chet Fortune; Leroy Reed; Debbi Hill; Bobby Harris; Perry Boyd; Roger Terry; Raeford Gerald (aka Ray Godfrey); Terry Huff; Reginald Ross

Act 1   1974 Spring SPR 6704 Producer: Raeford Gerald

The wholly uninspiring cover to this LP belies both the quality of the music and the complexity of the history of Act 1. It would be virtually impossible to say now who was actively part of the group on their one LP but I think I can say with some confidence that Terry Huff wasn't singing any of the leads and that Raeford Gerald was the biggest contributor to the artistic vision of the group. Philly influenced ballads such as "Friends Or Lovers" (#22 as a single) and "You Didn't Love Me Anyhow" are highly competent and "Party Hardy People" and "Tom The Peeper" are good funk sounds by way of variety, although there are two or three tracks of the utmost mediocrity.

Another single, "It Takes Both Of Us", was a small soul hit (#90) in the summer of 1973 but it was not included on the LP. Parker, Fortune, Huff and Ross all went on to form Special Delivery while Gerald moved on to work with the likes of The Determinations.

Arthur Adams

It's Private Tonight   1973 Blue Thumb BTS 43 Producers: Tommy Lipuma & Arthur Adams

Home Brew 1975 Fantasy F–9479 Producers: Arthur Adams & Wayne Henderson

Midnight Serenade 1977 Fantasy F–9523 Producer: Wayne Henderson

I Love Love Love Love Love Love Love My Lady 1979 A & M SP 4752 Producers: Stewart Levine & Rik Pekkonen

Over the course of a long career Arthur Adams (real name: Arthur Lee Reeves) straddled the line between soul and blues but cut enough soul sides - including the winning 1967 outing "Let's Get Together" by Arthur and Mary - to warrant inclusion in the book. And anyway, on these four albums the blues element is often completely absent. Unfortunately, the soul one is often absent too. These are, by and large and the debut excepted, fairly anonymous jazz-funk outings which is a shame, as he is a talented singer and guitarist and was capable of leaving us with a better vinyl legacy.

The Blue Thumb record (with a gatefold sleeve) is easily the best of his four LPs listed here and features a great title track written by Adams and Jimmy Lewis. It is a re-cut of a single he released in 1969 on Chisa (although the 45 didn't credit Lewis) and is probably the best thing on what is - a couple of instrumentals apart - a commendable release. A laid-back West Coast vibe pervades the record although he waxes indignant on "I've Got To Help My People". It's certainly not an obvious soul release for 1971, however, and has the same rather idiosyncratic approach as the work of Allen Toussaint.

Back in 1969 Adams had cut a couple of songs for Motown, which remained unreleased until the CD age. One of them, "Let Me Love You Tonight", was great and much stronger than anything on his next three albums. If only he had continued to go in that direction.

Homebrew chose to opt for a somewhat half-hearted funk, with a lesser emphasis on songs than we saw on the Blue Thumb release. It's not great: "That's The Way You Move" is lyrically mundane and "Keep On Dancing" and "First Class Lady" are just throwaway instrumentals from a set that lacked a single compelling side, although "We Got An Understanding" is probably the best on show.

I feel even less enthusiastic about *Midnight Serenade* due to the inclusion of an unspeakable side in "Reggae Disco" and the fact that the whole thing is just unremittingly dull.

And I can't be much more positive about the final LP, with its ridiculous title, either, I'm afraid, as guitar solos within long instrumentals are not to my taste at all, and neither are songs entitled "Boogie With Me".

Adams never used anything other than top-class musicians on these recordings but I suspect for many of them, they were not sessions that will be readily recalled. Nothing sold very well and he never had any hits on any national charts although must have come close in 1981 with his popular "You Got The Floor".

In the new century he has continued to record and releases CDs, but almost invariably in a blues style.

Gayle Adams

Gayle Adams 1980 Prelude PRL 12178 Producers: Rodney Brown & Willie Lester

Love Fever 1982 Prelude 14104 Producers: Rodney Brown & Willie Lester (Billboard soul charts: 55)

Gayle Adams came from Washington DC and, if she has any kind of reputation at all, it would be as a disco singer, which is unfair and restricting. Anyone who has possibly avoided Adams in the past (or avoided Prelude releases altogether) because of perceived disco associations really should give her a second chance as these are fine records by a fine singer and we should be pleased she gave up her other potential career of car racing.

Both of these albums are well worth owning, as, while they include a large number of uptempo tracks, she could also deal most capably with slightly more restrained material as well. And the uptempo cuts are generally all fine, anyway, arranged with a great deal of verve and energy. Certainly it is hard to resist something like "Your Love Is A Life Saver" (although the general public could: it failed as a single) from the first set which also includes a fine reading of Ed Townsend's "For The Love Of My Man". It proved beyond doubt for anyone who wants to know if she could sing more demanding material. "Stretch' In Out" was a small hit (#75) in the summer of 1980 but it wasn't the best representation of the LP.

Love Fever contains a highly impressive interpretation of the Four Tops "Baby I Need Your Loving", typically adroitly arranged by Al Johnson, and if nothing else on the album quite matches this standard, although "Don't Jump To Conclusions" a nice ballad comes closest, there is little filler to avoid. The title track went to #24 in early 1982, representing her biggest success on 45.

She continued to record throughout the 80s but without any more success or any more LPs and presumably then left the music industry as I haven't heard anything of her for ages.

Johnny Adams

Heart & Soul 1970 SSS International 5 Producer: Shelby Singleton

Stand By Me 1976 Chelsea CHL-525 Producer: Senator Jones

After All The Good is Gone 1978 Ariola America SW-50036 Producer: Senator Jones

The Many Sides Of Johnny Adams 1980? Hep' Me 158 Producer: Senator Jones

Sweet Country Voice 1981? Hep' Me 160 Producer: Senator Jones

The Tan Nightingale 1984 Charly (UK) CRB 1058

South Side of Soul Street 1986 P-Vine PLP302 (Japan)

Christmas In New Orleans 1987 Maison De Soul LP-1023 Producer: Senator Jones

Greatest Performance 1991 Ace 2043 Producer: Senator Jones

Old Flames 19?? P-Vine PLP732 (Japan)

Laten John Adams from New Orleans was one of the greatest of all soul singers but that fact never earned him much commercial success or even that much acclaim outside of a small hardcore of devoted fans and a few knowledgeable people in the music industry. Which was probably why his style moved increasingly away from soul as time moved on, and his later albums listed below saw him adopting a more blues/jazz/sophisticated approach and I can only hope he made more money as a result. Throughout his long career three things remained pretty constant: the wide range of his beautiful voice; his ability to choose (or have chosen for him) top-class songs; his sunglasses (although I never heard or read that he had eyesight problems.) He was also a noticeably "grown-up" singer; I imagine his teen appeal, even from his first records, was about nil. This was partly due to the fact that he wasn't particularly photogenic but his music unfailingly led me to the conclusion that he put away childish things at a very early age

He had scuffled around New Orleans for a few years making a number of singles - some of which were startlingly good, if not successful, apart from "A Losing Battle" in 1962 which went to #27 on the soul charts - before his first LP, *Heart & Soul,* came out in 1970. This high quality debut contained four of the only six records he ever posted on the *Billboard* soul singles charts, even if one, "I Won't Cry", was a much earlier version and not the "hit" while another, "I Can't Be All Bad", was simply too much of a copy of his only genuinely big success, the great "Reconsider Me", which became his one Top 30 pop entry in the summer of 1969. Not surprisingly therefore, the LP stands as one of the highest points in his career from both an artistic and pecuniary perspective. Listen to the similarly titled "Release Me" (yes, that song) and the aforementioned "Reconsider Me" to hear excellent examples of the diversity of his wonderful voice.

Sadly, Adams was not to record and release another long player for six years. In that time he put out a handful of singles for Atlantic, but they never favoured him with an LP release. That next set, *Stand By Me*, was somewhat disappointing in that, for once, the song choices were not particularly imaginative and he sounded as if he was going through the motions on one or two cuts. Not so, however, on "Don't Let The Green Grass Fool You" where he whoops with his habitual flexibility. A clue that maybe Chelsea's heart was not in the release can be discerned from the cover as they couldn't be bothered to give us a photograph of Johnny. Because Johnny Adams' thrilling voice was always worth hearing, the record cannot be described as bad, but it was heartily overshadowed by *After All the Good Is Gone* in 1978, his masterpiece, and one of the greatest soul LPs ever put out.

There will be few examples in this entire book of vocal performances over the course of an album that can beat Adams on this sort of form. Particularly inspired cover choices too: "After All The Good Is Gone", "Selfish"; and "One Fine Day" are GREAT songs, while his take on "Somewhere" is devastating. Couple all this with excellent musicians which included the New Orleans Symphony and it culminated in his finest hour, as well as being one of the strongest testaments to the fact that New Orleans wasn't quite dead as a recording location by the end of the decade. The magnificent title track managed to struggle to #75 on the soul charts in the middle of 1978, the last time Johnny Adams ever posted on a national chart.

He then disappeared slightly underground to record for Senator Jones' Hep' Me label where a lack of funds became apparent given the rather cheap packaging on these releases (the sleeve notes on *The Many Sides Of* are frankly illiterate) and the fact that the orchestra from the Ariola release had vanished. The music was still fine though and *The Many Sides Of* is a most meritorious record as is *Sweet Country Voice* (the horrible "When I Need You" excepted) although the latter LP will doubtless be too country for many. (It is hard to be precise about the release date of some of his later releases as they weren't offered up on the sleeves.)

"Hell Yes I Cheated", a typically powerful version of a country song, was probably the finest moment from *The Many Sides Of* which, apart from lacking the superior musicianship and stronger songs that graced the *After All The Good Is Gone* LP, didn't sound ALL that different from that earlier release.

The Tan Nightingale (embarrassingly mis-titled: his real nickname was "The Tan Canary") is a UK only release that is a collection of many of his best sides recorded over the course of his career and is worthwhile for including a number of tracks that cannot be found on any other of his LPs. The same sort of comments would also apply to the Ace release, which is another collection, many tracks on which also can't be found elsewhere. These range from an enjoyable and well-judged version of The O'Jays' "Stairway To Heaven" to the unedifying and luckily exceedingly rare example of Johnny "doing disco" on "Feel The Beat"). He also recorded a Christmas LP, and one tends to either like or loathe such excursions. I would class it as much better than most as it features a spellbinding version of "The Lord's Prayer".

South Side Of Soul Street is a Japan release well worth hunting down as it features no fewer than ten cuts from the SSS days which are not to be found on *Heart & Soul* while *Old Flames* is another Japanese release consisting of the entire *Many Sides Of Johnny Adams* plus the previously unreleased title track.

From The Heart 1984 Rounder 2044 Producer: Scott Billington

After Dark 1986 Rounder 2049 Producer: Scott Billington

Room With A View Of The Blues 1987 Rounder 2059 Producer: Scott Billington

Walking On A Tightrope 1989 Rounder 2095 Producer: Scott Billington

Boston's Rounder Records rather rescued Johnny and would appear to have almost certainly treated him better than any other company with which he was associated. Indubitably, they were the only one who ever provided him with a coherent career strategy: they dispensed with any danceable songs, moved him up-market by ensuring he was dressed better on the record covers and concentrated entirely on LPs rather than on singles. (The Rounder albums also marked a move away from Senator Jones after many years of his producing Johnny.) The intent was made clear from the first Rounder release, *From The Heart*, which opened up with "Breaking Up Somebody's Home", a venerable soul standard, thus establishing a clear link with Adams' recording style to date, but track 2, "Why Do I", a scat/jazz song, moved him into new territory. By the time *Walking On A Tightrope* came along five years later the shift in emphasis was complete. It was, like all the Rounder LPs, enjoyable and good, but it wasn't truly a "soul" record and there was no reason why it should have been, of course. His sixties and seventies work had not generated anything other than intermittent success so one could hardly blame Johnny for his new approach, which garnered him more acclaim (e.g. a W C Handy award) and recognition than he had ever enjoyed before.

He continued to releases jazzy and bluesy CDs up to his death in 1998 and his legacy is secure among soul connoisseurs. He was never a big name and never enjoyed big success but he was a consummate performer and leaves behind a most impressive body of work.

ADC Band (see also Black Nasty and Nazty)

Michael Judkins; Audrey Matthews (aka Kaiya Matthews); Curtis Hobson; James Maddock; Artwell Matthews (aka Kublah Khan); Mark Patterson; Pervis Johnson; Demont "Dee" Knighton; Gregory Johnson; Bryant "Sparky" Lawson; Al Harrison; John Calhoun; Charles Hawkins; McKinley Cunningham

Long Stroke 1978 Cotillion SD 5210 Producer: Johnnie Mae Matthews (Billboard soul charts: 16 ; Billboard pop charts 139)

Talk That Stuff 1979 Cotillion SD 5216 Producer: Johnnie Mae Matthews (Billboard soul charts: 62)

Renaissance 1980 Cotillion SD 5221 Producer: Mass Production (Billboard soul charts: 69)

Brother Luck 1981 Cotillion SD 16041 Producer: Mass Production

Roll With The Punches 1982 Cotillion SD 5232 Producers: Bill Curtis & Gerry Thomas

The ADC Band (which stands for, somewhat bizarrely but admirably, "Aid to families with Dependent Children", so you can see why they abbreviated it) represented the third attempt by Audrey Matthews, Artwell Matthews and Mark Patterson to become a successful recording act. While the ADC Band did sell a lot more records than Black Nasty and Nazty (the first two groups in which they were members) ever managed, they never attained the trio's much desired prosperity.

The title track of the first LP was the only big single they ever had (# 6 in the soul charts at the end of 1978) but was so blatantly derivative of Parliament that it was either demeaning or splendidly opportunistic depending on your point of view. The rest of the LP was more varied but was still not particularly distinctive and contained tracks entitled "Reggae Disco" and "More And More Disco" that weren't great. Better was "Fire Up" with some wailing female vocals buried too low in the dance mix; it became a #72 soul chart entry.

The title song from *Talk That Stuff* also borrowed heavily from P-Funk but could only manage #69 on the soul charts; virtually everything else within was pretty hard edged and funky with good horns to the fore on "ADC Is Back". "I Just Want To Hold You" was a welcome attempt to slow things down and although the band's singing was fine it was not a great song.

For the next two albums they were no longer produced by the legendary Johnnie Mae Matthews (mum to Audrey and Artwell) and moved under the wing of Cotillion stablemates, Mass Production. The mildly intriguing "In The Moonlight" kicked off *Renaissance* and Audrey' Matthews' powerful vocal made one wish she had been given more of a chance to show what she could do on the group's LPs. A truncated version went to #75 on the soul charts and, despite being no masterpiece, it demonstrated that the band were not mere copyists. A second funky 45, "Hangin' Out", was pretty decent too, thanks to a crunching bass line, and came to rest at #67. "Everyday" was also the best downtempo side the band had recorded thus far, and even on moments like the rather routine "Work That Body", I can't help admiring the band's drive and energy. I feel confident in opining that this LP was the finest ever served up by the ADC Band and if one likes the funk sound from the early eighties this is about as good as it got.

Brother Luck was possibly their most varied LP but also the lowest commercial point of the group: neither it nor singles taken from it charted anywhere. "Nothing You Can Do" sounded unlike anything they had recorded thus far while the slow "Waiting For You" was the best track. "Nuclear Funk-Out" should have been awful with a title like that, but wasn't, employing their by now customary vigour and addictive horns.

The ADC Band finished their vinyl career with *Roll With The Punches*, from which the title track became their sixth and final chart entry, even if, like all the others apart from "Long Stroke", a placing of #46 was modest rather than exciting. It was also another track that borrowed from P-Funk, but one that has dated rather better than much of Clinton's stuff. "So Good" and "Girls" were other strong funk outings that owed much to Mark Patterson's bass and while it was another set that will have little appeal to those who think soul died in 1970 or thereabouts, I really rather like it.

There were to be a few more unsuccessful singles from the ADC Band on small labels like Fat Boy and Uhuru International throughout the eighties - as well as a handful of solo 12" singles from Kaiya Matthews - and it seems as if there has been a recent attempt for them to reform.

Afrique

Soul Makossa 1973 Mainstream MRL 394 No producer listed (Billboard soul charts: 33 ; Billboard pop charts 152)

No such band as Afrique ever really existed and this one album, full of some genuinely funky instrumentals, was a one-off concoction by a number of top session men, including David T. Walker, Paul Humphrey, Arthur Wright, King Errison and Chuck Rainey. As a single, the title track vied with Manu Dibango's original, and both versions entered the soul charts on June 23rd 1973. Dibango's ended up as the slightly bigger hit but Afrique's version did pretty well at #33 soul and #47 pop. It's hardly an essential LP and one's attention wanders before it's over but I well remember buying the 45 and enjoying it a lot as a teenager.

Afro – American Ensemble

Free The Black Man's Chains 1972 GSF S1007
Producers: Fred DiSipio, Jerry Gross & Mitchell Rowe

This rather obscure outing is classed somewhat grandiosely as a "Black Rock Opera", and certainly tells a compelling story, but can also be enjoyed if one is not paying particular attention to the lyrics. Featured singers are L C Grier, Junior Grier and Novella Edmonds. It was recorded in Philadelphia but isn't as lush as most music emanating from that city at the time. One fine track, "Fair Skin Man", also came out on single as by the Capri's (sic) and The Broad Street Gang while another, "Gone Is The Laughter Of You", slipped out on the tiny Sunshine label by L C Grier. I mention these things as Mitchell Rowe knew he had some good material and wanted to get it out there as often as he could, once it was clear that the LP wouldn't sell. (Not that the singles sold in any quantity, either).

Afterbach

Matinee 1981 ARC / Columbia 37472 Producers: Beloyd Taylor & Verdine White

Afterbach comprised brothers Michael and Robert Brookins (who went on to cut solo LPs) from Sacramento and they came up with this routine but listenable and danceable set. They are generally better on faster material as "I Thank You Heaven" is a somewhat cheesy and weak ballad, although the midtempo "Me, Myself And I" is the best thing on here. The repetitive "It's You" was a small hit on the soul charts at #38 in summer 1981.

Tony Aiken & Future 2000

Unity (Sing It, Shout It) 1976 Kimsha 2000 Producers: Tony Aiken, Bill Kamarra & E Nichols

Tony "Big Red" Aiken was born in Jamaica but moved to New York when he was ten (thus justifying his inclusion in the book) and while he also worked in the reggae field, there is no doubt that this is a bona fide, if short, soul album.

An undeniably good one as well, with four good tracks outclassing the mediocre "Time Tunnel". Best of all is the sweet soul of "She Loves You", an exemplary way to create a compelling quasi-orchestrated sound from a synthesiser; so often such attempts sound rather cheap and nasty. Not this one, and the singing is gorgeous, too. "Unity, (Sing It Shout It)" and "Better Days" are rousing dance invitations, even if they are possibly slightly over long; no such reservations attend "Good Things", a stirring and well-judged melodic midtempo romp of great appeal. The LP did not do well at the time of release, but has come to be appreciated in the last few years.

Jewel Akens

The Birds And The Bees 1965 Era EL110 Producer: Don Ralke

Houston's Jewel Akens worked very much at the "poppy" end of soul - although he had sung lead in a couple of R&B groups and released a fine single on Icepac in 1973 - and *The Birds And The Bees* is unlikely to appeal to those who believe a soul man should evince passion or pain. He could sing, however, sounding like a slightly distracted Sam Cooke. The title track was a big hit for him, but, tellingly, much more so on the pop charts (#3) than the soul charts (#21). Other tracks include "The Vegetable Love Song", "Georgie Porgie" and a version of "King Of The Road" which, while all being pure hokum, are somehow quite fun. He was never able to follow up the success of the big hit even though he put out singles at regular intervals for the next decade or so. He passed away in 2013.

Arthur Alexander

You Better Move On 1962 Dot DLP 3434 Producer: Noel Ball

Arthur Alexander 1972 Warner Brothers BS 2592 Producer: Tommy Cogbill

A Shot Of Rhythm and Soul 1982 Ace CH 66 (UK)

Soldier Of Love 1987 Ace CH 207 (UK)

Arthur Alexander 1989 Ace CH 270 (UK)

Arthur Alexander was one of those singers, like Little Sonny of The Intruders or Barbara Mason, who, while not blessed with the strongest voice technically, can convey a thrilling sense of warmth and inclusiveness and it is therefore sad that he only bequeathed a relatively small legacy on LP; especially as 50% of the tracks on the Dot album can be found on the UK releases from Ace.

By all accounts both a lovely and troubled man, Alexander has a treasured place in the hearts of many and he left us with some great records. "You Better Move On", for example, is a masterpiece, and the first important record out of Muscle Shoals. It takes some doing to convey such determined and quiet menace and most singers would not have the artistry or subtlety required to pull it off and it's also interesting to be reminded that while "You Better Move On" made it to #13 on the *Cashbox* soul charts, it didn't register on the *Billboard* listings. On the other hand "Anna (Go To Him)" did (#10), but, sadly, it doesn't feature on the LP. It must also be said that Alexander did cut some "filler" throughout his career, some of which is certainly found on the Dot release, in the guise of "A Hundred Pounds Of Clay" and "The Wanderer". Filler notwithstanding, I love Alexander's voice and I could happily listen to the LP for hours on end. As it seems, could The Beatles and Rolling Stones: they both recorded his songs.

After he left Dot he cut a number of singles for Sound Stage 7 and Monument including the heart-wrenching "I Need You Baby" but none of them hit and an LP was not forthcoming.

By the time the Warner Brothers release came along Arthur was pretty much a footnote in history (although he did chart with one more single in 1976 on Buddah.) It's absolutely splendid, though, and should be sought out as its commercial failure does not obscure its overall excellence. (Given what a superb writer he was it is interesting to note that the LP, like the debut on Dot, features less Alexander songs than might have been expected.) The best tracks are probably an entirely convincing reading of the great Dan Penn and Donnie Fritts tale, "Rainbow Road", "It Hurts To Want It So Bad" and the marvellous "In The Middle Of It All" but it's all compelling in that unassuming southern way he managed so effortlessly. The LP owes nothing at all to other soul records of the time: there are no screaming vocals, no funk, no dance material and no teen appeal whatsoever but that's all to its credit, and it demands attention.

Evidence of this songwriting prowess can be found on the three Ace retrospectives which also demonstrate - as do pretty much all his records - just how idiosyncratic an artist he was. (The 1989 Ace LP is exactly the same as the Warner Brothers release plus two tracks - "Lover Please" and "They'll Do It Every Time").

He released a lovely new CD in 1993 but, somehow typically of Arthur, he couldn't capitalise for the most unanswerable of reasons: he died the same year. He was certainly not a hard soul shouter, nor a man blessed with any great range, but he occupies a niche all by himself on the fringes of the country-soul genre with a tone redolent of reflective thinking and sad regrets under humid summer nights somewhere in deepest Alabama.

J W Alexander

Raw Turnips and Hot Sauce 1970 Thrush 2006 Producers: J W Alexander & Carol Alexander

The title is clearly designed to make the record sound funky. It doesn't work as this is one of the dullest records imaginable. JW Alexander worked extensively with Sam Cooke and for that he earns a significant place in soul music history but this record, which I assume was a "vanity" product, can be bypassed, despite the high quality of the musicians employed.

Ray Alexander Technique

Ray Alexander; Douglas Wilkerson; Ron Mack; Holley Jones; Chris Bartley;

Let's Talk 1974 Harlem Sound SA 001 Producer: Lucy Williams

This is a superb LP, which reminds me a bit of the equally beguiling one by Harlem River Drive from three years earlier, as both perfectly capture aurally the essence of New York City and where Harlem River Drive had Jimmy Norman as a guest vocalist, the Ray Alexander Technique employ one Chris Bartley, although I'm not convinced it is the man of "The Sweetest Thing This Side Of Heaven" fame.

It's also an obscure record, appearing to no acclaim or sales at all, and it is only over the last few years that word has spread as to its desirability. Funky and highly energetic, but tuneful and thoughtful throughout, it's a set in which the needle can be placed anywhere with pleasing results, but if favourites are required I would cite the title track, "Taking The Long Way Home", "I Don't Bite" and, best of all, "My World", where the frenzy, alienation and heat of New York is impeccably conjured up.

Alfonzo

Alfonzo 1982 Larc LR 8101 Producer: Clay McMurray (Billboard soul charts: 50)

Champion of Love 1988 Angel City ACL 10000 Producer: Wayne Henderson

Alfonzo Lee Jones out of Los Angeles had the dubious honour of being seen as little Larc records' answer to Michael Jackson. The cover to his first album makes that abundantly clear, as does a listen to "Your Booty Makes Me Moody" (not a title guaranteed to win any literary awards) or indeed any track on here. It became, together with "Girl, You Are The One" and "Change The World", one of three singles from the set to reach the soul top 50 charts but Larc were out of business by the end of 1983 and his career was thus stalled for a while. Anyone who likes Michael Jackson would doubtless have opinions one way or the other as to the merits of Alfonzo's stance. I find it all a little amusing.

Doubtless realising there was no real career path in so doggedly copying Jackson, Alfonzo reappeared in 1988, but he was now billed as Alfonz Jones. Although he no longer mimicked Michael, which was a good thing, he actually sounded even younger than he did six years earlier, which was not so good. Nor was an excruciating version of "Ain't No Sunshine", bad almost beyond belief.

Doris Allen (see Big John Hamilton)

Rance Allen Group

Rance Allen; Steve Allen; Tom Allen

The Rance Allen Group 1971 Gospel Truth GTS 2701 Producers: Dave Clark & Toby Jackson

Truth Is Where It's At 1972 Gospel Truth GTS 2709 Producers: Dave Clark & Toby Jackson

Brothers 1973 Gospel Truth GTS 3502 Producers: Dave Clark & Toby Jackson

A Soulful Experience 1975 Truth TRS 4207 Producers: David Porter, Ronnie Williams & Toby Jackson (Billboard soul charts: 35)

Sanctified 1975 Stax STX 1036 (UK)

Monroe, Michigan's The Rance Allen Group will be the most conspicuously religious group to be found in this book but given their appeal outside of strictly gospel circles, the fact they recorded on Stax and associated labels and because Rance Allen is one of the most incredible and soulful singers who ever drew breath they have to be included. Regardless of one's beliefs there is almost a duty to listen to the music recorded by Rance, Tom and Steve Allen as the passion evinced by Rance has rarely been equalled on vinyl by anyone at any time since recording singers became possible.

After releasing one single as the Rance Allen Singers they were picked up by Stax who provided them with a slight name change and a fair deal of attention over the next few years. An impassioned twist on "Just My Imagination" was released as a single in 1972, and while it didn't hit, it would have been the first time a number of people got to hear the big man's voice for the first time and it was one of the high points from the group's debut album which also included a bluesy "What Is This?" and the optimistic and driving "Everything Is Gonna Be Alright".

After having tackled The Temptations the group turned to Archie

Bell & The Drells whose "There's Gonna Be A Showdown" was transformed into an impassioned whoop-out although sadly failing to hit when issued as a single from the excellent *Truth Is Where It's At* LP, on which sits the remarkable "That Will Be Good Enough For Me". This is nothing less than a brilliant song: profound and moving in Rance's message that disregarding material things and experiences is of no consequence so long as he reaches heaven. Stax put out no end of great records over the years but even an atheist like me has no hesitation in proclaiming this to be a masterpiece. Amazingly, a second track equalled it: a simply astonishing version of Delia Gartrell and The Mighty Hannibal's "See What You Done Done", one of the greatest anti-drug/Vietnam songs ever written. Nothing else could top these two cuts but "God Is Wonderful" and "Heartaches" certainly tried hard enough. To prove the group didn't need to rely entirely on Rance either Tom or Steve took the majority of the lead vocals on an enjoyable and fairly "straight" take on "To The Other Man". I found "Mama " to be one cut I don't particularly care for, but this is a seriously impressive LP.

In June 1973 the Rance Allen Group finally had their first hit when "I Got To Be Myself" reached #31 on the soul charts but it was far from their best record, or indeed even the best cut on the *Brothers* LP, being entirely eclipsed by the impassioned "He Will See You Through", the beautiful "Heaven Is Where The Heart Is", the funky "Hot Line To Jesus", the almost danceable "I Know A Man Who" and a superb and imaginative adaptation of "For Once In My Life".

By 1975 Stax was in dire trouble but did manage to put out the group's second best LP (and biggest selling), *A Soulful Experience*, which contained their next charting single, the lovely "Ain't No Need Of Crying" (#61 soul in January). David Porter and Ronnie Williams had been drafted in to help Toby Jackson on production and their experience in working with soul acts undoubtedly helped in making the LP sound less "religious" and more accessible ("The Painter" and "Just Found Me" are examples) to a wider audience but it was slightly at the expense of Rance's more uninhibited vocal flights; make no mistake, he is still streets ahead of virtually everyone else in range and passion, but he's not *quite* at his most extraordinary.

The group had meant virtually nothing in Britain so it was great to see an effort made - which sadly failed - to break them to a wider audience by the UK Stax label with *Sanctified*, a marvellous 12 track compilation of their best work with only one rather glaring omission: "That Will Be Good Enough For Me".

Say My Friend 1977 Capitol ST-11613 Producer: Larry Mizell & Fonce Mizell

After Stax collapsed The Rance Allen Group recorded one album for Capitol and, frankly, it wasn't their best as I don't believe the rather florid strings helped things and the songs meander somewhat. Having said that, it was in no way a poor effort, and listening to "Reason To Survive" is hardly a chore, but overall it's not the LP that best showcases the group's power and ardour. "Truth Is Marching On" only reached #100 on the soul charts for a week, proving that even a powerhouse like Capitol had trouble breaking a group who refused to compromise their message.

Straight From The Heart 1978 Stax STX 4109 Producer: Henry Cosby (Billboard soul charts: 74)

Smile 1979 Stax STX 4127 Producer: Henry Cosby Billboard soul charts: 69)

I Feel Like Going On 1980 Stax STX 4136 Producers: Rance Allen and Ronnie McNeir

The group then "returned" to the newly formed (and Fantasy distributed) Stax label where they did fairly well: The gentle "I Belong To You" (with beautiful backing vocals) from *Straight From The Heart* was their highest ever soul charting single (#24) and deserved its success, but the album lacked strong material and is not up to the standard of the earlier Gospel Truth work, Allen being rarely pressed into the need to unveil his stratospheric range.

Smile was better not least because it contained the wonderful "Where Have All Your Friends Gone", the best thing they did in their later years, a cautionary tale for the ages, and one which played down the explicit religious lyrics of much of the work, employing a more general moral tone, a shift in emphasis much along the lines we had previously seen from The Staple Singers. On the other hand "I'm Going Home" and the frisky "I'm Thankful" were unashamedly straight gospel. The title track became a #41 soul hit as a single in the late summer of 1979 and bounced along on a most contemporary sounding rhythm track.

The last Stax set was a pretty good one, co-produced beautifully in an uptown soul style by Ronnie McNeir and the whole LP has a smoothness they didn't attain before or since and it suits them surprisingly well. The title track, "Can't Get Enough" and "Where Did I Go Wrong" were particularly strong, but may not appeal to die-hard gospel fans and it must be said that Allen's voice is buried too far in the mix.

Hear My Voice 1983 Myrrh MSB - 6736 Producer: Rance Allen

I Give Myself To You 1984 Myrrh WR - 8243 Producer: Rance Allen

Phenomenon 1991 Bellmark D1-71806 Producers: Khaliq Glover, Michael McCurtis, Trevor Lawrence & The Rance Allen Group (Billboard soul charts: 33)

These last albums returned the group to a mainstream gospel approach with the ten track *Hear My Voice* being the strongest and most enjoyable of the three, sounding much like the early seventies work in its stripped-down sound. "Life Is What It Is" and "It's Your Time" are striking cuts, but it's all worth hearing.

I Give Myself To You features a rare Steve Allen vocal on "I've Been Searching" and an even rarer example of employing a choir on "I'm So Satisfied". *Phenomenon* is mainly interesting to hear how Rance's singing had changed since the debut twenty years before, He had certainly gained in richness of tone with a deep resonance to his voice but the manic falsetto had pretty much gone and its absence makes the disc one of his least interesting.

The brothers are still going strong today, after nearly fifty years of recording together and new gospel CDs appear at irregular intervals. They have never had, nor ever will have, a large group of fans, but anyone who is prepared to dig below the surface will discover a man who could outsing anyone. In this entire book no other male singer will be named who has the range and power of Rance Allen on his Gospel Truth recordings.

Vee Allen

All About Love 1983 MCA 5398 Producer: Al Hudson

Vee Allen is the sister of Al Perkins, both a successful DJ and artist in his own right (and who died in 1983), and she charted with a fair size hit, "Can I", #26 soul, in 1973 on the Lion label but had to wait ten years before she had a chance to make what became her one and only vinyl LP. It was, as were all of her releases, recorded in or around Detroit, but by 1983 that city barely had a soul music industry anymore and despite the effort and attention lavished on the recording of *All About Love* it didn't chart. There is no aural evidence that leads one to conclude there was any particular injustice in its commercial failure but it remains a worthwhile and enjoyable release nonetheless, particularly the tracks "I'm Still Your Lady", "I'm So Crazy" and "Ain't No Easy Way".

She has returned to recording in the last ten years or so, with a couple of new CDs.

Alley & The Soul Sneekers

Alley & The Soul Sneekers 1979 Capitol SW-11913 Producer: Jack Nitzsche

This very odd release snuck out almost unnoticed and unheralded in 1979 which is a shame as it deserves to be much better known given it features on vocals on the majority of tracks one of the best of all soul singers: Carl Hall. In fact, it remains the only secular LP on which one will find his marvellous singing (he recorded gospel albums for The Raymond Rasberry Singers) and one can only speculate as to the thinking behind the uninspired band name and awful record cover which doomed it to failure. There are many lovely tracks within, particularly "I'm Coming Down With A Thrill", "Love Breakdown" and "Let The Music Begin" which is a showcase for some mesmerising singing by Hall. All songs were written by pop veteran Alan Gordon who has a fine "pop sensibility" as these are not really hard soul tracks, but ones which play up the elements of tunefulness and fulsome production (reflecting producer Nitzshe's background). I recommend it unreservedly, however, and there were not many other soul records that sounded like this in 1979. (Note: It originally came out in Canada as by Alan Gordon entitled *Alley & The Soul Sneekers*. I said it was an odd release). Hall died in 1999 and Gordon in 2008.

Gene Allison

Gene Allison 1959 Vee Jay VJLP 1009 Producer: Ted Jarrett

It appears that Gene Allison was an alcoholic which might account for the fact he only released this one LP, and given it contains three big hits on the soul charts - "You Can Make It If You Try" (#3), "Have Faith" (#11) and "Everything Will Be Alright" (#19) - he obviously had the potential to have done much better. This will be one of the earliest recorded LPs to be covered in this book, but it is, to my ears at least, a perfect example of how "R&B" was mutating into something new. Allison had a clean, clear voice which is highlighted to good effect by the straightforward and uncluttered arrangements, some of which emanate from Nashville, but the majority of the LP was cut in Chicago.

He continued to record, without further success, right up to the end of the sixties but then left the music industry and passed away, almost completely forgotten, in 2004.

Allspice

Deborah Shotlow; Doug Thomas; Ned Perkins; Esau Joyner; Saundra Alexander

Allspice 1977 At Home AH-401 Producer: Wayne Henderson

There is nothing particularly original about this record, sounding much like one would expect from Wayne Henderson's polished productions of the time, but it is nonetheless appealing, with its above average vocals from a group of this type and slapping bass. It didn't sell too many copies though and the group disbanded soon afterwards. "Destiny" and "Hungry For Your Love" are notable highlights and either should probably have been chosen as a single rather than "Slipped Away" which failed to sell many copies.

Gerald Alston (see also The Manhattans)

Gerald Alston 1988 Motown 6265 Producers: Stan Sheppard & James Varner (Billboard soul charts: 18)

Open Invitation 1990 Motown 6298 Producers: James Carmichael, Stan Sheppard & James Varner (Billboard soul charts: 14)

Always In The Mood 1992 Motown 530 134 Producers: Douglas Grisby, Eric Mercury, Ira Antelis, Nick Martinelli & Stan Sheppard (UK)

Gerald Alston was the lead singer of The Manhattans between 1970 and 1988. They were abundantly successful years with the group posting no fewer than thirty 45s in the Top 50 of the US soul singles chart while he was with them. It was probably no surprise when the lure of a solo career became too tempting, given how many other distinctive lead singers had also opted to go out alone. And make no mistake, Alston is a distinctive singer, probably a great one in fact, and I rate him highly.

I remain firmly convinced though, that his best work was with The Manhattans (who he subsequently rejoined) as I really miss the Bobby Martin arrangements and the exquisite harmonies of his former group. Nevertheless, these solo records are well executed and the debut album is both respectful of his past and sensibly restrained in tempo. His singing is as beautiful as ever and he really stretches out on a version of "We've Only Just Begun". "Take Me Where You Want Me" was the lead-off single and made it to #6 on the soul charts (although missing the Hot 100 altogether and was followed up by "You Laid Your Love On Me" (#41) and "I Can't Tell You Why" (#52).

Open Invitation did even better business and continued the sound of the earlier LP, with stand-out tracks being the two successful singles "Slow Motion" (#3) and "Getting Back Into Love" (#6). A third single, a duet with Brenda Russell, "Tell Me This Night Won't End", could only manage a much more modest placing of #69. On the less acceptable front "Any Day Now" was an overwrought and heavy-handed version of the old Jackson hit.

Mind you, "Any Day Now" sounded quite good when compared to Alston's version of "Love And Happiness" from *Always In The Mood*, which I believe only came out as an LP in the UK, with the U.S. sticking to CD only. The Ron Kersey and Sam Dees written "Send For Me" was much better, reaching #40 on the soul charts, twelve places lower than the first single, "Hell Of A Situation". He was certainly well served with high quality backing vocalists on the set, as they included Betty Wright, Dee Dee Wilde, Eugene Wilde, Cynthia Biggs and Jeanette Holloway and although I can't pretend I am much enamoured of this style of soul music Alston is always a pleasure to listen to.

He has continued to sing and record as a solo artist as well as together with The Manhattans again over the last twenty five years or so.

Shirley Alston / Lady Rose (see also The Shirelles)

With A Little Help From My Friends 1975 Prodigal PLP-10008 Producer: Randy Irwin

Lady Rose 1977 Strawberry 6004 Producer: Randy Irwin

Sings The Shirelles Greatest Hits 1977 Strawberry 6004 Producer: Randy Irwin

An original Shirelle, Shirley Alston (born Shirley Owens in North Carolina) stayed with the group until the early seventies, when she left and recorded three solo LPs, two of which, on Strawberry, came out under her alternative name, Lady Rose.

I haven't heard much from these albums but two of them, the first and last, seem to be pure examples in nostalgia and can hardly have been expected to sell in great quantity, which they almost certainly didn't. The biggest disappointment for me from the Prodigal LP was the fact that it doesn't contain her excellent single for the same label, "Can't Stop Singing ('Bout The Boy I Love)". Wouldn't it have been better to continue in that vein rather than cut an updated version of "Silhouettes" with Herman's Hermits or "Sincerely" with Danny & The Juniors? (It also bears, for one of those inexplicable reasons, an entirely different front cover on the U.S. and U.K. releases).

I would also add that re-recording ten songs you had helped to make famous fifteen or so years earlier (as she did on the "Shirley Alston Sings The Shirelles Greatest Hits" set) was never likely to revive her fortunes.

She released a horrible seven minute disco record in 1981 and seems to have recorded little since then but remains singing live in concert to this day under the name of Shirley Alston Reeves.

Billy Always

Billy Always 1982 Waylo TAS-12114 Producer: Willie Mitchell

Billy Always 198? Always Publishing BA-51779 Produced by Billy Always

Watch Out 1988 Epic E 44332 Producers: Willie Mitchell, Daryl Duncan, Charlie Singleton & Eric Morgeson.

Let's Get Personal 1990 Waylo 269520 1 Producer: Willie Mitchell (Europe)

Billy Always (real name, William Lewis Moore) was one of Willie Mitchell's last serious attempts to find a singer who could provide him with some semblance of the success he had enjoyed with Al Green, Otis Clay, Syl Johnson and Ann Peebles. Unfortunately, it didn't work out like that and Billy and Willie had to settle for just two charting singles - both at a lowly level. Always is the godson of Mahalia Jackson so had some exemplary pedigree with which to help him and over the years he demonstrated that he was a very good songwriter (for Barrett Strong among others) with strong high register vocals.

He had cut a couple of singles in 1980 before starting to work with Mitchell and although "Didn't We Do It", which managed to get to #74 on the soul charts, "It's Just Not Enough" and "Suddenly" were impressive performances, the rest of *Billy Always* was somewhat disappointing with "My First Love" being a particular low spot. It was also surely a mistake for Always to have cut a version of "Let's Stay Together" as it just invites competitive comparisons and Green simply trounces him.

A self - produced and possibly self-distributed LP slipped out some time in the eighties to little avail, despite endorsements on the back cover from Jackson, Aretha Franklin and Gloria Gaynor. I do not remember seeing or hearing about it at the time and have still heard none of it to this day.

A couple of nondescript singles saw Billy through 1986 and 1987 before he moved to Epic for another uneven outing which ranged from pretty good ("Emergency Love" and "A Little Misunderstanding") to pretty dire ("Back On Track" - which did reach #43 on the soul charts as a single - and "Take 2"). *Watch Out* didn't do anything as regards sales, and the association with the label quickly came to an end.

Somewhat against the odds, he returned in 1990 to put out the distinguished *Let's Get Personal* (apt title, he finally did forge an identity) which concentrated almost exclusively on slow and midtempo songs, many of which were excellent with one, "No More Rodeo", being of special note. It sounds as if it could be a standard recorded by others and I'm amazed that hasn't happened but this may simply be a result of the fact that the LP wasn't released in the U.S. In addition, the fine single, "Ain't Nothing But A Heartache", "I Need You" and "I Don't Understand it" (covered by Otis Clay) were of a higher than average quality. The whole thing deserves to be much more widely heard and it was good to see that his LP career came to a close on such a high.

Ambassadors (see also Creme D'Cocoa)

Herley Johnson; John Johnson; Bobby Todd; Calvin Todd; Ben Speller

Soul Summit 1969 Arctic 1005 Producer: Jimmy Bishop

There were at least seven soul groups called The Ambassadors but only this one ever got to cut and release an LP. It's good but could have been better and I thus find it to be ever so slightly disappointing. This is largely due to the material on show, 50% of which consists of cover versions of songs often performed better by others ("I Dig You Baby" and "You've Lost That Loving Feeling"). The group were talented and harmonise beautifully throughout but they would have been better served by a few more original songs. Arctic did get good mileage from the record though, with seven of the eleven tracks appearing as a or b-sides on singles, although only one of them, "I Really Love You", became a hit, #43 soul in early 1969.

The group disbanded in 1971 but Johnson, Oliphant and Bobby Todd all re-surfaced as part of Creme D'Cocoa some years later.

Amuzement Park

Aaron Jamal; Darryl Ellis; Fred Entesari; Norval Don Hodges; Paul Richmond; Rico McFarland; Ruben Locke Jr

Amuzement Park 1982 Our Gang Entertainment OGI 30001 Producer: Dunn Pearson

All Points Bulletin 1984 Atlantic 80126 Producer: David Wolinski

Amuzement Park is a perfect example - all too often in soul - of an LP where the sleeve does not inform us who comprised the group, but does tell us who provided photography and art direction, and for that reason I'm not totally confident I have correctly identified the band members. The set was recorded in Chicago and New York and provided two small soul hits in "Groove Your Blues Away" and "Do You Still Love Me". It's not a bad record but is a tad predictable in as much as it features some token ballads amid a host of dance tracks that do little to engage or surprise the listener.

By the time Atlantic issued the second LP the group's name had changed slightly to Amuzement Park Band and the personnel was seemingly slimmed down to a quintet. A third and final charting single (#62), a so-so ballad entitled "No", was lifted from what was another decent outing, much in the same style as the first. Two more 45s, "Squeeze Me" and "A.P.B.", were released but neither charted.

Anacostia

Tony Boyd; Tommy Williams; Ron Sinclair

Anacostia 1977 MCA-2269 Producer: Charles Kipps

Anacostia 1978 Tabu JZ 35570 Producer: Charles Kipps

Anacostia is a neighbourhood in Washington D.C. so it isn't too difficult to determine from where this group originated. They first recorded for Columbia, issuing a handful of singles, one of which, "On And Off", managed to reach #41 and #90 pop in late 1972. One member, Tony Boyd, was formerly the lead singer with The Presidents, another Washington based group, and moved to front Anacostia after The Presidents broke up.

The MCA *Anacostia* release, an impressive and beautifully produced LP, boasts nine tracks, five of which were written by the group themselves. "Heartache In Disguise" was one of their best, a dance record which wasn't overwhelmed by disco tricks, and the more sedate "We Can't Live Life Alone" was also entirely enjoyable, although it was clear that The Spinners were an obvious influence. Possibly best of all, though, was the utterly delightful "I Can't Stop Loving Her" (with a Chi-Lites' feel) which was released as a single, but as it sounded more like a recording from 1972 or 1973 than 1977, it failed to attract much attention. Of the "outside" songs, Charles Kipps' "Looking Over My Shoulder" and Van McCoy's "Baby I'm Available" were best. The LP has always been unfairly neglected and ignored but I recommend it without reservation.

The Tabu album had exactly the same unimaginative title as its predecessor, and also shared much the same feel and approach as well: the majority of songs being provided by Boyd, Williams and Sinclair with Kipps and McCoy also chipping in. This consistency of approach - and same Media Sound New York recording venue - ensured that it was another immensely enjoyable outing, but once again I was dismayed that the LP and the two singles that were released from it meant so little to so many, and just imagine how Anacostia felt. All ten tracks are worthy but "Baby Don't Ever Leave Me", "Another City Morning" and "I Don't Need" are as good as soul group singing got in 1978.

Both LPs are marvellous, and exude a stately sense of dignity, and I can't help feeling a bit nonplussed that such artistry is even to this day so roundly ignored by almost everyone: these are not rare, expensive albums but they are vastly better than 90% of those which are.

Carol Anderson

Ain't Givin' Up 1983 Coup CR-LP 2008 Producers: Floyd Jones, George Anderson & Essie Anderson

Detroit's Carol Anderson had released around ten singles between 1969 and 1979 but none had charted nationally, although I assume one or two did ok in Michigan and surrounding areas. It was therefore a great surprise and pleasure to see her enjoy an LP release in 1982, on which a lot of talent was brought to bear. Songwriters of the quality of John Glover, James Dean, Floyd Jones, Will Hatcher and Barrett Strong provided the majority of the songs, and veteran Detroit musicians such as Rod Lumpkin and Bruce Nazarian supplied the music. *Ain't Givin' Up* has two or three fairly disposable numbers but some very good stuff too: "Sad Girl" (which has a marked Chicago lilt despite all the Detroit personnel on show), the tuneful "Come On Over Tonight" and the fine and heartfelt "I'll Get Off At The Next Stop", all of which had featured on 45s, are the three standout cuts.

Sadly, the LP didn't enjoy strong distribution and it wouldn't have sold many copies, but has maintained a good reputation ever since it appeared. Even more sadly, Anderson died only a year or so after its release.

Roshell Anderson

Introducing 1974 Sunburst SU 1098/1099 Producers: Cornelius E Faison IV & Roshell Anderson

Nature's Way 1988 Ichiban 1021 Producer: Roshell Anderson

Sweet 'n' Sour Rhythm 'n' Blues 1989 Ichiban 1035 Producer: Roshell Anderson

Stepping Out 1990 Ichiban 1053 Producers: Roshell Anderson & Adam Davis

The Outlawwh Casanova 1991 Ichiban 1113 Producer: Roshell Anderson

Roshell Anderson is not your average soul man: firstly because he is, for most of the time, a well-known T.V. anchor man, Mike Anderson, and second, because he owns a truly extraordinary voice, once heard never forgotten.

Raised in New Orleans, he released his first single on Excello in 1973, the doomy "Snake Out Of Green Grass", and, although it didn't hit, it presumably helped in securing a deal with Sunburst.

The debut LP is quite simply one of the most bizarre I have ever heard. On the one hand, it features three excellent tracks ("Know What You're Doing When You Leave", complete with a dreadfully cheap synthesiser sound some years before it became *de rigueur*; "Grapevine Will Lie Sometimes" and "What Do You Expect Of Me"). Amazingly, given how uncommercial they were and how Sunburst must have operated on a shoestring budget, the first two tracks hit the soul charts at #77 and #69 respectively. On the other hand, the album has three successive tracks on side two, "Moonlight Trip", "Jealous Hearted Women" and "I'm Pushin' On" which require a great deal of fortitude to listen to. They seem to be deliberate exercises in Anderson trying out as many variations of his voice as possible which, at best, sound like Roy C tossing and singing in his sleep, and, at worst, as if he were trying out for a part in a horror movie.

He released a handful of other singles in the seventies - without any repetition of chart success - but had to wait until 1988 for his second LP to appear, after which a few more tumbled out in quick succession. All appeared on the Ichiban label which had a great reputation for salvaging the careers of soul artists fallen on hard times, but less of one for releasing good records.

I have heard little from these four albums, but what I have heard was sadly uninspiring. Take, for instance, *Sweet 'N' Sour Rhythm 'N' Blues*. The musicianship is perfunctory and the best cuts are remakes of his strongest work on Sunburst. He covers well known soul songs such as "Leavin' Me", "Stop Doggin' Me" and "Choking Kind" and it would be true to say that they are not the definitive versions.

H. Andrews Congregation (see also The California Playboys)

Harold Andrews; Delmar Young; Jackie Rogers; Kelvin Dixon; Edgar Cabezas; Julien Vaught; Ken Dunaway; Victor Adra;

Inner Thoughts Of 1974 B.R.I. 1,000,00 Producer: H Andrews

This is a rare LP that tends to sell for a lot of money and, as a result, has also been bootlegged. In my experience such records are often highly disappointing and it is all too easy to see why they failed to sell. This is not such an example. While certainly not a lost classic or anything like that, it is well performed, sung and produced but I imagine Balance records simply didn't have the wherewithal to market it properly. The music is mostly pretty funky, which is what one might expect from what appears to be a nine member self contained band (only eight of whom are name-checked on the sleeve), but there is also included an excellent eleven minute slow track, "One More Chance" and an elegant Smokey Robinson influenced ballad entitled "I've Got To Find Myself Another Girl". Four of the group went on to help form the California Playboys.

Ruby Andrews

Everybody Saw You 1970 Zodiac ZS 1001 Producers: Ric Williams, Fred Bridges, Richard Knight & Robert Eaton

Black Ruby 1972 Zodiac ZS 1002 Producers: Robert Eaton, Fred Bridges, Richard Knight & Ric Williams

Genuine Ruby 1977 ABC AB 1002 Producer: Ronald Dunbar

Kiss This 1991 Ichiban 1104 Producers: Swamp Dogg & Michael Lockett

Ruby Andrews (born Ruby Stackhouse) is usually thought of as a Chicago artist but although she has spent most of her life there all of the tracks on her two Zodiac LPs were recorded in either Detroit or Memphis.

Her first two singles did not achieve much, but her third did and "Casanova" became a #9 soul and #51 pop hit in the fall of 1967. She found this level of success difficult to maintain, however, and of her next six 45s on Zodiac only two charted, "The Love I Need" and "You Made A Believer (Out Of Me)". It also wasn't until the end of 1970 that she was blessed with her first album, *Everybody Saw You*, the title track of which had hit #34 a few months earlier. The set does feature "Casanova", but this was a re-make, not the original, and a number of the earlier, nearly always good, singles are not included in any shape or form. It is, though, a noble work, and sees Andrews, always a passionate and committed singer anyway, delivering the eleven songs with a good deal of fire. The songs are almost all strong and I love the nice arranging touches such as the unusual horn (or keyboard ?) lines on "Can You Get Away" and "Tit For Tat", the high flourish of the strings on her version of "I Guess That Don't Make Me A Loser" and the hot crackle of the guitar lines throughout. It's a set that perfectly fuses the production values of what had gone in the sixties and what was to come in the seventies and is highly recommended.

The March 4th 1972 edition of *Billboard* magazine carried a small advert for her second LP, *Black Ruby*, which proudly - but entirely mistakenly - proclaimed that the lead-off track "(I Want To Be) Whatever It Takes To Please You" was one of the nation's fastest breaking singles. It didn't even chart, unlike another track, "You Ole Boo Boo You", which did (at #47 soul). It's another LP to thoroughly enjoy, and just looking at the colourful record label is a pleasure, but it pointed up looming problems for Zodiac as older singles in "You Made A Believer Out Of Me" and "Just Loving You" were pleasingly included. It was great to hear them, but the fact they were four and five years old respectively meant that it seemed likely that the record label wasn't about to last much longer. Because of the disparity in age between some of the tracks there was a slight unease about listening to the sixties material against newer, funkier stuff such as her tough and unrecognisable take on "Hound Dog" where her uncompromising and feisty stance might well have been influenced by what Laura Lee was doing at the time. It's for that reason that *Black Ruby* didn't *quite* match up to *Everybody Saw You*.

Andrews had to wait for quite a few years before she recorded again, when she returned to Detroit to record an excellently catchy 45 for ABC in "I Got A Bone To Pick With You", which unbelievably missed out on chart action entirely. Annoyingly it does not appear on her third LP which includes another great track, "Merry Go-Round", which sounds as if it should have been a smash, but the company went with "I Wanna Be Near You" and "Queen Of The Disco" as singles instead, both of which were inferior and both of which also failed. Another top moment on the LP was Ruby's excellent offering of "A Change Is Gonna Come", beautifully sung and arranged until it was unwisely speeded up for the last minute. A good album, certainly, but lacking the vitality of the finest Zodiac work.

Her last outing on vinyl came in 1991 when she recorded down in Baton Rouge with Swamp Dogg. The cover shows off her beauty but the record is only mediocre. I bow to no-one in my admiration for Jerry Williams but his grip is too strong here for any of Andrews' individuality to wriggle free and I would defy most people to even guess it was Ruby Andrews singing were they to listen to the record blind, so to speak.

A new - mostly engaging - CD appeared in 1993, followed by another in 1998 and over the last few years a couple of good retrospectives of her music have also popped out, but she remains underappreciated and needs to be remembered for what she was: one of the finest of all Chicago soul singers.

Anglo-Saxon Brown (see also Silk)

Debra Henry; Clemente Burnette; Carlton Robinson; Charles Manns; Dwight Smith; Joe Jefferson; Anthony Ingram; Alvin Brown; Larry Washington; Tyrone Durham

Evolution 1976 Atlantic SD 18192 Producers: Joe Jefferson & Charles Simmons

Anglo-Saxon Brown were another act who recorded under different names. At first they were known as Ujima when they cut some fine singles but no albums. They then became the group who put out this LP, before a handful of the band carried on under the name of Silk at the end of the seventies.

Unsurprisingly, given the producers, the Philadelphia recorded *Evolution* sounds pretty much like The Spinners records of the time and anyone who loves them should love this. Apart from one or two indifferent tracks, I rate it as a highly solid effort. "Straighten It Out" was released as a 45, but although it is a good enough album cut, it lacked the immediacy to have become a hit. (As an aside the LP cover shows eight people but lists ten musicians and I question if Larry Washington and Joe Jefferson were truly in the group.)

Anthony & Imperials (see Little Anthony & Imperials)

Apollo

Kerry Gordy; Cliff Liles; Benny Medina; Lenny Greene; Larry Robinson

Apollo 1979 Gordy G7-985R1 Producer: Ray Singleton

This is one of a number of LPs from the end of the seventies that had a cover with a space theme, which usually made it hard to guess at what kind of music one would find inside. The answer here, apart from the ten minute "Astro Disco" and "Space Cannibals", is not too bad. As so often in 1979 there was a nod to Earth, Wind & Fire, but also towards more classic Motown vocal groups and most soul fans could enjoy "Right In Front Of You", "Never Learn" and "Hungry Eyes" although they would need to understand that they are light and quite "poppy" rather than out and out soulful fare. Ray Singleton, ex-wife of Berry Gordy, produced, but neither the album nor the 7" or 12" version of "Astro Disco" made any impression in the market-place and Apollo disbanded.

Aquarian Dream (see also Sylvia Striplin)

Jacques Burvick; Claude Bartee; Gloria Jones; Jimmy Morrison; Mike Fowler; Pete Bartee; Valerie Horn; Pat Shannon; David Worthy; Winston Daley; Ernie Adams; Connie Harvey Sylvia Striplin;

Norma Connors Presents 1976 Buddah BDS 5672 Producer: Norman Connors (Billboard pop charts: 154)

Fantasy 1978 Elektra 6E-152 Producer: Norman Connors, Don Mizell, Elzy White & Aquarian Dream

Chance To Dance 1979 Elektra 6E-205 Producer: Jeff Lane

Norman Connors will not feature in the book as I believe he is first and foremost a jazz man, but he certainly worked with many genuine soul artists and he was the producer and mentor for this outfit's first two albums. The debut features vocals throughout by Gloria Jones, but it is not *the* Gloria Jones although this one can emote well enough and Connors always had a good record of working with excellent singers. However, the LP is fairly weak to my way of thinking, with as much "disco" as "soul" on show, although a pretty decent version of "Let Me Be The One" is worth a listen. The uptempo and peppy "Phoenix" became a small soul hit (#83) in early 1977.

The follow-up, *Fantasy*, is slightly better with a hotter production sound and sharper horns, although it is still a little bland on too many occasions, as on "Yesterday (Was So Nice Today)". Sylvia Striplin had joined the group at this point, by the way, and she went on to record a solo LP in 1981. A couple of singles were released but they didn't make it.

However, the first two sets sound like *What's Going On* in comparison to the unspeakable *Chance To Dance*, which has, with "Are You Ready For Love" just about excepted, precious little to do with soul music.

Chuck Armstrong

Shackin' Up 1976 R & R 910 Producers: Maria Tynes & George Kerr

Seemingly one of the most peripatetic of all soul men - for instance, he recorded in Florida (where he spent most of his time), New Jersey (the location for this LP) Nashville, Cleveland, and Chicago - Armstrong slightly surprisingly got a welcome opportunity to record a solitary album, and bracing and engaging it is too.

His first single had come out in 1966 as by "Little Charles" and he recorded a handful more under his real name before he moved to R & R. He was already an "old-school" singer in 1976 and he either could not or would not soften his style sufficiently enough to make this a commercially successful release, although one track, the meritorious "Give Me All Your Sweet Lovin'", did manage to scrape into the soul charts at #75 for a few weeks. The LP must have sold in dismayingly small quantity but George Kerr's usual mastery is evident, and "I'm A Lonely Man" and "I'm Coming Home" are just two example of how much of a reconstructed soul man Armstrong was. This is tough music, with a touch of Syl Johnson to his voice.

In later years he seemingly drifted away from the business with only two more singles emerging in a six year period - the last thirty years ago now - and I do not know if he is still alive.

Tal Armstrong (see also The Ascots)

The Tallest Man In Love 1980 Love LO 0112 Producer: Tal Armstrong

Talmadge Armstrong was formerly one of the lead singers in the Texas based group The Ascots and he recorded his one solo LP in California in 1980 although much of it sounds as if it were recorded earlier, with tracks such as "You've Got So Much Feeling" having a distinct mid seventies feel. Despite a rather irritating synthesiser throughout, it's a pretty good LP, much in demand for its rarity these days, but it was a strictly local affair, and neither it, nor the two singles pulled from it, would have escaped far beyond the California state line in any quantity. (The front cover is misleading, which suggests it is probably a jazz album, which it isn't, despite the odd jazzy flourish here and there.)

Artistics

Marvin Smith; Robert Dobyne; Curt Thomas; Larry Johnson; Jessie Bolian; Aaron Floyd; Tommy Green; Fred Pettis; Morris Williams; Jimmy Short; Bernard Reed

Got To Get My Hands On Some Loving 1964
Okeh OKM 12119 Producer: Carl Davis

The Artistics recorded six LPs, all under the tutelage of Carl Davis, and not one of them told you who they were. Having said that, both Davis and Brunswick clearly persevered with the group, even if they did not have a great deal of success: none of their albums charted and they could only really claim one single - "I'm Gonna Miss You" - as being a bona fide hit despite their being granted over twenty releases. Possibly the problem was that their music sometimes leaned too heavily on what was coming out of Detroit rather than exhibiting a stronger sense of their Chicago roots.

Got To Get My Hands On Some Loving was arguably their best LP as nearly all the songs were strong, and the flirtation with Detroit was already apparent. Lead singer Marvin Smith did a terrific job throughout and the title track became a small soul hit on the *Cashbox* listings in the late summer of 1964, while "This Heart Of Mine" became the first time the name of The Artistics was seen on the *Billboard* soul listings when it stalled at #25 in early 1966. (In between the much more traditional Chicago sounding "Patty Cake" had not made it as a single.) All three songs were to be found on the Okeh set which for years was my number one "want" and I was delighted to track it down in a New Jersey record fair in the mid nineties.

I'm Gonna Miss You 1967 Brunswick BL 754123 Producer: Carl Davis

The Articulate 1968 Brunswick BL 754139 Producer: Carl Davis

What Happened 1969 Brunswick BL 754153 Producers: Carl Davis & Eugene Record

(I Want You To) Make My Love Over 1970
Brunswick BL 754168 Producers: Carl Davis, Eugene Record & Willie Henderson

Look Out 1973 Brunswick BL 754195 Producer: Carl Davis

By the end of 1966 the group had migrated to Brunswick where they hit right away with the previously mentioned "I'm Gonna Miss You" (#9 soul and #55 pop). A gorgeous record, and it was followed onto the soul charts by the equally good "Girl I Need You" which also did well (#26 soul and #69 pop). Smith was apparently falling out with the rest of his colleagues around this time and left for a solo career (cutting, among other sides, the scandalously underrated "Time Stopped", #26 on the *Cashbox* soul charts in late 1966), and the rest of the group took to singing lead such as Tom Green on the beautifully orchestrated. "Glad I Met You". These three songs were the picks from the fine *I'm Gonna Miss You* set but the Detroit-influenced "Hope We Have" was also a stormer.

Virtually all the tracks from *The Articulate Artistics* are too content to sound as if they were recorded at Motown. Given the stiff competition coming from Berry Gordy's empire it was an interesting approach and one that didn't really benefit the group. "Hard To Carry On" and "You Left Me" were put out as singles but they were average songs and did not succeed. The album is ok, but certainly inferior to the previous two.

What Happened hedged its bets, mixing up some reasonable Eugene Record songs on side one with standards such as "That Lucky Old Sun" and "I Wish You Love" on side two. Record could do much better than "reasonable" though as he was proving with his work for Barbara Acklin and his own Chi-Lites, and it's a second successive no more than "ok" LP from the group, and once again, the two singles pulled from it did not hit; it was now over two years since The Artistics had reached the national charts.

Unfortunately, things were to get even worse for although *I Want To Make My Life Over*" contained, in its title track and "Just Another Heartache" two singles that did finally return the group to the soul charts, both at #48, Brunswick got up to their tricks of repeating material from previous sets and it contained four cuts that can be found on previous LPs. Furthermore another track, "Nothing But Heartaches (Keep Haunting Me)", was a two year old single. Worst of all, it was the third long player in a row that did include a genuinely great track.

As if to prove beyond any doubt that Brunswick no longer saw the Artistics as any sort of priority their final LP, *Look Out*, once again featured the group's two finest sides from the label in "I'm Gonna Miss You" and "Girl I Need You", both now six years old. The previous set's title track was also included once again but there were at least a few good new tracks: "Being In Love" (despite sounding more or less exactly like The Chi-Lites); "She's Heaven" and, best of all, an excellent rendering of Phillip Mitchell's "It's Those Little Things That Count", that did not deserve to fail as a 45, but which did. It was the last straw and the group broke up.

Although their career can hardly be called an untrammelled success, they had some brilliant moments, and it should also be noted that The Artistics could boast some decent songwriters - Marvin Smith, Larry Johnson, Jesse Bolian and Robert Dobyne (who also had a solo career) in particular - and a large number of songs on the albums came from these sources.

Ascots (see also Tal Armstrong)

Talmadge Armstrong; AC Guillory; James Kelly Duhon

Color Me Soul 1978 Crazy Cajun CCLP-1024 Producer: Huey P Meaux

Given this LP was obviously put out as a tax scam by the despicable Huey Meaux it must have sold in paltry fashion but, despite its lack of quality control (the sleevenotes state that "A Few Feet From The Gutter" is included when in fact it is not), it has a number of worthwhile moments. The stand-out cut is "You're My Salvation" which is a wrenching deep soul performance of particular power. Because of the desultory approach to the LP, many of the tracks came out years earlier and at least one, "The Graveyard Creep", was originally released as by James Duhon rather than The Ascots. (Another common name for a group, by the way, there were many others.)

Jack Ashford

Hotel Sheet 1977 Magic Disc MD-116 Producers: Jack Ashford & Art Stewart

Jack Ashford was one of Motown's funk brothers, and as it is only recently that these extraordinary musicians have got some of the respect they always deserved, he was used to staying in the background. I imagine he felt that the chances of recording a solo album were slim given that arguably the most famous funk brother of all, James Jamerson, never managed to achieve such a release, and I would also hazard a guess that Ashford never expected this record to attain much success. In fact, it didn't, but it is not without its attractions: "I'll Fly To Your Open Arms" and "Get Right On Top" are the best cuts (not surprisingly the musicianship is of a very high quality - other funk brothers such as Earl Van Dyke, Uriel Jones, Eddie Brown and Robert White play on the record) but much else is fairly inconsequential, and ultimately the record needed a stronger vocalist than Jack himself (who also wrote all the songs.) Oddly, *Hotel Sheet* came out with two different covers, only one of which credited Art Stewart as a producer.

He re-appeared with a second solo set on CD a few years back, only thirty five years or so since his first.

Ashford and Simpson (see also Valerie Simpson)

Gimme Something Real 1973 Warner Brothers BS 2739 Producers: Ashford & Simpson (Billboard soul chart : 18 ; Billboard pop charts: 156)

I Wanna Be Selfish 1974 Warner Brothers BS 2789 Producers: Ashford & Simpson (Billboard soul charts: 21 ; Billboard pop charts: 195)

Come As You Are 1976 Warner Brothers BS 2858 Producers: Ashford & Simpson (Billboard soul charts: 35 ; Billboard pop charts: 189)

So So Satisfied 1977 Warner Brothers BS 2992 Producers: Ashford & Simpson (Billboard soul charts: 30 ; Billboard pop charts: 180)

Nick Ashford and Valerie Simpson are true soul aristocracy and should be revered as American national treasures. The only other man/woman composing teams in popular music history that can sensibly be compared to the writers of such imperishable songs as "Ain't No Mountain High Enough", "I'm Every Woman","California Soul", "Ain't Nothing Like The Real Thing" and "I Don't Need No Doctor" would be Gerry Goffin & Carole King and Barry Mann & Cynthia Weil. I don't know exactly how many versions of songs that Ashford and Simpson composed have actually been recorded but it will be something close to a thousand. So quite apart from the fact that they recorded a series of magnificent LPs in their own names their legacy is, just as they said, solid as a rock.

Both had made records before: Nick with a handful of singles in the sixties and Valerie with two albums for Tamla in 1971 and 1972, but these all seemed like dabbling sidelines to their songwriting and it was thus clearly a conscious effort from 1973 onwards to forge out a sustainable career as a duo. And at first it was somewhat slow going for their solo LPs - just look at those lowly pop chart placings for the first four Warners releases. They were not selling in the quantities that they would be used to as songwriters, but they were nonetheless a series of beautifully composed and performed records.

Gimme Something Real housed two charting singles in "(I'd Know You) Anywhere" and "Have You Ever Tried It" at #37 and #77 respectively, but in all honesty, any of the nine tracks could have been put out as 45s, as each and every one of them was memorable, and although its hard to pick a stand-out I may have to plump for the lovely and uplifting "Ain't That Good Enough".

I Wanna Be Selfish also contained two fine charting singles: "Main Line" (#37) and "Everybody's Got To Give It Up" (#53). Possibly even better was the lovely orchestrated original of "I Had A Love" with which Ben E. King had a medium sized hit two years later. One or two songs are merely good rather than very good and they render the LP slightly inferior to *Gimme Something Real*, but it's a close run thing.

Puzzlingly, Warners delved back into the first album for the fifth single, "Bend Me", which was another lowly chart entrant (#73) but the next two, "It' ll Come, It' ll Come, It' ll Come" (#96) and the gorgeous and amazingly arranged "Somebody Told A Lie" (#58) both came from *Come As You Are*. Clearly A & S still could not sell singles in significant quantity, but the music remained of the highest quality and two more excellent tracks this time around were "Sell The Car" and "Believe In Me".

By now it was 1977 and therefore hard to ignore disco (although A & S had pretty much done so thus far) so their records did start to speed up with the excellent "Tried, Tested And Found True" and "Over And Over" both charging along; they also both charted, at #52 and #39 respectively; but "So So Satisfied", a slow and soothing and truncated version of the next LP's title cut did even better at #27. It was another set were virtually anything would have made a decent single, not least "Maybe I Can Find It", with a typically strong chorus.

Send It 1977 Warner Brothers BS 3088 Producers: Ashford & Simpson (Billboard soul charts soul charts: 10 ; Billboard pop charts: 52)

Is It Still Good To Ya 1978 Warner Brothers BSK 3219 Producers: Ashford & Simpson (Billboard soul charts: 1 ; Billboard pop charts: 20)

Stay Free 1979 Warner Brothers HS 3357 Producers: Ashford & Simpson (Billboard soul charts soul charts: 3 ; Billboard pop charts: 23)

A Musical Affair 1980 Warner Brothers HS 3458 Producers: Ashford & Simpson (Billboard soul charts soul charts: 8 ; Billboard pop charts: 38)

Performance 1981 Warner Brothers 2WB 3524 Producers: Ashford & Simpson (Billboard soul charts soul charts: 45 ; Billboard pop charts: 125)

Finally, with the luxurious title track from *Send It* (a #15 soul hit) A & S started to sell respectable numbers of records with both single and LP attaining decent chart placings. There was no obvious reason why they suddenly started to register with a greater audience although there was marginally more snap to their productions from here on in. The out and out funky "Don't Cost You Nothing" did even better as a 45 at #10 and while "By Way Of Love's Express" had to settle for only #35, it just might have been the best of the three. Considering *Send It* also housed another lovely ballad in "Love Let Use Me" and the original of Collins and Collins revered "At The Top Of The Stairs" it should it be clear that it is a set of rare quality.

The duo continued their upward momentum with *Is It Still Good To Ya* which went gold (as indeed had *Send It*) as well as all the way to #1 on the soul charts. This may be a good time to make a comment on Ashford's voice, as it is generally recognised that he didn't have the vocal talent of his wife, and I would concur, but just listen to his passion on the last minute of the great title track (a #12 soul single) - I would cite this as one of the most moving and heartfelt vocals ever recorded. Interesting too, to note that, despite the lack of "blackness" that some felt was characteristic of A & S (I'll return to this subject), how little they meant to a pop audience. The majestic "It Seems To Hang On" became a #2 soul single but couldn't even crack the Hot 100.

Finally, with "Found A Cure" Ashford and Simpson placed a single on the Pop Top 50, the first time they had ever managed to do so but its rather paltry #36 position contrasted poorly with #3 on the soul charts. The song was very much the acceptable face of disco (it was highly danceable) and as A & S always used such excellent musicians it is equally good to listen to; In fact, it is hard to think of any other act who adjusted so impressively to the "disco era". Their records, if anything, got even better from what was already a particularly high benchmark and I can't think of anyone else who managed that particular trick. It was the stand-out track on the consistent *Stay Free* set, from which "Nobody Knows" became their 18th soul charting single.

A Musical Affair incorporated three more soul charting singles, of which the best and most successful was "Love Don't Always Make It Right" (#6). There weren't many slow tracks on Ashford and Simpson LPs in these days, but strong choruses and verses were never in short supply.

With the double LP *Performance* Ashford and Simpson succumbed to the temptation to make a live album, but at least there were a few new studio songs on view, and one, "It Shows In The Eyes", became a rather disappointing soul hit at only #34, and this might be because it doesn't appear as if Valerie Simpson is singing it. Good song, but why did she sound so different?

We'd Like You To Meet 1982 Capitol SPRO 9769 / 9770

Street Opera 1982 Capitol ST 12207 Producers: Ashford & Simpson (Billboard soul charts soul charts: 5 ; Billboard pop charts: 45)

High Rise 1983 Capitol ST 12282 Producers: Ashford & Simpson (Billboard soul charts: 14 ; Billboard pop charts: 84)

Solid 1984 Capitol ST 12366 Producers: Ashford & Simpson (Billboard soul charts: 1 ; Billboard pop charts: 29)

Real Love 1986 Capitol ST 12469 Producers: Ashford & Simpson (Billboard soul charts soul charts: 12 ; Billboard pop charts: 74)

Love Or Physical 1989 Capitol C1 46946 Producers: Ashford & Simpson, David Frank & Mic Murphy (Billboard soul charts soul charts: 28 ; Billboard pop charts: 135)

After nearly ten years with Warners, Ashford and Simpson moved to Capitol with - initially - little diminution in artistic or commercial success, and "Street Opera" was both a top ten single and top ten album on the soul charts. The set also marked a move away from the more overt dance material that had characterised their music over the previous couple of years and the title track, "Love It Away" (a #20 single) and the wonderful "I'll Take The World On" could have appeared on those early Warner Brothers releases.

On the other hand, not much on *High Rise* could have, and this was the first time I ever felt indifferent to an Ashford and Simpson LP and "It's Much Deeper" was the first of their sides I actively disliked. 1983, you see, a bad year for soul, and the harder edged musical backing was not at all to my taste. Thanks then for "My Kinda Pick Me Up", the best thing on the set and one which maintained their normal quality.

A last hurrah arrived with the glorious "Solid", a #1 single (and #12 pop, easily their biggest ever hit) and album on the soul charts. In fact, it was their fourth gold album, a milestone it shared with *Send it, Is It Still Good To You* and *Stay Free.* Unfortunately it was the first set on which the accursed Linn drum appeared and it did not do cuts like "Babies" and "Outta The World" any favours.

Real Love was another huge disappointment with the programming on too many tracks snuffing out the delicacy of the compositions, a process that went even further on *Love Or Physical*, on which we find the single example of when they were produced by others ("Comes With The Package" by Frank and Murphy) and I really wish they hadn't bothered. However, because nothing can completely subdue Ashford and Simpson a track like "I'll Be There For You" (a #2 soul single) from the latter album was still better than pretty much anything else that came out in 1989.

There were no more LPs - strangely, no "Greatest Hits" or "Best Ofs" ever appeared on vinyl, if we ignore the *We'd Like You To Meet* promo - but a new CD arrived in 1996 before Nick Ashford's death in 2011 brought a sad end to a marriage and a partnership with the beautiful Valerie Simpson that created some of the greatest music of the twentieth century. It might be difficult for people to remember what rock critics were like back in the seventies and eighties but, believe me, few of them had any time for such a conspicuously middle-class couple as Ashford and Simpson, and, as a result, they have never had the positive critical acclaim as Marvin Gaye, Curtis Mayfield, Isaac Hayes and James Brown but this is simply a foolish prejudice; one doesn't need "authenticity" or "edge" to be important. Ashford and Simpson were brilliant.

A Taste Of Honey

Donald Johnson; Janice Marie Johnson; Hazel Payne; Perry Kibble

A Taste Of Honey 1978 Capitol ST 11754 Producers: Fonce Mizell & Larry Mizell (Billboard soul charts: 2; Billboard pop charts: 6)

Another Taste 1979 Capitol SOO 11951 Producers: Fonce Mizell, Larry Mizell & A Taste Of Honey (Billboard soul charts: 26; Billboard pop charts: 59)

Twice As Sweet 1980 Capitol ST 12089 Producer: George Duke (Billboard soul charts: 12; Billboard pop charts: 36)

Ladies Of The Eighties 1982 Capitol ST 12173 Producers: Al McKay, Ronald LaPread, Janice Marie Johnson & Hazel Payne (Billboard soul charts: 14; Billboard pop charts: 73)

Golden Honey 1984 Capitol ST-12354

"Boogie Oogie Oogie" was played everywhere in 1978 and you couldn't avoid it; it drove me slightly mad, to be honest, but does sound better today, in fact better than virtually everything else recorded by the short-lived but successful A Taste Of Honey.

If there was anything unusual and marketable about the original quartet, it would have been the fact that Janice Johnson played bass and Hazel Payne, guitar. Whether this was a factor in helping to guide both debut single and album to platinum status I cannot recall, but it was indisputably a most impressive start to a recording career. There is little on the first LP, apart from possibly "You're In Good Hands" and the hit single, to retain the interest of a soul fan in 2016 and the weakness of the material was summed up by the fact that the follow-up 45, "Distant", didn't even chart while a third single, the quite dreadful "Disco Dancin'" could only manage to reach #69 on the soul listings, a remarkable piece of inept strategy of how to build on a million seller.

Another Taste was also beset by weak material and although "Do It Good" managed to attain #13 on the soul charts, "Race" failed to do anything. It was a good thing that sales of the LP were respectable.

Two singles, "Rescue Me" (not the Fontella Bass hit) and "I'm Talkin' Bout You", had been pulled from *Twice As Sweet* in 1980 to limited acclaim (#16 and #64 respectively on the soul charts) before a third 45, "Sukiyaki", became their second 45 to reach the soul summit as well as #3 pop. It was an old Japanese song, and thus a rather odd choice to cover, and it's success was rather baffling, particularly as it lacks any soul. By now A Taste Of Honey were down to a duo, with Donald Johnson and Perry Kibble having departed.

Ladies Of The Eighties was the fourth and final LP, on which they finally got to cover a good song in Smokey Robinson's "I'll Try Something New", which did get to #9 soul and #41 pop. It's certainly my favourite of all their records, but there was nothing else on board to entice me.

Golden Honey was a "Greatest Hits" collection from 1984, and to be fair, five records on the soul top twenty was not a bad return, the year in which A Taste Of Honey broke up and Janice Marie Johnson went on to a brief solo career, cutting an LP for Capitol, also in 1984.

Atkins

Ronald Atkins; Shirley Atkins; Rancella Atkins; Reliant Atkins; Stinal Atkins

Atkins 1982 Warner Brothers BSK3659 Producer: Freddie Perren

Atkins were a quintet of brothers and sisters from California who had a remarkably short-lived career. Their one album displayed a good but pretty standard line in dance grooves - "Feel It, Don't Fight It" made it to #79 on the soul charts and is much better than average of its type - but they also didn't neglect ballads which sounded as if the Stylistics had been an early influence. This side of the group will be too twee and soft for many but I like it and the splendid "Do You Have A Friend" and "Baby You're The One" could have come out in 1972, the heyday of the orchestrated soul ballad. They deserved to have recorded much more but *Atkins* (and its singles) was all there was.

Ben Atkins

Patchouli 1971 Enterprise ENS-1021 Producers: Bobby Manuel & Duck Dunn.

Ben Atkins was a "blue-eyed" soul singer, entirely convincing on his 1967 and 1968 singles, "I'll Step Aside" and "Love Is A Beautiful Thing" respectively. He recorded this LP in 1971, which must win some award for the most misguided sleeve design in history. Quite why Enterprise thought photographing Atkins sitting on an outhouse toilet was going to attract record buyers will doubtless remain a mystery. The record is also very disappointing from a purely soul point of view, as apart from "Cross My Mind" and "Holding On To Friends", it is a rock/pop LP. Given Dan Penn, Roger Hawkins, Barry Beckett, Jimmy Johnson, David Hood, Bettye Crutcher, Duck Dunn, Bobby Manuel, Carson Whitsett and Al Jackson are all listed in the credits one might have hoped for an Eddie Hinton style masterpiece but that's not what we get.

He continued to record a few singles of mixed quality throughout the remainder of the seventies, including another superb soul side in "Baby Now That I've Found You". He died in 2013.

Sweet Pea Atkinson

Don't Walk Away 1982 Island / Ze 90007 Producers: Don Was, David Was & Jack Tann

Sweet Pea Atkinson is a fine artist, probably better known as a session singer and member of Was (Not Was). Sadly he gets overwhelmed by the insensitive production on his one solo LP. Just listen to "Should I Wait" where excellent singing and the typically inventive string arrangement by Paul Riser are both sacrificed on the altar of the horribly intrusive Linn drum. The best tracks on the album are a spirited version of General Johnson's "Don't Walk Away" and a short and sweet rendering of The Tymes "So Much In Love". Much of the rest is unlistenable. I can see that Don Was is talented and that "Girls Fall For Me" is a sharp song. I just don't want to ever have to listen to it again, and for my money, Atkinson's best work is to be found on the marvellous 2004 CD by Pat Boyack.

Atlantic Starr (see also Newban)

Wayne Lewis; David Lewis; Jonathan Lewis; Sharon Bryant; Clifford Archer; Porter Carroll; Barbara Weathers; Porscha Martin; Joseph Phillips; Damon Rentie; William Sudderth; Koran Daniels; Joey Phillips; Barbara Weathers

Atlantic Starr 1978 A & M 4711 Producer: Bobby Eli (Billboard soul charts: 21 ; Billboard pop charts: 67)

Straight To The Point 1979 A & M 4764 Producer: Bobby Eli (Billboard soul charts: 65 ; Billboard pop charts: 142)

Radiant 1981 A & M 4833 Producer: James Carmichael (Billboard soul charts: 5 ; Billboard pop charts: 47)

Brilliance 1982 A & M 4883 Producer: James Carmichael (Billboard soul charts: 1 ; Billboard pop charts: 18)

Yours Forever 1983 A & M 4948 Producer: James Carmichael (Billboard soul charts: 10 ; Billboard pop charts: 91)

Atlantic Starr were one of the biggest soul groups for a period of nearly ten years which was some achievement, and in that time, they exhibited a series of different styles which was smart as it kept them in the public eye before people got too bored. Before they became Atlantic Starr, however, a number of the band cut two LPs under the name of Newban, which, given they came out on the tax write-off Guinness label, meant they were guaranteed for obscurity.

The debut under the new name was pretty impressive and sold encouragingly. It was also democratic in that it featured no fewer than four of the group taking lead vocal duties - the best of whom was Sharon Bryant. The funk tracks stay (sometimes, only just) on the right side of cliché and the slower material has echoes of Philadelphia, doubtless the influence of producer Eli. "Stand Up" (funk) and "Keep It Comin'" (ballad) were the fine and well-selling singles but "(I'll Never Miss) The Love I Never Had" and "With Your Love I Come Alive" have also nicely withstood the test of time.

The follow-up, *Straight To The Point,* was a real step backwards, however, consisting of a poor collection of tracks apart from the final two, "Fallin' In Love With You" and "Losin' You", but they couldn't compensate for the dreadful memory of too much of what had come before and Eli was jettisoned as producer. "(Let's) Rock 'N' Roll" was a #46 soul chart entrant, but "Kissin' Power" failed completely.

James Anthony Carmichael - a highly respected, experienced and talented arranger and producer - was drafted in and it proved to be a great move as he delivered the three finest LPs of Atlantic Starr's career. One of Carmichael's best decisions was to bring in songs from the great Sam Dees, two of which, "Am I Dreaming" and "Send For Me" (#16 soul as a 45), featured on "Radiant". His other winning strategy was to employ Sharon Bryant on many more tracks than had hitherto been the case as she was obviously a gifted and charismatic lead singer and "When Love Calls" (a #5 soul single), "Does It Matter" and, especially, "My Turn Now" were all good showcases for her.

The next LP, *Brilliance* (an apt title), was possibly even better due particularly to the uplifting #2 soul hit "Circles" (a wholly convincing dance record on which Bryant was superb), "Let's Get Closer" and the majestic Dees' song, "Your Love Finally Ran Out". "Love Me Down" and "Perfect Love" were two further good 45s from the set and did ok at #14 and #32 respectively. The LP had a strong claim to be the finest from any soul group act in 1982.

Carmichael then delivered a hat-trick with *Yours Forever,* which was also excellent. "More More More" was the Dees song this time around (and a #11 soul hit single) and I shall never forget hearing it playing in a cab when I visited New Orleans on my first ever USA visit in 1984. "Touch A Four Leaf Clover", with another captivating performance from Bryant, became their second biggest hit to date at #4 soul. "Second To None" was a third single, and its lowly position of only #50 is no indication of lack of quality.

As The Band Turns 1985 A & M 5019 Producers: Wayne Lewis, David Lewis, Joey Gallo, Calvin Harris & Wardell Potts (Billboard soul charts: 3 ; Billboard pop charts: 17)

Secret Lovers…The Best Of Atlantic Starr 1986 A & M SP-5141

Budweiser Concert Hour 1986 Westwood One BC 86-26

All In The Name Of Love 1987 Warner 25560 Producers: David Lewis & Wayne Lewis (Billboard soul charts: 4 ; Billboard pop charts: 18)

We're Movin' Up 1989 Warner 25849 Producers: David Lewis & Wayne Lewis (Billboard soul charts: 26; Billboard pop charts: 125)

Love Crazy 1991 Reprise 7599-26545-1 Producers: David Lewis, Wayne Lewis & Daniel Sembello (Billboard soul charts: 25; Billboard pop charts: 134) (Europe)

Everything then changed with the release of *As The Band Turns* (which stayed on the album charts for 18 months and went gold) as both Carmichael and Bryant left, the latter for a solo career which, strangely, took a few years to take off. (Drummer Porter Carroll had also departed by this time and he put out a decent album in 1986.) It's also a piece of work that perfectly sums up my alienation from the way in which soul music was developing as, despite its huge success, and apart from "If Your Heart Isn't In It" and "Silver Shadow", I find it depressing listening. Barbara Weathers had taken over from Bryant and she was the reason why I like the two songs named above but nothing could redeem the terrible "Freak-A-Ristic" - but this was doubtless my problem as it reached #6 on the soul charts - or "Cool, Calm and Collected" which reduced Atlantic Starr to sounding the same as so many other faceless bands.

A *Best Of* and *Live* set appeared before a second gold LP arrived and *All In The Name Of Love* was even weaker than the first to these ears: "Always" was a massive hit, #1 on both soul and pop charts, but is a schmaltzy thing of little merit. The title track (a #51 single) was pretty good, though, as it had a definite feel of Carmichael-era Atlantic Starr but just when you think things may have been getting better a track like "One Lover At A Time" came along. Others liked it just fine though as it went to #10 on the soul charts, and the set was milked for a fourth 45, "Thankful", but it could only manage #65 soul.

By the time *We're Movin' Up* appeared interest was gradually drifting away from the group as it was their lowest charting LP since *Straight To The Point* ten years before. However, it did produce their second saccharine #1 soul single in "My First Love" (which, interestingly didn't even make the top 100 on the pop chart). It was not a bad album, with an emphasis on slower material, but compare the songs to those they had received in the past from Sam Dees to see what they had lost.

Love Crazy, which I have not heard, only came out as an LP in Europe remaining as a CD in the U.S. It contained three more soul chart singles, bringing their total up to 26, and there were more CDs to come as the nineties progressed.

Aura (1)

Aura 1979 Fusion Music FMI 1004 Producer: Gary Shimabukuko

Many sub-genres within soul music have had an "underground" tag from time to time. One such strand retains it to this day: soul from Hawaii. There will be a few examples within the book, and I can assure anyone that they barely made it out of the islands, and certainly I have never seen a single one in any of the shops I have frequented over the years.

Aura were a band comprised of, I believe, eight Mendoza siblings, Beverly, Dennis, Brian, Del, Christine, Clifton, Michael and Vincent, but I am unsure exactly which of them featured on their one album. The tracks I have heard are good enough, pretty funky with a fine brass section, but there is nothing to differentiate the sound from similar records coming out of Florida, California or indeed anywhere else in the States.

Aura (2)

Paulette Collins; Eddie Weiss; Robin Kutulas; Rick Kutulas; Cobe Haskell; Al Taylor; Jeff Ervin; Jean Hintermann

Aura 1977 Chakira CH 001 Producers: Eddie Weiss & Reggi Weiss

It might seem unlikely that two soul bands would share this name, but the above are an entirely separate outfit from the one in Hawaii. This Aura (out of San Francisco) feature rather strident, rock-influenced uptempo numbers which are not really my cup of tea and indeed tracks such as "Don't You Worry" and "Skyrocket" have little to do with soul music. The funky "You Got Something" and "Sativa" and the slower "Trying To Hold It Down" are more palatable. The album has many admirers and is apparently held up as a "Psych-funk classic". Lead singer Paulette Collins still performs today with The Taylor P Collins Band.

Aurra / Déjà (see also Slave)

Starleana Young; Curt Jones; Mysti Day; Steve Washington; Mark Adams; Steve Arrington; Charles Carter; Philip Fields; Jennifer Ivory; Tom Lockett; William Young; Mike Young; Buddy Hankerson

Aurra 1980 Dream DA3503 Producers: Steve Washington, Charles Carter & Tom Lockett

Send Your Love 1981 Salsoul SA 8538 Producer: Steve Washington (Billboard soul charts: 22 ; Billboard pop charts: 103)

A Little Love 1982 Salsoul SA 8551 Producer: Steve Washington (Billboard soul charts: 12 ; Billboard pop charts: 38)

Live And Let Live 1983 Salsoul SA 8559 Producer: Steve Washington (Billboard soul charts: 36 ; Billboard pop charts: 208)

Bedtime Story 1985 Next Plateau NPS1001 Producers: Starleana Young, Curt Jones, Eban Kelly & Jimi Randolph

Dayton, Ohio's Aurra have a pretty interesting history, too convoluted and time consuming to go into here, but it has echoes of the New Birth story. Cutting it very short, Steve Washington put Aurra together with Starleana Young and Curt Jones as the featured singers. All three came out of Slave.
  "In The Mood (To Groove)" was a lyrically challenged side of slender merit that got no higher than #86 on the soul charts in 1980, and on the strength of it, or an album cut like "When I Come Home", one couldn't have guessed that Aurra (or Déjà as they were to become) would go on to record seven LPs. Both sides were housed on *Aurra,* a six tracker with impressive bass playing from Buddy Hankerson but little else to commend it.
  Things improved slightly with *Send Your Love* as the music was better and "Are You Single" had enough drive and presence to reach #16 on the soul charts in spring 1981. "Forever" was a fair ballad and "Kingston Lady" marginally better than the title suggested, but the LP still lacked material of any true distinction.
  Released right at the end of 1981, "Make Up Your Mind" was the only genuine hit the group ever enjoyed under the name of Aurra, at #6 soul and #71 pop. It was the best cut on *A Little Love,* another I'm struggling to say anything particularly nice about. As with the previous two, there was little that was truly poor, just equally little that was inspired.
  If I was indifferent to the first three albums, then I'm actively disinclined to listen to the rest based on the brief snippets I have heard. A couple more charting singles, "Baby Love" and "Such A Feeling", sat on the *Live And Let Live* LP, but *Bedtime Story* (entitled *Like I Like It* in the U.K.) had no hits within at all.

Serious 1987 Virgin 90601 Producer: Monte Moir (Billboard soul charts: 27 ; Billboard pop charts: 186)

Made To Be Together 1988 Virgin 91060 Producers: Teddy Riley & Gene Griffin (Billboard soul charts: 96)

By the time of *Bedtime Story* Aurra were down to a duo of Starleana Young and Curt Jones and they made the decision to change their name to Déjà. It was a good one as a single from the *Serious* LP, "You And Me Tonight" went to #2 on the soul charts and #54 pop, a bigger hit than any cut by Aurra, On the second Déjà album Mysti Day had replaced the solo-bound Young and the new duo enjoyed two more reasonable hits from it. Both sets are pretty heavy going for anyone brought up on sixties soul music. In 2013 a new CD appeared under the name of Aurra.

Donald Austin

Crazy Legs 1973 Eastbound EB9005 Producers: Woody Wilson, Donald Austin & Bernie Mendelson

The fine title track of the one and only LP from guitarist Donald Austin should not be confused with the even better record of the same title by Albert Washington as they are entirely different compositions. Not much appears to be known about Austin other than he is from Detroit. The LP itself is entirely instrumental but is sparse and funky and deserves its in-demand status. His version of Funkadelic's "Can't Stand The Strain", as with the original, has an intro highly similar to that on "Sweet Home Alabama". I wonder which song came first? Both were recorded in 1973.

Geno Austin

Come Back Tomorrow Night And Try It Again 1982 Jasmine GA-1180 Producer: Geno Austin

Good-Bye My Love 1987 Jasmine 108 Producer: J James Jarrett

In 2008 Geno Austin released a CD that included re-cuts (I think, I haven't heard all of the originals) of six of the eight tracks on this little known West Coast LP, showing that he obviously believed in them. His new style is a mix of soul, country and blues but on the LP it seems as if he was aiming more at the dance floor as "Boogie Skating" proves.
  He cut a second LP in 1987 but none of these songs appear on the CD. The slow "Lonely Man" doesn't sound like a recording from that year, making me think he may have sat on it for a while. On the other hand, everything else does and the tracks range from the sedate but pop-influenced "Just One Kiss" to the more danceable "Breach Of Contract".

Baby Brother

Arthur Williams; Ricky Ward; Gary Strothers; Karl Cousin; James McNeal; David Paige; Ronald Hardy

Baby Brother 1981 Cotillion SD5225 Producer: Rick Hall

This LP was recorded in Muscle Shoals and sounds a million miles away from what Rick Hall was producing in the "golden age" at that studio. It is all rather nondescript I'm afraid and one tries in vain to hear anything that would distinguish its having been cut in the south as opposed to anywhere else. Even the normally unimpeachable Tommy Tate fails to deliver with his one song on here, "You Asked For It (You Got It)". Cotillion tried to break the band with two singles being pulled from the LP but both stalled and Baby Brother were never heard of again.

Baby Huey

The Baby Huey Story / The Living Legend 1971 Curtom 8007 Producer: Curtis Mayfield (Billboard soul charts: 38 ; Billboard pop charts: 214)

One of the most "in your face" soul LPs I have ever heard, there is palpable commitment on show, ranging from Baby Huey's effusive vocals to the magnificently aggressive horns on "Listen To Me" and the singular take on "A Change Is Gonna Come". While I applaud such an approach, I'm not sure it all works. "California Dreamin" is a waste of time and I don't really care for his reading of "Change" when compared to the dignity of many better versions. I'm also a bit leery of the "living legend" approach which seems a bit rich for someone who recorded so little, although I do appreciate that it was based on his stage shows. There are two classic cuts though that make the LP worthwhile: a great take on "Hard Times", a Mayfield song which Curtis was also to later record and the aforementioned "Listen To Me" which is a brilliant way to start an LP.

This enormous man (real name: James Ramey, and he weighed around 350 lbs) sadly died in 1970 before the record was even released. It came out as only credited to "Baby Huey" but singles were attributed to "Baby Huey and the Babysitters" and so I'd like to try and list those Babysitters who I think played on the LP: Melvin Jones, Othello Anderson, Rene Smith, Byron Watkins, Rick Marcotte, Alton Littles, Dan O'Neil, Dan Alffando, Plato Jones, Jack Reene, Philip Henry and David Cook.

Backlash

Backlash 1981 Strata Sphere 1001 Producer: E Ennis

Here's an album about which I know almost precisely nothing other than it came out in 1981 on a small Washington label and is so obscure that it wasn't even blessed with a proper cover, merely a plain white sleeve. It therefore follows that I do not know who comprised Backlash and the one track I have heard, "Hang With The Gang", is entirely routine funk.

1619 Bad Ass Band

Kalid Abdul Shaheid (aka Lee Khalid); Carl Harris; Phyllis Harris; Ogden Lee

1619 Bad Ass Band 1976 TSG 801 No producer listed

As this record came out on the New York based "tax scam" label TSG it is in great demand and all records on this label cost a lot of money nowadays assuming they can even be tracked down. That doesn't mean to say it is particularly good, though, and I would argue that there were countless better LPs than this one released in 1976. Having said that, it does straddle the right side of the soul/disco divide and the vocals are strong. Because of its obscurity I am not 100% sure about the band members, either, or even if there WERE any band members at all. (It appeared again, with a different cover but the same track listing on Graham International GIR-1980 in 1978.)

Perk Badger

The Mighty Perk Badger 198? Universal Love Sound Records ULSR 1300 Producer: Perk Badger

This is another exceptionally rare LP. Perk Badger aka Pearstine Badger or Mr. Percolator from South Carolina was an obscure but reasonably prolific artist putting out singles on small Miami labels in the sixties but none even came close to being successful, and therefore it was amazing to hear about the existence of this LP which I, like virtually everyone else in the world, have never been fortunate enough to hear. He was a talented singer so hopefully it maintained the quality of his other releases. He passed away in 1996.

Arlene Bailey

I Got My Game Plan Working Baby 1987 AGB 10-3-7517 Producers: Arlene Bailey & George Bailey

This LP came out of Boston but Arlene Bailey had earlier recorded a couple of songs that were released on Chicago labels, including a version of Ashford and Simpson's "Ain't That Something". She had a soft breathy voice and I suspect she may have seen herself as a jazz rather than a soul singer although the album is without doubt in scope for this book. The "Let's Stay In Love" track sounds as if it was probably cut years earlier than, say, the title song.

J. R. Bailey

Just Me 'N' You 1974 MAM 9 Producers: J.R. Bailey, Ken Williams, Jerome Gasper & Mel Kent

Love & Conversation 1977 United Artists LA815-G Producer: Buddy Scott

James Ralph Bailey had a distinguished musical career before he passed away in 1980. He was once a member of The Cadillacs but I think his real strength lay in songwriting, often in collaboration with Johnny Northern, Ken Williams or Rudy Clark. He also recorded a number of solo singles in the sixties, although only one, "Love Won't Wear Off", was any kind of a hit.

Just Me 'N' You is a deeply revered record, particularly in the UK and so I will doubtless upset many by saying that I have always found it to be somewhat overrated, featuring some rather watery Marvin Gaye soundalike tracks like "After Hours" and "Heaven On Earth". I do like "All Strung Out Over You" and would certainly not call the LP in any way poor or sub-standard but I will leave it to others to extol its virtues. (It would have helped had a really good record he recorded around the same time, "Too Far Gone To Turn Around", been included on the album). Three tracks from it, "Love Love Love", the aforementioned "After Hours" and "Everything I Want I See In You" all reached the soul charts as singles.

Another 45, a rather bizarre version of Scott Joplin's "The Entertainer (If They Could Only See Me Now)", was a small soul hit (#77) in 1975 and it set the tone for his second and final set, which was also a little peculiar.

Peculiar in as much as *Love and Conversation* cedes control to Buddy Scott and Phil Medley who produced, arranged, conducted and wrote all the songs bar one: Bailey's self-written "That's Love". I suspect the LP was released as some sort of contractual requirement on someone's behalf, as certainly neither Bailey nor UA seemed to believe in it, given that no singles emerged. Stylistically, it must have cost a fortune to record, so copious are the arrangements and production, but only "That's Love" and "Stella By Starlight" wouldn't have sounded out of place *Just Me 'N' You*. The rest is much more in a "sophisticated" bag, with "Live Love And Play" and "A Million To One" having little to do with soul music, while "The Coming Of Your love" is based on "The Battle Hymn Of The Republic". As I said, all a little eccentric.

Philip Bailey (see also Earth, Wind & Fire)

Continuation 1983 Columbia 38725 Producer: George Duke (Billboard soul charts: 19 ; Billboard pop charts: 71)

Chinese Wall 1984 Columbia 39542 Producer: Phil Collins (Billboard soul charts: 10 ; Billboard pop charts: 22)

The Wonders Of His Love 1984 Myrrh 701 6796 06x Producer: Philip Bailey

Triumph 1986 Myrrh 701 6834 069 Producers: George Duke, Jerry Peters & Philip Bailey

Inside Out 1986 Columbia 40209 Producers: Nile Rodgers & Philip Bailey (Billboard soul charts: 30 ; Billboard pop charts: 84)

Family Affair 1989 Myrrh 701 6877 612 Producers: Oliver Wells & Philip Bailey

Philip Bailey has enjoyed an impressive career, in which he has worn a number of hats: member of Earth, Wind & Fire during their glory years, excellent singer, gifted writer, performer of a massive selling single, "Easy Lover", with Phil Collins, creator of a number of well selling gospel records, winner of several Grammys and even, I believe, a sideline as an actor. His place in soul music history is thus thoroughly assured but did he make good solo records? Yes and no, in my book. His best track is a superb version of "Children Of The Ghetto" (written by the Amoo brothers from the UK soul band, The Real Thing and tucked away as a b-side to "Photogenic Memory") which was used to great effect in the film, *Clockers*, and "For Every Heart That's Been Broken" is mighty decent, too. Both can be found on *Chinese Wall.* On the other hand, so can "Easy Lover" which, despite its success, is a very irritating pop record.

On the gospel front the Leonard Caston written "God Is Love" from *The Wonders Of His Love* is excellent too, and notable for the fact that Bailey sings it in a much lower register than we are used to hearing from him. "I Will No Wise Cast You Out" from the same LP is also well worth hearing as is "All Soldiers" from *Triumph*.

Phylliss Bailey

Phylliss 1978 Americom S-6380 Producers: Marlo Anderson & Marvin Lewis

I know virtually nothing about this record (which I have reason to believe IS a soul outing) apart from the fact it is extremely rare, was recorded on the West Coast, and sells for a lot of money.

LaVern Baker

Let Me Belong To You 1970 Brunswick BL 754160 Producer: Carl Davis

This is where the book becomes difficult. LaVern Baker (who died in 1997) was undoubtedly a great black music singer, and hugely popular and successful in the fifties, scoring any number of hits. But when did what she record become "soul"?

It is therefore a purely personal and subjective assertion that she hadn't really moved into the soul era with any of her Atlantic sides. Even the later LPs like *See See Rider* from 1963 still sounded much like her great hits of the fifties (which were definitely "pre-soul") and so I am only including her LP on Brunswick from 1970 and ignoring the seven she recorded earlier. But even here LaVern couldn't be unshackled from her past. From a distance of forty plus years it is a nice LP to listen to, but, frankly, the stand-out cut "I'm The One To Do It" apart, it sounds dated compared with virtually everything else that was "hot" in 1970 and one has to wonder why Brunswick thought it would sell. Unsurprisingly, it didn't and it was to be twenty years before she recorded again.

Randolph Baker

Reaching For The Stars 1982 J & R JR-0001 Producer: Jim Erickson

Another highly obscure record, which mixes together rather functional elements of disco, funk and jazz. What makes it worthy of consideration is the fine Eddie Kendricks styled vocalist on "Getting Next To You". Is this Randolph?

Sam Baker

Sometimes You Have To Cry 1977 Seventy-Seven 77-108 Producer: John Richbourg

Bringing You Some Soul 1986 Charly CRB1137 (UK)

Sam Baker was born in Jackson, Mississippi, and recorded around twenty singles from 1960 until the end of the decade, including at the key Memphis locations of Stax and American. Despite most of them being thoroughly appealing and soulful, not a single one was any kind of a national hit.

These are two marvellous LPs which, unfortunately, brought no initial benefit to Sam Baker seeing as how they both appeared after he had finished recording. Nevertheless, they are important in helping to ensure that he will be more than a mere footnote in history as they are essential southern soul of the highest quality, and despite a fair bit of track duplication across the records, there are enough differences to ensure that anyone who loves this kind of music would wish to own both.

As with most artists, there are a few mundane tracks - his up-tempo records are not a patch on his slower ones - but the good easily outweighs the mediocre. He was a singer of great power and subtlety, best emphasized by his version of "That's All I Want From You" which is even better than Aretha's, "Sometimes You Have To Cry" and "Something Tells Me" (both cut at Stax) and the dead slow "I Love You" and "I Believe In You" (which can each be found on both LPs.) One song that can only be found on the Charly release is "Sugarman" a Kris Kristofferson composition of drug despair, and this is one that should be heard due to its inventive arrangement and sympathetic Baker delivery.

It doesn't appear that he recorded after 1969 and, given his low profile, I am not sure if he is still alive or not.

Ballads

John Foster; Leslie Palmer; Nate Romerson; Rico Thompson; Nate Harris; John John; Arthur Creggett; Stan Harris; Pamela Harris

The Gift Of Love 1968 Venture VTS4004 **Producers: Clarence Paul, Willie Hutch, Jesse Mason & Leon Ware**

Confessin' The Feeling 1980 Vivid Sound VS1023 **Producers: Ray Dobard, Wally Cox, The Ballads & Leroy Jackson (Japan)**

The Venture set was recorded in California but has many echoes of Detroit: Clarence Paul, Stevie Wonder, Micky Stevenson, Holland-Dozier-Holland, Susaye Green, Harvey Fuqua, Morris Broadnax, Marvin Gaye, Johnny Bristol, Leon Ware and soon to be Motown man Willie Hutch wrote 9 of the 12 songs on *The Gift Of Love* while " My Baby Knows How To Love Her Man"" is straight from a Tamla template. There were also distinct echoes of the doo-wop era, particularly noticeable on "Goodnight My Love" and "God Blessed Our Love" (the only single they released which ever reached the soul charts, # 8 in 1968, and also the best track on the LP.) "I Wish I Knew" was later recut by the group but re-titled as "Butterfly" (where Susaye Green lost her writing credits). It is a consistent and good work but possibly lacks a little bit of sparkle in the production which is surprising given the quality of those involved. Certainly their version of "Just A Little Misunderstanding" cannot compare with The Contours rendering, for example, and "Forever" probably loses out to The Marvelettes.

The Japanese only Vivid Sound LP pulls together a collection of singles that came out on such small labels as Balja, Soul Beat, Music City, Kimberly and Happy Fox over a period of a few years and so is somewhat disjointed and I would not like to even hazard a guess as to exactly which singers are involved on each track, but it does prove that the Ballads were a very talented group, even if they didn't always get the best material. Most soul vocal group lovers will derive much pleasure from listening to the LP but nothing, apart from "Confessing A Feeling" (and Tony Owens' version is better in my opinion), really screamed out hit record.

Hank Ballard

A Star In Your Eyes 1964 King K-12-896 No producer listed

You Can't Keep A Good Man Down 1968 King KSD1052 Producer: James Brown

Hanging' With Hank 1976 Stang ST1031 Producers: Harry Ray, Al Goodman & Walter Morris

Hank Ballard was born as John Henry Kendricks in Detroit and joined The Midnighters as their new lead singer in 1953, after which he and they enjoyed huge success in the black market until 1961. However, their popularity waned alarmingly for the next couple of years and in 1964 Ballard was marketed as a solo artist by King for the first time. (Hank Ballard and The Midnighters produced a whole host of great records but as these nearly all occurred back before soul was a recognised musical genre they fall outside the scope of this book and I will therefore only focus on Hank Ballard after he went out alone.)

The first album tended to hedge its bets, as while two of the sides from it appeared on a 45 under Hank's name only, a couple of others had already been released as by "Hank Ballard & The Midnighters". Moreover, the songs remained wedded to the earlier "R 'n' B" sound with which the Midnighters had been so successful, rather than embracing the new "soul" ethos. For example, "Don't Let Temptation (Turn You 'Round)", although a most enjoyable track, sounded as if it had been recorded in 1958 rather than 1964. Anyway, regardless how the LP came across, it failed to revive Ballard's fortunes and neither did a 1965 single, "Do It Zulu Style", (which also sounded dated). It was time for James Brown to take Ballard in hand.

You Can't Keep A Good Man Down unquestionably updated Ballard's music into the soul era; the only problem was that it was also so obviously Brown's, including a number of rhythm tracks that had been used by Mr. Please Please Please in the past. The result of which was to reduce a distinctive performer like Ballard to one who was pretty much anonymous. Let's face it, no-one did James Brown better than James Brown. But who's to say this strategy wasn't to Ballard's taste? After all, it gave him his first hit record in over seven years when "How You Gonna Get Respect" reached #15 on the soul charts in late 1968. I enjoy the album a good deal, thanks to my passion for J.B., but it's not the best example of Hank Ballard's music and falls short of the best of his fifties output.

His association with Brown continued up until 1972 (apart from a fabulous single on Silver Fox, "Sunday Morning Coming Down", in 1970) when "From The Love Side" entered the soul charts in November of that year at # 43 but he had to wait eight years before his next long player, which was notably different in sound. But, ironically, not in approach; Sylvia and Joe Robinson's All Platinum/Stang empire also had a highly distinctive formula as well as recycling backing tracks all the time and Hank was thus once again obliged to sing over rhythms that been heard before. This time there were few redeeming features; three singles from the set failed to sell and a great artist like Hank Ballard had to sing songs called "Hallelujah Disco" and "Have You Been Good To Your Nose?" Mind you, he co-wrote the latter, so maybe he didn't mind.

Not much else happened for Ballard as regards recording after this but he did re-form The Midnighters for live performances. He passed on in 2003.

Band AKA

The Band AKA 1981 PPL PP-9505 Producer: J James Jarrett

Men Of The Music 1983 Bouvier BO-0102 Producer: J James Jarrett

Master Of The Game 1987 Bouvier BO-0110-2 Producer: J James Jarrett ?

So far as I can tell, The Band AKA weren't a band as such, but really a solo vehicle for Jaeson James Jarrett who seemed to do all the producing, arranging, composing and singing. It is stirring stuff, too, as Jarrett seemed to focus on all these things more than merely the beat. In fact, the first two records sound as if they owe much more to the seventies than to the eighties, which, as should be clear by now, or will certainly become clear, is a good thing from my perspective. To single out a couple of tracks that were much loved in the UK: "Grace" (from the debut) is uplifting and positive while "Joy" (from the second LP) sounds like somewhat of a cross between Maze and Atlantic Starr but still sounds fresh. I must confess to not being acquainted with the final LP.

Band Of Thieves

Napoleon Crayton; Donald Breedlove; Wilbur Cole; James Vasquez; Orville Shannon; Jeffrey McGraven; Bill Gaskill; Gary McKeen; Mark Maxwell

Band Of Thieves 1976 Ovation OV-1727 Producers: Crosby Napune, Napoleon Crayton & Donald Breedlove

This most enjoyable, entirely band composed, record out of Minneapolis is something of a "lost classic", seeing as how it must have barely made it out of Minnesota. Band Of Thieves were blessed with an excellent lead singer in Napoleon Crayton and, as he was so good, it is a bit of a mystery why he never turned up anywhere else other than singing gospel and with a capable but short-lived vocal group, The Amazers. The whole album is mid-tempo in pace, luxuriant in sound and full of admirable tracks such as "Love Me Or Leave Me", "Sweet Lady" and the cautionary "City Slicker".

Darrell Banks

Is Here! 1967 Atco SD33-216 Producer: Revilot Record Company

Here To Stay 1969 Volt VOS-6002 Producer: Don Davis

Darrell Eubanks had a sadly short (he was shot to death in 1970) but impeccable career, not recording for long enough to produce any sub-standard work. He also hit first time out, with the dazzling "Open The Door To Your Heart", a record as respected as any in soul music circles in England. It was well-loved in America too, reaching #2 soul and #27 pop in the summer of 1966, and that great blaring intro can never fail to move any soul fan in the world. "Someone (Somewhere) Needs You" with its tremendous rattle of drums was a highly meritorious (and pretty successful) follow-up too, and although both singles came out on Revilot, the LP that housed them, *Darrell Banks Is Here!*, appeared in July 1967 on Atco.

It is an undoubtedly classic album, and one to play to anyone who wants to understand a little bit of what "Northern Soul" is all about. "Angel Baby" and "Our Love (Is In The Pocket)" (a b-side better than 90% of any other a-sides anyone could care to name) almost equal the hits in quality and all are all dazzling examples of that genre at its best. However, Banks is such a tremendous singer that he could also stretch out on heart rending ballads such as "Here Come The Tears" and "I'm Gonna Hang My Head And Cry". In fact, forget the "Northern Soul" bit, just play this LP to anyone who wants to know what soul music is all about. A magnificent record with no weak tracks at all. (The LP states the production as by "The Revilot Record Company" but those responsible were George Clinton, Sidney Barnes, Mike Terry, Don Davis and LeBaron Taylor).

After such a tremendous debut it could be expected that the up would not reach the same heights and it doesn't. However, that is only because the debut was so exceptional, as *Here To Stay* is another superb LP. The Don Davis imprint is clear and slightly cramps Banks' style (e,g "No-One Could Be Blinder" could easily be a Johnnie Taylor track) but this is a minor quibble in the face of great tracks like "My Love Is Reserved", another fabulous deep soul outing, and "Don' t Know What To Do" a lovely illustration of the confusion arising from a broken heart.

Patryce "Chocolate" Banks (see also Graham Central Station)

She's Back And Ready... 1980 T-Electric MCA 3243 Producers: Bruce Gray, Dunn Pearson, Jim Tyrrell & Patryce Banks

Back from vocal duties with Graham Central Station in case you were wondering. Banks sounds a little bit like Deniece Williams on "I'm In Love" and most of her vocals are in that high register. The LP is pretty good - "I Waited For Love" is excellent - but didn't really have enough to lift it out of the pack, and neither did a single she released in 1989, "Keep Lovin' Me".

She doesn't appear to have recorded any more solo records but is obviously multi-talented as she wrote a couple of tracks for Ren Woods' *Azz Izz* LP and has also had a couple of books published.

Ron Banks (see also The Dramatics)

Truly Bad 1983 CBS AL 39148 Producer: Ron Banks (Billboard soul charts: 62)

I've always found the title of this LP to be amusingly apt, though I realise it wasn't meant to be taken in a literal sense. Banks is one of the former lead singers of The Dramatics, one of the greatest of all soul groups, but too much of this LP is frustratingly mediocre and doesn' t play to his strengths: he is one of the finest of falsetto singers. However, all is forgiven by his breathtaking version of "Make It Easy On Yourself" on which he duets with Belita Woods (and she never sang better). Not only do I maintain that this is the best version ever of this great song, and I realise that is saying something when one considers how brilliantly Jerry Butler and Cissy Houston delivered it, but it is one of my favourite sides of all time. The long note he holds at the end of the song is the sort of ineffable moment that makes life worth living. "Let Love Flow" is also nice, and, like "Make It Easy", beautifully arranged, but he could have done so much better.

He released a CD in 1994 with another former Dramatic, L.J. Reynolds, before passing away in 2010.

Rose Banks

Rose 1976 Motown M6-845S1 Producers: Jeffrey Bowen & Hamp "Bubba" Banks

Rose Banks was aka pianist and singer Rose Stone, a member of brother Sly's great group at the time of "Dance To The Music" and was still there for 1974's *Small Talk*. In 1976 she left to go solo, turning up, somewhat surprisingly, on Motown.

In truth her one solo offering wasn't strong enough to have broken out, and also didn't get much of a marketing push from the company. Banks wasn't a particularly distinctive singer (compare her version of "Darling Baby" to those by The Elgins or Jackie Moore) and the songs she had to deal with were pretty nondescript: four of the five songs on side two were written by Eric Robinson and Victor Orsborn and none linger in the mind. "Whole New Thing" reached #50 on the soul charts.

A single turned up in 1980 on Source but since then she appears to have left the music business

Banks & Hampton

Passport To Ecstasy 1977 Warner Brothers BS 2993
Producer: Brad Shapiro

Carl Hampton and Homer Banks were two of the finest songwriters to ever have come out of the sub-genre that is "southern soul"; virtually all the best songs they wrote - often together with Raymond Jackson - which include If Loving You Is Wrong" and "If You're Ready (Come Go With Me)" - were for artists who recorded for Stax and other southern based record labels.

Homer Banks had previously released a few notable singles in his own name but Carl Hampton never followed that route. The biggest disappointment of *Passport To Ecstasy* is that it doesn't include any of the great single sides they also recorded for Warner in 1976, "It's Gotta Be This Way", "Wonderful" and "Caught In The Act (Of Gettin' It On)". Still, it contains a typical Banks/Hampton song in "I'm Gonna Have To Tell Her" (a small soul chart entrant at #80) which is one in a long line of top class cheating tales which they could turn out seemingly at will and a lovely, heartfelt "Believe".The other disappointment is that it simply contains too much filler: "Shake It" and "Get On Up, Shake Some Butt" are totally unworthy of their talent, "Passion And Promises" is just slushy, and the title track sounds as if The Love Unlimited Orchestra were moonlighting down south.

The album was possibly something they simply wanted to do as a one-off, as after this, they once again turned back to writing and producing, notably for Randy Brown. Banks died in 2003.

Richard Barbary

Soul Machine 1968 A & M SP-3010 Producer: Creed Taylor

I'm not sure if there will be many more mysterious singers discussed in the entire book than Richard Barbary. He produced this one LP - which must have been at considerable expense given the array of premium quality session musicians involved and its gatefold sleeve - and then seemed to fade away into obscurity. I've never seen any article about him at all and even Google throws up nothing about him whatsoever. What a shame. The LP is likeable and maybe some sort of minor "lost classic". The first cut, "Poor Side Of Town" is a beautiful - and definitive - delivery of the Johnny Rivers' song with a gorgeous horn arrangement. Nearly all the songs are covers in fact, "Nature Boy", "What's Your Name", "Please Stay" and "Call On Me" are all much loved songs and "Nature Boy" apart, are all handled exceedingly competently.

Sandy Barber

The Best Is Yet To Come 1977 Olde World 7701 Producer: Clyde Otis

Given this LP was produced and almost completely written by Clyde Otis, it is not surprising that it is of a high musical quality. "Don't You Worry Baby" demonstrates that Barber is confident enough in her vocal talent - which is considerable - to pull off the odd Aretha lick, and "Stay Here With Me" proves conclusively that she could also handle slow material. On the downside, the set also contains the execrable "Wonder Woman", but generally it is a most impressive and recommended release. After this, she disappeared from music for years before re-appearing in the late eighties and nineties, although the album's title has yet to become true.

Bar-Kays

Ben Cauley; James Alexander; Jimmy King; Carl Cunningham; Phalon Jones; Ronnie Caldwell; Willie Hall; Vernon Burch; Michael Toles; Ronnie Gordon; Barry Wilkins; Alvin Hunter; Winston Stewart; Harvey Henderson; Charles Allen; Larry Dodson; Lloyd Smith; Michael Beard; Frank Thompson; Roy Cunningham; Mark Bynum; Sherman Guy

Soul Finger 1968 Volt S417 Producer: Booker T Jones

As is reasonably well known, four members of the band - Jimmy King, Carl Cunningham, Phalon Jones and Ronnie Caldwell - died in the same plane crash that killed Otis Redding. I doubt if anyone thought in the immediate aftermath to that dreadful day of December 10th 1967 that the Bar-Kays would re-emerge to become one of the most successful soul bands of all time.

The *Soul Finger* LP was clearly not pushed by Stax/Volt as, despite the title track becoming a massive hit on both the soul and pop charts (#3 and #17), not bad for a band's first ever single, the album didn't chart at all. It is all instrumental (apart from some chanted vocals here and there) and close to what one would expect from listening to a Booker T and M.G.'s offering of the time. Relatively endearing, but hardly essential.

Gotta Groove 1969 Volt VOS-6004 Producer: Allen Jones (Billboard soul charts: 40)

Black Rock 1970 Volt VOS-6011 Producers: Allen Jones, Al Bell & Tom Nixon (Billboard soul charts: 12 ; Billboard pop charts: 90)

Do You See What I See? Volt VOS-8001 1972 Producer: Allen Jones (Billboard soul charts: 45 ; Billboard pop charts: 212)

Coldblooded 1973 Volt VOS-9504 Producer: Allen Jones

Money Talks 1978 Stax 4106 Producers: Allen Jones & Phil Kaffel (Billboard soul charts: 21 ; Billboard pop charts: 72)

Best Of The Bar-Kays 1988 Stax MPS 8542

Gotta Groove was the first LP from the post-1967 and re-constituted Bar-Kays group and started to set in train some of the characteristics of what would follow consistently for years to come: Allen Jones producing and big selling LP success. However, apart from the obviously Sly Stone influenced "Don't Stop Dancing To The Music Part 1", which failed as a 45, most of the tracks are not far removed from those on "Soul Finger" in sound and style.

Black Rock, though, branched out into definite new territory, clearly under the influence of what Funkadelic had been doing up in Detroit, as well as continuing to keep an eager eye on where Sly was going. Much of the record will be anathema to many soul fans and certainly it is as close to rock music as anything else, particularly the opening track, an unrecognisable take on Aretha's "Baby I Love You", which has lengthy guitar solos, time changes etc. that one wouldn' t normally encounter in soul. There are a couple of songs which start off in reasonably straightforward style ("I've Been Trying" and "How Sweet It Would Be" but guitar workouts then break in. Interesting also, that Stax did not release any of the tracks (other than "Montego Bay" as a b-side) on singles; clearly they already saw the group as one whom they hoped to break as album sellers.

The next LP, *Do You See What I See?*, consisted of a number of tracks written by Allen Jones and Harvey Henderson, whereas *Black Rock* had been entirely comprised of songs from outside the group, and saw another slight shift of emphasis, with a somewhat reduced rock influence, in favour of funk and a reflection on the ills of the world. Two "outside" compositions, "I Was Made To Love Her " and "Your Good Thing Is About To Come To An End", were both enjoyably different from the originals. Volt were evidently prepared to lavish money and time on the group given the record's gatefold sleeve, but such expenditure couldn't help two singles "It Ain't Easy" (patently Bill Withers' influenced) and "You're The Best Thing That Ever Happened To Me" become hits.

It may also be worth mentioning that, for a time, there seemed to be almost a separate strategy for the group as regards singles. For instance, between 1969 and 1972 the group put out 13 different sides (both a and b) on single and 8 of these - including the big hit, "Son Of Shaft"(#10 soul) - cannot be found on their LPs, which is a high percentage. I assume it was probably co-incidence, but intriguing nevertheless.

As was becoming somewhat of a pattern, the sound changed again for *Coldblooded*, which placed more conventional songs, rather than musical experimentation, at its core as well as playing up the always enjoyable lead vocals of the flamboyant Larry Dodson. It was by far their best LP to date as a result (and also significantly better than anything than their hero, Sly Stone, was doing at the time) but, sadly, didn't chart at all, although this was much more to do with the problems Stax were having in late 1973.

In 1978, on the revived Stax label, the group had a pretty big hit with the powerful "Holy Ghost", from the *Money Talks* LP which contains tracks recorded from the timeframe of 1972-1975 when they were originally with the label and is without weakness from start to finish. All tracks are strong including a delightful and shameless rip-off in the title track where the group ape both Earth, Wind & Fire AND The Ohio Players (the group certainly never shied away from borrowing from others.)

Too Hot To Stop 1976 Mercury SRM -1-1099 Producer: Allen Jones (Billboard soul charts: 8 ; Billboard pop charts: 69)

Flying High On Your Love 1976 Mercury SRM -1-1181 Producer: Allen Jones (Billboard soul charts: 7 ; Billboard pop charts: 47)

Light Of Life 1978 Mercury SRM -1-3732 Producer: Allen Jones (Billboard soul charts: 15; Billboard pop charts: 86)

Injoy 1979 Mercury SRM -1-3781 Producer: Allen Jones (Billboard soul charts: 2; Billboard pop charts: 35)

After Stax went bankrupt, the Bar-Kays found their way to Mercury, which proved big enough to accommodate them as well as the Ohio Players and both groups did extremely well at the label. The Bar-Kays hit immediately with "Shake Your Rump To The Funk" which became - and remains - only their second single to hit the pop top 30 (at #23) as their uncompromising music ensured that they always meant much more to the soul music audience than they did to most pop music buyers. It was the showpiece to *Too Hot To Stop* which contained more self-written compositions than before (as well as many more Sly homages) although the title track also performed well as a single, reaching #8 on the soul charts.

Flying High On Your Love continued the successful approach of *Too Hot To Stop* and by this time the Bar-Kays sounded nothing like the group who were flirting with rock at the turn of the seventies. "Spellbound" (#29), "Attitudes" (#22) and the title track (#11) were all pulled from the set, and all could not fail to be enjoyed by anyone who liked The Ohio Players.

Light Of Life didn't change the band's sound much, and although "I'll Dance" and "Shine" were the soul chart entries, the best thing on show was the funky as hell "Give It Up" which is one of the few tracks I can think of with syndrums that still sounds good today.

Injoy was the group's most successful LP ever, going gold (as had *Flying High On Your Love*) and "Move Your Boogie Body" was their joint biggest ever hit on the soul charts as well (#3, the same position as "Soul Finger") but perhaps more interesting was the second single, "Today Is Your Day", which did rather less well at only #25. Interesting because it pointed up a long held belief of mine about The Bar-Kays: they didn't do ballads very well, unlike contemporaries Earth, Wind & Fire, Tower of Power and The Ohio Players. No, for my money, this was a band who were at their best being funky, and I can't name a single ballad side of theirs I would unreservedly recommend.

As One 1980 Mercury SRM -1-3844 Producer: Allen Jones (Billboard soul charts: 6; Billboard pop charts: 57)

Nightcruising 1981 Mercury SRM -1-4028 Producer: Allen Jones (Billboard soul charts: 6; Billboard pop charts: 55)

Propositions 1982 Mercury SRM -1-4065 Producer: Allen Jones (Billboard soul charts: 9; Billboard pop charts: 51)

Dangerous 1984 Mercury 422-818478 M1 Producer: Allen Jones (Billboard soul charts: 7; Billboard pop charts: 52)

Banging The Wall 1985 Mercury 422-824727 M1 Producer: Allen Jones (Billboard soul charts: 11 ; Billboard pop charts: 52)

Contagious 1987 Mercury 422-830305 Q1 Producers: Allen Jones & R J Rice (Billboard soul charts: 25 ; Billboard pop charts: 110)

Animal 1989 Mercury 422-836774 Q1 Producers: Trevor Gale, James Mtume, Kenni Hairston & Jerry Goldstein (Billboard soul charts: 36)

Budweiser Concert Hour BC 86-06 1986? No producer listed

"Boogie Body Land" and "Body Fever" were the two funk singles pulled from *As One*, the latter doing much the better, but they were atypical of a set which was more subdued than normal, although this didn't harm the sales at all.

Nightcruising sold impressively too, going gold in fact, and its second track "Hit And Run", became their eighth top ten single. As before, they wore their influences on their sleeve and the second single "Freaky Behaviour", was absurdly close to Rick James' "Super Freak". Other cuts within made it clear that the band had been listening to Cameo, as well.

Propositions was the last Bar-Kays LP I enjoyed (this time around a discernible Prince influence was apparent) and they still served up more effective funk that virtually every other band around, although one still didn't want to listen to the lyrics too closely. For example, "Do It (Let Me See You Shake)" certainly didn't ask any questions in the manner of *Do You See What I See?* all those years before, but it certainly had a effective rhythmic drive, good enough to carry it to #9 on the soul charts.

In 1984 the band scored their biggest ever soul single when "Freakshow On The Dancefloor" reached #2, and although good and tough enough of its kind, it sounds pretty predictable in 2016. It can be found on the *Dangerous* LP, as can be one of their best ever ballads, "Lovers Should Never Fall In Love".

I can't find much to enjoy in their last few albums and towards the end of the eighties the two most significant events for years within the group took place. Firstly, after *Banging The Wall*, bassist James Alexander left the group (although he later returned) after having been a member of the Bar-Kays right back to the "Soul Finger" days and in May 1987 mentor and producer Allen Jones died which meant, obviously, that the last records, were, for the first time in nearly twenty years, produced by someone else. The sound, probably wisely, didn't change significantly, however, and "Struck By You" off *Animal* in 1989 was still recognisable as a Bar-Kays record with a great Dodson vocal.

CDs were to appear in the nineties and noughties, and, because the group were rather one-dimensional and never meant much to the pop world, they have been rather neglected over the years - even U.S. Mercury didn't bother with a "Best Of" during their years of big sales - and while no-one needs to own all their stuff their best work is pretty impressive.

Gloria Barnes

Uptown 1971 Maple 6006 Producer: Johnny Brantley

There is a sub-genre of soul music known as "deep soul". It is much misunderstood and, as often as not, misrepresented, but this LP defines it perfectly for anyone who really wants to know what it is. For a record to be described as true "deep soul" emotion takes precedent over commercial considerations and, frankly, everything else. Take, as evidence, the opening track, "Old Before My Time", which is desperation captured on vinyl and, to the uninitiated, such unfettered pain can be hard to take. Or, alternatively, consider "Home". The lyric is completely positive but the desolate delivery entirely contradicts this; it as if Walker realises only too well that things will end in tears and it is chilling to listen to her have to put herself through the charade of fleeting happiness. Johnny Brantley was a perfect producer for this LP as he had a history of delivering highly uncompromising music and the fact that it sounds muffled and as if it were recorded in a bathroom somewhere is entirely besides the point. The sales for this LP must have been tiny, and the potential audience, even today, to rediscover it would be miniscule but if anyone ever wanted to make a case for "soul" being art, and, as I've already said, it would generally be a pretty weak case, then this LP would have to be a prime exhibit. (She also recorded as Towanda Barnes under which name she delivered some similarly soulful records.)

J J Barnes

Rare Stamps (with Steve Mancha) 1969 Volt VOS6001
Producer: Don Davis

Groovesville Masters 1975 Contempo CLP520 (UK)
Producers: Don Davis & J & J Productions

Detroit's talented James Jay Barnes had a voice which was at the same time both his strength and weakness given how close he sounded to Marvin Gaye. Although he recorded many fine singles in Detroit in the sixties, only one, "Real Humdinger" (#18 soul), was a hit, and he was not especially well represented on LP.

That is not to say that his albums were all poor, as they certainly weren't, but two of them were retrospectives that would have done him little good. The first, *Rare Stamps*, was a shared release with fellow former Groovesville artist Steve Mancha, and although it appeared on Volt, all the ten tracks (five each) were sixties' Detroit recordings. "Baby Please Come Back Home", Barnes' biggest ever hit (#9 soul and #61 pop), was pleasingly included and though all the cuts were strong, they had little in common with most of what else was coming out of Stax at the time, not to mention that the material was over two years old. It was listed as a new release in the August 2nd 1969 issue of *Billboard* but no advertising was taken out, and it fared poorly when compared against the albums of the same name by Johnnie Taylor and Eddie Floyd.

Four of the five Barnes' tracks from *Rare Stamps* also found their way onto a 1975 UK only release with the unambiguous title, *The Groovesville Masters*. The record's appearance was a reflection of the fact that Barnes meant more to an English audience than an American one at this time of his career, and once again, all the tracks have that characteristic smooth yet powerful sound that Don Davis favoured at the time. Its an LP I can recommend without much reservation, but it obviously bears no musical resemblance to any other LPs from 1975, and would not have made Barnes' fortune.

Born Again 1973 Perception PLP-39 Producers: David Jordan & Patrick Adams

Sara Smile 1977 Contempo CLP604 (UK) Producer: Gerry Shury

Sandwiched in between the two Groovesville based releases was a genuine "new" LP from Barnes, but one that sadly did not sell many copies. It also moved him away from Detroit to New York and Philadelphia, and has a much more lush sound as a result, boasting full orchestration he had not enjoyed before. Actually, while it is a good record, I find it to be a bit TOO lush, with Tony Bell's arrangements not quite compensating for the loss of the crispness of the earlier sides, although "You Are Just A Living Doll" (a failed single) is certainly pretty intoxicating.

His last excursion on an LP came out in 1977, recorded a long way from all of his previous records: in London. It wasn't the pinnacle of his career. "The Errol Flynn" was probably the worst record he had ever made and his version of "How Long" wasn't a patch on the original by Ace. (To be scrupulously fair it did contain a really good take on "We Can't Hide It Anymore"). Still, few artists have completely unblemished careers and J J gave us three good LPs out of four.

Singles (and a new CD in 1991) continued to appear from time to time in the late seventies and eighties, and while he always retained a small and loyal audience in Great Britain he had long since been a forgotten man in the States.

Ortheia Barnes

Person To Person 1985 Michigan Satellite 508017 Producers: Sylvia Moy & Paul Riser

Believe 1992 Michigan Satellite 00120X Producer: ?

Sister to J J Barnes, and one time member of Cut Glass and disco outfit Hott City!, Ortheia released a handful of singles in the sixties which attracted little attention. She only ever got to cut a couple of LPs, both appearing on the tiny MSR label out of Detroit and these also did not do too much business. The best thing on the record, by far, is Barnes' vocal performance. She had a tremendous vitality and richness in her singing and it was a shame that she had such underwhelming material with which to work and that was a big surprise as virtually all of the songs were at least part-composed by Sylvia Moy, who has an enviable catalogue as a writer. I've played this record a few times over the years and not a single song has stuck with me, I'm afraid.

I have not heard her second album, which was a pure gospel set, and just before this she had released a fine single "'Til You Use It". She passed away in 2015.

Sidney Barnes

Foot Stomp'n Music 1978 Parachute RRLP 9009 Producer: Sidney Barnes

Sidney Barnes is a significant player in black music history with a long and intriguing story which can only be merely hinted at here. He was an important member of two groups, The Serenaders and Rotary Connection (with Minnie Riperton), who could hardly have been more dissimilar in style, made many stirring singles in his own name, hung out and worked with George Clinton, and produced and wrote for a whole host of others.

Surprisingly, then, it wasn't until as late as 1978 that he finally got the chance to issue his one and only LP under his own name, which, an unrecognisable version of "Hold On, I'm Coming" apart, was entirely self-written. It's pretty good, too and much less in thrall to disco then titles such as "Get On Up And Dance" (actually, that one is), "Disco Queen Dance With Me" and the title track might suggest. It didn't sell many, though, and nor did the two singles pulled from it.

Barrino Brothers

Livin' High Off The Goodness Of Your Love 1973 Invictus ST-9811 Producers: Ronald Dunbar, William Weatherspoon, Winford Terry & Raynard Miner

Four brothers: Pete, Nate, Bobby and Perry. Given their talent, and given the fact they recorded for Invictus, it is not surprising that one hears echoes of both The Temptations and The Four Tops on this album. The array of supporting talent brought to bear is impressive, and the result is a solid effort which carries the high production sheen of so many records emanating from the HDH empire. The highpoint is a seven minute song, "It Doesn' t Have To Be That Way" which is delivered elegantly by the brothers. Somewhat surprisingly, they disappeared completely from the industry within a few months of this release, and that wasn't for lack of trying on the part of Invictus who put out six singles on the group over a couple of years.

Keith Barrow

Keith Barrow 1972 Jewel LPS-0075 No producer listed

Keith Barrow 1977 Columbia PC34465 Producer: Bobby Eli

Physical Attraction 1978 CBS JC35597 Producer: Michael Stokes

Just As I Am 1980 Capitol ST12112 Producer: Ralph Affoumado

A talented singer from Chicago with a beautiful falsetto, but a very disappointing career, and the fact that he could never stay with a single producer for long probably didn't help.

The first LP can be ignored as it is a straight, bloodless religious affair. I hesitate to even append the description "gospel" as that implies a passion which the record resolutely lacks. He then cut his first secular album which I think suffered somewhat from an overwrought Bobby Eli production which makes me feel as if I need to go and lie down after listening to too many of the tracks and I don't much care for the re-working of Wilson Pickett's "Mr. Magic Man". The set does include more thoughtful moments in "Precious" and "Questions" but he still hadn't realised his potential.

In 1978 he recorded his best known, most successful (#26 on the soul charts), and by far his most impressive, record in "You Know You Want To Be Loved " which is glorious, and was the centrepiece of *Physical Attraction*. This is his finest work if still marred by filler like the title track and slightly "torchy" songs such as "Overnight Success" but for the first time I felt as if he consistently received production which enhanced rather than overshadowed his singing. The majority of the songs were written by Stokes and Ronn Matlock who were not to work with him again.

Unfortunately, it was downhill again after that as I find his final LP, *Just As I Am*, to be desperately poor without many redeeming features, although "Tell Me This Is Heaven" is decent. He died in 1983.

Chris Bartley

The Sweetest Thing This Side Of Heaven 1967 Vando VA60,000 Producer: Van McCoy

Chris Bartley, who died in 2009, was taken under the wing of Van McCoy who conducted, arranged and produced this LP, as well as writing every song. Anyone familiar with McCoy's work will know that such total involvement would almost guarantee that the record will be tuneful, competent and eminently listenable. And thus it proved. Bartley had a high, appealing tenor which conveyed the fragility of many of the songs beautifully. Tracks like "You Get Next To My Heart" and "Gotta Tell Somebody", on the other hand, epitomised the uptown New York sound of the times. As was McCoy's way, a number of these songs would see (or had seen) service elsewhere but Bartley's version of the title track, as well as being a big hit (#10 soul and #32 pop), remains the best ever take.

A number of other singles appeared over a period of eight years but none were hits, and he never recorded another album, although a fine four track 12" single (played at 45 rpm, so can't count as an LP) was issued by the U.K. company Move in 1986. (There is also speculation that the Chris Bartley who sings on the superb Ray Alexander Techniques' LP, *Let's Talk*, is our man, but it doesn't sound like him to me.)

Fontella Bass

The New Look 1966 Checker 2997 Producers: Billy Davis, Raynard Miner & Carl Smith (Billboard soul charts: 6 Billboard pop charts: 93)

Free 1972 Paula LPS-2213 Producer: Oliver Sain

Fontella Bass was a highly talented, well connected (daughter of Martha, wife of Lester Bowie and sister of David Peaston) and versatile singer from St. Louis but could never shake off her slightly unfair tag of "one-hit wonder", so closely is she associated with her massive - and only - worldwide hit, "Rescue Me". In fact, she placed six more singles - a couple with Bobby McClure were particularly excellent, with "Don't Mess Up A Good Thing" reaching #5 on the soul charts - on the soul top 50 in the years of 1965 and 1966. It is also surprising to note that she was never favoured with a second LP by the Chess organisation, especially as the debut did well enough. Maybe they just wanted to push Etta James instead.

As for the LP itself, it simply contained too many covers: ten of the twelve songs were best known by other singers and although her interpretations were never less than worthy, none of them were as strong as "Rescue Me", which was also the only one of her seven chart entrants that was included.

After having moved to Paris to sing jazz, she returned to soul in 1972 recording the largely ignored and little known *Free* LP for Paula. Frankly, it is better than the Checker release as it is much more personal and distinctive, although it had no significant commercial success. Splendid tracks like "My God, My Freedom, My Home", "Wiping Tears", "I Want Everyone To Know" and "I Need Love" all deserve to be much better known than they are.

She put out a wonderful single in 1977, "Soon As I Touched Him", and a poor one, a cover of "Hold On I'm Coming" two years later, but neither revived her fortunes and she thereafter turned her back on soul music, recording jazzy albums and CDs that are out of scope for the book. She died in 2012.

Joe Bataan

Gypsy Woman 1967 Fania SLP 340 Producer: Jerry Masucci

Subway Joe 1968 Fania SLP 345 Producer: Jerry Masucci

Riot! 1968 Fania SLP 354 Producer: Jerry Masucci

Poor Boy 1969 Fania SLP 371 Producer: Jerry Masucci

Mr. New York & The East Side Kids 1970 Fania SLP 395 Producer: Jerry Masucci

Singin' Some Soul 1972 Fania SLP 375 Producer: Jerry Masucci

For the vast majority of his career Joe Bataan (real name Peter Nitollano) successfully and skilfully juggled two different types of music on his albums: boogaloo / latin and soul. This was a conscious approach which developed as time went on, but had its origins in the first two LPs which are both enjoyable, but had he only ever recorded tracks like "Chickie's Trombone", "Fuego" and "Juanito" he would have been firmly outside the scope of this book. But included on those first releases were a small handful of tracks, for instance "Ordinary Guy" and "Special Girl", which had a hint towards the more recognisable soul music of the time, and he thus kept his options open. (The title track of *Subway Joe* was a humorous and presumably true story, and Bataan certainly always seemed entirely comfortable at relaying details from his life for all to hear.)

The third Fania LP, *Riot!*, took a much bolder step forward along the soul road with tracks like "My Cloud", "Daddy's Coming Home", "For Your Love" and, most significantly, a revised and beefed up version of "Ordinary Guy" (eloquent, heartfelt and humbling), being more accessible to soul music record buyers.

Poor Boy, the cover of which was certainly unpretentious, carried on the approach adopted on *Riot!* with "Obatala" and "Pajarito" supplying the boogaloo and "Sad Girl" and the title track the soul. A mixture of the two styles was well evidenced in "Uptown", his most autobiographical song to date.

Mr. New York And The East End Kids continued the format of the earlier LPs with a number of latin tracks outnumbering the soul although it does contain another deeply personal outing in the lovely and entirely unsentimental "My Opera"; his unforgettable take on The Lord's Prayer, and his latest homage to The Intruders: "When We Get Married". (It was perhaps to be expected that Bataan would have an affinity for this group's music as he had a somewhat similar singing style to that of "Little Sonny", marvellously affecting, but always at potential odds with melody lines.)

As might be imagined from its title, *Singin' Some Soul* was much more of a conscious move towards a straight soul LP and it is simply magnificent. If anyone ever doubted that he could be classed as a true soul man he or she should listen to this. It contains ten tracks and all are worthy but I'll put in a special word for "Under The Street Light" which is a classic and "Crystal Blue Persuasion" (a Tommy James' song particularly well suited to soul interpretations) which was only one of two singles he ever posted on the US Soul chart Top 50.

It should also be mentioned that Fania LPs didn't always come out in logical number order as I'm pretty sure *Singin' Some Soul* succeeded *Mr. New York*, even if the catalogue numbers don't suggest as much.

Sweet Soul 1972 Fania SLP407 Producers: Jerry Masucci & Joe Bataan

The Song Of Joe Bataan 1971 Fania SLP411

Saint Latin's Day Massacre 1972 Fania SLP420 Producers: Jerry Masucci & Joe Bataan

Mr. New York 1989 Hot 122 (UK)

Sweet Soul signalled a return to the format of *Singin' Some Soul* as well as employing Bataan as co-producer for the first time, although it wasn't quite so good. It included an unrecognisable version of The Beatles' "This Boy", a fairly straight one of "Shaft" and two excellent Bataan original songs, the lovely "You' re Driving Me Right Out Of My Mind" and the spirited "Johnny's No Good" which had backing vocals that sounded like The Dramatics (but probably wasn't.).

The final Fania LP, *Saint Latin's Day Massacre*, appeared in 1972 but it held the least soul content of nearly all his LPs, a winning ballad, "If I Were A King", excepted.

(*The Song of Joe Bataan* and the UK Hot release are both compilations, the former containing an excellent essay about Bataan's life.)

Salsoul   1974   Mericana XMS-124   Producers: Joe Cayre & Joe Bataan

Afrofilipino 1975 Salsoul SA33471   Producer: Joe Bataan

Mestizo   1980   Salsoul SA8534   Producer: Joe Bataan

Joe Bataan II 1981 Salsoul SA8549 Producer: Joe Bataan

After the Fania sojourn, Joe pitched up at Mericana and the *Salsoul* album at once signalled a new approach: fewer soulful ballads and funkier instrumental workouts such as "Latin Strut" and "After Shower Funk" even if a brand new - and unidentifiable - take on "Ordinary Guy " but in Spanish this time, kept a link with the past.

Afrofilipino heralded another label move, and contained one of his best-known records, the instrumental version of Gil Scott-Heron's "The Bottle" (his second single to reach the national soul charts, at #59) which boasted a great Gordon Edwards bass line, as well as yet another (and good) version of "Ordinary Guy" and fine new tracks like "Hey Girl" and "When You're Down". However, the disappointing "X-Rated Symphony" showed Bataan wasn't averse to travelling a disco route, either.

There was then a five year lull before his next, and penultimate, LP vinyl release and as could probably be imagined, disco now pre-dominated although his vocals were as identifiable as ever. *Mestizo* hosted "Rap-O, Clap-O" which I think is absolutely dreadful but certainly sold tons of records when released as both a 45 and 12 inch single, even if it failed to chart nationally, thus proving once again that charts and sales don't necessarily co-incide. "Sadie (She Smokes)" is an update of sorts to "Gypsy Woman" and despite having lots of irritating disco flourishes it does feature a highly committed guest vocal by Jocelyn Brown and a great guitar line.

His final vinyl outing came out in 1981 and apart from nonsense like "Ling Ching Tong" there were still some salvageable moments within "He Don't Really Love You" and "Forever". .

Joe Bataan has re-appeared in the last few years with some excellent new CDs and it seems as if he might finally be getting the recognition he has always deserved. He might have worn a suit and black tie back on the cover of the *Gypsy Woman* LP from 1967 but his music has always been much more characterised by an earthiness and down home approach that has made him a hero to many of the dispossessed of the world.

Batiste Brothers Band

Freeze 1982 Dynasty DR-181952 Producer: The Batiste Brothers

There are even more Batistes than there are Barrinos. Six, in fact:

David, Paul, Michael, Peter, Russ and Damon. Listening to music on their website, it is clear they have a great facility for playing the music so redolent of their hometown, New Orleans. You wouldn' t have thought so from this LP, however, as It features the same type of fairly generic funk that was coming out from many cities in 1982. The title track is probably their best known track which does boast a nice line in rhythm guitar, but also relies overmuch on a vocoder.

Bazuka

Bazuka 1975 A & M SP-3406 Producer: Tony Camillo

Tony Camillo has a great c.v. as a writer and producer for numerous soul artists over the years and was responsible for writing, arranging and producing this one-off LP. It's clear that no group called Bazuka ever existed, but it's an outing that has some fine moments, particularly on the two mid-tempo and soulful tracks sung by Kenny Kerr, a singer of some talent who does not appear to have done anything else. "Dy-No-Mite" was a rather tedious and moderately funky tune that managed to make #29 on the soul charts, a whole 63 places higher than the similar "Love Explosion".

BB & Q Band

Lucious Floyd; Abdul Walli Mohammed; Kevin Nance; Pee-Wee Ford; Dwayne Perdue; Kevin Robinson; Chelli Minucci; Tony Bridges; Ike Floyd; Curtis Hairston; Mauro Malavasi; Paolo Gianolio; Terry Silverlight; Timmy Allen; Bernard Davies; Ullanda McCullough; Michael Campbell

The Brooklyn, Bronx and Queens Band   1981 Capitol ST12155 Producer: Jacques Fred Petrus (Billboard soul charts: 19 ; Billboard pop charts: 109)

All Night Long 1982 Capitol ST12212 Producer: Jacques Fred Petrus (Billboard soul charts: 32)

Six Million Times 1983 Capitol ST12285 Producers: Jacques Fred Petrus & Mauro Malavasi

Genie   1986 Elektra / Pretty Pearl 60497-1 Producers: Jacques Fred Petrus & Kae Williams

I'm stretching the criterion a bit here about only including USA artists as The BB & Q band were as much Italian as American but much of the recording was done in the U,S, featuring U.S musicians and singers (including Luther Vandross on backing vocals) so it seems churlish and unnecessarily dogmatic to leave them out. The music was also entirely in keeping with what else was being played in the eighties and no-one listening to the music would have heard it as anything other than American soul music of the time.

The first album is the best, glossy, danceable and accomplished, while showing some versatility in the fine Ike Floyd led downtempo "Lovin's What We Should Do" and "Don't Say Goodbye". "On The Beat" was the big hit from it (#8 soul) and was compelling in its Chic styled momentum.

The other albums had entirely different personnel, thus confirming that the BB & Q Band were really just a means of expression for Jacques Fred Petrus rather than a group who naturally developed. It also meant that the sound didn't change in any significant way (although *All Night Long* had a "drier" sound). It also contained their second biggest hit, "Imagination", which made it to #21 on the soul charts.

The B B and Q Band closed out their career with *Six Million Times* and *Genie*, the latter featuring vocals from Curtis Hairston. Both albums are predominantly uptempo, of course, and they are ok, but nothing really stands out, although "Minutes Away" on *Genie* is a fair ballad.

Carl Bean & Universal Love

Carl Bean; Craig Pearson; Jackie Cannon; Royal Anderson; Alahaundra Romeo

All We Need Is Love 1974 ABC Peacock PLP 59208
Producer: Lee Young

Three years before Carl Bean put out his version of the gay anthem "I Was Born This Way" he was in this little known group. It is a bit of a mishmash containing love songs, pleas for universal peace and a couple of fairly straight gospel tracks. It also isn't helped by somewhat murky production which doesn't always make it easy to hear the words being sung. On a more positive note, the group don't obviously sound like anyone else and there are two fine tracks on show: the title song and "Love You Ain't Got".

The Beck Family

Anthony Beck; Mendy Beck; Tyrone Beck; Joanna Beck; Nick Mundy; Donald Wilson

Dancing On The Ceiling 1979 LeJoint 17001 Producers: T Life & Bill Greene (Billboard soul charts: 72)

What is it about the letter "B"? I'm blowed if there isn't a clan of Becks as well. Not entirely surprisingly, there are echoes of the Jacksons in their music, not least on "Can You Feel It" (they even share a song title) where the vocals sound ever so close to Michael J. "Can' t Shake The Feeling" was the reasonably successful 45 from the album (#43 soul) but it sounds dated today.

James Becton

Butter & Toast 1979 C-Bird SC3013 No producer listed

This is just about the only LP in the book that came out of Connecticut a state that, for some reason, never really managed to produce much in the way of soul music. Side one is a waste of vinyl in the shape of the 15 minute title track but side two is much better with three pretty good songs, of which "Time Will Tell" is the best. James Becton had a somewhat unusual voice, sounding a little bit like another rather unknown soul man, Robert Tillman. The sleeve does not offer up any information about who produced the record but as Becton wrote and arranged all the songs, one may assume it was him.

Jimmy Bee

Live 1973 ALA LP-1975 Producers : Jimmy Bee & Jimmy Simpson

Jimmy Bee (real name, Jimmy Brunsen) only ever recorded on the West Coast as a solo artist and as a member of a number of groups dating back to the fifties but this "live" album was apparently captured at the Club, Long Island. Call me sceptical, but I'm wondering if the crowd noises come from a studio instead. Either way, the approach doesn't really help *Live* which is, to say the least, all over the place. Many of the tracks sound quaintly dated for 1973 and are predominantly solid songs frequently performed over the years such as "Stormy Monday" and "I Need Your Love So Bad"; one would have to be a much better singer than Jimmy Bee to get anything new from them. He also sings a more restrained version of his single from 1966, "Talking About Love", before finishing the LP off with the best track by far, which sounds totally unlike anything else on it, a great version of Marvin Holmes' "Find Yourself".

He had a tiny soul hit in 1976 with a version of "Breakin' Up Is Hard To Do" but apparently moved into music promotion soon after this, and gave up singing. I believe he died in 1993.

Beginning Of The End

Raphael Munnings; Leroy Munnings; Frank Munnings; Fred Henfield; Peter Humes; Rudolph Pinder

Funky Nassau 1971 Alston SD33-379 Producer: Beginning Of The End

Beginning Of The End 1976 Alston LP-4403 Producer: Teddy Randazzo

"Funky Nassau" was a huge success as a single in 1971 (#7 soul and #15 pop) but it didn't lead to the LP of the same name charting and this is doubtless because the 45 had a pop appeal that is all but absent in the rest of the album, apart from "Monkey Tamarind" which was a noticeably weak soundalike follow-up single. There are few "songs" as such on *Funky Nassau* but it does feature good funk tracks in "Pretty Girl" and "When She Made Me Promise".

The biggest surprise of the second release - which also sold disappointingly - was that it was produced by Teddy Randazzo, given that his illustrious musical history was founded on music highly different from this. I assume it is his involvement that makes the record softer than the debut, and although it has a handful of good tracks in "Super Woman" "That's What I Get" and "I've Got The News", the rawness of "When She Made Me Promise" is absent.

Band member Raphael Munnings issued a couple of unsuccessful solo singles in 1972 before re-appearing in 1979 but Beginning Of The End will have to remain defined by their big hit.

Archie Bell & The Drells

Archie Bell; Lee Bell; James Wise; Lee Pernell; Billy Butler; Charles Gibbs; Joe Cross; Lucious Larkins

Tighten Up 1968 Atlantic SD 8181 Producer: LJF Productions (Billboard soul charts: 15 ; Billboard pop charts: 142)

I Can' t Stop Dancing 1968 Atlantic SD 8204 Producers: LJF Productions and Kenny Gamble & Leon Huff (Billboard soul charts: 28)

There's Gonna Be A Showdown 1969 Atlantic SD 8226 Producers: Kenny Gamble, Leon Huff & LJF Productions (Billboard pop charts: 163)

Few groups have got off the mark so quickly as Archie Bell and the Drells when only their third ever single, "Tighten Up", went to #1 on both the pop and soul charts. Great record too, and one that still sounds fresh today. The first two albums were recorded in Houston under the auspices of Skipper Lee Frazier, who was the man behind LJF productions. So although they had a relatively untroubled start, they were handicapped by Archie's stint in the army which meant it wasn't easy to capitalise on their success.

Tighten Up was obviously put together quickly as evidenced by such uninspired song choices as "Knock On Wood" and "In The Midnight Hour" but it also contained some tracks which have stood the test of time pretty well in "I Don't Wanna Be A Playboy" and "A Soldier's Prayer". Certainly nothing else on the album sounded like the title track, and the fact that Atlantic didn't even put out a second cut from the set as a 45 to follow-up the million seller, means they were also unconvinced or caught on the hop by Bell's draft.

The most significant songs on the follow-up LP, *I Can't Stop Dancing*, were the title track and "Do The Choo Choo" as they were the first records produced for the group by Gamble and Huff. Their subsequent relationship was to prove very fruitful indeed for everyone involved. They were also the two cuts selected as singles to follow-up "Tighten Up" and by reaching #5 and #17 respectively on the soul charts, they were the right choices, too. The album also rather strangely included three Curtis Mayfield songs (strangely, because they never recorded any more of his work) which presumably was another legacy of Archie's army service leading to a desperate need to get songs onto the LP and certainly three of the four tracks Bell wrote himself were of average quality. The other cut worth hearing, purely for the way in which it is tailored to Archie's own military experiences, is a version of "Dock Of The Bay".

There's Gonna Be A Showdown had some brilliant moments, though, and that was largely due to Gamble and Huff. I have always felt that they were better at writing and producing for groups rather than solo singers, and the best tracks, both released as 45s, "Girl You're Too Young" (#13 soul) and "Showdown" itself (#6), are magnificent records that suited Archie Bell and the Drells perfectly. I should also say that Earl Young's performance on the latter is one of the greatest examples of soul drumming ever captured on disc. Nothing else on the LP matched these two songs, although third and fourth charting singles, "I Love My Baby" (#40) and "My Balloon's Going Up" (#36) came close, but the filler was kept to a minimum. (In the U.K. the LP was entitled "Here I Go Again" - and had a different cover - as that fine track had become a big seller on the Northern Soul scene and charted over here.)

Dance Your Troubles Away 1975 TSOP PZ 33844
Producers: Kenny Gamble, Leon Huff, Bunny Sigler, John Whitehead, Gene McFadden & Victor Carstarphen (Billboard soul charts: 11 ; Billboard pop charts: 95)

Where Will You Go When The Party's Over
1976 P.I.R. PZ 34323 Producers: Bunny Sigler, John Whitehead, Gene McFadden & Victor Carstarphen (Billboard soul charts: 47)

Hard Not To Like It 1977 P.I.R. PZ 34855 Producers: John Whitehead, Gene McFadden, Victor Carstarphen & Roland Chambers

Strategy 1979 P.I.R. JZ 36096 Producers: John Whitehead, Gene McFadden, Kenny Gamble, Leon Huff, Archie Bell, William Bloom, Douglas Brown, Terry Price, Mark Mitchell & Roger Meltzer (Billboard soul charts: 37)

Artists Showcase 1986 Street Sounds Music 8 (UK)

The seventies did not start well for the group as although "A World Without Music" and "Wrap It Up" reached the soul charts, neither were backed up by an album, and the next three Atlantic singles bombed. A short-lived move to Glades generated nice music but no LPs. It was also no con-incidence that the majority of these records were neither written nor produced by Gamble and Huff.

It must have been a huge relief for the group, when G & H expressed a willingness to resume the relationship and the next four LPs moved the group squarely into the P.I.R.empire, all of them coming out on their record labels, although Kenny and Leon only wrote one more song for the group after this: "Show Me How To Dance" on *Strategy*. *Dance Your Troubles Away* unashamedly played up the group's terpsichorean legacy and features splendid uptempo outings such as "Let's Groove" (a #7 soul single) and "The Soul City Walk" (#42) but also had time for a nine minute ballad, "I Won't Leave You Honey, Never" a Bunny Sigler and Ron Tyson song where Archie phrases a lot like Eddie Levert of the O'Jays, and it could well be Bunny and Phil Hurtt providing the wonderful background vocals as it has been alleged that most tracks recorded at P.I.R. seldom featured anyone in a group other than the lead singers. It was their best selling LP ever.

Where Will You Go When The Party's Over followed the same template, with "Right Here Is Where I Want To Be" as the slow and gorgeous ballad (even if it failed to sell as a single when paired with "Nothing Comes Easy") with the remainder of the songs all aimed at the dance floor, the best of which was "Don't Let Love Get You Down" a much loved side in Britain. Worryingly, although another track, "Everybody Have A Good Time" charted, it was at a lowly #68.

Hard Not To Like It followed, which I would question as a title as it is not a particularly robust outing, although "I've Been Missing You" (a #56 soul single) and "There's No Other Like You" are solid enough efforts. By this time it was the slower tracks which most appeal as the dance tracks have none of the verve and sparkle of the earlier work. "Glad You Could Make It" followed "I've Been Missing You" as a 45 but could only limp to #63..

The final Archie Bell and the Drells album, *Strategy*, had a popular title track (#21 soul) and also saw the first recordings back down in Houston since the turn of the decade, with "Tighten Up At The Disco" (not quite as bad as the title might suggest) and "We Got 'Em Dancin'" being cut in Texas. It was a decent release and "We've Got Something" is an exciting dance track, but could not be classed as spectacular.

The UK set from 1986 is a fair retrospective (although misses much of their best work) and includes one track, "Don't Wait For The World", which does not exist on any other LP.

The group broke up soon after *Strategy* with Bell electing to go the solo route, and although their rather unusual name (just what *is* a Drell?) has possibly led to unnecessary mirth and a resultant lack of critical acclaim, they made a handful of brilliant records as well as placing ten singles on the Hot 100, and so they should not be ignored. And were they really The Houston Outlaws, another group who made some excellent singles in the early seventies?

Archie Bell

I Never Had It So Good 1981 Becket BKS013 Producer: Brothers United Together Inc.

Bell recorded his one and only vinyl album without any Drells in 1981, and it rather unjustly escaped notice. It has a number of highly worthwhile moments, namely: "Don't Wait For The World", "Harder And Harder" and the title song which is a classy country-tinged ballad written by Paul Williams and Roger Nichols that has also been recorded by artists as diverse as George Perkins and Barbra Striesand. "Any Time Is Right" was pulled to become a small soul hit (#49) and although no more records were to appear apart from one on WMOT in 1982 it seems as if he has continued to work up until the present day.

Arlene Bell

Two Sides To Every Coin 1979 Velvet VL-19 22 Producer: Aaron Johnson

This is a nice, unpretentious, noticeably West Coast, record but I suspect *Two Sides* contains some tracks that were recorded slightly earlier. Take, for example, "There's Something Wrong With You" which also came out on a single in 1977 but it sounds to me to have been recorded in the first half of the decade. Certainly there is little concession to disco on the LP and that gives it a timeless quality, even if some of the songs, on side one particularly, were not noticeably memorable. Mel Alexander was heavily involved in the whole thing and I believe it may well be him duetting with Arlene on "Did You Mean It" which has a horn line reminiscent of BT Express. Four singles from the album exist, but none would have garnered any but local sales.

Jerry Bell

Winter Love Affair 1981 MCA 5180 Producer: Michael Wycoff

Jerry Bell was a member of the Dazz Band, a younger brother to Archie Bell, and, according to Wikipedia, a one-time member of The New Birth, a piece of information that is resolutely missing from all their LP covers and CDs, and very much news to me. (A biography I have seen has also claimed he is related to Thom Bell, Al Bell, William Bell and Robert Bell of Kool and The Gang.) *Winter Love Affair* owed a great deal to Michael Wycoff, who wrote all the songs, played piano, and sang background vocals in addition to arranging and producing it. The whole thing is classy and tuneful and Bell can undoubtedly sing, with traces of Stevie Wonder and DJ Rogers (most noticeably on "Call On Me") in his voice. However, it didn't sell many copies and only generated one low level "hit" ("Love Will Make It All Right", #88 on the soul charts). He seemed to vanish without much trace afterwards.

Reuben Bell

Blues Get Off My Shoulders 1983 Port City 1002 Producer: Allen Orange

Shreveport's talented Reuben Bell made a number of lovely records - but only ever scored one hit, "I Hear You Knocking (It's Too Late)", in 1972 - in the late sixties and seventies including one of the greatest of all time in 1975 with the highly soulful, intelligent and entirely believable "Asking For The Truth" but sadly no album was ever built around that masterpiece. It was nevertheless a most welcome surprise to see this fine LP appear years later on the tiny Port City label out of Shreveport, produced by long time Bell associate, Allen Orange. The songs are well chosen and good (apart from a dull instrumental, "Rapid Fire") and include a re-cut of his "All The Time" single from 1972 but the whole thing was obviously done on the cheap and it had little or no chance of making it in a crowded and competitive market place as, apart from some cities down south, no radio stations would have played this sort of music in 1983. His voice was still impressive and I love the fact that a Reuben Bell LP exists but his earlier work was undeniably stronger. He died in 2004.

William Bell

The Soul Of A Bell 1967 Stax S719 Producer: Booker T Jones

Bound To Happen 1969 Stax STS-2014 Producer: Booker T Jones (Billboard soul charts: 49)

Wow 1971 Stax STS-2037 Producers: Al Bell, Tom Nixon & Booker T Jones

Phases Of Reality 1972 Stax STS-3005 Producer: William Bell

Relating 1973 Stax STS-5502 Producers: William Bell & Al Jackson

Do Right Man 1984 Charly CRB1076 (UK)

The Best Of 1988 Stax MPS-8541

Somehow, it always seemed as if local boy William Bell was underappreciated at Stax. As evidence, given he had been at the label virtually from the beginning, and having recorded and released a number of successful singles over a few years, it wasn't until 1967 that Stax favoured him with an album. But what a lovely piece of work it was, even if a handful of the tracks were rather obvious covers of other people's hits. The overwhelming quality that nearly always characterised William Bell as an artist was his stately dignity and understated delivery, perfectly instanced by tracks on *Soul Of A Bell* such as the marvellous "Everybody Loves A Winner" (a #18 soul single hit) and a re-make of "You Don't Miss Your Water". Only the likes of Arthur Alexander can rival Bell for "under-souling" in such a beguiling way. But he could also deliver hot dance tracks such as the great "Eloise", which has Bell somewhat amusingly phrasing like Levi Stubbs for the last minute or so. (The LP was entitled *A Tribute To A King* in England with the addition of the title track (a #16 soul single hit and homage to Otis Redding) and "Every Man Oughta Have A Woman".)

In addition to his vocal talents, Bell was also a gifted writer, sometimes working by himself, but most often with Booker T Jones and "I Forgot to Be Your Lover" from *Bound To Happen* was a highly successful example of what they could produce when they composed together. It became his biggest hit single to date when released right at the end of 1968 (#10 soul, #45 pop).

In fact, the quality of the songs on the second LP is high and I really like his interpretation of "I Got A Sure Thing". He can't match the passion of Ollie Nightingale and doesn't attempt to, delivering a reading that is equally valid in a different way. Mind you, undertaking Sly's "Everyday People" was a dire mistake. (It's also a shame Stax didn't see fit to include his two coruscating duets with Judy Clay, "Private Number" and "My Baby Specialises", as both were pretty decent hits around the same time.)

Wow rang a number of changes in as much as most of it was

recorded in Muscle Shoals, Al Bell (no relation) moved into the producer's chair for the first time and William provided fewer songs than on the first two LPs. The result of all this was a solid and worthy record, but not one quite up to his best standard. The fact that three failed singles were pulled from the set could either be put down to their lack of absolute top quality, or as further evidence of Stax's periodical indifference to Bell.

Things certainly improved with *Phases Of Reality*, arguably not only his best ever LP but also one of the best ever put out by Stax. I don't believe it was co-incidence that it also happened to be the first LP he ever produced himself as well as seeing his writing feature more prominently once again - six out of the eight excellent tracks are from his pen, a number of which had a stronger social theme than had hitherto been the case, possibly best evidenced by the splendid "Man In The Street" but the sunny and vibrant "Lonely For Your Love" was also a particular winner. The set also epitomises quality over quantity; it comes in at 26 minutes and not a second was wasted, but Stax again failed to get away a Bell single when "Save Us" did little in the market.

He bowed out on his Stax career with another strong LP, *Reality*, which saw him return to recording at Stax; the previous two had been largely cut at Muscle Shoals. "Lovin' On Borrowed Time" is quintessential Bell, restrained yet anguished, and it became one of Stax's finest ever singles when released from the album; it returned Bell to the soul charts for the first time in 4 years when it attained #22, and that success was continued by another track, "Gettin' What You Want (Losin' What You Got)" which became the twelfth and final William Bell single to hit the soul charts as a Stax artist. Most of the songs were co-written by James McDuffie, who seemed to appear from nowhere, and the whole has a softer, warmer feel than Bell's previous work which would be the result of Al Jackson's involvement.

The 1984 and 1988 release are two thoughtful and generous compilations, which did not duplicate any material at all, for the simple reason that the first one concentrated on early "blue" Stax material with the latter opting for the "yellow" period. .

Coming Back For More 1977 Mercury SRM 1 1146 Producers: William Bell & Paul Mitchell (Billboard soul charts: 15; Billboard pop charts: 63)

It's Time You Took Another Listen 1977 Mercury SRM 1 1193 Producers: William Bell & Paul Mitchell

It was ironic that when Bell put out his very first post-Stax single after having left the company he distinguished for the best part of fifteen years, it became easily his biggest single of his entire career. And I'm not really sure why. "Trying To Love Two" was typical Bell in composition and delivery and is certainly likeable enough, but I feel he had released a number of 45s in the past that were just as strong. This is in no way to begrudge him his deserved success but just points up the random nature of the music business. The single was obviously the centrepiece of *Coming Back For More* which was recorded in Detroit, New Orleans and Atlanta. The title track has an Al Green influenced lope and a splendid hook (although it could do no better than #66 on the soul charts) while one cut that worked surprisingly well was his interpretation of "I Wake Up Crying", and if one felt that hearing another version of this revered old song in 1977 was not required, then play it again; it suited Bell beautifully.

The follow up, *It's Time You Took Another Listen,* was topped and tailed well in the lead-off cut "Easy Comin' Out" (a reasonably successful single at #30 soul) and the closing track, "Let It Shine" but what sat in between was not the strongest set of songs found on Bell's albums. Even Paul Kelly contributes one, "Hollywood Streetwalker", that is slightly below par. I hesitate to say this is a weak release, as it isn't, and I admire the fact that Bell was going his own way in a disco era, but it just wasn't his finest work.

Survivor 1983 Kat Family FZ 38643 Producers: William Bell & Michael Allen Stewart

Passion 1986 Wilbe 3001 Producers: William Bell, Mike Stewart & Albert Burroughs (Billboard soul charts: 39)

On A Roll 1989 WRC WIL- 3007 Producers: William Bell & Michael Stewart

After the Mercury stay William moved to the new Kat Family label, although I am unclear why there was a six year gap in between. Apart from an unappealing and boring title track *Survivor* is generally a likeable record. He revisits "Private Number" with one Rubi Burt and I assume it is also her duetting on "Trying To Get To You" but the cover rather ungallantly fails to credit who it is. "Bad Time To Break Up" (a #65 soul hit) and "I Might As Well Be In Love" are decent compositions, and are vintage Bell in artistry.

Passion does contain a number of pretty good Bell songs, but it is beset by horrible programming and a handful of tracks, like the title, which are clichéd and formulaic and place the elegant Bell in a setting that sounds alien to him - it as if one has caught a favourite maiden aunt stumbling drunk out of the local pub. Objectivity suggests that it would have sounded ok had it been recorded at Stax twenty years earlier and "I Don't Want To Wake Up (Feelin' Guilty)" is a fine duet with Janice Bulluck but the LP has not aged well.

On A Roll was Bell's third successive LP co-produced with Mike Stewart - who really needed to have made his mind up about what he wanted to be called - and apart from three tracks: the smart "Gettin' Out Of Your Bed", "I Need Your Love So Bad" (not the old Willie John number) and "Holding On To Love" it is the most dispiriting work Bell ever did.

When one takes into account how good most of his records were, and then factor in his compositional skills, and the stirring records that were released on his own Peachtree label, the conclusion has to be that William Bell is one of soul's most impressive artists, even if a depressingly high number of music fans have probably barely even heard of him.

Bell Brothers

Alex Bell; Leroy Bell; P.C. Bell

At Last 1982 HAH 1001 Producer: Jim Qualley

The Bell Brothers put out three really good singles in the sixties on Houston's Sure Shot label and one rather assumed that we would hear no more from them, especially as none of the three were hits. It was a great surprise, therefore, when this LP suddenly appeared in the early eighties. So unheralded (and rare) is the LP that I have neither heard nor seen it so I can do no more than list its existence.

Bell & James

Bell & James 1978 A & M SP 4728 Producers: Casey James & Leroy Bell (Billboard soul charts: 17; Billboard pop charts: 31)

Only Make Believe 1979 A & M SP 4784 Producers: Casey James & Leroy Bell (Billboard soul charts: 36; Billboard pop charts: 125)

In Black And White 1981 A & M SP 4834 Producers: Casey James & Leroy Bell

Given that Leroy Bell is the nephew of Thom Bell, it was no surprise that Bell & James' records played up the elements of melody and production over mere danceability. The duo also have an enviable c.v. as writers for others, including Elton John, Phyllis Hyman and The O'Jays, so they would never have been solely dependent on the success of their own LPs. Their big hit was "Livin' It Up (Friday Night)" in 1978 (#7 soul, #15 pop) but in fact it is rather atypical of what will be found on these three records all of which are worth owning, even if it must be said that the duo are not the most distinctive singers imaginable.

Most of their songs feature a lush instrumental passage before the vocals come in, a winning formula and indicative of a cerebral approach to their music. Try "You Never Know What You've Got" from the first set as evidence. There are elements of Hall and Oates in the first two LPs and faint echoes of Steely Dan or Michael Macdonald on *In Black And White*, and while I imagine that a die-hard fan of southern soul would dismiss their work easily enough, anyone who loved Philadelphia soul will find them most palatable.

Jo Jo Benson (see Peggy Scott)

Brook Benton

Do Your Own Thing 1969 Cotillion SD 9002 Producers: Arif Mardin, Gary Illingworth, Jerry Leiber & Mike Stoller (Billboard pop charts: 189)

Brook Benton Today 1970 Cotillion SD 9018 Producer: Arif Mardin (Billboard soul charts: 4; Billboard pop charts: 27)

Home Style 1970 Cotillion SD 9028 Producer: Arif Mardin (Billboard pop charts: 199)

Gospel Truth 1971 Cotillion SD 058 Producer: Arif Mardin

Story Teller 1972 Cotillion SD 9050 Producer: Arif Mardin

Brook Benton was one of the most important, talented and successful black singers of the twentieth century. But was he a soul man? That is really the only question I need to answer for the purposes of this book and I have concluded, that until he moved to Cotillion in 1969, the majority of his recordings fall outside the scope of what I am trying to do, so I will only list his albums from that year onwards. This is not a comment on the quality of his earlier records, and I can see that many of them were most impressive, not least "A House Is Not A Home" and "Where Does A Man Go To Cry", but I would contend that they were somewhat isolated examples of soulful records in a much greater mass of straight MOR recordings.

Do Your Own Thing was recorded in New York and Muscle Shoals and Benton sounds at home from the moment the title track kicks things off. It is an LP of consistent strength with intelligently chosen songs, but if I had to pick a stand-out track it would probably be Mac Rebennack and Jesse Hill's " She Knows What To Do for Me", although his cover of "Nothing Can Take The Place Of You" was the hit single, moving smoothly up to #11 on the soul charts, his first notable success for four years. It was also slightly surreal to see that he covered a Phil Trim song entitled "Oh Lord, Why Lord", only a year or so before Parliament did. More disparate black acts would be hard to imagine.

He then returned to the big-time with the *Brook Benton Today* LP, which was built around the massive success of "Rainy Night In Georgia" (#1 soul and #4 pop), the brilliant Tony Joe White song that has been recorded by so many but never so evocatively as here. "Life Has Its Little Ups And Downs", another superb song covered by numerous artists, is also delivered magnificently as is "Desertion" but a number of other tracks on the Miami and New York recorded album veer off into the uninspired. Nobody apart from Aretha could salvage the horrible "My Way", no-one in the world could redeem "I've Gotta Be Me" and "Can't Take My Eyes Off You", while effortless, lacks the flow and release inherent in better versions.

Home Style, as with *Today*, cut in Miami and New York, was probably slightly top-heavy with songs better known by others, one of which, "Don't It Make You Want To Go Home", had to settle for #31 on the soul charts.

Story Teller probably moved away a little too far from recognisable soul music for some listeners (try "Big Mabel Murphy") but also included the handsome Don Covay and George Soule composition, "Shoes", which became a pretty fair sized hit as a single (#18 soul), even if no-one realised at the time that he wouldn't visit the charts again until 1978. .

Sandwiched in between these two LPs he cut *Gospel Truth*, which, although obviously different in subject matter, musically sounds pretty identical to the others.

Something For Everyone 1973 MGM 4874 Producer: Billy Davis

This Is Brook Benton 1976 All Platinum 3015 Producers: Al Goodman, Harry Ray, Sammy Lowe & Walter Morris

Makin' Love Is Good For You 1977 Olde World 7700 Producer: Clyde Otis

Soft 1984 Sounds Of Florida SOF5001 Producer: Clyde Otis

After the Cotillion stay came to close Benton became something of a nomad, recording for four different record labels over a period of ten years or so. The MGM and All Platinum releases reached back into his past, and sound like his work from the early to mid sixties but "Makin' Love Is Good For You" (that final soul chart entrant from 1978) adopted a much more up to date approach, with songs such as the title track (another Tony Joe White song) and "Bayou Babe" incorporating aspects of disco, while the slower tracks would not have been out of place on the Cotillion outings. Finally came *Soft*, which I suspect was all cut at the same time as the Olde World LP not least because both albums share a number of tracks.

Brook Benton died in 1988, his fame and artistry not in doubt.

Charles Berry

Neighbor Neighbor 1978 Crazy Cajun CC-1060 Producer: Huey Meaux

Another LP, like the Ascots', which exists as a tax scam by Huey

Meaux, this one by the mysterious Charles Berry reaches way back into the sixties for excellent cuts like "Neighbor, Neighbor" and "Time" as well as equally fine ones that sound of more recent vintage such as "You Wouldn't Recognise Me". Unfortunately, and consistent with the lack of care Meaux brought to bear on these albums, side two has four successive cuts that are sung entirely accapella, being unacceptably rough demos which don't belong on a released LP.

Best Of Both Worlds

Winfield Parker; Major Boyd; Joseph Conway; Ralph Fisher; James Gallon; Scott Johnson; Gary Langston, George Parrish

I Want The World To Know 1975 Shakat LPS5003
Producer: Clayton Roberts

Given that one obvious function of an LP cover is to attract potential buyers, you do have to ask what Shakat records were thinking when they came up with the design on this one. It could just as well be a classical record inside. As for the music itself? Not bad and this is a pretty solid release from an obscure group who were fronted by the fine singer, Winfield Parker, and he delivers the two best tracks, "Lost In A Shuffle Of Love" and "I Want The World To Know" itself, but the rest of the songs are routine.

Harmon Bethea

One Eye Open (as The Mask Man) 1969 Dynamo DS 8004 No producer listed

Got To Find A Sweet Name 1972 Musicor MS3239
Producers: James Burston & Harmon Bethea

One hope I have for this book is that it will alert people to artists they may not know or have disregarded. I suspect the great Harmon Bethea (aka The Mask Man) fits into this category. He put three singles into the soul charts but remains one of the most under appreciated artists in soul music history; I don't recall ever reading anything about him until he died in 2010 at the age of 86. He first started singing way back in the forties and made a number of recordings as a member of the Cap-Tans vocal group before adopting the Mask Man persona and making some marvellous music.

One Eye Open was his first LP, recorded under the name of The Mask Man, but he was ably supported by The Agents, Johnny Hood, Paul Williams and Tyrone Gray. Many soul artists obviously grew up listening to jazz, gospel or blues and bring these influences to bear in their music, but Bethea went beyond that and one can trace vaudeville and theatre as well, and he also liked to impart wit and wisdom in the manner of Joe Tex. He didn't often sing about enduring love or hopes for a better tomorrow; he was more concerned about workplace altercations, losing all his paycheck in a craps game, or his battles with tough women, and everything is imbued with great humour: when a judge enquires why he hit his wife with a chair, his answer is that the table or the fridge were too heavy to pick up. Gloriously, the title track became something of a hit when released as a single, reaching #20 soul and #95 pop in early January 1969; it's one of his finest ever moments with genuinely amusing asides about his tangles with his spouse, her attempts to poison him and his giving away his supper to his cat to avoid such a fate. "Roaches" and "Wigs" are also delivered in the same humorous vein, with the former using "Shout" as a musical reference, although nobody - including The Isley Brothers - would sing "kill it" with such relish as a vocal aside as The Agents do here. Bethea COULD play it safer when he wanted to and a handful of tracks are more conventional but all are blessed with great musical accompaniment and a sense of Sam Cooke and Otis Redding in his phrasing here and there.

A number of other singles followed in the late sixties and early seventies but only one, "My Wife, My Dog, My Cat", managed to chart (at #22 soul.) He moved to Musicor to try and resurrect his fortunes and was rewarded when "Talking About The Boss & I" made it to #59 on the soul charts in early 1974. In anyone else's hands the song would doubtless depict an extra marital affair, but Bethea spins an enthralling tale about being disrespected at work, and his subsequent forthright response. He also weaves in a serious point about black power amid all the fun. It became the cornerstone of the superb *Got To Find A Sweet Name* LP (which does duplicate two tracks from his first album) on which the band is tough and full of zest; it should be actively sought out by anyone who likes to laugh with records.

Betty & Dee

The Girls... 1976 Buddah BDS 5688 Producer: Larter Enterprises (Larry Gordon)

Now here we have one of the most mysterious releases in soul music LP history. The record looks like a bootleg, but isn't, but I think it is likely that it was never meant to be issued for sale as it appears to be solely a vehicle for showcasing songs by Jim Weatherley, as all the tracks were written by him. No-one seems to have any idea who Betty and Dee were, but they do the songs proud and this is a lovely LP. Weatherly compositions could veer off into the "poppier" end of soul, and some songs here do just that, but the girls are excellent vocalists and I would love to know who they were.

Charles Bevel

Meet Mississippi Charles 1973 A & M SP 4412 Producer: Calvin Carter

The emergence of Bill Withers as a highly successful artist led to a handful of other singers working the same sort of themes and adopting a similar musical approach. Charles Bevel was one such man. His one and only LP from 1973 contains thoughtful, intelligent and, in the case of the outstanding "Sally B White" (a small soul hit as a 45), angry songs throughout and also benefits hugely from the outstanding Chicago musicians who play on the LP. Even though the style Bevel favoured was much more in a "singer/songwriter" mode than nearly all soul music of the time, the horn section on "Keep On Stepping" is fat and full and play riffs that could have come from any Tyrone Davis 45 of the time.

It seems that in recent years he has combined singing with a move into the theatre.

Charles Beverly

In The Mood 1992 Torrid TRN90703 Producers: Lynette Clay & Charles Beverly

Charles Beverly (who died in 2008) worked almost exclusively out of St. Louis throughout his career although he also fronted the

Final Decisions group from Detroit. There was obviously not much money around at Torrid records as all copies of this LP came in a plain black sleeve. That frugal approach also extended to the music as much of which was programmed, including a re-cut of one of his better records from the eighties, "Hollywood". Beverly had talent but to hear him at his best, one would need to track down singles like "Stop And Think A Minute" from 1975, rather than listen to this LP.

Beverly & Duane

Beverly & Duane 1978 Ariola America SW50051 Producer: Will Hatcher

This Detroit recorded LP by Beverly Wheeler and Duane Williams has always had somewhat of a cult following in the UK. Certainly it benefits from employing stalwart Motown musicians such as Robert White, Eddie Brown and Joe Hunter and Beverly and Duane were rewarded with two minor entries in the soul charts in "Glad I Gotcha Baby" and "Living In A World", two of the better tracks on here. The whole thing is tuneful, accomplished and well sung, as well as being blessedly free from any disco influences, although it could have done with some variety in tempo.

A further two non-album singles also exist, but no more seems to have been heard from the duo.

B-H-Y

B-H-Y 1979 Salsoul SA 8524 Producers: Ronnie Baker, Norman Harris & Earl Young

Ronnie Baker, Norman Harris and Earl Young were three key members - arguably THE three key members - of the tremendous rhythm section out of Philadelphia that played on no end of brilliant and successful records, and all of them rank highly among the best ever practitioners within soul music on their respective instruments of bass, guitar and drums. They also wrote and produced countless other sides too, so had no compelling need to make this LP, which I suspect was just something they wanted to do because they could. It's pretty average stuff, with only one track "I Just Want To Funk (With You)", really worthy of a second listen. It was also the b-side of their small hit (also on here) "We Funk The Best" (#86 at the end of 1979). Some of the tracks are purely instrumental, while others employ the good singers Ron Tyson and Bruce Gray. Earl Young is still with us, but Baker and Harris have since passed on.

Big Maybelle

What More Can A Woman Do 1962 Brunswick BL754107 No producer noted

The Soul Of Big Maybelle 1964 Scepter SRM522 Producer: Tony Bruno

Got a Brand New Bag 1967 Rojac RS122 Producers: Bob Gallo & Jack Taylor

Saga Of The Good Life And Hard Times 1968 Rojac RS123 Producers: Robert Stepheny & Jack Taylor

The Gospel Soul Of 1968 Brunswick BL754142 No producer listed

The Last Of Big Maybelle 1973 Paramount PAS1011

The Amazing Big Maybelle 1973? UpFront UPF-162

Mabel Louise Smith was another important artist who straddled the pre-soul era and the "golden age", starting her recording career in the forties. As with other artists, then, I have chosen to focus on only a selected number of albums and, in her case, I will highlight her recordings from 1962 onwards, which kicked off with a set for Brunswick, *What More Can A Woman Do?*, badly marred by the overemphatic strings that make it uneasy listening.

The most pertinent thing to say about Big Maybelle, of course, is that she was an extraordinary singer. Just listen to "I Will Never Turn My Back On You" from the Scepter LP. While essentially a song of devotion and loyalty, the ingrained pain in her voice makes the first 90 seconds or so sound much more like a lament than an affirmation, until she changes to defiance just before the two minute mark, a stance much more in keeping with the sentiments of the song, before climaxing with an astonishing octave leap. It is such an adroit performance that it could obscure the truth of the album, which is that it is somewhat of a ragbag, with no style predominant. We have corny choruses, swing arrangements and marvellous early New York soul in the other great track, "Oh Lord, What Are You Doing To Me?"

If such an eclectic mix was true of the Scepter release, it is even more apparent on her first Rojac set, which makes the earlier album sound like a model of consistency and coherence. Hearing her tackle songs like "Cabaret", "I Can't Control Myself", "The Eggplant That Ate Chicago" and "There Must Be A Word" is not an enjoyable experience. On a more positive note, her driving and small hit version of "96 Tears"(#23 soul), demolishes the original and she could interpret "Love Is A Hurtin' Thing" with a great deal of conviction. Predictably, the sleevenotes play up the versatility angle of the LP, but in truth it is a bit of a mess, and really should have included her magnificent "Don't Pass Me By" (#27 - her first hit in ten years) which had hit the soul charts just before "96 Tears".

It would be most unfair to call *Saga* a mess but it is still a bit schizophrenic. Tracks like the superb "Old Love Never Dies" (recorded in Miami) and "It's Been Raining In My Heart" sound in tune with 1968; the ferocious "Maybelle Sings The Blues" and the mournful "Gloomy Sunday" do not. Still, it is probably her best LP of the sixties.

The Last Of Big Maybelle, a double album, does not contain "all unreleased material" as the sleeve erroneously tells us but, in fact, consists of the entire *Saga Of The Good Life* LP and, ironically, what would have been her best ever soul long player had the ten genuinely unreleased songs contained within ever have been issued at the time they were recorded. They range from a excellent Mack Rice composition, "Winnie Widow Brown", which owes something to "Harper Valley PTA", to the beautifully orchestrated "Blame It On Your Love" which would have fit in musically with what Bobby Bland was doing on *The California Album*. There are also shades of Etta James on a couple of the sides and it is all well worth hearing.

The Amazing Big Maybelle came out circa 1973 and is in fact the Scepter set minus three tracks. (I should also have mentioned the *Gospel Soul Of* LP which didn't have the mawkish strings of its Brunswick predecessor, but did have rather overbearing backing vocals to contend with.)

Big Maybelle died in 1972 and the desultory nature of her albums symbolised her rather messy and sad life but she was a huge talent, in every sense of the word.

Big Mouth (see also Stu Gardner)

Big Mouth   1971 Spindizzy Z 31024 Producer: David Briggs

Not a very flattering name for an artist (and would you believe eight or nine people have chosen it) and Stu Gardner, for he is the driving force, and I'm pretty sure, singer behind Big Mouth, is obliged to open wide for the cameras on the cover. This mysterious record, recorded on a CBS subsidiary, has received scant attention in the forty five years since it was released. The entry for Stu Gardner under his own name will elaborate a bit more on his career and his records but I would put out a big caveat emptor around this LP. It is stodgy, rocky music, of limited appeal.

Billion Dollar Band

Vernon Maddox; Charles Harris; Roosevelt Demps; Winston Stubbs; Reginald Polk; Taras Kowalchuk

Billion Dollar Band   1977 Good Sounds GS102 Producers: Stephen J Nicholas & Steve Gursky

This group came and went in 1977, which was when this album and the two singles from it were released. The second 45 particularly deserved to have made it as it coupled probably the best two tracks from the LP: "Get In The Groove" which has a fantastic chorus of release after fairly mundane verses, and the excellent "Let's Just Be Friends", the one track that highlights the lovely falsetto voice of Roosevelt Demps. The rest of the songs are delivered by Vernon Maddox. There are also a number of other good cuts with "Love's Sweet Notions" being probably the best-known but despite some predictable filler this is an LP worth seeking out.

Birdlegs and Pauline & Their Versatility Birds

Birdlegs   1963 Cuca K-4000 No producer listed

This charmingly named duo had one hit, "Spring", which even sounded a bit dated in 1963, and it, and its fine b-side, "In So Many Ways", are both featured on the LP. Birdlegs was Sidney Banks and Pauline, his wife, Pauline Shivers who also had a handful of releases under her own name. This is an almost unknown and/or totally forgotten LP and I think it is fair to say that it will be the only one in the book to have been recorded in Sauk City, Wisconsin. The record sleeve - which must have taken three minutes to design - does not tell us who produced the album but I think I am right in saying that The Versatility Birds were Antoinette Henry and Shirley Scott.

Edwin Birdsong

What It Is   1971 Polydor 24-4071 Producers: Edwin Birdsong & Ted Cooper

Super Natural   1973 Polydor PD5057 Producer: Edwin Kramer

Dance Of Survival   1975 Bam-boo GR004 Producer: Edwin Birdsong

Edwin Birdsong   1979 P.I.R. JZ 35758 Producer: Edwin Birdsong

Funtaztic   1981 Salsoul SA8550 Producer: Edwin Birdsong

The early seventies were a time when many artists were moving away from mere expressions of love, and tackling subjects of wider social implication. Los Angeles' Edwin Birdsong welcomed this change and only one of the eleven cuts on *What It Is* could be classed as a love song. Other topics were welfare, God, race, future hopes and inertia. (Some of the record was cut in FAME in Muscle Shoals but is very atypical of that studio.) Polydor at least tried to get Birdsong a hit by releasing two tracks as singles, but they had little commerciality with which to catch the ears of prospective record buyers.

The second Polydor LP employed a similar eclectic and wide-ranging approach as the first, right down to two failed singles and while one can applaud Birdsong for his refusal to conform to preconceived ideas of what a soul man should be, I'm afraid to say that both these releases sound very dated today and lack any melodic sensibility. And the same can be said of the Bam-Boo set which moved into more spiritual and mystical territory.

He then turned up, of all labels, on Philadelphia International with a set that celebrated dance. The social commentary had all gone. This was also true for his final LP on Salsoul but at least this one yielded up his only two singles ever to hit the soul charts ("Rapper Dapper Snapper" and "She's Wrapped Too Tight" at #65 and #55 respectively.) These latter two albums also sound significantly different in musical approach from the first three, but one still searches in vain for any tunes. (His work with Roy Ayers over the years proved he could do more "commercial" when he chose, however.).

Birdsong has to be classified as an "acquired taste", I think, and he was certainly unafraid to experiment in his music but I tend to think of his work now as interesting rather than vital, and all of it will have virtually no appeal whatsoever to anyone who worships at the altar of sixties' soul.

Blackbyrds (see also Keith Killgo and Blair)

Joe Hall; Keith Killgo; Kevin Toney; Barney Blair Perry; Allan Barnes; Perk Jacobs; Stephen Johnson; Orville Saunders; Wesley Jackson; James Garrett; Dan Stewart

Blackbyrds   1974 Fantasy F-9444 Producer: Larry Mizell (Billboard soul charts: 14 ; Billboard pop charts: 96)

Flying Start   1974 Fantasy F-9472 Producer: Donald Byrd (Billboard soul charts: 5 ; Billboard pop charts: 30)

Cornbread, Earl and Me   1975 Fantasy F-9483 Producer: Donald Byrd (Billboard soul charts: 19 ; Billboard pop charts: 150)

City Life   1975 Fantasy F-9490 Producer: Donald Byrd (Billboard soul charts: 3 ; Billboard pop charts: 16)

Unfinished Business   1976 Fantasy F-9518 Producer: Donald Byrd (Billboard soul charts: 29 ; Billboard pop charts: 34)

Action   1977 Fantasy F-9535 Producer: Donald Byrd (Billboard soul charts: 28 ; Billboard pop charts: 43)

Night Grooves   1978 Fantasy F-9570 (Billboard soul charts: 43 ; Billboard pop charts: 159)

Better Days 1981 Fantasy F-9602 Producer: George Duke (Billboard soul charts: 40 ; Billboard pop charts: 133)

The Blackbyrds out of Washington D.C. were a successful group right from their start until their end: note that every one of their eight LPs charted. It would be hard to imagine what would have happened without Donald Byrd, however. He inspired them, produced them, taught some of them at Howard University, and gave them use of his name. "Walking In Rhythm", and "Happy Music" were the two big records for the group, both reaching the US Pop Top 20, and they tended to favour two distinct styles: funky or dreamy. I much preferred the former.

Blackbyrds was a good one, establishing their jazz influenced funk approach, which was slightly more melodic and less hard-edged than what we heard from contemporaries like Kool & The Gang or The Ohio Players. It was also largely instrumental and it must be said that the group never had a lead vocalist of any great distinction. "Do It Fluid " was both the best track and their first hit, when it lodged at #23 on the soul charts in the summer of 1974.

Flying Start contained "Walking In Rhythm", which remains possibly their best known track and certainly their biggest ever hit: #4 soul and #6 pop. Personally, I find much of the album to be pretty bland ("Love Is Love" and Future Children, Future Hopes") and would have preferred more in the slightly edgier vein of "Spaced Out".

Next up they were given the opportunity to score the theme to a movie, *Cornbread, Earl And Me*, which accordingly sounds a little different with a number of tracks only being two minutes or so long but it is a good example of the genre.

They then really hit their stride with their best LP in the form of the superb *City Life* with its key track being "Rock Creek Park" which, helped significantly by the soulful vocals of Merry Clayton, brilliantly evoked a time and place: Washington DC, summer, mid-seventies. It is still revered in the city to this day. The flip-side to the carefree evenings spent in Rock Creek Park was addressed in the title track, which cautioned against the dangers to be found on the steamy urban streets. Another fine track, "Hash And Eggs", was just about breakfast, while the excellent "Happy Music" became their second biggest hit ever at #3 soul and #19 pop.

Unfinished Business was slightly disappointing - "Party Land" used the irritating "whoah whoah" disco call - when compared to *City Life* and the sense was that they had peaked (and maybe it was telling that nothing from the set appeared on *Night Grooves* which is a compilation of most of their best work) although the good and driving "Time Is Movin'" became their third single to enter the soul top 20.

Action was a return to better form in 1977 with two biggish singles in "Soft And Easy" and "Supernatural Feeling" but the slower tracks were still rather too soft for my taste. "Something Special" has surely been played in elevators, for example.

Last up was *Better Days*, where, for the first time someone other than Larry Mizell or Donald Byrd produced them: George Duke. The sound did change, things were a bit more melodic and there was more focus on singing than in the past, but it was still noticeably The Blackbyrds. "What We Have Is Right" and "Love Don't Strike Twice" were two more singles to hit the soul charts, the tenth and eleventh times this had happened.

Over the eight years or so that the Blackbyrds put out records they were very well served by Fantasy who didn't stint on investing in them - the group had their own logo as well as almost invariable gatefold sleeves for their albums.

The group broke up after *Better Days* with Keith Killgo and Barney Blair Perry going on to cut solo LPs, and although some of their many fans won't want to hear it, I will always consider The Blackbyrds to be a group of excellent musicians who never really managed to do their talents full justice.

Black Heat

Brad Owens; Phil Guilbeau; Johnell Grey; Esco Cromer; Naamon (Chip) Jones; Raymond Green; Ray Thompson; Rodney Edwards; James Duval

Black Heat 1972 Atlantic SD 7237 Producer: Joel Dorn

No Time To Burn 1974 Atlantic SD 2987 Producers: Joel Dorn & Jimmy Douglass (Billboard soul charts: 58 ; Billboard pop charts: 201)

Keep On Running 1975 Atlantic SD 18128 Producer: Jimmy Douglass (Billboard soul charts: 51)

Black Heat out of Washington DC were one of the more unheralded "street funk" bands that proliferated from 1972 until about 1974 or so when the music softened somewhat to reflect the burgeoning disco scene, but, for my money, they were also one of the best. This quality was driven by their adaptability as, unlike some funk bands, they could really sing, as evidenced by the lost classic "Street Of Tears", "You'll Never Know" and "Time Is Gonna Catch You" all from the splendid debut LP.

They followed up with another superb platter, *No Time To Burn*, which has a first side that is entirely funky and entirely excellent, including a socially conscious "Check It All Out", an aggressive reading of Kool and the Gang's "Love The Life You Live", and their only ever national hit in the title track when it reached #56 on the soul charts as a single. Side two doesn't quite match up as it has one throwaway cut in "Rapid Fire" but "Times Have Changed" is another fine publically spirited funk workout and "Things Change" is the album's one - and good - slow track.

The third and final LP kicked off with a real departure: a version of The Beatles' "Drive My Car", which - apart from a fine sax break by Ray Thompson - doesn't really impress. However, it does symbolise the variety of this third LP, which is more diverse than the first two with tracks like the great "Questions And Conclusions" and "Feel Like A Child" employing some highly soulful singing by Chip Jones. They had also toned down their assertiveness from *No Time To Burn* in favour of a more dreamy take on cuts like "Prince Duval" and only "Zimba Ku" and "Live Together" reprise the earlier energy.

Black Heart

Jigsaw 1977 Guinness GNS 36025 Producer: Paul Whitehead

Guinness was a mysterious label, set up, allegedly, by Prelude records for beneficial tax reasons, and the albums were thus never designed to be sold but, as is the way with vinyl, a number slipped out anyway to end up with collectors. It is anyone's guess as to who played or sang on *Jigsaw* and also debateable as to whether or not Black Heart existed for any longer than it took to record the LP but it does have some good moments, all of which are on side two, as side one is utterly forgettable with no redeeming features at all save a so-so ballad in "Side Effects".

"Feel The Need In Me" (not the Detroit Emeralds' hit) has a soulful delivery and Curtis Mayfield's "So In Love" is a worthy version, actually pretty damn close to the original, as is their take on Eddie Kendricks' "Happy" but this was never a paticularly strong song. *Jigsaw* ends with a cover of, for some reason, The Sunshine Band's "Shotgun Shuffle".

Black Ice

Antone Curtis; Gerald Bell; Cleveland Jones; Frank Willis; Ralph Lars; Robert Sherman

Black Ice 1976 Amherst AMH-1006 Producer: Hadley Murrell

I Judge The Funk 1979 HDM 2003 Producer: Hadley Murrell

Black Ice 1982 Montage ST-72003 Producer: Hadley Murrell

Three LPs on three different labels, but in fact Black Ice (a highly popular name for bands, there are a number of others) had a consistency driven by the same handful of key individuals who worked with them throughout: Hadley Murrell (producer, songwriter and mentor), Ray Jackson (arranger and songwriter) and Eddie Horan (songwriter).The first LP mixes up ballads and dance tracks (untouched by disco) and is certainly nice enough, if lacking in enough distinction to allow them to compete with The Dramatics, O'Jays, Dells etc. who were the key soul congregations of the time. Having said that, "Making Love In The Rain" is terrific. "Shakedown" was pulled as a 45, and scraped into the charts.

I Judge The Funk is more of the same, with "Fantazise" being the best ballad this time round, and even an eight minute track, "Play More Latin Music", retains interest throughout. Only the title track sounds dated today.

The final LP, also confusingly and unimaginatively called *Black Ice*, is generally excellent, particularly in the light of what most other soul vocals groups were serving up in 1982. Side two is uniformly good with "I Just Wanna Hold You" (their second soul chart entrant, #64) and "This Time" being exemplary sweet soul. Side one is more problematic as it features three dance tracks that are OK, but pretty dated, and a much better one in "(Sergios) I Want To Be With You".

Black Ivory

Russell Patterson; Stuart Bascombe; Leroy Burgess

Don't Turn Around 1972 Today 1005 Producer: Patrick Adams (Billboard soul charts: 13 ; Billboard pop charts: 158)

Baby, Won't You Change Your Mind 1972 Today 1008 Producers: Patrick Adams & David Jordan (Billboard soul charts: 26 ; Billboard pop charts: 188)

Black Ivory were a much loved trio from New York, who delivered two highly pretty albums on Today records. They sold strongly to a soul audience but could not cross over to a pop one. I can understand if anyone were to find their records a little "soft" as sweet soul is not for everyone, but I think they are lovely and still sound fresh today. Most of the leads were handled by the talented Leroy Burgess who left the group in the late seventies to work with other acts (most notably Aleem), although Stuart Bascombe also contributed significantly.

Don't Turn Around boasted three soul chart entrants in the title track, "You And I" and "I'll Find A Way" as well as a sweet take on "Got To Be There" and when the group stayed at this slow pace they were at their best. For variety it probably made sense to increase the pace here and there but "Our Future" and "I Keep Asking You Questions" were not distinguished songs.

The charming "Time Is Love" and "Spinning Around" were further moderate hits (#37 and #45 respectively) when pulled from *Baby Won't You Change Your Mind,* the title track of which would surely have been another success had it been featured as a single. Once again the emphasis was firmly and rightly on slow material, and if it was the second set in a row that lacked a genuinely great song, it was still highly enjoyable listening.

Feel It 1975 Buddah BDS 5644 Producers: Robert John, Mike Gately, Patrick Adams & Black Ivory

Black Ivory 1976 Buddah BDS 5658 Producers: Black Ivory, Robert John & Mike Gately

Hangin' Heavy 1979 Buddah BDS 5722 Producers: Lenny Adams, Stuart Bascombe & Russell Patterson

By 1975 the group had moved on to Buddah after a short stop at Kwanza (where no albums materialised, only one single, the atypical but enjoyable "What Goes Around (Comes Around)", their sixth soul chart entry), and they delivered three LPs.

Feel It by and large continued the approach of the Today material (examples being "Warm Inside" and the gorgeous "Will We Ever Come Together" which was the best track, and yet another soul hit at #40) although the sound was slightly fuller and featured more uptempo material, including the title track, somewhat of a "Rock Your Baby" clone.

Black Ivory changed things significantly and the group were no longer obviously identifiable as the one who made the Today sides. That's not to characterise it is a poor record (although the "Mandy/Could It Be Magic" medley was a huge misstep) and "Making Love In My Mind" was the finest uptempo song they had recorded thus far. However, the ballads on which they had made their reputation were in scarce supply, the beautiful "You Mean Everything To Me" and "Can't You See" apart.

By the time of *Hangin' Heavy* Burgess had departed, although he still wrote a handful of the tracks as well as taking care of some of the arrangements. "Mainline" was an anthemic dance outing of considerable power although "Big Apple Rock" and "Get Down" sounded like so many other uptempo records. "Rest Inside My Love" and "You Turned My Whole World Around" have one Diane Ransom sharing vocals with Bascombe and Patterson and she should have been utilised more often as they are stand-out tracks.

Then And Now 1984 Panoramic PLP-10001 Producers: Lenny Adams, Russell Patterson & David Hart

I, like many, had assumed that Black Ivory had finished their recording career on Buddah, but *Then And Now* surprisingly turned up in 1984. The "Then" side featured four original tracks from the early work whereas "Now "showcased four new songs. Bascombe had also left by this time and so it is conceivable that these cuts were actually solo outings by Russell Patterson. Whatever their origin, I'm afraid they weren't vintage Black Ivory. "Words" was a so-so ballad, and whereas "You Are My Lover" and "All The Right Moves" were no more than OK dance tracks, "Hold On Tight" was simply weak.

Black Merda

Anthony Hawkins; Charles Hawkins; V C Veasey; Tyrone Hite

Black Merda 1969 Chess CH1551 Producer: Swan

Long Burn The Fire 1972 Janus JLS 3042 Producer: Gene Barge

Black Merda claimed proudly and entirely accurately to be one of the first ever bands to use the word "black" in their name in order to reflect the growing militancy of the late sixties. The four members of the group originally met up in Detroit and performed as the Impacts and The Soul Agents, backing up big stars of the time.

Their new name clearly reflected their awareness of and interest in the music of Jimi Hendrix, but in fact the first album is much nearer in sound to the early Funkadelic sets, but that still means of course that it should be approached with caution by anyone who does not care for that style. It was not a success, selling few copies, but it has been recently re-discovered by a small but enthusiastic audience, to the extent that it was re-issued on CD in 1996. "Ashamed", "Good Luck" and "Reality" are good funk/rock tracks, much more to my taste that the guitar work-outs on "Over And Over" and "Windsong".

By the time of the second LP, drummer Tyrone Hite had been replaced by Bob Crowder, but the picture on the back of the record cover only shows the Hawkins brothers and Veasey suggesting that Crowder was never "in" the band. *Long Burn The Fire* was no more successful than the first as regards sales, and while the better tracks still recalled Funkadelic, others such as "Sometimes I Wish" had an extremely tenuous link with soul music.

Black Nasty (see also ADC Band and Nazty)

Audrey Matthews; Terry Ellis; Jackie Cosper; Thomas Carter; Mark Patterson; Artwell Matthews

Talking To The People 1973 Enterprise ENS-1031 Producers: Mack Rice & Johnnie Mae Matthews

A rock-influenced funk bank emanating from Detroit, it was no surprise that Black Nasty also (like Black Merda) sounded pretty similar to Funkadelic on many of the tracks on this LP which sadly did not sell many copies for the Stax empire. The band would have to wait until they morphed into Nazty and, later, The ADC Band before they could enjoy seeing their name on the soul charts. The funk tracks like "Getting Funky Around Here", "We're Doing Our Thing" and the title track are all much more enjoyable to me than the rockier cuts such as "Booger The Hooker". Best of all is a nice soulful ballad, "I Must Be In Love".

Black Satin (see also Fred Parris & The Satins)

Fred Parris; James Curtis; Richard Freeman; Nate Marshall Mosely

Black Satin Featuring Fred Parris 1976 Buddah BDS 5654 Producers: Marty Kugell & Al Altman

The Five Satins were one of the best-loved and most successful black vocal groups of the fifties. Like so many similar aggregations they had some difficulty in adapting to the soul era and recorded without much commercial reward for a host of different labels in the sixties. They decided to change their name for the one album on Buddah, which was a little patchy, but contained some good things. The best tracks are those which open each side, namely "Tears, Tears, Tears" and "Everybody Stand And Clap Your Hands" (also a #49 soul single), and a faithful and inevitable re-working of their best known and most successful record, "In The Still Of The Night".

Black Velvet

Jesse Kirkland; Joe Greene

Love City 1969 Okeh OKS14130 Producer: Jackie Mills

I think I might be right in saying that this was the last LP ever put out on the venerable Okeh label but it wasn't a glorious exit. If you can imagine, on one end of a spectrum, The Everly Brothers' approach to duet singing and, on the other, Sam and Dave's, consider where Black Velvet's Jesse and Joe might fall? Actually, probably nearer The Everlys, if truth be told. In other words, this is pretty soft, pop-oriented soul singing with a truly hideous version of "Hey Jude" thrown in. On the more positive side, they make a pretty decent fist of Sly's "Love City" and their harmonic sense is solid throughout.

J Blackfoot (see also The Soul Children)

City Slicker 1983 Sound Town ST-8002 Producers: Homer Banks & Chuck Brooks (Billboard soul charts: 16)

Physical Attraction 1984 Sound Town ST-8013 Producers: Homer Banks & Chuck Brooks

U Turn 1987 Edge EDLP-001 Producer: Homer Banks (Billboard soul charts: 67)

Loveaholic 1991 Platinum Blue PB4101 Producers: Homer Banks & Lester Snell

John "Blackfoot" Colbert was a lead singer in The Soul Children, one of the greatest of all soul groups, but it was quite a surprise when he re-surfaced - seemingly out of nowhere - at the end of 1983 to score a huge soul hit with "Taxi" (#4 soul), a record that became the showpiece of *City Slicker*. It was also, together with the follow-up single, "I Stood On The Sidewalk And Cried" (#63 soul), by far the best thing on the LP. He demonstrated on these excellent Banks and Brooks songs just what a superb artist he was, and what we had been missing while he was not recording. There were singers with better range than Colbert but few could convey pain as convincingly. "One Of Those Parties" was fun and presumably exactly the sort of get together that mama told her son not to come to, but most of the other tracks, while not bad, were slightly dull.

Physical Attraction - like *City Slicker* - was recorded at Ardent studios in Memphis and did not rely so much on Banks / Brooks songs, a tactic that had mixed results. Harlan Howard's "I Don't Remember Loving You" was a worthy addition to the many glorious country-soul songs recorded down the years, and "Don't You Feel It Like I Feel It" (a #62 soul hit) is an admirable tale of seduction but tackling Sam and Dave's "You Got Me Humming" didn't work and "Kum Ba Ya" (yes, that one) should have been left well alone.

Blackfoot then moved to Edge, but continued to work with

Homer Banks although Lester Snell replaced Chuck Brooks. *U-Turn* has its moments, with worthwhile songs like "Breaking The Monotony" and "Tear Jerker" but the title track, "Warning" and "Don't Get Funny With My Money" are very poor indeed.

Loveaholic was better than the Edge release given it featured consistently stronger songs by Banks and Snell with "She's Only Human" being particularly good. Nevertheless, it is another of many LPs from this era which would have sounded so much better had they been afforded the opportunity of a proper band. I don't think this is just nostalgia on my part as I imagine most people would agree that a proper horn section sounds more fulfilling than the ersatz on show here.

Colbert had recorded as a solo artist to no great acclaim a few years before he even joined the Soul Children, and he passed away in 2011.

Don Blackman

Don Blackman 1982 Arista GRP 5509 Producers: Dave Grusin & Larry Rosen

Another record with a big cult following but one whose appeal has always somewhat eluded me. Clearly talented in many disciplines, pianist Blackman has an impressive c.v. but not much about this album really stands out as being particularly good or bad, although "Holding You, Loving You" is sweet enough.

BlackSmoke

Michael Fisher; Tony Fisher; Arnold Riggs; Rodney Thompson; Bradley Henry Thoelke; Clifford Ervin; Buddy McDaniel; Raymond Genovese

BlackSmoke 1976 Chocolate City CCLP 2001 Producer: Wayne Henderson

A likeable LP that got lost in the shuffle. There is nothing particularly original about BlackSmoke, an eight piece band who generally sound like Kool/Tower of Power/ EWAF etc., but they were at least as good as any number of other bands who did attain some success. The standout tracks for me would be the two that are least typical: a nicely arranged "You Needn't Worry Now" which demonstrates they had a fine lead singer in Arnold Riggs and "Sunshine, Roses And Rainbows" a smooth and beguiling dance item.

The album originally came out as by "Smoke" and I imagine they changed their name to avoid confusion with another group of the same name. I am listing them under "BlackSmoke" as opposed to "Smoke" as their one single success on the soul charts, "(Your Love Has Got Me) Screamin'" (albeit at only #96), which is included on here, was under the new name.

Blair (see also The Blackbyrds)

Nightlife 1979 Solar Sound Records SS 001 Producer: Barney Blair Perry

Barney Blair Perry was a former guitarist of The Blackbyrds leaving them to record his one and only LP. The record has traces of the smooth sound of The Blackbyrds but precious little of their funk and I'm afraid to say that its rather disco approach does not thrill me, but the LP is in demand so others will doubtless disagree with my assessment.

Barbara Blake & The Uniques

Barbara Blake & The Uniques 1975 20th Century T-462 Producer: Jimmy Vanleer

Barbara Blake was born in Atlanta as Barbara Livsey, later moving to Chicago where she recorded some fine sides in the sixties as one half of The Du-ettes. When the Du-ettes called it a day Barbara teamed up with her sister Gwen to release a couple of singles before a third girl, Doris Lindsey, was added to form "Barbara And The Uniques" and it was under this name that a few singles were issued on the Arden and Abbott labels. However, on her one and only LP she used her full name. Barbara Blake was one of all too many soul singers: highly talented but almost completely unknown. This is an accomplished LP, which I recommend almost unreservedly. The "almost" is only appended because the songs could have been a little more memorable, but that is only a minor quibble given how much there is to enjoy in simply listening to Blake sing. Her best performances are probably on "Teach Me" and "I Need Your Love So Bad" (each released as failed 45s) but all the tracks are worthwhile. The music behind Blake is well orchestrated and sympathetic for which the somewhat enigmatic producer Vanleer should be applauded. (The album was released with three unnamed male singers supplanting Gwen Livsey and Doris Lindsey.)

Cicero Blake

Too Hip To Be Happy 1988 Valley Vue DI - 72920 Producers: Cicero Blake & Rico McFarland

Jackson Mississippi born Blake released a fair number of good singles in the sixties and seventies, some under his Christian name Cicero and some under his middle name, Corey, but none of them achieved any national success and his one LP, arriving years after his best work, was disappointing, mainly due to two factors: firstly, many of the tracks are in fact routine blues songs, and, second, too much of it is programmed, despite the presence of real musicians on a couple of tracks. The only cut that is definitely worth hearing is his interpretation of Tommy Tate's impressive "School of life" but even this can't compete with the original. The title cut is reasonable, but he delivers an entirely routine version of "I've Got To Use My Imagination" while, most oddly, "Oh Pretty Woman" is credited to Orbison, Nelson and Rush despite being an entirely different song from what one would expect. His biggest regional success, "Dip My Dipper", originally released in 1978, is re-cut here.

Blake has gone on to do fairly well in the last twenty years or so releasing a number of CDs.

Bobby Bland

Blues Consolidated (with Junior Parker) 1958 No producer listed

Two Steps From The Blues 1961 Duke DLP 74 No producer listed

Here's The Man! 1962 Duke DLP 75 No producer listed (Billboard pop charts: 53)

Call On Me / That's The Way Love Is 1963 Duke DLP 77 No producer listed (Billboard pop charts: 11)

Ain't Nothing You Can Do 1964 Duke DLP 78 No producer listed (Billboard pop charts: 119)

The Soul Of The Man 1966 Duke DLP 79 No producer listed (Billboard soul charts: 17)

The Best Of Bobby Bland 1967 Duke DLP 84 (Billboard soul charts: 29)

The Best Of Bobby Bland Volume 2 1967 Duke DLP 86

Bobby "Blue" Bland was one of the greatest of all soul singers and, like the Temptations, Aretha Franklin and James Brown, was revered by a black audience. Unlike them, however, he never really crossed over to a pop world. He has the astonishing statistic of only ever placing one single ("Ain't Nothing You Can Do", and that at number 20) in the US pop top 20 singles. Conversely, on the US Soul singles charts he put no less than *thirty nine* records in the top twenty, an almost unbelievable discrepancy, and somewhat of a damning indictment on how he was handled by Duke records.

That first LP was shared with Junior Parker, each artist having six tracks per side, with the highlight from Bland being his first ever #1 soul single, "Further On Up The Road", but it was the second, the magnificent *Two Steps From The Blues,* that really started to make his name. Featuring six top ten soul chart singles, it stands as one of the best albums in the history of black music, assiduously bridging the past with the future. "I'll Take Care Of You" and "Don't Cry No More" are poles apart in tempo and delivery but aligned in artistry, "Lead Me On" is a genuinely profound song, "I Pity The Fool" (his second #1) is one of soul's greatest moments and even the cover photo is a classic, conjuring up a land, which may indeed have been unfriendly, but which clearly had sunshine, the like of which never seemed to percolate through to cold and damp England. There is not even close to a weak track on the LP.

It was followed up by *Here's The Man*! which was kicked off by the thrilling "36 22 36" (now that's a band) one of so many tracks in the Duke years that showcases the superb production and arranging of Joe Scott, a man who, like Bobby's guitarist, Wayne Bennett, was crucial to his success. (Scott was the sole producer of all Bland's first four LPs, even if Duke declined to mention the fact on the sleeves.) It was now clear to most people who cared about popular music what a truly great singer Bland was, with his ability to convey passion or regret with impeccable timing. "Stormy Monday Blues","Turn On Your Lovelight","Who Will The Next Fool Be" and "Ain't That Loving You" were four more hits to be pulled from the set, which once again had no weak moments.

His third solo LP yielded a mere three hits in the shape of "Share Your Love With Me" and the two title tracks with "Call On Me" being his second ever biggest pop success (at #22), while "That's The Way Love Is" became his third, and final, #1 soul hit. However, changes were clearly afoot and "Share Your Love With Me" featured strings and a girl chorus that we were unaccustomed to hearing on Bobby Bland records, and in general, while the album is once again highly meritorious it doesn't have quite the drive and ardour of the previous two, and advertised a couple of songs on the front cover that were not in fact included.

Ain't Nothing You Can Do was slightly disappointing as it had a rather cheesy cover, only two hits, a further softening of style ("After It's Too Late" and "If You Could Read My Mind") and the odd merely Ok song such as "Today" but it did have a magnificent title track and the old toughness was back in "Blind Man", "I'm Gonna Cry", "Black Night"and "Reconsider".

There was a couple of years gap before *The Soul Of The Man* appeared (which meant that a number of charting singles in 1965 and 1966 don't appear on it) and it only included one hit in the shape of "Back In The Same Old Bag". Musically, it was harder than the previous two releases, with the strings absent once again. He also duets with Vi Campbell on "Dear Bobby (The Note)" which was a departure for him as was recording some of the tracks in Detroit with Joe Hunter and others in Houston with Gil Caple - both men helping Joe Scott with production duties, even if none were credited on the sleeve. (All the tracks on his previous LPs had been recorded in Los Angeles, Nashville or Chicago). Please also note that although it was the first of his LPs to appear on the soul charts it certainly doesn't mean it sold better than the previous four in the black market. It was simply that *Billboard* didn't start producing a separate Soul LP listing until January 1965.

Duke also put out a couple of *Best Of* sets before Bland's next "real" LP, but they both missed the opportunity to pick up (apart from "Poverty") big selling Bland 45s such as "Dust Got In Daddy's Eyes", "Yield Not To Temptation", "These Hands (Small But Mighty)" and "I'm Too Far Gone To Turn Around" which therefore remained unreleased on album at the time.

A Touch Of The Blues 1968 Duke DLP 88 No producer listed (Billboard soul charts: 38)

Spotlighting The Man 1969 Duke DLP 89 No producer listed (Billboard soul charts: 24)

A couple of the Caple/Scott Houston produced songs found their way onto *A Touch Of The Blues*, as did a couple of Memphis recorded tracks produced by Willie Mitchell (the thrilling title track, for example) but most of it was recorded in Chicago including the magnificent and utterly ferocious "That Did It" (a #6 soul hit, but much too "black" to bother the pop chart listings at all) which I think has a claim to be his finest ever record, although it is a surprise that such a quintessential Bland side was actually produced by Pearl Woods, not Joe Scott. (As ever producers were not listed on the sleeve). It's a really good set, his best since *Here's The Man!* and much loved tracks such as "Shoes" and "Road of Broken Hearted Men" can be found on it.

The next Duke outing, *Spotlighting The Man*, was also recorded in different locations (and produced by Andre Williams, Oscar Perry, Henry Boozier, and Joe Scott) and mixed up "standards" such as "Chains Of Love" (a #9 soul hit) which juxtaposed soaring strings with biting guitar from Bennett, with new songs like "Ask Me 'Bout Nothing" where Bland demonstrated that he had not lost one iota of his vocal skill over the years. "Rockin" In The Same Old Boat" and "Gotta Get To Know You" were two further big hits to be found on here, and although he went on to place a number of further singles on the charts for Duke, it was to be his last LP for them.

His California Album 1973 Dunhill / ABC DSX -50163 Producer: Steve Barri (Billboard soul charts: 3 ; Billboard pop charts: 136)

Dreamer 1974 Dunhill / ABC DSX- 50169 Producer: Steve Barri (Billboard soul charts: 5 ; Billboard pop charts: 172)

Together For The First Time…Live (and BB

King) 1974 Dunhill / ABC 50190 Producer: Steve Barri (Billboard soul charts: 2 ; Billboard pop charts: 43)

Get On Down With Bobby Bland 1975 ABC 895 Producers: Don Gant & Ron Chancey Producer: (Billboard soul charts: 14 ; Billboard pop charts: 154)

Together Again...Live (and BB King) 1976 ABC 9317 Producer: Esmond Edwards (Billboard soul charts: 9 ; Billboard pop charts: 73)

Reflections In Blue 1977 ABC 1018 Producer: Steve Barri (Billboard soul charts: 47; Billboard pop charts: 185)

Come Fly With Me 1978 ABC 1075 Producers: Al Bell & Monk Higgins (Billboard soul charts: 31; Billboard pop charts: 185)

ABC acquired Bland's contract in 1973 and the move meant that for the first time Bland found himself with a record label who were prepared, and could afford, to push him towards pop stardom (even if time was to prove that it didn't work) and certainly the records were more successful than they had been for a long time, with the excellent Oscar Perry song "This Time I'm Gone For Good", from the *His California Album* becoming his biggest single for nearly ten years (#5 soul, #42 pop). Steve Barri was entrusted with production for the first handful of LPs and the songs were generally well chosen and ensured that Bland's loyal audience would not be short-changed. The one slight disappointment from *His California Album* was firstly that strings predominated over horns and second, that "Goin' Down Slow" was a rather dull choice of follow-up single, probably expressed in the fact that it only made it to #17 soul and #69 pop.

Dreamer was a strong encore featuring big singles in the great "Ain't No Love In The Heart Of The City" (#9 soul) and "I Wouldn't Treat A Dog"(#3) and a third lesser hit but still highly enjoyable side in "Yolanda", a smart song from Daniel Moore, and even if the Duke albums did not exist, these first two on ABC/Dunhill alone would have ensured Bland was a soul man of the highest order.

Someone came up with the commercially inspired idea to release a live set of Bland together with BB King. Not only was it Bland's most successful ever LP, it was one of the biggest of King's career as well. In fact so well did it prosper, that ABC issued a follow-up two years later, which also flourished. Both outings are fine if a little bit predictable and more likely pitched towards crossover audiences than the chitlin circuit. It must be said, though: I wonder who still plays them today?

Slotted in between the two live albums was *Get On Down With Bobby Bland* an entirely misleading title which suggested Bobby had gone "disco". He hadn't, but he HAD gone country. If it was undoubtedly the most unusual of all his LPs, it was also a good one, not least because of the high standards of the songs he covered, from writers as accomplished as Dan Penn, Donnie Fritts, Conway Twitty and Merle Haggard. The record really needs to be listened to at 3 in the morning. although Bergen White's rather soporific string arrangements won't help to keep you awake. "Today I Started Loving You Again (good, but not as good as Bettye Swann's version) and "I Take It On Home" both hit the soul charts as singles but at #34 and #41 respectively, were hardly of a magnitude to make record company or singer deliriously happy.

Steve Barri returned to produce *Reflections In Blue*, another album characterised by strong songs including one of the very few co-penned by Bobby himself, "The Soul Of A Man", (nothing to do with the LP from 1966) which became a pretty big single in 1977 at #18 soul. On the other hand, the excellent "Sitting On A Poor Man's Throne" struggled to get any higher than #82, which meant beyond much doubt that Bland's audience was finally dwindling.

The final ABC record moved Bland into the hands of Al Bell and Monk Higgins who were to remain his producers across his entire stay at MCA. Bell and Higgins had just launched the ICA logo and the sound of *Come Fly With Me* was, not surprisingly, the same as the releases on their label. "Love To See You Smile" was a successful single from the set and became the last ever 45 from Bobby Bland to hit the Soul top 20 chart (#14).

I Feel Good, I Feel Fine 1979 MCA 3157 Producers: Al Bell & Monk Higgins (Billboard soul charts: 34; Billboard pop charts: 187)

Sweet Vibrations 1980 MCA 5145 Producers: Al Bell & Monk Higgins (Billboard soul charts: 29)

Try Me, I'm Real 1981 MCA 5233 Producers: Al Bell & Monk Higgins (Billboard soul charts: 52 ; Billboard pop charts: 207)

Here We Go Again 1982 MCA 5297 Producers: Al Bell & Monk Higgins (Billboard soul charts: 22 ; Billboard pop charts: 201)

Tell Mr. Bland 1983 MCA 5425 Producers: Al Bell & Monk Higgins (Billboard soul charts: 50)

You've Got Me Loving You 1984 MCA 5503 Producers: Al Bell & Monk Higgins (Billboard soul charts: 35)

ABC was sold to MCA in 1979 which resulted in Bland's records appearing on a new label and things began alarmingly, as the first LP, *I Feel Good, I Feel Fine*, had as its title track (and lead off cut, no less) a six minute plus dance track of no merit and, what's more, no Bland: he didn't sing a note. When one considers that two other tracks on side one employed coo-ing disco ladies it was time to fear for Bland's dignity and it was all as unseemly as, say, Joe Scott's having been cajoled into writing a rap song. Luckily, it was just a false alarm and sanity was restored on side two and, indeed, pretty much the entirety of the rest of the MCA LPs, even if they represent the least interesting period of his career. The fact that "Tit For Tat" managed only a paltry #71 on the soul charts, though, suggested at the time that his commercial decline might have been terminal.

The *Sweet Vibrations* set was dedicated to Scott, which is probably why I feel it to have been Bland's strongest MCA release and whereas most of the other sets for the label had more in common with his ABC period, this one echoed right back to the Duke days, and featured a band of power, verve and skill. It sounds great today in fact, with a lovely tender version of "Over The Rainbow" and a collection of grown-up songs, but "You'd Be A Millionaire", when released as a single was going up against the likes of Yarbrough & Peoples' "Don't Stop The Music". That went to #1, Bland's record to #92.

Try Me, I'm Real included two Bland songs, a highly unusual occurrence, and, in truth, neither was great, and the same has to be said for his interpretations of "What A Difference A Day Makes" and "I Cover The Waterfront", and the disappointing LP contained no soul charting singles at all, the first studio album of his entire career where this was the case.

Here We Go Again, the excellent "You're About To Win" and "Recess In Heaven" (#40 soul as a 45, and a lovely trombone solo by George Bohanon) excepted, toned down the brass from *Sweet Vibrations* in favour of strings and a more contemporary touch in the rhythm section here and there as well as featuring, for the third time in a row, an LP cover which omitted Bland himself in favour of a pretty woman. Doubtless MCA realised that in an era of increased marketing awareness, trying to sell records by a 50 year old man usually singing music out of step with pretty much everyone else, needed all the help possible.

Tell Mr. Bland at least had Bobby back on the front cover and no-one could have accused MCA in skimping on costs as the orchestration was fulsome throughout, but it was ultimately another rather lacklustre outing with Bobby playing no part on the "What Is It?" track, some mediocre songs and a heavy-handed take on "Fever". It wasn't awful, no Bland LPs ever were, but it is rather dull.

No hits of any sort could be found on *Tell Mr. Bland* and they were equally elusive on *You've Got Me Loving You*, but it was a more spirited set, particularly on side two which displayed a great deal of verve in the musical department with the kind of blaring horns that recalled his best days. It was also, though, probably the set on which he started to overdo his famous "squall" for the first time.

Members Only 1985 Malaco 7429 Producers: Tommy Couch & Wolf Stephenson (Billboard soul charts: 45)

After All 1986 Malaco 7439 Producers: Tommy Couch & Wolf Stephenson (Billboard soul charts: 65)

Blues You Can Use 1987 Malaco 7444 Producers: Tommy Couch & Wolf Stephenson (Billboard soul charts: 71)

Midnight Run 1989 Malaco 7450 Producers: Tommy Couch & Wolf Stephenson (Billboard soul charts: 26)

Portrait Of The Blues 1991 Malaco 7458 Producers: Tommy Couch & Wolf Stephenson (Billboard soul charts: 50)

Years Of Tears 1993 Malaco 7469 Producers: Tommy Couch & Wolf Stephenson (Billboard soul charts: 80)

In 1985 Bland moved on again, to an admirable independent record label. Throughout the eighties Malaco records out of Jackson Mississippi became the last company to market and sell soul music to an audience who still appreciated its history and heritage and they deliberately signed up artists who would feel comfortable with such an approach. Who better than Bobby Bland to become your "flagship" artist? While Malaco never had massive success they certainly did extraordinarily well and consistently released fine music for over a decade. The label has attracted a fair degree of opprobrium from those who felt that the arrangements and production were a little formulaic but it offered a genuine alternative to pretty much everything else that was marketed under the name of soul in the rather bleak musical decade that was the eighties.

Members Only was a strong start for Bland on Malaco with the title track being a sharp Larry Addison song as well as becoming the last single (out of a total of over sixty) he ever posted onto the soul singles top 100 chart, when it reached #54. The album also set the tone for, as with the MCA records, what would be a consistent approach: Wolf Stephenson and Tommy Couch producing, Harrison Calloway arranging and a consistent stable of strong writers providing the majority of the songs.

After All carried a handful of memorable compositions in "Angel", "Second Hand Heart" and "There Ain't No Turnin' Back" and an overlooked yet excellent version of "I Stand Accused" and was solid throughout. It was becoming clear that his Malaco records might not offer much in the way of genuine excitement but plenty as regards understated and sustained enjoyment.

"Get Your Money Where You Spend Your Time" was a typically striking song from Tommy Tate and it became the lead-off cut from *Blues You Can Use* as well as featuring in the Jim Jarmusch film, *Mystery Train*. The closing song was Frank Johnson's excellent countrified "There's No Easy Way To Say Goodbye" and in between were a collection of compositions that were slightly more blues-oriented than had been the case in the past.

But then came *Midnight Run*, which just kept selling and selling. It might have peaked at only #26 but it remained on the soul charts for an astonishing 70 weeks, which is almost exactly the same length of time as his other five LPs on the label put together, and longer than Karyn White's eponymous debut which was the biggest selling "soul" album of the entire year. *Midnight Run* was certainly a beauty: "You've Got To Hurt Before You Heal" was the best song Larry Addison ever wrote, and the same can be said for Joe Medwick and "If I Don't Get Involved"; Frederick Knight and Bettye Crutcher's wry and true "Take Off Your Shoes" is a delight and if Bland's covers of "Ain't No Sunshine" and "Starting All Over Again" can't quite match the originals, they are still highly enjoyable.

Portrait Of The Blues contained no more or less "blues" songs than his other Malaco outings, but it did include two songs from one of the finest soul writers of them all: Tommy Tate. "When Hearts Grow Cold" and "I Can Take You To Heaven Tonight" (co-written by Richard Kuebler) would surely have been hits in another time and place for someone. And did Willie Clayton borrow aspects of the horn line from George Jackson's excellent "Hurtin' Love" for his great "Three People"?

Years Of Tears came out as a limited run as an LP, with the majority of the pressings being in the CD format and while there was little to distinguish it from his other sets, there was no reason to rate it any lower, either. "I Just Tripped On A Piece Of Your Broken Heart", "Years Of Tears To Go" and "You Put The Hurt On A Hurtin' Man" are not merely great song titles, but great songs as well.

There were to be no LPs on Malaco from Bland but a couple of CDs did appear. The Duke years must remain Bland's best ever for the sheer brilliance of his output, but the Malaco stay yielded up a rare consistency that any artist could be proud of.

Given the scope of the book, it is impossible to do justice to any artist but one particularly feels the lack when discussing the likes of Bobby Bland. In truth, I like all his albums and think they all deserve to be owned and loved. As with any artist, some are much better than others, but he maintained a constancy over a recording career of more than fifty years that is probably unmatched by any singer in any field, and he should be remembered as one of the greatest singers of the twentieth century. He died in 2013.

CL Blast

I Wanna Get Down 1980 Cotillion SD5222 Producer: Frederick Knight

Made In Africa 1982 WEA WIC8008 Producer: Keith Hutchinson (South Africa)

CL Blast 1984 Park Place PPR416 Producer: Frederick Knight

Birmingham Alabama's Clarence "Junior" Lewis had been singing and recording for twenty five years before he got to cut his first album. In that time he had put out a series of excellent singles under variations of his own name (i.e. Clarence "Junior" Lewis, Jr. Lewis and Junior Lewis) on labels big (Atco) and small (Pearl Tone) before continuing the good work after the change of identity to CL Blast. Unfortunately, none of them were hits, but nearly all are worth hearing.

Although it was pleasing to see that he was finally given a chance to cut *CL Blast*, a major disappointment must be that it didn't contain his best side for the Juana label, the fearsome "Hard To Get The Feelin' Again", but there was still plenty to enjoy. That CL Blast was a highly committed singer has always been beyond any serious debate and the last sixty seconds or so of "Our Love Will Last " and the whole of the nearly six minutes long "Love Don't Feel Like Love No More" where he started at full throttle and didn't move down the gears at all, are clear proof of that. He also more than holds his own on "Share Your Love With Me", unsurprisingly the best song on the entire set. The title track became his first ever charting single, after years of trying, even if only at #93. (Note: The *I Wanna Get Down* LP also came out in the UK in 1987 on Timeless records (TRPL111) with one extra track: "Beautiful Lover").

He also released an eight track album in South Africa (only) which is pretty much unknown and reportedly somewhat uneven in quality but that is rumour, as I have never heard it myself. That he turned up there at all was apparently due to the local success of the Cotillion LP, which was more than could be said of it in America.

His last LP came out on the short lived Park Place label which was recorded in a number of studios, including Muscle Shoals Sound. "Lay Another Log On The Fire" was probably the stand-out cut although it really was a little too close to Latimore's "Let's Straighten It Out" to qualify as a classic. I also admire "Somebody Shot My Eagle", not a reference to the death of a pet bird, but an oblique way to convey that he was stone broke. He also sang beautifully and with soulful conviction on "Never Let Me Go", "Drown In My Own Tears" and "I Just Don' t Know", while the fine "50/50 Love" became his second chart entrant at #81 at the end of 1984. There was some filler like "Let Me Entertain You", but it remains a worthwhile set and it's a pity that he has never released any further music since.

Bloodstone

Eddie Summers; Willis Draffen; Harry Williams; Charles McCormick; Roger Durham; Charles Love; Melvin Webb; Harry Wilkins; Darryl Clifton; Ronald Wilson; Ronald Bell

Bloodstone 1972 Decca TXS 110 Producers: George Braunstein, Ron Hamady & Bloodstone (UK)

Natural High 1972 London XPS 620 Producer: Mike Vernon (Billboard soul charts: 2 ; Billboard pop charts: 30)

Unreal 1973 London XPS 634 Producer: Mike Vernon (Billboard soul charts: 6 ; Billboard pop charts: 110)

I Need Time 1974 London XPS 647 Producer: Mike Vernon (Billboard soul charts: 13 ; Billboard pop charts: 141)

Riddle Of The Sphinx 1974 London XPS 671 Producer: Mike Vernon (Billboard soul charts: 22 ; Billboard pop charts: 147)

Train Ride To Hollywood 1975 XPS 665 Producer: Mike Vernon

Do You Wanna Do A Thing? 1976 London PS 671 Producers: Mike Vernon, Bert DeCoteaux & Tony Silvester (Billboard soul charts: 51)

Lullaby Of Broadway 1976 Decca SKL 5238 Producer: Mike Vernon (UK)

The most striking thing about Bloodstone when being produced by Mike Vernon was how prolific they were: eight albums between 1972 and 1976 reveals a serious work ethic. Luckily, quantity did not outweigh quality. They came out of Kansas but also out of nowhere (apart from one single as The Sinceres) and had to fly to London to get the first LP recorded and released. While the group were also accomplished musicians, their strength lay in their voices, particularly Harry Williams', a singer of immense and thrilling range, and one who has never got the dues he deserved. The same can be said of the equally impressive Charles McCormick who sported a creamy and mesmerising falsetto. Charles Love and Willis Draffen could also deliver at a high calibre and it would appear that generally speaking whoever wrote the songs on the LPs also got to sing them.

That debut set was solid, but generally unspectacular, ranging from the funky, forceful and melodic "Sadie Mae", through the slow, sweet and censorious "Dumb Dude", to the rather mediocre "This Thing Is Heavy" and an unnecessary nine minutes worth of "Little Green Apples". It also established them as writers of most of their material, which would be a constant ingredient in the majority of their work (apart from the one-off Motown LP and the two peculiar releases of showbiz material, on which more later).

The utterly beautiful "Natural High" (McCormick on mesmerising lead) was an absolute smash, going gold, reaching #4 soul and #10 pop and became the title track of their second set from which the fantastic follow-up single, "Never Let You Go" (Williams on lead, this time), also did very well at #7 soul and #43 pop. A third wonderful song can be found in the sweet McCormick-led "Who Has The Last Laugh Now" and it was clear that they were becoming one of the classiest new bands of the seventies. They did have another side, though, one which sought inspiration in music from the fifties, and even earlier, and therefore we had Bo Diddley tributes on this LP (and a Coasters homage on the follow-up, *Unreal*). This aspect of the group was of less interest to most, however, and didn't play to their considerable strengths.

In listening to their records today it is evident that they really did have their own sound - a claim often made for groups, but isn't usually true - and one should recognise that this was due to the fact that many of their tracks continued to be recorded in England, which was certainly not the location for many other American soul groups. Mike Vernon and all the musicians who played at the Chipping Norton studios should be proud of the part they played in helping to make Bloodstone such an impressive recording act.

Unreal had a standout track in the Williams led "Outside Woman" (#2 soul and #34 pop) and an interesting (if overlong) cut in "What Did You Do To Me?" where Draffen took the lead vocals. If soul groups must cover Beatles' songs then "Something" was probably as good as it gets, but overall I would say it was a slightly disappointing LP.

Similarly, *I Need Time* reminded me of the debut in its consistency (it doesn't have a bad track, but also not a brilliant one) with the stand-outs being the Draffen-led "That's Not How It Goes" which went to #22 soul and #82 pop as a single (and remains a totally forgotten record these days) the simple but sweet "Closer Together", and another McCormick winner in "We Did It".

And then came *Riddle Of The Sphinx*. In all the history of soul music there are not many true "concept" albums and this was one of the few, tracking the path of one's life from birth to death, contemplating regrets and loss on the way. In other words, the big topics, and most impressive it is too, being both thoughtful and moving, and also contains just about the only track I can think of from this period when Bloodstone sounded like someone else: "My Little Lady" (#4 soul and #57 pop) is pure Chi-Lites. Even a concept needs tracks that can stand on their own, though, and in "For The First Time" and "Save Me" the LP delivered on that as well.

Around this time, the group cut two atypical LPs: *Lullaby Of Broadway* and *Train Ride To Hollywood*, with the latter being a soundtrack to a movie (with the band playing themselves) which seems to have disappeared into the murk of time. In some ways it was a logical move for the band as it allowed them to indulge in their obvious love for fifties styled music, which they performed impeccably as ever, but the record had nothing to do with soul. The same can be said for *Lullaby Of Broadway* which was stylistically similar to *Train Ride*. It was a long way from Bloodstone's finest hour, and it is hard to imagine anyone ever playing the record by choice. Only one track. "On The Street Where You Live", was recognisably Bloodstone, and, accordingly, it is by far the best thing on show.

Sanity returned with *Do You Wanna Do A Thing* which had two classic tracks: "Give Me Your Heart" (#18 soul) and "Just Like In The Movies", both beautifully performed by Charles McCormick. The latter song was also the last one to be produced by Mike Vernon, with the rest of the LP moving the group into the hands of Bert DeCoteaux and Tony Silvester for the first and last time. Other fine efforts were "If You Wanna Be My Baby" and Willis Draffen's "This Is It" where the vocals were shared around, but, and for the first time ever, Bloodstone recorded a couple of highly mundane dance tracks, "Shake The Building" and "Stand Up, Let's Party".

Their time with London had now come to an end, and despite recording no end of wonderful tracks, they never delivered an entirely satisfying LP; they deserved a "Best Of" or "Greatest Hits" set from the label, but never got one.

Don't Stop 1978 Motown M7 -909R1 Producer: Winston Monseque

We Go A Long Way Back 1982 T-Neck FZ38115 Producers: McKinley Jackson & The Isley Brothers (Billboard soul charts: 11 ; Billboard pop charts: 95)

Party 1984 T-Neck FZ39146 Producer: McKinley Jackson

Greatest Hits 1985 T-Neck PZ40016

It seemed that the band were a bit lost post-Vernon and Silvester/DeCoteaux as they pitched up on Motown for one LP, which was also notable for the fact that they didn't write a single song on it. They sung as beautifully as ever, of course, with Williams spectacular on "I'm Just Doing My Job" and there is a charming effort on "Just Wanna Get The Feel Of It" where all the group share vocals if I'm not mistaken. Motown should be congratulated for eschewing mindless dance cuts, but it was a little bit dull with no-one being able to write as well for Bloodstone as the group themselves.

There was a triumphant return to form on the first T-Neck album in 1982 even if Charles McCormick was no longer around (although he subsequently returned) with three marvellous tracks on side one, "How Does It feel", "Go On And Cry" (#18 soul) and "We Go A Long Way Back" (Williams in fantastic form and their biggest single for years at #5 soul.) Unfortunately, side two was markedly inferior with four tracks that did Bloodstone no favours. They were just another group/band here.

The follow-up, *Party*, had a similar approach, although this time it was side one that was close to unlistenable with side two being much more thoughtful with good tracks like "Instant Love" (#42 soul) and "I Adore You", even if they didn't sound much like classic Bloodstone. On the other hand, "Why Be The First One Home" did, and seeing as how it was the last track on side two it was a fitting way to bring the curtain down on a superb recording career on vinyl (although a T-Neck *Greatest Hits* set did follow and a couple of new CDs have appeared in the last ten years.)

In hindsight, and at the remove of three decades and more, I would rate Bloodstone as one of soul's most impressive groups, who could do it all: write, sing and play, and, for years at least, entirely avoid cliché and convention. That they have left the merest whisper of a touch on soul music history in the minds of most chroniclers is a shame and an injustice.

Blossoms

Darlene Love; Fanita James; Jean King

Shockwave 1972 Lion LN 1007 Producers: Arthur Munson & Joe Reed

The Blossoms story is long, involved, important and interesting but their one album is not representative of what they did best, which was to provide backing vocals to an extraordinarily large number of artists over a long period of time, and in that capacity, they remain one of the finest of all. They did, however, record a number of singles in their own right, with one minor hit in 1967, "Good Good Lovin'", but only got to cut the one LP, which is poppy and bright, typically West Coast, and frankly a little overproduced and breathless for my own tastes, typified by the overwrought reading of "Fire & Rain". Lion did try to get a hit on the group releasing three singles from the set including a reading of Freda Payne's "Cherish What Is Dear To You" which was pretty similar in sound to the original, but none succeeded.

Darlene Love is also well-known in her own right, of course, but she stayed with the Blossoms for well over a decade, and both she and Jean King recorded solo sets, although I consider them to be out of scope for the book.

Peggi Blu

I Got Love 1980 MCA 3223 Producer: Jerry Ragovoy

Blu Blowin' 1987 Capitol 12550 Producers: Nick Martinelli, Nick Johnson, Chuck Jackson, Christopher F Dixon, Paul Gurvitz, Ron Kersey & Jeff Barry (Billboard soul charts: 71)

She was called Peggi Blue on the first album and dropped the "e" thereafter. The most pleasing aspect of the debut was that it was one of the relatively few occasions around this time when the highly talented Jerry Ragovoy produced an entire LP. Presumably he was excited by Peggi's talent, which is not in doubt (she subsequently appeared on "American Idol" as a vocal coach), even if she does blur her identity by sounding a little too much like Chaka Khan on occasion. *I Got Love* was entirely written by Ragovoy, apart from a horrendous remake of "Dancing In The Streets", and tends to be upbeat and bright throughout with only one ballad on show. Nothing on here would be included in a list of Ragovoy's finest moments but it was a fairly good start for Peggi Blue as an artist in her own right (she had sung background vocals for others previously.)

Her follow -up record, which came years later, had no fewer than seven producers. Good idea or bad idea? In the end, it didn't really matter as most people wouldn't even realise and the whole LP had a consistency of sound anyway. There is nothing on here (apart from "Mesmerize Me") that I would not want to ever hear again and it is probably overall slightly stronger than the debut album."Tender Moments" and "All The Way With You" were pulled as 45s to become minor hits on the soul charts at #91 and #44 respectively.

Blue Magic

Ted Mills; Vernon Sawyer; Richard Pratt; Wendell Sawyer; Keith Beaton; Michael Buchanan; Walter Smith

Blue Magic 1973 Atco SD 7038 Producers: Norman Harris, Alan Rubens & Steve Bernstein (Billboard soul charts: 4; Billboard pop charts: 45)

The Magic Of The Blue 1974 Atco SD 36-103 Producers: Norman Harris, Bobby Eli & WMOT Productions (Billboard soul charts: 14 ; Billboard pop charts: 71)

Thirteen Blue Magic Lane 1975 Atco SD 36-120 Producers: Norman Harris & Ron Kersey (Billboard soul charts: 9 ; Billboard pop charts: 50)

Mystic Dragons 1976 Atco 103 Producer: Bobby Eli (Billboard soul charts: 44 ; Billboard pop charts: 170)

Live! (with Major Harris and Margie Joseph) 1976 WMOT 2-5000 Producers: WMOT Productions, Blue Magic, Major Harris & Margie Joseph

Message From The Magic 1978 Atco SD 38-104 Producer: Skip Scarborough

Soul is nothing if not a broad church; on the one hand we encounter "hard soul" singers such as Otis Clay and Jimmy Robins and right out on the other end of the scale is where groups like Philadelphia's Blue Magic are to be found. Listening to them in 1973 and 1974 was always a great pleasure, listening to them in 2016 is remarkable. No-one has sung with this sort of naked and unselfconscious devotion for years and imagine anyone reciting the rap in the middle of "What's Come Over Me" from *Blue Magic* these days! No-one would be prepared to do it. I can understand why some would find the music just too soft, insipid even, but for me, Blue Magic at their best (nearly always Norman Harris produced sides, I might add) produced music of surpassing beauty and, in Ted Mills, had the greatest falsetto singer in the history of soul music apart from Eddie Kendricks.

Having said all that, I submit that the majority of their greatest moments are heavily concentrated on the first three albums. The debut (which had a different cover in the UK from the US) houses "Sideshow" (#1 soul and #8 pop, a gold record), "Look Me Up" (#36 soul) "Spell" (#30 soul), "Stop To Start" (#14 soul) and "What's Come Over Me", and that's five magnificent sides, right there."Just Don't Want To Be Lonely" and "Tear It Down" are merely very good with only "Welcome To The Club" and "Answer To My Prayer" falling below the highest of standards. In short, it's one of the finest sweet soul LPs of them all, and one which spent 43 weeks on the soul charts.

The Magic Of The Blue is not of quite the same quality although "Three Ring Circus" (#5 soul , #36 pop), "Talking To Myself" and "When Ya Coming Home" are all sublime. "Love Has Found Its Way To Me" made it to #45 on the soul charts but it, "Let Me Be The One" and "Stringing Me Along" are no more than average to good Philly dance sides. Given the other four sides are all commendable enough, the conclusion is this was another sterling set.

Thirteen Blue Magic Lane might have been slightly patchy (who needed the instrumental "Magic Of The Blue"? And why did "Stop And Get A Hold Of Yourself" have to be speeded up?) but it also included the ineffable "Chasing Rainbows" (#17 soul) on which Ted holds two notes where the world stops and "The Loneliest House On The Block": simply two of the finest falsetto performances ever to emanate from Philadelphia."Haunted By Your Love" (a rare non Mills-led track) "Born On Halloween" and "I Like You" are also enchanting and the addition of Margie Joseph to "What's Come Over Me" certainly didn't hurt in making it a #11 soul hit. Given "We're On The Right Track" was the equal of the versions from Ultra High Frequency and South Shore Commission, it all added up to the third delightful LP in a row by the group.

After *Thirteen* their moment had passed, both commercially and artistically, although there were still plenty of isolated moments to cherish. Take *Mystic Dragons*, for example, which was the first album on which the group recorded music patently not right for them: "Rock N Roll Revival", "Freak-N-Stein" and "Mother Funk" sat uneasily alongside much better songs like "Summer Snow" and "Making Love To A Memory" but there is nothing on here that could compete with the glories on the first three sets.

The *Live!* outing is, as with virtually all such recordings, a bit of a bore and hardly calls out to be listened to repeatedly but Blue Magic do render, together with Joseph, a pretty good version of "I'm Gonna Make You Love Me" that cannot be heard elsewhere.

Message From The Magic was produced by Skip Scarborough and played up Ted Mills' considerable song-writing talents more than in the past (although he had always written at least two songs on each of the previous four studio releases.) The result is both commendable and consistent. If there isn't a track on here that would be in the top ten best tracks they ever recorded nothing would be in the bottom ten, either. One single from it, "I Waited", failed to even reach the soul charts, a reminder that falsetto-led "sweet" soul (unless you were Earth, Wind & Fire) was seen as old hat in 1978.

Welcome Back 1981 Capitol ST-12143 Producers : Norman Harris & Ron Tyson

Magic # 1983 Mirage 90074-1 Producer: Butch Ingram (Billboard soul charts: 52)

From Out Of The Blue 1989 Columbia 45092 Producers: Vincent Bell & Alvin Moody (Billboard soul charts: 48)

Blue Magic then left Atco and moved to Capitol. *Welcome Back* re-united the group with Norman Harris and it was surely no accident that the lead off cut was their best for years. "The Oscar" would have fit perfectly onto one of the LPs from the glory days and is utterly delightful with a perfect vocal from Mills. In fact the whole album is a strong one and the best since *Thirteen Blue Magic Lane*, but, sadly, became the second LP in a row not to chart. It should also be noted that *Welcome Back* also welcomed back the Sawyer brothers who had been replaced on *Message From The Magic* by Walter Smith and Michael Buchanan.

It was no surprise, therefore, that a new approach was deemed appropriate and Butch Ingram was entrusted with production duties on *Magic #*, which did chart. It was a most respectful record and not one to do any harm to the Blue Magic "brand" but, apart from a faithful version of the Dramatics' "In The Rain" and "Sit Alone Again", not much of the material was particularly memorable. It may be time to talk about the rest of the group's vocals here as another lead singer shares duties with Mills on "In The Rain" but it is difficult to ascertain who it was. Ted is so readily identified with the group that everyone else is overshadowed and it has even been alleged that the backing vocals on the records were handled by the likes of Bunny Sigler and Phil Hurtt.

There was then a lull of a few years before Blue Magic returned in 1989 with *From Out Of The Blue*. In fact the set seems to rather corroborate my point about the vocal contribution of the rest of the group as two tracks are credited as additional lead vocals having been provided by one Gordon Dukes, rather than by the Sawyers or Keith Beaton. Anyway, side one is excellent, the title track particularly so, and the last two songs on side two are worth hearing as well. The LPs cover sees the group looking resplendent in suits, while the back cover has them attired in hideous yellow outfits, doubtless meant to endear them to a young audience and the first three songs on side two are the manifestation of that approach and desire. Predictably, the tracks are as awful as the clothes.

Blue Magic occupied a very specific place in a soul universe: a building of love. They never sang about man's injustice to man, economic woes or anything else at all apart from adoration of their ladies or the heartbreak of losing them. It was a good place to live and Ted Mills was the perfect architect to have built it.

The Blue Notes (see also Harold Melvin)

Lloyd Parkes; Bernard Wilson; Lawrence Brown; John Atkins

The Truth Has Come To Light 1977 Glades 7512
Producer: George Perry

In 1975 Harold Melvin and The Blue Notes split acrimoniously. Teddy Pendergrass went one way and Harold Melvin another, leaving the two remaining Blue Notes, Wilson and Brown, stranded. They dealt with their poor hand as best they could by re-recruiting former member Parkes, and a new lead singer in Atkins, and signed with TK Records (of which Glades was a subsidiary) down in Florida where producer George Perry and talented arranger Mike Lewis tried as hard as they could to make the new Blue Notes sound like the Pendergrass / Melvin group that were still world famous. It was a sensible and understandable ploy, and I would have done the same. It has been claimed that the Blue Notes did not always sing on the Philadelphia International sides but, interestingly, the harmonies on tracks like "Memories" sure sounded much the same as the big hits, so maybe the full truth *hasn't* come to light. Atkins bellowed like Pendergrass and was a forceful singer but he simply wasn't Teddy and the LP was not a hit. Which is not at all the same thing as being poor, as it wasn't, mixing up good dance records like "Standing By You Girl" with good slow ballads sounding, as I said, as if they were recorded at Sigma Sound rather than down in Miami. Sadly, and probably bewilderingly, for the likes of Wilson and Brown that was about it. They did record a handful of unsuccessful singles for Fantasy later on but had to sit back and watch Pendergrass (particularly) and the re-constituted Harold Melvin and The Blue Notes go on to further success.

Eddie Bo

Check Mr. Popeye 1988 Rounder 2077

Vippin' and Voppin' 1988 Charly CRB 1195 (UK)

The Other Side Of 1977 Bo Sound EB 55379 Producer: Eddie Bo

Watch For The Coming 1980 Bo Sound EB 55379 Producer: Eddie Bo

Edwin Bocage recorded an almost limitless amount of singles, which generated precisely one hit on the *Billboard* soul charts ("Hook And Sling" in 1969), but he is now regarded, quite rightly, as one of the key figures in the history of New Orleans soul music. Sadly, though, he is as poorly served on album (as regards quantity) as he was excellently served on singles. One reason for this, however, was that New Orleans soul artists tended to be generally under represented on LP anyway, as the city always tended to favour 45s and even Irma Thomas had fewer long players issued than her massive local popularity might have suggested.

Check Mr. Popeye was a retrospective LP of singles (plus two unreleased songs) that range from 1959 through to 1962, and is thus right on the cusp of the birth of soul but don't let that put you off as this is marvellous stuff and should lift the lowest of spirits. Three songs on here DID make the *Cashbox* soul charts: "Dinky Doo", "It Must Be Love" and the title song.

Vippin' And Voppin was another superb collection of his work, this time concentrating on his work on the Blue Jay and Seven B labels in the mid-sixties.

The two releases on his own Bo-Sound label, which have the same issue number, are incredibly hard to track down, and are softer and jazzier than his late sixties and seventies funk sides, many of which have only started to appear on CD for the first time in recent years. The first is marginally better than the second, but both contain a number of colourless instrumentals, and neither include anything as funky as, say, "Check Your Bucket".

It is very little to show for such a prolific artist. Even the success of "Hook Or Sling" couldn't generate enough interest for anyone to record an album on him at the time, and, indeed, many of his singles would have barely made it past the New Orleans city limits. He died in 2009 and it is sad that I don't have the space to write more than a handful of paragraphs about him, given his importance and contribution to so many other New Orleans artists.

Bo & Ruth (see Mike James Kirkland)

Bob & Earl (see also Jackie Lee and Jay Dee)

Harlem Shuffle 1964 Tip 9001 Producers: Fred Smith & Bob & Earl

Harlem Shuffle 1967 Sue ILP 951 Producer: Fred Smith (UK)

Bob & Earl 1969 Crestview CRS-3055 Producer: Fred Smith

Bob & Earl 1969 B & C BCB1 Producer: Fred Smith (UK)

Bob and Earl had an almost unbelievably convoluted recording career which has been both hard and interesting to try and track down. The key facts, though, are these: "Bob" was Bobby Relf (who also made solo records under his real name of Bobby Garrett as well as the name Bob Relf) and "Earl" was Earl Lee Nelson (who also recorded hits under the name of Jackie Lee and Jay Dee and non-hits under the name of Earl Cosby) and they had a big success at the end of 1963 called "Harlem Shuffle". (The original "Bob" was Bobby Day, but he did not feature on these LPs.)

The first album came out on Tip and played heavily on the hit with no fewer than four tracks having the word "shuffle" in the title. Next, an LP was released only in the UK with the same title as the Tip release but with an almost completely different track listing. Thirdly, an LP came out on Crestview which had more or less, but not exactly the same, listing as the fourth and final LP on the UK B and C label. Just to make things even more confusing different versions of "Harlem Shuffle" could be found across the LPs. Oh, and the LPs also included many tracks that had come out as solo releases. Thus, the B & C set has four tracks on it that came out as by Jackie Lee or Earl Cosby (including his biggest hit, "The Duck") and two that were released as by Bobby Garrett.

But what about the music? Most people know "Harlem Shuffle" so I won't dwell on that but Bob and Earl could also convey deep emotions with confidence and skill, and the outstanding "Baby It's Over" is proof of that. (It can be found on both the UK only issued LPs.) Further evidence came in the shape of "Don't Ever Leave Me" which was on the first two albums. Much of the rest of the music is up-tempo, typical West Coast Fred Smith fare, for those who know such things; for those who don't, it can best be described as almost quintessential "Northern Soul". (By the way, if anyone wants to hear a good example of how the Blossoms sounded as backing singers, then listen to them on "Oh Baby Doll" from the debut LP.)

Body And Soul

Glenn Brooks; Charles Green; Doc Shervington; John Barnes

Body And Soul 1971 National General NG2002 Producer: Freddie Piro

It would appear that Body and Soul never really existed as a group, but were in fact a team of session musicians, predominantly the four listed above, who worked at the Valley recording studio in North Hollywood. Doc Shervingon and Glenn Brooks share the lead vocals on the album, and, frankly, it sounds like a group of session musicians making an LP as there is no real identity or mood created and the songs, most of which come from Body and Soul, are generally pretty ordinary, The Shervington led downtempo cuts such as "Unhappy Man" do have charm, and that might have been the way to go on the whole LP, but too many cuts are nondescript funk tracks like "Things". I certainly would not dismiss the release out of hand, and I know some people who make great claims for the quality of *Body And Soul*, but there is little on here that has ever made me perk up and listen more attentively.

Hamilton Bohannon

Stop and Go 1973 Dakar DK 76903 Producer: Hamilton Bohannon

Keep On Dancin' 1974 Dakar DK 76910 Producer: Hamilton Bohannon (Billboard soul charts: 49)

Insides Out 1975 Dakar DK 76916 Producer: Hamilton Bohannon (Billboard soul charts: 28)

Bohannon's Best Brunswick BRLS 3017 (UK)

Bohannon 1975 Dakar DK 76917 Producer: Hamilton Bohannon (Billboard soul charts: 21)

Dance Your Ass Off 1976 Dakar DK 76919 Producer: Hamilton Bohannon (Billboard soul charts: 47)

Gittin' Off 1976 Dakar DK 76921 Producer: Hamilton Bohannon

Bohannon's Greatest Disco Hits 1976 Dakar DK 76922

Tyrone Davis excepted, Hamilton Bohannon was easily Dakar's most prolific and successful artist. By all accounts somewhat of an assertive personality, he certainly went his own way on these releases, on which he didn't sound obviously like anyone else recording at the time even if some feel he was strongly influenced by Bo Diddley.

I find his music much too repetitive to listen to at long stretches at a time, but some tracks, if heard in isolation, are excellent. The first LP set the scene for what was to follow for the majority of all the Dakar sides: instrumental tracks of hard unremitting rhythm (by, predominantly, Bohannon himself, Leroy Emmanuel, Mose Davis, Rod Lumpkin and Fernando Sanders) with the odd vocal aside thrown in. Dakar pulled a number of sides from the set as singles, but none troubled any national charts.

The follow-up LP, *Keep On Dancin'*, adopted the same approach as the debut ("Have A Good Day" excepted) but did bear his first ever hit in "South African Man" when it charted at #78 on the soul listings. It did well in the U.K. too, and in fact the album was renamed after the hit and given a different sleeve for issue over here.

Dance material kicked things off on *Insides Out* as well but it also featured some much softer tracks like "Happy Feeling" and "Thoughts And Wishes" which don't have much to do with soul music. "Foot Stompin' Music" and "Disco Stomp" had entirely descriptive titles and both came to settle in the mid regions of the soul charts when pulled as singles.

Bohannon offered little in the way of surprises and included possibly the most obvious Diddley influence to date on "The Funky Reggae" but did introduce, for the first time, the vocals of ex-Motown singer Carolyn Crawford, even if she didn't have anything very taxing to do. The other side of his music was getting even softer, if anything, and "Gentle Breeze" was eight minutes of wallpaper. Alternatively, "The Day To Remember" had a bluesy note which had not been heard before. "Bohannon's Beat" went on for seven minutes, and a more palatable cut-down version at half the length became his latest middling size hit.

Dance Your Ass Off rang some more subtle changes, as evidenced by "Spread The Groove Around", which provided the first example of strings on a Bohannon dance record. On the other hand, "The Groove I Feel" sounded as if was entirely made up of licks and rhythms played a number of times before. In sum, the album was undoubtedly his hardest edged since "Keep On Dancin'".

Gittin' Off, the last Dakar LP, had another Diddley-esque title track of funky power but, to be honest, it was all sounding so familiar by now and it was no surprise that it didn't chart.

Phase II 1977   Mercury SRM 1 1159 Producer: Hamilton Bohannon (Billboard soul charts: 46 ; Billboard pop charts : 203)

On My Way 1978   Mercury SRM 1 3710 Producer: Hamilton Bohannon

Summertime Groove 1978   Mercury SRM 1 3728 Producer: Hamilton Bohannon (Billboard soul charts: 14 ; Billboard pop charts : 58)

Cut Loose 1979 Mercury SRM 1 3762 Producer: Hamilton Bohannon (Billboard soul charts: 34)

Too Hot To Hold 1979   Mercury SRM 1 3778 Producer: Hamilton Bohannon

Music In The Air 1980 Mercury 3813   Producer: Hamilton Bohannon (Billboard soul charts: 72)

The move to Mercury, while retaining a link to the past in the shape of the likes of Emmanuel and Davis from The Counts still playing on the records, kicked off with *Phase II* which was an accurate title symbolising what was indeed a new aspect of his career. Ben Picone and The Atlanta Strings saturate the disc and it is somewhat of a trial to listen to. There is certainly nothing on here that competes with the hypnotic quality of his best Dakar sides. "Bohannon's Disco Symphony" (the fourth time he had name-checked himself) made it to #67 on the soul charts.

The strings, while still evident, were somewhat less intrusive on the funkier follow-up, *On My Way,* but the lack of vocals still palled over the length of an album, which was also devoid of any hit singles.

Bohannon had easily his biggest ever success with "Let's Start The Dance"(#9 soul) in the summer of 1978 and it kicked off *Summertime Groove*, which also became his best selling LP by far. There will be plenty who love this single but I always found it to be a tiresome mess and it doesn't sound any better to me in 2016. Caroline Crawford was back on the LP but she still just throws in asides rather than really sings. The title track with its obvious echoes of the Dakar sides is the cut I felt stood up best.

Cut Loose and *Too Hot To Hold* carried on in much the same manner as the previous Mercury records but the odd track did stand out such as "Groove Machine" from *Too Hot* which is hard to resist in its unstoppable and string-less momentum.

Music In The Air was a Bohannon album that finally featured a track on which a female singer could sing properly but it was another ex-Motowner, Liz Lands, rather than Carolyn Crawford, who was given the honour and she is very good on a version of the Originals' "Baby I'm For Real" (a #54 soul single), "Spring Is In The Air" and, particularly, "Thoughts And Wishes", a significantly improved re-cut of a track from *Insides Out*. I should also make fleeting reference to the photo on the back cover of the LP where Bohannon looks absurdly youthful. All that dancing evidently did him a lot of good.

One Step Ahead 1980 Phase II JW 36867 Producer: Hamilton Bohannon

Goin' For Another One 1981 Phase II JW 37076 Producer: Hamilton Bohannon

Alive 1981 Phase II AL 37699 Producer: Hamilton Bohannon

Fever 1982 Phase II AL 38113 Producer: Hamilton Bohannon

Make Your Body Move 1983 Compleat / Phase II CPL 1 1003 Producer: Hamilton Bohannon

The Bohannon Drive 1983 Compleat / Phase II CPL 1 1005 Producer: Hamilton Bohannon

Here Comes Bohannon 1989 MCA MCAD 42310

Although Bohannon was never to chart again after he left Mercury he remained prolific as we can see from the above. It was good to see that he never forgot his Detroit years (he moved there in the sixties) and yet another ex-Motown lady, Louvain Demps, turns up on *One Step Ahead* but again it is Lands, with her incredible range, who comes out best on tracks like "April My Love". (In fact, people from Detroit would continue to turn up on his records with possibly the most unlikely of all being Thomas "Hit Man" Hearns on "The Gang's All Here" from the *Here Comes Bohannon* LP.) *Goin' For Another One* recruited The Originals to help out on "Do The Everybody Get Down" where they sit atop the familiar rhythm patterns.

The *Alive* and *Fever* LPs see members of the P-Funk clan such as Fred Wesley, Maceo Parker, Gary Shider and Ray Davis recruited to the cause. Good tracks across these LPs are "A Happy Song For You" and "You're The One" from *Alive* and "What Is A Dream" from *Fever* but too much else is hard going.

Carolyn Crawford finally got the chance to sing properly on "Tell Me You'll Wait" from *The Bohannon Drive* (it is a praiseworthy track) but she had already recorded it on her own 1978 LP, *My Name Is Caroline*.

The MCA set is probably of most interest to soul fans as the featured vocalist this time is Altrina Grayson, better known for her work with Bobby Womack. She provides a deeply soulful take on "Over The Rainbow" for example but it hardly felt like a Bohannon LP at all. In fact, the overwhelming reason to listen to pretty much all of Bohannon's records once he left Dakar is because of the excellence in the vocalists he chose to work with. He became a bit like Norman Connors in this regard, a harvester of talent, rather than a front man.

It is a surprise to be reminded of how many LPs Hamilton Bohannon put out and I can see that he was in many ways years ahead of his time in his understanding and use of rhythm and he has been highly influential but he was essentially someone who I feel was much better represented on single than on LP. Everyone should own some Bohannon music but no-one needs to own all twenty one albums listed here (and there were further "Best Of" type collections which are not.)

Angelo Bond

Bondage 1975 ABC ABCD-889 Producers: Angelo Bond & McKinley Jackson (Billboard pop charts:179)

Angelo Bond came out of the Invictus / Hot Wax stable, for whom he was an incredibly fruitful writer, penning such massive hits as the 8th Day's "You've Got To Crawl " and Freda Payne's "Bring The Boys Home". He then decided he wanted to make a record of his own, an itch he managed to scratch, as he subsequently once again returned to writing and arranging for others.

   This is an unfairly neglected record - even if it scraped into the pop charts - and might well be one of the great pleasures of this book for anyone who has so far not had the good fortune to hear it. Blessed with musicians such as Ray Parker, Ed Greene, Melvin Ragin and Scott Edwards, it has a lushness and vitality that was true of a number of other albums that came out around this time where the focus was on making a record that one would listen to, not dance to. Such an approach, of course, also requires good songs. And writing good songs was what Angelo Bond did best "He Gained The World" and "Reach For The Moon" (a #32 soul single) are the stand-out tracks and both talk to social and philosophical challenges, not mere love tangles, although he covers that side of things as well. All the songs are literate and tuneful, delivered by Bond's pleasing high tenor voice, and the LP deserves to be re-discovered.

Lou Bond

Lou Bond 1974 We Produce XPS-1904 Producers: Jo Bridges, Lester Snell & Tom Nixon

It was appropriate that Lou Bond (real name: Ronald Edward Lewis) should cover Bill Withers' "Let Me In Your Life" on this LP as Bond was following in the footsteps of the famous singer/composer by recording an album that fit into the niche of the time where a small "singer/songwriter" movement could be found in soul. Bond's highly impressive outing was a worthy addition to that genre.

   His earliest discs sounded significantly different. Recorded in Chicago, they were typical sixties songs that were OK, but without particular distinction, and gave no indication that he would one day re-appear taking such a dissimilar approach. It is truly an LP of riches: from the long note he holds at the end of "Lucky Me", to the socially conscious and thoughtful "Why Must Our Eyes Always Be Turned Backwards", all delivered against some outstanding arrangements by Bridges, Snell and Nixon. It is not a perfect piece of work: he misses some notes on "Lucky Me" and "To The Establishment" goes go for too long but it is still one of the best "unknown" soul LPs ever recorded. Sadly, it failed comprehensively in the marketplace and nothing else from him ever came out on Stax or any other label and he returned to obscurity.

Booker T & The M.G.s (see also Booker T Jones)

Booker T Jones; Al Jackson; Steve Cropper; Donald "Duck" Dunn; Lewie Steinberg; Bobby Manuel; Carson Whitsett; Willie Hall

Green Onions 1962 Stax S 701 No producer listed (Billboard pop charts: 33)

Soul Dressing 1965 Stax S 705 No producer listed

And Now 1966 Stax S 711 No producer listed (Billboard soul charts: 18)

In The Christmas Spirit 1966 Stax S 713 No producer listed

Hip Hug- Her 1967 Stax S 717 No producer listed (Billboard soul charts: 4 ; Billboard pop charts: 35)

Back To Back (with The Mar-Keys) 1967 Stax S 720 No producer listed (Billboard pop charts: 98)

Doin' Our Thing 1968 Stax S 724 No producer listed (Billboard soul charts: 17 ; Billboard pop charts: 176)

Stax could never quite make their mind up about how to write out the name of the Memphis Group: on LP covers we got the following variations: MGs, MG's, M.G.'s and M.G.s, but the record company were never in the slightest doubt as to their importance to the label. And nor should there be any doubt, as Booker T and the M.G.s (I'm going with that one) were one of the three or four greatest rhythm sections in the history of soul music, even more important for what they did for others, rather than what they did for themselves. Incredibly talented musicians, they played on countless hits, many of which they also wrote (or at least Jones and Cropper did) in conjunction with others. Their importance and influence cannot easily be overemphasized.

   All the albums listed above came out in the "blue Stax" phase and as with most all-instrumental LPs they are quite taxing to listen to attentively for any period of time and for that reason I won't discuss them individually; for most of us they are best digested in small chunks. For aspiring and actual musicians, however, they are doubtless all essential. Everyone knows "Green Onions" and many tracks across these LPs are very similar to that massive hit (#1 soul and #3 pop), but great joys are to be found in tracks that are less typical: "Summertime" from *And Now!*, for example. However, I think it fair to say that, despite the musical excellence of everything they cut, not one of the LPs above could be classed as "a must have". If I had to recommend one only, it would be *Soul Dressing* which is crisp and economical. Their truly necessary and required recordings, of course, from the 1962 to 1968 period can be found on lots of LPs by Otis Redding, Carla Thomas, and William Bell.

   None of the albums have producers listed but it is pretty clear that the group produced themselves. I should also note that, while never officially a member of Booker T & The M.G.s, Isaac Hayes played on a number of these tracks, deputising whenever Jones was unavailable. (Lewie Steinberg featured on bass for the first two LPs, after which he was replaced by "Duck" Dunn.)

   Finally, in this section, I should mention the cover to *Hip Hug-Her* which captures the "Swinging Sixties" look as well as any I can think of. (It also included their two biggest post- "Green Onions" hits before 1968 in the title track (#6 soul) and "Groovin'"#10.)

Soul Limbo 1968 STS 2001 Producer: Booker T & The M.G.s (Billboard soul charts: 14 ; Billboard pop charts: 127)

The Best Of 1968 Atlantic SD 8202 (Billboard pop charts: 167)

Uptight 1968 STS 2006 Producer: Booker T Jones (Billboard soul charts: 7 ; Billboard pop charts: 98)

The Booker T Set 1969 STS 2009 Producer: Booker T & The M.G.s (Billboard soul charts: 10 ; Billboard pop charts: 53)

McLemore Avenue 1970 STS 2027 Producer : Booker T & The M.G.s (Billboard soul charts: 19 ; Billboard pop charts: 107)

Greatest Hits 1970 STS 2033 (Billboard soul charts: 18; Billboard pop charts: 132)

Melting Pot 1971 STS 2001 Producer: Booker T G The M.G.s (Billboard soul charts: 2 ; Billboard pop charts: 43)

Union Extended 1976 STX 1045 Producer : Booker T & The M.G.s (UK)

The next batch of LPs were issued when Stax concluded the Gulf and Western deal but little changed, apart from the fact that they began to have more and bigger hit singles. In the period from 1962 until the summer of 1968 they only posted three singles on the Top 40; from late 1968 until September 1969 alone they managed a further four.

One of those four, "Soul Limbo", will for ever be associated with cricket by Englishmen of a certain age, as it was the BBC's Test Match theme for years. The rest of the LP carried on the approach that had been the case for all of the albums after the first two, lots of cover versions and less original music.

Uptight was a soundtrack to a movie and featured the mighty "Time Is Tight" (#7 soul, #6 pop), a record where (as so often) Jackson's drumming is mesmerising. We also had a first, vocals on a Booker T and M.G.s LP, delivered by Judy Clay on "Children Don't Get Weary". As with virtually everything she ever sang, it is compelling.

The Booker T Set went the whole hog: every single track was a cover version of well-known songs; Cropper was most impressive on "Light My Fire". Next up was the *McLemore Avenue* LP, the cover of which parodied The Beatles' *Abbey Road* and the music was instrumental versions of all the songs on the Beatles' LP. I find it to be extremely tedious, I'm afraid, and, as much as I like The Beatles, I have never felt that their songs lent themselves to soul interpretations.

Much, much better was "Melting Pot", a single version of which went to #21 soul and #45 pop). I submit that the full length title track was the best record the group ever cut (In fact, I'd go further and say it is maybe the best soul instrumental that ANYONE has ever cut.) All of the band are magnificent, with Cropper displaying a lovely line in dirty James Brown riffs. He simply was the best rhythm guitarist in soul music. The whole set was a real return to roots as the covers were disregarded and every song was composed by the group, and the result was the toughest since *Soul Dressing* back in 1965. It was a fitting way for the classic group to exit, as shortly after it was released Jones and Cropper were gone from Stax. (I will cover Jones' LPs in the book but feel that Cropper's fall out of scope.) By the way, *Union Extended* consists of unreleased - and pretty typical - material.

The M.G.s 1973 STS 3024 Producers: Al Jackson & Duck Dunn (Billboard soul charts: 56)

This was the one and only LP released by the group when it consisted of Jackson, Dunn and Bobby Manuel and Carson Whitsett, and the first ever to not be titled as by "Booker T and The M.G.s.".

It does not sound radically different to what had gone before but is all a little tepid.

Universal Language 1977 Asylum 1093 Producers: Booker T & The M.G.s & Tom Dowd (Billboard soul charts: 59; Billboard pop charts: 209)

This LP saw the return of Jones and Cropper, but sadly, Jackson was gone, murdered in 1975, and he was replaced on drums by Willie Hall. It was nice to see them back, but it was fairly routine and hardly sounded pioneering for 1977. "Sticky Stuff" managed #68 on the soul charts.

Dunn has also gone now but Cropper and the ever youthful looking Jones are still with us, but all four men are as important to the evolution and growth of soul music as anyone in this book.

Taka Boom (see also Dream Machine)

Taka Boom 1979 Arista 50041 Producers: John Ryan & Taka Boom (Billboard soul charts: 48 ; Billboard pop charts: 171)

Boomerang 1983 Mercury 812 376 1 Producer: Bob Esty (Holland)

Middle Of The Night 1986 Mirage 90290-1 Producer: Billy Rush

Taka Boom (real name Yvonne Brumbach, *nee* Stevens) is the sister of Chaka Khan a fact rendered indisputable by listening to the first few seconds of "Night Dancing" the only big single (#20 soul) she ever had, from her debut, *Taka Boom*. People might be surprised - as I certainly was - to find a Sam Dees song hidden away in this rather unlikely setting but Taka delivers his "Troubled Waters" admirably. So admirably, in fact, that it completely overshadows everything else on the LP which also includes an ok version of Lee Garrett's "You're My Everything".

She had a brief spell as joint lead singer with a group called Dream Machine (and she had previously provided vocals for The Glass Family's disco sides) before once again releasing solo records. *Boomerang* didn't come out in America and contains dance music with scant soul content.

Middle of the Night was her last LP, from which I quite like "Climate Of Love".

Bootsy's Rubber Band (see also James Brown, Funkadelic and Parliament)

William "Bootsy" Collins; Phelps "Catfish" Collins"; Gary Cooper; Leslyn Bailey; Robert Johnson; Frankie Kash Waddy, Frederick Allen, Maceo Parker, Fred Wesley,Rick Gardner; Joel Johnson; Richard Griffith; Larry Fratangelo; Carl Small ; David Lee Chong; Bernie Worrell; Jerome Brailey; Gary Shider; Larry Hatcher

Stretchin' Out In Bootsy's Rubber Band 1976 Warner Brothers BS 2920 Producers: Bootsy Collins & George Clinton (Billboard soul charts: 10 ; Billboard pop charts : 59)

Aah...The Name Is Bootsy, Baby! 1977 Warner Brothers BS 2972 Producers: Bootsy Collins & George Clinton (Billboard soul charts: 1 ; Billboard pop charts : 16)

Bootsy? Player Of The Year 1978 Warner Brothers BS 3093 Producers : Bootsy Collins & George Clinton (Billboard soul charts: 1 ; Billboard pop charts : 16)

This Boot Is Made For Funk-n 1979 Warner Brothers BS 3295 Producer: Bootsy Collins (Billboard soul charts: 9 ; Billboard pop charts : 52)

Ultra Wave (as Bootsy) 1979 Warner Brothers BS 3433 Producer: Bootsy Collins (Billboard soul charts: 30 ; Billboard pop charts : 70)

The One Giveth...The Count Taketh Away (as William Bootsy Collins) 1982 Warner Brothers BS 3667 Producer: Bootsy Collins (Billboard soul charts: 18 ; Billboard pop charts : 120)

What's Bootsy Doin'? (as Bootsy Collins) 1988 Columbia 44107 Producer: Bootsy Collins (Billboard soul charts: 58)

William "Bootsy" Collins made his mark as a bassist with James Brown at the turn of the seventies (not that many people realised it at the time, in those pre-internet and pre-information overload days) and was therefore playing a big part in creating some of the most exhilarating music in history. He had previously played with his brother Phelps in a band called the Pacemakers who morphed into The J.B.s when they started to play with Brown. After a couple of years he moved to join the Funkadelic/Parliament conglomeration before, in 1976, he put together Bootsy's Rubber Band and released their first LP which had a lot of impact. At the time, despite his musical credentials, it felt as if they had come out of nowhere. Two years later they were famous after having posted two successive number one albums on the soul charts, a feat managed by few.

Looking back now, it seems clear that much of the success was driven by the visual way in which the Rubber Band were presented, playing on Bootsy's charisma and sense of fun. No-one else in soul (apart from Isaac Hayes) was really paying attention to this now obvious and routine way to find an audience and that is credit to Collins' and Clinton's commercial savvy. There was also an almost insatiable public demand for George Clinton's brand of music back then so The Rubber Band were in the right place at the right time. The line-up of the band was fluid, as with so much of the P-Funk empire, and it is entirely likely that my listing of Rubber Band alumni is inaccurate. It is also interesting to note that Bootsy's Rubber Band never placed any singles at all on the pop 100 chart, despite posting eleven, including a #1 in "Bootzilla", on the soul singles chart which must have meant that they were afforded only limited radio play on more mainstream pop stations at their peak.

That Collins was important in the history of soul music is not in doubt, and his legacy is certain, but it has to be said, I think, that much of his music has dated badly and listening to all the albums above in their entirety today is a daunting prospect. In my defence, I bought all of them when they were first released and enjoyed them but their cartoonish and eclectic approach worked for my 20 year-old self in a way that they cannot for someone nearing the age of sixty. I well remember extraordinary claims being made for tracks like "Munchies For Your Love" by the UK's *Black Music* magazine at the time of their release and doubtless there are many people out there who will love this music for ever but I am certainly not the person to recommend that anyone should pull out or buy these LPs in 2016.

Having said the above, I am not immune to the charms of everything and an imaginary compilation consisting of more straightforward tracks such as "I'd Rather Be With You", "Mug Push", "Can't Stay Away", "Bootzilla", "Under The Influence Of A Groove", and "Music To Smile By" would work for me perfectly well. But listening to his amazing bass on James Brown's "Soul Power" would be better still.

Booty People

Mitch McDowell; Robert Palmer; Rick Hendrix; Ray Goodloe; Joe Phillips; Lemon Smyth

Booty People 1977 ABC AB 998 Producers: B B Dickerson and Jerry Goldstein

This short-lived funk band put out one LP, which delivered one minor "hit" on the U.S. soul singles chart in "Spirit Of '76", but it was not a particularly distinguished effort (although I do like "Anyway I'm Busted" and "Slappin' Five) and there was so much better around at the time. Mitch McDowell went on to form and front General Caine.

Boppers (see L.A. Boppers)

Tony Borders

Bordering on Love 1982 Brylen BN 4521

No-one really "produced" this album as it is a collection of ten tracks Tony Borders cut way back in the early sixties for the Delta and Smash labels, although about half of the songs were unreleased at the time. It certainly is far from the best of Borders, a fine singer who made some great records in Muscle Shoals at the end of the sixties, but it is the only Tony Borders LP in existence (apart from a Japanese bootleg) so it will have to do. Most of the songs are "poppy" midtempo tunes, and apart from two tracks which do give a nod to "black" music, "Can't Stand To See You Cry" and "Soft Wind, Soft Voice", there is really no need to want to listen to this record.

Bottom & Co.

Jesse Boyce; John Helms; Freeman Brown; Sanchez Hartley; Richard Griffith; George Woods; Fred Birdwell

Rock Bottom 1976 Gordy G 977 Producers: Clayton Ivey & Terry Woodford

Bottom & Co. (odd name, hard to see how they thought it would make them a success) recorded a nice and sought after single at the Muscle Shoals based Wishbone studios in 1974, "Gonna Find A True Love", but unfortunately it isn't on the LP, particularly as it would have been the best cut here by some distance.

The group's biggest asset was bassist, writer and vocalist Jesse Boyce, who has a long and respected series of achievements in the music industry both before and after the existence of Bottom and Co. He wrote every song on the LP, one of which, "Firefly", was also recorded by The Temptations at about the same time. It's hard to find much to get excited about on *Rock Bottom*; nothing is outstandingly bad, but Motown never really knew how to do funk particularly well (other than some tracks by The Commodores and Rick James), and there were just so many better albums out there in 1976 than this one.

Walter Bouligny

At Work 1978 ROI 2101 Producer: Joseph Leclair

This is an astonishingly rare record and I suspect few people in the world have even heard of it, let alone listened to it. Bouligny, a soul man from Louisiana, had already put out a handful of very obscure singles in the sixties and seventies, as either by Walter B or Walter Bee, which have attracted the interest of connoisseurs and they demonstrate that his failure to sell records was not because of any lack of talent. Sadly, the LP is not really up to scratch and lacks any strong material, although "I'll Go My Way" is probably the best thing on here, but Bouligny's voice remained intact and impressive.

Bobby Boyd

Bobby Boyd 1976 Tiger Lily TL 14066 Producers: Bobby Boyd, Harvey Fuqua & George Benson

I don't think this Bobby Boyd is the same man who fronted The Bobby Boyd Congress who recorded an in demand album in France in 1971 (which I've - without conviction, but because of their French connections - deemed out of scope) but this one created one of the best LPs on the Tiger Lily label, which I attribute to Harvey Fuqua's involvement, as he almost invariably produced good work. It's a shame the set wasn't released by another company as it therefore wouldn't have been restricted to a few hundred copies and no distribution. "Why Are You Crying" is the track that gets most people who know about *Bobby Boyd* excited but I think it is no more than ok and cuts like "Girl I Can Feel Ya" and "Good Woman" more eloquently demonstrate his undoubted soul credentials.

James Bradley

James Bradley 1979 Malaco 6358 Producer: Frederick Knight

Poor old James Bradley. Not only is he the merest punctuation mark in the book of soul but he didn't even warrant a mention in the six CD set (and 110 page booklet), *The Last Soul Company*, put out on the history of Malaco in 1999. But he had his moments, and all of them are on side two. This is one of those LPs split into dancing / listening styles and side one is pretty grim with Frederick Knight in his "Ring My Bell" mode, although it did deliver a minor soul hit with "I'm In Too Deep". However, the second side is more than acceptable, with five melodic and well produced and played tracks delivered by a genuine soul singer. For whatever reason Bradley never got to record again but soul fans who share my tastes will want this LP for side two alone.

Brainstorm (see also Lamont Johnson)

Belita Woods; Chuck Overton; Trenita Womack; Renell Gonsalves; Larry Sims; Deon Estus; Gerald Kent; Jeryl Bright; Lamont Johnson; Robert Ross; William Wooten

Stormin' 1977 Tabu BQL 1 - 2048 Producer: Jerry Peters (Billboard soul charts: 31 ; Billboard pop charts : 145)

Journey To The Light 1978 Tabu JZ 35327 Producer: Jerry Peters (Billboard soul charts : 53)

Funky Entertainment 1979 Tabu S TBU 83736 Producer: Jerry Peters

Brainstorm (another very popular name for a band) came out of Detroit and one of the more striking, and unacknowledged, facts about them was how many of the group members listed above have gone on to long and hopefully lucrative careers in the music industry. This is not the place to get specific, but a quick internet search will satisfy the curious. Possibly their best known member was their magnificent lead singer, Belita Woods. I have already praised her in my review of her duet with Ron Banks on his *Truly Bad* LP and she is terrific again on the best track on *Stormin'*, This Must Be Heaven". Mind you, so was co-lead singer Lamont Johnson (who also recorded a solo LP on Tabu which I will cover later.) The best known cut on that first LP, though, must be "Lovin' Is Really My Game" which became a pretty big hit single in 1977 (#14 soul) but is too fast and frantic for my tastes and if we are thinking about dancing, I much prefer "Wake Up And Be Somebody" (#48 soul) with its pummelling bass line and great drive. These are the three tracks most worthy of comment with the rest being ok but nothing special.

Journey To The Light was structurally similarly to *Stormin'* but sensibly placed Woods even more on the centre stage and she delivers "If You Ever Need To Cry", "Brand New Day" and "Lovin' Just You" beautifully. The rather mundane "We're On Our Way Home" was only a small hit as a single (#84), though, and whatever momentum the band may have had was lost.

The third and final LP, *Funky Entertainment*, was so markedly inferior to the first two LPs, that it was almost as if it were recorded by a different band, although the core members were still there and most everything within continued to be self-written. One cut which didn't come from the band was Sam Dees' "Case Of The Boogie" and it is the most inane thing he ever wrote, proving that no-one is infallible. Only one track can even be classed as a proper song, the graceful "You Put A Charge In My Life", as all the rest are faceless grooves.

As noted earlier many of the group went on to sustainable careers but Belita Woods' thirty five years in the industry sadly came to an end in 2012 when she died, aged only 63. (I should also have made earlier reference to Jerry Peters, who produced and arranged all the LPs, often with his trademark florid touches.)

Brand New Funk

Doug Wimbish; Seldon Powell; Cecil Powell; Hubert Powell; Bernard McDonald; Craig Derry

Brand New Funk 1978 Vibration VI 143 Producer: Sylvia Robinson

All Platinum had a distinctive sound to many of their records: cheap. This doesn't come across like that, though, and one would be hard pressed to identify it as having emanated from the New Jersey company. I don't believe Brand New Funk were anything more than a studio group (Seldon Powell, Bernard McDonald and Doug Wimbish played on hundreds of songs over the years, for example) and certainly they made no other records apart from this one. It's good, however, hard and funky and well played (particularly Wimbish's bass) throughout. The record sleeve does not tell us who does the singing (including a version of Bobby Patterson's "Fingers Do The Walking" which I recommend, and one of Boz Scaggs' "Lowdown" that I do not) but whoever he is performs well. One single was released from the set, "Jump Into Love". Etta James could only take her rendering of the same song to #92 on the soul charts. Brand New Funk couldn't even manage that.

Bill Brandon

Bill Brandon   1977   Prelude PRL 12149   Producers: Moses Dillard & Jesse Boyce

Like Tony Borders, Bill Brandon is a exceptional singer who recorded some great records in Muscle Shoals, but unlike Borders, he at least got the chance to record an LP that is reasonably representative of his best output. I add the qualifier, "reasonably", as while nothing can diminish the quality of Brandon's glorious voice, I find the LP to be somewhat overproduced with strings and backing singers unnecessarily prominent. Still, it is good and any record which lists the Muscle Shoals horn section, Sam Dees ("No Danger Of Heartbreak Ahead" is his song), and such fine musicians as Clayton Ivey, Roger Clark and Larry Byrom on the sleeve can't go drastically wrong, even if earlier 45s Brandon cut such as "Self Preservation", "Rainbow Road" and "Streets Got My Lady", are all better than anything on here. "We Fell In Love While Dancing" became only one of two records he ever placed on the soul charts, when it reached #30 in early 1978. but It would also have been nice if my favourite cut from his Prelude days, "Special Occasion", another Dees' song, had been included on the LP.

Brandye

Cynthia Douglas; Donna Davis; Pam Vincent

Crossover To Brandye 1979 Kayvette 804 Producer: Brad Shapiro

Like The Blossoms, Brandye were essentially a trio of excellent backing singers who got an opportunity to record an LP, but, as with the Blossoms' *Shockwave*, *Crossover To Brandye* is OK but nothing to get excited about. As with so many LPs. it might have helped if the record company had told us who Brandye were, but Kayvette did not think that necessary but did thoughtfully proclaim who provided their gowns.

Their vocal talent is not in doubt, which they show off a bit on the acappella cut that opens the LP and they have one great song with which to work: "One Woman's Trash Is Another Woman's Treasure". They perform this well enough but are eclipsed by Marion Love's fantastic version from 1972. "You Accuse Me" is the next best cut on here (and came out as their only single), with a splendid arrangement. Probably unavoidably in 1979, there are touches of The Emotions on tracks like "Mr. Mystery", and that lack of distinctiveness on the part of Brandye plus the overall lack of strong material stop this from being an LP that is lifted out of the pack.

Brass Construction

Randy Muller; Joe Wong; Wayne Parris; Morris Price; Larry Payton; Wade Williamston; Sandy Billups; Michael Grudge; Jesse Ward

Brass Construction   1975 UA LA 545   Producer: Jeff Lane   (Billboard soul charts: 1 ; Billboard pop charts : 10)

II   1976   UA LA6 77   Producer: Jeff Lane   (Billboard soul charts: 3 ; Billboard pop charts : 26)

III   1977   UA LA 775   Producer: Jeff Lane   (Billboard soul charts: 16; Billboard pop charts : 66)

IV   1978   UA LA 916   Producer: Jeff Lane   (Billboard soul charts: 24 ; Billboard pop charts : 174)

5   1979   UA LA 977   Producer: Jeff Lane   (Billboard soul charts: 18; Billboard pop charts : 89)

6   1980   UA LA 1060   Producer: Jeff Lane   (Billboard soul charts: 32; Billboard pop charts: 121)

Brass Construction came out of nowhere in a way that few records ever had, before or since. They had only issued one failed single before, on Docc Records, and, suddenly. they had a #1 LP and single ("Movin'") on their hands.

They were nothing if not terse in the early days as all the tracks on that first LP were one word titles and the first six album titles are hardly models of creative thinking. The other remarkable thing about the group was that their personnel was the same on all their work (except for Parris who didn't feature on "Conquest") which is an incredible achievement in itself when one considers the normal turnover in bands. (On the other hand, it must have contributed to their largely unvarying sound). Impossible, also, not to mention Randy Muller as their guiding force, as he arranged every one of the albums as well as writing the vast majority of the songs.

The UA sets were all produced by Jeff Lane, who, together with Muller, was also masterminding the rise of the similar sounding BT Express at the same time. Given that both bands were from New York, and enjoyed much the same success, it was sometimes difficult to tell them apart but Brass Construction's sound was generally a little less funky with more of an eye towards the rise of disco. I remember being as excited as most when *Brass Construction* became a big underground hit in the UK at the time of its release but I tired of the sound fairly quickly and stopped automatically buying the records after *Brass Construction IV*.

The first couple of sets do still have power though and probably deserved their success. All of the debut is danceable and funky and was played throughout the endlessly hot summer of '76 that everyone in England over the age of 50 remembers.The second set sounded more or less exactly like the first and it was already becoming clear that one wasn't going to buy Brass Construction LPs to be surprised or challenged. By the time *III* and *IV* appeared it was becoming impossible to tell the difference between one track and the next and the almost complete lack of melody that Muller and Lane served up was by now highly monotonous. *V* was more of the same and a track like "Shakit" could easily have come from the first album.

They bowed out of the UA years with *6*, which finally did vary the sound by virtue of featuring some ballads such as "I'm Not Gonna Stop" sung by one Eltesa Weatherby. Given their records were selling in ever diminishing numbers a new move was certainly needed.

Attitudes 1982 Liberty LT-51121 Producer: Randy Muller (Billboard soul charts: 21 ; Billboard pop charts: 114)

Conversations 1983 Capitol ST-12268 Producer: Randy Muller (Billboard soul charts: 29 ; Billboard pop charts : 176)

Renegades 1984 Capitol ST-12327 Producer: The Muller Organization (Billboard soul charts: 31)

Conquest 1985 Capitol ST-12423 Producer: The Muller Organization

1982 gave the opportunity for a fresh start: new label, no need to keep numbering the LP titles, and Lane had moved on. I'm not sure they really took it though, for while *Attitudes* certainly has a different sound, it is one that lots of other bands were also creating at the time and there was still no strong material on offer. Deciding, no doubt, that *Attitudes* wasn't the answer the band returned to the old approach on the opening cut on *Conversations*, "We Can Work It Out", and it was their best record for years. Other good cuts were "Easy" and "It's A Shame" and the whole album was generally a welcome if surprising return to form and I still listen to tracks from *Conversations*. Which is. sadly, more than I can say for *Renegades* and *Conquest* where the electronics are too prominent for me.

In summary, I admire Brass Construction for their single minded doggedness and longevity, which clearly brought them a fair degree of success, but I don't think they were inventive enough to have created too many releases that have stood the test of time.

Kenny Brawner & Raw Sugar

Chocolet Wright; Everett Brawner; Jeff Medina; Victor Seeyuen; Earl McIntyre; Bart McIntyre; Richard Trifan; Azzedin Weston; Courtenay Wynter

Kenny Brawner & Raw Sugar 1978 United Artists UA-LA928-H Producer: Horace Ott

Horace Ott has had a great career in the music industry, writing, producing arranging or playing on literally hundreds of records. Working on this LP was not his finest moment. It's all right, and just about plays up the funky side of this band's music at the expense of disco, and Brawner can sing pretty well, but it doesn't contain anything that I'd be dying to hear a second time. I believe Brawner is primarily an actor and has recently performed a show based on Ray Charles' music.

Breakwater

Kae Williams; Gene Robinson; James Jones; Linc Gilmore; Steve Green; Vince Garnell; Greg Scott; John Braddock

Breakwater 1978 Arista AB 4208 Producer: Rick Chertoff (Billboard soul charts: 36; Billboard pop charts : 173)

Splashdown 1980 Arista AB 4264 Producers: Kae Williams & Rick Chertoff (Billboard soul charts: 33 ; Billboard pop charts : 141)

Another funky aggregation, and there were so many such seven, eight or nine man bands in the seventies. Breakwater were not really any better or any worse than the others, and specialised in tuneful and gentle horn-led funk workouts. They did have the benefit of a pretty good lead singer in Gene Robinson and the musicianship of Kae Williams (who went on to play on no end of records by others) but could not quite forge a distinctive enough sound to compel Arista to have invested in them a little more. "Work It Out" had some success as a single (#71 soul) and was arguably the stand-out track from *Breakwater* which included a song, "No Limit", that was also performed in the same year by Jean Terrell. I'd call it a draw.

The best song from *Splashdown*, "Say You Love Me Girl", was sensibly released as a single (#79 soul) and the group's horn section is impressive on "Let Love In".

Brenda & Herb (see also The Exciters)

In Heat Again 1979 Drive 109 Producers: Steve Jerome & Lou Hemsey

Brenda Reid and her husband Herb Rooney were better known for being the mainstays of that excellent group, The Exciters, who put out some lovely records in the sixties and early seventies. This was their one and only LP as by Brenda & Herb and it wasn't helped by the awful, cheap looking cover. On actually listening to *In Heat Again*, it becomes apparent that they were still both highly gifted singers, and the best moments don't sound a million miles away from Ashford and Simpson recordings. The songs are, unsurprisingly, not up to A & S standards, but I do have a lot of time for "Look What They've Done To Our City", written by soul journeyman, Sam Culley. "Tonight I m Gonna Make You A Star " was a minor soul hit in 1978 (#70) but. together with a disco version of "I (Who Have Nothing)", it is one of the more uninteresting cuts to be found here. The best way to listen to much of the LP is to discount most of the songs and focus solely on the superb singing.

Brenda & The Tabulations

Brenda Payton; Pat Mercer; Deborah Martin; Jerry Jones; Eddie Jackson; Maurice Coates; Bernard Murphy; James Rucker

Dry Your Eyes 1967 Dionn 2000 Producers: Bob Finiz & Gilda Woods (Billboard soul charts: 19; Billboard pop charts: 191)

Brenda & The Tabulations 1970 Top & Bottom LPS 100 Producers: Gilda Woods & Van McCoy

I Keep Coming Back For More 1977 Chocolate City CCLP 2002 Producers: Gilda Woods, Norma Harris, Bobby Eli & John Davis

"Dry Your Eyes" was a big hit single (#8 soul, #20 pop) for this Philadelphia based group at the start of 1967 and thus became the title of their first LP. The song is charming but ever so close to "It's Gonna Take A Miracle" and remains probably their best known record. An even better cut (and single) from *Dry Your Eyes* is "Stay Together Young Lovers" (#44 soul) which is heartbreakingly beautiful in its naivety and yearning optimism. Generally. though, it's the sort of album that people might cite as typical of the times: a couple of hits and lots of filler in the shape of covers (it features no fewer than seven and all have been performed much better).

The follow-up, *Brenda & The Tabulations*, featured four singles that made the Top 50 of the soul charts but once again included a number of insipid cover versions. (It also most unusually provided no songwriting details on the sleeve or the record itself.) To be honest I found all the releases on Top and Bottom to be pretty uninteresting as the strings somewhat overwhelmed the rhythm and I don't think Payton's voice was suited to delivering social commentary material such as " A Child No-One Wanted". In early 1971 the group finally had another hit to match "Dry Your Eyes" in "Right On The Tip Of My Tongue" but, surprisingly, Top and Bottom didn't put out an album to capitalise on it although two further hit singles did follow. (Even more disappointingly, Epic Records didn't put out an LP around the excellent "One Girl Too Late" single from 1973.)

By 1977 I'm not sure if any Tabulations still existed and I suspect *I Keep Coming Back For More* is actually a Brenda Payton solo LP. As with all of Brenda and Tabulations' music it was recorded in Philadelphia and had a number of high points not least in the old Evie Sands' song "Take It Or Leave It" which was the best track she had recorded in years. Her voice seems to have an androgynous quality on this album, by the way, that I had not really noticed before.

Brenda Payton died, way too early, in 1992 and I don't think I'm being unkind in saying that no-one has ever made claims for her to be considered as a great soul singer but on a handful of sides she captured innocence as eloquently as anyone.

Brick

Jimmy Brown; Ray Ransom; Regi Hargis; Eddie Irons; Don Nevins; Ambric Bridgeforth

Good High 1976 Bang BLP-408 Producers: Jim Healy, Johnny Duncan, Robert E Lee & Brick (Billboard soul charts: 1; Billboard pop charts : 19)

Brick 1977 Bang BLP-409 Producer: Phil Benton and Brick. (Billboard soul charts: 1; Billboard pop charts : 15)

Stoneheart 1979 Bang JZ 35969 Producer: Bill Schnee (Billboard soul charts: 25 ; Billboard pop charts : 100)

Waiting on You 1980 Bang JZ 36262 Producers: Phil Benton & Brick (Billboard soul charts: 31 ; Billboard pop charts : 179)

Summer Heat 1981 Bang FZ 37471 Producers: Ray Parker & Brick (Billboard soul charts: 13; Billboard pop charts : 89)

After 5 1982 Bang FZ 38170 Producer: Phil Benton & Brick

Too Tuff 1982 Magic City MCR - 1001 Producer: Brick

Brick came barrelling out of Atlanta and sent the *Good High* set straight to #1 on the soul charts as well as top 20 pop, both based on the huge success of "Dazz"(#1 soul, #3 pop) as a 45. In truth, it is one of the most indifferent LPs to have ever reached the pinnacle as, outside of the hit, it contains a great deal of filler, including a handful of instrumental workouts. I like the simple and almost subliminal sixties piano on "Here We Come" and have always enjoyed "Music Matic", their first ever single (#82 soul) , but why it failed and "Dazz" scored is a bit of a mystery. (Note: I'm assuming the Robert E Lee production credit is a nod to proud southern roots.)

Brick, the follow-up, was just as big a success, thanks to another huge single, "Dusic" (#2 soul, #18 pop), and is a better realised record, no doubt because they had more time to think about it. There is only one semi-instrumental within and side two is nearly all down and mid-tempo with some soulful singing on "Good Morning Sunshine".

For some reason, it was then deemed necessary to move the recording location from The Web IV Studio in Atlanta to Studio 55 in Hollywood under a new producer. The approach and sound were little changed but *Stoneheart* was a pretty average LP and did not do so well as the first two, and nor did two singles pulled from it, languishing in the mid regions of the soul charts..

Waiting For You saw a return to Web IV but their fortunes continued to plummet, as it was their lowest charting - but ironically, possibly best - record they had issued. All Brick's music thus far had been self-written and it was therefore interesting to hear how an outside song like Paul Davis' "All The Way" lifted the LP as it had a melody their own songs could not match. It might have even stirred them to concentrate more on their own material as "Don't Ever Lose Your Love" and "Let Me Make You Happy" were probably the strongest songs they had produced.

It had been four years since Brick placed a single in the US soul singles Top 10 and so they were doubtless thrilled when "Sweat (Til You Get Wet)" made it there in the summer of 1981. It was their hardest (and thus, best) funk number to date and became the lead off cut on *Summer Heat* which had enlisted Ray Parker as co-producer and his pop sensibilities doubtless helped in the commercial upturn in their fortunes. He also served to improve their music as *Summer Heat* was the best LP they ever made, even better than *Waiting On You*. The songs were simply stronger and more memorable, and the fact he wrote 6 out of the 9 cuts was no co-incidence. A recommended outing for anyone who cares for this sort of thing.

Unfortunately for everyone, *Summer Heat* was the only Brick release on which Parker worked and it was back to Phil Benton for *After 5*, the first album of theirs which did not chart in any fashion. It was not a bad record at all with good tracks like "It's A New Day" but their time had gone.

The final vinyl outing was on the small Magic City label out of Birmingham and, once again, was not bad, but, by this time, the band were not able to get singles onto the charts, let alone LPs.

Brick were markedly successful for about 18 months, which was some going for a soul band from Atlanta, and generally softened their sound to became more versatile as time went on and if only they had composed more memorable material (or brought in more outside songs) they could have had an even more spectacular career.

Brides Of Funkenstein

Dawn Silva; Sheila Horn; Jeanette McGruder; Lynn Mabry

Funk Or Walk 1978 Atlantic SD 19201 Producers: George Clinton & William Collins (Billboard soul charts: 17; Billboard pop charts: 70)

Never Buy Texas From A Cowboy 1979 Atlantic SD 19261 Producers: George Clinton, William Collins & Ronald Dunbar (Billboard soul charts: 49 ; Billboard pop charts: 93)

Given my less then ringing endorsement for Bootsy's Rubber Band it might be expected that I will feel much the same way about the music made by The Brides Of Funkenstein and, to some extent I do, but their music had a slightly more serious side, such as on tracks like "Just Like You" or "When You're Gone" from

Funk Or Walk (where their one big selling single, "Disco To Go", #7 soul, can be found, which incidentally features one of the most amusing takes on an English accent since Dick Van Dyke's) and the Brides could certainly sing, so I believe their records have aged much better, but one still needs to have brought into the whole Mothership Connection concept to really "get" this music.

I'm surprised that I can still listen to the whole 15 minutes of "Never Buy Texas From A Cowboy" but I like the groove, the vocals and the title. "I Didn't Mean To Fall In Love" is good too, but entirely different from everything else they ever recorded. Given I also enjoy "I'm Holding You Responsible" I have to conclude that *Never Buy* is one of the best (or at least one of my favourite) P-Funk releases from about 1975 or so onwards.

Chuck Bridges And The L.A. Happening

Chuck Bridges And The L.A. Happening 1969 Vault SLP-132 Producer: Lucky Young

Chuck Bridges and The L.A. Happening were a multi-racial group who made a couple of singles and this one album, none of which came even close to "happening". It sounds very dated now and their style, which seemed to borrow from just about everywhere and mixed up jazz, blues, pop, rock, and soul, wasn't compelling enough to make them stand out from anyone else and they ended up sounding a bit like a poor man's Blood, Sweat and Tears. Most tracks are mid-tempo and some slower songs would have been welcome. The better cuts are "Keep Your Faith Baby" "Head Over Heels" and "Payin' Your Dues " all of which have good horn patterns. Despite coughing up for a gatefold sleeve and lengthy sleevenotes which waffle on, Vault records didn't seem interested in informing us who comprised the LA Happening.

Brief Encounter

Larry Bailey; Velmar Bailey; Montie Bailey; Gary Bailey; Maurice Whittington; Rufus Wilborn; Fredrick Alexander; Charles Graham; Michael Carter

Brief Encounter 1977? Seventy-Seven 102 Producer: John Richbourg

We Want To Play 1981 Music Town RSR 1205 Producers: Brief Encounter & Bob Holmes

Yet more brothers. North Carolina's Brief Encounter had the dubious honour of recording two albums which have always been in high demand and will thus not be found cheaply. They may be good news for collectors, but not for Brief Encounter as they did not sell well at all, and in fact, I'm not sure that the first album was ever commercially released, although copies clearly exist. Sadly, they are also examples of records whose rarity far exceeds their musical worth.

The group had put out a handful of highly enjoyable John Richbourg produced singles on Seventy-Seven in the early seventies, mainly delivered by the excellent lead singer Whittington, but none of these sides are included on the first LP, which, despite having been recorded in Muscle Shoals, is too heavy on synths and nondescript funk for my tastes. Best track is the rather lovely Whittington sung "In A Special Kind Of Way" which was a small soul hit (#78) in the summer of 1977 when it came out on Capitol.

We Want To Play contains some rather predictable and mundane dance tracks like the title cut and "Open Up Your Heart" but of much more interest is the surprising and appealing acoustic guitar driven "Now I Know I Love You" and the perky "Sweet Tender Loving" and "Just For Love". The latter two sound as if they were recorded earlier than 1981 (as well as being performed by an unnamed female singer.)

Kimberley Briggs

Who's Kimberley? 1971 Kimbrig KS 001 Producer: Freddy Briggs

Come And Get Me I'm Ready 1973 Chess CH 50040 Producer: Freddy Briggs

Kimberley is Dorothy Kimberley Tolliver, better known on record as Kim Tolliver, under which name she recorded some brilliant singles. She was married to Freddy Briggs, hence her name on this LP which was originally issued on Kimbrig with an incredibly cheap cover guaranteed to make any prospective buyers answer: "who cares?". It was then swiftly issued a second time (with merely a boring sleeve) under the title of *Passing Clouds* on Fantasy 8415, also in 1971. Both issues sank without the proverbial trace.

It is an interesting LP nevertheless; if one is of the opinion that soul music is all about the singer then he or she would have to conclude that this is one of the finest albums ever made, such is Briggs'/Tolliver's customary vocal commitment but if, like me, you believe that soul music is ultimately about the interplay between vocals, songs, production and accompanying music then you will possibly rate it somewhat less highly. While I do like the record and believe that she was one of the finest of all female soul singers, I have always found it to be a bit fussy and overproduced. Take "The Letter" for example. By the Box Tops this is a short and very sweet single and I genuinely much prefer their take to Kim's which is too drawn out, an interpretation which frankly acts against the spirit of the song, which is all about urgency. Kim Tolliver could sing rings around Alex Chilton but he had captured the song's essence much more adroitly.

For her second and only other LP she used her recording name of Kim Tolliver. I much prefer this one, which, although still a bit top-heavy on arrangements, has better and shorter songs which allow Kim's voice to take center stage, There are no weak tracks, but no absolute killers either, although the superb "The Other Side Of Town" (which has strong traces of Swamp Dogg's "She Kept On Talking") and "I'm Losing The Feeling" (also cut by Gwen McCrae) come closest, but sadly neither set ultimately contains anything as good as her finest ever moment on vinyl: "Where Were You" from 1980 where the naked pain she brings to the record is chilling and overwhelming. She passed away in 2007 without ever having reached the national charts

Brighter Side Of Darkness

Darryl Lamont; Ralph Eskridge; Randolph Murph; Larry Washington

Love Jones 1973 20th Century 405 Producers: Clarence Johnson, William Johnson & Johnny Cameron (Billboard soul charts: 35 ; Billboard pop charts: 202)

One of many groups that followed in the footsteps of The Jacksons, Chicago's Brighter Side of Darkness had a massive hit with "Love Jones" (#3 soul, #16 pop) as well as a reasonably good selling follow-up, "I Owe You", and released further singles up until 1978 at which point they disbanded. I like the arrangement, harmonies and production on the LP a great deal, but have always had trouble listening to pre-teen singers - which Lamont was at the time - regardless of how talented they were (and he was certainly gifted). I therefore listen with interest when the rest of the group take leads, but tune out somewhat when Lamont takes over, although "I'm A Loser" is a splendid side. For example, the b-side to the big hit, "I'm The Guy", has Murph on lead vocals and it is much more to my liking as a result.

Charles Brimmer

Expression Of Soul 1975 Chelsea CHL 508 Producer: Senator Jones

Soul Man 1976 Chelsea CHL 520 Producer: Senator Jones

Brimful Of Soul 1986 Charly CRB 1123 (UK)

Charles Brimmer had been making estimable 45s in New Orleans for a number of years before he had the good sense and fortune to cover "God Blessed Our Love", a song on Al Green's massively successful *Explores Your Mind* LP. Brimmer's version, while only making #43 on the US singles chart in 1975, was by some distance his most fruitful recording to date and on the back of it he was given the opportunity to put together the first two albums of his career by Chelsea records. *Expression Of Soul* has a nearly faultless first side with a spectacular version of "I Stand Accused" which is even better than his hit single. Side two is less impressive as, although it features two good songs in "Love Me In Your Own Way" and "Just Another Morning", both written by Brimmer, "The Music Is Funky" is poor and his take on "We've Only Just Begun" is the worst kind of "over-souling" when a much simpler interpretation would have been more beneficial.

Soul Man was more balanced than *Expression Of Soul*, with maybe nothing as good as "I Stand Accused", but with no bad tracks either, although he flirts with danger on "Dedicating My Life To You" where he just stays the right side of aping Al Green's phrasing in a slightly demeaning manner. But this is a small quibble: this is a very good LP, rooted in the grand tradition of assertive horn arrangements, sung by an underappreciated singer and it should not be as neglected as it always has been.

Brimful Of Soul comprised the whole of *Soul Man* plus "We've Only Just Begun".

Jimmy Briscoe & Little Beavers

Jimmy Briscoe; Robert Makins; Kevin Barnes; Maurice Pulley; Stanford Stansberry; Bobby Finch

My Ebony Princess 1974 Pi-Kappa 6000 Producer: Paul Kyser

Jimmy Briscoe & Beavers 1977 Wanderick WA 66000 Producer: Paul Kyser

This Baltimore based group delivered an album in *My Ebony Princess* that exemplified what East Coast "sweet soul" sounded like in the early seventies. Producer Paul Kyser always favoured a heavily orchestrated and tuneful approach - and the cover lists who played, among other instruments, harp, violin. viola, cello, glockenspiel, clarinets and horns of the French, English and Flugel variety - that was not unlike what Thom Bell did with the Delfonics, and I think it was lovely, but I can understand that some would find it to be an acquired taste. The group sang with a maturity that belied their tender ages, but just in case we were in any danger of forgetting who the main audience were for Jimmy Briscoe and his Little Beavers, the sleeve also told us their favourite colours and what they looked for in a woman, which I always enjoyed, seeing as how Makins and Barnes, particularly, looked about eleven years old.

Anyway, as I said, I think it was an utterly enchanting album, and one which slightly overshadowed their follow-up of three years later when the group were no longer "little" Beavers. The front of the Wanderick set makes this clear as we see the group walking down the road with unsmiling faces and large dogs in tow, although the back cover does provide much more reassuring images. It is not a poor release by any means, a fine one in fact, but fractionally lacks the quality of songs of the debut, didn't bring forth as many successful singles, and plays up the rhythm at the expense of the orchestration. Stand-out ballads are "True Love", "So Sweet The Way" and "More Than You Realise".

By the end of the seventies the group disbanded and all left the music industry, I believe, with Briscoe becoming a carpenter, for example. Clearly the group were put together as potential rivals to The Jackson 5 and while they never even came close to attaining that same level of success, they created some wonderful music and always managed to sound more "grown-up" than the Motown group until they became the Jacksons.

Johnny Bristol

Hang On In There Baby 1974 MGM 4959 Producer: Johnny Bristol (Billboard soul charts : 7: Billboard pop charts: 82)

Feeling The Magic 1975 MGM 4993 Producer: Johnny Bristol (Billboard soul charts : 29)

Bristol's Creme 1976 Atlantic SD 18197 Producer: Johnny Bristol (Billboard soul charts : 43: Billboard pop charts: 154)

The Best Of 1976 Polydor 2391 318 (UK)

Strangers 1978 Atlantic SD 19184 Producer: Johnny Bristol

Free To Be Me 1981 Handshake FW37666 Producers: Johnny Bristol & Gus Dudgeon

Johnny Bristol was a skilled and highly successful songwriter and producer for Motown for many years before he went the solo route, where he hit immediately with "Hang On In There Baby", a song known by everyone reading this book or with any interest in soul music. The album of the same name is musical, chock full of literate songs with hummable melodies and catchy hooks, but it is all a little....dull. Bristol was a good singer, sharing some of the same tonal qualities as Bill Withers, and he was an even better writer and producer, so it is a little surprising that I feel the way I do about it. Part of that might be the fact that one rather sickly song, "Love Me For A Reason", was a big hit for The Osmonds, and another could be that there are moments when he drifts close to Barry White territory, and it sits in my collection as earnest and respectable, but not one to dig out to play blind to someone who wants to know what "soul" is all about.

Despite changing arrangers from H B Barnum to Paul Riser, Bristol adopted the same format for *Feeling The Magic* and it sounds much like the debut. It contained two soul charting singles in "Leave My World"(#20) and "Love Takes Tears" (#72).

Subtle changes took place for *Bristol's Creme,* such as Willie Weeks and James Gadson being drafted in to play and Sonny Burke arranging the rhythms, and I feel more positive towards this album, which featured the second biggest single of his career, "Do It To My Mind" (#5 soul, #43 pop), while "You Turn Me On To Love" is soulful and heartfelt and "Have Yourself A Good Time" is genuinely catchy and employs an unnamed female vocalist which helps its flow.

Bristol was now established as a genuine solo artist rather than as a producer/writer just dipping his toe into the waters of going it alone and *Strangers* was my favourite of all his LPs. It boasted an uplifting title track, and a much crisper approach to rhythm than had hitherto been the case. Sadly it was his least successful LP to date, suggesting that Atlantic's promotional efforts were lacklustre, but a single from the set, "Waiting On Love" did reasonably well and reached #27 on the soul charts.

Free To Be Me was another excellent album which failed to sell in appreciable quantities but did house an anthemic track in "Love No Longer Has A Hold On Me" which was a big favourite in the UK. A number of tracks were cut in London and it is to the musicians and producer Gus Dudgeon's credit that they lose nothing in comparison to the ones recorded in L.A. The other noticeable departure on this LP was Bristol's willingness, for the first time, to bring in outside songs and one, "I Can't Stop You", was an inspired choice as no bad version of this exists. What I particularly liked about Bristol's latter work was that, apart from an irritating syndrum ping here and there, it disdained the disco beats that were overwhelming so many others at the time. The uptempo tracks were certainly good for dancing, but not at the expense of solid musicality and literate songwriting.

John William Bristol died in 2004 at the too early age of 65 but had a lengthy career of which he could be justly proud. There will not be too many artists covered in this book who will have outdone him in success and, hopefully, wealth.

Tina Britt

Blue All The Way 1969 Minit 24023 Producer: Juggy Murray

Tina Brittingham had a pretty short career, scoring one reasonably big, and likeable, hit single in 1965 with "The Real Thing", but has remained almost completely unknown ever since, and to the best of my knowledge, has never been tracked down and interviewed. Her one LP, while not blue *all* the way, is certainly heavily influenced by the blues and does include some venerable old songs such as "Bright Lights, Big City" and "Key To The Highway". I am somewhat lukewarm towards these tracks, much preferring the more obvious "soul" efforts like "My Lover's Prayer","Sookie Sookie" and "I Love You More Than You'll Ever Know", the latter being one of the superior versions of this oft-recorded song. Despite Britt's rather limited success in the industry Minit certainly did not stint on the album, bringing in good songs from many sources while the arrangements, mostly by George Andrews and Willie Bridges, are particulary creative and thoughtful and in perfect tune with the vocals and top class New York musicians. The lead off cut, "Who Was That", hit #39 on the soul charts at the end of 1968 and was the last time Britt's name appeared on any chart.

Broadway

Magic Man 1979 Hilltak HT 19225 Producer: Willie Henderson

This Chicago recorded LP by an outfit with a predictably popular name (a few "Broadways" exist) contained a couple of tiny soul hit singles in "Kiss You All Over" (#92) and "This Funk Is Made For Dancing" (#83) but they are two of four cuts on the album which are poor, dull disco dance tracks. In fact is it weren't for an ok midtempo cut in "I Can't Think Of Anything Better Than Lovin' You" and the best track on here by far, "Take Me In Your Arms", this would be a pretty tame effort. I don't know for sure, but strongly suspect that this Broadway didn't actually exist, and were in fact a studio band playing behind vocalist, Patti Williams. Nothing on here taxes her in the slightest, apart from "Take Me In Your Arms", on which she impresses.

Tom Brock

I Love You More And More 1974 20th Century T-430 Producer: Barry White

From 1973 up until the end of that decade Barry White's song titles tended to be longer than everyone else's, a little known observation of mine, and I note that this trait percolated down to his protégé, Tom James Brocker from Austin, as the eight song titles on his one LP are satisfyingly lengthy.

Brock, who died in 2002, would appear to have had a very short career on the other hand, with just this one LP and the two singles pulled from it to his name, and I suspect he might not have been aware of the esteem with which it has long been held in the UK. He was not an especially distinctive singer and he adopts a Marvin Gaye influenced tone throughout but the album is appealing thanks to its lush L.A. orchestration and Brock's skill at writing songs with strong hooks.

Brockingtons

Brockingtons 1971 Today TLP 1003 Producers: Terry Philips & Maurice Irby

This is not a typical soul release, and the music is a mixture of pop, soul and jazz which produces a slightly uneasy melange. I'm not sure who they were but the sleeve would suggest that it was a one man, one woman combination and I'm pretty certain they were related to jazz man Julius Brockington who also recorded for Today. They perform an interesting, and radically different, take on "Natural Woman" while "Eye Doctor" and "Jeremiah" were also recorded by Debbie Taylor on her own Today LP and I prefer her versions.

Ramona Brooks

Ramona Brooks 1978 Manhattan MR-LA909-H Producers: Neil Portnow & John Miller

Ramona Brooks looks extremely young and pretty on her one LP, which seems to be in demand from some quarters. Not mine, I'm afraid, as I find her breathless soft singing style to have scant appeal. "Skinny Dippin'" was a small soul hit (# 94) in 1977. Her "I Don't Want You Back" is also popular but it is not included here.

Ray Brooks

I'll Take Care Of You 1982 Castle CA 7082 Producer: Ray Brooks

Songs Within (with Full Fource) Timeless TRPL114 (UK)

Brooks put out a lovely Bobby Bland influenced soul/blues 45, "Walk Out Like A Lady", in the late seventies which is included on his fine Castle LP. It is the best thing on the set, but "Sweet Sixteen", "These Arms Of Mine" and "I'll Take Care Of You" are worthwhile too. Yes, these are all the famous songs of the same names, and maybe Brooks thought that by rendering the first two, particularly, almost unrecognisable by speeding up the tempos that no-one would notice that he also claimed to have written them all.

Timeless records also probably thought that they were safe from being sued by anybody as it seemed pretty clear that their LP (which includes four Brooks' tracks off the Castle LP and four from the group Full Force) would sell in negligible quantity, an outcome further guaranteed by the lack of sleevenotes and awful cover.

Brotherhood

Delbert White; Les Coulter; Nathan White; Dwight White; Tony Trevias; Scottie White; Don Delatorre

Brotherhood 1978 MCA 2373 Producer: Dwight White

Three of the Whites, Delbert, Dwight and Nathan (or Mathan?), recorded a highly sought after 45 round about 1970 under the name of Lil' Lavair & The Fabulous Jades which must have sold about 86 copies. They resurfaced in 1978 with four others to comprise Brotherhood. This time around they did at least have the satisfaction of attaining some modicum of success, as a single from the album, "Change Of Pace", made #77 on the soul charts in July of that year, but after the follow-up single did not make it they seemed to have disbanded and left the music industry. (Some discographies list the couple of records made by "Bobby Womack & Brotherhood" in 1976 and 1977 as by this "Brotherhood" but there was no connection whatsoever.)

It is not a bad outing at all, and "Change Of Pace", an insipid instrumental which sounds like a distant cousin of "The Hustle", is not typical of the rest on offer. They do not serve up anything original, content to borrow from here and there, such as a Commodores - era Lionel Richie snarl on "Together Alone", while it sounds as if Ernie Isley breezed in to dash off a guitar solo on "Given My Life", but the LP is generally better than merely competent. "Top 40 Band" is thoughtful, and they acquit themselves without mishap on a couple of slower tracks.

Brothers Johnson (see also Louis Johnson)

Look Out For # 1 1976 A & M SP 4567 Producer: Quincy Jones (Billboard soul charts: 1 ; Billboard pop charts: 9)

Right On Time 1977 A & M SP 4644 Producer: Quincy Jones (Billboard soul charts: 2 ; Billboard pop charts: 13)

Blam !! 1978 A & M SP 4714 Producer: Quincy Jones (Billboard soul charts: 1 ; Billboard pop charts: 7)

Light Up The Night 1980 A&M SP 3716 Producer: Quincy Jones (Billboard soul charts: 1; Billboard pop : 5)

Bassist Louis Johnson and guitarist brother George were another soul act who made it big with their first record and maintained a high level of success for a number of years. They first came to some sort of prominence by writing a couple of songs which were recorded by Billy Preston before being noticed by mentor and producer Quincy Jones. Not a bad man's attention to attract. They wrote most of the best tracks on Jones' *Mellow Madness* LP before producing their own debut LP, *Look Out For #1*. Given they were both highly talented (Louis particularly; he played bass on Michael Jackson's "Billie Jean" among numerous other credits), and given Jones' involvement which assured that the record was going to be classy and musically impeccable. it could hardly have failed to hit and did not. "Get The Funk Out Ma Face"(#4 soul as a 45) was nice and aggressive ("I'll Be Good To You" went all the way to #1 soul and # 3 pop) and the whole LP has a shimmer and gloss that has kept it looking and sounding good all these years later.

The follow-up, *Right On Time*, housed their masterpiece: "Strawberry Letter 23", a great Shuggie Otis song and one of the best pop/soul records ever recorded. It became their second #1 single on the soul charts ("I'll Be Good To You" from the first LP was the other). An ingredient which helped to give *Right On Time* an even fuller sound was the Tower of Power horn section on a handful of tracks, but, by and large, the first two albums are peas from the same pod.

For some reason, the two singles released from the third LP, *Blam!!*, failed to do well at all, which was odd, especially as one, "Ain't We Funkin' Now", despite borrowing the intro from the Ohio Players' magnificent "Fire", was one of their best and funkiest ever. (The other single, "Ride O Rocket", was an atypical Ashford-Simpson song.) For all their talent, they did have an Achilles' heel in their singing on slower songs which was functional but not inspired, as on "So Won't You Stay". The best lead vocal on the LP by far is taken by Alex Weir on "It's You Girl" which I think sort of proves my point. All in all, though, another strong LP deserving of its success.

While Jones could never be accused of failing to prepare for and deliver on his musical challenges, it did feel as if he took even more care than usual on *Light Up The Night* which was another huge success, as well as containing a single in "Stomp!" which returned the brothers to #1. If you recruit the likes of Michael Jackson, Merry Clayton, Susaye Greene, Jim Gilstrap, Augie Johnson, and Scherrie Payne just to deliver backing vocals you are taking a project very seriously indeed, and certainly their singing on "All About The Heaven" and "Treasure" was almost transcendentally beautiful.

Winners 1981 A & M SP 3724 Producer: Brothers Johnson (Billboard soul charts: 10 ; Billboard pop charts: 48)

Blast ! 1982 A & M SP 4927 Producer: Brothers Johnson (new tracks) (Billboard soul charts: 23 ; Billboard pop charts: 138)

Out Of Control 1984 A & M SP 4965 Producers: Keg Johnson, Leon Sylvers & Brothers Johnson (Billboard soul charts: 20 ; Billboard pop charts: 91)

Kickin' 1988 A & M SP 5162 Producers: Brothers Johnson & Bryan Loren

Winners was the first album cut by The Brothers Johnson without Jones as producer but most of it didn't sound that much different from what had come before, as many of the same musicians were used. An exception would be "Daydreamer Dream" a light pop confection that *did* sound highly different, with shades of Queen, of all people. One could start to see the Brothers' fingers slipping from the hitherto firm grasp of unbroken success, as it was their lowest charting LP thus far, by some distance, although it did house a #11 soul hit single in "The Real Thing".

Their slide was exacerbated by the release of *Blast!* a slightly dubious release in my opinion for it wasn't great value for money, containing five new songs on side 1 and five old songs, including three number one hits, on side 2. Guess which side I preferred? To be fair, the new tracks are not all that bad but inevitably lost a lot in comparison with the hits.

The brothers returned to outside producers in Leon Sylvers and Keg Johnson for a couple of tracks on *Out Of Control* which did revive their fortunes to some extent, and Louis Johnson's bass playing was still amazing, but it was a record I knew I would never listen to a second time after hearing it once. Ditto for *Kickin'* which literally gave me a headache last time I played it.

That they signed out with two sub-par albums is frankly of little consequence though, given the glories of much of their earlier career, and Louis and George Johnson ended up as two of the most successful artists ever to be associated with soul music.

Brother To Brother

Michael Burton; Billy Jones; Chuck Carrado; Bobby Palido; Leslie Booker; Danny Lattuca; Leslie Cunningham

In The Bottle 1974 Turbo TU-7013 Producers: Al Goodman, Michael Burton & Harry Ray (Billboard soul charts : 45)

Let Your Mind Be Free 1976 Turbo TU-7015 Producers: Billy Jones & Bernadette Randle (Billboard soul : 33)

Shades in Creation 1977 Turbo TU-7018 Producer: Billy Jones

Brother 2 Brother 1980 Sugar Hill SH-259 Producer: Billy Jones

A multi-racial band, Brother to Brother made an excellent record when covering Gil Scott-Heron's "In The Bottle" and two enjoyable albums in their debut and *Let Your Mind Be Free*, although the latter had a cover that has always baffled me somewhat as to its relevance to the record within.

In The Bottle suffered from the all too usual All Platinum offhand quality control approach with some tracks having the most abrupt endings I know of on vinyl but it did house other good moments apart from the title track (a 9 soul and #46 pop hit) including a totally different take on The Temptations' "I Wish It Would Rain". They were funky enough in that slightly thin way favoured by the Robinsons (Sylvia and Joe, record company owners) and lead singer Michael Burton had an appealing Sly Stone influenced vocal style.

Let Your Mind Be Free is also worth listening to, with the title track and "Chance With You" (a #30 soul hit) having a following to this day, but the follow-up, *Shades In Creation,* is not good, being dull and uninspiring and there is nothing more I can usefully say. Their last LP, which I have not heard, was on Sugar Hill in 1980. Given that their album covers did not always display a great deal of information it is entirely possible that I might have incorrectly stated the band's personnel.

Brothers Unlimited

Leon Aldridge; Curtis Johnson; Alvin Potts; John Harris; Ronald Echols; Jerry Jones; Lee Cox; Oscar Smith; Charles Allen; Charles Aldridge; Harold Johnson; Larry Lee

Who's For The Young 1970 Capitol ST-600 Producers: Earl Cage & Robert Owens

Not content with the typical seven or eight band members, Brothers Unlimited weighed in with a hefty twelve, and such an investment in people was definitely justified on this excellent LP, which was recorded at the great FAME studios in Muscle Shoals. It was a shame they only issued this one album, as they were a most interesting band. For instance, they included two former members of the Stax group The Astors in lead singer Curtis Johnson (also in another Stax group, The Chips) and his brother Harold, as well as former Astors associate and songwriter, guitarist Larry Lee (who had worked frequently with Jimi Hendrix.)

Given Brothers Unlimited featured four singers (and I think the raw voice which takes lead on most cuts belongs to Jerry Jones), there were echoes of the way in which The New Birth were constituted, but they don't sound like them, relying to a large extent, unsurprisingly, on Lee's guitar. It really is a collection of delights: some pulsating and earthy organ-driven funk in the title track and "Life, Dreams, Death"; a Lee - led version of "Spoonful", which sounds like early Funkadelic; a noteworthy and unusual version of "A Change Is Gonna Come" and much more mainstream soul songs in the superb "Got To Get Over" and "Take Me Back". A rare album without a single weak cut, this is one to seek out without delay, or slap on the turntable tomorrow if you already own it.

Brothers By Choice

Chuck Higgins; Patty Brooks; Petsy Powell

Brothers Of Choice 1978 Ala 1983 Producers: EJ Gurren, Barnett Williams & Stan Ross

This highly worthwhile LP is confusingly entitled on the record label as "She Puts The Ease Back Into Easy" after one of the singles that was released from it, whereas the cover merely lists the band's name as the title. There is also a lack of clarity as to who comprised Brothers by Choice and I have gone with some information I picked up in my research, but it wouldn't surprise me if there was no such group and it was really a solo outing by vocalist Chuck Higgins (Brooks and Powell are credited as back-up singers on the album). It is all mid-tempo or uptempo and much of it is typical of the kind of thing that was played on the dance scene in England known as "Modern Soul" although I'm not sure why Ala felt it was wise to split "Ease" Parts 1 and 2 across different sides.

Two singles pulled from the set reached the soul charts ("Ease at #79 and "Baby You Really Got Me Going" at #51) as did two others in 1980, although these latter were not included on here. That seemed to be it for Brothers By Choice.

Alex Brown

In Search Of Love Sundi SD 5001 1972 Producer: Monk Higgins

Alex Brown was another ex-Raelet and this is a highly in-demand

LP, which was only granted a distinctly limited release, leading to few known copies in the world. She was obviously talented - Raelets had to be - and the tracks I have heard (I don't own it) are all good, with one cut, "I'm Not Responsible", also being much prized when released as a single. (There also seems to be a question mark over the year of the album's release, but as it was reviewed in the April 1972 edition of *Billboard* I am assuming that must be the correct one.)

Charles Hilton Brown

Owed To Myself 1974 Ampex 3200-SD Produced by Charles Hilton Brown (Italy)

Here's one right out of left field. I know virtually nothing about Brown and have assumed he is an expatriate American serviceman who ended up in Europe. He is a talented and entirely convincing soul singer and serves up good covers of "Love Train", Try A Little Tenderness" and "Ain't No Sunshine". The LP was recorded in Milan and the musicians are competent and generally provide sympathetic and engaging backing if verging just now and then on the margins of bombastic. There are a couple of instrumentals here and the style throughout is funky with jazz tinges. I have covered another LP by an American in Europe: Donny Burks. This album is better.

Chuck Brown & The Soul Searchers

Chuck Brown; John Buchanan; Donald Tillery; Leroy Fleming; Jerry Wilder; Gregory Gerran; Curtis Johnson; Skip Fennell; Ricardo Wellman; LeRon Young; Rowland Smith; Glenn Ellis; Lino Druitt; Hilton Selton; Horace Brock; John Euell; Lloyd Pinchback; Kenneth Scoggins; Bennie Braxton

We The People* 1972 Sussex SXBS 7020 Producers: Carroll Hynson & Joe Tate

Salt of The Earth* 1974 Sussex SRA 8030 Producers: Carroll Hynson & Joe Tate

Bustin' Loose 1979 Source SOR-3076 Producer: James Purdie (Billboard soul charts: 5 ; Billboard pop charts: 31)

Funk Express 1980 Source SOR-3234 Producer: Wayne Henderson

Live '87 1987 Melt LP 3 Producer: Rio Edwards (UK)

Any Other Way To Go 1987 Rhythm Attack RT 501-1 (Germany)

Initially, they were just "The Soul Searchers" and the first two LPs above marked thus (*) came out under this name, "Chuck Brown" being added from *Bustin' Loose* onwards. Unquestioned heroes in Washington D.C., The Soul Searchers were always one of the best ever funk aggregations, as well as being the main architects of the local "go-go" style.

The three key individuals in the group were Brown, Buchanan and Tillery, who were the only ever-presents across all the albums above, also writing more than half of the songs. The band's style was clear from that first LP: lots of percussion and horns, seasoned by Brown's chicken-scratch guitar and his fast and hard vocals. If anyone has any doubt about how good they were listen to their take on James Brown's "Think" (a #43 soul single) which easily holds its own with the versions by Lyn Collins and Brown himself. And to prove they could do it all, they deliver a soulful eight minute version of "Your Love Is So Doggone Good" that fine song by West coast men Dee Ervin and Rudy Love. An absolutely tremendous album, it must be played loud, and is as good a debut as any funk band ever managed.

Amazingly, they nearly matched the quality of *We The People* with *Salt Of The Earth*. Once again, the funk was so HARD, but they did go soft on "We Share", which I found to be much too wishy-washy, and I can't make up my mind about their version of "Close To You" but the rest was all good or better. I am generally completely ignorant as to who has "sampled" what in music history, but even I know that "Ashley's Roadclip" is one of the most "borrowed" pieces of music of all-time and it is another great piece of funk driven along by Brown's incessant guitar line and Euell's bass, leading into the famous drum break by Scoggins.

After a short stay at Polydor - from which came a couple of singles but no LP - they turned up on Source and began the most commercially period of their entire career. "Bustin' Loose" became a #1 soul single and even hit 34 on the pop charts and, if it was even played on U.S. mainstream radio, must have startled and baffled people more used to listening to Olivia Newton-John. "Game Seven" was a slightly disappointing choice as a follow-up single (and only made it to #81), but "I Gotcha Now" and a re-make of "If It Ain't Funky" were as tough and nasty as anyone could want. Brown was not a particularly gifted vocalist but he worked within his limitations and never sounded less then completely sincere and involved on a fine version of Jerry Butler's "Never Gonna Give You Up" and the other slow cut, "Could It Be Love". "Berro e Sombaro" rounded things out on what was, as can be imagined by the title, a departure for the band.

The second Source LP was unsure about what it wanted to be called (it says *Funk Express* on the cover but not on the sleeve) but such confusion didn't matter in the face of what was another tremendously solid set. The Soul Searchers were consistently one of the best set of musicians of any funk band and this latest album was particularly notable for some astounding bass playing, but, sadly, no credits were provided and I'm therefore unsure if it was Jerry Wilder (who played on *Bustin' Loose*) or someone else. It's another outing with no weak cuts, mainly featuring ridiculously addictive uptempo strutting apart from the highly acceptable adaptation of David Oliver's "Who Are You" and another slow cut, "Time Has No Ending". It also pointed up that it didn't seem to matter who produced the band as their natural exuberance and energy couldn't be suppressed.

As good as The Soul Searchers were on record, they were apparently (I never saw them) even better in person and, as a result, there are a couple of "live" albums out there. The first, *Live '87* also came out as *Live - D.C. Bumpin' Y'all*, but I haven't heard the second, *Any Other Way To Go*, although it would appear to contain many of the same tracks from *Live' 87* (although not their tremendous hit from 1984, "I Need Some Money"). Having stated that the band were spectacular on stage, I have to say that I find *Live '87* to be a dull listening experience. Brown talks rather than sings, his guitar is virtually absent and the horn section are underemployed, apart from the odd jazzy solo. Drummer Ricardo Wellman and conga player Rowland Smith earn their money but it is a big let-down. One where you had to be there, I think.

Brown died in 2012 and only Kool & The Gang, Earth Wind & Fire, The Ohio Players, War, The J.B.'s and a couple of other bands can equal or surpass his band's achievements in the field of funk.

Genie Brown

A Woman Alone 1973 ABC DSX-50155 Producer: Dee Ervin

This LP, and the one single released from it, were, so far as I can tell, the only records ever made by the mysterious Ms. Brown. Recorded in LA with top musicians and produced by the prolific Dee Irvin, it is a tuneful affair, but I wonder if she possibly saw her career moving in a different direction, namely towards the supper clubs. I say this as her voice is slightly "torchy" and there are a number of tracks on here, such as "My First Night Alone Without You" that are firmly MOR. She serves up a good version of the Ervin song, "Can't Stop Talking", but it as not as good as the obscure Patty Hall's take on it. I also wonder if this LP suffered from limited distribution as my copy, and some others I have seen, are promotional issues only.

James Brown

Please Please Please * 1958 King 610 Producer: Syd Nathan

Try Me * 1959 King 635 No producer listed

Think! * 1960 King 683 No producer listed

The Amazing James Brown And The Famous Flames * King 743 No producer listed

James Brown Presents His Band 1961 King 771 No producer listed

Good Good Twistin' * 1962 King 780 No producer listed

Tour The U.S.A. * 1962 King 804 No producer listed

Where even to start on James Brown? I'll go with some surprising observations about his albums: 1) There was fierce debate with King as to the sales potential of *Live At The Apollo* LP, with the record company questioning the viability of a 'live' release. Brown had to finance it himself. It went to #2 pop, and stayed on the charts for 66 weeks. In his entire career he never again equalled such illustrious heights. 2) In 1968 he put out 7 albums, one every few weeks, an incredibly prolific output 3) He only ever had one #1 album on the soul charts, *The Payback*, and that not until 1973. Contrast that with The Temptations who had *seventeen* LPs that reached #1. (*The Payback* was also his only ever "gold album".)

I have been both looking forward to, and been daunted by, the task of trying to list all JB LPs as there were so many of them, often containing the same tracks, and merely changing record covers or names. But to start at the beginning....

In the 1950s James Brown was just another singer, having to find his own style and make his way like everybody else. In 1956 he placed a big single, "Please Please Please", on the soul charts and must have thought he was about to make it but it was two and a half years and ten singles later before "Try Me" became his second charting single, first ever #1 in fact, on the soul charts. He had to wait until 1958 for his debut LP, which, in what was to become typical Brown style, didn't stint on providing the public the chance to hear his voice as it contained no fewer than 16 tracks, including the majority of his singles up to "Try Me". The sound then, of course, was very different from how most people today think of Brown's music, being heavily influenced by gospel and the rolling r'n'b of the era. *Try Me* was another sixteen tracker, and like all his LPs of the time, was hugely reliant on, and all the better for, the Famous Flames: consisting at that time of Bobby Byrd, Bobby Bennett and Lloyd Stallworth and, on occasion, Johnny Terry and all albums in my list marked thus (*) were credited as performed by James Brown and his Famous Flames.

Think was when his LP covers started to become more interesting. The original version had a picture, entirely incongruously, of a baby, but was re-issued with pictures of Brown; he was starting to control his own destiny and only rarely from here on in would a U.S. album cover fail to feature him. The LP itself contained *six* top twenty singles in "I'll Go Crazy", "Baby, You're Right", "Bewildered", "This Old Heart", "You've Got The Power" (the version where he duets with Bea Ford) and the title track and it was clear that he was beginning to matter.

The Amazing James Brown And His Famous Flames outdid *Think* by having three versions of the cover issued. (Four, in fact, if we also consider the UK release on Ember EMB 3357 in 1964, entitled *Tell Me What You're Gonna Do*, which had yet another cover although the music was all the same.)

Now it was really getting complicated as King 771 (which also featured other artists) was likewise issued with three separate covers and three separate names: *James Brown Presents His Band Featuring Night Train", Twist Around* and *Jump Around*.

And, wouldn't you know it, King 780 also had three covers and three different titles: *Good, Good Twistin'*, *Shout And Shimmy* and *Excitement Mister Dynamite*. Moreover, it was an album (or albums) that contained a lot of previously released material, with only two new to LP tracks.

The *Tour The USA* LP surprisingly only came out in one cover and featured a number of instrumentals, a ploy he was to return to many times.

The Apollo Theatre Presents - In Person! 1963 King 826 Producer: James Brown (Billboard pop charts: 2)

Prisoner Of Love 1963 King 851 No producer listed (Billboard pop charts: 73)

Pure Dynamite! 1964 King 883 No producer listed (Billboard pop charts: 10)

The Unbeatable 16 Hits * 1964 King 919 No producer listed

By the spring of 1963 James Brown had scored fifteen top twenty soul chart singles, although none had gone higher than #33 ("Think") on the pop charts and he had deemed the time was right to record a live album and the result was, to give the record its proper title, *The Apollo Theatre Presents - In Person!*, or more colloquially, *Live At The Apollo*. It is one of the greatest and most important records in popular music history, showcasing the incredible power Brown could assert over an audience. I saw him live at the end of the seventies, but to have seen him in this show, or indeed at any show in the sixties, must have been an incredible experience. The music fairly jumps from the grooves but it is the little things that also make it, such as the way M.C. Fats Gonder pronounces the "hardest working man in show business" and, of course, *that* scream from the audience during "Lost Someone", one of the great moments on disc, brought about by Brown's incendiary delivery demonstrating that he was an undeniably great soul singer as well as the best purveyor of funk that ever lived.

Next up, Brown went the same route as so many others, and recorded an album, *Prisoner Of Love*, which wouldn't offend (white) parents; side one was replete with strings and rather unsoulful back-up singers, although his delivery remained untrammelled. It served its purpose as the title track became his first ever pop top twenty hit although side two was more robust and played the strings down.

Pure Dynamite was another live set, recorded at the Royal in Baltimore only six months after its famous predecessor but featured a couple of studio tracks, notably the excellent "Oh Baby Don't You Weep" which had that annoying trick where fake crowd noises were overdubbed. Lastly, in this batch of LPs came *Unbeatable 16 Hits* which was an exact reissue of *Try Me*.

In 1964 Brown fell out with King and there was a stand-off until June 1965 when he signed a new contract, the terms of which were to leave him much more in control of his own destiny and the music he recorded after that date reflected that new power in more ways than one.

Showtime 1964 Smash SRS 67054 No producer listed (Billboard pop charts: 61)

Grits and Soul 1965 Smash SRS 67057 No producer listed (Billboard soul charts: 9 ; Billboard pop charts: 124)

Out Of Sight 1965 SRS Smash 67058 No producer listed

Plays James Brown: Today and Yesterday 1965 Smash SRS 67072 No producer listed (Billboard soul charts: 3 ; Billboard pop charts: 42)

Plays New Breed 1966 Smash SRS 67080 Producer: James Brown (Billboard soul charts: 11 ; Billboard pop charts: 101)

Handful of Soul 1966 Smash SRS 67084 Producer: James Brown (Billboard soul charts: 24 ; Billboard pop charts: 135)

The James Brown Show 1967 Smash SRS 67087 Producer: James Brown

Plays The Real Thing 1967 Smash SRS 67093 Producer: James Brown (Billboard soul charts: 27 ; Billboard pop charts: 164)

Sings And Plays 22 Giant Hits 1969 Smash SRS 67109

When the stand-off with King was current, Brown at least found a way to keep his name out there and release new records, even if they were all mainly instrumental, apart from a few songs he managed to record (which can be found on *Showtime* and *Out Of Sight*) before King slapped an injunction on him, prohibiting his being able to record new vocal tracks. The key song from the Smash period, by a mile, was "Out Of Sight", a record also important for the arrival of Maceo Parker and his brother Melvin into the James Brown camp. It became a #24 pop hit but the album on which it was featured contained such safe songs as "Nature Boy", "Come Rain Or Shine" or "Mona Lisa", thus marking it out as an oddity and a reminder that, as with side one of *Prisoner Of Love*, even such a fiercely proud man as Brown wasn't immune to the need to compromise in order to search for a wide pop audience.

Albums such as *Grits And Soul*, *Plays New Breed*, *Plays The Real Thing*, *Handful Of Soul* and *Today and Yesterday* are all much of a muchness and to hear one is to really hear them all, although everyone should make the effort to hear at least one because they are fun with James on funky organ. And, now and again, as on "The King", from *Handful Of Soul*, we can see the genesis of what was to come to fruition years later as it sounds like a rudimentary version of a number of later grooves.

The James Brown Show was a rare - if rather dull - opportunity to hear others in JB's stable, namely The Jewels, Baby Lloyd, James Crawford and Vickie Anderson, while the rather odd release on Smash 67109, *22 Giant Hits*, was certainly misleading as it was simply a combination of two previous Smash albums, *Out Of Sight* and *Today And Yesterday*.

Papa's Got A Brand New Bag 1965 King 938 Producer: James Brown (Billboard soul charts: 2 ; Billboard pop charts: 26)

I Got You (I Feel Good) 1965 King 946 Producer: James Brown (Billboard soul charts: 2 ; Billboard pop charts: 36)

Mighty Instrumentals 1966 King 961 Producer: James Brown

It's A Man's Man's Man's World 1966 King 985 Producer: James Brown (Billboard soul charts: 11 ; Billboard pop charts: 90)

Brown moved into another gear when he resumed his King career. He had scored big selling 45s for a few years, but hadn't reached the pinnacle of the soul singles chart since "Try Me" back in 1958, but now had two #1 hits in quick succession with "Papa's Got A Brand New Bag" and "I Got You (I Feel Good)", two of his most famous ever recordings, of course.

However, and doubtless because Brown needed to record some new material, the first four albums of the second go-around with King contained virtually all previously released material. To furnish just one simple example: *I Got You* contained "Love Don't Love Nobody" - the fourth Brown LP to date on which it had appeared. Such shenanigans, though, didn't stop *Papa* and *I Got You* from being very successful, nor from having different versions of the album sleeves. Papa didn't have *quite* such a new bag as might have been assumed, in short.

"It's A Man's Man's Man's World" was Brown's fourth #1 single on the soul charts and in among the previously released stuff on the LP of the same name was one of my favourite and most underrated of his mid-sixties sides, "Ain't That A Groove", which became a #6 soul single.

Sings Christmas Songs 1966 King 1010 Producer: James Brown

Raw Soul 1967 King 1016 Producer: James Brown (Billboard soul charts: 7 ; Billboard pop charts: 88)

Live At The Garden 1967 King 1018 Producer: James Brown (Billboard soul charts: 5 ; Billboard pop charts: 41)

Cold Sweat * 1967 King 1020 Producer: James Brown (Billboard soul charts: 5 ; Billboard pop charts: 35)

Live At The Apollo Volume 2 1968 King 1022 Producer: James Brown (Billboard soul charts: 2 ; Billboard pop charts: 32)

Presents His Show Of Tomorrow 1968 King 1024 Producer: James Brown (Billboard soul charts: 13)

I Can't Stand Myself When You Touch Me 1968 King 1030 Producer: James Brown (Billboard soul charts: 4 Billboard pop charts: 17)

I Got The Feelin' 1968 King 1031 Producer: James Brown (Billboard soul charts: 8 ; Billboard pop charts: 135)

The batch of albums above demonstrate the next phase of Brown's career. Firstly, he released his first ever Christmas LP, but more significantly, *Raw Soul* was finally one consisting of all new material as well as being a brilliant muddle of a record. "Bring It Up", "Money Won't Change You", "Let Yourself Go" and "Don't Be A Drop-Out" were all big - and great - singles, with the latter also being the first instance of Brown using his fame and success to address his audience didactically, in this case as to the wisdom of staying in school, and however much he might have alarmed middle America over the years, he often exhibited such staunch conservative values. The album also contained an instrumental and some ballads, which alternated between tough and hopelessly overblown, as well as a snatch of a live recording in "Tell Me That You Love Me" which sounded almost avant-garde in its strangeness.

In this period Brown issued three more live sets with *Live At The Apollo - Volume II* being another massive seller, staying on the soul album charts for ten months. *Presents His Show Of Tomorrow* once again featured Crawford and Anderson, but this time also Bobby Byrd, Marva Whitney and Hank Ballard, while *Live At The Garden* was good but unspectacular.

Cold Sweat, apart from containing what was another #1 single in the title track, was another hotch-potch, mainly made up of show tunes and standards, many of which were also found on the Smash *Out Of Sight* release.

I Can't Stand Myself was finally another superb album, containing three hits ("Get It Together", "There Was A Time" and the title track, all top 15 soul and top 40 pop) and a less successful single in "You've Got To Change Your Mind" (only #47 soul) which was nevertheless a fine duet between Brown and Byrd. It was also a key set in Brown's career as it was the furthest he had yet ventured along the path of creating his revolutionary new funk sound where he concentrated less on traditional song structure and more on exhortations to dance, staccato and repetitive riffs and dialogue with his band members.

And then there was *I Got The Feelin'* which came out in England as *The King Of Soul* (with an entirely different LP cover, as indeed were the majority of UK-issued Brown albums in the sixties, so this was obviously a deliberate if rather odd policy by his record companies.) I need to spend a bit of time on this LP as it has highly personal connotations, being the first Brown record I ever bought. It was virtually impossible for me, as a young teenager in England, to hear Brown's music on the radio, or indeed anywhere else, and so I purchased it "blind" based on word of mouth. It sounded so fierce, so tough and so downright alien compared to what I was used to hearing that I had to take my time in absorbing it before succumbing unreservedly and it has played as big a part as any other record in fostering my lifelong love of soul music. I still worship it today and apart from a couple of so-so instrumen-

tals it has no weakness to my admittedly biased ears, with marvellous Jimmy Nolen guitar throughout. The title track and "Licking Stick Licking Stick" (wonderful and exotic title) were massive singles (#1 and #2 respectively on the soul charts), the new version of "You've Got The Power" has Brown egging on Vickie Anderson to sing herself to almost exhaustion, while the little-known, wonderful and insanely fast track, "It Won't Be Me", is an extremely rare example of Brown publically acknowledging other soul singers, in this case Otis Redding, Wilson Pickett and Arthur Conley.

Plays Nothing But Soul 1968 King 1034 Producer: James Brown (Billboard soul charts: 20 ; Billboard pop charts: 150)

Thinking About Little Willie John And A Few Nice Things 1968 King 1038 Producer: James Brown

A Soulful Christmas 1968 King 1040 Producer: James Brown

Say It Loud I'm Black And I'm Proud 1969 King 1047 Producer: James Brown (Billboard soul charts: 6 ; Billboard pop charts: 53)

Gettin' Down To It 1969 King 1051 Producer: James Brown (Billboard soul charts: 14 ; Billboard pop charts: 99)

The Popcorn 1969 King 1055 Producer: James Brown (Billboard soul charts: 4 ; Billboard pop charts: 40)

It's A Mother 1969 King 1063 Producer: James Brown (Billboard soul charts: 2 ; Billboard pop charts: 26)

Ain't It Funky 1970 King 1092 Producer: James Brown (Billboard soul charts: 5 ; Billboard pop charts: 43)

It's A New Day - Let A Man Come In 1970 King 1095 Producer: James Brown (Billboard soul charts: 11 ; Billboard pop charts: 121)

Soul On Top 1970 King 1100 Producer: James Brown (Billboard soul charts: 12 ; Billboard pop charts: 125)

Sho Is Funky Down Here 1970 King 1110 Producer: James Brown (Billboard soul charts: 26 ; Billboard pop charts: 137)

The period from August 1968 until the end of 1970 when all the albums above came out was characterised by, on the one hand, a further distillation and honing of his funk sound and on the other, by a series of experiments into new musical areas.

Plays Nothing But Soul was a short all-instrumental LP, *Willie John* was a loving tribute to a favourite singer of Brown's, *A Soulful Christmas* is self-explanatory, while, most unlikely of all, was *Gettin' Down To It*, where he sang standards and new versions of some of his songs with the Dee Felice Trio. There are even a couple of tracks where Brown seems to take no part at all, which is surprising, to say the least. for a man of his notorious ego.

There were a further two experimental sets, *Soul On Top* and *Sho Is Funky Down Here* , the first of which was similar to *Gettin' Down To It* as regards material and jazz influence, but it employed a much larger band which certainly swung, and thus eschewed the stripped down sound of the earlier album. *Sho Is Funky Down Here* is important for the fact that it emphatically demonstrated that not all James Brown music sounded the same. It was another all-instrumental disc, but with a rock music bent, complete with long guitar solos by Kenny Poole. Nobody, on hearing this played 'blind', would guess it was a record that came out as by James Brown, and it predictably only lasted on the charts for four weeks.

In between all of these were a handful of more genuinely "new" Brown LPs, but many of them were less that satisfying for one reason or another. *Say It Loud* may well have included a title track that reached #1 soul and #10 pop, as well as being the first one to include Fred Wesley as a JB band member, but it also featured a number of tracks that had appeared on previous Brown sets. *The Popcorn* was largely enjoyable enough, but once again relied on numerous instrumentals, while *It's A Mother* was all over the place. "The Little Groove Maker Me" and "Mother Popcorn" were irresistible (the latter being JB's ninth #1 soul single) but "Mashed Potatoes Popcorn" was uninspired while "Any Day Now" and "If I Ruled The World" were delivered "straight" and sounded out of step with the funky stuff.

My favourite two sets from the period were *Ain't It Funky* and *It's A New Day - Let A Man Come In*. The former contained two more big soul chart singles in the title track (#3) and "Give It Up Or Turnit A Loose" (#1), both uncompromisingly indestructible, while album only cuts like "Fat Wood" and "Use Your Mother" might not be the absolute best from the man, but they were funky enough and not rather pointless standards. The latter once again dipped into his back catalogue but it did house four more hit singles (including the great "It's A New Day" and "Let A Man Come In And Do The Popcorn") and rather good but completely overlooked sides such as the thoughtful "Man In The Glass" and "I'm Not Demanding".

Sex Machine 1970 King 1115 Producer: James Brown (Billboard soul charts: 4 ; Billboard pop charts: 29)

Hey America! 1970 King 1124 Producer: James Brown

Superbad 1971 King 1127 Producer: James Brown (Billboard soul charts: 4 ; Billboard pop charts: 61)

The last three albums on King were an important break with what had gone before as Bootsy and Phelps Collins were now on board, to supplant the previous band, who had been fired or quit (depending on what version you wish to believe) just before a series of concerts in Georgia. *Sex Machine* was a 'live' set recorded in Augusta as part of that tour (or at least that was how it was marketed; some of it was live and some was recorded in a studio) but it has some electric moments where Clyde Stubblefield's drums and Bootsy's bass set up some incredible grooves proving that the new band, called the J.B.s for the first time, were one of his best. The ten minute take on the title track *is* live, and it's interesting to note that the studio version of "Sex Machine", after all one of his two or three most famous sides of all, was never featured on one of his "new" LPs.

Hey America! was Brown's third Christmas LP, although it had a good deal of general peace and love messages thrown in as well. In truth, it is a dull LP but had a great title track, which I well remember dancing to in UK discos where it would be played most years at Christmas until the mid seventies or so.

Superbad was yet another "live" LP, although, again, it wasn't really live and was not one of his finest hours and the King era ended on somewhat of a low point.

Hot Pants 1971 Polydor 4054 Producer: James Brown (Billboard soul charts: 4 ; Billboard pop charts: 22)

Revolution Of The Mind - Live At The Apollo Volume III 1971 Polydor 3003 Producer: James Brown (Billboard soul charts: 7 ; Billboard pop charts: 39)

Soul Classics - Volume 1 1972 Polydor 5401 (Billboard soul charts: 13; Billboard pop charts: 83)

There It Is 1972 Polydor 5028 Producer: James Brown (Billboard soul charts: 10; Billboard pop charts: 60)

Get On The Good Foot 1972 Polydor 3004 Producer: James Brown (Billboard soul charts: 8 ; Billboard pop charts: 68)

Black Caesar 1973 Polydor 6014 Producer: James Brown (Billboard soul charts: 2 ; Billboard pop charts: 31)

Slaughter's Big Rip-Off 1973 Polydor 6015 Producer: James Brown (Billboard soul charts: 15 ; Billboard pop charts: 92)

Soul Classics - Volume II 1973 Polydor 5402 (Billboard soul charts: 30; Billboard pop charts: 202)

The Payback 1973 Polydor 3007 Producer: James Brown (Billboard soul charts: 1; Billboard pop charts: 34)

Hell 1974 Polydor 5401 Producer: James Brown (Billboard soul charts: 2; Billboard pop charts: 35)

Brown started releasing his records on Polydor in 1971 (and label and star never hit it off, to say the least) but for the first two or three years of the association Brown continued to put out no end of brilliant releases.

One was "Hot Pants", his eleventh soul #1 and fourteenth time he reached the pop top 20, and it was the proud title track to one of his most best-selling albums of all but also one of his shortest at under thirty minutes. "Escape-ism" was another hit from the set, which was ok rather than inspired; "Blues And Pants" lasted nine minutes but probably didn't deserve to.

The Polydor period also heralded yet another new band, the Collins brothers having already moved on, and these latest J.B.s were another tremendous ensemble having a number of hits in their own right. They can be heard on the third episode of Apollo live albums, *Revolution Of The Mind*, which was very tight, and did well, even if not quite so triumphantly as the previous two.

There It Is was another winner, and his best LP for a while, containing four top ten soul chart singles in the title track (#4), the magnificent and surely most quintessentially symbolic Brown song in "I'm A Greedy Man"(#7), the defiant "Talkin' Loud And Saying Nothing" (#1) and the poignant and atypical "King Heroin" (#6), a fine example, as was "Public Enemy", of the socially conscious and cautionary messages Brown put forth throughout his career. People listened, too, and Brown had single handedly stopped rioting in Boston in 1967 when he exhorted them to come and see him on stage rather than tear up the city.

Within a few months came another generally top-class LP, *Get On The Good Foot* which was the third double album he had put out in two years, containing three more brilliant top 3 soul singles in the title track, "I Got A Bag Of My Own" and "Make It Funky", and "Your Love Was Good For Me" (co-written by J.J. Barnes) a good and much more "mainstream" sounding side than Brown usually put out. Elsewhere, it must be said, was some filler and less than essential re-castings of old songs.

The early seventies were characterised by the "Blaxploitation" movie movement and Brown was hardly the sort of man to sit and idly watch while the likes of Curtis Mayfield and Isaac Hayes were enjoying huge selling soundtrack albums, and thus in 1973 he released two successive such sets in *Black Caesar* and *Slaughter's Big Rip-off* and although they both sold reasonably well, nowhere near the quantity the other two stars had enjoyed. They didn't contain any big hit singles either although I have always enjoyed "Sexy Sexy Sexy" from *Slaughter* as it was such an exact copy of "Money Won't Change You" that you had to admire his cheek.

Brown regained the momentum he had perhaps lost with the release of the soundtracks with yet another double album, *The Payback,* his only gold-accredited LP (although this was reportedly partly due to an unwillingness on his behalf to always be completely open about the number of records he actually sold.) It might be patchy and overlong but the magnificent title track was yet another #1 soul single with its slowed down tempo matching Brown's own waning powers, and it boasted a completely uncompromising lyric seemingly aimed at his record company and indeed anyone who had ever crossed or had even thought about crossing him. "Stoned To The Bone" was another highly worthwhile track, a truncated version of which became another big hit, but there was little else on board that ranked among his best work.

Another uneven double followed in *Hell* which sold strongly and contained two more #1 soul singles in "My Thang" (ok, but not his best) and the tough "Papa Don't Take No Mess", and a number of other re-workings of earlier songs, but this was very much Brown's last hurrah as a consistently big selling artist. It should also be noted that, on the whole, Polydor couldn't sell him to a wider audience in the way his previous label had. King managed to get thirteen James Brown singles onto the Top 20 pop charts, Polydor managed a mere two.

After *Hell*, James Brown, for the first time in over ten years, was no longer the biggest black artist, to whom everyone else had to play second fiddle, and he was now forced to follow trends rather than dictate them, as new acts like Earth, Wind & Fire and The Ohio Players were selling many more records than J.B. as well as crossing over pop.

Reality 1974 Polydor 6039 (Billboard soul charts: 5; Billboard pop charts: 56)

Sex Machine Today 1975 Polydor 6042 Producer: Charles Bobbitt (Billboard soul charts: 10; Billboard pop charts:103)

Everybody's Doin' The Hustle & Dead On The Double Bump 1975 Polydor 6054 Producer: James Brown (Billboard soul charts: 22; Billboard pop charts: 193)

Hot 1976 Polydor 6059 Producer: James Brown (Billboard soul charts: 25)

Get Up Offa That Thing 1976 Polydor 6071 Producer: James Brown (Billboard soul charts: 14; Billboard pop charts: 147)

Bodyheat 1977 Polydor 6093 Producer: James Brown (Billboard soul charts: 20; Billboard pop charts: 126)

Mutha's Nature 1977 Polydor 6111 Producer: James Brown (Billboard soul charts: 31)

Jam / 1980's 1978 Polydor 6140 Producer: James Brown (Billboard soul charts: 30; Billboard pop charts: 121)

Take A Look At Those Cakes 1979 Polydor 6181 Producer: James Brown (Billboard soul charts: 58)

Despite the mutual disaffection of Brown and Polydor they slogged on for a further thirteen LPs, with ever diminishing returns, although there were still some good and interesting moments. For instance, after three highly average albums - there are tracks on *Sex Machine* and *Hustle* where even he seems bored, and these are really highly disappointing outings - Brown put out *Hot* which was notable for two things: the furore surrounding the fact he used exactly the same riff on the title track as David Bowie had used on "Fame" (ironic, really, when one considers how often others had ripped-off Brown) and the autobiographical nature of much of the album, on which he was rejoined by some of the Famous Flames for the first time in a decade and their beautiful harmonies make it one of his most enjoyable later releases.

Get Up Offa That Thing was the powerful title cut and single (#4 soul) from a reasonably decent album and "I Refuse To Lose" showed the old defiance was still intact, but it was one of a series of LPs which suffered from the earlier departure of Bobby Byrd and Maceo Parker, thus robbing them of a certain spirit.

Bodyheat, the title track aside, was largely dull as was *Mother's Nature,* mainly notable for a rare Martha High duet on "Summertime."

Jam is worthy of a mention as it was one of his funkiest for years and was pretty uncompromising in its call to dance and would have been a revelation by most other artists, whereas by Brown it was merely very good. *Take A Look At Those Cakes*, on the other hand, was one of his worst ever, bereft of any particular merit, with one track, "Spring", being genuinely awful.

The Original Disco Man 1979 Polydor 6212 Producer: James Brown (Billboard soul charts: 37; Billboard pop charts: 152)

People 1980 Polydor 6258 Producer: Brad Shapiro (Billboard soul charts: 68)

Live ! Hot On The One 1980 Polydor 6290 Producer: James Brown (Billboard pop charts: 170)

Nonstop! 1981 Polydor 6318 Producer: James Brown

The Original Disco Man used a new producer, Brad Shapiro, which was the first time, the 1975 *Sex Machine Today* LP aside, Brown had entrusted production to someone else for over a decade and it was a good move with "It's Too Funky In Here" becoming his biggest (#15 soul) and best single in three years, while "Let The Boogie Do The Rest" was much richer and slower than the title might suggest. In summary, recording in Muscle Shoals was an all-round excellent idea and Shapiro was duly granted a second opportunity in producing JB on "People" but it was an uneven work, and, more to the point, a poor seller and that was the end of his association with Brown. It did have its moments, though, not least a fine Barbara Wyrick country song in "Regrets" which was one of the best things he had done in years.

As so often in the past James decided what he needed to do

next was record a live double album, and *Hot On The One* was his first from Japan, cut in Tokyo. It stacks up pretty well with most of his previous live offerings, with a seriously good band, which includes Jimmy Nolen, even if it is a bit odd to hear female backing voices on "Try Me".

His last Polydor album was *NonStop!* and it was not a high point of his career. Three of the seven tracks were (yet again) re-cuts of old favourites and, while ok, do not match up to the originals, thus rendering them somewhat pointless. The most interesting cut is a complete one-off in "You're My Only Love" which has beautiful backing harmonies of the type only normally heard on "sweet soul" records.

Soul Syndrome 1980 TAK 615 Producer: James Brown

Bring It On 1983 Churchill / Augusta CAS 22001 Producer: James Brown

Gravity 1986 Scotti Brothers 40380 Producer: Dan Hartman (Billboard soul charts: 39; Billboard pop charts: 156)

James Brown & Friends..Soul Session Live 1987 Scotti Brothers 7461 45164 Producer: Johnny Muss

I'm Real 1988 Scotti Brothers 44241 Producer: Full Force (Billboard soul charts: 15; Billboard pop charts: 96)

Love Overdue 1991 Scotti Brothers 75225 Producer: James Brown (Billboard soul charts: 51)

Universal James 1993 Scotti Brothers 514 329-1 Producers: Ricky Crespo, Jazzier B, Charles Sherrill & James Brown

After the Polydor liaison mercifully ended Brown recorded one-offs for TAK and Churchill/Augusta before signing with Scotti Brothers were he remained for years, albeit recording for them sporadically by his standards.

Soul Syndrome was a poor start to his new recording life, with three of the six cuts being re-makes of previous glories, and as so often they were markedly inferior to the originals with "Rapp Payback", for example, having not one ounce of the power of the celebrated song from 1974. "Smoking & Drinking" was even worse with someone thinking that having JB cough on the song for the last thirty seconds or so was a good idea.

Bring It On was much better, despite its horribly cheap and tacky sleeve. It was never going to be a hit with its focus on decades old songs like "Tennessee Waltz" and "For Your Precious Love" but he sang them superbly and at least there were no re-workings this time around of his old hits. The title track was hard and funky as well, and while it is a fairly minor note in his career it was nonetheless a small triumph.

Then, against all reasonable odds, he came back into prominence right at the end of 1985 when "Living in America", due entirely to its being featured in the film *Rocky IV,* became a massive hit, reaching #4 on the *Billboard* top 100. Only "I Got You" at #3, had ever posted higher. He was presumably delighted but maybe chagrined by the fact it had become more successful than so many of his vastly better sides. Brown would have been entirely comfortable with the sentiments of the song, as he had always been intensely patriotic and, to say the least, he deserved the success. I can do without its rather bombastic style to be honest but I know I was delighted for him when it did so well. It obviously became the showpiece of the first Scotti Brothers LP, which featured a fine song and performance in "How Do You Stop", but also some typical eighties stuff like "Goliath" which does not stand up remotely as well today when compared to the vast majority of his records of twenty years before.

The follow-up was one of those tiresome and immensely boring all-star gatherings when Joe Cocker, Robert Palmer, Wilson Pickett and Billy Vera appeared on the *Soul Session* LP.

I'm Real delivered two big soul singles in "Static" (#5 and not bad) and the title track (#2 and very disappointing) but tellingly, they meant nothing whatsoever pop, proving that "Living in America" was an aberration. Most of the rest of the album is unlistenable from my perspective, and I will quickly pass over *Universal James* as well for similar reasons, although it did have more going for it artistically than *I'm Real* with at least three or four tracks I like, but it did not generate any hits.

Squeezed in between these two records, however, was *Love Overdue* which does bear investigation. It sported a particularly "dry" sound and the band was nowhere near his best ever, but was still good, and songs like "Teardrops On Your Letter" and "It's Time To Love" were the best things he had recorded in years.

James Brown came back into fashion in a big way in the mid-eighties or so and a whole host of LPs were released to capitalise on this new found popularity and there are simply too many to usefully include in the book here, especially as so many were more or less identical to each other. The only compilations I have therefore listed in the section under Brown are the two *Soul Classics* sets which were current (and charting) releases when they were issued.

James Brown died on Christmas Day 2006 leaving the world as arguably the most important and influential black artist of the 20th century. No-one who cares for popular music can be unaware of him, whether one likes his music or not, and for my money the sheer excitement of his records eclipses anyone else's. For ten years or so he was the biggest solo male singer in soul music and made some of the most magnificent records anyone has ever made or ever will. This book has consciously been about LPs rather than CDs but as I will break my rules, just this once, as seems appropriate with a man who broke them frequently, to recommend a CD only track that captures Brown's vitality on stage better than anything on vinyl. It is the near 13 minute version of "Cold Sweat" from the 1998 *Live In Dallas* release of a show he played there in 1968. If anyone has ever recorded a more exhilarating piece of music I haven't heard it.

Jocelyn Brown

Somebody's Else's Guy 1984 Vinyl Dreams VNDLP 1 Producers: Greg Carmichael, Patrick Adams, Fred McFarlane, Allen George, Louis Valdez & John Lagana

One From The Heart 1987 Warner 25445 Producers: Jellybean, James Batton, Rob Mounsey, Russ Titleman & Hubert Eaves (Billboard soul charts: 65)

Turn On The Hits 1991 Bellaphon 260 07 166 Producer: ? (Germany)

Absolutely Jocelyn Brown! 1992 Capital City JOLP 1 Producer: ? (Germany?)

Two solo albums, eleven producers, which sounds like overkill to me, particularly as it was obvious to anyone that Brown was a gifted singer who should have just been left alone to belt them out. After all, she had been in demand as a session singer in the late seventies. The debut has a number of good tracks, but is overwhelmingly a "dance" record and it was a shame she wasn't permitted to deliver a slow song as she would have nailed it conclusively as on her Possee single from 1981, "If I Can't Have Your Love". The stand out cuts are the big hit title track (#2 soul) and her version of "Ain't No Mountain High Enough".

One From The Heart is a much more varied record, with Warners obviously realising she was not merely a purveyor of dance music, and "Living Without Your Love", "I Cry Real Tears" and "Whatever Satisfies You" allow her to stretch out and sing from her heart, even if the backing is too "poppy" and synthetic to entirely win me over. Of the uptempo cuts "Love's Gonna Get You" is compulsive and likeable and even such a clichéd title as "Ego Maniac" doesn't portray the horror one might have expected. In fact, it is a solid album and placed four singles on the US soul singles chart.

I have never seen nor heard the *Turn On The Hits* or *Absolutely Jocelyn Brown!* LPs which I believe only came out in Europe so I cannot comment any further other than to note that Oliver Cheatham and Heatwave helped her out on vocals, and that they contained many of the same songs.

Keisa Brown

Keisa Brown......Live! 1974 Little Star LSLP 1001 Producer: H.B. Barnum

Keisa Brown 1986 Park Place PPR-417 Producer: Frederick Knight

Keisa 1988 Park Place PPR 1714 Producer: Frederick Knight

Mississippi-born Keisa (pronounced Key-sa) Brown recorded a James Brown influenced single, "The Dance Man", at the end of the sixties which is in-demand but almost completely unrepresentative of the rest of her recorded work. Her first LP, *Live*, largely consisted of standards and a lot of talking and is most definitely one of those "you had to be there" LPs.

In the eighties she released two Frederick Knight produced LPs which are neither essential nor poor, but are both worth owning. Knight was a good songwriter - he wrote everything on both albums - and Brown gets to interpret his own two biggest hits, "I've Been Lonely For So Long" and "I Betcha Didn't Know That", on *Keisa Brown* although the former is beaten hands-down by the latter. "I Tripped On A Piece Of Your Broken Heart" is as good as its title suggests and the whole album contains about 50% hits and 50% misses which wasn't a bad ratio for 1986.

The second Park Place album, *Keisa* (she certainly wasn't blessed with wildly inventive LP titles) was possibly marginally better than the first and proves again that she was an accomplished soul singer, entirely at ease with slower material. It started poorly with the dull "Full Time Love" but got better as it progressed. "Is It Love Or Is It Memorex?" has a rhythm pattern almost exactly like Clarence Reid's "Nobody But You Babe" but I doubt if there was much chance of being sued given the relative obscurity of both songs and the twenty year gap between them.

She died in 2006 without ever having posted any singles or albums onto any charts but she did record a fair number of records over a thirty year period and everyone should make an effort to hear the superb "I Tripped On A Piece Of Your Broken Heart" and the entire second side of the *Keisa* album.

Lattimore Brown

This Is Lattimore's World 1977 Seventy-Seven 77-106 Producer: John Richbourg

Everyday I Have To Cry 1986 Charly CRB 1157 (UK)

Lattimore Brown 1987 P-Vine PLP 315 (Japan)

Lattimore Brown's history reads like a series of clichés on how tough life can be: left home at 12 due to one too many beating, father at 15, years of poverty, contracting cancer, losing his home to Hurricane Katrina and his wife to a heart attack, left for dead in a horrendous mugging in 2007 and then killed while crossing the road by a passing car in 2011. But even with all this to contend with, and it requires a minute's silence just to type it, he was by all accounts a lovely man, and, by any standard at all, a superbly gifted and moving singer.

His recording career somewhat mirrors that of stable mate Sam Baker, and they were both much more impressive on slower material than uptempo dance music, and sadly, as with Baker, none of Brown's albums were released at a time when he could capitalise on them as he was not doing much at all in the music industry from the mid seventies onwards until he was literally re-discovered in 2008. All three albums are, by and large, the same, as all the 14 tracks on the Seventy Seven LP are also duplicated on the other two albums which each then add a couple of further songs, so there is no reason to own or track down all three, but there is every reason to make sure you hear at least one. Songs such as "I Know I'm Gonna Miss You", and "It's Such A Sad Sad World" are heart rending ballads anyway, but listening to them in the light of how his life developed is almost unbearable. Then also consider other superb deep performances such as "I'm Not Through Lovin' You", "Nobody Has To Tell Me" and "It's Gonna Take A Little Time" and we can make a case for "Sir" Lattimore Brown (he was ennobled in 1966 as a gimmick that did little to help him sell any more records) to have been one of the greatest of all the "unknown" soul men. Credit should also go to Allen Orange who wrote the majority of Brown's songs, and nearly all of his best ones.

Maxine Brown

Sings (with Margie Anderson) 196? Spin O Rama S 144 No producer listed

The Fabulous Sound Of 1963 Wand 656 No producer listed

Spotlight On 1965 Wand 663 No producer listed

Saying Something (and Chuck Jackson) 1965 Wand 669 Producer: Stan Green

Hold On! We're Coming (and Chuck Jackson) 1967 Wand 678 No producer listed

Greatest Hits 1967 Wand 684

One In A Million 1984 Kent 028 (UK)

Like Never Before 1985 Kent 047 (UK)

Diana Ross fans might disagree, but no soul singer has had quite the same aura of Hollywood glamour as South Carolina's Maxine Brown. She has always looked like a star, even years after she had any big hits.

The first two albums were really just collections of her records that happened to be put out on an LP. *Sings*, for example, was released on a budget label to capitalise on her growing success, and collected Maxine's five Nomar releases from 1961 on one side with the other consisting of performances by Margie Anderson. *The Fabulous Sound Of* included three of the Nomar sides as well as a handful of singles from her short stay at ABC. The LP cover does not denote a producer but most of her songs at the label were produced by Mal Williams or Clyde Otis. (She also had another long player - together with tracks by Irma Thomas and Ronnie Dickerson on the Grand Prix label, which, given it is more a less a various artists compilation, is out of scope.)

So, her first 'real' LP with all songs recorded for the label on which she had her biggest successes, Wand, was *Spotlight On*, a winning set with no fewer than ten of the twelve tracks having come out on singles over an 18 month or so period, so I suppose an argument could be made to say it wasn't a pure album concept. Again, no producer was listed but Stan Green, Ed Townsend and Luther Dixon were responsible. The brilliant "Oh No, Not My Baby", an imperishable Goffin-King song, was the stand-out, as well as being one of her biggest ever hits (#24 pop), but the LP also included such spotless sides as "Little Girl Lost", "Since I Found You", and "It's Gonna Be Alright" (#26 soul) and helped to establish her as one of the most distinctive of all female soul singers. You can't hear a Maxine Brown record 'blind' without knowing it is by her.

Wand teamed her up for two duet albums with Chuck Jackson, the first of which is a particular favourite, the second of which is not. I attribute the success of *Saying Something* to the fact that Ashford, Simpson and Armstead wrote half the tracks and it sounded as if it was created for Brown and Jackson, with only two sides, "Something You Got" (nevertheless a decent sized hit as a single at #10 soul and #45 pop) and "I Need You So", more readily known by other versions. Contrast this with *Hold On!* which almost entirely consists of songs that are indelibly associated with different artists, as well as duplicating three tracks from the earlier album. My one quibble with *Saying Something* was the sleeve. Despite having two chances to get it right - it had a different cover in the UK and the US - neither showed a picture of Maxine or Chuck, opting in England for a photo and in America for a drawing of unnamed white people. Despite this rather crass approach (and I do realise that Wand were hardly alone in not wishing to alienate potential caucasian buyers), it should be tracked down by anyone who hasn't heard it.

The two Kent records brought her name back into circulation with their two LPs from 1984 and 1985 (both from her Wand period). The second is the more interesting (the first contains all previously issued material) as it presented the world with a dozen unreleased cuts, including two, "Baby Cakes" and "Slipping Through My Fingers" which were recorded at FAME, a real departure for such a consummate uptown singer. They worked too.

Out Of Sight 1968 Epic BN 26395 Producer: Mike Terry

We'll Cry Together 1969 Commonwealth United CUR-LPS 10,001 Producers: Charles Koppelman, Don Rubin & Bob Finiz (Billboard pop charts: 195)

Despite their also issuing a *Greatest Hits* LP it was clear that Scepter/Wand was not big enough to accommodate Maxine Brown as well as Chuck Jackson and, particularly, Dionne Warwick, both of whom were favoured with substantially more than the handful of LPs put out on Brown. She therefore moved to Epic for a short spell - one album and two singles, but no hits - under the production lead of Mike Terry in Detroit. Even if the change didn't bring about much commercial reward there was plenty to enjoy on *Out Of Sight* which was a good one with stirring versions of "I Wish It Would Rain" and "I'm In Love", as well as the original of "Don't Leave Me", a great Lorraine Chandler and Jack Ashford song. Maxine delivers a storming version, but she was not to know that the little-known Ray Gant would eclipse her with a magnificent rendition a few years later.

Her next stay, with another one-off LP, was on the short-lived Commonwealth United, recorded once again in New York but one which showed how much times had changed since 1965 as it had a completely different feel from the Wand classics, with only one track, "I Can't Get Along Without You" (a #44 soul hit), that would not have sounded out of place on the earlier LPs. There was a more stately, piano-led feel on this beautifully produced album, which sounds so clear, and Brown delivers up a superb country-soul song in "You're The Reason I'm Living" as well as the best sung version I know of "Reason To Believe", and, what's more, one of the biggest (and best) hits of her entire career in the shape of the title track when it reached #15 on the soul charts in the autumn of 1969.

She moved on again, to Avco, who put out three singles in 1971 and 1972, but no album, and that was that as far as new vinyl recordings go, and she sustained her career by live performance and acting roles.

Maxine Brown might have only placed ten records on the *Billboard* singles charts over a relatively long recording career but that is a misleading statistic as she was one of the finest of all soul singers and, what's more, she is still around, and I saw her live in London as recently as 2007 where, as ever, she looked like a million dollars with her star quality entirely undiminished by time.

Mel Brown

Actor Of Music 1978 ABC AA - 1103 Producer: James Gadson

The first track on *Actor Of Music* is entitled "I A Man And You A Woman" whose "Me Tarzan, You Jane" connotations don't bode well, but one shouldn't be fooled: it is terrific. Any LP that employs James Gadson on drums has a big advantage and his typically crisp, unfussy playing, combines brilliantly with David Shields' guitar and Bernorce Blackman's bass to drive this forward relentlessly. Gadson and Blackman are alumni of the great Watts 103rd Street Rhythm Band and it was lovely to hear them once again in 1978. But that opener is not typical of the rest of the LP, which is more thoughtful in composition and restrained in tempo. Mel Brown is a functional rather than a great singer, but what he lacks in vocal dexterity he more than makes up for in songwriting ability and he and co-writer Chuck Green have penned an album's worth of music that is all worth hearing. The tempo changes on "Reality" (and I admire the string riff straight out of "Dancing In The Street" that drifts in and out; indeed the string arrangements throughout - by Gadson and Ray Jackson - are a delight) are impressive but everything on here is first class and this is another LP that I recommend highly. It had no success, is not "rare" or in-demand and has never had received any acclaim at all so far as I can recall but hopefully I am redressing that here in some small way. (I am reasonably - but not 100% - sure he is not the jazz guitarist of the same name.)

Randy Brown

Welcome To My Room 1978 Parachute RRLP 9005 Producers: Homer Banks & Carl Hampton (Billboard soul charts: 46)

Intimately 1979 Parachute RRLP 9012 Producers: Homer Banks & Chuck Brooks (Billboard soul charts: 48)

Midnight Desire 1980 Chocolate City CCLP 2010 Producers: Homer Banks & Chuck Brooks (Billboard soul charts: 50)

Randy 1981 Chocolate City CCLP 2017 Producers: Homer Banks & Chuck Brooks

Just look at the titles above: there was a clear plan to present Randy Brown as the south's main man in the bedroom, the heir to Isaac Hayes and the young gun challenger to Barry White and Teddy Pendergrass. It was, in truth, a challenge that was brushed off fairly easily as Brown never sold a vast amount of records, and his solo career was of a short duration, but he certainly made some fine music, not all of which is contained in the five LPs put out under his name.

His first recording was made as a member of the Newcomers, but it appears he only featured on one single before leaving to try and forge a solo career, which manifested itself in a handful of mostly worthwhile 45s under the name of Randolph Brown and Company on both the Truth and IX Chains labels.

The first album came out in 1978 and it is generally held to be an excellent debut. While I can undoubtedly see the merit in such an opinion, I do find the whole "love man" thing to be a little tedious which is why I prefer his love songs, which to me are more soulful; as evidence I propose his splendid remake of a great Banks - Hampton song originally cut by The Newcomers, "Too Little In Common", the excellent "I'd Rather Hurt Myself" and the tender "Sweet, Sweet Darling". I should also mention that "I Wanna Make Love To You", a reasonably big hit single for Brown at #22 soul, has an intro clearly modelled on "Keep That Same Old Feeling" by Side Effect.

The rather less acclaimed follow-up, *Intimately*, thankfully plays down the "lurve" side and also houses some perfect examples of what an excellent singer he was: particularly "I'm Here" which has a double-track vocal of his "normal" voice with a seldom used falsetto.

Both releases sold pretty well - apparently the debut did some 300,000 or so - but he was then moved by parent company Casablanca to the Chocolate City label on which he delivered two more good albums. *Midnight Desire* contained his only top 20 soul success in "We Oughta Be Doin' It" and lovely ballads in "You're So Good" and "The Next Best Thing" but I thought that *Randy* had the slight edge.

Brown recorded one of the best Christmas songs in 1985 for Sound Town ("At Christmas Time") and "Tomorrow" from *Randy* was its clear prototype while "If I Don't Love You" (#31 soul) and "Leave The Bridges Standing" were two more exemplary ballads, while "I Was Blessed" was a tuneful uptempo track to offset just about the only downright poor cut he had thus far submitted in "Right Track".

All four sets were beautifully played, produced and arranged and proved that Casablanca believed in Brown as an artist and were prepared to get behind him. It was a shame for everyone that it didn't quite work out as planned.

Check It Out 1981 Stax MPS 8512 Producers: William Brown & Henry Bush

Back in 1973, Brown recorded some songs for Stax which were not released at the time. When Fantasy (who then owned Stax material) realised in 1981 that Randy was a reasonable marketable name, they issued the eight songs as the *Check It Out* LP, which had a cover that was truly tacky. The music was pretty good, but not as luxurious as on his other LPs, and most tracks are at least recognizable as Brown recordings, although "Sweet To The Bone" would be hard to identify. It is not "classic" Brown but his diehard fans would doubtless own or want it.

Sheree Brown

Straight Ahead 1981 Capitol ST-12153 Producer: Richard Rudolph

The Music 1982 Capitol ST-12229 Producers: Alexander Thomas & Andre Fischer

Sheree Brown comes from the high-voiced traditions of such singers as Deniece Williams and Syreeta Wright (who provides some background vocals on *Straight Ahead*) and indeed her first album was produced by the ex-husband and producer of the highest voiced singer of them all: Minnie Riperton. It should be understood, then, that these are not LPs even remotely in the tradition of hard, punchy, aggressive soul, but their tuneful, bright and pop-tinged approach brought them many admirers, if not many sales. I personally prefer the second album, which plays the horns up and the acoustic guitar down. Which, by the way, was strummed by Brown, which puts her in the small but admirable circle of female soul singers who played guitar. *The Music* also featured my favourite cut by her in the excellent "Got To Get Away". She should also be commended for writing every single song on both sets and anyone of a certain age who has a penchant for beautifully played and arranged jazzy mid-tempo soul of the time, will doubtless already own both records. Newer listeners with the same tastes would do well to seek them out.

Shirley Brown

Woman To Woman 1974 Truth TRS 4206 Producers: Jim Stewart & Al Jackson (Billboard soul charts: 11; Billboard pop charts: 98)

Shirley Brown 1977 Arista 4129 Producers: Bettye Crutcher & Jeff Stewart

For The Real Feeling 1979 Stax STX-4126 Producers: David Porter & Lester Snell

Despite having released a single on the small A-Bet label Shirley Brown was pretty much completely unknown when she hit massively with "Woman To Woman" in 1974 on the Stax subsidiary, Truth, which went all the way to #1 on the soul singles chart and a respectable #22 on the pop listings. (Brown had been signed to the label and had her records produced by Jim Stewart, the first time for years he had become so actively involved in making music.) The hit single was obviously the centrepiece of the album, which was a complete artistic success, although its uncompromising soulfulness made it rather difficult to be marketed across the board as its measly showing on the pop charts proved. Added to which was Brown's misfortune that Stax were sliding into bankruptcy and did not have the funds to spend on marketing, anyway. The LP is a treasure though, in the classic Stax tradition of spare, unfussy playing featuring excellent songs from the likes of Frederick Knight, Bettye Crutcher, Al Jackson and Mack Rice. One of only two "outside" song was a lovely understated version of Lorraine Ellison's "Stay With Me Baby" but most of the ten tracks are strong, and none more so than the follow-up hit, "Ain't No Fun", which reached #32 soul. It was impossible to ignore the similarity between Brown's voice and that of Aretha Franklin, although Shirley was higher pitched and slightly more nasal, but Aretha wasn't doing anything particularly exciting in 1974, and so there was an opportunity to exploit.

Because of the Stax demise, however, Brown could not capitalise on the opportunity for a while and it was not until early 1977 that she was once again a visitor to the U.S. soul singles charts with the excellent "Blessed Is The Woman" (#14) on her new label, Arista, An album followed, once again recorded in Memphis and mostly written by Betty Crutcher, using many of the old Stax musicians so there was a continuity of sound, but despite the presence of another small - but wonderful - hit with "I Need Somebody To Love Me" (#50), the LP did not become a commercial success which was a great shame as it is pretty much the equal of the Truth debut.

After another tiny hit on Arista in the summer of 1978, Brown was re-signed to the resurrected Stax label, who put out the *For The Real Feeling* LP which, despite not containing any Crutcher songs, was again recorded in Memphis with more ex-Stax musicians. It was her third fine LP in a row, if a tad less distinctive than the previous two, but after the lead single, "After A Night Like This", only crawled to #73 on the soul charts it was obvious that it was not a move that would re-kindle any successes for singer or record company. Of all her LPs, this is the one where she sounds the closest to Aretha, particularly on tracks like "Crowding In On My Mind".

Intimate Storm 1984 Sound Town ST-8008 Producers: Homer Banks & Chuck Brooks

Fire And Ice 1989 Malaco 7451 Producers: Shirley Brown, Winston Stewart & Jim Stewart (Billboard soul charts: 66)

Timeless 1991 Malaco 7459 Producers: Shirley Brown, Winston Stewart & Bobby Manuel (Billboard soul charts: 63)

She returned again to limbo, which must have been frustrating for such a fine singer, and after a small hit on 20th Century in 1980, became one of a handful of artists signed to the commendable Memphis independent label, Sound Town. The *Intimate Storm* LP, beautifully produced by Homer Banks and Chuck Brooks, might actually be her best ever and housed four singles that sneaked - albeit not at very high placings - onto the soul singles charts and the album contains some of her best ever work: "This Used To Be Your House", "Boyfriend", "I Don't Play That" (which amusingly revisited her "Woman To Woman" hit) and the magnificent ballads "This Love" and "Leave The Bridges Standing" all have to be heard.

After four superb albums, cracks started to appear. Once again she had to wait a few years before releasing a new LP and Malaco seemed like a perfect label for Brown, given their ethos and approach. However, and presumably because she was younger, *Fire And Ice* utilised on a number of tracks a more contemporary musical backing than had been previously been the case when the label presented music by Bobby Bland, Little Milton and Johnnie Taylor, and it wasn't a success, as summed up by her horrible take on Rufus' "Tell Me Something Good". I was also a little perturbed by her rather demeaning - and totally unnecessary - aping of Anita Baker on "Take Me To Your Heart", but the album still contained some pretty rich fruit: the duet with Bobby Womack on "Ain't Nothin' Like The Lovin' We Got" (a #46 soul hit in early 1990), "If This Is Goodbye " and "I Wonder Where The Love Has Gone".

Her last vinyl outing, *Timeless*, more or less copied the cover from *Fire And Ice*, which didn't bode well, and it got off to a bad start with a mundane cover of Al Green's "I'm Still In Love With You" but despite another couple of poor cuts, it still had enough good things, such as "Time" and an elegant take on Mitty Collier's "I Had A Talk With My Man" to place it into the "good but not great" category.

Shirley's still around but has gone rather quiet after releasing a handful of new CDs in the nineties, but she will always be chiefly remembered for "Woman To Woman" which was the last ever big hit on a Stax record label as well as prompting a large number of answer and/or related songs.

Brown Sugar (see also Clydie King)

Clydie King; Jim Gilstrap; Melissa McKay

Brown Sugar Featuring Clydie King 1973
Chelsea BCL1-0368 Producer: George Tobin

Clydie King sang on no end of estimable records in her career, many in her own name but even more when she was a backing singer for some of the biggest names in the music industry and I will of course cover her own albums later. This one, however, was not a particularly stellar effort. Typically West Coast, it bears as many traces of pop and rock as it does soul and despite having a single released from it, "Loneliness", which went to #44 on the soul singles charts in the summer of 1973, and despite all the undoubted talent of those involved in its creation, it comes across as "just another session".

Don Bryant

Precious Soul 1969 Hi SHL-32054 Producer: Willie Mitchell

What Do You Think About Jesus 1987 Faith ADC 4242 Producer: Don Bryant

Don Bryant played an important part of the history of Memphis soul, for not only did he release many commendable records in his own right but he also wrote a number of classic songs for his wife, Ann Peebles. His first foray into recording was with The Four Kings and he also recorded with Marion Brittnam as 1 + 1 but nothing sold in startling numbers. Hi certainly persevered with him as he put out ten singles as a solo artist between 1964 and 1969 which ranged from good to truly excellent, but not one of them reached the national charts.

His one album for the company came at the end of 1969 and

was, rather disappointingly, made up entirely of cover versions of well-known soul hits. It's hard to know at such a remove of years why Mitchell opted to release such an LP, as it would have had little chance of becoming a success. The record is solid and enjoyable enough, as Bryant was a highly gifted singer, but it was simply not his best work and nothing on it topped the originals. The album also missed a trick by not including one of Bryant's best covers, a reading of "Shop Around" which demolished the Miracles' hit. He then pretty much stopped recording (until 1981 when he put out an unsuccessful duet with Peebles) and, instead, concentrated on writing material for Ann which included "I Can't Stand The Rain".

His only other LP - a straight gospel album - sneaked out in 1987 and while it is always good to hear Don Bryant singing, it was frankly a little dull. The problem is twofold, really: a) the songs are nearly all too long and b) the musical backing is sparse and there is little compelling reason to pull the LP out a second or third time.

So, all in all, Don Bryant was not particularly well represented on long players, but he is a superb artist and his singles and CDs (which include all his 45s) should be sought out instead.

Leon Bryant

Leon Bryant 1981 De-Lite DSR 8501 Producer: Jhon (sic) Christopher

Finders Keepers 1984 De-Lite DSR 8507 Producer: Leo Graham

Not much seems to be known about New York's Leon Bryant, and his musical career appeared to span only from 1980 to 1986, in which time De-Lite put out these two albums. He was a good singer, although perhaps did not have that magic ingredient (or the luck) that would have provided a longer lasting legacy. *Leon Bryant* contains three fine ballads in "You Can Depend On Me", "Come And Get It" and "Can I" as well as a dance track in "Mighty Body (Hotsy Totsy)" that is more popular than its miserly soul chart placing (#81) would suggest. It also has a limited amount of filler, and is overall a good effort.

Finders Keepers generally finds him singing in a lower, deeper manner than on the debut and is strong throughout, with other worthwhile ballads in "I Can See Me Loving You" and "You're My Everything" amid a number of non-clichéd, enjoyable and tuneful dance tracks. In fact, it is an excellent LP and one that suggests he was yet another soul artist who received scant reward for considerable talent. (Another thought on "You're My Everything": it sounds awfully similar to The Manhattans' "Shining Star". But as Leo Graham and Paul Richmond wrote both songs there is a reason for that.)

Peabo Bryson (see also Moses Dillard)

Peabo 1976 Bullet BT-7000 Producer: Peabo Bryson (Billboard soul charts: 48)

Reaching For The Sky 1978 Capitol ST-11729 Producers: Peabo Bryson & Richard Evans (Billboard soul charts: 11; Billboard pop charts: 49)

Crosswinds 1978 Capitol ST-11875 Producers: Peabo Bryson & Johnny Pate (Billboard soul charts: 3; Billboard pop charts: 35)

We're The Best Of Friends (and Natalie Cole) 1979 Capitol SOO-12019 Producers: Mark Davis, Marvin Yancy, Peabo Bryson & Johnny Pate (Billboard soul charts: 7; Billboard pop charts: 44)

Paradise 1980 Capitol SOO-12063 Producers: Peabo Bryson & Johnny Pate (Billboard soul charts: 13; Billboard pop charts: 79)

Live And More (and Roberta Flack) 1980 Atlantic 7004 Producers: Peabo Bryson & Roberta Flack (Billboard soul charts: 10; Billboard pop charts: 52)

Turn The Hands Of Time 1981 Capitol ST-12138 Producer: Peabo Bryson

I Am Love 1981 Capitol ST-12179 Producers: Peabo Bryson & Johnny Pate (Billboard soul charts: 6; Billboard pop charts: 40)

Don't Play With Fire 1982 Capitol ST-12241 Producer: Peabo Bryson (Billboard soul charts: 28; Billboard pop charts: 55)

Born To Love (and Roberta Flack) 1983 Capitol ST-12284 Producers: Michael Masser, Carole Bayer Sager, Burt Bacharach, Bob Crewe, Bob Gaudio, Peabo Bryson & Roberta Flack (Billboard soul charts: 8; Billboard pop charts: 25)

Straight From The Heart 1984 Elektra 60362 1 Producers: Peabo Bryson, Michael Masser, Richard Feldman & Rick Kelly (Billboard soul charts: 12; Billboard pop charts: 44)

The Peabo Bryson Collection 1984 Capitol ST-12348 Producer: (Billboard soul charts: 55; Billboard pop charts: 168)

Take No Prisoners 1985 Elektra 9 60427 1 Producers: Arif Mardin & Tommy LiPuma (Billboard soul charts: 40; Billboard pop charts: 102)

Quiet Storm 1986 Elektra 60484 1 Producer: Peabo Bryson (Billboard soul charts: 45)

Positive 1988 Elektra 60753 1 Producers: Sir Gant & Michael J Powell (Billboard soul charts: 42; Billboard pop charts: 157)

All My Love 1989 Capitol C1-90641 Producers: Sir Gant, Nick Martinelli, Peabo Bryson & Dwight Watkins (Billboard soul charts: 27)

Can You Stop The Rain 1991 Columbia C 46823 Producers: Barry Mann, Walter Afanasieff, Dwight Watkins, Sir Gant, Peter Bunetta, Rick Chudacoff & Peabo Bryson (Billboard soul charts: 1 Billboard pop charts: 88)

Peabo Bryson's first recorded effort was as part of Moses Dillard's Tex Town Display where he sang a couple of songs on their highly sought after LP from 1969, and he was also the featured singer on Michael Zager's "Do It With Feeling" hit from 1975. I don't think anyone could have foreseen back then that he would become one of the most successful soul singers of all time, selling millions of records over the next couple of decades, culminating in a massive (and ghastly) pop #1 in 1992 when he duetted with Regina Belle on "A Whole New World (*Aladdin's Theme*)". In fact, as we shall see, his forte was the duet, and he had much joy in singing with Roberta Flack and Natalie Cole, as well as with Belle.

But for all his success he has never been particularly hip and vital and I'm pretty sure the words, "have you heard Peabo Bryson's great new record?", have never been uttered to or by me. I am doubtless being unfair, and I realise his audience was mainly women, not the likes of me, and his talent is not in doubt, as he could sing beautifully in a voice and style with strong echoes of Donny Hathaway, but I cannot stop my mind wandering when I try to listen to his music for any length of time.

His first album, back on Bullet in 1976, was pretty good though, and It still sounds fine today even if the first track, "Just Another Day" sounded EXACTLY like what the Spinners were doing at the time. An amazing piece of chutzpah, but one which was never followed up. It just paved the way though, and *Reaching For The Sky* was big. Massive, in fact, going gold, as did the follow-up, *Crosswinds*. He wrote everything on the LPs and produced them too, so he liked to keep in control of things, and their appeal is not hard to understand, and there is nothing sloppy or trite within, and they benefit from the superb skills of Johnny Pate, but nearly all the tracks come in around the five minute mark, and would have been improved by being shorter and sharper.

We're The Best Of Friends was his first of his duet LPs and one can understand why Capitol would have gone this route, in pairing two big name stars in order to consolidate their increasing success in the soul music market. "What You Won't Do For Love", a much-loved Bobby Caldwell song was the lead-off single but did not sell as well as might have been suspected, but Capitol would have been more than pleased with the success of the album, which I found (and still find) to be uninspired. *Paradise* was more of the same, although the songs were by now even longer.

Bryson was next teamed up with Roberta Flack with whom he recorded two long players. *Live And More* was a double album, no less, and most people will know "Tonight I Celebrate My Love" from the follow-up LP, *Born To Love*, which simply took Bryson further along a road which led him unerringly into that bland place where "adult contemporary music" is to be found. By this time, I found his connections with what I term to be soul music to be almost non-existent, and I have listened to very little of his music from the years of 1983 onwards and thus will content myself with merely listing these latter works. (By the way if anyone is wondering why *Turn The Hands Of Time* did not reach the charts it is because it is a collection of previously recorded and unreleased material.)

B.T. Express (see also Kashif)

Louis Risbrook; Terrell Wood; Barbara Joyce; Richard Thompson; Bill Risbrook; Dennis Rowe; Carlos Ward; Leslie Ming; Michael "Kashif" Jones; William Robinson; Tyrone Govane; Gene Ghee

Do It 'Til You're Satisfied 1974 Scepter SPS 5117 Producers: Jeff Lane & Trade Martin (Billboard soul charts: 1; Billboard pop charts: 5)

Non - Stop 1975 Roadshow RS-41001 Producer: Jeff Lane (Billboard soul charts: 1; Billboard pop charts: 19)

Energy To Burn 1976 Columbia PC 34178 Producer: Jeff Lane (Billboard soul charts: 11; Billboard pop charts: 43)

Function At The Junction 1977 Columbia PC 34702 Producer: Jeff Lane (Billboard soul charts: 39; Billboard pop charts: 111)

Shout It Out 1978 Columbia JC 35078 Producers: Billy Nichols & BT Express (Billboard soul charts: 16; Billboard pop charts: 67)

1980 1980 Columbia JC 36333 Producers: Morrie Brown & BT Express (Billboard soul charts: 29; Billboard pop charts: 164)

Greatest Hits 1980 Columbia JC 36923

Keep It Up 1982 Coast To Coast FZ 38001 Producer: Glen Kolotkin (Billboard soul charts: 49)

As noted earlier, B.T. ("Brooklyn Transit") Express were contemporaries of Brass Construction, with both bands being led to success by Randy Muller and Jeff Lane. *Do It 'Til You're Satisfied* did extraordinarily well, going gold, and generating two #1 soul singles in the title track and "Express". It is certainly funky and danceable, with some extraordinarily resonant bass, but has dated a little over the decades in a way in which some other bands of the time have not. I put this down to the disco strings and the slightly too chirpy girl backing singers but a track like "Do You Like It" retains all its power to this day.

They could never have hoped to follow up the initial burst of success with a relatively small player like Scepter (as they were by the mid-seventies) and it was no surprise when *Non-Stop* failed to achieve *quite* the same commercial prosperity as *Do It* but it still did well enough, although it did not bear any more #1 singles. "Give It What You Got" (#5 soul) and "You Got It, I Want It" carried on the sound, unsullied, from the first LP but it was the Carpenters song, "Close To You", that showed us a hitherto unseen side of the band as Richard Thompson and Barbra Joyce slowed it down and delivered a faithful version, with Joyce emoting powerfully. It was a shame it didn't do better as a single, stalling at only #31. Overall, though, the album was somewhat of a disappointment with few high points.

Energy To Burn was their most varied outing yet with another admirable vocal by Joyce, this time on Gamble and Huff's "Now That We Found Love", but "Herbs" was an inconsequential reggae tune and "Energy Level" sounded almost exactly like Brass Construction. "Can't Stop Groovin" mined the familiar BT Express groove and became a big hit single (#6 soul). The set was also notable for the fact that Michael Jones joined the group, before going on to have solo success a few years later when he changed his name to Kashif.

Function At The Junction must have alarmed Columbia (and the group) as not only did it do markedly less well than the three previous albums but the one single lifted from it did not even reach the soul top 100. It may or may not have been significant that it was the band's first LP without Barbara Joyce, or simply it could have been that the group were changing but were not quite sure what to change into. The second side was saturated with ballads, a pretty big departure from what had gone before, but none were particularly memorable with "The Door To My Mind" being the strongest, whereas the funk on side one was somewhat tired and lacking in zest.

After the failure of *Function* the band, together with the experienced Billy Nichols, produced *Shout It Out* which somewhat revived their fortunes, with both album and title track single going top twenty soul, but in all honesty, that was somewhat of a surprise as it was not a strong record. Overall, the sound on the LP was not especially different from what had gone before and the band pretty much slew off all the slower stuff and returned to what they were known for but the LP was no more interesting to listen to than *Function*.

1980 DID sound different from the group's earlier work, doubtless due to Morrie Brown's production, but B.T. Express were now utterly indistinguishable from any number of similar aggregations of the time. Paradoxically, that wasn't a bad thing and it was the most spirited they had sounded in years.

Their last record with Columbia was a *Greatest Hits* package which was stingy with only seven cuts, but it should be noted that three of them do not appear on any other LP, and one of them, "Stretch", was the last single they ever posted on the soul singles chart.

There was one final LP, *Keep It Up*, in 1982 but it did not restore the band to prosperity although they now featured their best lead singer since Barbara Joyce in William Robinson who duly delivered their best ballad in years in "It's Got To Be You".

Buckeye Politicians

Larry Almon; Rosco Almon; Jay Almon; Ronnie Threatt; Ron Farthing; Bobby Marsillio

Look At Me Now 1976 Utopia BUL1-1823 Producer: Jeff Barry

It's not the greatest name for a band is it? They should have stuck with The Soul Partners or The Vondors - actually, maybe not - other monikers under which the bulk of this band recorded. They hailed from Ohio (the "Buckeye" state) and despite releasing discs under these three different designations nothing became even close to a hit, but they were certainly not without talent or merit as fine singles "Look In The Mirror" (Vondors) and "Girl I Could Love You More" (Buckeye Politicians) from 1969 and 1971 respectively demonstrate.

Given this lack of success it certainly didn't seem likely that by the middle of the seventies they would a) record with Alan Parsons at Abbey Road in London and b) release an album that was afforded the luxury of a gatefold cover. The tapes from the Abbey road sessions were apparently lost on a plane journey and the unlucky band had to cut the songs all over again in Los Angeles with Jeff Barry, and it was from these latter sessions that *Look At Me Now* was created.

Sadly, it is not as good as the singles I have mentioned and that is due to a lack of genuinely strong material and a sense that they didn't quite know what they wanted to be; the music is reasonably soulful (and Rosco Almon was a singer in the great "throaty" mould of a David Ruffin) but there are also elements of pop and rock in here too, and while all this means that The Buckeye Politicians didn't sound like anyone else in particular, there is little to get excited about. There's the merest hint of War and Sly and The Family Stone in places but not enough slow material and not enough emphasis on Rosco's voice, as four tracks feature other less distinctive members of the band taking lead vocals. Nothing really mattered in the end as it was not a strong seller and apart from a couple of singles in the eighties and a brand new CD a couple of years ago, nothing more was heard of the group.

Thomas Bucknasty

Thomas McNeil; Michael Davis; Lawrence Newton; Clayton Johnson; Bobby Byrd; Michael Saunders; Chuck Lee

Blast-O-Funk 1980 RCA AFL1-3430 Producer: T. Life

This rather oddly named band put out a perfectly titled album which really does live up to its name: there are no ballads on here at all and in fact nothing that falls short of a rush of super-charged adrenalin. I rather admire them for it and they do not admit to any particularly obvious influences although I suppose there are touches of Slave on here. Thomas McNeil is "Bucknasty" and either he or producer T. Life have a songwriting credit on all the tracks. If you do not like funk, this is one to be avoided at all costs, but if you do then check it out.

Vernon Burch

I'll Be Your Sunshine 1975 UA LA-342-G Producers: Denny Diante, Spencer Proffer, Tom Wilson & Vernon Burch (Billboard soul charts: 46)

When I Get Back Home 1977 Columbia PC 34701 Producer: Vernon Burch

Love- A-Thon 1978 Chocolate City CCLP 2005 Producer: Vernon Burch

Get Up 1979 Chocolate City CCLP 2009 Producer: James Gadson

Steppin' Out 1980 Chocolate City CCLP 2014 Producer: James Gadson

Playing Hard To Get 1982 SRI SW-70005 Producer: Vernon Burch (Billboard soul charts: 50)

Washington D.C. born Vernon Burch is an ex-guitarist of the Bar-Kays, leaving them to forge a solo career in the early seventies. As can be seen, he released a respectable amount of albums, but not for a particularly high rate of return. Only two of them lodged onto the top 50 soul charts, and although he placed ten singles on the soul charts, only a couple, "Changes" (from the debut) and "Do It To Me" (from *Playing Hard To Get*), broke into the top twenty.

By all accounts the proverbial "whiz-kid", he reputedly played on Delfonics sessions as early as age 13 before briefly becoming part of the Bar-Kays. His voice was clearly strongly influenced by Stevie Wonder, which tended to mean that his records often lacked any distinct sound of their own, and I think it is fair to say that, while he was consistent enough, he never cut any "killer" sides. (It has also been stated on a few occasions that he played that famous guitar part on Isaac Hayes' "Shaft", but it appears that it was really the work of Skip Pitts.)

I'll Be Your Sunshine was the only one of Burch's LPs to be released in the UK and I suspect UA were rewarded with very meagre sales although it deserved better, with the afore-mentioned "Changes " being the stand-out track. He wrote everything on the album (which, apart from a so-so cover of "Try A Little Tenderness" from *Get Up*, held true for all his other records as well.)

When I Get Back Home was probably the set on which the Wonder influence was most pronounced, but it didn't do well, and only spawned a meagre soul "hit" in "Leaving You Is Killing Me" at #95 while *Love-A-Thon* was another fair but unspectacular LP with a good melody on "Mama" and some impressive drive on "Brighter Days".

Get Up, despite all the talent on board helping him - Gadson, Tom Tom Washington, Tony Coleman, Richard Evans, The Waters, Fred Wesley - was a most disappointing LP, sounding uninspired at the time of release and even more lacklustre now. Simply, none of their skills could overcome the fundamental challenge of trying to render an LP worth listening to when the songs served up were so ordinary.

Steppin' Out was an improvement with memorable tracks in "Family And Friends" and "Baby Love" and the dance tracks are crisper and tighter than they were on *Get Up* but it does contain "Stiffin' Stuffin', Ain't Sho Nuffin" which is every bit as atrocious as its spectacularly dreadful title would suggest.

Burch's last album was on the small SRI label and it was a good move, stirring him into producing his best since *I'll Be Your Sunshine*, underpinned by his best songs for ages and a crunching dance groove.

It was a shame that following his best and most successful LP in years there were to be no more vinyl releases but he is still recording today - but now only gospel as The Reverend Vernon Burch.

Keni Burke (see also Invisible Man's Band and Stairsteps)

Keni Burke 1977 Dark Horse DH 3022 Producer: Keni Burke

You're The Best 1981 RCA AFL1-4024 Producer: Keni Burke

Changes 1982 RCA AFL1-4226 Producer: Keni Burke

Artists Showcase: Cult Cuts From A Genius 1986 Street Sounds Music 9 (UK)

Kenneth M Burke was another whiz-kid, first recording with his sister and brothers in the Five Stairsteps at the age of 12 in 1966. The group had a lot of success over a period of years, but disbanded in 1977, the year in which Kenneth (now "Keni") put out his first solo album, on which he sang, wrote and produced everything as well as playing bass. Dark Horse was George Harrison's label, which had no soul pedigree whatsoever, a factor which doubtless played a part in the set's modest success, although it is generally listenable and likeable, despite a couple of nondescript instrumentals and one or two ordinary songs.

After a break from issuing his own records for a few years when he made his living from doing things like playing bass for Bill Withers and re-grouping with his brothers to put out a couple of LPs by The Invisible Man's Band, he released two more albums on RCA and it is these for which most people remember his name, although, once again, they did not sell particularly well.

First up was *You're The Best* which included "Let Somebody Love You", one of his best-loved sides and one which reached #66 on the U.S. soul singles charts, as well as the sumptuous "Gotta Find My Way Back In Your Heart", and "Never Stop Loving Me". It is an excellent album, well named to reflect its quality and Burke's voice had evolved to sound something like a fine but rather obscure soul singer from Tennessee, Freddie Waters.

But if "Let Somebody Loves You" was merely loved, "Risin' To The Top" - easily Burke's best known track - was absolutely cherished although it only made it three places higher on the charts as a single. It was the highlight of *Changes* and deserves all its fame, for it is a superb record, apparently having also been "sampled" countless times since. "Who Do You Love" is another pretty track, on which he sings with a trace of Ronald Isley to his voice, adding to the feeling that he was somewhat of a chameleon when it came to singing. It was another good LP but in "Shakin'" and the title track it had two throwaway tracks of the type that *You're The Best* had managed to avoid.

I mentioned how Burke put out records that were "loved" and "cherished" and the title of his 1986 UK only compilation album rather bears this out.

Solomon Burke

Solomon Burke Apollo ALP-498 1962 No producer listed

Blues Before Sunrise 1964? (with Ray Charles) Grand Prix KS-406

A huge man with huge talent and a huge family, Burke, until his death in 2010, pretty much outlived all of his contemporaries from the days when soul was first born, as well as continuing to outdo them in productivity by releasing new music. This native son of Philadelphia was one of the most gifted, colourful and entertaining - both on and off stage - individuals to be covered in this book. Many people will know some of his more amusing stories - such as selling food at his own concerts - and it is a shame that I can only scratch the surface of his amazing life.

His earliest recordings appeared on the Apollo label in 1956 and his first few sides from that label can be found on his debut LP, put out in 1962 to capitalise on his growing success with Atlantic. It is fairly sedate, orchestrated music, untouched by too much gospel passion, although there is the odd moment where his future promise can be easily discerned. Similarly, the Grand Prix set contains a handful of sides Burke recorded in 1959 or so before he was well-known, but it does not duplicate any of the songs from the Apollo set.

Greatest Hits 1962 Atlantic SD 8067

If You Need Me 1963 Atlantic SD 8085 Producer: Bert Berns

Rock N' Soul 1964 Atlantic SD 8096 Producer: Bert Berns

I Almost Lost My Mind 1964 Clarion 607

The Best Of 1965 Atlantic SD 8109 (Billboard soul charts: 6; Billboard pop charts: 141)

King Solomon 1968 Atlantic SD 8158 Producers: Bert Berns, Jerry Wexler, Bob Gallo, Dan Penn & Chips Moman

I Wish I Knew 1968 Atlantic SD 8185 Producer: Tom Dowd

Take Me 19?? Atlantic P-8622 (Japan)

Cry To Me 1984 Charly CRB 1075 (UK)

It was Atlantic records on which Burke really made his name, and his stay with them covered his most satisfying years both artistically and commercially. Not only were most of his best loved songs on Atlantic, but of the nine singles he posted on the pop top 50 in his career, eight of them were on this label. It is also sobering and highly surprising to note that Burke was never a big seller of LPs - even if it must be recognised that his earliest appeared at a time when *Billboard* did not provide a soul album chart - and he actually only managed to get a meagre three of them onto either soul or pop album chart in his entire career, a frankly astonishing statistic, and no soul artist in history has had a bigger disparity between single and LP success.

Not too many artists either have had, as their first album on a new label, a *Greatest Hits* package, but it was an accurate title with four of the tracks ("Just Out Of Reach", "I'm Hanging Up My Heart For You","Cry To Me" and "Down In The Valley") having reached the soul top 20. Back in these days Burke was saddled with some fairly unsympathetic backing, which he always had to struggle against, and it was his beautiful voice and strong songs which overcame the often wooden instrumentation and sickly backing singers, but the sides mentioned above were among the best of the emerging "soul" style.

If You Need Me had a rather dull cover and also contained its fair share of soft, poppy type sides such as "Tonight My Heart She Is Crying" and "This Little Ring" (one of two tracks on the album that had previously come out on other labels) although cuts like the title track, a #2 soul hit and a much better seller than Wilson Pickett's version, and "Home In Your Heart" were more exciting and hinted at what was to come.

His best LP so far, and one of his best ever, the virtually flawless *Rock 'N' Soul*, did re-cycle some material, but proved beyond any reasonable doubt that Bert Berns was one of Burke's greatest collaborators and this is also the only LP on which one will find the top selling "Goodbye Baby (Baby Goodbye)" (#33 pop) and great but unheralded sides such as "Hard Ain't It Hard", "You Can't Love Them All" and "Someone To Love Me". Listen also to "Can't Nobody Love You", one of a number of songs Burke recorded in his career which was unadorned with nothing other than the most basic instrumentation so that his voice could surge free. This was one artist who was never in need of any studio trickery to cover up any vocal inadequacy.

Atlantic followed this up with a *Best Of* collection, which duplicated four songs from the earlier *Greatest Hits* as well as including his only ever soul #1 single in "Got To Get You Off My Mind", the # 2 hit, "Tonight's The Night" and the magnificent "The Price", a #57 pop hit at the time when *Billboard* did not provide a separate soul chart.

King Solomon was another superb LP, with the apposite "It's Been A Change" kicking things off with a distinct new sound provided by Memphis & Muscle Shoals musicians (although recorded in New York) and one of the Sweet Inspirations' fiercest and best ever backing vocal performances. "Take Me Just As I Am" was another truly thrilling record, with a brilliant churchy arrangement and Burke was now recording in a "southern" style for the first time ever, and it suited him perfectly. Other top-notch tracks on the album were "Detroit City", "It's Just A Matter Of Time", "Baby, Come On Home" and "Someone Is Watching", even if the latter two fared slightly disappointingly when issued as singles at #31 and #24 respectively.

Atlantic clearly recognised that Burke was at home recording in the looser southern mode and took him down to American in Memphis for the whole of the *I Wish I Knew* LP, which was good, but the somewhat lacklustre song choices ("By The Time I Get To Phoenix", "What'd I Say") and the fact that the title track only made it to #32 on the soul charts as a single suggested that Atlantic were losing interest in him. "Get Out Of My Life Woman" is funky and fun and "Shame On Me" is an overlooked gem but it was not one of his absolutely best sets, although it should still be heard.

Take Me and *Cry To Me* are later compilations which contain only Atlantic material, and are thus listed in this section. The Clarion - a short-lived budget subsidiary label of Atlantic - release came out in 1964 and was really another *Best Of.*

Proud Mary 1969 Bell 6033 Producers: Solomon Burke & Tamiko Jones (Billboard pop charts:140)

The Bishop Rides South 1988 Charly CRB 1187 (UK)

After Burke left Atlantic he joined Bell, a short stay that resulted in only one album, but one that was satisfying in every way, as the title track became his biggest hit in about four years (#15 soul, #45 pop), and the Muscle Shoals recording location was another that was perfect for Burke. His intensely soulful reading of "Uptight Good Woman" also did some business as a single (#47 soul) while the uptempo "I Can't Stop" is irresistible and "Don't Wait Too Long" and "What Am Living for" are essential Burke slow burners.

The Bishop Rides South contains the entire *Proud Mary* LP plus four other Shoals recorded sides. Indeed, anyone who argued that this was his finest ever work would have a case.

Electronic Magnetism 1972 MGM SE 4767 Producers: MBM Productions & Ted McQuiston

We're Almost Home 1972 MGM SE 4830 Producers: The MBM Staff, Solomon Burke, Gene Page, Jerry Styner & Michael Lloyd

Cool Breeze 1972 MGM 1 SE 35 ST No producer listed

The History Of 1972 Pride PRD-0011 Producer: Solomon Burke & Elec Burke

The MGM stay was decidedly odd. (In fact the seventies in general was not his best decade.) After recording some classic southern soul at Bell, *Electronic Magnetism* was a shock. There is nothing wrong with versatility but Burke's talents were wasted on this LP, which was too much of a straight pop album, characterised by an Elton John medley and jaunty backing singing. It has never received a lot of plays in my home, although I do like "PSR 1983" and its title track did fairly well as a 45, by reaching #26 on the soul chart.

We're Almost Home was better although I don't care too much for his celebrated version of "Drown In My Own Tears", and my favourite cut is an excellent version of an old Valentinos record, "Everybody Wants To Fall In Love". The title track could do no better than reach #42 on the soul charts as a single.

Cool Breeze was the soundtrack to a "Blaxploitation" film that appears to have had a limited release and cuts like the title track and "The Bus" showed that Burke could master the genre with ease. It also duplicated a couple of tracks from the previous MGM albums, and featured his highest soul charting single in five years in "Love's Street And Fool's Road", at #13.

The History Of LP came out on the MGM subsidiary, Pride, and rounded out a year, which, above all else, was certainly busy. The album contained a mixture of old Atlantic sides and MGM recordings, one of which, "My Prayer", not having appeared on LP previously.

I Have A Dream 1974 ABC-Dunhill DSX-50161 Producers: Solomon Burke, Gene Page, Jerry Styner & TKI Production Staff

A new label, but *I Have A Dream* maintained much the same sound as on the MGM releases. The album was inspired by, in fact dedicated to, Martin Luther King and his vision and I can only assume it was a particularly personal project for Solomon. Apart from the title track becoming the b-side to "Midnight And You" (taken from the next LP) no singles appear to have been released from the LP which adds to the suspicion that it was a labour of love rather than a labour of commerce. It is therefore an easy record to admire, but not a particularly easy one to listen to with a great amount of enthusiasm, as too much of it sounded as if it could have been recorded in 1962, rather than 1974, what with its chirpy and sanitised backing singers and overbearing string section.

Music To Make Love By 1975 Chess CH- 60042 Producers: Solomon Burke, Jerry Styner & TKI Staff (Billboard soul charts: 54)

Back to My Roots 1976 Chess ACH-19002 Producer: Solomon Burke

I clearly remember the release of the *Music To Make Love By* LP and the dismayed review by *Black Music* magazine's Cliff White as he bemoaned its Barry White influence, a charge that, while understandable, seems a tad misjudged on re-appraisal. To be sure, it has a lot of tender rapping and lush production, but Burke had been employing such techniques for years and he didn't need White to teach him how to suck eggs. My own feeling is that it did contain a fair amount of nonsense (like the title track) and it is a long way from being my favourite Burke record but it also featured a number of catchy and tuneful songs, something that had more or less been extinct in Burke's MGM and ABC work. "Midnight And You" and "You And Your Baby Blues" both went top twenty soul as singles, the first time in seven years a Burke album had managed to contain two big sellers.

Back To My Roots moved Burke away from the West Coast as he tried to benefit from the success All Platinum were reaping in their Englewood, New Jersey studios and it was also the first time in years that Gene Page had not worked on a Burke LP. The result was his most stripped-back record since his Bell days ("Night And Day" apart, the first time Burke did "disco") but it also sounded pretty much out of step with virtually everything else being recorded in 1976 and was a bit puzzling that he would move so far away from a sound that had just given him his biggest success in years. Having said all this, it remains a likeable, if not essential, LP,

Sidewalks, Fences And Walls 1979 Infinity INF 9024 Producers: Jerry "Swamp Dogg" Williams & Michael Stokes

From The Heart 1981 Charly CRB 1024 Producer: Jerry Williams (UK)

1979 saw yet another label and further new producers, both of whom worked with Burke for this LP only. Michael Stokes was a "hot" producer of the time and so Burke must have been pleased to get the chance to work with him but the eight minute, disco influenced "Yes I Love You" was neither man's finest hour. Luckily, Stokes redeemed things significantly with his other two tracks, "Heavenly" and "Does Life Have A Meaning", which were both splendid. The Williams' produced side was predictably strong, apart from a slightly pointless remake of "Hold On, I'm Coming", with the title track being a lost Burke classic. All in all it was one of the best LPs of 1979.

From The Heart reprised the Swamp Dogg produced tracks from *Sidewalks* together with four more previously unreleased sides, the best of which is "The More", an excellent country-soul song by Williams, although the record's production is muffled.

Lord, I Need A Miracle Right Now 1981 Savoy SL-14660 Producers: Robert Wilson & Jean Wilson

Into My Life You Came 1982 Savoy SL-14679 Producer: Solomon Burke

Take Me, Shake Me 1983 Savoy SL-14717 Producer: Milton Biggham

This Is His Song 1984 Savoy SL-14738 Producer: Milton Biggham?

Burke went back to church for these four albums - although some would argue he never left it anyway. They are, however, straight gospel, not church-influenced soul music. As with most gospel music of the time, that meant minimal instrumentation, which at least had the benefit of leaving the focus of the music entirely on the glories of his voice. In truth, they do not sound markedly different from the more sacred of his Atlantic recordings and so long-time Burke fans would feel at home here. *Take Me* is a live LP, with the others being studio recordings.

Soul Alive! 1984 Rounder R 2042/2043 Producer: Solomon Burke

A Change Is Gonna Come 1986 Rounder R 2053 Producer: Scott Billington

Although it did not feature on any charts, I believe that *Soul Alive!* was in reality a surprisingly healthy seller for Rounder and it was certainly one of the records that helped to re-ignite world-wide interest in "classic" soul music in the middle of the eighties (helped also by Peter Guralnick's necessary and overdue *Sweet Soul Music* book.) Not only was it superb - indeed, one of the few 'live' albums that actually matter and bears repeated listens - but it was such a pleasant surprise to see him back again after years when he was out of the spotlight. Recorded in Washington, it consists almost entirely of medleys and inspired monologues, a recipe that few could carry off so convincingly. It was if everyone had been transported back into the sixties when soul was burning at its brightest.

Not content with having just come up with one of the finest albums of his career, Burke then gave us another with the magnificent "A Change Is Gonna Come", shot through with great songs by some of the finest songwriters in soul music history: Paul Kelly, Dan Penn, Spooner Oldham. Sam Cooke, Jimmy Lewis and Burke himself. Many artists have attempted the title track, of course and I contend that Burke's version is as good as any. The whole thing was recorded just outside New Orleans, yet another new recording location for Burke.

Love Trap 1987 Isis Voice IV 21336 Producers: KHS Burke & Solomon Burke (Switzerland)

A really odd release by Burke. He certainly refused to be pigeon-holed. I do not know the story behind this LP and why it only came out in Europe but it was an uneasy way to close out his album catalogue, being very pop-oriented in sound and nature. In fact, apart from two lovely mid-tempo tracks in "Do You Believe In The Hereafter" and "Only God Knows", I consider it to be some of his most average work and it certainly slipped out without much fanfare..

Burke continued to record prolifically on CD right up until his death in a variety of styles and will be remembered as one of the greatest of all soul men; indeed, the greatest of them all, in the opinion of Jerry Wexler. He has certainly left us with some magnificent music and, together with Joe Tex, he was the most accomplished "talker/rapper" of them all before rap came along and meant something else.

Donnie Burks

The Swingin' Sound Of Soul 1969 Europa E 326 No producer listed (Germany)

Although Donny Burks was born in New York, and had released a single on Decca in the mid-sixties (as Donnie Burkes) and went on to cut singles in the seventies on such labels as Dakar and Metromedia (the fine "I Was Satisfied"), his one LP only came out in Europe, which I used to see from time to time sitting, unloved, in cut-out bins in odd places. That's probably because the cover gave off an unmistakeable whiff of K-Tel, while the track listing was rather uninspired - who wanted to hear "Amen", "C.C. Rider" and "Stagger Lee" in 1969? The sound was rather dated too, with a competent if rather thin sounding band (recorded in Europe?) playing in the manner of one from 1966 or so. Burks wrote three of the songs himself including the unpleasant "Hattin' Up" where he regrets not "busting" his woman's lip for daring to speak her mind.

Harold Burrage

The Pioneer of Chicago Soul 1979 P-Vine PLP-9003 (Japan)

A minor soul man, perhaps, as regards fame and fortune but he meant a lot in Chicago in the early sixties, strongly influencing the likes of Tyrone Davis and Otis Clay, and it was a real shame that he died so young - only 35 - in 1966. He never got the opportunity to record a long player in his lifetime and this lovely P-Vine release from 1979 is the only vinyl example at 33⅓ of his soul sides. (An album also exists on the UK Flyright label FLY LP 579 but consists of his work from the fifties in the pre-soul days and is thus out of scope.)

Burrage was known as a "hard soul" singer which meant that he tended to deliver heartfelt and soulful songs over tough and uncompromising backing tracks, usually unadorned by strings or woodwinds, which sounded much less bright and upbeat than the work produced in the same city by the likes of Carl Davis. He was also apparently a piano player of some skill and it might well be him playing on "That's A Friend". But above all he was a tremendous singer, and on cuts like "Faith" his passion and power cannot be denied. The only single he ever posted on the soul top 100 in the late summer of 1965, "Got To Find A Way" (#31) is included on the LP as is its similar sounding "More Power To You" and both demonstrate that he could deal equally skilfully with more up-tempo material.

Jenny Burton

In Black And White 1984 Atlantic 80122-1 Producer: John Robie (Billboard soul charts: 50; Billboard pop charts: 181)

Jenny Burton 1985 Atlantic 81238-1 Producers: Fred McFarlane, Allen George, John Robie, Peter Link & Maurice Starr (Billboard soul charts: 45)

Souvenirs 1986 Atlantic 81690-1 Producers: Alan Glass, Preston Glass, John Luongo & Peter Link

The first album is simply awful electric music with no redeeming features at all from my perspective, and if that was all that Jenny Burton recorded then she would fall outside the scope of this book but she also put out some good stuff too, not least the excellent "Bad Habits" and "Let's Get Back To Love" from the sophomore LP, the former going to #19 on the soul charts in early 1985. Similarly, on "Souvenirs " she serves up a good stab at "Until You Come Back To Me" but the rest leaves me fairly cold.

Years before she had recorded with Dooley Silverspoon on songs like "Am I Losing You?" when she spelt her name as "Jeanne" so she did have some pedigree from an earlier era, and there is no doubt that she can sing. Shame about too much of the material.

Burton Inc.

L.A. Will Make You Pay $$$ 197? Charli-Barbara 1617 Producers: Charles Burton & Barbara Burton

Oklahoma has hardly been a hotbed of soul music over the years and it was therefore no surprise that the home state of husband and wife team Charles and Barbara Burton could not propel the album into any sort of prominence, and it is likely that the LP was pressed up in minimal quantity. Barbara had tried for success a few years earlier when, as Barbara Burton and The Messengers, she recorded a fine country-soul single for King, "Too Much For Me To Bear", but it appears not to have been released at the time and when one also considers that the Messengers went on to release an album, *A Soulful Proclamation*, which also made no waves whatsoever, it is clear that she must have found the industry tough going, particularly as she was a talented singer.

This is a good LP, breezy and bright in sound, with a biting title track, although a strong ballad or two rather than the slightly "torchy" "Sincerely Yours" would have improved it further. I am unsure about year of release (the label doesn't provide this information) but the presence of syndrums would suggest late seventies.

Angeline Butler

Impressions 1970 Co Burt 1000 Producer: Tommy Cogbill

This one will be new to most people, including me recently. Butler's LP slipped out almost apologetically and its therefore good that she has accomplished a great many things in her life including ending up as Professor Angeline Butler at Fisk University in Nashville.

Produced by Tommy Cogbill for AGP down in Memphis, it was thus guaranteed musical quality, and does contain a number of cover versions which range from "Yours Until Tomorrow" (a spirited rendering) to "When You Wish Upon A Star", a song not to be found on too many soul albums. In truth, it is a set which sits on the fence between soul and pop, and I much prefer side one to side two, so it may not be for everyone, but I think it has many charms and I have no qualms about featuring it here.

Billy Butler

Right Track 1966 Okeh OKS 14115 Producer: Carl Davis

Right Track 1985 Edsel ED 147 (UK)

Hung up on You (as Billy Butler and Infinity) 1973 Pride PRD-0018 Producers: Billy Butler & James Blumenberg

Sugar Candy Lady 1977 Curtom CU 5015 Producers: Billy Butler & Rufus Hill

Six years younger than his much more famous brother, Jerry, Billy Butler made no end of marvellous records in his own right, virtually all of which were recorded in his home town of Chicago. The fact that he only ever posted one single on the *Billboard* Hot 100 pop chart - "I Can't Work No Longer" - is no indication whatsoever of the quality of most of his output, much of it being uptown soul of surpassing beauty (the best of the lot, and sadly, not on an album was his swooningly lovely Blue Rock cut, "Let Her Love Me".)

The Okeh LP is an undoubted classic - ten tracks all coming in at two and half minutes or less with not a single second wasted. It includes one of the biggest "Northern Soul" records in history in "The Right Track" (which reached #24 soul) as well as heart-melting slower songs such as "Tomorrow Is A Brighter Day" and "Can't Live Without Her". Predictably, many of the songs were written by Curtis Mayfield, but Butler contributed four himself, and when one considers that he also played guitar, it becomes clear that he had more than just the talent to sing. One reason why the LP is so good is that all ten tracks came out on 45 as either a or b-sides and it would be remiss not to point out that the majority of them came out as billed by Billy Butler and either The Chanters, The Enchanters or The Four Enchanters. The group members were Jesse Tillman, Errol Banks, Alton Howel and John Jordan. They were not best amused to see later singles such as "Right Track" come out as under Billy's name only, and neither were they credited on the Okeh LP.

The UK album of the same name that came out in 1985 contains all of the Okeh record plus six additional tracks. It is simply one of the best soul LP compilations of all time and is totally and unreservedly recommended.

Butler moved to Brunswick after Okeh and put out a number of good singles from 1967 onwards, although none matched the best of his earlier work. No album was forthcoming, however, and Billy had to wait a few years for the next one when the new group he formed at the end of the sixties called Infinity (members: Phylis Knox, Errol Batts and Larry Wade) put out a highly commendable release on the Pride label. It was much more ornate than his previous work even though some of it was cut in Chicago, with the remainder being recorded in Memphis. Butler and Wade, together with help from Chuck Jackson and Terry Callier, wrote most of the tracks, the stand-outs being "What Do You Do When Your Baby's Gone", "I Don't Want To Lose You" (a #38 soul single), "Now You Know" and the title track (#48), all of which are gorgeous sweet soul.

His last album was 1977's rather disappointing *Sugar Candy Lady* which was simply not strong enough to get much attention from his record company or the public. It was virtually all self-composed and hinged on two long cuts, "Alone At Last", where he phrased uncannily like Curtis Mayfield in the latter part of the song, a temptation he had hitherto avoided, and "The Saga Of Sadie Lee", an ambitious song which I felt didn't quite work.

He passed away in 2015, sadly largely forgotten, and if his voice may not have had quite the resonance and command of his brother, he could communicate a palpable apprehension quite superbly.

Freddie Butler

A Dab Of Soul 1967 Kapp KL-1519 Producer: Pied Piper

Pied Piper productions are revered within the world of "Northern Sou"l but their output was normally confined to singles and a Pied Piper album is unusual. The company consisted of businessman and owner Shelley Haims and musical men Jack Ashford and Mike Terry who were the ones who really produced the records. Freddie Butler could certainly carry the melodies that were such a feature of Terry's and Ashford's work and these are for the most part catchy and strong songs, and his voice has a smooth and pleasing uptown timbre that could erupt into something more forceful where appropriate. I like the LP a lot and listening to it is a pleasant way to spend around twenty seven minutes - a fairly miserly total - but I don't care for the discordant "This Thing!" and "Deserted" makes it clear that Butler would have been just as much at ease in a supper club setting as he would have been in front of a more youthful audience. The latter would certainly have been more attuned to a track like "You'd Better Get Hip Girl", but in the end whatever plans Kapp or Haims had in mind for Butler didn't matter a great deal as the album was not a big seller (the same fate as his singles from the early sixties) and he never recorded again before passing away in 1998.

George Butler

Doin' It Doin' It 1977 Dellwood DLD 56003 Producer: Scotty Moore

Yet another tax-write off label. This LP does contain commercially released material for once, though, and Butler's "Betty Lou" on the Million label was even advertised as a new single in *Billboard*'s June 24th 1972 edition. I haven't heard any of the album at all but an internet review suggests it is reasonably varied. I assume he is not the same person as bluesman George "Wild Child" Butler, but imagine that producer Moore was indeed the same man who played with Elvis Presley.

Jerry Butler

Jerry Butler, Esquire 1959 Abner 2001 No producer listed

He Will Break Your Heart 1960 Vee Jay 1029 No producer listed

Love Me 1961 Vee Jay 1034 No producer listed

Aware Of Love 1961 Vee Jay 1038 No producer listed

Moon River 1962 Vee Jay 1046 No producer listed

The Best Of 1962 Vee Jay 1048

Folk Songs 1963 Vee Jay 1057 No producer listed

Need To Belong 1963 Vee Jay 1076 No producer listed

Delicious Together (and Betty Everett) 1964 Vee Jay VJS-1099 Producer: Calvin Carter (Billboard pop charts:102)

More Of The Best 1964 Vee Jay VJS-1119

Another of the greatest soul singers of all time, Sunflower Mississippi's Jerry Butler has always carried himself with great dignity, both on and off record, and it is this aplomb which is at the heart of the great personal success he has achieved for well over fifty years and counting. One of the few soul singers for whom a nickname had resonance and made sense, "The Iceman" will always be one of the most loved members of the soul community.

The first LP, although issued under his own name, actually contains sides recorded and released when he was a member of The Impressions. It includes the song he wrote with Richard and Arthur Brooks, "For Your Precious Love", which, owing to its beauty, has become one of the most covered and most enduring compositions soul music has produced. He must have made a fortune from it. It was also a smash hit (#3 soul, #11 pop) and hastened Butler's move to become a solo performer. The cover of that Abner LP was smart. too: Jerry looking very much the urbane man about town, an image nobody has ever felt compelled to change. "Come Back My Love" was lovely as well, but the LP significantly also contained a version of "September Song", one of a whole host of standards Jerry delivered for years to come.

"He Will Break Your Heart" was another all-time classic soul song, this time composed with the help of Curtis Mayfield and Calvin Carter, and was an even bigger hit (#1 soul, #7 pop) than "Precious Love", and the first really big seller Jerry had enjoyed as a solo artist. The album it fronted contained virtually all standards - and even the other two Butler and Mayfield songs on the record sounded like standards - and the smash hit was really the only track that had much connection with the emerging soul music sound. The set was also the first in a run of three where Vee Jay, rather disgracefully, didn't see fit to show a picture of Jerry on the cover, going instead with unknown caucasians.

Love Me was a straight re-issue of the Abner LP while *Aware Of Love* contained two more excellent Mayfield and Butler songs, "Find Another Girl" and "I'm A Telling You", both of which also became sizeable hits.

Breakfast at Tiffany's was a highly acclaimed film in 1961 and famously featured the song, "Moon River". Vee-Jay thus rather astutely reached back in time and released Butler's version and were rewarded with a pop smash (#11) although, tellingly, because of its rather unhip sound it was not so successful on the soul charts (#14), the one and only time in Butler's career this ever happened. It goes without saying that Butler delivered it faultlessly but he has made literally dozens of better sides for my money. *Moon River,* with one or two changes, was the same as the *He Will Break Your Heart* LP.

Next up was *Folk Songs*, a rather bewildering release by Vee Jay that contained precisely no hits and no good tracks. It was clearly issued as a result of the briefly popular folk music revival (and I wonder how many people know that Peter Paul & Mary's "Puff The Magic Dragon" reached #10 on the soul charts around the same time?) but it was simply misguided.

It was back to sanity with *Need To Belong* (re-released in quick succession as *Giving Up On Love)*, by some distance his best LP to date, containing five charting singles, including the estimable title track and two all-time Butler masterpieces in the swooningly gorgeous "Giving Up On Love", and "Make It Easy On Yourself". The latter has one of the all-time great moments in recorded music when Jerry sighs just before he starts singing while that off-key note that follows would never have been allowed to remain by producers in later years. Furthermore, the LP also includes his great interpretation of "Message To Martha", which did not come out as a single.

Vee Jay decided to match Butler up with Betty Everett and the resultant album, *Delicious Togethe*r, became the first from Jerry ever to chart nationally. Much more significantly the duo had a massive single with "Let It Be Me" (# 5 pop) but it is a song I have always hated and I much prefer their take on Gene Chandler's "Just Be True" but I found it to be a disappointing LP, with both artists delivering much better work on Vee Jay when performing alone. (It was re-released by UK's Charly records in 1981 (CRM 2022) with the addition of the "Smile" track.)

Jerry (together with brother Billy) then wrote yet another soul standard in "I Stand Accused" which amazingly only reached a lowly #61 on the pop charts in the summer of 1964 and one would have had to have bought the *More Of The Best* LP if you wanted to own it on an LP. The same also goes for his great take on Randy Newman's spectacular song, "I Don't Want To Hear It Anymore" (which was also the b-side to "I Stand Accused" on the 45.) The next eighteen months or so were not good for Vee Jay, however, and they went bankrupt before Butler could deliver any more albums for them.

For some years after Vee Jay went bust there was seemingly an absolute free for all as regards releasing their material and I have tracked down about nineteen compilation albums that contain Butler's work for the label, most of which were almost identical. Only a completist or a mad man would want them all and, as with James Brown's numerous retrospectives I am not listing any of them in the book, preferring to concentrate on his "genuine" LPs.

Soul Artistry 1966 Mercury SR 61105 Producer: Jerry Ross (Billboard soul charts: 23)

Mr. Dream Merchant 1967 Mercury SR 61146 Producers: Jerry Ross, Kenny Gamble & Leon Huff (Billboard pop charts: 154)

Golden Hits Live 1968 Mercury SR 61151 Producer: Dick Corby (Billboard soul charts: 40; Billboard pop charts: 178)

The Soul Goes On 1968 Mercury SR 61171 Producers: Cal Carter, Kenny Gamble & Leon Huff (Billboard soul charts: 25; Billboard pop charts: 195)

The Ice Man Cometh 1968 Mercury SR 61198 Producers: Kenny Gamble & Leon Huff (Billboard soul charts: 2; Billboard pop charts: 29)

Ice On Ice 1969 Mercury SR 61234 Producers: Kenny Gamble & Leon Huff (Billboard soul charts: 4; Billboard pop charts: 41)

The Best Of 1969 Mercury SR 61281 (Billboard soul charts: 31; Billboard pop charts: 167)

Jerry now needed a new label and found one in Mercury, who did not have a particularly strong presence in the mid-sixties marketplace as regards soul music. The *Soul Artistry* LP was good enough, with some typically smooth fare in "You Don't Know What You Got Until You Lose It" and the Magnificent Men's "Peace Of Mind" and a reasonably big selling single in "I Dig You Baby" (#8 soul), but it lacked the verve to restore Butler's fortunes to the type of success he had enjoyed a few years earlier.

The *Dream Merchant* LP was generally a big disappointment with some appallingly dull song choices ("Yesterday" and "When A Man Loves A Woman") and an ok title track (which was completely eclipsed by New Birth's version nearly ten years later) but it did contain two very important tracks: "Lost "and "Beside You". They weren't the greatest sides that Butler ever recorded but they were the first written and produced for him by Kenny Gamble and Leon Huff. It was a combination that was to provide him with just about the most sustained period of success in his entire career. (The *Dream Merchant* LP was also issued in the UK on Mercury 6855006 in 1969 entitled "The Stuff Dreams Are Made Of".)

But before the Gamble and Huff combination truly flowered, along came an inessential *Live* album and *The Soul Goes On* which only included two Philadelphia recorded tracks, the lovely "Never Gonna Give You Up", his biggest pop hit for four years (#20), and a rather throwaway cover of "Respect". In fact, "Never Gonna Give You Up" apart, all of *The Soul Goes On* consisted of soul or doo-wop songs previously recorded by others. The most significant track on the rather dull release was "I've Been Loving You Too Long", written by Butler with Otis Redding, yet another example of Butler's ability to compose all-time classic soul songs covered by many others.

Butler was then fully "handed over" to Gamble and Huff and flown down to Philadelphia where he recorded two of the greatest of all soul albums. *The Ice Man Cometh* was the first LP for a long time that put Butler right at the forefront of the "happening" soul sound of the day rather than sounding as if he was a couple of years behind the pace, and the reward was two soul #1 singles, "Hey, Western Union Man" and "Only The Strong Survive", the latter becoming the biggest record of his entire career when it went gold and also climbed to #4 on the pop charts. Moreover, the set included another soul top ten hit in "Are You Happy" and such strong LP only cuts as "Go Away-Find Yourself" and "I Stop By Heaven", excellent enough to have been hits in their own right had they been released as singles.

Mercury quickly followed up with *Ice On Ice*, another magnificent LP without weakness containing two more huge soul singles, "Moody Woman" (#3) and "What's The Use Of Breaking up" (#4), as well as a b-side, "A Brand New Me", which might just have the greatest arrangement that Bobby Martin and Thom Bell ever conjured up. When one also considers that Butler co-wrote twenty one of the twenty two songs on these two classic albums, we have further evidence that he was one of the best singer/songwriters to be covered in this book.

Sadly for all concerned, but particularly for Butler, Mercury and Gamble and Huff couldn't agree mutually satisfactory financial terms for future sessions and the men from Philadelphia did not record with Butler again for the best part of a decade, by which time Jerry was way past his commercial and artistic peak.

The Best Of LP contained 12 tracks of Mercury material, wisely heavily slanted towards the Gamble-Huff productions.

You & Me 1970 Mercury SR 61269 Producers: Kenny Gamble, Leon Huff, Donny Hathaway & Jerry Butler (Billboard soul charts: 10; Billboard pop charts: 172)

Sings Assorted Sounds With The Aid Of Assorted Friends And Relatives 1970 Mercury SR 61320 Producers: Gerald Sims & Billy Butler (Billboard soul charts: 25; Billboard pop charts: 186)

One & One (and Gene Chandler) 1971 Mercury SR 61330 Producers: Jerry Butler & Gene Chandler (Billboard pop charts: 143)

The Sagittarius Movement 1971 Mercury SR 61347 Producers: Gerald Sims & Jerry Butler (Billboard soul charts: 25; Billboard pop charts: 123)

The Spice Of Life 1972 Mercury SRM 7502 Producer: Samuel Brown (Billboard soul charts: 17; Billboard pop charts: 92)

The Love We Have, The Love We Had (and Brenda Lee Eager) 1973 Mercury SRM 660 Producer: Bobby Bowles (Billboard soul charts: 43; Billboard pop charts: 201)

Power Of Love 1973 Mercury SRM 689 Producer: Johnny Bristol (Billboard soul charts: 22)

Sweet Sixteen 1974 Mercury SR 1006 Producer: Calvin Carter (Billboard soul charts: 55)

Life had to go on, of course, and *You And Me* did pretty well in the spring of 1970. The best performing single from the album, "I Could Write A Book"(#15 soul), was an "in the can" Gamble and Huff production that sold in satisfying rather than spectacular fashion, but the LP was primarily a Donny Hathaway production to usher in the new era. Paradoxically, though, despite Hathaway's youth, the sound of the album was less aggressive and hip than the G and H sides and Butler once again seemed a little out of step with the current trends in soul, although the LP did also feature one of his better loved post G and H sides, "Ordinary Joe".

Despite its unwieldy and frankly absurd title, *Sings Assorted Sounds* was a strong album, and one which decisively and confidently broke the Philadelphia ties, and I liked its economy in only containing songs of 2 and 3 minutes in length: for example, "If It's Real What I Feel", a #8 soul single and the first instance of Brenda Lee Eager singing with Jerry on one of his records.

Mercury followed up with *Sagittarius Movement*, which contained the last really big single of Butler's career in "Ain't Understanding Mellow" (#3 soul, #21 pop), another duet with Brenda Lee Eager and somewhat of a surprise hit - another gold record, no less - as it was an unusual song construction with a long delayed hook. It sat atop, however, a sumptuous bass line from Cleveland Eaton, whose work throughout the entire LP was first class. The album could also boast one of Terry Callier's best and most immediate melodies in "Sail Away", a gorgeously smooth "The Girl In His Mind" and a confessional and entertaining" Windy City Soul".

Possibly feeling particularly pleased with the success of the single, Mercury then permitted Jerry to record a double album, *Spice Of Life*, which mixed up well-known and oft-recorded songs - six or so of them - with a couple more Eager duets. Perhaps the most interesting track, though, was Butler's take on the O'Jays' brilliant Gamble and Huff song,"One Night Affair". Interesting, because Butler had always eschewed "cheating" songs in favour of declarations of love, and while "One Night" wasn't about deceit it certainly wasn't about commitment either. In addition, it did well for him when released as a single, #6 soul, #52 pop.

The logical move was for the record label to put out an entire album of Butler and Eager duets and therefore *The Love We Have* LP appeared. Despite its quality and charm it did not sell very well, nor did it bring forth any big selling singles. I assume Brenda Lee Eager was happy with her work with Butler but nearly all her tracks sounded suspiciously as if she was singing in a key that forced her to strain somewhat, even if the result was always a soulful and pleasing contrast with Jerry's deep and resonant tone.

The last two Mercury albums really affirmed what was then patently obvious to most people: he could still sing beautifully, he could still deliver some great tracks but his days as a big selling artist were now long gone. In addition, despite their quality, the inclusion of three tracks on *Power Of Love* that had just featured on brother Billy's LP with Infinity did not suggest rampant creativity on anyone's part. The title of *Sweet Sixteen* acknowledged Butler's number of years in the music business, but it was recorded at a time, as Butler himself has attested, that did not fill him with any great joy, and he moved on - to Motown.

Three final things about the Mercury stay: One, he put out a joint album with Gene Chandler which did not do well - oddly, as both men were marketable enough in 1971. It was neither man's finest moment which doubtless is the simple enough reason for its modest showing. Second, a soundtrack to a film entitled *Joe* (Mercury 1-605) came out in 1970 with songs credited to "Jerry Butler and Exuma", but as he only sings on three of the tracks it falls outside my definition of a Butler album, hence its omission in my listing of his records. Similarly, a second soundtrack album, *Melinda* on Pride PRD0006, came out in 1972 with "music by Jerry Butler and Jerry Peters", and is also absented from my list for the same reasons (four tracks on this one). Third, I will discuss the album by his musicians, "The Ice Man's Band", in a section of their own.

Love's On The Menu 1976 Motown M6-850 Producers: Mark Davis, Sam Brown, Hal Davis, Michael Sutton, Michael Smith, Clayton Ivey & Terry Woodford, (Billboard soul charts: 49)

Suite For The Single Girl 1977 Motown M6-878 Producers: Jerry Butler & Paul Wilson (Billboard soul charts: 22; Billboard pop charts: 146)

It All Comes Out In My Song 1977 Motown M6-892 Producers: Jerry Butler, Homer Talbert & Paul Wilson

Thelma & Jerry (and Thelma Houston) 1977 Motown M6-887 Producers: Hal Davis, Jerry Butler, Michael Sutton & Homer Talbert   (Billboard soul charts: 20; Billboard pop charts: 53)

Two To One (and Thelma Houston) 1978 Motown M7-903 Producers: Hal Davis, Michael Sutton, Van McCoy, Willie Hutch, Clayton Ivey, Terry Woodford & Sam Brown

Sadly, the Motown period was to be no more fulfilling than the latter part of his time with Mercury and he had no real commercial success at the new label other than a top ten soul single in "I Wanna Do It To You" in 1977. Perhaps the writing was on the wall from the start: seven producers on *Love's On The Menu* did not suggest the undivided attention he had enjoyed with Gamble and Huff was going to be extended to him by Berry Gordy. That hedging the bets approach was reflected in the sound of the LP, which, while hardly a disaster, was a little dull. "The Devil In Mrs. Jones" was put out to become a #56 soul single for Jerry, but it was an exceedingly weak song and barely sounds like him singing.

I preferred the next one, *Suite For The Single Girl*, which was a slightly sentimental concept album but did have more vibrancy that its predecessor and was more consistent and "I Wanna Do It To You" and "Chalk It Up" were both decent efforts and decent sized soul hits (#7 and #28 respectively), even if still falling far short of his best work .

Butler's other solo Motown LP, *It All Comes Out In My Song*, was also worthy but my attention has always wandered somewhat while it is playing. It contains a compelling song in "That Train", but Jerry's reading is easily eclipsed by an unreleased version by The Friends of Distinction which captures the forward momentum inherent in the title much more effectively.

And then there were the two albums with Thelma Houston, recorded in an obvious attempt to re-create the success generated with Brenda Lee Eager. Sadly, it didn't work as there were no big selling singles whatsoever although the first LP performed respectably enough. I like "And You've Got Me" from the *Thelma and Jerry* LP and while it is all performed in the best possible taste, and disco is avoided, I find it too MOR for my unalloyed enjoyment.

Two To One differed from *Thelma And Jerry* by only containing two duets (neither of which I much like; again too MOR) and three solo cuts each from Butler and Houston. Jerry's "Chicago Send Her Home" (also recorded by Willie Hightower) is downright funky, not a style often associated with Butler, but it worked just fine, and proved his versatility.

Nothing Says I Love You Like I Love You 1978 P.I.R. JZ 35510 Producers: Kenny Gamble, Leon Huff, Joe Jefferson & Jack Faith (Billboard soul charts: 42; Billboard pop charts: 160)

The Best Love 1980 P.I.R. JZ 36413 Producers: Kenny Gamble, Leon Huff, John Usry, Jerry Butler, Dexter Wansel, David Williams & Dennis Williams, (Billboard soul charts: 71)

Butler's return to Philadelphia to once again work with Gamble and Huff was heralded as exciting news, and so it was, but times had clearly changed since the late sixties. The suspicion that reunions do not often work proved to be the case. "Cooling Out" did reach #14 on the soul singles charts but did not even reach the top 100 pop. First time around with G and H, Butler hit the pop top 100 TEN times. That being said, the LPs were both good, indeed the best things he had recorded in years. "I'm Glad To Be Back" was the symbolically important track from *Nothing Says I Love You* on which seven of the eight tracks were written by the Gamble/Huff/Butler combination. It's hard to pick out highlights as both albums were consistently strong with no obvious weaknesses - even a dance version of "Reach Out For Me" came across ok - but the title track of the former and "Tell Me Girl" from the latter should be acknowledged as particularly strong Butler ballads. Debra Henry from Silk provided the seemingly now obligatory female duets on a couple of tracks from *The Best Love*.

Ice 'N' Hot 1982 Fountain FR 2 821 Producers: Jerry Butler, Lawrence Hanks & Fred Perren (Billboard soul charts: 60)

After the disappointing sales figures of the two P.I.R. albums, Butler more or less retired from active recording, re-surfacing only a handful of times again, one example being this album which turned out to be his last new vinyl release. Given his unimpeachable history, a brand new LP in 1982 from Butler was never going to be his best ever work, but it did house one notable track in "No Fair (Falling In Love)" but it sat uneasily alongside minor Jerry cuts in "Ask Me" and "Night Life".

I know somebody who went to hear Jerry Butler sing live in Washington,D.C. in 2013 - a mere 55 years after his first records appeared. Unsurprisingly, it appears that he was great. This is an astonishing example of staying power in an industry not noted for taking a long term view and when one also considers his other accomplishments - in politics, for example - it becomes clear that Butler is one of the most important, gifted and dogged soul men of them all. Everyone needs to own some LPs by the "Ice Man".

Jesse Butler

Free To Be Me 1984 Bound Sound BS-1008 Producer: Clarence Reid

This is NOT the same Jesse Butler who put out an album entitled *Memphis Soul* (which falls into enough jazzy territory to warrant exclusion from the book.) This Jesse Butler hails from Muscle Shoals and recorded a couple of obscure solo 45s before cutting what was to become a popular single on the "Northern Soul" scene under the name of ZZ and Co. Following its sales failure Butler reverted to once again recording under his own name and the album above was one of the results. Butler is an excellent "gritty" singer in the Wilson Pickett mould and this unashamedly tough LP will appeal to soul traditionalists who grew up on the harder soul music of the sixties. The song choice is a little tired, but all is delivered exceedingly soulfully and there were few LPs being issued in 1984 that sounded like this one. It includes a longer re-cut of "Getting Ready For The Get Down", the aforementioned ZZ and Co. track.

Tommy Butler

Tommy Butler 1974 Zardaeo ZDS 16001 Producers Tommy Butler & Dale Frank

I bought this a few years ago on the hope that it might be a "lost gem" of some sort. Sadly, it isn't. It is a dull LP of limited merit, by a singer who sounds a little bit like Swamp Dogg but without any semblance of his wit or ability to write strong songs. I quite like "Seven Days-Seven Nights" which is gently funky but you could vigorously shake this LP and not a single tune would fall out.

Bobby Byrd

I Need Help (Live On Stage) 1970 King 1118 Producer: James Brown

Hot Pants (I'm Coming, Coming, Coming) 1989? Polydor PLP-7701 Producer: James Brown (Japan)

On The Move (I Can't Get Enough) 1993 Soulciety ME 018/94 Producers: Bobby Byrd & Soulciety

Got Soul The Best Of 1995 Simply Vinyl SV 205 (UK)

Many people will have heard Bobby Byrd's voice - even if they have no idea who he was. For example, it was Byrd who intoned "get on up" over and over again on James Brown's "Sex Machine", and as he provided many more vocal assists over the years (not least as a member of The Famous Flames) as well as being married to another long-time Brown associate, Vicki Anderson, his roots within the Godfather's dynasty were solid and deep..

I Need Help was one of those fake "live" jobs that contained mainly studio tracks with applause dubbed on, but it is a marvellous LP, showcasing what an underrated singer he was. If Byrd is known for anything it is for his funk, but there are six excellent example of straight soul singing on the album: "I Found Out", "I'm Not To Blame", "My Concerto", "I'll Lose My Mind" the excellent duet with Brown, "You've Got To Change Your Mind" and, best of all, a splendid country-soul performance in "It's I Who Love You".

Sadly, we had to wait for nearly twenty years before another Byrd LP appeared and this time only in Japan. It does duplicate some tracks with the first album but mainly features the singles he put out on the Brownstone label in the early seventies, as well as two Anderson solo cuts. As with the first Byrd LP, it is recommended.

Byrd did benefit from the re-appraisal of Brown's music in the nineties and he got the chance to record a superb new album "On The Move"; this really should be heard, and features a surprising choice of songs in "Sunshine" as well as recuts of a number of his earlier records.

It was also delightful to see the release of a comprehensive double LP in 1995 which included seven of the nine singles he posted on the soul singles charts between 1964 and 1975, with the biggest being "I Need Help (I Can't Do It Alone)" which had reached #14 soul and #69 pop towards the end of 1970.

Byrd died in 2007 but never got the acclaim - or money, by all accounts - he fully deserved. Every one of the four LPs he put out is well worth hearing and much better than average. (I haven't listed the 1988 LP, "Finally Getting Paid", as it is, to my mind, a various artists album, rather than a Byrd solo record.)

John Byrd

Your Thing And My Thing 1974 20th Century T-436 Producer: Joe Wilson

This winsome and melodic LP was produced by Joe Wilson down in Muscle Shoals but is not really typical of most of what emerged from that city, being much lusher in approach than normal, with strings being emphasised more than horns. John Byrd was - and remains - somewhat of a mystery man and I have never read a thing about him. He sings well, if lacking any particular distinguishing tone, and although the LP did not do particularly well it is ripe for re-appraisal now and would be perfect for certain sections of the UK dance scene who adore records of this ilk. Byrd gives us fine covers of "Sunshine" and " I'll Be Your Everything" while most of the other cuts are Joe Wilson, George Byrd (is this John?) and Henderson Huggins songs, with the excellent "I've Got What You Need" being the best of them.

A single from the set, "I Can't Stop Loving You, Girl ", failed and so did another, "There's No Cold In Me" although this one wasn't included on the album. Neither 20th Century, nor anyone else, recorded John Byrd again to the best of my knowledge.

Calendar

Donna Ahjuder; Stanley Haygood; William Jones; John Barbee; Michael Barbee; Hurlie Fair; Gerald Fair

It's A Monster 1976 Pi Kappa PKS 4001 Producer: Paul Kyser

I always liked "Hypertension", a tale of woe that used to get a lot of play in the clubs of my youth, but one which was more of a turntable hit than a big seller. It had an unmistakeable B.T. Express influence which is true of most of the rest of the album as well, and there was nothing else on here strong enough to break the group out of the large pack of soul aggregations of the time. Given Paul Kyser's expertise with ballads it was disappointing that there were none on the album. And "Calendar" was an awful name for a band.

California Playboys (see also H Andrews Congregation)

Lennell Salone; Julian Vaught; Ken Dunaway, Jackie Rogers, Kelvin Dixon and Will Smith

Trying to Become A Millionaire 1976 Loadstone LLP-13956 Producer: ?

An excellent, if hideously rare, LP by a San Francisco based group who arose from the ashes of the H Andrews Congregation. Most tracks are uptempo and the style is gently funky and jazzy with lots of instrumental passages but "Double Loving" and "Just Say A Four Letter Word" show that the boys were no mean vocalists either. Shame the cover is so dull.

Terry Callier

The New Folk Sound Of 1968 Prestige PRLP-7383 Producer: Samuel Charters

Occasional Rain 1971 Cadet CA 50007 Producer: Charles Stepney

What Color Is Love 1972 Cadet CA 50019 Producer: Evelyn Greco

I Just Can't Help Myself 1973 Cadet CA 50019 Producers: Charles Stepney, Larry Wade & Terry Callier

Fire On Ice 1978 Elektra 6E-143 Producer: Richard Evans

Turn You To Love 1979 Elektra 6E-189 Producer: Reginald "Sonny" Burke

With the exception of Ray Charles, no artist in this book has taxed me as much as Terry Callier. Is he or isn't he a soul artist? I must have changed my mind about ten times. In the end I have included him, because of the esteem in which he is held by so many people whose opinions I admire. I have never been in any doubt as to his ability or talent, by the way, just purely as to whether or not he falls into scope.

With regard to *The New Folk Sound Of Terry Callier*, there is no debate; it is not a soul record in any shape or form. It is good, though, and I can happily listen to "900 Miles" and "I'm A Drifter" if I want to hear something different.

Occasional Rain is another album that wanders around the boundaries of soul music, looking in. It needs to be heard in its entirety as it is structured with a number of segues leading into lengthy songs, one of which is "Ordinary Joe", possibly his best known and best loved composition.

What Color Is Love is by and large in a similar style to the Prestige set, with acoustic guitars, sparkling arrangements and long and thoughtful songs to the fore. But something more obviously "soulful" breaks through from time to time and the beautifully melodic "Just As Long As We're In Love" (which The Dells also recorded) is the best example on show. The Dells also cut "You Don't Care" and their power is at odds with Callier's own largely instrumental version.

One other thing was not in doubt: Callier was not selling many records and presumably was making a living purely as a result of a number of his songs being covered by others. *I Just Can't Help Myself* was a marginally more straightforward set than the previous three - "Gotta Get Closer To You" and the title track were commercial and memorable - but "Until Tomorrow" and "Satin Doll" continued the acoustic and jazzy sound Callier had established for himself.

Callier released no music for a few years and then re-appeared at the end of the decade with a couple of sets for Elektra which undoubtedly played down the jazz and folk influences in seeking a more immediate sound. It worked in as much as both LPs are much loved and a single from *Turn You To Love*, "Sign Of The Times", hit the soul charts at #78 in the late summer of 1979. "Be A Believer", "African Violet" and "Turn You To Love" itself would be the tunes across the two sets that are of most appeal to Callier's loyal fan base.

In the last twenty years Callier has finally received the recognition he has deserved. He has always been his own man and refused to compromise his art for which I much respect him. A number of new records have come forth in the last three decades and in fact he has cut more CDs than he did LPs.

Cameo

Larry Blackmon; Gregory Johnson; Tomi Jenkins; Nathan Leftenant; Arnett Leftenant; Eric Durham; William Revin; Kurt Jetter; Wayne Cooper; Gary Dow; Aaron Mills; Thomas Campbell; Jeryl Bright; Stephen Moore, Charlie Singleton

Cardiac Arrest 1977 Chocolate City CCLP 2003 Producer: Larry Blackmon (Billboard soul charts: 16; Billboard pop charts: 116)

We All Know Who We Are 1978 Chocolate City CCLP 2004 Producer: Larry Blackmon (Billboard soul charts: 15; Billboard pop charts: 58)

Ugly Ego 1978 Chocolate City CCLP 2006 Producer: Larry Blackmon (Billboard soul charts: 16; Billboard pop charts: 83)

Secret Omen 1979 Chocolate City CCLP 2008 Producer: Larry Blackmon (Billboard soul charts: 4; Billboard pop charts: 46)

Cameosis 1980 Chocolate City CCLP 2011 Producer: Larry Blackmon (Billboard soul charts: 1; Billboard pop charts: 25)

Feel Me 1980 Chocolate City CCLP 2016 Producer: Larry Blackmon (Billboard soul charts: 6; Billboard pop charts: 44)

Knights Of The Sound Table 1981 Chocolate City 2019 Producer: Larry Blackmon (Billboard soul charts: 2; Billboard pop charts: 44)

Alligator Woman 1982 Chocolate City 2021 Producer: Larry Blackmon (Billboard soul charts: 6; Billboard pop charts: 23)

Anyone listening to the *Cardiac Arrest* LP back in 1977 would probably not have forecast that Cameo would go on to become one of the biggest funk bands of all time, registering three #1 soul albums and soul singles as well as numerous other massive hits. Not surprisingly, given it was a debut from a band making their way, the first album was a stew of influences, about three parts Kool and The Gang, Earth Wind & Fire and Parliament with a soupcon of Ohio Players added in. When one also considers the atypical cut "Find My Way" (originally released as by "The Players") the conclusion was that *Cardiac Arrest* lacked any particular distinction.

But the group were learning, and on the possibly significantly entitled *We All Know Who We Are* the only discernible influence left was that of EWAF, but, more importantly, Cameo's own sound was coming to the fore. That sound was a relentlessly driving rhythm attack with a pronounced bass line, emphasised just as much as the horn section. In short, Cameo's records were starting to be the most rhythmically dynamic of all the funk bands, doubtless exactly the intention of leader, producer, main songwriter, and drummer, Larry Blackmon. "It's Serious" and "It's Over" were both released as singles and both entered the soul charts.

Ugly Ego was an enjoyable third LP, spawning the band's biggest single hit to date in "Insane" (#17 soul), which is a perfect example of how tough and tight they could sound. The same could also be said of "Anything You Wanna Do" while "Friend To Me" was by far the best ballad they had delivered to date.

Secret Omen was the album that indicated how far they had come: it showed they had shaken off other influences, was their first to go Top 50 pop, and contained their first two top ten soul singles in "I Just Want To Be" (#3) and "Sparkle" (#10). However, honesty compels me to note that I didn't care much for the album (which also contained a re-make of "Find My Way") as I felt the songs were weak.

I preferred *Cameosis*, their first #1 LP, as although I remain lukewarm about tracks like "Shake Your Pants" and the title track (utterly routine to my ears), "On The One" is taut and funky with an excellent bass line and side two contains three decent ballads.

In fact, the group were gravitating more towards slower material and once again the ballads from *Feel Me* (title track) and "Better Days" were good as was the thoughtful and midtempo "Is This The Way". "Keep It Hot" was funky, enjoyable and successful (#4 soul) even if it sounded a little dated for 1980, in its mid seventies Ohio Players-like groove.

Knights Of The Sound Table was, for my money, easily the best ever Cameo album with a number of excellent tracks: one of their finest ever funk tracks in "Freaky Dancin'" (#3 soul) a tuneful and appealing midtempo number in "Use It Or Lose It" , the wry "Don't Be So Cool" and fine ballads in "I Never Knew" and "I'll Always Stay" as well as a jazzy "The Sound Table". In fact, the only throw away is the discordant "Knights By Nights" but this was Cameo's best work and is an album every soul fan should own, or at least try and listen to. It deservedly did very well and was also the first

album on which Charlie Singleton had joined the band, and I suspect its quality was not unrelated to this fact.

Just when I was getting excited about Cameo my hopes were rather dashed by *Alligator Woman* a pretty different beast from its predecessor. The band were now down to just five, and the sound was changing, to a much more pronounced pop/rock influence on the title track and "Secrets Of Time", neither of which appeal at all, and while most of the other cuts were reasonably solid it is not an LP I play frequently and it ended their association with Chocolate City. As so often, though, my own tastes can easily be ignored as it secured their highest ever placing on the pop charts, thus justifying that they were still making the right commercial moves.

Style 1983 Atlanta Artists 811072 Producer: Larry Blackmon (Billboard soul charts: 14; Billboard pop charts: 53)

She's Strange 1984 Atlanta Artists 814984 Producer: Larry Blackmon (Billboard soul charts: 1; Billboard pop charts: 27)

Single Life 1985 Atlanta Artists 824546 Producer: Larry Blackmon (Billboard soul charts: 2; Billboard pop charts: 58)

Word Up! 1986 Atlanta Artists 830265 Producer: Larry Blackmon (Billboard soul charts: 1; Billboard pop charts: 8)

Machismo 1988 Atlanta Artists 836002 Producer: Larry Blackmon (Billboard soul charts: 10; Billboard pop charts: 56)

Real Man...Wear Black 1984 Atlanta Artists 846297 Producer: Larry Blackmon (Billboard soul charts: 18; Billboard pop charts: 84)

Emotional Violence 1992 Reprise 7599-26734-1 Producer: Larry Blackmon (Germany)

The shift towards a more mainstream, crossover, appeal continued with the first Atlanta Artists album, *Style,* with a ballad like "Heaven Only Knows" sounding much more radio friendly then their earlier work while "You're A Winner" had Steely Dan overtones. It also included the first ever example of Cameo using outside material in a rather startling version of "Can't Help Falling In Love". Play this one to someone 'blind': they would never guess it was Cameo in a million years.

In early 1984 I visited New York City for the first time. Two songs seemed to be playing all the time and everywhere: Cheryl Lynn's "Encore" and Cameo's "She's Strange". As a result, the Cameo song will always have a positive nostalgic effect on me but, despite the variety and musicianly quality of the album from whence it came, it does not appeal these days, sounding much too rocky, rappy and eighties for my tastes.

By now, Cameo had reasonable claims to be the biggest soul band in the States and *Single Life* was another massive success even if the band were now down to three: Blackmon, Tomi Jenkins and Nathan Leftenant. The title track and "Attack Me With Your Love" both went top three on the soul singles chart. And then came "Word Up!", easily their biggest ever record, with the single going to #6 in the pop charts, the only time they reached the top twenty, while both single and LP went to #1 on the soul charts. By this time, it had been a while since I could enjoy their music and the last few albums didn't change this trend.

Regardless of my unenthusiastic feelings about their later work,

Cameo were a highly successful group, and hardly any soul act in history can match their feat of placing every single album they ever cut (apart from the last one) into the top twenty soul albums chart.

G.C.Cameron

Love Songs & Other Tragedies 1974 Motown M6-819S1 Producers: Stevie Wonder, Willie Hutch, Terry Woodford, Clayton Ivey, Winston Monseque, Frank Wilson, Larry Brown, George Gordy & G.C.Cameron

Sailing With Soul 1975 Navy Recruiting Command Series 13 (not commercially available)

G.C.Cameron 1976 Motown M6-855S1 Producers: Terri McFadden, T-Boy Ross, Leon Ware, Hal Davis, Winston Monseque, James Carmichael, Freddie Perren, Larry Brown, Iris Gordy, Mark Davis & G.C.Cameron

You're What's Missing In My Life 1977 M6-880S1
Producer: Brian Holland

Rich Love, Poor Love (with Syreeta) 1977 M6-891S1
Producer: Michael L Smith

Cameron - from Jackson, Mississippi - had been in the Spinners (a group with a legacy of extraordinary lead singers) for a while before he stepped out with a mesmerising lead on "It's A Shame", a record which, in truth, he seldom matched again despite the invariable quality of his singing down the years.

The first two Motown albums, as can be seen, featured a whole host of producers (and an equally large number of songwriters) and despite Cameron's excellent vocals throughout, and as enjoyable as the records are, there was not much (with one exception) that really stood out as a "must play" song on either LP to compare with "It's A Shame". If there had been more belief in him from Motown he was capable of doing great things but he never really stood a chance of competing with the big Motown stars while he was being shunted around so many different producers. That one exception was "Include Me In Your Life", from *G.C. Cameron*, a magnificent vocal performance. In fact, his virtuosity might have been a problem: on "Share Your Life" , for instance, he declaims throughout in a high tenor, a style he hadn't really used before and, even though he could do it all, he couldn't necessarily do it in an instantly recognizable style to your average record buyer.

Cameron's next LP had the benefit of one producer only - Brian Holland - and the title track from *You're What Missing* became the biggest single he ever had when it reached #24 on the soul singles charts in the first half of 1977. It is not a bad album at all, boasting some nice cuts such as "I'll Love You Forever", a good version of "Nothing Sweeter Than Love" and the rather Invictus sounding "Don't Tear Down What Took So Long To Build" but also included things like "Let's Run Away Together" where Cameron may as well have stayed in bed.

Back in 1974 Cameron had provided guest vocals on Syreeta Wright's second album when they sang together on "I Wanna Be Your Side" which was easily the most impressive track on the LP. No doubt mindful of this, plus coming at a time when the record company were actively putting out male/female duet albums, Motown released the Cameron and Wright *Rich Love/Poor Love* platter. It did little commercially and is not really to my taste artistically, as it was over-orchestrated to a degree that somewhat detracted from the vocals - quite an achievement with a singer of Cameron's talent. (The odd album, *Sailing With Soul*, contained Cameron solo cuts as well as Spinners tracks, some of which he didn't even sing on. For further details on this series see the entry under Odia Coates.)

Give Me Your Love 1983 Malaco 7413 Producers: Wolf Stephenson, Tommy Couch, Vasti Jackson & G.C. Cameron

In 1983 Cameron was to produce the only truly satisfying album of his career with the excellent *Give Me Your Love* set, one of the best ever from the admired Malaco record label, even if it sounds little like the work done there by Bobby Bland, Johnnie Taylor etc. The reason for my enthusing was primarily because the material was simply much stronger than had been the case in the past but sadly it sold no better than his previous records and maintained G.C.'s run of lack of exposure on any album charts. I recommend this record unreservedly which covers a wide range from an obviously "What's Going On" influenced "Hearts And Flowers", a trawl back into his own back catalogue with a re-make of "It's So Hard To Say Goodbye To Yesterday", and some lovely horn-driven southern soul in "Caught In Your Love Trap" and "Hold You To Your Promise" as well as "Night Like This In Georgia", probably the best track he had cut since "Include Me In Your Life" all those years before.

He has been reasonably prolific in recording and releasing new material in the last twenty five years.

Rafael Cameron

Cameron 1980 Salsoul SA 8535 Producer: Randy Muller (Billboard soul charts: 18; Billboard pop charts: 67)

Cameron's In Love 1981 Salsoul SA 8542 Producer: Randy Muller (Billboard soul charts: 29; Billboard pop charts: 101)

Cameron All The Way 1982 Salsoul SA 8553 Producer: Randy Muller (Billboard soul charts: 43)

There are 21 songs across Rafael Cameron's three LPs and Randy Muller wrote twenty of them. Which says one thing at least: if you don't like Brass Construction or dancing then there is absolutely no reason to listen to one second of any of them. Fortunately for Cameron enough fans did buy in to Muller's rather one-dimensional but determined brand of funk to make him - Cameron - a reasonably big selling artist for a couple of years and he placed seven singles from the LPs on the charts as well.

I'm not going to pretend that these are records I would ever play by choice but I suspect that his voice was good enough to have done more interesting work had he been given the chance to record in different styles.

Choker Campbell

Hits Of The Sixties 1965 Motown MT 620 No produced listed

Street Scene 1977 Candy Apple RC10744 Producer: Choker Campbell (Canada)

Saxophonist Walter Luzar Campbell has tended to be almost entirely overlooked in the deserved rehabilitation and belated acknowledgment of the Funk Brothers but he warrants recognition for the work he and his 16 piece band performed for so many Motown artists, particularly when on the road, in the early days of the label's revues. It is not a great LP - not even really a "soul" album, featuring big band versions of well loved hits from the Gordy empire - but it must have been gratifying for him that at least his name got out there on a record from the most successful indie of all time, however briefly.

The *Street Scene* LP only came out in Canada and has, if anything, an even more tenuous link with soul, though might work for fans of "Blaxploitation" soundtracks.

Capitols

Donald Storball; Richard McDougall; Samuel George

Dance The Cool Jerk 1966 Atco 33-190 Producer: Ollie McLaughlin (Billboard soul charts: 10; Billboard pop charts: 95)

We Got A Thing 1966 Atco 33-201 Producer: Ollie McLaughlin

Their Greatest Recordings 1984 Solid Smoke SS-8019

That Detroit's Capitols would probably not sustain a long career was evident from the sleevenotes to the *We Got A Thing* LP where Storball was called "Norman" and McDougall, "Mitchell". If one then also considers that both their albums from 1966 consisted almost entirely of covers of other artists' big hits it should be clear that they were hardly at the top of Atlantic/Atco's priority list. But the group should not be dismissed: "Cool Jerk" was an infectious and entirely deserved massive hit (#7 on the Hot 100) and the group had a warmth and sense of fun that could be palpable (like the little laugh that ran throughout "Wild Thing" - the group *knew* it wasn't a great version but clearly enjoyed cutting it anyway.) They could also sing just fine: as later singles like "I Thought She Loved Me" and "When You're In Trouble" (both on the *Greatest Recordings* LP) proved. Such songs, like "Cool Jerk" and "We Got A Thing" (their second biggest hit at #26 soul) were written by the talented Storball.

Greatest Recordings is the best of their albums as it dispenses with most of the cover versions, adds in later singles, as well as four previously unreleased songs. As expected though, the group didn't survive past the sixties and a sad footnote was the murder of George in 1982.

Captain Sky

Adventures Of 1978 AVI 6042 Producer: Daryl Cameron (Billboard soul charts: 30; Billboard pop charts: 157)

Pop Goes The Captain 1979 AVI 6077 Producer: Daryl Cameron (Billboard soul charts: 49)

Concerned Party # 1 1980 TEC 1202 Producer: Daryl Cameron (Billboard soul charts: 69 ; Billboard pop charts: 210)

The Return Of Captain Sky 1981 AVI 6100

Captain Sky is Daryl Cameron and if one can get past the rather silly and dated aspects of his music - Parliament induced space trivia, syndrums and the comic book graphics - then there are things to be enjoyed, nearly all of which are to do with a driving and hard rhythm section, particularly on "Moonchild" from the second album or "Bubble Gum" from the third. Cameron's voice is ok, too, without being spectacular but this brand of Chicago music, as evidenced by the esteemed Robert Pruter's dislike of it, will always have to be approached with care.

The last album contains only tracks from the other LPs, and is thus rather mis-leadingly titled. He made no more albums after this but did continue to release records, the most unlikely of which was a version of Bloodstone's "Natural High". (Bloodstone won hands-down.)

Caress

Caress 1977 P&P PAP3301 Producers: Patrick Adams, Ed Carpenter & William Scholl

This record sneaked out without any success to speak of, which was not too surprising given its lacklustre cover and lack of promotion. It has also been difficult to track down any information about the group but these things should not obscure the fact that it is an excellent Philly sounding album, even if it was recorded in White Plains, New York.

One of Patrick Adams' strengths was his ability to write melodic songs of a high standard and he wrote everything on here, and I think it may be his most satisfying piece of work. It's a decidely underrated record, in fact, and anyone who loves vocal singing of the seventies must track it down as it beats any of the records that even such a great group as the Dramatics, for example, was releasing at the time. Despite my ignorance of Caress the sleeve doesn't help) "Just Like In The Movies" and "Family Man" are entirely acceptable ballads while the uptempo tracks pump along entertainingly.

Carl Carlton

Can't Stop A Man In Love 1973 ABC / Back Beat BBLX 71 Producers: Jay Wellington, Dave Crawford, Mike Terry, Monroe Pastrel & William Webb

Everlasting Love 1974 ABC 857 Producer: Bob Monaco (Billboard soul charts: 22; Billboard pop charts: 132)

I Wanna Be With You 1975 ABC 910 Producer: Bunny Sigler (Billboard soul charts: 49)

Drop By My Place 1988 Charly CRB 1198 (UK)

Carl Carlton was born in 1952 in Detroit and originally was propelled along as an alternative to "Little" Stevie Wonder when both singers were cutting records as young boys. Indeed, on the "Why Don't They Leave Us Alone" Back Beat single Carlton was billed as "Little Carl Carlton, 14 Year Old Sensation", a variation on his "Nothin' No Sweeter Than Love" Golden World side when he was "The 12 Year Old Wonder". I have to say that CC did ok, as I find most records by youngsters are close to unlistenable, but "Competition Ain't Nothing" is good stuff, fairly charging along and is the archetypal "Northern Soul" record.

The first LP spanned a long period of time from "Competition" (a #36 soul single hit in 1968) to "Can't Stop A Man In Love" (# 81 in 1973) and, unsurprisingly, his voice had deepened and matured across the stretch of the album, which was poorly annotated with missing producer credits on a number of the tracks. One of his best singles (which is on the album) was the endearingly entitled "I Won't Let That Chump Break Your Heart", which must be one of the last known instances in the English language of anyone actually using that particular term of disparagement.

Carlton had enjoyed a quietly successful career - 8 singles on the soul chart over a six year period - but he then - out of nowhere - moved into an entirely different gear when he had a massive hit with a cover of "Everlasting Love" which scored at #6 pop in 1974. An album was inevitably built around the single, but it was a fairly average affair, consisting mainly of covers of well-known songs which had been performed better elsewhere and, on some cuts, for example, "Hurt So Bad", it was clear that his voice was somewhat limited and lacking in character. My favourite cut on the LP was a typically melodic offering from Paul Kelly, "I Wanna Be Your Main Squeeze", the only known recording of this song.

Disappointingly for Carlton, he could not immediately follow up his success as the Bunny Sigler produced LP *I Wanna Be With You*, did not contain any big hits. It also, I think, underscored my comments about his voice as all of the Sigler-penned tracks on the album have Carlton clearly following the phrasing Sigler would have employed on his demo versions of the songs. I deeply admire Bunny Sigler, but have always found him erratic, and this is generally not his best work and Carlton couldn't do a lot with it.

Drop By My Place was an anthology of his work with ABC / Back Beat and is worthwhile as half of the sixteen tracks are not to be found on the earlier three albums.

Carl Carlton 1981 20th Century 628 Producer: Leon Haywood (Billboard soul charts: 3; Billboard pop charts: 34)

The Bad C.C. 1982 RCA AFL1-4425 Producers: David Rubinson, Narada Michael Walden, Larry White, Gavin Christopher & Greg Levias (Billboard soul charts: 21; Billboard pop charts: 133)

Private Property 1985 Casablanca 422 822 705 Producers: Allen Jones & Sam Dees (Billboard soul charts: 36)

After a failed single on Mercury, Carlton bounced back in the summer of 1981 with the second big success of his career, "She's A Bad Mama Jama", #2 on the soul charts and #22 pop, which turned the *Carl Carlton* LP into a genuine hit as well. Life was good for Carlton at this time, reflected in the fine physique he exhibited on the LP's cover. It was a competent affair too, benefitting from an assured Leon Haywood production and still sounds appealing in 2016.

He moved on quickly from 20th Century to RCA to place a version of "Baby I Need Your Loving" off the *Bad C.C* album into the top twenty soul singles charts but it was not a patch on Gayle Adams' interpretation, let alone the Four Tops' original. The rest of the album wasn't particulary distinctive either and he moved on again, for his last vinyl outing, onto Casablanca. The good news was that all of side two was written and produced by Sam Dees; the bad news was that it was possibly the weakest work Dees ever did. "Mama's Boy" is a smart song, but can't escape its awful musical backing whereas tracks like "Hot" and "Free, Fine And 21" are just poor in all respects. The Allen Jones produced side was no great shakes either and it was an inauspicious end to a long and respectable career.

Sadly, recent reports suggest that Carlton is now back in Detroit, in straitened circumstances.

Jean Carn

Jean Carn 1976 P.I.R. PZ 34394 Producers: Kenny Gamble, Leon Huff, Dexter Wansel, John Whitehead, Gene McFadden & Victor Carstarphen (Billboard soul charts: 46; Billboard pop charts: 122)

Happy To Be With You 1978 P.I.R. JZ 34986 Producers: Kenny Gamble, Leon Huff, Dexter Wansel, Jack Faith, William Bloom, Douglas Brown, Thomas Wallington & Sherman Marshall (Billboard soul charts: 55)

When I Find You Love 1979 P.I.R. JZ 36196 Producers: Jerry Butler, John Usry, Eddie Levert, Dennis Williams, Dexter Wansel, Phillip Pugh, John Faith, Teddy Wortham & Cynthia Biggs (Billboard soul charts: 42)

Sweet And Wonderful 1981 TSOP FZ 36775 Producers: Norman Connors, Jean Carn, McKinley Jackson, Billy Bloom & Frankie Smith (Billboard soul charts: 38; Billboard pop charts: 176)

Artists Showcase 1986 Street Sounds MUSID 7 (UK)

Philadelphia International Records (P.I.R.) was extraordinarily lucrative in the 1970s but, the Three Degrees apart, all the success was deriving from male singers and there was therefore an obvious gap and opportunity for someone to come along and be the P.I.R. equivalent of Diana Ross and Carla Thomas at Motown and Stax respectively. That person proved to be Jean Carn, even if she only ever enjoyed a modicum of their success.

Sarah Jean Perkins (Carn's real name) from Atlanta, Georgia had already recorded a handful of jazz albums with husband Doug (which are out of scope for this book) as well as providing some vocals on the first two Earth, Wind & Fire LPs (uncredited on the first one) before moving on to work with Norman Connors at which time she posted a top ten single on the soul charts (late 1975) when she sang on his "Valentine Love" with Michael Henderson. With such a rich background she was hardly a newcomer when she signed with P.I.R. in 1976.

The first album is excellent, one of the best the company issued from that year onwards. Most people seem to prefer Carn's slow or mid-tempo work (and "No Laughing Matter" and "I'm In Love Once Again" are fine examples) but I also found her to be a great interpreter of dance music and "If You Wanna Go Back" and the title track from "Free Love" (#23 soul) were magnificent singles, although the former inexplicably failed in the marketplace.

Happy To Be With You maintained the same level of quality as the debut, and featured one of her best-loved tracks, "Don't Let It Go To Your Head" (#54 soul), a charging "There's A Good Shortage Of Good Men" as well as my favourite slow cut of hers in Dexter Wansel's "Together Once Again" - the only song I have highlighted thus far not written by Gamble and Huff. In fact, the main men backed off from working with her at this point and didn't write for her at all on her last two albums with P.I.R./TSOP.

As a result of G&H's distance I felt the quality did dip a little, but this is relative, as *When I Find You Love* and *Sweet And Wonderful* are still good records. The former includes two splendid songs in "Lonely Girl" and her revered "Was That All It Was" as well the oddity, "All I Really Need Is You", when she sounds almost exactly like Karen Carpenter. Bizarre and far from her best.

Sweet And Wonderful included lovely takes on the Spinners' "Love Don't Love Nobody" (#35 soul) and Martha and The Vandellas' "Love Makes Me Do Foolish Things" (wonderful harmonies on this one). (In between these albums she scored a #26 soul single in early 1981 with yet another of her duets: "I'm Back For More" with Al Johnson).

The Artists Showcase UK release is a good way to catch up with her work at P.I.R. and Motown as it is notably generous with 21 tracks.

Trust Me 1982 Motown 6010ML Producers: Norman Connors & Jean Carn (Billboard soul charts: 37; Billboard pop charts: 210)

Closer Than Close * 1986 Omni 90492-1 Producers: Grover Washington, Dexter Wansel & Maurice Starr (Billboard soul charts: 9; Billboard pop charts: 162)

You're A Part Of Me * 1988 Atlantic 81811 Producers: Nick Martinelli, Grover Washington, Jean Carne, Bobby Eli, Ken Thomas, Terry Price & Bryan Williams (Billboard soul charts: 40)

Albums marked thus* were released as by Jean Carne

Carn moved to Motown after P.I.R. where she put out just one album. Again, the best cuts were re-workings of old tunes: "If You Don't Know Me By Now", backed by gorgeous harmonies by The Temptations, went to #49 on the soul singles charts while a dazzling "My Baby Loves Me" recruited High Inergy and The Jones Girls to help out. Another track, "Completeness", reached back into her previous jazz work, but "Super Explosion" was just a poor song.

Carn had not posted any singles at all on the Hot 100, and that didn't change when she moved to Omni. Amazingly, in fact, since "Closer Than Close" became a #1 soul single, easily her biggest hit ever, but if even that couldn't cross over.....It is a fine record but not noticeably better than many of her earlier 45s and once again points up the difficulty in trying to predict anything in the record industry. The album was ok, with a good reading of "Break Up To Make Up" but the uptempo tracks, like a tepid "Anything For Love", were woefully short of the verve of earlier cuts like "If You Wanna Go Back".

She then moved on yet again to Atlantic for her last vinyl LP. As usual for me, the best cut was old and distinguished: Aretha's "Ain't No Way" on which Carn(e) acquits herself very well. I was also quite pleasantly surprised by the rest of the LP, which, while hardly her best work, was much better than most other "soul" records appearing in 1988.

Jean Carne is still performing today, never short of work it seems, and she remains one of soul's heroines, particularly in the U.K.

Barbara Carr

Good Woman Go Bad 1989 Bar-Car 1001 Producers: Willie Mitchell, Harrison Calloway & George Jackson

This was a loving LP, which includes excellent and indeed, definitive, sleevenotes on Barbara's career by long-time Carr associate Bill Greensmith but I fear it probably made a loss. She is a most gracious woman, as I know from phoning her up out of the blue many years ago to ask if I could buy a number of copies of this LP from her. She said yes.

St. Louis based Carr had put out a number of singles on Chess in the sixties and early seventies as well as releasing a handful of songs on obscure local labels before forming the Bar-Car label in 1982. The songs on this album were recorded in 1984 and 1985 so she had to wait a few years for it to appear. Despite my initial enthusiasm for the record, it has to be said that it was ultimately disappointing, Firstly, because it features Barbara's solo rendering of "Not A Word" rather than the superior version where she duets with songwriter George Jackson and second, because too many tracks, such as "Summer Nites", "See Saw" and "Let Me Entertain You", are weak. Nevertheless there are three fine tracks well worth hearing: the title track, "Messing With My Mind" (which both came out as the two sides of a single on the Gino's label) and "Oh What A Price", a song I first encountered on a James Govan LP.

Since this album came out Ms.Carr has released a number of CDs which have kept her active in the industry.

James Carr

You Got My Mind Messed Up 1967 Goldwax GW 3001 Producers: Quinton Claunch & Rudolph Russell (Billboard soul charts: 25)

A Man Needs A Woman 1968 Goldwax GW 3002 Producers: Quinton Claunch & Rudolph Russell

Freedom Train 1977 Goldwax VG-3006 (Japan)

At The Dark End Of The Street 1987 Blueside 60008-1

No disrespect intended to Vikki Carr, but she posted 12 LPs on the Hot 200 pop chart, whereas James Carr, a singer of immensely greater talent, posted precisely none. Anyone who knows and loves soul music will probably deeply revere James Carr, and his wider critical reputation has soared since the mid-eighties when he was featured fairly prominently in Peter Guralnick's *Sweet Soul Music* book. In fact, there are a number of sane people who will attest to Carr's being the best soul singer of all time.

It is somewhat of a pleasant surprise to recall that this most soulful and uncompromising singer actually posted 6 singles on the top 100 pop charts, even if none went any higher than #63. Four of them were included on his first magnificent LP, including his biggest ever hit, the wonderful title track (#7 soul), and the song which most people know him for: "Dark End Of The Street". This justly famous Moman-Penn song was a second big hit for Carr - #10 soul in early 1967 - but I feel he recorded a handful of even better sides. One of which is "Forgetting You", a b-side to the equally glorious "Pouring Water On A Drowning Man" (#23 soul), where, for the last few seconds of the song he exhibits some of the most desperate pain ever committed to wax. Both songs were included on the first album which is a undoubted masterpiece and one of the greatest LPs in the history of soul music. There is not even close to weakness on any of the twelve tracks, recorded, like virtually all his work, in Memphis. When one considers that another shattering side, the desperately sad "I Don't Want To Be Hurt Anymore" didn't make it onto a single as even a b-side, it becomes evident just how strong *You Got My MInd Messed Up* is.

A Man Needs A Woman reprised "Dark End" and "Mind Messed Up" but also introduced nine more superb Carr tracks on an album that was only marginally less impressive than the debut. Both title track and "I'm A Fool For You" (which benefitted from the joint vocals of the great Betty Harris) did well as singles (#16 and #42 respectively), but sadly the wonderful "Life Turned Her That Way" did not. Listen out also for the rather unheralded "A Woman Is A Man's Best Friend" where he delivers another example of perfect soul singing. It should also be noted that the UK release of the album (Bell MBLL 113 in 1968) was even better as it included five extra tracks that were not on the U.S. album. One was Penn and Oldham's "Let It Happen" which only just missed out on becoming another Hot 100 hit. Special mention should also go to O.B. McClinton who provided more songs on the two LPs than anyone else.

As has now been well documented elsewhere on many occasions Carr started to betray some alarming and erratic behaviour as the sixties progressed which would have been a significant reason for his not recording another new album (and hardly any more singles) for 23 years but in 1977 the Japanese P-Vine label reached back into the Goldwax vaults and put out a Carr album, *Freedom Train*, which included some more marvellous music ("What Can I Call My Own" for example, even if it does sound a lot like Percy Sledge's "Out Of Left Field") without ever reaching the heights of the first two LPs. The title track was one of the relatively few dance tracks Carr recorded - he was simply much better on slower material - and had reached #39 on the soul singles chart at the start of 1969, while other tracks such as "Search Your Heart" despite Carr's usual highly emotive reading, were not fully finished and required a horn section.

The Blueside LP was the first ever proper retrospective of Carr's music and is important for that reason alone, but it also includes three superb tracks - "To Love Somebody", "That's The Way Life Turned Out For Me" and "Everybody Needs Somebody" - that were not featured on any of the first three albums thus far mentioned.

The Japanese Coldwax label also put out a "live" LP, *Oriental Live And Living*, which I haven't listed as it is obviously a bootleg.

Take Me To The Limit 1991 Ace CH310 Producers: Quinton Claunch, Roosevelt Jamison, John Rutherford & Ricky Ryan

This album was better than we had a right to expect from Carr, and was thoughtful and faithful to his previous work as regards style, song selection and sound. But it wasn't as good. The musicians simply were not as gifted - not a criticism, hardly any set of musicians were - as the American crew and a fake horn section grated. But it was still great to hear him back in a studio, particularly in light of his challenges. Ace went on to release more new Carr material, but not on vinyl.

Carr finally attained some peace when he passed away in January 2001 but pretty much all his music is readily available for anyone who has yet to sample his magnificent singing.

Jerry Carr

This Must Be Heaven 1981 Cherie CR 19330 Producer: William Talbert

This Must Be Heaven was the only LP that Jerry Carr ever released and it could not have done much for the declining Michigan record industry, despite being picked up by Atlantic for distribution. Apart from one track, "Stay With Me", it is rather undistinguished funky music, even if the title cut managed to sell enough to make it to #69 on the soul charts. He did record a decent single in "Love Recession" for the same label, but unfortunately it is not included on the LP.

Linda Carr

Cherry Pie Guy 1976 Roxbury RLX 104 Producer: Kenny Nolan

Carr recorded a number of singles for a variety of different labels in the sixties, all in the lighter pop-soul style of a Dionne Warwick or a Diana Ross. It was therefore no surprise that her one LP consists of unashamedly pop-soul fare and parts of it - the catchy "High Wire" for instance - are reasonably satisfying to listen to once, but repeated plays would require some stiff resolve. What WAS surprising is that she cut some sides in the sixties at FAME in Muscle Shoals, that most soulful of locales.

Carter & Chanel

Midnight Love Affair 1981 Sweet City 7862 Producer: Carl Maduri

Al Carter and Patrice Chanel got to release their one LP on the tiny Sweet City label out of Cleveland. It's the epitome of the sort of music often described as "classy" in soul music circles, and certainly sounds more like a set from a major label rather than a tiny one in Ohio. The duo are talented and the songs, generally mid-tempo in approach, are almost invariably well-constructed with good melodies and memorable choruses. There are no mindless "boogie" things on here either and anyone who likes the music of artists such as Ashford and Simpson or Anita Baker should enjoy this easily enough.

Clarence Carter

This Is 1968 Atlantic SD 8192 Producer: Rick Hall (Billboard soul charts: 49; Billboard pop charts: 200)

The Dynamic 1969 Atlantic SD 8199 Producer: Rick Hall (Billboard soul charts: 22; Billboard pop charts: 169)

Testifyin' 1969 Atlantic SD 8238 Producer: Rick Hall (Billboard soul charts: 35; Billboard pop charts: 138)

Patches 1970 Atlantic SD 8267 Producer: Rick Hall (Billboard soul charts: 18; Billboard pop charts: 44)

The Best Of 1971 Atlantic SD 8282 (Billboard soul charts: 11; Billboard pop charts: 103)

Soul Deep 1984 Edsel ED125 (UK)

Once married to Candi Staton, Montgomery Alabama's Clarence Carter was one of the most successful soulmen ever to have based a career on recording (almost) entirely in the south. Blind from the age of one, he was possessed of much the same wit and playfulness that made Joe Tex's music so compelling. And while Joe certainly had a better giggle, no-one has ever matched Clarence's deep, salacious chuckle that seemed to shake his entire body.

He had recorded a number of singles with another blind singer, Calvin Scott, before hooking up with Rick Hall and cutting at FAME. It took two years of middling success before he hit very big indeed with "Slip Away" (#2 soul, #6 pop), a good enough record, to be sure, but bettered by "Looking For A Fox" (his previous single and #20 soul) which has a marvellous intro and great lyrics. Both singles were included on his debut Atlantic album as was the deeper "I Can't See Myself" (later to be featured on the soundtrack to a Larry Clark film, *Another Day In Paradise*) and it is an overall excellent set. mixing up Carter originals with songs from other top-class writers, a pattern he was to replicate on all his other Atlantic LPs.

The Dynamic album did even better than the debut, which was a little surprising as it only included one charting single, albeit another big one for him in the superb "Too Weak To Fight". The set also featured a version of Staton's "Sweet Feeling" although here entitled "That Old Time Feeling". (Candi's is better which only reinforces a feeling I have always had about Carter: while he seldom delivers less than respectable and creditable cover versions, he doesn't often top the original. His best records tend to be ones he cut himself first.) Having said that, I will immediately point up a possible exception: one of the strongest cuts on *The Dynamic* was a tremendous version of Mann and Weil's "You've Been A Long Time Comin'". I say "possible" as I'm not sure if Carter's was the original or not: I know other versions exist.

1969 brought about a further Carter album in *Testifyin'* which is one to treasure. There are three weak tracks from my perspective: two Wayne Carson Thompson songs which simply don't suit Clarence and a rather tedious version of "Dark End Of The Street", which didn't come within a million miles of James Carr's original. Everything else, though, was fantastic. It boasted three top ten soul singles in "Doin' Our Thing", "The Feeling Is Right", and the gloriously tough "Snatching It Back" with its delightfully bellicose horn section, some of his best ever chortles on "Bad News" and "Back Door Santa", and a b-side of the quality of "I Smell A Rat". Much was written by the great George Jackson and this is an album to play at high volume in the sweltering heat of a southern summer.

Even more success was to accrue to Carter with "Patches", the record for which he is probably best known, and certainly its huge success as a single (#2 soul and #4 pop) helped to propel the album of the same name to much greater heights than the previous three but it is a lesser work. "Patches" is a love-hate song (I'm in the latter camp) and as its spoken section was deemed to be a winning formula it was repeated on the follow-up single "It's All In Your Mind" (#13 soul). *Patches* also gives us another song where Carter was beaten hands down by Candi Staton as his rendering of her "I'm Just A Prisoner" was too polite, attempting The Beatles "Let It Be" was an obvious misstep, and I'm not sure that a suave song like "Till I Can't Take It Anymore" really suited him. But not all was lost: "I Can't Leave Your Love Alone" and "Getting The Bills " are good Jackson songs and "Changes" is possibly the earliest example of a Sam Dees song on any album. In summary, though, the LP contains 12 songs and I wouldn't place one of them in Carter's all-time best top ten.

The two Carter collections of the Atlantic work are different in scope: *The Best Of* concentrated on the hits and actually performed extraordinarily well, becoming his highest ever charting LP on the soul charts. The UK Edsel release shone a light on lesser known Carter work.

Sixty Minutes With 1973 Fame FM-LA186 Producers: Rich Hall & Clarence Carter (Billboard soul charts: 41)

For reasons that are not clear to me, Carter had to wait for three years before he released another studio album and *Sixty Minutes With* became one of the few LPs to be issued on the Fame label. In that time he had chalked up five more top 50 soul chart singles, three on Atlantic, and two on Fame, and none were to be found on LPs. *Sixty Minutes With* is a highly likeable album, beautifully and clearly produced, and a return to form after *Patches*. George Jackson and Carter again wrote the majority of the songs and there are no awkward covers this time around. "I'm The Midnight Special", which had an intro much like The Doobie Brothers' "Long Train Runnin'", was a pretty big single (#15) for Clarence and in fact was the last 45 he ever posted on the soul top twenty. Another excellent track, "And They Say Don't Worry", was also recorded by Jackson himself as "Things Are Getting Better", and there is no filler aboard.

Real 1974 ABC ABCD-833 Producer: McKinley Jackson

Loneliness & Temptation 1975 ABC ABCD-896 Producer: Clarence Carter (Billboard soul charts: 58)

A Heart Full Of Song 1976 ABC ABCD-943 Producer: Clarence Carter

Carter moved to ABC for three albums, the first of which was atypical of the rest of his output as it was recorded in LA, rather than in Georgia or Alabama where all his other studio work took place. *Real* also featured no Carter songs at all, the only LP he ever issued where this was the case, other than the mysterious Brylen releases. It is ok, but sounds more like a fairly generic West Coast record of the time than a Clarence Carter outing, and would have been more at home on the Invictus or Hot Wax labels. As a commercial experiment, things didn't work either, as neither it, nor the two singles lifted from *Real*, charted anywhere.

He therefore rather sensibly returned to recording in the south and the excellent *Loneliness & Temptation* LP was produced by Carter himself at his Future Stars recording studio in Atlanta. It was mainly a return to using a number of his own songs - as well as a couple from George Jackson - and he also chose outside material more astutely than had sometimes been the case in the past. For example, a version of Roger Hatcher's "I Was Caught" returned Carter to the top fifty on the soul singles charts and he also delivered a nice, soulful and drawn out interpretation of Otis Redding's "Just One More Day". I also enjoyed his humorous "Take It All Off" (with its great line about having to make sure that his woman's legs didn't look like scrambled eggs), much more of a typical Carter song than the rather corporate atmosphere that had infused *Real*. Lastly, the album profited from the arranging talents of Mike Terry, the only time he worked with Carter.

A Heart Full Of Song generally continued the approach from *Loneliness*, even if Terry was no longer on board, but it was a little softer, as evidenced by a cut like "That's What Your Love Means To Me". "Jennings Alley", with a lovely arrangement by Ted Stovall and Alfred Cook, and a very belligerent (by 1976 standards) interpretation of Ray Charles' "Come Back Baby" were the standout tracks, and overall it was another good Carter release..

Let's Burn 1980 Venture VL-1005 Producer: Clarence Carter (Billboard soul charts: 28; Billboard pop charts: 189)

In Person 1981 Venture VL-1009 Producer: Clarence Carter

Livin' The Life 1982 Brylen BN 4527 No producer listed

Patches 1982 Brylen BN 9939 No producer listed

Carter began the eighties uncertainly. He had waited for four years before a new album arrived, and then two came in fairly quick succession on the Venture label. Neither were great. The songs were longer and less interesting than usual and the sound was stripped back and sounded much thinner as a result. There is not much to recommend about *Let's Burn* - for it contained a really poor version of a fine song, "Scratch My Back", and some rather dispirited singing from Carter - apart from a tuneful "She's Out To Get Me".

In Person was an improvement - "Can We Slip Away, Again?" and "I Love You" (the same version as on the *Sixty Minutes With* LP) are good tracks, Clarence is singing with more heart, the musicianship and production are fuller and more rounded, and "It's A Monster Thang" became the 23rd (and last) Carter single to hit the soul top 100 chart. But it still failed to match up to his Atlantic and ABC output.

The two albums on Brylen were just plain odd. They consisted pretty much entirely of songs that had been big hits for others (e.g. "Back Stabbers", "Use Me", "Brick House" and "Finally Got Myself Together") and were completely bereft of any information, and, in the case of "You Don't Have To Say You Love Me", a total absence of any emotional engagement from Carter. *Livin' The Life* didn't even feature a picture on Clarence on either front or back cover. I can only imagine it was some sort of tax write-off deal as neither album is well known and must have sold few (if indeed they were even offered for sale.) It would be nice to know where and when the songs were recorded but given that in all cases the originals were better it is really just of academic interest.

Live in Johannesburg 1982 Bullet BU 588 No producer listed (South Africa)

Love Me With A Feeling 1982 Big C AG 8214 No producer listed

Singing For My Supper 1984 Big C BC 114 No producer listed

And then things improved. The *Live* album, while flawed ("I Got Caught" really didn't need to be 13 minutes long) and not all "live" (the excellent "Girl From Soweto" is a studio recording), is actually pretty decent but was eclipsed by the excellent *Love Me With A Feeling*, the best album he had recorded in years. The title track is an x-rated blues, tough as hell for 1982, while the song selection is sure-footed and wise. Penn and Oldham's "Wrong Too Long" is delivered in wry fashion, "Trying To Keep My Head Above Water" is one of Carter's best ever cover versions, "It's All In Being In Love" has a lovely country burr and there are two fine (but uncredited) duets with Pat Cooley in the shape of "You And Me Baby" and "We Are A Good Act Together" but the whole set is good, no bad tracks at all.

Singing For My Supper was equally impressive. The stand-out track was the fantastic "What Was I Supposed To Do" (he had recorded an earlier version as a single), one of the best songs he ever wrote, a tale of helpless yet justified anger and the logical conclusion of what would happen if the other man failed to heed the warning of Arthur Alexander's "You Better Move On". He had another go at "Sweet Feeling" (and Candi still came out on top) and "Hot Stuff" wasn't enthralling, but the rest was more than acceptable. "Messing With My Mind" was a peppy way in which to open an album and "I Was In The Neighbourhood" and "So You're Leaving Me" were simple and heartfelt, while Sam Dees placed his first song ("Mama Used To Sing The Blues") on a Carter LP for 14 years.

Messin' With My Mind 1985 Ichiban 1001 Producer: Clarence Carter

Dr.C.C. 1986 Ichiban 1003 Producer: Clarence Carter (Billboard soul charts: 20)

Hooked on Love 1987 Ichiban 1016 Producer: Clarence Carter (Billboard soul charts: 34)

Touch of Blues 1988 Ichiban 1032 Producer: Clarence Carter (Billboard soul charts: 52)

Between A Rock And A Hard Place 1990 Ichiban 1068 Producer: Clarence Carter (Billboard soul charts: 48

The Best Of 1991 Ichiban 1116 (Billboard soul charts: 74)

Have You Met Clarence Carter..Yet? 1992 Ichiban 1141 Producer: Clarence Carter (Billboard soul charts: 73)

Carter kicked off his Ichiban career with the best album he ever recorded for the label, even if *Messin' With My Mind* consisted entirely of tracks to be found within the two albums on Big C, both of which were recorded in Muscle Shoals, incidentally.

While the later Ichiban albums produced ever diminishing returns the label did provide him with a massive hit with "Strokin'" easily the biggest record he had enjoyed in years even if it did not feature on the soul singles charts. The fact that the album made it as high as it did on the album listings was entirely due to the song. I find all of the later Ichiban albums almost impossible to listen to attentively given their d.i.y musical approach and the fact that he often recorded new versions of old glories ("I Stayed Away Too Long" on *Dr. C.C* and "I Can't See Myself" on *Hooked On Love*) merely pointed up how much better his earlier music was.

He is still around, releasing new CDs every so often, and one feels that his due respect is still to arrive and maybe his good but not great voice is the reason he has not yet received the acclaim accorded to contemporaries such as Solomon Burke. But make no mistake, he is a fabulous soul man, with bags of personality and a genuine talent for writing strong songs.

Earl Carter & The Fantastic Six

Make It With You 1974 Princess PR 1112 Producer: George Penn

Earl Carter and the Fantastic 6 were an obscure group from Virginia who released a couple of singles and this one LP. I know producer Penn played the drums and Carter delivered the vocals (and I think played guitar or bass too) but further information about the Six has been hard to find, and the album cover provides little help. There is no dominant style on the LP, which features good funk in "Shake Your Poo Poo", soulful balladry in a worthwhile version of "Make It Easy On Yourself", a bright, nimble and danceable take on "Make It With You" and a number of "lounge" ballads. If I were to sum up the overall feel of the album, though, I would posit the purely fanciful thought that the band probably enjoyed a six night a week residency somewhere down in Roanoke and the track listing is the set they always played. Certainly, on a cut like "Make The World Go Away", with its cheap-sounding keyboards and hushed drum brushes, I can imagine Carter crooning the words to the last handful of customers staring into their drinks at 3 am in the morning wondering why life had gone so wrong.

Alvin Cash & The Registers

Twine Time 1965 Mar-V-Lus MLP -1827 Producers: Andre Williams, Otis Hayes, Harold Burrage & Milton Bland

The Philly Freeze 1966 President PTL 1000 Producers: Andre Williams, Otis Hayes, Harold Burrage & Milton Bland (UK)

Alvin Cash was born in St. Louis (and died in 1999) and based his entire career around dance moves, a choice guaranteed to ensure he would never be taken especially seriously as an artist.

His first sides came out as by 'Alvin Cash & The Crawlers', and he hit straight away with "Twine Time" in March 1965, one of those crude and enjoyable semi-instrumentals that emerged from time to time in the sixties. Its chart placing of #4 soul and #14 pop was by some distance his biggest ever hit. It was followed into the soul singles charts over the next 18 months or so by "The Barracuda", "The Philly Freeze" and "Alvin's Boo - Ga - Loo", the latter two of which were credited to 'Alvin Cash & The Registers'.

Both LPs are pretty inconsequential, consisting invariably of short upbeat tracks, most of which sound pretty much the same as the big hit. "Twine Time" might have been tagged as by 'The Crawlers' as a single but the LP went with 'The Registers', demonstrating that no-one at Mar-V-Lus was losing any sleep over trying to build a sustainable career for Alvin Cash.

The albums are not quite identical as regards tracks with two cuts on the UK release that are not on the Mar-V-Lus outing and four on the US album that are not on the President issue.

Cash did not release any more LPs, nor did he hit the charts again after a typical single in 1968, "Keep On Dancing", but he continued to cut dance 45s right up until the early eighties.

Sharon Cash

He Lives Within My Soul 1970 Mothers Records MRS 74 Producer: H B Barnum

Sharon Cash 1973 Playboy PB 114 Producer: George Tobin

Sharon Cash is a singer of great power, obviously derived from a gospel background, and she made these two albums, as well as a one-off single on A & M, before briefly becoming lead singer of a re-formed Honey Cone in 1976.

Jerry Wexler used to use a term, "oversouling", to describe a surfeit of emotion and over the top vocal pyrotechnics from a singer and that is how virtually all of Cash's recordings come across to me but if one is disposed to this type of performance these albums should be sought out. The debut contains all covers, while the Playboy LP consists of mainly new material. A handful of singles were put out from the LPs but not one of them became any sort of a hit. One was "Fever" from *He Lives Within My Soul* and is my favourite of all her sides.

Cashmere (see also Heaven & Earth)

Dwight Dukes; McKinley Horton; Daryl Burgee; Keith Steward

Let The Music Turn You On 1983 Philly World PWRL 2001 Producers: Bryan Loren, Nick Martinelli & Bruce Weeden

Cashmere 1985 Philly World 90243-1 Producers: Ron Dean Miller, Bobby Eli, Donald Robinson, Michael Forte & Bunny Sigler

Dukes and Steward came out of Heaven and Earth, a Chicago based vocal group who recorded some beautiful records. These two albums have their moments - a fair version of "Tracks Of My Tears", "We Need Love" and "Cutie Pie" - but their biggest hit was "Do It Any Way You Wanna",(#35 soul) a dance track, and like so many of their other uptempo cuts, it is predictable and obviously highly influenced by Michael Jackson.

Jimmy Castor

Gerry Thomas; Jeffrey Grimes; Paul Forney; Langdon "Lenny" Fridie; Ellwood Henderson; Douglas Gibson; Bobby Manigault; Harry Jensen; Leburn Maddox

From The Roots 198? Paul Winley 111 No producer listed

Hey Leroy 1967 Smash SRS 67091 Producer: Luchi De Jesus

Jimmy Castor has a highly interesting background which cannot be related here in any detail but his story goes back as far as the fifties when a song of his, "I Promise To Remember", became a big hit for Frankie Lymon and The Teenagers. His recording career has also been extraordinarily eclectic and has covered many bases. A soul man, yes, but by no means a typical one.

The Paul Winley LP, which came out some time in the 1980s, contains early Castor material dating back to the sixties. It is not a great album, consisting of some inconsequential instrumentals, some average songs, and a no better than fair sound quality. "It's What You Give", "Soul Sister" and "Fabulous New York" are worth hearing but it is an album for a Castor completist only - assuming such people exist.

In early 1967 he had his first hit with the latin influenced "Hey Leroy, Your Mama's Calling You" which was big enough (#16 soul and #31 pop) to spawn an LP of the same name. Almost completely instrumental, it mixed up hot dance material such as "Leroy" and a cover of "Bang Bang" with some dreary tracks such as "Our Day Will Come". More importantly, the LP contains five tracks written by Castor with Johnny Pruitt, a long time friendship that turned into a musical partnership that was to last for well over a decade.

There is also another album knocking around as by Jimmy Castor, *I Remember Yesterday* from 1981 on Crystal Ball 104, but it is actually a compilation, featuring work by other artists as well as from Jimmy Castor and the Juniors, the group he fronted in the fifties.

It's Just Begun 1972 RCA LSP-4540 Producer: Castor Pruitt Productions (Billboard soul charts: 11; Billboard pop charts: 27)

Phase Two 1972 RCA LSP-4783 Producer: Castor Pruitt Productions (Billboard pop charts: 192)

Dimension III 1973 RCA APD1-0103 Producer: Castor Pruitt Productions (Billboard soul charts: 49)

Troglodyte: The Best Of 1975 RCA ANL1-0877

The RCA years were some of the most diverse of Castor's career, and his records were now credited to "The Jimmy Castor Bunch".

"It's Just Begun" had come out as a single on the Kinetic label to little notice but the superb LP version has become one of the most sampled records in history. However, it was "Troglodyte" that became the big success at the time, reaching #6 on the pop charts in mid 1972, and that was sufficient to drive the LP to highly respectable sales (over 100,000 apparently). A track like "Psyche" reprised Castor's love of latin music, while "My Brightest Day" was a pure pop song, thus confounding anyone who felt that Castor should produce recognisable "soul music". The group also re-cut "I Promise To Remember" in original doo-wop style while "Bad" was another funk track in the mould of the title track. Pigeon-holed they would not be.

Phase Two could not consolidate the success of *It's Just Begun* and had a rather tiresome "Troglodyte" sound-alike in "Luther The Anthropoid" which couldn't even hit the top 100 soul or pop singles charts, as well as a Jimi Hendrix tribute which I even preferred to the bloodless cover of "The First Time Ever I Saw Your Face". My favourite tracks on a disappointing album were "Party Life" which would not have been out of place on a Joe Bataan LP and the funky and driving "When".

But if *Phase Two* was disappointing, then *Dimension III* was downright awful. There is not a cut on the LP I would want to listen to again, and it is hard to know who it was even aimed at, given its lack of character, energy and relevance to what other "black" records sounded like at the time. Not surprisingly, it was to be the final RCA release apart from a surprisingly hard to track down *Best Of* compilation.

The Everything Man 1974 Atlantic SD 7305 Producer: Castor Pruitt Productions

Butt Of Course 1974 Atlantic SD 18124 Producer: Castor Pruitt Productions (Billboard soul charts: 34; Billboard pop charts: 74)

Supersound 1975 Atlantic SD 18150 Producer: Castor Pruitt Productions (Billboard soul charts: 30)

E-Man Groovin' 1976 Atlantic SD 18186 Producer: Castor Pruitt Productions (Billboard soul charts: 29; Billboard pop charts: 132)

Maximum Stimulation 1977 Atlantic SD 19111 Producer: Castor Pruitt Productions

Despite a move to a new label, the Bunch couldn't shake their penchant for instrumental versions of well-known songs that had rendered *Dimension III* so bland and boring. The first Atlantic LP, despite the obvious intent of the title to label Castor as a renaissance man, contained too many instrumental doodlings ("Walk On The Wild Side", "Didn't I Blow Your Mind", "Love's Theme" etc.) to justify such a claim. As ever his funk was far better and "Maggie" is good stuff, but it is another LP that I will never play again.

Butt Of Course had a greater funky quotient than the previous few albums and was thus much stronger and "The Bertha Butt Boogie" even hit the Top 20 pop singles chart (#16, six places higher than in fared on the soul charts) in early 1975. The lazy and appealing swagger of "Potential" reached #25 on the soul charts as a follow-up 45.

Supersound had the most vitality of any Castor album for years with only one track, "Drifting", being a meandering instrumental. "King Kong" did ok as a single (#23 soul, #69 pop), but "Bom Bom", a Caribbean-flavoured thing, did not. Best track was "A Groove Will Make You Move" with an intro similar to that of "For The Love Of Money" by the O'Jays.

E-Man Groovin rather sweetly invited Sherman Garnes from Lymon's Teenagers to come and intone in his deep rumble on a couple of tracks and it is one of his more varied albums, as well as being the last one to chart anywhere.

Maximum Stimulation, despite not doing particularly well commercially, is one of his best records, featuring an atypical "Magnolia" based on the old "Mannish Boy" riff, through some of his best hard funk on "E-man Par-tay", "Mind Power" and the title track. I wish he hadn't covered "Mandy", though.

Let It Out 1978 Drive 107 Producer: Castor Pruitt Productions

The Jimmy Castor Bunch 1979 Cotillion SD 5215 Producer: Castor Pruitt Productions

I Love Monsters 1979? Little Monster LDR 6601

C 1980 Long Distance 1201 Producer: Jimmy Castor

The Return Of Leroy 1983 Dream DA 6001 Producers: Jimmy Castor, John Pruitt & Gerry Thomas

As the seventies turned into the eighties Castor jumped around on a number of different labels, even popping back to Atlantic on their Cotillion subsidiary. *Let It Out* was a pretty good effort - despite having no truly outstanding cuts - but received no promotion and no sales. The afore-mentioned Cotillion album was poor, and apart from the "I Just Wanna Stop" instrumental, didn't even sound like a Jimmy Castor LP.

I have never seen a copy of *I Love Monsters*, so can't comment, but I think it is a compilation, while *C* and *The Return Of Leroy* were albums released as just by "Jimmy Castor", i.e. no "Bunch". The former contains a version of "I Can't Help Falling In Love With You" which became a miniscule hit (# 92) on the soul top singles chart in 1980 as well as a predictable "Godzilla"; he just couldn't break away from the monsters theme.

The Dream label album is not bad at all, with a good breezy reworking of "Leroy" although a new version of "It's Just Begun" doesn't come close to the power of the original. Side 2 has a good driving track in "(Tellin' On) The Devil" and a tuneful poppy song in "Hold On To Me". That was it for Jimmy Castor vinyl albums although he somewhat surprisingly got his name out there again by playing saxophone on Joyce Sims' version of "Love Makes A Woman" which did pretty well in 1988.

Jimmy died in 2012 and while he might not have made my favourite records of all-time he was funny, durable, talented, versatile and, by virtue of having made "It's Just Begun", a hero to the hip-hop crowd.

C.A.T.

C.A.T. 1977 Magna Glide MGS 323114 Producers: T.K.Murray, D Blair & J Durkin

This obscure album is mainly the work of one T.K. Murray who sings all the songs, and wrote and produced most of them. It did next to nothing on release but has become "in-demand" in recent years. Interestingly, the executive producers were Kasenetz and

Katz, kings of the sixties bubblegum pop sound. Luckily, the album sounds nothing whatsoever like the 1910 Fruitgum Company but it is also far from the "masterpiece" that someone somewhere always claims for rare records. In fact, I find it to be an undemanding and not particularly interesting platter. The background vocals are too prominent for my taste, the songs are not memorable and Murray does not have a distinctive voice. I am not sure what C.A.T. stands for, either.

Chairmen of The Board (see also General Johnson and Danny Woods)

General Johnson; Danny Woods; Harrison Kennedy; Eddie Custis; Ken Knox

Give Me Just A Little More Time 1970 Invictus ST 7300 Producer: HDH Productions (Billboard soul charts: 27 ; Billboard pop charts: 133)

In Session 1970 Invictus SVT 7304 Producers: William Weatherspoon, Greg Perry & Raynard Miner (Billboard soul charts: 16 ; Billboard pop charts: 117)

Bittersweet 1972 Invictus ST 9801 Producer: General Johnson and Greg Perry (Billboard pop charts: 178)

Greatest Hits 1972 Invictus SVT 1009 (UK)

Salute The General 1984 HDH LP 001(UK)

A.G.M. 1985 HDH LP 006 (UK)

Soul Agenda 1989 HDH LP 007 (UK)

In 1969 Holland-Dozier-Holland were searching for strong, experienced singers to create a new group, to be called Chairmen of the Board, one which would enable the famed producers and writers to continue the same level of success they had enjoyed at Motown, They found four, Norman "General" Johnson (a previous member of The Showmen), Danny Woods (who had released the odd unsuccessful single), as well as Eddie Custis and a Canadian, Harrison Kennedy. And for a while, at least, the plan clicked perfectly. "Give Me Just A Little More Time" hit #3 pop in early 1970 and, over the next twelve months or so, they had four more top 50 pop entries. And nearly every one of their singles was excellent - even the ones that didn't become big hits. It was the albums that didn't work so well.

Take the debut for example: everyone knows the title track, "You've Got Me Dangling On A String" and "Patches" (a Ron Dunbar and General Johnson song that became a huge smash for Clarence Carter). But I submit that there isn't too much else on there - apart from "I'll Come Crawling" - that is particularly strong. There were too many cover versions of songs I don't like at all: "My Way", "Didn't We", "Come Together" and "Feeling Alright" and I always have had a challenge with listening to too much HDH Invictus/Hot Wax material at one sitting. It too often lacks light and shade, being indisputably brilliantly and glossily produced, but it is nearly all the same tempo with slow songs never getting much of a look-in.

The same concerns hold true for *In Session*. I don't want to hear "Bridge Over Troubled Water" or "Twelfth Of Never" but I love "Everything Is Tuesday", "Chairman Of The Board" (a rare Kennedy lead vocal) and the Danny Woods-led "Pay To The Piper" - all released as singles, with the latter perhaps surprisingly becoming their second ever biggest pop hit at #13.

After the first two albums Eddie Custis left the group and, luckily, the "standards" went with him, as *Bittersweet* featured only songs by Greg Perry, Johnson and HDH. It was a much better album as a result, even if the lack of variety in tempo remained. "Men Are Getting Scarce" and "So Glad You're Mine" are strong LP only tracks and the singles remained superb: "Working On A Building Of Love", "I'm On My Way To A Better Place" particularly, but even the rather hokey "Elmo James" had charm.

The Chairmen had always been popular in England and it was therefore no particular surprise that a *Greatest Hits* package came out in the UK only which I rate as a magnificent pop-soul effort. All the favourites are on there and nearly every one of these songs are part of a soundtrack to any young soul fan's life - definitely including mine - who was growing up in Britain at the time. The three HDH compilations from the 1980s all feature material from the first three years of the group's existence.

As 1972 progressed it seemed as if HDH were growing bored with the group; a feeling that was given more prominence by the fact that Johnson, Woods and Kennedy all produced solo albums, none of which were particularly successful and in the case of the one from Kennedy, had not even a passing acquaintance with soul music. When the next Chairmen Of The Board album appeared it sounded significantly different from what had come before.

Skin I'm In 1974 Invictus 32526 Producer: Jeffrey Bowen (Billboard soul charts: 52)

Skin I'm In was described by *New Musical Express* at the time of release as sounding something like a funky version of Yes. They meant it as a compliment. In reality, it was Parliament musicians supporting Jeffrey Bowen's vision for C.O.B., with large chunks of it rendering the members of the group redundant (such as "Morning Glory" and "White Rose") and although I don't think it has aged notably well it did have two essential cuts: another excellent single in "Finders' Keepers", their last ever hit (#7 soul) with Woods again on lead and a very rare example of a C.O.B. ballad with Johnson delivering "Love At First Sight" in wonderful style.

However, soon after this the group fell apart although the breakup did allow Johnson to finally have some joy as a solo artist. (A single, "You've Got Extra Added Power In Your Love", came out under the C.O.B. name in 1976, as did another in 1978 on the ICA label, but neither featured anyone from the original group. And neither did well, either.)

Success 1980 Surfside SR 1001 Producer: General Johnson

A Gift Of Beach Music 1983 Surfside SR 1003 Producer: General Johnson

The Music 1987 Surfside SR 1007 Producer: General Johnson

They returned in 1980, or at least Johnson and Woods did, joined by Ken Knox. By the eighties a big revival music scene was prominent in the Carolinas, under the name of "Beach Music" and this audience took the newest version of the group to heir hearts as the strong tunes that characterised the best work of vintage C.O.B. were exactly the sort of things that appealed to them. The musicianship and production is not what it was during the glory years but the tunes remained strong and while it isn't the most challenging music ever recorded there is plenty to enjoy on these three albums even if my favourite song of theirs from the "Beach Music" period, the lovely, laid-back, "Gone Fishin'" doesn't appear.

Johnson died in 2010 but a new version of Chairmen Of The Board (which I don't believe includes Kennedy or Woods these days) are still out there performing to enthusiastic crowds.

Tony Chambers

Can't Let This Moment Go 1981 Mopres MP 1302
Produced by Dean Chambers

I know nothing about Tony Chambers. He released a couple of singles before this LP but I believe all three were local affairs, and I doubt if anything was pressed up in quantity. Chambers is hardly a tough soul singer and this is rather 'easy listening' stuff but does have a reasonably full sound. "Don't Wait Too Long" is catchy and would surely have caught on had it received enough radio play.

Champaign

Michael Day; Pauli Carman; Rena Jones; Leon Reeder; Rocky Maffit; Dana Walden

How 'Bout Us 1981 Columbia FC 37008 Producer: Leo Graham (Billboard soul charts: 14 ; Billboard pop charts: 53)

Modern Heart 1983 Columbia FC 38284 Producers: George Massenburg & Champaign (Billboard soul charts: 9 ; Billboard pop charts: 64)

Woman In Flames 1984 Columbia FC 39365 Producer: Champaign (Billboard soul charts: 45 ; Billboard pop charts: 184)

Champaign IV 1991 Malaco 7461 Producers: Michael Day & Rocky Maffit (Billboard soul charts: 72)

Champaign is a city in Illinois, about 130 miles south of Chicago and for a brief couple of moments in the early eighties - when "How 'Bout Us" (in early 1981) and "Try Again" (spring 1983) both reached the top thirty pop charts - it looked as if this group might single-handed revive that state's soul music fortunes but it wasn't really to be.

"How 'Bout Us" was a very pretty pop-soul record, entirely deserving of its success, delivered nicely by Carman and Jones, and is, as might be expected, the best thing on the debut album. "I'm On Fire" was a good follow-up single but inexplicably failed almost entirely to emulate the success of "How 'Bout Us". Many of the other tracks on the first album are dance songs, with unpromising titles such as "Party People", "Whiplash" and "Spinnin'" but all are just about worth a listen.

Modern Heart was more or less a straight pop record with very little soulful content. I quite like "Love Games" but the rest of the LP isn't to my taste at all.

Woman In Flames had a tad more of a soulful edge than *Modern Heart* but was still predominantly a black pop record and fared worse than the previous LPs.

Malaco was a surprising choice of a record label for Champaign to move to, given the label's roster of long established southern soul stars. However, the music continued to continue along the tuneful pop path that Champaign had mapped out and it sounds unlike other Malaco records. "Teardrops Fall" is a nice slow track but the album is still one likely to sit, unplayed, on a shelf of many who bought it.

Pauli Carmen went on to a brief solo career during which he released two pop styled LPs.

Gene Chandler

The Duke Of Earl 1962 Vee Jay 1040 Producer: Bill Sheppard (Billboard pop charts: 69)

Greatest Hits 1964 Constellation C-1421 Producer: Bill Sheppard

Just Be True 1964 Constellation C-1423 Producer: Bill Sheppard

Live On Stage 1965 Constellation C-1425 Producer: Bill Sheppard (Billboard soul charts: 5 ; Billboard pop charts: 124)

The Duke Of Soul 1967 Checker 3003 No producer listed

Duke of Earl 1968 Upfront UPF 105

Just Be True 1980 Charly CRB 1007 (UK)

Walk On With The Duke 1984 Solid Smoke SS 8027

Chicago's Gene Chandler (real name Eugene Dixon) tends not to feature on those lists of "best soul singer of all time" but he would be right near the top of my list of "best *uptown* soul singers ever". Chandler was not a deep soul man out of the southern soul tradition like Otis Redding, James Carr or Percy Sledge but had few peers when it came to interpreting songs of life in the big city and, at his best, could communicate brilliantly with the listener about the joys and despair that life bestows on us all.

His first records were released when he was a member of the Dukays vocal group who issued a number of good but not particularly successful songs before recording the huge #1 hit "Duke Of Earl". The record (and rights to issue it) came to the attention of Vee Jay records but the problem was that the Dukays were still contracted to Nat records. The solution was for it to be released as by Gene Chandler, a great break for him, but one which doubtless didn't make the rest of the Dukays deliriously happy. Most listeners of a certain age know the record well enough, but age has withered its charms for me, and I feel it was eclipsed by other tracks on the Vee Jay LP, such as "The Big Lie" and "Festival Of Love". The album is early soul, with strong doo-wop echoes, but was not as essential as what was to come later. (The LP was re-released in the UK in 1969 on Joy 136 as *A Gene Chandler Album* and then again in 1977 minus "Kissin' In The Kitchen" as *The Best Of* on Vee Jay International VJS 1198)

Chandler recorded for Constellation for a few years before they followed Vee Jay into bankruptcy but they were years in which he delivered some of his finest ever sides. The *Greatest Hits* LP was a little misleading, and optimistic, as only three of its twelve tracks had even reached the soul top fifty charts but it had some marvellous moments, particularly in the shape of some Curtis Mayfield compositions - "Think Nothing About It", "Man's Temptation" (#17 soul) and "Rainbow" (#11 soul) - appearing on a Chandler long player for the first time. The LP also duplicates a couple of tracks from the Vee Jay album as well as containing a couple of forgotten singles: a duet with (I think) Shirley Johnson on "Wish You Were Here" and "Soul Hootenanny" (really a version of "Big Boss Man".)

Just Be True was a strong album - more for its consistency than for a surfeit of brilliant tracks - but housed another Mayfield killer in the title track which became one of his biggest ever hits, #19 pop.

Live On Stage followed in 1965 (when re-released by UK's Charly records in 1986 it was retitled as *Live At The Regal*) and became the only Chandler album ever to hit the soul top ten. It is a particularly atmospheric 'live' album and boasted a fine band who were nicely showcased on "A Song Called Soul" but, as is often the case on stage, some songs were unnecessarily speeded up although it remains a good historical record of how popular he always was in Chicago.

The Duke Of Soul, despite appearing on the Checker label, was composed entirely of earlier Vee Jay and Constellation tracks and rather disappointingly did not include his big hits on the same label, "I Fooled You This Time" and "To Be A Lover".

The Upfront, Solid Smoke and UK Charly releases are all retrospective compilations that only contain Constellation and Vee Jay material.

The Girl Don't Care 1967 Brunswick BL 54124 Producer: Carl Davis

There Was A Time 1968 Brunswick BL 54131 Producers: Carl Davis & Gene Chandler

Two Sides Of 1969 Brunswick BL 54131 Producers: Carl Davis & Eugene Record

60's Soul Brother 1986 Kent 049 (UK)

Although *The Girl Don't Care* LP came out on Brunswick it also contains predominantly Constellation material. If all you know of Gene Chandler is "Duke Of Earl", "Groovy Situation" or "Get Down" I beg you to listen to this utterly magnificent album, which is, side one particularly, his masterpiece and a brilliant showcase of vibrant Chicago music. "Nothing Can Stop Me" (#3 soul) and the ineffable "Good Times" (#40 soul) are wonderful evocations of being young, happy and carefree, with the latter's narrative specificities making it one of Mayfield's and, indeed, soul music's, greatest ever songs. As evidence of Chandler's ability to cover a wide emotional range we also get "You Can't Hurt Me No More" (#40 soul) a splendid piece of defiance wrapped up in a truly winning Sonny Sanders arrangement, the exquisite pain of the title track (#16 soul) and the masterly "Here Come The Tears". And then there is also "Fool For You", "Bet You Never Thought" and "To Choose", all much better than average. The LP didn't chart but that is mainly a result of Brunswick's indifference to the album market at the time.

The Girl Don't Care, for all its excellence, wasn't really a "true" LP, recorded specifically as an LP, but more of a collection of singles that had been released over a two year period; *There Was A Time* was much more of an album recorded as an album, if you catch the difference. And it was not as good. The main and simple reason for this is that it did not contain any Curtis Mayfield songs. It did harbour six of Chandler's own compositions, and he was a fair writer, as "Those Were The Good Old Days" and "Pit Of Loneliness" prove, but it also contained a handful of covers that were not particularly memorable, with one exception: "There Was A Time" was an inspired choice of song for him to attempt, even if it sounded unlike anything else he ever recorded, and it did reasonably well when released on 45 at #22 soul.

The final Brunswick LP, *The Two Sides Of*, was mediocre and it sounded as if Brunswick couldn't really be bothered with him any longer. "This Guy's In Love With You", "Eleanor Rigby, "This Bitter Earth" and "Honey" were unimaginative and dismaying covers and the album yielded no hit singles at all. The best two tracks were the ones written by Chandler with Kenny Lewis: "Familiar Footsteps and "Suicide".

The Kent album is a fine Brunswick / Constellation compilation, containing many of his finest sides as well as a handful of superb tracks which do not appear on his albums (such as the stupendous "Tell Me What Can I Do"), and a beauty of an unreleased track in "My Baby's Gone".

The Gene Chandler Situation 1970 Mercury SR 61304 Producer: Gene Chandler (Billboard soul charts: 35 ; Billboard pop charts: 178)

One & One (and Jerry Butler) 1971 Mercury SR 61330 Producers: Jerry Butler & Gene Chandler (Billboard pop charts: 143)

Chandler did not let Brunswick's nonchalance stifle his creativity as he started managing and producing acts, firstly on the Bamboo label, on which he turned out two big hits for Mel and Tim, "Backfield In Motion" and "Good Guys Only Win In The Movies", and secondly on his own Mister Chand label which did not yield anything like the same level of success.

He returned to releasing records under his own name and enjoyed the second biggest hit of his career when "Groovy Situation" went to #8 on the soul charts and #12 on the pop charts in the summer of 1970. The album built around the hit, *The Gene Chandler Situation*, was ok (side one, particularly, I don't care for the MOR approach on side two at all) and a step up from the final Brunswick album but was not a patch on his sixties work.

He placed six singles in the soul top 50 while he was with Mercury so it was not a disaster by any means, unlike his subsequent short stay on Curtom where he more or less completely vanished from any public awareness. This was a dark time in his life and one reason he recorded so little between 1973 and 1978 was his arrest and brief incarceration for selling heroin.

Get Down 1978 Chi-Sound T-578 Producer: Carl Davis (Billboard soul charts: 12 ; Billboard pop charts: 47)

When You're #1 1979 20th Century T-598 Producer: Carl Davis 1981 (Billboard soul charts: 50 ; Billboard pop charts: 153)

'80 1980 20th Century T-605 Producers: Carl Davis & Gene Chandler (Billboard soul charts: 11; Billboard pop charts: 87)

Here's To Love 1981 20th Century T-629 Producer: Gene Chandler

Given his difficulties, it was great to see him back with a big hit with "Get Down" even if the single was pretty much your standard boogie tune. The album on which it was contained holds considerably better cuts, however, not least of which is the intriguing "I'm The Travelling Kind". When I first heard this, I assumed it was some sort of decades old folk tune, passed down across the ages. But no: it is an original co-written by Chandler with long-time writing partner James Thompson. It is an extraordinary song and performance, clearly deeply personal, and unlike anything else he ever recorded. "Tomorrow I May Not Feel The Same", "Greatest Love Ever Known", "Please Sunrise", "Give Me The Cue" and a really good re-make of "What Now" are also fine tracks - and anyone, like me - who originally passed on the album because of a lack of enthusiasm for the title track should hunt it down.

It was therefore with a fair degree of disappointment when I first encountered the *When You're #1* album given it was grossly inferior to *Get Down*, relying on a mixture of long and uninspired dance tracks and a handful of ballads, all of which were considerably softer than in his heyday, given that horns were pretty much entirely absent and strings were to the forefront. One for completists only.

However, he was to bounce back with a much better set, a very good one, in fact, with *Gene Chandler....80*. "Does She Have A Friend" (#28 soul, his last visit to the top 30) and "All About The Paper" were better songs than he had been receiving for a while, "Rainbow '80" was an inspired update with a terrific arrangement, "I'll Be There" was a nice duet with former Lovelite, Joni Berlmon, and the words "dance" and "disco" do not feature in any song title on the LP.

Sadly, though, *Here's To Love* was another let-down with the paucity of good material shown up by the fact that a re-make of "God Bless Our Love" was the best song on show. Even Sam Dees' "For The Sake Of The Memories" wasn't his best.

Chi - Sound, after promising beginnings, was in trouble by late 1983 and Chandler's last good single for the company, "I'll Make The Living", was not supported by a new LP. In 1984 the label was closed down and Gene was once again looking for a new outlet for his music.

Your Love Looks Good On Me 1985 Fast Fire FFL 7000 Producers: Gene Chandler, Archie Russell & Donald Burnside

He found it on the small independent, Fast Fire, but the one collection they issued was patchy. By which I mean it contained, in two long dance cuts, "Be Mine For Tonight" and "Something's Got My Body", among the worst sixteen minutes of music Chandler had ever committed to wax, a title track that sounded about eight years out of date, but also the best thing he had cut for years in an excellent slow duet with Shawn Christopher "Haven't I Heard That Line Before?". When released as a single it was the 35th time Chandler had placed a record on the soul singles chart and "Lucy", a Lionel Richie song, became his 36th, and last.

There's no doubt in my mind that Gene Chandler is one of the most successful and finest soul singers ever to come out of Chicago, one of the crucial cities in the history of the music. His work from 1970 onwards certainly needs to be approached with care but for a golden six years or so in the sixties he recorded some of the greatest music it has ever been my privilege to hear.

Change

James Robinson; Toby Johnson; Mike Campbell; Timmy Allen; Vince Henry; Jeff Bova; Rick Brennan; Debra Cooper; Rick Gallwey

The Glow Of Love 1980 RFC 3438 Producer: Jacques Fred Petrus (Billboard soul charts: 10 ; Billboard pop: 29)

Miracles 1981 Atlantic SD 19301 Producers: Jacques Fred Petrus & Mauro Malavasi (Billboard soul charts: 9 ; Billboard pop charts: 46)

Sharing Your Love 1982 Atlantic SD 19342 Producers: Jacques Fred Petrus & Mauro Malavasi (Billboard soul charts: 14 ; Billboard pop charts: 66)

This Is Your Time 1983 Atlantic 80053-1 Producers: Jacques Fred Petrus & Mauro Malavasi (Billboard soul charts: 34 ; Billboard pop charts: 161)

Change Of Heart 1984 Atlantic 80151-1 Producers: Jimmy Jam, Terry Lewis & Timmy Allen (Billboard soul charts: 15 ; Billboard pop charts: 102)

Turn On Your Radio 1985 Atlantic 81243-1 Producers: Jacques Fred Petrus & Timmy Allen (Billboard soul charts: 64 ; Billboard pop charts: 208)

If The BB & Q Band are included in the book, then the same has to go for Change, another group who mixed Italian song writers, musicians and producers with American singers and musicians.

At first they weren't a group as such, more of a studio ensemble, and the first album includes vocals by Luther Vandross and Jocelyn Brown, but I'm not sure that they can be accounted as members of Change, who didn't really take shape until the third LP, when the names of the group appeared on an album sleeve for the first time. Despite whatever or whoever they were, the first album was a massive success, spawning three top fifty soul singles with one, "A Lover's Holiday", reaching #5. I find the LP to be way too shiny sounding and soulless for my own tastes, although "Searching" does have a good melody and was the type of song that Vandross would place on his own albums over the next few years.

Miracles did well too, housing a #7 soul hit in "Paradise" and an impressive title track, sung with power by James Robinson, the first song of theirs I liked unconditionally. "Heaven Of My Life" sounds like what Chic were producing at the time, driven by a notable bass line. They also finally got around to recording a ballad, "Stop For Love" a schmaltzy thing with good Robinson vocals.

The sound changed on *Sharing Your Love* which was, unlike the first two LPs, recorded only in New York. Apparently "Take You To Heaven" features ex-Volt recording artist Roz Ryan on vocals. and I liked the Robinson-led "You're My Girl", their best ballad yet.

This Is Your Time had a reasonably good selling title track as a 45 (#33 soul), with a chorus almost identical to Chic's "Good Times" but the follow-up, the ok "Don't Wait Another Night" sold poorly as a single. The sound was by now very generic eighties dance music.

"Change Of Heart" was another big soul single hit for the group, reaching #7 in the first half of 1984 and a well received LP was built around it with production now coming from the hot team of Jam and Lewis. *Turn On Your Radio* saw a return to recording in Italy but the album did not sell well and Change were soon no more.

Change Of Pace

Greg Jackson; Luis Farinas; Tony Matthews; Doug Green

Bring My Buddies Back 1972 Stone Lady SL-1001 Producers: David Sheffield, Chesley Holmes & Art Wilson

Another odd LP. Tiny Stone Lady records out of East Orange (who only seemed to last for a year or so) spared no expense in the production of the album cover, which was a gatefold, with photos of the group and the lyrics of all the cuts proudly printed. But it seems as if so much effort went into the cover that little energy was left for the songs, as this seven tracker comes in at only 25 minutes. Alas, the grandiose plans did not come to fruition: the album did not do well, nor did it contain any hit singles (two were issued from it.)

No matter, though, for some of the album is lovely. The title track is an answer record to Freda Payne's "Bring The Boys Home" and is a worthy and moving addition to the many excellent records written about the Vietnam war. "Our Fore Fathers" is probably the stand-out cut, with some beautiful harmonising on a strong song. When they go uptempo (such as "People" and "Blood's Much Thicker Than Water") things get less interesting but the LP ends on a good note with "Hello Darling" and its doo-wop roots.

Chanson (see also David Williams)

David Williams; James Jamerson Jnr.

Chanson 1978 Ariola America SW-1-50039 Producers: David Williams & James Jamerson Jnr. (Billboard soul charts: 23 ; Billboard pop charts: 41)

Together We Stand 1979 Ariola America SW-1-50065 Producers: David Williams & James Jamerson Jnr.

James Jamerson Snr., was one of the greatest bassists in the history of popular music, even if this fact has only really been generally recognised over the last 25 years or so. What remains less well-known is the fact that he had a son, also a bass player, who put out two LPs as a member of the duo, Chanson.

"Don't Hold Back" sold strongly in the autumn of 1978, managing to reach #8 soul and #21 pop, and it was certainly right in the dance groove of what people wanted that year. Accordingly, the debut album on which it is to be found featured other long uptempo work-outs and nearly forty years on they lack much in the way of distinction. But the duo did have something going for them, apart from their obvious proficiency on their respective instruments (Williams was a guitarist), and that was the ability to sing. I believe it may have been Jamerson who employs a high tenor on occasion, but whoever it was helps to raise one's listening pleasure and using Linda Evans on "I Can Tell" was a good idea, too, even if it only managed to scrape along at #72 soul as a follow-up to the big hit.

The second LP, like the first, had an uninspired cover and expectations weren't raised by seeing a song entitled "Rock Don't Stop" on the track listing. (Someone really should have copyrighted that title, they would have made a fortune.) It's a pretty unappetising album in my view, consisting of six lyrically uninspired dance tracks that skirt closer to out and out disco than anything on the debut, It also dispenses with any compelling singing.

The duo split up after this but both men went on to considerable success as session musicians, with Williams playing on "Billie Jean", no less.

Chapparrals

Jay Nation; Sandy Allen; Horace Henry; Leroy Dunlap; Robert Rawles; Andrew Stephens; Timothy Steed; Cecil Sparks; Larry Powell

Shake Your Head 1978 Maximillion MR 1000 Producers: Morris Ogletree & The Chapparrals

This one is a rare but excellent LP out of Atlanta from a nine piece funk band who had what it took to have been much bigger than they were. They sounded as accomplished as many other groups of the same era who maybe had better management, larger record labels or just more luck. The album mixed up excellent funk like the title track and "Hittin' it" which were heavy on synths and horns (bass player Allen deserves a special mention) and good ballads like "Country Girl" and "My Lady".

Chapter 8

Derek Dirckson; Michael Powell; Allan Nance; Courtlen Hale; Anita Baker; Gerald Lyles; Scott Guthrie; David Washington; Van Cephus; Valerie Pinkston; Vernon Fails;

Chapter 8 1979 Ariola SW-50056 Producers: Derek Dirckson & Michael Powell (Billboard soul charts: 70)

This Love's For Real 1985 Beverly Glen BG 10007 Producer: Michael Powell

Forever 1988 Capitol C1-46947 Producer: Michael Powell (Billboard soul charts: 54)

Chapter 8 didn't have a great deal of commercial success, but did have a degree of fame for the simple reason that Anita Baker was a member of the group for a while before she left and went onto solo stardom. The first album, and the only one on which Baker features, is not bad of its type and has a good duet between her and co-lead vocalist Gerald Lyles in "Ready For Your Love", a fair hit at #38 on the soul charts. But it also has tracks entitled "I Go Disco", "Come On And Dance With Me" and "Come And Boogie", nonel of which tax the mind. Most of the other cuts are mid-tempo in construction but ultimately the LP can't escape the fact that the material is simply not strong enough, and, in the case of the opening track, "Don't You Like It" which sounds a lot like The Emotions' "Best Of My Love", is also derivative.

The Beverly Glen album from 1985 deserves credit for staking out a claim for the "lush and classy" market and avoiding the horribly mechanical and sterile sound of all too much eighties music but it failed to sell in appreciable volume. Valerie Pinkston was an able replacement for Baker and the songs were better this time, even though I will contend they were still much too long. My favourite cut is "How Can I Get Next To You", which sounds a little like a George Jackson song of the same name. Whether one will like, love or be indifferent to this LP depends, I suspect, on what one thinks about this type of "penthouse" soul music which is undoubtedly tasteful, well performed and produced.

The final album carried on the sound of *This Love's For Real* and the standout was a particularly strong Pinkston vocal on "Give Me A Chance", which was beautifully arranged by Paul Riser and is possibly the best thing they ever did (and certainly their biggest ever hit on the soul charts at #20), but "So In Love" and "Long Time To Love" are not to be sneezed at either.

Ray Charles

No artist has caused me as much anguish as Ray Charles. One part of me says that not to include him in a book on soul artists that covers a range from The Hues Corporation to Cameo is almost certainly a grievous error. The other part insists on saying that he wasn't really a "soul" singer at all given that such a high percentage of his records are clearly jazz, country or pop based. I also suspect he would have resented being "pigeon-holed" as well. After much thought I have decided to compromise and treat him differently from every other singer or group in the book as I recognise that his importance and influence within "black" music make him impossible to leave out but I have no appetite to cover all of his albums, not least the sixty or seventy compilations alone, particularly as so many of them have a tenuous connection with soul music. The endless Gershwin songs, the overblown arrangements; the heart sinks. I will therefore just concentrate on a handful of his albums which I think - even more subjectively than normal - easily fall in scope.

I should also declare a long-held view here: I think there tends to be an "Emperor's New Clothes" aspect to his output and the "genius" tag has been unthinkingly applied to his music too often. I wouldn't dream of trying to deny his talent, utterly distinctive and "black" voice, and unquestionable influence on any number of other singers but don't see why it should be *verboten* to point out that he made a large number of safe and uninteresting records.

Crying Time 1966 ABC S-544 Producer: Joe Adams (Billboard soul charts: 1 ; Billboard pop charts: 15)

A Portrait Of Ray 1968 ABC S-625 Producer: Joe Adams (Billboard soul charts: 5 ; Billboard pop charts: 51)

Doing His Thing 1969 ABC S-695 Producer: Joe Adams (Billboard soul charts: 34 ; Billboard pop charts: 172)

Love Country Style 1969 ABC S-707 Producer: Joe Adams (Billboard soul charts: 34 ; Billboard pop charts: 192)

Through The Eyes Of Love 1972 ABC X-765 Producer: Ray Charles (Billboard soul charts: 43 ; Billboard pop charts: 186)

By the time *Billboard* started printing a separate "R&B" album chart, January 30th 1965, Ray Charles had already posted thirteen LPs in the pop Top 20, including such huge sellers as *Modern Sounds In Country and Western Music* (both *Volume 1* and *2*) and *Ingredients In A Recipe For Soul.*

After the above date Charles only ever hit the pop Top 20 once again - with *Crying Time* - and such a significant falling off in popularity says, I think, a fair bit about how Charles' greatest days as an artists were already behind him as the soul era kicked in. That being said, *Crying Time* contains some superb tracks, unmistakably soulful and rewarding: "Let's Go Get Stoned" (#1 soul, #31 pop as a single), "No Use Crying", "You're Just About To Lose Your Clown" and "Peace Of Mind". In fact, it's a most worthwhile set and pretty much every track is worth hearing.

A Portrait Of Ray was only slightly less gratifying with "Never Say Naw", "Understanding" (a #13 soul 45), "Eleanor Rigby" (a Beatles' cover I DO like), "Sweet Young Thing Like You" and "I Won't Leave" leading the charge of enjoyable tracks, nearly all featuring The Raelets in top form. (The UK issue of the LP on Stateside 10269 has a slightly different track listing.)

My favourite Ray Charles album is undoubtedly *Doin' His Thing*, and that is because it is as much Jimmy Lewis' thing as Ray's; Lewis wrote or co-wrote all ten tracks and provided joint vocals to "If It Wasn't For Bad Luck" (a #21 soul and #77 pop single). I won't call out any more cuts as I think they are all great and this LP is Charles finest ever soul offering in my opinion. If only all his work sounded like this.

Lewis also provides "If You Were Mine", the excellent lead-off song on *Love Country Style*, which also includes such other winners as "Your Love Is So Doggone Good" and its imaginative quasi-classical arrangement, "Ring Of Fire", "Sweet Memories" (despite the backing vocals), "Show Me The Sunshine" and "Don't Change On Me". It's a set characterised by the strength of the largely contemporary songs (no Gershwin, Berlin or Hammerstein on here) and Charles' singing.

Charles last ABC album, *Through The Eyes Of Love*, sported a dreadful cover but also some of his best stuff from the seventies in a singular take on "Rainy Night In Georgia", "My First Night Alone Without You" and the wonderful "I Can Make It Thru The Days (But Oh Those Lonely Nights)" (a #21 soul single).

Renaissance 1975 Crossover CR 9005 Producer: Ray Charles (Billboard soul charts: 34 ; Billboard pop charts: 175)

True To Life 1977 Atlantic SD 19142 Producer: Ray Charles (Billboard soul charts: 23 ; Billboard pop charts: 78)

Love And Peace 1978 Atlantic SD 19199 Producer: Ray Charles (Billboard soul charts: 35)

Charles started cutting for his own CrossOver label in 1973 but his first album, *Come Live With Me*, was disappointing, other than another Jimmy Lewis song, "Where Was He". Better was *Renaissance* with its fantastic, sweaty version of "Living For The City"(#22 soul), even better than Stevie Wonder's original, and a highly enjoyable take on "We're Gonna Make It". I'm not mad on side two, apart from "Sail Away" but it's still his best LP for a while.

I find his 1977 Atlantic LP to be uneven - "Let It Be " and "Oh What A Beautiful Morning" are not much fun - but I love his subtle take on "The Jealous Kind" and the greasy "Game Number Nine", while "Anonymous Love" and " I Can See Clearly Now" (a #35 soul single) are both deftly rendered.

Lewis provided two more typically smart songs for the excellent *Love And Peace* LP, "Take Off That Dress" and "Give The Poor Man A Break" but it wasn't a two-track album as "Ridin' Thumb", "Is There Anyone Out There?" and "We Had It All" are also first-rate and only "20th Century Fox" sounds a little below Charles' dignity. The uncredited musicians on here also deserved to have been called out.

Since 1978 Ray Charles released many more albums, enjoyed a credit on a Quincy Jones' #1 soul hit from 1989 and garnered no end of further awards and acclaim. His longevity in the music industry alone was a wonder before he passed away in 2004. Despite showing my hand in declaring that he was never one of my favourite singers it is abundantly clear that he was one of the most important artists of the 20th century, and with eleven #1 r'n'b or soul singles to his name, one of the most successful too.

Sonny Charles (see also The Checkmates Ltd)

The Sun Still Shines 1982 Highrise HR 102 Producer: Bobby Paris (Billboard soul charts: 14 ; Billboard pop charts: 136)

Not many people would have bet that Sonny Charles (Charles Hemphill from Indiana) would come back with a big hit single in 1982, nearly twenty years after he first appeared on vinyl, and more than a decade after the appreciable success of "Black Pearl" when he was lead singer of The Checkmates Ltd. But that is exactly what happened with "Put It In A Magazine", a most appealing and tuneful song that hit #2 on the soul charts, and the standout on what is a worthwhile album, containing a second particularly good track in "Weekend Father Song", not a subject that crops up very often on soul albums. Paris also manages to get Charles to cover his old "Northern Soul" favourite, "Per-so-nal-ly".

Charles made no more solo records after the Highrise stay, but has remained in the music industry, most recently as a member of The Steve Miller Band.

Charnissa

Charnissa 1978 Zeus S1009 Producer: Bud Reneau

Charnissa 1979 Robox EQAD 7919 Producer: Bud Reneau

They will not win any awards for inspired album titles but the first of these two highly obscure records by Charnissa Jones is worth tracking down as it was among the last country-soul LPs to have been made. Her first vinyl outing appears to be when she sang back-up for Aretha Franklin on the 1968 *Live In Paris* set and she was also, I think, briefly a Raelet before making her first ever album, which I absolutely love.

It is not going to be to every soul fan's taste, that is for sure, as it also has strong pop echoes, and is largely the work of Bud Reneau, a man who has written songs for the likes of Waylon Jennings, John Denver and Dr. Hook (as well as Gladys Knight, I should add) but he can write fantastic hooks as well as having a strong sense of melody. "I've Been There Before","We're Not Gonna Make It" and "Ease Me To The Ground" are all excellent Reneau songs, but if one is not convinced, then maybe try the Phillip Mitchell penned " When Can We Do This Again" or a great re-make of a George Soule part-penned song also covered so well by Arthur Alexander, "She'll Throw Stones At You".

Unfortunately the second set is almost completely bereft of any soulful content and is a pretty mediocre pop album with much inferior songs, which is a bit puzzling given Reneau once again wrote nearly everything on show. The inadequacy of the album is best summed up by Charnissa's take on "All I Need Is Time" which is so markedly inferior to Gladys Knight's version as to be almost embarrassing. I do not recommend this one at all. In 1984 she recorded two more excellent Mitchell songs on a single on the CRP label but made no more records thereafter.

It should be noted that Charnissa also sang on a disco LP in 1979 by a group called Frisky, which isn't covered in the book.

Oliver Cheatham (see also Round Trip)

The Boss 1982 MCA 5325 Producers: ADK & Oliver Cheatham

Saturday Night 1983 Producer: ADK (Billboard soul charts: 52)

Go For It 1987 Champion 1006 Producer: Rob Davis (UK)

Oliver Cheatham was both a stalwart of the Detroit recording scene and a most accomplished singer with an extraordinary range. He featured as lead singer in five Michigan based groups, including Gaslight, The Young Sirs and Round Trip, all of whom made terrific records despite attaining no hits. (He was also a member of Sins Of Satan, but I do not believe he was with them for either of their two albums.)

For his first LP, he was merely called "Oliver" but there was no mistaking the voice. It's well worth hearing/owning for his virtuosity, particularly on cuts such as "I Gave Myself To You" and "I Want Your Love, I Need Your Love" where he duets with Vee Allen. The music is typically what one expects from the Al Hudson/Dave Roberson/Kevin McCord stable and the songs are often not especially memorable but it is all solid enough.

The follow-up LP, *Saturday Night,* did contain a song of enduring worth in the title track which did even better in England than in his homeland and doubtless contributed to his deciding to live in the UK in later years. It remains a dance record of crisp power, thirty years on. As before one can only admire his vocal range and it could easily be (but isn't) two different singers on "Do Me Right" and "Never Gonna Give You Up".

His last album was recorded in London with Rob Davis (ex-Mud) producing and Peter Waterman helping out and one shouldn't be snobbish about such associations for it was often as good as what had gone before and, indeed, "Wish On A Star" is a much better song than nearly everything on the MCA LPs. On the other hand, the title track and "S.O.S" are definitely not, even if the latter did reach #35 on the soul charts.

Cheatham died in 2013 after having helped out Jocelyn Brown on a couple of her albums in the nineties and releasing a new CD of his own in 1995 and a second one in 2002.

Checkmates Ltd (see also Sonny Charles)

Sonny Charles; Bobby Stevens; Harvey Trees; Bill Van Buskirk; Marvin Smith; Joe Romano; Paul Maturkanic; Mario Panvani; Regina Warfield; Chip Steen; Clint Mosley; Lou Gonzales; Gene Wing

Live At Harvey's 1965 Ikon IER S 121/122 No producer listed

Live! At Caesars Palace 1968 Capitol ST- 2840 Producer: Kelly Gordon (Billboard soul charts: 36)

Love Is All We Have To Give 1969 A & M SP-4183 Producer: Phil Spector (Billboard pop charts: 178)

Life 1971 Rustic RR-2001 Producer: Bobby Stevens

F/S/O 1974 Rustic RR-2004 Producer: Sonny Charles

We Got The Moves 1977 Fantasy F-9541 Producer: Richie Rome

The Checkmates Ltd (or Checkmates Inc. as they were called on the first album) were originally a mixed race quintet from Indiana who did not conform to the standard soul group format, and were a most eclectic bunch, appealing as much to pop as to soul audiences, and are possibly a rather acquired taste; certainly I have never met anybody who classes them as a favourite group. This is to do them a disservice as their records - although indubitably uneven - could be very good.

I must confess to never having heard either of the live albums but the track listings do not look compelling and I imagine them to be fairly standard cabaret type offerings. My first experience, therefore, of the group was with the third LP, which was produced, most surprisingly, as he wasn't doing much work at the time, by

Phil Spector in his usual towering and dynamic style. That style could be considered heroic or bombastic, depending on taste, but it certainly sustains my interest through side one, and "Black Pearl" is just a lovely song, becoming a big hit in the summer of 1969 at #8 soul and #13 pop. Side two, on the other hand, is not for me, consisting of a suite of material from the musical "Hair". (All three albums were subsequently re-released on Rustic. the Checkmates own label.)

The reason for the creation of Rustic was the dissatisfaction of the group with the lack of payment from previous record companies. But owning a label also permitted a degree of artistic licence, and the early seventies were a time when doing one's own thing was more accepted anyway and *Life* was an example of that approach. Each track is preceded by a poem, and it reeks of the early seventies, but is as much a pop/rock LP as a soul one and is not to my taste at all. Songs like "I Am I Said", "Sweet Caroline" and "God, Love And Rock & Roll" would surely suggest a degree of caution is needed. (It was later reissued as *Sould Out* on the Gucci label G301.)

Similarly, as regards artistic freedom, the *F/S/O* album - despite the silly name, which stood for "Furnishing The Services Of" - is very diverse and very interesting, Ranging from the latin groove of "Got To See "U" Soon", through the meandering river of "I Must Be Dreaming", to the driving and funky "Run Nigger Run", it is a lost gem, that's for sure, as it did next to nothing in the marketplace. The album cover listed a number of musicians as a part of The Checkmates Ltd beyond the original quintet.

A couple of singles filtered out in the mid-seventies (one, the excellent "All Alone By The Telephone", scratched the soul charts at #96) and by the time *We Got The Moves* came along, a much more traditional soul record, the group was credited as down to just three, Charles, Smith and Stevens. Apparently, however, the LP, essentially a Charles solo set, came out without his knowledge. Regardless of the origins of the record, I like it a lot, and it was a strong album to end out the career of one of the most singular soul groups of all time.

Chee Chee & Peppy

Chee Chee & Peppy 1972 Buddah BDS-5116 Producer: Jesse James

Super You 1981 Branding Iron BI-333 Producer: Jesse James

Keith Boiling and Dorothy Moore (not the solo singer) from Pennsylvania were Chee Chee and Peppy respectively and the duo scored two soul hits in 1971, one of which, "I Know I'm In Love", was pretty big reaching #12 soul and #49 pop. On the back of these successes an album came out on Buddah. I'm not really in a position to comment on it, as the two were young teenagers at the time, and while they had an undoubted appeal to other young teenagers I find it all too twee to listen to.

They returned in 1983 with a second set, but it had severely limited distribution and barely escaped outside Philadelphia. The only track I have heard, a dance side called "Super You", did not sound exciting.

Cheyenne's Comin'

Cheyenne Fowler; Danny Jacob; Steve Schindler; Dave Amper; Larry Aguerro; Bruce Fowler; Clarence Bell; Bill McCrary; Kim Joey Jo

Cheyenne's Comin' 1976 Shadybrook SB33 - 002 Producer: Gene Russell

Cheyenne Fowler, a native American, was the leader of this band who produced this one LP back in 1976. It's all rather polite; gently funky from time to time with more of a jazzy slant at others. I do like the slow and fairly soulful "I Love You But I Gotta Go" and "Dream Street" gets up a nice groove in a manner vaguely reminiscent of Tower of Power but it isn't hard to see why the set didn't sell strongly.

Chicago Gangsters (see also Ivy & Rumple-Stilts-Skin)

Leroy McCants; Chris McCants; James McCants; Sam McCants; Anthony Amos; Dave Yuhasz; Ralph Flemm; Sammy Bryant; Scooter Evans; Paul Ware

Blind Over You 1975 Gold Plate GP 1011 Producers: Mac & Mac

Gangster Love 1976 Gold Plate GP 1012 Producers: Mac & Mac

Life Is Not Easy Without You 1979 Heat HTH-002 Producer: The Gangsters

Gangsters 1982 Montage ST-72005 Producers: Mac & Mac

An oddly ignored group, in as much as they do not appear to have ever been represented on CD, nor had any articles written about them. Their fame, such as it is, would appear to be largely based on the popularity of their "Gangster Boogie" track as a source of sampling. Although their early albums were recorded in Chicago, the group hailed from Ohio and were originally known as The Harmonics. Under the new name they were built around four McCants brothers, and generally adopted a nice balance between funk and sweet ballads.

The first side of the debut album contains their first two soul charting singles: a long, sultry version of Willie Hutch's "I Choose You" (#74) and the winning "Blind Over You" ballad (#67), but side two has some discordant moments such as "Why Did You Do It" where music and vocals don't appear to be quite in sync.

The most sought-after of their LPs is *Gangster Love* which houses good ballads in "I'm At Your Mercy" and "On The Way" as well as a so-so rendering of "Feel Like Making Love". On the tougher side of things, "Michigan Avenue" sounds as if it should have been the title track for a "Blaxploitation" film, while "Music For The People" just about trickled into the soul charts at #97.

I'd always felt that the band's name was a little awkward and they possibly came to the same conclusion as the "Chicago" was in much smaller letters on the third album and dispensed with entirely by the Montage release. *Life Is Not Easy* is a good enough album, thanks to the excellent title track (albeit sounding somewhat similar to EWAF's "That's The Way Of The World"), possibly their best ever ballad in "I Feel You When You're Gone" (a reasonably large soul hit at #36) and the funky "Wop That Wandy" (#77), a title that has completely bemused me for nearly forty years.

The *Gangsters* album adopts a minimalist stance on the dance tracks - which predominate - stripping them back to basics, but unfortunately, they lack interest as a result, but all is not lost as "Precious" and "I Just Can't Go On" are slow tracks of distinction.

They released no more records as the Gangsters, but two of the brothers, Chris and Sam, went on to form two new bands, firstly Rumple-Stilts-Skin and then Ivy.

Chi-Lites (see also Eugene Record & Danny Johnson)

Eugene Record; Robert Lester; Creadel Jones; Marshall Thompson; David Roberson; Willie Kensey; T.C. Anderson; David Scott; Danny Johnson; Vandy Hampton; Anthony Watson; Aaron Floyd

Chi-Lites / Romanceers 1971 Pickwick SPC - 3319 No producer listed

One of the finest groups - and not just soul groups - of all time, the Chi-Lites are also one of the most under appreciated in the annals of opinion and comment on popular music, doubtless because their strengths - of which there were many - fall outside received wisdom as to what constitutes a great act. In Eugene Record they had a singer and writer of immense skill and the group's harmonic flourishes were often truly beautiful. Only The Impressions and The Dells have an equally strong claim to be the best group to ever come out of Chicago.

In the beginning they - Record, Lester, Thompson and Jones, the four mainstays of the group - were the Hi-Lites, releasing just two singles before adding the "C" to their name. Their first records under their new name appeared on the Blue Rock label where they issued three singles. All six of these sides are included on the *Chi-Lites And Romanceers* LP, issued to capitalise on the group's success in the late sixties and early seventies. It is fascinating to listen to a side like "I'm So Jealous" which is an unashamed Impressions rip-off and compare it to "Never No More" which has a number of the elements already in place that were to make the group so successful for a period of five or six years.

Give It Away 1969 Brunswick BL 754152 Producers: Carl Davis & Eugene Record (Billboard soul charts: 16; Billboard pop charts: 180)

I Like Your Lovin' (Do You Like Mine) 1970 Brunswick BL 754165 Producer: Eugene Record

(For God's Sake) Give More Power To The People 1971 Brunswick BL 754170 Producer: Eugene Record (Billboard soul charts: 3 ; Billboard pop charts: 12)

A Lonely Man 1972 Brunswick BL 754170 Producer: Eugene Record (Billboard soul charts: 1 ; Billboard pop charts: 5)

Greatest Hits 1972 Brunswick BL 754184 (Billboard soul charts: 4 ; Billboard pop charts: 55)

A Letter To Myself 1973 Brunswick BL 754188 (Billboard soul charts: 4 ; Billboard pop charts: 50)

Chi-Lites 1973 Brunswick BL 754197 (Billboard soul charts: 3 ; Billboard pop charts: 89)

The first "proper" Chi-Lites LP, *Give It Away*, appeared on Brunswick in 1969 and consisted of seven Record compositions and four rather mundane covers (apart from "I'm Gonna Make You Love Me", a song that suited them well). "Let Me Be The Man My Daddy Was" and the title track were both pretty big soul hits for the group and are the highlights of the album. The former was a perfect example of Record's lovely voice and his willingness to compose songs that were somewhat left-field in subject matter, while the latter mined the midtempo seam that was to prove so successful for them. "24 Hours Of Sadness", despite its similarity to the title track, still retained enough charm of its own to also hit the soul charts, although more modestly.

Unfortunately, Brunswick were soon up to their old tricks of recycling material as the *I Like Your Lovin* set duplicated a dismaying seven tracks from *Give It Away* with only three new songs to tempt buyers. Two of them were successful singles on the soul charts - "Are You My Woman" (#8) and the title track (#11) but they were heavily influenced by Norman Whitfield (as was the third new track "Troubles A Comin'") and while all have merit, they lack the distinctiveness of premium Chi-Lites' music. Not surprisingly, the LP was a poor seller but it didn't really matter as the group were about to become massively popular.

The first sign that the group were moving up to another level came with the title song from the third Brunswick LP and "(For God's Sake) Give More Power To The People" with its inspired siren intro and traded vocals in the manner of Sly and The Family Stone and The Temptations, might have had a rather naïve (and dated nowadays) lyric but it was catchy and instantly memorable and fully deserved its #4 soul and #26 pop placing, by some way their biggest hit to date. It was followed into the charts by "We Are Neighbours", either a witty and true or distasteful (depending on your politics or point or view) depiction of race relations but its rhythm brooked no argument and the third single from the set, "I Want To Pay You Back" (#35 soul) was a beautiful example of Record's romantic leaning where he sings as if he wishes to give every girl in the world a red rose. However, it was precisely the sort of song that has caused a blind spot in some misguided critics, as they can't see the beauty behind the soft and fluffy exterior. The LP also included exquisite versions of two of Record's best ever compositions, "Love Uprising" and "You Got Me Walkin'" and another brilliant example of his taking on unusual and neglected topics in "Yes I'm Ready (If I Don't Get To Go)" which is one of the only songs I know on the subject of busing. And all this without even mentioning "Have You Seen Her" which was the fourth single to be released from the LP, becoming not only a massive worldwide hit (#1 soul and #3 pop in the US) but probably the record the group are still best known for. The legendary UK DJ John Peel even named it as one of his records of the year in 1971. Brunswick helped things by only duplicating two tracks from previous albums, and overall it is one of the finest LPs to be covered in the book.

The Chi-Lites were now one of the biggest vocal groups in the world and "Oh Girl", another superb single (and one that even brought a tear to Tony Soprano's eye), became an even bigger hit than "Have You Seen Her" when it went all the way to #1 on the pop charts (the only time the group ever achieved this) in the early summer of 1972. The album built around it, *A Lonely Man*, was another highly accomplished set, containing the magnificent eight and a half minute version of the epic "The Coldest Days Of My Life" and it did well when released as a truncated single (#8). The title track itself became the third hit from the set (#25) but another glorious side, "Living In The Footsteps Of Another Man", one of the group's few not written by Record, was relegated to the b-side of the inferior "We Need Order" single. Even unheralded tracks such as "Love Is" and "Being In Love" could have been hits in other hands, while they even gave us a thoroughly decent version of "Inner City Blues" which I think features "Squirrel" Lester taking lead.

Brunswick then put out a marvellous hits package before *A Letter To Myself* became another strong seller. The title track borrowed much from all their biggest hits to date and came close to self-parody but is so exquisite that it breaks down any resistance easily, and captured enough hearts to make it to #3 soul and #33 pop. The album overall, however, was not quite so compelling as the previous couple. "Someone Else's Arms" is a lovely song done well, Marshall Thompson (I think) gets a rare outing on "Too Late To Turn Back Now" which is welcome, but generally the songs are slightly too long and "Love Comes In All Sizes" is too repetitive, and "Sally", too slight. The previously mentioned "We Need Order" harked back to a Norman Whitfield sound and "My Heart Just Keeps On Breaking" was simply plain awkward in its C&W style (although it was commendable for the group to try something so different) and clearly didn't strike a chord with fans as it was their least successful single in years (#46 soul, #92 pop.)

They bounced back superbly, though, with their second best ever album, the dully entitled *The Chi-Lites* which had a different sleeve in the UK from the US, which was a good thing as the U.S. one was dreadful. "Stoned Out Of My Mind" (#2 soul, #30 pop) was a marvellous song with great lyrics; the slightly slushy but still lovely "Homely Girl" was another totally deserved smash (#3 soul); "I Found Sunshine" (#7 soul) and "Too Good To Be Forgotten" were delightful slices of pure pop, and, indeed, a throw away version of "One Man Band" apart, I'd say the album, which fizzes with constantly impressive musical flourishes, has no weak tracks at all. I should also make specific reference to "I Never Had It So Good" which is the type of song to justify why albums exist. Not having enough obvious impact to make it as a single, it takes its time, with precise lyrics, to point out the pathos of a man looking back on a divorce from a year ago, which initially he welcomed. It is great popular song writing and one should give credit to Stan McKenny who co-wrote it with Record, along with three other album cuts.

Toby 1974 Brunswick BL 754200 Producer: Eugene Record (Billboard soul charts: 12 ; Billboard pop charts: 181)

Half A Love 1975 Brunswick BL 754204 Producer: Eugene Record (Billboard soul charts: 41)

Chi-Lite Time 1976 London SHU 8520 (UK)

Greatest Hits Volume 2 1976 Brunswick BL 754208

Greatest Hits 1983 Epic PE 38627

Most acts can expect a relatively short time at the top and the Chi-Lites best moments were mostly behind them by the time of *Toby*, and not only because bass singer Jones had also left the group by this time. While it was by no means a disaster it sounded rather workmanlike to my ears without any particular stand-out tracks (although it was home to three top twenty soul singles in the title track, "You Got To Be The One" and "There Will Never Be Any Peace", with the latter being another example of the sort of song that alienates most rock critics.) It was also another which had different sleeves in the US and the UK.

Surely nobody could have been happy with *Half A Love* - once again using different covers on each side of the Atlantic - as Brunswick, no doubt mindful of their serious financial difficulties, started to once again reprocess earlier songs. The U.S. version of the album (with another terrible cover) featured ten tracks (the U.K. one had two more) and four had appeared before. Luckily, though, there were three new songs of great appeal: the title track, "Here I Am" and "It's Time For Love", the latter being the last great Chi-Lites side in the first Eugene Record era. His vocals on this one are spectacular, one of the best performances he ever delivered, although as it only managed to reach #27 soul, making 1975 the first year of the decade in which the group did not post at least one single in the top 20, it was clear that the group's audience had diminished to an alarming degree.

Two compilations of Brunswick material followed in 1976 as did a very stingy one on Epic in 1983 which only included ten tracks.

Happy Being Lonely 1976 Mercury SRM 1-1118 Producer: Marshall Thompson

The Fantastic Chi-Lites 1977 Mercury SRM 1-1147 Producer: Richard Rome

Disaster soon followed when Record left the Chi-Lites (and, rather mysteriously, did not fare particularly well as a solo artist) and their fortunes plummeted immediately, seeing as how the *Happy Being Lonely* LP featured on no charts at all, although the likeable title track (with new lead vocalist Danny Johnson) scraped into the soul top thirty as a 45. It was strange seeing a Chi-Lites album without a single Record composed song, although the fine Marshall Thompson led "Don't Blame The World" did its best to sound like one.

The Fantastic had one of those bemusing pictures of the group jumping up and down but it can't have been for joy as it was another album that stiffed, and the two singles from it could only reach lowly levels on the soul charts. The glory days were really gone by now. That is not the say the album, like *Happy Being Lonely*, did not have its moments, for example "My First Mistake" and "Stop Still", and it is likeable and competent enough, but they were no longer distinctive at all, and it was hard to imagine anything on it being strong enough to be a hit.

Heavenly Body 1980 Chi-Sound T-619 Producer: Eugene Record (Billboard soul charts: 42 ; Billboard pop charts: 179)

Me & You 1981 Chi-Sound T-635 Producers: Eugene Record & Carl Davis (Billboard soul charts: 31 ; Billboard pop charts: 162)

The big news for the Chi-Lites was the return of Eugene Record in 1980, and he also persuaded Creadel Jones back as well. Given the involvement of Carl Davis, it must have seen like old times. However, the industry had changed significantly, of course, and the Chi-Sound albums, despite for the first (and last) time being billed as "The Chi-Lites featuring Eugene Record" did not return the group to prosperity, although they did register a commercial improvement over the Mercury years. I don't have strong feelings either way about these albums, which are, as ever, musical enough with the trademark strong harmonies, but the songs are generally not Record's best and I can see no reason why one would pick them off the shelf to play in preference to the Brunswick LPs. Having said that, "Give Me A Dream" and, particularly, "Super Mad" from *Heavenly Body* are nice enough. Perhaps the most telling comment on the LP is that the re-make of "Have You Seen Her" was the best cut.

"Hot On A thing" from the *Me And You* LP hit #15 on the soul charts in early 1982, thus becoming their biggest hit in seven years but is not a record I can warm to. I prefer their reading of "Tell Me Where It Hurts", also cut by Walter Jackson, the fine slow-drag "Never Speak To A Stranger" and "Whole Lot Of Good Good Lovin'", with its trademark Chi-Lites lilt.

Love Your Way Through 1981 Excello EX-8032 Producers: Heyward Collins & Jay Kessler

This puzzling record with an absurdly dull sleeve escaped into the market in 1981, but contains old tracks recorded before Record re-joined the group and exactly who sings on the record will probably remain a mystery although it certainly does involve bona-fide Chi-Lites members, possibly including Thompson, Lester and Hampton, and it sounds to me like Danny Johnson on most leads. None of the music or songs emanated from Chicago and I suspect the group were unaware it ever came out. It is all rather boring, without any spark at all and it is hardly surprising that two singles that are included on the LP did absolutely nothing.

Bottom's Up 1983 Larc LR-8103 Producer: Eugene Record (Billboard soul charts: 15 ; Billboard pop charts: 98)

Budweiser Concert Hour 1983 Westwood One 83-18

Steppin' Out 1984 Private I PZ 39316 Producer: Eugene Record

Live 1988 Super Power HTLP 3311 Producer: Marshall Thompson

The Larc LP (entitled *Changing For You* in the UK), went even further in re-establishing the group as an economically feasible act, with the title track even becoming a soul top ten hit. Jones had once again left, and it was notable that a number of the songs, including the hit, did not come from Record's pen. I like, a great deal, their version of Black Ice's "I Just Wanna Hold You", and "Making Love" is sweet and soulful, but I remain indifferent to the rest of the album, which all too often deals in dance grooves heard a million times before.

The Larc label morphed into Private I in 1984 and the *Steppin' Out* album yielded two smallish soul hits but it is puny stuff consisting almost entirely of uninspired dance tracks that besmirch the great name of the Chi-Lites. I understand of course why they recorded it - their golden era sound was never going to work in 1984 - but it was an album by men in their mid-forties covering the same ground as groups twenty years younger and it was un likely to be an inspired outcome.

The *Live* album is no more essential or interesting or worse than most other "live" albums and features seven of their well-known tracks, a version of EWAF's "You And I" and their then current single "Nothing Lasts Forever" (I haven't heard the second "live" album, *Budweiser Concert Hour.*)

Just Say You Love Me 1990 Ichiban ICH 1057 Producers: Robert Lester, Anthony Watson, Buzz Amato & Wayne Stalling (Billboard soul charts: 77)

The last vinyl album from this great group came out on Ichiban, a label that offered a safe haven for artists from the golden years of soul, and it was good to hear the famed harmonies on the excellent "Solid Love Affair", a record also put out by new member Anthony Watson under his own name. Eugene Record had once again left by this time, but it must be said that this cut was the best thing they had done for years, and the whole LP is solid.

Marshall Thompson is the only living member of the original four, and despite the rather uninspired last years of The Chi-Lites they must be regarded as one of the soul outfits who really mattered.

Chimere

Let's Take The Time 1982 Pot Of Gold No number Producer: Virgil Ginyard

This is light pop-soul from a five-woman group who employ a bit of The Emotions and a bit of High Inergy in their upbeat and glossy sound. It's an obscure LP, and despite the clear visual appeal of the group on the front cover, the back doesn't bother to tell us who they are. Things get really grim on "Save A Little Love For Me" when we are nearly in Spice Girls territory, and if nothing else quite gets as poor as that it remains a set of very limited appeal to me.

Chocolate Clay

Clay Cropper; George Perry

Chocolate Clay 1977 Cat 2610 Producers: Clay Cropper & George Perry

Cropper - guitar and keyboards - and Perry - bass - were first and foremost session musicians for Henry Stone's empire of Florida based record labels, playing on, as well as sometimes writing, sides for the likes of Betty Wright, Latimore and Gwen McCrae. Their place in the history of soul from the Sunshine State should thus be recognised, but more in the capacities above than for their one LP, which neither sold enough, nor is good enough, to rank with records issued by the three artists above. The duo wrote all of the eight songs, but none really establish an identity for Chocolate Clay, although they were funkier than K.C. & The Sunshine Band.

Chocolate Milk

Amadee Castanell; Ernest Dabon; Robert Dabon; Joe Smith; Frank Richard; Dwight Richards; Mario Tio; Ken Williams; Lloyd Harris; David Barard; Steve Hughes; Joe Foxx;

Action Speaks Louder Than Words 1975 RCA APL1-1188 Producers: Allen Toussaint & Marshall Sehorn (Billboard soul charts: 34 ; Billboard pop charts: 191)

Chocolate Milk 1976 RCA APL1-1399 Producers: Allen Toussaint & Marshall Sehorn (Billboard soul charts: 18)

Comin' 1976 RCA APL1-1830 Producers: Allen Toussaint & Marshall Sehorn

We're All In This Thing Together 1977 RCA APL1-2331 Producer: Allen Toussaint (Billboard soul charts: 34; Billboard pop charts: 171)

Milky Way 1979 RCA AFL1-3081 Producer: Allen Toussaint (Billboard soul charts: 52 ; Billboard pop charts: 161)

Chocolate Milk were a New Orleans group who, after the first album, didn't much sound like one. Which may have been a smart commercial move, as music from that city wasn't selling strongly by the mid-seventies. They were adept though, even if they meant virtually nothing to white America: the title track from the debut album is the only single that ever made it to the top 100 pop, and that at only #69, whereas they posted eleven singles on the soul listings.

The debut album employed a highly appealing laid-back and fluid funk groove that was singular enough to render them somewhat different from most of the other 8 or 9 man groups of the time. All the material was self-penned apart from a version of America's "Tin Man" (also covered winningly by John Edwards) and I like all of it, apart from the uninspired "Confusion" and the one downtempo cut, "Out Among The Stars" - at this time slow tracks were not their forte. By 1975 funk had arguably peaked but no one told Chocolate Milk.

Chocolate Milk was also good listening, consistent and funky, sensibly eschewing any slow stuff, with another compelling rhythm section performance from Dwight Richards on drums and Ernest Dabon's bass even if the traces of New Orleans had been pretty much eradicated. "How About Love" could surprisingly only manage #79 on the soul charts when pulled as a single.

RCA certainly couldn't be accused of not trying with the group and the UK release of *Comin'* even included an album insert with photos and information about the group but I suspect the sales were still trifling (and it also became their only non-charting album in the US). This could all be simply down to the fact that the album was far from their best, as the funk was watered down in favour of jazzier excursions, apart from "I Refuse" which sounded a fair bit like Sly and The Family Stone's "Frisky".

We're All In This Thing Together featured, for the only time, a number of Allen Toussaint songs, one of which, "Girl Callin'", (which Kool and the Gang must have heard before they recorded "Ladies Night") became a pretty decent sized hit - their second biggest ever - for the band (#14 soul) even if was atypical of the rest of the album which continued the process of smoothing out the sound and slowing the tempo.

The last set they recorded with Toussaint was *Milky Way*, which was kicked off by "Save The Last Dance" and I would have defied anyone hearing it for the first time to guess it was by Chocolate Milk, as it was a catchy poppy tune they would never have cut a few years earlier. Nevertheless, it was one of their best albums with stronger songs than had sometimes been the case and the best vocals lead singer Frank Richard had thus far delivered. "Groove City" (#59 soul) had a mesmerising mellow flow, at odds with what its title might suggest and "Doc" is another example of how far they had improved in delivering slower material.

Hipnotism 1980 RCA AFL1-3569 Producer: George Tobin (Billboard soul charts: 69)

Blue Jeans 1981 RCA AFL1-3896 Producer: Allen Jones (Billboard soul charts: 22 ; Billboard pop charts: 162)

Friction 1982 RCA AFL1-4412 Producer: Allen Jones (Billboard soul charts: 50)

After the Toussaint association ended they recorded one album with George Tobin which moved the group even further in a pop direction and it included one of my absolute favourites of theirs in "I'm Your Radio". Catchy, poppy and bright, I have always loved it and am at a loss to understand why it wasn't a massive hit. Or even a small one, as it didn't sell at all. The one single from the set to reach the soul charts was "Hey Lover" which was ok, as was most of the LP, but there was little funk on show and the single's failure to rise higher than #40 presumably made it unlikely that Tobin would be retained.

Blue Jeans employed the Bar-Kays long-time producer Allen Jones, and he moved the band back in a much funkier direction where they sounded a bit like - surprise - the Memphis based outfit and they were rewarded when the title track reached #15, becoming their third biggest hit ever. The groove of the song is appealing enough, but the lyrics are cliched in the extreme and it is amazing that it took eleven people to write it. "Honey Bun" was a crunching dance side and was another reminder of the band's rhythmic power when it was called upon. On the other side of the coin, we also had to endure the execrable "Video Queen" a title guaranteed to make one's heart sink. To balance that, the album featured a first rate version of Otis Redding's "I've Been Loving You Too Long", the one and only time they recorded anything like this, and I assume it was due to Jones' Memphis background.

The last album, also recorded in Memphis by Jones, was a no-nonsense dance affair of no lyrical profundity whatsoever but was a testament to their togetherness as they were now into their eighth album without adding any new members at all, even if a handful had by now left. The melodic "Don't Make Me Wait" was the final track on the LP, a neat enough bookend to demonstrate that in some ways they had improved since that fine debut back in 1975.

Choice Four

Bobby Hamilton; Ted Maduro; Peter Marshall; Charles Blagman;

Finger Pointers 1974 RCA APL1-0643 Producer: Van McCoy

Choice Four 1975 RCA APL1-0913 Producer: Van McCoy

On Top Of Clear 1976 RCA APL1-1400 Producer: Van McCoy (Billboard soul charts: 43)

The Choice Four were a talented Washington D.C. group, taken under the wing of Van McCoy, but - and for no discernible reason, sometimes these things just happen - they never really made it big in a highly competitive market.

The debut album is enjoyable, but sadly did not burden any charts, and only generated two lowly soul charting singles, both y reminiscent of the music coming out of Philadelphia, the uptempo lope of "The Finger Pointers" (#85) and the slow and sweet "You're So Right For Me" (#63). Elsewhere, "Ready, Willing And Able", the Chi-Lites influenced "I Need Your Love To Keep Me Warm", and the melodic "The Woman I'm Being True To" all demonstrated that the group were versatile and equally at ease with fast or slow material, and not entirely in thrall to Philly.

Choice Four was similar to the debut as regards songs, tempo and quality of the singing and it was nice that RCA provided details of who was taking lead on each track. The album contained a pleasing and relaxed version of one of McCoy's signature tunes, "When You're Young And In Love", which did ok when released as a single, as well as what I believe to be the original of "Walk Away From Love", performed so brilliantly by David Ruffin later in the same year. "Hook It Up" was a warm and catchy dance record that should have been a hit, and the whole LP sounded intoxicating to lovers of mid-seventies soul vocal groups.

On Top Of Clear was a slight step down, as it couldn't escape the sticky embrace of disco and tracks started getting longer, particularly the dull "Hey, What's That Dance You're Doing" (#57 soul). I preferred "Just Let Me Hold You For A Night" (#76), another song they got to before Ruffin. "Come Down To Earth" was also performed with the dance floor in mind, and on this occasion they did not get to it first, the New Censation having taken it into the soul charts two years before. The album is not a bad one, but the other two should be sought out first by anyone interested in finding out more about The Choice Four.

Choice Reunion

Wilbur Stewart; Victor Green; George Jones; James Battle; Timothy Outten

Free & Easy 1986 Les-Wes LW-10001 Producers: Leon Stewart & Wilbur Stewart

A talented singing group out of Maryland, it was a shame they couldn't have put this LP out ten years earlier, as they would have received much more sympathetic musical backing than is the case here. But I don't wish to be too harsh on anyone involved in the making of the LP as it can't have been easy to record and release anything with such a throwback vocal approach in 1986. The excellent title track is by far the best thing on show, and only "On My Own" comes close to it in quality, as most of the other songs are fairly routine. There are eight tracks on show, and two of these are merely the instrumental backing tracks to the vocal takes, so it is not an overwhelmingly generous LP, but again this was doubtless due to the company having to cut their cloth accordingly. Two 45s and a 12" single were pulled from *Free & Easy* but they did not become successful. (I'm only sliding this album into the book by the way as I believe Green was the same man who had a single out in 1980 and Stewart was in All Points Bulletin Band who had two minor soul hits on the LCR label in the 70s.)

Chosen Few

Roy Handy; Gerald Perry; Mac Williams

Takin' All The Love I Can 1971 Maple M-6000 Producer: Johnny Brantley

Maple was a small label distributed by All Platinum, so don't expect the sound of this record to come jumping out of the speakers in crystal clear purity. It was also produced by Johnny Brantley, a man who worked at the uncompromising end of the scale and so the commercial attributes of this record, all told, were about nil. Which is not the same as saying that is poor and parts of it are very attractive to me indeed: "Something Bad" and "I Can't Take No More Chances" are exemplary vocal group soul and the title track and "Birth Of A Playboy" have been danced to down the years by discerning soul fans. It contains a few highly ordinary tracks as well, but overall it is a record I am happy to own. (There were a large number of groups who went under the name of The Chosen Few but I am pretty confident that none of the others were anything to do with this one.)

Gavin Christopher

Gavin Christopher 1976 Island ILPS-9398 Producers: Eric Malamud & Gavin Christopher

Gavin Christopher 1979 RSO RS-1-3052 Producers: Bobby Eli & Gavin Christopher

One Step Closer 1986 Manhattan ST-53024 Producers: Carl Sturken & Evan Rogers (Billboard soul charts: 36; Billboard pop charts: 74)

Gavin 1988 EMI-American E1-46998 Producers: David Frank, Mic Murphy, Steve Thompson, Michael Barbiero & Gavin Christopher (Billboard soul charts: 48)

Brother of Shawn, Gavin Christopher is another singer who has had little or no coverage over the years. He started out in small local groups in his native Chicago, one of which, Lyfe, also included Chaka Khan, while another, High Voltage, encompassed other Rufus members. Those associations were to prove fruitful for all concerned as Christopher penned such hits for the band as "Dance Wit' Me" and "Once You Get Started". He also worked with Mariah Carey, Herbie Hancock and many others and I believe him to be a more talented writer, musician and producer than singer.

In fact, his vocals put me off that debut Island album as he comes across as heavily influenced by Stevie Wonder on tracks like "Treasure Every Moment" and "Return The Love" and, as a result, it all sounded highly derivative. "Sightings" provides a showcase for his musical prowess but it is not an album I turn to with any regularity.

I much preferred his second LP, which, despite sharing the same title as the first, proved he had come into his own vocally and I could relate more easily to the sophisticated dance flow of tracks like the excellent "This Side Of Heaven" and "Feelin' The Love", the first time he ever placed on the soul singles chart.

He hit the big time, briefly, with "One Step Closer" which made #22 on the Hot 100 in 1986. It is, without doubt, a pop record with a catchy hook, and its success is easy to understand, but is not one for me, and the same goes for much of the album which includes his take on "Once You Get Started" although I would be unfair to dismiss "Back In Your Arms" which sounds as if it could and should have been another hit.

Gavin was the last LP, which was slick and bright and featured "You Are Who You Love", the only single of his that ever reached the soul top ten. It deserved it as it proved once again he was talented enough to write catchy songs with strong melodies and it also showed how far his vocals had improved since 1976.

Circle O' Fire (see also O'Conner)

Donald O'Conner; Gregory McIntosh; George Jounigan; Tim Dancy; Walter Person; William Kirkwood; John Sangster; Larry O'Neil Johnson;

Escape Hatch 1978 Stax STX-4108 Producer: David Porter

One of a number of albums that was released during the re-birth of Stax, this one, despite its quality, didn't do much to help resurrect the label to a position of strength. Lead singer Donald O'Conner had a pleasing voice (and managed a solo LP release on Bearsville in 1981) and he, guitarist McIntosh and producer Porter were responsible for most of the material on here. The group's musical style is split between gently funky uptempo numbers and orchestrated slower songs like "Nobody Loves You Like I Do" and "(You're A) Winner" and is generally much softer than other groups of the time also working out of Memphis - such as The Bar-Kays and Con-Funk-Shun - were producing. Other tracks of note: "Ray Of Sunshine" sounds not unlike a Rance Allen track and "Have It Your Way" has a number of fans. There is nothing on here that sounded like a hit, but it is a consistent, competent and enjoyable outing, one of the better efforts from Stax second time around.

Chuck Cissel

Just For You 1979 Arista AB 4257 Producers: Skip Scarborough & David Crawford (Billboard soul charts: 39)

If I Had The Chance 1982 Arista AL 9581 Producers: John Barnes, Kenny Nolan, Jimmy Simpson & Benjamin Wright

Oklahoma native and former dancer and actor, Cissel looked very dapper on the front cover of his debut album which seemed as if it might launch him into a career of significance but it didn't really happen for him although Arista were obviously prepared to back him up as an artist by assigning the highly talented Skip Scarborough to co-producer duties.

Just For You is easy to listen to with a warm accomplished sound throughout and a blessed absence of disco influence - one track excepted - and Cissel is a highly gifted singer who has somehow escaped critical notice. In fact the album, the first side particularly, is inspired, with excellent arranging, singing and songs and is one of the best things to have come out in 1979. He covers the great Holland-Dozier-Holland song, "Forever", with taste and skill, while "River Of Love" and "I've Been Needing Love So Long" demonstrate his impressive vocal range and "Don't Tell Me You're Sorry" and "Emergency" are compelling dance tracks. The LP also features the track for which he is best known, the minor hit "Cisselin' Hot", and it is the one disco track on show and I must confess that its energy is hard to resist even though as a song it is mediocre.

He had to wait three years for a follow-up and it was somewhat disappointing, although his dress sense was still immaculate. His voice was gloriously intact, but the songs were not as strong and Scarborough had moved on. "Possessed" and "Dance Away The Pain" were not up to the level of the uptempo cuts on the debut and the title track, despite the excellence of Cissel's and Marva King's vocals, was too "torchy" for my tastes, as was "Understanding Man" and "Love's Grown Deep". But there was good stuff: "Love Is Missing From Our Lives" is a fantastic Tony Hester song and if the arrangement is not as good as in the definitive Dells and Dramatics version, the track benefits from some glittering back-up singing and an inspired Cissel vocal. "All I See Is You" also has enough quality to have fitted effortlessly on the debut LP.

It appears that in recent years Cissel has returned to Oklahoma where he works as the CEO of the local Jazz hall of fame and it was a shame his "soul years" were so brief as he had the talent to have become a household name.

City Limits (see also Terri Wells)

Ron Richardson; Terri Wells; Clayton Wortham; Vicki Lyn Richardson

Circles 1976 TSOP PZ 34110 Producers: Bruce Hawes & Joseph Jefferson

I have a deep and abiding love for most soul music that came out of Philadelphia and the sight of the TSOP label still gets me excited all these years later, but this LP, while enjoyable enough, lacked that special something to permit it to be a success and sustain a career for City Limits (though later on, Terri Wells did ok as a solo singer). That "something" is truly memorable material and if everything on here was as good as "Words Without Love" or the seven minute plus version of "Circles" they could have made it big, especially as their vocal talents were not in doubt.

City Streets

Joe Havis; Paul Easley; Allan McCrary; Donald McCrary; Felton Ward

Livin' In The Jungle 1979 RCA AFL1-3429 Producer: Ron Haffkine

This is a most intriguing album. I cannot think of too many other bands that sounded like City Streets, as the music is almost pop/funk in nature. A couple of cuts aside, these are not mere exhortations to dance, but songs with storylines, and not from the usual suspects either; two are from the pen of Dr. Hook's Dennis Locorriere, and another is provided by Vic McAlpin, a Nashville country songwriter of note. But what makes it all work is the incredibly tough rhythm section of Tommy Cogbill on bass and Roger Hawkins and Hayward Bishop on drums. Other southern soul musicians of the quality of Bobby Wood and Bobby Emmons also play on the set, which, sadly and unfairly, did nothing at all as regards sales. "Layin' Down Too Low Too Long" sounds not unlike what War were doing at the time and "Work Song", the blunt "Get It Up Get It In" and the title track all drive along in a manner that few other albums of the time were doing. I like *Livin' In The Jungle* a lot, but can easily understand that it may be an acquired taste.

Alice Clark

Alice Clark 1972 Mainstream MRL 362 Producer: Bob Shad

Clark released an excellent single in 1968 which bore a lung-pumping dance side "You Hit Me" on one side and a slow and intense piece of soul, "Heaven's Will" on the other but it failed to attract much interest at the time, and nor did her one album of four years later.

It's a somewhat puzzling release as it pits her emotional delivery (and she sometimes sounds rather as if the key she sings in is set too high for her, adding to the tension) against songs which mainly come from distinctly non-soul sources: one from Petula Clark, one from *Cabaret*, one from Jim Webb and three from Bobby Hebb, a man I have deemed out of scope as regards his own work. It all works though as Mainstream releases were always beautifully played and arranged and the dance side "Don't You Care" is absolutely irresistible while Leonard Caston's "Don't Wonder Why" (also cut by Stevie Wonder) has a production that brooks no argument at all.

Clark is a mysterious singer and virtually nothing is known about her but this is an LP that has had a loyal if small following for around twenty five years now.

Chris Clark

Soul Sounds 1967 Motown MT-664 No producer listed

C.C. Rides Again 1969 Weed WS-801 Producer: Deke Richards

Clark could be considered to be Motown's Dusty Springfield and certainly the two women shared similarities in looks and singing style. The debut album makes no particular concession to the fact that she was a white singer and is typical of what came out of the hit factory, although Clark herself didn't share in the usual success and only "Love's Gone Bad" reached any charts, and only #41 soul and #105 pop at that. She delivers a sultry version of that great song, "From Head To Toe", and "Do Right Baby, Do Right" is an excellent and rather unknown Berry Gordy song. Other Motown standards such as "Sweeter As The Days Go By" and "Whisper You Love Me Boy" are also handled competently but I don't particularly care for her take on "Put Yourself In My Place" which lacks the flow of other versions. The album does not list a producer but the majority of the tracks were actually the work of Holland and Dozier, Berry Gordy and Marvin Gaye. A good LP.

The same could not be said of the bizarre follow-up. Weed was a short-lived Motown subsidiary label and the album mainly consisted of well-known hits by others, such as "Spinning Wheel" (with tuba accompaniment), "Get Back" (awful), "In The Ghetto" (a good stab) and "You've Made Me Very Happy" (sensual and engaging). It bombed completely, despite the fact that it had a gatefold sleeve, so money and time was expended, but she was hardly a big enough star to warrant not having her name on the front or back cover. For once, it was hard to understand what Berry Gordy was thinking.

Dee Clark

Dee Clark 1959 Abner SR 2000 No producer listed

How About That 1960 Abner ABLP 2002 No producer listed

You're Looking Good 1960 Vee-Jay 1019 No producer listed

Hold on...It's Dee Clark 1961 Vee Jay 1037 No producer listed

The Best Of 1961 Vee Jay 1047

Wondering 1968 Sunset SUS- 5217

Keep It Up 1980 Charly CRB 1010 (UK)

His Best Recordings 1984? Solid Smoke SS-8026

The Delectable Sound Of 1986 Charly CRB 1113 (UK)

This Arkansas native moved to Chicago where he became, for a few years, one of the first soul singers to have some sustained national success, placing six singles on the pop top 40 between 1958 and 1961. Those first records are highly pop flavoured but his vocals are purely those of a soul man and he has also been sadly underrated, probably because his best years came before the "golden era" of soul which arguably started in 1963.

His first album, on Abner, contained three of those hit singles in "Nobody But You" (#3 soul), "Just Keep It Up" (#9) and "Hey Little Girl" (#2), all highly attractive with the soaring backing singers unable to suppress the soulfulness of his high pitched delivery. The first hit also established his credentials as a songwriter, and if anyone felt he could only tackle unthreatening material then "Blues Get Off My Shoulder" would dispel such a theory. On the other hand, this WAS 1959 and so the album contained the likes of "Whispering Grass" and "Nature Boy".

The follow-up album, *How About That,* bore in the title track his fourth hit (albeit slightly smaller than the first three at #10; it also just missed the pop top 30, which the previous three had not) and has a swinging take on "At My Front Door" but the rest is fairly tame stuff and is not so good as the debut. Both albums, incidentally, were re-released on Vee Jay as numbers 1026 and 1028 respectively.

The first "proper" Vee Jay album, therefore, was *You're Looking Good* which contained a number of songs that had been cut when Clark was a member of the Kool Gents in the second half of the fifties. It also contained "Little Red Riding Hood" which was more fun than one might imagine and the amusing Little Richard take-off "24 Boyfriends". All in all, better than *How About That*.

The *Hold On* album contained his biggest (#2 pop, #3 soul) and best hit to date in "Raindrops". An excellent record, its last ten or so seconds leave no doubt that Clark was a soul man of the highest class. "Your Friends" (#30 soul) was also first-rate, not least because the Dells helped out on backing vocals and "Hold On", despite sounding somewhat like "He Will Break Your Heart" was also beautifully sung. Unfortunately, the album also contained some tracks that had previously appeared on the earlier LPs.

And that was just about it as original albums went. He recorded many more good singles in the sixties, mainly on Constellation, but none made it to LPs, and none, "Crossfire Time" excepted, achieved much success. He scored, out of nowhere, a small hit in England in 1975 with "Ride A Wild Horse" but it led to nothing (other than Clark's apparently pocketing and absconding with some upfront money to tour on the strength of it.) The Sunset LP is all previously released material and is more or less the same as the "You're Looking Good" LP. The Charly LPs are typically well thought out retrospectives while the Solid Smoke release delves back into his past including early tracks when he sang with the Kool Gents and Upsetters.

Hey Little Girl 1982 Brylen BN4542 No producer listed

Which leaves us with another mystifying Brylen set. Given the inclusion of a track like "Bad Bad Leroy Brown" it seems that it must have been recorded at least as late as 1973, the year that hit came out. Most of the tracks are re-makes of Clark's biggest hits and apart from a version of "Barefootin'" that features some horns, the sound is basic and sparse with a simple rhythm section.

Delecta Clark died, almost entirely forgotten, in 1990 when only 52 years old but he was a singer of immense class and skill, a fact that seems to have also been largely forgotten.

Classic Example

Classic Example 1972 GSF S-1006 Producers: William Stevenson & Curtis Colbert

Although this is a laudable record it was let down badly by its muffled and muddy production, surprising from such an experienced record man as William "Mickey" Stevenson. Classic Example were a man and woman team but, once again, the sleeve does not tell us who they are, and it has proved challenging, even in this internet age, to find out more. It seems they might be Curtis Colbert and Harriet Hurst but this has yet to be confirmed.

The West Coast recorded album is uptown, rather than "southern" in style, and has hints of other male/female teams like Marvin and Tammi but somehow does not sound obviously like anyone else. "That's Groovy" (an unsuccessful 45) had been previously cut by Stevenson's former wife, Kim Weston, "Just Another Lonely Night" was performed, among others, by The Temptations and "Punish Me" was recorded by Margie Joseph so some thought has gone into the material. I also really like "Hey There Little Girl" with its "I Had It All The Time" bass line. Another group of the same name recorded in the nineties but there is no link between the two at all.

Class-Set

Michael Quinn; Lloyd Jenkins; Tommy Thomas; Malcolm Smith

My Style 1975 Mod-Art MALP-675 Producer: Chuck Sibit

It's hard to imagine that this obscure but utterly charming album ever made it outside of Chicago's city limits but at least the sleeve gives us plenty of information about the group, who made a few singles before cutting this LP.

Their style is smooth and slow harmony soul, although the budget didn't run to sophisticated musical backing, and it sounds a bit dated for 1975, but I love it all the same. Only two of the eight tracks move above a crawl and even the spurious live audience noises on "I'll Do What My Heart Tells Me" fail to ruin it. "I'll Never Be Your Friend Again" sounds a trite and naive title in these more cynical times but is sweet and soulful as indeed is everything here, especially the gorgeous "Julie". Fans of soul harmony singing will love this and for them it will be the proverbial lost classic.

Judy Clay

Storybook Children (and Billy Vera) 1968 Atlantic SD 8174 Producers: Ted Daryll & Chip Taylor

I shouldn't complain about this LP as it's the only one that exists bearing Judy Clay's name, and that fact alone is annoying enough, but it's a most disappointing release. Facts won't support the claim that she is one of the finest of all soul singers, but ears will. It must have been galling for her to see lesser talents attain much more success, and of the five singles she placed on the soul charts between late 1967 and early 1970, four of them needed help from others, two from William Bell and two from Billy Vera. Only one single by herself, the ineffable "Greatest Love", ever made it and that only at #45 in 1970. This is also to ignore the many excellent sides she made earlier for other labels, most notably Scepter, not to mention her membership of the gospel group The Drinkard Singers and the numerous backing vocals she added for other people.

So, what's the problem with *Storybook Children*? In short, the songs. Of the former, three are too hackneyed to afford much pleasure, while the songs by Chip Taylor and Billy Vera are unexciting and far from their best work and these, Taylor in particular, were gifted writers. It must also be said, with no disrespect meant to Vera, a talented man, that Clay can sing rings around him, and all the best moments come from her. It's therefore a bit exasperating to see that Vera gets two solo outings here, while Clay gets none. The title track, with on overly florid string arrangement, reached #20 soul and #54 pop while another single from the duo, "Country Girl-City Man", managed #41 soul and #36 pop but that one is not on the first edition of the album but IS on the second which appeared a few months later.

She left the music industry in the early seventies after cutting some more good things for Stax and was sadly killed in a car crash in 2001. I would have to rate her as one of the most underrated, for pure singing ability, of all soul singers who cut at least a fair number of records.

Otis Clay

The Beginning - Got To Find A Way 1979 P-Vine Special PLP-9002 (Japan) No producer listed

For anyone dipping their toes into the sea of soul, and wants to know what a "deep" or "hard" soul singer sounds like, go and seek out some Otis Clay records. He was born in Waxhaw, Mississippi and was a renowned performer in the gospel field in his younger days, so it was therefore a reasonably seamless transition from spiritual to secular as the passion he brought to his singing remained constant.

His early soul records were cut for George Leaner's One-derful! label out of Chicago, the city where Clay lived for most of his life. They are almost invariably excellent and exciting records with little thought about crossing over into a pop market. One amusing exception to this, given that the approach of Clay and the darlings of Motown could hardly be more different, was when he quoted from The Supremes' "Back In My Arms Again" on his fine ballad "I'm Satisfied". Clay put out eight singles on the label and two of them, the startling "That's How It Is" and "A Lasting Love" made it into the soul top 50 in 1967 at #34 and #48 respectively. One-derful! was concentrating entirely on the singles market and so no album was forthcoming at the time and fans had to wait until 1979 when P-Vine in Japan put out a marvellous collection of his work on Leaner's label. It contains twelve tracks though not, surprisingly, "A Lasting Love", and is worth tracking down not merely for its artistry but also for the fact that five tracks were previously unissued. No producers are credited on the LP but Eddie Silvers, Bernie Hayes, Morris Dollison and Otis Hayes were certainly involved.

Trying To Live My Like Without You 1972 Hi XSHL 32075 Producer: Willie Mitchell

I Can't Take It 1977 Hi HLP 6003 Producer: Willie Mitchell

Trying To Live My Like Without You 1987 Hi 406 (UK)

One-derful! went the way of virtually all small record companies - bust - in 1968 and Clay moved to Cotillion and Dakar where he cut some more great stuff, but was not favoured with an LP. His first ever album was released in 1972 which he recorded for his new label with Willie Mitchell and the Hi crew down in Memphis. His style remained tough and was not markedly different from his Chicago work although the production was marginally slicker with more strings than he was accustomed to working with. It was a undoubtedly a good move artistically and commercially and the title track went to #24 in the soul charts, nowhere near the success Hi were attaining with Al Green, of course, but good for Clay. The LP features a slightly unnecessary and inferior re-make of "That's How It Is" but overall is an excellent piece of work, and it was good to hear a label afford him the opportunity to stretch out on a track like "I Love You, I Need You". He delivers stringent takes on Jackie Moore's sublime "Precious Precious" and a typically excellent Betty Crutcher song in "Home Is Where The Heart Is", but everything on it is worth hearing. It certainly isn't an LP for dancing to, but sit down to listen in the dark with a glass of whisky to hand and it sounds just perfect.

The next Hi album came out three years later, after he had also recorded for Elka, Echo and Glades - of which more later - and it is nearly the equal of the first set, with some inspired moments, not least of which was the superb title track, an almost unbelievably hard and uncompromising song for 1977. "House Ain't A Home" is another must-hear song, as is a peppy re-make of "I've Got To Find A Way" and apart from "Home Is Where The Heart Is" being repeated on the set, there are no irritations or shortcomings. (I assume it was "in the can material", given he presumably left Hi to cut for Elka etc.)

The second *Trying to Live My Life Without You* album was a compilation that picked up the entire first set and added three non-LP songs, "Brand New Thing", "I Didn't Know The Meaning Of Pain" and "Let Me Be The One".

The Only Way Is Up 1985 Blues R&B BRB 3602 Producers: Otis Clay, Troy Thompson & Benjamin Wright

As mentioned above, Clay recorded for a few labels in the mid-seventies, not very successfully if chart positions are the sole criterion. However, the music was typically good and in 1985 much of this material was released on a long-player for the first time. *The Only Way Is Up* contains ten tracks and picks up virtually all the Elka, Echo and Glades material as well as some later Echo releases such as "Messin' With My Mind" and some previously unreleased things like his versions of "Cheatin' In The Next Room" and "I'm Gonna Hate Myself In The Morning". The excellent title track, of course, became a worldwide smash for Yazz, and as Clay didn't write it, the benefit he received was fairly negligible. The music on here is not as vigorous as his One-derful! or Hi work but is a first-rate LP, nonetheless. (Incidentally the album does not contain the two singles he recorded for Kayvette.)

Live ! 1978 Victor VIP 5042 Producer: Kaname Tajima (Japan)

Live Again 1984 Yupiteru YR38 - 8001 Producer: Hiroshi Asada (Japan)

Clay had always had a following and in Japan, and saw two live albums - both doubles - released from his tours there. The first one featured American musicians who I do not believe he had worked with on record before, and is composed of material spread across most of the labels he had previously recorded for. The second LP, also released in the US and UK as *Soul Man, Live In Japan*, employed the Hi Rhythm section as well as horn players he had cut with in the past, and has a broader range of songs, including some he never recorded elsewhere such as "Love Don't Love Nobody", "Love And Happiness" and "Ellie". Both are fine and capture the energy and commitment of his act very well, but only die-hard fans would want both as being given the opportunity to cut two double live albums is swaggeringly generous and off the top of my head I can't recall any other soul man apart from James Brown who has been afforded such an honour.

Watch Me Now 1989 Waylo W-13008 Producer: Willie Mitchell

Clay was re-united with Willie Mitchell in 1989 and while the album could never hope to match the earlier Hi albums given the original rhythm section were not used and drum programs were never going to match Howard Grimes, "I Don't Understand It" was a scorcher, a real stand-out and a cut that holds up well with nearly everyone else he ever did. "I Know I'm Over You" was another strong side and "Soap Opera Blues" was quite a witty song but overall it is not really Clay's best work. For most other singers this would be an LP to be fairly proud of but Clay had much higher standards than most.

Seven albums is not really an acceptable return for a singer of Clay's longevity and talent, but he did put out a number of good CDs over a long period of time before passing away in early January 2016.

Merry Clayton

Gimme Shelter 1970 Ode SP-77001 Producer: Lou Adler

Merry Clayton 1971 Ode SP-77012 Producer: Lou Adler (Billboard soul charts: 36; Billboard pop charts: 180)

Keep Your Eye On The Sparrow 1975 Ode SP-77030 Producer: Gene McDaniels (Billboard soul charts: 50; Billboard pop charts: 146)

Emotion 1980 MCA 3200 Producer: Steve Tyrell

Merry Clayton, despite her undoubted and in-demand talent, seemed never quite sure if she was a rock or soul singer, and was also never quite able to make the difficult transition from world-class backing singer to front-line solo performer. Her c.v. is outstanding as regards who she worked with and to cite The Rolling Stones, Ray Charles (as a Raelet), Sisters Love (as a member) Bobby Womack and BB King is merely to skim the surface but she has never seemed come up much in conversations I have had with soul fans over the last forty years or so. This is possibly due to her willingness to cover songs such as "Gimme Shelter", "I Got Life" and "Bridge Over Troubled Water" on the debut album alone, although, on the other side of the coin, she did release a couple of highly collectable singles back in the first half of the sixties. In fact , like so many others in this book, her musical history is diverse and fascinating, and worthy of anyone's time in checking out.

As mentioned above, the first album was content to borrow songs from pop/rock rather than from the soul tradition although there were a handful of exceptions, including Billy Page's "Good Girls" which sounds much more like a sixties recording than the rest of the LP. The whole set is typically efficient and skilled West Coast music, but I must confess it to be a bit rich (overproduced?) for my tastes.

The follow-up was more of the same with songs by writers of the calibre of Carole King, James Taylor, Leon Russell and Neil Young and once again, despite all the undoubted talent on show, it doesn't really appeal to me. "After All This Time", when released as a single, put her name on the soul charts for the first time ever (#42 in early 1972) and this one I do like a lot, and wouldn't have sounded out of place on an Aretha album of the same era. She also covers Bill Withers' "Grandma's Hands" but I much prefer Bill's simpler take of this intimate song.

The last Ode album was her only one to hit the soul albums charts and also contained in the title track the first time she ever took a single (under her own name) into the pop top fifty.

After a gap of a few years she returned with *Emotion*, a somewhat more "typical" soul album than had been the case in the past. It is patchy: a "Sly Stone Medley" doesn't work for me, her version of "Armed And Extremely Dangerous" is good but can't match the original, but the title track is a massive production job that works particularly well, and "Let Me Make You Cry A Little Longer" is arguably her best ever vocal performance.

Perhaps fittingly, given my preference for her collaborative work, my personal favourite piece or work of hers remains her singing on the Blackbyrd's "Rock Creek Park".

Willie Clayton

Forever 1988 Timeless TRPL 127 Producers: Willie Clayton, Andre Miller, Cornell Ward & Jim Sims (UK)

Never Too Late 1989 Polydor 422 839 935-1 Producer: Lionel Job

Open The Door 1992 About Time ATLP 020 Producers: Willie Clayton, General Crook, Paul Richmond & Jim Sims (UK)

Willie Clayton was and is a big cheese on the US "soul/blues" scene that developed in the late eighties or so, as well as having a small but loyal following in the UK, and he has been steadily releasing CDs for years. He is not so well represented on vinyl albums and he had been recording for nearly two decades, most notably on the Hi subsidiary, Pawn, before a record company finally put out an LP of his work.

That label was Timeless in England who should be commended for taking a chance on Clayton and releasing a set of Chicago recorded material although, in all honesty, it doesn't stand up particularly well today owing to its muffled drum beats and fake horns. Clayton's career from the eighties onwards has always been characterised by his willingness and ability to cover well chosen songs and "Rocking Chair", "One Nite Stand", "Stone Good Lover" and "Can I Change Your Mind" (where the production is unfortunately at its worst) were all such examples but much better by far than all of these was "Your Sweetness" a compelling dance record which allows Clayton's impressive vocal range to impose itself.

The next year, and for a fleeting moment, it looked as if Clayton's time might have come when a major label showed interest. His name was shortened to "Will" and Polydor put out a truly execrable album that was the worst thing - and remains the worst thing - he ever did, totally wasting his talent.

Blessedly he moved back to recording infinitely better work on smaller labels, and the UK again came to the rescue releasing the last vinyl album on this fine singer. It was a compilation of many of the excellent singles he had put out over the previous few years for labels like Compleat and Kirstee. "Tell Me" (#78 soul) and "Best Years Of My Life", both top-notch General Crook songs, prove again what a really good vocalist Clayton is and "Love Pains" was always a record I liked, but do beware of his version of "Open The Door To Your Heart" which showed that when he got a re-cut of an esteemed old song wrong, he really got it wrong.

Clem

Just In Time 1983 Hep' Me 153 Producer: Senator Jones

Memory is a sensitive and unreliable thing, but I seem to recall that, unbelievably, this LP was reviewed as a new release by the UK's *New Musical Express* magazine. Quite why the NME would assess what seemed at the time, and has definitely proved to be, such an obscure album, is anybody's guess.

"Clem" is Clementine Easterling, who is, so far as I can ascertain, no relation to Skip Easterling, a slightly better known artist from New Orleans (as is Clem). It is a slightly eccentric LP in a way, as side one is entirely composed of fifteen year old (at the time of this LP's release) Diana Ross and The Supremes songs, one of which, "Someday We'll Be Together", had been put out as a single to no acclaim at all in 1982. The sleevenotes tell us that Diana was Clem's heroine, so covering those songs is understandable in that sense, but it did not seem to be a strategy to sell the LP in any great quantities. Side two houses the best two cuts on *Just In Time*, "The Blue Side" and "Half The Way", but it also includes a version of Stevie Wonder's "All In Love Is Fair"' where Clem goes for the big, all-out vocal assault so beloved of every contestant on TV talent shows over the last few years and the result is about as interesting.

Carrie Cleveland

Looking Up 19?? Cleve/Den BC 14 Producers: Bill Cleveland & Norris Snowden

Another incredibly scarce one here, this album was pressed up in small quantity and apparently only sold at Carrie's concerts which were mainly in the Bay Area of California. There is no year of release printed anywhere but I would put it at the mid to late seventies. She has a high light voice which would not have stood out in the crowded market of the time and the music is notably thin too, relying largely on an organ which brings to mind Timmy Thomas. But the set it is not without a certain charm and based on its contents I would have gone to see her had I ever found myself in Oakland with time to kill.

Linda Clifford (see also Curtis Mayfield)

Linda 1977 Curtom CU 5016 Producers: Gil Askey & Leroy Hutson

If My Friends Could See Me Now 1978 Curtom CUK 5021 Producers: Gil Askey & Curtis Mayfield (Billboard soul charts: 9; Billboard pop charts: 22)

Let Me Be Your Woman 1979 RSO RS-2-3902 Producer: Gil Askey (Billboard soul charts: 19; Billboard pop charts: 26)

Here's My Love 1979 RSO RS-1-3067 Producers: Norman Harris, Ron Tyson & Curtis Mayfield (Billboard soul charts: 47; Billboard pop charts: 117)

The Right Combination 1980 (and Curtis Mayfield) Producers: Curtis Mayfield, Gil Askey, Norman Harris & Bruce Gray (Billboard soul charts: 53; Billboard pop charts: 180)

Greatest Hits 1989 Curtom CUR-2007

Native New Yorker Linda Clifford was Curtom's disco star, and, as a result, has never received much of a following among the soul cognoscenti, who have tended to be unimpressed with her rather unimaginative dance sides and her lack of soulful ballads.

She had released a couple of obscure and unmemorable singles in the sixties under her maiden name of Linda Cumbo as well as a good one in 1973 on Paramount, "A Long Long Winter", before he first album, *Linda*, came out in 1977. Like all her LPs until her final one, it sensibly played up her beauty on the front cover, but lacked a little focus and it seemed as if Mayfield was maybe unsure what to do with her, given the songs came from a variety of outside sources. My favourite track is a spirited take on "Tonight's The Night" where she delivers the most committed vocal on the LP, but she brings nothing new to "Still In Love With You". Interestingly, there is only one out and out dance track on view, Bunny Sigler's "From Now On".

Everything was to change with *If My Friends Could See Me Now* which made a respectable showing on both soul and pop LP charts as well as housing her best ever track, "Runaway Love" which hit # 3 as a single on the soul charts in the middle of 1978. This excellent uptempo cut sees her adopting a sassy Marlena Shaw-like delivery and the record sizzles funkily as opposed to simply adopting mindless disco beats and deserved every bit of its success. Sadly, nothing else on the album approached its quality, with the title track opting for a much more standard disco approach and there were no ballads of particular quality on display.

Encouraged by the success of the LP, Mayfield and Gil Askey, went the whole dance hog next time around with a double LP, *Let Me Be Your Woman* (Curtom now had a deal with RSO), which also sold in good numbers but included tracks like a ten minute dance version of "Bridge Over Troubled Water" and one simply likes or hates such things. When the tempo DID drop on, for example, the splendid "I Can't Let This Good Thing Get Away", the results were much more congenial.

As the decade ended, Clifford turned away from a Gil Askey produced album for the first time and sales slipped backwards somewhat: "I Just Wanna Wanna" a perfectly respectable single from *Here's My Love* stalled at # 36 soul and the album didn't reach anywhere near the sales heights of the previous couple. Despite the change of producers the set continued in the vein of what had gone before with an uptempo slant and a marked absence of any compelling slow cuts. All in all, it sounded not unlike what Gloria Gaynor was doing at the same time.

In 1980 label boss Mayfield decided to cut an album with Clifford and, as senior partner, so to speak, it was not surprising that the result sounds more like one of his albums with Clifford assisting, rather than the other way around and is probably thus better discussed in the Mayfield section.

The *Greatest Hits* LP came out much later under an Ichiban distribution deal but contained a rather miserly six tracks only and unsurprisingly failed to catch on.

I'm Yours 1980 RSO RS-1-3087 Producers: Gil Askey, Isaac Hayes & Michael Gore (Billboard soul charts: 47; Billboard pop charts: 160)

I'll Keep On Loving You 1982 Capitol ST-12181 Producers: Leo Graham & Michael Gore

By the 1980 the RSO/Curtom tie-up was coming to an end and *I'm Yours* can be found on both the RSO and Capitol - her new record company - labels, the latter re-releasing it on ST-12131. Isaac Hayes was entrusted with the production of virtually all of the LP but sales didn't particularly revive although "Shoot Your Best Shot" and "Red Light" (from the *Fame* film) did at least enter the soul top forty charts and a superb cover of "I Had A Talk With My Man" - the best thing she ever did - also fared surprisingly well hitting #53 soul at a time when it sounded more soulful and out of step with pretty much everything else in vogue at the time.

I'll Keep On Loving You saw another change of producers but, despite good moments like "Never Say Never" and, particularly, "Only The Angels Know", neither the album, nor any singles from it, breached any charts. (It also contained the original of "All The Man I Need", a big hit later on for Whitney Houston.)

Sneakin' Out 1984 Red Label RA-10000 Producers: Gary Lee Jones, Billy Osbourne, Zane Giles, Benjamin Wright & Lee Young (Billboard soul charts: 49)

My Heart's On Fire 1985 Red Label ST-73104 Producer: Bobby Daniels

Her next move was to the Red Label and her tenure there proved that her best vinyl days were certainly in the past as regards both sales and listening pleasure, although *Sneakin' Out* did at least contain her last two singles to ever hit the soul singles charts in the title track and "A Night With The Boys".

The record label couldn't even be bothered to put a picture of this beautiful woman on the cover of *My Heart's On Fire*, a strange decision to say the least and whereas *Sneakin'* contains largely unmemorable dance tracks, the new one seemed to be a play for the straight pop market.

She did not cut any more LPs but has continued to record from time to time, often guesting on CDs by others.

George Clinton (see also many related)

Computer Games 1982 Capitol EST- 2246 Producers: George Clinton, Bootsy Collins, Gary Shider, Junie Morrison & Ted Currier (Billboard soul charts: 3; Billboard pop: 40)

You Shouldn't-Nuf Bit Fish 1983 Capitol ST-12308 Producers: George Clinton, Gary Shider & Junie Morrison (Billboard soul charts: 18; Billboard pop charts: 102)

Some Of My Best Jokes Are Friends 1985 Capitol ST-12417 Producers: George Clinton, Bootsy Collins, Thomas Dolby, Gary Shider, Tracy Lewis & Steve Washington (Billboard soul charts: 17; Billboard pop charts: 163)

R & B Skeletons (In The Closet) 1985 Capitol ST-12481 Producers: George Clinton, Andre Jackson & Steve Washington (Billboard soul charts: 17; Billboard pop: 81)

The Best Of 1985 Capitol ST-12534

The Mothership Connection-Live From Houston 1986 Capitol MLP-15021

The Cinderella Theory 1989 Paisley Park 1-25994 Produced by George Clinton (Billboard soul charts: 75; Billboard pop charts: 192)

George Clinton is undoubtedly one of the most important figures in the history of soul music. One of the most prolific, too, releasing a bewildering array of records under myriad names. As should be clear by now, this book is not the place to do any more than merely kiss the skim of the surface of Clinton's history but, in brief, he was born in North Carolina, grew up in New Jersey and wrote, recorded and produced lots of records out of Detroit, initially in fairly typical soul styles before he began wandering off down increasingly idiosyncratic roads as time went on. His greatest success and legacy came out of the twin attack of Funkadelic/Parliament and, precisely because they were so distinctive, his music and approach has alienated some soul fans who prefer their soul music straight.

As for his solo LPs, *Computer Games* owed more to Funkadelic than to Parliament and much of the music on the album (apart from the drum machines) would not have sounded out of place on the *One Nation Under A Groove* LP. Clinton's highly attuned sense of fun and rhythm made for an excellent debut album, although I have to be in the right mood to listen to it. "Atomic Dog" is a striking record that totally deserved its #1 showing on the soul singles chart, but stalled at # 101 pop, which says all that one needs to know about how uneasy the mainstream usually felt about his music (apart from a few years in the late seventies when he conquered all.) He also, probably more than any other soul artist, spent a lot of time thinking about his album sleeves, and one must give recognition to Pedro Bell, who illustrated virtually all of them. They are more often than not amusing and full of information and remind us of his deep love of soul singing given that he recruited the likes of Sandra Feva, Hugh Boynton, Joe Harris, Pat Lewis, and Jessica Cleaves to help out.

Fish included two fairly big singles in "Nubian Nut" and "Last Dance" although a third, "Quickie" didn't do so well. The approach had changed a fraction and The LP sounded more like Parliament this time around with "Silly Millameter" being the funkiest cut on show. So many other bands tried to imitate Clinton and his superb musicians but hardly anyone got even close to the brilliantly dense rhythm of a cut like this. For way of variety, "Stingy" is vocally impressive and it is another worthwhile LP.

I have more trouble with *Jokes* as the sound is more compact and, to me, less intricate and interesting than on the two previous records and I attribute this to the involvement of Thomas Dolby. In fact, it is not a record I particularly care for and it took the great single "Do Fries Go With That Shake" (his second most successful at #13) from *Skeletons* to resurrect my interest in Clinton. It also sports the funniest of his album sleeves which is worth reading. "Hey Good Lookin'" is another excellent funky cut with some engaging Steve Washington bass playing and the loose and jazzy "Cool Joe" is one of the best things Clinton ever did. On the other hand "Mix-Master Suite" and "Electric Pygmies" are best avoided.

A *Best Of* compilation and a *Live* set saw out his time with Capitol before he moved to Paisley Park with the *Cinderella Theory* album, which performed worse than his previous works. Given it came out in 1989 it was unsurprisingly more "electronic" than the Capitol output but it at least remained recognisably Clinton-esque.

There are also numerous albums released as by "George Clinton Family Series", "George Clinton Presents Our Gang Funky" etc. etc. but as these are actually various artists collections (with Clinton the obvious common denominator) they fall out of scope.

He's still active and as recently as October 2015, when I was driving around California, I noticed that he and his latest collection of musicians were playing a show in some obscure little town.

Bruce Cloud

California Soul 1969 Capitol ST-343 Producer: Phil Wright

Bruce Cloud comes out of the same tradition as Jewel Akens (and they both recorded for Era) in as much as he is right on the border line - or he is to my ears - between soul and pop. This album and a couple of the tracks certainly have their adherents but too many of the tracks are safe, rather hackneyed standards, although I do have a soft spot for the tuneful "Why Can't I Be Born Again".

Odia Coates

Odia Coates 1975 UA LA228-G Producer: Rick Hall

Sailing With Soul 1975 Navy Recruiting Command Series 19 (not released commercially)

Because ex-Raelet and Sisters Love member Odia Coates had such a massive and mawkish #1 pop hit with Paul Anka on "You're Having My Baby" she has tended to be disregarded by the soul fraternity and her debut album is one of the celebrated FAME studio's less celebrated records. But that is to miss out on much excellent music as this is a good, if slightly uneven, LP. The "uneven" bits first: "Having My Baby" and its follow-up," One Man Woman. One Woman Man" are both on here (although *sans* Anka), "Do I Love You" is pure and poor pop and "Showdown" is not a great song choice. But the rest is pleasing. "Heaven And Hell" and "Don't Leave Me In The Morning" should meet with favour from any demanding southern soul fan, "The Charmer" is an excellent dance record with a lyric in the "Armed And Extremely Dangerous" mode and two George Jackson songs, "I'll Just Keep On Loving You" and "Thief" are up to his usual standard. "The Woman's Song" is superior pop/soul as well with a lovely arrangement. Sadly, the LP got lost and even more sadly, Coates died of cancer at only 49.

There was a second album in her name, one of a rather odd series of LPs that were not commercially available and here is as good a place as any to explain how they worked. On behalf of the U.S. Navy Lou Rawls hosted four fifteen minute radio shows a month which consisted of Lou advertising the service as a great place to work as well as interviewing a singer or group of choice. In September 1975 that singer was Coates and Series #19 is a double album containing the four shows that were devoted to her. Every track on her UA album (some of which were slightly truncated) is included as well as a couple of then current tracks by Rawls, and another Paul Anka record, "I Don't Like To Sleep Alone" on which Coates sings two lines only. All in all, there is no need for anyone - apart from those who *must* have everything - to track any LPs in this series down.

Wayne Cochran & His C.C.Riders

Robert Gable; Don Capron; Allyn Robinson; Buzz Troy; Bob Scellato, Dennis Wilson; Charles Brent; Mike Katz; Harold Pierce; Michael Palmeiri; Skip Weissner; Randy Emerick; Bob Brawn; Artie Goleniak; Stuart Aptekar; Tony DeCaprio; Wayne Hurst; Dan Michler; Chalky Morehouse; Jeff Van Der Linden; Chester Mass; Mike Verbois; Greg Chesson; Harry Hann; Rudy Valenti

Wayne Cochran! 1968 Chess CLPS 1519 Producer: Abner Spector (Billboard pop charts: 167)

Alive And Well 1970 King KS-1116 Producers: Wayne Cochran & Charles Brent

High and Ridin' 1970 Bethlehem BS10,002 Producers: Wayne Cochran & Hal Neely

Cochran 1971 Epic BL 30989 Producers: Larry Cohn, Charles Brent & Roy Segal

Wayne Cochran was probably the most flamboyant white soul singer who ever lived, with, in the mid-sixties, the most astonishing haircut it has been my privilege to see, but despite his undoubtedly powerful image and often engaging music, chart success almost completely eluded him. Indeed, his biggest triumph was when one of his songs was recorded by someone else: "Last Kiss" covered by J.Frank Wilson and the Cavaliers, was a huge hit in 1964.

The man from Georgia had released a number of excellent singles over the years - notably on Mercury - but had not been rewarded with an LP until he moved to Chess in 1967. The company could not be faulted for any lack of interest or investment in him, given the album sported a gatefold sleeve and was recorded in such legendarily fertile studios as Criteria in Miami and FAME in Muscle Shoals but it never became the big hit everyone would have hoped for and maybe even expected. Possibly, in hindsight, that could be put down to the material which was somewhat predictable in too many cases ("Boom Boom", "Little Bitty Pretty One", "You Don't Know Like I Know" and "You Can't Judge A Book By Its Cover") but there were three excellent cuts aboard to sweeten the pill: "When My Baby Cries", the exciting "Some-A Your Sweet Love" and the stand-out track - and arguably the best thing he ever did - in the marvellous reading of Eddie Hinton's "Big City Woman", a 6/8 southern ballad of the highest class.

Calling an album *Alive And Well* would suggest a need to reassure the audience as to the robustness, and possibly even continuing existence, of an artist, always a worrying sign. This feeling was compounded by the full album title, *Alive And Well And Living In A Bitch Of A World*, and his take on "If I Were A Carpenter" where he does not sound in good health. All in all, it is more of a rock album than a soul one, but it sank without much trace as did the *High And Ridin'* jazz instrumental album which has precious little to do with soul music, but at least pointed up his refusal to be pigeon-holed..

Much better was his last vinyl outing, *Cochran*, on Epic in late 1971, which, while typically patchy, did contain three glorious cuts: "Somebody's Been Cuttin' In On My Groove", a two-speed version of Little Milton's "We're Gonna Make It" and "Sittin' In A World Of Snow" which may just be about Cochran himself.

Given his travails throughout life it is good to report that at the time of writing he is indeed alive and well, which he would doubtless attribute to his having "found religion" a few years ago.

Finally, I would not stake a lot on my having got the C.C.Riders from the four albums correct. They seemed to come and go quickly and I'm not sure that Tubby Zeigler, despite being listed on the Chess album, was ever really in the band.

Bill Coday

Bill Coday 1978 Vivid Sound VC 1001 Producers: Bill Jones & Denise LaSalle (Japan)

This is, plain and simple, a fantastic record. Coday released a string of tough as hell singles in the early seventies and most of them are on this 12 track LP. Sadly he was never honoured with an album at the time when the singles were extant and it is thanks to the Japanese that this collection was put out in 1978.

He was born in Mississipi but it was a move to Chicago which was to prove fortuitous as this is where he met Denise LaSalle and husband Bill Jones. They quickly saw his potential and sent him down to Memphis to record at Hi with Willie Mitchell. They were all rewarded with a pretty big hit (#14 soul) by the magnificent "Get Your Lie Straight" and the follow-up "When You Find A Fool Bump His Head" did well at #48, also. The titles of these sides give a good sense of the uncompromising approach of the music and there is not one second of weakness in any of the twelve songs. LaSalle wrote most of them herself and they are compelling proof as to my estimation of her as one of the finest and most underrated of all soul songwriters.

Bill Coday put out a series of CDs at the end of the last century and into this one, before passing away in 2008, but none got remotely close to the power and artistry of this LP.

Coffee

Elaine Sims; Gwen Hester; Dee Dee Bryant

Slippin' and Dippin' 1980 De-Lite DSR 9520 Producers: Clarence Johnson & Riccardo Williams

Second Cup 1982 De-Lite DSR 8503 Producer: Tony Valor

By 1980 the once vibrant Chicago record industry was struggling, but there were still a few outposts of activity and producer Clarence Johnson - who had a distinguished history of making fine music in the city - was the driving force behind this excellent trio, who did not sound unlike Motown's High Inergy.

The stand-out from *Slippin' And Dippin'* was a vivacious and worthy remake of a hit by the Lovelites back in 1969, "How Can I Tell My Mom And Dad", and Coffee also acquitted themselves admirably on another venerable Chicago hit, "Casanova". Of the new songs "Slip And Dip" and "Can You Get To This" were red-blooded dance items and "A Promise" was a dreamy slow number of merit. Only "I Wanna Be With You" lowered the quality a tad, but overall it is a highly recommended album.

Despite a lack of sales the group did get the chance to make a second LP, which was recorded in New York with a different production team. They were rewarded with two singles on the soul charts this time around: "Take Me Back" a ho-hum dance record and "If This World Were Mine", a tremendous reading on which they were helped by Leon Bryant (who I do not believe had any relationship to Dee Dee.). Other good things on what was another strong album were "Fantasy", "Purpose" and "I Wouldn't Give You Up" (the old Ecstasy, Passion and Pain mini-hit.)

After this release Coffee broke up and have been scarcely received any recognition whatsoever which is an injustice for such a talented group. Their most successful moment, in fact, was singing backing vocals on Kool and The Gang's "Celebration".

Cold Fire

Warren Petty; Roland Jennings, Ronald Rillera; Jimmie Weaver; Michael Loatman; Douglas Stevens; Ray Towns Sr.; Ray Towns Jr.; William Reese

Too Cold 1981 Capitol ST-12096 Producer: Cecil Hale

Cold Fire had the briefest of stays in the music business: a couple of earlier singles on small West Coast labels, this album and the one 45 that was pulled from it. And nothing sold well, either, which was understandable as Cold Fire did not have much to distinguish them from the crowd of similar self-contained funk groups. The

LP is pleasant enough listening but seemed destined to be played once or twice and then more or less forgotten.

Coldwater Stone

Defrost Me 1973 GSF S -1010 Producer: Freddy Briggs

Every so often an album comes along where the cover is so stunningly tasteless and ugly that you simply have to wonder why *anyone* could ever have thought it was a good idea. Thus it was with *Defrost Me*, which, thanks to the cover, had no chance of becoming a hit. And not only did the sleeve look horrible, but "Coldwater Stone" hardly conjures up soul music, either. But in fact the album was a strong one musically and even had somewhat of a cult following for a while.

Coldwater Stone is actually a *nom de plume* for Freddy Briggs who had a distinguished career in writing for many top soul artists before he passed away in 2006. The LP is generally of a fairly lugubrious and heartfelt nature, agreeable to afficionados but having no pop appeal whatsoever. Briggs himself sings in a mournful tone somewhat reminiscent of Jerry Butler and conjures up true emotion in "Without The One You Love", a genuine "deep soul" offering. There is the hint of homage to Al Green in "You're The One" but the album is really all down to Briggs, who wrote every track bar one - which came from his former wife, soulstress Kim Tolliver - and arranged the songs in an intricate and satisfying way with John Brinson. A single, "Outside Love Affair", was pulled from the set but did not become a success.

Natalie Cole

Inseparable 1975 Capitol ST-11429 Producers: Chuck Jackson & Marvin Yancy (Billboard soul charts: 1; Billboard pop charts: 18)

Natalie 1976 Capitol ST- 11517 Producers: Chuck Jackson, Marvin Yancy, Gene Barge & Richard Evans (Billboard soul charts: 3; Billboard pop charts: 13)

Unpredictable 1977 Capitol SO-11600 Producers: Chuck Jackson, Marvin Yancy and Gene Barge (Billboard soul charts: 1; Billboard pop charts: 8)

Thankful 1977 Capitol SW-11708 Producers: Chuck Jackson, Marvin Yancy & Gene Barge (Billboard soul charts: 5; Billboard pop charts: 16)

Natalie...Live! 1978 Capitol SKBL-11709 Producers: Chuck Jackson, Marvin Yancy & Gene Barge (Billboard soul charts: 9; Billboard pop charts: 31)

I Love You So 1979 Capitol SO-11928 Producers: Chuck Jackson, Marvin Yancy & Gene Barge (Billboard soul charts: 11; Billboard pop charts: 52)

We're The Best Of Friends (with Peabo Bryson) 1979 Capitol SOO-12019 Producers: Mark Davis, Marvin Yancy, Peabo Bryson, Johnny Pate (Billboard soul charts: 7; Billboard pop charts: 44)

Don't Look Back 1980 Capitol ST-12079 Producers: Marvin Yancy, Gene Barge & Michael Masser (Billboard soul charts: 17; Billboard pop charts: 77)

Happy Love 1981 Capitol ST-12165 Producers: George Tobin & Mike Piccirillo (Billboard soul charts: 37; Billboard pop charts: 132)

By 1975 Aretha was flailing a little, her best days behind her, and Capitol seized the opportunity to propel Natalie Cole into arguably taking on the mantle of the top female soul singer of the latter half of the decade. The statistics would bear this out as Cole placed ten top 10 singles - including five at #1 - on the soul charts between 1975 and the end of 1979 whereas Franklin's figures were three and two respectively. My own feeling on Ms. Cole is that she was talented, photogenic and tough but lacked the genius of Aretha and never allowed herself to show the pain that permeated so many of Franklin's sides.

Both women had famous fathers, of course, but Natalie's lineage was particularly impeccable, and it clearly helped enormously in getting her a record deal. *Inseparable* was her first ever LP and "This Will Be" was her first ever single - no paying dues here - and both went #1 soul and top twenty pop. An extraordinary achievement. She was clearly strongly influenced by Franklin and "This Will Be" itself sounds VERY similar to "You Send Me" from Aretha's *Now* album of some years earlier. To be fair to Cole, she increasingly evolved her own style, and made some fine records as a result. The first album was the work of Chuck Jackson and Marvin Yancy, pretty hot writers and producers in 1975, but I don't find it to be a particularly inspiring piece if work, despite its huge success, and I feel they were producing better songs for The Independents. Nothing is poor, but not much is exciting, either.

Entirely predictably and appropriately, *Natalie* followed the same basic pattern as its predecessor but it did have a slightly jazzier feel than the debut. "Sophisticated Lady" (#1 soul) and "Mr. Melody" (#10) became the hits this time around with "Can We Get Together Again" being the "This will be" re-write.

A third big album - her biggest in fact, and platinum where the first two had been merely gold - followed in *Unpredictable* which was hardly an apposite title but it did include the first time she had ventured out on an emotional limb in the excellent "I'm Catching Hell". "I've Got Love On My Mind" was a really good single as well, deserving to become another #1. The album was also the first instance of where a couple of Cole's own songs were featured.

The fourth album, *Thankful*, was recorded in LA, the first time one of her LPs hadn't been cut in Chicago, but the sound and feel were much the same, and "Our Love" was another impressive #1 single. There were some subtle changes: "La Costa" was a bossa-nova style cut and a departure from much of what had gone before while "Annie Mae" and "Keeping A Light In My Window" were examples of Cole's increasing confidence as a songwriter. "I Can't Stay Away From You" was a particularly good Jackson-Yancy offering but all in all, the album seemed to play up, rather than down, the vocal similarities with Franklin which seemed a bit odd now Cole was so popular in her own right.

And then came the inevitable *Live* album, a double no less. It had the effect that "live" albums so often do: of slowing down the momentum of an artist and Cole never hit the top twenty pop charts again with an LP. In some ways it is a schizophrenic record, in as much as apart from all the obvious hits, she also serves up "Something's Got A Hold On Me" and "Cry Baby" (the old Garnet Mimms hit) which see her singing in an out and out soulful style, completely at odds at anything on any of her studio albums, as if in response to criticisms that she couldn't sing "real" soul. The problem was that this mode didn't suit her in the slightest, and neither did a version of "Lucy In The Sky With Diamonds" which performed disappointingly when released as a single.

Cole ended the decade with two albums in 1979, the first of which was *I Love You So*, which had some good moments, including "Oh Daddy", a song which I thought was going to refer to Nat, but it doesn't, and is in fact a good song from Fleetwood Mac. Much of the LP is poppy in construction but at least kept up her policy of refusing to go down a dance / disco route. The second LP of the year was the duet with Peabo Bryson.

Don't Look Back saw Michael Masser arrive on the scene, a ploy guaranteed to send me in the other direction and by now I found her records increasingly hard to take - although I did and do like "Hold on" from the album a great deal, a record that deserved to go much higher than #38 on the soul charts - so I will freely admit that from here on in she had a large audience out there that did not include the likes of me.

Happy Love continued the transition to pop/adult contemporary music as evidenced by "Nothing But A Fool", a single from the set, or "Love And Kisses", neither of which are soulful in any way.

I'm Ready 1983 Epic FE-38280 Producers: Chuck Jackson, Marvin Yancy, Chuck Bynum & Stanley Clarke (Billboard soul charts: 54; Billboard pop charts: 182)

Unforgettable (and Johnny Mathis) 1983 CBS 10042 Producer: Jim Danguglia (UK)

Dangerous 1985 Modern 90270 Producers: Eddie Cole, Gary Skardina, Harold Beatty, Marti Sharron & Natalie Cole (Billboard soul charts: 48; Billboard pop charts: 140)

Everlasting 1987 EMI-Manhattan ST-53051 Producers: Aaron Zigman, Jerry Knight, Dennis Lambert, Reggie Calloway, Vincent Calloway, Bibi Green, Marcus Miller, Paul Jackson, Eddie Cole & Natalie Cole (Billboard soul charts: 8; Billboard pop charts: 42)

Good To Be Back 1989 EMI E1-489102 Producers: Andre Fischer, Dennis Lambert, Michael Masser, Narada Michael Walden, Lee Curreri, Ric Wake & Eddie Cole (Billboard soul charts: 21; Billboard pop charts: 59)

Unforgettable With Love 1991 Elektra 7559-61049 Producers: Andre Fischer, Tommy LiPuma & David Foster (Billboard soul charts: 5; Billboard pop charts: 1)

Cole moved labels in 1983, but initially continued to be rather on the margins of acclaim, commercially and artistically, and the Epic stay was brief in the extreme, and the time at Modern didn't last much longer. The title track from *Dangerous* (predictable, boring and misleading title) did at least put her back in the soul top twenty but it is a poor record in a "Footloose" style, and it is another album that traditional soul fans had little time for. If you doubt me listen to "Billy The Kid Next Door", a record of depressing awfulness.

But then, with *Everlasting* she bounced back with her best selling album for nearly ten years. The reason for this could be traced to "Pink Cadillac" one of the biggest singles she ever had, #9 soul, #5 pop. I don't care for it at all, but can at least see that it is a well-constructed, tuneful and catchy song. I much preferred "In My Reality" with its gentle swing and overall it was much more satisfying than her previous four of five efforts.

Good To Be Back made sense as a title and built on the previous album's high profile. It housed the first soul single #1 (it also made #7 pop) she had enjoyed in twelve years, "Miss You Like Crazy", another adult contemporary ballad.

An album with Johnny Mathis had come out in the UK in 1983 which saw Natalie singing her father's songs but a much bigger deal came in 1991 when she put out a double LP of Nat's best loved sides which was a massive hit, her biggest ever. Shame it was nothing to do with soul music, but could be argued to be the record she was born to sing, of course.

Cole had an undeniably rewarding and fruitful career and made music in the new century, including the best thing she ever did in my opinion with her excellent *Leavin'* CD from 2006, before passing away on New Year's Day 2016.

Collage

Lee Peters; David Agent; Richard Aguon; Albert De Gracia; Larry White; Emilio Conesa; Ross Wilson; Ruben Laxamana; Dean Boysen ; Melicio Magdaluyo; Kirk Crumpler

Do You Like Our Music? 1981 Solar S-23 Producer: The Whispers

Get In Touch 1983 Solar 60240 -1 Producers: Nicholas Caldwell, Grady Wilkins & Larry White

Shine The Light 1985 Constellation MCA-5564 Producers: Dana Meyers, William Zimmerman, Larry White & Collage

I'll avoid the obvious answer to the question posed by the first set, but it must be said that Collage were a rather bland act in an era where originality was generally at a premium anyway. They released three albums and a handful of singles, but apart from "Get In Touch With Me" which did reach the Cashbox soul charts, nothing sold in any quantity.

One of those singles was a version of "Groovin'", and while it was certainly pleasant enough, it's no better than many of the others that exist. It sat on the first album, which also featured rather colourless ballads in "When You Smile" and "Special Occasion" and a six minute take on the dull standard, "Feelings". The rest were nondescript dance tracks. Lee Peters was not a bad singer, but he was either told to keep it light or he couldn't muster up much passion anyway.

Get In Touch sported a harder, more aggressive style, which was probably fair enough seeing as how the more relaxed approach on the debut set hadn't resulted in many sales. "Love Is For Everyone" did keep the tempo down but the title track, "Punk Me Off" and "Alien ZZZ" were more representative of the general tone of the album.

I must admit that I expected very little from the *Shine The Light* set, but it certainly houses by far my favourite track of theirs in the commendable "Winners And Losers" which has a genuine tune, and some of the group's (and Peters') best ever singing. The rest of the LP, while not featuring much to my personal taste, was well constructed and quite nicely varied and I can see why anyone would like it.

Mitty Collier

Shades Of A Genius 1965 Chess LPS 1492 Producer: Billy Davis

The Warning 1972 111 AM 1022 Producers: David Peay, Mitty Collier & Charles Pikes

Hold The Light 1977 Gospel Roots GR 5020 Producer: Kevin Yancy

I Am Love 1987 New Sound 8214827 Producers: Mitty Collier & David Peay

I rate Mitty Collier as one of the finest of all female soul singers with a marvellous throaty and fruity contralto and it is therefore a shame that of the four albums she put out, three were fairly routine gospel sets and the one soul LP that exists - while superb - does not contain some of her best sides.

She was born in Birmingham, Alabama and made the move north to Chicago where she soon got a record deal with Chess. Over a seven or eight year period she put out fifteen singles on the label and all of them were good. In 1965 *Shades Of A Genius* was released, the title of which referred to Ray Charles, as three of his songs feature. The album contains what are probably her best known hits: "I Had A Talk With My Man" (#41 pop) and "No Faith, No Love" (#29, soul), the latter having one of the most lovely and arresting arrangements (from Riley Hampton) of all soul records. These are magnificent pieces of artistry and while the whole album is exceptionally strong Chess royally screwed up by first issuing it with a lady on the cover who was not Ms. Collier, resulting in its being hastily withdrawn and reissued with an awful sleeve design of no merit or distinction and such shenanigans could not have helped sales. Listening to the album again now for the umpteenth time I am almost struck dumb by the brilliance of her phrasing, the musicianship and arrangements and the lyrical skill of songs such as "I've Got To Get Away From It All" (astonishing in its maturity and content) and "Little Miss Loneliness" which are exquisite and profound. Even the "hackneyed" material (like "Drown In My Own Tears" and "Let Them Talk") is delivered beautifully.

After releasing a number of other brilliant singles for Chess, including the tremendous "Sharing You" (#10 soul) and "Everybody Makes A Mistake Sometimes", she signed to William Bell's Peachtree label in 1968 where she put out a number of yet more extraordinarily good 45s, none of which sadly ever found themselves onto a Collier album, although they do exist on a Japanese various artists compilation. One more secular single followed before she apparently completely lost her voice in late 1971. She attributed its return to a sign from God and therefore dedicated the rest of her career to singing only gospel.

The gospel albums in their starker simplicity cannot compare with her soul sides but her voice had indubitably returned as a listen to, at random, "He Brought Joy Into My Life" from the *Hold The Light* LP proves conclusively.

Collins And Collins

Collins And Collins 1980 A & M SP-4806 Producer: John Davis

Brother and sister team, Bill and Tonee, put out this one and only LP in 1980, which has remained in demand ever since, no surprise as it is full of memorable tunes and none more so than Ashford & Simpson's "At The Top Of The Stairs", and it remains hard to understand why such an absurdly catchy song did no better than only reaching #68 on the soul charts in June 1980. The duo also perform a good cover of the old Harold Melvin and Blue Notes' side "You Know How To Make Me Feel So Good" which sits atop a rhythm pattern remarkably similar to that from "Be Thankful For What You Got". These two and "I'm Feelin' Your Love" are the stand-outs from an impressive set. Not many other acts were releasing such confident, tuneful and lush albums in 1980, apart from Ashford and Simpson themselves, of course. Despite the quality, though, the LP didn't do a great deal of business and Tonee and Bill stopped making any more records together.

Lyn Collins

Think (About It) 1972 People PE 5602 Producer: James Brown (Billboard soul charts: 34)

Check Me Out If You Don't Know Me By Now 1975 People PE 6605 Producer: James Brown

I don't think there can be any serious doubt that working for James Brown was challenging in the extreme, but it could also have its rewards and the success Lyn Collins achieved with her immortal "Think" (#9 soul in summer 1972) doubtless owed much to the public's willingness to embrace the Brown groove.

Collins was one of a number of women who worked with the JB review but not many of them went on to record a couple of LPs. Originally from Texas, she hooked up with The Godfather in early 1970 and a couple of singles didn't really take off before "Think" did so well. The first album has its moments as Collins was a soulful and satisfying singer although she could sometimes overpower a song when a softer approach may have paid higher dividends: "Ain't No Sunshine" and "Fly Me To The Moon" for example. On the other hand, her feisty reading of "Never Gonna Give You Up" contrasts nicely with Jerry Butler's cooler interpretation. "Women's Lib" owes a lot to the attitude of Laura Lee and the melody of "I Don't Want To Do Wrong".

Check Me Out contained three singles that made the soul top 100 but omitted two more that could have been included given they were released between 45s that were on the album. Never mind, it is another worthwhile LP with the marvellous "Rock Me Again And Again And Again And Again And Again And Again" (#53 soul) taking centre stage. The album opened up with, surprisingly but charmingly, "A Foggy Day", a George Gershwin song, and she also performs more than adequately on other covers such as "If You Don't Know Me By Now" (#82 soul) and "Mr. Big Stuff". Conversely, "Backstabbers" and "Try A Little Tenderness" do not get close to equalling the better known versions. "How Long Can I Keep It Up" from *Slaughter's Big Rip-Off* is also included and is a plaintive cry that had done well for her as a single in the summer of '73 (#45 soul).

She didn't record much after the mid seventies and passed on in 2005.

Willie Collins

Where You Gonna Be Tonight? 1986 Capitol ST-12442 Producers: Billy Nichols, Willie Collins, Gene McFadden, John Whitehead & Rahni Harris (Billboard soul charts: 59)

Willie Collins is (or was on here) an unreconstructed soul man working within the smoother confines of what record labels were looking for in 1986 and the mundane nature of much of the musical backing and the songs themselves could not entirely subdue his gospel passion and this is a good album, if a little too imbued with the "love man" spirit. He made his first record back in the early seventies on the Geneva label with the involving and deep

"Two Lives" but had to wait a long time for his one and only LP to come out. Nothing on the set sounds remotely like the earlier single which was to be expected but the title track was good of its type and "Let's Get Started" - also good, with a Freddie Jackson flavour - became the one and only single he ever placed on the soul top fifty. Some cuts are not great - like the Billy Ocean-ish "Determination" - but all in all not bad.

Commodores (see also Lionel Richie and Thomas McClary)

Lionel Richie; Ronald LaPread; Thomas McClary; William King; Milan Williams; Walter Orange; J D Nicholas

Machine Gun 1974 Motown M6-798S Producers: James Carmichael & Commodores (Billboard soul charts: 22; Billboard pop charts: 138)

Caught In The Act 1975 Motown M6-820S Producers: James Carmichael & Commodores (Billboard soul charts: 7; Billboard pop charts: 26)

Movin' On 1975 Motown M6-848S Producers: James Carmichael & Commodores (Billboard soul charts: 7; Billboard pop charts: 29)

Hot On The Tracks 1976 Motown M6-867S Producers: James Carmichael & Commodores (Billboard soul charts: 1; Billboard pop charts: 12)

Commodores 1977 Motown M7-884R Producers: James Carmichael & Commodores (Billboard soul charts: 1; Billboard pop charts: 3)

Sailing With Soul 1975 Navy Recruiting Command Series 12 (not released commercially)

Given how terminally unhip Lionel Richie is - although he addressed that to a large extent with a Glastonbury performance in 2015 - it would be easy for a hardcore soul fan to dismiss the Commodores as a pop band of no consequence but it would also be wrong. Not only were they exceptionally successful for a number of years but some of their early records still hold their appeal all these years later. It should also be remembered that initially The Commodores were a funk band on a label that didn't really do funk and thus were a departure for the biggest black owned record company of all time.

The group formed in Alabama and after Swamp Dogg did some work with the band (which was unreleased at the time, but came out on the Intermedia album in 1983) they cut a handful of tracks in Muscle Shoals, a couple of which were featured on their first, excellent, LP, *Machine Gun*. They were a most democratic band as every member of the group had at least one song on every single album they put out up to *Heroes*. Side one of *Machine Gun* is particularly good as it is excitingly funky with snarling vocals, stabbing horns, resonant bass and drums that were hit immensely hard by Walter Orange. "Young Girls Are My Weakness" would doubtless raise an eyebrow or two in today's politically correct world and only "Rapid Fire" and "Gonna Blow Your Mind" are substandard. I even like "Superman", an enjoyable piece of fluff.

Caught In The Act took the band to another level as regards sales, with "Sllppery When Wet" becoming the first of seven #1 singles they posted on the soul charts. "Wide Open" and "Look What You've Done To Me" were more good hard funk but "I'm Ready" was a "Machine Gun" clone which sounded flimsy when compared with the thoughtful and inspirational song, "This Is Your Life" (#13 soul). "Better Never Than Forever" also concentrated on hard social realities, demonstrating a willingness to look beyond the need to dance or romance.

Movin' On featured "Sweet Love" which became their first ever top five pop success as a single and it was the first sign of what would come later in that it was melodic enough but softer than previous ballads and more accessible to a larger audience. The majority of the album was still funky in nature but I must confess that I was already starting to become slightly bored with the derivative vocals which borrowed so heavily from Sly and The Ohio Players.

Hot On The Tracks was their biggest album to date and was similar in style to *Movin' On* with "Just To Be Close To You" being the slow cut and huge hit (#1 soul and #7 pop) while most of the rest of the LP kept the tempo up.

Commodores (entitled *Zoom* in the UK) proved the band could still do hard funk when they wanted to as it included the irresistible "Brick House" (#4 soul, #5 pop) but it also featured the estimable "Easy" (#1 soul, #4 pop) and this was clearly the path the band would increasingly take, given its immense sales.

Live! 1977 Motown M9-894A Producers: James Carmichael & Commodores (Billboard soul charts: 2; Billboard pop charts: 3)

Natural High 1978 Motown M7-902R Producers: James Carmichael & Commodores (Billboard soul charts: 1; Billboard pop charts: 3)

Greatest Hits 1978 Motown M7-912R (Billboard soul charts: 24; Billboard pop charts: 23)

Midnight Magic 1979 Motown M8-926M Producers: James Carmichael & Commodores (Billboard soul charts: 1; Billboard pop charts: 3)

Heroes 1980 Motown M8-939M Producers: James Carmichael & Commodores (Billboard soul charts: 3; Billboard pop charts: 7)

In The Pocket 1981 Motown M8-955M Producers: James Carmichael & Commodores (Billboard soul charts: 4; Billboard pop charts: 13)

All The Great Hits 1982 Motown 6028ML (Billboard soul charts: 12; Billboard pop charts: 37)

Anthology 1983 Motown 6044ML (Billboard soul charts: 50; Billboard pop charts: 141)

From 1977 until 1982 The Commodores were one of the biggest bands in the world with *Natural High, Heroes* and *In The Pocket* all attaining platinum selling status although they did start to record some awfully slushy songs like "Three Times A Lady" and "Still". Both might have made it to #1 on both the soul and singles charts, but they are sickly and sentimental outings, utterly devoid of the spirit of even the most throwaway genuine soul side.

That is my problem, though, not the band's and they could even place a double "Live" album high on the charts; they were good live, too, as I saw them In Brighton in 1977 and they were certainly far funkier than the likes of "Still" would suggest.

Listening again now to the *Natural High* set, I'm surprised why it was so successful; it's by no means poor stuff, but what did it have that so many other funky dominated LPs did not? I'd suggest very little and the band simply had the good fortune to record for Motown and tap into an audience that were losing interest in The Ohio Players. ("Say Yeah" was a far better ballad to my ears than "Three Times A Lady" proving that the group could be more soulful on album cuts than singles.)

Midnight Magic was another big success of course but the title track was a completely throwaway item, characterising an appallingly dull set, with nothing of any lasting appeal at all. I don't wish to be disrespectful to a million selling band but we had by now reached a point where we were better off well apart.

Nevertheless, I did and do like "Lady (You Bring Me Up)" from *In The Pocket* which reached #5 soul and #8 pop and had more drive and excitement than anything from them in years.

Uprising 1983 Intermedia QS-5047 No producer listed

Commodores 13 1983 Motown 6054ML Producer: Commodores (Billboard soul charts: 26; Billboard pop charts: 103)

Nightshift 1985 Motown 6044ML Producer: Dennis Lambert (Billboard soul charts: 1; Billboard pop charts: 12

United 1986 Polydor 422 831 194-1 Producers: Dennis Lambert, Jeremy Smith, Greg Mathieson, Lloyd Tolbert, James Carmichael & Milan Williams (Billboard soul charts: 17; Billboard pop charts: 101)

Rock Solid 1988 Polydor 422 835 369-1 Producers: Steve Harvey, Walter Orange, Tony Prendatt, William King, Sandy Torano, Marti Sharron, Howie Rice, Howard Hewett, Hawk Wolinski, J D Nicholas, Milan Williams & Walter Orange

By the time *Commodores 13* arrived Richie had left but "Only You" showed that Milan Williams was determined to carry on with writing the sort of ballad Lionel was known for. Much better was the title track to *Nightshift,* the band's biggest hit for four years and a record that proved they could forge a new sound in the post-Richie era.

In 1986 the group moved to Polydor for a couple of last vinyl albums, which are very much of their time - pop/synth stuff - but to be fair, "Goin' To The Bank" from *United* was a big hit (#2 soul) and did get the new label off to a good start in that respect.

More recently the band continue to perform live around the world although they do not appear to have released much new music in the last twenty five years or so.

Congress Alley

Lee Andrews; Karen Briscoe; Jacqui Andrews; Richard Booker

Congress Alley 1973 Avco AV-11009-598 Producer: Vinny Testa

Congress Alley starts well with the Norman Whitfield influenced opening track, "Are You Looking?", which also turned up on the Tymes' *Trustmaker* album, but after that it all does downhill for me, veering off into Fifth Dimension territory and songs by Graham Nash, Donovan and Lennon and McCartney demonstrate that this is not going to be the most soulful of albums.

Looking again at that Tymes LP, I note that Jacqui Andrews and Briscoe sing backing vocals and Lee Andrews arranged it. Lee Andrews and Booker were formerly in Lee Andrews & The Hearts.

Con-Funk-Shun (see also Michael Cooper)

Michael Cooper; Felton Pilate; Louis McCall; Danny Thomas; Cedric Martin; Paul Harrell; Karl Fuller; Melvin Carter

The Memphis Sessions 1980 51 West Q 16106 Producer: Ted Sturges

Organized 1978 Pickwick BAN-90081 Producer: Ted Sturges

Con-Funk-Shun 1976 Mercury SRM-1-1120 Producers: Ron Capone &nd Con-Funk-Shun

This reassuringly solid and consistent self-contained band were formed on the West Coast but moved eastwards in order to seek their fame and fortune. The Bar-Kays are the biggest soul/funk band ever to have come out of Memphis and Con-Funk-Shun sought to emulate that success when they recorded a number of sessions in the city, the first fruits of which could be seen on a really good 45 in 1974 entitled "Clique" on the small Fretone concern but it didn't really make it, and neither did a bizarre version of "Mr. Tambourine Man" on the same label.

The tracks on the *Memphis Sessions* LP were cut back in 1973, even before the Fretone recordings, and released on an album in 1980 when the group had triumphed and become one of the biggest funk bands in the world. The few tracks I have heard from the LP are all in a soft, ballad vein, including a take on Marvin Gaye's "You Sure Love To Ball", and there was nothing so compelling about them to be able to accuse anyone of missing an opportunity in not releasing the tracks at the time.

Organized is similar in as much as it was released a couple of years after the cuts were recorded in order to take advantage of the group's later success. (Neither album contains the Fretone sides). It includes the first ever single they placed on the soul charts in "Sho Feels Good To Me" and the funk tracks utilise the horn section more fully than would be the case in later years. "Do You Really Know What Love Is For" was also a precursor of what would come later regarding the quality of their ballads.

For their first Mercury LP they continued to record in Memphis but remained unable to crack the market. Nevertheless it was a highly competent and attractive album and showed they were equally at home with slow and uptempo material and the lovely "Never Be The Same" is almost a "sweet soul" side, The intro to "Another World" recalls "What's Happening Baby" by the Soul Children, which given Con Funk Shun once backed them up might not be so surprising.

Secrets 1977 Mercury SRM-1-1180 Producer: Skip Scarborough (Billboard soul charts: 6; Billboard pop charts: 51)

Loveshine 1978 Mercury SRM-1-3725 Producer: Skip Scarborough (Billboard soul charts: 10; Billboard pop: 32)

Candy 1979 Mercury SRM-1-3754 Producers: Skip Scarborough & Con-Funk-Shun (Billboard soul charts: 7; Billboard pop charts: 46)

Spirit Of Love 1980 Mercury SRM-1-3806 Producer: Skip Scarborough (Billboard soul charts: 7; Billboard pop : 30)

Their big break finally came when they moved under the tutelage of Skip Scarborough and relocated to California to record *Secrets* which contained a #1 soul single in "Ffun", though it was not a particularly outstanding 45 and its huge success always baffled me somewhat. By now their sound was beginning to take shape and it was a shape that owed much to Earth, Wind & Fire with Felon Pilate's high, ethereal vocals recalling Philip Bailey while Michael Cooper provided a tough voiced alternative. EWAF had the edge with their horn section (although Con-Funk-Shun's was not bad at all) and also tended to write stronger songs but the newcomers had an enviable consistency and were probably even better than the Maurice White's band on ballads.

That consistency was evident in all the four albums that were produced by Scarborough. Not many tracks jump out of the speakers demanding instant attention but hardly any require a raising of the stylus, either. If one is a fan of skilled seventies funk/ballad bands then there is no reason whatsoever not to seek out and enjoy all of these albums, although *Candy* is weaker than the others. Having said the above some cuts *are* worthy of a special mention: "Tears In My Eyes" and "Who Has The Time" from *Secrets*; "Wanna Be There" and the lovely "Make It Last" from *Loveshine*; "Honey Wild" and the title cut from *Spirit Of Love*.

Touch 1980 Mercury SRM-1-4002 Producer: Con-Funk-Shun (Billboard soul charts: 7; Billboard pop charts: 51)

Con-Funk-Shun 7 1981 Mercury SRM-1-4030 Producer: Con-Funk-Shun (Billboard soul charts: 17; Billboard pop charts: 82)

To The Max 1982 Mercury SRM-1-4067 Producers: Con-Funk-Shun & Gordon DeWitty (Billboard soul charts: 9; Billboard pop charts: 115)

The next chapter in the band's career saw a parting of the ways with Scarborough and a series of self-produced albums. As usual it was on the slow material where the band's strengths lay and "Give Your Love To Me" from *Touch* maintained the standard while uptempo cuts like "Too Tight" (the second biggest single they ever had at #8 soul and #40 pop) proved the market could still stand two Earth Wind & Fires.

Fever 1983 Mercury 422-814- 447-1 Producer: Eumir Deodata (Billboard soul charts: 12; Billboard pop charts: 105)

Electric Lady 1985 Mercury 422-824-345-1 Producers: Maurice Starr, Billy Osborne & Larry Smith (Billboard soul charts: 9; Billboard pop charts: 62)

Burnin' Love 1986 Mercury 422-826-963-1 Producers: Attala Zane Giles, Leon Ware, Billy Osborne, Denzil Foster, Thomas McElroy, Billy Valentine, J King & Bryan Loren (Billboard soul charts: 25; Billboard pop charts: 121)

After seven well-selling LPs (or at least in the soul market, Con Funk Shun never really "crossed over") the group now entrusted production duties for *Fever* away from themselves or Scarborough and yet retained the usual quality in slow cuts such as "Baby I'm Hooked" which was typically big on the soul charts (#5) as well as becoming only the fourth ever single they managed to post on the Hot 100. Worryingly, though, the uptempo material was entirely predictable and generic, and as it heavily outnumbered the slower stuff, I find it to be one of their least interesting albums.

Mind you, it sounded a lot better than *Electric Lady* where all the songs, for the first time, came from outside the band and there is not a track on it I would ever want to hear again.

The last vinyl album, *Burnin' Love,* was significant because it was the first one without Pilate although the rest of the band remained intact - an incredible achievement to stay together for so long. It was also somewhat of a return to form as someone recalled that the group were at their best on slower material and "You Make Me Wanna Love Again", "It's Time Girl" and "How Long" are all good, although much else remained grim.

Strangely, for a group that placed 26 records on the soul singles charts, a *Greatest Hits* or *Best Of* LP did not come out at the time in the U.S, although CD collections appeared in due course.

Michael Cooper went on to release solo LPs while Felton Pilate has long been an in-demand producer.

Arthur Conley

Sweet Soul Music 1967 Atco 33-215 Producer: Otis Redding (Billboard soul charts: 10; Billboard pop charts: 93)

Shake, Rattle & Roll 1967 Atco 33-220 Producer: Otis Redding (Billboard pop charts: 193)

Soul Directions 1968 Atco 33-243 Producers: Otis Redding & Tom Dowd (Billboard pop charts: 185)

More Sweet Soul 1969 Atco 33-276 Producer: Tom Dowd

Best Of 1973 Atlantic K20062 (UK)

Many people will only know Arthur Conley for his massive worldwide hit, but he made many better records in a career of unusual complexity.

It started in Atlanta where he was a member of the Corvets, before moving to Baltimore and becoming the lead singer in The Harold Holt Band who issued a single entitled "I'm A Stranger" which found its way to Otis Redding. The great soul singer agreed to become Conley's mentor. The song was re-cut and appeared on his debut album, which came out in 1967, named after the big hit. There are no weak tracks on this tremendous LP, most of which was cut at FAME in Muscle Shoals, with the remainder being recorded at Stax. "Sweet Soul Music" (basically a re-make of Sam Cooke's "Yeah Man") went to #2 on both soul and pop charts as a single but the re-cut of "Stranger" and "Let Nothing Separate Us" are far superior indications of Conley's prowess as a soul man of skill and subtlety. "I Can't Stop" is a better dance record, too. The album is probably his best.

It was quickly followed by *Shake, Rattle & Roll* which was a little disappointing as too many of its songs were lacklustre, having been performed better by others. The title track is one such example but did ok as the follow up single to "Sweet Soul Music", (#20 soul, #31 pop). I preferred Conley's performances on his own "Hand And Glove" and his excellent reading of Penn and Oldham's "Keep On Talking" but the two stand-outs were both superb slow sides: I'll Take The Blame" and "You Don't Have To See Me" which has great horns.

In December 1967 Otis Redding died and Conley was, understandably, devastated but it didn't stop his releasing a much improved LP in *Soul Directions*. It included the last two Conley songs to have been produced by Redding, one of which, "Love Comes And Goes" is of high quality. It also contained his second big hit, "Funky Street" (#5 soul, #14 pop), a success that has been almost forgotten in the public's perception of him as a "one hit wonder". The album was all cut at American in Memphis and is sadly under appreciated. "Get Yourself Another Fool" was an inspired song choice, which Conley delivers beautifully, "You Really Know How To Hurt A Guy" and "This Love Of Mine" are lesser known Penn-Oldham songs, but easily up to their normal standard, while the emotion in "Otis Sleep On" is evident and genuine.

But if *Soul Directions* was two steps forward, *More Sweet Soul* was five steps back. It did have a good cut in "Is That You Love" but too much of the material was sub-standard and the tempo was too often too fast to hear Conley at his best. "Ob La Di, Ob La Da" was simply a disaster, "Speak Her Name" suffered from an over-wrought production and even George Jackson dipped below his usual quality with "Stuff You Gotta Watch". One to avoid, really.

After this it was more or less all downhill with Atco and despite the release of a handful more singles there were no more albums (apart from a Best Of) and only one more hit.

One More Sweet Soul Music 1988 P-Vine PJ-122
Producer: Jerry Williams (Japan)

Soulin' (as by Lee Roberts & The Sweaters) 1987 Blue Shadow BS 4703 Producer: Dick Baars

In the early seventies Conley started to work with Jerry "Swamp Dogg" Williams and the last "hit" referred to above (it only reached # 33 soul and #107 pop) was Williams' "God Bless". In 1978 the Japanese P-Vine label put out an 8 track album of the work the two men created together. When I played it again recently I thought "that's not Arthur Conley!" before realising it has to be played at 45 rpm. It is a good LP, despite containing possibly the worst song Williams ever wrote in the unspeakable "Do It Shake Your Booty". Most of it was unreleased before the album appeared and it is typical of Swamp Dogg's work of the time: lots of piano and horns. "God Bless" is included and despite its obviously child-like lyrics has a beautiful rolling flow. The other strange thing about the record is that it *doesn't* contain the single he put out on Capricorn entitled "More Sweet Soul Music".

In some ways the most extraordinary twist of Conley's life came in the mid seventies when, disenchanted with life in general and the music industry in particular, he relocated to Brussels before moving to Amsterdam where he became, of all things, a carpet designer. He then changed his name to Lee Roberts and refused to talk about - maybe even think about - his previous life as Arthur Conley. In 1979 he obviously had the urge to sing again and started performing in small clubs under his new name. A concert was recorded in January 1980 but wasn't released until 1987. It frankly isn't the greatest 'live' album in the world with very predictable sixties soul covers but is fascinating in as much as the sleevenotes make it clear that no one knew this was Arthur Conley, and even when the record came out it was still a secret, and Arthur certainly wasn't going to spill the beans.

He died in Holland in 2008, having gained a measure of happiness in his later years denied him for too long after Otis died. .

Bennie Conn

Soul Music 1980 Groove Time GTR-1003 Producers: Art Stewart & Bennie Conn

West Coast soul man Benjamin McConner released a handful of excellent 45s at the end of the sixties, the best of which was possibly "Satisfy My Hunger" on Wand. Another fine outing, "I Don't Have" on Soultown, is re-cut here as the first track on this truly excellent LP, which was nonetheless doomed to be a commercial failure. No one else was cutting music like this in 1980, as it was a pure throwback to the sixties, with the focus on songs and singer, not big productions and dancing. But credit to all involved and experienced musicians like Sonny Burke and Cash McCall must have been surprised to be asked to play in this style so many years after it had a major audience. I won't highlight tracks, as all are good, but must chide Conn for claiming to have written "Help Me Lord" as it is in fact an Ingram-Tate-Baylor-Gregory song, "Help Me Love", which was the b-side of a Tommy Tate single from 1971. The record label obviously thought no-one would notice and there is at least a certain irony in Johnny Baylor being ripped-off.

Continental Four

Fred Kelly; Ronnie McGregor; Larry McGregor; Anthony Burke

Dream World 1972 Jay Walking JWL 1020 Producer: Bobby Martin

An utterly lovely album. "Sweet" soul may not be for everyone, given its heavy orchestration, falsetto singing and the outfits that most groups who sang in this style used to wear, but, at its best, it has surpassing beauty in delivery and melody and a number of tracks on this LP show the genre at its best.

"I Don't Have You" was a gorgeous single from 1971 that reached the soul top 50, but it was the follow-up, "Day By Day (Every Minute Of The Hour)" that did even better (#19) and is the cream cut on display. It is a record I used to play over and over again as I was starting to learn that soul music meant more than just Motown or James Brown and I can hardly hear it even now without being overwhelmed. Fred Kelly was a magnificent high-voiced vocalist and he can also be heard on the other perfect cuts: "How Can I Pretend", "Running Away (From Love)" and the title track. Some of the other material is of lesser quality but the group do render an excellent take on "Heaven Must Have Sent You".

The group came out of Harrisburg and the album was recorded at Sigma Sound with Bobby Martin in the producer's chair but after three more unsuccessful singles on other labels they broke up.

Contours (see also Dennis Edwards)

Leroy Fair; Billy Gordon; Billy Hoggs; Joe Billingslea; Sylvester Potts; Hubert Johnson; Huey Davis; Dennis Edwards; Joe Stubbs; Council Gay; Jerry Green; Alvin English; Arthur Hinson; Charles Davis; Darrel Nunlee

Do You Love Me 1962 Gordy 901 Producer: Berry Gordy

Baby Hit & Run 1974 MFP 50054 (UK)

Flashback 1990 Motor City MOTCLP 26 Producer: Ian Levine

For a group who placed eight singles on the soul top 50, including one #1 and three other top 20 hits, the Contours have been poorly served on LP, and their best ever side, the extraordinary "That Day When She Needed Me", doesn't exist at 33⅓ speed.

Based in Detroit, they were one of the first groups to be signed to Motown and were rewarded with "Do You Love Me", a massive hit in the USA. An LP was hastily built around it but 1962 was not a year in which Motown were paying any attention to albums and apart from the similar "Shake Sherrie" (#21 soul) and the slow "Funny" there were not many other cuts that stand out but nevertheless it is a good snapshot of how early Motown was developing. It is also notable for "The Old Miner", a Smokey Robinson song, the best for which can be said is that he was still learning as a writer. The album cover was fairly tacky, but it has a certain nostalgic charm, all the same.

Much better was *Baby Hit And Run*, primarily a 'Greatest Hits' collection, but unfortunately it didn't come out until years after the group had disbanded so they would have received no benefit from it at all. We had the cheapline UK label, MFP, to thank for this one and it also included two excellent previously unreleased cuts, "It's Growing" and the title track, both sung by Dennis Edwards, at a time when unreleased Motown was seldom trickling out. It is simply an excellent album, essential for anyone who loves Detroit soul, and sides like "Just A Little Misunderstanding", "Can You Jerk Like Me" and "First I Look At The Purse", all of which reached the soul top 20, epitomize excitement.

The group reformed for their last album in 1990, at which time only Billingslea and Potts remained from the early days. "Gonna Get You Back" was my favoured cut from an album which shows the group to be still in good voice.

One reason that they didn't record as many LPs as other vocal groups might simply be due to the rather rapid turnover they experienced in personnel; there was never really a "definitive" Contours line-up.

Controllers

Reginald McArthur; Larry McArthur; Rickey Lewis; Leonard Brown

In Control 1977 Juana JA 200001 Producer: Frederick Knight (Billboard pop charts: 146)

Fill Your Life With Love 1978 Juana JA 200002 Producer: Frederick Knight

Next In Line 1979 Juana JA 200005 Producer: Frederick Knight (Billboard soul charts: 47)

Controllers 1987 Timeless TRPL 106 (UK)

My Love Is Real 1987 Timeless TRPL 112 (UK)

Group soul singing was predominantly mastered by groups from big cities, New York, Philadelphia, Detroit, Chicago and Los Angeles in particular, and outstanding groups from the south were relatively few in number. One such exception, for a while anyway, were the Controllers out of Birmingham, Alabama. After a couple of tiny singles as the Soul Controllers they shortened their name and following two ok singles on Juana they scored big with "Somebody's Gotta Win, Somebody's Gotta Lose" in late 1977. This was a soaring ballad of soulful intensity and while it hit #8 on the soul charts it fell just short of the Hot 100, as it was too authentic to cross over. They followed this up with another brilliant single, "Heaven Is Only One Step Away" which also did well on the soul charts. These two tracks utterly dominated their first album, which also contained a couple of reasonable dance cuts and three tracks of mediocrity. Main lead singer Reginald McArthur possessed a gruff, commanding voice and he delivered the two big records superbly, both of which were elongated on the LP so the singles will not really suffice.

At the time of release I found *Fill Your Life With Love* to be rather a disappointing follow-up, but in retrospect this is a harsh view as it did include many nice slow cuts such as "If Somebody Cares" (with fine dual vocals by McArthur and Lewis), "Getting Over You" and "Castles In The Sky", and it was probably their most consistent LP, as well as being a fine antidote to disco, but there was nothing quite to match "Somebody" or "Heaven".

Next In Line mirrored the first LP, in that it contained some great stuff as well as others of a much lower quality. "If Tears Were Pennies" was a dazzling single, written, like virtually all their best sides, by David Camon, but it unaccountably failed to make the soul charts. But "We Don't", another tremendous ballad, did, making it to #43 in early 1980. The third wonderful cut was "I Just Don't Know", a typically strong Joe Shamwell and Tommy Tate song, but things like "I Can't Turn The Boogie Loose" and "Ankle Chain" were weak.

These three LPs comprised the Frederick Knight years and he should be commended for doing such a fine job with the group. Timeless records in the UK put out two compilations in 1987, comprised entirely of tracks from the first two albums, apart from "This Love Is Real", another excellent 45 that became their last ever charting single on Juana. It does not exist on the other albums.

Controllers 1984 MCA 5514 Producer: Nick Johnson (Billboard soul charts: 47)

Stay 1986 MCA 5681 Producers: Barry Eastmond, Ralph Benatar & Galen Senogles (Billboard soul charts: 25)

For The Love Of My Woman 1987 MCA 42043 Producers: Ralph Benatar & Galen Senogles (Billboard soul charts: 72)

Just in Time 1989 Capitol C1-91100 Producers: Donnell Spencer, Sam Sims, Vassal Benford & Ollie Brown

West Coast soul man Jimmy Bee took over mentorship of the group after they moved on from Knight and the MCA years were successful commercially as the group posted six more singles on the soul charts but they were less satisfying from a musical perspective. The first MCA album did at least keep the focus on their harmonies and slow sides, two of which, "Crushed" and the likeable "Just For You", became charting singles but the vocals were ratcheted down in a manner that resulted in a loss of their previous distinctiveness. One could no longer tell a Controllers record by listening "blind".

1986's *Stay* was their best-selling LP and boasts a pretty good version of "Distant Lover" (#34 soul) but also houses routine songs such as "Big Bad Jama", "So Glad" and "Got A Thang", and the title track itself, even if it did climb to #12 on the soul charts.

For The Love Of My Woman was interesting in that most of its tracks were slow ballads, the style which suited the group best, but the compositions were almost uniformly dull and even a Sam Dees song, "Play Time", was far from his best. "Sleeping Alone" was ok, though. None of the MCA albums are bad as such, but I would still always reach for one of the Juana albums by choice. Just compare" Knocking At Your Door" from *For The Love*

Of My Woman with "Somebody's Gotta Win" for example - both are ballads but "Knocking" lacks the soulfulness of the big hit.

One last album snuck out in 1989 on Capitol, most of which is not to my taste at all - too much electronics - although the title track is nicely sung and produced. They re-emerged at the end of the nineties with a CD on Malaco.

James Conwell (see also Smoked Sugar)

Let It All Out 1977 Guinness 36007 Producers: Hank Graham & Leonard Smith

This is not the first time we have encountered the notorious Guinness label. It was allegedly a tax shelter scam set up by Prelude and the many LPs that came out on the label - in a bewildering array of styles - were never intended to be made available to the public. Given this, it is fascinating to me that somebody went to some trouble with this record. To wit: Conwell was the lead singer in two decent groups, The Exits and The Light Drivers, and some of the tracks on this LP are taken from when he was singing with them, so it is in some ways a sort of (albeit incomplete) anthology of his work. But why go to this trouble for a record that wasn't even going to be for sale? All very mysterious, but it is a most enjoyable LP as Conwell was a highly gifted vocalist of easy charm and "Another Sundown In Watts", "Dreams Of A Shoeshine Boy", "Second Hand Happiness" and "I'm So Glad" are all delightful.

He had also recorded as Jimmy Conwell and Richard Temple and sung in a number of other groups as well but the only other album he recorded was after he became the lead singer of yet another one, Smoked Sugar.

L.C. Cooke

Sings The Great Years Of Sam Cooke 1965 Blue Rock MGB 24001 Producer: Andre Williams

L.C. (so far as I can ascertain, his actual Christian name) Cooke was Sam's younger brother and, unsurprisingly, his career was but a shadow of his famous sibling's. L.C. recorded a few singles over a number of years for various labels and this one album, on which he was on a hiding to nothing: there was no way he was going to serve up superior versions of Sam's songs. Having said that, it is an enjoyable LP, and, in one case, at least, he *does* better Sam and that is on "That's Where It's At", a tremendously gritty, deep soul reading with lovely piano and horns. In the end, though, the aural experience of the LP is the difference between listening to a good singer, which L.C. undoubtedly was, and a great one, which Sam indubitably was.

Sam Cooke

Sam Cooke 1958 Keen A-2001 Producer: Bumps Blackwell (Billboard pop charts : 16)

Encore 1958 Keen A-2003 Producer: Bumps Blackwell

Tribute To The Lady 1959 Keen A-2004 No producer listed

Hit Kit 1959 Keen 86101 No producer listed

The Wonderful World Of 1960 Keen 86106 No producer listed

I imagine all committed soul fans have their view of what constituted the "golden age". And let's say, just as an exercise, that a golden age can only last for ten years. In which case, my own vote would be from 1965-1974. Sam Cooke was shot dead in a motel in December 1964. Just imagine what he would have created had the murky events of that night never come to pass. As it was, he delivered much music of enduring worth, was one of the most charismatic and handsome soul men who ever lived, a possessor of one of the purest voices captured on vinyl and a good businessman, as well. And still there is a massive sense of what riches were denied us all.

He first came to prominence as a member of the Soul Stirrers, when he was still Sam Cook, although he also sang with a couple of other gospel groups before that, but as the fifties progressed the temptation to record secular music grew and grew until he finally succumbed, first as Dale Cook, and then as Sam Cooke. (I haven't listed the gospel LPs, deeming them to be out of scope.)

All the albums on Keen can fairly safely be ignored by soul fans. "You Send Me" was his first big hit, #1 pop and soul. no less, and it was and is charming (and sits on the first LP) but the records are overloaded with entirely predictable and safe standards and were aimed at an audience that felt at ease with Nat King Cole, Johnny Mathis or Ella Fitzgerald. It goes without saying that Cooke sang impeccably, and the musicianship was of high quality, and there were some good tracks that transcended the ordinary such as "You Were Made For Me", "Let's Go Steady Again" and "That's Heaven To Me" but there is little that is vital when compared to, say, what Bobby Bland was producing at the same time.

Cooke's Tour 1960 RCA LPM 2221 Producers: Hugo and Luigi

Hits Of The 50's 1960 RCA LPM 2236 Producers: Hugo and Luigi

Swing Low 1960 RCA LPM 2293 Producers: Hugo and Luigi

My Kind Of Blues 1961 RCA LPM 2392 Producers: Hugo and Luigi

Twistin' The Night Away 1962 RCA LPM 2555 Producers: Hugo and Luigi (Billboard pop charts : 72)

The Best Of 1962 RCA LPM 2625 (Billboard soul charts: 5 ; Billboard pop charts : 22)

Mr. Soul 1963 RCA LPM 2673 Producers: Hugo and Luigi (Billboard pop charts : 94)

Night Beat 1963 RCA LPM 2709 Producers: Hugo and Luigi (Billboard pop charts : 62)

Ain't That Good News 1964 RCA LPM 2899 Producers: Hugo and Luigi (Billboard pop charts : 34)

At The Copa 1964 RCA LPM 2970 Producer: Al Schmitt (Billboard soul charts: 1 ; Billboard pop charts : 29)

Keen was never going to be a record label capable of bringing out the potential of Cooke and so he made the move to RCA.

The first three albums on the new label were, if anything, even more MOR than the ones on Keen. Apart from "Chain Gang" on

Swing Low, there is very little on any of them I would ever choose to listen to again.

It wasn't until *My Kind Of Blues* that we were blessed with an album that was filled with material worthy of a singer of Cooke's stature. It is easily the best of his early albums and parts of it are fully satisfying: "Trouble In Mind", "Nobody Knows You When You're Down And Out" and "Baby Won't You Please Come Home" for example, even if the album, to be pedantic, was still not really indicative of the burgeoning soul sound.

Twistin' The Night Away was. in some ways, the first true Cooke album as it featured his own songs on more than 50% of the tracks, whereas in the past he had to deliver other writers' work. More than this, it is clearly a "soul" record, as hip and contemporary as anything else that was issued in 1962. "Somebody Have Mercy", "Whole Lotta Woman", "Soothe Me", "Somebody's Gonna Miss Me", "Movin' And Groovin'" and the title track are all wonderful sides, although it has to be said that "Camptown Twist" certainly was not.

A *Best Of* LP sold very well, and so it should have done, seeing as it contained seven soul top ten smashes, but *Mr. Soul* was a disappointing backward step, in as much as it returned, in the main, to standards like "Cry Me A River", "I Wish You Love" and "Willow Weep For Me", a more jazzy style and few Cooke original songs. An exception was the magnificent "Nothing Can Change This Love", which is far superior to all else on the record.

Much, much better was *Night Beat*, with four Cooke original songs, and seven other impeccably chosen sides. It is the first *great* Cooke album. Right from the first few bars with "Nobody Knows The Trouble I've Seen", through the brilliant "Little Red Rooster" (#7 soul, #11 pop) to the frankly astonishing, in the light of what was to come, "Fool's Paradise", Cooke is in magnificent voice and only a rather pointless take on "Shake, Rattle And Roll" is throwaway. Billy Preston, Ray Johnson, Hal Blaine and Clifford Hills are crucial on organ, piano, drums and bass respectively.

Most of *Ain't That Good News* was also excellent and Cooke was by now a superstar. The title track, "Good Times", "Rome (Wasn't Built In A Day)" and "Meet Me At Mary's Place" were the stand-out tracks from a nearly perfect side one. Side two was markedly inferior - all reverting to the mush he was too often compelled to record - except for the song which is now, by common consent, one of the most important and greatest compositions of the twentieth century, "A Change Is Gonna Come". I have lost count of the number of other soul singers who have also covered this song, but none can match Cooke's voice on his own recording which had to transcend the rather pompous musical backing he is saddled with here. Somehow this discrepancy between soulful expression and overbearing accompaniment makes the performance even the greater.

The last album released before his death was *Live At The Copa* which was his most successful to date. I can't pretend to be overwhelmed by a record that features such "safe" material and staid backing, but the artistry of his delivery cannot be gainsaid.

Shake 1965 RCA LPM 3367 Producer: Al Schmitt (Billboard soul charts: 1 ; Billboard pop charts : 44)

Best Of Volume 2 1965 RCA LPM 3373 (Billboard soul charts: 7 ; Billboard pop charts : 128)

Try A Little Love 1965 RCA LPM 3435 Producers: Al Schmitt & Hugo and Luigi (Billboard pop charts : 120)

The three LPs above came out posthumously and, *Best Of Volume 2* included, contain material not available on his earlier albums. Given its release date just about coincided with his death, it is not surprising that "Shake" contained a fair number of new songs although it did also include a couple of songs that had appeared way back on the *Hit Kit* LP. The best and most interesting of the new songs was the light-hearted and swinging "Yeah Man", more or less the original of Arthur Conley's "Sweet Soul Music", and "Somebody (Ease My Troublin' Mind)" a mournful and soulful number that Bobby Womack was to cover decades later.

Live At Harlem Square Club 1985 RCA AFL-1 5181
Producers: Hugo and Luigi

Finally, in 1985, we were blessed with a "new" Sam Cooke LP although it was recorded in 1963 in Miami. In the near twenty years since its release it has attained near legendary status, and is certainly one of the relatively few live albums I frequently play by choice. particulary to hear him sing "Somebody Have Mercy", a magnificently thrilling version. As a piece of history, as well, it is impeccable, particularly when contrasted with Live At The Copa, a radically different Cooke show.

Since 1966 there have been no end of Sam Cooke compilation LPs released, at least forty in fact, and as stated in the introduction, I see no real point in trying to list them all.

There are plenty of people who would contend that Cooke was the greatest soul singer who ever lived and such an opinion is not fanciful.

Pat Cooley

Double Talk 1987 Ichiban ICH 1010 Producer: Clarence Carter

Cooley was Clarence Carter's protégé, and the blind singer/producer issued a couple of admirable singles for her on his Future Stars imprint in 1975. Sadly, they went nowhere and it was thus somewhat of a surprise when she re-surfaced in the mid eighties, firstly with two 45s and then this LP. It is not one that soul fans need to unduly worry about in tracking down if it has not already been heard as its shortcomings are manifest. Firstly, too much of the musicianship is of the synthesised/programmed style and second, Cooley was not really strong enough a singer to tackle material such as "I've Never Loved A Man" or "Something Is Wrong With My Baby", not to mention "Can I Be Your Main Thing" which Margie Alexander delivered more effectively. Lastly, songs such as "Borrow Me" and the title track do not repay repeated listening. To end on a more charitable note though: "I'm Giving It All I Got" is a cut of much charm which is far better suited to her light soprano voice and the lyrically and melodically strong "I'm Gonna Trade You In" is the best of the new Carter songs on show.

Michael Cooper (see also Con - Funk - Shun)

Love Is Such A Funny Game 1987 Warner Brothers 25653-1 Producers: Jay King, Michael Cooper, Ron Everette, Felton Pilate, Benjamin Wright & David Agent

Just What I Like 1989 Reprise 1-25923 Producers: Larry White, Cornelius Mims, Michael Cooper, Robert Brookins, Skylark, Tony Valera & Les Edwards

I saw Michael Cooper live about ten years ago, as a support to the Ohio Players in Phoenix. As his music had completely passed me by since he left Con-Funk-Shun, I didn't know his material but he was a good singer and engaging performer and the crowd loved him. That doesn't mean I have suddenly started to enjoy these two LPs though. Seven singles across the two sets reached the soul charts with "To Prove My Love" from *Love Is Such A Funny Game* and the enjoyable "My Baby's House" from *Just What I Like* being by the biggest at #3 and #7 respectively.

Cornelius Brothers And Sister Rose (see also Prince Gideon)

Eddie Cornelius; Carter Cornelius; Rose Cornelius; Billie Jo Cornelius

Cornelius Brothers And Sister Rose 1972 UA 5568 Producer: Bob Archibald (Billboard soul charts: 12 ; Billboard pop charts : 29)

Big Time Lover 1973 UA-LA121-F Producer: Bob Archibald (Billboard soul charts: 32)

Greatest Hits 1976 UA-LA593-G (Billboard soul : 32)

A family of brothers and sisters out of Dania Beach. Florida, they had a short-lived burst of success when "Treat Her Like A Lady" and "Too Late To Turn Back Now" went to #3 and #2 respectively on the pop charts in the summers of 1971 and 1972. Both of these songs as well as two more hits in "Don't Ever Be Lonely" (#23) and "I'm Never Gonna Be Alone Anymore"(#37) can be found on the debut album. What was interesting about all four singles is that they fared better on the pop charts than on the soul charts, demonstrating black audience ambivalence towards this rather soft styled group.

For my part, despite the undoubtedly poppy tone of their music, I thought their best records had a great deal of charm and "Too Late" and "Don't Ever Be Lonely" still sound good and fresh forty years later. Not surprisingly, the first LP performed impressively but their time in the limelight was spectacularly brief as *Big Time Lover*, the follow up disc, despite a proud gatefold cover, couldn't even reach the top 100 pop albums charts and only housed two minor hits as singles: "I Just Can't Stop Loving You" (#104 pop and #79 soul) and the title track (#88 soul). Sister Billie Jo had not sung on the first LP but she augmented the others in 1973 and Eddie continued to write most of the songs. Both albums were arranged by the excellent Mike Lewis but listening to the group's music for any length of time is a slightly saccharine experience and one feels a need for some Bill Coday or James Brown afterwards to restore equilibrium.

The *Greatest Hits* album was a bit of a con in as much as it included a whopping six tracks from the first LP, a mere two from *Big Time Lover* and only a couple that could not be found on either: "Since I Found My Baby" (a record that got a savage review from England's *Black Music* magazine on release, and it's actually not bad at all) and "Got To Testify (Love)".

Cornelius Brothers and Sister Rose disbanded in 1976 but both brothers were to return. For more on Eddie see immediately below, while Carter changed his name to Prince Gideon and released two albums in the late eighties.

Eddie Cornelius

My Hands are Tied 1982 Audiograph AG 7785 Producer: Jesse Butler

For You 1982 Audiograph AG 7794 No producer listed

Eddie Cornelius released these two LPs in quick succession on Nashville's Audiograph records in 1982 to audience indifference (assuming they were even properly released) and subsequent record collectors' interest: both are in-demand these days.

As might be imagined the three biggest hits of Cornelius Brothers and Sister Rose are recut across the albums, as are many well-known soul standards. The massive string arrangements of the Sister Rose days are long gone and the more stripped down sound holds its own appeal and listening to the first album particularly is a pleasant way to spend 42 minutes. The title track sways along nicely, "All In The Game" and "I'll Carry A Torch" are skilfully sung slow workouts and "Talk To Me" (another old song) makes it clear how influenced he was by Sam Cooke. In fact only "Let's Fool Around" is obviously second-rate but listening again to "Treat Her Like A Lady" reminds me how patronising the lyrics are. The opening cut to side two, "Release Yourself" is a duet between Eddie and an unnamed female singer who sounds much like Chaka Khan, presumably one of the backing singers: Debra Carter, Vickie Newsom or Barbara McCoy.

For You duplicates three tracks from *My Hands Are Tied* and is not so good given it reprises "Let's Fool Around" and Cornelius' versions of "Try A Little Tenderness", "Sunny" and "What's Going On" are poor. Much better is "Still On My Mind", which owes a lot to Bobby Womack's work of the early seventies, and is possibly the best side he ever cut as a solo singer.

He issued a well regarded single on the UK GB label in the eighties, "That's Love Making In Your Eyes", before retiring and becoming a pastor.

Frank Cornelius

Tender Love 1989 SoundShine 1SSA-89-FC Producer: Frank Cornelius

Bass player Frank Cornelius had a P-Funk influenced single out in 1982, "This Groove Is Bad", which was ok, before issuing a stream of other singles, all of which presumably convinced someone to cut an LP on him which issued forth in 1989. His voice is capable, if not distinctive, and the LP, while generous at 12 tracks, had nothing to make it stand out.

Corner Gang

Stone Out Of Your Mind 1976 TSG 815 Producer: ?

TSG was a subsidiary of Lloyd Price's LPG label, and was, allegedly, set up for tax shelter reasons. As a result, all the releases are very rare, very expensive these days and very variable in quality. It is anyone's guess who comprised the Corner Gang - although I've heard speculation that another TSG artist, Eric Dunbar, may sing on it - and all I know of it are the handful of tracks I have heard on the internet and they are pretty decent in a light and tuneful funk style.

Cortez (see also One Way)

All About Love 1990 Tezru CH006 Producers: Cortez Harris & Ruth Ward

In Love...But Seriously 1991 Tezru CH 007 Producers: Ruth Ward & Cheryl Byrd

(Enjoy) Your Fantasy 1992 Rise High BAM-001 Producer: ?

Cortez Harris was a singer and guitarist with Al Hudson and The Soul Partners and he continued with them after they morphed into One Way. The two LPs he released on the Tezru label as a solo artist came as a welcome surprise, as they revived a dying art: a soul man singing in a high tenor.

On *All About Love* this style was mainly to the fore on side one, but side two sees him revert to what I imagine he saw as his normal range. That first side is entirely downtempo, and even side two hardly rushes along at a gallop, and if these are not the strongest songs ever recorded, the record should still be tracked down by fans who liked listening to Eddie Kendricks, Ted Mills etc. Even the programming is unobtrusive. Yes, a nice one.

In Love only had four tracks and was therefore maybe as much as an EP as an LP, but they are all enjoyable as he once again employs his falsetto throughout on the four downtempo tracks.

Similarly, his last album, *(Enjoy) Your Fantasy,* only really has four tracks as all of them are repeated as instrumentals to bring the set count up to eight. It's not as good as the other two albums as he plays down the falsetto and the musical backing is less sympathetic and more intrusive. (On this release his name was very slightly changed to Corte'z.) He died in 2006.

Hayes Cotton

Secret Lover 1980 Act 1 TBS 101 Producer: Hayes Cotton

Hayes Cotton was born in Texas, and throughout his life juggled making records with working in the aerospace industry. He cut a bluesy and atmospheric single in the sixties entitled "Black Wings Have My Angel" on which his deep baritone vocals sounded a little like Screaming Jay Hawkins'. It gained plays in England on the "Northern Soul" scene, but no-one would have got rich from it at the time of release.

He re-cut the song in 1980 for his one LP, *Secret Lover,* which was in a totally different style to the sixties' single, being recorded in Oklahoma in a fuller, more contemporary manner. It is another record that has admirers, but like or dislike of the album will almost certainly pivot around Cotton's voice which had become more idiosyncratic over the years. I'm afraid to say I am not a fan. He died in 2015.

Clifford Coulter

East Side San Jose 1970 Impulse! AS-9197 Producer: Ed Michel

Do It Now, Worry About It Later 1971 Impulse! AS-9216 Producer: Ed Michel

The Better Part Of Me 1980 Columbia JC 35786 Producers: Bill Withers & Clifford Coulter

Star keyboard player and guitarist Coulter is a difficult artist to pin down; issuing two albums on the Impulse! label might suggest he was a unreconstructed jazz man; work with John Lee Hooker exposed an affinity for the blues; his third LP was straight up soul. There is also the puzzle that the two tracks he sings on his *East Side San Jose* set sound as if they were performed by a completely different singer from the one on *The Better Part Of Me.*

After some thought I decided to include him and will state that those two songs, "Do It Again" and "Sal Si Puedes", are both excellent downtempo and soulful sides, even if the rest of the debut LP consists of instrumental funk tinged jazz that would account for his absence from the book if all his music were in that vein.

The second set included three vocals, and "Before The Morning Comes", bridged the vocal gap between the first and third sets, as he did venture into the higher register that he used exclusively for the final LP. "Mr. Peabody" was the funkiest item on show but overall the album was "jazzier" than the first.

The Better Part Of Me saw Coulter team up with Bill Withers for a record that was significantly different in approach than the first two: firstly it is entirely composed of proper songs rather than instrumentals; second, the jazz element is more or less completely absent; and third, as stated earlier, Coulter sings in a high tenor throughout. If someone tells me that I have got it wrong and there were TWO Clifford Coulters I would not be in the least surprised. On the other hand, to re-invent yourself in this matter is most impressive. It's an accomplished set, tuneful and relaxed, with no disco touches at all, with an emphasis on articulate well-constructed songs - all from Coulter - and has always had admirers

Counts (see also Moses)

Mose Davis; Andrew Gibsont; Jim White; Demo Cates; Raoul Mangrum; Leroy Emmanuel; Les Daniels; Byron Miller; Riccardo Rankins

Jan Jan 1969 Cotillion SD 9011 Producer: Richard Popcorn Wylie

What's Up Front That Counts 1971 Westbound 2011 Producer: The Counts (Billboard soul charts: 35 ; Billboard pop charts : 193)

Love Sign 1973 Aware AA2002 Producers: Leroy Emmanuel & Marlin McNichols (Billboard soul charts: 45)

Funk Pump 1975 Aware AA2006 Producers: William Bell & James McDuffie (Billboard soul charts: 58)

Originally they were The Fabulous Counts and were accredited as such on the first LP but afterwards they dispensed with the adjective. Out of Detroit, they were surprisingly initially more influenced by Booker T. and the M.G.'s than The Temptations as many of the tracks on the debut album made clear. "It's A Man's Man's Man's World" could easily have come from the Stax band and only a much more liberal use of horns by the Michigan outfit makes the differences between the two groups transparent. The title track did well for the Counts, reaching #42 soul in early 1969 when released on the local Moira label, but I find it to be a routine workout, as indeed are most of the cuts - anyone for "Hey Jude"? - on what is a wholly instrumental record, apart from the penultimate track, "Girl From Kenya", which throws in some chants. (The sinuous "Get Down People" also reached the soul charts on Moira in 1970, but did not feature on any album.)

The Westbound LP was a marked change, and improvement. Firstly, all the songs were now self-composed; second, it was much more of a vocal album and third, the focus fell on the rhythm section whereas sax men, Demo Cates and Jim White, had been more in the spotlight on the Cotillion set. Overall, it was simply funkier. The excellent "Why Not Start All Over Again" is the standout track and inexplicably failed as a single but there are no real clunkers and I recommend it for all funk fans.

In 1973 the band had condensed to four - Emmanuel, Davis, Cates and Gibsont (sic) - and moved to a new label, Aware, where their sound changed once again. While there were still some funky cuts like "Riding High" that would not have been out of place on the Westbound LP, there was generally a looser, jazzier feel, and a track like "Love Sign" itself was much softer than had been the case with their music in the past.

By the time of their final LP, *Funk Pump*, they had increased to a quintet with only Emmanuel and Davis from the original band still left. The sound, once again, had slightly shifted and a number of cuts, "Jazzman" , "Flies Over Watermelon" and "Magic Ride", for instance, would not have been out of place on the albums that War were issuing at the time. although other tracks were a continuation of the music on *Love Sign*. "Since We Said Goodbye" is a good soulful ballad, and was another string to their bow, unlikely at the time of the Cotillion sides.

The band then broke up but Davis (who returned to lead a band called Moses), Cates and Emmanuel have all continued to make a good living in the music business, recording on countless sessions for other musicians and singers as well as fronting jazz combos in more recent times.

Courtial

Bill Courtial; Errol Knowles; David Kempton; Edward Williams; Geoffrey Whyte; Jose Najera;

Don't You Think It's Time 1976 Pipeline 2001 Producers: Bill Courtial & Steve Whiting

Courtial were a mixed race band whose limited recording career resulted in this album and a single. Unmistakably West Coast in sound and vibe, the LP should appeal to anyone who liked Maze as it shares their same mellow yet gently funky approach to music. There are no horns in earshot and most of the action is generated by Bill Courtial's guitar and David Kempton's keyboards. Errol Knowles is a really good vocalist about whom I can find little information and he is prominent on the best cuts, "Losing You", "Time To Explain" and the title track. There are a couple of rather dull instrumentals but those apart, it is a most worthwhile LP, best listened to late at night.

Lou Courtney

Skate Now Shing A Ling 1967 Riverside RM 2000 Producer: Robert Bateman

I'm In Need Of Love 1974 Rags/Epic BL 33011 Producers: Jerry Ragovoy & Lou Courtney

Buffalo Smoke 1976 RCA APL1- 1696 Producer: Lou Courtney

Courtney was born Louis Pegues in Buffalo, New York in 1944, and often used his real name in the numerous compositions he has written over the years for other artists. His first singles came out in the first half of the sixties on labels such as Imperial and Philips but it was not until he moved to Riverside - a rather odd move, given their overwhelming focus on jazz - that he finally placed some 45s - three - on the soul singles charts. Two of these, "Skate Now" and "Do The Thing", can be found on the debut LP, on which Riverside brought to bear their usual quality control as it has unquestionably the thickest cardboard of any LP in my entire collection, as well as a gatefold cover, some interesting photos and some sycophantic waffle from Ted Williams as sleevenotes. The only problem was that nobody thought to bring any tunes to the party. The songs - possibly wisely - were not credited on the album but I think they were all written by Courtney himself or in tandem with Bob Bateman. Not to put too fine a point on it, the record is pretty awful, thin sounding, bereft of melody and variety in tempo and even Courtney sounded bored. After leaving Riverside he released a handful of other singles for a variety of different labels.

The transformation on his next album, given my lack of enthusiasm for his debut, was startling as *I'm In Need Of Love* is a magnificent record. All the eleven Courtney compositions this time around are strong, with some much more than that, such as "Just To Let Him Break Your Heart" and the title track. I have probably listened to "What Do You Want Me To Do" as frequently as any record ever made and it and the equally excellent "I Don't Need Nobody Else" were reasonably successful singles for him in 1973 and 1974 respectively but the album needs to be heard in its entirety, as it has a richness, consistency and strength of purpose that is uncommon, and certainly lacking on the Riverside release. It undeniably has shades of what Marvin Gaye had been doing over the previous few years but was in no way a mere copy, and much credit should also go to the great Jerry Ragovoy and Leon Pendarvis for their sumptuous arranging throughout.

The RCA album was a little odd as it didn't really make it clear if Buffalo Smoke was a new *nom de plume* Courtney had adopted or if he was now fronting a group of this name. If the latter, I remain uncertain as to who the others members were unless it was the backing singers, Dorothy Cooley, Gladys Freeman and Mary Johnson, who were really good, by the way, on "Amen For Good Music", one of the better tracks on what was a rather disappointing set. Disappointing because after the melodic strengths of *I'm In Need Of Love* the LP reverted somewhat back to the Riverside debut in the sense that the focus was once again on dancing and not on songs. However, I like "Call The Police" and the whole LP does have a pronounced live, hot feel which is to Courtney's credit as he produced it all. His Marvin Gaye vocal similarities were particularly marked on "Come To Me", the one slow cut.

Courtney/Buffalo Smoke were later to put out an unappealing disco version of "Stubborn Kind Of Fellow" (although it didn't sound like him on vocals, but I assume it was) before Courtney had seemingly had enough of going it alone and joined The Fifth Dimension for what I think was possibly a short spell but information on what he has been doing for the last thirty years or so has been hard to find.

Don Covay

Don Covay & Brook Benton 1965 Grand Prix K-429

I have always been a massive admirer of Don Covay, that highly distinctive singer and even better songwriter, and believe him to have been one of the most talented, impressive and underrated soul men that ever lived. And don't just take my word for it: Mick Jagger clearly rated him a great deal as well.

He was born in Orangeburg, South Carolina before moving to Washington D.C. where he helped to form a vocal group, The Rainbows, who also included Billy Stewart and Marvin Gaye in their ranks. It wasn't long before he became a solo singer, though, and he recorded a whole host of singles for many labels, although only one of them, "Pony Time", became any sort of a hit. That track and "Love Boat" are his only two songs on a budget line LP that the Grand Prix label put out in 1965, with all the rest of the album consisting of songs performed by Brook Benton.

Mercy! 1964 Atlantic SD 8104 No producer listed

See Saw 1966 Atlantic SD 8120 No producer listed

The House Of Blue Lights 1969 Atlantic SD 8237 Producer: Don Covay

Mercy 1984 Edsel ED 127 (UK)

Covay had already started to make somewhat of a name for himself as a song writer by the time his first two Atlantic albums were released. The *Mercy!* set, his first proper LP, and marketed as by Don Covay and The Goodtimers, featured 12 tracks, nine of which were written by Covay alone or in collaboration with Horace Ott or Ronald Miller. While certainly enjoyable enough, it does feature a number of tracks that sound too close to the title song, with one of them, "Daddy Loves Baby" being more or less an exact copy. One of the most interesting cuts to me was "Can't Stay Away" which lifted great chunks (unattributed) from The Swan Silvertones' astonishing "Saviour, Pass Me Not". The track also featured Covay singing in two entirely different ranges, a trade mark of his. "Mercy Mercy" became a reasonably big hit (#35 pop) although the follow-up, the similar sounding "Take This Hurt Off Me", performed much worse.

See Saw was a stronger collection, a fair bit of it of it recorded at Stax, with both the title track and "Please Do Something" doing well in the soul charts as single releases (#5 and #21 respectively in 1965). "A Woman's Love" and "The Usual Place" are gorgeous ballads, "Sookie Sookie" is one of his best-known and loved compositions, and even the inclusion again of "Mercy, Mercy" can be understood and forgiven.

He had to wait for over three years until his last and final album, the radically different *House Of Blue Lights* which was a straight blues album and not really to my taste at all. It did not yield any charting singles and seemed to possibly arise as a result of Atlantic's not being quite sure what to do with Don. The fact had to be faced that they had released nearly twenty singles on him and, despite their quality, only four of them had ever charted.

The UK Edsel label collected six tracks from the first album, seven from the second, and three non-album tracks (all good) to create a fabulous compilation of the cream of his best Atlantic work in 1984, although, sadly, it omitted two of his greatest achievements: "I Stole Some Love" and "It's In The Wind", the second of which is one of the most magical songs and performances in the history of soul music, a transcendently great record.

Different Strokes 1971 Janus JLS 3038 Producer: Don Covay

Super Dude 1 1973 Mercury SRM-1-653 Producer: Don Covay (Billboard soul charts: 45 ; Billboard pop charts : 204)

Hot Blood 1974 Mercury SRM-1-1020 Producer: Don Covay

Checkin' In With 1988 Mercury 422 836 030-1

Covay moved onto the Janus label for the next phase of his career, where he released the typically quirky, if wildly uneven, *Different Strokes* which was nonetheless a marked improvement on *The House Of Blue Lights* and a portent in what was to come in style, song content and recording location - much of it was cut in Muscle Shoals. The album carried on the credit of *House Of Blue Lights* - Don Covay & The Jefferson Lemon Blues Band - but it was back to soul, especially in tough tracks like "Sweet Thang", "Ain't Nothing A Young Girl Can Do" and "Bad Luck" but did lack a truly outstanding stand-out cut. As usual, the vast majority of the compositions were penned by Covay but he really should have resisted the temptation to cover the pop song, "Hitching A Ride". Also interesting was "If There's A Will, There's A Way", the only time I can recall Covay writing with Donny Hathaway (not great, actually) and "In The Sweet Bye And Bye", which started out peacefully and arrestingly before collapsing into rock histrionics. (The album was re-released on the UK Top Line label, Top 137, in 1985 entitled *Sweet Thang*.)

But then came *Super Dude 1*, Covay's *magnum opus* and a set that is one of the best twenty soul albums ever made. Everything came together here: uniformly strong material, great vocals, playing and arrangements and commercial acclaim, all mixed in with the usual Covay audacity, best evidenced by his outrageous take on "Money", the old Motown song funked up out of all recognition, and a reggae version of "Memphis", the Chuck Berry hit. He really surpasses himself on the dance tracks here: "Bad Mouthing" is lyrically brilliant, as is "I Stayed Away Too Long" (an overlooked Vietnam song) while "Overtime Man" is a worthy addition to the string of "Jody " tales. But if the uptempo tracks are amazing - and they are - then it is the slow material that is the real clincher of the album's quality: "I Was Checkin' Out. She Was Checkin' In" (his biggest ever hit, #29 pop), "Somebody's Been Enjoying My Home", "Don't Step On A Man When He's Down" and "Leave Him" (inexplicably split across both sides of the LP) all have me shaking my head in wonder even today, forty plus years after first playing the LP.

He couldn't realistically hope to match *Super Dude* but made an extremely good fist of it, all the same, with *Hot Blood*, another superb LP, and one which, shamefully, and bizarrely, didn't even make the soul charts. "It's Better To Have (And Don't Need)" was a single of rare quality, doing well on both sides of the Atlantic but the follow-up, the rather trite "Rumble In The Jungle", did not do much business despite sporting an inspired bassline. Elsewhere we could enjoy the surprising and irresistible hoe-down of the title track, while "A Mind Is A Terrible Thing To Waste" was the cream cut, social commentary of power and grace. "Gangster Strut" was no more than so-sot, and if "Enjoy What You Have" didn't boast a good chorus it would have been an exact replica of "Better To Have". All the other sides are good, if not absolutely top drawer Covay.

In 1988 Polygram put out a welcome collection of his work, which was a pleasant surprise. Ten of the twelve tracks are culled from *Super Dude* and *Hot Blood*; of the other two sides one, "Dungeon #3", a tribute to Angela Davis, had been the b-side to "Overtime Man" in 1972, while the other was a rather uninspired version of "There's Something On Your Mind". The album was let-down, though, by a rather silly assertion on the sleeve: that he "discovered the Muscle Shoals rhythm section", which he did not.

Travellin' In Heavy Traffic 1976 P.I.R. PZ 33958 Producer: Don Covay

God knows how Covay ended up on P.I.R. of all labels, but possibly it was as a result of Tony Bell having done a number of string arrangements in Philadelphia on *Hot Blood*. It was another wildly eccentric outing ranging from the enjoyable and danceable "No Tell Motel", through the soaring and anthemic title track and the wry "You Owe It To Your Body" to the completely unsuitable "Feelings", the disco based "Chocolate Honey "and "Six Million Dollar Fish" a totally bizarre tribute to Jaws. You really do have to ask what he was thinking on these three awful tracks.

Funky Yo Yo 1977 Versatile NED 1123 Producer: Don Covay

Apart from the Mercury retrospective, this was Covay's last ever album, on the small Versatile label out of New York, and by this time he was an almost totally forgotten figure. *Funky Yo Yo* is almost certainly a collection of sixties demos, showing what he was reduced to issuing. There are no horns, no strings and a rather primitive sounding drummer. It is interesting in as much as it includes "Three Time Loser", which Wilson Picket cut in 1966 as the b-side to "Mustang Sally" and "Love Is Sweeter On The Other Side" which would have made a great single for somebody. All in all though, it can hardly be classed as essential Covay.

Covay's last outings on vinyl were a single, "Back To The Roots", in 1977 which did not revive his fortunes and the unspeakable "Badd Boy", a record unworthy of his talent, but it did at least put him back on the soul charts in 1980. Since then his star rose as people with influence finally realised his talent and he started to receive the acclaim he had long deserved, although it occurred at much the same time as he suffered a stroke. He died in 2015.

Matt Covington

Matt Covington 1978? Zip F/W 18651 Produced by Odean Pope

Although I've stated that I want to try and keep away from discussing prices of records, there is no way I can ignore mentioning that one would need deep pockets to purchase this LP. Only a handful have come up for sale in the last few years and the cheapest price attained was over £500. In fact, I suspect only a handful have EVER come up for sale as few copies were pressed up in the first place and Zip records were certainly not P.I.R.

It's all rather a shame as Covington has a beautiful falsetto as he proved on a number of sides in the early to mid seventies when he was the lead singer for The Philly Devotions and there are some lovely slow cuts on the album, and none better than "If Love Can Be Magic" and, best of all, "Philadelphia Dreaming" which is really a love letter to the city of his birth. The mid-tempo songs "Country Folks" and "Finally Got Over On You" are perfectly cooked, too, and only the well-meant "Muhammad Ali" really requires the needle to be swiftly lifted.

He recorded a few more solo sides in the eighties but although The Philly Devotions managed three small soul hits in their career, Covington never saw his own name up in lights on any charts.

Caroline Crawford

My Name Is Caroline 1978 Mercury SRM-1-3742 Producer: Hamilton Bohannon

Nice And Soulful 1979 Mercury SRM-1-3792 Producer: Hamilton Bohannon

Heartaches 1990 Motor City MOTCLP 42 Producers: Ian Levine & Rick Gianatos

There were a number of singers in the sixties on Motown who, despite undoubted talent, just couldn't garner enough attention from the people who mattered at the label to make the time there as rewarding as they would have hoped. One such singer was Caroline Crawford who only had three singles released - and no LPs at all - while with the company. In the seventies she joined three other singers to put out two 45s, the second of which laboured under the rather ridiculous name of "The Firm of Hodges, James, Smith and Crawford". This trio went on to enjoy some acclaim as soon as Caroline left them. She also cut a handful of fine - but failed - singles in Philadelphia for P.I.R.

Her first ever album was written, arranged and produced by Hamilton Bohannon and is more varied than one might suspect from listening to his music. The record's title was doubtless a reference to her Motown days when her records were released as by "Carolyn" Crawford. The tracks alternate between funky and dead slow, the latter of which are vastly superior, showcasing what a fine singer she was, albeit one who was heavily influenced by Aretha Franklin. "Coming On Strong", one of the funky cuts, became a small hit in early 1979, her first for fourteen years.

The same approach - funky, then slow - was retained for her second LP and it is thus rather interchangeable with the debut. I'm pleased I own both albums as the slow songs are all good, all well produced and arranged and very competently delivered but none of them are *killers*. The uptempo tracks are not to my taste and no better (or worse) than what one would find on Bohannon's own albums from the late seventies.

She was one of a number of artists given the chance to record again by Ian Levine on his Motor City label at the end of the eighties on an album that was full of well loved soul songs, including a good remake of Loleatta Holloway's "Cry To Me".

In more recent years she has released little in the way of new music, but has turned to acting as well as still singing on stage from time to time, as her means of making a living.

Dave Crawford

Here Am I 1977 LA DCP-1909 Producer: Dave Crawford

Dave Crawford was best known as a songwriter and producer of great skill and commercial astuteness and anyone who could write and produce "Young Hearts Run Free", "Precious Precious" and "I Don't Know" (for Baby Washington) is more than all right with me. His one album was, ironically, not a success at all and, on reading an interview with Candi Staton, this was something that caused him a fair degree of distress. One of the tracks came out in 1975 on the small Scorpio label as by "David" with a slightly different title of "I'd Be A Millionaire" and it wouldn't surprise me if that was precisely what he could have been, had he not allegedly had a bad drug habit. The album certainly has some good moments, the best of which by far was his stirring slow re-cut of "I Don't Know", radically different to Washington's. It has to be said that he was not a particularly gifted vocalist, but he certainly sounded involved emotionally in what he was singing, although dragging the title track over two sides seemed misguided.

Sadly, his life continued to spiral downwards after the hits dried up and I understand that he was murdered some time in the 1980s and found in a ditch.

Randy Crawford

Everything Must Change 1976 Warner Brothers BS-2975 Producer: Stewart Levine

Miss Randy Crawford 1977 Warner Brothers BS-3083 Producer: Bob Montgomery

Raw Silk 1979 Warner Brothers BS-3283 Producer: Stephan Goldman (Billboard soul charts: 63)

Now We May Begin 1979 Warner Brothers BS-3421 Producers: Wilton Felder, Stix Hooper & Joe Sample (Billboard soul charts: 30 ; Billboard pop charts : 180)

Secret Combination 1981 Warner Brothers BS-3541 Producer: Tommy LiPuma (Billboard soul charts: 12 ; Billboard pop charts : 71)

Randy Crawford is one of those singers who straddle the line between, soul, pop and jazz, and were it not for her records above she would possibly fall outside my definition of who qualifies for this book.

Her early musical efforts demonstrated that she wouldn't be your typical soulstress, given she worked with the likes of Cannonball Adderley and George Benson and her first records came out on Columbia, and, indeed, her first Warners LP was almost entirely composed of pop songs, and only "Soon As I Touched Him". also recorded by Fontella Bass, really appealed to me.

Her next two albums, despite once again being wildly catholic in style are sung so beautifully that there are enough moments to keep me entranced, such as "This Man", "At Last" and the two Paul Kelly songs,"Take It Away From Her" and "I'm Under The Influence Of You", all from *Miss Randy Crawford*, and "Endlessly" and her towering take on "I Stand Accused" from *Raw Silk,* one of the best versions I know.

In 1979 she teamed up with the Crusaders, with whom she delivered the song for which she is probably sill best known, "Street Life" (#17 soul, #36 pop), although this does not feature on the *Now We May Begin* LP. What are present are other famed Crawford songs such as "Tender Falls The Rain" and "One Day I'll Fly Away" which are indisputably compositions and performances of enduring quality, although they appeal more to my head than my heart. The last album of hers that I went out and bought was *Secret Combination*, and I retain a great deal of affection for the title track (a #70 soul entrant as a 45) and her lovely take on "Rainy Night In Georgia".

Windsong 1982 Warner Brothers 1-23687 Producer: Tommy Lipuma (Billboard soul charts: 24 ; Billboard pop charts : 148)

Pastel Highway 1982 Warner Brothers P-11178 (Japan)

Nightline 1983 Warner Brothers 4-23976 Producer: Tommy Lipuma (Billboard soul charts: 41 ; Billboard pop charts : 164)

Abstract Emotions 1986 Warner Brothers 25423 Producers: Reggie Lucas, Hawk Wolinski & James Newton Howard (Billboard soul charts: 53; Billboard pop charts : 178)

Rich And Poor 1989 Warner Brothers 1-26002 Producers: Robin Millar & Michael Powell (Billboard soul charts: 19; Billboard pop charts : 159)

Through The Eyes Of Love 1992 Warner Brothers 7599-26736-1 Producers: Michael Powell, Sadao Watanabe & Corrado Rustici (Billboard soul charts: 49) (Europe)

Don't Say It's Over 1993 Warner Brothers 9362-45381-1 Producer: Misha Segal (Europe)

From 1982 onwards it was clear, merely from the titles of her albums, that she was now fully committed to other directions than soul and these are not records on which I am going to dwell. Her talent is not in any doubt, and I rate her as a great singer, but not as a great soul singer.

Crack Steppin'

Crack Steppin' 1982 Get Down GD 1002 Producer: Barry Hankerson

Subtitled, not very snappily, *A Comic Book Operetta In Rhythm And Blues By Ron Milner*, the album is obscure, and thus "in-demand". Barry Hankerson has been active in politics, married to Gladys Knight and manager to the likes of Toni Braxton and R Kelly, so the low profile of this LP is a little surprising. It features an army of musicians and singers and it seems to me unlikely that a band or group called "Crack Steppin'" ever existed outside of this LP. Donald Albert is a talented soul singer who once put out a superb and little-known single called "The Hardest Part" and he takes a number of the vocals on here as do Lisa Stone and Kellie Evans. Hankerson also chips in. There are four uptempo cuts, all almost laughably devoid of melody or interest, and the first three best tracks - and "best" is relative, none of them are THAT compelling - are the more restrained "Will You Be Mine", "Is Love Worth The Pain" and "What We Gonna Do With This Feeling".

Creation (See Leon's Creation)

Creative Source

Don Wyatt; Celeste Rhodes; Steve Flanagan; Babara Berryman; Barbara Lewis

Creative Source 1973 Sussex SRA-8027 Producer: Michael Stokes (Billboard soul charts: 21; Billboard pop charts : 152)

Migration 1974 Sussex SRA-8035 Producer: Michael Stokes (Billboard soul charts: 28)

Pass The Feeling On 1975 Polydor PD 6052 Producer: Michael Stokes (Billboard soul charts: 49)

Consider The Source 1976 Polydor PD 6065 Producer: Brad Shapiro

Creative Source were a West Coast soul combination who sounded not unlike The Friends of Distinction on much of their first LP, which was graced with a gatefold sleeve. The key cut from the set was their twelve minute version of Bill Withers' great song, "Who Is He And What Is He To You", which features a splendid Paul Riser arrangement and which used to be played in its entirety at Brighton clubs I frequented in 1974. It reached #21 soul and #69 pop when chopped down for single release.

The group was apparently assembled by Ron Townson of The Fifth Dimension and didn't really have to pay any dues as such, as the first album was also their initial collective foray into a studio, although some of them had sung with other outfits in the past. The remainder of the debut album was not particularly compelling, apart from two other good singles in "You're Too Good To Be True" (#88 soul) and what I believe is the original of "You Can't Hide Love" (#48 soul). The rest was a little bit too flimsy for my tastes, particularly their cover of "Wild Flower" which was trounced by New Birth's vastly superior version of around the same time.

Migration followed the same pattern as the first LP, again using songs from Withers and Scarborough with the focus being more on the excellent musicianship and arranging and production than on the singers, especially on long cuts like "Corazon" and " I Just Can't See Myself Without You". While enjoyable enough to listen to, it could be pretty much anyone delivering the vocals and the whole thing is redolent of those albums one could once buy that showed off the stereo qualities of a good record player.

The group moved labels to Polydor but retained Michael Stokes as producer and he introduced some subtle changes on the *Pass The Feeling On* LP, by moving away from long instrumental passages and allowing the group to sing more freely. Nevertheless, the best track was the funky yet smooth title song which has a beautifully flowing momentum. Many compositions were provided by Earl Thomas, who I don't believe is the same singer/writer who has released a series of CDs from the nineties onwards, but none of them were overwhelmingly compelling, and the group sounded no "tougher" than they had on the first sides they had cut.

 Changes were in order for the next album as Brad Shapiro moved into the producer's chair and he persisted with the greater emphasis on the songs, the best of which was a winning country/soul composition by Tony Joe White and Donnie Fritts, "I Never Thought It Would Come To This", recorded at Muscle Shoals and delivered well by Don Wyatt. The musicianship remained of the highest quality, however, and Shapiro also pitched a song, "Singin' Funky Music Turns Me On", that turned up on a Jackie Moore LP the same year. "Good Lovin' Is Good Livin' " was another nice track, one of Thomas' better efforts, with the band employing their trademark Fifth Dimension-ish floppy harmonies, all underpinned by a captivating guitar line.

This was their last album, doubtless as the two years at Polydor had only resulted in one minor "hit" ("Pass The Feeling On" at #92 on the soul charts), and the group disbanded. None of the LPs are essential and it is a shame that a 'Best Of' does not exist, as, by taking the two or three best cuts from each album, it would have been well worth having. (There is talk that a compilation of their Sussex work WAS released in France but I've not seen it.)

Creme D' Cocoa (see also The Ambassadors)

Jenny Holmes Johnson; Herley Johnson; Orlando Oliphant; Bobby Todd; Brenda Bailey

Funked Up 1978 Venture VL-1001 Producers: Tony Camillo & Cecile Barker

Nasty Street 1979 Venture VL-1004 Producers: Tony Camillo & Cecile Barker

Three ex-Ambassadors joined Jenny Johnson, formerly of The Ebonys, to create this elegantly named group who recorded two lovely albums, the second of which, I believe, saw Brenda Bailey replacing Holmes.

 They had the good fortune to work with Tony Camillo, a man who really understood how to write, produce and arrange soul music although it is interesting that the best track from the first album, the glorious "Waiting For The Last Goodbye", was cut by Ms. Johnson when she was with The Ebonys and the version for Creme D'Cocoa sounds identical to me in every respect. Similarly with "Mr. Me, Mrs You", another highly appealing ballad, which does appear to have a different lead vocal, but the rest of the track also sounds exactly the same as The Ebonys' effort. Nothing else on the first album quite matches up to these two cuts but, apart from "Toe Jam", which is poor, everything else is highly listenable.

Nasty Street is even better, despite containing "Mr. Me" again, and I happily confess to greatly enjoying all the three marathon dance tracks as the vocals of the group are so strong. The Chic-influenced "Doin' The Dog" would be tedious if it were not for the fierce male lead (sadly uncredited on the typically unhelpful sleeve) and the even tougher eight minute "Gimme Your Love" has to be heard. But, once again, it is the ballads that really stand out and "I Don't Ever Wanna Love Nobody But You", "Baby Please Don't Go" and "I Will Never Stop (Lovin' You)" are all better than anything virtually any other soul group was producing in 1979. Each album served up two singles that made the soul top 100, but, unfortunately, none were big hits, with "Doin' The Dog" faring best at #30.

They made one more record, a version of "I Will Survive", a song I cannot abide in any form, which is not on these albums, and then they were never heard of again. Bobby Todd died in the mid-eighties.

General Crook

General Crook 1974 Wand WDS 697 Producer: General Crook

It seems - as unlikely as it sounds - that the real name of this great favourite of mine was General Columbus Crook so he shouldn't have wanted in confidence but he was yet another gifted artist who has been completely ignored by virtually everybody throughout his entire career.

That career started in 1969 with a couple of excellently soulful singles for Capitol, "In The Warmth Of My Arms" and "When Love Leaves You Crying", but they didn't do much and so he moved up to Chicago and switched to an entirely different style - James Brown influenced - for "Gimme Some", and "Do It For Me" which both saw soul chart action at #22 and #37 respectively in 1970. "What Time It Is" - another reasonable hit - moved Crook away from the JB sound into a gentler, more personal expression of funk which was often continued on his one LP which appeared in 1974.

 The album - on which Crook wrote or co-wrote all tracks bar one as well as playing keyboards and arranging and producing the whole thing - is more or less split into two distinct styles: a continuation of the style of "What Time It Is" as evidenced by "Fever In The Funkhouse" (#59 soul), "Reality" and "Lying Cheatin' Woman" and beautifully constructed and immensely pleasureable slow soul: the instantly memorable "The Best Years Of My Life" (#71 soul), the lyrically impressive "I'm Satisfied", the gorgeous "Tell Me What'cha Gonna Do (#57 soul, (later on covered admirably by Willie Clayton), and an excellently long drawn-out take of "If This World Were Mine" which benefits from a lovely arrangement and backing vocals from The Kitty Haywood Singers, good enough to compensate for the lack of an answering female vocal which one expects from other versions. The only "renegade" cut on view which doesn't fall into the two categories outlined above is "Thanks But No Thanks" a most acceptable mellow dance cut of lasting appeal. I bought the LP as a new release and have probably played it at least once every year ever since.

General Crook released no more LPs and enjoyed no more hits

but was still releasing the odd excellent record as late as 1987 with "In This Thing Called Love".

Crowd Pleasers

Delbert Payne; Craig Moreland; Donald Payne; Earl Davis; Al Carey; Michael Roberts

Crowd Pleasers 1979 Westbound WT-6110 Producers: Bernie Mendelson & Leroy Emmanuel

Take a bit from Parliament, a bit from Sly, a bit from The Ohio Players and a bit from most every other funk band who ever existed. The result is the Crowd Pleasers' album. Neither inspired nor contemptible, it made little impression at the top of release and doesn't sound amazing these days, but the group did bear lead vocalists who were more than half decent, even if I don't know who was singing on which tracks.

Crown Heights Affair

William Anderson; Raymond Reid; James Baynard; Arnold Wilson; Phil Thomas; Raymond Rock; Harry Boardley; Bert Reid; Howie Young; Muki Wilson; Julius Dilligard; Darryl Gibbs; Stan Johnson; Tyrone Demmons

Crown Heights Affair 1974 RCA APL1-0492 Producers: Freida Nerangis & Britt Britton

Dreaming A Dream 1975 De-Lite DEP 2017 Producers: Freida Nerangis & Britt Britton (Billboard soul charts: 28 ; Billboard pop charts: 121)

Do It Your Way 1976 De-Lite DEP 2022 Producers: Freida Nerangis & Britt Britton (Billboard soul charts: 41 ; Billboard pop charts: 207)

Dream World 1978 De-Lite DSR-9506 Producers: Freida Nerangis & Britt Britton (Billboard soul charts: 56 ; Billboard pop charts: 205)

Dance Lady Dance 1979 De-Lite DSR-9512 Producers: Britt Britton, Crown Heights Affair & Freida Nerangis (Billboard soul charts: 40 ; Billboard pop charts: 207)

Sure Shot 1980 De-Lite DSR-9517 Producer: Bert Decoteaux (Billboard soul charts: 50 ; Billboard pop charts: 148)

Think Positive! 1982 De-Lite DSR-8504 Producer: Bert Decoteaux

Struck Gold 1983 De-Lite DSR- DX-1-510 Producers: Raymond Reid & William Anderson

Hailing from The Crown Heights area of Brooklyn this self-contained group looked young and fresh-faced on their early albums, the first of which came out on RCA in 1974. It is excellent, too. with many of the tracks sounding as if they should have been on a soundtrack to some "Blaxploitation" movie, given all the chattering wah-wah guitar and dramatic swoops of sound. What is more surprising is the "Special Kind Of Women" track, virtually country-soul in construction with a subtle pedal steel strum. Julius Dilligard could really sing, too, but only lasted for this one LP.

The band moved to De-Lite in 1975 where they were to stay for the rest of their career and hit first time out with "Dreaming A Dream" which went to #5 soul and #43 pop, and an album was built around it. The sound had changed dramatically, though, with the funky soundtrack style being supplanted by a much more straightforward disco approach, which thrilled many, but left me disappointed. There are some reasonably appealing ballads on side two, sung well enough by a decent new lead man, Philip Thomas. and mixing what almost sounded like samples of "Tubular Bells" into "Foxy", was a neat touch, but I was underwhelmed with the whole thing. (The album was re-released entitled *Foxy Lady* as De-Lite DEP 2021 in the late summer of 1976 and reached #59 on the soul charts.)

Do It Your Way was also pretty successful as an album, with "Dancin'" going to #16 soul and #42 pop and was an interesting nod back to their early days as the instrumental portion of the song sounded not unlike - to say the least - "Theme From Shaft". The majority of the album was even more geared to the discos than *Dreaming A Dream*, and there are no slow cuts at all, but "Music Is The World" and "Far Out" took on some of the musical elements of stablemates Kool and The Gang.

Dream World included a side, "Galaxy Of Love", which managed to hit in the UK but not in the US, but I must confess I tended to leave the dance floor whenever it was played in my younger days, disliking its flimsiness and silly *Star Wars* associations. The US managed to put "Say A Prayer For Two" on the soul charts but only at a measly #41. Despite the impressive horn section throughout *Dream World*, I cannot find too much that has stood the test of time, apart from "I'm Gonna Love You Forever" which has good vocals.

Dance Lady Dance is somewhat misleading as the title would suggest rather more somewhat faceless disco but there are two tracks that should be heard. Firstly, "You Don't Have To Say You Love Me" (not the sixties song) has another fine (either Thomas or Harry Boardley) lead as does "Empty Soul Of Mine" which is excellent, with a melody not unlike "Neither One Of Us", and is completely unlike everything else they ever did. However, it was the title track which became their fifth (and last) single to reach the top twenty of the soul chart.

"You Gave Me Love" became another UK hit, but rather failed in the U.S. when it was issued as a single from *Sure Shot,* maybe owing to its rather dated chant on top of what sounded like The Mamas and The Papas on backing harmonies. There was only one slow track this time around, the rather enjoyable "Tell Me That You Love Me", which was a shame, and the LP is mostly notable for a lovely pair of legs on the front cover.

By the time of *Think Positive!* it was clear that they had adapted fairly significantly over the last few years. Gone was the overt disco, replaced by a much richer sound, heard to best effect in a fine single off the set, "Somebody Tell Me What To Do" (#31 soul), and "Heart Upside Down", an alluring ballad, although there were still too many uninteresting cuts on show and the title track really sounded way too much like an unwelcome cross between Grandmaster Flash and "Oops Upside Your Head".

The last album, *Struck Gold*, an optimistic title for a band who were no longer selling records, was a mediocre finish to a fairly lengthy career and contained no cuts of any particular merit, nor any successful singles.

Dillard Crume And The Soul Rockers

Singing The Hits Of Today 1969 Alshire S-5168 Producer: Glen Pace

Dillard Crume had a long and diverse career in the music business for many years, singing with a number of esteemed gospel groups before issuing this one low-key set under his own name.

He didn't really record many out and out soul records, although this is indisputably one of them. As might be inferred from the album title there are a number of covers of well-known hits of the time within, but he was an adroit songwriter himself and four cuts on here are his. It is a captivating outing, even if it employs a number of different styles which range from the plaintive and heartfelt slow numbers, "Wait For Me" and "Come Back Baby", which have something of a Roy C feel, through to out and out funk like "Let A Woman Be A Woman", the Dyke and The Blazers hit, and a fantastic version of James Brown's "Mother Popcorn". Hardly anyone could ever hope to match JB on his own material but Dillard Crume does here. Other really good covers are of "Polk Salad Annie", "Your Good Thing Is About To End" and "That's The Way Love Is". I would love to know who the Soul Rockers were, as well, as they are superb throughout. Crume died in 2008 after singing with the Soul Stirrers for a number of years.

Bettye Crutcher

Long As You Love Me 1974 Enterprise ENS-7505 Producers: Bettye Crutcher & Mack Rice

A quite marvellous songwriter, who had immense success with Stax and boasts a portfolio of compositions unmatched by most other women who worked in the field of soul music (Johnnie Taylor's "Who's Making Love" and Otis Clay's "Home Is Where The Heart Is" are but two examples), she obviously wanted an opportunity to try her luck at singing, but the failure of *Long As You Love Me* meant she did not bother again. The album has always divided opinion with those people who know it, as many remain unconvinced by her voice. I'm a big fan, though, being easily won over by the set's late night feel, captivating songs, superb arrangements and typically excellent musicianship. It has to be said though that she is certainly not a tough "southern soul" singer and it is also undeniably an album for an album's sake, if you see what I mean, not a set on which some sub-standard tracks were going to be built around strong singles (although "Sugar Daddy" was put out - to sadly little acclaim - as a 45 in the UK.)

Crystal Winds

Paul Coleman; Morris Cortez Brown

First Flight 1982 Cash Ear 9255 Producers: Morris Cortez Brown & Paul Coleman

By 1982 the soul music scene in Chicago was moribund, with records selling in vastly smaller quantity than had been the case fifteen years earlier although good ones still appeared if you knew where to find them.

Such is the album from Crystal Winds, a rather obscure outfit who would appear to really only consist of two men, although nine musicians were listed on the back cover. Some of these musicians, as well as Paul Coleman, had been members of Rasputin Stash, another Chicago group who recorded a couple of albums in the seventies. What makes the LP appealing are the vocals and low-key but gently funky backing and arrangements, rather than the songs, which are serviceable rather than memorable. Teresa Davis (who cut some singles in her own right) helps out here and there and my favourites are "So Sad" and "Love Ain't Easy" which feature charming high vocals from (I think) Coleman, so characteristic of much of the best of the music from the city over the years, and the impressive and imaginative "Signs Of Winter's Time", although this one did not manage to attract any interest as a 45. There are one or two rather throwaway tracks but this is still an above average set for 1982.

The Cult

Cholly Williams; Billy Ray Morris

The Mail Must Go Through 1976 Starburst SLT-500 Producers: Giac Ungaro, Larry Thorpe & Marc Ungaro

I'm not quite sure who the members of The Cult were but I do know that this LP came out with two separate covers, which seems to be a fair bit of trouble to go to for a record that remains terminally obscure, although, as a result, in demand of course. There are only seven tracks, some of which are instrumental, and the style is West Coast light funk with jazzy overtones. "Back Pay" is an urgent plea of charm, probably the best track, and had what it took to have been a hit.

Clifford Curry

Greatest Hits Then And Now 19?? Wood Shed WS 001 Producer: Rob Galbraith

Clifford Curry had sung with a number of obscure doo-wop and soul groups before he went solo, and he should not be confused with the singer of the same name who was a member of The Notations. In recent years he has done well for himself on the "Beach Music" scene in the U.S. but he had earlier recorded some good soul singles in the sixties and seventies, although only one of them, the ridiculously catchy "She Shot A Hole In My Soul", was ever reasonably widely well-known, making it to #95 pop in 1967. That track is on here, as are four others from his earlier career (although it may be that "Our Love Goes Marching On" was previously unreleased, and it sounds as if it was cut later than the others), while side two of this album has six of his new sides. Unfortunately, the album, while welcome, is hardly definitive and his in-demand sides like "Ain't No Danger", "I Can't Get Hold Of Myself" and "Good Humor Man" are not included.

Side two is dedicated to Curry's "Beach Music" oeuvre, which I find to be pleasant but undemanding and if that sounds patronising, it is nothing compared to the lyrics of "I Love Women", believe me. I'm also not sure that "Moving In The Same Circles" shouldn't have been on side one, as it came out on Buddah in 1977.

He is still releasing new music these days and remains in-demand as a live performer.

Ray Dahrouge

Rendezvous with Destiny 1979 Polydor PD-1-6189
Producers: Billy Terrell & Ray Dahrouge

Dahrouge is a caucasian soul man of impeccable taste and skill; he wrote some great songs over a long period of time, most notably every composition on Street People's fine LP from 1976 as well as lovely singles for Timothy Wilson, Barbara Jean English and a number of others based on the East Coast.

His one and only LP came out in 1979, although it was a little coy in as much as it hedged some bets by featuring an unidentifiable black man on its cover. With all due respect, Dahrouge is a better writer than singer and the LP's finest moment was his own take on his well-known song (in soul circles, anyway), "I Can See Him Making Love To You Baby". There is nothing poor on here, even if the slower songs are not especially "soulful", but I'm not sure there was ever any intention for them to be so, anyway.

Damion & Denita (see also Hodges, James and Smith)

Damion & Denita 1980 Rocket PIG - 3232 Producer: William "Mickey" Stevenson

I'm sure I've already said it a few times, and I'm sure I will say it again, but there is NO excuse for singers not to be credited on their own LPs. Who were Damion and Denita? God forbid that the record sleeve (or lyric insert sheet) would tell us. (Actually, Denita James was one third of Hodges, James & Smith and former solo singer and member of the Naturelles. I know no more about Damion.)

A man-woman team will inevitably invite comparison with Ashford & Simpson and while this LP could have done with some A & S material, Damion and Denita acquit themselves impressively vocally; they were both highly accomplished singers. Their best performances come on songs I know from other versions; firstly, "I Really Want To See You Tonight" is nearly as good as David Sea's marvellous reading from 1987 (and Damion raises the stakes by singing "I really want to sleep with you tonight") while "Love Your Sexy Ways" (originally cut by Hodges, James and Smith) does sound steamy and passionate rather than clichéd and silly. The majority of the rest of the songs - including some from Al Johnson and some from Mickey Stevenson - are better suited to being LP tracks rather than singles as they tend to lack impact, but all in all this is a good LP, worthy of investigation.

Damn Sam The Miracle Man & The Soul Congregation

O.C.Tolbert; A.J. Branham; Rudy Thompson; Tony Trice; Greg Whitfield; Ben James; Jonathan Scott; Wallace Childs; Lewellen Sutherland; Ben Littles; Richard Dilligard; Dave Newton; Good Sister

Damn Sam The Miracle Man & The Soul Congregation 1970? Tay-ster TS-0001 Producer: Jack Taylor

Rather silly name for a band, but a superb record, not least because O.C. Tolbert was possibly the strongest, most huskily soulful singer ever to front a funk group. The harrowing "Poor Mary" and the pleading "Let Me Be Your Only Man" showcase his ferocious gospel-based delivery but are atypical of most of the rest of the album which is funky in the extreme. "Smash", "Sonny B" and "BJ" are compelling in a way that so much funk from the early seventies could be. Only a slightly overwrought and overlong version of "Rainy Night In Georgia" misses the mark, and even then, not by much. A rare and in-demand LP which really deserves its cult status.

Sarah Dash

Sarah Dash 1979 Kirshner AL 35477 Producers: Gary Knight, Gene Allan, Jay Siegel & Wally Gold (Billboard pop charts: 182)

Oo - La - La 1980 Kirshner AL 36207 Producers: Jay Siegel, Wally Gold & Tom Anthony

Close Enough 1981 Kirshner AL 37659 Producer: David Wolfert

You're All I Need 1988 EMI Manhattan E1-90036 Producers: Sarah Dash, Daryll Duncan, Randy Klein, Ernie Poccia, Vaneese Thomas & Wayne Warnecke

Despite decades in the music industry, Dash has not meant a great deal to hard-core soul fans. This is in no way a reflection on her vocal abilities, more the fact that for many years she was a member of Patti Labelle and the Bluebelles, who were, particularly when they morphed into Labelle, often an acquired taste, working at the margins of what most people consider to be "soul". She left Labelle in 1977 and went solo, issuing a series of albums which, because they freely mixed pop and dance into the stew, did not particularly endear her to the soul community. None of the LPs rested on the soul charts (the first one did hit the pop equivalent) and only the debut contained singles that made the soul listings and then in fairly minor fashion: "Sinner Man" (#70) and "Candy From Your Baby" (#91).

I must confess to being pretty lukewarm about her records myself. The ballads are generally too "torchy" for my tastes, such as "You" on the debut album or "Let's Put Our Things Together" from the follow-up. "I Can't Believe", also from *Sarah Dash*, proves her talent beyond much doubt but it's all a bit rich for my blood. But I will rise up from my fence sitting position as regards her version of "You're All I Need To Get By", sung with Patti Labelle, on her final album. It is horrible.

Angela Davis

Please Don't Desert Me (At The Altar) 1982 Flaming Arrow FA 3320 Producers: Eugene Davis & Henry Bola Martins

Not to be confused with the political activist of the same name, this Angela managed a fairly lengthy career with the small Flaming Arrow concern, who put out singles by her over a period of a few years, none of which attained much success. It was thus rather a surprise to see the release of this album in 1982. (Earlier singles make reference to an album entitled *The Answer* but it never materialised.) And what an odd LP it was.

Gloria Walker had recorded Flaming Arrow's only hit back in 1968 with "Talking About My Baby", which featured a lengthy rap before she broke into "I'd Rather Go Blind". Davis reprises this, with more or less exactly the same rapped intro before launching into a song with "Blind's" same melody but different words. She also covers another Walker single, "Please Don't Desert Me". The problem is that Walker's sides beat Davis' hands down, for Walker was a superior singer. It's as if the record company were well aware of this as well, for although this LP has a running time of around 33 minutes, probably only half of it actually features Davis singing. The rest either features her spinning her raps or ignores her completely in favour of long instrumental breaks; exciting on "Congratulations", excruciating on "Take A Little Time With Me". The final cut, "Billy John", even has a touch of country about it.

Betty Davis

Betty Davis 1973 Just Sunshine JSS-5 Producer: Gregg Errico (Billboard soul charts: 54 ; Billboard pop charts: 202)

They Say I'm Different 1974 Just Sunshine JSS-3500 Producer: Betty Davis (Billboard soul charts: 46)

Nasty Gal 1975 Island ILPS 9329 Producer: Betty Davis (Billboard soul charts: 54 ; Billboard pop charts: 202)

Can someone of obviously limited vocal ability make excellent soul albums? If, like me, you believe that soul is as much about the musicians as the singer, then the answer would be "yes". Betty Davis was beautiful, forthright and charismatic, but when compared to an Etta James or an Aretha Franklin there is absolutely no contest whatsoever as regards talent. However, Davis was astute enough to assemble some stellar musical accompaniment on all her work and the result was that I have enjoyed the best parts of these albums for forty years or so.

"Stepping In Her I Miller Shoes", "If I'm In Luck, I Might Get Picked Up" (#66 soul) and "Game Is My Middle Name" are all titles from her debut album, and should make it plain that she was not coming from the same direction as your average soul singer, and a listener would probably need to enjoy early Funkadelic sides to get satisfaction from *Betty Davis*.

They Say I'm Different dispensed with the rocky approach of the debut and moved into a much more funky groove, exemplified by "Git In There", an irresistible outing. I have also always wondered how her erstwhile husband Miles Davis felt about the lyrics to "He Was A Big Freak" (assuming it was about him at all, of course) which now mainly amuses with its talk of her wielding a "turquoise chain". "Shoo B Doop And Cop Him" is also great fun, where Davis sounds like a female Sly Stone and just confirms my feeling that if anyone wishes to discover her music then *I'm Different* is the LP to seek out. (Just Sunshine kept trying to break her - five singles in all - but to no avail, as only two reached the soul charts and both at lowly positions.)

"Nasty Gal" and "Talkin' Trash" from her last LP - very funky in parts and somewhat rocky in others - have always seemed to me to be sung with her tongue placed firmly in cheek, so I'm not sure why she felt the need to defend herself in "Dedicated To The Press". "You And I" also demonstrated a surprisingly softer side to her personality; she should have tried to do more work in this vein.

So, Betty Davis, very much an acquired taste, one I like to indulge every so often but I can understand why anyone wouldn't want to be in the same room as her voice.

Geater Davis

Sweet Woman's Love 1971 House Of Orange HOS-6000 Producers: William Crump & Allen Orange

Sad Shades Of Blue 1986 Charly CRB 1132 (UK)

Better Days 1983 MT 0001 Producer: James Bennett

Vernon Geater Davis was a somewhat mysterious - and certainly woefully underappreciated - southern soul man who recorded the songs on his first LP at Little Rock, Arkansas and Birmingham, Alabama, locations that have yielded few hit records over the years. It's still a thrill for fans of such "underground" sounds to be reminded that Davis' first ever single, "Sweet Woman's Love", hit #45 on the soul charts (and must have sold by the truckload in the southern states), doing well enough to encourage House Of Orange to splash out on an album (which certainly did not sell in anything like the same quantities.) Cursory and lazy listening has led to some dismissing Davis as a poor man's Bobby Bland but such a conclusion is insulting and wrong. Geater was not only a fine writer, but also a skilled singer in his own right with a lighter timbre than Bland, even if there are some undeniable similarities in their overall delivery.

Sweet Woman's Love is a treasure of an LP, with a charmingly amateurish cover that rather symbolises the almost complete lack of ostentation in the music - apart from a possibly misguided latter few minutes on "Cry Cry Cry", which sound as if Vanilla Fudge had suddenly and bizarrely entered the studio to take over backing duties. That cut stretches out to over seven minutes as does a splendid version of "For Your Precious Love" but nearly everything else is short, sharp and tough. Drums, bass, plaintive guitar, a few swathes of organ and a handful of horns take on the task of providing a backdrop against which Davis pours out his soul. These are uniformly strong songs too, even if liberties were sometimes taken with songwriting credits.

House Of Orange never stood much of a chance of lasting long and after a handful of non-charting singles, Davis needed a new outlet for his records, finding it in John Richbourg's set of labels. 14 tracks from this period, spanning 1972 and 1973, and including his only other national hit, "Your Heart Is So Cold", were collected on an excellent and highly recommended compilation by Charly in 1986.

Davis had to wait until 1983 for his second "proper" LP to appear, a stripped to the bone collection that made the House Of Orange records sound positively Spector-esque in comparison. 1983 was a tough time for fans of "real" soul and there were a handful of us who lapped up the few releases from James Bennett's labels but, in all honesty, although it was great to hear Davis' voice again, the album has not really stood the test of time apart from "The Children" and "I Got To Know". The album had no chance of resurrecting his career to any substantial degree, but even if it had done, he sadly died, aged only 38, the following year.

Larry Davis

Satisfaction Guaranteed 1970 Perception PLP 11 No producer listed

This Larry Davis was neither the bluesman from Kansas of the same name, nor the Larry Davis who recorded for Kent. In order to really like this LP though, it would probably help to be a fan of the Kansan, given there is a fair degree of prominent guitar playing on show. It is another "in-demand" set which can only really be accounted for by the title track which is much more peppy, tuneful and obviously soulful then the rest of the cuts which are a little too eclectic for my taste: a bit of rock, pop, blues and southern soul all somehow mixed in together. Davis is a fine "black" sounding singer, mind you, so he carries some emotional heft, but the songs could do with being stronger.

Mary Davis (see also The S.O.S. Band)

Separate Ways 1990 Tabu Z 40978 Producers: Bernard Terry, Howie Rice, Daryl Simmons, Kayo, Royal Bayaan, John Lee, John Johnson, LA & Babyface (Billboard soul charts: 50)

This album is only in the book as a) Davis is an excellent singer who had a couple of singles released back in the "golden era" for soul b) she was the lead singer of the S.O.S. Band c) the title track is nice. Other tracks such as "Some Kind Of Lover" and "Don't Wear It Out" are, to say the least, not my idea of any kind of soul music.

Tyrone Davis

Can I Change My Mind 1969 Dakar SD 9005 Producer: Willie Henderson (Billboard soul charts: 12 ; Billboard pop charts: 146)

Turn Back The Hands Of Time 1970 Dakar SD 9027 Producer: Willie Henderson (Billboard soul charts: 9 ; Billboard pop charts: 90)

I Had It All The Time 1972 Dakar DK 76901 Producer: Willie Henderson (Billboard soul charts: 42 ; Billboard pop charts: 182)

Greatest Hits 1972 Dakar DK 76902 (Billboard soul charts: 42)

Without You In My Life 1973 Dakar DK 76904 Producers: Willie Henderson, Richard Parker & Monk Higgins (Billboard soul charts: 24 ; Billboard pop charts: 174)

It's All In The Game 1973 Dakar DK 76909 Producers: Willie Henderson, Richard Parker & Leo Graham (Billboard soul charts: 28)

Home Wreckers 1974 Dakar DK 76915 Producers: Willie Henderson, Richard Parker, Leo Graham, Carl Davis, Otis Leavill & Monk Higgins (Billboard soul charts: 55)

Turning Point 1975 Dakar DK 76918 Producer: Leo Graham (Billboard soul charts: 10)

The Tyrone Davis Story 1985 Kent 037 (UK)

Greatest Hits 1983 Epic PE 38626

A native of Mississippi, Davis moved to Chicago in the late fifties, where his first introduction to the music scene would be as a valet and chauffeur to Freddie King. His first singles came out in the mid-sixties as by "Tyrone (The Wonder Boy)", a hopelessly inaccurate title at first, given their poor sales, but prescient in the long run, as both artistically and commercially, he was one of soul music's most notable artists. It is also interesting to observe how almost completely his success was confined to a black American audience: he never had a sniff of a hit in England (or any other country so far as I'm aware) and only two of his records went top 20 pop. Contrast that with the twenty one records he placed on the U.S. soul charts top 20.

He had released six moderately selling 45s before finally placing a single on those soul charts and what a success it was too. The brilliant "Can I Change My Mind" climbed to #1 (and #5 pop) and was the pillar around which his first LP was built. As with so many albums of the sixties, covers were sprinkled liberally throughout and no fewer than 6 of the 11 tracks had been big hits for others. But riches could be found : "A Woman Needs To Be Loved", the b-side to the hit, was engaging with its typically uplifting Chicago brass section and one of the toughest vocals Davis ever laid down; "Have You Ever Wondered Why" and his version of "Just The One I've Been Looking For" were lovely too, but the fact that a follow-up single was not released from the album is surely compelling evidence as to its rather hasty appearance in the marketplace.

The eventual follow-up single - and another big hit - "Is It Something You've Got" - appeared on the second Davis album, *Turn Back The Hands Of Time*, which was much more of a carefully constructed offering, given that it featured only one cover: Johnnie Taylor's "Love Bones". What it did contain was soul hits, with four top ten soul singles: "Something You've Got", the superb title track (his second #1 and #3 pop hit), "I'll Be Right Here" and "Let Me Back In". In fact, every one of the eleven tracks on the LP appeared as either an a or b-side for Davis, so there was a minimum of throwaway material.

Dakar were by now putting out 45s on Davis at a rate that even James Brown would have admired, and by the summer of 1972, when his third LP, *I Had It All The Time*, hit the stores, he had already been favoured with 14 singles by the company. Four of these were to be found on the album, with two of them, "Could I Forget You" (#10) and the title track (#5) becoming big soul hits. His style was also firmly set by now, mid-tempo songs of regret and longing, brassy and rhythmically pungent, although it must be said that quite a few of them did sound remarkably similar. What a title cut, though: the tumbling breakdown into the music after his conciliatory spoken plea to his woman is one of the most thrilling in all soul music.

A well-named *Greatest Hits* followed as 1972 ended before the mighty *Without You In My Life* appeared, arguably his best ever LP. It did incorporate "I Had It All The Time" and "You Wouldn't Believe" again - Brunswick/Dakar up to their usual trick of duplicating songs across albums - but also had a great title cut (#5), unusually powered by a simple yet totally compelling horn line, rather than by a sung chorus, the irresistible drive of "There It Is"(#9) and the more romantic "Wrapped Up In Your Warm And Tender Love" (#19). The album was also notable for its inclusion of that rarest of beasts: a Tyrone Davis song. "I'm Just Your Man", a gentle and subtle offering, was penned by Davis together with Monk Higgins and turned up again years later on Bobby Bland's *Come Fly With Me* LP.

Davis' last really good album on Dakar appeared in *It's All In The Game* which had many exultant moments: a nine minute take on "I Wake Up Crying" (it was highly unusual for David to venture out above four minutes or so while on the label), two more great singles in the slow and forlorn "I Wish It Was Me" (#11) and the uptempo but equally wistful "What Goes Up (Must Come Down)" (also #11). Unheralded but worthy Davis'' performances in "You Don't Have To Beg Me To Stay" and "When Lovers Meet" are also tucked away on here as are two more reasonably successful 45s, "Happiness Is Being With You" and "I Can't Make It Without You".

Sadly, the *Homewreckers* LP was a bit of a disgrace, and pointed up the severe financial problems facing the record company at the time. Only two of the ten tracks had not already been included on a Davis LP so it was scandalously poor value for money. It was a shame as both of the new songs, which had Davis as co-writer, were pretty strong with the title track (on which Sam Dees was a co-writer) becoming a minor soul hit.

The last Dakar album wasn't much better. At least there was no duplication of tracks but the songs were almost uniformly dull with only the outstanding "Turning Point" itself (Davis' third and final #1 soul hit) ranking with his best material. The "Turn Back The Hands Of Time" cut on the album was a re-make, not the original.

Two compilations came out in the eighties of Dakar material with, as usual, the UK release being more generous in playing time than the U.S. one.

Love And Touch 1976 Columbia PC 34268 Producer: Leo Graham (Billboard soul charts: 12; Billboard pop charts: 89)

Let's Be Closer Together 1977 Columbia PC 34654 Producer: Leo Graham (Billboard soul charts: 17)

I Can't Go On This Way 1978 Columbia JC 35304 Producer: Leo Graham (Billboard soul charts: 18)

In The Mood 1979 Columbia JC 35723 Producer: Leo Graham (Billboard soul charts: 9 ; Billboard pop charts: 115)

Can't You Tell It's Me 1979 Columbia JC 36230 Producer: Leo Graham (Billboard soul charts: 40)

I Just Can't Keep On Going 1980 Columbia JC 36598 Producer: Leo Graham (Billboard soul charts: 39)

Everything In Place 1981 Columbia FC 37366 Producer: Leo Graham

The Best Of 1982 Columbia FC 37979

In The Mood Again 1989 Charly CRB 1214 (UK)

Davis never enjoyed the same level of success on 45 at Columbia that he had known at Dakar, mainly because he could never come to terms with disco, but he did at least release a number of satisfying albums and it was good to see a major label with resources and money get behind him for a while; the results of which were that he could now count on bigger selling LPs.

The first Columbia album (all the first three in fact) was recognisably Tyrone Davis to anyone who had followed his Dakar career, but the strings were increasingly played up at the expense of the horns, and while it was polished and consistent and contained one of his biggest hits in "Give It Up (Turn It Loose)"(#2 soul, #38 pop), it lacked the vibrancy of his best work. The follow-up single "Close To You" was a decent record, but was short of enough impact to fare any better than #33 on the soul charts, although it was hard to see any other potential hits within.

The best cut from *Let's Be Closer Together* was "This I Swear" and it did well as a 45 (#6 soul) but once again the set failed to house a second obvious hit and "All You Got" could only get to #32. Leo Graham was by now writing virtually all of Davis' material, whereas in the past he had to be content with a song or two on each album, and he was not a man to baulk at stretching out tracks to five minutes plus.

He extended one song to nearly ten minutes on *I Can't Go This Way* in "Get On Up (Disco)". It was one of the worst things either man was ever involved with and it didn't deserve to place as high as it did (#12) on the soul charts. But that was 53 places higher than the mundane "Can't Help But Say" could manage. The rest of the set was easy to listen to and enjoy without ever being close to vintage Tyrone. It was by now clear: Davis had moved from a singer who enjoyed big selling singles to one who relied upon album sales.

In The Mood was a more uneven outing than the previous three, with a mixture of very good tracks equalled by sub-standard ones. The good: The title track, a big soul hit for Davis (#6) in early 1979, the follow-up single, "Ain't Nothing You Can Do" (which did not do very well), "I Can't Wait" and "We Were In Love Then". The less good: "You Know What To Do" and "Keep On Dancing".

There was a definite plan for *Can't You Tell It's Me*: slow songs on side one and fast songs on side two. Guess which I prefer? The dance side seems to go on for ever, but the other is a success, with the title track, in particular, being one of my favourite cuts from Davis. Its gentle country burr is unlike anything else he ever did and it really suits him. One of Graham's best ever compositions, it nonetheless failed as a single (only #58) and I can only imagine his long-term fans were simply not prepared for this change of approach.

Davis' last two albums for Columbia came out at the time he was no longer enjoying big selling singles, and as he had sold vast quantities of 45s over a ten year period it was probably inevitable that he and the record company would have a parting of the ways. *I Just Can't Keep On Going* was not a bad album at all, though, and his version of "How Sweet It Is", while not improving on the versions by Marvin Gaye or Junior Walker, at least swung nicely and certainly didn't embarrass Tyrone. It reached #36 on the soul charts. The title track and "Overdue" were also fine cuts and he rang the changes again with "I'm Glad You're Here With Me Tonight" which, while not really working, was at least an interesting attempt at a pop styled song. Two dance tracks on side two were throwaway but all in all it was a pretty good album.

Everything In Place was a less convincing LP. It started in excellent fashion with "Just My Luck" which overcame its unpleasant drum sound by virtue of a truly catchy chorus and fine male backing vocals to become one of his strongest singles in a long time. Alas it only made #62 on the soul listings. "Love (Ain't Over There)" and "Headed For Love" weren't bad either but it was all downhill from there. "Let's Be Closer Together" was yet another example in Davis' music of a track being recycled from an old album while side two, most unusually, featured no Leo Graham songs at all. Sam Dees' "Leave Well Enough Alone" was not one of his best songs, "Turn Back The Hands Of Time" was re-cut in an ok but ultimately rather pointless fashion while "You Made Me Beautiful" and "You're Heaven Sent" were simply syrupy supper club outings.

Can I Change My Mind 1980 Manhattan 5034 (UK)

I have pulled out this album on the decidely weird Manhattan label for a specific comment as, despite the accreditation, it is not by Tyrone Davis at all. It is in fact entirely performed by a West Coast soul man, Rudy Love, and as such will be discussed in his section.

Tyrone Davis 1982 Highrise HR103AE Producer: Leo Graham (Billboard soul charts: 10 ; Billboard pop charts: 137)

At first, Davis' move to a new record label seemed to be the tonic he needed. "Are You Serious" was a really excellent single, his biggest hit in six years (#3 soul), and the album from which it came did well too, but the label fell into financial difficulty and went bust. In all honesty, it is a little difficult to understand the album's success as the single was vastly superior to all the other tracks apart from "Overdue", and that was yet another re-cycle anyway. Money was obviously tighter, as evidenced by the lack of strings, and tracks like "A Little Bit Of Loving" and "The Fool In Me" were just too poppy while "Let Me Be The One" was simply weak.

Something Good 1983 Ocean-Front OF 101 Producer: Leo Graham (Billboard soul charts: 46)

Pacifier 1987 Timeless TRPL 104 (UK)

Ocean Front proved to be another short-lived venture but the album Davis put out was solid. It didn't stand much of a chance of becoming a big hit as its style was in keeping with his Dakar period circa 1974 but it did ok and produced two top forty soul singles in "I Found Myself When I Lost You" and "Let Me Be Your Pacifier". "Turning Point" was re-cut and it was good to see him cover such a strong song as George Jackson's "All Because Of Your Love".

Seven of the tracks on the UK only *Pacifier* album came from the Highrise and Ocean Front LPs, with two more to be found on the Sexy Thing release.

Sexy Thing 1985 Future FR1001 Producer: Leo Graham

Man Of Stone (In Love Again) 1987 Future FR 1002 Producers: Leo Graham, Sam Ray Mosley & Bob Johnson

Flashin' Back 1988 Future FR 1003 Producer: Leo Graham (Billboard soul charts: 37)

Come On Over 1990 Future FR 1004 Producer: Leo Graham

Doubtless fed up to the back teeth with record companies going broke on them, Davis and Graham started up Future records which put out the four albums above (*Sexy Thing* also came out on Prelude PRL 14115). There were two problems though: Davis was by now pretty cold as regards hit singles (although *Flashin' Back* did contain three modest soul charts entrants, the last of which, the title track, being the 43rd time he had placed a 45 on the listings) and the music was generally less than enthralling anyway. *Sexy Thing* contained a fair number of tracks pressed into service for a second or even third time, and if *Man Of Stone* at least contained new songs, they generally weren't particularly good, being too long in each and every case. Davis could still sing well enough but he now also had to contend with an awful programmed drum sound of high irritant value. As noted above, *Flashin' Back* did at least provide some success, but once again re-cast previous songs as did *Come On Over*, mercifully the last Davis Future LP. The "One In A Million" track didn't even sound like Tyrone singing, and was probably the nadir of a real barrel-scraping exercise.

I'll Always Love You 1991 Ichiban ICH 1103 Producers: Leo Graham & Paul Richmond (Billboard soul charts: 39)

Something's Mighty Wrong 1992 Ichiban ICH 1135 Producer: Leo Graham (Billboard soul charts: 53)

For The Good Times 1994 Life LR 78002 1 Producer: Leo Graham

By the end of the eighties the Ichiban label was becoming somewhat of a refuge for battered old soul singers who could no longer shift many records, so it was no surprise to see Davis pitch up there. At least there was a glimmer of extra effort and interest from all involved and *I'll Always Love You* had three tracks that were pretty decent: "Let Me Love You"; "Do U Still Love Me "(despite its title) and "Mom's Apple Pie".

Something's Mighty Wrong wasn't bad, either, with stronger songs than had been the case for a while but the out of focus cover shot was symbolism enough for a man who was no longer commercially relevant.

Also symbolically interesting was his last, mediocre, album of cover versions and songs he had cut before, *For The Good Times*. Hardly anyone was still putting out vinyl in 1994 and it summed up how much Davis seemed a man out of time and step with the marketplace.

Davis continued to put out CDs until his death in 2005 and if none of them were much good, it is still a significant achievement to have been releasing music forty or so years after his first 45s came out. Like most artists, his commercial and artistic highpoints were finished long before he stopped making music but Tyrone Davis only just fell marginally short of being one of the best twenty or so soul men who ever drew breath, and he is certainly a great favourite of mine. Ironically, given how sensational he and his band were on stage throughout most of the seventies, no 'live' album was ever forthcoming.

Dawn Of Beige

Dawn Of Beige 1981 Loretta L08131H Producers: Billy Hinton, Beverly Hinton & Curtis Hinton

Lightning Strikes Twice (by Beige) 1982 Loretta L0282 Producers: Billy Hinton & Curtis Hinton

Hard And Soft (by Billy Hinton) 1984 Loretta L03BH4891 Producer: Billy Hinton

Some more highly obscure Chicago albums and there must be a fascinating story behind Billy Hinton and Dawn Of Beige, even if it was another name I wouldn't have chosen for a band and shortening it to just "Beige" for the second set wasn't a vast improvement. I know very little - actually, nothing - about this group but would like to know more as they certainly had something, as well as a pleasingly funky bass player in Charles Hosch.

Most of the tracks on the first two sets found their way onto a third album, this time as by Billy Hinton himself on which "Friends", "A Challenge", "Give Her Up", "Don't You Know Heart" and "What You Thought" were all admirable slow numbers with nimble guitar from Keith Henderson. Hinton achieved that rarest of things on these songs: he sounded like no-one else, although a Smokey Robinson influence is certainly in there. I'm very impressed. Unravelling the story behind all of this and reissuing the music seems to be a job tailor made for that excellent reissue company, The Numero Group.

Cliff Dawson (see also Zenith)

Cliff Dawson 1982 Boardwalk NB-33254-1 Producer: Lionel Job

Never Say I Do (If You Don't Mean It) 1983 Boardwalk NB-33264-1 Producer: Lionel Job

Dawson first came to my attention with a fairly decent single, "Somehow", in 1981 and he was also a member of a group called Zenith who put out an album the same year. But neither of those records prepared me for the excellence of his first set. *Cliff Dawson* was punchy, well-produced and thoroughly enjoyable. While he didn't sound anything like Luther Vandross it appealed to the same people who were buying Vandross' records, or would have done if enough people had had the chance to hear Dawson's offering. On the record cover he looks young and fresh faced and therefore the rather deep voice that greets us on the really good "It's Not Me You Love" (#39 soul) was a bit of a surprise. As proof of his impressive vocal range, the next best track, "Love Is Just A Dream", is largely sung in a sweet falsetto more in keeping with his youthful appearance.

Beware the second album though, as it is exactly the same as the first apart from the fact that the worst track, "I Can Love You Better" is excised to make way for "Never Say I Do", a duet with Renee Diggs that made the top twenty soul charts in early 1983 but it is the type of "Disney" ballad that is anathema to me.

After seemingly recording no more solo records for decades he re-appeared in 2014 with a new CD.

Dayton

Jenny Douglas; Chris Jones; Dean Hummons; Derrick Armstrong; David Shawn Sandridge; Kevin Hurt; Craig Robinson; Rachel Beavers; Justin Gresham; Michael Dunlap; Evan Rogers; Jenny Matthews; Rahni Harris; Elaine Terri

Dayton 1980 UA LT-1025 Producers: David Shawn Sandridge & Rich Goldman

Cutie Pie 1981 Liberty LT-1093 Producer: David Shawn Sandridge

Hot Fun 1982 Liberty LT-51126 Producers: David Shawn Sandridge, Rahni Harris & Ted Currier (Billboard soul charts: 36)

Feel The Music 1983 Capitol ST-12297 Producers: David Shawn Sandridge, Rahni Harris & Roger Troutman

This Time 1985 Capitol ST-12412 Producers: David Shawn Sandridge, Rahni Harris & David Cole

The first album from these obviously proud sons and daughters from Ohio got rather lost in the shuffle, but it was competent enough, even if the quality of the lyrics was negligible. All up-tempo, apart from "So Glad", funky tracks like "Dank", "Dayton (Jam)" and the more melodic but still danceable "Eyes On You", were particularly good. In fact, only "Tonight" was genuinely substandard.

Cutie Pie at least generated a charting single in the title track (but only # 62) but both it and the other faster tracks were more routine than on the debut and therefore it was good to hear a melodic if light and poppy cut in the charming "You Lift Me Up". "Wanna Be Your Man", "Let Me Know" and "Fool Was He", songs rather than grooves, were impressive too, but I wonder how many tracks over the years have been recorded called "Piece Of The Rock"? Clichéd title, clichéd record.

The band had not used any outside material at this point and it was therefore a departure when they recorded Sly and The Family Stone's "Hot Fun In The Summertime" as the title track and lead-off single for their third LP. It did pretty well too (#17 soul and # 58 pop) and they made a much better fist of it than I had feared. Jennifer Matthews delivered an impressive vocal on "We Can't Miss" and further evidence that the group were by now much more confident as singers than most of their rivals in this congested era of self-contained soul groups, came in the slow and intricately arranged "Patiently". But the real gem was "Never Repay Your Love" an arresting ballad. On the funkier side, "Krackity-krack" featured, obviously, Bootsy Collins and it sounds as much like one of his own records as Dayton's. Not bad at all, despite the title, and "Gunch " was also much harder and compelling (and a minute too long) than it sounded as if it had a right to be. I wasn't mad on "Meet The Man" or "Movin' Up" but overall, this is Dayton's finest by some distance and was one of the best soul / funk albums of 1982.

The introduction of Rahni Harris was a major factor in the band recording more radio-friendly and accessible songs and he was responsible for co-writing and singing the three best tracks on the *Feel The Music* LP: "It Must Be Love" (#54 soul), "Promise Me" and "Caught In The Middle" - all excellent, with the latter sounding like Atlantic Starr at their best. I am also partial to the Roger Troutman produced "Love You Anyway" but was not moved by the rest of the album.

This Time sounded as if it had been made by an entirely different band eschewing the earlier funk and soulful ballads in favour of a vaguely entertaining brand of pop-soul. It's certainly better than a lot of the mind-numbingly predictable albums other soul/funk aggregations were turning out in 1985 but it palled when compared to the *Hot Fun* album.

Dazz Band

Wayne Preston; Les Thaler; Ed Myers; Bobby Harris; Michael Wiley; Michael Calhoun; Isaac Wiley; Reggie Stewart; Kenny Pettus; Sennie Martin; Pierre DeMudd; Eric Fearman; Kenny Kendrick; Steve Cox; Keith Harrison; Marlon McClain; Juan Lively; Jerry Bell

Kinsman Dazz ** 1978 20th Century T-574 Producers: Philip Bailey, Tommy Vicari & Ralph Johnson (Billboard soul charts: 52 ; Billboard pop charts: 203)

Dazz ** 1979 20th Century T-594 Producers: Tommy Vicari & Pat Glasser (Billboard soul charts: 62)

Dazz, like Dayton, were another Ohio band, although this time from Cleveland. The two albums above marked thus (**) came out under the name of Kinsman Dazz. From the third album onwards the band changed their name to The Dazz Band. They were heavily influenced by Earth, Wind & Fire on the first couple of albums which was no great surprise given Philip Bailey's and Ralph Johnson's production involvement. The first album was much better than the second with good tracks like "Saturday Night" (not the EWAF song), "I Might As Well Forget About Loving You" (#46 soul) and "(Don't Want) To Stand In Your Way" but the second was uninteresting; six lengthy tracks of minimal merit, although, one, "Catchin' Up On Love", was a small soul hit at #36.

Invitation To Love 1980 Motown M8-946M1 Producer: The Dazz Band

Let The Music Play 1981 Motown M8- 957MI Producers: Dazz Band & Reggie Andrews (Billboard soul charts: 36; Billboard pop charts: 154)

Keep It Live 1982 Motown 6004ML Producer: Reggie Andrews (Billboard soul charts: 1 ; Billboard pop charts: 14)

On The One 1982 Motown 6031ML Producer: Reggie Andrews (Billboard soul charts: 12; Billboard pop charts: 59)

Joystick 1983 Motown 6084ML Producer: Reggie Andrews (Billboard soul charts: 12; Billboard pop charts: 73)

Jukebox 1984 Motown 6117ML Producers: Bobby Harris & Reggie Andrews (Billboard soul charts: 18; Billboard pop charts: 83)

Hot Spot 1985 Motown 6149ML Producer: Bobby Harris (Billboard soul charts: 24; Billboard pop charts: 98)

As Kinsman Dazz the band had placed two singles on the soul charts at fairly lowly placings, and this sort of performance continued with *Invitation To Love* when the band had made the move to Motown and truncated their name. "Shake It Up" was one of those "hits" (#65 soul) and its repetitive nature eventually overcomes listener resistance. The other was the title track (#51), a pretty decent ballad. All the songs on the album were written by the band and despite a handful of sub-standard cuts it was a big improvement on *Dazz*.

Let The Music Play carried on the sound and flavour of *Invitation To Love*, right down to a middling hit - "Knock Knock" at #44 soul in the summer of 1981. "This Time It's Forever" was a satisfying slow workout, but "I Believe In You" was much too sloppy and poppy. Their fine horn section excelled on "Don't Stop" and all their better uptempo cuts had interesting things going on in the upper register.

And then they suddenly hit the big time with "Let It Whip" a #1 soul and #5 pop hit in the spring of 1982. It helped the album on which it sat, *Keep It Live*, to become easily their biggest. Shame it was such an uninspiring record. The title track also became a reasonably big soul hit for the band (#20) but far more appealing to my ears was "Gamble With My Love" a good ballad with nice harmonies. There was nothing about the album that was obviously better or different from what had gone before so it is just one of those good strokes of fortune that conjures up a hit where none existed before.

The momentum was continued with another big selling album, *On The One*, from which a #9 soul hit, "On The One For Fun" came forth. Much more interesting and surprising were a take on "Bad Girl" one of the earliest Miracles singles, and "Stay Awhile With Me", a Van McCoy song. The former has the edge for me, but Dazz acquit themselves without mishap in both cases.

No such surprises were forthcoming on *Joystick*, an album of meagre aural delights and a most suggestive cover. Horns were by now sacrificed for unappealing synth flourishes and even the ballads were not up to their previous standards. A cut like "To The Roof" was just awful, not an adjective I have felt compelled to use with regard to their earlier work. Luckily for them, many people disagreed with me and "Joystick" and "Swoop" were big soul singles.

"Let It All Blow" and "Heartbeat" were two more very healthily selling 45s from the next album, *Jukebox*, but I could no longer listen to their music as it was now firmly cast in that mid-eighties rock/pop/dance/synth mixture that drove me crazy.

Their Motown sojourn ended with *Hot Spot*, an album that contained a track entitled "Paranoid". I'd rather listen to Black Sabbath's song of the same name than sit through this one again. The whole thing, though, sounds dreadfully dated in a way that so much soul from earlier decades simply never does.

Wild And Free 1986 Geffen 924 110-1 Producer: Bobby Harris (Billboard soul charts: 37; Billboard pop charts: 100)

Rock The Room 1988 RCA 6928-1-R Producers: Eumir Deodato, Ish Ledesma & Bobby Harris (Billboard soul charts: 91)

The Dazz Band closed out their vinyl album career with these two albums. Jerry Bell had now joined the group as lead singer and the Geffen LP contained two singles that became soul chart entrants, while the RCA set housed three. After ten years they still retained a large following.

Dealers

Stanley Johnson; Pametricia Johnson; Elton Johnson; Rickey Townes; Darrell Hunter; George Wilburn; Kenneth Blackwell

Dealers 1985 CBS BFZ 40065 Producers: Michael Zager, Roger Hawkins & Stanley Johnson

In 1977 this band covered Minnie Riperton's "Lovin' You" to pretty decent effect with wailing and charmingly naïve vocals from a male and female lead, and bettered it a year later with "I'm For You, You For Me" on the tiny Muscle Shoals Sound label. Neither sold and nor did a much worse dance thing, "Love Maker" from 1979. As might be expected, given it was 1985, their one album chose to build on "Love Maker" rather than the earlier ballads and I'm afraid I don't care for it at all. Titles selection : "Party All Night", "Hump", "Sexy Operator" and "Miss Foxy".

Snoopy Dean

Wiggle That Thing 1977 Blue Candle 55057 Producer: Horace Straws

I Can Read Between The Lines 1992 Hot Blues HTLP 3352 Producers: Snoopy Dean & Sam Early

Consider this choice: you could buy the best 25 LPs ever put out by Marvin Gaye, James Brown, Curtis Mayfield, The O' Jays and Aretha Franklin or for the same amount of money you could purchase an original copy of Snoopy Dean's *Wiggle That Thing*. What's it to be? And consider this as well: would you ever play the Dean more than once? For it is a highly mundane affair.

Dean issued an acclaimed single in 1974, "Shake 'N' Bump", and that repetitive style is reprised on a number of tracks on *Wiggle That Thing*. He is not a great singer (although he performed well enough on "Been So Long", a single he cut while part of a group entitled The Third Guitar in the sixties), and melody is a stranger to most of the tracks. The funk itself is not hard enough to sustain interest either and only the gentle "Walking On Air" and "We'll Try Again, which he sings in a higher register, provide something to challenge my torpor.

On the other hand, I retain a soft spot for *Between The Lines*. It is not a great record a little bit shoddy and of no relevance whatsoever to what large numbers of record buyers wanted in 1992, but there *was* a small audience for it out there: long-time soul fans like me. We can instinctively feel at home with these types of songs - all written by Snoopy - which have more of a link to "classic" sixties soul than anything ever put out by Freddie Jackson, Robert Brookins or singers of that ilk. There is plenty of dross on here - "Whipped And Whipped", for example - but "Back Door Lover" continues the tradition of "cheating" songs that go back decades in soul and all of side one was the sort of thing that just about kept the flame alive twenty four years ago. He died in 1998.

Debarge

Eldra DeBarge; Randy DeBarge; Mark DeBarge; James DeBarge; Bunny DeBarge

The Debarges 1981 Gordy G8 1003MI Producers: Bobby DeBarge, Bunny DeBarge & Eldra DeBarge

All This Love 1982 Gordy 6012GL Producers: Iris Gordy, Eldra DeBarge, Curtis Nolen & Raymond Crossley (Billboard soul charts: 3; Billboard pop charts: 24)

In A Special Way 1983 Gordy 6061GL Producer: Eldra DeBarge (Billboard soul charts: 4; Billboard pop charts: 36)

Rhythm Of The Night 1985 Gordy 6123GL Producers: Bobby DeBarge, Bunny DeBarge, El DeBarge, Richard Perry, Jay Graydon & Giorgio Moroder (Billboard soul charts: 3; Billboard pop charts: 19)

Bad Boys 1987 Striped Horse SHL 2004 Producers: Carlo Nasi & DeBarge

DeBarge proved one of the eternal truisms of pop music; release records by people with pretty faces and they will sell. It's the oldest trick in the book.

 I believe there were ten children in the DeBarge family. Two of them, Tommy and Bobby, had been members of the band Switch before Bobby turned his attention to working with a new group comprised of four more of his brothers and a sister, Bunny. The first four albums from DeBarge had carefully concocted covers of neatly scrubbed siblings smiling at their chosen age group of potential buyers: 8 to 18. (The fifth provided another truism of the industry: the safest acts imaginable just can't resist releasing records with edgy titles; DeBarge duly followed this tradition with "Bad Boys".)

 For some reason, the first album (as by "The Debarges") didn't sell in great quantity but did include one or two tuneful and enjoyable tracks ("Saving Up (All My Love)" and "What's Your Name") which had echoes of the early seventies' sweet soul sound.

 The group dropped the "s" and enjoyed three successive big selling LPs in a row, on which were included six top ten soul singles including two #1 hits, "Time Will Reveal" and "Rhythm Of The Night". There were by now only the most distant echoes of early seventies' soul and it was all antiseptic pop music guaranteed not to offend. And why not? It was after all the ethos of Motown's early days, although those did of course have the bonus of brilliant music at the same time.

 El Debarge went on to considerable success as a solo singer in the mid eighties onwards while Bunny also got the chance to cut some sides on her own.

Leon Debouse

A Fine Instrument 1977 Bold 303 Producers: Clay Cropper, Roger Hattfield & Norman Lotterer

Bold records was a subsidiary of T.K. but this one LP from the unknown Leon Debouse struggled to make its way out of Florida. It deserved to be better known, though, for it is competent and enjoyable throughout, and at least as good as plenty of other records that sold well. Debouse was an adept if not inspired singer and while most of the set contains midtempo songs of decent quality the jazzy "Same Old Changes" and the ballad "What Do We Do About Our Love" are the stand-outs, with "Every Fella's Girl" not far behind.

 He returned briefly in 1985 with a 12" single, "We Go Better Together", that is inferior to every track on the LP.

David Dee

Going Fishing 198? Vanessa 2001 Producers: Gene Norman & Oliver Sain

Sheer Pleasure 1986 Edge ED LP- 003 Producer: Don Davis

Goin' Fishin' 1991 Ichiban 1114 Producer: Gary Coleman

David Dee (real name: David Eckford) was one of those artists who managed to happily straddle the fence that lies between soul and blues without discomfort, and there are obvious parallels between him and another man who recorded in a similar style, Little Milton Campbell: both were born in Mississippi, both recorded in St. Louis. But while Milton moved on, Dee stayed put. He released singles sporadically, and sustained a career by gigging in the city, before anyone thought to cut him on an album.

 That first LP on the local Vanessa label (later to be re-issued on Edge ED LP-009 entitled *Portrait Of The Blues)* was solid enough, with a mixture of fairly contemporary soul sides such as "Sweet Loving Baby" and a re-cut of his nice ICA single from 1977, "Give Me Some Air", sitting alongside straight blues tracks like "Blues Jam". Dee/Eckford wrote most of it, and the title track was probably as close as he ever came to having a "hit" single as it sold very well locally, by all accounts. Also, just to underline the Little Milton comparison, Dee offered up a version of Campbell's small hit from the spring of 1977, "Just One Step".

 The next album, though, was pitched at a much higher level of quality and *Sheer Pleasure* is one of the best soul LPs of the eighties, as well as being almost totally forgotten. The reason for this was manifest: the quality of the musicianship and production. I would wager Don Davis and the magnificent Detroit band he assembled (although one track was also cut at Muscle Shoals, not a bad second location) saw it as a rare opportunity to stretch out and really show what they could do. Hardly any soul LPs from the mid-eighties were blessed with this sort of musical verve. "Your Sweet Word" is probably the best example of a band in peak form but "Working Blues Man" was exhilarating too, while "Don't Leave Me On Hold Too Long" was a deep soul cut in the grand tradition of the sixties' "golden age". Sadly, though, this was not what many people wanted to hear or buy thirty years ago; nor now, it would seem, as copies sit unwanted and unloved on ebay for pitifully small asking prices.

  David Dee's final LP came out on Ichiban, and was another good effort. Much of Ichiban's output could be thin or synthetic sounding but this was a red-blooded affair, which, although leaning more to blues than soul, included more than acceptable versions of "Lean On Me" and "Rainy Night In Georgia" while "If I Knew Then" made for a fine single when released from the set.

Jay Dee (see also Bob & Earl)

Come On In Love 1974 Warner Brothers BS 2820 Producer: Barry White

I gave a brief breakdown of the convoluted recording career of Bob and Earl in the section under their albums, and it wouldn't have been apparent to any record buyers that the one LP by Jay Dee was from the same man who was "Earl". One may have thought Warner Brothers (or Earl Lee Nelson himself) would have played up this point, but they did not.

Or maybe it isn't so surprising as this LP is really more about Barry White than Jay Dee. The big man produced and arranged it, dreamed up the concept (even if it's unclear just what that is), and wrote most of the songs and at no time does the album suggest that Jay Dee's presence was critical; almost anyone else could have delivered the vocals. In fact, on the first and last tracks there aren't even any vocals to deliver and these instrumentals are markedly similar to the music White released on The Love Unlimited Orchestra which means their link to soul music is rather tenuous. And even on the second track, the small soul "hit", "Strange Funky Games And Things" (#88), Jay Dee doesn't appear until we are three minutes or so in. When we finally do get to hear him sing he is up to the task, and it's a pity he didn't get a chance to stretch out on some more challenging material. White was always gifted at writing catchy hooks and the title track certainly features one, even if it is hammered home over and over again. Those who love highly orchestrated and crisply played and produced rhythm tracks from that classic year of 1974 should get on perfectly well with the LP, but it's not one for anyone who likes a bit of rough.

Jimmy Dee & The Mighty Dee-Jays

James Dudley; Skip Pearson; Frank Stevens; 'Lil' Buddy McKnight; Pete Minger; Bill Campbell

Memorial Tribute To Sam Cooke 1965? Hear Me 64-25 No producer listed

James Dudley was a fine singer who cut some good singles in the sixties under his own name and that of "Jimmy Dee" but even soul experts have had difficulty in documenting all his work, so obscure were most of his recordings. It was to my astonishment that I recently became aware of an album he recorded around fifty years ago in tribute to Sam Cooke.

The sleevenotes inform us that the LP was recorded within a matter of hours of Cooke's death, but given that was on December 11th 1964, it would have taken a significant effort to get it issued in the remaining 20 days of that year and I therefore deduce that 1965 seems a more likely year of release. The LP is obviously heartfelt, but does drag a little to listen to as the sound is pretty rudimentary, and the songs so well-known. It's recorded "live" but whether in a church, a nightclub or a studio is hard to ascertain and the audience seems rather small judging by how they react to a song. It's not solely Cooke covers as a trio of gospel songs can be found on side two, but it is definitely an album for the hardcore collector rather than a general soul enthusiast.

Joey Dee's

Music Is My Life 1986 Mazel Express MXLP 001 Producers: Joey Dee's & Lawrence Henry

I have no idea why Joey decided his surname needs an apostrophe - given it wasn't present on a single he issued in the early seventies - but that's how it is spelt on the record cover and record itself. It should also be pointed out that the album has possibly the most difficult to read sleevenotes I have ever encountered. Light brown on dark brown is not a good design idea.

Joey was born Joe Dorgan in Mississippi and despite this LP being the merest blip on the soul landscape it is definitely worthy of investigation. The record, heavily sixties influenced both in the musical arrangements and structure, had not a chance in hell of becoming a hit in 1986, but was a real find for those of us who missed the more abrasive side of soul in the age of synths and drum machines. The band, with real horns, are fine, the songs are generally good and Joey's vocal debt to Otis Redding is obvious and welcome. "Here Stands Your Fool" is the stand-out cut and if the two covers - "Bring It On Home To Me" and "Funny" - are not the best of all time, they merely serve to further root the record in a much earlier time and place.

Sam Dees

The Show Must Go On 1975 Atlantic SD 18134 Producer: Sam Dees

Secret Admirer 1989 Pen Pad PP 1002 Producer: Sam Dees

The Homecomings 1991 Pen Pad PP 1007 Producer: Sam Dees

The name of Sam Dees won't mean anything to the average music fan, but to a small number of us, most of whom probably live in the UK, he is a master, a genius, and one of the most talented artists ever to work in the field of soul music. A physically imposing man, he could write, sing and produce better than just about anyone else. When he came to perform for the first time in London in 1989, everyone present was overcome with emotion not least Sam, himself. That big frame trembled on stage as he realised - as he certainly had not before - how much he was loved by those who had been lucky enough to discover his music.

In the early seventies he made a handful of singles, heavily rooted in the southern soul tradition - to be expected from someone born in Birmingham, Alabama - as well as providing songs for the likes of Clarence Carter. Nothing sold particularly well, but the quality was already glaringly evident. By 1973 he had turned up on Atlantic, who put out his first - genuinely brilliant - album in 1975. *The Show Must Go On* is an album to rank with *What's Going On* for breadth of topic, sheer soulful emotion and iconic cover photo.

One of the few albums where it could be vigorously argued that every track was strong, the LP divided into three categories: social commentary, loving bliss and loving despair. "Child Of The Streets", led off by an eerie sheet of sound, is a totally convincing depiction of the hell some people have to endure and "Trouble Child" provides little respite, with Dees laying out cold reality in chilling cries while "What's It Gonna Be" is a plea to embrace self-respect rather than self-pity, a welcome stance and not one that will be found on many other records. When he turned to affairs of the heart he was just as compelling: the magnificently orchestrated "Just Out Of My Reach" shows us a tortured man who can't let go of the woman he loves, while "Worn Out Broken Heart" - astonishingly, in retrospect, for such naked emotion, a #15 soul hit in 1974 – is a shattering evocation of pain, as good as anything Smokey Robinson wrote. The title track is an updated version, lyrically, of "The Tracks Of My Tears" and every bit as good, and just when one could find it all too much to take, he provides us with the joy and pleasure of being in love with "So Tied Up" and "Good Guys" as well as the stoicism of "Come Back Strong". All that is left is the impeccably southern brew of "Claim Jumpin'" which would doubtless have provided another smash hit for Johnnie Taylor had he ever recorded it.

"So Tied Up", "Just Out Of My Reach" and "The Show Must Go On" all made relatively minor showings on the soul charts as well, and apart from issuing a handful of singles at irregular intervals, Dees was to turn to song-writing as the main way to make a living for the rest of the decade and much of the next. It was, on the face of it, a smart move as many artists were to benefit from his songs and many became big hits, but it seems as if little of the money trickled back to Dees. Doubtless bitter about this, he put out a second vinyl LP on his own label in 1989.

Initially disappointing, as much for a lack of a proper cover and a last track on side two by one Freddie "Rap attack" Jones which brought to mind Raymond Chandler's remark about a tarantula on an angel food cake, the album did contain the song that arguably even surpassed everything on the debut. "After All" is simply one of the greatest songs ever written - in any field, at any time - about a marriage break-up. If ever a song should be played to those who feel popular music is trivial, this is it. It deserved to sell a few million, but its devastating bleakness and honesty could never have been programmed on mainstream radio. Time has also shown just how good most of the rest of the LP is as well and hardly anything from 1980 onwards can compare with *Secret Admirer* even if it doesn't have the depth and breadth of *The Show Must Go On*. Dees updated his 45 from the late sixties, "Lonely", and apart from "After All" there are seven other new songs which are generally up to Dee's almost peerless standards, while his confidence and artistry even extended to a lovely and too short one minute instrumental interlude, "Heart". "Say It's Only A Rumour", "All The World To Me", "Expert" and the title track were surely missed hits for someone.

The Homecomings was barely an LP: it only had six tracks, one of which was instrumental, and another which wasn't by Dees at all, but so starved have fans been of Dees albums that it must be included. The title track, "Get The Message Out" and Alfreda James' "Personal Man" are all excellent while "You've Been" and "I'll Be A Man" are merely good. Once again, it had no cover, and so must have been cut on a tight budget, and only sold to real devotees, I suspect. It is not vintage Dees and is the least essential of his three albums, but it still contains more skill, love and passion than hundreds of other albums in this book.

Delfonics (see also Major Harris)

William Hart; Wilbert Hart; Randy Cain; Major Harris; John Johnson

La-La Means I Love You 1968 Philly Groove PG 1150 Producers: Stan Watson & Thom Bell (Billboard soul charts: 15; Billboard pop charts: 100)

Sound Of Sexy Soul 1969 Philly Groove PG 1151 Producers: Stan Watson & Thom Bell (Billboard soul charts: 8; Billboard pop charts: 155)

Super Hits 1969 Philly Groove PG 1152 (Billboard soul charts: 7; Billboard pop charts: 111)

The Delfonics 1970 Philly Groove PG 1153 Producers: Stan Watson & Thom Bell (Billboard soul charts: 4; Billboard pop charts: 61)

Tell Me This Is A Dream 1972 Philly Groove PG 1154 Producer: Stan Watson (Billboard soul charts: 15; Billboard pop charts: 123)

Let It Be Me 1972 Sounds Superb SPR 90078

Alive & Kicking 1974 Philly Groove PG 1501 Producers: Stan Watson, William Hart & Wilbert Hart (Billboard soul charts: 34; Billboard pop charts: 205)

The Best Of 1976 Kory KK 1002

The Best Of 1984 Arista AL5-8095

Symphonic Soul 1988 Charly CRB 1184 (UK)

Black music has a long history of providing a showcase for pretty singers: doo-wop and gospel could boast any number of young men who thrilled their audiences with the beauty and purity of their voices. So the Delfonics had come from a long and proud tradition. What Thom Bell brought to the table for late-sixties Philadelphia soul was his familiarity and facility with instruments that had hitherto played a small part in soul music such as the flugelhorn and the oboe, and he cloaked the Delfonics in great swathes of orchestration. It wasn't a style that found favour with those who believed that soul should be tough and emotional but it obviously appealed to many and from early 1968 until the end of 1971 the group had eleven hit singles that reached the soul top ten, with all eleven also hitting the Hot 100 pop.

William Hart was the lead singer and only Blue Magic's Ted Mills or The Temptations' Eddie Kendricks could equal Hart in the grace of a high tenor delivery. He could write too, and the six songs he composed with Bell on the *La-La Means I Love You* album were all exquisite. The title track was the big hit (#2 soul and #4 pop) but "I'm Sorry" and "Break Your Promise" are heartbreakingly lovely, too. Bell always the good sense to counter the sweetness at the top of his music with a tough rhythm section in order to keep things from being just *too* sickly, and the thud of the drums could have been recorded nowhere else in the world but Philadelphia. There, was, though, a definite sense of a rush to complete the album and the five non-original songs range from ok - "Hurt So Bad" - to boring - "Shadow Of Your Smile".

The *Sound Of Sexy Soul* LP followed the same pattern as the debut: six Hart–Bell originals and six "outside" songs. The best of the originals, the magnificent "Ready Or Not, Here I Come", was paired with the next best cut, "Somebody Loves You", on a superb double headed single (both sides made the charts), but all of them were good, with the exception of the dull "Hot Dog". Of the "standards" the Spector-esque "With These Hands" should be heard for the sheer joy of its unremitting sound while "Face It Girl, It's Over", was marvellous and a less obvious choice than the others.

Bell and the group realised that their strongest suit was with self-penned songs and the third album, *The Delfonics*, dispensed with any covers - apart from Barry Mann's "When You Get Right Down To It" - and boasted seven Bell-Hart cuts and two Hart solo compositions. There has long been a conceit in the music press that true creativity was the province of pop and rock groups with soul's strengths lying in a more emotive appeal to the senses. *The Delfonics* demolishes such an argument. It is a brilliant album, with staggering layers of musical complexity, and Thom Bell achieved undeniable greatness in his arranging, best exemplified by the titanic "Didn't I Blow Your Mind This Time" which became a #3 soul and #10 pop hit. Another shift of emphasis in the album was a greater willingness to let Wilbert share some of the vocals with his brother and it adds an extra dimension to what was already a winning strategy. "The Delfonics Theme" might have been self-indulgence on Bell's part but fit in perfectly with the feel and texture of the whole set, the strength of which could be further seen by the fact that five successful singles were pulled from it.

Unfortunately for the group, Thom Bell decided it was time to move on and the Delfonics never posted a 45 on the pop top 50 again. However, they were still capable of making exquisite records and the loss of Bell brought Wilbert further to the forefront and he contributed five tracks to the *Tell Me This Is A Dream* LP including the gorgeous "Round And Round" with its ingenious arrangement. The title track, "Walk Right Up To The Sun" and "Hey Love" were all top twenty soul hits from this excellent LP but an ominous note was detectable in "Looking For A Girl". There was nothing wrong with the track at all but it sounded very much like the Chi-Lites. The Delfonics were now copying instead of being copied. (I think *Tell Me This Is A Dream* is the album on which Major Harris joined the group to replace Randy Cain, but the sleeve keeps us in the dark.)

There was a wait of a couple of years before the next (and last) Philly Groove LP, during which time a compilation came out in the UK which was composed of the debut album minus a couple of tracks plus the addition of "Round And Round". That last album was a real beauty, however, with no filler at all. Four singles were to be found on *Alive And Kicking:* the uptempo "I Told You So"(#26 soul) holding its own against the more typically tender and slow "Lying To Myself" (#60), "Think It Over" (#47) and "I Don't Want To Make You Wait" (#22). In fact, only *The Delfonics* can surpass *Alive And Kicking* for sheer beauty, inventiveness and consistent quality of songs.

Three compilations came out after the demise of the Philly Groove label in the mid-seventies. All comprise previously released material, and all are good, with the UK release containing the most tracks.

The Return Of 1981 Poogie P121680 Producers: William Hart & Wilbert Hart

It might have been a return, but one wonders if they should have bothered. The voices were still there, as beautiful as ever, and this is not a bad record at all, but it falls well short of all the Philly Groove LPs and could not return the group to prosperity. It is a brief work of only six songs, and all four of William's are better than Wilbert's two, but nothing on here can match the perfection of so many of their greatest sides. The cover is cheap in the extreme, and it is therefore a surprise to hear that the musical backings is fulsome and rather nicely arranged by the Harts, who clearly were highly talented in this field and I understand they always felt that Bell's skills had unfairly obscured their own. There were to be no more returns on vinyl but the Delfonics' place in history as one of the greatest soul vocal groups should be secure, but I still feel they have not fully received the credit they deserve.

Frank Dell

Yesterday's People 1977 Guinness GNS 36001 Producers: David Blake & Phil Medley

Two Faces Of 1985 Valise FD 430 Producer: Franklin Murphy

Daily Loving 1989 Valise FD 432 Producer: Franklin Murphy

Frank Dell (or Franklin Delano Murphy) was a mysterious New York based soul man who once invited me, a total stranger, to his wedding - I couldn't go - but that is another story. He put out a handful of singles, one of which, "He Broke Your Game Wide Open", is much desired as well as being available on the first of his three albums. He must have had a small but loyal audience - or an unquenchable desire to make it - to sustain this number of releases (and there were more on CD) as he had no hits whatsoever.

The Guinness label was, of course, a tax write-off sideline and so Frank, assuming he knew the record existed, would have made no money from it at all, and even had it been commercially issued the material within was clearly a decade or so older than the 1977 release date. It was such a shame it didn't make his name as he was a superb singer of great power and personality and three tracks, "I'll Go On Loving You", "Love's Battle" and, particularly, "I Want What I Want" were in the great soul tradition of high class New York ballads as performed by the likes of Solomon Burke or Hoagy Lands. "He Broke Your Game Wide Open" was full of beans and vitality too, but it wasn't as good as the slow stuff. There are other ballads on the album as well but tended to be more poppy and less satisfying.

 He originally came from North Carolina and recorded singles as "Big Frank Murphy" and "Big Frank and The Essences" but these sides did not find their way onto the Guinness release. When he finally put a "valid" LP on his own in 1985 it only featured six tracks, nearly all covers of well-known songs like "Taxi" and "Pledging My Love". It is an interesting album as although it is not billed as a 'live' set, that is how it comes across; long raps preceding some of the songs and exhortations to the band are standard stage devices, and I wondered if it was indeed cut "live" in the studio. Webster Lewis' "Tell Me Love" was a somewhat surprising choice but he performs it well although his strength remained at a more sedate tempo and he delivers "I Stand Accused" beautifully and soulfully. Synth strings grate a little, but the band is really good, and pleasingly includes The Pazant Brothers on horns.

Daily Loving retained the impressive band but did sound about ten years out of date for 1989. This helped to ensure that the album could never expect to sell many copies but was good news for listeners like me, who preferred the music to feel alive, rather than conjured up on computers. The best track was a wonderful six minute plus take on Walter Jackson's "Welcome Home" which also name checked The Originals' "Baby I'm For Real", but nearly all the cuts are worth hearing as they provide irrefutable proof that terrific if obscure soul singers could still cut it at the end of a dark decade like the eighties.

Dells

Marvin Junior; Johnny Carter; Chuck Barksdale; Michael McGill; Verne Allison

It's Not Unusual 1965 Vee Jay VJS-1141 No producer listed

Oh What A Night / Stay In My Corner 1970 Buddah BDS 5053 No producer listed

In Concert 1974 Vee Jay Intnl. VJS 7305 Producer: ?

From Streetcorner To Soul 1985 Charly CRB 1055 (UK)

Who was the greatest soul group of all-time? It's a game fans play all the time. The Temptations would get a lot of votes, as indeed would the Four Tops, Impressions and O'Jays - and The Dells. It wouldn't be just because they made many marvellous records over a forty year plus time frame; it's also because they made them with the same personnel. Labels changed, producers and arrangers changed, but the five men singing the songs didn't. In the early days they were the El-Rays (Johnny Funches and Lucius McGill were other members of the group back then) before cutting their first records as The Dells in 1955. They issued lots of singles with only one, "Oh What A Nite", becoming a hit, a big one too: #4 soul (or "R&B", as it was then) in 1956. These early pre-soul sides can be found on a number of albums from record labels such as Vee Jay, Upfront, DJM, Solid Smoke and Charly but fall outside the book's remit. Carter was a newcomer, by the way, joining the Dells in 1960, a number of years after the other four had started singing together, but there were no more changes in personnel after that.

The first LP in the soul era was cut in 1965 for Vee Jay, unfortunately at a time when the company were running into serious financial difficulties but "Stay In My Corner" from the album at least became the first time in nearly ten years that the name of The Dells was back on the soul singles chart. Overall, it was a highly eclectic set, with tracks like "Lil' Darling" and "My Baby Just Cares For Me" showcasing a facet of the group which they often exploited: a "whitebread" harmony style which owed as much to the Four Freshmen as to the Swan Silvertones. On the other hand their take on "I Got A Woman" was closer to pure gospel then they usually allowed themselves. I have a soft spot for "What Do We Prove" a simple mid-tempo song of deceptive and lasting charm. (The LP was re-issued in 1970 on Buddah, with two tracks, "Jeeper's Creepers" and "Alexander's Ragtime Band", being omitted, replaced by "Oh What A Night" and "I Wanna Go Home".).

In 1974 Vee-Jay International put out a set, *In Concert* which I have neither seen nor heard, but is highly unlikely to be a 'live' album. My reason for saying this is because in 1985 Charly in the UK put out a compilation that contains the majority of the tracks that were on the *In Concert* album and they are studio rather than stage recordings. It is worth tracking down, despite its absurdly ill-advised sleeve design: placing black type on black flecked background makes reading the notes very difficult. Side one is from the pre-soul era but side two is definitely in scope and all the songs - cut between 1961 and 1965 - are good.

There Is 1968 Cadet LPS-804 Producer: Bobby Miller (Billboard soul charts: 4; Billboard pop charts: 29)

Always Together 1969 Cadet LPS-822 Producer: Bobby Miller (Billboard soul charts: 9; Billboard pop charts: 146)

Greatest Hits 1969 Cadet LPS-824 (Billboard soul charts: 9; Billboard pop charts: 102)

Love Is Blue 1969 Cadet LPS-829 Producer: Bobby Miller (Billboard soul charts: 3; Billboard pop charts: 54)

Like It Is, Like It Was 1970 Cadet LPS-837 Producer: Bobby Miller (Billboard soul charts: 7; Billboard pop charts: 126)

Freedom Means 1971 Cadet 50004 Producer: Charles Stepney (Billboard soul charts: 4; Billboard pop charts: 81)

Sing Dionne Warwicke's Greatest Hits 1972 Cadet 50017 Producer: Charles Stepney (Billboard soul charts: 32; Billboard pop charts: 162)

Sweet As Funk Can Be 1972 Cadet 50021 Producer: Charles Stepney (Billboard soul charts: 33)

The Best Of 1972 Checker 6467 303 (UK)

That first Cadet LP, *There Is*, was magnificent and virtually faultless, arranged with winning effervescence by Charles Stepney. It included four big hits, with one of them, a six minute re-cut of "Stay In My Corner", becoming the first of their two #1 smashes on the soul charts. (It also became their biggest ever pop hit at #10.) Wholly satisfying, the track has a mesmerising moment when Marvin Junior holds a note for fifteen seconds but it is only one sublime moment in an album that is a perfect example of soul harmony singing. The Dells proved they could do it all, here: fast songs such as "There Is" (#11 soul and #20 pop), "Run For Cover" and "Wear It On Our Face" (#27 and #44) are handled with great assurance, while other exquisite slow songs, "Please Don't Change Me Now", "O-o I Love You" (#22 and #61), "Love Is So Simple" and the oft-recorded "Close Your Eyes" showed what an obvious debt soul owed to doo-wop. Only "When I'm In Your Arms" lowers the standard to merely highly competent and all in all, it was one of the greatest soul vocal group LPs to emerge from Chicago - in fact, anywhere - in the sixties.

Always Together was a much more problematic set. Stepney's arrangements on "There Is" had been impressive; here they veered towards the bombastic and on poor tracks like "I Want My Momma" the results were raucous and unappealing. Four tracks saved the album: the touching Vietnam song "Does Anyone Know I'm Here" (a #15 soul hit), and three subtle and intelligent Bobby Miller compositions about the complexities of human relationships and passing time: the title track (also a #3 soul hit), "I Can't Do Enough",(a # 20 soul hit) and "Make Sure (You Have Someone Who Loves You)" the b-side to "Does Anyone Know I'm Here".

Cadet put out a Greatest Hits album which did well, consisting solely of tracks that could be found on *There Is* or *Always Together*.

I don't care, though, for the next LP, *Love Is Blue*, where Stepney's arrangements became ever more flowery, and, to these ears at least, pretentious. "A Whiter Shade Of Pale", "A Summer Place", and a dreadful rendition of "Dock Of The Bay" did the group no favours at all and even the better cuts such as their second #1 soul hit, "Oh What A Night", "Love Is Blue/I Can Sing A Rainbow" (#5 soul) and "Glory Of Love" (#30) were saddled with (or blessed with, depending on your taste, of course) towering orchestration. Interestingly, producer Miller contributed no songs at all this time around, after having penned every single cut on *Always Together*.

Like It Is, Like It Was restored my equilibrium as the orchestration was subordinated to the singing, rather than the other way around. The concept here was new songs on side one, and older songs on side two. There was little difference in style, however, and the whole album is a masterclass of harmony singing. A particular favourite was "Open Up My Heart" which reached #5 soul in the spring of 1970 when truncated as a single. But it is only the six and a half minute album version that truly satisfies with the rest of the group humming soulfully and hypnotically behind Marvin Junior's typically committed vocal. "Come Out, Come Out" should also be heard as another particularly good example of their "straight" harmony style. The exuberant "Oh What A Day" was also a successful single (#10 soul) although "Long Lonely Nights" did less well (#27).

Freedom Means was a pleasant album, too, even if side one had a distinct advantage over side two. Much of its appeal can be attributed to the songwriting team of Terry Callier and Al Wade who provided most of the songs, including the two that became successful singles, "The Love We Had (Stays On My Mind)" (#8 soul and #30 pop) and "It's All Up To You" (#23 soul). The latter had an irresistible bright and uncluttered Stepney arrangement, and, indeed, the whole album had a lighter and fresher feel than some of his previous work with the group.

Unfortunately this was to change on a very dull LP: *The Dells Sing Dionne Warwicke's Greatest Hits.* Bacharach and David are rightly famous for writing delicate and memorable melodies, but on too many cuts here the overwhelming arrangements render the songs unrecognisable and not a single one was any better than Warwick(e) had already delivered. It all seemed rather pointless and the LP generated no hits at all.

And neither did the last album the Dells made with Stepney, *Sweet As Funk Could Be*. It was a messy affair featuring a number of segues that made no discernible sense and tunes were absent without leave. One cut saved it from total disaster: "Just As Long As We're In Love", a marvellous Callier - Larry Wade song, perfect for the group, but one which disappointingly stalled at only #35 soul when released as a single at the end of 1972.

Checker in the UK put out a superb *Best Of* set but the group clearly needed a new approach and, luckily, were to get it when they teamed up with Don Davis.

Give Your Baby A Standing Ovation 1973 Cadet 50037 Producers: Charles Stepney, Don Davis & Bobby Miller (Billboard soul charts: 10; Billboard pop charts: 99)

The Dells 1973 Cadet 50046 Producer: Don Davis (Billboard soul charts: 15; Billboard pop charts: 202)

The Dells 1973 Cadet CADJ-3 (Promo-not for sale)

The Dells Vs The Dramatics (with The Dramatics) 1974 Cadet 60027 Producers: Don Davis & Tony Hester (Billboard soul charts: 15; Billboard pop charts: 156)

The Mighty Mighty Dells 1974 Cadet 60030 Producers: Don Davis & Charles Stepney (Billboard soul charts: 13; Billboard pop charts: 114)

Greatest Hits Volume II 1974 Cadet 60036 (Billboard soul charts: 47; Billboard pop charts: 210)

The Mighty Mighty Dells 1974 Chess 9109 100 (UK) Producer: Don Davis

We Got To Get Our Thing Together 1975 Cadet 60044 Producers: Don Davis, Tony Hester, John Roach & Charles Stepney (Billboard soul charts: 31; Billboard pop charts: 207)

The Dells 1982 Chess CH-8400

Charles Stepney had not quite finished with the group, though, and he did produce the majority of the better than average *Standing Ovation* album. Of the Stepney cuts, "You Don't Care" is a gorgeous ballad, one of the Dells' best kept secrets, while "Share" was a most intriguing Terry Callier song, almost country in construction, and most unlike pretty much anything else they ever cut. The one Miller produced track was "Glory Of Love", rather cheaply reprised from *Love Is Blue* of four years earlier. But Davis got the hit. The title track - a Marv Johnson and Henry Williams song - played up Carter's voice to share equal lead billing with Marvin Junior and reached #3 soul and #34 pop, their biggest smash since 1969.

No doubt thrilled by the success of *Standing Ovation*, Cadet entrusted Davis with exclusive production duties for *The Dells* LP, their first ever to be recorded entirely outside of Chicago. The recording locations were Detroit and Muscle Shoals but the whole set is seamless and anyone would be hard pressed to say which tracks were cut where exactly. As usual, the best cuts were the singles and "I Miss You" and "My Pretending Days Are Over" had truly engaging arrangements by Wade Marcus and reached #8 and #10 respectively on the soul charts. But there were other winning sides as well: "If You Move, I'll Fall" and "Don't Make Me A Storyteller" were both cut by others but these were strong interpretations. Davis' confidence could be seen in the fact that "Let The Feeling Talk To You" and "I Hear Voices" were both more than seven minutes long - too long, in fact - but there were no real duds on show.

Davis - or someone - then had the inspired idea to put together a joint album by The Dells and The Dramatics. The result was an utter triumph, the best LP ever put out by The Dells with the possible exception of *There Is*. The Dramatics had four cuts to themselves, The Dells three, while two more glorious tracks featured both groups singing together. Every cut is a winner, so I won't go into much detail other than to exhort everybody to hear the album, but I will say that "Love Is Missing From Our Lives"(#46 soul), one of the collaboration cuts, is simply one of the most heart-stoppingly perfect examples of soul arranging and singing ever captured on disc and "I Wish It Was Me You Loved" (#11 soul) a Dells' "solo" cut with meltingly exquisite Reggie Young guitar on a tale of desolation, features arguably Marvin Junior's best ever vocal, with the contempt in his voice a thing of wonder.

Another excellent LP followed in the shape of *The Mighty Mighty Dells*. After a slightly worrying start to "Bring Back The Love Of Yesterday", which clearly aped Barry White's music of the time, it settled into a typical Dells album of this era: fine songs, marvellous arrangements, and great singing. To take this album as representative of soul music in 1974: listen to that unobtrusive and sympathetic drumming and compare it to the overwhelming and insensitive cacophony that all too often prevailed from the early eighties onwards. Only "The Way We Were" was unnecessary and album only cuts like "Nothing Can Stop Me" (an even better version by Cissy Houston exists) and "Since I've Been In Love" should be heard.

Highly confusingly, the UK arm of Chess also put out a *Mighty Mighty Dells* album in 1974, with an identical cover to the U.S. Cadet release, but it was a significantly different album with six tracks from the U.S version not making the UK LP. It's quite possible that not many people know this.

Cadet also put out a second Greatest Hits compilation in 1975 but it was a little odd in as much as it included four tracks that were in no way hits, and omitted two that were: "I Miss You" and "I Wish It Was Me You Loved".

We Got To Get Our Thing Together, The Dells last album for Cadet, was a worthwhile effort, even if the two best tracks ("You Don't Care" and "Love Is Missing From Our Lives" (with a truncated and inferior arrangement) had been pressed into service on previous albums. The title track was excellent, too, and performed well as a single reaching' #17 soul. I also liked "The Power Of Love" (a not very successful single) and "Reminiscing" but "Strike Up The Band" was a jazzy swing thing I didn't care for. (The LP was also re-pressed and released as SRM-1-1059 on Mercury.)

The 1982 compilation features exclusively Cadet material, as did the 1973 "promo" LP, and both are OK, if not overwhelmingly generous with the number of tracks.

No Way Back 1976 Mercury SRM-1-1084 Producers: Bobby Miller & Andrew (Mike) Terry (Billboard soul charts: 47)

They Said It Couldn't Be Done, But We Did It! 1976 Mercury SRM-1-1145 Producer: The Harris Machine (Billboard soul charts: 40; Billboard pop charts: 208)

Love Connection 1977 Mercury SRM-1-3711 Producer: The Harris Machine (Billboard soul charts: 45; Billboard pop charts: 204)

By 1976 The Dells had a new label to go with their new recording locations, Chess/Cadet having gone broke. *No Way Back* was a mediocre first effort, largely cut at All Platinum in New Jersey, with rather uninspiring material from fine writers like Mike Terry, Bobby Miller and Ivy Hunter. Predominantly uptempo, the album did feature a couple of slower songs, the best being the languid "Slow Motion" but neither it nor the title track did well when released as singles (#49 and #68 soul respectively).

Mercury sent the group down to Philadelphia for the next two albums in an effort to revive their fortunes, but The Philly sound had lost a degree of its magic by this time and *They Said It Couldn't Be Done* was another average offering. There were no obvious big hits on the LP and only the ordinary "Our Love" reached the top twenty soul as a single. Having said the above, "Waiting For You" was a fine slow burner. And therein lay the dilemma: no-one could doubt the skill of The Dells' slower offerings but the uptempo material was too often uninteresting in the Mercury period.

Things certainly improved, however, at least in quality, if not in chart success, on the *Love Connection* release. "Private Property" (#57 soul) was a lovely ballad that would surely have been a smash ten years earlier, and "Wasted Tears" was a wonderful homage to their past. Apparently written in 1966 by Junior it had sat dormant for over ten years and featured one of those ineffable long notes from Marvin at the end. Finally, too, the faster songs were of a higher quality and "Don't Trick Me, Treat Me" and "How Can One Man Be So Lucky" were tuneful and memorable.

New Beginnings 1978 ABC AA-1100 Producers: Al Perkins, Eli Fountaine, George Clinton & The Dells (Billboard soul charts: 55; Billboard pop charts: 169)

Face To Face 1979 ABC AA-1100 Producers: Al Perkins, Calvin Carter, Rudy Robinson & The Dells (Billboard soul charts: 71; Billboard pop charts: 203)

Another label move came about in 1979 when the group shifted to ABC, for whom they recorded two albums in Detroit. The first of them included two old Parliament tracks, "I Wanna Testify" and "All Your Goodies Are Gone", interesting choices and both produced by George Clinton, a man who had always loved harmony singing, even if his image suggested otherwise. Unfortunately, they didn't really suit The Dells, but the rest of the album was really good. "Superwoman " reached #24 on the soul charts and its b-side, "My Life Is So Wonderful" was an excellent dance side while "Call Me", "Drowning For Your Love" and "Cherish" are all unjustly neglected album cuts that never get mentioned in any discussions about the group.

Face To Face was markedly inferior with only the single "(You Bring Out) The Best In Me" (#34 soul) being really worthy of the group, although "Thought I Could" and "Plastic People" weren't bad. Worryingly, it was also the third successive LP where the Dells weren't even shown on the front cover (and this time around, they didn't even make the back.)

I Touched A Dream 1980 20th Century T-618 Producers: Carl Davis & Eugene Record (Billboard soul charts: 23; Billboard pop charts: 137)

Whatever Turns You On 1981 20th Century T-633 Producers: Carl Davis & Eugene Record

In 1980 The Dells returned to Chicago. No expense was spared on the *I Touched A Dream* LP which welcomed them back. The orchestration was lavish and impressive, they once again graced the cover of one of their albums, and it was their biggest seller for a number of years, as indeed was the title track when released on 45 (#17 soul). The album also boasted "All About The Paper" and "Your Song", much-loved club tracks, and "Passionate Breezes" a classy Jackson-Yancy tune.

The follow-up, *Whatever Turns You On,* had the misfortune to suffer from one of those periodically alarmingly misguided moves by a record company as someone decided that placing a picture of a huge toucan on the front cover was a good idea. Once again one of the most eminent groups in soul music history had to be content with a tiny picture on the back. As marketing it was a disaster: the LP became their first in 15 years to fail to reach the soul charts. However, the record itself wasn't half bad with a pretty good cover of Mystique's " It Took A Woman Like You" and the nice if exhaustingly-titled "How Can We Find The Love We Lost When We Don't Know How It Got Away" to enjoy. But the real beauty came right at the end: an update of "Stay In My Corner". It isn't radically different from the 1969 hit, but this time Marvin Junior holds a note for thirty seconds; a thrilling half minute of virtuosity from one of the greatest lead singers who ever lived.

One Step Closer 1984 Private I BL 39309 Producers: Chuck Jackson, Marvin Yancy, David Williams, Danny Johnson & Archie Russel (Billboard soul charts: 49)

The Second Time 1988 Veteran VR-1988 Producers: Cornell Ward & Andre Miller (Billboard soul charts: 92)

One Step Closer had noticeably stripped-down musical accompaniment when compared to the 20th Century records but the singing was as impeccable as ever and the majority of songs were not bad at all, three of them charting soul, with the best of them, the excellent "You Just Can't Walk Away", going the highest at #23. The best track on the LP though, was a super old Ashford and Simpson song, "I Am Your Man", which had once done some business for Bobby Taylor and The Vancouvers. Dells fanatics should certainly not ignore this LP.

The Dells bowed out on vinyl with a miraculously good LP. They had now moved to the unflattering if accurate Veteran Records and *The Second Time* was as good an album as could be found in 1989. "Can We Skip That Part?", a tremendous Verne Allison song, was beautifully arranged and sung and genuinely bears comparison with all their finest sides. "No Win Situation", "That's How Heartaches Are Made", and "Thought Of You A Little Too Much" were all highly meritorious ballads and a cover of Willie Clayton's uptempo "Sweetness" also worked. In fact only "Hott" (as one could tell from the title) was mundane.

The Dells had not quite finished with making hits as they managed to put a fine single, " A Heart Is A House For Love", as high as #13 soul in 1991 but it came from *The Five Heartbeats* movie rather than a Dells album; two further singles also reached the soul charts in 1992 from a CD they issued on P.I.R.

The voices of Marvin Junior and Johnny Carter have now been stilled for ever, and it seems inconceivable that Allison, Barksdale and McGill would ever contemplate drafting in replacements so we can assume that The Dells will never record or appear on stage again but the glory of their talent, and the fact they placed 46 singles on the soul charts over a 36 year time-frame, can never be denied.

Sugar Pie DeSanto

Sugar Pie 1961 Checker 2979 No producer listed

Lovin' Touch 1987 Diving Duck DD 4310 (Holland)

Down In The Basement 1989 Chess CH-9275

Born in New York, but raised in San Francisco, Sugar Pie had a great recording name, an inspired and much needed change from her real one, Umpeylia Marsema Balinton. Standing just under five feet tall she also had a visual impact that one would not easily forget, particularly by anyone lucky enough to witness her highly charged live shows. Unfortunately, her chart showing is meagre and her LP legacy very poor, factors that contribute to her continued lack of current and retrospective acclaim.

The only genuine hit she ever had was "I Want To Know" on Veltone in 1960 which reached #4 soul. Its success was enough to attract Checker and for the remainder of the sixties the majority of her records came out on Chess associated labels. Her only "true" album was the *Sugar Pie* set from 1961 which was built around the hit. Released at a time when "R&B" was changing to "soul", the LP didn't have a dominant style as the company decided how best to record her. Not surprisingly other tracks - such as "Can't Let You Go" - sounded suspiciously similar to the hit but the nicest surprise was a sultry and appealing - rather than overblown and sickly - take on "The Twelfth Of Never".

Most of her best sides were released in the years between 1964 and 1966 and it is both a great shame and mystery why Chess never released another LP on her. It would have been quite something as sides such as "Soulful Dress", "I Don't Wanna Fuss", "Slip In Mules" (her second biggest hit at #48 pop) and the fiery duet with Etta James, "In The Basement" (her third, #37 soul), are all tremendous and brilliantly conjure up smokey and sweaty sixties'

clubs. Fortunately all of these, and more, can be found on the two excellent compilations from 1987 and 1989, each generous at 16 tracks. Both are needed, too, owing to little track duplication.

Hello, San Francisco 1984 Jasman JR121829 Producer: James Moore

This album was also retrospective in nature and is both of merit and completely different in style from her sixties sides. She pitched up on the Jasman label after short and unsuccessful sojourns at Brunswick and Soul Clock and recorded for them - Jasman - over a period of time. The cuts on here range from the blues-based title track to in-demand and sharp funk cuts like the splendid "Git Back" but the real gem is the frankly astonishing "Strange Feelings" (also the b-side to "Git Back" when it was put out as a 45) which I take to be autobiographical. It is rare to hear such naked self-confession, even in soul music, and it is not easy listening; it's such a shame that no-one knows it and it has never been mentioned in any dispatches I have seen but is that rare beast: a genuine "lost classic". Almost its equal in world-weariness is "How Many Times" and both tracks are troubling in the best way. They proved that she is one of the best "deep soul" singers around when she wanted to be or was allowed to be.

Gloriously, she is still going strong in 2016, albeit by singing live rather than releasing much new music, but she has recorded new material in the CD age.

Determinations

Roosevelt Powell; Irwin Powell; Nathaniel Valentine; Leonard Coleman

One Step At A Time 1976 Event 7001 Producer: Raeford Gerald

This is another extremely rare LP. In fact I have never even seen a copy of the original and, believe me, that is not for a lack of looking. I can only assume few copies were pressed up and it must also have experienced from very limited distribution.

There were a number of soul groups called The Determinations, nearly all of whom only got the chance to record a solitary 45; at least this one also got to make an album. In truth, it is not a great set and my hunt for it has been more as a record collector than a soul lover. I certainly do like the two tracks that ape the then current Philly sound, "That Ain't The Way" and "But Not For Me", and the group also serve up an interesting and quite tough slant on Aaron Neville's "Tell It Like It Is" but too much of the rest is mediocre and there were plenty of other vocal groups at the time who put out finer discs. (One track, "Come And Get These Memories", is not even a Determinations recording: it also came out as a 45 by producer Ray Godfrey (aka Raeford Gerald) and is nowhere near as good as Martha and The Vandellas' original.)

Detroit City Limits

98c Ninety-Eight Cents Plus Tax And Other Hits 1968 Okeh OKS 14127 Producer: Mike Terry

This LP is really only in the book as a) it was produced by Andrew "Mike" Terry, one of the more important "back-room" men in soul music, b) contains covers of a number of big soul hits and c) some may be curious as to what it sounds like as it does appear to have fans. The answer to c) is "moderately assertive elevator music",

All instrumental, the LP fails to meet the exacting standards set by the likes of Booker T. & The M.G.s and can be pretty safely ignored.

Detroit Emeralds

Abe Tilmon; Ivory Tilmon; James Mitchell; Marvin Willis; Carl Johnson

Do Me Right 1971 Westbound WB 2006 Producers: Abe Tilmon, James Mitchell & Bernie Mendelson (Billboard soul charts: 23; Billboard pop charts: 151)

You Want It, You Got It 1972 Westbound WB 2013 Producers: Abe Tilmon, James Mitchell & Bernie Mendelson (Billboard soul charts: 37; Billboard pop charts: 78)

I'm In Love With You 1973 Westbound WB 2018 Producers: Abe Tilmon, James Mitchell & Bernie Mendelson (Billboard soul charts: 27; Billboard pop charts: 181)

Abe, James & Ivory 1973 Westbound 6309 101 (UK)

Feel The Need 1977 Westbound WB 302 Producer: Abe Tilmon

Let's Get Together 1978 Westbound WT 6101 Producers: James Mitchell, Abe Tilmon, Marvin Willis & Mike Theodore

Way back, Abe and Ivory Tilmon were part of a gospel group, The Tilmon Brothers, while James Mitchell sang with a doo-wop group, The Five Rockets. None were Detroit natives, but they met and grew up there. The Detroit Emeralds first recorded for Ric-Tic with one single, "Show Time", doing well on the soul charts (#22) in 1968. Although Ric-Tic was acquired by Motown, the group were not part of the deal, and this allowed them to move to Westbound where they had a highly successful few years. Their best work is characterised by strong, catchy songs, crisp rhythms and soaring string arrangements but a lack of top-class ballads has probably hindered them from receiving the critical acclaim afforded to other groups.

After a typically pounding Detroit recorded 45, "Holding On", didn't have the desired sales impact, Westbound sent the group down to Memphis to record a couple of appealing songs, one of which, "If I Lose Your Love", reached #32 soul in early 1970. Both singles were included on the *Do Me Right* LP as were other Memphis-recorded sides, "I Can't See Myself" and "Just Now And Then", which became a smallish soul hit (#41) when released together on a single that summer. However, a big one was around the corner and "Do Me Right" reached #7 soul and #43 pop in early 1971 which enabled Westbound to build the first album around it. It remains an irresistible side: tuneful with clear lyrics and a winning arrangement, fully deserving of its success. Apart from a rather misguided attempt at "And I Love Her" all of the album is good - "Long Live The King" is an absolute killer neglected track with wonderful string charts - and still sounds pretty fresh forty plus years later.

Abe Tilmon had written most of the tracks on the first album, but nearly all were in collaboration with others, whereas on *You Want It You Got It* he wrote everything himself apart from one track with Mitchell. The group's style was now instantly recognisable and the album included two big hits, and perfect examples of how to arrange pop-soul sides, in the title track (#5 soul) and "Baby Let Me Take You In My Arms" (#4 soul and #24 pop - the only time they made the top thirty) as well as the song that made their name once and for all in England: "Feel The Need In Me". It is impossible to imagine any British soul fan who went out clubbing in 1973 not dancing to this record and there are few sides that transport me so instantly as this one to that carefree and exciting time. There was nothing else on the LP to dismiss out of hand, but equally, nothing even remotely of the quality of the three singles.

I'm In Love With You continued the formula of cutting rhythm tracks in Memphis and then adding strings in Detroit and at first things continued to go well for the trio as "You're Getting A Little Too Smart", a typical Tilmon song / arrangement, and lead-off single from the set, reached #10 soul in the summer of 1973. But it was a false hope as the follow-up, which coupled "Whatcha Gonna Wear Tomorrow" with an old song, "Lee" from the debut set, only reached #79. Both songs were "typically" Emeralds in sound but the public had become bored. There were other good tracks like the underrated and atypical "Heaven Couldn't Be Like This" and, particularly, "I Think Of You", which became another UK hit for the group. (The UK didn't release *I'm In Love With You*, preferring to put together a "Best Of" collection - *Abe, James & Ivory* - instead.)

Things really fell apart - and became rather confusing - in 1974 when Abe Tilmon left the group to form a new outfit, AC Tilmon & The Detroit Emeralds. Ivory Tilmon and James Mitchell carried on, together with a new singer, Carl Johnson, to create a new group with a frankly awful name: Now. After the release of some unsuccessful singles for both aggregations, the first album for four years under the name of "The Detroit Emeralds" was released. *Feel The Need* was much more the work of Abe Tilmon rather than Now as he wrote all the songs but only a beefed-up and partially newly recorded version of the title track reached the soul charts in the U.S. but only limped to # 73. In the U.K, the group and song still meant something, though, and it became a hit for the second time.

A reconciliation took place in 1978 when the three original members got back together, with the addition of a new one, Marvin Willis (Carl Johnson was no longer around), to record a final album, *Let's Get Together*. It was a reasonable, if not outstanding, effort and included just about the best slow side they ever delivered in their version of The Masqueraders' "(Call Me) The Travelling Man". A fairly catchy single, "Turn On Lady", failed, though, and other than a 45 in the 80's there were no more new recordings and Abe Tilmon passed away in 1982.

William DeVaughn

Be Thankful For What You've Got 1974 Roxbury RLX-100 Producer: John Davis (Billboard soul charts: 10; Billboard pop charts: 165)

Figures Can't Calculate The Love I Have For You 1980 TEC SA 1200 Producers: Frank Fioravanti, Lou Delisle & Pal Rakes (Billboard soul charts: 74)

It wasn't much of a career, really, considering what a smash (#1 soul) the first hit had been, and there are only the two albums to remind people about Washington's William DeVaughn. He had no background in music and a bit like Bill Withers, went straight from a regular salaried job to test out the uncertainty of the entertainment business. His misfortune, really, was to have recorded for a small label like Roxbury. The immense charm and obvious hit-making potential of "Be Thankful For What You Got" propelled the song to #4 pop as a single in early 1974, but there was no marketing machine to push the resulting LP beyond a derisory #165. It also didn't help that the album was rather painfully one-paced, containing a number of songs that sounded exactly like the hit, and DeVaughn himself - again like Bill Withers - never demonstrated much affection for the industry. His obviously Curtis Mayfield-influenced voice had appeal and the Philadelphia musicians are impeccable as ever but only "You Can Do It" and "We Are His Children" really bear second listening from the album cuts. "Blood Is Thicker Than Water" reached #10 soul and #43 pop as the follow-up single.

Surprisingly, he was tempted back into a studio in 1980 but the results have always seemed a bit half-hearted to me. The title track was gentle and reasonably captivating, and a small hit (#37 soul), but there was also a somewhat inevitable and pointless remake of "Be Thankful", an awful thing called "Boogie Dan" and versions of "You Send Me" and "I've Never Found A Girl" added little to the originals. On a more positive note: "Hold On To Love" was the best thing on the album and "Love Comes So Easy With You" was dreamy and satisfying.

He tried one more time with a single on the HCRC label in 1982, but it failed to attract any buyers and he returned to corporate life.

Moses Dillard

Now! (as by Moses Dillard and Tex-Town Display) 1969 Tex-Town TT-921 Producer: Moses Dillard

We're In This Thing Together (as by Dillard & Boyce) 1980 Mercury SRM-1- 3826 Producers: Moses Dillard & Jesse Boyce

Moses Dillard is an interesting and talented singer, guitarist, writer, producer and arranger with a long career so it is ironic that the only time he has ever had a record on the charts was with a group on which his name doesn't appear. The Saturday Night Band, a rather awful disco studio band and out of scope for the book, had some success at the end of the seventies, but few people know that Dillard arranged and produced and played on their albums. As I've stated frequently, this book is not the place to provide detailed overviews of artists but suffice it to say that Dillard has released many fine singles in his own name over the years and a comprehensive overview one day would be welcome.

Now! is one of the most in-demand soul long-players in the world and is almost unique in its approach: one side is excellent southern soul and the other, instrumental jazz. As might be imagined, my overwhelming preference is for side one, which really deserves to be more widely known and available. The vocals are shared and the best two cuts are sung by Bill Wilson, "Are You For Real", a strutting horn-driven dance side, and the more restrained "Won't Somebody Help Me". Dillard sings two cuts himself, the first of which, "You Can't Laugh It Off", was re-cut (and improved) as a duet with Martha Starr in 1972. Lastly Peabo Bryson gives us "Cry Like A Baby" (yes, that one) and "Bring Your Dreams To Me" years before he became famous. Other members of the Tex-Town Display were Art Leo Adams, Johnny Goldsmith, Preston Robinson, James Madison and Tony Waldrop. Significantly, Jesse Boyce played bass on the album and the two men were to work together for more than a decade.

Moses and Jesse decided they should finally issue a record in their own name and We're In This Thing Together was the result. Unsurprisingly much more palatable than their work with The Saturday Night Band (and the Constellation Orchestra and Frisky, other nondescript disco outfits) it was nevertheless pretty ordinary and left barely a ripple in 1980. There were three ballads, all well sung, but rather lacking in melody, and five uptempo cuts that had little to make them stand out from a very crowded field. If anyone really needs or wants to sample the best work from Dillard and Boyce it will be found on Lorraine Johnson's first LP.

Directions

Earl Haskin; Willie Morrison; Kenneth Perry; Howard Hopgood; Lawrence Wooden

Directions 1976 Brunswick BL 754209 Producers: Benny Clark & Willy Bridges

Brunswick struggled throughout the latter half of the seventies and before things finally imploded they adopted a rather odd strategy of putting out LPs by wholly unknown bands/groups - such as The Directions. And it wasn't as if the label's heart wasn't in it; the inner sleeve of this LP has a photograph and name check for the Directions Band so time and trouble were taken. Unfortunately none of the records came even close in becoming successful but nearly all have their moments.

This one, while rather haphazardly mixing up vocal tracks and instrumentals, has five tracks I like a great deal. "If You Ever" is a slow song with an interesting array of vocals, "I Love You So" soars, "I Want To Be Your Special Man" is an enjoyable mid-tempo romp and "We Need Love" and "She'll Never Say It" are good examples of a popular sub-genre in the UK, "Modern Soul". But despite their appeal to committed soul fans like me it was plain that none of them remotely had what it took to become hits, and a casual listener would not find much here to get too excited about. Lastly, although the LP was cut in Chicago, it doesn't really sound like it, having little of the obvious musical trademarks of that city.

Dirte Four

Funky Soul 1968? Charay 1004-C Producer: Major Bill Smith

This album bears similarities from the one discussed above by The Detroit City Limits in as much as it is all instrumental and not wildly exciting; where it differs is that it doesn't concentrate on covering hits (apart from "Ode to Billy Joe") and, more importantly, was never, I believe, properly released and the few known copies do not bear album covers. One track, "On The Move", was certainly released as a single as by "Willie Hobbs and The Dirte Four" and is the only instance I know of a record by that fine singer not actually featuring his voice at all.

Larry Dixon

I'm So In Love 1980 Vanity LD 8002 Producer: Larry Dixon

Can't Price Love 1985 Lad Productions 8408 Producer: Larry Dixon

Chicago's Larry Dixon managed to release two LPs - two more than many much more established soul singers - but remained and remains almost totally unknown. That both albums are now "in-demand" would be scant reward indeed for Dixon, who is still out there plying his trade to this day with a number of recent CDs. The first set was apparently recorded live at The Copherbox (sic) club on Chicago's south side but it doesn't sound live at all. The best track is "Show Me The Way", a very appealing jazzy shuffling tuneful song which demonstrates that Dixon can really sing, in a style reminiscent of a young Smokey Robinson. It's just a shame that he lowered his register for the other cuts, which are more ordinary if still not bad at all.

The five year gap was kinder to *Can't Price Love* than I would have expected, given how swamped so many records were by inappropriate technology in 1985, but Dixon continued to play with a proper band and he even managed to make a cut entitled "Dance To The Beat" sound much better than the title might suggest. "Make Up Your Mind" was tuneful and sweetly soulful, while other cuts are in the danceable mid-tempo style that makes them highly appealing to a small number of soul fans in the UK.

Jimmy Dockett

My First Edition To You 1973 Flo-Feel 33,000 Producer: Jimmy Dockett

Beauty & Soul 1976 Image IM-302 Producer: Jimmy Dockett

Different Moods 1979 Star Vision SVI 11000 Producer: Jimmy Dockett

Tender Moments (and Barbara Stroman) 1985 Star Vision SVI 1205 Producer: Jimmy Dockett

Jimmy Dockett, who died in 2013, must be one of the most mysterious soul men of all. He released over twenty singles and four albums but has never received any plaudits or attracted any interest: I have yet to see a single article about him or any of his music.

I have also not seen or heard any of his first album from 1973 apart from the throw-back sound of "When We First Met", which sounded like a cross between doo-wop and sweet soul but his second on Image is almost completely uninteresting. Side one comprises rather weak and watery disco styled music while side two contains rather weak and watery ballad material, but at least includes the one reason to listen to the album in "Count Your Blessings" a rather lovely slow song that became his one and only national chart entry when it reached #87 in the summer of '73. He sings it beautifully and if only the rest of the material matched his high tenor voice he might have had more of a career.

Star Vision International Records sounds grandiose and impressive but the reality was that the third album had a rather cheap, do-it-yourself feel: the label's address seemed to be a P.O Box in Jamaica, New York and a talented singer called Kacy was apparently invited to sing a duet with Jimmy when she turned up for the front cover photo shoot. That track, "You're Mine, I'm Yours" is good enough, as is the doo-wop influenced "I Hear A Melody" where Dockett is backed up by the Persuasions, but not much else bears a second listen. In fact upbeat tracks like "Love Dance" (which lasts for the whole of side one) and "I Need Your Love" don't even bear a first. "Tae Kwon Do" could have been good as it has a chorus that is sung with angelic purity but it can't make one forget the subject matter of the song.

I am pretty sure that Barbara Stroman was Dockett's wife and the two of them were credited together for the final album. I have only heard a handful of tracks from it so can't really comment, but what I have heard, including a re-make of Jimmy Briscoe and The Little Beavers' "Where Ever You Go", is all nice enough, if pretty soft and undemanding.

Dr. York

New York 1985 Passion PRC-786 Producers: Dr.York and Kashif

Re-New 1986 York YRC-786-36 Producer: Dr.York

As I think I have made abundantly clear, this book can only scratch the very surface when discussing anything other than LPs. Were I able to expound on the individuals behind the music it is fair to say that no-one would have such an extraordinary background as Dr. Malachi York. Apparently this is only one of his many aliases, and he is currently serving a 135 year prison sentence - he is due for release in 2122 - as well as being the founder of a creed called Nuwaubianism.

Given that, his albums are but the merest blips in his life, and it is surprising he found the time to cut them. He actually had rather a lovely light voice and if one can ignore the apparently unsavoury aspects of his behaviour, these are nice enough LPs. Clearly influenced by the "sweet soul" movement, they are a mixture of original songs by Dr. York and well-known tunes such as "Love Won't Let Me Wait", "Mona Lisa, "You Are Everything" and "It's All In The Game". The music, while largely programmed, has at least been undertaken with thought and skill, and complements the songs, rather than overwhelming them. The majority of the tracks are down-tempo and "It's Only A Dream" from the debut is my favourite. (He is in the book owing to his recording a 12 inch single in 1980.)

Lee Dorsey

Ya ! Ya ! 1961 Fury FULP 1002 Producer: Bobby Robinson

The Best Of 1965 Sue ILP 924 (UK)

Irving Lee Dorsey was not a great singer, barely ever cut a song that was profound or introspective, and had his biggest hits with titles like "Ya! Ya!", "Do-Re-Me" and "Holy Cow", so he shouldn't matter much, right? Wrong. He made some of the most exhilarating music ever to come out of New Orleans and even though, like most artists from the city, his LP career was a bit of a mess, he did place nine singles in the soul top 50 between 1961 and 1970. He never seemed to set much store by making it in the music business either, seemingly equally happy in his auto repair shop, and, sadly, he died in 1986 before soul became "hip" again, and so could not benefit from the renewed interest in performers from the "golden age".

The first album, almost certainly produced by Allen Toussaint despite the Bobby Robinson credit, housed two top thirty pop hits in the title track (his biggest ever hit, it also went to #1 soul) and "Do-Re-Mi" and was a combination of cheerful nonsense ("Yum Yum", "Ixie Dixie Pixie Pie") irresistible calls to dance ("Behind The 8 Ball"), and rueful common sense ("People Gonna Talk"). Not one of the eleven tracks went on for longer than two and a half minutes so, even if you didn't care for a cut, one was bound to come along soon enough that you did. In 1965, Sue records in the UK put out a *Best Of* set that contained all of the *Ya! Ya!* tracks as well as five others which had only come out on singles, including the great "Hoodlum Joe".

Lee Dorsey 1966 AMY 8010 Producers: Allen Toussaint & Marshall Sehorn

The New Lee Dorsey 1966 Amy 8011 Producers: Allen Toussaint & Marshall Sehorn (Billboard soul charts: 13; Billboard pop charts: 129)

The Best Of 1969 Regal Star Line SRS 5023 (UK)

Rightly realising that novelty songs would only take Dorsey so far, Toussaint switched to more mainstream compositions for the Amy label and some of Dorsey's best loved and finest sides can be found on the *Lee Dorsey* set from 1966. "Get Out Of My Life Woman" (#5 soul) and "Ride Your Pony" (#7 soul) were big – and superb - hits and an excellent reading of "The Greatest Love" proved Lee could handle more challenging material. "Hello Mama" and "Can You Hear Me" were typically lovely rolling New Orleans sides while "Work Work Work" was a sly and amusing tale of failing to find any. The LP cover photo, by the way, couldn't help but remind one of its similarity to that on the sleeve of Bob Dylan's *Freewheelin'* album.

Dorsey was now hot again, and *The New Lee Dorsey* was the only album of his that ever charted. It was rather a misleading title, however, seeing as how four tracks had seen duty on the previous LP. New hits within were the immortal "Working In The Coalmine" (#5 soul) and "Holy Cow" (#10). "Confusion" did much less well but both it and its b-side, " Neighbour's Daughter", are enjoyable as is the sharp "Don't You Ever Leave Me". There was some filler though: "Mexico" is one of Toussaint' s worst efforts and " A Little Dab A Do Ya", although not without charm, was ultimately disposable.

He managed two more reasonably sized hits on Amy, "Go Go Girl" and "Everything I Do Gonh Be Funky", but no album was built around them, although each can be found on the worthy UK collection from 1969.

Yes We Can 1970 Polydor 24-4042 Producers: Allen Toussaint & Marshall Sehorn

Dorsey 's output on 45 was prolific in the second half of the sixties and for every hit there were two or three failures, but from 1968 his music took a new turn when he was backed by The Meters. This didn't do much to change the pattern of his success/ failure ratio but did lead to some great sides like "Four Corners".

In 1970 Lee moved to Polydor and they put out his best ever LP. The title track from *Yes We Can* is now justly famous (and did ok at the time as a single when it reached #46 soul at the end of that year) and is one of the funkiest records ever committed to wax, coming at a time when the Meters were almost without equal as a rhythm section. Entirely written by Toussaint - apart from a version of "Games People Play" that, while not bad, just feels completely out of place - the album has many other high points: the original of "Sneakin' Sally Through The Alley" and other titanic funk workouts in "Who's Gonna Help Brother Get Further", and the incredible "Gator Tail". Seriously, only James Brown was as funky as this in 1971. Variations on the funk theme were "When The Bill's Paid", "Riverboat" and "Occapella" - all good.

Night People 1978 ABC AA-1048 Producer: Allen Toussaint

Night People, annoyingly underrated, was Lee Dorsey's last outing on a "true" LP. All the songs were written by Toussaint, and the album has a overall consistency and purpose that is impressive. It is not a collection of strong singles and mere filler and demands to be taken in at one sitting with total concentration for then the quality of the songs and playing become readily apparent. This is a more sedate Dorsey, singing grown-up songs rather than the "novelty" sides on which his reputation rather unfairly rests. The title track bombed at a pitiful #93 on the US soul charts when released on a single so nothing about *Night People* can be considered a commercial triumph but for anyone wishing to hear what great soul music from New Orleans sounded like in 1978, this is as good a place as any - apart from Johnny Adams' *After All The Good Is Gone* - to find out.

Gonh Be Funky 1980 Charly CRB 1001 (UK)

All Ways Funky 1982 Charly CRB 1036 (UK)

Am I That Easy To Forget ? 1987 Charly CDX 21 (UK)

From 1980 onwards many compilations of Dorsey's work exist but I will only list three as they almost certainly the best. While *Gonh Be Funky* and *All Ways Funky* are both excellent and generous in playing time, and each includes a handful of cuts unavailable elsewhere on Lee Dorsey LPs, *Am I That Easy To Forget?*" has to be the one to go for. Weighing in at a bumper 27 tracks with 17 of them previously unreleased, it is a fascinating collection including early cuts, Coca-Cola commercials, live recordings, New Orleans goes Motown on an "It's The Same Old Song" sound - alike in "A Place Where We Can Be Free" and two beautifully delivered country-soul sides in the title track and "Before The Next Teardrop Falls".

Kenny Doss

Movin' On A Feeling 1980 Bearsville BRK 6997 Producer: Willie Mitchell

By 1980 Al Green had quit the secular scene and Willie Mitchell obviously missed the long line of hits that Green had delivered. A replacement was needed and I assume Mitchell thought Kenny Doss would be that man. He sounded - or more likely, was made to sound - much like Green and looked photogenic enough to maybe succeed. But despite the immense likability of this fine album it just didn't happen, although "Sugar" did reach #43 soul in early 1980. Three obvious barriers to the master plan existed: a) This sort of southern music no longer had a large audience b) Bearsville was not a label with any experience in issuing soul music c) "Kenny Doss" just doesn't sound like the name of someone who is going to cut hit records.

He didn't deserve to fail, though. He could certainly sing, at ease with all tempos, and the songs were nearly all of a high calibre. But then almost any record recorded down at Hi in 1980 with world-class musicians was going to sound great when compared to most of what else was coming out back then.

Double Exposure

Leonard "Butch" Davis; Charles Whittington; Joseph Harris; James Williams

Ten Percent 1976 Salsoul SZS 5503 Producers: Ronnie Baker, Norman Harris & Earl Young (Billboard soul charts: 40; Billboard pop charts: 129)

Fourplay 1978 Salsoul SA 8501 Producers: Norman Harris, Ron Tyson, Bunny Sigler, Ron Kersey & Bruce Hawes

Locker Room 1979 Salsoul SA 8523 Producers: Ronnie Baker, Bunny Sigler, Ron Kersey & Bruce Hawes

The term "disco" to describe a certain type of music started to be pretty widespread by 1975, and by the end of the decade there was a discernible difference between "disco" and "soul" for those of us who cared about such appellations. For instance, any hard-core long-term soul fan in 1978 could, and probably did, distinguish between discs by Musique on the one hand and the O'Jays on the other. I know I did. And as far as this book is concerned, I have continued to make such a distinction of course. But records such as the first Double Exposure LP could be problematic for the stickler. Was this an acceptable face of "disco" or was it simply a new and exciting trend in soul? After all "Ten Percent" was one of the first ever commercially available "12 inch" singles, a new type of disc, and a record totally aimed at dance floors. But first things first....

In the early seventies the group were known as United Image and recorded two singles that bombed totally. There was then a lull before they re-surfaced on Salsoul, one of the most famous "dance/disco" (call it what you will) labels of all and recorded "Ten Percent" with all those great Philadelphia musicians like Earl Young, Ronnie Baker, Norman Harris, Larry Washington, Bobby Eli et al. In short, the very men who made the "Philly Sound" what it was and brought us countless great records. So, for me, there was never much doubt: "Ten Percent" was a most exciting disc, and so was the majority of the album from which it came, and all of it was still clearly "soul music" to these ears. For anyone who didn't care for six minute plus dance tracks - and three of the seven tracks on the debut album fell into this category, all of which also charted as singles, albeit in a minor manner - there should still be things to enjoy such as a version of the Four Tops' "Baby I Need Your Loving" where lead voices are switched adroitly, "Just Can't Say Hello" a nice ballad which sounds a bit like "Neither One Of Us" and "Pick Me" which would have sounded just fine on a Teddy Pendergrass or Detroit Spinners LP of the time. (And let's not forget one more of those long dance tracks: "Everyman" was a "thinking man's" call to the floor with a clear message of self-reliance that caused a good deal of controversy at the time.)

Interestingly, *Fourplay* moved the group away from a dance-oriented approach and saw them somewhat re-invented as a much more mainstream "soul vocal group" but the ploy didn't work for them commercially: neither the LP nor the two singles pulled from it sold well. Lead singer James Williams sounds a great deal like Eddie Levert on "Perfect Love", an excellent slow track, and together with the pretty and beautifully sung and harmonised "There's Something Missing", is the best thing on the LP, but most of *Fourplay* should be enjoyed by anyone who loves Philadelphia soul, even if one might have hoped for a slightly stronger batch of songs.

Doubtless stung by the failure of the album Salsoul returned to the dancefloor for inspiration and were rewarded when "I Got The Hots For Ya" reached #33 soul, their biggest hit, but it was a dull record, and not representative of the *Locker Room* album on which it was included. For example: although "Ice Cold Love" and "I Wish That I Could Make Love To You" were also dance tracks they carried on the tradition of "Everyman" in being songs one could also listen to. The standout though was "Why Do We Have To Go Our Separate Ways", a tremendous ballad with Ernie Isley-ish guitar.

And after one more single in 1981 on the Gold Coast label they did indeed go their separate ways, which included James Williams joining another famous Philly group, The Trammps.

Don Downing

Doctor Boogie 1978 Roadshow BXL1-3392 Producers: Tony Bongiovi & Lance Quinn

Don Downing only made this one album and information about him is hard to come by. I know he's from Oklahoma and is the brother of Al but that's about it. (By the way I am not including Al Downing in the book, as although he made some impressive soul records one of his two albums is straight country and the other is rock and roll.)

I'm not sure why Don made his best tracks, "Dream World" and the minor hit "Lonely Days, Lonely Nights" (#65 soul), in 1973 and then had to wait five years to see them appear on an LP. Any small momentum his career might have had was well and truly over by the time this set came out. It's also a shame we haven't heard more from Downing as he was a virile and resonant singer who I imagine would have been good on ballads, but none are to be found on *Doctor Boogie*. It's an ok album in that "recorded in New York but trying to sound like Philadelphia" way that was true of a few records in the mid seventies, but needed more songs in the vein of "Dream World" and less in the way of the dull title track and "Playtime" to have enabled it to sell in any quantity.

Gene Dozier And The Brotherhood

Blues Power 1967 Minit 40010 Producer: Gene Dozier

Can instrumental records be "soul music"? There are many who would answer "no", and I can certainly see the point, but my own default position would be for an album such as this one: it's not blues, it's not jazz, it's not rock and it's not pop, so what is it ? I'm voting for soul and anyway, Ugene Lloyd Dozier released undoubted soul records such as the excellent "The Best Girl I Ever Had" (under the name of Gene Dozier and The United Front) and produced, arranged, wrote and played on many soul sides over the years, most notably for Wilson Pickett and the Solar label.

I believe the Brotherhood may have comprised Dozier on piano, James Gadson on drums, Al Mckay on guitar and James Wesley Smith on bass - some band then - but the sleeve gives little away. A single from the album, "A Hunk Of Funk", made #46 on the soul charts at the end of 1967 and was one of the two tracks Dozier wrote under a pseudonym, Billy Jackson. Most of the other tracks are well-known soul songs such as "Cold Sweat", "Soul Man", "I Wanna Testify" and "How Sweet It Is". The LP is enjoyable enough when played in the background but there is no compelling reason to pull it out repeatedly.

Lamont Dozier

Out Here On My Own 1973 Producer: McKinley Jackson (Billboard soul charts: 11; Billboard pop charts: 136)

Love And Beauty * (Holland-Dozier tracks) 1974 Invictus BL 33134 Producers: Eddie Holland, Brian Holland, Lamont Dozier & Richard Wylie

Black Bach 1974 ABC ABCD 839 Producer: McKinley Jackson (Billboard soul charts: 27; Billboard pop charts: 186)

No relation to Gene, Lamont Dozier was one third of the Holland-Dozier-Holland team and the hands-down winner out of the three of them when it came to making solo records. There is no need to dwell on his years of writing and production at Motown or Invictus/Hot Wax as these were so phenomenally successful as to now be thoroughly well known and documented so I will confine myself to the records he released as a singer.

He had first sung with doo-wop groups the Romeos and Voice Masters back in the late fifties and early sixties before releasing a solo single on Anna as Lamont Anthony. Once this failed to do any business he put out a single as Lamont Dozier, "Dearest One", which was mainly notable for the fact it was one of the earliest compositions from the H-D-H team. Certainly there was little indication in 1962 that he would be involved in some of the biggest and most enduring records in popular music history. We will now fast forward to 1973 when he once again started to release records in his own right. He can't have needed the money, but seemed to have an itch he needed to scratch that passed the Holland brothers by as their own solo careers were much more half-hearted and short-lived.

Having said that, there was a brief period when Brian Holland and Lamont sang together as "Holland-Dozier" and the team released a handful of singles, two of which, "Why Can't We Be Lovers" and "New Breed Kinda Woman", hit the soul charts in 1972 and 1973 respectively and it is a number of these singles that make up the *Love And Beauty* set from 1974. Confusingly, it was released as "The New Lamont Dozier Album" but didn't fool too many people - as well as not being marketed strongly - as it failed to chart. It is an excellent set throughout with a couple of real standouts: "Why Can't We Be Lovers" is a gorgeous record (and a #9 soul hit) with one of the strongest hooks imaginable and "Baby Don't Leave Me" (not to be confused with "Don't Leave Me Starving For Your Love", another Holland-Dozier single that was NOT on the LP) was a superb two-part cut with the years-ahead-of-its-time instrumental - it could have been recorded in the nineties - easily matching the vocal take. It is a highly orchestrated album so isn't for anyone who likes their soul to be a bit more down home and edgy but is classy in the good sense of the word.

However, the first genuine Lamont Dozier solo LP had appeared at the end of 1973 and achieved considerable success, with two singles from it, "Trying To Hold On To My Woman" and "Fish Ain't Bitin'", making the top 30 U.S. pop charts. The title of the album, *Out Here On My Own*, was easy enough to understand, but what was slightly surprising was that Dozier neither produced nor wrote any of the songs on it. This situation was to change in a few years when he took much more control over his albums, but it's still interesting to note that his biggest success came when he did the least amount of work. And the songs were definitely catchy, sticking in the mind after only a couple of plays, while the playing from the West Coast's finest session men guaranteed musical quality. And yet... and yet...I must own up here to say that I am not a particular fan of Dozier's voice and it is this no doubt purely personal quirk that has tended to mean that, while recognizing his brilliant musical talent, I do not consider him to be one of the great soul singers.

Black Bach was proof that the man didn't lack self-confidence and was a set that divided opinion when it came out, with many loving the long orchestrated instrumental passages and its desire to try something different, while others found it all a bit pompous. "Let Me Start Tonite" from the LP - nearly all written by Dozier this time around - had a nice gentle country feel and did very well on single (#4 soul) but from here on in his records started to sell in noticeably lesser quantities.

Right There 1976 Warner Brothers BS 2929 Producer: Lamont Dozier (Billboard soul charts: 59)

Peddlin' Music On The Side 1977 Warner Brothers BS 3039 Producer: Stewart Levine (Billboard soul charts: 59)

Bittersweet 1979 Warner Brothers BSK 3282 Producer: Frank Wilson

Dozier moved to the Warner Brothers label for his next three LPs, but he had almost completely lost his audience by now and the lead-off single from *Right There*, "Can't Get Off Until The Feeling Stops", only managed to reach the derisory position of #89 soul, despite its being a tuneful song in a Johnny Bristol vein. In fact, it is a good record, more subtle and soulful to these ears than some of the work on ABC, and it is also the only one of his LPs where he permitted himself the indulgence of re-cutting one of the old H-D-H hits, a nice lush take on "It's The Same Old Song".

But his best work was to follow in the *Peddlin' Music On The Side* album which is a much more rhythmically assertive set driven by the keyboards of Ronnie Colman and Joe Sample. For unfathomable reasons, though, WB couldn't even get a hit out of the much-admired "Going Back To My Roots" track although it must be said that the ten minute version on the album was the one to hear. (Odyssey did make it a minor hit a few years later). "What Am I Gonna Do About You Girl" had a majestic arrangement to go with its fine lyric and "Sight For Sore Eyes" evinced an appealing world weariness well communicated by Dozier. But there is no real need to pick out tracks, it is a most cohesive and strong collection of songs.

So what do you do if you are Lamont Dozier or Warner Brothers? You have just received a beautifully constructed album which has failed to do any business. Do you do more of the same or do you swallow your pride and go "disco"? The answer seemed to be that they would do both. Some of these tracks, like "Fly Away Little Birdsong" and "I Got It All With You", wouldn't have been out of place on *Peddlin'* whereas "Boogie Business" and "We're Just Here To Feel Good" were aimed squarely at the dance floor. Overall, I think this is an album that would only really strongly appeal to anyone who was already a committed Dozier fan.

Working On You 1981 Columbia BL 37129 Producer: Lamont Dozier

Lamont 1981 M&M MM-104 Producer: Lamont Dozier

Bigger Than Life 1983 Demon Fiend 12 Producer: Lamont Dozier (UK)

Inside Seduction 1991 Atlantic 7567-82228-1 Producer: Lamont Dozier and Phil Collins (Billboard soul charts: 28) (Germany)

For the next ten years, Dozier moved from label to label in an attempt to revive his fortunes but there were to be no more hits. The Columbia album had some nice moments - "Why (Ain't My Love Enough" and "Too Little Too Long" instantly stick in the mind - but side two did seem to meander somewhat. While Dozier was to be applauded for nearly always avoiding mindless dance tracks, an album like *Working For You* rather called out for the incisiveness that had informed the big hits he wrote for Motown in the sixties.

Lamont went some way to addressing my concerns as the album had more of a zip and a sharper feel than the last two LPs and "You Oughta Be In Pictures" was surely a missed hit. There was one small chart entry, "Shout It Out" - his first for nearly six years - but it only crawled to #61 soul. However, it was a dullish dance number, as was "Help Is On The Way", but they are not representative of the rest of the LP.

By the time of *Bigger Than Life* he didn't even have a U.S. record deal and the LP only appeared over here. It has the same feel of his previous couple of albums and features more or less the same musicians. I'm not sure why the U.S. felt it was unworthy as "Right Where I Wanna Be", "Round Trip Ticket" and "Call The Wagon" rank among the best songs from his solo career.

I think I am right in saying that *Inside Seduction* only came out on vinyl in Europe, while it appeared on CD in the States. It contained the last single Dozier ever scored on the U.S. soul chart in "Love In The Rain" but it was hardly a hit, only reaching #60. The fact that Phil Collins played drums and Eric Clapton played guitar just showed how esteemed Dozier continued to be. It is not music that appeals much to me, being more pop-oriented than his previous solo sets, although it remained recognisably the work of Lamont Dozier.

In more recent years he has finally come to terms with the need to put out a CD containing nothing but his versions of the biggest hits he wrote as part of H-D-H with *An American Original*.

Charles Drain

Dependable 1976 RCA APL1-1414 Producers: Kent Washburn & Michael L Smith

St. Louis as a soul music centre has never received the acclaim of other cities such as Chicago and Philadelphia but it always managed to sustain a small but impressively talented number of artists which included the likes of Little Milton, Fontella Bass, Ike & Tina Turner and Oliver Sain. A relatively unknown member of that club was Charles Drain. He had previously recorded as a member of the group The Tabs, as well as releasing a couple of singles to considerable public indifference in the sixties, and it was a pleasant surprise to see that RCA were prepared to invest in an album on him. And very enjoyable it is too. There is nothing on here that sounded like a massive hit - and none of the three singles released from the set even became small ones - but it's hard to imagine that any fan of melodic, well produced and arranged seventies soul music would not like it. The songs are nearly all well chosen with strong hooks and stand-outs would be Drain's take on Willie Hutch's "I'm Gonna Stay", the instantly memorable "Is This Really Love" and Van Morrison's "I've Been Working" where Drain's vocal is noticeably tougher and more aggressive than before.

The album did not do well and Drain was only ever heard on vinyl one more time when he released a good single, "When You Say You Love Me", on a tiny St. Louis label in 1985. He passed away in 1995.

Dramatics (see also Ron Banks, L.J. Reynolds and Wee Gee)

Ron Banks; William "Wee Gee "Howard; Larry Demps; Willie Ford; Elbert Wilkins; L.J.Reynolds; Lenny Mayes; Eldridge Bryant; Steve Barnett; Craig Jones

Whatcha See Is Whatcha Get 1972 Volt VOS-6018 Producer: Tony Hester (Billboard soul charts: 5 ; Billboard pop charts: 20)

A Dramatic Experience 1973 Volt VOS-6019 Producer: Tony Hester (Billboard soul charts: 11; Billboard pop charts: 86)

Dramatically Yours * 1974 Volt VOS-9501 Producers: Don Davis & Jimmy Roach (Billboard soul charts: 36)

The Dells Vs The Dramatics (with The Dells) 1974 Cadet 60027 Producers: Don Davis & Tony Hester (Billboard soul charts: 15; Billboard pop charts: 156)

Best Of 1974 Volt VOS-9506

Sailing With Soul 1975 Navy Recruiting Command Series 14 (not released commercially)

Best Of 1984 Stax MPS-8526

Live 1988 Stax MPS-8545 No producer listed

Almost universally regarded as the finest soul group to have ever come out of Detroit who didn't record for Motown (and some might say *including* Motown), they were also one of the most commercially successful, placing 12 singles on the Hot 100, and 36 on the soul charts.

They first recorded for small labels like Top Ten, Wingate and Sport, shedding a few group members on the way, before settling on the Banks, Howard, Demps, Ford and Wilkins combination that recorded the *Whatcha See Is Whatcha Get* album. Before this time they hadn't meant a lot, only placing one single on the soul charts, on Sport at the lowly number of #43 back in 1967. Everything was to change for The Dramatics when "Whatcha See" was a massive hit in the summer of 1971, reaching #3 soul and #9 pop. An utterly brilliant single, its magnificent breezy intro captured the sense of a blistering hot day as well as any record I know, and Howard proved himself to be one of the most soulful, aggressive lead singers, more than ably supported by the high tenor counterpoint of Banks and the wonderful harmonies of the rest of the group. Although they released their records on Volt, at this time they recorded everything in Detroit. "Get Up And Get Down" was a good if slightly less outstanding follow-up single before "In The Rain" became their biggest single ever, hitting #1 soul and #5 pop in early 1972. Completely different from "Whatcha See", this was a slow and mournful tale of woe, but shared many of the characteristics of the earlier hit: a majestic Johnny Allen arrangement, imposing Tony Hester production and compelling singing. The album that emerged in support of these three singles was a good one, with a number of fine tracks, all written by Hester, but there was nothing on there that could compare with "Whatcha See" and "In The Rain".

Volt took a surprisingly long time - about 20 months - to follow up the first LP, and it was an ambitious effort although one had to question the wisdom of placing a singularly unattractive devil on the front cover, which must have lost some sales."The Devil Is Dope" "Beware Of The Man With The Candy In His Hand" and "Jim, What's Wrong With Him" were stern admonitions against drugs and Hester is to be applauded for tackling a subject that most soul acts avoided (although, ironically, he had his own drug problem), but the emphasis was still on love songs and the two hits from the album, "Hey You! Get Off My Mountain" (#5 soul) and "Fell For You" (#12), were affairs of the heart rather than the vein. The latter was particularly beautiful as were two other tracks, "Now You Got Me Loving Me" and "You Could Become The Very

Heart Of Me" and a convincing claim could be made for *A Dramatic Experience* as the best album the group ever released. Certainly I rate it as their most consistent. It was also significant in that it marked the departure of Howard and Wilkins who were replaced by L.J. Reynolds and Lenny Mayes respectively. The two departees must have regretted their decision as their own group, (initially also called The Dramatics but afterwards A Dramatic Experience), were conspicuously less successful than the "real" Dramatics continued to be. Reynolds was an excellent replacement for Howard with a similar fire and attack in his vocal style.

The next album, *Dramatically Yours*, alluded to the departure of Howard and Wilkins in as much as it was the first LP on which the group were promoted as "Ron Banks and the Dramatics". I have marked it thus (*) above to highlight this and the same went for the *Dramatic Jackpot* LP which had the same billing. Unfortunately, Stax/Volt were now beginning to encounter significant financial problems and the album and the two singles from the set all suffered as a result. *Dramatically Yours* sold much more modestly than the previous two LPs and it's hard to imagine that such a fine single as "And I Panicked" would not have done better than #49 soul if Stax still had money to spend on promotion. The second single, a most appealing but atypical gospel-influenced side, "Highway To Heaven", failed to chart at all. The fact that the album also included an 18 month old single, "Toast To A Fool", just underlined the problems and it also marked the temporary end of the Hester hegemony as he only contributed one typically excellent song, "You Got Me Going Through A Thing". It should not be assumed, though, that its poor commercial showing means that the LP is sub-standard as it is not, although it falls short of the previous two. (By the way, the track "Trying To Get Over You" is the same song as The Dells' "Learning To Love You Was Easy".)

I have wildly enthused over the collaborative album with the Dells earlier, and so will only add here that the four Dramatics' "solo" cuts are all superb, with the extraordinarily arranged "Door To Your Heart" (yet another Tony Hester masterpiece) being one of my favourite records of all time.

Two *Best Of* sets of the Volt material exist on vinyl although neither were over-generous in their number of tracks. More interesting was a set that came out under the rather odd Naval recruiting command series, hosted by Lou Rawls. There were about twenty releases in this series and The Dramatics effort was a double album with ten Volt-era tracks and six from the collaborative album with The Dells.

Lastly, Fantasy put out a retrospective "live" set, recorded in 1972 and 1973, on the re-vamped Stax label in 1988. It is an important historic document in demonstrating how the group sounded back then, and is also the only album on which Eldridge Bryant is featured (a man who also briefly sang with The Temptations), but it is not compelling listening. Songs like "Respect Yourself" and "This Guy's In Love With You" are not associated with the group and a then current single, "Toast To The Fool", was not one of their best. Obviously the big hits are also included but can't match the album versions. The vocals are switched around nicely but I can't see my listening to it again.

The Dramatic Jackpot * ABC ABCD-867 Producers: Don Davis, L.J. Reynolds & Ron Banks (Billboard soul charts: 9; Billboard pop charts: 31)

Drama V 1975 ABC ABCD-916 Producers: Don Davis, Tony Hester, Michael Henderson, Ron Banks & L.J. Reynolds (Billboard soul charts: 10; Billboard pop charts: 93)

Joy Ride 1976 ABC ABCD-955 Producers: Don Davis, Tony Hester, Michael Henderson, Ron Banks, Jimmy Roach & L.J. Reynolds (Billboard soul charts: 11; Billboard pop charts: 103)

Shake It Well 1977 ABC AB-1010 Producers: Don Davis & Tony Hester (Billboard soul charts: 10; Billboard pop charts: 60)

Do What You Wanna Do 1978 ABC AA-1072 Producers: Don Davis, Ron Banks & L.J. Reynolds (Billboard soul charts: 6 ; Billboard pop charts: 44)

Anytime, Anyplace 1979 ABC AA-1125 Producer: Don Davis (Billboard soul charts: 15)

Their Greatest Recordings 1978 At Ease MD-11103 (not released commercially)

After Stax/Volt collapsed The Dramatics moved to ABC where they cut six albums, kept their personnel intact, and enjoyed a great deal of success. The lead-off album, *A Dramatic Jackpot*, was blessed with a gate-fold sleeve as a demonstration of ABC's commitment to the group. It housed two fine singles, "(I'm Going By) The Stars In Your Eyes" (#22 soul) and "Me. & Mrs. Jones" (#4) which did well, the latter maybe surprisingly so as it only came out a couple of years after Billy Paul's original, and the company were to be congratulated on picking the two strongest songs as 45s. None of the other compositions or performances were by any means poor, but they were all best left as album tracks.

The two best things on *Drama V* were yet again Tony Hester songs and Johnny Allen arrangements: "You're Fooling You" (another top ten soul single) and "She's A Rainmaker" which had more than a hint of the Dells about it. But there was plenty more to admire on what was probably their best ABC album. "I Was The Life Of The Party" was a beauty and the two Michael Henderson songs, "Dramatic Theme/Treat Me Like A Man" and "Just Shopping (Not Buying Anything)" were intricate and enterprising. Only "Things Are Changing" had the whiff of the mundane.

Joy Ride, the third ABC album in a row with a gate-fold sleeve, had a slight change from all the group's previous work when one track, "Sundown Is Coming", was recorded down in Muscle Shoals rather than in Detroit. It wasn't a compelling song, but did feature some nice baritone singing by Larry Demps. "Finger Fever" was an adequate lead single but didn't get higher than #23 soul and it was left to two superior tracks, "Be My Girl" and "I Can't Get Over You", to do much better on 45: #3 and #9 respectively. The latter had a spectacular performance from Reynolds, one of his best ever. Even these excellent tracks were trumped though by "Say The Word" a perfect example of soul group singing and once again a Hester/Allen collaboration. "I Get Carried Away" was also a good one, but there were a handful of mediocre things, too.

The title track from *Shake It Well* introduced a new era for the group. Unlike anything they had recorded before, it sold in quantity, reaching #4 soul as a single, but lacked distinction as a song. Some of the album was recorded in Los Angeles too, another departure, and all in all I rate it as the first Dramatics LP to lack a truly outstanding track. Most of it is good, particularly "My Ship Won't Sail Without You" and "Ocean Of Thoughts and Dreams", but none of it is *great*.

Do What You Wanna Do was their least impressive yet as for the first time ever really mediocre songs started to appear on a Dramatics LP. "Jane", "Disco Dance Contest" and "California Sunshine" were not worthy of this great group and only "Stop Your Weeping" kept up their standards, but even that could get no higher than #22 on the soul chart whereas the next single, Hall and Oates' "Do What You Want To Do" a cut-down version from the long album track, only reached a dismaying #56. In truth, the group's best years were already behind them.

The group bowed out of the ABC era with *Anytime Anyplace*, another largely disappointing collection, although it was at least slightly better than the previous set. Cecil Womack had come onboard to provide a handful of good songs but things like "I Just Wanna Dance With You" and "Get With The Band And Dance" were rather grim.

In 1978 a 12 track LP of some of their best ABC sides was issued, but once again only for Navy personnel.

10½ 1980 MCA 3196 Producers: Ron Banks & L.J. Reynolds (Billboard soul charts: 14; Billboard pop charts: 61)

The Dramatic Way 1980 MCA 5146 Producers: Ron Banks & Don Davis (Billboard soul charts: 38)

10½ denoted the fact that this was the tenth and a half album (the equation includes the shared album with the Dells) the group had released and it was an accurate figure if one ignores the Volt *Best Of* in 1974 and the sets that were not made for general release. It provided further evidence of how ill-suited The Dramatics were at recording dance-oriented material. It is not difficult to understand why it was felt that in order to continue to be relevant the group needed to record dance sides; what is much harder to forgive is why they were so inept at it. Cuts like "If You Feel Like You Wanna Dance, Dance" and "I Just Wanna Dance The Night Away" are as uninspired as the titles suggest. Fortunately, there were four good tracks which saved the album from disaster with the best being "Welcome Back Home", a classy ballad which reached #9 soul at the beginning of 1980 - proof that their slow material sold best, and the last real hit they ever enjoyed, while "It Ain't Rainin'" and "Love Is Here" were only slightly behind. "Be With The One You Love" proved they could record interesting uptempo songs on occasion.

The Dramatic Way, another hodge-podge of an album, was significant as being the first recording in over a decade when the Dramatics were not a quintet: Reynolds and Demps had left and Craig Jones had arrived. The change was possibly best demonstrated by "Givin' Up My Love" which sounded like a different group altogether. Some awful dance tracks again marred a Dramatics LP and only one track showed off the group at their best: the lovely "You're The Best Thing In My Life", a beautiful Banks-led song that did ok as a single, reaching #26 in early 1981.

New Dimension 1982 Capitol-12205 Producer: Ron Banks (Billboard soul charts: 40)

Somewhere In Time (A Dramatic Reunion) 1986 Fantasy F-9642 Producers: F.L. Pittman, Claytoven, Ron Banks & L.J. Reynolds

Positive State Of Mind 1989 Volt V-3402 Producers: Don Davis, Ronnie McNeir, N.Berman, Ben Crosby, Ron Banks & L.J. Reynolds (Billboard soul charts: 80)

Stone Cold 1990 Volt V-3407 Producers: Don Davis, Ben Crosby, Ron Banks, Dave Robertson, L.J. Reynolds & The Maestro

So, to Capitol. The Dramatics only cut one LP for their new label and the *New Dimension* title was accurate: The Dramatics no longer sounded like The Dramatics, lacking a powerhouse lead like Reynolds or Howard. It is not a bad LP at all, and at least the faster tracks were no longer automatically inept: "I Can't Stand It" and "She's My Kind Of Girl" were pretty decent. But as ever, it was a more sedate song which was best: "I Don't Want To Lose Your Love".

1986 promised a potentially exciting development: the return of L.J. Reynolds and William Howard (at the expense of Jones) which also meant they would sing together for the first time. The album also helpfully annotated who was singing which track and this allows me to acknowledge Lenny Mayes as a talented lead voice who has been rather glossed over to date. But there was bad news: the fact that production duties had been largely passed on to F.L. Pittman and Claytoven. As ever with this duo, it signalled the introduction of DMX programming which overwhelmed and spoiled about 60% of the LP. Three cuts are listenable: "One Love Ago","When Love Is Over" and a five song medley of some of the group's finest moments where the quality of the singing reminds us that The Dramatics simply were one of the greatest soul groups of all time.

Two more albums on the revived Volt logo saw out the group's vinyl era, but Howard had once again left to be replaced by Steve Barnett. "Please Say You'll Be Mine" and "Come On And Stay" from *Positive State Of Mind* were the highlights of a dull set which also hosted a rather horrible rendering of "Bridge Over Troubled Water", a measly chart entrant (#93) in the middle of 1989.

To call an album *Stone Cold* when the group palpably were was either an act of bravado or unthinking ineptitude and it was another average offering with only one cut bearing repeated listens. "No Place To Live", an obviously old Tony Hester song (he was shot to death ten years earlier) was, fittingly, the last track of their last vinyl album and reminded us that no-one had ever written so many excellent songs as he had for The Dramatics.

Some new CDs followed in the next few years and Mayes, Banks and Howard are key members of the group who have now passed on.

Dream Machine (see also Taka Boom)

Yvonne Brumbach (Taka Boom); Joe Harris; Melvin Stewart; Lloyd Williams; Lafayette Trey Stone; James McKinney; Ron Artis; Pete Carr

Dream Machine 1981 RCA AFL1 4079 Producer: Norman Whitfield

Some record covers give no indication what the music within will sound like, others make it obvious. I would put this one firmly in the second category. Seven individuals resplendent in uniforms concocted from the Stars and Stripes can perform nothing other than soul/funk. Equally clearly, the music will divide into good and poor. Tracks like "The Force " and "Shakedown " are an unspeakably bad way to start an album with Taka Boom at her strident worst and Norman Whitfield rarely produced stuff this weak, but perseverance will deliver better results and "All My Love" is a good ballad and Boom is much better on the gentle "Don't Walk Away". "Simple Love Song" is a big ballad which doesn't really appeal to me but "Just Say When" is a not bad mid-tempo offering. Nothing on here cries out to be heard and the group never enjoyed any hits but they remain interesting for housing both Boom and Joe Harris, formerly of The Undisputed Truth.

Patti Drew

Tell Him 1967 Capitol ST 2804 Producers: Don Carone & Pete Wright

Working On A Groovy Thing 1968 Capitol ST 2855 Producers: Don Carone & Pete Wright

I've Been Here All The Time 1969 Capitol ST 156 Producers: Don Carone & Pete Wright

Wild Is Love 1970 Capitol ST 408 Producers: Don Carone & Pete Wright (Billboard soul charts: 49)

Patti Drew was born in South Carolina but like so many others made her way north with her family to Chicago where she grew up. Together with Carlton Black and two of her five sisters Patti cut records as The Drew-Vels, one of which, "Tell Him", reached #90 on the Hot 100 in early 1964. Other singles followed before the group broke up in 1966. Shortly thereafter Drew started to record as a solo artist. She has always been a strangely neglected singer, never receiving much recognition or approval despite releasing four LPs and placing the same number of singles on the top 50 soul chart. Her voice has a little bit of Baby Washington, Maxine Brown and Barbara Lewis in it, although without quite their range, but she had a most appealing uptown style and deserves more appreciation.

She re-recorded "Tell Him" in 1967 and had a hit (#22 soul) with it the second time around. It became the title track of her first album, which was a varied affair as regards style and approach. More of a "soul" album than she was to record again, it featured a rare song written by The Dells in "Turn Away From Me", the old Golden World tune, "I Can't Shake It Loose" ,and throwaway versions of "Knock On Wood" and "Show Me".She was never remotely a passionate southern soul type singer but she made a good if refined fist of "Tired Of Falling In (And Out Of) Love" and "My Lover's Prayer" previously recorded by Otis Clay and Otis Redding respectively. More representative of what she was to record in the future were the jazzy "You've Changed" and the poppy "Stop And Listen".

"Working On A Groovy Thing" may owe a lot to Maxine Brown's "Oh No Not My Baby" but it is nevertheless an excellent song and fully deserved to become Patti's next hit, #34 soul and #62 pop, in the summer of 1968. It also became the title of her second album, which contained the instantly memorable follow-up single, "There'll Never Be Another", which unaccountably failed to hit any charts. It goes without saying that the Capitol musicians were of the highest class but they were probably more at home with jazz or pop music rather than soul and this was the direction in which this LP was aimed. There were no soul songs on show this time around. This is not to denigrate what is a tuneful and accomplished record, merely to point out what it sounds like.

I've Been Here All The Time reverted somewhat to the approach of the debut LP and included good versions of Jerry Butler's "Just Can't Forget About You Baby" and Redding's "Hard To Handle" (her third chart entrant on single). Also on board were enchanting and intriguing versions of "Fever" and the Rascals' "A Guy Like You" as well as her fourth and final soul chart entrant, "The Love That A Woman Should Give To A Man" (#38). The remainder of the tracks were in her pop/jazz style.

Somewhat ironically, the only of her LPs to reach the soul charts, was her last, *Wild is Love*. I say this as it has preciously little to do with soul, being a big band jazz outing that was previously recorded by Nat King Cole; I mean this literally: he cut an album in the same name in 1960 with all these tracks included. Musically it is impeccable, but simply not a soul record.

By 1971 she had some bad drug experiences and departed the music business until she re-appeared in 1975 to cut a tribute single, "The Mighty O.J", which sounded as if it should have been the title track to a 'Blaxploitation' film. It bombed and, although she was to sing in the eighties with a group called Front Line, I don't believe she ever recorded again.

The Drifters (see also Ben E. King & Bill Fredericks)

Ben E. King; Johnny Williams; Charlie Thomas; Dock Green; Elsbeary Hobbs; Rudy Lewis; Tommy Evans; Billy Davis; Eugene Pearson; Johnny Moore; Johnny Terry; Butch Leak; Grant Kitchings; Clyde Brown; Bill Fredericks; Butch Mann; Billy Lewis; Joe Blunt

Save The Last Dance For Me 1962 Atlantic SD 8059 Producer: Mike Leiber and Jerry Stoller

Up On The Roof - The Best Of 1963 Atlantic SD 8073 (Billboard pop charts: 110)

Under The Boardwalk 1964 Atlantic SD 8099 No producer listed (Billboard pop charts: 40)

The Good Life 1965 Atlantic SD 8103 No producer listed (Billboard pop charts: 103)

I'll Take You Where The Music's Playing 1966 Atlantic SD 8113 No producer listed

Golden Hits 1968 Atlantic SD 8153 (Billboard soul charts: 33; Billboard pop charts: 122)

The Drifters seem to have been around for ever, as comfortable and welcome as a favourite old pair of slippers, singing a perpetual series of "Golden Oldies", and without being in any way threatening or challenging. It has been both their strength and weakness.

They first started to score big hits in 1953 and remained on or near the top of the tree until about early 1965 when they went into steep commercial decline - or at least in the States; they had a second successful career in the early seventies in England which lasted for a few years. So many of their best sides were in the "pre-soul" days that I have chosen to start discussing their LPs from 1962 onwards and it is interesting to note that the only one of their albums to ever hit the soul charts was the *Golden Hits* package in 1968. And this sums up a great deal of debate about The Drifters: were they just a pop outfit? After about 1972 or so, I would answer such a question as "yes" and certainly they meant nothing to me or my soul friends in the seventies, but to deny the group's excellence and "black" appeal in the early sixties seems perverse. Brilliant songs like "Up On The Roof" and "On Broadway" were big soul hits in 1963. Also, I have been true to my stance of only listing those individuals who were in the group at the time these LPs were released; I am well aware there were a number of other singers I have not highlighted.

Save The Last Dance For Me contained five top ten soul singles including their last ever #1 in the title track and one would imagine therefore, that it must have sold a few copies itself. However, it failed to reach the top 100 of the pop chart (soul album charts didn't exist in 1962) which seems extraordinary. The strength of the music lay in the songs and the voices; there was not much for a soul fan to latch onto as regards the music which was too often saturated in strings atop polite rhythm sections.

The *Up On The Roof - The Best Of* album was obviously named after the imperishable Goffin-King song and apart from that single, a rather forgotten failed 45, "What To Do", and their respective b-sides it was all previously released songs. "What To Do", by the way, was rather tougher fare than one had come to expect from the group.

"Under The Boardwalk" was another huge hit for the group (#4 pop) and the album of the same name also contained five hit singles, the best of which was "On Broadway" (#7 soul, #9 pop) one of the greatest and smartest pop/soul songs ever written. The strings were still oppressive but songs like the oft-recorded "Let The Music Play" are fine examples of what is now known as "uptown soul".

The Good Life LP, on the other hand, veered alarmingly away from anything that could be classed as "uptown soul", or, indeed, *any* soul, and, apart from "Saturday Night At The Movies", another big hit and well-loved song, it was show tunes all the way.

I'll Take You Where The Music's Playing was certainly an improvement on *The Good Life* and contained more of the group's best known songs - "At The Club", "I've Got Sand In My Shoes", "Come On Over To My Place" - but, despite the quality of all the songwriters involved, and The Drifters seldom used any but the best, the pop-soul sound was starting to wear a bit by then and the album does sound dated today.

Now 1973 Bell 219 (UK)

Love Games 1975 Bell 246 (UK)

There Goes My First Love 1975 Bell 260 (UK)

Every Nite's A Saturday Night 1976 Arista ARTY 140 (UK)

Something Old & Something New 1979 Sounds South SO 16089 Producer: Harold Thomas

Too Hot 1982 51 West Q 16242 Producer: Paul Whitehead

Live At Harvard 1985 Showcase SHLP 124 (UK)

I do not intend to review the rest of the albums as all the UK releases were straight pop music to my ears, and frankly, to most others too: other than "Kissin' In The Back Row Of The Movies" reaching a paltry #83 soul in late 1974, the Drifters never placed a single record on the U.S. soul charts after 1967. By the way, needless to say, none of the Drifters albums above from 1973 to 1985 provide any details on the sleeves as to group personnel.

There were no end of Greatest Hits and Best Of collections that came out in the seventies and eighties but I have no heart or appetite to track them down and list them, especially as so many of them were cheap and nasty or were more or less exactly the same.

D Train

D Train 1982 Prelude PRL 14105 Producer: Hubert Eaves

Music 1983 Prelude PRL 14109 Producer: Hubert Eaves

Something's On Your Mind 1984 Prelude PRL 14112 Producer: Hubert Eaves

You're The One For Me - The Very Best Of 1985 RCA ZL70885 (UK)

The Best Of 1986 Prelude PRL 14116

D Train were a duo, James Williams, who sang (well), and Hubert Eaves, who played much of their music, and who had already issued a jazzy LP in his own name in 1979. They were a straight ahead, no nonsense dance team, who hardly made any sides that couldn't be gyrated to. They certainly had a following, large enough to ensure that the group placed eight singles on the soul charts between early 1982 and mid 1985, as well as supporting a couple of Greatest Hits collections.

The first LP is their best, as it contained their best down-tempo track, the agreeable "Lucky Day", as well as their finest dance cut, a spirited take on "Walk On By", and two pretty big hits, "You're The One For Me" and "Keep On".

Music followed the same template with only one slow track amid the dance sides, but there were no stand-outs this time around.

"Something's On Your Mind" was their biggest hit, #5 soul and #79 pop at the very start of 1984 and it became the title of their last LP. Slower than most of their other music, but not really a ballad, it was perhaps a surprise that it did so well. The most startling track, by far, because it sounded nothing whatsoever like D Train, was an acoustic guitar driven version of Carole King's "So Far Away".

The duo split up in 1986 with Williams releasing a couple of solo albums and Eaves going on to work with many other artists.

Doris Duke

I'm A Loser 1970 Canyon 7704 Producer: Swamp Dogg (Billboard soul charts: 39)

A Legend In Her Own Time 1973? Mankind 200 Producer: Swamp Dogg

Woman 1975 Scepter SPS 5124 Producer: The Contempo Family

Doris Duke's music was about as far removed from The Drifters' and D Train's as can be imagined. She was born Doris Curry in Georgia, and, after becoming a talented and in-demand session singer in New York and releasing a couple of singles in her married name of Doris Willingham that flopped spectacularly, had the good fortune to hook up with Jerry "Swamp Dogg" Williams when he was at the peak of his artistic and commercial powers. She cut two long players with him and the first is one of the greatest soul albums of all.

I'm A Loser is a concept LP of great power and artistry, one of those entirely adult sets like Gloria Barnes' *Uptown* or The Soul Children's *Friction* that defines "deep soul", and it is a shock to be reminded that it actually reached the soul charts, and might even have done better than it did had Canyon not dissolved into bankruptcy. It is also fascinating to understand that Doris Duke herself retains no fond memories of the record, claiming it made her no money whatsoever and forced her to sing in a style in which she felt uncomfortable. The album doesn't bear a track called "I'm A Loser", but doesn't need to, given that the harrowing and relentless storylines make it all too clear that coming second was the inevitable fate of this woman. The LP cover sets the tone with Duke photographed against total blackness, and the opening cut, "He's Gone", demonstrates that this is going to be an LP of uncommon ingenuity when we hear a drum pattern that I don't think has ever been repeated, and a bass line of such resonant profundity that it seems to have come from deep down in a canyon somewhere, maybe a subliminal echo of the record label. All the songs are unremittingly bleak, with the slight exception of Clarence Carter's "The Feeling Is Right", but even here her man seems somewhat unreliable and feckless. To just highlight a few more of the brilliant tracks: "Congratulations Baby" is an extraordinary song with Duke expressing first bitterness against and then hope for the baby inside her that is forcing her into a marriage against her will; "Divorce Decree" is self-explanatory and unavoidable; "How Was I To Know You Cared" a lament against the inability of her man to express his feelings, thus driving her away. And then there is "I Don't Care Anymore". This tale of a young woman coming to the city in search of her fortune, but instead finding a broken marriage, hopeless jobs, and being sold into prostitution, is the magnificent centrepiece of the album. Hard to listen to, but entirely in keeping with the album's concept, it stands as one of soul's greatest moments. Two more superb tracks, "Feet Start Walking" and "To The Other Woman" (with a devastating, sneering vocal), did very well as singles reaching #36 soul and #7soul (and, amazingly, in the case of the latter, #50 pop) respectively. Swamp Dogg productions are generally liberal in their use of blaring horns but they are eschewed completely here, with the focus laying on a taut and stark rhythm and strings which often seem to be used in an ironic sense when they soar against the misery of the lyrics.

Williams and Duke wouldn't have reasonably expected to match *I'm A Loser*, and I'm not sure anyone could have taken another set of such anguish, but the follow-up, *A Legend In Her Own Time*, was indeed rather disappointing. The cover showed Duke standing in a desert, for no clear reason, and the acknowledgments on the back cover were hard to read. It is also much more muddled than the previous set, with one side - the better one - containing original songs while the other consists of fairly mundane cover versions. There *are* good things here and "If She's Your Wife" and "I Wish I Could Sleep" wouldn't have sounded out of place on *I'm A Loser*. Overall though, the strings are often a little too overblown in places and her version of "By The Time I Get To Phoenix" almost sounds as if it were sung by someone else, so different is it in style and tone. Her time her come and gone: the LP and two singles pulled from it failed to sell.

A short and unsuccessful stay with Mainstream followed before Duke pitched up in London of all places to cut her third and final album with producer John Abbey, a man with a long and abiding love of soul music.

It is by no means a bad album at all, and proved again that proper soul records could be cut on proper soul singers in the UK, however much any soul purist may wish to turn up his or her nose. The songs were generally well chosen - apart from Bunny Sigler's "Grasshopper", possibly the worst song he ever wrote - and even included one, "Hey Lady", from two members of staff on the English *Blues And Soul* magazine. It is a decent song, suited to Duke, although like the other cuts on side one it is at least a couple of minutes too long. Once again the LP didn't sell, though, and that was the end of her recording career.

Some readers might be aware of an LP that came out on the decidedly peculiar UK label, Manhattan, in 1980 with a credit of *Doris Duke and Friends*. Like the Tyrone Davis LP they also put out, it is an entirely misleading title and there is not one single note of music on it sung by Doris Duke. The tracks are by Mamie Galore, Tyrone Davis (ironically) and Bobbie Jean Bland.

Eric Dunbar

Freeway 1976 TSG 814 No producer listed

Another TSG LP, and another that has a number of good tracks, some funky, some less so, but also therefore another album that never got a proper release thus making it become more coveted in the last few years. It appears from research that Eric Dunbar was based in New Orleans but that's as much as I know.

Duncan Sisters

Helen Duncan; Phyllis Duncan

The Duncan Sisters 1979 EarMarc EMLP 4001 Producers: Ian Guenther & Willie Morrison

Gonna Stay In Love 1981 Malaco MAL 7405 Producers: Ian Guenther & Willie Morrison

Two sisters from Mississippi, the Duncans found themselves in Memphis in the mid seventies and got the chance to release one single on the Hi label, "It's You That I Need", which was a most untypical offering from Willie Mitchell's label and although the 45 states that it was recorded in Memphis I'm assuming not at Royal. Anyway, it didn't do much and the girls then sang on a couple of disco LPs by Sticky Fingers and The THP Orchestra before getting a chance to record their own album on the Casablanca subsidiary, EarMarc. It's by and large a rather anonymous disco set, with minimal soul content, but "You Give Me Such A Feeling" is not too bad and "Rock Along Slowly", was a surprisingly decent downtempo song which even managed to reach #89 on the soul charts at the end of 1979 when released as a single (a second 45, "Sadness In My Eyes", reached #94 a few months later).

Given the sisters' career had been largely confined to recording out and out disco music it was rather startling to see them pitch up on Malaco, a quintessentially "southern" record label, although one which had tried hard to get into the dance market at the end of the seventies and early eighties. Recorded, as had been much of the debut, in Toronto rather than Jackson, Mississippi (where Malaco was based) there was nothing on the LP to excite anybody who expected a set in the Dorothy Moore style although it wasn't all out and out disco. The title track, for example, was a pop-slanted ballad which, apparently, became some sort of hit in Canada, although it certainly didn't in the U.S.A. and that was therefore it for the recording history of The Duncan Sisters although they kept their hand in, so to speak, by recording backing vocals for a number of other artists over the years.

Dunn & Bruce Street

Official Business 1982 Devaki DKI 300003 Producers: Dunn Pearson & Bruce Gray

Cleveland, Ohio, is a bit like St. Louis in as much as it sustained a talented soul music community for years without receiving the credit it deserved and Dunn Pearson and Bruce Gray contributed a half decent LP to add to the city's achievements, even if it was recorded in New York. (For anyone baffled about the duo's name, it was modelled, for some obscure reason, on Dun and Bradstreet, a leading U.S credit risk company.) They had already released a 45, "Moment Of Truth", which adopted a style based on the Philadelphia sound; perhaps not surprising given that Gray had worked with no end of groups from there in the past, including The Trammps and Love Committee. Sadly, it is not included on the LP. Although the album didn't chart, it must have done tolerably well, given that it did produce three singles that reached the soul charts: the melodic and pleasing Vandross-ish "If You Come With Me" (#45), the so-so "I Owe It To Me" (#63) and the thoroughly clichéd "Shout For Joy" (#35). "Let Me Learn" and "Take Me Away" were good LP tracks, showcasing Gray's passionate singing.

They went their separate ways after this one LP and Pearson released a pleasing single in 1986 as by Dunn Street, "Even A Fool".

Dyke & The Blazers

Arlester "Dyke" Christian; Alvester Jacobs; JV Hunt; Bernard Williams; Richard Cason; Rodney Brown; Clarence Towns; Alvin Battle; Elmer Scott

The Funky Broadway 1967 Original Sound OSR LPS 8876 Producers: Arthur Barrett & Austin Coleman (Billboard pop charts: 186)

Greatest Hits 1969 Original Sound OSR LPS 8877 Producers: Arthur Barrett & Art Laboe

So Sharp! 1983 Kent 004 (UK)

Arlester Christian had a short but eventful life: born in Buffalo, NY, in 1943; placed eight singles on the soul charts with his band; wrote "Funky Broadway"; heroin addict; shot to death in 1971. By all accounts a man for whom fame and money was irrelevant, he made some refreshingly unsophisticated and intensely funky music for a few years. He remains one of my favourite "funk" artists and his music is interesting as on the one hand it sounds very much of its time but, on the other, has not really aged at all. I only wish he had made more of it.

His first excursion on disc was with the miniscule combo, Carl La Rue & The Crew, cut in Buffalo, after which he relocated to Phoenix where he was to remain for the rest of his life. His first disc with the Blazers was "The Funky Broadway" which hit immediately: #17 soul and #65 pop in early 1967 and he would have made a lot of money later that year when Wilson Pickett had a huge hit with it. An album was built around the two-part single which featured three wholesome looking young ladies (or the same lady) on the cover, wholly at odds with the "dirty" music within as evidenced by "City Dump", the most perfect title for a Dyke and the Blazers' track. This is fairly rudimentary music, with Dyke's limited voice declaiming over repetitive riffs and it is not difficult to understand if some find it not to their taste at all. There is little variety, apart from a number of modifications on the hit, no ballads of any stripe or any fine singing, but the LP's unpretentiousness is what makes it so much fun. All the songs are short apart from "The Wrong House" a compelling and amusing tale of domestic mishap that ran for ten minutes. "So Sharp", a second single from the LP, also hit the charts but in a smaller way, at #41 soul.

From 1968 onwards the music behind Dyke improved a great deal as members of the Watts 103rd Street Rhythm Band started to back him but the spirit remained the same: Dyke wasn't about to go uptown for anyone. In fact, if anything, he got even funkier and a James Brown influence became much more pronounced. "Funky Walk", "We Got More Soul" and his biggest ever hit, the #4 soul hit, "Let A Woman Be A Woman – Let A Man Be A Man", owe a great deal to Brown and nothing at all to political correctness. All became substantial successes. As did, surprisingly, the 3 year old "Uhh" from the debut album, which was released in the spring of 1970 due to heavy radio play. All of these tracks can be found - and should be - on his *Greatest Hits* album which also includes a good take on The Isley's "It's Your Thing" and an unrecognisable version of "You Are My Sunshine" which became The Blazers' penultimate soul hit at #30..

The final chart entrant was the excellent "Runaway People", which even featured strings but was hardly soft, in the summer of 1970 ; his last single was Stuff", an anti-drug song, the message of which he was to personally ignore, and then, a few months later, he was dead.

Kent records put out an LP in 1983 which includes all eight hits, and was a welcome way to get his name back out there. (Note : band member Richard Cason is the same man who went on to work at Malaco as well as fronting Formula IV.)

Dynamics

Isaac "Zeke" Harris; George White; Fred Baker; Samuel Stevenson

First Landing 1969 Cotillion SD 9009 Producers: Tommy Cogbill & Chips Moman

What A Shame 1973 Black Gold BG-5001 Producers: Ronnie Shannon & George White (Billboard soul charts: 52)

There were a number of soul groups called The Dynamics but only one of them got to record an LP. This excellent Detroit group had a complex and long career, recording for a number of labels with two stand-out moments before they pitched up on Cotillion: a fairly big hit on Big Top in 1963 with "Misery" and the magnificent "Lights Out" on RCA in 1967 (the lead singer on that record, Zerben Hicks, had left the group before the Cotillion and Black Gold days, but he did contribute a handful of songs on their albums.)

Even allowing for the brilliance of "Lights Out", the *First Landing* set was much better than anyone had a right to expect from a debut album. For a start it was all recorded down at American in Memphis which guaranteed the quality of the music (listen to Gene Chrisman's drums on "Ain't No Love At All") and the group were also provided with some excellent songs, the best of which came from Ronnie Shannon, a genuinely gifted writer who could even make a title like "Dum-De-Dum" worthy of a listen. Lastly, these were really good singers with the forceful Harris taking most of the leads, although George White was every bit his equal with his dreamy high tenor. The quality of the composing could be ascertained from the fact that 8 of the 12 tracks came out on singles as either a or b-sides. Indeed, two songs, both from Shannon, attain classic status: "Ice Cream Song" belied its odd and unpromising title to make #17 soul and #59 pop as a single and has an exquisite mid-tempo flow and sweet lyrical logic. "What Would I Do" may have been tucked away as a b-side on a 45 but it is of surpassing beauty, so fragile in White's hands that you think it might break. If I had to be harsh I would say that "Since I Lost You" goes on a tad too long, and "Fair Love" and "The Love That I Need" are routine but these are minor quibbles; splendid album.

Remarkably, the next LP, despite a four year gap, was just as good as the first. I believe it was recorded in New York this time around with White taking the majority of the lead vocals and all but one of the songs being provided by Shannon. Heart meltingly beautiful tracks like "You're The Only One", "Voyage Thru The Mind", "Let Me Be Your Friend" and the title track proved their mastery of slow material but uptempo cuts like "She's For Real (Bless You)","You'll Never Find A Man Like Me" and "Shucks I Love You" were all delightful too. "Funkey (sic) Key" proved they could cut convincing funk, and as with the title track and "She's For Real", reached the soul charts when released as a 45.

Sadly they only recorded another couple of singles which didn't sell very well, the last coming out in 1977, and that seemed to be it for this outrageously underrated group.

Dynamic Five

Robert Ahed; James Clemmons; Wayne Stevens; Robert Ursery; Don Patton

Love Is The Key 1978 UA MR-LA899-H Producer: Joe Reed

Over the years, I have often been asked which is the rarest soul LP known to man. The answer would probably be this one by the totally unknown Dynamic Five. Apart from a single from it, "Lover's Lullabye", which I know well, every other piece of information I have ever been able to find about the album is from the internet. I have certainly never seen a copy of the actual thing, and I am pretty sure it was never properly released, hence its staggering rarity. Again, thanks to the internet, one can listen to most of the tracks and it is up to scratch, in the Enchantment bag, making it hard to understand exactly why it was never issued. It seems a bit odd to review a record that is so scarce and so my tip is to simply go on You Tube and listen for yourselves.

Dynamic Superiors

Tony Washington; George Spann; George Peterback Jr.; Michael McCalpin; Maurice Washington.

Dynamic Superiors 1975 Motown M6-822S1 Producers: Nick Ashford & Valerie Simpson (Billboard soul charts: 36; Billboard pop charts: 201)

Pure Pleasure 1975 Motown M6-841S1 Producers: Nick Ashford & Valerie Simpson (Billboard soul charts: 36; Billboard pop charts:130)

You Name It 1976 Motown M6-875S1 Producers: Hal Davis, Michael Sutton, Marilyn Mcleod, Pam Sawyer & Don Daniels

Give & Take 1976 Motown M6-879S1 Producer: Brian Holland

Following in the footsteps of The Miracles, Four Tops, Marvelettes and Supremes,The Dynamic Superiors is just such a Motown name. What is more surprising is that there were other, unrelated, Dynamic Superiors combos who cut records. This particular one came out of Washington D.C. and made a record on Sue as The Superiors before beefing their name up and being signed by the giant Detroit company. If they are known for anything, it is probably due to lead singer Tony Washington being openly gay at a time when this was unusual. Their timing was not great: signing for Motown when the label was in clear decline and framing their first LP largely in the sweet soul style that had also passed its peak,

It's a good thing that you can't *always* judge a record by a cover otherwise hardly anyone would want to listen to that first album. Its sleeve is tacky almost beyond belief, but the contents within made it a worthwhile purchase. Written almost entirely by Ashford and Simpson, the fun is in hearing just how clearly tracks like "Leave It Alone" and "Star Of My Life" follow the test vocals of the great duo. "Leave It Alone" also did well as a 45, reaching #13 soul but was eclipsed by the rather lovely "Shoe Shoe Shine" which went to #16 soul, but also #68 pop. It should go without saying that there were no bad songs here, but by and large A & S were keeping their premier material for their own albums in this period. Incidentally, the LP also includes a version of "Don't Send Nobody Else", but Ace Spectrum and Millie Jackson did it better.

The follow-up album followed some of the same patterns of the first: the songs were nearly all written by producers Ashford and Simpson with arrangers Paul Riser, Leon Pendarvis and Richard Tee all contributing again. But the tempo was increased with an obvious eye on the dance floors. Both charting singles, "Nobody's Gonna Change Me" and "Deception", were fast songs but their lowly positions, #51 and #53, suggested what was actually going to happen: the group had already peaked. The best slow song on the LP was "A Better Way" but they also essayed an interesting and dead-slow take of "Ain't Nothing Like The Real Thing" even if it didn't entirely work. It also seemed apparent that the interest of Ashford and Simpson was waning as "Face The Music" and "Hit And Run Lovers" were as close to scraping the barrel as they ever got. Finally, Motown also still lacked a great deal in the marketing department. The album cover this time around just showed a pair of knees and there was no attempt to forge any identity for the group whatsoever. Not one of their LPs ever told us who was in the group. Given Tony Washington's obvious flamboyance and talent it seems a clear opportunity was missed. (The UK version of the album included "Shoe Shoe Shine" and "Leave It Alone", doubtless because the debut was not released over here.)

At least the group got their picture on the cover of *You Name It*. What they didn't get, Ashford and Simpson having moved on, is any outstanding songs or any hit singles. The long disco tracks are without interest and the slower tunes lack hooks or distinction. Nothing is shocking, but it's one of those LPs you play two or three times and then struggle to remember any of it a few months later.

Much the same could be said of the last album, *Give And Take*, apart from the group's once again being banished from the cover of their own LP. The Hollands had returned to Motown and provided a handful of songs, but none were memorable, sounding quite dated even at the time of release. Martha and The Vandellas said more in nine seconds of "Nowhere To Run" than The Dynamic Superiors did on their nine minute version here. Washington sang Stevie Wonder's "All In Love Is Fair" well enough, and this version has its fans, but it is not a song I much care for. The LP was entitled *Nowhere To Run* in the UK.

In 2004 a CD by the Dynamic Superiors came out in Japan, *The Sky's The Limit,* but I suspect none of the original group were still around. Certainly Tony Washington wasn't, having died in the early eighties.

Dynasty

Kevin Spencer; Nidra Beard; Linda Carriere; William Shelby; Leon Sylvers

Your Piece Of The Rock 1979 Solar BXL1 3398 Producer: Leon Sylvers (Billboard soul charts: 72)

Adventures In The Land Of Music 1980 Solar BXL1 3576 Producer: Leon Sylvers (Billboard soul charts: 11; Billboard pop charts: 43)

The Second Adventure 1981 Solar S 20 Producer: Leon Sylvers (Billboard soul charts: 42; Billboard pop charts: 119)

Right Back At Cha ! 1982 Solar ST-60176 Producers: Leon Sylvers, Foster Sylvers, William Shelby & Kevin Spencer (Billboard soul charts: 54)

Daydreamin' 1986 Solar ST-72550 Producers: Fenderella, Lathan Armor, LA Reid, Babyface, Kevin Spencer & William Shelby

Out Of Control 1988 Solar D1-72559 Producers: Bill Wolfer, Todd Cochran, LA Reid, Babyface, Kevin Spencer, Fenderella, Lathan Armor & William Shelby (Billboard soul charts: 68)

Dynasty recorded for the Solar label for about ten years from 1979 onwards. I was well aware of them and their music at the time but must confess that they left the scantest of impressions and when I started this section I realised that I could not recall a single one of their tunes. This may be due to my forgetfulness, but I suspect is also rooted in their rather faceless approach. Listening again, it is clear that their clean-cut dance music was determined not to offend, and nor does it, but there is little spark and their one big hit, "I've Just Begun To Love You" (#6 soul), is utterly routine.

The first album had six tracks only, and was competent and professional, but would have been better had the songs been shorter. "Satisfied" sounds pretty good for the first three minutes but meanders on for another four. "When You Feel Like Giving Love" shows the group to have a nice line in harmony but is not a particularly strong song. All in all, a completely typical Solar release.

Adventures did extremely well for the group and does have some nice moments, not least some notably astute arranging from Gene Dozier, but songs like "Ice Breaker" and "Something To Remember" were beyond redemption.

The group had increased to five by the time of *The Second Adventure*, which includes the first side of theirs I really liked, "You're My Angel", beautifully arranged and sung. The dance tracks continued to be rather formulaic, but if one loved the Solar sound, there remained no reason not to like this LP as much as the previous two. The songs were somewhat shorter this time around, too, which was a good move.

Dynasty had hardly been a "hard" soul act, but *Right Back At Cha!* moved them even further in a pop direction than before and two singles from the set became minor soul hits.

Leon Sylvers was no longer producing by the time of the *Daydreamin'* set, and the group were now a trio of Spencer, Beard and Shelby. The album didn't chart, nor did it generate any hit singles, thus proving that I wasn't the only person who found it to be exceedingly poor.

Their last set, *Out Of Control*, reprised three tracks from *Daydreamin'* as well as its front cover, which did seem to suggest that interest in the group was no longer what it was, but the set did at least generate two small soul hits in "Don't Waste My Time" (#41) and "Tell Me" (#56).

Clifton Dyson (see also Dyson's Faces)

Slow Your Body Down 1981 Afterhour LU-200 Producers: Clifton Dyson, Rodney Brown, Butch Bonner & Greg Millerton

There is evidence to suggest that Clifton was either the brother or half-brother to Ronnie Dyson but I have not seen positive proof to confirm this. What I am sure about was that he was once the lead singer of The Differences group who cut a super disc on Mon'Ca and that he died in 2003.

This platter out of Washington D.C. just about qualifies as an album although with only five tracks and coming in at a mere 28 minutes, it is not generous. Side one consists solely of the interminable title track, which did reach #51 soul in the summer of '82, and is entirely overshadowed by a most acceptable second side. "Hypnotize" (with an accomplished co-lead vocal from Debra Wilson) and "So Lonely" are winning slow drag songs which show off Dyson's committed and satisfying voice while "I'm Giving Up" is a dance effort worth hearing. His last known vinyl waxing was a duet with Rick Webb in 1988.

Ronnie Dyson

(If You Let Me Make Love To You Then) Why Can't I Touch You? 1970 Columbia C 30223 Producer: Billy Jackson (Billboard soul charts: 12; Billboard pop charts: 55)

One Man Band 1972 Columbia KC 32211 Producers: Billy Jackson, Stan Vincent & Thom Bell (Billboard soul charts: 34; Billboard pop charts: 142)

The More You Do It 1976 Columbia PC 34350 Producers: Chuck Jackson & Marvin Yancy (Billboard soul charts: 30)

Love In All Flavors 1977 Columbia PC 34866 Producers: Chuck Jackson & Marvin Yancy (Billboard soul charts : 45)

If The Shoe Fits 1979 Columbia JC 36029 Producers: Eugene McDaniels & Michael Zager

Ronnie Dyson was born In Washington and died in Philadelphia in 1990, aged only 40. His background to becoming a soul singer was somewhat unusual as he rose to fame and prominence as a result of his lead part in the hit musical, *Hair*. That he was a gifted singer is in no doubt, but I always felt he could never really shake off his show business roots and his voice, while beautiful, never had an edge and it always appealed more to my head than my heart.

His first album, with its unwieldy title, made it clear that Columbia thought it would be best if he went a pop route. It's full of well-known and well-loved songs and is accomplished, but sounded a little dated in 1970. The title track, with its gentle latin tinge, could have been recorded and released back in 1965, but clearly struck a chord with listeners anyway, as it hit both soul and pop top ten; and even if tracks like "Bridge Over Troubled Water", "Make It With You" and "Fever" were hardly daring in 1970 when compared to James Brown or the emergent Philly sound, they didn't stop the album from selling strongly to both black and white audiences. (The album came out in the UK in 1971 (CBS 64779) entitled

When You Get Right Down To It with the addition of the song of that name only.)

Aligning himself with that incipient Philly Sound was exactly, and happily, what Dyson did for his next album, even if, for some reason, it did not appear for more than two years after the debut. It contained standout Philadelphia songs like "I Think I'll Tell Her", "When You Get Right Down To It" and "Just Don't Want To Be Lonely" and was all arranged by Thom Bell. Side two hedged its bets, though, and followed the approach of the first album in containing covers of pop songs like "Something" and "A Wednesday In Your Garden". Because the LP took so long to appear the singles within had been released over a wide time period; the biggest success of which was the title track which reached #15 soul and #28 pop in March 1973.

Dyson had another long wait before his next album came out, and only a small (not on any album) hit in the shape of "We Can Make It Last Forever" had kept his name out there in the meantime. (Around this time, 1975 in fact, he also recorded another non-album single, "Lady In Red", that became popular on the "Modern Soul" scene in England, but which failed in the States).

The More You Do It paired Dyson with Chuck Jackson and Marvin Yancy, then hot producers for Natalie Cole. It did push Dyson in a slightly different direction as he was cajoled to sound more urgent and involved although two covers were still included: "Jive Talking" and "A Song For You" and neither was great. The title track became a #6 soul hit and deservedly so, as it was by far the strongest song on show. Another track, "(I Like Being) Close To You" did relatively poorly as a follow-up, only reaching #75 soul. It is not a worthless album, but was hardly filled with great material.

Columbia continued with Jackson and Yancy for *Love In All Flavors*, and were rewarded with a reasonably successful album and reasonably successful lead-off single in "Don't Be Afraid"(#30 soul). "Sara Smile" was the only well-known cover on show and it was one of his best, with a thoughtful and involving arrangement, although Ronnie also delivered a take on The Independents' "I Just Want To Be There". I much preferred the original. As with the previous set, it was all ok and competent but hardly enthralling, but I will single out "I Want To Be Where You Are" as a fine uptempo dance side that probably should have been put out as a single and "Ain't Nothing Wrong", a good ballad where his voice takes on some elements of Donny Hathaway's.

By the end of the decade Dyson was no longer a successful recording artist and his hit-making days were long behind him but Columbia did persevere with one more album, even if they decided he couldn't grace the cover of the *If The Shoe Fits* set. It was the first LP of his to fail to reach the soul charts and heralded no hit singles either which was no surprise to anyone listening to the overblown and dull ballad "Familiar Strangers", or the clichéd "Couples Only", a dance song of no merit at all.

Phase 2 1982 Cotillion SD 5234 Producer: Bobby Eli

Brand New Day 1983 Cotillion 90119-1 Producer: Butch Ingram (Billboard soul charts: 53)

Columbia dropped the singer after this and Cotillion became his new label, on which he put out two albums. *Phase 2* was an improvement over *If The Shoe Fits* and contains "Say You Will", and "Even In The Darkest Night" quintessential Dyson ballads. He sings them beautifully but cannot shake off their essential pop sensibility which means that even while I want to love them, I can't. When released as a double-sided single "Bring It On Home" and "Heart To Heart" became small hits.

Dyson had never been known for recording dance material but that was to change with "All Over Your Face" from the *Brand New Day* set. Not a bad effort at all, it became his biggest single for about seven years reaching #23 in the fall of 1983. However, despite also being the first album to contain a couple of Dyson's own songs, *Brand New Day* didn't revive his fortunes in any significant way and he was never to record another LP although in 1991 he had a small posthumous "hit" when a duet with Vicki Austin, "Are We So Far Apart" reached #79 on the soul chart.

Dyson's Faces (see also Clifton Dyson)

Clifton Dyson; Gretta Kent; Walter Johnson; Michael Chandler;

Dyson's Faces 1975 DMC DMC-SLP-76331 Producer: R Jose Williams

Dyson's Faces 1977 Dy Rich DRL 10017 Producer: Clifton Dyson

Before Clifton Dyson went solo he recorded two LPs with a group under the name of Dyson's Faces. Both suffered from poor distribution and there must have been few copies pressed and even fewer sold. Which is a shame, because these are good records. The first album mixed up dance tracks and slower songs, and all seven cuts are worth hearing apart from the poor "Nosey People". The material tended to be tuneful and stuck in the mind after only two or three spins and the music, arranged by Eddie Drennon, complements the fine singers rather than overwhelming them.

The second LP reprised two songs from the first set, "Welcome To All This Love Again" and "Don't Worry About The Joneses", but also contained seven new tracks. The sound is slightly more dense this time around, with an excellent arrangement on "Working My Way To Something Better", but the uptempo tracks stay firmly the right side of "disco" and the slower cuts like "Cry Sugar" and "Try Me Baby" are soulful and memorable.

Brenda Lee Eager (see Jerry Butler)

Earth, Wind & Fire (see also Philip Bailey & Maurice White)

Maurice White; Wade Flemons; Don Whitehead; Sherry Scott; Verdine White; Michael Beal; Phillard Williams; Chester Washington; Leslie Drayton; Alex Thomas; Yackov Ben Israel; Roland Bautista; Philip Bailey; Jessica Cleaves; Larry Dunn; Ronnie Laws; Ralph Johnson; Al McKay; Andrew Woolfolk; Johnny Graham; Fred White;

Earth, Wind And Fire 1971 Warner Brothers WS 1905 Producer: Joe Wissert (Billboard soul charts: 24; Billboard pop charts: 172)

The Need Of Love 1972 Warner Brothers WS 1958 Producer: Joe Wissert (Billboard soul charts: 35; Billboard pop charts: 89)

Another Time 1974 Warner Brothers 2WS 2798 (Billboard soul charts: 29; Billboard pop charts: 79)

One of the genuine "supergroups" within the soul (actually, any) genre, Earth, Wind & Fire (EWAF) were one of the biggest bands in the world from 1975 until 1981, an amazingly long time to remain so popular. They put eight albums in the pop top ten, the same amount as The Supremes, and only The Temptations and Stevie Wonder can beat that number. They also had eight #1 singles on the soul charts, and there are only a handful of soul artists or acts who can top that including Aretha Franklin, Marvin Gaye, The O'Jays, Kool & The Gang and James Brown. (The Supremes, again, can equal it.)

Ex-Chicago session musician and Ramsey Lewis Trio member Maurice White was always the driving force behind the band, just as he was in their earliest form as The Salty Peppers who put out two rather nondescript singles on Capitol in 1969. Shortly afterwards the band increased their personnel to nine, changed their name to Earth Wind & Fire and moved to Warner Brothers, who put out their first album in 1971. That first LP, while not great, already had large elements of the distinctive EWAF sound that was to become so successful: unison vocals on choruses, use of a kalimba, complex time changes within the music and a prominent and superb horn section. What they didn't have, though, at this time was Philip Bailey whose falsetto vocals were to become so important later on. The album was also fractionally more "rocky" than later records. The best track, which was also their first ever charting single, albeit modestly at # 43 soul was "Love Is Life".

The Need Of Love could so easily have taken EWAF in another direction as the opening track, the nine-minute long "Energy" was more or less straight jazz, with no commercial possibilities and while they did record again in this style on a handful of occasions, it is not recognisable as coming from a group who were to become a household name. Given the LP also closed with a jazzy /rocky version of the oft-recorded "Everything Is Everything" it could almost been seen as a regression from the debut set. While interesting, *The Need Of Love* is not one of their best, with my favourite track being "I Think About Lovin' You", sang and composed by Sherry Scott, a reminder that an important aspect of their music in these early days was the incorporation of female singers within the band.

Warner capitalised on the later success of the band by issuing the *Another Time* double album in 1974 which includes *Earth,* *Wind And Fire* and *The Need Of Love* in their entirety plus one other track, "Handwriting On The Wall".

Last Days And Time 1972 Columbia C 31702 Producer: Joe Wissert (Billboard soul charts: 15; Billboard pop charts: 87)

Head To The Sky 1973 Columbia KC 32194 Producer: Joe Wissert (Billboard soul charts: 2; Billboard pop charts: 27)

Open Our Eyes 1974 Columbia KC 32712 Producers: Joe Wissert & Maurice White (Billboard soul charts: 1; Billboard pop charts: 15)

That's The Way Of The World 1975 Columbia PC 33280 Producers: Maurice White & Charles Stepney (Billboard soul charts: 1; Billboard pop charts: 1)

Gratitude 1975 Columbia PG 33694 Producers: Maurice White, Joe Wissert & Charles Stepney (Billboard soul charts: 1; Billboard pop charts: 1)

Spirit 1976 Columbia PC 34241 Producers: Maurice White & Charles Stepney (Billboard soul charts: 2; Billboard pop charts: 2)

All 'N All 1977 Columbia JC 34905 Producer: Maurice White (Billboard soul charts: 1; Billboard pop charts: 3)

The Best Of, Volume 1 1978 ARC / Columbia FC 35647 (Billboard soul charts: 3; Billboard pop charts: 6)

I Am 1979 ARC / Columbia FC 35730 Producer: Maurice White (Billboard soul charts: 1; Billboard pop charts: 3)

The band shifted to Columbia and really moved on to another level, both commercially and artistically with *Last Days And Time* which was their finest LP to date by far. The quality of the album was in large measure due to the arrival of Bailey, Larry Dunn and Ralph Johnson, all of whom were to become key members of the group in the glory days. The other factor was the stronger material: "Mom", "They Don't See" and "Time Is On Your Side" were the best songs the band had written to date, "Power" had great drive and "Make It With You" and "Where Have All The Flowers Gone" were covers that worked well.

Head To The Sky welcomed other new and key group members in Al McKay, Andrew Woolfolk and Johnny Graham and the building blocks were all now in place: Bailey's ethereal leads, the twin threat of the Whites as alternative vocalists, soaring choruses and the relentless positivity of the band, which was their real trademark. Compare the optimism of EWAF with the nihilism of so many rap bands today; the contrast is telling. Many foolish rock writers of the day rather mocked EWAF's spiritualism but so many of their best songs from 1973 to 1977 have brilliantly stood the test of time. The title track absolutely soars (#23 soul as a 45) and they contrasted it beautifully with "Build Your Nest", a nasty piece of street funk. For those who liked the jazzier and more experimental side of the band, there was the 13 minute "Zanzibar" to keep them happy. This cut, which had slight echoes of what War were doing back then, is also a reminder of a time when 13 minute cuts were for listening, not dancing.

The band were still not enjoying big hit singles at this time, but that was to change with "Mighty Mighty" a funky track from *Open Our Eyes* which reached #4 soul and #29 pop, appreciably the biggest success they had enjoyed thus far. Two other excellent cuts, the exultant "Devotion" and the irresistible "Kalimba Story" were also released as singles and the three 45s were the stand-outs from a slightly uneven LP. The remainder of the set sounded a bit like in the can material, ranging from the jazzy "Spasmodic Mood" to the title track which was an old gospel song but all were definitely album only cuts; nothing else could have been profitably released on 45.

Earth Wind and Fire finally broke through with *That's The Way Of The World*. The LP came out at much the same time as the lead-off single, "Shining Star", and both went to #1 on the pop charts. The title track remains one of their best-loved sides and also sold exceptionally well when released as a follow-up 45 (#5 soul, #12 pop) but it was in no way a two track LP: "Happy Feelings" was a frothy and danceable slice of joy with the horn section coming on like Tower Of Power's on a good day; "Yearnin' Learnin'" has that snarling Sly/Ohio Players vocal atop a great Larry Dunn piano line and "Reasons" was arguably their best ever ballad and Bailey's best ever vocal. A complete triumph, it stayed on the pop top 100 for over a year.

And so did the follow-up album, *Gratitude,* a double consisting of three "live" sides and one containing four impressive new studio cuts: "Sing A Song"(#1 soul, #5 pop), "Gratitude" itself, "Celebrate" and "Can't Hide Love". The confidence of the band was now palpable, and the musicianship was as faultless as ever, witness Verdine White's striking bass line on the title track, and if, as usual, I cannot get up much enthusiasm about the live sections, the album still sold in great quantity. Anyway, EWAF were a band to *see* live, not listen to.

Next up, another massive success, *Spirit* , which contained "Saturday Nite" a record with an incredibly hot feel, and one which had me dancing like a lunatic in 1976. It rose to #4 soul as a single, which was three places lower than "Getaway" another great side with fabulous riffing horns (a good time to mention Don Myrick, Louis Satterfield and Michael Harris, who while not officially part of the group, played on many albums). It was another impeccably strong collection with no clunkers and the title track had Bailey singing in an impossibly high register. The album was dedicated to the memory of Charles Stepney who had recently died after having contributed so much to the band's development and was their first to feature a pyramid on the sleeve, a sign of the band's growing mystical bent.

The platinum selling *All 'N All* followed *Spirit* and mixed up songs that promulgated the band's spirituality such as "Jupiter" and "Fantasy" with more straightforward love songs all encased in a package that consisted of unimpeachably solid rhythms at the bottom and their tremendous horn section on top. For those who cared to take the time to read the inner sleeve, the words to "Magic Mind" bordered on nonsense, and it was an example of an increasing number of compositions where it was probably better to enjoy the driving music rather than listen to the lyrics too closely. The lead-off single, "Serpentine Fire", was another massive #1 soul hit in the winter of 1977. The only LP EWAF issued in 1978 was a huge-selling *Best Of* which also contained two more #1 soul singles that cannot be found on the other albums: the great "September" and the disappointing "Got To Get You Into My Life".

I Am became the band's third successive platinum album in 1979 and was where two more impressively successful singles, "Boogie Wonderland" and "After The Love Has Gone", could be found, records I must confess to having become rather sick of.

There were absolutely no chances taken on this album which sounded rather like the last two. If one loved EWAF this was of no consequence, and the band remained as solidly loved and commercially dependable as ever.

Faces 1980 ARC / Columbia KC2 36796 Producer: Maurice White (Billboard soul charts: 2; Billboard pop charts: 10)

Raise! 1981 ARC / Columbia TC 37548 Producer: Maurice White (Billboard soul charts: 2; Billboard pop charts: 10)

Powerlight 1983 Columbia TC 38367 Producer: Maurice White (Billboard soul charts: 4; Billboard pop charts: 12)

Electric Universe 1983 Columbia QC 38980 Producer: Maurice White (Billboard soul charts: 8; Billboard pop charts: 40)

Touch The World 1987 Columbia FC 40596 Producers: Maurice White, Preston Glass, Phillip Bailey, Wayne Vaughn & Bill Meyers (Billboard soul charts: 3; Billboard pop charts: 33)

The Best Of, Volume II 1988 Columbia FC 45013 (Billboard soul charts: 74; Billboard pop charts: 190)

Heritage 1990 Columbia C 45268 Producers: Maurice White, Frankie Blue, Les Pierce, Robert Brookins, Ian Prince, Bill Meyers & Butch Stewart (Billboard soul charts: 19; Billboard pop charts: 70)

Millenium 1993 Reprise 9362-45274-1 Producers: Maurice White, Frankie Blue, Bill Meyers & Freddie Ravel (Germany)

EWAF entered the eighties with *Faces*, a double album, and their first for years to not contain any big hits: "Let Me Talk","You" and "And Love Goes On" all performed well enough on the soul charts, but none reached higher than #44 on the pop listings thus making 1980 the first year since 1973 when they didn't post a 45 on the pop top 30. Most of the 15 tracks were instantly recognisable as EWAF but it was not one of their most inspired works and the increasingly pop sounding songs like "You Went Away" were rather dull. The most interesting track, by far, was the seven minute long title cut which harked back to their jazzy roots.

As if stung by the lukewarm reaction to *Faces* - mere gold, rather than platinum - EWAF returned with *Raise!* another huge success as was the major single from the set, "Let's Groove", yet another #1 soul single. Listening to tracks like" You Are A Winner" or "I've Had Enough" (great horn lines) demonstrate how little their sound had changed over the years and they wouldn't have sounded out of place on the mid seventies LPs they were putting out. So why change? They had captured a worldwide audience who loved what they were doing. The status quo was maintained on *Powerlight* which contained three more singles, although one,"Spread Your Love", was their poorest selling in for over a decade (#57 soul).

But time catches up with everyone and EWAF's turn came with *Electric Universe*. The singing and songs hadn't changed much but the music had, moving away from their trademark crispness into something which was discordant, brash and unappealing on poor pop singles like "Magnetic " and "Moonwalk". This was their first LP I ever passed on.

After a break of over three years EWAF were back, and with a bang as the single "System Of Survival" became their eighth and final #1 on the soul charts. Tellingly, though, it only made #60 pop. Their enormous audience had gone, although the *Touch The World* LP that housed the single did pretty well. It was a good enough album, but the magic, like the global audience, had slowly trickled away.

I can't report on the *Heritage* or *Millenium* albums as the little I have heard has been unappealing to my ears, other than to say that the latter only came out on vinyl in Europe, with the U.S. plumping for a CD release. I have also ignored the numerous later compilations.

Writing a section on a group like Earth, Wind and Fire is both the easiest and the hardest part of a book like this. Easy, because information is simple to come by and I know the music so well, but hard, because most other people know it so well too.

East Coast (see also Cameo and Gwen Guthrie)

Larry Blackmon; Gwen Guthrie; Pat Grant; Michael Harris; Gregory Johnson; Melvin Whay; James Wheeler

East Coast 1973 Encounter EN 3002 Producer: Larry Clement

For anyone interested in beginnings: Larry Blackmon and Gregory Johnson went on to form Cameo and Gwen Guthrie forged a pretty successful solo career ten years later.

East Coast as a group, though, left little trace. The LP boasts a gatefold sleeve but lacks definition; what did they want to be? The LP has elements of funk, jazz, pop and rock but fails to gel together into something particularly coherent and memorable. The opening track, "I Found You" is the best, as there is a good song structure but it is rather marred by some unsubtle rock guitar. Most of the other compositions lack melody and despite the obvious talents of East Coast it is not surprising the group didn't last for long. In summary, it remains a somewhat reasonable curiosity, rather than a must have LP.

This East Coast were no relation to a disco ensemble who put out a couple of small hits on RSO at the end of the seventies.

East Harlem Bus Stop

Get On Down! 1976 D & M Sound DML 4 Producers: Dave Miller & Marty Wilson

A pretty much completely instrumental album which just strays the right side of funk, but with obvious disco touches, this is another set that scrapes into the book. D & M was a budget label and Miller and Wilson had a career in the business stretching back a long way. There was no group called East Harlem Bus Stop, and this LP was the work of session musicians. As the album sleeve states, the obvious model for comparison is Brass Construction and the string arrangements are certainly similar to those dreamt up by Randy Muller. So, if you like Brass Construction, track this one down. If not, don't.

Ebo (see also Harold Melvin & The Blue Notes)

I'd Rather Be By Myself 1986 Domino DS 15001 Producers: Allan Felder & David Ebo

One criticism that is often made of LPs is that they sometimes contain one track that completely overshadows everything else. This is a perfect example. The title track, even at 8 minutes long, is magnificent; nothing else is.

David Ebo replaced Teddy Pendergrass in Harold Melvin and The Blue Notes, and one can see - or hear - why. His voice had much the same throaty attack as the more famous singer and he stayed with the group for a few years before striking out on his own. His one solo album suffers from that typical mid-eighties overpowering Linn programming, which renders the dance tracks dated and uninteresting while his version of "Always And Forever" is rather schizophrenic. It starts off as if it is in the wrong key and Ebo sounds ill at ease, but by the time it reaches its climax he had produced an impressive level of vocal dexterity. But everything *is* overwhelmed by that title song, which reached #37 in the soul charts in early 1986. The finale is superb with Ebo holding a note for over twenty seconds in the grand manner of the Dells' Marvin Junior.

I don't think he put out any more records after this one and he died, aged only 43, of bone cancer in 1993.

Ebonee Webb

Michael Winston; Thomas Brown; Gregg Davis; Charles Liggins; Kenneth Ray Coleman; Roy Munn; Leon Thomas; Ronald Coleman;

Disco Otomisan 1978 Seven Seas GP 644 Producer: Motohiko Takawa (Japan)

Ebonee Webb 1979 Seven Seas GP 728 Producer: Motohiko Takawa (Japan)

Ebonee Webb 1981 Capitol ST-12148 Producers: Allen Jones & Anthony Taylor (Billboard soul charts: 21; Billboard pop charts: 157)

Too Hot 1983 Capitol ST-12250 Producers: Allen Jones & Anthony Taylor (Billboard soul charts: 45)

The background to this group is rather confusing. At first, there was a band called Ebony Web who recorded a handful of 45s for Hi records in the seventies. Most people would expect that Ebony Web simply became Ebonee Webb but it is not quite so simple. In fact, while a couple of members of Ebony Web, Winston and at least one of the Colemans, *did* indeed join Ebonee Webb, the majority of Ebony Web eventually became Kilo, another Memphis band.

To add to the saga: the band recorded two albums in Japan which are incredibly rare: certainly I have never seen them and only know of their existence due to my research. I believe they might have been recorded directly for the Japanese market and do not bear much resemblance to their other records.

Which sound quite a bit like what Prince was doing. Given Ebonee Webb were from Memphis and were produced by Allen Jones it would have been understandable if they aped the Bar-Kays but this was not really the case; they were a little smoother and less frenetic and Michael Winston's light tenor voice was radically different from Larry Dodson's snarls. The first Capitol set did rather well in the marketplace and provided three singles that hit the soul charts with the biggest being "Something About You" at #16. The album is aimed very squarely at the dance floor and was good of its kind. When they slowed things down as with "Woman" and "Do Me Right" they got a little soft and poppy, although "Stop Teasing Me" is sweet enough.

Too Hot was a bit harder edged than the previous album, and reduced the number of slow songs on offer to one, while Michael Winston had seemingly decided he now wanted to be known as Chico. "Are You Really Ready" and "Too Hot To Be Cool" (a small hit as a 45) were even closer to Prince than anything on the debut and that Minneapolis feel permeates the set, which is heavy on keyboards and synths and light on horns. Both Capitol albums are well worth owning if one is a funk fan, but those who like their southern soul to be of a more traditional bent need not bother to investigate.

Ebony Jam Band

Glenn Colbert; Melvin Jenkins; Dirke Tolson; Tony Newsom; Ernie Cooper; Dave Young; Cathalene Tolson

Ebony Jam Band 1981 Starbound STB-1001 Producer: The Ebony Jam Band

I believe The Ebony Jam Band were from Oakland, but they never managed to attain a fraction of the success that neighbours Tower Of Power enjoyed. The band comprised seven individuals and the little of the LP I have heard would suggest they had a reasonable line in funk.

Ebony Rhythm Funk Campaign

Pam Tanner; Anthony Roberts; John Jackson; Master Boobie Townsend; Lester Lamonte Johnson; Matthew Watson; Sean Hendrick; Henry Miles; Dwayne Garvin; Lloyd Thomas Jones; Michael Woods; George Dennie

Ebony Rhythm Funk Campaign 1973 Uni 73142 Producer: Wayne Henderson

Watchin' Me Watchin' You 1976 Chi-sound CH-LA657-G Producer: Carl Davis

Ebony Rhythm Funk Campaign only ever had one (minor) hit, "How's Your Wife", which was also by far their best ever record. Frustratingly, it does not appear on either of their albums. The band was from Chicago but the first set was recorded on the West Coast and, frankly, is immensely dull and sounds like a rather second-rate rock band with soulful pretensions. One to avoid.

Watchin' Me Watchin' You was cut in their home town and was much better although it was a funk set with little to set it aside from the rest of the myriad other groups who performed in a similar mode around the same time. Tony Roberts' vocals aped the Ohio Players/Sly Stone style then in vogue and the material was rather weak, apart from a worthy title track well delivered by Pam Tanner. There are instrumentals, slow songs and fast songs and it is enjoyable for anyone like me who grew up with this type of music but it really can't be recommended to anyone wishing to hear something out of the ordinary.

Ebonys

Jenny Holmes Johnson; Clarence Vaughan; David Beasley, James Tuten

Ebonys 1973 P.I.R. KZ 32419 Producers: Kenny Gamble, Leon Huff, Phil Terry, Talmadge Conway & T.Life (Billboard soul charts: 33)

Sing About Life 1976 Buddah BDS 5679 Producer: Tony Camillo

This excellent group from Camden, New Jersey put out two singles (on Avis and Soul Clock) to resounding indifference before being one of the first signings to the fledging Philadelphia International Records (P.I.R.) label. They only released two albums and disbanded shortly after the second one appeared.

The P.I.R. set is undeniably good, but is not perfect. This is firstly due to the fact that it contains a number of singles recorded over a period of time and "Sexy Ways" sounds from a different era when compared to, say, the sweet "I'll Try" and second, some of the tracks, "Nation Time" for instance, go on a little longer than necessary. Third, why wasn't "Determination", a reasonable hit for the group, included? But these are quibbles, the good stuff is essential: "It's Forever" (#14 soul) is a crushing ballad, the old warhorse "I Believe" suits them perfectly, and "You're The Reason Why" is one of the finest records ever to come out of Philadelphia, featuring a magnificent arrangement from Thom Bell on a wonderful Gamble-Huff song which had become the first ever hit on P.I.R. (#10 soul) when it was released as a single in 1971. They could also deliver uptempo songs and "I'm So Glad I'm Me" is punchy and addictive, but I just wish we could have been told who delivers which of the marvellous leads: the dark brown powerhouse (James Tuten?) and the soaring tenor.

The Buddah album almost sounded like a different group, not least because Holmes took a number of lead vocals, an honour not extended to her on the debut set, while the forceful male lead was much less prominent (although he delivers a fine version of the old Mann/ Weil song, "Nobody But You"). It's also a rather unusual set in as much as most albums tend to have the title track as the strongest or one of the strongest cuts. On here, it is just about the weakest. Ms. Holmes didn't always get the best material to work with, as evidenced by "Neighborhood Gossip", but "Waiting For The Last Goodbye" is gorgeous (and an identical version also appeared on a Creme D' Cocoa LP). Tony Camillo, as ever, provides us with some stirring arrangements and the set is worthwhile, but inexplicably does not include their only "hit" on Buddah, the charging "Making Love Ain't No Fun" (#83).

A couple of CDs under the name of the Ebonys came out in the last decade or so, but none of the original members remained.

Ecstasy, Passion & Pain

Barbara Roy; Althea Smith; Carl Jordan; Joseph Williams; Jimmy Clark; Ronald Foster

Ecstasy, Passion & Pain 1974 Roulette SR 3013 Producer: Bobby Martin (Billboard soul charts: 38)

A great Philly album. Ecstasy, Passion & Pain were unusual in featuring two ladies who also played instruments, Barbara Roy and Althea Smith, and it is the former's distinctive, if rather nasal, vocals which provided a focal point, and it helped that she wrote almost everything on here. Roy's real name was Barbara Gaskins and she had recorded a number of singles with her niece as Barbara and Brenda in the sixties.

Three cuts hit the soul top twenty: "I Wouldn't Give You Up", "Good Things Don't Last Forever" and "Ask Me" - all uptempo, peppy and memorable. But the group were just as impressive on slower material and "I'll Take The Blame", "Born To Lose You" and "Don't Burn Your Bridges Behind You" are deeply soulful, Roy declaiming in a manner more generally associated with Memphis or

Muscle Shoals rather than Philadelphia. Despite the fact that EP & P all played instruments - and Foster is the same Ronnie Foster who has released many jazz albums - it is clearly the usual P.I.R. session men who provide all the music on the album.

The group disbanded in 1977 after having posted a further three singles on the soul charts although they re-formed briefly in 1981. Roy continued in the business for a number of years but now only releases gospel CDs.

Edge Of Darkness

James Carrington; Robert Glover; Cornelius Cade; Harry Coleman; Jamal Jahal Nubi; Willie Williams; McArthur Duncan; Robert Cole; Larry Griffin;

Eyes Of Love 1979 Bohannon's 005074 No producer listed

Because Edge Of Daybreak consisted entirely of inmates from the Powhatan prison facility in State Farm, Virginia they were allotted five hours to record this LP. In the circumstances, they did a remarkable job. When played purely as an album rather than a curiosity, however, its obvious shortfalls become apparent.

As the musical accompaniment is competent rather than inspired, and the tiny budget would not run to employing strings and horns, the responsibility for providing aural enjoyment falls firmly onto the songs and the singing and it is the latter which most impresses. On the title track, "Let Us" and "Let's Be Friends" the harmonies are of a surprisingly high quality and it is hard to imagine that this was not the work of a seasoned professional outfit. These three melodic tracks bear repeated play; the other four do not, being uptempo workouts of limited appeal.

The LP was pressed up in a quantity of 1000 on a label which had nothing to do with the Detroit drummer, Hamilton Bohannon. It was never going to be any kind of hit but did draw some attention at the time of release.

Candye Edwards (see also One Way)

Candye 1982 MCA 5329 Producers: Irene Perkins, Kevin McCord, Al Hudson & Dave Roberson

Right Now 1986 Presents CA 100 Producer: Kevin McCord

Endless Nights 1988 Chance 1000TC Producer: Kevin McCord

The "house style" of ADK productions (Hudson, Roberson and McCord) was fairly distinctive in the early eighties: taut rhythms, the odd stab of horns and not much truck with frills like strings. It was also recognisably soul music of the time, with no concession to pop or post-disco dance indulgence and it suited Candye Edwards just fine. (Note: all three LPs were issued as by "Candye").

Edwards had worked with the trio before as all four of them were members of the group One Way and she continued to be produced by McCord until she stopped making records. (I also believe they got married.) The MCA album is a most acceptable platter from the difficult year of 1982 when great soul records were starting to become an endangered species. Edwards was an adroit singer with a good range and she receives lovely backing vocal support on "If You Want Me To Stay" (not the old Sly Stone song). Hudson also chips in with two duets and I enjoyed the record when it came out and I enjoy it now. There were no obvious hits or true stand-out tracks but it all adds up to a good offering by a rather underappreciated team from Detroit.

She had to wait three years before her next release which was a departure from the debut. Edwards had written none of the songs on her first set but wrote almost everything on *Right Now*, which was split into "dance" and "romance" sides, hardly a novel concept. It surely goes without saying which I prefer and her voice is impressive on "Where Did Our Love Go" and the title track.

By the time the *Endless Nights* LP arrived, things were getting rather tight financially and the small Chance label could not run to a proper cover. It was once again split into "dance" and "romance" sides but in fact the romantics easily won out as the first side included a ballad, "The Only One", and it would have taken some ingenuity to boogie along to "Let's Celebrate" thus leaving two tracks only as uninhibited calls to the floor. On the slower side "I Want You" and "Take Me Where You You're Going" are the best and both feature, I think, Kevin McCord, helping out on vocals.

Dee Edwards

Heavy Love 1979 Cotillion SD 5212 Producer: Floyd Jones

Too Hearts Are Better Than One 1980 Cotillion SD 5223 Producer: Michael Zager

Born Doris Jean Harrell in Alabama, Dee Edwards had recorded a number of good singles on numerous Detroit labels throughout the sixties and seventies without any of them ever hitting any national charts (although a handful did well locally) and she must therefore have been delighted when Cotillion took a chance on issuing a couple of albums for her. It's just a shame that they didn't really do her justice.

Heavy Love, which was produced by her husband, Floyd Jones, had a lacklustre and overly pop-influenced side one, which also carried onto the first track on side two, "Loving You Is All I Want To Do", which sounded not unlike the dreaded "Hustle" by Van McCoy. "Don't Sit Down" was boring disco (and a minor national soul hit at #78, her first ever) and "Stranger On The Shore" (the Acker Bilk record) is something I cannot take in any form. So it was a blessed relief to hear the final three tracks where Edwards' tremendous voice at last came to the fore. "I Wanna Be Your Woman" was a superb slow track, much more soulful than anything else on display and if "No Love, No World" was also a little "poppy" it could not restrain the exuberance of her voice. Lastly, there was the title song, a dance track above which she declaimed in emotional and satisfying style.

For the second set she was produced by Michael Zager who tended to allow her voice to sound too light and airy, as exemplified by the title track and "Baby, This Time". She had never been a "hard" soul singer but could do much better than this. And she did on "Don't Walk Away" and "Mr. Miracle Man" (another minor hit, #64 soul) but they were merely the best of an average bunch.

There were to be no more albums, but a handful more singles came out once she had left Cotillion. She died in 2006.

Dennis Edwards (see also The Contours and The Temptations)

Don't Look Any Further 1984 Gordy 6057GL Producer: Dennis Lambert (Billboard soul charts: 2; Billboard pop charts: 48)

Coolin' Out 1985 Gordy 6148GL Producer: Dennis Lambert (Billboard soul charts: 36; Billboard pop charts: 205)

Like so many other soul singers a native of Alabama, Dennis Edwards had cut one barely released solo single on a tiny Detroit label in the sixties as well as becoming a member of the Contours for a relatively brief spell before he got a huge break in 1968 when he was selected to replace David Ruffin in The Temptations. He stayed with the group for nine years, and his distinctive and fierce vocal attack can be heard on many of their greatest records, before leaving in 1977, re-joining in 1980 and leaving again in 1984.

This time, his solo career went notably well for a short while as he hooked up with the extremely successful pop producer Dennis Lambert and "Don't Look Any Further", on which he duetted with Siedah Garrett, hit #2 on the soul charts in early 1984. A record which owes a little to Lionel Richie's "All Night Long", it left me almost entirely cold, but I could at least understand why it became a hit. The album of the same name was highly disappointing even if a second single, "You're My Aphrodisiac", partly written by Sam Dees, also did well as a single, but Dees had done much better work. These were at least the two best tracks, the remainder - "I Thought I Could Handle It" apart, which was not bad - being either pop dance music or "Disney" ballads, miles below the quality of the work Edwards had performed with The Contours, let alone The Temptations.

Lambert also handled Edwards' second LP and, again, it was a record I couldn't get excited about. The producer had always infused a strong pop element into all his work with soul artists, and when he got it right - as in Tavares' "It Only Takes A Minute" - the results were entirely satisfying but by the eighties his work became more predictable and less soulful. Like the first LP, *Coolin' Out* was well sung, competent, cleanly produced, musically impeccable - and entirely unexciting. The title track reached #23 soul, after the first single from the set", "Amanda", rather deservedly failed to do much business.

There were to be no more LPs and it all got rather complicated after this. Edwards rejoined and left The Temptations yet again, released a few more records and CDs, and put together his own version of the famous group, which not surprisingly prompted a legal battle with Otis Williams who was still out there with his own Temptations ensemble. I will be much kinder to Edwards when I get to the section on the world famous group.

Gloria Edwards

Anything You Want 1977 Crazy Cajun CCLP-1071 Producer: Huey Meaux

It's a Crazy Cajun LP so the backing is hardly going to be luxurious but this is one of the labels' better efforts, with backing vocals and horns appearing on most of the ten tracks, half of which appeared as singles in the early seventies and I would guess that everything here was recorded in a period from about 1968 to 1973.

Edwards was born in Texas and has sung for decades but with precious little to show for it if one is judged by the quantity of releases or hit records. Her voice sounds more suited to the output of labels from the northern U.S. cities and there is thus quite an appealing tension between her singing and the obviously southern backing on the majority of these songs. "Real Love" could have been recorded in Detroit, while the excellent Vietnam-based story of "Something You Couldn't Write About" or "Blues Part 2" are much more down-home.

John Edwards (see also The Spinners)

John Edwards 1973 Aware AA 2005 Producer: Floyd Smith

Life, Love & Living 1976 Cotillion SD 9909 Producer: David Porter

This man was one of the most gifted of all soul singers. And who has heard of him? John Edwards was born in St. Louis and moved to Chicago where he recorded a handful of highly impressive singles in the late sixties and early seventies but none sold in any appreciable quantity.

His fortunes changed in 1973 when he was contracted to the Atlanta based Aware record label. For whatever reason, this time around everything clicked and he started to post singles on the national soul charts. It wasn't as if the records were any better, and it would be hard to get any better than his Weis single, "There Will Never Be Another Woman", but trying to gauge why some records sell and others fail is as often as not a fruitless exercise.

What is not in doubt is the quality of the songwriters who contributed the songs to the Aware album: Sam Dees, Frank Johnson, Jimmy Lewis, Bobby Womack, Bill Brandon, David Camon, Terry Woodford and Clayton Ivey. The astute reader may deduce from such a list that the record was in the "southern soul" style and indeed it was. "Spread The News" and "Messing Up A Good Thing" might have been smooth and urbane, but "Claim Jumping" and "Careful Man" were no nonsense numbers that mixed up a down-home ambience with Edwards' unreconstructed soul man screams. The latter, when released on a 45, became his biggest ever success, amazingly reaching #8 on the soul charts in the late fall of 1974. I say "amazingly" because it was a record that sounded out of place and out of time, and not even much of a song, just a cautionary chat really, that had much more of a sixties' vibe that anything else that was hitting in the mid-seventies. The main thing about Edwards though, is that he was a marvellous singer, and he really needed slow songs on which he could stretch out and mesmerise the listener and in "It's A Groove", "I'll Be Your Puppet" and "Exercise My Love" he found them. His range was extraordinary and not many soul singers would not have fancied following him on stage. In summary, there were nine cuts on *John Edwards* and all were good and it is one of the best LPs from the seventies.

Aware was owned by Michael Thevis, an unsavoury man who once made it to the FBI's ten most wanted list, so it was never a label destined for longevity and after Edwards posted one more small hit on the national soul charts in early 1975 ("Vanishing Love", not on the LP) he needed to find a new record label. That turned out to be Cotillion and the resultant LP was a little mixed but did feature some more lovely moments. It was produced by David Porter and split into a "meat side" and a "sweet side", the latter being by far the better as all four songs were excellent and this was as good a place as any to find unadulterated southern soul on album in 1976. "Nobody But You" and "Baby, Hold On To Me" were both charting singles, but at the fairly lowly levels of #85 and #59, and "You, Trouble And Me" and "(You've Got) My Mind Working Overtime" were equally as good. Side one was more problematic, particularly on "The Key To My Life" and "Sister Rose" where Edwards was forced (presumably) into an Al Green bag. There was no need for this as Edwards was an even better singer than Green, and it diluted and demeaned his own vocal talent. Nothing was actually bad on that first side, but it was the least impressive of the four he recorded across the two LPs.

Apart from a couple of Christmas songs Edwards recorded no more solo singles, but that didn't really matter as he became the latest in a long and honourable line of superb front men to join The Spinners (in 1977), with whom he stayed until illness meant he could no longer carry on in 2002. Sadly, he has not sung since which is why I have extolled his talent in the past tense.

Lee Edwards

Shades Of Love 1981 Seawind AR 6081 Producers: Robert Evans & Vera Jenkins

I'm assuming that Lee Edwards is the same chap who once recorded a 45 as Lee Edward & The Continentals (the voices certainly sound similar) but *Shades Of Love* didn't sell anywhere near enough copies for him to become famous and make such possible connections clear cut.

The LP originated from Detroit and includes a single - "I Found Love/ Equal Love Opportunity" - that was released to help support its sales, but that floundered too, and no more was heard of from Lee Edwards as a singer. I love the chutzpah of the annotation on the front cover - "includes the million seller, "Ingredients Of Love" - which even in an industry famous for outlandish and wholly inaccurate claims, is a pretty good one. Edwards sings nicely in a high tenor (although he could apparently adapt his voice at will) and it's a pleasant enough set to listen to, even if the musical backing suffers somewhat from a clearly low budget.

Edwards Generation

In San Francisco "The Street Thang" 1976 Tight TLPS 401 Producers: Chuck Edwards & Carolyn Barnett

Chuck, Irene, Ronald, Jeffrey, Myron, Leslie and Charlene Edwards (actually all Edwins, "Edwards" was a stage name) were a family unit apparently "world famous" for performing at Fisherman's Wharf in San Francisco in the seventies. It's another claim to be taken with a pinch of salt, but the album is a really good one, although tiny Tight Records was the family's own and they simply sold the LP when they were performing live, which is one reason why it is scarce and in demand today.

Chuck Edwards (the father) recorded some impressive solo singles throughout the sixties with "Downtown Soulville" and "I Need You" being two of the best, and he brought his skill, professionalism and experience to bear on the *Street Thang* LP. There were clearly limited funds available for recording and the sound is somewhat rudimentary but that matters not one whit in the face of "You're The One For Me" and "Starlite Starbrite", highly appealing ballads, sung with passion by Chuck. It's funk cuts such as "Smokin' Tidbits" that have led to a recent and belated appreciation of the album - sadly denied to Chuck Edwards who passed away in 2001 - and while I can see their appeal, the slow tracks are even better.

8th Day

Tony Newton; Steve Mancha; Carole Stallings; Anita Sherman; Melvin Davis; Michael Anthony; Bruce Nazarian; Lynn Harter; Jerry Paul; Lymon Woodard; Larry Hutchison; Tyrone Douglas; Virginia McDonald; Barrington Henderson; Denzil Broomfield

8th Day 1971 Invictus ST-7306 Producers: Eddie Holland, Lamont Dozier & Brian Holland (Billboard soul charts: 42; Billboard pop charts: 131)

I Gotta Get Home (Can't Let My Baby Get Lonely) 1973 Invictus ST-9809 Producers: Eddie Holland, Lamont Dozier, Brian Holland, Melvin Davis & Tony Newton

8th Day 1983 A & M SP-6-4942 Producers: Brian Holland & Harold Beatty

The history of The 8th Day is rather complicated and impossible to cover in the right level of detail here. Suffice it to say that when they enjoyed two big hits, "She's Not Just Another Woman" (#3 soul and /#11 pop) and "You've Got To Crawl (Before You Walk)" (#3 and /#28), both in 1971, there was not really any such outfit as the 8th Day. Clyde Wilson (aka Steve Mancha) sang on the former and Melvin Davis on the latter and these esteemed Detroit singers were effectively making solo records but Holland-Dozier-Holland wished to market a group, even if one didn't then exist. It wasn't until the second album that a handful of people were actively assembled to work under the chosen name.

The first album featured an ugly cover, reminiscent of The Dramatics' *A Dramatic Experience*, and this may simply have been a ploy to disguise the fact that there was no "8th Day" of whom a photograph could have been taken. The album was grand, however, if lacking in overall cohesion. "Crawl " has a vocal of tremendous power from Davis and is one of the best things ever to have come out of Invictus/Hot Wax. He also showed his vocal prowess on much slower material, such as "I'm Worried" and "Just As Long", whose long running times do not outstay their welcomes by one second. Proof that the album was rather cobbled together lay in tracks like "She's Not Just Another Woman" and "Too Many Cooks", both of which had appeared on an LP by another Invictus/Hot Wax group, 100 Proof Aged in Soul, a member of whom was...Clyde Wilson. Furthermore, contrast the nursery rhyme poppiness of "Eeny Meeny Miny Mo" with the soulful, heavily Sam Cooke influenced "La-De-Dah". They sounded worlds apart and it is for all these reasons why the album comes across as a collection of excellent cuts, rather than one with a plan.

The second album didn't have much in the way of continuity, either, but it certainly sounded different from the debut. It was looser, funkier and rockier, and not so obviously the work of a H-D-H act. It also didn't have any songs as strong as "Crawl" and "Shes Not Just Another Woman". "Cheba" was a jazzy instrumental workout, "Rocks In My Head" and "Get Your Mind Straight" featured guitar solos, and "Good Book" sounded a bit like a Sly and Family outtake circa 1968. There were no ballads on show and only the title track and "Faith" sounded as if they could have been on the first album. All in all, It is a fascinating hotchpotch and I enjoy it, but it was rather out of left field. There were no hits onboard (the debut set had included four) and the eight individuals who now comprised the group broke up soon after.

In 1983 the 8th Day were back, but in name only as the new group had nothing to do with the Invictus records. Now a quartet of talented singers - Barrington Henderson later sang with The Temptations, while Tyrone Douglas and Virginia McDonald had been with The Undisputed Truth - they nonetheless served up a woefully poor offering. It is for the most part entirely nondescript uptempo pop music in a "Footloose" style and I wouldn't wish it on anyone. If my thumbs were being screwed I might confess to being prepared to listen to "(He Put Me In) The Right Mood" one more time, but hope I could remain stoical about holding out and refusing to listen to the rest.

Eight Minutes

Ricky Goggins; Hank Goggins; Ronald Goggins; Hedda Sudduth; David Sudduth; Wendell Sudduth; Juwanna Glover; Carl Monroe

An American Family 1972 Perception PLP-27 Producer: James Porter

The LP cover of *An American Family* makes it clear that The Eight Minutes are a "kiddie" group, one of a number that appeared in the wake of the success of the Jackson 5. They came out of Chicago and the highest compliment I can pay the LP is that I can listen to it all the way through without wincing. I normally cannot abide music from sub-teens at all, regardless of how talented they may be, but at least The Eight Minutes were given some decent songs and arrangements from James Porter and Patrick Adams and one track, "Oh Yes I Do", does transcend the genre and is lovely. A number of the cuts can also be found on singles but nothing broke nationally and the Eight Minutes soon disbanded. (They also had one record which was well-known on the UK "Northern Soul" scene, "Looking For A Brand New Game", but it is not included on the LP.)

Donnie Elbert

The Sensational Donnie Elbert Sings 1959 King 629 No producer listed

Poor Donnie Elbert. His musical career was a bit of a shambles, his LP legacy a tawdry, cheap mess. What makes it even sadder is that he was genuinely talented and made my favourite record of the entire 1950s: the dazzling "What Can I Do".

Born in New Orleans, he moved to Buffalo at an early stage and cut some sides with a group called The Vibraharps before going solo and hitting big first time out with "What Can I Do" which went #61 pop in 1957. It is an extraordinary record, crystal clear in production with a lovely dirty sax solo above which Elbert's totally distinctive voice weaves magical patterns. Two years later his first LP was released and even if it appeared in the pre-soul days it included the single, another lovely side in "Have I Sinned" and an inevitable "What Can I Do" soundalike in "Tell Me So". The whole LP sounded ahead of its time and could easily have been recorded in the early sixties. (It was re-released, minus two tracks, as *Have I Sinned* on Deluxe 12003 in 1972.)

Tribute To A King 1968 Polydor 236 560 Producer: Donnie Elbert (UK)

He then recorded singles for a whole host of labels throughout the sixties without ever hitting the national charts again although he did have some success in England (with the much-loved "Little Piece Of Leather") and became known as a man who would happily cover the work - it sometimes seemed like the entire works - of other well known artists and /groups. For instance, his next outing at 33⅓ came in 1968 with the *Tribute To A King* set, that king being Otis Redding. The album didn't even come out in the USA and was, as with so many of his LPs, re-released: as *Introducing Donnie Elbert* (once again only in the UK) in 1972 on Contour 2870 162). It's surprisingly pretty good, with Elbert singing for the most part in his natural voice rather than the sky-high falsetto he is best known for and if you were listening to many of these tracks without knowing the identity of the singer you would be hard pushed to guess it was Elbert. The best track was probably "Good To Me", a song that no-one ever seems to mess up.

Where Did Our Love Go 1971 All Platinum AP-3007 Producer: Donnie Elbert (Billboard soul charts: 45; Billboard pop charts: 153)

Despite the quality of a number of his singles, the fact was nothing had really sold in quantity for over a decade but that was to finally change when he joined the All Platinum label, and he scored his first national hit for thirteen years when "Can't Get Over Losing You" made it to #26 soul in early 1971. It was a most appealing song (despite its overcooked string arrangement) and deserved its success. An album followed in its wake, which was named after the biggest record of his career by far, a cover of The Supremes' "Where Did Our Love Go" (#6 soul and #15 pop). It was a thin sounding effort and its success was bit baffling but he had clearly paid his dues and the album also included further hits in "Sweet Baby", which sounded like another Detroit recording circa 1964, and the much better "If I Can't Have You", both reaching #30 soul.

In between these last two hits he had also scored in a pretty big way (#14 soul and #22 pop) with another Motown remake: The Four Tops "I Can't Help Myself", an old recording put out by Avco to capitalise on his success. Cue yet another Elbert re-issued LP: *Donnie Elbert Sings* on Trip 9514, which consisted of the entire *Where Did Our Love Go* set plus the Four Tops song.

The Real Me 1973 Ala 1973 Producers: John Cevetello & Donnie Elbert

Stop In The Name Of Love 1972 Trip 9524 Producer: Donnie Elbert

Ala were the next label to try and trade on the Elbert bandwagon and this LP consisted of the singles he put out on the Gateway label in 1964 and 1965. There was nothing wrong with the music and it was nice to have these tracks on LP for the first time but they cut no mustard at all in 1973. It also came out in the UK the same year entitled, more accurately, *The Roots of Donnie Elbert,* on Ember EMB 3421. (And came out yet again on an LP entitled *A Little Piece Of Leather* on the Klik label, KLP 9012).

Trip also put out the rather excruciating *Stop In The Name Of Love*, Elbert's covers of eight massive Motown hits, all of which were better performed by the original performers. DJM put out the same set (with one extra track) in the UK in 1975 (DJSLM 2014) and it is hard to say which version has the cheapest looking cover.

Dancin' The Night Away 1977 All Platinum AP-3019 Producer: Donnie Elbert

Somehow, despite all the re-issues, All Platinum had managed to keep Elbert's career going and he had three further singles hit the soul charts between 1974 and 1977 before the label decided to give him a new LP release. It was not memorable, being yet another collection of covers, this time of other songs that were then current such as "You Should Be Dancing", "Don't Leave Me This Way" and "Free". Once again, his versions were inferior and it was sad to see him reduced to such a release. Predictably, the LP was re-released as *From The Gitgo* on Sugar Hill SH-256 in 1980.

There were to be no more hits and - finally - no more LPs. For a man who had released countless singles, placing nine of them on the soul charts, his LP haul only really amounts to six different records over a twenty year period. He died in 1989.

Electric Indian

Keem - O - Sabe 1969 United Artists UAS 6728 Producer: Len Barry (Billboard soul charts: 46; Billboard pop charts: 104)

If you have an all-consuming interest in the birth of Gamble and Huff's take on Philadelphia soul music, you might want this one as Electric Indian (a studio band) contained many of the musicians who went on to form MFSB and play on so many of the huge hits on P.I.R. On the other hand, this is highly bland instrumental music, with a tenuous link with soul, and I urge great caution for anyone who may be curious but hasn't heard it.

Elgins

Saundra Edwards; Johnny Dawson; Cleotha Miller; Norbert McClean; Jimmy Charles; Yvonne Vernee Allen

Darling Baby 1966 V.I.P. 400 Producers: Brian Holland & Lamont Dozier

Take The Train 1990 Motor City MOTCLP 39 Producers: Ian Levine & Rick Gianatos

Johnny Dawson and Cleotha Miller had been members of an obscure Motown group, The Downbeats, and when they were joined by Edwards (who had also cut for Motown under the name of Sandra Mallett) and McClean the Elgins were born. They didn't last long, releasing just this one album (on which another former singer within the Downbeats, Robert Fleming, was credited but he did not sing with The Elgins) and four singles.

The album is in some ways the epitome of the LP where successful singles are surrounded by "filler", in this case five thoroughly well-known songs that had been big hits for others such as "The Midnight Hour" and "When A Man Loves A Woman". None of The Elgins versions are worth much, other than they give the male members of the group the opportunity to take some leads, and so the strength of the LP must rely totally on the 45s. Luckily, "Darling Baby"(#4 soul) ,"Put Yourself In My Place", "Heaven Must Have Sent You" (# 9) and "It's Been A Long Long Time" (#35) are all excellent, showcasing Edward's light but charming vocals. Unusually, the LP was produced by only two thirds of the HDH team, with Eddie Holland not involved.

The Elgins re-appeared in 1990 with original members Dawson and McClean and two newcomers to the group in Jimmy Charles and Yvonne Allen as part of Ian Levine's huge Motor City project.

Eliminators

Jonathan Robinson; Calvin Rhodes; Robert Burris; James Funches; Carl Johnson; Levon Meyers; Clifford Little; Godosakahi Jordon; Nathaniel Williams; Donald Clark; James Anderson

Loving Explosion 1974 BRC 77001 Producer: Alonzo Tucker

Despite this album coming out on a Brunswick subsidiary, BRC, and despite its production by Alfonzo Tucker, a man with longstanding Chicago associations, The Eliminators hailed from Winston-Salem, North Carolina, rather than the Windy City. As with so many similar albums it got rather lost and neither it nor any singles from it attained any national chart action. But I like it a lot.

Back in the pre disco-excess days of 1975 there were many albums that employed a variety of styles and demonstrated some originality; thus it isn't clear from the first five seconds of many of the cuts on *Loving Explosion* exactly how they would unfold over the next few minutes. Exhibit #1 would be a cover of a fairly forgotten David Ruffin track, "Blood Donors Needed". It's not the best cut on the LP but at least they didn't go for something banal. The title track is excellent, a record that is danceable and instantly memorable after only one listen with a fiery lead vocal by either Levon Meyers or Donald Clark, and they could also do mellow convincingly as "Taking Love And Making Love" soaringly proves. But more than anything else it is a funky set and the crucial men producing such a satisfyingly tight mesh on the tremendous "Get Satisfied" and "Give It Up" are bassist Williams, rhythm guitarist Burris and drummer Johnson. They came and went with this one LP but I'm glad they did.

Shirley Ellis

In Action 1964 Congress CGL-3002 Producer: Hutch Davie

The Name Game 1964 Congress CGL-3003 Producers: Hutch Davie & Charles Calello

Soul Time With Shirley Ellis 1967 Columbia CS 9479 Producer: Charles Calello

No one ever has or ever will make any claims for Shirley Ellis (birth name: Shirley Marie O'Garra, not a surname that will pop up in the book very often) to be a great soul singer given that two of her biggest hits, "The Name Game" (#3 pop), and "The Clapping Song" (#8), are mildly enjoyable pop soufflés but the third, "The Nitty Gritty" (#8), was just that bit tougher and hinted that there might to more to her music that initially met the eye.

Her first two albums on Congress were more or less the same, with the second one adding three songs that didn't exist on the debut at the expense of three that did. The albums are mainly composed of well-known songs, "Bring It On Home To Me", "C.C. Rider", and "Stagger Lee" are examples, but she was a fair writer too and "Shy Guy" is an appealing ballad that stands out on what are pretty decent records, anyway.

Her final LP was noticeably different as it dispensed with cover versions and novelties (for the most part: "Birds, Bees, Cupid and Bows" was pretty excruciating) in favour of a more contemporary soul style and "Soul Time" (#31 soul) and "Sugar, Let's Shing-A-Ling" were atmospheric and exciting uptown calls to dance. Barbara Mason's "Yes I'm Ready" also got a splendid interpretation, one which proves that Ellis could do yearning perfectly well, while "Truly Truly Truly" is unrecognisable as being from the same singer who sang "Ever See A Diver Kiss His Wife While The Bubbles Bounce About Above The Water?" She died in 2005.

Lorraine Ellison

Heart Of Soul 1966 Warner Brothers WS 1674 Producer: Jerry Ragovoy

Stay With Me 1969 Warner Brothers WS 1821 Producer: Jerry Ragovoy

Lorraine Ellison 1974 Warner Brothers BS 2780 Producer: Ted Templeman

Best Of 1976 Warner Brothers K56230 (UK)

Ellison was born in Philadelphia and first started singing gospel with her sisters in the Ellison Singers. Her first secular records were on the Mercury label, with whom she had her first chart success in late 1965 with "I Dig You Baby" (#22 soul). But any discussion about her quickly turns to "Stay With Me", the record with which she has always been and will continue to be associated. It was a pretty big single in 1966, #11 soul & #64 pop, and has often been cited as the perfect example of a "deep soul" record, a view which has often divided soul fans, some of whom consider it to be "overrated". Personally, I think it is a magnificent side, one where her sometimes overwrought vocals make perfect sense.

The album on which it could originally be found, *Heart And Soul*, was a huge disappointment though, placing Ellison in a jazz setting in a manner which gave the strong impression that the label didn't know what to do with her. My earlier comment about "overwrought vocals" applies to tracks such as her version of "A Change Is Gonna Come" where employing Sam Cooke's dignity and restraint would have served her better.

Although "Stay With Me" had been a reasonable hit, it had also become a cult record. On the strength of that acclaim Warners were moved to put out a new album on Ellison, titled after the hit, but the problem was that it wasn't really new at all. More a collection of sides she had cut over the previous two and a half years. This is not to denigrate the quality of *Stay With Me*, the album, as it is a wondrous example of late sixties uptown soul which is a showcase of sheer talent, with exquisite arrangements from Ragovoy, Bert De Coteaux and Garry Sherman. In such a setting, "Stay With Me" was surrounded by performances cut from the same cloth, and it faced steep competition in being the best cut on show from "Heart Be Still", "You Don't Know What Love Is", "I Want To Be Loved" and "No Matter How It All Turns Out", which features irresistible drumming. This cut, like five others on the album, had already come out as a single by the time the LP appeared, and in a country with an insatiable appetite for the newest sounds, and on a label like Warners, which persisted in being a bit mystified by soul music for a few more years to come, it fizzled our rather to everyone involved's intense disappointment. It seems that "Stay With Me" could never get off the ground in the way it deserved to.

She seemingly went to ground for a number of years before returning in 1974 with an LP that sounded almost totally out of step with what was happening in the soul world at that time. It is a remarkably austere recording with a strong emphasis on Mark Jordan's keyboards and brooding string arrangements and its horn-free singularity meant it had no chance whatsoever of making any noise in the marketplace. No matter. It was a superb LP and still sounds lovely today.

A *Best Of* album appeared in the UK in 1976, which included two tracks, "You've Really Got A Hold On Me" and "He Ain't Heavy, He's My Brother", which were neither fantastic nor available on her other LPs.

Lorraine Ellison's talent and commitment are not in dispute and she made some marvellous music but in the final analysis she could be seen as perhaps an acquired taste, sharing some of the same attributes of Linda Jones, another singer whose all-out emotionalism can alienate some. She died as so often, too early, at only 51 in 1983.

Elusion

Limon Wilson; Derrill Jackson; Joe Williams

All Toys Break 1981 Cotillion SD 16040 Producer: Michael Zager

Show And Tell 1982 Cotillion SD 5235 Producer: Michael Zager

There isn't much to say about this group: they apparently came from Ohio, made a single as The Elusions, shortened their name, released two LPs, and then were never heard of again.

The first LP started off as if it could be something special. The title track is a lovely ballad, beautifully sung, and scraped into the soul charts at #84 when released as a single, and the second cut, "Didn't You Know (I Didn't Mean It)", displays class, but then it all went rather downhill. "Living On The Verge Of Leaving" and "I've Never Been In Love Before" are clean-cut dance tracks that do not offend, but "When The Bell Rings" and a version of Sly's "I Want To Take You Higher" certainly do. A dull ballad, "Lord", rounded out the album.

On the first LP Wilson was "Lyman" and Jackson was "Daryll" so Cotillion had a slight issue in the quality control department, and that concern filtered through to a lot the music on *Show And Tell*, which entitled the group as 'Elusion Featuring Limon Wilson'. As ever, I preferred the slower material but there was precious little of it, apart from the good "Now That I've Made It With You" and the so-so version of "Love Hurts". The title track was a jerky rather disappointing take on the old Al Wilson hit, and I defy anyone to make songs with titles like "Computer Lover" and "Lady Of The Night" worth listening to.

Emotions

Sheila Hutchinson; Wanda Hutchinson; Jeanette Hutchinson; Pam Hutchinson; Theresa Davis

So I Can Love You 1969 Volt VOS-6008 Producers: Isaac Hayes & David Porter (Billboard soul charts: 43)

Untouched 1971 Volt VOS-6015 Producers: David Porter & Ronnie Williams

Sunshine 1977 Stax STX-4100 (Billboard soul charts: 39; Billboard pop charts: 88)

Heart Association 1979 Stax STX 3008 (UK)

Chronicle 1979 Stax STX-4121

Stax had lots of things by 1969. What they didn't have was a big selling female vocal group; this opportunity was perfectly exploited by The Emotions who went on to place 12 singles on the soul charts for the company between 1969 and 1974. Originally known as the Hutchinson Sunbeams when they were singing gospel at an early age in Chicago, they became The Emotions and made fine local singles like "Somebody New" for the Twin Stacks label, sides which demonstrated that their sound was already more or less set: breathy lead vocals from Sheila with piercing and soulful back-up from her sisters. As good as those early records could be, they weren't blessed with a Hayes and a Porter and the Stax/Volt musicians to take the group to another level altogether.

They hit first time out on Volt, with "So I Can Love You" reaching #3 soul and #39 pop in 1969. It remains a marvellous disc, written and delivered by the precocious Sheila at barely 15 years of age, with an unusual and totally compelling arrangement, which allowed wisps of sound to fade in and out. An album followed, and became a reasonable success. "The Best Part Of A Love Affair" was another good single (#27 soul) from the LP, which was short on filler and long on quality. The disarming lyrical simplicity of "I Like It" belied its sophisticated arrangement, while "Somebody Wants What I Got" and "Got To Be The Man" unleashed the deeper and more soulful Wanda on the world.

For some reason, and despite placing another three singles on the soul charts in the meantime, Volt waited until 1971 to release the next Emotions LP, *Untouched,* which was neither as good as nor did as well as their first LP. Apart from the superb "Show Me How", a genuinely touching and heartfelt plea from a young girl to an older man on how to make love, and its mesmerising arrangement and great testifying from Sheila, there were no real stand-outs this time around. "Show Me How" became a big single (#13 soul, #52 pop) for the group, and performed considerably better than the lead-off 45 from the set, "If You Think It (You May As Well Do It)" which didn't even reach the charts. One reason for my lack of all-out enthusiasm for the LP was that it seemed to be aimed at a younger audience, a ploy which saw Wanda's lead vocal duties kept to a minimum. Jeanette had left the group by the time of the LP, being replaced by a cousin, Theresa Davis.

It seems that Volt were on the verge of issuing a third LP, *Songs Of Innocence And Experience*, (not the old William Blake smash hit), but for some reason it did not materialise so the group had to content themselves with the fact that they did post six more singles on the soul charts before Stax imploded. After the group's successes on Columbia the revised Stax label put out the *Sunshine* set which not only contained the admirable "Shouting Out Love", (which charted in early 1978) but three of those last six hits and some unissued material as well, but it was a little parsimonious at only nine tracks. The UK compilation, *Heart Association*, was much more generous at sixteen tracks, while the *Chronicle* set weighed in at fourteen.

Flowers 1976 Columbia PC 34163 Producers: Maurice White & Charles Stepney (Billboard soul charts: 5; Billboard pop charts: 45)

Rejoice 1977 Columbia PC 34762 Producers: Maurice White & Clarence McDonald (Billboard soul charts: 1; Billboard pop charts: 7)

Sunbeam 1978 Columbia JC 35385 Producer: Maurice White (Billboard soul charts: 12; Billboard pop charts: 40)

Come Into Our World 1979 Columbia JC 36149 Producer: Maurice White (Billboard soul charts: 35; Billboard pop charts: 96)

New Affair 1981 Arc / Columbia JC 37456 Producers: Billy Meyers, Wayne Vaughn, Wanda Hutchinson & Maurice White (Billboard soul charts: 46; Billboard pop charts: 168)

A number of artists who had to find a new label once Stax collapsed did ok for themselves in the aftermath. Johnnie Taylor, The Dramatics, The Staples and Isaac Hayes all had big hits in the immediate post-Stax years but they had all experienced huge selling records in the past. For The Emotions, though, success now arrived at a level that was entirely new, and mainly due to hooking up with Maurice White from Earth, Wind & Fire.

White brought his production skills, not to mention his group, to the assistance of his fellow Chicagoans for four LPs and the first two were generally sumptuous, sparkling affairs, with that almost palpable confidence that EWAF exuded at the time. If *Flowers* was the appetiser, *Rejoice* was the main course, as it housed "Best Of My Love", a record of widespread fame, and one which went to #1 soul and pop as a single, attaining gold status in the process. I won't dwell too much on the two sets as they are somewhat of a highly polished piece, other than to make a few observations. 1) Columbia messed up in releasing "I Don't Want To Lose Your Love" and the fabulous title track as a and b-sides of the same single as they were the two strongest cuts on *Flowers* 2) "How'd I Know That Love Would Slip Away"(also cut by Deniece Williams) from *Rejoice* had a fearsome groove 3) "Don't Ask My Neighbours" (another big hit: #7 /#44 and also from *Rejoice*) was gorgeous.

Sunbeam, the third album under the wing of White is much less known than the previous two LPs which is in the right order of things as it is inferior. The Emotions' music was starting to sound a bit too predictable by this time, and although the unremarkable "Smile" did well as a single (#6 soul), two further singles "Walking The Line" and "Whole Lot Of Shakin'" fared more modestly. Furthermore, cuts like "Time Is Passing By" and "Love Vibes" sounded rather like everyone was going through the motions.

Nevertheless, the group were to enjoy further massive success when "Boogie Wonderland" reached the top ten on both soul and pop charts in the summer of 1979 although as it was billed as "Earth Wind & Fire with The Emotions" rather than the other way around, it did not feature on any of their albums. *Come Into Our World* was the final LP produced by White and the Emotions' large audience was by now slipping through their fingers: the album fared less well than the previous three and the lead-off single, "What's The Name Of Your Love?" (a rare outing from Wanda, I believe) could get no higher than #30 soul, although this was still at a higher position than all their subsequent singles. The album, like *Sunbeam*, is not bad, just rather dull and predictable.

The last album in the group's ARC/Columbia career had new producers in Billy Meyers, Wayne Vaughn and Wanda although as White was still listed as co-producer and produced one track a continuity of sound remained. So much so, in fact, that it was no better or worse than the previous two sets and if you like one you'd like them all or, alternatively, would be indifferent to all three. For my part I must confess to no particular anticipation when *New Affair* came out in 1983. It spawned two modestly selling singles with one, "Turn It Out", sporting a - mercifully - brief rap.

Sincerely 1984 Red Label RLLP-001-1 Producers: Wanda Vaughn, Wayne Vaughn, Benjamin Wright, Billy Osborne, Attala Zane Giles & Lee Young; (Billboard soul charts: 33; Billboard pop charts: 206)

If I Only Knew 1985 Motown 6136ML Producers: W W Productions, David Cochrane, Benjamin Wright, Billy Osborne, Atala Zane Giles & Lee Young (Billboard soul charts: 54; Billboard pop charts: 203)

The Emotions resided at Red Label for one LP, which sported a remarkably boring cover photo of a melting cake in the shape of a heart, but it did at least bear three singles that climbed into the lower reaches of the soul charts, although my favourite track was "You Know I'm The One", sultry and pitched at a slower tempo than the relentless diet of mid-tempo songs that they fed on while at Columbia. For 1984, there was also the good news of a real drummer battling it out with programming to end in a 50/50 draw.

The Emotions' last album saw them move again, making them

one of the select few who recorded at both Stax and Motown. They looked great on the front cover, a reminder that they were still young women, despite having been recording for nearly twenty years. The title track and "Eternally" were good enough, but like so many tracks in the mid eighties and beyond, could have done with being half the length, while the lead-off cut, "Supernatural" was a poor pop record. It took five people to write this? Best of all, though, was "The Good Times" and overall all concerned were to be congratulated on bucking some trends and refusing to release an album which overdosed on frenzied dance material. It remains my favourite album of theirs since *Rejoice*.

There were to be no more Emotions' vinyl records after this although Sheila did put out a solo record in 1990, but the group are still active in 2016 and remain much loved.

Enchantment

Emanuel Johnson; David Banks; Joe Thomas; Ed Clanton; Carl Cotton; Bobby Green

Enchantment 1976 UA LA682-G Producer: Michael Stokes (Billboard soul charts: 11; Billboard pop charts: 104)

Once Upon A Dream 1977 Roadshow / UA RS-LA811 Producer: Michael Stokes (Billboard soul charts: 8; Billboard pop charts: 46)

Journey To The Land Of 1979 Roadshow BXL1-3269 Producer: Michael Stokes (Billboard soul charts: 25; Billboard pop charts: 145)

Enchantment were a five man vocal team out of Detroit. They placed ten singles on the soul charts over an eight year period and were proof that from the mid-seventies onwards the Motor City could still produce good and successful records even if you did not record for Motown or were not called The Dramatics. Their main assets were a fine lead singer, Emanuel Johnson, a skilled producer in Michael Stokes and the arranging of Johnny Allen.

Their first single came out on Polydor in 1975 (and was also featured on the soundtrack of an obscure film, *Deliver Us From Evil*, in 1977) but it was "Come On And Ride" on the small Desert Moon label that first took them onto the soul charts in 1976 (#67). The track found its way onto their first LP, the cover of which suffered from an uninspired drawing of a frog, hardly conducive to communicating with prospective buyers about what the content of the music inside would be. In fact it was two things: rather uninspired uptempo dance tracks (of which "Come On And Ride" was one) and vastly superior ballads. The best of these was entitled "Gloria", a song title that has been used on many occasions down the years, but this was an original composition by Stokes and Johnson and it did exceptionally well when put out on 45: #5 soul and #25 pop in early 1977. A second fine ballad, "Sunshine", did good business as well, reaching #3 and #45 and these two tracks together with "My Rose" and "Thank You Girl For Loving Me" completely overshadowed the other four.

Their biggest success was to arrive in 1978 though, when "It's You That I Need" reached #1 soul and #33 pop. It is their best record, precisely constructed and arranged, and the longer version was the showpiece of the group's second album. As with the debut set the dance tracks were devoid of any long-term interest and leaned more towards pop than disco or funk, which was somewhat unusual for the times. "Silly Love Song" was another exquisite slow workout but it was the speedier "If You're Ready (Here It Comes)" which became the second soul hit (#14) from the LP and was presumably an attempt to make sure the group were not pigeon-holed merely as purveyors of top class balladry.

Journey To The Land Of Enchantment was a slightly disappointing record: the ballads were not quite as strong as in the past and the uptempo cuts had not got any better. That being said, side two boasted three downtempo tracks which made the album bearable: "Let Me Entertain You", "Forever More" and "Where Do We Go From Here" which reached #29 soul on single.

Soft Lights, Sweet Music 1980 RCA AFL1-3824 Producer: Don Davis (Billboard soul charts: 65; Billboard pop charts: 202)

Enchanted Lady 1982 Columbia FC 38024 Producers: William Anderson & Raymond Reid

Utopia 1983 Columbia FC 38959 Producer: Michael Stokes

Enchantment moved on to RCA for *Soft Lights, Sweet Music*, produced by Don Davis, and it was possibly their most consistent offering to date. It might not have had the highs of "Gloria" or "It's You That I Need" but apart from "Setting It Out", an unpleasant dance thing, it didn't have any lows, either. Davis had improved the uptempo cuts, making them more punchy, and if there were no absolutely top-class ballads this time around there was a superb mid-tempo song, "I Can't Fake It", to compensate. The album didn't sell particularly well though, and only served up one charting single, the tender and underrated "Moment Of Weakness", but only at #47.

Their last label was Columbia, and the first album was overseen by William Anderson and Raymond Reid from Crown Heights Affair. Tracks like "I Know Your Hotspot", "Only You" and "Toe Jammin'" bore the CHA imprint and were hardly prime Enchantment although the latter song was better than the title might suggest. As ever, the ballads were what distinguished the group and "Enchanted Lady", "Adora" and "I Can't Forget You", although all probably longer than they needed to be, kept fans happy enough.

Somewhat surprisingly, Michael Stokes returned to produce and arrange the last album the group ever made. It was a thoroughly contemporary sounding record, thick of sound, and highly uneven. It would have been unreasonable to expect an LP full of ballads in 1983 and if the dance cuts had all been as invigorating as "Give It Up" I wouldn't have had too much cause for complaint but tracks like "Come Be My Lover", "Get It While It's Hot" and "Here's Your Chance" were completely faceless and clichéd. The really good things from the set were Johnson's "I'm Dreaming", a Sam Dees and Ron Kersey song, "Love Struck" and, best of all, "Don't Fight The Feeling", which also became the last ever charting single for Enchantment at #64 soul.

If ever a group needed a 'Best Of' LP, it was Enchantment but we would have to wait for the CD age for such a thing to appear. None of their six LPs were wholly satisfying, and none were bad, but if one vinyl LP could have scooped up their best twelve slow cuts it would have been magnificent.

Energetics

Melvin Franklin; Roscoe Mills; Joey Lites; Herbert Jackson; John Border

Come Down To Earth 1979 Atlantic SD 19224 Producer: Brian Holland

The Energetics came out of Boston. They were well named as virtually the whole of this LP features careering disco tracks of great speed and little subtlety. In fact, there are only three things that redeem it: the compelling and insistent guitar line on "Beat The Heat", the good EWAF influenced track, "You're My Guiding Light", and the one ballad on view, "Let's Say Goodbye To Goodbye". The album didn't do a great deal and the title track could only muster the derisory heights of #98 on the soul charts as a single. (By the way, this is a different Melvin Franklin from the one in The Temptations and he two of the others went on to form Planel Patrol, the hip-hop band.)

Barbara Jean English

So Many Ways 1972 Alithia AR-9102 Producer: Lou Toby

Barbara Jean English 1973 Alithia AR-9105 Producer: George Kerr

Experience 1989 Blue Chip BJLP1 Producer: Kevin Roberts (UK)

Barbara Jean English was born in South Carolina and eventually moved to New York where she performed in a handful of groups in the early sixties, the most notable of which were The Clickettes and The Fashions, before going the solo route. None of her singles in the sixties made much noise, so it was good, if surprising, to see that she got a chance to record two albums in the early seventies.(Her first singles came out as by Barbara English and she added the "Jean " later.)

The first one, *So Many Ways*, is a distinctly pop-oriented record and not one I care for a great deal. "I'm Living A Lie" had a number of spins on the UK "Northern Soul" scene, but thousands of better records have graced that particular genre while "Lil' Baby" sounded as if it could have been sung by Mary Hopkin. "All This" and "I'm Sorry" were ok but there was not an outstanding track on the entire album.

Much better was the slow and soulful "You're Gonna Need Somebody To Love" which was the only single she ever placed on the soul charts, at #65 in the autumn of 1973. It was also the lead-off cut for the much improved second album, which benefitted from the arrangements of Bert Keyes, the production of George Kerr and some very nice back-up vocalising but was once again hardly a "hard soul" affair, and one track, "Guess Who", was about a stray cat. Also onboard were breathy versions of "Key In The Mailbox" and "Breakin' Up A Happy Home", both songs performed by others, but ones for which I have a good deal of affection. The album was also released in the UK, and I imagine sales must have been almost non-existent.

Once Alithia went bust she recorded a few more singles in the late seventies, none of which sold well. She did return to release one more album, in the UK, in 1989 which seems to have come and gone without much acclaim at all. I have only heard the title track - a dance thing - and I'm afraid it didn't make me want to hear more.

Eon

Raymond Orta; Daniel Anderson; Jay Borrero; Robert Remming

Eon 1975 Scepter SPS 5122 Producers: Haig Palanjian & Fred Frank

Eon 1978 Ariola SW-50038 Producer: Allen Richfeild

What an odd group Eon were. I used to see their debut album in second-hand shops in England all the time in the seventies but ignored it as the front cover gave the strong impression that it was a heavy rock LP. It is certainly not that, but it has an unmistakeably pop influence with a big production approach and is unquestionably different from the "average" soul LP from 1975. Given that many of the songs come from Mark Barkan, a man who wrote for the Archies and The Monkees, this should not be surprising and the best way to describe the majority of the tracks on the set is that they have "pop" verses and "soul" choruses. So just when you have been twitching uncomfortably at the start of the song, and wondering what is going on, in comes a section of sweeping soul purity, delivered by true soul men. They could certainly sing. The one track that is excellent throughout, though, is "We'll Go On" a seven minute dance workout of uncommon quality. There are also a couple of things that simply don't work in any way at all, like "Sing A Happy Song", but we can skip over those.

The second album, also cunningly called *Eon*, was more varied and less intriguing. Five of the eight songs were written by Michael Burton from Brother To Brother, and this means that his work was more recognisably "soulful" than the offerings of Barkan, and he even managed to get them onto the soul singles charts with "Biggest Joke In Town", one of the best tracks, which reached #72 in 1978. On the other hand the album contains the two worst cuts by the group: a heavy handed and unlistenable version of America's "Horse With No Name" (they couldn't shake their pop tendencies) and "The Force" a *Star Wars* derived thing of no merit, which is a real renegade: they cut nothing else like it.

That was it. There were no more recordings so far as I know and they left few traces. I've never seen a single word written about them. They could have done with a top-class ballad or two to really raise the bar but I would commend the first LP to anyone who wants to hear something that doesn't sound obviously like anyone else.

Eramus Hall

Marvin Williams; Michael Gatheright; Joe Anderson; Bernard Provost; William Tillery; James Wilkerson; Grady Smith

Your Love Is My Desire 1980 Westbound WB-5000 Producers: Rudy Robinson & Joel Martin

Gohead 1984 Capitol ST-12376 Producers: George Clinton & Joel Martin

An odd name for a group: firstly, Eramus Hall is (or was) an old building in Chicago and the cover of the debut album suggests it was a solo singer at work. In fact, Eramus Hall were a funk congregation from Detroit.

The first album has "cult status" as it seems as if not many copies were pressed up and it has always commanded a high price. The title track is somewhat redolent of Earth, Wind & Fire and deserves its cult status while "Just Me And You" is a good cover of an old J.R. Bailey song, sounding much earlier than a 1980 release, however. "She Shined A Light" and "Will You Love Me Tomorrow (As You Do Today)" are two further tracks of smooth and sensual intent, but the remaining seven tracks are run of the mill funk outings and certainly the overall LP has never thrilled me enough to want to pay out the reasonable sum of money required to have it nestled away in my collection.

Gohead was co-produced by George Clinton and sounds totally different from the debut set. Many traditional soul fans will abhor the whole thing but the rhythm of "I Can't Keep My Head" is impressive stuff with an inspired bass synth line; this was as good as P-Funk got in the eighties, as well as being the right choice as a lead-off single even if it only crawled to #83 on the soul charts, the only time the group ever posted a disc on a national listing. There are a couple of the same songs across the two sets, but in both cases they are re-recordings. In fact, there is little need to go on: if you love Clinton/P.Funk you will either have this or definitely want it.

Dee Ervin (see also Dave Williams)

Swinging On A Star (and Little Eva) 1964 Golden Guinea GSGL 10497 Producer: Gerry Goffin (UK)

Sings D. Ervin 1972 Signpost SG 4256 Producers: Eric Malamud & Peter Tevis (UK)

Big Dee Irwin's "Swinging On A Star" is one of those songs that everyone seems to instinctively know but was hardly his most soulful moment; indeed it didn't even hit the soul charts, and despite the fact that he recorded some fine singles for many different labels over the years the one and only time he placed a record on the soul listings was under his real Christian name, "Difosco", in 1976 with the unremarkable "Face to face" on the Roxbury label. He had also, back in the fifties, been the lead singer of the acclaimed group, The Pastels, but none of his background had prepared anyone for the truly weird one and only album ever put out on him (apart from the *Swinging On A Star* set with Little Eva, which need not detain us here given it has nothing to do with soul music).

It wasn't weird because it was musically poor or odd, just that it only came out in the UK on the almost completely unknown Signpost label with a truly dreadful cover, under a name, Dee Ervin, that had no widespread recognition at all. I shudder to think how few copies it would have sold and it took me nearly forty years to track one down. I can only presume that the LP's *raison d'etre* was to shop around Ervin's songs given that he wrote everything on it. He was arguably a better writer than singer and "Seems Like I Gotta Do Wrong" had already been a big hit for The Whispers, while Ripple would take "Willie Pass The Water" into the soul top thirty in early 1974. On the other hand the absurdly obscure Richie's Room 222 Gang had not been able to turn "I'd Rather Stay A Child" into any kind of a hit and even Sam and Dave failed with "One Part, Two Part". Musically, the LP comes across as not very "black" and despite being recorded down in Muscle Shoals, it had as much in common as the sound the Swampers were concocting for the likes of Paul Simon and other visiting pop artists back in 1972 as it did for what they produced for The Staple Singers.

Anyone interested in Ervin might wish to know that he provided all the lead vocals on a good LP that came out in 1978 from Dave Williams entitled *Love Is Free*, thus almost qualifying it as another Ervin album. He died in 1995.

Escorts (see also Reginald Haynes)

Laurance Franklin; Reginald Haynes; Robert Arrington; William Dugger; Stephen Carter; Frank Heard; Marion Murphy; George Byers; James Green; Frank Harris; Grover Troutman

All We Need Is Another Chance 1973 Alithia AR-9104 Producer: George Kerr (Billboard soul charts: 41)

3 Down 4 To Go 1974 Alithia 1973 Alithia AR-9106 Producer: George Kerr (Billboard soul charts: 57)

There have been a number of groups or singers over the years who have been recorded while in prison but the best-known by far in soul circles was The Escorts, a genuinely talented group whose singing made you instantly forget the sordid realities of their background. This is certainly not the place to debate the morality or otherwise of whether prison inmates should be granted the chance given to The Escorts, and I will focus solely on the music.

The first album came about as a result of the persistence of George Kerr to prevail upon the powers that be at Rahway prison to allow him to record and produce an LP on The Escorts, who had formed while inside. After the permission was finally granted a seven song LP emerged, which lacked nothing in presentation including a gatefold sleeve and lots of photos and newspaper cuttings about the project. The attendant publicity helped propel the LP and two singles from it, "Look Over Your Shoulder" and "I'll Be Sweeter Tomorrow" into the soul charts at #45 and #83 respectively The only minor criticism I would aim at the set was that it consisted entirely - apart from the title track - of non-original songs some of which, "Little Green Apples" for example, seemed rather out of place. But this is indeed a minor carp: the singing throughout is little short of magnificent. Reginald Haynes took the tough, husky leads, while Stephen Carter provided the high tenor counterpoint and such an arrangement worked particularly superbly on "Ooh Baby Baby" which just pipped the two singles as best track on show.

The title of the second LP was self-explanatory and Haynes was one of the three who had left prison and needed to return to Rahway as a visitor to cut the follow-up. Ten tracks were on show this time around, with originals slightly outweighing covers. A so-so Norman Whitfield influenced track, "Disrespect Can Wreck", reached the soul singles charts (at #61) as did its follow-up, "Let's Make Love (At Home Sometimes)" (#58), a brilliant ballad, delivered gloriously by Carter. It remains the best track they ever cut. Covers of "I Can't Stand To See You Cry", "We've Come Too Far To End It Now" and "La-La (Means I Love You)" were all vastly better than the original songs "Corruption" and "The Shoo Nough".

The Haynes and Kerr inspired Escorts were to make no more records, and, indeed, most of the group who were released eventually found their way back behind bars, apparently leading to great disillusionment on the part of the producer.

Escorts 1981 Knockout KO-1500 Producer: Herschel Dwellingham

Back To Love 1992 Soul Vibes SVLP 07 Producers: George Kerr & Reginald Haynes

In 1981, Franklin and Arrington, two members of the original group, recruited four others to form a new Escorts sextet who put out an album on the Knockout label. Anyone seeing the cover would assume, as I did, that it was an entirely different group, one consisting of four women. Fortunately, there was an awareness of history on board and "Let Love Walk Into Your Heart" and, even better, "Heart Of Gold", bore glorious echoes of earlier days. "Sing A Happy Song" was a reasonable effort at a dance track, although "Make Me Over" was a seven minute uptempo cut that seemed to go on for seven hours. The album did nothing, however, and the group disbanded.

That was until 1992 when Haynes returned with a new Escorts LP. The cover shows three men but as so often a piece of information that seems pretty important - the identity of the other two - is ignored. I believe they may be William Martin and La Grant Carlos Harris but cannot be sure about this. It often sounds more like another Haynes solo album rather than a group outing, and indeed three tracks are repeated from Haynes' *On The Wings Of Love*, but it's all rather enjoyable. The musical backing is rudimentary but the song selection is well judged - The Whispers' "There's A Love For Everyone" and "Somebody Loves You", Randy Brown's "The Next Best Thing" and Linda Jones' "Hypnotized" are examples - and the singing is excellent. Only a poor execution of "Superstition" really raises the tempo and lowers the engagement and it was not a bad way to conclude the Escorts' career.

Esquires

Gilbert Moorer; Alvis Moorer; Shawn Taylor; Sam Pace; Mill Evans

Get On Up And Get Away 1967 Bunky BS 300 Producer: Bill Sheppard

Chi-Town Showdown (with The Marvelows) 1982 Solid Smoke SS-8017

The Esquires were one of the few soul groups to have come from Milwaukee and achieve some sort of national prominence. And they also hit first time out with "Get On Up" which went to #3 soul and #11 pop in late 1967.

Their one album is likeable enough in the grand Chicago tradition without any poor tracks, and the group were certainly talented, with a great falsetto lead in Gilbert Moorer, but it somehow lacks genuine distinction, which I put down to the lack of ballads, the similarity of tempo across the whole set, and an absence of a genuine killer cut. Two tracks, "When I'm Ready" and "Things Won't Be The Same, were actually Mill Evans solo releases. The album's follow-up single, "And Get Away", became a second big hit (#9 and #22) and although they were to post a further six singles on the soul charts between 1968 and 1976 and went on to record many more singles for an extraordinary number of labels they never got the opportunity to record a second album.

The *Chi-Down Showdown* outing was a retrospective set, comprising six songs by The Marvelows, and seven from The Esquires, three of which could be found on the debut album. The other four were "You Got The Power", "I Know I Can", "Part Time Angel" and "I Don't Know".

Ethics

Ron Tyson; Joe Freeman; Andy Collins; Carl Enlow; Larry Richardson; Norman Frazier; Michael Bell

The Ethics Sing 1969 (?) Love 1003 No producer listed

Law & Order (as Love Committee) 1978 Gold Mind GA 9500 Producers: TAN Productions; Baker-Harris-Young Productions & Ron Tyson

Love Committee 1980 T Electric MCA - 3233 Producers: Ron Tyson, Terry Stubbs, Cheryl Tyrrell & Mike Jackson

I have avoided including patently obvious bootlegs in this book, but it is not always easy to tell. One such dubious album is this one by The Ethics. There are no credits whatsoever on the record label or sleeve, merely the names of the ten tracks, but I remain unconvinced it is definitely a "dodgy release" because the question has to be asked: who was the audience it would have been bootlegged for?

The Ethics were a quartet out of Philadelphia and they recorded one single for the Wales label, five for Vent and, much later on, one for Golden Fleece. All the Wales and Vent sides are included on the LP and two of them, "Farewell" and "Tell Me" both reached the soul charts in 1969. Given my uncontrollable weakness for late sixties Philadelphia music there is no way I could not love this album. Tyson is one of the great falsetto singers (later joining The Temptations) and the songs - a number of which were written by him - are nearly all of a high standard, and all blessedly short at between two and three minutes. The content is a mixture of pounding and red-blooded dance material like "Standing In The Darkness", "Searching" and "Look At Me Now" and heart melting ballads such as "That's The Way Love Goes", "Tell Me" (#43 soul), "Farewell" (#32) and "Sad Sad Story". In truth, it is one of my most cherished LPs.

In 1974 they changed their name to Love Committee and made some excellent singles (for Golden Fleece and Ariola America) and two albums, one of high quality, one less so. The good one turned up in 1978 and is one of the better LPs of the latter half of the seventies. Salsoul could spend too much time on instrumental breaks (and they probably did here on the nevertheless still good title track from *Law And Order*) but the quality of the songs (all co-written by Tyson) and singing couldn't be suppressed and the twin vocal attack of Tyson's fragile tenor and the caustic gospel based power of (I think) Joe Freeman was contrasted beautifully. "Cheaters Never Win" (#57 soul) is one of the most exhilarating dance sides of the disco era, "Tired Of Being Your Fool" has an instantly memorable hook, and "If You Change Your Mind" and "Give Her Love" are ballads of class that nearly matched the best work of the group when they were still known as The Ethics.

Love Committee was disappointing and that is primarily due to a lack of Tyson; he was rationed on both songs and vocals, only co-writing two of the seven tracks this time around and played a much more subdued role in singing, and we hardly hear him. The same goes for Frazier too, as I believe it is new man Michael Bell who takes most lead vocals this time around. He is good enough, but not so distinctive as the others. Eddie Levert and Walter Williams from The O'Jays provided three of the songs and while there is nothing actively poor on show, it is only the dance tune, "I Made A Mistake", that really sticks in the mind, even it if surprisingly failed to become any sort of a hit when released as a 45. It certainly sounded like a smash.

Linda Evans

You Control Me 1979 Ariola American SW 50045 Producers: David Williams & James Jamerson Jr.

Linda Evans provided lead vocals for Chanson on their "I Can Tell" track, and the duo repaid the favour by producing her first (and only?) LP. It's not a bad outing - despite having little in the way of light and shade and varied tempos - and the fact that it doesn't sound especially compelling thirty-six years later shouldn't be held against it; it was recorded for people to dance to in 1979, not for posterity. Evans is a strong singer and it's easy to see why she was in demand to help out on the works of others, including

Quincy Jones and Margie Joseph. "Don't You Need" was pulled from the set as a single and reached #70 on the soul charts.

A gospel LP was released by a Linda Evans on Good News Records in 1984 but aural evidence suggests to me that this may be a different singer. What seems more likely is that the Linda Evans who cut *You Control Me* was the same as the one who released a fine single on Watts Sound Records in the seventies.

Betty Everett (see also Jerry Butler)

You're No Good 1963 Vee Jay VJS-1077 No producer listed

Delicious Together (and Jerry Butler) 1964 Vee Jay VJS-1099 Producer: Calvin Carter (Billboard pop charts:102)

The Very Best Of 1964 Vee Jay VJS-1122

Hot To Hold 1986 Charly CRB 1006 (UK)

Betty Everett, yet another native of Mississippi who moved up to Chicago, was one of the more consistent female soul singers for well over a decade and cut records in many styles, some of which were surprisingly tough given her somewhat "young" voice. She didn't have the range or power of many more esteemed stars - which has tended to mean she lacks acclaim - but she made no end of excellent sides, the earliest of which dated back to the late fifties.

You're No Good - which was shortly re-titled and re-released as *It's In His Kiss (Shoop Shoop)* - was a truly fine LP, unencumbered, as so many albums were back in 1963, with pointless and sugary cover versions of standards. "You're No Good", "Hound Dog" and "Hands Off" were assertive and tough; "The Prince Of Players" borrowed shamelessly from "He Will Break Your Heart" and there was no denying the unstoppable exuberance of the big hit, "It's In His Kiss". But she could also do vulnerable: "Chained To Your Love" and the bluesy "It Hurts To Be In Love". There were few soul LPs before 1964 better than this one.

However, my enthusiasm drained away with *Delicious Together* with Jerry Butler, a tired and unimaginative set, which was re-released on Buddah at the end of the sixties and then again by Charly (with one extra track) in 1981.

The Very Best Of was not great value, as it only contained two tracks that hadn't been on the *You're No Good* or *Delicious Together* sets, but as one of them was the magnificently atmospheric "It's Gettin' Mighty Crowded" (#65 pop) it needed to be owned. Better collections later appeared - lots of them in fact - but I have not listed these apart from the best of the lot on Charly which contains 16 tracks, nearly all good.

There'll Come A Time 1969 Uni 73048 Producers: Archie Russell, Leo Austell & Hillery Johnson (Billboard soul charts: 44)

The first twenty eight seconds of "There'll Come A Time" can lay fair claim to be the most brilliant intro to any soul record: eight seconds of tumbling, swirling horns and strings followed by twenty more of heavenly backing vocals and all this before Everett breaks in with one of her most affecting and desperate vocals. It is a masterpiece and arranger Tom Tom Washington, writers Eugene Record and Floyd Smith and the producers surpassed themselves here. Luckily, its quality was well recognised by the general public who propelled it to #2 soul and #26 pop when released as a single. On the other hand, it was far superior to anything else on the LP which overall lacked a little focus. "Hold On" seemed too aware of the existence of Aretha for its own good, the rather raucous "Sugar" had her straining a little and songs like "Is There A Chance For Me" and "Take Me" were no better than ok.

Love Rhymes 1974 Fantasy F-9447 Producers: Johnny Watson, David Axelrod, Willie Mitchell, Charles Chalmers & Calvin Carter

Happy Endings 1974 Fantasy F-9480 Producer: Gene Page

Everett placed another couple of non-album track singles on Uni on the soul charts in 1970 but she had to wait until 1974 and another new label, Fantasy, before her next LP was forthcoming. It was recorded in Los Angeles, Chicago and Memphis (and contained music cut over a period of a few years) so was a little lacking in overall cohesion but included many excellent moments. If her version of "I'm Afraid Of Losing You" wasn't *quite* up to the one by Quiet Elegance it was a close run thing while a second Memphis track, "It's Just A Matter Of Time", and "I Gotta Tell Somebody" a Dee Ervin song of instant charm, were also splendid. The latter, like "Sweet Dan", another album track, reached top forty soul. "Wondering" was a nicely lazy and effortless slow number and she delivered Charlie Rich's "Who Will The Next Fool Be" in surprisingly bluesy style.

Sadly, her next set, *Happy Endings*, was somewhat ironically titled given it was her last ever LP (barring retrospective collections), and was anything but a happy ending to her album career. Almost entirely spoiled by some awful MOR production by Gene Page, it appeared to be an attempt to move her into Diana Ross territory but failed in every way. On one hand it lacked hit records and on another completely stripped away any zest and excitement from a woman who had given us such life-affirming sides as "It's In His Kiss, "There'll Come A Time" and "Gettin' Mighty Crowded".

There were to be a handful of further singles after she moved on from Fantasy but she stopped recording round about 1980 and died in 2001. I continue to rate her highly and feel miffed about her lack of a higher profile.

Everlife

Dwayne Lomax; Rod Williams; Delores Whyte; Don Whyte; Eddie Taylor; Larry Johnson; Ron Payton; Lloyd Collier; Leander Saunders

Everlife # 1 1981 Jibaro JLP2-10-4401 Producer: Jim Roach

The awfully dull cover of this LP did not cause one's heart to leap at the prospect of unimaginable musical riches within, and that feeling was borne out by a handful of listens. This is not dreadful by any means but it is one of those albums where you look at the track listing a few months (maybe even days) later and can't recall what a single song sounds like.

They hailed from Detroit and had talent. The sound is full: strings and horns up top and cowbells and other rhythm enhancers down below but there are only two modes on the LP: uptempo dance material such as "Have A Good Time" and ballads like "You Are My Lucky Star". And I submit that every track is too long. Shorter, more telling songs would have delivered a better LP. Best composition: "Money's Only Paper".

Everyday People

Milton Carpenter; Curtis Davis; Laforest Jinkins; Douglas Hayes Pinkney; Harley Tyler; Joseph White; Hartwell Clifton Williams

Everyday People 1972 Red Coach RCL 6000 Producer: Gene Redd

This stuff can get confusing. Firstly, there was a band out of Canada called The Everyday People who recorded a track called "I Like What I Like". And then a band from America, the one above, also called Everyday People, cut a version of it as well. Anyway, it is not on their one album, which owes a lot to early Kool and The Gang.

An awful lot, in fact, including two songs previously cut by Kool, "Funky Granny" and "Who's Gonna Take The Weight", and a shared producer in Gene Redd. This all meant great, aggressive in- your- face horns and a busy rhythm section. But as much as I really like "Weight", and "Funky Generation", it is two slower, more restrained tracks that make Everyday People a cut above the average: a version of Stevie Wonder's "Superwoman" and arguably the best thing on here: "Do Re Mi Fa So La Ti Do". Anyone who can make a listenable song from a title like that must have something going for them. And The Everyday People certainly did. It is an essential LP for fans of early seventies funk. It was just a shame it did nothing and when a couple of later singles also failed the band was heard of no more.

Exciters (see also Brenda & Herb)

Brenda Reid; Carol Johnson; Lillian Walker; Herbert Rooney

Tell Him 1963 United Artists UAL 3264 Producers: Jerry Leiber & Mike Stoller

Exciters 1966 Roulette R-25326 No producer listed

The Exciters were one of the best mixed (i.e. boy/girl) quartets to have ever graced soul music, but have somehow escaped unadulterated critical acclaim. They were from New York, a fact eminently clear from just a few seconds of listening to their records, and thus could call on writers of the calibre of Bert Berns, Van McCoy and Ellie Greenwich, although they always contributed their own songs as well.

Tell Him has a great cover, one that, in its bold colours and lettering, captures the exuberance of the sixties perfectly. I'd want to own such an album even without listening to it. Fortunately, the music is dazzling too, even if it veers maybe more closely to New York power pop than some soul fans would like. But it's just fine with me as Brenda Reid's voice is so big, so enthralling, that she demolishes any cravings I might have for soul of a deeper hue. Who could resist her on "So Long, Goodnight" or "It's Love That Really Counts", a Bacharach-David song that has been somewhat overlooked? The title track was a huge hit, #5 soul and #4 pop in early 1963, but the follow-up "He's Got The Power" did less well, doubtless because it had a chorus that was just too close to "Tell Him". I really like all of this charming LP, apart from "I Dreamed", which is just a little cringe-worthy.

They had to wait until 1966 for their second LP (after having also cut the original of "Doo Wah Diddy" in the gap between the two albums) and as a number of the tracks had come out on singles in 1964 and 1965 the set did sound dated when it appeared but it was still a great opportunity to enjoy Reid's tremendous voice all over again. She is just marvellous on "That's How Love Starts" and "There They Go". "Talkin' 'Bout My Baby" was probably the only track that sounded contemporary while another cut, "I Want You To Be My Boy", only managed #98 on the pop charts when it had come out in early 1965, but was nevertheless the must successful 45 on the LP. ("Run Mascara" was the renegade track this time around: not great.)

Caviar & Chitlins 1969 RCA LSP-4211 Producers: Paul Robinson, Larry Banks & Herb Rooney

Black Beauty 1971 Today TLP 1001 Producer: Herb Rooney

After a few not very successful singles on labels like Shout and Bang, The Exciters pitched up on RCA where they delivered a much tougher LP than the first two. It was also noticeably more of a personal effort, seeing as how all but one song was written by the team of Reid and Rooney who were by now married. The LP, still New York recorded and resolutely uptown in style, sounded in step with much else what was coming out of the city or Detroit in 1969, but sadly didn't make much noise in the marketplace and only generated one small soul hit in "You Don't Know What You're Missing"(#49) but that is no slur on the undoubted quality of the LP which is unjustly neglected outside of collecting circles. Top tracks: "I Don't Have To Worry (No More), a delightful mid-tempo lope, and "You Got Me", a radically different take on the immortal Jaibi song with a rare Herb Rooney lead. There were no weak cuts, just one slightly eccentric one: "A Year Ago" which sounded as if it was recorded way more than a year before the rest of the set.

Given the lukewarm response to *Caviar & Chitlins*, The Exciters moved on to the Today label who issued one LP, a short one, clocking in at only about 23 minutes. The stand-out cut, "Leaving Him Tomorrow", proved beyond any reasonable doubt Reid's credentials as a deep soul singer and showed how far the group had come from songs like "Run Mascara". The great Debbie Taylor also performed this excellent song but Reid 's version is every bit as good. There is nothing else to match it and, not surprisingly, no hit singles were forthcoming as it was not an album full of instantly memorable tunes and also unfortunately contained rather poor efforts like "Soul Sister Annie" and "Don't It Make You Just Feel Good?".

Heaven Is Wherever You Are 1976 20th Century BT-472 Producers: Herb Rooney & Ian Levine

Exciters 1977 TVI 141 Producer: Herb Rooney

Producer Ian Levine made a number of records in the seventies. They were steeped in "Northern Soul" history and were slanted overwhelmingly towards dance music. I admire the time and trouble that went into making them but they were not records I bought at the time and not ones that sound particularly alluring forty years on either. The Exciters were doubtless pleased to get some attention, though, at a time when no-one else was interested.

Some of the tracks on the two albums above are duplicated and Levine's name is missing as producer for the TVI set.

Executive Suite

Charles Conyers; Billy Tyler; Vincent Unto; Henry Tuten

Executive Suite 1 1974 Polydor 2310-400 Producers: Bobby Martin, Norman Harris, Ronnie Baker, Earl Young, Ken Lewis, Stanley Lucas & Howard Jennings (UK)

This is one of those baffling LPs which was released in the UK but not in America for reasons I have been unable to discover. It's not as if the group had any success over here.

They surfaced from Camden, New Jersey, and all four members had sung in other groups before coming together to form Executive Suite in 1970. The album was recorded at Sigma Sound in Philadelphia (apart from "You Believed In Me" which was cut in New York) with the usual suspects writing, producing and arranging. It is not a generous album with only seven tracks (two of which are "Part 2") and it would be inaccurate to assert that the quartet had anything to distinguish them from all the other vocal teams working the same sort of field but "I'm A Winner Now" and "Your Love Is Paradise" are sumptuous ballads that rendered their unoriginality completely irrelevant. Furthermore,"When The Fuel Runs Out" is a churning dance side of warmth and class. Only the dull "You Got It" deserves to be entirely forgotten. "Winner", "Fuel" and "Paradise" all hit the mid reaches of the soul charts in late 1973 and 1974.

There was to be a further single on UA in 1975 but that was to signal the end of their recordings. (Other records did come out later under the name of "Executive Suite" but I don't believe they have any connection to this group at all.)

Exit 9

Hollis Googe; David Lavender; Michael Pelzer; Enoch Jappa; James Davis; Eric Hoosier; William McCormick; Solomon Jappa

Straight Up 1975 BRC 7-7006 Producers: John Jenkins, Alonzo Tucker & Modeste Clarke

Another obscure LP from a Brunswick subsidiary label, but a better than average one; cut in New York by an impressive combo with all the necessary ingredients in place for a satisfyingly funky outing: chanking rhythm guitar, tough bass and drums, and a commendable horn section. But it's the welcome and unusual addition of Enoch Jappa's congas that helps to ensure that attention does not wander elsewhere. Johnny Rios could sing pretty well too. Cuts range from the jazzy instrumental "MFB" through the decent ballad, Thoughts Of You" to the strutting "Jive Man" which Kool & the Gang would surely have been proud to cut.

Exoutics

Darrel Vaden; Van Brailsford; Michael Pennick; Andrew Williamson; Leon Martin; Ron Walker; Thomas Hall; Annette Batia

The Exoutic Touch 1980 Dee Gee 41341 Producers: Christopher Gaines, Leon Martin & Ron Walker

A pleasing single, "Here We Go Again", by this Buffalo based group, came out in 1978 on the small EP label. Unfortunately, it is not to be found on their one and only LP. And the album could have done with the single as it is a rather disappointing set. "(If You Shuffle) You've Got To Deal" meanders along nicely until you realise it is going to last for nine minutes, and "If You Can't Find The Funk" and "Groove Move Ya" sound pretty much as you would imagine from their titles. "That's Me" perked up my ears but that's maybe because it recalls The Stairsteps' "From Us To You".

The Exoutics are still active and a new CD came out not too log ago.

Experience Unlimited

Anthony Easton; Gregory Elliott; Donald Fields; Philip Harris; Michael Hughes; Greylin Hunter; Andre Lucas; Clarence Smith; David Williams

Free Yourself 1977 Black Fire BF 19757 No producer listed

The debut set from Washington D.C.'s Experience Unlimited is startlingly good, better than virtually every other funk LP of that year (in fact any year) and it remains bemusing that it utterly failed to sell. I can see that Black Fire Records were small fry, but couldn't a big company have leased it? The album is dedicated to "the spirit of Jimi Hendrix" but in fact generally plays down guitar pyrotechnics and is much closer to the thick rhythmic patterns to be expected from Sly, War, Kool and The Gang or The Ohio Players. *Free Yourself* stands up every bit as well nearly forty years on as the records from the more famous bands as well as other neglected classics of the genre from The Ray Alexander Technique or Harlem River Drive. There are seven tracks here lasting forty minutes in total and I love every second; it's such a well co-ordinated set that pulling out favourites isn't really necessary but I must particularly highlight Melva Adams' vocals on "Peace Gone Away" and the fantastic, driving "Hey You".

By 1982 Experience Unlimited were re-born as E.U. with only Gregory Elliott left from the Experience Unlimited days. The new sound they played was "Go-Go" a sub-genre of funk originating in the D.C. Area. E.U., together with Chuck Brown and Trouble Funk, were the most successful and best practitioners of "Go-Go" and while I am partial to the style, I am going to deem it out of scope as virtually all the records made by the new bands (Chuck Brown's excepted, but his had a rich history years before "Go-Go" was identified) were cut after 1982 and I also don't feel well qualified enough to talk about it.

Exportations

Arthur Gibson, Willie Gibson, Bernard Gibson, Anthony Pilgrim, Luician Thomas

Meet The Exportations 1978 United Artists LA872-H Producer: Clarence Rome

Living Proof 1987 G.E.M.C. GEM 4002 Produced by Elron

The Exportations were an accomplished vocal group from a city with a history of accomplished vocal groups, Detroit. They didn't last long as The Exportations, just releasing this one LP, a 45 from it, and two in-demand singles a coon a small local label, Vir-ro, before changing their name to Living Proof.

Side one of *Meet The Exportations* is certainly the better. All four cuts, "Kiss Me Love", "Main Ingredient", "Strange Sensation" and, best of all, "Fell In Love Too Late" switch vocals along nicely and all featured singers are strong, with pleasing contrasts between falsetto and driving tenor. This is an excellent example of a late seventies vocal group ignoring the imperatives of disco. The same cannot be said of side two, though. An instrumental take of

"Strange Sensation" is rather a waste of vinyl, "Music" is a mundane track and "You've Been A Long Time Coming" while ok, shouldn't have taken such a long time in ending.

I'm not sure why they opted to change their name (and another soul group called Livin' Proof already existed) but the second album is nearly as good as the first which was quite an achievement for 1987 and it revived the moribund art of soul harmony singing. Only two tracks out of eight are a waste of vinyl, and apart from these and an appealing skipping "Fell In Love Too Late" (an updated version of the best cut from the *Meet The Exportations* set) all is slow and sedate and requires to be heard by anyone who cares for top class group soul. Best track here is probably "Hold On To Your Dreams", also cut by William "Wee Gee" Howard a few years earlier.

Fabulous Waller Family

Harry Waller; Chris Waller; Karen Waller; Sandra Waller; Bruce Waller

Love Moods 1980 Dynamic Artists DA 1010 Producer: Joe Carter

This family from Richmond, Virginia, issued a scarce LP in 1980 which would probably have done much better had it come out in 1972 as it is based unashamedly on the "sweet soul" style that was so popular back at that time. By the turn of the decade this style was seen as a bit outdated by most people and the group never managed to catch a large audience.

They had released an execrable single as "The Waller Family" back in 1977 entitled "Sweet Disco Daddy" and fortunately there was only the odd horror such as "Can You Dance Like Me" on the LP in a similar style; no, it was much better when they simply sang their slow ballads, and even if the production and arrangements couldn't quite hope to match those of eight or nine years earlier, Dynamic Artists certainly tried hard enough, and listening to "What Good Is Love" and "Without You Tonight" remains a pleasure.

I believe the family still sing together today as The Wallers.

Facts Of Life

Chuck Carter, Jean Davis; Keith Williams

Sometimes 1977 Kayvette 802 Producer: Millie Jackson (Billboard soul charts: 33; Billboard pop charts: 146)

A Matter Of Fact 1978 Kayvette 803 Producer: Millie Jackson (Billboard soul charts: 54)

This trio first recorded as The Gospel Truth, a name which erroneously suggested a spiritual bent and they therefore changed it to the more worldly Facts Of Life. They all had pedigree: Carter had released solo records, Williams had sung with a number of groups including The Flamingos, and Jean had a famous brother in Tyrone Davis. Being produced by and associated with Millie Jackson didn't hurt either. They didn't record for long, only four years in total, but did have two big soul hits in that brief time.

The first album was, rather touchingly and optimistically in retrospect, also released in the UK and I imagine sales must have been soberingly low. Soul of an adult and deep nature in 1977 was being swamped and sidelined by the incessant demands of disco and had precious little appeal to the vast majority of British record buyers. Fortunately, that wasn't quite the same situation in the States and "Caught In The Act (Of Gettin' It On)" and "Sometimes" were magnificent records that reached #13 and #3 respectively on the soul charts. Both are to be found on that debut set which had rhythm tracks recorded in Muscle Shoals with horns and strings cut at Criteria in Miami. Not surprisingly, they rather overshadowed everything else on the LP, which would have been worthy but a little uninspired without them. The beautifully sung and arranged (by the always excellent Mike Lewis) "Love Is The Final Truth" is probably the next best track, and certainly more suited to them than Barry Manilow's "Looks Like We Made It".

Millie made a vocal contribution to one of the two stand-out songs on *A Matter Of Fact*, "Did He Make Love To You". The other winner was "We Can't Hide It Anymore" a top-class composition by Barry Murphy which had also been cut by a number of singers including Ben E. King, but sadly failed when put out as a 45. All the other eight cuts are enjoyable to listen to if you like unadulterated soul music from the southern states but none of them are essential.

Yvonne Fair

The Bitch Is Black 1975 Motown M6-832S1 Producers: Norman Whitfield, Harvey Fuqua, Pam Sawyer, Gloria Jones & Clay McMurray

Flora Yvonne Coleman learned a thing or two about the power of image when she worked as a member of the James Brown Revue in the early sixties. And image was what she flaunted on the cover of her one LP, which also borrowed in more than one way from Betty Davis.

But to return to the sixties. Under her new stage name of Yvonne Fair she was briefly a member of The Chantels, as well as recording a number of singles on the King label, none of which did particularly well. Her second break came when she left Brown's stable and joined Motown where she got rather lost, only releasing one single in 1970 and then having to wait until 1974 for her next 45. Trading on the "bitch" image, and sounding (and even looking) very much like Betty Davis - although Fair was a far superior singer - she did manage to post three small hits on the soul charts between the summers of 1974 and 1975. All of them - "Funky Music Sho Nuff Turns Me On" (with vocal help from Marvin Gaye), "Love Ain't No Toy" and "Walk Out The Door If You Wanna - were produced by Norman Whitfield as was her one and only UK hit, the splendid "It Should Have Been Me". Whitfield could be an acquired taste with his attitude and ego-driven music but his productions suited Fair in her "tough" persona and I think the songs generally work pretty well. The album also trawled the vaults and included that 1970 single, "Stay A Little Longer", and a distinctly average cover of Barbara George's big hit, "I Know", which Fair cut back in 1968, where it had lain unreleased until now. Another enjoyable side was the big, blowsy "It's Bad For Me To See You", produced by Pam Sawyer and Gloria Jones, which was one of my favourite tracks on the LP, as well as appearing, as with virtually every song on the album, on a 45 (in this case in 1975 and failing to hit the charts.)

And that was pretty much it for Yvonne Fair. She worked with Dionne Warwick for a while but released no more of her own records before dying aged only 51 in 1994.

Faison

Love Fire 1981 Erect EPLP 504 Producer: Jim Porter

Producer Jim or James Porter did a fair bit of work in Chicago in the seventies and eighties including the LP from The Eight Minutes. He also produced this one from Joyce Faison. I know little about her other than she sang backing vocals on the first Rockie Robbins LP and appears to be another woman who has combined singing and acting over the years. It's not a bad set, with rather expansive and expensive arrangements for 1981 and Joyce can sing sweetly enough as well evidenced on "Talking 'Bout Love". The cover is poorly executed, however, with a picture of a fireplace being favoured over a shot of the singer herself.

Faith, Hope & Charity (see also Zulema)

Zulema Cusseaux; Albert Bailey; Brenda Hilliard; Diane Destry

Faith, Hope & Charity 1970 Maxwell ML-88002 Producers: Van McCoy & Joe Cobb

Heavy Love 1972 Sussex SXBS 7019 Producers: Van McCoy, Joe Cobb & Michael Stokes

Faith, Hope and Charity had come up from Florida (where they had recorded as The Lovells) to New York where they had the good fortune to work with Van McCoy for the whole of their career. Zulema Cusseaux and Brenda Hilliard were tremendous singers and McCoy only ever worked with the best musicians. But I must confess to indifference to most of their music. There was something rather earnest about Faith Hope and Charity. There was the name itself, of course, which led to the religious overtones of the first album's front cover and the first two LPs all too often sounded like musicals of the time. If one cared for *Godspell* these records would have sounded great, I expect.

The first album's music dripped with pomp and circumstance and "Baby Don't Take Your Love" (#36) and "So Much Love" (#14) both fared well as singles on the soul charts and the threesome were thus off to a good commercial start.

Heavy Love appeared at about the same time Zulema left to go solo. No-one could accuse Sussex of not trying to break the threesome as five singles were released from the set but not one of them hit. "No Trespassing" was a change from their usual fare sounding like an Invictus track and "Come Back And Finish What You Started" was the original of a song later cut by Gladys Knight & The Pips.

Faith, Hope & Charity 1975 RCA APL1-1100 Producer: Van McCoy (Billboard soul charts: 24; Billboard pop charts: 100)

Life Goes On 1976 RCA APL1-1827 Producer: Van McCoy

For a brief moment in 1975 it looked as if the trio might finally have made it, when "To Each His Own " hit #1 on the soul singles charts in the late summer of that year, and while the LP on which it could be found also did fairly well, the set was just too frenetic to be convincing. It contained nine tracks and all of them zipped along. The set has a strong odour of hastiness with routine re-workings of venerable old songs like "Rescue Me" and "Just One Look" as well as one of McCoy's own compositions, "Little Bit Of Love", all being pressed into service once again. I also imagine that such a talented writer as McCoy must have knocked off tunes like "Let's Go To The Disco" and "Disco Dan" in the car on the way to the studio. What was undeniable, though, was that musically they had certainly moved on.

Life Goes On is an almost entirely forgotten album today but I think it was probably their best to date. Virtually everything was still uptempo (and generally, too long) but "Positive Thinking" and "You're My Peace Of Mind" stuck in the mind after only one play and "You've Gotta Tell Her" was a rare (and good) slow track, sounding a bit like "Neither One Of Us (Wants To Be The First To Say Goodbye)". On the other hand, a medley of "Cherish" and "Monday Monday" reminded me of why so much disco was so awful. The title track and "Peace Of Mind" both made the soul charts as singles, albeit in unspectacular style at #65 and #83 respectively.

Faith, Hope & Charity 1978 20th Century T-560 Producer: Van McCoy

They recorded one last album on a new label, 20th Century, which was notable for the fact that it had an Ernie Barnes cover strikingly close to the one he produced for Marvin Gaye's *I Want You* LP. It was a decent effort musically as well, kicking off with an exuberant" How Can I Help But Love You" and keeps its head above water until the end, with some more welcome slower material in "Keep Me Baby" and "Don't Pity Me"(their last ever charting single at #20 soul.) No clunkers were in sight, Hilliard was in great voice throughout and they went out on a fairly high note, being unusual in as much as their records got better as the decade went on, when the opposite was true for most other groups.

Falcons (see also Eddie Floyd & Wilson Pickett)

You're So Fine: The Falcons Story Part 1 Flick 8005

I Found A Love: The Falcons Story Part 2 Flick Lu-Pine 8006

The Falcons proved to be one of the best breeding grounds for future singers of all the groups in the pre-soul era of around 1958-1962. Wilson Pickett, Eddie Floyd, Mack Rice and Joe Stubbs all sang for them, while Willie Schofield was another important member, particularly as a writer. Their biggest hits came in 1959 with "You're So Fine" (#2 soul and #17 pop) and in 1962 when " I Found A Love" landed at #6 soul and #75 pop. Because the group broke up in early 1963, right at the time "soul" was becoming the recognised new sound of Black America and because their only albums are long after the event compilations, I have not dwelt on them much here. Which is not the same as saying they were unimportant or failed to make excellent records. Far from it, in fact.

Fame

Andrew Chamberlain; Erwin Leader; Johnny Lambert; Clarke Smith; Quinton Raynor; Barry Fitzsimmons

Introducing 1977 Strawberry STW 6008 Producer: Randy Irwin

Fame was not an inspired name for a group but their one LP was released on the in-demand Strawberry logo, the same label on which a couple of Family Circle LPs can be found, and thus attracts some interest these days. While both groups shared the same producer, Fame's set is more varied, and is nothing like the ballad-heavy approach of their stablemates. On some tracks they provide straight-ahead funk while "Release Me" has a verse that reminds me of Barry White's music. Overall, it is a reasonable enough outing but cannot have generated many sales.

Fame Gang

Junior Lowe; Harrison Calloway; Jesse Boyce; Aaron Varnell; Ronnie Eades; Mickey Buckins; Harvey Thompson; Clayton Ivey; Freeman Brown

Solid Gold From Muscle Shoals 1970 Fame SKAO-4200 Producer: Rick Hall

The Fame Gang were the third great band from Rick Hall's esteemed Muscle Shoals studio and record label. They had already recorded three obscure singles which had not really gone anywhere, including to this LP which consists of 16 well-known songs. I doubt if anyone thought it would sell but at least it afforded the musicians some recognition at a time when recognition for studio band personnel was more or less unknown. As an album it is anodyne and apart from the odd chanted vocal here and there is entirely instrumental too.

Family

Tyrone Brunson, Milton Bond; Reginald Marsh; Reginald McNair; William Jackson

Music-Let It Thru 1977 Little City LC-1502 Producer: Leon Stewart

My first reaction on seeing this record's front cover was, "another example of not making it clear what lies within". Yet, after having listened to it I'm not so sure the cover wasn't apt. It is a particularly difficult record to describe. Certainly urban, but not really funk, powerfully vocally, but not classic vocal soul, it really does occupy a small niche of its own. There is a sprinkling of Ohio Players and Sly here, a nod to Funkadelic and white rock, but none of that really captures the essence of Family who were certainly their own men. Ultimately, though, what really characterises the album is the backing music. It is not merely adorned by synths and string ensembles, but utterly *engulfed* by them, which becomes a wearying distraction in pretty short order.

The title track became a small soul hit (#70) in the summer of '77 but the Washington D.C. based group soon disbanded. Tyrone Brunson and Reginald Marsh (as Osiris) went on to record solo records in the eighties. (Family were also no relation to a Minneapolis based group of the same name who hit in the eighties.)

Family Brown

Gary Brown; Anthony Brown; Joseph Brown; Renee Brown; Donny Lewis

Imaginary World 1977 UA LA828-G Producer: George Daly

This group should not be confused with one of the same name who were a country outfit. Other than this album, and a couple of singles in the eighties, this Family Brown committed little to vinyl and little to the coffers of the United Artists company. It is a good LP, though, based on the bedrock of soul music: good singing. I'm not sure which of the four Brown men handles the majority of the lead vocals but whoever he is has a splendid voice. The music is orchestrated West Coast fare, falling just short of out and out danceable in most cases, but rarely failing to engage the listener. An exception is "When I Need You", sung impeccably, but nothing can erase the fact that it is a Leo Sayer song, and not one I particularly want playing over and over in my brain. Donny Lewis - a lady - also shows her chops on "When Your Love's Not There".

Family Circle

Charles Simmons; Don Simmons; James Simmons; Mary Simmons; David Simmons

Family Circle 1973 Sky Disc SKD 301 Producer: Randy Irwin

Love Bound 1976 Strawberry STW 6002 Producer: Randy Irwin

Let's Give Each Other Love 197? Strawberry STW 6007 Producer: Randy Irwin

The Family Circle were yet another group of brothers (and a sister) and despite their tender ages and lack of a big record label behind them, nevertheless managed to attract star musicians like Bernard Purdie, Billy Vera, Gordon Edwards and Cornell Dupree to play on their debut set. Which is lovely floaty and dreamy New York soul, heavy on ballads. Apart from on the excellent "If You Really Want To Make It" there is a marked absence of huge string sections (although a slightly intrusive string synthesiser of some sort is utilised on one or two other tracks) or much brass and so the emphases fall squarely on the stellar rhythm section and the exquisite Simmons' vocals. The songs could also be stronger, and it is this drawback which really stops this from being an album absolutely out of the top drawer but it is nevertheless more or less worth the high price it always commands, a result of its failure to sell many copies at the time of release.

Love Bound replicated four tracks from the Sky Disc set, but we were still provided with seven new ones, the best of which were probably "Barbara Ann" from a dance point of view, and "Stop Turn Around" and "You Are The Love Of My Life" for those who craved ballads.

But if the second album duplicated some songs, the third was no value for money at all. Firstly, it only comprised eight tracks, and second, because six of those had appeared previously leaving only the title track and "Baby I'm Hooked (On Your Sweet Love)" as new to market but that hasn't stopped it attracting high prices these days every time it comes up for sale; it certainly wouldn't have done so initially as hardly anyone knew it even existed.

Charles Simmons released a couple of 12" singles in the eighties as by "Chaz" and I think he is possibly the same man who put out an album in 1990 with a female singer as by "Chaz and Trinna".)

Family Players

Mark Raphael; Derrick Lewis; Willie McMiller; Brian Lewis; Joey Porter; Kevin Hayes

I Love Funk 'N' Roll 1982 MCA 5356 Producer: Isaac Bolden

This album was produced by the respected veteran Isaac Bolden at Sea-Saint in New Orleans, but the few tracks I have heard could have been recorded anywhere, so fully devoid were they of any of the spirit of that city's distinctive music. Song titles such as "We're Live In Video", "Let's Do It, Let's Freak", "Mini-Skirts" and the title track also made it clear that the band were more interested in appealing to those who liked The Bar-Kays or Con-Funk-Shun rather than Johnny Adams.

Family Vibes

Warren Dawson; Soko Richardson; Jackie Clark; Claude Williams; Mack Johnson; Ed Burks; Jimmy Smith; J.D. Reed; Larry Reed;

Strange Fruit 1972 UA UAS-5560 Producer: Ike Turner

Confined To Soul 1973 UA UA-LA051-F Producers: Ike Turner, Jackie Clark & Claude Williams

The Family Vibes - formerly known as The Kings Of Rhythm - were to Ike Turner as were The J.B.'s to James Brown. Not only did they play on numerous Ike & Tina Turner records, but they were "allowed" out on their own from time to time, cutting the two LPs above.

Strange Fruit need not detain us long. Its eleven tracks are all instrumental (apart from about ten seconds of cooing background vocals) and while it undoubtedly showcases the skills of the musicians there is not a single cut that demands to be heard again. Anyone looking for funk would be disappointed too, as there is precious little here, with the three styles on show being slow and dreamy, rock influenced or reaching way back into the forties and fifties in a fond re-creation of the jump-blues mode.

Confined To Soul is also effectively a jam session, which makes it another inessential record to own. Again mainly instrumental, although this time there are a couple of vocal tracks, taken by Claude Williams, it's pleasant enough to listen to, as the Family Vibes were excellent musicians. It's also quite tough, without any strings, but doesn't ape the funk stylings of The J.B.'s, Kool and The Gang or The Ohio Players, with Turner opting instead for a slightly more fluid, guitar and keyboard driven sound. Doubtless never cut to sell in any great quantity, it was also the last record ever released by The Family Vibes

Fantastic Four

James Epps; Joseph Pruitt; Ralph Pruitt; Wallace Childs; Ernest Newsome; Cleveland Horne; Paul Scott

Best Of 1969 Soul SS-717

This excellent Detroit group had been formed in 1965 and had enjoyed some hits on the Ric Tic label with five singles reaching the soul charts between the spring of 1967 and the early summer of 1968. Berry Gordy acquired Ric Tic in September of that year and its acts and thus all five singles can be found on the *Best Of* set (which was called just *The Fantastic Four* in the UK, but both releases shared the awfully uninspired and dull cover.) They had their first success on the Motown subsidiary, Soul, with "I Love You Madly" (#12 soul, #56 pop) in late 1968, which is also included on the LP and therefore the 'Best Of' tag was fully justified. It was an imperative for Motown groups to have strong lead singers and The Fantastic Four had one of the strongest of all in the excellent "Sweet" James Epps and so when they moved across to Gordy's empire they were never going to have a problem fitting in as regards style. (They certainly also had a trademark Motown name; the company always liked superlatives in a group's title.) Whether or not they got the attention they deserved, though, is another question entirely and certainly given they only managed this one LP and four singles it was maybe the case that they did rather get neglected. They probably owed more in the way they approached songs to The Temptations than The Four Tops, but any Motown fans would get a great deal of pleasure from this cool and generally relaxed LP as would lovers of male soul harmony groups in general. "Can't Stop Lookin' For My Baby", an early (Ric Tic) single which did not chart, is a particularly strong song, specific in its urban desperation. (It is also interesting to hear them interpret a Bobby Bland hit, "Share Your Love With Me", as I cannot, off the top of my head, recall any other Bland covers by Motown groups.)

Alvin Stone (The Birth And Death Of A Gangster) 1975 Westbound W-201 Producer: Al Kent (Billboard soul charts: 33; Billboard pop charts: 99)

Night People 1975 Westbound W-226 Producer: Al Kent

Got To Have Your Love 1977 Westbound WT-306 Producers: Dennis Coffey, James Epps, Joseph Pruitt, Cleveland Horne & Al Hamilton

B.Y.O.F. (Bring Your Own Funk) 1978 Westbound WT 6108 Producers: Dennis Coffey & James Epps

Given they could not emulate their Ric-Tic success at Soul they moved on again, this time to the Eastbound/Westbound company, with whom they remained for a few years, placing a further six 45s on the soul listings, even if none were smashes.

Alvin Stone looked as if it was going to be an ambitious concept LP with its arresting cover based on that of an imaginary newspaper, but in fact the "concept" didn't extend past the tremendous title track with its great arrangement by Paul Riser (his work is terrific throughout). But the feeling was not one of a lost opportunity as it is an excellent LP in its own right, with strong generally downtempo songs and an improved vocal armoury now that Cleveland Horne had also joined the group. The set only fielded six cuts, but all carried their weight in a collection strikingly devoid of filler. Put the needle down anywhere for pleasure, but maybe linger on "My Love Won't Stop At Nothing" or "Have A Little Mercy".

The next album, *Night People*, also went with a recipe of only a handful of tracks but was less convincing. "Night People/Lies Divided By Jive" was just too long at 11 minutes and also flirted too unashamedly with disco, as did its coquettish fellow tracks, "If I Lose My Job" and "Hideaway". Better by far was the tremendous "They Took The Show On The Road", and the sedate "By The River Under The Tree" was also, as they say, a cracker.

There was a return to form with *Got To Have Your Love*, which once again bore some good songs; "She'll Be Right For Me", "Ain't I Been Good To You" and "Mixed Up Moods And Attitudes" coaxed fine leads from Epps while the title track always straddled the right side of disco for me with its vivacious arrangement and attacking vocal (it went to #30 soul when released on 45). It was a shame about "Disco Pool Blues" and "Cash Money" though.

And shame too, about the *B.Y.O.F* LP which was pretty awful. It had a first side that could have been delivered by anybody, given its total focus on dance which rendered any individuality superfluous."Cold And Windy Night" was good enough, and raised hopes for better when the album was flipped, and these hopes intensified with the excellent "Realize (When You're In Love)", a trademark ballad, but were then dashed by the other two cuts: it was almost guaranteed that a song called "Sexy Lady" in 1978 (which staggered to #96 soul) was going to be very poor indeed and it was equalled in mediocrity by the title track (#77).

The group were not heard of again until 1989 when they re-surfaced to cut a 12" single and three years later for a CD - both for Ian Levine's organisation. (Epps had released a couple of excellent solo singles in the early eighties, which didn't sell many copies unfortunately.) Both Pruitts, Horne and Epps have all since passed away.

Fantastic Johnny C

Boogaloo Down Broadway 1968 Phil L.A. Of Soul 4000 Producer: Jesse James

The obviously confident Johnny Corley had his five minutes of fame when the rather staid and mechanical dance side "Boogaloo Down Broadway" became a big hit at the tail-end of 1967 reaching #5 soul and #7 pop. He could never build a sustained career around it though, and the equally repetitive follow-up, "Got What You Need", only managed #32 and #56, suggesting that the world wasn't about to succumb to Fantastic Johnny C fever.

The LP on which both singles sat would be a prize exhibit in any prosecution for the charge against an "album containing a big hit and lots of filler" as half of its twelve tracks were so-so covers of well known songs. It was all a bit of a wasted opportunity as Corley could actually sing pretty well in a manner vaguely reminiscent of Otis Redding as tracks like "New Love" and "Baby I Need You" demonstrated.

He went on to cut a further handful of singles up until the mid seventies, although only one of them, "Hitch It To The Horse", managed to return him to the charts. He was not to be favoured with a second LP, though, and doesn't appear to have recorded at all in the last forty years.

Fantasy

Carolyn Edwards; Rufus Jackson; Ken Roberson; Tamm E Hunt

Fantasy 1980 Pavillion AL 37151 Producer: Tony Valor

Sex And Material Possessions 1980 Pavillion AL 37945 Producer: Tony Valor

Fantasy were a group pitched precisely on the dividing line between disco and light funk, and if the (very) marginally tougher and funkier second set didn't exist they would have to be ignored for the book. "You're Too Late" and "(Hey Who's Gotta) Funky Song" from the debut album both reached the soul charts but I'm afraid that I don't really care for any of their sides at all.

Mikki Farrow

Mikki 1982 Emerald International EIR-1001 Producers: The Harris Machine & Mikki Farrow

Mikki Farrow is not a name known to the casual soul fan, let alone the general public. But she does rate a note in the history of the music for what she achieved before her premature death in early 2002 which included releasing an in-demand "Northern Soul" 45 on the Karate label in 1966, becoming a high-class background singer on Philadelphia sessions for the likes of Wilson Pickett and Jerry Butler, and being married to both Mike Terry and Billy Butler.

Her one album was a seriously patchy affair, though. Sporting a truly awful cover, it had a first side to match. "Itching For Love" may well have made people dance in 1982 but it goes on for sixteen minutes here, and the other track, "Right In The Middle", is from the "Footloose" school of pop music. Side two, however, recovers nicely with five Philly recorded tracks that hold up that city's impeccable soul traditions admirably; or at least the first three tracks do where Farrow brings to bear her great vocal range on decent songs. Anyone who liked what Jean Carn was doing in the early eighties should feel at home here.

F. A.T.

Funky And Tough 1977 Bold 305 Producer: Willie Clarke

This is another LP, like Leon Debouse's, on the T.K. subsidiary Bold, which has its fans these days. Eric "Fat" Gallon is the deep-voiced singer and drummer behind the record's title. The engaging and relatively relaxed "How Can I Explain" is the best cut and overshadows an uninspired instrumental like "Satan's Dream". Overall it's hardly essential but not bad at all, even if it made no impression on release.

Fatback Band

Johnny King; Johnny Flippin; George Adams; George Williams; Earl Shelton; Bill Curtis; Wayne Wilford; Warren Daniels; Billy Hamilton; Richard Cornwell; Gerry Thomas; Calvin Duke; Kenny Ballard; Fred Demery; Tom Copolla; Cobra Butler; James Skelton; Sam Culley; Billy King; George Victory; Michael Walker; Herb Smith; Ed Jackson; Robert Damper; Linda Blakely; Wesley Watson; Elaine Lockley; John DeBerry; Vernon Lloyd; Edward Walker; Abdul Hameed Zuhri

Let's Do It Again 1972 Perception PLP-28 Producer: Fatback Records

People Music 1973 Perception PLP-43 Producer: Fatback Records

Feel My Soul 1974 Perception PLP-46 Producer: Fatback Records

Who would have guessed that The Fatback Band (or Fatback, to use their latter name) released over twenty studio LPs? Certainly not me, but I did stop listening fairly early on in their career. They were a band, just like Kool & The Gang, who probably wisely smoothed out their music to gain a wider audience and a longer lifespan, but who lost their early vitality in the process.

Proudly from New York, they were led by Bill Curtis who created a Fat Back record label before forming the band who released their first single back in 1968, but it was the move to the Perception label that got them established, albeit only in a rather underground fashion; they were popular with black audiences and hip young white kids, but continued to mean bugger all to the pop audience at large. (This never changed: they eventually ended up posting 31 singles on the soul charts and not a single one of them reached the pop top 100, an extraordinary case of musical ghettoisation.)

The "paarty paarty" street funk sound was wildly popular around 1972 and 1973 and The Fatback were right at the forefront of this movement, which relied heavily on chanted vocals, bass, drums, horns and whistles. "Street Dance" was the quintessential "street funk" single and sold enough copies to make it to #26 soul. It was the lead-off cut on their first LP, *Let's Do It Again*, which, like their other Perception sets, was a mixture of tough funk (which worked) and rather soft instrumentals (which didn't). "Free Form", "Take A Ride (On The Soul Train)", "Goin' To See My Baby" and the title track were all good examples of the former while "Baby I'm A Want You" and "Wichita Lineman" were typical of the latter.

And so it went with the follow-up album, *People Music*. "Njia Walk" and "Soul March" were two more funky charting singles while "To Be With You" and "Baby Doll" brought out their fluffier side. Three things were already clear about The Fatback Band: you didn't listen to their music if you wanted to hear top-class vocals, they were great for a party, and they were better represented at 45 than at 33⅓.

They turned all those preconceptions on their head though with *Feel My Soul* where they decided they didn't want to be good for a party, after all. It was a somewhat admirable but rather misguided attempt to re-invent themselves as more of a "thinking person's" band with the nine minute title track leading the charge. They hadn't recorded anything like this before, with its time changes, prominent organ and metaphysical vibe. The album was subtitled as *Featuring Brother Johnny King* and to be honest he wasn't the greatest singer in the world and couldn't carry a whole LP, and there wasn't even any funk to fall back on, given nearly all the tracks were soporific in feel. An interesting curiosity but hardly essential.

Keep On Steppin' 1974 Event EV-6902 Producer: The Fatback Band

Yum Yum 1975 Event EV-6904 Producer: The Fatback Band

Raising Hell 1975 Event EV-6905 Producer: The Fatback Band (Billboard soul charts: 37; Billboard pop charts: 158)

Curtis, King and the rest of the band must have realised that they had slipped up with *Feel My Soul* as *Keep On Steppin'* celebrated a return to a funkier style as well as a move to a new record label. There was a pronounced Kool & The Gang influence at play this time around while Johnny Flippin's bass remained a key element of their music. They hadn't utterly forsaken the slower things though, as "Love", "Can't Fight The Flame" and "Breaking Up Is Hard To Do " proved and the latter was probably as good as they had so far managed in this vein. But it was "Wicki Wacky" and the title track which most people will remember. Both made it to the soul charts as singles (#94 and #50 respectively) but still nowhere near as high as everyone would have hoped for.

It was slim business as usual for *Yum Yum* as well, their fifth to date, none of which had managed to chart and the title track only crawled to a paltry #80 as a single but musically things were slowly evolving again as "Trompin" and "Gotta Learn How To Dance" had a pop sheen that didn't exist back on the Perception LPs and the sedate "If You Could Turn Into Me" sounded as if it was performed by an entirely different group.

Finally, in 1976 their luck changed. "(Are You Ready) Do The Bus Stop" hit #37 as a single, while the disco tinged but clearly catchy "Spanish Hustle" went to #12 - easily their best showing to date - and they even managed to have a charting album with *Raising Hell* from whence came both 45s. It was also the last album I ever bought by The Fatback Band as their music was reducing its funk quotient in favour of disco and as they still couldn't deliver any decent ballads I simply lost interest. The nadir of this album was a take on The Four Tops' "I Can't Help Myself" which they really shouldn't have attempted.

Night Fever 1976 Spring SP-1-6711 Producer: The Fatback Band (Billboard soul charts: 31; Billboard pop charts: 182)

The Best Of 1976 Polydor 2391 246 (UK)

NYCNYUSA 1977 Spring SP-1-6714 Producers: The Fatback Band & Gerry Thomas (Billboard soul charts: 54)

The three albums above were the last released as by "The Fatback Band" with *Night Fever* taking them further into pure "disco" style than ever before. A brief spark was provided on "Double Dutch" from *NYCNYUSA* which wisely employed an (uncredited) female singer to help out. The fact that a *Best Of* LP appeared in Europe and not the U.S. was also telling, as if Spring still couldn't make up their minds about the band. They would have been glad they persevered though, as the band were shortly to do significantly better.

Man With The Band 1977 Spring SP-1-6717 Producers: The Fatback Band, Gerry Thomas & Henry Ellerbee

Fired Up 'N' Kickin' 1978 Spring SP-1-6718 Producers: The Fatback Band, Bill Curtis & Gerry Thomas (Billboard soul charts: 17; Billboard pop charts: 73)

Brite Lites, Big City 1979 Spring SP-1-6721 Producers: The Fatback Band, Bill Curtis & Gerry Thomas (Billboard soul charts: 57)

Fatback XII 1979 Spring SP-1-6723 Producers: The Fatback Band, Bill Curtis & Gerry Thomas (Billboard soul charts: 16; Billboard pop charts: 89)

Hot Box 1980 Spring SP-1-6726 Producers: Bill Curtis & Gerry Thomas (Billboard soul charts: 7; Billboard pop charts: 44)

14 Karat 1980 Spring SP-1-6729 Producers: Bill Curtis & Gerry Thomas (Billboard soul charts: 16; Billboard pop charts: 91)

Tasty Jam 1980 Spring SP-1-6731 Producers: Bill Curtis & Gerry Thomas (Billboard soul charts: 17; Billboard pop charts: 102)

Gigolo 1981 Spring SP-1-6734 Producers: Bill Curtis & Gerry Thomas (Billboard soul charts: 68; Billboard pop charts: 148)

On The Floor With Fatback 1982 Spring SP-1-6736 Producers: Bill Curtis & Gerry Thomas (Billboard soul charts: 28; Billboard pop charts: 204)

Is This The Future? 1983 Spring SP-1-6738 Producers: Bill Curtis & Gerry Thomas (Billboard soul charts: 27)

With Love 1983 Spring SPR-33-6741 Producer: Bill Curtis & Gerry Thomas (Billboard soul charts: 64)

Phoenix 1984 Cotillion 90168-1 Producers: Bill Curtis & Gerry Thomas (Billboard soul charts: 67)

So Delicious 1985 Cotillion 7 90253-1 Producers: Bill Curtis & Gerry Thomas

Live 1987 Start STL 12 (UK)

To-Nite's An All Night Party 1988 Start STL 16 (UK)

They abbreviated their name to "Fatback" with *The Man With The Band* LP, finally had three top ten soul singles, "I Like Girls", "Gotta Get My Hands On Some Money" and "Backstrokin'" between the summers of 1978 and 1980, had a highly popular record in the

U.K. with "I Found Lovin'" in 1983 and carried on with Curtis and Thomas as the core of the band for decades more. But I really have nothing else to say, other than to admire their industry and to genuinely applaud their feat of sustaining success in the industry for so long. Many people loved Fatback's later records but I was not one of them.

Father's Children

Sadik Abdul Hagg; Malik Abdul Khabir; Qadir Abdul Mateen; Tony Vaughn; Raheem A Khabir; Hakeem Abdul Ghani; Khalik Abdul Hanif; Yah Yah Abdulla

Father's Children 1979 Mercury SRM-1- 3755 Producers: Wayne Henderson & Augie Johnson

What a boring cover. It's the most obvious thing to say about this one LP from Father's Children, an eight piece band from Washington D.C. The music within is competent and gently jazzy and funky in that mid to late seventies groove that was true of a number of bands who were produced by Wayne Henderson but ultimately it is all rather faceless in a way that, say, Side Effect, were not. "Hollywood Dreaming" is the best cut and rather inexplicably failed as a single. As might be inferred from the names of the group members, they embraced Islam, but it didn't help them to become stars.

Fat Larry's Band

Larry James; Art Capehart; Erskine Williams; Ted Cohen; Larry LaBes; Darryl Grant; Terry Price; Freddie Campbell; Alfonso Smith; Douglas Jones; Jimmy Lee; Frank Williams; Anthony Middleton; John Barry; Arthur Austin; Butch Harper; Charles Kennedy; Ed Martin; Tony Chambers; Alton Clark; George Fairbanks; Steve Garand; Doug Slick

Feel It 1976 WMOT WM 625 Producer: Vince Montana

Off The Wall 1978 Stax STX-4103 Producers: Larry James, Steve Bernstein, Alan Rubens & Erskine Williams

Spacin' Out (as F.L.B.) 1978 Fantasy WMOT F-9565 Producers: Larry James & WMOT Productions

Lookin' For Love 1979 Fantasy WMOT F-9587 Producers: Larry James & WMOT Productions

Bright City Lights: The Best Of 1978 Fantasy FT-564 Producers: Larry James & Vince Montana (UK)

Stand Up 1980 Fantasy F-9599 Producer: Larry James (Billboard soul charts: 72)

Breakin' Out 1982 WMOT FW 37968 Producers: Larry James & Nick Martinelli

Philadelphia was not really a funky town. Its soul musical legacy was built overwhelmingly on vocal groups and it is not surprising, therefore, that Larry James' outfit produced records that were overshadowed in just about every way by those from the O'Jays, Intruders, Delfonics, Blue Magic etc. It was with the latter two, however, that James cut his musical teeth, playing drums for their bands, before forming one of his own in 1976 in which year "Center City" became an undeniably popular club record, but nevertheless failed to reach the soul charts. It is the best track on their *Feel It* LP debut, which shared the vocals around with a particularly gruff lead (James himself?) on the dated sounding title track and "We Just Want To Play For You". Anyone who liked funk should be reasonably impressed by the album, but it lacked that "something" that would have endeared it to a wider audience.

For some reason the follow-up album turned up on the re-constituted Stax label, but was once again produced and performed in Philadelphia. The atypical "Peaceful Journey" from the set became their first ever single to reach the soul charts, although it can hardly be regarded as a "hit" given it only reached #98. "Castle Of Joy", "Sparkle" and "Passing Time" were more representative of the funk they favoured and also provided proof that Fat Larry's Band were certainly accomplished musicians.

The group had by now released two albums and a handful of singles to no great acclaim and it was decided to abbreviate their name to "F.L.B." for the third LP (the only time this happened) and it may or may not have been a co-incidence that one of the 45 releases from it, "Boogie Town" reached the top 50 of the soul singles charts. Whatever, it was a clichéd and forgettable record, as, to be frank, was the entire LP - the sweet and slow "Countryside" and "We Just Can't Get It Together" both beautifully sung by Darryl Grant excepted - which signally failed to stand out from any other funk LP from 1978.

Lookin' For Love contained two more top forty soul singles in the shape of the title cut and "Here Comes The Sun" (not the Beatles song) as well a contender for the worst song title of 1979 in "Hey Pancho It's Disco" which was every bit as bad as it suggests. "How Good Is Love", a fine ballad, was infinitely better and became the third charting 45 from the set at #75.

Every now and then James reminded us of his vocal group roots and the best track of the not bad and rather smooth sounding *Stand Up* LP was a faithful and enjoyable take on The Stairsteps' "You've Waited Too Long". Rather oddly, given it housed no hits, it was the only album that ever charted for the band.

In 1982, Fat Larry's Band released the single that anyone in England over a certain age will always associate them with: "Zoom". It became a sizeable hit here, despite its rather cloying lyrics, but undeniably had a memorable melody. It also sounded nothing like anything they had ever recorded before, and proved that writers Bobby Eli and Len Barry knew how to compose hits (they had enjoyed plenty of others in the past). "Zoom" featured on *Breakin' Out* from which the "hit" in the U.S was "Act Like You Know" at #67. (The U.S. didn't see "Zoom" chart until 1986.) The whole album had much more of a pop flavour than had been the case in the past as a quick listen to "House Party" or "Traffic Stoppers" would prove.

Straight From The Heart 1983 Virgin V2289 Producer: Larry James (UK)

Nice 1986 Omni 90510-1 Producers: Eumir Deodato, Larry James, Terry Price, Dave White, John Madara, Len Barry, & Alan Rubens

After a few years on WMOT, the group moved to a new label, Virgin, in 1983 and the first album delivered pretty decent versions of Marvin Gaye's "Stubborn Kind Of Fellow" and Jean Carne's "Don't Let It Go To Your Head" (she sings on it, which helped). What didn't help was a cheap looking cover, which could not have enticed prospective purchasers. And there were no more pretty decent tracks, either.

Fat Larry Band's last ever album came out on Omni in 1986, a year in which drum programming was as ubiquitous and unwelcome as kudzu vines, and the whole brazenly unsubtle thing would require a better man than me to listen to in its entirety.

James died, aged only 38 in December 1987, and never managed to enjoy a true hit in his home country.

Faze-O

Keith Harrison; Tyrone Crum; Ralph Aikens; Roger Parker; Robert Neal

Riding High 1977 She SH 740 Producer: Tight Corporation (Billboard soul charts: 19; Billboard pop charts: 98)

Good Thang 1978 SH 741 Producers: Clarence Satchell, Billy Beck & Keith Harrison (Billboard soul charts: 40; Billboard pop charts: 145)

Breakin' The Funk 1979 SH 742 Producers: Clarence Satchell & Keith Harrison (Billboard soul charts: 48)

Faze-O were produced by Satch from The Ohio Players and, unsurprisingly, there is some similarity in the sound of the two bands. Unfortunately for Faze-O though, the Players were past their best by the end of the seventies and there is little of enduring worth on the three albums above. It's also the case that Faze-O were much more appreciated by American audiences than they were in England. None of the LPs were released over here and I cannot recall hearing any of their music in the clubs I visited.

Their style was set as almost invariably long funk work-outs with "I Still Love You", "I'm Thankful" and "See You Through The Night" (with co-lead vocals from an uncredited woman) from the *Breakin' The Funk* album being just about the only conventional songs they ever cut. I think that they would have been better served by keeping their tracks shorter and tighter and I simply see no good reason why "Who Loves You" on *Good Thang* went on for over twelve minutes, especially as it wasn't a showcase for any soloing. The three singles they placed on the soul charts followed the unusual pattern of being the title track from each LP, with "Riding High" (one of their more mellow grooves) being the biggest by some distance at #9 soul.

Keith Harrison went on to join another Ohio funk aggregation, The Dazz Band, after Faze-O disbanded in 1979, while Roger Parker ended up in Steve Arrington's Hall Of Fame.

Norman Feels

Norman Feels 1973 Just Sunshine JSS-8 Producer: Sal Scaltro

Where Or When 1974 Just Sunshine JSS-3502 Producer: Sal Scaltro

Some readers of this book might recall an excellent English magazine, *Black Music*, which was absolutely required reading for the first few years of its existence. I was still learning a lot about soul music in 1974 and for a while *BM* used to run a list of editor Tony Cummings' favourite singles and LPs of the previous year. Back then, most of the records he highlighted were unknown to me and one of his favourite LPs of 1973 was Norman Feel's debut on Just Sunshine. This sounded impossibly obscure and alluring to me back then and I made a concerted effort to track a copy down. It was a great decision, for it was (and is) a wonderful album, and the only sorrow is that Norman Feels remained obscure for the whole of his short career.

His real name was Norman Solomon and he had sung with the New York Preludes in the early sixties and wrote the odd song for other groups before re-surfacing with the two albums above. The debut was a lovely thing of almost fragile music, symbolised by the hand on the cover which seemed to be having difficulty holding on to the wispy and ethereal sounds that were contained within. Drums were placed way back in the mix and strings took pride of place, which could have been a problem, were they not arranged by the excellent David Van De Pitte. Recorded in Detroit, with legendary players like Jack Brokensha, Eddie Brown (lovely to hear congas on a soul album) and Robert White onboard, it was an album made entirely for listening rather than dancing, with a continuity and overall feel that only seemed possible in that post - *What's Going On* era. Feels was a skilled song-writer, with a great sense of melody, and he wrote everything save for a startling slowed down version of The Supremes' "My World Is Empty Without You". His voice, delicate and keening, was perfect to interpret these songs, of which "Something About You (Makes Me Love You)" is probably the best and most representative of his talent. Two singles were released but neither were a success.

The follow-up, *Where Or When*, is another splendid album, but perhaps lacks the distinctiveness of the debut and this I put down to a more pronounced Marvin Gaye feel on some of the cuts, (particularly "Movie", and the title track) and a sense that Feels' very best songs had been used on the earlier set. On the other hand there is more variety this time around: "Mr. Wanna Be" sounds like a superior theme tune for a "Blaxploitation" movie and "You Made Me Feel Better" is even nearly danceable. Everything else is resolutely set just below mid-tempo and the Detroit musicians and Van De Pitte do another sterling job. Feels sings in a slightly lower register than before and Aretha's "Until You Come Back To Me" gets a lovely makeover. Sadly, though, the album fared no better than the debut and it seemed that Just Sunshine didn't have the necessary clout to make it in the marketplace (the only charting albums the label ever had were with a soulful sounding white group, The Fabulous Rhinestones, and then only at the rather pitiful #193 pop).

Feels left the music industry after this and died in the 90s of an aneurism. He deserves to be remembered as a soul mant of consummate taste and talent. Apparently, he used to drive a bus before he passed on: I hope he used to sing to his passengers.

Sandra Feva

The Need To Be 1979 Venture VL-1002 Producers: Tony Camillo & Cecile Barker

Savoir Faire 1981 Venture VL-1008 Producers: Tony Camillo, Cecile Barker & The Wizards

Fever All Through The Night 1990? Grandstand 900 No producer listed

Sandra Arnold was born in Los Angeles, but moved early to Detroit from where she issued her first records as Sandra Richardson (her married name) and her later ones as Sandra Feva. The records under the Richardson name didn't chart but many soul fans will cherish her original version of Gladys Knight & The Pips' "I Feel A Song In My Heart" which was the closest she came to a hit at the start of her career.

Feva's first album didn't come out until 1979 and it was a patchy affair, with the tracks seeming to go in two by two. By which I mean: there were a couple of disco tracks; a couple of rather horrible MOR tunes ("Sometimes When We Touch" and "Three Times A Man"); revisited oldies in "Expressway To Your Heart" and "The Choking Kind" and two ballads that can't but help bring Gladys Knight to mind: the title track and "Love Me For What I Am", which were the best things on show. Also good was the one cut that stood out alone, a medley of "Pain In My Heart", "These Arms Of Mine" and "I've Been Loving You Too Long". These last three cuts prove that Feva was a vocalist of great talent, with superb range and timing, but I could understand why Tony Camillo wanted to hedge his bets on a singer who remained fairly unknown.

Nothing she had done to date, though, prepared us for the excellent, almost classic, *Savoir Faire* set in 1981. It contained ten tracks, none of which were poor, and profited from some inspired writing and producing from Camillo, excellent musicians and glorious singing from Feva. "Leaving This Time" was magnificently arranged, and featured a genuinely inspired little trail of guitar notes, while "Let The Roses Die" was simply the best country-soul performance of the decade. "Here Now" also boasted a vocal of uncommon quality and, like the equally splendid "Tell 'Em I Heard It", returned Feva to the soul charts when released as a single (although in the former's case, she had to wait until a beefed-up new version appeared in 1987). Disastrously, Venture collapsed soon after and Feva went on to sing back-up for Aretha Franklin from 1982 for a number of years, a period of time in which, rather ironically, Aretha produced not a single album of the same quality as *Savoir Faire*.

She returned in 1986 as the featured singer for a short-lived (and non-existent) group, Epicenter, who placed the superb "You Can't Come Up Here No More" on the soul charts at #76 that same year. An album did not materialise, though, and she had to wait until the early nineties for her final LP to appear.

Which was another inconsistent set, revising three tracks from the previous two LPs: "Choking Kind", "Fade Away" and "Leaving This Time" and predictably all were inferior to the originals. But they were mere irrelevancies; what really hurt was a thing called "Sexyonic". Cutting a singer of Feva's quality on a mess like this was a bit like using Chateau Lafite to make the gravy for a Sunday roast. Much, much better was the lilting "Boy What You Gonna Do" and "Making Up My Own Mind" was good, too. But in the end, none of it really mattered as the LP didn't receive great distribution outside its Detroit origins and is not very well known.

A last single sneaked out in 1996 but there were to be no more trips to the recording studio although she continued (and continues) to sing live. Her rather scant commercial rewards were in no way a reflection of her talent. She is a magnificent singer and everyone should listen to *Savoir Faire* at every opportunity.

Alvin Fields

Special Delivery 1981 A & M SP-4890 Producer: Michael Zager

Fields is a highly talented singer and writer (The Manhattans, Gladys Knight and Cissy Houston are just three examples of who has cut his songs) who has always seemed to be content to lurk in the background, which presumably accounts for the fact that he only released this one album and remains rather unheralded.

His wide-ranging voice reminds me a little of David Lasley's and the LP is a pretty good one with an emphasis on upbeat songs, all of which are underpinned by the fine bass-playing of Francisco Centeno and Jolyon Skinner. It's just a shame that there is nothing outstanding on board as I believe Fields has the talent to have had a great LP in him.

Lee Fields

Let's Talk It Over 1979 Angle 3 A3-4-28-79 Producer: Lee Fields

North Carolina's Lee Fields has been recording and releasing records for over forty years but it is only in the last five or six that he has finally begun to receive recognition, good reviews, repeat live bookings and hopefully decent sales.

His only ever vinyl album was released back in 1979 on the tiny Angle 3 records out of Plainfield, New Jersey. It's another with an entirely uninspired cover (yellow roses) but it's utterly captivating nevertheless, with a wide array of styles. Both "Your My Weakness" and the tremendous slow-drag title track sound as if they were cut in Memphis circa 1966 (and just about *no-one* was cutting sides like these in 1979); "Mighty Mighty Love" rolled along winningly; the instrumental "Flim Flam" belied its title in its solid funkiness; "She's A Love Maker" is a terrific James Brown rip-off; "Everybody Gonna Give Their Thing Away" was a re-cut of a single he had released a few years before.

None of this quality availed it any however and it bombed completely. But it does prove that what goes around comes around: there was no audience for this sort of un-reconstructed hard soul in 1979; in 2016, and without greatly changing his style, there is.

Richard "Dimples" Fields

Two Are Better Than One 197? Jo Jo JLP-101 Producer: Richard "Dimples" Fields

It's Finger Lickin' Good 1973 Dat Richfield Kat DRK 196273 Producer: Richard "Dimples" Fields

Spoiled Rotten! 1974 Dat Richfield Kat DRK ?#1? (sic) Producer: Richard "Dimples" Fields

Ready For Anything 1977 Dat Richfield Kat DRK 3-21-41B Producer: Richard "Dimples" Fields

Richard "Dimples" Fields was an extraordinarily good looking man. He released records for over twenty years. His time in the spotlight lasted just over a year. It is therefore hard to shake the feeling that the record companies of America really missed a trick with him before he died in 2000, aged only 57.

He had recorded the odd single back in the sixties but it was the four albums for his own labels that at least kept his name out there in the seventies. Someone of means must have been behind him, too, as the second album, *It's Finger Lookin' Good*, boasted a gatefold sleeve and a number of colour photographs, all of which would have cost money for a singer who had never hit any national charts despite years of trying. I can also attest to the fact that the albums cannot have received great distribution as none of them ever turned up in Brighton at the time of release, or indeed, even afterwards.

The Jo Jo album was his first and one cannot discuss it without also mentioning Smokey Robinson, who clearly had a massive influence on Fields' singing, although the Motown star was frankly more talented and had an ache and purity to his voice which Fields couldn't quite match. The record also has a strong doo-

Johnny Adams
AFTER ALL THE GOOD IS GONE

ASHFORD & SIMPSON
GIMME SOMETHING REAL

Darrell Banks Is Here!
ATCO

WILLIAM BELL
PHASES OF REALITY

got to find a sweet name
HARMON BETHEA
THE MASK MEN AND THE AGENTS

MEET "MISSISSIPPI CHARLES"
BEVEL

STEREO
Bobby Bland
TWO STEPS from the BLUES

Blue Magic Thirteen Blue Magic Lane

ANGELO BOND
BONDAGE

Lou Bond
Lou Bond

brothers unlimited
who's for the young

Polydor
KING OF SOUL
JAMES BROWN
AND THE FAMOUS FLAMES

CHUCK JACKSON
MAXINE BROWN
SAYING SOMETHING
stereo
wand

MEL BROWN
FOR PROMOTION ONLY
Ownership Reserved By ABC
Sale is Unlawful

The King of Rock n' Soul
Solomon Burke
Goodbye baby (Baby goodbye) Cry to me Won't you give him (One more chance)
You're good for me You can't love them all Someone to love me Beautiful brown eyes

OKeh STEREO
BILLY BUTLER
RIGHT TRACK

THE ICE MAN COMETH
JERRY BUTLER
mercury
FEATURING: ARE YOU HAPPY
HEY WESTERN UNION MAN • NEVER GIVE YOU UP • LOST

jean carn

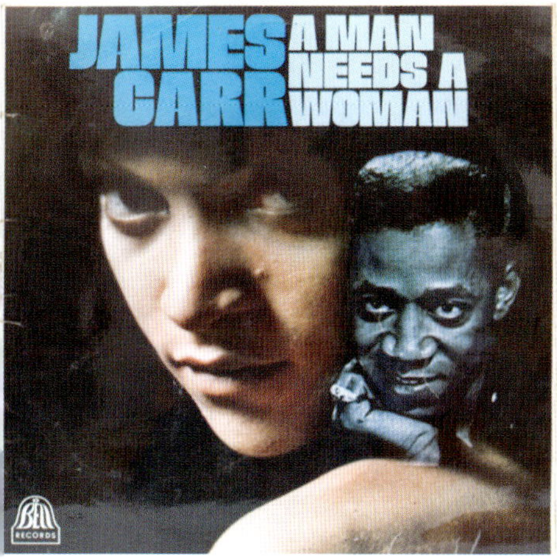
JAMES CARR
A MAN NEEDS A WOMAN

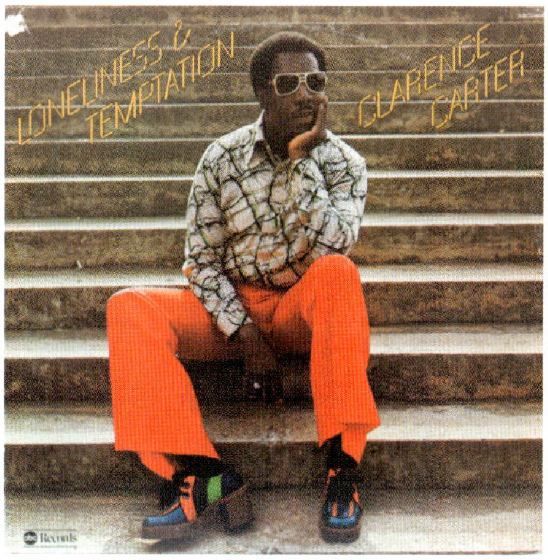
LONELINESS & TEMPTATION
CLARENCE CARTER

Brunswick
gene chandler
"the girl don't care"

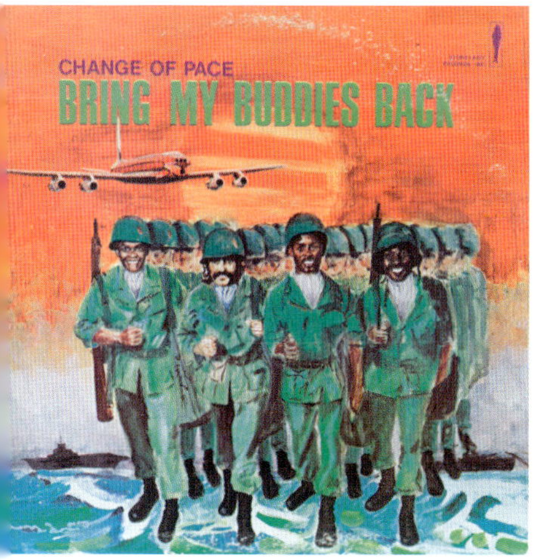
CHANGE OF PACE
BRING MY BUDDIES BACK

RAY CHARLES
DOING HIS THING
EMI

Charnissa

Chi-lites
Stoned out of my Mind
I Found Sunshine

CHUCK CISSEL
JUST FOR YOU
Featuring the full length Disco Mix of the Smash Hit
"CISSELIN' HOT"
ARISTA

MOD-ART
The Class-Set
MY STYLE

Trying to live my life without you
Otis Clay

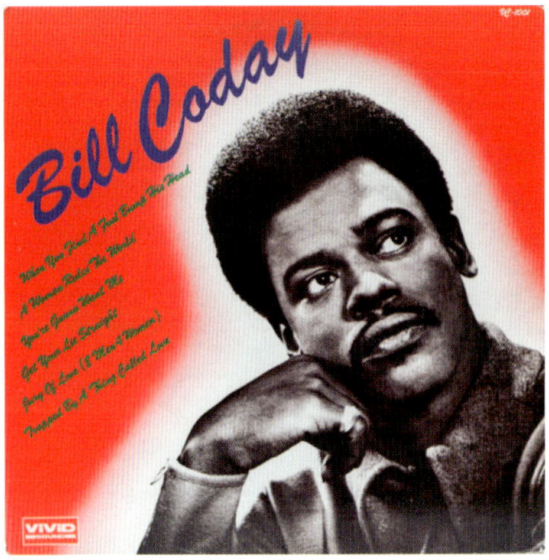
Bill Coday

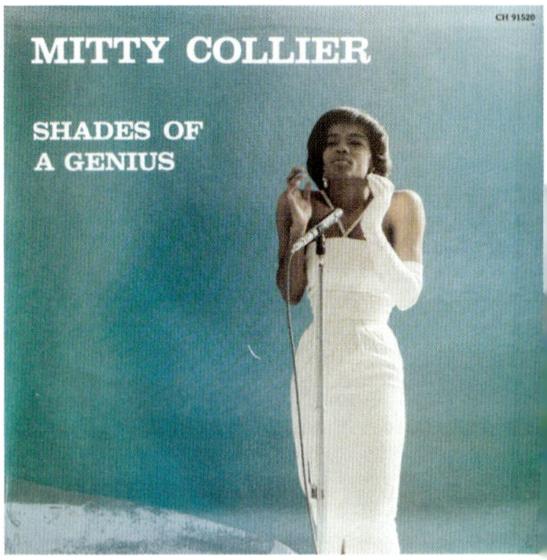
MITTY COLLIER
SHADES OF A GENIUS

BENNIE CONN
Soul Music

I'm in need of Love
Lou Courtney
Epic Records Radio Station Service
Not For Resale

DON COVAY
SUPER DUDE I

CREME D' COCOA
Nasty Street

General Crook

Long As You Love Me
Bettye Crutcher

SWEET WOMAN'S LOVE
Cry, Cry, Cry
My Love Is so Strong
GEATER DAVIS
HOUSE OF Orange
STEREO HOS-6000

WITHOUT YOU IN MY LIFE
Tyrone Davis
DAKAR

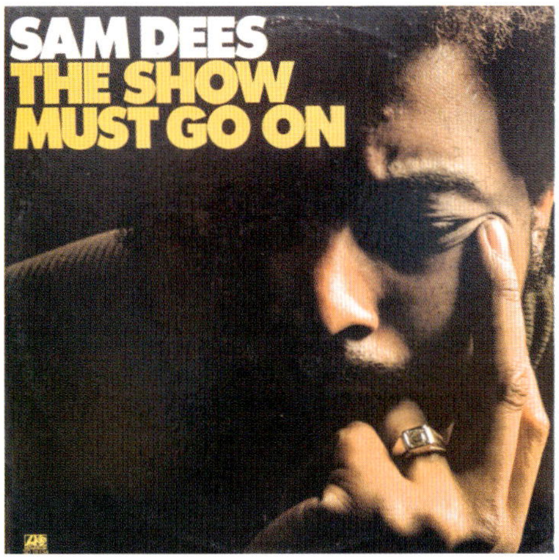
SAM DEES
THE SHOW
MUST GO ON

THE DELFONICS
INCLUDING: DIDN'T I (BLOW YOUR MIND THIS TIME) ■ TRYING TO MAKE A FOOL OF ME
bell

LPS 804
STEREO
CADET RECORDS
THE DELLS
THERE IS

The Dells vs. The Dramatics

The Dramatics · A Dramatic Experience
including: Hey, You! Get Off My Mountain.

I'm a Loser
DORIS DUKE

STEREO
THE DYNAMICS
FIRST LANDING

THE EBONYS

Ecstasy, passion & pain

JOHN EDWARDS

THE ETHICS SING
stereo

"TELL HIM"
AMERICA'S NUMBER ONE HIT
GOLDBLATT'S RECORD RIOT
$1.29
E EXCITERS
UNITED ARTISTS
PLUS TEN MORE NEW SONGS

Family Circle
LOVE BOUND
STRAWBERRY

Norman Feels
2933 401

Sandra
FEVA
SAVOIR FAIRE

BRUCE FISHER
Red Hot

FLASHLIGHT

THE FOUR MINTS
STEREO
Capsoul

FOUR TOPS
ASK THE LONELY · WITHOUT THE ONE YOU LOVE · BABY I NEED YOUR LOVING
WHERE DID YOU GO · TEA HOUSE IN CHINA TOWN · DON'T TURN AWAY · LOVE HAS GONE
YOUR LOVE IS AMAZING · LEFT WITH A BROKEN HEART · SAD SOUVENIRS · CALL ON ME

Funk
INC.

Past, Present and The Futures

the best of luck to you
don't take my kindness for a weakness
earl gains

TO SOUL WITH LOVE
STU GARDNER
Revue

"THAT STUBBORN KINDA' FELLOW"
MARVIN GAYE
INCLUDED IN THIS ALBUM
HITCH HIKE
SOLDIER'S PLEA
I'M YOURS, YOU'RE MINE
HELLO THERE ANGEL
GET MY HANDS ON SOME LOVIN'
TAKING MY TIME
PRIDE AND JOY
WHEREVER I LAY MY HAT
IT HURT ME TOO

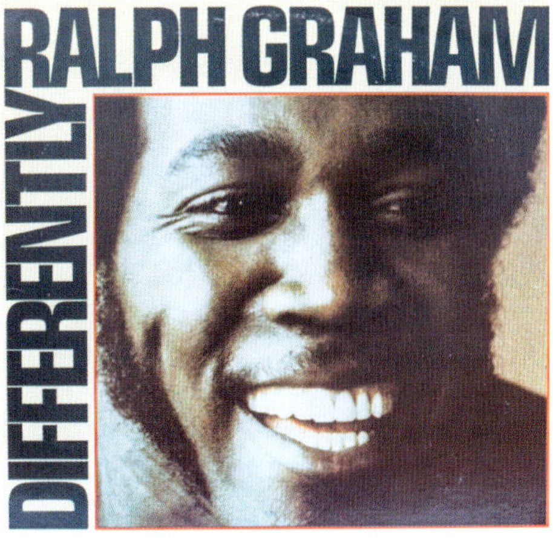
RALPH GRAHAM
DIFFERENTLY

AL GREEN
I'M STILL IN LOVE WITH YOU
LONDON

GARLAND GREEN
Jealous Kind of Fella
Jealous Kind of Fella
Don't Think That I'm a Violent Guy
You Played on a Player
Angel Baby
UNI

Deep Soul Classics Vol. 2
BIG JOHN HAMILTON DORIS ALLEN
STEREO
Big John Hamilton & Doris Allen

CLAY HAMMOND
taking his time

DONNY HATHAWAY
LIVE

Action
ACLP 6007
SOUL PERFECTION
RIDE YOUR PONY•CAN'T LAST MUCH LONGER
MEAN MAN • WHAT A SAD FEELING
NEARER TO YOU • I'M EVIL TONIGHT
LONELY HEARTS•I'M GONNA GIT YA
12 RED ROSES•SHOW IT•BAD LUCK
WHAT'D I DO WRONG • SOMETIME
I DON'T WANNA HEAR IT•HOOK LINE 'N SINKER•TROUBLE WITH MY LOVER
BETTY HARRIS

STAX RECORDS/STEREO
ISAAC HAYES
Hot
Buttered
Soul
stax

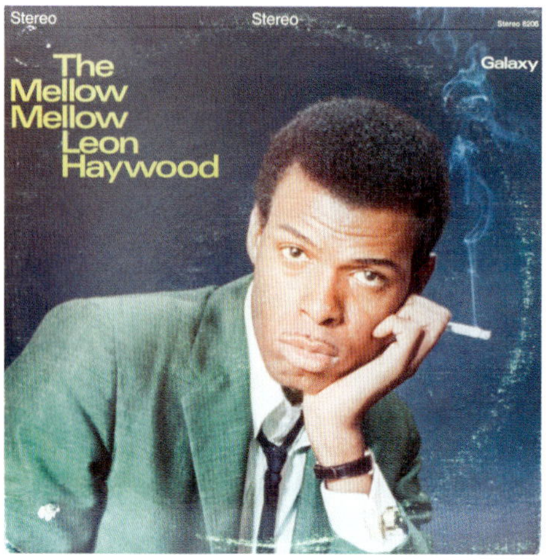
Stereo
Stereo
Stereo 8206
Galaxy
The
Mellow
Mellow
Leon
Haywood

Walter Heath
you know your wrong
dont ya brothe

HEAVEN AND EARTH
I CAN'T SEEM TO FORGET YOU

Michael Henderson
In The Night-Time

The HESITATIONS
Soul Superman

If I Had A Hammer
Willie Hightower

Z.Z. HILL
THE BEST THING THAT'S HAPPENED TO ME

electrified
ernie hines

EDDIE HINTON
VERY EXTREMELY DANGEROUS

HITCHHIKERS

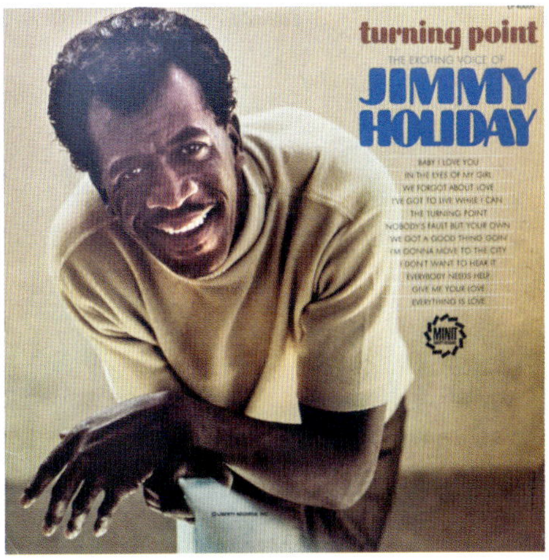
turning point
JIMMY HOLIDAY

The Artistry of Brenda Holloway

LOLEATTA HOLLOWAY
CRY TO ME

EDDIE HOLMAN
A NIGHT TO REMEMBER

Frank Hooker and Positive People

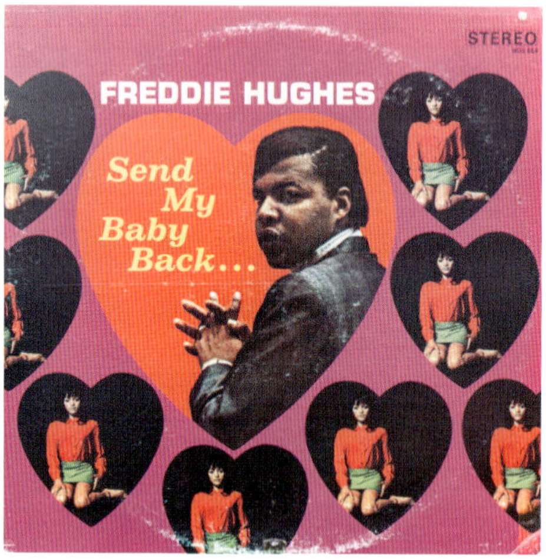
STEREO
FREDDIE HUGHES
Send My Baby Back...

Jimmy Hughes
Why Not Tonight?
ATLANTIC
MONO ATLANTIC 587068

IMPACT

THE IMPRESSIONS
THIS IS MY COUNTRY

THE INCREDIBLES
HEART & SOUL
STEREO
AUDIO ARTS

LUTHER INGRAM
Do You Love
Somebody
KoKo

Save The Children

MILLIE JACKSON
CAUGHT UP

SPEAK HER NAME
Walter
Jackson
SHE'S A WOMAN
NOT YOU
MY ONE CHANCE TO MAKE IT
SPEAK HER NAME
TEAR FOR TEAR
A CORNER IN THE SUN
THEY DON'T GIVE MEDALS
I'LL KEEP ON TRYING
IT'S AN UPHILL CLIMB TO
THE BOTTOM
AFTER YOU THERE CAN
BE NOTHING

Tell Mama
ETTA
JAMES

janice

Fred Wesley and the J.B.'s
"Damn Right I Am Somebody"
people

Norma
Jenkins
Patience Is A Virtue

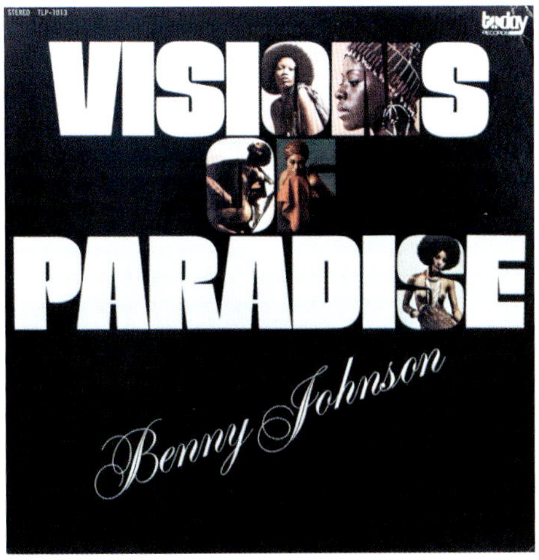
PARADISE
Benny Johnson

SYL JOHNSON
BACK FOR A TASTE OF YOUR LOVE
LONDON

Charlie Jones
(Mr. Master Voice)
EVERYBODY'S BUSINESS IS NOBODY'S BUSINESS

THELMA
JONES

margie joseph
feeling my way

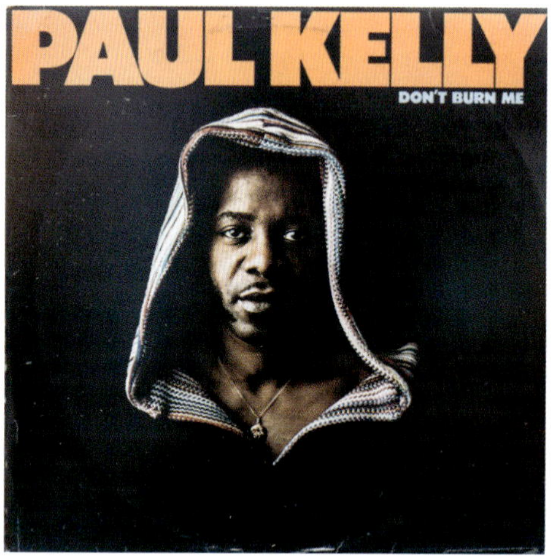
PAUL KELLY
DON'T BURN ME

EDDIE KENDRICK
VINTAGE 78

HI-FI STEREO
PHILIPS
back to soul
ANNA KING
MAKE UP YOUR MIND / IF SOMEBODY TOLD YOU
COME ON HOME · SITTING IN THE DARK · THAT'S WHEN I CRY · I FOUND YOU · I DON'T WANT TO CRY · NIGHT TIME IS THE RIGHT TIME
TENNESSEE WALTZ · BABY, BABY, BABY · COME AND GET THESE MEMORIES · IF YOU DON'T THINK
PHILIPS

TRUTH
KING HANNIBAL
AWARE

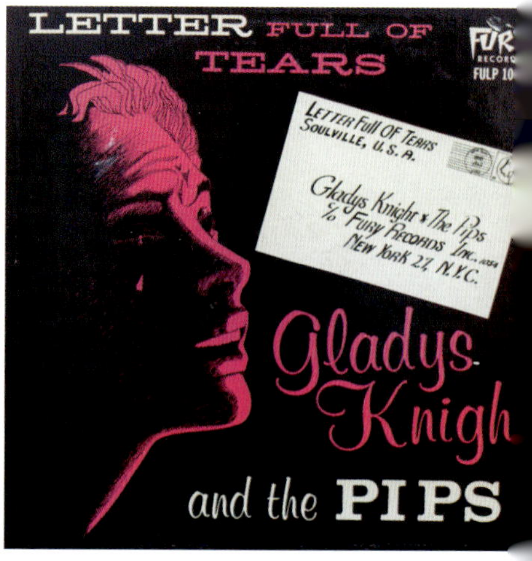
LETTER FULL OF TEARS
Letter Full Of Tears
Soulville, U.S.A.
Gladys Knight & The Pips
% Fury Records Inc.
New York 27, N.Y.C.
Gladys Knigh
and the PIPS

wop feel and is a little flimsy in sound, despite the assistance of talented arrangers like Ron Carson and Art Freeman. Nevertheless, it has some nice moments: "Tears Big As Canteloupes", "The Handwriting On The Wall" and "Tag Along" being the best of the slower tracks and "And Then Along Came Belinda" and "Honest To Pete" being the pick of the faster.

The entire Jo Jo album, minus two tracks, appeared again on the experimental, eclectic, varied and only just short of fascinating *It's Finger Lickin' Good* double LP. When things were good - the arrangements on "Tag Along" and "So Glad I'm Your Top Kat", Clydene Jackson's churchy organ on "You Do Something To Me" and the superb bass players throughout - it was a pleasure to listen to; but the 12 minute long title track or the not much shorter "Snake In The Grass" suggested that too much was simply thrown into an LP that wanted to try on as many styles as possible.

Spoiled Rotten ran for around forty-five minutes but sitting down and listening intently leads me to conclude that it is over-long rather than generous. A somewhat uneasy mix of jazzy sides and a couple of funk workouts ("Sassy" being the best of these), the LP also features some rather irritating and cheap sounding synthesiser which doesn't help the songs on which it is employed. The album is mainly notable for containing a decent cover of The Miracles' "I'll Try Something New" and the original version of Fields's one and only big hit, "If It Ain't One Thing...It's Another".

The last of his "indie" albums, *Ready For Anything*, reprised a couple of tracks from *Finger Lickin' Good* and kicked off with the old Carla Thomas hit, "Gee Whiz" which rather summed up his LPs and music of the time; nice, but somewhat out of step with what was going on in the mainstream. It's hard to imagine he got much airplay in an era where hits needed to be more immediate and "in your face". Fields may have employed some of the politest drummers in soul music history across these albums and there was just not enough "oomph" for them to have been successes or to stand up marvellously well forty years later.

Dimples 1981 Boardwalk NB1-33232 Producers: Richard "Dimples" Fields & Belinda Wilson (Billboard soul charts: 5; Billboard pop charts: 33)

Mr. Look So Good! 1982 Boardwalk NB1-33249 Producers: Richard "Dimples" Fields & Belinda Wilson (Billboard soul charts: 3; Billboard pop charts: 63)

Give Everybody Some! 1982 Boardwalk NB-33258-1 Producers: Richard "Dimples" Fields & Belinda Wilson (Billboard soul charts: 40)

After a break of a few years Fields turned up on Boardwalk, a label big enough to give him a national push, and although the two singles from it didn't do much, the album was a notable seller with "She's Got Papers On Him", a track on which he was helped out by a sassy Betty Wright, possibly being the stand-out cut. He also did a good job on the old classics, "Earth Angel" and "In The Still Of The Night", which both showcased his doo-wop roots. *Dimples'* success was somewhat surprising at the time, as it was an album from a fairly unknown singer that spent more time on songs than dance grooves, even if it did have some uptempo moments.

And then he had his BIG record: a re-make of "If It Ain't One Thing...It's Another" which went all the way to #1 soul (and #47 pop) in early 1982. It deserved its success and could thank the way in which its memorable melody was picked out by a much more assertive arrangement than on the original. In fact, the arrangements by Hense Powell were excellent throughout the whole of the album on which the hit could be located: *Mr. Look So Good!*. Rhythmically too, things were much crisper than on the early albums, with more prominent drumming, and its a shame there were no musician credits. Fields was by now attracting a similar audience to Luther Vandross, which would have included a large middle class black fanbase. But if Fields certainly had it over Vandross in the looks department, it has to be said that Luther could sing rings around Fields and it was this lack of a distinctive voice which I believe probably sealed "Dimples" fate as his records became less impressive, selling in ever decreasing numbers.

By the time of *Give Everybody Some!* the crossover audience had almost completely vanished: look at its chart performance compared to the two previous LPs. I can imagine why too, as it was quite easy to get a bit bored with his records around this time and *Give Everybody Some!*, while not being in any way "bad", was simply a bit dull and doesn't sound particularly thrilling thirty five years later either. The usual Fields' trademarks are all here: a cover of an old song ("You Send Me"); too much talking on too many tracks; impressive arrangements; trawls from his back catalogue ("Moody's Mood").

Mmm 1984 RCA AFL1-5169 Producers: Richard "Dimples" Fields & Belinda Wilson (Billboard soul charts: 51)

Dark Gable 1985 AFL1-5482 Producers: Richard "Dimples" Fields & Belinda Wilson

Tellin' It Like It Is 1987 Columbia FC 40859 Producers: Richard "Dimples" Fields & Belinda Wilson (Billboard soul charts: 58)

Dimples 1990 Bellmark D1-71804 Producer: Richard "Dimples" Fields

The move to RCA started off well. *Mmm* is filled with songs with strong hooks, and the whole thing has a bright, poppy feel that is to its credit. "Your Wife Is Cheating On Us" and "Jazzy Lady" were singles that charted but not in any substantial way. I should also add that "Dear Mr. God" was a bit cringe-making but is clearly a song that would play much better in America than in England.

I am not familiar with his last three LPs which continued his downward commercial spiral but I think he did a decent job on Aaron Neville's "Tell It Like It Is" which was the title track (and his second most successful single at #22 soul) from his penultimate album. I was also gently amused to see that the final track on his final LP was entitled "I'm Outta Here". (However, he did return with a new CD in 1994.)

Fiesta

Johnny Burton; Thomas Wiley; Thomas Bullock; Carl Sims; Wesley Lee

Fiesta 1978 Arista AB 4196 Producers: Randy Stewart & Marvell Thomas

The Fiestas cut numerous singles for the Old Town label in the late fifties and sixties, including one huge hit in "So Fine" (#3 soul, #11 pop) but never got to release an album, a state of affairs that was to continue for the handful of labels for which they recorded in the seventies. They shed and added a few singers, dropped the second s in 1978, and - hey presto! - an album finally appeared. A likeable one too, even if no-one could quite work out what Fiesta should sound like.

As my evidence: their one modest hit on single under the new name, "E.S.P." (#53), was surely hoping to emulate the huge success of the Bar-Kays, the likable "Everyday Housewife" clearly had the Spinners in mind and "Hold On" had faint echoes of "Hang On In There Baby". The best tracks were ones that didn't obviously sound like anyone else: "Thanks For The Sweet Memories" and "Baby If You Love Me" were lovely ballads which featured husky lead vocals (Tommy Bullock?) and excellent arrangements from Stewart and Thomas. All in all it was a very acceptable LP, and good to hear a Memphis record in 1978 that didn't seem to be aware that there was something called "disco" out there.

Carl Sims went on to make some acclaimed solo sides and The Fiestas finally got an album of their own in 1986 when Ace put out a compilation of their Old Town material which I have not included here as it contains their early work from the pre-soul era.

Fifth Avenue

a) Carol Lynn Townes; Sam Credell; Herb Duncombe; Roger Mimms; Jimmy Solomon b) Darren Durst; Mark Sligh; Derek Organ; Gamal Smalley; Joe Foxworth

Carol Townes And Fifth Avenue 1976 Sixth Avenue AWL1-1671 Producer: Lou Courtney

Miracles 1981 Lyon's L-572 Producers: Alvin Few, Joe Foxworth & Fifth Avenue

Given the desirability of Fifth Avenue as an address, it is not surprising that more than one group chose to use it for their name and the two groups above have nothing to do with each other.

The Carol Townes led group delivered a fine set, produced deftly by Lou Courtney. It mixed up dance (but not disco) sides like "Bring Your Body" and "One Hand Washes The Other" with slower efforts such as the outstanding "The Best Thing A Man Can Ever Do For His Woman" which proved that Ms.Townes was more than just a pretty face (she was apparently a six times beauty pageant winner.) The album is worth hearing and has always been a rather unfairly ignored work. Townes herself had some success as a solo artist in the mid eighties but with records in the hi-energy vein that I have deemed out of scope.

The group on Lyon's gave us a decent set as well, although I remain a bit bemused why it has become "in-demand" given that it is by and large a standard funky album with a discernible EWAF influence. The record is better when the tempo is speeded up and a ballad like "You Are My Life" is rather routine. I do think that the dreamy title track is nice enough but I don't care at all for the pure pop of "Everything's Gonna Be Alright" or "God Has".

As if to prove the durability of the name, a third group called Fifth Avenue put a single onto the soul charts in 1987 but I am pretty sure they had no connection to the two above.

Fifth Dimension

Marilyn McCoo; Florence La Rue; Ron Townson; Lamonte McLemore; Billy Davis; Danny Miller Beard; Terri Bryant; Mic Bell; Lou Courtney

Up, Up And Away 1967 Soul City SCS-92000 Producers: Johnny Rivers & Marc Gordon (Billboard soul charts: 10; Billboard pop charts: 8)

The Magic Garden 1968 Soul City SCS-92001 Producer: Bones Howe (Billboard soul charts: 43; Billboard pop charts: 105)

Stoned Soul Picnic 1968 Soul City SCS-92002 Producer: Bones Howe (Billboard soul charts: 10; Billboard pop charts: 21)

The Age Of Aquarius 1969 Soul City SCS-92005 Producer: Bones Howe (Billboard soul charts: 2; Billboard pop charts: 2)

Greatest Hits 1970 Soul City 33900 (Billboard soul charts: 8; Billboard pop charts: 5)

The July 5th Album 1970 Soul City SCS -33901 Producer: Bones Howe

I bow to no-one in my admiration and passion for the magnificent "Wedding Bell Blues" and "One Less Bell To Answer" but, until a much more recent re-acquaintance with their music, I would have been compelled to say that they were the only two records by The Fifth Dimension I had ever loved. For the most part, I always found their music to be much too light and pop-oriented although that isn't to say that I was unaware of the talent they had, the calibre of the musicians that worked on their music or the quality of their best songs. They certainly had success with both "soul" and "pop" audiences: of their eleven biggest selling singles a telling nine of them were bigger hits on the pop charts than on the soul charts. On the other hand, they had eight top twenty LPs on the soul charts, with five of them performing less well on the pop listings. Despite such undoubted commercial conquests, however, there has also been a feeing that they were not really loved by black audiences in the same manner as The Temptations, James Brown, Bobby Bland or Curtis Mayfield and it was possibly the whiff of the middle class good life their music exuded that alienated some. Singing for Richard Nixon at the White House didn't help either.

They recorded a single back in 1966 as The Versatiles before being "discovered" by Johnny Rivers and changing their name to the more exotic Fifth Dimension. The first LP set the scene: top class musicianship, complex arrangements and tempo changes, lots of Jim Webb songs. Interestingly though, despite the undoubted success of the LP, it yielded no hit singles at all, and it can thus be seen as one of the earliest attempts to aim a black group at the album rather than singles market. As such it was fairly important, but the music didn't persuade me and it all sounds as polite now as it did then.

The second album, however, didn't even garner LP success, let alone bring forth any top selling 45s. There is no reason at all why a black group should confine themselves to making soul music and, believe me, this LP certainly wasn't soulful. There are those who rate this LP highly and it was nothing if not ambitious, though many also called it pretentious as the titles of three of the tracks might suggest: "Orange Air", "Dreams/Pax/Nepenthe" and "Requiem: 820 Latham".

Webb's influence was much less marked on the *Stoned Soul Picnic* album although it remained a resolutely "pop" album for the most part. The title track became their first (and biggest ever) soul single success when it reached #2 in the summer of 1968 and two further tracks also breached the soul top fifty.

Age Of Acquarius was the real big one for the group though. A worldwide hit, the single went to #1 on the pop chart and the album was also a huge seller. I find the song to be tedious in the extreme, but that's just me. At least this is the album where "Wedding Bell Blues" can be located and that also went to #1 pop when put out on a 45. They had a good stab at "Working On A Groovy Thing", another top 20 pop single, and "Dont'cha Hear Me Calling To You" was a fine track, atypical of their normal sound but I wonder what Cream fans made of their take on "Sunshine Of Your Love".

The quintet rounded out their time with Soul City by the release of a top-selling *Greatest Hits* set and another compilation entitled *The July 5th Album* before moving to Bell where they initially continued to sell a lot of records.

Portrait 1970 Bell 6045 Producer: Bones Howe (Billboard soul charts: 6; Billboard pop charts: 20)

Love's Lines, Angles And Rhymes 1971 Bell 6060 Producer: Bones Howe (Billboard soul charts: 10; Billboard pop charts: 17)

Live 1971 Bell 9000 Producer: Bones Howe (Billboard soul charts: 13; Billboard pop charts: 32)

Individually & Collectively 1972 Bell 9000 Producer: Bones Howe (Billboard soul charts: 21; Billboard pop charts: 58)

Greatest Hits On Earth 1972 Bell 1106 Producer: Bones Howe (Billboard soul charts: 10; Billboard pop charts: 14)

Living Together, Growing Together 1973 Bell 1116 Producer: Bones Howe (Billboard soul charts: 25; Billboard pop charts: 108)

Soul & Inspiration 1974 Bell 1315 Producer: John Florez (Billboard soul charts: 55; Billboard pop charts: 202)

The first Bell album, *Portrait*, featured the excellent "One Less Bell To Answer" which was sung every bit as sweetly and authoritatively by Marilyn McCoo as had been the case on "Wedding Bell Blues". It went to #2 pop and #4 soul on single as a very successful follow-up to the lead-off single "Save The Country" which only reached a rather disappointing #27 pop and #41 soul. I didn't particularly care for this album either, which had a deeply ponderous thing on side two entitled "The Declaration" but they also did deliver a better than I would have expected take on "A Change Is Gonna Come".

Next up was the rather unwieldy sounding "Love's Lines Angles And Rhymes", but the title track was a good song and another top twenty pop hit when released on 45. A winning Billy Davis-led version of "What Does It Take To Win Your Love" is on the set, as are the usual number of pure pop sides.

A double "Live" album followed, before the swansong of their hit-making days with the rather good "(Last Night) I Didn't Get To Sleep At All" reaching #8 on the pop charts in the first half of 1972 when it was pulled off the *Individually & Collectively* set. This was an interesting affair, as a number of the tracks permitted all the singers to perform solo, with the exception of the deep-voiced McLemore. Ron Townson upstages everyone by his superb job on the gorgeous "Band Of Gold" (not the Freda Payne song), one of their first truly soulful cuts.

From here on in The Fifth Dimension would not have any more big selling records but they still had their moments: "Everything's Been Changed", "Ashes To Ashes" and "Let Me Be Lonely" were all pretty good cuts from *Living Together, Growing Together*, despite sounding almost completely out of step with how other "soul" records sounded in 1973.

Bell obviously realised this and John Florez moved into the producer's chair for the *Soul & Inspiration* set. Songs from Bill Withers, Ralph Graham and Teddy Randazzo appeared on a Fifth Dimension for the first time and "Harlem" with its tough Billy Davis vocal was the first ever side where the word "funky" could have been used to describe the group's music. The title track, the old Mann & Weil song, was good too even if it sounded about ten years out of date (so Bell hadn't fully worked it out). But the best cut of all was the marvellous "No Love In The Room", which I have even played in clubs in my absurdly short-lived deejay career.

Earthbound 1975 ABC ABCD-897 Producer: Jimmy Webb (Billboard soul charts: 30; Billboard pop charts: 136)

Star Dancing 1978 Motown M7-896R Producers: Harold Johnson, Michel Rubini, Marc Gordon, Pam Sawyer & Marilyn McLeod

High On Sunshine 1979 Motown M7-896R Producers: Harold Johnson, Michel Rubini, Marc Gordon, Pam Sawyer & Marilyn McLeod

Jimmy Webb came back for *Earthbound* which didn't really work in any way at all. It was once again a work of no soulful content whatsoever, apart from the "Don't Stop For Nothing" and "Lean On Me Always" cuts, and didn't have the consolation of selling many copies either. I'm frankly a bit astonished it reached #30 on the soul charts as I cannot imagine any U.S. soul stations playing any of it; certainly I never heard any of it on U.K. radio at the time. Their best work, by far, though, for ABC was their version of "Love Hangover" which reached #39 soul in the spring of 1976 and I would challenge anyone who ever heard it "blind" to realise it was by The Fifth Dimension. Sadly, it didn't appear on any LP.

By the time of their next album, in 1978, not only had Webb moved on again, but so had Townson, McCoo and Davis. Married for some years now (no more Wedding Bell Blues), the latter two left the group to go out as a duo in 1976 and enjoyed some success for a while. Three new members ensured that Fifth Dimension retained the number of personnel their name demanded.

Motown needed to find a way to fuse the traditional approach of the group with something more contemporary and they didn't do too badly, even if the emphasis - probably correctly - was on the latter rather than the former. "We Could Fly" is unusual in featuring a baritone lead vocal and "You Are The Reason" was a pretty fair falsetto led dance track that became their last ever soul charting single at #66.

There was one more change of personnel for their last ever album release and it was an exciting one too, as Lou Courtney joined the group, delivering a typically deft vocal on Ashford and Simpson's "Everybody's Got To Give It Up". Mic Bell could sing well too, and he did a good job on "Magic Man", which I think must be the original of the song that co-writer Robert Winters had some success with in early 1981. Unfortunately, side two was very dull indeed.

The only time the group seemed to re-surface after the Motown days was in 1983 when a decent version of Diana Ross' "Surrender" slipped out to more or less total indifference. I have ignored the majority of the large number of compilations that exist.

Fillmotions

Young Girls In Motion 1980 Young Girls YGP-1001
Producer: Paul Breed

In 1979 an obscure Bay Area group called Fillmotion put out an exquisite sweet soul ballad entitled "Young Girl" which sounded as if it was recorded a few years earlier. It did little but a re-cut and slightly inferior version of the same song was still the standout cut from the one LP by the four or five men (I think) who added an "s" to their name and saw their dreams of the big-time fail to materialise. "Last Night" is lovely too, but the dance tracks, "Let's Party" and "Star Rise", are dull and predictable. It's a short album, with only six tracks (and one of these is simply the instrumental backing to "Young Girl") and I suspect was pressed up in limited quality as not many copies ever turn up.

Fingers

Chris Adams; Michael Ford

Searching For A Love 1979 RCA AFL1-3311 Producers: Chris Adams & Michael Ford

An album devoted to dancing, and almost a perfect example of a so-called "one track" set. "Fingers", the nickname of keyboard player Adams, served up some generally highly underwhelming disco music and if it wasn't for Foster McPhees's soulful and husky lead singing on "Searching For A Love", the best track on here by an extraordinary distance, I'm afraid this record would not stand up to much scrutiny. McPhee sings "Wanna Get A Piece Of Your Love" as well, but a number of other cuts are instrumentals or sung by Michael Ford, who does not have McPhee's power.

Finished Touch

Kenny Stover; Larry Brown; Harold Johnson; Michael McGloiry; Brenda Sutton; Michael Sutton

Need To Know You Better 1978 Motown M7 906R1
Producers: Kenny Stover, Larry Brown, Terry McFaddin, Harold Johnson, Michael McGloiry, Brenda Sutton & Michael Sutton

Research and the back cover suggest Finished Touch comprised the six individuals listed above but it wouldn't surprise me to one day discover that there was really no such group as The Finished Touch i.e. one that ever went out on the road.

The ten tracks within are all aimed at the dance floor and the only real light and shade is provided by a couple of jazzier songs and the two instrumentals that are a little more restrained than the rest of the disco-oriented ones. There is only one cut I will ever ly play again: "Sticks And Stones", a good Funkadelic clone that reached #88 on the soul listings in late 1978 as a 45.

First Choice (see also Wardell Piper)

Rochelle Fleming; Debbie Martin; Annette Guest; Joyce Jones; Ursula Herring; Wardell Piper

Armed & Extremely Dangerous 1973 Philly Groove PG 1400 Producers: Stan Watson & Norman Harris (Billboard soul charts: 55; Billboard pop charts: 184)

The Player 1974 Philly Groove PG 1502 Producers: Stan Watson & Norman Harris (Billboard soul charts: 36; Billboard pop charts: 143)

The Best Of 1976 Kory KK 1004

So Let Us Entertain You 1976 WB BS 2934 Producers: Stan Watson & Norman Harris (Billboard soul charts: 53; Billboard pop charts: 204)

Was Rochelle Fleming the best female singer in a Philly group? It's certainly a possibility. Her distinctive voice helped to make First Choice one of the best loved and more successful of all the numerous girl groups that emanated from the City of Brotherly Love. At first, though, they were known as the Debronettes and The Silver Rings before having their name changed to the much more memorable First Choice. After a flop single on Scepter they moved to Philly Groove and hit straight away (#28 pop) with "Armed And Extremely Dangerous" a bundle of joyous energy with a brilliant Fleming vocal and unremitting rhythm section.

Both these singles can be found on the debut LP as can the successful follow-ups, the slightly too cutesy "Smarty Pants" and "Newsy Neighbors", which both also reached the soul top forty. The LP is good enough but could have done with more slower tracks of the quality of "Wake Up To Me" rather than so-so covers of "Love And Happiness" and "Running Out Of Fools".

The follow-up album, *The Player*, (the title track became their biggest hitting soul single at #7 and had obvious echoes of "Armed", including its superb effervescence), was a little disappointing with a track like "Hustler Bill" taking the "Armed/Player" theme just a little too far. "Guilty", a cover of a UK hit by The Pearls (although with different writer credits, I notice), was a song I never really cared for and certainly doesn't need a five minute instrumental version either, while Norman Harris and Allan Felder hardly bothered to write a new melody for "Guess What Mary Jones Did" so similar was it to "Armed". Much better was an excellent take on "All I Need Is Time" which if maybe not *quite* up to the version by Gladys Knight certainly trounces the Charnissa offering, while "You've Been Doin' Wrong For So Long" wins out for me over the other interpretations I know.

They had one more charting single on Philly Groove, "Love Freeze", (which didn't appear on any of their albums) before their records started coming out on the Warner Brothers logo, even though Watson and Harris remained as producers. By and large *So Let Us Entertain You* did its stated job although the overlong "Ain't He Bad" mined the "hustler" theme one more time. The album is not a classic, and contains no hits or genuinely standout tracks, but just about everything is perfectly enjoyable. Encouragingly, there were also three good slow tracks on show: "If The Sun Shines", "Don't Fake It" (complete with vocal asides from Stan Watson) and "Let Him Go" while the album's best song was "I Got A Feeling", which had just been a big hit for Al Wilson.

Delusions 1977 Gold Mind GZS 7501 Producers: Ron Baker, Norman Harris & Earl Young

Hold Your Horses 1979 Gold Mind GA 9502 Producers: Tom Moulton, Norman Harris, Thor Baldursson & McKinley Jackson (Billboard soul charts: 58; Billboard pop charts: 135)

Breakaway 1980 Gold Mind GA 9505 Producers: Norman Harris, Carl Gilbert, T.G. Conway, Allen Felder, Mervin Steals, Marvin Steals, McKinley Jackson & Ron Tyson

The girls then moved to the Salsoul/Gold Mind label but the sound didn't change much. Stan Watson may have vacated the producers chair but the musicians remained much the same as had played on all their previous records. Probably unsurprisingly uptempo dance tracks were the order of the day on *Delusions* with only "I Love You More Than Before" and "Do Me Again" moving along at a less than brisk pace. "Doctor Love" was a fair sized hit for them (#23 soul and #41 pop) but it is a surprise to recall that one of their most famed tracks, "Let No Man Put Asunder", was not released on 45 although (it did come out as a 12" single.

Hold Your Horses had an unforgivably cheesy front and back cover, and was very patchy indeed, in fact their worst LP to date by some distance. The slow songs were totally absent and given most of the set was recorded in Munich, it obviously sounds much more Euro disco oriented than anything they had released in the past. "Let Me Down Easy" and "Love Thang" are better than the rest but it is still an LP I will never play again. Two singles from it reached the lower end of the soul charts.

Mercifully, it was back to the U.S. for their final LP and Fleming was granted more licence to sing, which she did to typically good effect on virtually all the tracks on here with "House For Sale" and "I'm The One" even being slow songs. Despite containing much of their best work in years, there were no hits at all on board, and the album saw no chart action either.

That was it for First Choice, although Fleming did cut some records as a solo singer.

First Class

Harold Bell; Sylvester Redditt; Tony Yarborough; Fred Brown

Going First Class 1976 All Platinum AP-3018 Producer: Tommy Keith

Together (with The Softones) 1979 Parkway International PA1001 Producers: George Kerr, Marvin Brown & Rod Armstrong

First Class 1980 Sugar Hill SH-255 Producers: Tommy Keith, George Kerr & Sylvia Robinson

Coming Back To You 1989 P-Vine PLP-6513 Producers: Tommy Keith, George Kerr, Sylvia Robinson & Donnie Elbert (Japan)

First Class were maybe not quite that, but they were certainly good enough. They hailed from Baltimore and released a handful of excellent singles on a number of different labels with the best of them probably being "What About Me", a gorgeous sweet soul ballad on the Today label which made the national soul charts at #85. It wasn't until they moved to All Platinum that they were rewarded with an album, though.

That set owes a great deal to Tommy Keith: he wrote or co-wrote all seven songs as well as producing it and playing guitar. Anyone hoping for a collection of "What About Me" soundalikes would be disappointed and only the fine "Let's Make Love" sounds remotely like that earlier disc. Everything else is summery, peppy and uptempo which was to be expected really in 1976 but it is all agreeable enough. "This Is It" and "Me And My Gemini " made it onto the soul listings at #89 and #54 respectively.

Their next album was a joint effort with another Baltimore group, The Softones. First Class sung on three tracks of varying quality: "Tell Me What You Want " was a decent cover of the Jimmy Ruffin original and "Laying My Heart On The Line" was a nice ballad but the danceable "Candy" was mediocre. The album didn't really break out of the Eastern seaboard area leading to its becoming a sought after set these days.

The outing on Sugar Hill has become a rare and sought after one as well and *First Class* contains some of their best ever work. It consists of a number of covers but the group acquitted themselves well on all of them, with "I Wasn't There", "Hypnotized" and "Lucky Me" being the pick of the bunch. It was a really good effort, one of the best of 1980, with a lovely emphasis on slow tracks but it failed to revive their commercial fortunes and they broke up soon after.

In 1989 an LP appeared in Japan that consisted of ten tracks: two from the All Platinum album, five from the one on Sugar Hill and three that had not appeared anywhere before, all good covers: "Nothing You Can Do", "Give Him Up" and "I Do".

First Gear

Larnelle Harris; Russ Gregory; Terry Haschman; Jerry Idle; Wally Gilmour; Don Perry; Billy Sanders; Rick Everitt; Rick Brunermer; Tommy Wells; Randy Hammel; Ken Cooley

First Gear 1972 Myrrh MST 6505 Producer: Thurlow Spurr

Caution! Steep Hill 1972 Myrrh MST 6516 Producers: Billy Ray Hearn & Paul Riser

Not typical outings from Myrrh, normally a label dedicated exclusively to gospel, and it's a good thing First Gear employed the gifted Larnelle Harris as their lead singer, as he keeps these albums just about enjoyable.

There's a little bit of early Sly, Average White Band, Tower Of Power and Blood, Sweat & Tears in the music served up here, but not much that is genuinely funky along the lines of Kool, EWAF or The Ohio Players. Songs such as (yet again) "He Ain't Heavy, He's My Brother", "Mr. Bojangles" and "Sudan Village" are dotted across the sets and show how familiar the group were with the pop and rock songs of the day. The only cut I unreservedly love is Carole King's "I Feel The Earth Move" which can be found on *First Gear* and while nothing is downright awful, I have listened to hundreds of better sets in the writing of this book.

Harris subsequently went out on his own and has cut a number of gospel albums over a period of years.

First Love

a) Anne Le Sear ? Albert Eatmon ? b) Denise Austin; Demetrice Henrae; Martha Jackson; Lisa Hudson

The First Love 1981 HCRC HCI-2007 Producer: Albert Eatmon

Love At First Sight 1982 CIM FZ 38374 Producer: Donald Burnside

Another instance of two entirely different groups with the same name, and in the case of the former, yet another album with a front cover that gives no indication as to the music within.

The HCRC album was recorded in Texas, not a source of many soul LPs by 1981, and it should appeal to anyone who liked the sound of soul groups from the seventies. Sadly, the sleeve doesn't tell us who comprised the group but it clearly contained both sexes within the ranks, and I believe Anne Le Sear may be the female vocalist. As is usually the case with me, I am more persuaded by the slower tracks, of which there are two that were as good as it got in 1981: "Dry Your Eyes" and "Strive For Understanding". "You'll Love Me" is also striking, with a most appealing re-creation of the sound of the old Impressions' harmonies. The uptempo cuts are more ordinary, but none are actually poor.

As for the *Love At First Sight* group, think The Emotions or The Jones Girls and you will know what they sound like. But this is not to suggest that they are second-rate imitators serving up a poor offering as it is by and large pretty good stuff, recorded in Chicago, with a worthy and zestful rendering of "Lady Marmalade" thrown in. "It's A Mystery To Me" and "Stop What'cha Doing" are highly acceptable mid-tempo outings, with the former hitting the soul singles chart at #68 in early 1983. (They had earlier also posted "Don't Say Goodnight" (at #67) on the charts as well, but that one isn't on the LP.)

Bruce Fisher

Red Hot 1977 Mercury SRM-1-1168 Producers: Jerry Schoenbaum & John Lee

He co-wrote "Body Heat", "Will It Go Round in Circles" and "You Are So Beautiful" but hardly anyone knows who Bruce Fisher is and I've certainly never talked about him to anyone else, nor read anything about his career. I imagine he has always been content to stay in the background but emerged briefly in 1977 for this one solo LP (though he also cut a CD in 1996), on the cover of which he looked much younger than his then 26 years. It's first rate and I recommend it as its singular stance and refusal to play the disco game reminds me a bit of other good LPs in the book such as Lou Bond's, Norman Feels' and Walter Heath's. His own version of "Body Heat" doesn't quite measure up to Quincy Jones' but "Money's Funny" is compellingly funky and "Fly In The Window" is a fascinating cut, seemingly covering about twenty musical bases during its six minutes. "When Will I See You?", like many tracks on here, boasts an arresting arrangement from John Lee and gives Fisher a chance to show off his decent voice. "Starlite Starbrite", "Daring Me Closer" and "In My Life" are all really good ballads and this LP deserves to be much better known than it is. Tawatha Agee, Cheryl Alexander and Ace Spectrum help out on backing vocals.

5 Du-Tones

Andrew Butler; Frank McCurrey; James West; LeRoy Joyce; Willie Guest; David Scott

Shake A Tail Feather 1979 P-Vine PLP-9004 (Japan)

The 5 (or Five) Du-Tones are one of those groups who had a big hit with a "dance" record, and could never really live it down. If they are remembered at all, it is for that hit, "Shake A Tail Feather", and certainly not for failed follow-ups like "The Flea", "The Cool Bird" and "Woodbine Twine". Slow gospel influenced songs such as "Please Change Your Mind" are even more forgotten.

Originally out of St. Louis, they made the trip to Chicago from where a healthy number of singles came out on the One-derful! label. This was not an operation that was really equipped for or interested in releasing LPs and the group had to wait until 1979 when an album finally appeared in Japan - well over a decade after they had broken up. It obviously contained the hit and its novelty b-side, "Divorce Court", as well as a handful of unreleased tracks. There is some pleasingly tough early soul on here: "My World", the afore-mentioned "Please Change", "Don't Let Go" and "That's How I Love You" should satisfy anyone who likes his soul neat, and proved they weren't just an anonymous dance outfit.

Scott and McCurrey went on to join South Shore Commission, with the former later becoming a member of The Chi-Lites.

Five Special

Steve Boyd; Bryan Banks; Mike Pettilo; Steve Harris; Greg Finley

Five Special 1979 Elektra 6E-206 Producer: Ron Banks (Billboard soul charts: 20; Billboard pop charts: 118)

Special Delivery 1980 Elektra 6E-270 Producer: Ron Banks (Billboard soul charts: 46)

Trak'n 1981 Elektra 5E-553 Producer: Ron Banks

Proving once again that there was still life in Detroit after Motown decamped to the West Coast, Five Special had a big soul hit (#9 in mid 1979) with "Why Leave Us Alone" which is stretched out to over eight minutes on their debut set, and its undoubted appeal is not diminished one bit by such a marathon workout. Before this, this worthy group, featuring Bryan Banks, brother of Dramatic Ron, had put out two well-regarded but unsuccessful singles on TEAI and Mercury.

The first album mixed up bass and falsetto voices in a way reminiscent of The Dramatics but Five Special lacked a tenor with the power of L.J. Reynolds or "Wee Gee" Howard and also relied more on dance material than did their more famous Detroit neighbours."You're Something Special" was the only slow track on the debut set and it, together with the hit and the summery "It's A Wonderful Day", stood out from the rest of the material which lacked any real distinction.

Special Delivery contained their third and final soul charting single in the long, funky and relatively routine, "Jam (Let's Take It To The Streets)" (#29), and while it was a collection that lacked anything of the quality of the obviously superior, "Why Leave Us Alone", it was probably a slightly more consistent set, with the last three tracks on side two closing out proceedings in a painless and enjoyable manner. "Heaven (You Are To Me" on side one was worth a listen as well.

Five Special's race was pretty much run by 1981 and *Trak'n* neither charted in its own right nor hatched any hit singles but it did house the finest ballad the group ever cut in the truly excellent "Spread Love All Over The World", which like another good cut, "Now And Then", reminded me of what Ray, Goodman and Brown were cutting at the time. Most of the rest of the album consisted of the typically tight yet highly orchestrated and crisply produced uptempo cuts they favoured.

Five Stairsteps (see The Stairsteps)

Roberta Flack (see also Donny Hathaway)

First Take 1969 Atlantic SD 8230 Producer: Joel Dorn (Billboard soul charts: 1; Billboard pop charts: 1)

Chapter Two 1970 Atlantic SD 1569 Producers: Joel Dorn & King Curtis (Billboard soul charts: 4; Billboard pop: 33)

Quiet Fire 1971 Atlantic SD 1594 Producer: Joel Dorn (Billboard soul charts: 4; Billboard pop charts: 18)

Roberta Flack & Donny Hathaway 1972 Atlantic SD 7216 Producers: Joel Dorn & Arif Mardin (Billboard soul charts: 2; Billboard pop charts: 3)

Killing Me Softly 1973 Atlantic SD 7271 Producer: Joel Dorn (Billboard soul charts: 2; Billboard pop charts: 3)

Feel Like Makin' Love 1975 Atlantic SD 18131 Producers: Rubina Flake & Leon Pendarvis (Billboard soul charts: 5; Billboard pop charts: 24)

Blue Lights In The Basement 1978 Atlantic SD 19149 Producers: Rubina Flake, Joe Ferla & Eugene McDaniels (Billboard soul charts: 5; Billboard pop charts: 8)

Was Roberta Flack a soul singer? Four #1 soul singles and about thirty other charting 45s would certainly suggest so. On the other hand, like Ray Charles, Randy Crawford, Stevie Wonder, Michael Jackson and Diana Ross she easily transcended the limits of what one might consider to be obviously "soulful". Certainly, she never seemed to sweat, was at ease with singing material from pop or rock writers and tended to avoid melisma, but her beautiful voice and tasteful piano playing have been undeniably influential and if she may seem irredeemably "middle class" to some commentators, or often not really to my own personal taste, then I never had any doubt about including her in the book.

Right from the beginning, Atlantic pushed her as an album artist and were rewarded with huge sales for *First Take*, an extraordinary achievement for a new singer, especially one who didn't have a big selling single to wrap the LP around. (Even though the LP did include "The First Time Ever I Saw Your Face", it wasn't to be issued as a single until well over a year later.) Tracks like "Compared To What" and "Tryin' Times" could have sat fairly easily on albums by other soul artists; "Hey That's No Way To Say Goodbye", "Angelitos Negros" and "Ballad Of The Sad Young Men" could not. There was no denying the purity of her vocals or the superb musicianship and the slow, sad laments that poured forth were best enjoyed by listening in a darkened room with total concentration.

Chapter Two was a continuation of the formula from the debut: all tracks at least four minutes in length, a willingness to tackle a diverse range of material, no fears about interpreting them in her own style, and a heavy emphasis on downtempo and melancholy songs. "Reverend Lee" was another failed single, but singles were not the point of Roberta Flack at this time.

That was to change in 1971. Atlantic had paired up Flack with Donny Hathaway (they had been classmates at Howard University and he had contributed songs and arrangements to her first two albums) and they were pushed as a duo who could sell 45s: "You've Got A Friend" reached #8 soul in the summer of that year and "You've Lost That Lovin' Feelin'" followed it into the soul top 30 in the winter of 1971. Both songs were included on the *Roberta Flack & Donny Hathaway* album that came out in the wake of these hits, and it pushed the next single to untold of heights: "Where Is The Love" hit #1 soul and #5 pop. The album was more "up" by some distance from Flack's solo work to date and also, tellingly, had a number of tracks of running times at three and a half minutes or less.

However, also in 1971, and after the first two singles with Hathaway had hit the charts, came *Quiet Fire,* Flack's third solo set. It followed the path of her first two albums, rather than that of the collaboration with Hathaway. The singing was still a thing of great beauty - particularly on Van McCoy's "Sweet Bitter Love" and King and Goffin's "Will You Still Love Me Tomorrow" - but it didn't seem so surprising or new any more. And a seven minute version of "Bridge Over Troubled Water" just didn't seem to be such a wise or interesting choice of material as many of her earlier tracks. Anyway, that's clearly just a personal observation: the album still sold in large quantities, and once again went gold, a landmark all her first five LPs were to achieve.

As a result of its exposure in the Clint Eastwood film, *Play Misty for me*, "The First Time Ever I Saw Your Face" had been rushed out as a single and it went to #1 pop and #4 soul in the spring of 1972. Flack was by this time close to being a superstar, one of the biggest selling female artists in the world, and this situation was consolidated by the release of "Killing Me Softly With His Song", another #1 pop single (and #2 soul). I must confess to being very indifferent to it, and felt much the same about the follow-up, "Jesse", which also fared significantly less well - #30 pop and #19 soul. On the other hand, the LP did feature a welcome change of pace from Flack in the perky "No Tears In The End" while the "trademark" cut was probably the nine minute long version of Leonard Cohen's "Suzanne".

No new album appeared in 1974 but the year did see another #1 pop and soul single in "Feel Like Makin' Love" which became the title track of her next album that came along in 1975. It was the first not to go gold, but still sold respectively enough. It was also the first one she had produced herself, demonstrating a hitherto well-hidden levity when she pronounced herself as "Rubina Flake". It was an atypical record for Flack, by the way, being soft and submissive in a way she had not attempted before, but it was a style she was to reprise for "Feelin' That Glow", the not as successful follow-up single. She was clearly still not intimidated by recording lengthy tracks and Stevie Wonder's "I Can See The Sun In Late December" clocked in at just shy of thirteen minutes.

As the world turned into 1978, Flack had her first failure in years when her new single, the unremarkable "25th Of Last December", failed comprehensively when it crawled to #52 soul and missed the pop top 100 completely. It was a mere blip though as the follow-up re-united Flack with Hathaway and "The Closer I Get To You" became another #1 soul single as well as hitting #2 pop. Both singles sat on the *Blue Lights In The Basement* album, which returned her to gold status. It was a slightly more conventional "soul" set than most she had recorded in the past in the sense that there were no long songs, nor any re-cuts of famous rock or pop "standards" with the possible exception of the Box-Tops "Soul Deep", which was delivered in a brash, up-beat manner that sounded most un-like her.

Roberta Flack 1978 Atlantic SD 19186 Producers: Rubina Flake, Joe Ferla & Joe Brooks (Billboard soul charts: 37; Billboard pop charts: 74)

Roberta Flack Featuring Donny Hathaway 1979 Atlantic SD 16103 Producers: Joe Ferla, Arif Mardin, Roberta Flack & Eric Mercury (Billboard soul charts: 4; Billboard pop charts: 25)

Live & More (and Peabo Bryson) 1980 Atlantic SD 2-7004 Producers: Roberta Flack & Peabo Bryson (Billboard soul charts: 10; Billboard pop charts: 52)

A somewhat fallow period was to follow, in which the dull *Roberta*

Flack album became easily her poorest performing set, containing such insipid MOR songs like "Come Share My Love" and "If Ever I See You Again", which somehow made it to #37 soul in the summer of 1978. It did better on the pop charts, which made sense, hitting a respectable #24. Of the rest: there was a take on "You Are Everything", but The Stylistics did it better, while "Independent Man" was even a dance track. Times really had changed and the austere, thoughtful music of the early albums had by now gone.

Atlantic then did what it had done a few times before in order to secure some success: matched Flack up with Donny Hathaway and it certainly restored her fortunes, with the collaboration resulting in yet another gold album as well as containing two well performing singles, "You Are My Heaven" at #8 soul and "Back Together Again", #18. Both also hit the pop top 60. Very sadly, at the time the album was being recorded, Hathaway committed suicide and Flack had to finish much of the album herself. It was easily her most "soulful" LP yet, if one uses the term in the sense by which most people recognise "soul music" with the excellently melodic "God Don't Like Ugly" and "Back Together Again" being contemporary dance outings - sharp horns and popping bass on Roberta Flack records, whatever next? - and entirely in step with what a number of others had been doing.

Fortunately for Flack, but unfortunately for me, Atlantic needed to pair her up with a new partner and chose Peabo Bryson. This was an astute move commercially, and made sense, and the two achieved much success, but I found the music to be without any interest and I pretty much stopped listening from here on in and so can only offer limited comments for the rest of her records.

Bustin' Loose 1981 MCA 5141 Producer: Roberta Flack (Billboard soul charts: 48; Billboard pop charts: 161)

I'm The One 1982 Atlantic SD 19354 Producers: Roberta Flack, Ralph MacDonald, William Salter & William Eaton (Billboard soul charts: 16; Billboard pop charts: 59)

Born To Love (and Peabo Bryson) 1983 Capitol EST 7122841 Producers: Michael Masser, Carole Bayer Sager, Bob Crewe, Bob Gaudio, Peabo Bryson, Al Johnson & Roberta Flack (Billboard soul charts: 8; Billboard pop charts: 25)

Oasis 1988 Atlantic 81916-1 Producers: Marcus Miller, Michael Omartian, Jerry Hey, Andy Goldmark & Barry Miles (Billboard soul charts: 24; Billboard pop charts: 159)

Set The Night To Music 1991 Atlantic 7867 82321 1 Producers: Arif Mardin, Joe Mardin & Ahmet Ertegen (UK)

Bustin Loose came out on MCA because it was the soundtrack to a film, but it certainly didn't sell many copies. A fine version of Luther Vandross' "You Stopped Me" was the stand-out cut and reached #32 soul when put out as a single. "Children's Song" was the nadir.

It was back to the parent company for *I'm The One* from which "Making Love" became her first top 20 pop single in four years. "I'm The One" also did well on 45 and it must be said that, while I don't care for the style of either record, her beautiful singing hadn't deserted her. There was another successful pairing with Peabo Bryson before the title track from the *Oasis* LP became her fourth soul #1 single but it was interesting to note that it didn't even reach the pop top 100. At this late stage in her career, she had finally "failed to cross over".

Her last vinyl outing was in 1991 but I think I am right in saying that this only took place in Europe: in the U.S. the release was CD only. As with a number of other artists, I have ignored the large number of compilations that exist.

She is still active today and will be remembered as one of the most successful and influential of all black female singers.

Flakes

1980 1980 Magic Disc MDLP-118 Producers: Mel Bolton & Marilyn McLeod

Flakes 1981 Salsoul SA 8540 Producers: Mel Bolton & Marilyn McLeod

I have a great love of falsetto singing and *1980* had a really good practitioner - Cornell "Flakes" Matthews. He serves up an imposing version of "Hey There Lonely Girl" and, maybe more importantly, transforms songs like "Miss Fine Lover" and "Sugar Frosted Lover" into much more enjoyable outings than possibly they warranted. "No One (Can Love You Like I Do)" and "Your Love's Too Strong For Me" were decent compositions anyway and Matthews' singing just makes them even better. The music is performed at a nicely funky standard throughout and all in all it's a really good set, neglected at the time and forgotten now with only "Flakes Rap" falling below the high standard.

Salsoul picked up on the LP and re-released much of it the next year, omitting three tracks, adding three more and changing the artist's name (*1980* had come out as by "Flakes 1") to merely "Flakes". "Love On The Hour" was the finest addition, another lovely slow performance. (Disgracefully, the name of Cornell Matthews is only seen in the smallest of print on the back of the album and then misspelt as "Carnell")

Because all five members of the Elektra group Mighty Fire had helped out in one shape or another on the LPs it seems to have become accepted wisdom that Flakes and Mighty Fire are one and the same (or that Flakes morphed into Mighty Fire) but this is not the case and certainly Matthews is not involved on the two albums by the group. He died in 1990, aged only 40.

Flamingos

Zeke Carey; Jake Carey; Douglas McClure; Julien Vaught; Jacob Carey; Alan Fontaine; Billy Clarke; Clarence Bassett;

Their Hits Then And Now 1966 Philips PHS 600-206 Producer: Ted Cooper

Color Them Beautiful 1971? Ronze RSLP 1001 Producer: Zeke Carey

Today 1972 Ronze RSLP 1002 Producer: Zeke Carey

In Touch With You 197? Ronze RSLP 1003 Producers: Zeke Carey, Billy Nichols, Jack Sontag & Johnny Worlds

The Flamingos were a great doo-wop group but rather a half-hearted soul one. By the time the sixties progressed and "soul" was the pre-eminent music of Black America their best days were already well behind them, and they never really came to terms with the newer musical form. (I would argue that their finest record in their later days was the excellent "Buffalo Soldier" on Polydor in 1970, but an album never appeared on which it was featured).

Nevertheless their place in history had already been assured by classic records such as "I Only Have Eyes For You" which had a massive influence on the "sweet soul" movement that was to occur in the early seventies. To recap about the scope of book: I am only including their four albums made in the "soul era" and am only listing the personnel of group at the time of those albums. I am well aware there were other famous singers in the group in the early days including Tommy Hunt and Johnny Carter.

The Philips LP consisted of updates of their most enduring sides from the fifties as well as a couple of up-tempo attempts to move with the times, such as "Boogaloo Party" which made it to #22 on the soul charts when released as a single in spring 1966. That 45 has many fans, but I'm not one of them, finding it to be rather mechanical and repetitive. It was not a very successful album, and I believe it would have had more impact had one side been devoted to the "old" material and the other one to "new" stuff, rather than mixing it all up together.

They formed their own label, Ronze, out of Brooklyn in the early seventies but their albums still continued to favour doo-wop tracks and where "soul" cuts did appear they could be rather messy things like "Why Can't Susie Go To School With Lucy" from the *Today* LP. (Which, despite its gatefold cover, didn't really sound like "Today" at all).

The *Color Them Beautiful* LP kicked off with two contemporary sounding sides, "She's Gone" and "Gotta Have All Your Lovin", and also included a single that had appeared on the Julmar label in 1969 and created a little noise, "Dealin' (Groovin' With The Feelin'), but also made sure to insert some "standards" like "I Need You So", "Too Young" and "Goodnight Sweetheart".

The final Ronze LP, *In Touch With You*, was full of over-long dull songs and provided final confirmation that the Flamingos really couldn't "do" soul properly; it's a bit like listening to someone pretend to be English when clearly speaking it as a second language.

The Flamingos still carry on today, but their soul records are almost completely forgotten: even the group's own website makes no mention of the Philips and Ronze records at all.

Flashback Band

Toby Domino; Joe Parker; David DeCuir

Flashback Band 1982 Rocker International 333/334 Producer: Joe Parker, David Decuir and Traci Borges

I have heard little of this eight track funk LP from New Orleans which was subsequently re-released with a further eight added. What I have heard is utterly routine and without wishing to be unkind, completely understand why it failed and why bigger labels did not pick up on it.

Flashlight

Howard Smith; William King; Willard Hines; Bunny Bailey; Patty Webb

Flashlight 1978 Philly Groove PG-8000 Producer: Adam & Eve for Garden Productions

Anyone looking at the uninspired cover of this LP could be forgiven for thinking that it was "just another disco album". They would be wrong: it was one of the best soul albums of 1978, although arriving at such a judgment does require a love of the music of Philadelphia - and dancing.

Flashlight had a brief if interesting history. They were the same group known as The Quickest Way Out who placed a single on the soul charts, "Thank You Baby For Loving Me", in early 1976 and also released a second 45, "Who Am I", which didn't do so well. Both sides are included, unadulterated, on the album. The only disappointment for me is that the b-side to "Who Am I", the lovely "I Don't Want To Lose Your Love", isn't here. There was no clear reason for the name change to Flashlight, by the way..

It is a really good set, performed with great energy and zest by talented singers (Smith went on to record solo gospel albums), and to bring up two further mysteries surrounding it: a) The "Adam and "Eve" production credit hides the identity of Stan Watson b) How and why didn't "Beware, She's Pulling My Strings" become a hit given its memorable hook? Most of the cuts are uptempo but "Every Little Beat Of My Heart" and " Don't Feel Nothin' ('Til You Hear From Me) "proved they could handle ballads with ease.

Flavor (see also Livin' Proof, Skool Boyz and Triple "S" Connection)

Stan Sheppard; Chauncey Matthews; Fred Brown

In Good Taste 1976 Ju-Par JP6-1002S1 Producer: Ron Rancifer and Stan Sheppard

Flavor comprised three young men who put out a nice single, "Don't Freeze Up", on the Bunky label in 1975 which was picked up by the Motown subsidiary Ju-Par but neither it nor the album on which it is included, *In Good Taste,* managed to reach any national charts. The trio deliver the contents confidently throughout on an LP that is generally enjoyable (although the backing vocals on "Magnifico" grate). The style within is predominantly uptempo although not really "disco" or "funk".

Flavor soon disbanded after which things got a little confusing as Sheppard went on to join two other groups, Living Proof and Triple S Connection (on whose LP Matthews played guitar), before Sheppard, Brown and Matthews re-united (with a fourth member Bill Sheppard) to form Skool Boyz.

Flirtations

Earnestine Pearce; Shirley Pearce; Viola Billups

Nothing But A Heartache 1968 Deram DES-18028 Producer: Wayne Bickerton

Love Makes The World Go Round 1975 RCA SF 8448 Producers: Colin Frechter & John Goodison

The Flirtations' two LPs may have been cut in England but the trio were all Americans and had cut singles in the States as by both The Flirtations and their previous name, The Gypsies, under which they placed a single, "Jerk It", onto the soul charts in 1965.

There are some who profess indifference to soul music cut in this country and while it was all too often undoubtedly lacking in comparison to that recorded in the U.S. there are good examples and the atmospheric and danceable "Nothing But A Heartache" is one of them. Sadly, the rest of the LP on which it sits is all too often dreary pop music, which the good singing can't rescue. The LP was entitled *Sounds Like The Flirtations* in this country with a different sleeve from the U.S. version.

Sadly, the follow-up album which appeared six years later is even worse, lacking a "Nothing But Heartaches" to pull it through.

As a pure pop record it's not too bad, but any soul content is entirely absent.

The trio have continued to release records every so often over the last forty years including a new CD in 2015.

Floaters

Larry Cunningham; Paul Mitchell; Charles Clark; Ralph Mitchell; Robert ? ; Shu-Ga; Jonathan Murray

Floaters 1977 ABC AB-1030 Producers: James Mitchell & Marvin Willis (Billboard soul charts: 1; Billboard pop charts: 10)

Magic 1978 ABC AA-1047 Producers: James Mitchell & Marvin Willis (Billboard soul charts: 27; Billboard pop charts: 131)

Float Into The Future 1979 MCA 3093 Producer: Eugene McDaniels

Get Ready For The Floaters & Shu-Ga 1981 Fee WW711 Producers: James Mitchell & Marvin Willis

One thing that has to be said about soul music over the last thirty years or so is that it has been critically accepted and respected. It is not a music that is often ridiculed. Only one exception springs to mind: "Float On" by The Floaters. Not only did it occasion a "joke" record in response in the shape of "Bloat On" by Cheech and Chong, but it is one of the few soul records that most people would never own up to actually liking. It's also the perfect example of a song earning a group a "one-hit wonder " tag, given how it performed so much better than every other record they released.

Ralph and Paul Mitchell were brothers to producer James, who was also a member of The Detroit Emeralds (as was co-producer Marvin Willis) and certainly there were moments on the debut album where The Floaters sounded rather like The Emeralds. The first side contains the hit - all twelve minutes of it - and the follow-up single, a rather dull version of "You Don't Have To Say You Love Me", but there are a couple of tracks on side two that show the group in a much better light: "Take One Step At A Time" is an excellent dance record and "I Am So Glad I Took My Time", an excellent slow one, and they had already been coupled together for The Floaters' first single at the end of 1976. It went nowhere, so everyone involved must have been amazed when "Float On" became such a massive hit (#1 soul, #2 pop).

The follow-up set was not much to write home about with the nine minute title track doubtless meant to be the "Float On" this time around. It just meandered on and on without ever really going anywhere while the palpably weak "I Just Want To Be With You" somehow made it to #36 on the soul charts in June 1978, and it was perhaps inevitable that the group would cover Boby (sic) Franklin's small hit from 1975, "Whatever's Your Sign". There were *some* good moments and "Let's Try Love (One More Time)" was a perfectly decent ballad with some fine singing but The Floaters had already slipped from public consciousness.

Into The Future provided the next proof that The Floaters were not built for a long-term career. It is an awfully colourless affair, with little to be said for it. Most tracks were fast, some were slow, but there was no strong material at all, and not surprisingly both it, and the one single that was released, failed to sell.

One Shu-Ga joined the remaining three male members of the group for the final album and she provided some variety to their sound with her appealing voice adding value to the only three half-decent things on here. "Back Home", "For Your Love" and "Not Enough For Me" were not much as songs but all had some good vocal interplay. As for the other cuts: "Show Time" and "Make It Hot" were dull dance fodder while "Get Ready", a ten minute plus cut, was not the Smokey Robinson song but I wish it had been.

It was probably too much to expect from record companies that an identity could have been built up for the group - after all they told us their Christian names, star signs and likes on the hit - but their LPs usually neglected to tell us who the members were.

Eddie Floyd (see also The Falcons)

Knock On Wood 1967 Stax 714 No producer listed

I've Never Found A Girl 1968 Stax STS-2002 Producer: Steve Cropper

Rare Stamps 1969 STS-2011 (Billboard soul charts:49)

You've Got To Have Eddie 1969 Stax STS-2017 Producer: Steve Cropper

California Girl 1970 Stax STS-2029 Producers: Eddie Floyd, Booker T Jones, Al Bell & Tom Nixon (Billboard soul charts: 41)

Down To Earth 1971 Stax STS-2041 Producers: Steve Cropper & Eddie Floyd

Baby Lay Your Head Down (Gently On My Bed) 1973 Stax STS-3016 Producers: Al Bell, Dale Warren, Al Jackson & Eddie Floyd

Soul Street 1974 Stax STS-5512 Producer: Eddie Floyd

Chronicle 1979 Stax STX-4122

The Best Of 1988 Ace SX 010

Eddie Floyd is an underrated soul man of pedigree and talent - both as a singer and a writer - who scored a number of big hits but was always somewhat in the shadow of fellow Stax artists, Otis Redding and Johnnie Taylor and to this day he has not received the acclaim he deserves.

He was born in Alabama but was raised in Detroit from where he became a member of one of the best of the pre-soul groups, The Falcons, staying with them for a number of years before recording some solo singles on Lu-Pine and forming the Safice label with Chester Simmons and Al Bell, which provided an outlet for his soulful compositions for the likes of Grover Mitchell. His big break came when he co-wrote those classic hits for Wilson Pickett, "634-5789" and "Ninety-Nine And A Half (Won't Do)", with Steve Cropper.

Flushed with confidence, he and Cropper collaborated again on the record by which a casual music fan might only know Eddie Floyd: "Knock On Wood". It is a record that has become over-familiar over the years but Floyd won't mind. It must have earned him a fortune, but it is surprising to note that despite hitting #1 soul it could do no better than #28 pop in 1966, a reminder that Stax could never "crossover" as easily as Motown. Not surprisingly, it became the title track of his debut LP, the fate of which also proved that Jim Stewart's heart wasn't in promoting and selling LPs back in 1966; it didn't chart anywhere. It was also a typical album of the time: throw in a lot of covers, eight in all, including "High Heel Sneakers", "I Don't Want To Cry" and "I Stand Accused" with four Floyd originals. Apart from the hit and another pretty successful single, "Raise Your Hand" (#16 soul) , these were the superb "Got To Make A Comeback" and "I've Just Been Feeling Bad", both glorious and dignified reminders of how good Stax was in the mid-sixties.

He released four more singles that didn't find their way to albums of the time before 1968 brought him two more big and excellent hits, "Bring It On Home To Me" (his biggest ever pop hit, in fact at #17) and "I've Never Found A Girl", with the latter becoming the title track of his second LP. The format was a little different this time around as only three covers were used, while eight more Floyd songs were featured, most of which continued to be written with Cropper. I don't believe anything was quite up to the quality of "Comeback" or "Just Been Feeling Bad" but "Water" and "Girl, I Love You" were both good enough.

Stax put out a fine and thoughtful Floyd compilation in 1969 entitled *Rare Stamps* which picked up quite a few non-album sides (including the marvellous and atypical "Big Bird" which had flopped as a single in 1968) and became his first ever charting LP. Shortly after this, the "new" Floyd album arrived, *You've Got To Have Eddie*. The positive title belied the contents, which reverted to mainly cover versions and, rather insultingly, only two new Floyd songs, although one of these, the latin-tinged "Don't Tell Your Mama", became his sixth soul top twenty hit. It was rather dispiriting to hear him cover songs like "Can I change your mind", "Proud Mary" and "It's Not Unusual", none of which were a patch on the originals. "Seagull" and "That's All" are certainly both worth hearing but all in all it was still probably his weakest album to date.

California Girl restored Floyd as the main songwriter on his own LPs: seven of the eleven tracks were co-written by him but, again, the covers had an unmistakeable smell of filler, rather than songs carefully selected for him. Was he ever going to bring anything new to "Didn't I Blow Your Mind This Time" or "Rainy Night In Georgia"? And "Hey There Lonely Girl" was spectacularly ill-suited for him. The title track did very well as a single in reaching #11 soul and #45 pop but it was to prove the last big record he ever had and from here on in he really became a "second-tier" artist for Stax, trailing behind the likes of Taylor, Isaac Hayes and The Staple Singers as a singer on whom the company were prepared to lavish time and money.

A number of non-album singles followed *California Girl* before the release of the decidedly odd *Down To Earth* LP. Odd in as much as it appeared to have support from Stax, as it was Eddie's first (and last) gatefold sleeve, but the company then seemed to backtrack by not releasing any singles from it. Odd in that it featured musicians - other than Cropper - who did not play often on Stax releases and oddest of all in that it was as close to a "rock" record as a "soul" one. I can't imagine who it was thought it could possibly sell to and it would be interesting to know what Eddie Floyd thought of it all.

Baby Lay Your Head Down saw a return to a much more traditional approach and was all the better for it. The LP contained two small hits (the title track and "Check Me Out"), but, more importantly, featured stronger songs than had been the case on the previous two or three albums, as well as completely jettisoning cover versions. The best track was the slow and beautifully orchestrated "I Hear Footsteps (Coming Closer)" which was performed with soulful dignity by Floyd. There was also a bit of reggae, but no hint of the rockiness that marred *Down To Earth.*

His final Stax album, *Soul Street,* received a rather savage review at the time of release in England's *Black Music* magazine, but on listening again forty years later it sounds just fine. It certainly didn't contain any hits but the title track is warm, loose and inviting and "Stealing Love" (not the same song as cut by The Emotions) is a worthy addition to the cheating genre. One of my least favourite songs ever, "Guess Who", is included and there are a couple of instances where Floyd flirts with Al Green-isms but I think it is one of his most consistent sets of all.

A retrospective album, *Chronicle*, came along at the end of the seventies, but the U.K. version (Stax 7005) should be chosen as it had a generous eighteen tracks, whereas the U.S. release only had twelve.

Experience 1977 Malaco 6352 Producers: Eddie Floyd & Mack Rice

Eddie sadly missed out on the post-Stax success that quickly came to the likes of Isaac Hayes, William Bell, Johnnie Taylor, The Emotions and The Staples. He did place a single on Malaco on the soul charts in 1977, a duet with Dorothy Moore, but that was his last ever visit, and a lowly one at that in only reaching #74. It didn't help, either, that the single, "We Should Really Be In Love", was not included on his one and only album release for the label, and *Experience* slowly slid into obscurity. Which is a shame as the sound and approach was not that far removed from his later Stax albums and should appeal to anyone who has always cared for his work. Only "Feel My Body" was sub-standard and "Your Love Is Heavy" was excellent, bringing to bear a mixture of jaded joy and world weariness of a seasoned and experienced performer. Completely different was "It's Got To Be That Way" which had what it took to be a hit had it been released on a 45, being danceable and memorable, without crossing over into mindless "disco".

Try Me 1985 Easy Street ESA 9001 Producers: Marshall Sehorn & Eddie Floyd

Flashbacks 1988 Wilbe WIL 3005 Producers: William Bell & Eddie Floyd

Two unsuccessful singles came out on Mercury and it wasn't until 1985 that Floyd got another shot at an LP, which, intriguingly, was cut down in New Orleans. Unfortunately this was almost twenty years after that city had a thriving record industry and so it had no chance of being anything other than a curiosity in his career but at least it was an opportunity to get his name back out there in some shape or form. It is not a great LP, to be honest, and certainly has no Crescent City atmosphere at all. The relatively tuneful "Our Love Will Survive" is the best thing on here with the other extreme being reached by "I'm So Funkful", which doesn't even sound like it bears an Eddie Floyd vocal.

His last album slipped out on William Bell's Wilbe label. Floyd wrote all the songs and two of them. "Love's Gonna Get To You" and "You Don't Say No" are certainly worth a listen. "Daddy's Coming Home" is one of those things that probably sounded fairly good live but, and I mean no disrespect to the musicians on the album, it's hard to imagine anyone listening to *Flashbacks* in the twenty first century when an option is playing any number of Floyd sides where he is backed up by the M.G.'s.

He is still going strong today, gigging all over the world, and this likeable and seemingly unassuming man had a warmth on his best sides that was his own recognisable trademark.

King Floyd

A Man In Love 1969 Pulsar AR-10602 Producers: Harold Battiste & Mac Rebennack

King Floyd 1971 Cotillion SD 9047 Producer: Elijah Walker (Billboard soul charts: 19; Billboard pop charts: 130)

Think About It 1973 Atco SD 7023 Producer: Elijah Walker

It would be easy to assume that King Floyd came from Jackson, Mississippi, as four of his five albums were recorded there and also easy to assume that the name "King" denoted a grandiose self-bestowed title such as with "Sir" Mack Rice or, indeed, "King" Curtis. Both assumptions would be wrong; he was born in New Orleans and his real name was King Floyd III.

He recorded a handful of singles in the sixties, and given the fact that none of them made any noise, it was surprising to see that he was afforded the opportunity to cut an LP on the small L.A. based Pulsar label. One of the most overworked adjectives to describe a singer's voice is "unique", but it really did apply to Floyd: he genuinely sounded like no-one else, employing, particularly on his early records, a soft rather feminine tone which I have always thought of as "floppy". This is not a bad thing, as I like his singing a great deal, but I can imagine it would not be to everyone's liking.

That debut album was rather undistinguished and fared no better than any of his singles. Floyd wrote or co-wrote every song and most cuts were mid-tempo with a "girlie chorus" employed on a number of occasions. The only track I think warrants repeated plays is "This Is Our Last Night Together", a nice unhurried exercise in sadness. However, despite the failure of the set in pretty much every way, it wasn't the last time it was seen. For more details, see below.

In 1970 Floyd got the opportunity to work with the great Wardell Quezergue up in Jackson and the resulting session brought him his biggest ever success, and pretty much by accident. A number of songs had been recorded and his new label, Chimneyville, put out a 45 with the a-side being touted as "What Our Love Needs". It was, though, the presumed b-side, the simple, funky and irresistible "Groove Me", that caught people's attention and went on to reach #1 soul and #6 pop at the end of the year. Clearly, an album was needed to capitalise on the single's success and the King Floyd set appeared in 1971. It might have been expected that there would have been a host of other tracks on board that sounded much like the hit, but this was not the case, with only the successful follow-up single "Baby Let Me Kiss You" (#5 soul, #29 pop), based fair and square on "Groove Me". His voice had matured and deepened and he was now even more capable of imbuing genuine emotion into his compositions, which was most apparent on "Don't Leave Me Lonely" and "Day In The Life Of A Fool". It is not close to being an all time great album but Elijah Walker's crisp production, Quezergue's astute arrangements and the splendid rhythm and horn sections added enormously to Floyd's raw material and I enjoy it a good deal, and it was a big improvement on the Pulsar set. (Atlantic's distribution also contributed in a significant way to more sales for the LP than would otherwise have been the case if Chimneyville had gone it alone.)

Speaking of the Pulsar set, it surprisingly now re-appeared on the Motown subsidiary V.I.P (number VS407), (Gordy's company had purchased the original tapes in the wake of the success of "Groove Me") when it was re-titled for no apparent reason as *Heart Of The Matter*. It fared no better this time around either and V.I.P even released a single from it, the utterly routine "Heartaches". That was it for the Motown connection, a throw of the dice that didn't work but it would have been fascinating had Floyd ever had the chance to record up in Detroit.

A third (non- album) single, "Got To Have Your Lovin'", fared much worse than the earlier two had, and a fourth failed completely so Chimneyville, rather hopefully it at first seemed, delved back into *King Floyd* to release "Woman Don't Go Astray", another fine Floyd song. Luckily, it became a smash on the soul charts reaching #3, but its modest performance on the pop listing (#53) proved that King Floyd's music did not have lasting appeal to a wider audience.

Floyd's third LP came out in 1973 with "Woman Don't Go Astray" once again included, but the album was named after Otis Redding's *Think About It*, one of three Redding songs onboard ("My Girl" was stretched out to over six minutes which was a novel approach even if it doesn't come close to the quality of Redding's own version, let alone The Temptations'), although Floyd was as usual the composer for much of the material. "Think About It" went to #49 on the soul charts and was a highlight from a likeable LP, even if a sense of quiet desperation was aboard with some straight "Groove Me" clones wheeled out: "Here It Is" was at least a good one; "Do Your Feeling" and "It's Not What You Say" were not. Lastly, "You've Got Me" sounded nothing like anything else on this or the previous LP, proving that Floyd could do much more than just revisit his biggest hit.

Well Done 1975 Chimneyville 201 Producer: Malaco Staff

Body English 1977 Chimneyville CH-202 Producers: Tommy Couch, James Stroud & Wolf Stephenson

He was now to release his three best ever sides, ironically from my point of view, as none of them are to be found on any of his LPs. The first, the gently funky Norman Whitfield influenced "So Much Confusion" scraped into the soul charts at a pitiful #95 but stands up just fine against any of the "social commentary" records that existed in soul music in the early seventies; next a one-off on Dial, the superb "Can You Dig It?" with a wonderful Buddy Killen production (the crispness of the hi-hat on the drums is notable) and, finally, best of all, the magnificent "Handle Me With Care", a genuine deep soul side with a guitar intro very reminiscent of Bobby Womack's "Love, The Time Is Now". (It was notable that Floyd wrote all three, by the way, once again proving his worth as a songwriter).

Another excellent side that DID make it to an album was "I Feel Like Dynamite", which somehow transcended the fact that it was once again suspiciously close to "Groove Me". It reached #35 soul as a single and was the cream funky cut on the *Well Done* set. Apart from "Dynamite", side one was pretty average stuff, with everything sounding much the same with only Vernie Robbin's bass playing raising much interest. Side two, however, aside from "Try Me", was the best LP side King Floyd ever recorded. His sense of melody was strong here, with beguiling compositions like "I'm Gonna Fall In Love With You", "If I Lie To You, "I Don't Think I Could Face It" and "I'm For Real" all being fully satisfying. As usual the set was recorded in Jackson, but by this time the connections with both Quezergue and Atlantic had ended and Floyd and Chimneyville had to go it alone.

And go it alone they did for a while longer, with two more "non-album" singles hitting the lower reaches of the soul charts in 1975 (one of which was an excellent duet with Dorothy Moore, "We Can Love") before his last - and worst - album appeared in 1977. "Body

English", the title track, did become his biggest hit for five years reaching #25 on the soul listings, but it was heavily influenced by "disco" and not in a good way. Other nondescript dance tracks also littered the LP, and, worst of all, two tracks were included that had appeared on the *Well Done* set and "Baby Let Me Kiss You" was re-cut to no great effect at all. It wasn't all bad, though: his re-make of Frederick Knight's "Trouble" was just fine (if a tad over-long) and "I Really Do Love You" could be played out on a dance-floor to this day to good acclaim.

A few more singles came out in the late seventies but none breached the national soul charts and he thus retired from the business before re-surfacing in 2000 for a highly forgettable CD which preceded his passing away in 2006.

I really like the best of King Floyd but he was another artist who was probably better served by singles rather than albums; if only a "Best Of" LP had come out; it would have been spectacular.

Force Of Nature

Ronald James; Donald Harmon; John Faison; Harry Dixon; Warren Patterson; Rozell Randolph; Cleveland Brunson; James Walker; Gerald James; Brian Evans

Force Of Nature 1974 Tommy KZ 32758 Producers: Joseph Jefferson, Bruce Hawes & Bunny Sigler

Unemployment Blues 1976 P.I.R. PZ 34123 Producers: Jimmy Bishop, Jerry Akines, Johnnie Bellmon, Victor Drayton & Reginald Turner

Force Of Nature were one of a handful of groups based on the P.I.R. group of labels who offered up an alternative to the more typical vocal group sound with which the city of Philadelphia is associated. The first album, on Thom Bell's short-lived Tommy label, was a pretty good one, even if it is hard to pin down. There were some dreamy vocals here and there on some decent songs, even if things meandered somewhat on the rather "rocky" "Simba", and the overblown "Ie Man Ja", but matters improved with the centre-piece of the set being the rather good nine minute long "Signs Of Our Times" which ebbed and flowed quite nicely. In truth, Force Of Nature didn't really sound like anyone else on their debut LP, and that was to their credit.

For their second LP the sound changed somewhat: "If You Decide" and "Baby I'm Yours (And I'm Glad)" could have sat fairly unobtrusively on a set by The O'Jays but they are not typical of the album which is generally more funky than its predecessor. "Do it (Like You Ain't Got No Backbone)" employed an Ohio Players style vocal, while a handful of other rather inconsequential cuts employ no vocals at all. The title track is worth listening to though, a fine inner city lament.

Neither of the albums, nor a handful of singles that were pulled from them, had any success and Force Of Nature quickly disbanded as a result.

Reginald Forch

Reginald Forch (with Jesse Harrison) 1978 Crazy Cajun CCLP-1057 Producer: Huey Meaux

Another cheap Crazy Cajun outing. Reginald Forch had one single released in the sixties as by "Reggie Forch" and both sides, "Love Wars" and "Filled Up To My Neck", are on the LP. Mind you, I suspect the versions released on the 45 were more fully realised than the ones on here, which are sparse and unfinished. The other three Forch tracks are also basic demos too, and, all in all, it adds up to a exceedingly poor first side of an LP. Not Forch's fault, of course, and he had a nice voice but it's almost impossible to imagine anyone ever listening to this side of the album by choice. (The Harrison tracks are much better and I will review them in the section under his name.)

Dee Dee Ford (see also Don Gardner)

I Need Your Lovin' (with Don Gardner) 1962 Fire FLP 105 Producer: Bobby Robinson

In Sweden (with Don Gardner) 1965 Sonet SLP-39 No producer listed (Sweden)

In Sweden (with Don Gardner) 1966 Sue 1044 No producer listed

Rhythm & Blues Dance Party (with Don Gardner) 1965 Sonet SLP-47 Producer: Don Gardner (Sweden)

Dee Dee Ford was really Wrecia Holloway out of Louisiana and so one can see why she adopted a stage name, a name that was as inescapably linked to Don Gardner as salt is to pepper; she went on to record more singles with Gardner than she ever did by herself. And on some of the best of these duets - like the monumental "Bitter With The Sweet" - she wasn't even credited.

She had cut her first sides as Dee Dee Ford back in the late fifties but it wasn't until she met up with Gardner that she had any kind of chart triumph. "I Need Your Lovin'" and "Don't You Worry" were both as enjoyable as they were successful, even if the latter was virtually a solo Gardner record. (For more on the album on which they featured, see the section on Gardner).

Ford was not only a spirited and talented singer but she also played keyboards (and wrote Betty Lavette's "Let Me Down Easy", one of the greatest of all soul records) and it was as much in her capacity as an organist as it was as a vocalist, that she features on no less than three albums recorded "live" in Sweden with the Don Gardner Quintet. There is not much on these to satisfy a Ford enthusiast as only a handful of tracks showcase her singing: "Shiney (sic) Stockings" (on which, frankly, she struggles a bit), "I Don't Need You Anymore" and "A Man" and that's about it apart from some vocal assists to Gardner. (Oddly, they don't sing "I Need Your Lovin" on any of the albums). Please also note that the track listing on the two identically entitled LPs, "In Sweden", is slightly different.

As improbable as it sounds, Ford also played organ on a FOURTH Swedish LP, when she backed Freda Payne as part of the Gardner Quintet, and I believe put out one last single (without Gardner) on the Chattahoochee label in 1966 before leaving the record industry soon after.

Forecast

Amir Bayyan; Adil Bayaan; Armenta Richardson; Royal Bayaan; Greg Fitz; Huey Harris

Forecast I RCA NFL1-8031 Produced by Adil Bayaan, Royal Bayaan & Amir Bayaan

This youthful and good-looking team from Ohio placed a single, "Non Stop", on the soul charts in 1980 but it is not included on their one album. I cannot recommend *Forecast I* as it is really a pop album with a hint of soul rather than a soul album with a hint of pop and it does sound dated now. The lyrics are tired too, and the state of Ohio alone had any number bands who issued better LPs than this one. (I believe - but am not sure - that Amir Bayyan may be the man from the Kay-Gees.)

Formula 1

Hold On 1977 Guinness GNS 36003 Producer: Carl Palmer

Could the producer of another tax scam LP from Guinness be the same man who played drums for Emerson, Lake and Palmer? Seems unlikely, but who knows? The sleeve, as ever with this label, gives very little away, but a couple of tracks feature a decent lead singer.

Formula IV

Charles Richard Cason; Leon Kittrell; Ted Butler; Billy Ray Charles

Come Get Yourself Some 1974 Rocky Roads RR 3701 Producers: Steve Cropper, Richard Delvy & Formula IV

Formula V

Alfreda James; Charles Richard Cason; Leon Kittrell; Earl Esby; Billy Ray Charles; Tony Hithe; Tony Davis; Tony Delgado; Esther Jones

Phase 1 1977 20th Century T-530 Producers: Pete Peterson & Richard Cason

Determination 1985 Malaco MAL 7424 Producers: Rich Cason & Jimmy Lewis

On The Rise 1986 Malaco MAL 7433 Producers: Rich Cason & Jimmy Lewis

Formula IV became Formula V, with Rich Cason being the main driving force between both groups. He has had a long and distinguished career in the music industry and is probably better known for his writing, arranging and producing than his singing, but he does all four things across the first two sets before stepping away from the microphone as a lead singer for the two Malaco albums.

The one album performed as Formula IV is solid enough, and Cason must have been delighted when the title track, which he wrote, became a fair sized hit for Leon Haywood in the summer of 1975. The sound is lush, courtesy of some typical L.A. "sweetening", and the songs are generally good enough. the majority of which were delivered by Leon Kittrell's accomplished voice.

Three years were to pass before the next album appeared, with the slight name change simply denoting that the members of the group had increased by one. Alfreda James was a fine addition, as she is a singer of some distinction, going on to work with Sam Dees in later years. Tracks like "Dance All Night" and "Disco Funkinstein" threatened to waste her talents as they could have been sung by anyone, but luckily "We've Got Such A Good Love" a sultry mid-pacer, and "When Love Is Gone", a just below middling tempo song with striking arrangements, gave her every opportunity to prove her skills. "She's My Woman", a fine Billy Ray Charles song, with lead vocals by, I think, Kittrell, was the third excellent cut on a patchy album.

Cason stuck with the Formula V name for the two Malaco albums, but they comprised a completely new set of personnel, Cason excepted, with James, Kittrell and Charles no longer involved. At the time Malaco was having some success with throwback classic singers like Bobby Bland, Johnnie Taylor and ZZ Hill and I remain a bit puzzled by the music and approach of the revamped Formula V. The songs were mostly obviously "southern" in sound and so would have appealed to the traditional Malaco audience but by placing it in such a thinner synth driven musical setting they fell between two stools, neither fully satisfying Bland and Hill hardcore devotees nor a younger audience who wanted a more "now" sound. "Full Time Lover, Part Time Fool" was the choice cut with a great Esther Jones vocal, and any album which has a significant contribution by Jimmy Lewis (writing, background vocals and producing) can't be all bad.

I have not heard much of the final album, *On The Rise*, as the lead-off cut was a thing of unremitting awfulness called "Killer Groove" which led to my shunning the LP. It does contain more Lewis songs though,so might have some good moments.

Cason then chose to close down the project called Formula V and spent the next few years enjoying commercial success ("Bill" by Peggy Scott, for example) and annoying soul purists with his computerized productions.

Millie Foster

Feels The Spirit 1973 MGM SE 4897 Producer: Leo Kulka

Millie Foster cut a handful of sides on the West Coast in the early to mid sixties which are uniformly appealing, suiting her expressive if rather "innocent" voice and it's a shame that none were hits, as this might have led to an album at the time; the only LP she ever cut was the straight gospel set above, which I haven't heard.

Four Jewels

Sandra Bears; Margie Clark; Carrie Mingo; Grace Ruffin

Loaded With Goodies 1985 BJM 001 Producers: Lawrence Berry, James Owens & J. "Mac" Alsobrooks

The four women named above originally recorded as The Impalas (not the "I Ran All The Way Home" group), before changing their name to The Four Jewels which was further truncated to The Jewels when Carrie Mingo left and they became three. They recorded a number of singles under these various group names, and hit only once with "Opportunity" (as by The Jewels) in late 1964. It appears that BJM wished to licence the original recordings in order to put out a compilation of the Impalas / Four Jewels / Jewels work, but that proved troublesome, and so they decided that an alternative was to get the four singers back into a Washington D.C. studio and re-record ten of their original songs and the result is the album we have here. (Martha Harvin aka Martha High was also a member of the Jewels for a few years and was featured on the original "Opportunity" for example, but I haven't listed her above as she did not participate in the making of this LP.)

The album consists of mainly charming songs, recreated in loving and authentic fashion and it is a splendid record to listen to if you are a fan of early sixties girl group soul singing although it is a style which is somewhat of an acquired taste. (It is certainly a much softer style than was required when the group became part of the James Brown Revue for a few years.)

The LP obviously stood no chance in the marketplace of 1985 but then selling huge numbers was never the intention of BJM records and they should be applauded for their determination to get this music out there once again.

Four Mints

Ben Caldwell; James Brown; Donald Russell; Jimmy Harmon

Gently Down Your Stream 1973 Capsoul CSLP 370
Producers: Jeff Smith, Dean Francis, Dana Middleton, Erwin Cochrane & Norman Whiteside

Little Capsoul records out of Columbus, Ohio, didn't last very long and only ever had a couple of small hits but they did manage to put out a couple of fine albums, with this one being a beautiful example of early seventies soul harmony singing. (It has been difficult to establish exactly who comprised the group on the LP but the best bet seems to be the four gentlemen I have listed above.)

Two of those small hits are contained on the album: "Do You Really Love Me" and "You're My Desire" which hit the soul charts in late 1973 (# 84) and early 1974 (#80) respectively. The label couldn't afford the quality and quantity of the musicians in Philadelphia or Los Angeles and this is therefore not an album of symphonic and pungently lush arrangements but no-one has a monopoly on beautiful voices and The Four Mints acquit themselves superbly, while the slightly lo-fi production has a charm all of its own. When they up the tempo the group become a little less interesting as with, say, "Too Far Gone" but the two "hit" singles, "Can't Get Strung Out", "Row My Boat" and, best of all, "Why Did I Go", are all lovely.

Four Tops

Levi Stubbs; Lawrence Payton; Renaldo "Obie" Benson; Abdul Fakir

Four Tops 1964 Motown MT-622 Producers: Brian Holland, Eddie Holland & Lamont Dozier (Billboard soul charts: 1; Billboard pop charts: 63)

Second Album 1965 Motown MT 634 Producers: Brian Holland, Eddie Holland & Lamont Dozier (Billboard soul charts: 3; Billboard pop charts: 20)

On Top 1966 Motown MT 647 Producers: Brian Holland, Eddie Holland & Lamont Dozier (Billboard soul charts: 3; Billboard pop charts: 32)

Live ! 1966 Motown MT 654 No producer listed (Billboard soul charts: 1; Billboard pop charts: 17)

On Broadway 1967 Motown MT 657 Producer: Frank Wilson (Billboard soul charts: 15; Billboard pop charts: 79)

Reach Out 1967 Motown MT 660 Producers: Brian Holland, Eddie Holland & Lamont Dozier (Billboard soul charts: 3; Billboard pop charts: 11)

Greatest Hits 1967 Motown MT 662 Producers: Brian Holland, Eddie Holland & Lamont Dozier (Billboard soul charts: 2; Billboard pop charts: 4)

The Four Tops started off life in Detroit in the fifties as the unheralded Four Aims. They ended up as one of the best loved, most successful and greatest soul groups of all time. They were similar to the Dells in as much as they also survived decades without a single change of personnel, an astonishing state of affairs in the volatile music business.

Success wasn't instantaneous as The Four Tops either, with singles on such labels as Chess and Riverside faring very poorly. In the early sixties their direction was somewhat confused, veering between doo-wop and straight up supper club fare and a proposed jazz based album for a Motown subsidiary (which was scrapped) would have doubtless merely served to blur their identity even further. Luckily, Berry Gordy saw their potential and summoned them to the studio to cut the tracks which were included on *The Four Tops* LP, a true great, and one they possibly only matched once again in all of the years they recorded. "Baby I Need Your Loving" (#11 pop) and "Without The One You Love" (#43) were fine songs and successes when released as singles but the key track - and another top selling 45 - was "Ask The Lonely" (#9 soul, #43 pop), a magnificent record where Levi Stubbs achieved greatness as a singer. It is one to play to anyone who wants to know what soul is "all about", and should be a hundred times better known than it is (outside of soul circles)."Where Did You Go", "Your Love Is Amazing" and the ridiculously underrated "Left With A Broken Heart" are all top class as well, and the same can be said for the backing vocals throughout from The Andantes. Given that Motown didn't really focus on LPs back in 1964 they did a remarkable job here. (The album sleeve gave producing credits to Holland and Dozier, but Marv Johnson, Ivy Jo Hunter and William Stevenson also produced tracks on it.)

The *Second Album* was first rate too, containing the massive and famous hits "I Can't Help Myself" (#1 pop), and "It's The Same Old Song" (# 2) while "Something About You" was a third top twenty pop entry and album only tracks like the careering "Helpless", "I'm Grateful" and the Smokey Robinson co-penned and (uncredited) produced "Is There Anything That I Can Do" ensured that it was not just an album of hits and filler.

A noticeable change took place on the third Motown set, *On Top*, which married a superb and hard driving first side with a more worrisome second. "I Got The Feeling" kicked things off in pounding style while "Shake Me, Wake Me" (#5 soul,#18 pop) and "Loving You Is Sweeter Than Ever" (#12 and #45) were the hits this time around. All was just fine. However, Gordy always had an eye on the night club audience and thus The Four Tops were given "Michelle", "In The Still Of The Night" and "Bluesette" to sing on side two. The results were not pretty for fans of soul music, but, to be fair, the LP was as successful as the previous two.

The next one was their biggest to date, a *Live!* album that predictably mixed up hits with standards. but that was just a taster for the *On Broadway* set, which I found to be a complete disaster and was Gordy going way too far in courting a new audience at the expense of the old.

Fortunately, sanity returned for the excellent *Reach Out* LP, which, despite continuing the tradition of ignoring other producers on the sleeve (Smokey Robinson and Clarence Paul should have been credited), contained an astonishing SIX top twenty pop hits, which is reaching Beatles' proportions and I can only think of one soul album - *Thriller* - that can beat this; it contained seven top 20 pop hits. And *Reach Out* contained not just big hits but all-time classics: "Reach Out, I'll Be There"; "Bernadette"; "Seven Rooms Of Gloom"; "Standing In The Shadows Of Love". The Monkees covers were regrettable but the collection still vies with the debut as their best ever. It stayed on the pop charts for over a year.

And so did their next LP, a *Greatest Hits* collection that was aptly named: 12 tracks, and every one of them had hit the Top 50 pop charts as singles. But now, at the peak of their commercial and artistic success, disaster struck: Holland Dozier and Holland left Motown. The impact was dramatic for The Four Tops. While still maintaining a level of success that would have been the envy of 99% of all soul groups, they never enjoyed the same number of huge hits on the label again. Nine of the tracks on the *Greatest Hits* set had reached the pop top 20; for the remaining four years that the Four Tops remained with Motown they posted only two more singles at the same level.

Yesterday's Dreams 1968 Motown MS 669 No producer listed (Billboard soul charts: 7; Billboard pop charts: 91)

Now! 1969 Motown MS 675 No producer listed (Billboard soul charts: 18; Billboard pop charts: 74)

Soul Spin 1969 Motown MS 695 Producer: Frank Wilson (Billboard soul charts: 30; Billboard pop charts: 163)

The first post-HDH album was *Yesterday's Dreams* and it proved to be, probably to be expected in the circumstances, a confused set, with covers outnumbering new songs. The best track was an "in the can" song by HDH, "I'm In A Different World" (a disappointing #23 soul), which only highlighted the challenge the group would face in overcoming the loss of the great songwriters, and could have been taken symbolically. The worst, and it has a case for the worst record they ever made, was "The Sweetheart Tree".

Things weren't to get much better in the short term either and the record buying public and (I assume) the group themselves had to endure the haphazard and unthinking way in which Motown now treated the Four Tops albums. *Now!* and *Soul Spin* between them included some dreadfully hackneyed and uninspired choices of songs for a group of this stature to cover, including "Eleanor Rigby", "California Dreamin'", "This Guy's In Love With You" and "The Fool On The Hill". They were entirely bereft of true emotion and excitement and, given the albums didn't even have big hits on board to sweeten the blow, their disastrous performance on the pop charts can hardly have been a surprise.

Still Waters Run Deep 1970 Motown MS 704 Producer: Frank Wilson (Billboard soul charts: 3; Billboard pop charts: 21)

Changing Times 1970 Motown MS 721 Producer: Frank Wilson (Billboard soul charts: 20; Billboard pop charts: 109)

The Magnificent 7 (and The Supremes) 1970 Motown MS 717 Producers: Nick Ashford & Valerie Simpson (Billboard soul charts: 18; Billboard pop charts: 113)

The Return Of The Magnificent 7 (and The Supremes) 1971 Motown MS 736 No producer listed (Billboard soul charts: 18; Billboard pop charts: 154)

Greatest Hits Volume 2 1971 Motown MS 740 (Billboard soul charts: 22; Billboard pop charts: 106)

Dynamite (and The Supremes) 1971 Motown MS 745 Producer: Frank Wilson (Billboard soul charts: 21; Billboard pop charts: 160)

Nature Planned It 1972 Motown M748L Producer: Frank Wilson (Billboard soul charts: 4; Billboard pop charts: 50)

The Best Of 1973 Motown M 764D (Billboard soul charts: 35 ; Billboard pop charts: 103)

Anthology 1974 Motown M9-809A3 (Billboard soul charts: 42; Billboard pop charts: 203)

At the sixties turned into the seventies The Four Tops' fortunes changed for the better. Frank Wilson was still producing but there was a subtle change afoot. The covers were not quite so prevalent and higher quality new songs finally started to appear, not least some from Wilson himself.

While I would not claim that *Still Waters* and *Changing Times* were great albums they were certainly improvements on the previous post-HDH sets and at least Motown showed that they were once again prepared to take time on long players from the group. The Smokey Robinson and Wilson penned title track from the former LP was the best song they had cut for a long time and "It's All In The Game" was a cover that actually suited them, rather than sound as if it were force fed. Both tracks were released as singles, reaching #6 and #4 respectively on the soul charts, as well as hitting the pop top thirty. In short, their biggest hits since 1968.

Changing Times was close to being a concept album with a number of songs reflecting on the fickleness of life, and while it really should have done away with a pointless version of "Raindrops Keep Fallin' On My Head", most tracks were solid enough, four of them being co-written by Wilson, and "Just Seven Numbers" became their fourth single in eight months to reach the soul top ten at #9. The Tops were back as a commercial force.

The other track that reached the top ten was a collaboration with The Supremes, "River Deep Mountain High", which was pulled from the next Tops album, *The Magnificent Seven*, which paired up the two famous Motown groups. It was a formula that the record company milked, releasing three combined LPs with ever decreasing returns.

The first album with the Supremes was produced by Ashford and Simpson, rather than by Wilson, and sadly reverted to a staid, safe and ultimately rather pointless approach of lots of covers. Listening to totally ill-advised songs like "Everyday People" is frankly rather painful. "River Deep" performed very well indeed as a single (hitting #14 pop and #7 soul) but no other 45 with The Supremes came remotely close to matching this.

The Return Of The Magnificent Seven featured songs from The Motown stable of songwriters with the exception of Tony Hatch's "Call Me". I did rather take to the version of Tammi Terrell's "I Can't Believe You Love Me" but found most of the songs, while certainly tuneful enough, to be rather lightweight and it's hard to stop the mind from wandering while the set is playing.

The final set with The Supremes, *Dynamite*, was once again dominated by covers. It also suffered from the main shortcoming of the whole concept: Levi Stubbs and Jean Terrell just didn't have very compatible voices. I liked the harmonies on "Hello Stranger" but there is nothing else on the album I would ever particularly want to hear again.

A second *Greatest Hits* appeared in late 1971, and had 12 tracks whereas the UK version had a more generous 14, which included "A Simple Game" which had been a much bigger hit in England then in the States plus "I Can't Help Myself" which had recently hit for a second time over here.

The final album The Four Tops recorded for Motown was a good one in *Nature Planned It*, which, mercifully, spared us any covers apart from a rather inspired choice in Todd Rundgren's "We Got To Get You A Woman"; for once one that was not all too obvious. It was also the first time studio musicians were listed on a Four Tops LP, and reminded us, if any reminding were indeed needed, that James Jamerson was a magnificent bass player while the rest of The Funk Brothers had never let themselves down, even when asked to play on so many drab Tops tracks in the last few years. "If You Let Me", a smallish hit by Eddie Kendricks, gave Lawrence Payton a rare lead, "You Got To Forget Him Darling" harked nicely back to the sixties, while the slick and stylish title track fully deserved its placing of #8 on the soul charts. It was to be the last time they saw a single released on Motown reach those listings for eleven years.

Two compilations - one a double LP and one a triple - charted on Motown after the group had departed for ABC/Dunhill.

Keeper Of The Castle 1972 Dunhill DSX-50129 Producers: Steve Barri, Dennis Lambert & Brian Potter (Billboard soul charts: 6; Billboard pop charts: 33)

Main Street People 1973 Dunhill DSX-50144 Producers: Steve Barri, Dennis Lambert & Brian Potter (Billboard soul charts: 8; Billboard pop charts: 66)

Meeting Of The Minds 1974 Dunhill DSD-50166 Producers: Steve Barri, Dennis Lambert & Brian Potter (Billboard soul charts: 22; Billboard pop charts: 118)

Live & in Concert 1974 Dunhill DSD-50188 Producers: Steve Barri, Dennis Lambert & Brian Potter (Billboard soul charts: 22; Billboard pop charts: 118)

The Four Tops had been disenchanted with life at Motown for a while and it was no great surprise when they jumped ship in 1972 and joined ABC/Dunhill. It was to be an inspired move for a few years as despite the excellence of much of the *Nature Planned It* Motown swansong, there was a definite sense that ABC welcomed the Tops and lavished more time and effort on them than Gordy's empire was ever going to. Time and effort that was rewarded with their biggest run of hits for years.

The early Dunhill albums had a coherence and confidence that had not often been seen in the previous five or six years and were typically tuneful and well played sets, and permitted songs to be included which were written by members of the group themselves (as to be fair, had a couple of later Motown albums). The main writers were Lambert and Potter, and what you got from them was a superb pop sensibility that manifested itself in instantly catchy melody lines and a keen eye on hit singles but the group did have to sacrifice a certain soulfulness. One wasn't going to get an "Ask The Lonely" from L and P.

Keeper Of The Castle typified the focus on hit 45s. It had no poor tracks at all, but the two massively successful singles, "Ain't No Woman (#2 soul and #4 pop), and the title track, (#7 soul and # 10 pop), were clearly the best tracks on offer.

Much the same seemed to be said for *Main Street People* as well, which housed its best cuts in "Are You Man Enough", "Sweet Understanding Love" and "I Just Can't Get You Out Of My Mind", all of which were excellent, and all of which reached the soul top 20 and the pop top 70. On reflection though, it was a stronger album than its predecessor as it also included a handful of estimable album cuts too: the title track, "Am I My Brother's Keeper" and "Whenever There's Blue". One last good cut worth mentioning: "One Woman Man" which had a touch of "Love Makes The World Go Round" to it and which was sung by Lawrence Payton and indeed released as a single under his name. Without the magical Four Tops credit though, it stalled at a lowly #63 soul.

Pleased with all this success, Dunhill afforded the group a gatefold cover - the first ever for a quartet of this importance - on *Meeting Of The Minds*, another highly worthwhile set. It had some variety too: "One Chain Don't Make No Prison" was an atypical and superbly driving Lambert and Potter song while "Midnight Flower" (an almost completely forgotten record) was the first time Lamont Dozier had provided a song for The Tops in a very long time. It is clearly from his pen. Both tracks, when released as 45s, hit the soul top five, but, ominously, did no better than #41 and #55 respectively on the pop chart, a clear indication that their commercial peak was once again about to pass. Lawrence Payton's "Tell Me You Love Me" was released as his second single but failed completely, which was a shame as it was a nice song in a J.R. Bailey style, and had an even better b-side in "I Found The Spirit". "The Well Is Dry", another hard pushing cut, clearly acknowledges "Reach Out I'll Be There" which was a wry touch.

A *Live* album came out towards the end of 1974 which sensibly mixed up their most recent hits with a smattering of Motown classics after which the group were moved to the main ABC label, which coincided with the fact that their albums got progressively less interesting.

(I have not included *Shaft In Africa* under their Dunhill releases as while they had a big hit with "Are You Man Enough"? (#2 soul, #15 pop) from the soundtrack they contributed nothing else and I do not think it can be considered to be a Four Tops LP.)

Night Lights Harmony 1975 ABC ABCD-862 Producers: Steve Barri & Lawrence Payton (Billboard soul charts: 24; Billboard pop charts: 148)

Catfish 1976 ABC ABCD-968 Producer: Lawrence Payton (Billboard soul charts: 26; Billboard pop charts: 124)

The Show Must Go On 1977 ABC AB-1014 Producer: Lawrence Payton (Billboard soul charts: 54)

At The Top 1978 ABC AA-1092 Producers: Norman Harris, Ron Tyson & Bruce Gray (Billboard soul charts: 73; Billboard pop charts: 208)

To lose one set of key songwriters (HDH) may be regarded as a misfortune, to lose two (L&P) looks like carelessness, but this is what happened, disastrously again, when The Four Tops had to make do without Lambert and Potter from the *Night Lights Harmony* LP onwards. With L & P The Four Tops had placed six singles on the soul top ten and six on the pop top sixty. Without them, the tally became one and zero.

The lead-off single from *Night Lights Harmony*, "Seven Lonely Nights", adopted a back to the future approach with its distinctly sixties construction while the follow-up, "We All Gotta Stick Together", was led by Lawrence Payton, the first I can think of where Stubbs didn't play the major role on a Four Tops single. Both 45s reached the soul top twenty which was a respectable performance but both fell well short of past glories and there were no hidden gems lurking within the rest of the LP, either.

Catfish bore a title track which inexplicably - it wasn't great - made it to #7 on the soul charts but the whole LP was somewhat uninspired with nothing to stir the soul. A track called "Disco Daddy" didn't bode well, even if it wasn't really even a "disco" cut.

By the time of *The Show Must Go On* LP it was obvious that ABC could do nothing more with the group, and it certainly didn't remotely match up to the Sam Dees' set of the same name. Its chart performance was woeful and the title track hit the derisory #84 spot on the soul charts when released on a 45. Four tracks were stretched out to six minutes or more and only one -"Love Is A Joy" - was even worth half that length. The lack of quality on the LP was summed up on the final cut, a cover of The Brothers Of Soul's "Candy". An interesting song choice, it was spoiled by the fact that the lead vocal by, I believe, Renaldo Benson, rare enough in itself, was almost inaudible and one couldn't have guessed in a million years that it was a track by The Four Tops.

At The Top took the group down to Philadelphia for the first time and the upbeat billing belied the fact that the group were anything but. A more pertinent title would have been the first single from the set: "H.E.L.P". It reached # 38 soul. It wasn't too bad as a dance record, but the next 45, "Put It On The News", didn't make the soul top 100 at all. Most of the LP was upbeat without being uplifting - apart from the reasonably satisfying slower cuts, "Seclusion" and "Just In Time" - and even if it was superior to *The Show Must Go On*, it still brought the ABC era to a low-key end.

Tonight! 1981 Casablanca NBLP 7258 Producer: David Wolfert (Billboard soul charts: 5; Billboard pop charts: 37)

One More Mountain 1982 Casablanca NBLP 7266 Producer: David Wolfert (Billboard soul charts: 45)

Happily, the third flowering of The Four Tops occurred in 1981 on a new label and it was probably as unexpected as it was welcome. In truth, the album was not something I listened to a lot. The massive single, "When She Was My Girl", was their first soul #1 for 15 years (!) and also made it to #11 pop. I was delighted for the group but the track still sounded like a slightly better than average cut from any one of the last few LPs, and the whole set was bright, upbeat eighties pop music. Restoring Levi to sing the vast majority of the leads was plainly a good move, though. It was all somewhat of a flash in the pan though as the next two singles to be released from the album fared significantly less well.

A fate that was even more true with the second Casablanca set, *One More Mountain*, which sold few copies and contained little of lasting value.

Back Where I Belong 1983 Motown 6066ML Producers: Brian Holland, Eddie Holland & Lamont Dozier (Billboard soul charts: 47; Billboard pop charts: 202)

Magic 1985 Motown 6130ML Producers: Willie Hutch, Benny Ashby, Kerry Medina, Reggie Lucas, Johnny Bristol & Hal Davis (Billboard soul charts: 33; Billboard pop charts: 140)

In 1983, The Four Tops returned to Motown. Hence the LP title. On the surface, it was as if nothing had changed; HDH produced and Berry Gordy oversaw the whole thing as "Executive producer". One thing clearly had changed, of course: it was no longer 1965. The LP sold poorly and a single lifted from it, "I Just Can't Walk Away", reached no higher than #36 soul and #71 pop. Gordy was astute enough to realise that things may not have panned out triumphantly, and so persuaded Aretha Franklin and The Temptations to lend their talents to the project. Sadly, the respective results, "What Have We Got To Lose" and "Hang", were not very thrilling. Stubbs did a trademark good job on my favourite track, the old classic "The Masquerade Is Over", when he rolled back the years, but nothing else was in its class.

By the time of the follow-up Motown LP, HDH and Gordy had all quietly disappeared leaving Willie Hutch and Reggie Lucas to do most of the producing. Despite a disconcertingly average title track and a shaky cover of "I'm Ready For Love" it was not a bad album at all ; in fact probably their strongest of the eighties. "Don't Tell Me That It's Over" and "Easier Said Than Done " were strong ballads and Phyllis Hyman guested to good effect on "Maybe Tomorrow". Another good cut, "Sexy Ways", made it to #21 on the soul charts, the last time they ever posted a 45 so high.

Indestructible 1988 Arista Producers: Bobby Sandstrom, Narada Michael Walden, Jerry Knight, Aaron Zigman, Albert Hammond, Phil Collins, Lamont Dozier, Steve Barri, Huey Lewis & Tony Peluso (Billboard soul charts: 66; Billboard pop charts: 149)

Oh dear. Ten producers, never a good recipe for success. And so it proved. Two singles - one being a sugary duet with Aretha - briefly hit the soul charts but the album sold poorly. I was excited to see a Paul Kelly song called "Change Of Heart" on the album but it was not one of his best with rather clumsy lyrics. The LP also included "Loco In Acapulco", a thing of horror. It apparently featured in a film, as did the boring title track. And so the Four Tops vinyl LP career came to an undistinguished end.

They are all - apart from Abdul Fakir - gone now. But history will record The Four Tops as one of the greatest of all soul groups. 27 pop top 50 singles and no end of "household known" songs will ensure that. (I have ignored countless compilations that exist.)

Tony Fox

The Beginning 1981 Blaster L.V.C. 50142 Producer: Larry Capel

Tony Fox had a fascinating and varied career and released a large number of excellent singles, some under different names like Larry Hale and Larry Cappell (sic), on lots of different labels. As ever, I can't go into the details of his story but given that not a single one of his near twenty singles made it onto the Billboard soul charts it was somewhat of a shock to see that he did get the opportunity to cut an LP, one that has always been in-demand due to its limited distribution around New York.

It's a good one, too, with "A Tear Fell" being probably the standout. This is a country-soul song of immense charm that matches Solomon Burke's version from fifteen years earlier and is almost equalled by "Hurtin' Hurt So Much" another country-tinged item. However, these are not typical of most of the LP, which has more of a concern with danceable tracks, and "Love Let love And Be Loved", "I Wanna Get Next To You" and "Lay Some Lovin' On Me" are all fine examples of potent dance tracks from the turn of the decade. Only "Love And Care" is a bit peculiar; not only is a renamed version of "Try A Little Tenderness" but it is a rudimentary sounding song, almost a demo in fact.

It was ironic to call the set *The Beginning* when it was actually the end as I know of no further records from Fox, under that name or any other. Interesting too, that the sleevenotes make reference to Tony Fox AND Larry Capel when there is speculation that they were one and the same person. Maybe it was a ploy to throw unwanted creditors off the scent? Who knows, but Tony Fox was a splendid singer and this album deserves to be far better known than it is.

Inez And Charlie Foxx

Mockingbird (as by Inez Foxx) 1963 Symbol 4400 Producer: Juggy Murray

Mockingbird 1964 Sue ILP 911 No producer listed (UK)

Inez & Charlie Foxx 1966 Sue 1037 No producer listed

Mockingbird: The Best Of Charlie & Inez Foxx 1986 EMI-America SQ 17243

Another confusing act in many ways. In the summer of 1963 a record by Inex Foxx called "Mockingbird" was a huge hit, hitting #2 soul and #7 pop. In the small print on the 45 were the words "accompaniment by Charlie Foxx". On the back of this success Symbol issued an LP, named after the hit, also as by Inex Foxx. In 1964 Sue records in the UK issued an LP, also called "Mockingbird", but credited to Inez & Charlie Foxx. Seven tracks were the same. From here on in, until Inez definitely went solo on Volt in the early seventies all records were to be credited as by "Inez and Charlie Foxx". Unless it was the LP called "Inez and Charlie Foxx's Swinging Mockin' Band", a set by the duo's road band.

Most people know the big hit and it has become something of a "standard" over the years and its obvious nod to Ike and Tina Turner was perpetuated on the *Mockingbird* Symbol LP on cuts like "Confusion". Other tracks like "Talk With Me" and "I See You My Love" brought out Inez' individuality somewhat better. There were no more hits on the Symbol album but three more were contained on the UK "Mockingbird" issue: the very poor "Hi Diddle Diddle" (absurdly close to the big hit) and the considerably better "Ask Me" and "Hurt By Love".

In 1966 Sue put out the *Inez & Charlie Foxx* LP, but Sue's day was done and it was all "in the can" material, much of which had come out before, It's still full of good stuff, though and listen to it for "La De Da I Love You" which was, to say the least, close to The Supremes' "Where Did Our Love Go".

The *Best Of* release from 1986 is generous in including 16 tracks, but there is nothing on it that hadn't already appeared on the LPs from the sixties.

Come By Here 1967 Dynamo DS 8000 Producer: Luther Dixon

Greatest Hits Past And Present 1968 Dynamo DS 8002 Producer: Charlie Foxx

Swinging Mockin' Bird (by Inez & Charlie's Road Band) 1968 Dynamo DS 8003 Producer: Charlie Foxx

By 1967 the duo had moved to Dynamo where they did their best work. *Come By Here* was led off by a title track (a re-make of "Kumbaya") which had been the b-side to their mini-hit, "No Stranger To Love" in late 1966. It is a song I find hard to take in any form and if it sounded clunky in 1967, there was better fare on board in "Tightrope" and "Never Love A Robin", both great dance records, and the rather hammy but perfectly enjoyable "I Stand Accused" - a small soul hit (#41) when issued as a two part 45. In fact, title track apart, it is a splendid "uptown" album.

Nearly as good was *Greatest Hits, Past And Present* with the emphasis much more on the "present" as only "Mockingbird" was trawled from the past. Inez Foxx acquits herself superbly on "You Are The Man" and the splendid two-sided, "Vaya Con Dios"/"Fellows In Vietnam", one of the best of all the songs about that sad conflict. Another fine track, "Count The Days", became a decent hit when released on 45 at #17 soul.

The *Swinging Mockin' Bird* set, apart from the inevitable inclusion of the big hit, is entirely instrumental and includes versions of big soul hits like "Hard To Handle" and "Midnight Mover".

A word should be said here about Charlie Foxx, as he was a strong songwriter, and has never really received the credit he deserves, In truth, the Foxx duo (brother and sister, by the way) have tended to be viewed as an "Ike And Tina-lite" a horrible phrase, and an unjust one as well.

Inez Foxx

At Memphis 1973 Volt VOS-6022 Producers: Randy Stewart & Willie Hall

In the seventies, Charlie once again took a back seat and Inez' solo "You Shouldn't Have Set My Soul On Fire" was a small soul hit (#50) in early 1971. In 1973 she had signed a deal with Stax/Volt, a perfect fit, given her rootsy appeal and approach, and the adept *Inez Foxx At Memphis* was the one album that resulted from the deal. There are no absolute classics on display, but nothing is weak either; the one oddity is "Mousa Muse", which is an interview with the lady. Her voice is slightly more nasal in places than her sixties' sides but she proves again that, among the lush arrangements provided by Wade Marcus and James Mitchell, her singing cannot be subdued and she remains a most underrated artist. She takes on three songs for ever associated with other legendary soul singers, "I Had A Talk With My Man", "The Time" and "Let Me Down Easy", performed by Mitty Collier, Baby Washington and Betty Lavette respectively. While she may not top the originals, she doesn't get disgraced either and all three are well worth a listen. The former was a small soul hit in early 1974 as was the tough and sassy "Circuit's Overloaded" (NOT on the LP).

Aretha Franklin

Aretha 1961 Columbia CL 1612 No producer listed

The Electrifying 1962 Columbia CL 1761 Producer: John Hammond

The Tender, The Moving, The Swinging 1962 Columbia CL 1876 Producer: Robert Mersey (Billboard pop charts: 69)

Laughing On The Outside 1963 Columbia CL 2079 Producer: Robert Mersey

Unforgettable - A Tribute To Dinah Washington 1964 Columbia CL 2163 Producer: Robert Mersey

Runnin' Out Of Fools 1964 Columbia CL 2281 Producer: Belford Hendricks (Billboard soul charts: 9; Billboard pop charts: 84)

Yeah !!! 1965 Columbia CL 2351 Producer: Clyde Otis (Billboard soul charts: 8; Billboard pop charts: 101)

Soul Sister 1966 Columbia CL 2521 Producers: Clyde Otis, Bob Johnston & Robert Mersey (Billboard soul charts: 8; Billboard pop charts: 132)

Aretha. One of the few for whom a Christian name is enough to grant universal recognition. Even if she had been called "Susan", it might still have worked, such was her talent. The facts are well-known and oft-repeated and her story isn't over yet, but the sister from Memphis is the greatest singer in the history of soul music.

There are two schools of thought about her Columbia material: firstly, that the label had no idea what to do with her and the material was vastly inferior to her Atlantic work or second, that she recorded some very good things indeed, that have been underrated and overlooked for too long. If pushed, I veer towards the second opinion, although I agree that too many of the Columbia years were somewhat wasted when compared to what was to come along later.

One of the best Columbia LPs was the first where Aretha is backed by the Ray Bryant trio. Most of the elements of her future greatness are already apparent: the beauty of her voice, her piano playing and a sympathetic bunch of musicians. It is an undeniably "black" record from the pre-soul era and benefits tremendously from the absence of strings that often smothered her Columbia sides. "Sweet Lover", for one, could easily have sat on an early Atlantic album without being out of place at all. It even contained two top ten "R &B" singles: "Today I Sing The Blues" and" Won't Be Long". John Hammond produced this excellent album, even if the sleeve did not credit him.

The strings and a big band approach arrived for the second set, *The Electrifying*, but some cuts like the lovely "Nobody But You" (another that could easily have been on Atlantic) managed to do just fine without them. And if anyone doubts the continuity in her music, listen to "It's So Heartbreakin'" which has a piano intro that she lifted, more or less intact, for "Don't Play That Song" a decade later. Tracks like "I Surrender Dear" and "Blue Holiday" are not to my taste but it is still a beautifully performed and sung LP.

The *Tender, Moving And Swinging* set put her on the album charts for the first time, but it was her jazziest and most string-laden effort to date, with a predominance of "standards", with only one song from her own pen, "Without The One You Love", which has a magnificent vocal, as does the "toughest" (the term is relative in this context) track on here, "Don't Cry Baby".

The *Laughing On The Outside* collection had precious little to do with the emerging soul sound, as it continued the approach of the prior release: lots of standards wrapped up safely and snugly in a bed of strings. No question though about her singing, which was once again amazing.

Columbia shifted their stance on *Unforgettable -A Tribute to Dinah Washington* which provided Franklin with the opportunity to go for a much tougher sound, which she clearly relished on "Evil Gal Blues", "Soulville" and "Cold Cold Heart". This was her best LP since her first, even if it remained somewhat of a mystery as to which audience Columbia were trying to push her towards. It was not a "hip" album for 1964, and was too committed for the supper club set. Not surprisingly, therefore, it failed to chart and did not bring forth any hit singles.

Runnin' Out Of Fools, with a lovely cover photograph of the young Aretha, was the most obvious attempt yet by the label to market her to a much younger audience. It was more or less a complete triumph. Maybe "My Guy" was a bit perfunctory, maybe "You'll Lose A Good Thing" and "Every Little Bit Hurts" couldn't *quite* match Barbara Lynn's and Brenda Holloway's originals but her version of "Walk On By" remains my favourite of all-time, her takes on "It's In His Kiss" and "I Can't Wait Until I See My Baby's Face" worked without reservation, the superb title track became her biggest pop hit to date (#57) and a lesser-known song like "One Room Paradise" (with the Sweet Inspirations on backing vocals) was marvellous as well. But most of all, it was an obvious "soul" album, in tune with what else was going on in late 1964.

Which made the *Yeah!!!* LP a bit puzzling as it was a return to "standards". "If I Had A Hammer", "Once In A Lifetime" and "Misty" were not what a younger audience wanted to hear from Aretha, and no hit singles were on board the LP, although, to be fair, it performed respectably enough when compared to her other Columbia sets.

At least Columbia went out on somewhat of a high on the last LP Franklin recorded for them before she moved to Atlantic. *Soul Sister* had a trendy title, and some more bona fide soul music within, even if the best tracks had to contend with - despite her fine singing - jazzy things like "Swanee" and "Ol' Man River". "Sweet Bitter Love" and "Until You Were Gone" brooked no vocal arguments and "Cry Like A Baby" became a fair-sized soul hit when released as a 45 (#27 right at the end of 1966). But nothing could compare to "No No I'm Losing You" which in addition to a desperate Franklin vocal had a magnificent "uptown" arrangement by Robert Mersey.

And then she went to Atlantic.

I Never Loved A Man The Way I Love You 1967 Atlantic SD 8139 Producer: Jerry Wexler (Billboard soul charts: 1; Billboard pop charts: 2)

Aretha Arrives 1967 Atlantic SD 8150 Producer: Jerry Wexler (Billboard soul charts: 1; Billboard pop charts: 5)

Lady Soul 1968 Atlantic SD 8176 Producer: Jerry Wexler (Billboard soul charts: 1; Billboard pop charts: 2)

Aretha Now 1968 Atlantic SD 8186 Producer: Jerry Wexler (Billboard soul charts: 1; Billboard pop charts: 3)

Live In Paris 1968 Atlantic SD 8207 Producer: Jerry Wexler (Billboard soul charts: 2; Billboard pop charts: 13)

Soul '69 1969 Atlantic SD 8212 Producer: Jerry Wexler and Tom Dowd (Billboard soul charts: 1; Billboard pop charts: 15)

Aretha's Gold 1969 Atlantic SD 8227 (Billboard soul charts: 1; Billboard pop charts: 18)

Over the years, the rock press has consistently hailed three LPs as the greatest soul has ever produced: *What's Going On, Otis Blue* and *I've Never Loved A Man The Way I Love You*. Given how often pop writers have got soul hopelessly wrong, it would be tempting to think they have made a crucial misjudgement here. But they haven't. Much of her work on Columbia had been very good indeed but the musicians, production, arrangements and songs that Atlantic brought to bear were perfect for Franklin, and when those key ingredients were added to her vocal and piano playing talents, everything and everybody else in the world of soul had to stand back in amazement at what they were seeing and hearing. It is impossible for me to play this without being deeply moved by its greatness and for recognising how briefly Aretha's star burned at this level. "Respect", an immense global hit, of course, is even, due to its over-familiarity, easily my least favourite song on the LP. The title track, like "Respect", went to #1 on the soul charts when released as a single and for all its brilliance, is eclipsed by some of the other, maybe lesser-known tracks. "Baby Baby Baby" and "Do Right Woman-Do Right Man" are so full of grace, so pure, yet so intelligent and worldly at the same time that "genius" really is the right word to use; "Don't Let Me Lose This Dream", with its bossa-nova beat, was unlike anything else she had done or was to do later and was simply glorious; "Dr Feelgood" had an unmatchable "three in the morning" feel while the sleepy "Soul Serenade", "Good Times","Drown In My Tears" and "A Change Is Gonna Come" were all perfect song choices for her. This was setting a standard that no-one else in the world could match. As far as I'm concerned, it's not just the best soul LP ever made, it's the best LP ever made in the history of popular music.

The follow-up, *Aretha Arrives*, was a huge disappointment artistically. It sold in vast quantities, so Atlantic would have been happy, but why on earth was she saddled with songs like "Satisfaction", "You Are My Sunshine", and "96 Tears"? These were the sort of song choices Columbia would have made, and the unerring instinct for inspired material that was so evident on the previous set was missing this time around. As were Aretha's own compositions, of which there were none, compared to four on *I Never Loved A Man*. "Prove It", "Ain't Nobody (Gonna Turn Me Around)" - a fine song from sister Carolyn - and "I Wonder" were all excellent and the super "Baby I Love You" was another huge hit on single (#1 soul, #4 pop), so it was hardly a shambles, but it is not classic Aretha, a mistake Atlantic were to shortly rectify.

I suspect Atlantic knew *Aretha Arrives* had slightly missed the mark, as it was surely no co-incidence that only one 45 was pulled from it. *Lady Soul* served up three, all classics, and all top five singles on the pop charts as well as huge soul smashes: "Chain Of Fools", "Natural Woman" and "(Sweet Sweet Baby) Since You've Been Gone". The third was co-written by Franklin, as was "Good To Me As I Am To You", a fine blues. The whole album was nearly up to the quality of the debut Atlantic set, with imported songs like "People Get Ready", "Come Back Baby" and "Groovin'" all delivered confidently and soulfully. Carolyn Franklin once again served up an excellent composition, "Ain't No Way" which went to #9 soul in its own right as a single after it was flipped from the b-side to "Sweet Sweet Baby". Musicianship was as ever of the highest class and an interesting addition to Franklin's sound were the "swampy" textures of "Chain Of Fools" and "Niki Hoeky".

Aretha Now was another tremendous set, housing "Think" and the soaring "I Say A Little Prayer", two more of her best-loved performances and two more top 3 soul hits on 45. "See Saw" was another strong single but its performance at only reaching #9 on the soul charts and #14 on the pop charts was almost a disaster by her own standards. It is also interesting to listen to her take on "You Send Me" and to be reminded how closely Natalie Cole's "This Will Be" was modelled on it. *Aretha Now* is possibly her "toughest" album of all, and the feisty singing of the Sweet Inspirations and the tremendous southern band (although recorded in New York) combine to make her come across as the quintessential earthy soulstress. All the LP lacked was a Carolyn Franklin ballad to pull at the heartstrings but is still absolutely essential. (It also contains her splendid and highly underrated single, "I Can't See Myself Leaving You", which, oddly, was not put out on 45 for over a year after the release of the album).

A *Live in Paris* album was next inevitably released (or the 'live' bit, anyway, not so much the location) and is no better or worse than the majority of such sets but I cannot see that many people still pull this one out to play in the twenty-first century.

There has often been a question as to whether it was Atlantic or Aretha herself who called the shots of what she recorded, and whatever version one chooses to believe, there was no doubt that her talent was too broad and sweeping to be confined on pure "hard soul" LPs such as *Aretha Now* as *Soul '69* was to conclusively prove. It was a full-blown return to the jazzier side of her Columbia tenure and sounded nothing like her previous Atlantic work in any way at all. A couple of the songs - "Tracks Of My Tears" and "Gentle On My Mind"- came out as b-sides but nothing was put out as an a-side which only confirmed that all concerned saw it as somewhat of a one-off, something that had to be done, rather than as a change of direction that would be continued in future. I'm sure there are plenty of people who love *Soul '69* - it was yet another #1 on the soul charts, after all - but it is my least favourite album of hers by some distance from the early Atlantic years.

A greatest hits compilation, *Aretha's Gold*, closed out the sixties and was the sixth of her seven Atlantic LPs from the decade to reach #1 on the soul charts. The other reached #2.

Take It Like You Give It 1967 Columbia CL 2629 Producers: Bob Johnston, Bobby Scott & Clyde Otis

Greatest Hits 1967 Columbia CL 2673 (Billboard soul charts: 10; Billboard pop charts: 94)

Take A Look 1967 Columbia CL 2754 No producer listed (Billboard soul charts: 22; Billboard pop charts: 173)

Greatest Hits Volume 2 1968 CL 9601

Soft And Beautiful 1969 Columbia CL 9776 No producer listed (Billboard soul charts: 29)

Today I Sing The Blues 1970 Columbia CL 9956 Producers: John Hammond & Billy Jackson

As can be imagined, Columbia had a lot of Franklin material in the vault and released much of it on the series of LPs above. The least worthwhile are *Today I Sing The Blues* as it contains work which had all been released before and the Clyde Otis produced (but uncredited) *Soft And Beautiful* which is certainly "soft" and completely MOR. *Take A Look* also contains a fair bit of previously released material so *Take It Like You Give It* is by far the best bet, especially as tracks like "Deeper" and "Only The One You Love" are genuinely soulful.

Just to confuse things, though, The UK put out an album entitled *Take A Look* (CBS 63269) but is entirely different from the U.S. release, and consists mainly of tracks from the *Runnin' Out Of Fools* LP.

This Girl's In Love With You 1970 Atlantic SD 8248 Producers: Jerry Wexler, Tom Dowd & Arif Mardin (Billboard soul charts: 2; Billboard pop charts: 17)

Spirit In The Dark 1970 Atlantic SD 8265 Producers: Jerry Wexler, Tom Dowd & Arif Mardin (Billboard soul charts: 2; Billboard pop charts: 25)

Aretha Live At Fillmore West 1971 Atlantic SD 7205 Producers: Jerry Wexler & Tom Dowd (Billboard soul charts: 1; Billboard pop charts: 7)

Greatest Hits 1971 Atlantic SD 8295 (Billboard soul charts: 3; Billboard pop charts: 19)

Young, Gifted & Black 1972 Atlantic SD 7213 Producers: Jerry Wexler, Tom Dowd & Arif Mardin (Billboard soul charts: 2; Billboard pop charts: 11)

Amazing Grace 1972 Atlantic SD 2-906 Producers: Jerry Wexler, Aretha Franklin & Arif Mardin (Billboard soul charts: 2; Billboard pop charts: 7)

Hey Now Hey (The Other Side Of The Sky) 1973 Atlantic SD 7265 Producers: Aretha Franklin & Quincy Jones (Billboard soul charts: 2; Billboard pop charts: 30)

Let Me In Your LIfe 1973 Atlantic SD 7265 Producers: Aretha Franklin, Jerry Wexler, Arif Mardin & Tom Dowd (Billboard soul charts: 1; Billboard pop charts: 14)

1970 opened with another disappointing LP, *This Girl's In Love With You*, and the slightly out of focus cover shot seemed to symbolise the efforts within. Her life had its challenges around this time and she seemed bored on routine versions of "Son Of A Preacher Man", "Dark End Of The Street" and "The Weight". "Eleanor Rigby" and "Let It Be" were much better left to The Beatles, and only "It Ain't Fair","Sit Down And Cry" and the rather lovely "Call Me" (her only composition on the entire album) are worth repeated listens. My comments count for little though: "Share Your Love With Me" and "Call Me" became her seventh and eighth soul #1 hits respectively and "Eleanor Rigby" made it to #5 as well.

Spirit In The Dark was a highly welcome return to form. As ever, it included lots of songs made famous by others, but the difference this time around was the zest with which they were tackled; "Don't Play That Song" absolutely demolishes any other version, for example,and equally importantly, five of her own songs were included making it one of her most personal LPs ever. It also features some of her most inspired piano playing. The title track and "Don't Play That Song" were yet two more smash hits on 45, and the whole collection hangs together beautifully with no real weak cuts.

Atlantic released a second live album on Franklin in 1971 which went gold, as well as becoming her best performing LP on the pop charts since her last gold set, *Aretha Now*. It was no more appealing to me than the *Live In Paris* set being overly raucous in sound and with some seriously disappointing song choices: "Make It With You", "Love The One You're With" and "Reach Out And Touch (Somebody's Hand)".The only thing really worth hearing twice is Ray Charles' appearance on "Spirit In The Dark" where he delivers some incredibly soulful piano work. If only he had performed like this all the time.

Her second hits collection came out in 1971, and listening to it again now reminds me that "Spanish Harlem" (a great record) and "Bridge Over Troubled Waters" (an overblown one) were not included on her other studio albums. They were both yet more #1 soul singles. "You're All I Need To Get By" hadn't been featured on an album, before, either. It was a #3 soul success.

Franklin released another near-masterpiece in 1972 with the generally brilliant *Young, Gifted And Black* set, arguably the last time she ever produced an LP of such consistently high quality. There are four tracks I don't care for including "Didn't I Blow Your Mind This Time" (a stripped down version that doesn't work at all) and "The Long And Winding Road", a song I can't abide, but the rest is marvellous. The title track is my favourite version of a magnificent song, while "April Fools" and "All The King's Horses " have wonderful Arif Mardin arrangements, with the latter being one of Franklin's greatest ever vocal performances: a throwback to the dignity of *I Never Loved A Man*. "Rock Steady" and the lovely "Day Dreaming" were two more huge hits when pulled as singles, and "The First Snow In Kokomo" proved again that she had a singular talent for composing a song.

A third Atlantic 'live' album came out in 1972 but *Amazing Grace* was different and more interesting. It is not only her solitary certified platinum album but the biggest selling gospel LP of all-time. Listening to a double album of live gospel is not to everyone's taste and it does require taking time to sit down and concentrate as it is not background music. But it is worth the perseverance as it does give a sense of her power and abandon when the spirit truly moved her. If taking it all in is simply too much, then do at least find a way to hear her impressive ten minute version of "Never Grow Old".

Hey Now Hey was an odd one: the only time she worked with Quincy Jones, nearly all songs strung out for four minutes or more and the first album in years that did not list all the musicians who played on it. It didn't really work. "Moody's Mood", "Somewhere" and "Just Right Tonight" can't sustain my interest and her overlong version of "That's The Way I Feel About Cha" didn't come close to the charm of Bobby Womack's original. But the LP did include one of the all-time great records in "Angel", with an astonishing vocal where her pain is all too palpable. Set up by an irresistible spoken intro the last minute features some of the greatest singing that will be covered in this entire book. When truncated for a single it became yet another #1 soul hit.

Let Me In Your Life was the first of a series of albums that had a flattering picture of Franklin on its cover, as if to assuage the fears of her fans that her personal life travails were damaging to her art. More importantly, it was a strong set and contained some particularly striking songs including one of her sweetest performances of all on "Until You Come Back To Me", one of two tracks that went to #1 on the soul charts (and #3 pop) when put out as a 45. The other one was "I'm In Love" a stately cover of an excellent Bobby Womack composition that had hit a number of years earlier for Wilson Pickett. It was good to see her covering an offering by the talented Eddie Hinton on his "Every Natural Thing" and she also had her second hit with an Ashford-Simpson number when "Ain't Nothing Like The Real Thing" became the third single to be pulled from the album. Elsewhere, the title track pointed up one of her few weaknesses: to sometimes sacrifice subtlety on the altar of over emoting. On hearing it in isolation it is a good enough performance but when compared to Bill Withers' original it lacks the pathos and yearning that he brought to the song.

With Everything I Feel In Me 1974 Atlantic SD 18116 Producers: Aretha Franklin, Jerry Wexler, Arif Mardin & Tom Dowd (Billboard soul charts: 6; Billboard pop charts: 57)

You 1975 Atlantic SD 18151 Producers: Aretha Franklin & Jerry Wexler (Billboard soul charts: 9; Billboard pop charts: 83)

Sparkle 1976 Atlantic SD 18176 Producer: Curtis Mayfield (Billboard soul charts: 1; Billboard pop charts: 18)

Ten Years Of Gold 1976 Atlantic SD 18204 (Billboard soul charts: 29; Billboard pop charts: 135)

Sweet Passion 1977 Atlantic SD 19102 Producers: Aretha Franklin, Lamont Dozier, Marvin Hamlisch, Carole Bayer Sager, Marty Paich & David Paich (Billboard soul charts: 6; Billboard pop charts: 49)

Almighty Fire 1978 Atlantic SD 19161 Producer: Curtis Mayfield (Billboard soul charts: 12; Billboard pop charts: 63)

La Diva 1979 Atlantic SD 19248 Producers: Aretha Franklin, Van McCoy, Charles Kipps & Skip Scarborough (Billboard soul charts: 25; Billboard pop charts: 146)

By the middle of 1974 and from *With Everything I Feel In Me* (rather a clumsy title) onwards Franklin's best days were behind her, both artistically and commercially. Never again would she release an LP I adore, and although she still had big smashes on 45 - 4 more #1 soul hits were yet to come - she had could hardly match the almost astonishing 15 she had enjoyed between 1967 and early 1974. And the LPs sold in ever fewer quantities: between 1974 and 1985 she had only three albums reach the pop top twenty; contrast this with the twelve in the period from 1967-1973.

With Everything is not a bad LP by any means, but it doesn't stand out when compared to her best work. The formula was much the same as usual, with Wexler, Dowd and Mardin helping Franklin to produce the usual slew of well-known songs and a couple of Carolyn Franklin originals. Maybe the fact that only one song by Aretha herself was onboard, the strangely lack-lustre title track, was the overriding reason as to why it the album was not a particularly strong outing. Having said all that, "Without Love" was a fine song, performing pretty well as a single, #6 soul and #45 pop.

You was an improvement on *With Everything* but once again the question has to be asked: why were the songs all so long? Ten tracks, the shortest of which was 3:44. Her earlier, better albums had more to say in much less time. That being said, there is much to enjoy here and "Without You", "You Got All The Aces" and "As Long As You Are There" are all unsung Franklin sides of merit. So is the admirable Frank Johnson song, "I'm Not Strong Enough To Love You Again" even if Sandra Wright put out an even better version some years later. The title track and "Mr.D.J" couldn't even breach the soul top ten as singles; a sign of the times for her mid-seventies career.

For the remainder of her stay with Atlantic a series of new producers were tried out but the results were never particularly satisfying even if certain moments still stood out. For the soundtrack to *Sparkle*, a film that certainly passed me by, Curtis Mayfield took over production duties but it was a case of two artists coming together who had both passed their peak. They were still much too talented to produce a genuine dud, but the whole thing comes across as "just another Franklin album".To be fair, "Giving Him Something He Can Feel " from the LP became her latest #1 soul hit but it doesn't particularly move me. It also reached #28 pop, the last time she would ever plant a single on the pop top thirty for Atlantic.

Franklin looked beautiful, radiant and happy on the cover of the *Sweet Passion* collection, for which five new producers came on board. It started off well: track 1 was the excellent "Break It To Me Gently", her last ever Atlantic soul #1 single, while track 2 was the exuberant "When I Think About You". It is a noticeably slight song but her unbounded double-tracked passion atop the bouncing rhythm has always made it just about my favourite record of hers from the last Atlantic days. The album did go somewhat downhill from there, although "Meadows Of Springtime" has some moments of the old magic. On the other hand "Touch Me Up" was definitely not her finest hour.

Mayfield was brought back for *Almighty Fire* which suffered from the same shortcomings as *Sparkle*: a whole LP of average material could not sustain her. She always needed work that stretched her and allowed her to delve into corners of songs that others could not find. Curtis Mayfield was one of the greatest songwriters of the twentieth century, but the work he did with Aretha fell a long way short of his finest compositions. To sum things up, "More Than Just A Joy" could only make it to #51 soul as a single, her worst performing 45 in her entire Atlantic history.

Franklin closed out her Atlantic tenure with the very poor La Diva which was surely her worst ever album. I can't imagine anyone loving this one and its chart performance doesn't lie. "Only Star" and "Ladies Only" were even disco and only "You Brought Me Back To My Life" and "Honey I Need Your Love" - an updated version of "You Send Me" from her *Aretha Now* album all those years ago - are worthy of her talent.

Aretha 1980 Arista AL 9538 Producers: Arif Mardin, Chuck Jackson & Aretha Franklin (Billboard soul charts: 6; Billboard pop charts: 47)

Love All The Hurt Away 1981 Arista AL 9552 Producers: Arif Mardin & Aretha Franklin (Billboard soul charts: 4; Billboard pop charts: 36)

Jump To It 1982 Arista AL 9602 Producers: Luther Vandross & Aretha Franklin (Billboard soul charts: 1; Billboard pop charts: 23)

Get It Right 1983 Arista AL 8-8019 Producer: Luther Vandross (Billboard soul charts: 4; Billboard pop charts: 36)

Who's Zoomin' Who? 1985 Arista AL 8-8286 Producers: Narada Michael Walden, Dave Stewart & Aretha Franklin (Billboard soul charts: 3; Billboard pop charts: 13)

Aretha 1986 Arista AL 8-8442 Producers: Narada Michael Walden, Keith Richards & Aretha Franklin (Billboard soul charts: 7; Billboard pop charts: 32)

One Lord, One Faith, One Baptism 1987 Arista AL-8497 Producer: Aretha Franklin (Billboard soul charts: 25; Billboard pop charts: 106)

Through The Storm 1989 Arista AL-8572 Producers: Narada Michael Walden, Arif Mardin, Jerry Knight, Aaron Zigman, Joe Mardin & Aretha Franklin

What You See Is What You Sweat 1991 Arista 211 744 Producers: Luther Vandross, Aretha Franklin, Narada Michael Walden, Burt Bacharach, Carole Bayer Sager, David Conley, David Townsend, Elliot Wolff, Bruce Roberts, Oliver Leiber & Michel Legrand (Germany)

Franklin made her first label move in thirteen years and there was thus a lot riding on the first Arista album. She was no longer a superstar, but remained an irresistible essence in American culture and her Christian name alone was once again deemed sufficient together with an attractive picture of her on the cover to try and reclaim her audience. Did it work? Yes, just about. It was certainly better and more cohesive than her last three or four Atlantic outings but did not completely restore her fortunes. Reaching #6 soul and #47 pop was respectable, no more. More promisingly, the lead-off single, "United Together" went to #3 soul and #56 pop, which was at least her biggest hit in three years. Musically, "School Days", "Together Again", "Love Me Forever" and the hit were blessed returns to form but ""Can't Turn You Loose" was a heavy-handed take on the Otis Redding hit and "What A Fool Believes" fell slightly short of its intended mark, too.

Love All The Hurt Away sold a little more strongly but started the trend that was to render too many of her post 1980 years somewhat boring from my point of view: the collaborations with other singers. The title track saw Franklin comprehensively out-sing George Benson but it is one of those overblown ballads - as was "It's My Turn" - I don't much care for. "Hold On I'm Coming" was even worse than "Can't Turn You Loose" and said a lot less in five minutes than Sam and Dave had said in two. It is in essence an urgent song, which did not need Aretha's vocal curlicues. If anyone ever wants to cite an example of Franklin "oversouling", then this would be a prize exhibit. A more interesting and surprising cover could have been the Rolling Stones' "You Can't Always Get What You Want" but it was delivered in a somewhat perfunctory manner. My obvious misgivings about the whole set can probably be laid at the door of the musicians and production. Not a single player on the set is anything other than highly talented but where the Muscle Shoals players brought a dignified and spare style to the early Atlantic sets, virtually the whole of *Love All The Hurt Away* has a glossiness and soaring pop ethic that was perfectly symbolised on the front cover.

Jump To It's title track gave Franklin her first #1 soul single (and first top 30 pop hit) in five years and Arista had made a smart move in bringing in Luther Vandross as writer and producer as he was at his commercial peak in the early eighties. Personally, while I liked the LP enough at the time, and still much prefer it to *Love All The Hurt Away*, I don't think Vandross' songs and Marcus MIller's popping basslines have aged particularly well over the years and it is another set that I can play and enjoy but not much on it makes me sit up in wonder. My favourite cut is, predictably, a Sam Dees' song, "If She Don't Want Your Lovin'", although she does sing the hell out of "This Is For Real".

Get It Right was the fourth Arista LP in a row that had Aretha glowing on the cover, and the second in succession that employed Vandross as producer. The title track was another #1 soul single which continued the significant upturn in her material rehabilitation. I must confess to finding the hit dull and the whole LP to be too imbued with Vandross' style at Franklin's expense. The only track I like unreservedly is "Better Friends Than Lovers" which has exquisite backing vocals.

Mind you, *Get It Right* sounded mighty good when compared to virtually everything on *Who's Zoomin' Who?* on which the only track I care for is "Integrity" .Her duet with Peter Wolf on "Push" was a career nadir, genuinely sad to hear. And I can't stand the horrible eighties' pop of "Sisters Are Doing It For Themselves" either. This was the album when Aretha and I finally parted company and I never bought another one. She would doubtless find that to be my loss rather than hers particularly as "Freeway Of Love", another straight pop record from the set, became yet another #1 soul single. More significantly it reached #3 pop and the title track followed up as #2 soul and #7 pop. Arista had triumphed; she was now having huge hits again; her biggest for ten years.

Rather boringly Arista called Aretha's sixth album exactly the same as her first one. It had a nice track in "Jimmy Lee". On the other hand, it also saw her singing "Jumping Jack Flash" as well as duets with George Michael and Larry Graham.

A return to gospel was next and I like it a great deal more - despite the overlong prayer segments - than the later Arista sets and it is touching to hear (if only just) Carolyn and Erma join their sister on "We Need Power" and "Packing Up, Getting Ready To Go" although it is The Mighty Clouds of Joy's Joe Ligon who really takes the honours on the latter. Best of all, to hear Aretha sing "Jesus Hears Every Prayer" is to be transported back to Muscle Shoals in the sixties when she had the world at her fingertips.This one makes me forget all those depressing duets and she is reborn as the greatest soul singer on the face of the earth.

There were two more Arista LPs (I have noted the second one as coming out in Germany as the U.S. release was a CD only) the first of which had the dismayingly unoriginal title of Through The Storm. Across these sets we found duets with James Brown, Elton John, Levi Stubbs, Whitney Houston and Michael MacDonald. And thus was the vinyl career closed out on a singer who had less need of singing duets than any other in this entire book. (I have ignored nearly all the numerous compilations that exist.)

She is, of course, still with us and there have been a number of notable commercial successes in the CD era. She is a national treasure, but for a while she was more than that: a great American artist to be discussed in the same breath as Louis Armstrong or Frank Sinatra.

<u>Carolyn Franklin</u>

The First Time I Cried 1970 Joy 180 Producer: Lloyd Price (UK)

Baby Dynamite! 1969 RCA LSP-4160 Producer: Buzz Willis

Chain Reaction 1970 RCA LSP-4317 Producers: Buzz Willis & Jimmy Radcliffe

I'd Rather Be Lonely 1973 RCA LSP-4411 Producers: Wade Marcus & Carolyn Franklin

If You Want Me 1976 RCA APL1-0420 Producer: Jimmy Radcliffe

Like Aretha, Carolyn Franklin was born in Memphis, moving north with other sister, Erma, and the rest of the Franklin clan at an early age. Her first records were released in the early sixties under the name of Candy Carroll. They went nowhere. When she started to record for RCA at the end of the sixties an album of her early work was put out on the eclectic UK Joy label but only "Easy Living" had been released before. The whole set is stripped back, three in the morning jazz, with not a string or a horn to be heard. It all sounds pretty similar, in fact, to the style employed by Julie London on "Cry Me A River", a song which Carolyn covers here.

Although RCA are to be commended for persevering with Carolyn for four albums over a six year period, the fact that her first LP had one title on the front and seemingly another (*This Is Carolyn*) on the back suggested that maybe they were not fully prepared to do whatever it took to turn her into a hit artist. In her entire time with the label she placed just two singles on the soul charts: "It's True I'm Gonna Miss You" and "All I Want To Be Is Your Woman" at #23 and #46 respectively.

The former was to be found on *Baby Dynamite!* which had sleevenotes provided by father C.L. Franklin. It is an album utterly bereft of any songs that could have become big hits and RCA did well to even get "It's True" on the charts as, like virtually every track on the set, it lacked a memorable hook-line. The whole LP is brassy and uptown in style but offers little enticement for it to be worn out by constant play. Perhaps more than one composition by Carolyn herself would have made it much stronger, given the number of exceptional songs she provided for Aretha over the years. Her singing, while now and again employing phrasing that recalled her more famous older sister, was tuneful and soft, without ever being suited for the multi-octave jumps that Aretha could deploy.

Her second RCA album adopted a markedly conservative approach: ten tracks, virtually all of which were covers. "I Ain't Got To Love Nobody Else", "Not On The Outside", "Chain Reaction" and "Goin' In Circles" had all been performed by soul groups and I must confess to preferring all of them to Carolyn's offerings. Other songs like " Everybody's Talking" and "Put A Little Love In Your Heart" were dull while her one original song, "Right On!", was rather messy and unmemorable. The production throughout the album was too fussy and stodgy for my liking and there was no lightness of touch anywhere on the set, a problem which had also been apparent on her debut.

I'm glad I can be more positive about *I'd Rather Be Lonely*, as it has stronger songs that were better suited to her and more immediate. The fact she wrote about 50% of them is clearly no coincidence. The title track for instance sticks in the memory after just one play, and her spoken intro sets up "As Long As You Are There" perfectly, on a song which has one of her best vocal performances. No wonder Aretha covered it. Carolyn even delivers a song entitled "Dad" which I had feared would be unbearably mawkish, but it works well. I could do without the covers of "Fire And Rain" and "Baby I'm A Want You" but Bill Withers' "Sweet Wanomi" was a more interesting choice. It was certainly my favourite LP of hers to date, but it still didn't sound compellingly cutting edge for 1973, being somewhat out of step with most other soul sounds from the era. While that can sometimes be a good thing, it didn't help *I'd Rather Be Lonely* to sell any more copies than her previous albums.

Her final LP rather shuffled out in 1976 with no big splash from RCA. Encouragingly, she wrote about half of the songs, but, once again, it didn't sound even remotely likely to be a success in that bicentennial American year. "Deal With It" was gently funky, for instance (with more than a hint of Aretha's "Mr. D.J") but sounded rather tame when compared to Earth, Wind & Fire or The Ohio Players. Much better was the sophisticated "I Can't Help My Feeling So Blue" which was a lovely song and performance to listen to, but RCA put it out on a 45 and its subtlety and understated charm had no chance of becoming a hit. "You Can Have My Soul" was another exceptional cut of decided attraction, but her version of "You Are Everything" was rather lightweight. If only she had eschewed the covers in her career and recorded a "Carolyn Sings Carolyn" LP we would have had something to treasure.

She made no more records in her own name after 1976 although she did appear on some of Aretha's from time to time. She stood out from most other female soul singers in that she wasn't funky, didn't do any disco, stayed the right side of MOR and was decidedly not a southern-soul style wailer either. Such a lack of a hook on which to hang and market her music doomed her to commercial backwaters but she was a highly gifted songwriter and a singer of poise and talent. She died, like sister Erma of cancer, in 1988, aged only 43.

Erma Franklin

Her Name is Erma 1962 Epic LN 3824 Producer: Al Kasha

Soul Sister 1969 Brunswick BL 754147 Producers: Carl Davis & Eugene Record (Billboard pop charts: 199)

Most music fans will know Erma Franklin's "Piece Of My Heart" but I wonder if they realise that a) it wasn't *that* big a hit, only reaching #62 pop in 1967 (although it did make #10 on the soul listings) and b) it, like all of her fine Shout material, does not appear on an LP by Franklin. She managed to average more or less a single every six months in a career spanning some eight years, but both she and Carolyn, even when their output is added together, released only a small percentage of the records put out by Aretha and father C.L. Franklin.

Erma's first LP, which proclaimed her identity to a largely indifferent world, is a terrific example of how to mix up the emerging soul sound with standards like "Time After Time" and "The Man I Love". An early Carolyn song, "Each Night I Cry", is both the "blackest" thing on the album and an early warning as to her precocious song-writing ability given she was only 17 when it was penned. "It's Over", "What Kind Of Girl", "Never Let Me Go" and "Saving My Love For You" would also have been thrilling to me had I been listening to such exciting fare when I was six years old. The album has stood the test of time exceedingly well, despite the "torchy" offerings, and there are not many other LPs in this book from 1962 that I prefer to this one.

She released some more good singles on Epic (who didn't really know what to do with soul music in the first half of the sixties) before moving to Shout where she recorded her best known-hit and a great reading of "Big Boss Man" but had to wait until she moved to the Brunswick label before her final album emerged.

Franklin was *tough* on this set. Contrast her new version of "Saving My Love For You" with the one on Epic; both beautifully sung but by 1969 soul was of course fully established so the arrangements on the new track were much more conducive to a singer emoting in the manner employed by Erma here. She also delivers her takes on Jackie Wilson's big hits, "Higher And Higher" and "I Get The Sweetest Feeling" with Brunswick skimping on studio time by simply letting Franklin emote over the existing backing tracks. She almost loses control at the end of the former but gives Wilson a run for his money in both instances. As indeed she does to Dusty Springfield on "Son Of A Preacher Man" but Sam and Dave wouldn't have lost any sleep on hearing Franklin tackle "Hold On I'm Coming". "You've Been Cancelled", one of two of Franklin's own songs on the LP has a great title, which is actually better than the song itself, but she delivers her second "hit" single (#40 soul in early 1969) superbly. "Gotta Find Me A Lover", is a great "lost" single on which Franklin roars atop the brassy orchestration that propels this irresistible record ever onwards. She does fight a losing battle on "By The Time I Get To Phoenix", though, where her undoubted passion is simply all but drowned out by the aggressive backing. Somewhat of a mixed bag, then, and possibly not quite as impressive as her debut but the good moments are really good and should be cherished.

Sadly, like Carolyn, she succumbed to cancer in 2002 leaving Aretha the only surviving Franklin sister at the time of writing. While she obviously was overshadowed by Aretha's fame and success, Erma Franklin was a tremendous singer in her own right and the world should not have dismissed her so lightly.

Frank-O

Flashbacks 1987 Traction T-0002 Producer: James Bennett

Pickin' Up The Pieces 1988 T-0004 Producer: James Bennett

Jealous 1990 T-0006 Producer: James Bennett

Frank Johnson was and is a great songwriter, with his most lucrative and best credits possibly being "We're Getting Careless With Our Love" and "Love Is So Good When You're Stealing It" for Johnnie Taylor and Z.Z.Hill respectively. I'm thankful he released a single in 1978 under the name of Le Frank O ("Keep On Gettin' Down" and not as bad as it may sound) as it thus renders him eligible for inclusion in the book and he deserves to be written about.

Flashbacks was his first ever album and it's a shame it didn't appear fifteen or twenty years earlier as it is full of songs that others would have eagerly chosen to cover and record back in an era when southern soul style singers could sell records in large numbers. "Ain't No Easy Way To Say Goodbye" (which Bobby Bland did cut in 1987), "Don't Lie To Me", "You Ain't My Daddy" and "It Don't Hurt Like It Used To" would have been lapped up like cream by singers of the calibre of Taylor and Hill in, say, 1972, rather than in the former's case in 1988; Johnson knows the world he writes about intimately and if his songs are often about pain and regret, well, he knows that's the way life goes. Nine of the ten tracks are either lightly sprinkled with an unmistakeable blues flavour or are out and out southern soul songs (the LP was recorded down in Memphis) with only the much more danceable "It's Too Late" standing out as something different; it's very good, too. Because the LP appeared in 1987, and because Traction records didn't run to big budgets, the musical accompaniment is rather cheap with synthesisers standing in for horns, but because the songs are so good, and as Johnson was also an accomplished singer it's a piece of work I still enjoy a great deal.

Johnson faithfully followed the same approach for *Pick Up The Pieces* with the title track, "Hell Became Heaven" and "Starting All Over" being the main standouts but I feel slightly less enamoured by it for three reasons: the production sounds even cheesier; Johnson phrases like Taylor throughout rather than adopting more of his own style; the pressing is rather poor on my copy - and presumably all copies - with crackles and pops galore à la All Platinum. But these fairly minor reservations and it's still a pleasure to hear how well he constructs a song with such seeming ease.

Jealous was Johnson's last vinyl album and it was by far my least favourite almost entirely due to the karaoke style backing which is almost impossible to listen to in one sitting without wincing. The songs are probably not so impressive either, and "She Just Came To Dance" is repeated from the previous set. "Tip Of My Tongue" is a striking song, probably another lost hit, but it doesn't sound like a typical Johnson composition, which probably only goes to prove his versatility and skill.

Frank O Johnson is still active today and has released a number of CDs over the last twenty five years or so. He doesn't quite have the in-the-know reputation of some other songwriters such as Sam Dees, Jimmy Lewis or George Jackson but anyone capable of writing such brilliant songs as Willie Clayton's "Three People (Sleeping In My Bed)" and Sandra Wright's "I'm Not Strong Enough" deserves to be taken seriously.

Freddie / Henchi & The Soulsetters

Fred Gowdy; Marvin Graves; Larry Wilkins; Arnold Andrews; Jesse Escoto; Epifanio Guerrero

Dance 1972? The Record Company 1001 Producer: Hadley Murrell

There was certainly a no-frills approach to this LP. A plain black cover with one word on it, on a label imaginatively named "The Record Company". Fred Gowdy ("Freddie") and Marvin Graves ("Henchi") were the main protagonists of this Phoenix-based band but it is guitarist Larry Wilkins who most clearly defines their style. Which is heavily rock-based and classic soul fans can look away now as there is nothing here that will be even remotely appealing. I remember Reprise records picking up on the "Funky To The Bone" track and putting it out as an ok single in 1973 but that's about as good as it gets and it is not an album for me either, and not a patch on the exuberant sides of fellow Phoenix residents, Dyke & The Blazers.

Bill Fredericks (see also The Drifters)

Love With You 1977 Polydor 2383-470 Producer: Peter Johnson (UK)

Fredericks was one of a whole multitude of ex-Drifters singers, joining them in 1967 and taking a rare lead vocal on their UK hit, "Like Sister And Brother". The group relocated to England in the early seventies at a time when they were enjoying more success here than in their native USA, and Bill presumably liked his new address so much that he stayed here until he died in 1999. This LP consists of entirely Bee Gees' written songs and there was no doubt they could write memorable tunes, the best of which is "To Love Somebody" which is covered by Fredericks here. However, I find the whole album to be very undemanding, gentle MOR / soul music although it is impeccably performed.

Freedom

Adolph Adams; Larry Addison; Tyrone Armstrong; Robert Black; Victor Mason; Joe Short; Ray Smith; David Thigpen; Lindsey Brooks; Wardell Chambers; Quintous Johnson; Richard Morgan;

Farther Than Imagination 1978 Malaco 6357 Producers: Jesse Thompson, Freedom, Vernon Weakly & Mike Daniel

Free 1980 Malaco 7362 Producers: Jesse Thompson & Freedom

Changes Of Time 1981 Malaco 7403 Producers: Freedom Productions & Jesse Thompson

Are You Available? 1984 Malaco 7418 Producer: Benjamin Wright

The Malaco label is best-known to soul fans as being a sort of "rest home" for legendary soul singers at the end of their careers. Think Bobby Bland, Johnnie Taylor, Little Milton and Denise LaSalle, for example. It also, however, provided a base for some self-contained funky bands who made music which sounded nothing like that served up by the artists named above. The most prolific of these groups was Freedom, who gave us four LPs. Interestingly, one of their members, keyboard man and lead vocalist, Larry Addison, went on to write any number of memorable songs for Bland and Taylor.

The first three albums are better than average when compared to the work of other self-contained groups of the same era, if pretty predictable in approach; Freedom never cut anything that surprised and any recognisable "southern" element is non-existent. The funky tracks - which predominate - are tight, punchy and to the point. It was virtually impossible for an ensemble in 1978 to not bear traces of EWAF or The Ohio Players, and, indeed, one of the best tracks across the albums, "Set You Free" from *Farther Than Imagination*, sounds quite a bit like EWAF's "Getaway". I'm reliably informed, though, that "Get Up And Dance" from the same set is the big one from the group, given that it has apparently been sampled on a number of occasions and that fact must have been much more lucrative for all concerned than its miserly chart placing at #82 when released as a single.

Free bears more slow cuts than the debut, and is also nice to see that a splendid if neglected Malaco artist, Jewel Bass, lends her voice to "Lovelight" even if it is not a particularly strong side.

By the time their best set, *Changes Of Time*, appeared Addison had moved on, to be replaced by two new lead singers in Short and Brooks, but the sound had not altered at all and a cut such as "Everlasting Love" still sounded as if it was created by an EWAF tribute band. "Stacked back" was the sort of bass-driven funk track that was *de rigueur* in 1981 and while I am not indifferent to its drive and mathematical precision I prefer slower songs such as "I Give You Love" and "Give Me A Moment" which were really rather good.

Are You Available? featured more of the same from what one had come to expect from Freedom in providing tough, four-square dance items, negligible melody and unchallenging lyrics as well as better singing than the material probably deserved.

No vinyl compilations exist but if one wants to sample Freedom, and there is no need to own all four albums, a *Best Of* CD did appear in 1996.

Free Life

Carl Carlwell; Julian Carey; Winston Ford; Spencer Bean; Wayne Stalling; Ernest Straughter; David Straughter; Robert Russell; Louis Russell

Free Life 1978 Epic JE-35392 Producers: Philp Bailey & Tom Vicari

Four of these musicians played on Blue Magic's *Message From The Magic* with a further two of them contributing to writing one of the songs on it. Free Life's one album, however, bears much more of their famous co-producer's influence and sounds similar to an Earth, Wind & Fire set rather than one from the great Philadelphia group. And not a great EWAF set, either. It is enjoyable and the group avoid any of the more egregious clichés but nine piece bands were two a penny in 1978 and a large slice of luck or an obviously different sound was needed to break any group out from the pack. Free Life had neither of these things.

Bobby Freeman

Do You Wanna Dance 1958 Jubilee JLP 1086 Producer: Morty Palitz

Twist With Bobby Freeman 1962 JGM 5010 No producer listed

Get In The Swim With Bobby Freeman 1964 Josie 4007

C'Mon And Swim 1964 Autumn 102 Cougar Production

Despite Bobby Freeman's rather unconvincing credentials to be considered as a soul rather than a pop singer, I've included him for two reasons: 1) I included Jewel Akens and Robert Knight 2) He made some good singles after his LP days were finished, some of which were undoubtedly more soulful than his early work.

None of his three albums on Jubilee are really worth much investment in time by soul fans, though, as there is virtually nothing included that could be classed as "R 'n' B", "soul" or anything that would suggest "black" music, although it must be noted that "Do You Wanna Dance" and "Betty Lou Got A New Pair Of Shoes" did make it to #2 and #20 respectively on the soul charts. There was some track duplication across the first two sets and whereas the third is subtitled as *Singing His Greatest Hits* it does include four tracks not available on the first two albums, including "Need Your Love" his first soulful side.

The Autumn LP was overwhelmingly better, without being overwhelmingly good. Firstly, it bore seven early Sylvester (Sly Stone) Stewart songs; second, some pretty tough guitar prevailed throughout; and third we heard some much more involved singing from Freeman, and he was more talented than some of his material suggested. It still all sounded fairly tame when compared to what was coming out of Detroit, Memphis and Chicago in 1964 but at least this time there was something for a soul fan to hang his hat on.

Louise Freeman

Listen To My Heart 1991 Ichiban ICH 1111 Producers: Buzz Amato & Jimmy O'Neill

Louise Freeman put out four lovely and soulful sides on single in the seventies, "How Could You Run Away","Save Your Love" (where she sounds remarkably like Aretha), "How Can I Forget" and "Tell Me A Lie", but had to wait until 1991 for her one and only LP, which was largely disappointing.

The album contains eight tracks, only a handful of which I can really listen to with any pleasure. The three uptempo cuts have a total playing time of just under 16 minutes and I can manage about 16 seconds of these before lifting the needle. Side two includes possibly the 67th best ever version of "Fever" and "Unchained Melody" is a dull song, regardless of how eloquently Freeman sings it. Which leaves the good news. Firstly, a well considered take on "I Don't Want To Talk About It"; second, "Love Is Gone", which Freeman co-wrote and, best of all, a new reading of "Save Your Love" which is only marginally different from the single she put out in 1978. She was a first-rate vocalist who had no success at all, and singers of her class and power were never going to make many waves in 1991, but there are a few of us out here who rate her very highly indeed.

Free Movement

Adrian Jefferson; Claude Jefferson; Godoy Colbert; Cheryl Conley; Jennifer Gates; Josephine Brown

I've Found Someone Of My Own 1972 Columbia KC 31136 Producers: Toxey French & Michael Omartian (Billboard soul charts: 26 ; Billboard pop charts: 167)

Free Movement was an unsung and short-lived outfit whose style was somewhat similar to Fifth Dimension or The Friends Of Distinction. They released the one LP, from which were pulled three singles, two reaching the soul top fifty: the title track and "The Harder I Try (The Bluer I Get)" at #20 and #49 respectively. In

1973 they put out one more single that failed and they were never heard from again.

Both the hit singles were tuneful and soothing, rather than electrifying, while elsewhere there were other influences on show such as gospel on "Love The One You're With" or gentle latin on "Comin' Home". It's definitely not a set for anyone who likes to take their soul neat, but it has moments of genuine charm.

Friends Of Distinction

Harry Elston; Floyd Butler; Jessica Cleaves; Barbara Jean Love; Charlene Gibson; Dianne Jackson; Dani McCormick

Grazin' 1969 RCA LSP-4149 Producer: John Florez (Billboard soul charts: 10 ; Billboard pop charts: 35)

Highly Distinct 1969 RCA LSP-4212 Producer: John Florez (Billboard soul charts: 14 ; Billboard pop charts: 173)

Real Friends 1970 RCA LSP-4313 Producer: Ray Cork (Billboard soul charts: 9 ; Billboard pop charts: 68)

Whatever 1970 RCA LSP-4408 Producer: Ray Cork (Billboard soul charts: 42 ; Billboard pop charts: 179)

Friends And People 1971 RCA LSP-4492 Producers: Ray Cork & Jerry Peters (Billboard pop charts: 166)

The Best Of Friends 1972 RCA LSP-4814

Love Can Make It Easier 1973 RCA LSP-4829 Producers: Ray Cork & The Friends Of Distinction

Reviviscence "Live To Light Again" 1976 RCA ANL1-0905 Producer: ??

Golden Classics 1988 Collectables DPL1-0862

The Friends Of Distinction made music that could only have come from the West Coast. Sunny, upbeat and with an emphasis on harmony and complex arrangements and songs from here, there and everywhere, they sounded like Fifth Dimension with a bit more attitude.

Elston and Butler had been members of two short-lived groups, The Hi-Fi's and The Versatiles, and the Friends of Distinction were formed when Cleaves (who went on to join Earth, Wind & Fire for a while) and Love joined to make up the foursome who were fortunate enough to score with their very first single, "Grazin' In The Grass", which, like Hugh Masekela's original, became a top 3 pop hit. It's a great giddy pop record, too, proving that soul doesn't have to be introspective, profound or hard-edged to make a connection with an appreciative audience. "Goin' In Circles" was an excellent follow-up as well, different enough from the first hit to make me admire such a refreshing and daring change of direction when there must have been pressure to make "Grazin' Part Two". It went to #15 pop and was also their highest ever placed 45 on the soul charts at #3. Both songs have since been covered countless times but I think the Friends' versions are still the ones to beat. Other album tracks I really enjoy are the peppy "Help Yourself (To All Of My Lovin')" and the sultry "Lonesome Mood" (but I bet "Eli's Coming" divides opinion; me, I like it) and the whole LP stands up to be counted today, by still capturing a time and place perfectly.

Highly Distinct was by all accounts a rushed follow-up and this feeling is reinforced by the fact that RCA didn't even put out a single from it (if you discount the fact that "This Generation" was a b-side). It is, frankly, a disappointingly poor set with only "Working On A Groovy Thing" (a song that suited them beautifully), "Why Did I Lose You" and "Let Yourself Go" being worth committing to vinyl. The rest ranged from dull (everything else) to nonsense ("Impression").

The *Real Friends* offering, despite a cheap looking cover, was a noticeable improvement on *Highly Distinct* with another big hit on board in "Love Or Let Me Be Lonely" (#6 pop and #13 soul) and other above average cuts were "Out In The Country" and "Long Time Comin' My Way". If the rest was fairly mundane, then it wasn't dreadfuln either. Charlene Gibson had now joined to cover for Barbara Love's maternity break and, as usual, the vocals were spread around all the four members of the group.

Whatever may have continued the pattern of ever decreasing sales for Friends Of Distinction albums but I think it is probably their most entertaining set and certainly contains the best singing ever served up by Floyd Butler on "Willa Faye", a mesmerising ballad, while Barbara Love gives a notable performance on "Didn't We", a Jim Webb song I don't usually much care for. The LP was also their most ambitious to date, with the group recalling no-one else on the lengthy "Soulful Anthem" and throughout there is a grace and lightness of touch they never quite attained again. They deliver the original of Tavares' first ever hit, "Check It Out", although another decent cut, "Great Day" is not the same song performed by The Whispers. I've never seen a review or heard anyone talk about *Whatever* (which got a UK release, the last of theirs to do so) in the forty plus years since it came out but it is worth a spin or two.

At 57 minutes long, *Friends And People* has a convincing claim to be one of the best value for money albums in the book. It also, as with parts of the *Whatever* set, appropriates some aspects of jazz - time changes and intricate instrumentation - before merging them into a soul album wrapped up attractively in an unmistakable West Coast package. The group were down to three by now if the front cover is any indication, but the sleevenotes gush about four individuals, and how creative and successful they are without ever deigning to tell us their names. To give a taste of the diversity within: three nine minute plus tracks; the winning unusual, double-tracked and dead slow "Dying To Live"; the rather charming verses and weak chorus of "Jenny Wants To Know; the pleasing momentum of "Down I Go"; a bossa-nova beat of "I Can't Get You Out Of My Mind"; some impressive singing on "Oh, How I Miss You".

In 1972 RCA put out a *Greatest Hits* collection. A second album, with exactly the same tracks and catalogue number, but called *The Best Of Friends,* also came out. I don't know why RCA did this or which came first, but it hardly matters.

The Friends recruited two new singers for *Love Can Make It Easier* in Dianne Jackson and Dani McCormick but this didn't slow the group down from continuing along their singular and unpopulated path. It was another set which sounded radio-oriented and uncommercial at the same time, but by now they really were singing to the converted only and the set was not a hit and neither was a single from it which yoked together the best known-songs on show in "Ain't No Woman (Like The One I've Got)" and "Easy Evil". I really liked the socially-conscious title song which had a beautiful flow and arrangement but didn't find too much else to be particularly diverting. (Exactly the same front cover photo as on *Love Can Make It Easier* was used by the Collectables label for their 12 track *Golden Classics* release in 1988.)

Their last LP slipped out with little fanfare and I don't recall ever seeing it as a new release which suggests limited distribution. I am not familiar with it at all - apart from one song, the smoothly undulating "When A Little Love Began To Die" - but titles such as "Terrie", "Rock And Stone" and "Reviviscence" itself suggest that it was likely to be one of their trademark idiosyncratic outings.

George Frye

Keep On Keeping On 1982 Beach City SF 16 Producers: John Vestman & Chris Wright

This independently released LP from 1981, out of Long Beach, contains six longish tracks and is really rather good. It was doubtless George Frye's one shot at stardom (he seems to have made no more records) and he deserved better than pretty much total obscurity. He is a limited singer with a light but nonetheless appealing voice and there are two excellent tracks on here: "You're All My Dreams" with addictive backing vocals and the memorable title cut which is pitched just above mid-tempo. Synthesisers detract from some parts of the LP but there is still enough going on musically elsewhere to sustain interest.

Full Fource

James Spencer; Douglas Brown; Willie Brown; Tyrone Young; Chaz Hollowell

A Long Way Together 1980 Castle CA 7080 Producers: Kondoo Dume Productions & Ray Brooks

I like this album from this Los Angeles based group for a number of reasons: 1) It includes two enchanting slow tracks in "(We've Come) A Long Way Together" and "A Song Within" 2) People were prepared to release tracks like this in 1980 when they would have had much more impact in 1972. 3) It's such an unpretentious offering. No flowery dedications, just a few thanks and the names of those who made the music, did the singing and worked out the arrangements. In short, just no-frills soul music. It starts inauspiciously, though, with "Broke Your Face" being almost laughably nondescript, but the other uptempo cuts are all ok. Not great, but certainly ok. Needless to say, the set did not become a hit, but it's an album I pull out every three years or so, and it's always a half hour reasonably well-spent. (Four of the tracks were also released on an LP shared with producer Ray Brooks entitled *Songs With In* on the UK Timeless label TRLP 114 in 1987.)

As for the group, I don't think James Spencer is the same person who recorded solo singles for the Taurus and Memphis labels but do suspect Willie Brown was formerly a member of the Intentions.

Funkadelic (see many other related entries)

George Clinton; Eddie Hazel; Billy Nelson; Tawl Ross; Tiki Fulwood; Mickey Atkins; Bernie Worrell; Tyrone Lampkin; Frank Waddy; Zaki Frazier; Harold Beane; Gary Shider; Phelps Collins; Bootsy Collins; Prakash John; Cordell Mosson; Ron Bykowski; Calvin Simon; Clarence Haskins; Grady Thomas; Ray Davis; Mike Hampton; Glen Goins; Jerome Brailey; Bobby Lewis; Walter Morrison; Rodney Curtis; Larry Fratangelo; J.S. Theracon

Funkadelic 1970 Westbound WB 2000 Producer: George Clinton (Billboard soul charts: 8 ; Billboard pop charts: 126)

Free Your Mind And Your Ass Will Follow 1970 Westbound WB 2001 Producer: George Clinton (Billboard soul charts: 11 ; Billboard pop charts: 92)

Maggot Brain 1971 Westbound WB 2007 Producer: George Clinton (Billboard soul charts: 14 ; Billboard pop charts: 108)

America Eats Its Young 1972 Westbound 2WB 2020 Producer: George Clinton (Billboard soul charts: 22 ; Billboard pop charts: 123)

Cosmic Slop 1973 Westbound WB 2022 Producer: George Clinton (Billboard soul charts: 21 ; Billboard pop charts: 112)

Standing On The Verge Of Getting It On 1974 Westbound WB 1001 Producer: George Clinton (Billboard soul charts: 13 ; Billboard pop charts: 163)

Let's Take It To The Stage 1975 Westbound W-215 Producer: George Clinton (Billboard soul charts: 14 ; Billboard pop charts: 102)

Greatest Hits 1975 Westbound WB 1004 (Billboard soul charts: 50)

Tales Of Kidd Funkadelic 1976 Westbound W-227 Producer: George Clinton (Billboard soul charts: 14 ; Billboard pop charts : 103)

The Best Of The Early Years Volume 1 1977 Westbound WB 303

Funkadelic were my favourite manifestation of the "Parlia-Funkadelicment Thang", George Clinton's sometimes demented, sometimes sane vision of how music should sound and life be lived. For soul fans, they were not a band one could be indifferent to; one either loved them or hated them and many people for whom I have the greatest respect make it a point of honour not to own any of their records. *Chacun à son gout*. I should also point out here that Funkadelic were one of the select few groups in the soul world who always placed much more importance on albums than singles and every one of their first eleven LPs (*Greatest Hits* excluded) hit the soul top thirty. They also quickly came to realise the importance of having a visual image. It is hard to think of any soul/funk band who understood this better than Clinton and his sleeve designer Pedro Bell.

"Mommy What's A Funkadelic?" the first track on their first album gave clear notice that we were not about to listen to a band who played by the rules that had been set down for soul groups, even ones who worked in the funk sphere. It was nine minutes long, druggy, spaced out, with time-changes galore and answered the question posed by the title pretty eloquently. There was an element of Sly and The Family Stone in some of the songs, and the way in which voices were bounced around, particularly on "What Is Soul", but Funkadelic were always much more of a guitar-heavy band than The Family Stone and at this early stage of their development would usually wish to take six minutes over a track where Sly would chose three. For all the wackiness and experimentation of their music it should not be forgotten that Funkadelic always meant much more to a black audience than a white one; they did not follow a Jimi Hendrix route in that respect. Look at the disparity in the soul placings of their albums when compared to the pop ones. Three singles from the debut hit the soul charts when issued on 45: "Music For My Mother", "I'll Bet You" and "I Got A Thing, You Got A Thing, Everybody's Got A Thing". The album was a startling arrival and one of the best they ever produced, even if, like virtually all their work, it was uneven: "Qualify & Satisfy" and "Good Old Music" don't do much for me.

And neither does virtually the entirety of the second LP, *Free Your Mind*. It sets out too clearly to ape heavy rock and has scant soul association. "I Wanna Know If It's Good To You" hit #27 on the soul charts when put out as a single and "Some More" has exactly the same guitar riff as Sly's "Sex Machine". Other than that, I have nothing to say.

I believe that the photograph on the inside cover of *Maggot Brain* was taken in Liverpool on a tour of Great Britain in 1971. I have looked up the details of where they played that year and see that Tunbridge Wells was on the list. I shudder to think how small the audience must have been, and what that genteel town would have made of the band. The title track is a fairly famous ten minute work-out by Eddie Hazel, which is not to my taste, as it, like "Super Stupid", is a pure rock cut, and I prefer the shorter and punchier "Hit It And Quit It", "Can You Get To That" (#44 on the soul charts) and "You And Your Folks, Me And My Folks" (#42). I liked "Wars of Armageddon", too. It had absolutely nothing to do with soul music, but was engagingly mad. The gatefold sleeve printed, for the first time on a Funkadelic album, the idiosyncratic sleevenotes by Clinton for which he would become famous. From here on in, some people anticipated Funkadelic sleeves as much as for the music within.

America Eats Its Young was the first double album Funkadelic issued. It was also rather more accessible to fans of soul with a greater emphasis on singing and the rhythm section at the expense of guitar solos. "We Hurt Too" and "Everybody Is Going To Make It This Time" were slow songs that did not sound anything like what had gone before and the excellent "Philmore" saw the introduction of Bootsy Collins to the band. Most songs bear close listening and if they could sometimes be playful and lascivious ("Pussy" and "Miss Lucifer's Love") there was a seriousness behind "Biological Speculation", "If You Don't Like The Effects" , and "Everybody's Going To Make It". Clinton had always had something to say, but on this album he said it a bit more unambiguously and in an era when any number of soul records had rather formulaic "peace and love" lyrics Funkadelic were much more political and committed than virtually everyone this side of Curtis Mayfield. "A Joyful Process" and "Loose Booty", were compelling funky workouts , and each hit the soul charts as a double sided single, but it was definitely an album to be heard in its entirety as its variety was invigorating and impressive and it has a claim to being their best ever LP.

Cosmic Slop has been a somewhat forgotten LP (although it was the first to be designed by Pedro Bell) as it contained no singles that reached the soul charts and the title track and the marvellous and important post-Vietnam song "March To The Witch's Castle" aside, no particularly well-known tracks either. It rewards listening though and it's somewhat of a surprise to be reminded that the opening bars of "Can't Stand The Strain" were suspiciously close to what was to follow a year later on Lynyrd Skynyrd's "Sweet Home Alabama". There is also a cover of an obscure doo-wop record by the Sonics, "This Broken Heart", from the late fifties, proving again that the band had a deep awareness of the roots of soul. "Nappy Dugout" and "No Compute" were also fun; no-one else in soul was as upfront and wry about sex as Funkadelic. Reading Clinton's latest treatise on the album sleeve was also amusing; the drugs were obviously still working.

The sixth Westbound LP, *Standing On The Verge Of Getting It On,* had a good title, a typically lurid sleeve which contained a genuinely amusing run down of the band amid increasingly non-sensical Clinton ramblings, and their biggest (although the term is relative) hit in four years in the title track when it reached #27 soul in the summer of 1974. It was a great record too, unstoppable and assertive which rather bucked up the album after a somewhat uneventful first side. "Good Thoughts, Bad Thoughts", another twelve minute long Eddie Hazel guitar workout closed out what is probably a pretty good LP for Funkadelic obsessives, but it is not one of my favourites.

On the other hand, *Let's Take It To The Stage* most definitely is. In fact side one is my favourite side of any P-Funk related album, ever. Six tracks, all short or shortish and not an ounce of fat on the lot of them. The singing was more upfront than usual and the lyrics were not buried in the mix as often happened with the band. Mike Hampton, Garry Shider and Eddie Hazel employed their usual guitar skills for those who needed them but there were numerous other little touches that made that first side so compelling: the percussion on "Better By The Pound"; the rhythm guitar and Bootsy's sleazy vocals on "Be My Beach" ; the good natured jeers at fellow funk bands on the superlative title track; the bass playing on the in-your-face assault of "Get Off Your Ass And Jam". And "No Head, No Backstage Pass" is one of the best "groupie" songs ever written. Other than the rather slight "Stuffs And Things" which would have fit better onto the first side, the album's flip was notably different - this was Funkadelic, after all - with the harpsichord playing by Bernie Worrell on "I Owe You Something Good" bringing yet another element to their music. "The Song Is Familiar" was an almost conventional soul song with only the background guitar and time signature reminding us who were performing it, while "Atmosphere" was an amusing piece of stoned naughtiness underneath some more Worrell virtuosity.

The Westbound era concluded with *Tales Of Kidd Funkadelic,* a set which suffered from almost illegible sleevenotes and a sense of marking time. The title track was one of their longest yet at nearly thirteen minutes and did and does sound ahead of its time as an early example of what would be called "chill-out" music today but it was one of the more interesting cuts on show .There was entertainment of a rather childish sort in listening to the first couple of minutes of "Take Your Dead Ass Home" before it got boring and "Undisco Kidd" had a swipe at the disco culture but the album was far from the band's best on which only "How Do Yeaw View You? " had any sort of philosophical bent and the earlier political comment was entirely absent.

Hardcore Jollies 1976 Warner Brothers BS 2973 Producer: George Clinton (Billboard soul charts: 12 ; Billboard pop charts : 96)

One Nation Under A Groove 1978 Warner Brothers BSK 3209 Producer: George Clinton (Billboard soul charts: 1 ; Billboard pop charts : 16)

Uncle Jam Wants You 1978 Warner Brothers BSK 3371 Producer: George Clinton (Billboard soul charts: 2 ; Billboard pop charts : 18)

The Electric Spanking Of War Babies 1981 Warner Brothers BSK 3482 Producers: George Clinton, Bootsy Collins and Sly Stone (Billboard soul charts: 41 ; Billboard pop charts : 105)

The Best Of 1976-1981 1994 Charly GRLPD 104 (UK)

The first Warner Brothers LP, *Hardcore Jollies*, came out almost concurrently with *Tales Of Kidd Funkadelic* and their chart performance was almost identical. There was little change in the sound of the band and look of the album and an unwary listener could be forgiven for not realising there was a label change. It was a rather ho-hum release from my point of view with nothing on show that I would class among their very best work although "Comin' Round The Mountain'", "Soul Mate" and "You Scared The Loving' Outta Me (almost an Ohio Players rip-off with a fine Glen Goins' vocal) were good enough.

Clinton also ran Parliament alongside Funkadelic of course, and the former had been much the more successful commercially with top ten singles and albums to their name by the time the latter joined Warner Brothers. But in 1978 this all changed. Funkadelic's "One Nation Under A Groove" became a huge worldwide hit and #1 soul and #28 pop as a single in the U.S. which was uncharted territory indeed for the band. It just showed what going for a mainstream groove could do: there were no guitar solos or awkward time changes to distract from the record's clean lines and although I did and can still appreciate its charm and appeal it reminds me of a time when the whole P-Funk show was rapidly beginning to pall for me. The fact it sat on a double album that clocked in at around an hour didn't thrill me, either, and after playing the LP two or three times I filed it away. Indeed, it is sobering to realise that I have just played the whole record for the first time in around thirty-five years. I'm not sure it will come out any time again soon, either. I do like the vocally impressive "Into You" a good deal and "Cholly" is satisfyingly funky but there are great swathes of the album that haven't aged as well as earlier collections like *America Eats Its Young* or *Let's Take It To The Stage*.

Uncle Jam continued the success and cleaner sound of its predecessor and also continued to pass me by in the sense of providing much enjoyment. "Knee Deep" did have a rather relentless fifteen minute groove, not quite as overlong as it might sound, and it was good - if strange - to hear ex-Spinner Phillippe Wynne singing along on the top of the beat. It also became another #1 soul single and was the last hit record the band ever had.

The Electric Spanking was most notable for me in employing ex-Family Stone members in Cynthia Robinson and Pat Rizzo as well as Sly himself on "Funk Gets Stronger". Not an accurate title; anything from the *Stand* or *There's A Riot Going On* albums were miles better than this. Committed Clinton fans have no reason not to like the album, however, as it contains all the usual stylistic traits and striking cover art that had characterised the group for the last near decade.

Connections & Disconnections 1981 LAX JW-37087 Producers: Grady Thomas, Greg Errico, Calvin Simon & Clarence Haskins (Billboard soul charts: 45 ; Billboard pop charts : 151)

The P-Funk collective - like all empires eventually do - fell apart in an acrimonious mess in the early eighties and this LP does not involve Clinton in any way at all; it is the spinning of former disillusioned band members. Just to be contrary, I prefer it to the last handful of bona fide Funkadelic albums, as although there are enough obvious musical touches to make anyone realise the P-Funk influences, it is more straightforward, less bloated and rock-influenced and well, *more funky*, than many of the later Clinton excesses. The title track and "Phunklords" are particularly to my liking.

Funk Inc.

Steve Weakley; Gene Barr; Jimmy Munford; Bobby Watley; Cecil Hunt; Michael Hughes; William Simmons; Rudy Turner

Funk Inc. 1971 Prestige PRST-10031 Producer: Bob Porter (Billboard soul charts: 45 ; Billboard pop charts: 211)

Chicken Lickin' 1972 Prestige PRST-10043 Producer: Ozzie Cadena

Hangin' Out 1973 Prestige PRST-10059 Producer: Ozzie Cadena

Superfunk 1973 Prestige PRST-10071 Producer: David Axelrod (Billboard soul charts: 31)

Priced To Sell 1974 Prestige PRST-10087 Producer: David Axelrod (Billboard soul charts: 30)

Acid Inc. The Best Of 1988 BGP 1011 (UK)

There will be those who refuse to countenance the fact that Funk Inc. could in any way be considered a "soul" band for two main reasons: the debut LP is entirely instrumental and it appears on the Prestige label, which is indelibly associated with jazz. On the other hand if you, like me, think that "funk" is a vital strand of soul, and that aggregations like Booker T. And The M.G's and The Meters made marvellous music, then you will be prepared to give this band the time of day. And I submit that you should for, at their best, they were one of the greatest funk bands ever, influenced more by Sly Stone than by John Coltrane.

Charging out of Indianapolis in early 1971 they got signed to Prestige on the strength of an audition tape and it's a blessing they did as the debut LP is an absolute classic of the funk genre. The five men who kicked off Funk Inc. - Watley, Barr, Weakley, Munford and Hall - are wonderful musicians and the whole LP demands to be played loud. The exhilarating collection consists of only five tracks, but all clock in at over five minutes each and I hesitate to pick one out as the best as it is a set best ingested whole. But if pressed, listen to the towering "Bowlegs".

Prestige always rather sniffed at 45s and Funk Inc. only ever put out three in the five year association with the label but they certainly were admirably served at the speed of 33⅓. *Chicken Lickin'* carried on the sound and attack of the debut set with a aggressive title track although the rest of the album rather toned things down and despite remaining undoubtedly enjoyable I think it falls a little short of *Funk Inc.* Watley and Munford even sing on the excellent and blissed-out "Let's Make Peace And Stop The War" the only side on which vocals are employed.

The band kept up the high standard on *Hangin' Out* which included one of their best known, and simply best, tracks in "Dirty Red". "Smokin' At Tiffany's " was a fine way to kick off a new album and "We Can Be Friends" (with vocals) sounded a bit like War, who of course came up with a similar title for one of their biggest hits a couple of years later. The only bad moments came with " I Can See Clearly Now", the first time that Funk Inc. had flirted with jazzy elevator music. Avoid this one.

Superfunk was Prestige's effort to break the group and it was quite the departure. Firstly, it featured a gatefold sleeve, the inside of which featured a long interview between the group and Ralph Gleason, but second and more importantly the music had changed significantly. David Axelrod had been brought in to produce for the first time and one aspect of his oversight was that the LP had more singing than the previous three put together. Indeed, the ""Honey I Love You" track sounded nothing like what one had come to expect from the group. Nonetheless, there were still enough of the long instrumental passages that had become associated with the band even if they went on rather too long on the nine minute plus version of Barry White's "I'm Going To Love You Just A Little More Baby". Overall, it is another decent album but despite the label's evident backing didn't sell significantly more copies than any of their others.

Axelrod was retained for the band's fifth and final album, but Munford and Weakley had now departed and three new members meant that Funk Inc. became a sextet for the first time. They were by now almost unrecognisable from the band who had so much fire and attack three years earlier. The songs were now much shorter and vocals increasingly had taken the place of long instrumental solos. A cover of "Gimme Some Lovin'" was rather a surprise and featured almost a gospel background while "The Girl Of My Dreams" was a mushy thing that would not have been allowed near the debut. Most of the rest of the set - which I do like - comes across a bit like what the Blackbyrds were doing at the time.

The group disbanded in 1976 and became forgotten until the UK based BGP label put out a best of set in 1988. It's generally judiciously chosen and it was great to see some new recognition for them but I would have put "Dirty Red" and "Bowlegs" on there.

Future Flight

Brynwood Tanner; David Swanson; Sy Jeffries; Anthony Patler

Future Flight 1981 Capitol ST-12154 Producer: Lamont Dozier

Lamont Dozier produced and wrote or co-wrote every track for the one and only LP by Future Flight but listening doesn't easily betray his influence and this smooth, gently funky but highly orchestrated outing could just as easily be mentored by Earth, Wind & Fire's Maurice White. There is nothing poor or outstanding on here and Dozier seldom penned such hook-less ditties, but it's a painless way to spend forty minutes or so. Tony Patler later joined General Caine.

Futures

James King; Kenny Crew; Harry McGilberry; Frank Washington; Jon King

Castles In The Sky 1975 Buddah BDS 5630 Producers: Jimmy Bishop, Jerry Akines, Johnny Bellmon, Reginald Turner & Victor Drayton

Past, Present And The Futures 1978 P.I.R. JZ 35458 Producers: Sherman Marshall, Joseph Jefferson, Charles Simmons, Kenny Gamble, Cynthia Biggs, Ted Wortham, Douglas Brown, Terry Price, William Bloom, Carl Gamble, Frankie Smith & John Usry

Greetings Of Peace 1980 P.I.R. JZ 36414 Producers: Sherman Marshall, Kenny Gamble, Cynthia Biggs, Ted Wortham, William Bloom, Frankie Smith & Leon Huff

In 1975 there were still a large number of excellent soul records being issued which meant that even one as good as the debut LP from The Futures could be easily lost. Obviously modelled on The Temptations and The Dramatics, this excellent Philadelphia based group had enjoyed a small hit on the Gamble label in early 1973 (the gorgeous "Love Is Here") but things never worked out for them on Buddah. They released four singles on the label, only one of which, "Make It Last"/ "We Got Each Other" (when they were paired up with Barbara Mason) reached the soul charts, at #35. Moreover, only one of the eight sides that were to be found on those singles - the strong title track which features a tough vocal from Frank Washington in the Dennis Edwards style - is to be found on the LP. The group were always adept at switching vocals around and they had a top class bass man in McGilberry as well as the magnificent falsetto of Kenny Crew who delivers the best track on the set: the ineffable "Love Lives On A Windy Hill". The much-esteemed writing team of Akines-Bellmon-Drayton-Turner wrote everything apart from the Mason penned and snappily entitled "Ninety Days (In The House Of Love Correction)", but not even their skills were sufficient to turn the LP into any sort of a hit.

The group had to wait another three years before their next record and despite the plethora of producers it was worth the wait as they maintained the high standard set by all their previous work. "Party Time Man" kicked off the album in marvellous fashion, being a fully orchestrated rich and satisfying dance track that unaccountably, only made it to the pitiful #94 on the soul charts as a single. Track 2 was also excellent, the "rare groove" favourite "Ain't No Time Fa Nothing" and hopes were being raised that we were in for something special. The feeling persisted as Crew was then to the fore on "Deep Inside Of Me" which made it 3-0 in only sixteen minutes. This level of mastery couldn't quite persist and if the other five tracks didn't match the quality of the first three they were still all worthy of at least a couple of spins.

Greetings Of Peace was not as good as the other two Futures' LPs. This was nothing to do with the quality of the singing which remained top class but is more a reflection of the material which was not as strong as it had been in the past. Even Gamble and Huff's four tracks were not their best while "Feels Like The First Time" is the kind of "schmaltzy" song that leaves me cold. The only unqualified success was "Silhouettes" which had been a been huge hit for The Rays back in 1957. The Futures' version was a considerably smaller success as a single when it reached only #79 in January 1981 but it's a gorgeous example of soul ensemble singing nonetheless. Because the group has attracted such little critical attention it is hard to be certain about who delivers the lead vocals on some occasions but I think the marvellous James King takes a few on here.

Other than a 45 on the tiny Warped label in 1982 there were to be no more releases by the group although they nearly all went on to do other things in the business, the most notable of which were a fine James King solo 45, "Memory" and McGilberry's joining The Temptations but sadly the angelic voice of Kenny Crew was never heard of again to the best of my knowledge, and I believe he passed away in 1982.

Fuzz

Val Williams; Sheila Young; Barbara Gilliam

Fuzz 1971 Calla SC-2001 Producer: Carr Cee Productions (Billboard soul charts: 43 ; Billboard pop charts: 196)

A few years ago I read an interview with an American soul enthusiast who explained one of the rules that governed his apparently magnificent collection: "no broads". To have no interest in the music of Aretha Franklin, Candi Staton, Etta James or all the other wonderful women who have so nourished soul music struck me as rather perverse, and I imagine he would be completely bemused by this one album by the former Passionettes which largely fits into that almost wholly neglected genre: "sweet soul by women".

While there is much too much in the way of spoken preludes on the album for my comfort, I submit that tracks like "I Love You For All Seasons", "Like An Open Door", "It's All Over", "Leave It All Behind Me" and their version of The Miracles' "Ooh Baby Baby" are wholly captivating and the Washington D.C. based trio of Sheila Young (who wrote nearly everything on the set), Val Williams and Barbara Gilliam have been desperately overlooked. The first two tracks listed above were big soul hits (#10 and #14 respectively) and the uptempo "I'm So Glad" from the set also hit the soul top forty. It was therefore sad and strange that after only one more entirely lovely single The Fuzz disbanded. (Footnote: Carr Cee productions consisted of Joe Tate and Carroll Hynson who also produced the first Soul Searchers LPs.)

Earl Gaines

The Best Of Luck To You 1966 Hanna-Barbera HLP 9508 Producer: Rogana Productions

Lovin' Blues 1970 De Luxe DLP-12002 Producer: Bill Allen

That's How Strong My Love Is 1979 Vivid Sound VS 7010 Producers: John Richbourg & Allen Orange (Japan)

Yearning And Burning 1986 Charly CRB 1142 (UK)

House Party 1989 Meltone 1517 Producer: Winton Cobb

I saw Earl Gaines live a few years ago. He didn't wear sharp clothes, conducted no fancy moves and generally avoided much communication with the audience. He just stood there stolidly and belted out his songs. It was great. What I witnessed that night is what I always hear on his records: an underrated and adult singer of great skill and power.

He was born in Alabama but moved to Nashville where he cut his first sides as far back as 1955 when he was the lead singer for Louis Brooks and The Hi-Toppers. Their single, "It's Love Baby (24 Hours A Day)" (#2 soul), was by far the biggest hit Gaines ever registered and he was to re-record the song a number of times in his later career. He cut a number of singles over the next few years but never got the opportunity to record an album until his single on the Hanna Barbera label, "The Best Of Luck To You", reached #28 soul in the latter half of 1966. Given that Gaines was a tough soul singer singing grown-up songs over the entire course of his career it has always amused me how he came to end up on the same label as Huckleberry Hound, Super Snooper and Blabbermouse. Never mind the incongruity; we should be grateful to that label for following up the single with an album of such high quality. However, the price Gaines had to pay for its release was to see his name spelt incorrectly on the cover ("Gains") and a search in vain for his own picture to be seen anywhere.

We are not so blessed with albums in the "deep soul" idiom that we can take them for granted as most singers who sang in Gaines's highly committed style had to make do with singles and the whole set sounds, frankly, wonderful today. There was a bit of Bobby Bland in Earl's output at the time, particularly on the "Poor Man Gotta Make It" track but he was much tougher than even Bobby "Blue" on occasion. For instance, Gaines' one self-composed song on here, the blues-based "Mercy On My Soul", is fearsomely robust. Or if the need is for something more obviously soulful then try "I Have Loved And I Have Lived" which is also ferocious. The material is strong throughout too, and "Don't Take My Kindness For Weakness" and "The Door Is Still Open" are genuinely excellent compositions.

I imagine sales of the LP must have been pitifully few and Gaines moved on to the King organisation where he recorded five singles on their Hollywood subsidiary in the late sixties including a couple under the rather curious pseudonym of "A. Friend". Sales were once again low but at least King persisted with him and he was shifted onto their De Luxe outlet where he recorded and issued his second album which, while good, was not quite up to the debut on HB. We didn't really need yet another update of "It's Love Baby" and although he delivered them well enough, "The Things I Used To Do" and "Every Day I Have The Blues" have come to be the kind of songs that the word "hackneyed" could have been invented for. He also re-cut "The Door Is Still Open" which was certainly fine; until one played the original again. This is all to carp a bit though as there were still some excellent sides on here which were attractive precisely because they showed a more sensitive side to Gaines as, without sacrificing one whit of soulfulness, he (or more likely the label) toned down the out and out fire of his previous LP. "My Woman", "Three Wishes For A Fool" and a marvellous version of "Don't Deceive Me" are all delectable while "Fruit From Another Man's Tree" and "From Warm To Cool To Cold" are only marginally inferior. A young Bootsy Collins played on "My Pillow Stays Wet" and it, as with many of the sides on the LP, which at least had his picture on the front cover and his name spelled correctly, was put out on 45 by King / De Luxe. None of them hit.

It was thus an astute move to try his luck elsewhere, and in 1972 Gaines joined John Richbourg's Seventy Seven record label, which, at the start of 1973, ensured that his name once more featured on the national charts when "Hymn #5" reached the lower reaches of the soul top 40. There were to be no more U.S. vinyl album releases for him, however, and we had to wait until 1979 when the Japanese Vivid Sound label put out an LP of 12 tracks from the Seventy Seven era, over 50% of which had never been released before although, oddly, it did not include "Hymn #5". It's a good album, but not quite up to the HBR standard, and I favour the cover songs within which included "A Certain Girl", "Turn On Your Lovelight", "Nine Pound Steel" and "Been So Long" among others. The talented Allen Orange co-produced the set and contributed half the songs but "Since I Lost You" and "Hello My Lover" were possibly his most nondescript compositions ever.

In 1986 the UK Charly label issued an even better LP of Gaines' Seventy Seven material, given it included all but three cuts from the Japanese LP as well as seven more which had not featured on the Vivid Sound release. On the downside, the sleevenotes were all but unreadable, so unnecessarily prominent was a map of Tennessee beneath the words, and songwriting credits were incomplete. Of the "new" tracks, "Hymn #5 " was the best, an astonishingly "black" sounding record for 1973, while the title track and "You're The One" were way above average as well. And if that isn't Allen Toussaint playing piano on "I Can't Face It", I will be amazed.

Gaines left the record business to drive trucks some time in the seventies but returned with *House Party* (more blues than soul on balance) in 1989 and recorded a number of CDs for the next eighteen years or so before passing away in 2009.

Galaxxy

Bruce Aikens; Perry Aikens; Curtis Aikens

Galaxxy Featuring Bruce Aikens 1982 Pop-Art P-8074 Producer: Butch Ingram

The little-known Galaxxy owe thanks to the brothers from Ingram for their one LP release as Butch produced while John, Timmy, Jimmy and John all contributed as well. I have only heard a handful of tracks from it which range from poor ("We're Here To Rock You") through OK ("Give Your Dog A Bone") to good ("Spend Some Time").

Gap Band

Charlie Wilson; Ronnie Wilson; Robert Wilson; Tommy Lokey; Roscoe Smith; O'Dell Stokes; Chris Clayton; Buddy Jones; James Macon; Rick Calhoun

Magicians Holiday 1974 Shelter SR-2111 Producer: Buddy Jones

The Gap Band 1977 Tattoo FL 12168 Producer: John Ryan

The Gap Band 1979 Mercury SRM-1-3758 Producer: Lonnie Simmons (Billboard soul charts: 10 ; Billboard pop charts: 77)

The Gap Band II 1979 Mercury SRM-1-3804 Producer: Lonnie Simmons (Billboard soul charts: 3 ; Billboard pop charts : 42)

The Gap Band III 1980 Mercury SRM-1-4003 Producer: Lonnie Simmons (Billboard soul charts: 1 ; Billboard pop charts : 16)

The Gap Band IV 1982 Total Experience TE-1-3001 Producer: Lonnie Simmons (Billboard soul charts: 1 ; Billboard pop charts : 14)

The Gap Band V – Jammin' 1983 Total Experience TE-1-3004 Producer: Lonnie Simmons (Billboard soul charts: 2 ; Billboard pop charts : 28)

Strike A Groove 1983 Passport PB 6026 No Producer listed

The Gap Band VI 1984 Total Experience TEL8-5705 Producer: Lonnie Simmons (Billboard soul charts: 1 ; Billboard pop charts : 58)

Gap Gold - Best Of The Gap Band 1985 Total Experience 824343 (Billboard soul charts: 46; Billboard pop charts : 103)

The Gap Band VII 1985 Total Experience TEL8-5714 Producer: Lonnie Simmons (Billboard soul charts: 6 ; Billboard pop charts : 159)

The 12" Collection 1986 Mercury 422-826 808-1M-1 (Billboard soul charts: 61)

The Gap Band 8 1986 Total Experience 2700-1-T Producers: Lonnie Simmons, Charlie Wilson, Rudy Taylor, Oliver Scott & Jimmy Hamilton (Billboard soul charts: 29)

Straight From The Heart 1988 Total Experience 2710-1-T Producers: Ronnie Wilson, Charlie Wilson & Robert Wilson (Billboard soul charts: 74)

The Shelter label was never known for its soul music output and I imagine that no-one at the company really know what to do with Oklahoma's Gap Band. What we got was an LP that sounded exactly how one might imagine a cross between Sly and The Family Stone and Stevie Wonder in 1974 would come out. I certainly prefer the cuts that have the greater Sly influence - such as "Fontessa Fame" - but it was all rather academic as the album bombed. One could not foresee back in 1974 how big the group was to become by the early eighties.

A single on A&M also failed and the band had to wait until 1977 for their next LP, on the small Tattoo label. The Wonder influence persisted but Sly's was superseded by that of EWAF. "Out Of The Blue (Can You Feel It)" and "Little Bit Of Love" both made small dents on the soul charts as singles but I must confess to finding the album generally as unappealing as the Shelter set. If one doesn't care for Stevie Wonder's voice Charlie Wilson's homages on songs such as "Thinking Of You" are going to be hard to take.

In 1979 the band moved to Mercury and finally had a big hit with "Shake" (#4 soul), which may or may not have been related to the fact that the Wilson brothers were now going it alone, having jettisoned all other band members. They followed up with another, "Open Up Your Mind (Wide)" which went to #13. Both were included on the snappily entitled *The Gap Band* LP as was "I Can Sing" which had a vocal incredibly reminiscent of D.J. Rogers but it seems it was indeed one of the Wilsons.

The Gap Band II (the group spent no more time on their LP titles than they did on their song lyrics) contained the famous "Oops Upside Your Head". I believe it is possibly illegal in England for anyone of a certain age not to have sat on the floor at a disco and undertaken the singular "dance" that always accompanies the record when it is rather unfortunately played. As ever with an act as huge as The Gap Band my indifference is irrelevant and the song became a worldwide hit, although only making #101 pop in America, but it did reach #4 soul. "Steppin' Out" also performed well on 45 on the soul charts. I'm pleased to say that I can finally be positive as I am enamoured of "Who Do You Call" as its appropriation of the style of the great Ohio Players is so obvious. To be fair to the Gap Band, they never worried in the slightest about flaunting their influences, which were to increasingly include the P-Funk stable.

The Gap Band III was a more varied, mellow, pop-oriented and radio friendly affair than before, and the results were that the group had now become one of the two or three biggest soul outfits in the world and "Burn Rubber (Why You Wanna Hurt Me)" from the set became their first #1 soul single.

For the next few years the band moved to the Total Experience label but sustained their chart pre-eminence until 1985. Commercially they scored hit after hit and attained a level of success very few soul bands in history have matched. *Gap Band IV*, as with *III* before it, went platinum and contained three massive soul hits: "Early In The Morning" (#1), "Outstanding" (#1) and "You Dropped A Bomb On Me"(#2). *Gap Band V - Jammin'* merely went gold and contained a big hit in "Party Train" (#3 soul) even if it was about one thousandth as good as the "Love Train" the O'Jay's took all those years before. I've said it before - probably ad nauseam - but is there any genre in soul that has aged as poorly as these thumping one beat tracks of the eighties?

The Passport album that appeared in 1983 contained a mixture of previously unreleased material and a handful of cuts that had appeared on the Tattoo LP from 1977.

A few more big hits were to be found on the *VI* and *VII* albums, and one of them was easily my favourite of theirs ever and it was as gratifying as it was surprising to see that they had covered The Friends Of Distinction's "Goin' In Circles" and took it all the way to #2 soul. If only they had covered more outside material.

By *Gap Band 8*, their audience had more or less vanished. As so often in soul music it was further proof than an artist or group can only really sustain a top level of success for a few years. The album couldn't even reach the top 200 pop LP list. Their sound had softened fairly significantly and Charlie Wilson's Stevie Wonder influenced voice delivered pop ballads like "I Can't Live Without Your Love" and "I'll Always Love You" well enough. *Straight From The Heart* was another commercial disaster and wasn't much fun to listen to, either.

Round Trip 1989 Capitol C1-90799 Producers: Ronnie Wilson, Charlie Wilson & Jon Gass (Billboard soul charts: 20; Billboard pop charts : 189)

It was probably a great relief for everyone that the band moved to Capitol for their final vinyl release and it did perform better than any of their albums since *Gap Band VII*. Not only that, but it contained a #1 soul single in "All Of My Love" (although, tellingly, it couldn't even breach the pop top 100). It was a "New Jack Swing" thing that was total anathema to me of course but to bounce back in this fashion is testimony to the band's resilience.

A few Gap Band CDs came out in the nineties and Charlie Wilson went the solo route and continues to release new material to this day. I wish I could have been more positive about the LPs made by what was after all one of the biggest soul bands in history- and certainly Tulsa, Oklahoma's biggest of all time by some distance - but their inability to truly create a sound of their own and a paucity of strong material means it would be dishonest of me to pretend that they moved me more than they ever did.

Don Gardner (see also Dee Dee Ford and Baby Washington)

I Need Your Lovin' (and Dee Dee Ford) 1962 Fire FLP 105 Producer: Bobby Robinson

In Sweden (and Dee Dee Ford) 1965 Sonet SLP-39 No produced listed (Sweden)

In Sweden (and Dee Dee Ford) 1966 Sue 1044 No produced listed

Rhythm & Blues Dance Party (and Dee Dee Ford & Beverly Glenn)1965 Sonet SLP-47 Producer: Don Gardner (Sweden)

Lay A Little Lovin' On Me (and Baby Washington) 1973 Master Five 901 Producer: Bobby Martin and Clarence Lawton

As pointed out in my introduction to this book, there are a number of artists who were palpably better served on single than on LP. Don Gardner was one of them. His dark, subterranean voice, which made him sound like a more excitable Chuck Jackson, was to be found to thrilling effect on a large number of singles, but none of the albums that bore his name really did him full justice. Indeed, he never even got to record an album in his own name as he was always paired up with someone else. (And, I should say, never had a single chart entry in his own right, either: his only hits came when he was teamed up with Dee Dee Ford or Baby Washington).

He was born in Philadelphia and was a drummer as well as a fine singer and I have excluded the LPs he made with Jimmy Smith in the fifties as they are truly out of scope and I have therefore only concentrated only on the handful of LPs he made in the sixties and seventies. His first big success came in the middle of 1962 - and it had taken him a long time to attain this success - when "I Need Your Lovin'", a great duet with Ford, made it to #4 soul and #20 pop. They followed this up with "Don't You Worry", another excellent side, which they took to #7 soul and #66 pop, and both of them can be found on the *I Need Your Lovin'* album. Which was, to say the least, a rush job; not only was the cover basic and unimaginative in the extreme, but a handful of tracks, most notably "Nobody But You", feature a male singer who is assuredly not Gardner himself. Ford and Gardner get a couple of songs on which they perform solo, but in all honesty there is little reason for anyone to own the LP; the hit singles are by far the best things on show.

The duo recorded a startling three "live" LPs in Sweden in the mid-sixties and I can't think of any other soul artists who opted for this country as the place to showcase their talents. None are really worthy of too much investigation but if you have to plump for one, make it *Rhythm And Blues Dance Party* simply because it has more singing than is featured on the first Sonet set, which consists largely of a number of jazzy instrumentals. By the way, the Sue LP that came out in the U.S. under the same name is considerably different: it has four tracks that did not appear on the Swedish Sonet album, which, in turn, has three that can't be found on the Sue release. The second Sonet LP features not just the voices of Gardner and Ford but one Beverly Glenn who provides vocals on a couple of forgettable songs.

There are not many cuts across the three LPs that really show Gardner at his roaring passionate best, and only "Ole Man River" (with a horn line identical to King Curtis' and Aretha Franklin's "Soul Serenade") from *In Sweden* (Sue release) and "Sticks And Stones", "People Get Ready" and "Some Good Some Bad" from *Rhythm And Blues Dance Party* warrant concentrated listening.

Gardner went on to record a number of singles in the late sixties and early seventies for a variety of labels but had to wait until 1973 for his next - and last - album to appear. It would have been difficult to have paired him up with a finer singer than the great Baby Washington but it is true to say that both artists were not as well known as they had been ten years earlier. It is a good LP, although is a little uneven, which isn't surprising as it was recorded in New York, Philadelphia and Detroit. Half of the ten tracks were duets, with only two being performed solo by Gardner. I really like their work together on "Forever" an obviously Philly recorded rendition of this great Holland-Dozier-Gorman song. It also has to be said that "Is It True I Fell In Love Again" sounds pretty dated for 1973, which makes me wonder about the time scale involved in the recording sessions. I'm also not sure how they got away with " I Just Want To Be Near To You" given it has an almost identical chorus to "Just As Long As You Need Me" by The Independents. As for the two Gardner solo cuts: "We're Gonna Make It Big" has become a sought-after record on 45 and while it is nice enough, he has done better work. The stately "Just Stand By Me" is also enjoyable but is another song that sounds as if it may have had an earlier recording date than 1973.

Stu Gardner (see also Big Mouth)

To Soul With Love 1968 Revue RM-202 Producers: Hugh Masekela & Stewart Levine

And The Sanctified Sound 1974 Volt VOS-9503 Producer: James Gadson

Bronx born Stu Gardner probably didn't make much money from releasing records in his own name, but I assume he did pretty well from his long association with Bill Cosby, for whom he wrote, produced, arranged, played keyboards and sang on any number of the comedian's album releases.

Gardner made a couple of singles in the sixties before appearing, according to the sleevenotes of his first LP, on the same bill as Hugh Masekela in the Whiskey A-Go-Go club in Los Angeles. So impressed was the South African that he exhorted his producer, Stewart Levine, to produce Gardner forthwith. One may be tempted to write this off as typical record label hype, but based on Gardner's performance in a nightclub scene in the great John Boorman film, *Point Blank*, it has the ring of truth.

That first LP is a divertingly good one, brassy and devoid of anything in the way of sweetening. Gardner is sweaty and engaged on the funky dance tracks, and invests deep emotion in the slow songs, such as "I Can't Make It By Myself", "Love Slipped Away" and "Love Lifted Me" which come across in the great southern soul tradition. Maybe best of all is an almost completely unrecognisable slowed down version of The Spinners' "I'll Always Love You" which is the only song on the LP not written by Gardner himself.

As a result of the Masekela connection Gardner then recorded a couple of singles for Chisa, the second of which was the magnificent "Expressing My Love", one of the most funky and exhilarating records ever made.

He then turned up on Stax / Volt, for reasons that remain unclear to me despite Bill Cosby's sleevenotes, on a one-off album in 1974. It was once again recorded on the West Coast with stellar musicians on board such as Truman Thomas, Al McKay and the great drummer James Gadson but it headed straight for the cut-out bins; there weren't even any singles released from it but one must remember that 1974 was hardly a good year for Stax. Despite its lack of success, though, it was a collection to make one sit up and take notice filled as it was with some highly autobiographical sounding songs (and others you hoped weren't reflections on Gardner's own life). The early seventies were a time when soul artists were often permitted to stretch out somewhat and muse in a philosophical manner and the whole album coheres superbly as a planned effort rather than as a mere collection of random songs. Gardner was obviously influenced by Ray Charles and this comes through strongly in his singing while the overall musical backing was a little more sophisticated than it was on the Revue set with strings and back-up singers employed here and there. The LP includes his take on the traditional song, "Home On The Range", which had been his first 45 on Chisa, with the album cut sounding pretty much identical to that single.

Jo Ann Garrett

Just A Taste 1969 Chess LPS-1548 Producer: Andre Williams

Chicago native Garrett had a big following in the city in the sixties, but this never translated to national success and she only got to record one album. Chess never stinted on productions and the whole set boasts some splendid arrangements which help to off-set the somewhat MOR nature of a couple of the songs - "This Bitter Earth" and "Unforgettable - and her rather "little girl" voice which is not to the taste of everyone. The best soul cuts on show are all compelling: "Foolish Me","Ain't No Way" (the Carolyn Franklin song), "Soul Town" and "It's No Secret". Finally, it should be noted that the album version of "A Thousand Miles Away" is not the same as the single Chess put out on her (it doesn't feature The Dells on backing vocals, for example) and her rendition of "Walk On By" copies Isaac Hayes' arrangement from *Hot Buttered Soul* so openly as to be amusing.

Lee Garrett

Heat For The Feets 1976 Chrysalis CHR 1109 Producers: Eric Malamud & Tom Sellers

Lee Garrett is a blind singer who recorded a handful of singles in Philadelphia in the sixties (none were hits) before working with Stevie Wonder to co-write such big Motown smashes as "Signed, Sealed Delivered" and "It's A Shame". He then went off the radar for a few years before re-surfacing with a loud, shiny, poppy LP called *Heat For The Feets.*

I think it is fair to say that Garrett is a far more gifted writer than singer (although Robert Taylor as co-composer of most of the songs must take credit as well) and the album contains nine songs which all stick in the memory after only two plays. His knack for melody and hook-lines was exceptional and his big UK hit single, "You're My Everything" is almost unfairly catchy. It was therefore no surprise when others plundered the set for songs to cover, the two best-known being "It's Better Than Walking Out" and "Heart Be Still" by Marlena Shaw and Carl Graves (or Jackie Moore) respectively. (I'm surprised, though, that no-one to my knowledge has chosen the excellent "Stop That Wrong" to cover thus far.) Some soul fans might be leery of the set as it has a pop construction and sensibility, with bright and full production, out of which electric guitars pop from time to time, and the whole thing, apart from the first two tracks on side two, is exhausting, given the relentlessly fast tempo of the songs.You could lose two pounds just listening to it. But it is an impressive piece of work nonetheless, and surely also the only soul record in history to give a name check to Zowie Bowie.

Garrett scored another hit when he started to work again with Stevie Wonder in the late seventies (Jermaine Jackson's "Let's Get Serious") and released another solo single in 1981 that went nowhere before appearing to leave the music business behind.

Vernon Garrett

Going To My Baby's Place 1975 Grenade SPGR-202

Crossroads 1982 California Gold CG5012 Producer: Joey Jefferson

Somebody Messed Up At The Crossroad 1987 White Records Enterprises J.W. 103 Producer: Jerry White

If You Can't Help Me Baby 198? White Records Enterprises J.W. 104 Producer: Jerry White

Vernon Garrett, a tough and uncompromisingly soulful singer from Omaha Nebraska has recorded for over fifty years, releasing nearly forty singles, the four albums listed above and a number of CDs from 1991 onwards, and yet remains unknown to all but committed soul fans.

His first recordings were as a member of a doo-wop group called the Sliders and he also made a number of fine sides with his wife Jewel, who sadly died of cancer decades ago. All his vinyl records were cut on the West Coast (he relocated to Atlanta studios in the CD era) and he released some excellent 45s on Kent and many other smaller labels but only one single - a duet with Marie Franklin on Venture entitled "Without You" - ever hit the national soul charts (#33 in early 1969). His first LP, Going To My Baby's Place", really a collection of earlier singles rather than a newly recorded album, has always been scarce and sought after and was a good antidote for anyone who might have been feeling a need for something a bit more bracing in 1975 after a listening session, for example, with the highly orchestrated music of Barry White or Marvin Gaye. *Baby's Place* contains abrasive soul music, eschews any strings, and concentrates on Garrett's committed vocals and a tough rhythm section and sparring horns. If it has a fault, it is that the pace isn't varied with everything recorded at a brisk mid-tempo and a really drawn out ballad or two would have been welcome. The two tracks that stir the recipe a tad are the bluesy and risqué "I Made My Own World" which features Garrett's best singing on the set and Billy Ray Charles' "To Be A Part Of You" which I could imagine Tyrone Davis recording. One Margaret Love provides a duet on the good "Satisfied Woman, Satisfied Man".

In 1977 Garrett recorded the first of three fine singles for Al Bell's ICA logo, and "I'm At The Crossroads" became a huge record for him, reaching #33 on the soul charts in the autumn of that year. However, sometimes relatively lowly placings can be misleading as the record stayed on the charts for 20 weeks apparently selling in the hundreds of thousands and remains the record for which he is best known today. Sadly, ICA never put out any LPs and we had to wait until 1982 when he put out a set on California Gold.

A "live" set, in fact, rather an odd choice in a way for an artist who was not exactly blessed with a huge back catalogue of albums. But it's a good one, with a couple of covers preceding a handful of songs he had put out on singles over the years. The band is fine, new wife J J Burton helps him out on "Baby You Got What It Takes" and the whole thing captures how adept and confident Garrett was in front of an audience, particularly on the longer, drawn-out cuts such as "Crossroads" and "Jody Can Ease The Pain".

Somebody Messed Up At The Crossroad was an unwieldy title for what was to prove to be his bluesiest and most musically synthetic (though not oppressively so) LP. Side one in particular will probably alienate a number of soul fans given it consisted of four Ray Agee songs. Side two is more typically "soulful" with a worthwhile version of Denise LaSalle's "Love Me Right" and a very good re-make of "I'm At The Crossroad", although a much inferior one of "I Got To Get Over To My Baby's Place" moves us a step back. As ever he sings with spirit and fire and there were plenty of lesser LPs around in 1987.

If You Can't Help Me Baby was an enjoyable LP, expertly produced by Jerry White and the music fairly hurtles out of the speakers in crystal clear sound. As usual, Garrett prefers to work in the mid-tempo resister with only "Aim To Please" slowing things down, and there are nearly as many blues tracks as there are soul ones, so it isn't a collection for everyone, but he brings to bear his usual power on all the songs and three are really tough horn-laden outings for the late eighties: "I Can't Work And Watch You Too", "Riches And Gold" and "Blood Of My Blood". There are no drum machines or other computerized stylings on show and it is an album that could just easily have been recorded in 1969.

He has gone quiet in the last couple of years but a number of his CDs have been pretty decent.

Rex Garvin & The Mighty Cravers

Rex Garvin; Clayton Dunn; Pete Holman

Raw Funky Earth 1968 Tower ST 5130 Producers: James Johnson & Sammy Vargas

This album by Rex Garvin and his two Mighty Cravers reminds me of Dyke & Blazers and not just because both bands recorded "Funky Broadway; it has the same no frills and funky approach adopted by the Phoenix outfit, and if the Blazers possibly had the edge as musicians, Garvin was a better and more soulful singer than Arlester Christian.

Rex Garvin had been cutting singles for a number of years before this LP appeared, and apart from "Sock It To 'Em J.B.", which must have sold quite a few, all of them fell far short from being any kind of hit. Back to the album; it contained ten short tracks ("By The Time I Get To Phoenix", excepted, which was, like "Boogaloo Down Broadway", not an inspired choice of song to cover) and it's a straight-forward and enjoyable set. Garvin died in 2013, having left the music industry decades earlier. (Tower was a highly eclectic label, by the way; the next album in catalogue after *Raw Funky Earth* was *A Saucerful Of Secrets* by Pink Floyd.)

Gaston

Randy Hudson; Jerry Reid; William Fewell; Quincy Huitt; Valentino Burroughs; Virginia Gaskin; Greg Thompson; Richard Butler

My Queen 1978 Hotlanta H-7804 Producer: Charles Howe

Gaston 1982 Chocolate Cholly's CC-4 Producer: Chocolate Cholly

The cover of Gaston's first LP was another in the "what were they thinking?" category and it gave no clues at all as to what would be found inside. Which is generally fairly tepid funk, with some slight jazzy overtones - a sax solo here, a flute solo there - but the three best tracks (the entire second side, in fact) are well worth hearing: "My Queen" for its funky and tough neo-Ohio Players groove; "The Clap Song" which may be long at nine minutes but has a cowbell, drum and bass driven beat that just will not be denied above which a synthesiser conjures up some intriguing and very slightly sinister touches; "Love And Affection" a unpretentious and sweetly sung ballad. It's an "in-demand" set today, but barely crept out of the southern states as a new release.

Their second album, no more successful than the first, is equally in demand these days. What I've heard of it is good, if marginally more "mainstream" than the debut, and once again the rhythm section has some especially good moments ("Broken Record" and their take on line dancing, "Here A Funk, There A Funk, Everywhere A Funk Funk", which is much more enjoyable than the title might suggest.) "Mind Sticker" is genuinely catchy, "You Don't Love Me" and "Love Is Gonna Getcha" are soulful in the Atlantic Starr style of the time and only "We Come To Take Control" sounds dull and predictable. The one cut I haven't heard is the one I wish I had: "Benny Hill". I know he had a cult following in the States but can this really be a song about Fred Scuttle? All in all I like what I hear and the whole thing is much better to my ears than anything the likes of Fatback, Commodores or other bigger names were issuing in 1982.

I'm reasonably sure they were named after Gaston, a city in South Carolina, from which I believe they hailed.

Marvin Gaye

The Soulful Moods Of 1961 Tamla TM 221 Producer: Berry Gordy

That Stubborn Kinda' Fellow 1962 Tamla TM 239 Producer: William Stevenson

Recorded Live On Stage 1963 Tamla TM 242 Producer: William Stevenson

When I'm Alone I Cry 1964 TM 251 Producers: William Stevenson & Clarence Paul

Hello Broadway 1964 Tamla TM-259 Producers: Hal Davis & Marc Gordon

Together (and Mary Wells) 1964 Motown MT 613 Producers: William Stevenson & Clarence Paul (Billboard pop charts: 42)

Marvin Gaye 1964 Stateside SL 10100 (UK)

We know a lot about Marvin Gaye. We know his records, we know how he died and we know how seldom he found peace in his life. We also know he was one of the greatest and most successful soul men that ever lived. As ever, I can't dwell on anything but his albums and, as so often in the early days of Motown, they began as hedge-betting exercises.

Four of his first six albums were stuffed full of classy standards and depending on one's viewpoint, were either rather bloodless affairs or beautiful examples of a nightclub sophistication. Across these albums, only the odd track such as "Let Your Conscience Be Your Guide" and "Never Let Me Go from the *Soulful Moods Of* LP cause the heart to beat a little faster as they were stirring examples of the excitement that the music of the emerging record labels from Detroit would bring to the world.

It was the second album, though, *That Stubborn Kinda Fellow,* which announced that we were in the presence of someone who was going to matter, particularly on side one which was clearly aimed directly at a young audience. I love the fact that his voice "breaks" on the title track and they left it in anyway. This was vital Motown. Side two was a little fluffier, perhaps, but at least all the songs on the album were "pop" songs rather than standards and it was therefore a bit of a shame that Motown felt the need to play it safe again for the next few albums. The title track, "Hitch Hike" and "Pride And Joy" (all to be found on side one, significantly) were the first hits Marvin Gaye ever had when they released as singles; all of them hit the pop top 50 and soul top 15.

Mixed in with the straight "standards" albums, *When I'm Alone I Cry* and *Hello Broadway*, were the not particularly inspired *Recorded Live On Stage* set and one with Mary Wells which was built around the appealing hit they had enjoyed together when "What's The Matter With You Baby"/"Once Upon A Time" became another pop top 20 hit. Unfortunately everything else on the LP was once again MOR material. It really seemed as if it were one step forward and one back as regards these early LPs. Gordy really couldn't work out what he should do with Gaye, who, in turn, wasn't sure what he wanted to be.

The UK Stateside release was not a straight copy of any of his U.S. LPs and was largely drawn from the *Stubborn Kinda Fellow* album as well as adding hit singles like "You're A Wonderful One" the brilliant "Can I Get A Witness" (#15 soul, #22 pop) and "Try It Baby" which had not featured on Gaye LPs before.

Greatest Hits 1964 Tamla TM 252 (Billboard pop charts : 72)

How Sweet It Is To Be Loved By You 1964 Tamla TM-258 No producer listed (Billboard soul charts: 4 ; Billboard pop charts : 126)

A Tribute To The Great Nat King Cole 1965 Tamla TM-261 Producers: Hal Davis, Marc Gordon & Harvey Fuqua

The Moods Of 1966 Tamla TS-266 No producer listed (Billboard soul charts: 8 ; Billboard pop charts : 118)

Take Two (with Kim Weston) 1966 Tamla T 270 Producer: William Stevenson (Billboard soul charts: 24)

Motown continued to squeeze the *Stubborn Kinda Fellow* album as dry as possible when they included seven of its ten tracks on a *Greatest Hits* set, not a very accurate title given that only five of the twelve tracks could be classed as such.

Finally, right at the end of 1964 came an undeniably great Gaye album. *How Sweet It Is To Be Loved By You* dispensed with any standards or indeed softness in any form. The cool, swinging title track was a huge smash reaching #4 soul and #6 pop and "You're A Wonderful One", "Baby Don't You Do It", "No Good Without You Baby" were hand-embossed invitations to any dance floor in the world. In fact, all twelve cuts were strong (listen to the marvellous backing vocals even on a little known cut like "Stepping Closer To Your Heart") and it remains, even fifty years on, one of the highlights of Gaye's career. No producers were listed but the work was carried out by Brian Holland, Lamont Dozier, Smokey Robinson, Clarence Paul , William "Mickey" Stevenson, Harvey Fuqua , Norman Whitfield, Berry Gordy and Gaye himself. (Note: the UK version of the album (Tamla Motown TML 11004) added "Witchcraft" and "Never Let You Go" at the expense of "You're A Wonderful One" and "Try It Baby")

Motown being Motown though, followed up this shining success with an album entitled *A Tribute To The Great Nat King Cole* which was not a success of any sort, and just serves to remind how assiduously Gordy worked to have his stars become palatable to middle white America.

It's best to move on from this to his next "proper" set, *The Moods Of*, on which we can forget the three standards that were included as they were overwhelmed by such prime Gaye magnificence as "I'll Be Doggone" and "Ain't That Peculiar". The former became his first #1 soul single and the latter became his second. They both rose into the pop top ten too. When one then considers that the uniformly excellent "One More Heartache" (#4), "Take This Heart Of Mine"(#16), "Your Unchanging Love"(#7), and "Little Darling (I Need You)"(#10) were included on the LP as well, we are faced with not only an LP that contained six hit singles, but one of the three or four best of Marvin's career. The uncredited productions were performed by the usual suspects of Robinson, Holland and Dozier, Fuqua and Paul with the addition of Pete Moore and Johnny Bristol.

(Given Gordy tried so hard and often with his artists to cut them on LPs that would widen their appeal, it is interesting to note how little time he spent on marketing his really good LPs: *Moods Of* and *How Sweet It Is* were brilliant sets, full of hits but look at their incredibly lowly pop chart positions. The 45 was still king for Gordy at this time.)

Back in 1964 Motown had paired Gaye up with Kim Weston for what appeared to be a one-off single and "What Good Am I Without You" made it to #61 on the Hot 100, which was not deemed good enough to take the relationship any further at the time but the label tried again at the end of 1966, when the much-loved "It Takes Two" became a big hit (#4 soul and #14 pop) and this led to an LP in 1967. It is an OK but not particularly inspired set (a so-so version of The Four Tops "Baby I Need Your Loving" and a really schmaltzy take on "Secret Love" are examples of what I mean) and was another instance where Motown issued a set where the UK release's cover differed from the one that had been used in the USA.

United (and Tammi Terrell) 1967 Tamla TS 277 Producers: Harvey Fuqua & Johnny Bristol (Billboard soul charts: 7; Billboard pop charts: 69)

Greatest Hits Volume 2 1967 Tamla TS 278 (Billboard soul charts: 19 ; Billboard pop charts: 178)

You're All I Need (and Tammi Terrell) 1968 Tamla TS 284 Producers: Harvey Fuqua & Johnny Bristol (Billboard soul charts: 4 ; Billboard pop charts: 60)

In The Groove 1968 Tamla TS 285 No producer listed (Billboard soul charts: 2 ; Billboard pop charts: 63)

M.P.G. 1969 Tamla T-292 No producer listed (Billboard soul charts: 1 ; Billboard pop charts: 33)

And His Girls 1969 Tamla S-293 No producer listed (Billboard soul charts: 16 ; Billboard pop charts: 183)

Easy (and Tammi Terrell) 1969 Tamla S-294 No producer listed (Billboard pop charts: 184)

That's The Way Love Is 1969 Tamla S-299 Producer: Norman Whitfield 1969 Tamla T-292 (Billboard soul charts: 17; Billboard pop charts: 189)

Super Hits 1970 Tamla TS-300 (Billboard soul charts: 19; Billboard pop charts: 117)

Greatest Hits (and Tammi Terrell) 1970 Tamla TS-302 (Billboard soul charts: 17 ; Billboard pop charts: 171)

Gaye had made good music with Mary Wells and Kim Weston but reached greater heights when he was teamed up with Tammi Terrell, a collaboration that made sense musically and emotionally. They really sounded as if they cared for each other, but the three albums they made together did contain plenty of filler. The first and best of these, *United*, housed three massive hits, "Ain't No Mountain High Enough", "Your Precious Love" and "If I Could Build My Whole World Around You"; all went top 3 soul and top 20 pop and all were fully deserving of such success. Less enthralling were songs like "Little Ole Boy, Little Ole Girl" and a cover of "Somethin' Stupid" but "Two Can Have A Party" was irresistible and best of all was the b-side to "Build My Whole World", "If This World Were Mine".

A second volume of Gaye's *Greatest Hits* came out between the first two sets with Terrell, and this time it was well-named: ten of the twelve tracks could indeed be considered to be hits of reasonable magnitude.

The *You're All I Need To Get By* album contained two genuinely brilliant records, both penned by Ashford-Simpson with the former featuring typically magnificent bass playing from James Jamerson: the title track and "Ain't Nothing Like The Real Thing"; both made #1 on the soul charts and #7 and #8 respectively pop when released as singles. Nothing else on the LP came close to the quality of these two sides and a third Ashford and Simpson written single from the set, "Keep On Lovin' Me Honey", was undeniably inferior to the earlier 45s and sold many fewer copies as a result.

Easy, the final album with Terrell, was filled with sadness as it was now apparent how ill she was, and on these sides, her final recordings before she died in March 1970, Valerie Simpson provided vocal support. Three singles were released - "Good Lovin' Ain't Easy", "What You Gave Mme" and "The Onion Song" (a tune that hardcore soul fans seem to particularly dislike) - but none hit anywhere near as big as had previous singles from the duo, and, indeed, the whole album fared worse too. The majority of songs on the set were penned by Ashford and Simpson and on "California Soul" Gaye and Terrell gave one of the best renderings of a composition that has now become something of a "standard".

In 1969 Motown put out the latest Gaye solo album, *In The Groove*. Nobody thought too much of it at first and it contained a couple of singles that sold well if not spectacularly so, neither of which were his best or his worst: "You" and "Chained". Tucked away as track 4 side one, however, was the song that remains his best known ever: "I Heard It Through The Grapevine". His version wasn't even the original of this song - Gladys Knight and The Pips had already had a massive hit with it at the end of 1967- but when Gaye's effort was played as an album cut on Chicago radio, the listener reaction was so great that it was pushed out as a 45 in late 1968. It became - and remains - his biggest and most successful record ever: 7 weeks at #1 soul, and even more incredibly, the same number of weeks at #1 pop. No introduction or explanation is needed for this record - a genuinely world famous recording - and Motown quickly re-packaged the *In The Groove* LP with a new cover and a new title: that of the huge hit. "Change What You Can" and "You're What's Happening In The World Today" were good, if relatively minor, Gaye cuts from elsewhere on the album but "Some Kind Of Wonderful" and "There Goes My Baby" added little to the originals.

Gaye was now a huge star and this exalted status was reflected when his next LP *M.P.G* (it stood for "Marvin Pentz Gaye") became his first to hit #1 soul as well as his first to breach the top 40 pop listing. More huge hits were aboard: "Too Busy Thinking 'Bout My Baby" and "That's The Way Love Is", #4 and #7 pop respectively, with the former also becoming Gaye's sixth #1 on the soul charts, as well as a smaller one, "The End Of Our Road". Among the lesser-known cuts I have always had a soft spot for "Seek And You Shall Find" and "Try My True Love" stomps along powerfully in quintessential Motown sixties style. It was also yet another Gaye album that omitted any producer details but much of it was the work of Norman Whitfield.

Whitfield WAS credited as producer on Gaye's last solo album of the sixties, *That's The Way Love Is*, the title track of which had also been on the *M.P.G* LP. Whitfield was highly driven and highly talented and he brought a great deal of success to Gaye, but the price one often had to pay to work with him was to cover songs that had been previously cut by others and that was certainly the case on this set which ranged from well-known compositions like "Yesterday, "Groovin'", "Cloud Nine" and "I Wish It Would Rain" to lesser ones like Jimmy Ruffin's "Don't You Miss Me A Little Bit Baby". The best cover on the set was his lovely take on "Abraham, Martin And John" which became a sizeable hit in the UK (it was not released on 45 in the U.S.A). Also included was the no more than adequate "How Can I Forget", and it is hard to recall a more forgotten single by Gaye in his pre - "What's Going On" days than this one, and its #18 soul position was notably disappointing for such a big name as Marvin in this period. His dissatisfaction with the label was now profound but changes were afoot and the next time anyone heard music from Marvin Gaye it would sound utterly different.

However, a couple of *Greatest Hits* sets appeared in 1970 to fill the void that existed because of Gaye's refusal to record any new material in the wake of Terrell's tragic passing. (An album, *Marvin Gaye And His Girls* had come out in 1969 which included work with Weston, Wells and Terrell.)

What's Going On 1971 Tamla TS 310 Producer: Marvin Gaye (Billboard soul charts: 1 ; Billboard pop charts: 6)

Trouble Man 1972 Tamla T-322L Producer: Marvin Gaye (Billboard soul charts: 3 ; Billboard pop charts: 14)

Let's Get It On 1973 Tamla T 329V1 Producers: Marvin Gaye & Ed Townsend (Billboard soul charts: 1 ; Billboard pop charts: 2)

Diana & Marvin 1973 Motown M 803V1 Producers: Hal Davis, Mark Davis, Berry Gordy, Margaret Gordy, Bob Gaudio, Nickolas Ashford & Valerie Simpson (Billboard soul charts: 7 ; Billboard pop charts: 26)

Anthology 1974 Motown M9-791A3 (Billboard soul charts: 10 ; Billboard pop charts: 61)

Live! 1974 Tamla T6-333S1 No producer listed (Billboard soul charts: 1 ; Billboard pop charts: 4)

I Want You 1976 Tamla T6-342S1 Producer: Leon Ware (Billboard soul charts: 1 ; Billboard pop charts: 8)

When Gaye finally presented Motown with a new album it just happened to be his masterpiece. *What's Going On* is a unique album in my experience in as much as I have never heard anyone, ever, say that they don't like it and it remains a piece of work as loved and admired as any in the annals of popular music. It is salutary to remember that Gordy disliked it intensely when he first heard it and it's also interesting to note from the distance of over forty years that it did not go gold at the time of release nor reach any higher than #6 on the pop charts, although it did reach #1 on the soul lists, a pinnacle it held on to for five weeks. Most people with an interest in music will know the album but, for me, its greatest achievement was to hear how completely Gaye had re-invented himself; it sounded nothing like his previous work at all. The title track, "Mercy Mercy Me" and the magnificent "Inner City Blues" all went to #1 on the soul singles charts as well as all reaching the pop top ten. Marvin Gaye was now a superstar, a situation that both thrilled and appalled him.

Gaye followed up the LP with a rather forgotten single, "You're The Man", which did not appear on any album at the time before his next set arrived, a soundtrack (nearly all the big soul artists were recording soundtracks in the early seventies) to a forgettable film entitled *Trouble Man*. The excellent title track was a big hit and Gaye has been quoted as saying that it was his favourite of all his albums but I'm not sure anyone else shared this opinion.

In 1973 Gaye served up what was really the proper follow-up to *What's Going On* and *Let's Get It On*, another brilliant album, was one of the most sumptuously arranged of all soul LPs, thanks to the work of David Blumberg, David Van DePitte, Gene Page and Rene Hall. It was also one of the most personal sets Gaye was ever to make and where *What's Going On* had been addressed to the world *Let's Get It On* was addressed to one young woman only: Janis Hunter. The title track (which I have now heard too many times to enjoy much anymore) became his second pop #1 as the lead-off 45 from the set but I much preferred other songs such as "If I Should Die Tonight", "Come Get To This" and "Just To Keep You Satisfied" which were all superlative.

In 1973 Motown had given the first signs it was starting to think properly about its legacy and illustrious place in music history when it put out an *Anthology* set on The Temptations. Gaye's own *Anthology* appeared in 1974 and this was a most handsome retrospective: a triple album consisting of 40 tracks, 21 of which had reached the pop top twenty, nine of which had reached #1 soul. At the time it was pricey, but it still sold well.

Motown then decided it was time for Gaye to record with yet another woman, Diana Ross, and typically called the resultant album *Diana And Marvin* when *Marvin And Diana* would have made more sense given how much more commercially prominent Gaye was at that time. It appears the artists were never even in the studio at the same time and the fact that seven producers were required just highlights what an unsatisfactory and unenthralling set it was. I didn't like it at the time of release and don't like it now.

I wasn't particularly enamoured of Gaye's next two solo LPs either although I did try very hard to like *Live* and *I Want You* at the time of release, particularly the latter. The former could not overcome my usual indifference to "live" sets (but *New Musical Express* loved it, I recall) whereas I simply felt that *I Want You* was devoid of much strong material as well as bearing an overly defined footprint by Leon Ware (he co-wrote all the songs as well as producing and arranging the entirety.) This is not to say that the outcome was anything other than wholly professional but *Let's Get It On* had a naked passion that I feel *I Want You* lacked. As so often, my qualms are entirely irrelevant: both albums performed exceedingly well.

Greatest Hits 1976 Tamla T6-348S1 (Billboard soul charts: 17 ; Billboard pop charts: 44)

Live At The London Palladium 1977 Tamla T7-352R2 (Billboard soul charts: 1 ; Billboard pop charts: 3)

Here My Dear 1978 Tamla T 364LP2 Producer: Marvin Gaye (Billboard soul charts: 4 ; Billboard pop charts: 26)

In Our Lifetime 1981 Tamla T8-374 M1 Producer: Marvin Gaye (Billboard soul charts: 6 ; Billboard pop charts: 32)

Maybe no-one knew it at the time but 1977 marked the last year that Marvin Gaye would remain a big selling artist for Motown. His demons continued to roil around in his head and getting him into the studio remained problematic. As so often, a *Greatest Hits* and another "live" album became a way to fill the gap and a noticeably stingy hits (a paltry 10 tracks) set came out at the end of 1976 (his sixth such collection) followed up by his third "live" set at the start of the following year. The latter contained one new studio cut and it was a very good - and long - one indeed. Produced by Art Stewart, "Got To Give It Up" filled the whole of side four of this double LP, clocking in at just short of twelve minutes. When released on 45 it went to #1 on both the soul and pop charts, the last time he would ever enjoy a big hit of any description until "Sexual Healing" in 1982, when Motown was but a distant and still bittersweet memory.

Gaye's next studio album was the extraordinary *Here My Dear*, much of which was a highly detailed and personal account of his time with his first wife, Anna Gordy, a woman seventeen years his senior. The record has become something of a critic's delight but I have always found it to be a fascinating mess, which was doubtless a good metaphor for much of Gaye's life. There are brilliant moments, but nothing is sustained and the overall lack of melody coupled with the four or five patently way overlong tracks deter my unbridled enthusiasm. I love the deeply touching and wrenching "I Met A Little Girl" and the cries of "Anna" on "Anna's Song" are among the most chilling and heartbreaking moments in all of popular music. The sardonic "You Can Leave, But It's Going To Cost You" just points up that the person who the album cost the most in emotional pain was Gaye himself. The rather trivial "A Funky Space Reincarnation" reached a not particularly impressive #23 soul when put out on a 45.

Every five years or so I pull out and play Gaye's last Motown LP, In Our Lifetime, to see if I "get it" yet. I'm afraid I never do. The album has an intriguing cover, cleverly denoting the warring facets of Gaye's tortured soul and the overall sound is lush and pungent but I always get bored, as the almost total lack of melody ("Praise" excepted) over the forty minutes or so of the album means it speaks to me less compellingly than Marvin did in three minutes in "Ain't That Peculiar". I'm aware that my dismissal of a set which has many fans will cause annoyance and affront but we're just going to have to agree to disagree on this one.

Midnight Love 1982 Columbia FC 38197 Producer: Marvin Gaye (Billboard soul charts: 1 ; Billboard pop charts: 7)

Dream Of A Lifetime 1985 Columbia FC 39916 Producers: Marvin Gaye, Gordon Banks & Harvey Fuqua (Billboard soul charts: 8 ; Billboard pop charts: 41)

Romantically Yours 1985 Columbia FC 40208 Producers: Norman Whitfield, Hal Davis, Marc Gordon, Bobby Scott & Marvin Gaye

Motown Remembers Marvin Gaye 1986 Motown 6172 TL Producer: Hal Davis (Billboard soul charts: 48 ; Billboard pop charts: 193)

A Musical Testament 1964 - 1984 1988 Motown 6255ML2 (Billboard soul charts: 69)

Midnight Love is another Gaye LP I am unable to warm to, given its predominantly computerised backing tracks which are - apart from on "Joy", where there is enough going on to break down my resistance - highly uninteresting to my ears, but the horns are good throughout and Gaye delivers one of his best vocals in years on "'Til Tomorrow". Much more to the point than my lukewarm comments are the facts that "Sexual Healing" became his thirteenth single to reach #1 on the soul charts and his first to reach the top 3 of the pop charts since "Got To Give It Up" five years before. The LP sold very well, too, being one of the biggest of his career, in fact "going platinum".

It is well-known that Gaye was shot dead by his father in 1984 and so a "follow-up" to *Midnight Love* was by no means a certainty, but *Dream Of A Lifetime* can be considered as such, even if much of the music within was recorded prior to the earlier LP. What a mixed-bag, though. The first three tracks were considered worthy of a lyrical content warning in case listeners found them offensive, and I was certainly offended by them, on the grounds that Gaye had seldom recorded such poor stuff, and, in the case of "Masochistic Beauty", genuine rubbish. In his defence, it seems highly unlikely he would ever have sanctioned their release had he survived. One of the three, "Sanctified Lady", even made it to #2 on the soul charts as a single in mid 1985 which I suspect shows how much people missed Marvin Gaye rather than loved the record. Much of the rest was much, much better, having been recorded back in the early seventies and wouldn't have sounded musically out of place on his great works like *What's Going On* or *Let's Get It On*. Best of all were the autobiographical "Life's Opera" and the title track, both of which were beautifully orchestrated and moving and fascinating to listen to when one understands the conflicts that drove him to an inevitable sad end.

Romantically Yours was a reprise of the style that had dominated early albums like When I'm Alone I Cry and Hello Broadway (as examples, "Maria" and "Shadow Of Your Smile" were included) but side two did contain four of Marvin's own songs and if they were played and arranged in the style of side one so as to achieve a stylistic whole, one, "Walking In The Rain", did stick in the mind thanks to its emphatic production.

The *Motown Remembers* LP was welcome because it presented us with twelve previously unreleased Gaye tracks, but unwelcome as the record company saw fit to meddle with the original tracks and impose "additional music overdubs" which were philistine and misguided. I suppose it should be said that the tinkering may have been even worse, but it still rankled. Nearly all the songs were exhumed from the sixties while one from the seventies, "I'm Going Home", included an unfortunate line about returning home to see his "dear old dad". We know how well that worked out.

I have listed *A Musical Testament* as it charted but have ignored the dozens of other Gaye compilations that came out over a long period of time.

Gloria Gaynor

Never Can Say Goodbye 1975 MGM M3G 4982 Producers: Tony Bongiovi, Meco Monardo & Jay Ellis (Billboard soul charts: 21 ; Billboard pop charts: 25)

Experience 1975 MGM M3G 4997 Producers: Tony Bongiovi, Meco Monardo & Jay Ellis (Billboard soul charts: 32 ; Billboard pop charts: 64)

I've Got You 1976 Polydor PD-1-6063 Producers: Tony Bongiovi, Meco Monardo & Jay Ellis (Billboard soul charts: 40 ; Billboard pop charts: 107)

Glorious 1977 Polydor PD-1-6095 Producers: Gregg Diamond & Joe Beck

The Best Of 1977 Polydor 2391-312 (UK)

Park Avenue Sound 1978 Polydor PD-1-6139 Producers: Tan, Conell Johnson, Al Stewart & Joel Diamond

Love Tracks 1978 Polydor PD-1-6184 Producers: Dino Fekaris & Freddie Perren (Billboard soul charts: 4 ; Billboard pop charts: 4)

I Have A Right 1979 Polydor PD-1-6231 Producers: Dino Fekaris & Freddie Perren (Billboard soul charts: 56 ; Billboard pop charts: 58)

Stories 1980 Polydor PD-1-6274 Producers: Dino Fekaris & Freddie Perren

I Kinda Like Me 1981 Polydor PD-1-6324 Producers: Gene McFadden, John Whitehead & Jerry Cohen

Greatest Hits 1982 Polydor 2482 573 (UK)

When this New Jersey born singer recorded an excellent single back in 1965 on the tiny Jocida label no-one could have forseen that nearly fifteen years later she would have recorded one of the biggest selling and best-known records of the entire seventies in "I Will Survive".

As ever I will be honest: Gaynor has never been an artist who has meant much to me as too many of her records have been unashamedly disco oriented but she was actually a much better singer than the majority of her records would suggest. Her debut single proved that as did the superb "This Love Affair" from *The Park Avenue Sound* LP .

After the Jocida 45 she didn't release any records for the best part of a decade and had her first taste of any success when "Honeybee" became a moderate soul hit (#55) in the first half of 1974. It is a side I liked well enough, sounding like a perfect cross between the things that Hot Wax and P.I.R were putting out at the time. The challenge for me as a listener came when it was added onto covers of "Never Can Say Goodbye" and "Reach Out, I'll Be There" to forge an unbroken eighteen minute first side of her debut LP which leaves me somewhat exhausted. Take a listen, instead, to "Sear*c*hin'" on side two for a much better dance track. This one sits on the right side of the soul/disco fence whereas side one is off limits to me. Even stronger is "Real Good People" which might not be a song of much merit but Gaynor's vocal is downright "sassy" and if played" blind" to someone they would be hard pressed to guess it was her.

The album did extremely well for Gaynor and MGM and it was therefore inevitable that a follow-up would have even more of a disco feel and "Walk On By" and "How High The Moon" got the full dance treatment. As did all of side one, in fact. I much preferred "Tell Me How " (even if it sounded in the wrong key for her voice) and, better still, "What'll I Do" which both showed that she was more than a disco diva.

Despite the popularity of her disco sides, none of her singles had sold in great quantities apart from "Never Can Say Goodbye" which reached #9 pop and this might have been a major reason why she and her producers moved to Polydor for her third LP. It didn't do anyone much good at all at first. The album was highly mediocre throughout with undistinguished disco sides mixed up with rather bloodless ballads and it sold poorly.

In fact, the album was so disappointing that Bongiovi, Monardo and Ellis departed to be replaced by Gregg Diamond and Joe Beck as producers. The problem was that *Glorious*, the follow-up, was anything but. If all Gloria's albums had sounded like this one, I'm afraid she would have been "out of scope" so entirely devoid of soul is the whole thing. It didn't sell many, being her first LP to miss the soul charts entirely and yielded no hit singles, either.

That was the end of Gregg Diamond and Beck as occupants of the producer's chairs which were next entrusted to Conell Johnson, Al Stewart, Joel Diamond and the rather mysterious Tan for "Gloria Gaynor's Park Avenue Sound" which was her best LP by some distance, helped immeasurably by the employment of many great arrangers and musicians from Philadelphia. The afore-mentioned "This Love Affair" is a marvellous record and even an uptempo version of "You're All I Need To Get By" is by no means to be dismissed while I can imagine First Choice performing "Kidnapped". Gaynor sings with much more power and fire than on all her previous LPs and there is nothing on here I actively dislike. Sadly, though, the album failed in the marketplace it was time to change producers yet again.

It was now up to Freddie Perren and Dino Fekaris to revive her fortunes with the 1978 set, *Love Tracks* and in early 1979 everything paid off when THAT single made it to #4 soul and #1 pop. It has become much beloved down the years and I can understand that the positive nature of the lyrics make it "empowering" (to use that horrible word) but I think it is fair to say that it is not my favourite record of all time. Nevertheless, its inclusion on *Love Tracks* pushed the album to dizzying heights hitherto unexplored by Gaynor's previous LPs. "Anybody Wanna Party?" reached the distinctly underwhelming position of 105 on the pop charts as the follow-up to "I Will Survive" thus completely derailing Gaynor's momentum as a big seller of records. A version of "Goin' Out Of My Head" on the set summed up the approach of Perren and Fekaris as producers and one could see their point in 1978 but Little Anthony and Baby Washington made immeasurably better records with the same song.

The decline of Gaynor's commercial fortunes continued with the poor *I Have A Right* set; three singles were released from it, with two missing the charts completely and "Let Me Know (I Have A Right)" only made it to #61 soul and #42 pop. "Can't Fight The Feeling" is the only track on the album I would ever play again by choice.

There were two more albums on Polydor but neither charted and neither contained hit singles. Stories passed me by completely but *I Kinda Like Me* (another title, like *I Have A Right*, clearly inspired by her "I Will Survive" image) was interesting in that it contained five songs by Gaynor herself while "Let's Mend What's Been Broken" was her best single in ages and deserved to reach higher than #76 soul. "Chasin' Me Into Someone Else's Arms" was good as well, and it was refreshing to hear her making soul rather than disco music once again.

Gloria Gaynor 1982 Atlantic 80033-1 Producers: Amir Bayyan, Linwood Simon, Rick Stevens, Ollie Brown & Yves Dessca

I Am Gloria Gaynor 1984 Silver Blue AL 39267 Producer: Joel Diamond

The Power 1986 Stylus SMR 618 Producer: Steve Rowland

Gloria Gaynor 90 1990 New Music International NMLP 1018 Producer: Pippo Sandro

Love Affair 1992 New Music International NMLP 1032 Producers: Pippo Sandro & Linwood Simon

Gaynor moved to Atlantic in 1982 and put out a set that contained a handful of cuts that proved again that she was a talented and underrated vocalist: I like "Love Me Real", "Even A Fool Would Let Go" and a decent cover of "Stop! In The Name Of Love" but it was not a commercial success and from here on in she parted company with soul music almost totally and her last handful of albums were all dance efforts that are of no appeal to me.

Frankie Gearing

Just Frankie 1980 Beale St. VS 1022 Producer: Dan Greer (Japan)

Frances Gearing was born in Florida in 1944 and had an interesting career, although the quality of the recordings on which she provided sultry and usually captivating vocals were neither rewarded by many sales nor showcased on anywhere near enough LPs.

One of her earliest outings on vinyl was as the lead singer of The Steinways' "Northern Soul" favourite "You've Been Leading

Me On" but her first taste of any sort of success at all was when she joined the Glories. This fine group put out eight singles but only the first, "I Stand Accused", reached the national soul charts at #48 in 1967. Given the quality of many of the Glories' sides it is a shame that they did not get the chance to ever record or release a vinyl LP. Even more of a shame was the absence of an album by Quiet Elegance (who The Glories more or less morphed into in the early seventies) as many of their 45s were brilliant.

So we have to console ourselves with her one LP, recorded as a solo artist and released in Japan in 1980. It is somewhat of a mixed bag, and a couple of cuts, most notably "Going Through The Motions Of Love", feature her singing with a much higher and lighter tone than she utilised on, say, the magnificent "I'm Afraid Of Losing You" by Quiet Elegance. "Spinning Top", another light-voiced excursion, has fans on UK dancefloors but the cream cut was the opener, "Teardrops", which is built around a wonderful and involving arrangement. She is also very good on the country song, "Bluer Than Blue", on which, as with a decent cover of "Tired Of Being Alone", she reverts to the soulful approach I much prefer. "Shine On My Superstar " is also well worth hearing but covers of "Endlessly", "Rock And Roll Waltz" and "California Dreamin'" don't do a lot for me.

A couple more singles (one being a superb take on "Tears On My Pillow") followed the release of the set but, although she is still out there singing, no new recordings have materialised for more than thirty years.

Gene & Bobby

Strike Again 1977 Guinness GNS 36008 Produced by ?

A few years ago Daptone records released a CD by Bob & Gene entitled *If This World Were Mine*, a collection of cuts from late 1967. Bob was Bobby Nunn (later to record for Motown) and Gene was Eugene Coplin. But were they also Gene and Bobby? Who knows. This Guinness LP, like all the others, is short on information but it is at least a reasonable assumption that they may be the same pair. The tracks include covers of big soul hits from 1974, "Hang On In There Baby" and "Happiness Is Around The Bend" so maybe that was when this was recorded. What I have heard, and it's not much, sounds pretty decent.

Gemini

Fred Sawyers; Karvin Johnson

Rising 1981 M & M 101 Producer: Sam Brown

By 1981 the number of albums that were built around soulful singing and sympathetic musical backing were increasingly hard to find and this outing from the L.A. based duo of Fred Sawyers and Karvin Johnson sounded good back then and still stands up strongly today. Executive Producer Freddie Perren brought his commercial flair to the proceedings as most tracks on the set sound as if they had what it took to have become hits, but "(You've Got) Something Special" failed on 45, and was possibly the wrong choice as the beautifully flowing "Can't Throw Away A Good Love" was better and more catchy. There is not a great deal of lyrical profundity on show but the singing more than compensates and a good take on Infinity's mini-hit from 1971, "I Don't Want To Lose You", was an inspired choice of song to cover. Top class musicians such as James Gadson, Ed Greene, Wah Wah Watson and Paulinho Da Costa were drafted in but the album was more admired than purchased.

Karvin Johnson had put out a so-so single, "If You Let Me" in 1980 while Fred Sawyers provided backing vocals on a number of records by others, but this was Gemini's one and only shot at making it.

General Caine

Mitch McDowell; David Chadwick; Trey Stone; Alga Thomson; Anthony Patler; Joe Blocker; Jimmy Carter; Tony Patler David Williams; Gary Metz; David Jarmillo; Timmy Lee; Robert Palmer; Rick Hendrix; Nathaniel Price; Danny Macon; Darrel Haywood; Kevin Goines; Herschell Kennedy; Johnny Carson; Leroy Williams; Ronald Jerry; Erik Jones; David Dobler; Jim Morrison; Alvino Bennett; Gerry Davis; Marion McQuery;

Let Me In 1978 Groove Time GTR-1001 Producers: Mitch McDowell & General Caine

Get Down Attack 1980 Groove Time GTR-1004 Producer: Mitch McDowell

The Best Of 1991 Groove Time GTR-1006

Anyone who likes to collect albums with sexually suggestive covers will want the debut set from General Caine which featured a shot of a young lady and a guitar in an embrace that the Ohio Players would have been proud of. The L.A. based group arose from the ashes of the Booty People and that debut was pretty good, being funky enough in style while McDowell had a rather laid-back and playful lead vocal which suggested he didn't take himself too seriously. The striking cover notwithstanding, the LP failed to sell, being released into a market place replete with self-contained funk bands.

Groove Time records gave the band a second chance at the big time with *Get Down Attack*, a collection which retained a provocative cover but moved the sound more into the Parliament/Cameo sphere. It's one of those albums which sounds good or derivative depending on what mood I'm in but it did have something about it; "Shake" certainly crunches along and "More Than A Do-Wop" was a thoughtfully constructed slow number. Nevertheless, it was another album that failed to sell well. (A *Best Of* set, containing six tracks culled from the two Groove Time albums came out in 1991.)

Girls 1982 Tabu FZ 37997 Producer: Mitch McDowell

Dangerous 1983 Tabu FZ 38863 Producers: Reggie Andrews & Leon Chancler

Seeing as how things hadn't really panned out so far for General Caine McDowell stripped the band back to a five piece and dispensed with the overtly "naughty" covers for their first album on new label Tabu which bore a more conventional sleeve. The title track did at least make it to #72 on the soul charts, which was something for a band desperate for hits. They retained their sense of fun on "Can We Warm It Up" and apparently the track "For Lovers Only" was a big one for the group in Cleveland and it is another appealing example of how funk bands could often serve up satisfying ballads. Overall it is another album that would make no sense to anyone uninterested in funk but plenty to those who love the genre.

For the second Tabu LP (with the utterly routine, dull and misleading name *Dangerous*) the band's personnel had swelled up again to eleven and new producers had been brought on board but the sound didn't appreciably change. "Bomb Body" was another small hit and "Upside Down" was the obligatory pleasing slow side.

General Kane

New members: Tim Heintz; David Z; Brenda Jackson;

In Full Chill 1986 Gordy 6216 GL Producers: Mitch McDowell & Curtis Anthony Nolen (Billboard soul charts: 46)

Wide Open 1987 Motown 6238 ML Producers: Mitch McDowell & Curtis Anthony Nolen (Billboard soul charts: 57)

General Caine had hardly set the world alight after four albums and a minor name change to General Kane was the latest attempt by McDowell to change the band's fortunes. It worked to a fair degree as a rap-based anti-drug number (I hesitate to call it a "song") entitled "Crack Killed Applejack" made it to #12 on the soul charts in late 1986 but both it and the entire heavily programmed *In Full Chill* LP are simply not to my taste at all.

It wasn't quite clear who comprised the band by the time of the *Wide Open* set (which contained a #33 soul hit in "Girl Pulled The Dog") but to be honest I didn't much care as it was clearly aimed at a wholly different audience from the likes of me.

Gentlemen And Their Ladies

Bobby Johnson; Mayland Etheridge; Jimmy Reed; Richie Cowell; Ronnie Johnson; Danny Mitchell; Gypsy Marie Griggs; Jeanette Cooper; George Jaswell

Party Time 1974 Jean JR 5000 Producer: George Kerr

Presented Live 19?? Co-Jo DS-001 Producers: Richard Cowell & Ronald Johnson

In early 1974 an eight man group, consisting of six gentlemen and two ladies, had a small soul hit with "Party Bump". Given it only reached #80 an arrival of an album was somewhat of a surprise (it even got a release in England) and its rather threadbare quality must surely have meant it sold in exceptionally limited numbers. The "hit" itself sounded much like a Junior Walker & The All-Stars record with whistles added on, and was enjoyable enough if pretty unrepresentative of what else was on offer. For example, much less enticing were long sax-led instrumentals of "Amazing Grace" and "Bridge Over Troubled Waters", not exactly thrilling song choices in the first place, with the latter having a soulful if rather uncertain lead vocal from one of the ladies in addition to an unintentionally rather amusing few bars from one very deep male voice indeed. Side two included more instrumentals including the backing track to Barbara Jean English's "You're Gonna Need Somebody To Love You" as well as the second best cut on show, "One More Time", where lead vocals are switched around quite adroitly.

A single came out in 1976, "Like Her", which made some noise on the UK "Northern Soul" scene, by which time the group were billed as "Gentlemen and Their Lady", Gypsy Marie Griggs having departed. It was under this slightly new name that the group put out their second LP, of such obscurity that it made the debut come across like *Thriller*. I have never heard it but know it consists of nine tracks, eight of which are covers with "Party Bump" being the only original on show. No year of issue is provided on the sleeve but I would hazard a guess at 1975 or 1976 given the songs that are included, and I also obviously assume it is a "live" album.

Gentle Persuasion

Leza Holmes; Renee Johnson; Sharon Williams

Gentle Persuasion 1978 Warner Brothers BSK 3164 Producer: Jerry Ross

Gentle Persuasion had a handful of singles and one LP issued over a period of ten years or so but never had any hits at all, probably because the people who mattered in the music industry decided there was only room for one successful group out of Philadelphia who sounded like The Three Degrees. And certainly the album cover would suggest Jerry Ross was not exactly wholeheartedly committed to providing the group with any sort of identity. The three women who comprised Gentle Persuasion may not have minded too much, though, as they provided backing vocals on many other recordings and doubtless made a living that way.

Not that they sounded exactly like The Three Degrees on this so-so album but there is certainly some of their flavour in here, as there is The Emotions'. It is not an introspective set, and everything is delivered with the dancefloor in mind although three subtly different approaches can be discerned: out and out disco ("Litterbug") light and breathy ("I'm Gonna Blow Your Mind") and my favourite, surging P.I.R. influenced soul ("Who Do You Love").

Barbara George

I Know (You Don't Love Me No More) 1961 A.F.O. Producer: Juggy Murray

One striking aspect of Barbara George's one and only LP was that it provided the names of the musicians who played on the set, which was highly unusual for a soul record back in 1962. Born in New Orleans, where the album was recorded, she is a perfect example of a "one hit wonder" as the title track had become a #1 soul and #3 pop hit at the end of 1961, and she never reached the *Billboard* charts again, although did place two more singles onto the *Cashbox* listings, albeit at a lowly level.

The charming hit sported that typically rolling sound that could only have come from the Crescent City, and about half the other tracks follow the same highly appealing pattern. The other thing that jumps out from the set is the fact that George wrote eleven of the twelve songs on show. Not only was this a noteworthy and unfamiliar achievement back then, but only "Hurted" (more or less "I Know part 2") and "I'm In A Strain" were below par; "I Never Knew" was a noticeably mature composition from a 19 year old. Her voice betrayed her youth, but had a slight tinge of toughness which suggested she could take care of herself. It's certainly a good example of the emerging soul style and is one of the better LPs from before 1964.

However, it bore a shoddy cover that was to be expected from a small label like A.F.O. ("All For One") and the next few of George's singles came out on Murray's Sue label. She was never a prolific artist, although she did release a wonderful 45 in the seventies called "Leave Me Alone" which sadly failed to get noticed outside her home town, and she passed away in 2006 almost completely forgotten.

Donny Gerrard

Donny Gerrard 1976 Greedy G-1002 Producers: Henry Marx & Robbie Buchanan

Canadian-born Donny Gerrard was the lead singer for Skylark when they had a big hit with "Wildflower" but he had already moved to L.A. to make it further in the music industry and over a two-year period from 1975 to 1977 he did manage to place six singles on the U.S. soul chart; the problem was that none of them went any higher than #37 and it all rather fizzled out for him.

The "biggest" of those hits, "Words (Are Impossible)" is on his one album, as are three of the others. Gerrard is undoubtedly an accomplished vocalist, but it's a very safe, smooth LP, verging on MOR much too often for my tastes and only the danceable "He's Always Somewhere Around" (with "He" being God, on a song where Gerrard is demonstrably influenced by the Spinners' Philippe Wynne) and a reasonable take on The Impressions' "You Must Believe Me" made my ears perk up a bit.

Giants

Giants 1978 LAX MCA-3188 Producers: Gregg Errico & Mike Carabello

Who thought up the name "Giants"? An awful name in my opinion for an ensemble who made a pretty average LP with a pretty average cover. I suspect that it came into being after a one-off session or sessions and no group called Giants ever existed. Producer Gregg Errico used to be in Sly and The Family Stone and their influence, particularly on Doug Rauch's bass, is discernible if not overwhelming. The album is mostly instrumental apart from some female backing vocalists chanting a few lyrics.

Gift Of Dreams

Michael Rochelle; Randolph Brownlee; Reginald Baskins; Bettye Jo Miller; Albert Trepagnier

The Gift 1982 Jam Power JP-002 Producer: Gift Of Dreams

Mandroid 1983 Jam Power JP-006 Producer: Gift Of Dreams

L.A. based Gift Of Dreams put out a fine and soulful dance record in 1982, "Better Days", which caught my attention at the time and so I was pleased to invest in an album when it appeared the same year although for some reason the 45 was not included. Luckily, a similar track, "Feel it", was, which went some way towards assuaging my disappointment. "Love Is All We Need", "By My Side" and "One In All " were all good sides too, somewhat in an EWAF vein, which also helped, as I was left cold by nondescript funk efforts such as "Funkincise" and "Spirit Of The Dancer".

A year later a second LP appeared, but when I saw it included song titles such as "Sneeky", "Mandroid" and "Video Sensation" my heart sank and I knew it would not be coming into my household. To this day, I haven't heard all of it so it might contain the odd good side but the cuts I listened to would suggest not.

Eddie Giles

I'm A Losing Boy 1979 Vivid Sound VS-1015 Producers: Jerry Strickland, Bobby Patterson & Allen Orange (Japan)

Modern "brand" marketeers would have despaired of the way in which Elbert Wiggins Giles' career was handled. He had singles issued in the following names: Eddy Giles, Eddy "G" Giles, Eddie Giles, Eddie Giles & The Numbers and Eddy "G" Giles and the Jive Five. Unsurprisingly, such an approach meant that he never enjoyed a record on any national charts and never had an LP released in his home country.

Still, it would be slightly misleading to suggest that the Louisiana born singer and former Pilgrim Jubilee did not have a brief moment of glory as his first - excellent - single, "Losin' Boy" (as by Eddy Giles), sold strongly regionally, and must have shifted a fair number of copies. Over the years he issued eleven singles in all, the best of which was a magnificent take on "That's How Strong My Love Is" on Silver Fox in 1969 which may just be my favourite ever reading of this famous song.

His one LP was released in Japan in 1979 and consists mainly of unissued material, only five of the twelve tracks having been previously put on 45s. It is a strong set, but does contain its fair share of average material including "Soul Bag", which seemed determined to have Eddie shout out more song titles of soul records than any other such track in history. Given some of the sides he declaims it is pretty safe to assume this cut dates from 1972 and equally safe to state that "There Must Be A Place" is squarely based on "I'll Take You There". "Baby I Care" is somewhat throwaway as well, while "Baby Be Mine" is just too close to "Losin' Boy" to have much merit.

But that leaves lots of good things. "Are You Living With The One You're Loving With" and "Married Lady" were yoked together on a particularly strong single on Alarm in March 1973 while the amusing "It Takes Me All Night" was the b-side to a re-cut and inferior version of "Losing Boy" (which is not on the LP; the original is) that Stax rather surprisingly decided to distribute to little effect in 1971. Giles liked being on Stax, but didn't care for the new version. Best of all the cuts on the LP, though, is the slow and stately "I Can't Get Over You", which is only pipped by "That's How Strong My Love Is" (sadly, not on the LP) as the best vocal performance of his entire career.

Joey Gilmore

Get All You Want 1977 Blue Candle 55059 Producers: Snoopy Dean & Horace Straws

So Good To Be Bad 1989 Pandisc PD-8807 Producer: Yosiah Israel (Billboard soul charts: 80)

Florida born Joey Gilmore shares a number of characteristics with Willie "Little Beaver" Hale: both sang; both played bluesy guitar; both recorded for Henry Stone's labels; both were members of Frank Williams' Rocketeers band in the sixties. Gilmore made a couple of pretty good singles at the start of the seventies but they didn't do much outside of the Sunshine State.

In 1977 he released his first album, which has become "in-demand" over the last few years despite being rather saturated with other influences: "Get All You Want" rolls along quite nicely, and bears a distinct George McCrae feel; "Give Me Your Love" filches the intro from Johnnie Taylor's "I Believe In You" and pretty much the rest - with one exception - is routine seventies funk. That one exception, "Funny Feeling", a delightfully breezy dance number with Gilmore singing in a seldom used but appealing high tenor, is by far the best cut on the LP, and, I assume, the reason why people want to track it down.

A handful of other singles crept out between 1978 and 1986 but none made any national charts and he had to wait until 1989 for the chance to cut a second LP, which, sadly, did not have a great deal going for it. The eight tracks were split 50/50 between straight blues cuts and more soul-oriented items, but all shared a rather thin-sounding synthesised sound and none of the songs (all from the pen of Yosiah Israel) were strong. Nevertheless, the LP did manage a 12 week run on the *Billboard* soul charts

In the 21st century Gilmore has been happy to be perceived as a straight blues man, in which guise he has released a number of well-received CDs and garnered a handful of awards.

Jim Gilstrap

Swing Your Daddy 1975 Roxbury RB 2013 Producers: Wes Farrell & Kenny Nolan (Billboard pop charts: 179)

Love Talk 1976 Roxbury RLX 105 Producer: Wes Farrell

Texan Gilstrap is another artist who has surely been much more financially successful as a backing singer than from cutting his own records; certainly he has been vastly more prolific in the former category.

He had cut a rare and ignored single for Bell in 1974 before enjoying a surprise hit in early 1975 called "Swing Your Daddy", which was a cross between "Rock Your Baby" and any doo-wop side from around 1959. It became the title track of his first LP, which was a pop-oriented affair, and proved that while Gilstrap was clearly talented, he didn't have enough of an identity to have sustained a long solo career; his versions of Marvin Gaye's "Ain't That Particular" and "One More Heartache" are dreadfully bloodless while he clearly is content to copy Lamont Dozier's vocal phrasing on "Put Out The Fire". "Take Your Daddy For A Ride" and "House Of Strangers" are my favourite cuts, given their catchiness, and the latter became a small hit (#64 soul, #93 pop) as a follow-up 45 to the title track.

Love Talk was a noticeably different set, comprising only four long tracks. All of side one was taken up by the title song, lasting over 13 minutes, characterised by the fussy and overblown arranging that Gene Page could sometimes fall prey to; it wasn't disco by any means but it wasn't enthralling either. Over on side 2, "Move Me" had a similar approach to "Love Talk" but only lasted for around eight minutes; "Never Stop Loving Me", a third song from Dee Ervin, was a bit more peppy while "Hello It's Me", the Todd Rundgren song, had a fine Page arrangement but I prefer the Isley's version. I can see the appeal of the album - it's certainly lush and musically competent - but the lack of edge and overlong performances mean I can't really warm to it.

Glass House

Scherrie Payne; Ty Hunter; Sylvia Smith; Larry Mitchell; Pearl Jones

Inside The Glass House 1971 Invictus ST-7305 Producers: Greg Perry, Eddie Holland, Brian Holland, Lamont Dozier & William Weatherspoon

Thanks I Needed That 1972 Invictus ST-9810 Producers: Eddie Holland, Brian Holland & Lamont Dozier

There seems to be some confusion about who comprised The Glass House, as although the cover of the second LP clearly states that Sylvia Smith was a member, none of the sleevenotes to the CDs I have from the group even mention her. I am therefore going to assume she was indeed a member and is also the same lady who issued the *Woman Of The World* LP in 1975. It's thus, I think, often hard to tell who sings on the tracks and as an example, is it Ty Hunter who has a nice line in Johnnie Taylor screams on "Giving Up The Ring" as well as providing the smooth tones on the lovely "I Don't See Me In Your Eyes Anymore"?

What I do know for sure is that the tough "Crumbs Off The Table" (#7 soul, #59 pop) was a pretty big hit in 1969 a couple of years before it was featured on *Inside The Glass House*, Hunter was a singer with an impressive pedigree before and after he joined the group and Scherrie Payne is Freda Payne's sister as well as a former Supreme. On what is a most enjoyable first LP it seems that the leads are taken by either Payne or Hunter, except for a couple of tracks where the vocals are switched around and "Touch Me Jesus" where an unamused Darlene Love is singing (she was never a member of the group and sued HDH.) The captivating "Look What We've Done To Love" is my favourite track on show (with Hunter on lead) sounding more like a "sweet soul" outing than an Invictus track. It also reached #31 on the soul charts as a single in late 1971.

Their singles release pattern was rather erratic as "I Can't Be You, You Can't Be Me" a vaguely influenced by Sly & The Family Stone single did ok for the group in 1970 but it doesn't feature on either LP, while "Stealing Moments From Another Woman's Life" (#42 soul) was issued *before* "Look What We've Done To Love" despite sitting on their second album. Which was another top class LP, with a well delivered title track (I think probably by Smith, the CDs say by Pearl Jones) reaching #47 soul, their fifth and last charting single. (More confusion later ensued as another cut, the catchy "V.I.P" was put out on a single as a Scherrie Payne solo release, and another, the afore-mentioned and gorgeous "I Don't See Me In Your Eyes Anymore", as a Ty Hunter 45.) Payne also delivers a solid interpretation of "A House Is Not A Home" while, and I assume it IS by Jones this time, as she wrote it, "The Man I'll Never Have" is also a winner.

The group broke up in 1972 and Hunter went on to join The Originals for a while, although he passed away in 1981.

Bobby Glenn

Shout It Out! 1976 Koala KST-5004 Producers: Glen Scott, Doug Gibbs & Ralph Johnson

Earth, Wind & Fire's Ralph Johnson was heavily involved in the creation of the one album by the Donny Hathaway influenced Bobby Glenn, which came and went without much impact in 1976. Not only did Johnson play, write, arrange and produce much of *Shout It Out!*, but he also cajoled fellow EWAF band members Philip Bailey, Al McKay and Larry Dunn into helping out as well.

It is all a little dull to my way of thinking, possibly because I have always been less moved than many by Donny Hathaway's music, and there is not a vocal passage, song or arrangement on here that compels me to listen to it a second or third time. Equally, there is nothing inept either and I can entirely see why someone would enjoy the album. The slower, longer cuts like "Sounds Like A Love Song" and "Put Yourself In My Place, Friend" are probably the ones that work best.

Garry Glenn

G. G. 1980 PPL 0201-2 Producers: J James Jarrett, Garry Glenn, Dave Pruitt & Robert Palmer

Feels Good To Feel Good 1987 Motown 6234ML Producer: Garry Glenn

Detroiter Gary Glenn (who died in 1991, at only 36) was a quietly successful songwriter providing material for the likes of The Dramatics and Phyllis Hyman from the mid-seventies onwards and his first LP contained a further eight of his own compositions.

It's accomplished and enjoyable, sympathetically arranged and produced, and nearly all mid-tempo, apart from the unremarkable dance side "Don't Stop The Music". "I Need You In My Life" was released as a single by PPL, but while being a perfectly acceptable album track, didn't have the spark required to become a hit. Glenn wasn't an especially distinctive singer, and a ballad or two would have been nice, but the album should be played in its entirety to be best enjoyed; it's not one to really dip into as no track stands out above any other.

His singing seemed much more confident and assured on his follow-up set and his performances throughout didn't sound like the same man from *G.G.* (Maybe his co-write of the previous year of Anita Baker's "Caught Up In The Rapture" had increased his self-esteem.) His duet with Sheila Hutchinson on the title track and "Do You Have To Go" were both pulled as singles, each making it to #37 on the soul charts. The most striking aspect of the album given its 1987 release date is its lack of programming, with only two and three cuts dipping their toes in electronic waters, and drummer John Bradley is well employed throughout. The album is similar to the debut as regards pacing and lack of anything standing out but it's a second good effort.

Godmoma

Cynthia Girty; Arnenita Walker; Carolyn Miles

Here 1981 Elektra 5E-552 Producer: Bootsy Collins

Cynthia & The Imaginations put out a handful of gorgeous records in the sixties on the Magic City and Blue Rock labels with Cynthia Girty's lovely lead voice supplying the right sort of pathos. It is hard to believe (and I suspect few realise) that she was the same person singing on the Godmoma LP, which was a fairly minor effort in the P-Funk canon, so radically different is the music, and I certainly know which sides I prefer. Two singles were pulled from the album, but did not sell strongly. Godmoma then dissolved, but Walker and Girty continued to add backing vocals on other projects from time to time.

Goodie

Call Me Goodie 1982 Total Experience TE -1- 3002 Producer: Lonnie Simmons and Jonah Ellis

I Wanna Be Your Man 1985 Total Experience TEL-8-5706 Producer: Cavin Yarborough, Robert Whitfield, Jonah Ellis and Oliver Scott

"Goodie" was the nickname of Robert Whitfield, and he put out an underrated and enjoyable LP in 1982 which was not as saturated with Gap Band influences as might have been supposed. Goodie sported a look on the front cover that suggested he may have been a moonlighting Coconut from Kid Creole's band but he had a good sense of soul's history and the unpromisingly titled "Puddin' Pie" has a really pleasing throwback arrangement. He also sings well on the nicely flowing yet restrained "You And I"

which reached #30 on the soul charts, 16 places lower than the dance item, "Do Something", which I don't much care for, preferring the more tuneful "Does Anyone Know Where The Party Is" and the thoughtfully arranged "L.A."

The second LP was fairly anodyne with only "I'll Scratch Your Back" falling into the "terrible" category. "Special Lady" was the best track and a good way to open an LP, while "Because Of You" was issued as a 45 to some acclaim at #67 on the soul charts. The album is slightly less heavy-handed than so many others from 1985 but on occasion Whitfield's voice seems a bit too low in the mix. It is yet another set, though, that sixties soul fans can ignore.

He had released a single in 1978 under his real name but seems to have never recorded anything after the two LPs - apart from possibly helping out on some hip-hop records in the nineties.

Cuba Gooding (see also Main Ingredient)

The 1st Cuba Gooding Album 1978 Motown M7-897R1 Producers: Dennis Lambert & Brian Potter

Love Dancer 1979 Motown M7-919R1 Michael L Smith

Cuba Gooding is a gifted and distinctive singer who recorded a number of excellent records as a lead singer of Main Ingredient but his first solo LP was a disappointing affair. It wasn't poor, but lacked songs of real quality and it must have been a tough choice for Motown to pull a single for release as no track was noticeably stronger than any other. They went with "Mind Pleaser". It reached #91 on the soul charts. "Ain't Nothin' To It" makes cheeky reference to the Main Ingredient's "Just Don't Want To Be Lonely" in the spoken intro, but the whole album - mainly mid-tempo in speed and fairly lush in sound - never provides any sense that Motown were committed to the project or that Lambert and Potter were serving up their best work.

Mind you, the debut contained nothing as weak as "Disco Royale" "Hey! The Party's In Here" and "Dance Floor Lover", all of which were located on the rather wretched *Love Dancer* album. He does sing impressively on "Tell Me How Long It's Been" (the best thing on the LP) and "How Long"(too MOR for my tastes) but Motown didn't even bother to go with a 45 this time around.

Gooding made a few more singles throughout the eighties but only one (a markedly inferior remake of "Happiness Is Around The Bend", one of Main Ingredient's best known songs) landed on the soul charts (#43) and he hasn't appeared to do much in the music industry over the last twenty five years or so. If he is known for anything these days it is because of a number of alleged misdeeds and as father to the well-known actor.

Benny Gordon & The Soul Brothers

Tighten Up 1968 Hot Biscuit ST 9100 Producer: Bob Finez

What Is Soul? 1969 RCA LSP-4063 No producer listed

For someone who managed to release around fifteen singles and two albums Benny Gordon has remained awfully obscure; and it's anyone's guess who comprised the Soul Brothers, but assuming the drawing on the front cover of the first album is in any way accurate there might have been five Brothers plus Benny. Just about the only information I have been able to glean is that Gordon came from South Carolina and recorded most of his music in New York (including a stirring version of "Gonna Give Her All The Love I've Got" on Wand).

The first LP came out in 1968 (I think, but information is scant) containing four Gordon originals and eight covers. It's very much a "Soul Brothers album" rather than a "Benny Gordon album" given that everything (apart from the dance exhortations on a good version of "Tighten Up", easily the best thing on show) is instrumental and the album palls pretty quickly. Most of it sounds like the sort of reasonably funky music that was played in the background of films of the late sixties and I know that will actually therefore be of great appeal to some, but others will wish to avoid this.

One label that did persist with Gordon and his group was RCA for whom they recorded four 45s, and all eight sides of these singles are included on an LP, which featured a picture of an unknown woman on its front and no information whatsoever on its back (such as who produced it - in fact Gordon himself and Paul Robinson) and the overall cavalier approach to the album begs the question as to why it was released in the first place. The record has always been scarce (and I used to think it might have only come out in Canada, but I'm not sure about this) and is lacking in anything that would help a listener get to grips with what Gordon had to offer or, indeed, what he looked like. Most of the songs are covers rendered in a pretty straightforward manner as with the title track and "I Can't Turn You Loose" and if "Midnight Hour" allows Gordon an element of improvisation, it is not much. He attempts a "deep soul" feel on "I'm In Love With A Woman" but doesn't quite have the vocal stature to pull it off ; "Greyhound Blues" may have been credited to Gordon but it sounds pretty much like "Since I Met You Baby" to me while "Up And Down" has a slight West Indian lilt.

Gotham Flasher

Gotham Flasher 1979 Keylock K2501 Producers: Peter Alves & Gino Soccio

This frankly rather awful disco LP is in the book for one reason only: the great soul man George Jackson sings on the best track (although the competition is pitiful) " I'm Never Gonna Leave You", and given he never had an LP released, it's the only way I can ensure he is at least included. He might even provide vocals on one of the three other cuts but as I can't listen to them for more than a few seconds I'm not sure. "Gotham Flasher" was clearly a made-up name for what is a one-off session and if there are worse versions of "Try A Little Tenderness" and "I Can't Turn You Loose" out there, I've not heard them. The great Muscle Shoals rhythm section provides the music and it must rate among the most peculiar records on which they ever played.

James Govan

I'm In Need 1987 Charly CRB 1162 Producer: David Johnson

1987 was a pretty bleak year for fans of "southern soul", which was not surprising as the genre's peak had long since been passed. The emergence, therefore, of an album from Mississippi-born James Govan, a man who had released two singles on Fame in the "golden age" as well as an excellent one in 1984 was a great tonic to those of us who thirsted after such music. Even better was the fact that the '84 release, "Uphill Climb", was included and the whole LP, which boasted session players of the prowess of Roger Hawkins, David Hood, Jimmy Johnson, Clayton Ivey and many more, was close to being a glorious one.

David Johnson originally cut the sides on the LP in 1982 but was hardly swamped with offers to release them, which was the main reason for the five year wait before *I'm In Need* eventually appeared and then only in England, a country that still had enough of a fan base for this sort of bedrock soul sound to make a release just about practicable. I loved the album when it came out, and still like it a great deal now, even if it must be admitted that southern soul created in 1982 was never going to be quite so good as southern soul from 1972. It's not a set for singling out individual tracks - I like them all - but the songs were intelligently chosen and Govan is an accomplished singer, even if I think he sounds less like Otis Redding than other good judges have suggested.

He was still singing live on Beale Street in Memphis in 2015, but I don't believe his repertoire includes any of the ten tracks on *I'm In Need*.

GQ

Emmanuel Rahiem LeBlanc; Sabu Crier; Herb Lane; Kenny Banks; Paul Service

Soul On Your Side ** (as The Rhythm Makers) 1976 Vigor VI 7002 Producers: Billy Terrell & The Rhythm Makers

The Rhythm Makers should be applauded for one thing straight away: they were on the Vigor label (a subsidiary of De-Lite) and were a funk band who DIDN'T sound like Kool & The Gang on their groovy debut LP in 1976, when it might well have been supposed that they would do. "Zone", one of a handful of instrumental cuts on the album, is the track for which they were best known and it holds up well today, even if it only managed to make it to #92 as a single on the soul charts. Personally, I prefer the excellent "socially conscious" title track and the sweet "You're My Last Girl" as it contained the seeds of how they would re-invent themselves three years later.

Disco Nights 1979 Arista AB 4225 Producers: Jimmy Simpson & Beau Ray Fleming (Billboard soul charts: 2 ; Billboard pop charts: 13)

Two 1980 Arista AL 9511 Producer: Jimmy Simpson (Billboard soul charts: 9 ; Billboard pop charts: 46)

Face To Face 1981 Arista AL 9547 Producers: Jimmy Simpson & GQ (Billboard soul charts: 18 ; Billboard pop charts: 140)

That re-invention was pretty spectacular. Vigor had gone out of business in the late seventies and the quartet (after replacing drummer Banks with Service) signed up with Arista, and changed their name to GQ (after the "Gentlemen's Quarterly" magazine) and their image to one drawn straight from the pages of that periodical.

And, immediately, they had a huge hit with "Disco Nights" (Rock Freak)" which climbed all the way to #1 soul as well as #12 pop in early 1979. As with many such cuts it has dated a little now, but still retains enough of a crisp punch to remind us why it became such a big favourite. The second success from the album, though, was more satisfying as the group chose to re-interpret the great record from the sixties by Billy Stewart, "I Do Love You", and were rewarded with another top five soul and top twenty pop hit. Their take could not match Stewart's original which was after all one of the most beautiful soul records ever cut, but GQ still sounded mighty fine for 1979. The soaring b-side, "Make My Dreams A Reality" was more than decent as well, and even though the album was heavily oriented towards the dance floor their vocal inventiveness and skill gave them an edge over most other funk bands of the time.

The follow-up, *Two*, wisely followed the path of the previous set including another worthy (but not as good as the original) Billy Stewart re-make in "Sitting In The Park" which, when it was released as a single, pointed up how difficult it was for dance/funk bands to retain the interest of the public at large as although it reached #9 soul it could only crawl to #101 pop. The second single, "Standing Ovation", was a poppy and peppy dance romp which made #12 soul. The whole set was bright, listenable and entertaining but the over-use of a synthesiser grates a little all these years later.

For the final GQ album the group dispensed with the Stewart songs as their choice of a customary sixties cover version and opted instead for Jay Wiggins' superb "Sad Girl" on which they acquitted themselves wonderfully well even if it only reached #39 soul. The first single from the set had been "Shake" which performed slightly better (#23) but it was a rather routine offering. Overall, the LP was a softer, less soulful outing than had been the case in the past, no doubt largely as a result of the fact that Kenny Nolan had been asked to provide three songs. Another cut, "You Put Some Love In My Life", even adopted a light reggae beat.

A couple of other 45s trickled out in the eighties and GQ continued to perform and release CDs for years to come but no more vinyl albums ever appeared.

Fredi Grace & Rhinstone

Fredi Grace; Ros Sweeper; Keith Rawls

Get On Your Mark 1982 RCA NFL1-8016 Producers: Ed Howard & Keith Rawls

Tight 1983 RCA MFL1-8505 Producers: Ed Howard & Keith Rawls

I know virtually nothing about this group other than they recorded these two albums and had a small hit with "Help...(Save This Frantic Heart Of Mine") in 1982. I like "Perfect Lover", a good song and vocal performance from the debut; every other track of theirs I have ever heard has been unappealing dance music.

Graham Central Station (see also Patryce Banks)

Larry Graham; Patryce Banks; Hershall Kennedy; Robert Sam; David Vega; Willie Sparks; Gaylord Birch; Gail Muldrow; Manuel Kellough; Tina Graham; Gemi Taylor

Graham Central Station 1974 Warner Brothers BS 2763 Producers: Larry Graham & Russ Titelman (Billboard soul charts: 20 ; Billboard pop charts: 48)

Release Yourself 1974 Warner Brothers BS 2814 Producers: Larry Graham & God (Billboard soul charts: 22 ; Billboard pop charts: 51)

Ain't No 'Bout A Doubt It 1975 Warner Brothers BS 2876 Producer: Larry Graham (Billboard soul charts: 4 ; Billboard pop charts: 22)

Mirror 1976 Warner Brothers BS 2937 Producer: Larry Graham (Billboard soul charts: 7 ; Billboard pop charts: 46)

Now Do U Wanta Dance 1977 Warner Brothers BS 3041 Producer: Larry Graham (Billboard soul charts: 12 ; Billboard pop charts: 67)

There aren't many bassists who have gone on to make decent careers as "front men" in soul music. In fact only three spring readily to mind: Bootsy Collins, Michael Henderson and Larry Graham. From Texas originally, Graham made his name as a member of Sly and Family Stone in the sixties and early seventies and is rightly considered as one of soul's finest and most innovative players. By 1972 Sly Stone's spectacular personal descent into drug-influenced paranoia and madness, and subsequent increase in underlying tensions within the Family Stone, compelled Graham to leave to form his own band. Originally and briefly called Hot Chocolate, they changed their name to Graham Central Station and had a fair amount of success for a few years. As one who believes that Sly and The Family Stone were one of the greatest groups in the history of popular music, I was always going to be particularly receptive to the music served up by Graham Central Station (henceforth "GCS") but that doesn't mean to say that I was entirely besotted with the first set. I really liked the way in which an acappella take on Frederick Knight's "I've Been Lonely For So Long" was contrasted with the manic intro to a cover of Al Green's "Ain't No Fun To Me" and the funky "Hair" carried on things in grand manner but, apart from the good single, "Can You Handle It?" (#9 soul, #49 pop), the rest of the tracks are OK but a little dull. Graham took most of the lead vocals with Patryce Banks taking over on "We Be's Gettin' Down" and "Why?". Not unreasonably, it sounded like a new band finding their feet.

Actually, I wasn't besotted with the second set, either, which, apart from the driving "Hey Mr. Writer" and a rather demented but entertaining take on "Feel The Need In Me" (#18 soul), has an absence of horns and an emphasis on Graham's bass and Hershall Kennedy's keyboards. This approach led to a pronounced drifting, trippy feeling throughout, and possibly suggested that the band were ahead of their time, but it doesn't make for exhilarating listening today. Graham rather waggishly gave God a co-production credit.

In 1975, after ditching God, the band suddenly hit big with "Your Love" which went to #1 soul and #38 pop. I submit that it is quite possibly the most neglected and forgotten #1 soul single of all time, as I have never heard it played on any radio station (or even mentioned) in the 40 years that have passed since. Which is a shame as although clearly heavily influenced by Sly's "Hot Fun In The Summertime" it is an excellent homage to early soul and doo-wop with Graham singing in a seldom-used falsetto well supported by Banks. It sounded nothing like previous GCS material whatsoever. Most of the rest of the *Ain't No 'Bout A Doubt It* album from whence it came did though, and "The Jam" and "It's Alright" were fearsomely driving funk tracks which both reached the soul top twenty as singles. Banks also covered Ann Peebles' "I Can't Stand The Rain"; good enough, but too long and lacking the gloomy atmosphere of the original. I also liked "It Ain't Nothing But A Warner Brothers Party", a slightly cheesy piece of marketing, as the Tower of Power horns were irresistible and all the players within GCS got to show off their considerable skills. "Ole Smokey" sounded like New Orleans jazz from the forties and sat well on what was the most playful set from the group to date. It was also their best.

Mirror was kicked off by "Entrow", which, as with all of their LPs, was an opening track designed to introduce the band and get listeners in the mood. A truncated version reached #21 in late summer of 1976 when released as a 45, whereas track two, "Love (Covers A Multitude Of Sin)" had previously been chosen as the first (rather ordinary) single from the album, and had climbed to #14 in the spring. Graham dusted off his falsetto for "I Got A Reason" and had surely listened to The Beatles' "Dear Prudence" before writing "Priscilla". I can't recall now if the title track caused any controversy at the time but it contained deeply religious and conservative lyrics which condemned homosexuality but frankly wasn't a good enough song to get very worked up about either way. "Save Me" and "Forever" were also straight religious songs; Graham had always made his beliefs fairly clear but here they got full rein. Each to his own, but I would rather he had worked harder on putting memorable tunes on what was a disappointing LP.

Things didn't get much better on *Now Do U Wanta Dance* either and the only track out of ten on the LP that I like without reservation is "Stomped, Beat Up And Whooped" which is another doo-wop pastiche in the manner of "Your Love". Graham chose two great songs to cover in "Love And Happiness" and "Lead Me On" but both suffer badly in comparison with the originals; "Last Train" sounds like any number of previous GCS cuts ; "Have Faith In Me" goes on for much too long and "Earthquake" would not have been out of place on an album by a heavy rock band. Budding and professional bass players probably lapped it up, as Graham remained an amazing player, and the title track reached #10 on the soul charts so GCS still had plenty of fans, but my affection was rapidly turning elsewhere.

My Radio Sure Sounds Good To Me 1978 Warner Brothers BSK 3175 Producers: Larry Graham & Benny Golson (Billboard soul charts: 18 ; Billboard pop charts: 105)

Star Walk 1979 Warner Brothers BS 3322 Producer: Larry Graham (Billboard soul charts: 44 ; Billboard pop charts: 136)

On the last two WB albums above the group changed their billing to "Larry Graham and Graham Central Station" on the former and to "Larry Graham with Graham Central Station" (with those last four words in very small letters indeed) on the latter. Frankly, I always wondered why it hadn't come sooner given Graham's dominance within the band.

The former album saw Benny Golson share producing duties with Graham and, while the music didn't sound startling different from the previous five sets, the odd change was on display: "Boogie Witcha Baby" bore definite elements of Bootsy Collins' music while "Is It Love?" had Gemi Taylor laying down guitar solos in the manner of Ernie Isley. The title track once again glanced back to the early sixties and the group were rewarded with a #18 soul hit in the summer of 1978 when it came out as a 45. All the other tracks are solid, and the set was probably stronger than the previous two, but it was still lacking in any genuine inspiration.

The commercial fortunes of GCs reached their lowest level with the release of *Star Walk*. The album performed more poorly then all the others and neither "(You're A) Foxy Lady" nor the title track could even breach the soul top 30 as singles. The former could not recover from its totally predictable lyrics while the latter employed Graham's falsetto on the most overtly "disco" track they had cut to date and interest waned well before its eight minutes were up. The most interesting thing about "Scream" was the fact that its spoken intro was delivered by sixties soul favourite Jamo Thomas as the song itself sounded awfully like Sly Stone's "Life And Death In G & A ". The best thing on the whole LP was Bobby Martin's string arranging on "Tonight" and that statement rather sums up what was another rather dispiriting outing.

Larry Graham

One In A Million You 1980 Warner Brothers BSK 3447 Producer: Larry Graham (Billboard soul charts: 2 ; Billboard pop charts: 26)

Just Be My Lady 1981 Warner Brothers BSK 3554 Producer: Larry Graham (Billboard soul charts: 8 ; Billboard pop charts: 46)

Sooner Or Later 1982 Warner Brothers BSK 3668 Producers: Larry Graham & George Duke (Billboard soul charts: 15 ; Billboard pop charts: 142)

Victory 1983 Warner Brothers 1-23878 Producers: Larry Graham & Charles Calello (Billboard soul charts: 52 ; Billboard pop charts: 173)

Fired Up 1985 Warner Brothers P-13129 Producers: Larry Graham, Eumir Deodato & Narada Michael Walden (Japan)

In 1980 the inevitable happened: Graham went solo. What could not have been foreseen, however, was that he would hit big right away with "One In A Million You" a song from the pen of the great Sam Dees; it went right to the top of the soul charts and even hit #9 pop and was a complete departure in sound with Graham's bass playing a subservient role to song, arrangement and vocal, the last of which saw Larry eschewing both his falsetto and his favoured dark brown tones in favour of a more neutral attack. It made perfect sense for WB to follow-up the big hit with another excellent song: the old Dreamlovers /Intruders number, "When We Get Married" (which I actually prefer to "Million") and it was great to hear such soulful quality - possibly Graham's best ever singing - stand out from so much dance material of the time and it did pretty well, too: #9 soul and #76 pop. "Stand Up And Shout About Love" was good as well, and interesting as I believe it is Graham singing all the vocal parts, showing off his impressive range. "There's Something About You Baby" was another good dance song that sounded nothing whatsoever like the funk outings of GCS and also drew huge benefits from Dees' help in writing it; despite its lasting five minutes Dees always knew how to maintain interest levels. Elsewhere, Graham once again decided to re-write "Hot Fun In The Summertime" with "I'm So Glad It's Summer Again" and I wonder how Sly felt about Larry's taking writer credits. The brief "Sunshine, Love And Music" was also a real departure and it sounds much like some of Richard Hawley's music thirty five years later. I will pass on the remaining three tracks, but overall, it was Graham's final vindication as a solo artist, both his most impressive work since leaving the Family Stone and by far his biggest financial success. It wasn't going to last for long, but he fully deserved it.

It is easy to understand the thinking behind the *Just Be My Lady* LP, but, as a mere listener, I was greatly underwhelmed with the outcome, and mourned the fact that Sam Dees had not been invited to provide any further songs. The title track owed more to Lionel Richie than to Dees and, although Graham's profile in the wake of "One In A Million" was sufficient to propel the single to #4 soul I found it to be dreadfully bland and soulless. Things didn't get much better on the rest of the album and even the one cover chosen, "Guess Who", is one of my least favourite songs. The only tracks that caught my ear positively were the best ballad on show, "Our Love Keeps Growing Strong", and the one cut on which Graham's bass playing was to the forefront, "Feels Like Love".

Despite my indifference, *Just Be My Lady* sold respectably, and it is therefore to the credit of Warners and Graham that they changed tack for *Sooner Or Later*. The ballads - Richiesque without exception - certainly did not change but a number of funkier efforts were attempted, two of which, the title track and "Don't Stop When You're Hot", reached the soul top thirty as singles. My preferred cut was the only one that sounded out of step with the others: "Hold Up Your Hand".

Sam Dees returned to co-write the uptempo "I'm Sick And Tired" on the *Victory* set and if it was not his greatest moment it was certainly, together with "I'd Rather Be Loving You", by far the best thing on show. "I Never Forgot Your Eyes", another schmaltzy ballad, got to #34 on the soul charts in mid 1983 while "Just Call My Name" sounded more like GCS than most of Graham's solo work. The rest of the set left me cold with some typical eighties pop-influenced things on show as well as Dees' own rather soppy ballad "You've Been" which showed that even the great man had his off days.

Graham had run his race by this time and his last vinyl album only came out in Japan. I have heard but two danceable tracks from *Fired Up* so can't add much comment but they did seem to be slightly above average when compared to most of the competition in 1985.

By the end of the eighties Aretha Franklin was singing duets with just about everyone and her turn with Graham came on "If You Need My Love Tonight", a dull song that only made #88 soul as a single. And that was pretty much it as regards Larry Graham releasing records until a new CD appeared in 2012. His records tended too often to be rather underwhelming, but his bass playing was inspirational.

Ralph Graham

Differently 1974 Sussex SRA 8033 Producers: Terry Woodford, Clayton Ivey & Jimmy Briggs

Wisdom 1976 RCA APL1-1918 Producer: Leon Pendarvis

Extensions 1977 RCA APL1- 2307 Producers: Ralph Graham & Neil Portnow

I should put out a warning here for anyone who doesn't like to stray too far from listening to "classic" soul music: Ralph Graham was certainly not a gospel-influenced soul singer. Although his own website chooses not to dwell much on his past, only noting that he began his singing career in Boston nightclubs at the age of 15, he had put out a handful of singles at the end of the sixties and early seventies one of which, "She Just Sits There", being keenly sought after today. While that side is ok (and has a better flip side), it can't compare in quality with, nor sounds anything like, his marvellous debut LP from 1974.

The early seventies saw a handful of soul performers work in the manner of Bill Withers which was almost an equivalent of the "singer/songwriter" genre made popular by the likes of James Taylor and Elton John and Graham's seventies' output should appeal to anyone who enjoys Withers. That first album even came out on Withers' label, Sussex, and was enhanced by the fact that it was all recorded down in Alabama, thus having a southern flavour

to season its appeal. Graham wrote all the songs, almost exclusively to do with love, and the lyrics were printed on an insert which was still a relatively unknown phenomenon on soul LPs in 1974. The title track was his masterpiece, and although it has already been recorded by a handful of others over the years I still believe it has the potential to be a worldwide hit to this day if recorded by a big name artist. I have played it to numerous friends in the last four decades and it has never once failed to elicit a great response. That excellent soul man, Bill Coday, also had the good sense to cover one of the best tracks on the LP, "I Don't Want To Play This Game", a wry tale of cheating love. Most of the songs were designed for listening rather than dancing but the impressive "Ain't No Need" has certainly had many people up "on the floor" over the years. The sleevenotes pointed out how everyone had worked long and hard to get things just right and for once this is not record label hyperbole, as it is a carefully conceived work to treasure.

There was only one problem with the Sussex LP: it sold modestly. Given this and the difficulties the label soon found itself in anyway, Graham needed to move on, and ended up on RCA, recording in New York with some of that city's finest session men. I must confess I immediately found *Wisdom* to be rather disappointing with only "Changes" sounding as if it would have fitted snugly onto *Differently*. The music was clearly of a high quality, and Graham's song writing topics were much wider than before, with philosophical musings on life taking over from "mere" love songs, but it wasn't really to my taste; it sounded as much like the sort of record James Taylor or Elton John could have made as it did like a soul offering. There is, of course, no reason why Graham should have been restricted to marching down the same path as everyone else and he should be applauded for being his own man but I instinctively preferred the Sussex album to this one and have done so for decades now.

It may be that Graham shared my reservations about *Wisdom* as *Extensions*, his final LP, was much better, returning to love songs and punchier and more accessible tunes. As ever he wrote everything, but also as ever, it did not sell strongly nor did it house any hit singles. "Changing Up My Life" and "What Am I To Do" could entice people onto the more discerning dance floors of the world, but they are not typical of the rest of the set which, as with all his work bears repeated listening and is best placed on the deck when one just wants to hear something different.

Graham retired from the music industry soon after this album appeared but returned with a new CD in 2003 and still sings live from time to time.

Rita Graham

Vibrations 1969 ? Tangerine TRCS-1507 Producer: Ray Charles

Rita & The Tiaras' "Gone With The Wind Is My Love" is one of the most exhilarating records ever made, with some of the coolest vocals, best drum rolls and heavenly "oohs" it has ever been my privilege to hear. Rita was Rita Graham and although she was not really a soul singer her great outing with the Tiaras means that her only vinyl album deserves a place in the book. "My Cup Runneth Over" is the one cut on the LP that would (and does) most obviously appeal to soul fans having had, like "Gone With The Wind", a big following on the UK "Northern Soul" scene, and the track is certainly the best thing on a set I cannot enjoy much. It's not bad music at all, it just is - "Cup Runneth Over" excepted - a straight jazz album.

Micki Grant

Lovin' Kind Of Woman 1973 Mercury SRM - 1- 683
Producer: Tony Camillo

Was actress, writer and composer Micki Grant really a soul singer? Possibly not. Is *Lovin' Kind Of Woman* a soul album? Just about, yes, but people who don't know it needn't rush to seek it out, even if I enjoy it more than a number of other LPs in this book. Grant wanders down the country-soul route, a road I enjoy travelling a great deal, and having the respected producer Tony Camillo on hand helps matters too as there are tracks on here that recall his work with Gladys Knight. Grant doesn't have the vocal capabilities of others who have sung in this style, such as Candi Staton or Bettye Swann, and even though the musicians are among the best, and include many who have played on scores of soul records, there is no overt "southern" feel here which is another reason to urge a bit of caution.

Carl Graves

Carl Graves 1976 A&M SP-3410 Producer: Spencer Proffer

Like his fellow Canadian Donny Gerrard, Carl Graves sang with Skylark, and, as had Gerrard, moved to LA to try and further his career in the record industry. It was a good move as he hit big with the utterly lovely sweet soul song "Baby Hang Up The Phone" (#18 soul, #50 pop) at the end of 1974. He followed this up with another highly appealing single, "The Next Best Thing", on which was printed the information that it was to be found on the *Carl Graves* album, catalogue number SP-3403. Sadly, no such album ever materialised, and when a *Carl Graves* album DID appear it bore the catalogue number SP-3410 and did not include "The Next Best Thing" (nor, sadly, "Baby Hang Up The Phone".)

It is not an especially distinguished set, consisting of a number of covers and a handful of original songs, with nothing coming up to the standards of the two earlier singles. Both of those had been written by Walter Pedroski and Pat McManus and they didn't have any new songs included on the LP, which didn't help. The best slow track on board was the Bee Gee's "Be Tender With My Love" while "My Whole World Ended " utilised a reggae rhythm which was at least different. A single that was pulled, "Heart Be Still", made it to #26 soul at the start of 1976 but, apart from another 45, "Sad Girl", in 1977 (not on the LP) no more records were ever released by Carl Graves.

R.B. Greaves

R.B. Greaves 1969 Atco SD 33-311 Producers: Ahmet Ertegun, Jackson Howe & Marlin Greene (Billboard soul charts: 24 ; Billboard pop charts: 85)

R.B. Greaves 1977 Bareback BB 3333 Producer: Stephen Metz & Helen Miller

R.B. Greaves was another rather mysterious singer who didn't attract much critical acclaim in a career which lasted from around 1965 (when he was based in England singing under the name of Sonny Childe) until 1980 when his last single under the name of R.B. Greaves was issued. He was born in Guyana as Ronald Bertram Aloysius Greaves so one can see why he shortened his name for recording purposes and was also, apparently, a nephew of Sam Cooke (although this fact isn't mentioned on either of his LP covers) and the relationship would seem to be clinched by the fact that his versions of "Cupid" and "Ain't That Good News" from his Atco album certainly betray strong vocal similarities between the two men.

The main reason, I suspect, that he rather slipped under the radar was that he was certainly not a "hard" soul singer at all, and his heyday - such as it was - came at a time, the late sixties, when "authenticity" was valued at a premium and Greaves' decidedly "pop" leanings made him appear somewhat lightweight. Tellingly, his huge hit "Take A Letter Maria" was a bigger hit (#2) on the pop charts than the soul ones (#10) in 1969. That hit, and its follow-up, a version of "There's Always Something There To Remind Me" (#50 soul and #27 pop - that pattern again) were absurdly catchy and memorable tunes, and both were included on his debut LP recorded in New York and Alabama. Articles and discussion on Muscle Shoals almost invariably omit what is a fine, and unjustly neglected, outing, including a couple of Greaves' songs "The Ballad of Leroy" and "Birmingham Alabama" which are both moving and mawkish at the same time. More impressive still is the rather startling "Home To Stay", presented and sung as if by Otis Redding while lying dead in his coffin.

After "There's Always Something There To Remind Me "slipped off the charts in early 1970 Greaves issued a further eight singles, but none charted and none were included on any LPs. He had to wait until 1977 when "Margie, Who's Watching The Baby" (a song he had previously cut back in 1972) became his third and final single to hit the *Billboard* soul charts (#66) as well as being the lead-off cut on his second LP. Greaves wrote all the ten tracks this time around, and stripped of the southern tones of its predecessor, it is much less satisfying and completely pop-oriented. Nevertheless, it was good to hear a singer prepared to be guided by the beat of his personal drum, and not be swayed by the disco sound that was so prevalent at the time. The album did not do well at all in the marketplace and was - rather surprisingly - subsequently re-issued with a new title, *Rock And Roll*, on Metromedia 5032.

He died in October 2012, a forgotten man - a fact made more apparent by the fact that no CDs on him seem to exist - but history should well note his Atco set.

Al Green

Back Up Train 1967 Hot Line Music Journal HL-1500 Producers: Palmer James & Curtis Rogers (Billboard soul charts: 37 ; Billboard pop charts: 162)

Green Is Blues 1969 Hi SHL 32055 Producer: Willie Mitchell (Billboard soul charts: 3 ; Billboard pop charts: 19)

Gets Next To You 1971 Hi SHL 32062 Producer: Willie Mitchell (Billboard soul charts: 15 ; Billboard pop charts: 58)

Gets Next To You 1971 London SHU 8424 (UK)

It's easy to forget now, given his worldwide fame, that Al Green had to struggle like virtually everyone else to make it in the music business, and that his earliest solo sides were issued when he was still calling himself Al Greene and he was not being produced by Willie Mitchell. And even before he went solo he had been a member of a vocal group called The Creations (and there is plenty of dispute as to whether or not this was the same Creations who recorded for the Zodiac label, but that's another story). What is not in dispute, though, is that the man from Forrest City, Arkansas was one of the most successful solo soul singers of all time.

He enjoyed his first hit right at the end of 1967, when "Back Up Train" by Al Greene & The Soul Mate's (sic) reached #5 soul and #41 pop, and even though the two follow-up singles didn't repeat the success, he still got a chance to release his first LP (which also came out in the UK in 1969 with a slightly different cover). "Back Up Train" was a ponderous, dreamy number on which Green's voice was instantly recognisable as the one which would propel him to superstardom five or six years later and it still sounds good today, as indeed do all the slow songs on the LP. They were encased in some highly idiosyncratic but charming string arrangements but even at this early stage it was clear that Green was a man who was much more comfortable with down-tempo material; nearly all the faster cuts were pretty average. The sleevenotes try to convince us that his voice was influenced by James Brown and Sam Cooke, but apart from the odd moment when the ghost of Cooke shimmers in, I only hear Al Green. Thirteen tracks, and still the LP only lasted thirty minutes; those were the days. (Please note that the chart placings for this album relate to its reissue in 1972 (on Bell 6079 and without "Lover's Hideaway" and "What's It All About".)

Hot Line Music Journal was not big enough to satisfy Green's ambitions, nor stable enough to survive, and Green made the move to Memphis to hook up with Willie Mitchell, who would make the young singer into a superstar. But it didn't happen straight away, not least because of a bizarre choice of song for Green's first single: The Beatles' "I Want To Hold Your Hand". Not only did it deservedly "stiff" as a 45, it wasn't even included on his first Hi album, *Green Is Blues,* decidedly a mixed bag. It's also instructive to be reminded that Green's early music on Hi was nowhere near as "soft" as it was to become in later years and no strings were utilised on a set on which Green mistakenly attempted a second Fab Four song, "Get Back", as well as some rather ordinary original material. What made the LP have some value were three tracks on side one, all covers. "I Stand Accused" is not the best version ever recorded, but does boast a splendid horn arrangement while "One Woman" and "The Letter" were seductive and heartfelt. (Again, the chart positions relate to when the album was re-issued in 1972. It did not chart on its first release in 1969.)

Everything came together on the third album, *Al Green Gets Next To You*, which had a brilliant first side and a merely excellent second one. This was by far the toughest music Green had ever recorded - or ever was to record - and "I Can't Get Next To You", "Are You Lonely For Me Baby", "God Is Standing By" and "Tired Of Being Alone" is just about as perfect a sequence of four tracks on any soul album, ever. Green also wrote five songs with two of them being put out as singles and each doing fairly well: "You Say It" (#28 soul) and "Right Now, Right Now" (#23). However, these were eclipsed by "I Can't Get Next To You" which went to #11 (and 60 pop). "Driving Wheel" became the fourth single from the album to reach the soul charts (#46) before "Tired Of Being Alone" smashed all resistance and hit #7 soul and #11 pop in the summer of 1971. As good as all these were, I also love a forgotten track from the album, "All Because", which despite being a decidedly average song, has punishing horns and exhilarating sections where Green just accelerates away, and no-one can catch him.

The UK LP from 1971, also entitled *Gets Next To You*, comprises all the ten tracks from the U.S. release as well as four from *Green Is Blues*.

Let's Stay Together 1972 Hi SHL 32070 Producer: Willie Mitchell (Billboard soul charts: 1 ; Billboard pop charts: 8)

I'm Still In Love With You 1972 Hi XSHL 32074 Producers: Willie Mitchell & Al Green (Billboard soul charts: 1 ; Billboard pop charts: 4)

Call Me 1973 Hi XSHL 32077 Producers: Willie Mitchell & Al Green (Billboard soul charts: 1 ; Billboard pop charts: 10)

Livin' For You 1973 Hi ASHL 32082 Producers: Willie Mitchell & Al Green (Billboard soul charts: 1 ; Billboard pop charts: 24)

Explores Your Mind 1974 Hi SHL 32087 Producers: Willie Mitchell & Al Green (Billboard soul charts: 1 ; Billboard pop charts: 15)

Greatest Hits 1975 Hi SHL 32089 (Billboard soul charts: 3 ; Billboard pop charts: 17)

Is Love 1975 Hi SHL 32092 Producers: Willie Mitchell & Al Green (Billboard soul charts: 1 ; Billboard pop charts: 28)

From here on in, it was all strictly big-time for the next four years: excluding the *Greatest Hits* album, which also did remarkably well, his next six albums each went to #1 soul and top thirty pop. The first of these was his weakest, though. *Let's Stay Together* has a title track everyone knows and which I have long since tired of, but it also lacked strong material, and of the seven Green originals the only two I like unreservedly are the tough "It Ain't No Fun To Me" with typically great playing from the Hi musicians, and "So You're Leaving" with marvellous drumming by Howard Grimes. I suspect Mitchell and Green realised this lack too, as "Let's Stay Together" was the only track pulled as a single, reaching #1 on both soul and pop charts.

Things were rectified with *I'm Still In Love With You,* another magnificent set, on which the "Al Green sound" all finally came together, matching up velvet with punch, and it includes some of his greatest ever moments: the title track and "Look What You've Done For Me" were huge hits as singles, while "Love And Happiness" must rank as the "most obvious hit in history not to be put out on a 45". "Simply Beautiful" had his most seductive singing to date, as if he were whispering in your ear, and if I am indifferent to his version of "Oh Pretty Woman" I wouldn't want to be without "For The Good Times". By the way, Grimes' and Al Jackson's drumming on this set (listen to "I'm Glad You're Mine" for instance) is worth a damn sight more than any drum machine ever created and the cover is one of the most striking in soul's history. Green's appeal was as much about his looks as his music and Mitchell was not about to miss this fact.

Amazingly, Green nearly matched the quality of *I'm Still In Love With You* with *Call Me* and the title track, "You Ought To Be With Me" and "Here I Am (Come And Take Me)" went to #2, #1 and #2 respectively as singles on the soul charts as well as all making the pop top ten although round about this time "it all sounds the same" jibes were starting to appear and in fact, Green's pop appeal had peaked with only one more top ten hit single left to come. He continued to select covers judiciously as "I'm So Lonesome I Could Cry" and "Funny How Time Slips Away" were particularly well-suited to soul treatments and rather forgotten album cuts like "Stand Up" and "Your Love Is Like The Morning Sun" still sound good today.

The quality definitely DID slip considerably on *Livin' For You* where even I could see that he was starting to coast on past glories and the title track itself, despite becoming yet another #1 soul single, was surely his weakest for a while. The well-known cover this time around was uninspired too: "Unchained Melody", a seriously dull song, while "Home Again", "So Good To Be Here" and "Free At Last" all sounded rather tired and predictable. Where *Livin' With You* did do well, was - unusually for Green - on its faster songs such as "Sweet Sixteen" and, best of all, "Let's Get Married" (#3 soul), one of my favourite of all his singles with a superb bridge. Also, "Beware" - an eight minute track which might have been conceived in the face of the "samey" criticisms. Not that it was especially different, it was just that Green had not stretched out quite like this before and it was a pleasure to listen to Grimes and Leroy and Teenie Hodges doing their enthralling thing.

Green was not through with making great albums though, and *Explores Your Mind* was a triumphant return to form and an almost unalloyed success, with only "School Days" being somewhat below par. The whole set was notable for the re-appearance of crisp, tuneful, memorable songs and that compositions of the calibre of "Hangin' On" (with some lovely strings touches), "I'm Hooked On You" and "Stay With Me Forever" were not even released as singles is proof of the quality of the album. Oddly, only one single *was* issued, "Sha La La (Make Me Happy)", which was classic Green and became his last ever pop ten hit at #7. The obvious follow-up single would have been the great "Take Me To The River", one of Green's best and most famous songs, but I can only assume that Mitchell figured if people wanted it badly enough they would have to buy the album, and certainly the LP was a big seller. But Green's loss was Syl Johnson's gain as he recorded the song in early 1975 and was rewarded with the biggest hit of his entire long career. Similarly, but at a much more modest level, Charles Brimmer cut and released another album track, "God Blessed Our Love", and enjoyed the biggest hit of *his* career too.

In October of 1974, the horrible grits incident occurred, which clearly had a traumatic effect on Green; enough, indeed, to be a major factor in his deciding to give up recording secular music for a number of years. Such a decision was still a while away but the episode must have had an impact on his output which now went into undeniable decline; in the meantime, a *Greatest Hits* set was wisely put out and although "How Can You Mend A Broken Heart" shouldn't have even been on there as it wasn't a single, it was hard to argue with a ten track LP that contained seven records that had reached the top 3 of the soul charts, including three #1's.

Al Green Is Love was another above average effort, if not quite re-capturing the magic of *Explores Your Mind*. " L.O.V.E. (Love)" was another irresistible #1 soul hit although the follow-up, "Oh Me, Oh My (Dreams In My Arms)" was one of his weakest singles for ages, not surprisingly becoming his poorest selling single (but still #7 soul) in four years. There were a number of excellent album only cuts too: "The Love Sermon" and "I Didn't Know" were two of Green's sleekest and slinkiest efforts, both drawn out meditations on which he was not going to be hurried; "Rhymes" was robust and fun while "The Love Ritual" was a rhythmic workout of a kind Green or Mitchell had not permitted before.

Full Of Fire 1976 Hi SHL 32097 Producers: Willie Mitchell & Al Green (Billboard soul charts: 12 ; Billboard pop charts: 59)

Have A Good Time 1976 Hi SHL 32103 Producers: Willie Mitchell & Al Green (Billboard soul charts: 12 ; Billboard pop charts: 93)

Greatest Hits Volume II Hi SHL 32105 (Billboard soul charts: 33 ; Billboard pop charts: 134)

Sailing With Soul 1974 Navy Recruiting Command 73263 (not released commercially)

Full Of Fire was the first album to be recorded after he recovered from the grits incident and also the first of his undoubted commercial decline. It started off tellingly with "Glory Glory" where he was singing to his God rather than to his woman and the lyrically ambiguous "That's The Way It Is" might well have been directed heavenwards, too. The rest of the album, "Full Of Fire", yet another #1 soul hit, and "Soon As I Get Home" more or less a straight gospel song, excepted, was pretty much standard Green fare and although I like it well enough, I can easily understand why others may find it unengaging and certainly a number of songs did sound interchangeable with much of what had gone before. The general public at large certainly took this view as the follow-up single, "Let It Shine", couldn't even reach the top 100 pop (and only managed #16 soul) and the album itself performed more modestly than Green and Mitchell were accustomed to.

Have A Good Time bore a front cover on which Green was scratching his head while looking a bit bemused as if to say, "here's more of the same and I know my day has passed". I like this album a fair bit too, and think it has some of his more tuneful songs from the mid - seventies but although "Keep Me Cryin'" did pretty well as a 45 (#4 soul and # 37 pop) , "I Tried To Tell Myself" sold very poorly indeed by Green's standards hitting a mere #27 on the soul charts.

A further sign of how far Green had fallen was apparent when a nine track second volume of *Greatest Hits* came out and four of the songs hadn't even been issued as singles.

The Belle Album 1977 Hi HLP 6004 Producer: Al Green (Billboard soul charts: 29 ; Billboard pop charts: 103)

Truth N' Time 1978 Hi HLP 6009 Producer: Al Green (Billboard soul charts: 44)

Tokyo...Live 1978 Hi HLP 6012 Producer: Kaname Tajima

In 1977 Green decided to work without Mitchell and the Hi rhythm section and horns for the first time since signing with the label. It worked in as much as it was mostly a pleasure to listen to (apart from the thin and intrusive synthesisers) but it did not restore Green to his previous commercial heights, although the title track did well as a single on the soul charts (#9). I'm not sure he especially cared, as much of the album still showed how pre-occupied he was with spiritual matters. It is neither my favourite nor my least admired Green LP but I certainly respected how he only made the odd sop to the disco audience (as with the disappointing "I Feel Good" and the occasional popping bass notes here and there) and it showed once again that he was a highly talented (and underrated) songwriter.

Truth N' Time was much more problematic, being undoubtedly the least impressive Hi album Green ever issued, clocking in at only about 26 minutes."To Sir With Love" and "I Say A Little Prayer" were not inspired song choices for Green to cover (although I can understand why their titles would have appealed to him), particularly as his take on the latter was almost embarrassingly inferior to Aretha's. The surprisingly funky "Wait Here" and "Blow Me Down" are the only tracks worth persevering with. The LP did not sell well, and neither did the singles pulled from it, and when a *Live* set from Tokyo also failed to attract much interest, Green finally decided that he would withdraw from making secular music.

The Lord Will Make A Way 1980 Myrrh MSB-6661 Producer: Al Green

Higher Plane 1981 Myrrh MSB-6674 Producer: Al Green (Billboard soul charts: 62)

Precious Lord 1982 Myrrh MSB-6702 Producer: Al Green

I'll Rise Again 1983 Myrrh MSB-6747 Producer: Al Green

White Christmas 1983 Myrrh SPCN 7-01-678006-6 Producer: Moses Dillard

Trust in God 1984 Myrrh SPCN 7-01-678306-5 Producer: Pail Zaleski

Green's gospel career started in 1980 and he steadily released albums throughout the decade. Although some of the songs he chose on the early Myrrh sets were sometimes rather obvious, "Amazing Grace", "Battle Hymn Of The Republic", "Precious Lord" and "Rock Of Ages" being examples, they were much more extravagant musically than most eighties gospel which was more often than not stripped down and basic. However, only the odd track really caught my ear such as the impressively arranged title track from *Higher Plane* and his super duets with Laura Lee and Margie Joseph on "People Get Ready" from the same album. He switched tack a little on the *Trust In God* LP, where he covered three famous soul songs, "Lean On Me", "Ain't No Mountain High Enough" and "Up The Ladder To The Roof" but I will stick with the originals, thanks.

Going Away 1985 A&M 395102-1 Producer: Willie Mitchell

Soul Survivor 1987 A&M SP 5150 Producers: Paul Zaleski & Errol Thomas (Billboard soul charts: 25 ; Billboard pop charts: 131)

I Get Joy 1989 A&M SP 5228 Producers: Al Green, Paul Zaleski, Eban Kelly & Jimi Randolph (Billboard soul charts: 60)

Really good news came in 1985 when Green re-united with Willie Mitchell (and the Hodges brothers) for the *Going Away* LP. It was still a gospel album, but anyone who enjoyed his seventies work could enjoy this one painlessly, and in fact I think it was one of the best LPs of the entire decade and it still sounds excellent today. Superbly produced throughout, it also featured nearly all new songs rather than rather tired staples, and Green's ability with melody did not desert him here. The only surprise was that it didn't chart in the U.S. in the same way some of his other gospel LPs did.

Such as the highly disappointing *Soul Survivor* for example, which surprisingly attained the highest position of any Al Green LP on the soul charts since *Have A Good Time* in 1976. It once again included well-known covers that had a spiritual bent, such as "You've Got A Friend" where Green's extended workout couldn't match earlier versions by Donny Hathaway and Carole King, and "He Ain't Heavy, He's My Brother", a song I do not care for. The title track and "Everything's Gonna Be Alright" (a pretty big hit as a single at #22 soul) sadly went the "electronic" route for the first time on a Green LP, but more disturbing than all the above was the fact that Green was not at his best vocally for some reason, sounding thinner and more nasal than he had in the past.

The *I Get Joy* LP did little for me but I should make note that one track, "As Long As We're Together", made it to #15 soul in the summer of 1989, the first time an Al Green single had lodged in the top 20 of that chart since "Belle" twelve years earlier.

Green wasn't to release any more vinyl albums but carried on recording for years to come and returned to recording secular music in the late eighties and early nineties, before enjoying another - once again very good - re-union with Willie Mitchell on the *I Can't Stop* CD in 2003.

There are those who contend that there were numerous soul singers better than Green, and on the Hi label alone, Otis Clay and Syl Johnson could certainly be considered as such, and I can see the merit of these claims, but Green had one magical thing going for him, that hardly anyone else has ever managed: he was a huge star, and a huge star who released great music. James Brown did it; Aretha did it; Marvin Gaye did it; The Temptations and Four Tops did it too, as well as a handful of others, but it is a devilishly difficult act to pull off.

Garland Green

Jealous Kind Of Fella 1969 Uni 73073 Producer: Joshie Jo Armstead

Love Is What We Came Here For 1977 RCA APL1-2351 Producer: Leon Haywood

Garland Green 1983 Ocean Front OF 100 Producer: Arleen Schesel

Garland Green 1990 Love LA Music Co. LLA 101 Producers: Garland Green, Arleen Green & Abe White

The Spring Sides 1990 Kent 097 Producers: Brad Shapiro & Raeford Gerald (UK)

Garland Green, Mississippi born and Chicago based for much of his life, is one of many artists in this book who means a great deal to soul fans, and virtually nothing to the music buying public at large. His recording career had its ups and downs in both quality and success but his finest sides stand up exceedingly well with the best work of his contemporaries.

In fact, it was never really to get as good again as how it started. His first three 45s were all of a notably high quality but they didn't do much other than sell fairly well in Chicago. However, his fourth release, "Jealous Kind Of Fella", was magnificent, a fact so clearly apparent that it reached #5 soul and #20 pop, lofty positions that he was never to come close to matching again in his entire career. His deep, earthy voice pleaded utterly convincingly, even breaking a couple of times, and came wrapped up in a compelling arrangement. The single's success resulted in an album of the same name, and the good news was heightened by the fact that all the a and b- sides from the three earlier singles were included on the set. On the majority of the songs he came across as a love-whipped man, but the controversial "Don't Think That I'm A Violent Guy" (which reached #42 soul as a single) showed that he could only be pushed so far. "Love Now, Pay Later" was the only track on an utterly convincing LP that fell below the standards of pretty spectacular (as well as being the only track that didn't appear as an a or b- side on a 45) and credit must go to Joshie Jo Armstead as producer, and it's a shame to be reminded that she never got to release an album in her own name.

In 1971 Green moved to the Cotillion label, where he recorded five singles with one of them, "Plain And Simple Girl", becoming the second biggest hit he ever enjoyed (#17 soul). Sadly, no album ever appeared on the label and nor did one appear on Spring (or at least at the time) either, which was even more surprising seeing that four of the five 45s he cut for them reached the soul charts. In 1990, however, the UK Kent label released a fine album on which not only were all the singles scooped up, but three unreleased sides were included too, including a gripping "Just What The Doctor Ordered". The LP mixed up fast and slow songs, including among the latter a take on the great Jerry Williams, Gary Bonds and Charlie Whitehead song, "He Didn't Know (He Kept On Talkin')" but it falls well short of Dee Dee Warwick's version. "Bumpin' And Stompin' did pretty well for him as a dance floor oriented single (#72 soul nationally, but apparently much more popular in Chicago) but is a tad heavy handed, and another uptempo 45, "Let The Good Times Roll", is a better side. I'm extremely happy this album exists but it can't match the quality of his Uni records.

However, in 1976, and years before the Kent album emerged, Green needed to find a new label after his time with Spring came to an end. One single, "I.O.U", a cover of a country song which one might love or hate given its rather mawkish subject matter came out on the small Casino label, before he pitched up for a short stay on RCA. A single, "Don't Let Love Walk Out On Us", became a tiny soul hit (#93) in 1977, but rather oddly was not included on his one LP for the label. I have always seen it as a fairly good rather than inspired set, which never really recovered from its mundane opening track, "Shake Your Shaker", although I am well aware that others rate it highly. Most of the other cuts are pitched at a brisk mid-tempo and my rather lukewarm response to the LP is shaped by the lack of a truly top-class slow cut (although "I Know What Love Is" and the title track do come close) and the fact that some of the midtempo tracks sound somewhat similar. On the other hand, it certainly was not a "disco" set at all, for which much thanks.

After two further singles from the RCA label rather flopped, Green left the label and had to wait until 1983 for his next LP to appear which was very much a "Garland Green Sings Lamont Dozier" affair, given that the great Detroit writer penned six of the eight songs within. It has not been a set that has attracted much critical acclaim with the word "cheap" appearing more than once in other reviews, which I feel is a bit unfair, unless that is a comment on the front cover which must have taken about thirty seconds to design. It is nowhere near as good as the *Jealous Kind Of Fella* platter but it does have its moments. One being the fact that Green managed to get his version of "Trying To Hold On To My Woman" onto the soul charts at #63 in the latter part of 1983, even if that was 59 places lower than Dozier had managed himself ten years earlier. There are also serviceable enough versions of Zingara's "Love's Calling" and Mary Wells' "You Make Me Feel So Good Inside" but the main drawback of the album for me is that, as so often from 1980 onwards, the songs are too long. Nothing clocks in at shorter than four minutes and there is not much on here that would not have received benefit from a trim.

Green's last LP sneaked out in 1990 on such a tight budget that it didn't even have a proper cover, being encased instead in a plain white sleeve. Given such an obvious scarcity of financial resource, it would be unreasonable to be too harsh on the record, but the fact is that it was his least impressive collection to date and the aural evidence that his voice was not what it was twenty years earlier could not be gainsaid. It was also in large part, a gospel set, as the track "Gospel Rap" made clear but other songs such as "You Came Along" and "If You Stand Beside Me" were ambiguous - when one could hear the lyrics in the rather muddy mix - and could be aimed at either his saviour or his woman.

Nothing else was issued by Green for over twenty years but in 2012 he put out a new CD which was well received and would have jogged the memories of people about a man who recorded one of the finest soul LPs from Chicago in the sixties.

Cortez Greer

Live At Scarlet O'Hara's 1973? Garner JM-1970 Producer: Joe Messina

Cortez Greer was a rather unknown artist from Chattanooga (who sadly died in 1976 from an accident where he was overcome by carbon dioxide) responsible for a handful of singles, including the likeable "Very Strong On You" for the Violet label in 1972. His one LP was undated but I think it may have come out in 1973 given he sang Looking Glass' "Jimmy Loves Maryann", a hit in that year. It's an obscure record, not even providing writing credits, and I suspect would have received minimal and local release only. It's not even really a "soul" record, either, with Greer - obviously at home and confident in a "live" setting - surely seeing himself as an "all-round entertainer" and thus providing renditions of such unsoulful songs as "Sweet Caroline", Joy To The World" and "Exodus". (By the way, I also assume that producer Joe Messina is the same man as the guitarist who played in the Funk Brothers behind all those Motown hits.)

Dan Greer

Not With Words 1982 Praise BSR-PR-1281-101 Producer: Dan Greer

Holly Springs, Mississippi born Dan Greer was an important figure in Memphis soul music in the sixties and seventies, writing and producing for a number of acts over the years, most notably The Ovations, as well as putting out a number of singles in his own name. Unfortunately he did not get to ever release a soul LP and his one outing at 33⅓ was a straight gospel set. It's a hard record to listen to, simply because it is so off-centre that the music is distorted and discordant (and I know other - maybe all? - copies are the same). Others might be more tolerant of this blemish, and if they listen all the way through will hear some good things like "The Story Of My Life" and some rather less good ones such as "Bubbles" which is about a wayward hippopotamus.

Grey And Hanks

You Fooled Me 1978 RCA AFL1-3069 Producers: Len Ron Hanks & Zane Grey (Billboard soul charts: 20 ; Billboard pop charts: 97)

Prime Time 1980 AFL1- 3477 Producers: Len Ron Hanks & Zane Grey (Billboard soul charts: 60 ; Billboard pop: 195)

These excellent songwriters provided big hits for the likes of LTD ("Back In Love Again") and Tavares ("Never Had A Love Like This Before") and given that Grey was also an accomplished lead vocalist, we had a right to expect a lot from their debut LP. It never quite happened though, despite selling healthily and bearing a big soul hit in "Dancin'" (#5), as their best songs had been - and continued to be - sent elsewhere. "You Fooled Me" is far from being a poor record, and is better than many others from 1978, but I feel they had the talent to have done even better, and had they not aimed all eight songs at the dance floor, might well have achieved more. Footnote: it was good to see sixties cult hero Darrow Fletcher involved as associate producer and backing vocalist.

Prime Time was mostly more of the same and while it was still good to listen to Grey's husky lead vocals there was nothing on board to get excited about. "Now I'm Fine" reached #57 on the soul charts as a single, the title track didn't (it failed) and "For The People" was the best song lyrically on show.

After years of silence Grey released a new CD in 2014. I'm not sure what Hanks is doing.

Roosevelt Grier

Soul City 1964 RIC M 1008 Producer: Bobby Darin

Committed 1986 Word WR-8342 Producer: Dick Tunney

Roosevelt Grier was once a "household" name in America - just not as a singer. It was as a highly successful American football player that he was best known but his other skills included being a bodyguard for Bobby Kennedy, an actor and - unbelievably - writing a book on needlepoint, so he was quite the renaissance man.

A number of pro or ex-pro sportsmen have tried their hand at singing but surely none were as gifted as Grier and he released many excellent records including a fine Muscle Shoals' recorded version of Bobby Womack's "Oh How I Miss My Baby". But that was a few years after his one Soul LP was released, back in 1964.

Recovering from their initial surprise that Bobby Darin wanted to record an album on Grier (even though he - Grier - had already issued a couple of singles back in 1960), RIC pulled out all the stops, so to speak, and not only ensured that top-class musicians would back the football star, but also provided a "concept" album, no less, back at a time when no-one had really coined the phrase. All twelve of the tracks are songs of the big city, expressing the joys and sorrows of the people that inhabit it. This was both the strength and the weakness of the LP, in fact: a strength because these were uniformly excellent compositions; a weakness, because Grier could never realistically hope to match the better known versions by the likes of The Drifters. But, apart from the odd moment where his voice wasn't quite up to the task, he acquitted himself well and it wasn't for any mere novelty value that he went on to release a fair number of other singles right up to the mid-seventies.

In 1983 he became an ordained minister soon after which he released his second LP, a gospel set, which I must confess I haven't heard. By all accounts a lovely man, he has gone on to do great things with under-privileged children and deserves his brief footnote in the history of soul music.

Billy Griffin

Be With Me 1982 Columbia BL 37745 Producer: John Barnes

Respect 1983 Columbia BL 38924 Producer: John Barnes (Billboard soul charts: 63)

Systematic 1985 Columbia AL 39907 Producer: Leon Ware and Todd Cochran

Billy Griffin is best known for being the man who replaced Smokey Robinson in the Miracles, and while their best years were behind them at his time of joining, the group certainly still had some memorable moments in the best part of ten years that he was to remain with them. In 1982 he left to go solo and, rather unexpectedly, he was to arguably do better in the UK than in his native U.S. as he placed "Hold Me Tighter In The Rain" onto the top 20 over here as well as later going on to produce a successful British group, The Pasadenas. I rate him as a notably capable high tenor in the classic mould, but he never quite reached the heights of the great singers of that ilk, as his voice was never really distinctive enough to make it instantly recognisable.

Unfortunately, his three LPs under his own name sold only modestly, as did all the singles pulled from them, and he was never to enjoy a single sizeable hit in America as a solo artist. The first LP, *Be With Me*, is where the afore-mentioned "Hold Me Tighter" resides and I remain puzzled to this day why it failed in the U.S. as it was both entirely in vogue with the sounds of 1982 and had one of the biggest record companies in the world behind it. It was a good LP, too: "Second Day Love Story" and "Stones Throw From Heaven" were dreamy and compelling, while "Love Is Not A Word" was even better, and all three still sound good thirty years later. So many eighties soul ballads adopted the overblown and soulless "Disney" formula, and it was good to see that Griffin - a fine songwriter - could avoid this temptation. The mid-tempo and jazzy "Understand" also worked well, and only the dull and predictable "The Beat Is Getting Stronger" pulled down the overall quality. There was a little of Marvin Gaye at times in Griffin's phrasing, but my ears tell me that *Be With Me* is a better LP than Gaye's *Midnight Love* on the same label in the same year.

However, the fact had to be faced that *Be With Me* had not sold well and *Respect* thus turned up the dance floor emphasis with a number of numbingly predictable cuts on board, including the title track, and I only really enjoy "Serious" a flowing dance track of some flair and the slower "Don't Stop Loving Me".

One can sometimes tell a lot from a record's title: it's called marketing. An LP in 1985 entitled *Systematic* was rather inevitably going to be filled with electronic touches and have a heavy bias of tracks that people could dance to. Thus it proved. The one well-known outside song included on the LP, "If I Ever Lose This Heaven", was performed better by virtually everyone else who ever recorded it given that Griffin couldn't compete with the backing which overwhelmed his sensitive vocals.

He has continued to write and release new music every so often in the last thirty years.

Reggie Griffin (see also Manchild)

Mr. Everything 1982 Sweet Mountain 1982 SM 300 Producer: Mr. Lucky

Hot Fingers 1984 Qwest 1-25123 Produced by Reggie Griffin

The title track of ex-Manchild member Griffin's first album, refers to the fact that he plays, arranges, writes and sings everything on show. It's a good effort too, as he can do all of these things well; he also mixes up ballads with worthy dance tracks throughout and there is nothing on here I need to skip over, apart from "Electric Love" and "Be Myself". "Can't You See" is probably the best example of his good singing, showing off his range.

You don't get signed to Qwest Records unless you have something going for you, and once again Griffin (and by now he was billing himself as just "Griffin") did virtually all the work on *Hot Fin-*

gers. "Mirda Rock" and "Throw Down" were mid-size hits on the soul charts but I can't get to grips with any of the LP and its pop/funk/electro approach, finding it to devoid of anything I associate with soul music.

Eddie Gross

Guantanamo Bay 1972 Queen G QGS-10772 Producer: Eddie Gross

On researching and writing this book, it's always nice to come across an LP from someone who had completely passed me by before, and if the album is really rather eccentric at the same time, with a hideously cheap cover, then so much the better. Thus Eddie Gross.

I have recently discovered that he sang lead on a disc by The Pinkertones as well as fronting a San Diego band, The Nobles, and based entirely on pure speculation derived from the information on the LP's sleeve, I would suggest that he was a sailor in the U.S. Navy and recorded the LP in Jamaica while his ship was passing through. It's a soul album, though, nearly all upbeat in tempo, and has nothing to do with any type of music normally associated with the Caribbean (apart from the lilting "Eddie's Jamaica"). It's also rather odd, and Gross must surely have recorded the LP as simply a "vanity project" with no real intention of selling many copies - apart from to other sailors? - a feeling reinforced by the fact that any interested purchasers are requested to write directly to Eddie in California should they want to buy it. That being said, I have also found out that in an April 1973 edition of *Billboard* the "Guantanamo Bay" song was, amazingly enough, a "hit pick", which must suggest the title track came out as a single. (It's fair to say that the prediction was wayward in the extreme.) That title track traces Gross' arrival into "Gitmo" while "In Puerto Rico" has a snatch of a spoken exchange between Gross and a local, with Eddie expressing his admiration for the quality of the weaving on local baskets before breaking into a song that borrows from "Ob La Di, Ob La Da". So far, so definitely bad, then, but all is redeemed by the best track on the album by some distance, the midtempo "It's Not Who You Are (But What You Can Do)" which is simply excellent (and also the b-side to the afore-mentioned Pinkertones single) and reminiscent of recordings by another obscure soul singer, Richard Caiton. Most of the other tracks are pretty decent as Gross is a gifted singer with a compelling tone and a good range, but I don't think he ever recorded again.

Ground Hog

Got To Get Enough 1971 Turbo TU-7005 Producer: Joe Richardson

Joe Richardson was a man who could never make up his mind about what he wanted to be called. His first singles were issued under the names of "Tender Slim" and "Fender Guitar Slim" over fifty years ago before he started to release a handful of 45s in both his own name and the slightly elongated "Tender Joe Richardson" but nothing ever sold and the South Carolina born session guitarist (he appears on Don Covay's *The House Of Blue Lights* as an example) then took the slightly bizarre decision to change his recording name to the surely not hit-guaranteed "Ground Hog" in the hope that this might change his fortunes. To a slight extent it did, for he went on to have his only LP issued under this new name but he continued to remain terminally obscure and the internet doesn't turn up much more about him at all. I don't know even if he is still alive or not, for example. (By the way, the Ground Hog who took a single called "Bumpin'" to #61 on the soul charts in 1974 is nothing to do with Joe Richardson.)

Anyway, the Turbo set is a typical offering from The All Platinum group: short playing time; a release from an artist with no fame or fortune; cheap looking cover. It also gives me no pleasure to say this, but it is very undistinguished indeed. The only track I could ever wish to listen to again is his cover of Roy C's "Got To Get Enough" which sounds much like the original and is therefore a good record (and also reached the top forty on the *Cashbox* soul charts for one week.) The rest range from the incredibly thin sounding "Right On With The Right On", through two inconsequential instrumentals, the more or less straight country song (but definitely not country-soul) "Sticking Because She's Stuck", some spoken passages on "Going Back Home" and the plain odd "Wig Wearing Mama". Trying desperately to be positive, I could say it is good-natured and I know All Platinum never really expected their LPs to sell in quantity anyway but this is taking things too far.

G.T.'s

Charlie Jackson; Larry Walker; Corlos Williams; Bobby Wilson; Ralph Hammie; Charlie Banks; Billy Eason; John Dixon

You Gave It Away 1977 Jeds SJM-3377 Producer: John Dixon

This is an absurdly scarce LP out of Las Vegas which certainly didn't hit the jackpot and I wonder how many copies ever escaped from Nevada. It's good though with much better vocals than one had a right to expect from funk based groups in 1977: check "Let's Do It Together" as good evidence. The slower things were even better: "Running Back" has lovely backing singing and a charming lead vocal (from Charlie Banks?) where his slight technical shortcomings are compensated by his heartfelt tone. "Don't Blame Me" is its equal with fine piano and guitar enhancing a more gospel-based lead by Banks, where no limitations are on show at all.

Lenis Guess

I Can't Leave Your Love Alone 1984 Guess GU 612 Producer: Lenis Guess

Throughout the sixties and seventies there was a small but reasonably vibrant soul music community in Norfolk, Virginia. It certainly generated lots of singles, but few hits and even fewer LPs. One of the more important players within this scene was Lenis Guess, a writer, singer, arranger and producer who eventually put out around fifteen singles in his own name over a twenty year period without ever reaching the national charts. His one LP came out in 1984 on his own label which guaranteed that he could make whatever kind of record he wanted to, even if it also ensured limited distribution.

And what it turned out he wanted was a record that appealed to two different types of record buyer. Side one had four good slow tracks that would sound compelling to anyone who was listening to soul music when Guess was releasing his first records back in the mid-sixties. "I Can't Leave Your Love Alone" and "I Keep Coming Back For More" were excellent sides, both showing off Guess' expressive vocals which would doubtless have been toned down if an outside producer was on board. Side two though, all uptempo material, was aimed at a much younger audience, an understandable, if slightly misguided, move given that this market already had the choice of hearing this sort of thing from any number of more well-known artists who were providing it in great quantity. So, if you like traditional soul music seek this record out and play side one. Just don't turn it over.

Gwen Guthrie

Gwen Guthrie 1982 Island 90004-1 Producers: Sly Dunbar, Robbie Shakespeare & Steven Stanley (Billboard soul charts: 28 ; Billboard pop charts: 208)

Portrait 1983 Island ILPS 9758 Producers: Sly Dunbar & Robbie Shakespeare

Just For You 1985 Island 90252-1 Producers: Eumir Deodato, Gwen Guthrie & Steven Stanley (Billboard soul charts: 55)

Good to Go Lover 1986 Polydor 829 532-1 Y-1 Producer: Gwen Guthrie (Billboard soul charts: 20 ; Billboard pop charts: 59)

Lifeline 1988 Warner Brothers 9 25698-4 Producer: Gwen Guthrie

Hot Line 1990 Reprise 26238-1 Producers: Gwen Guthrie & Brian Jackson

The highly talented Gwen Guthrie made a number of excellent and intriguing records, even if a number of them do require an open mind and a willingness to stretch the boundaries of what might be considered as soul music. She had already served notice of her ability back in the seventies when she had composed the likes of "Supernatural Thing", a massive hit for Ben E. King.

The first album is an example of what I mean about her music as its pop sheen should be borne in mind by anyone who looks for a more raunchy approach, but good things lay within. "God Don't Like Ugly" is an impressive composition (covered by Roberta Flack) and although "It Should Have Been You" repeats the chorus over and over and over it still has power and deserved its #27 placing on the soul charts.

The follow-up set, *Portrait*, was her best work, and one of the best of that year by anyone. "Oh What A Life" was possibly the finest cut within, demonstrating both her singing and writing abilities, and her versatility was highlighted by the vastly different and funky "Peanut Butter" (great guitar and bass) which was better than the title suggested and deserved to have landed higher than only #83 as a single. "Younger than Me" was another winner, lyrically impressive with more compelling rhythm and sustaining interest for over seven minutes. She couldn't hope to top Sly and The Family Stone's "Family Affair" but she certainly doesn't disgrace herself either. What helps to makes the album so impressive is the intelligent and interesting rhythms; so many other sides from this time sounded utterly predictable and safe; not here.

Just For You surprisingly only included two songs from Guthrie herself, one being the pretty "On Donny No". "Love In Moderation" became her biggest hit to date by reaching #17 on the soul charts and I like both chorus and her Aretha-tinged singing but was less enamoured of the rhythm for once. In fact it was not as gripping throughout as the programming had started to inevitably creep in.

Good To Go Lover was kicked off by a seven minute version of "Close To You" which has an unremittingly dull drum programme, but fortunately is saved by a great Guthrie vocal, sweet back-ups and some nice instrumental swirls; if only it had been cut three or four years earlier - it would have been spectacular. The album also contained her big hit, "Aint Nothin' Going On But The Rent" (#1 soul, #42 pop), which despite not really appealing to me has stood up better in 2016 than most other big hits of the year. The rest? Not much to interest me.

There is no point in my commenting on the last two albums, as ten seconds of listening to her version of "Too Many Fish In The Sea" makes it clear that there is no middle ground; but I was still impressed with her singing. She sadly died in 1999 at the age of only 49.

Delores Hall

Hall-Mark 1973 RCA APL1-0204 Producer: Billy Jackson

Delores Hall 1979 Capitol ST-11997 Producers: Robert Thiele & Mark Kamins

Delores Hall is another performer who has been pretty much ignored by soul fans over the years, possibly because she is an actress as much as a singer, even though her gospel background comes across strongly on nearly all her recordings which began in the sixties on Keymen records where she recorded as a solo artist in addition to duetting with Jackie Lee on one of his 45s.

Her first LP in 1973 is a rather curious affair and one which RCA did not seem to be sure how to market. First, there is the cover which looks for all the world like a straight country outing (it isn't at all) and secondly, because the compositions are rather unchallenging pop/MOR in a number of cases, particularly on a disappointing second side which bears little that sounded vital and "with-it" in 1973, nor indeed in 2016. Nevertheless, side one is interesting and pretty good. "Where Do We Go From Here", which sports a pleasing arrangement from Wade Marcus, is my favourite, while "Who's Gonna Make It Easier For Me" is a duet with a vocally unrecognisable Luther Vandross, one of his earliest ever outings on wax. Furthermore, "Sha La Bandit" is an excellent song, later performed by Aretha Franklin and Sandra Wright, and "The Weight Shifted (To My Side)" is sung with real gospel fire by Hall.

A handful of singles came out in the seventies, a couple of which were from her second LP, *Delores Hall,* which was marketed much more clearly: towards the dance floor. While it was good enough of its kind, and she sang throughout with her customary attack, there was little to make it stand out from everything else on sale at the time, and even though she had accomplished admirable work on the stage, she wasn't really well enough known to have a ready made fan-base anticipating its release. The stand-out cut for me was a good ballad: "Never Gonna Let You Go".

So far as I can tell, she did not release any more records in her own name after 1979, deciding instead to concentrate on acting.

Hamilton Affair

Myrna Hamilton; Ray Hamilton; Roy Hamilton Jnr.

For Roy 1976 Monument MG 7607 Producer: Clyde Otis

Roy Hamilton was a marvellous singer, even if few of his records could really be classed as "soul", although the handful of songs he recorded for AGP in Memphis in 1969 were brilliant and most certainly were. For that reason I have excluded him from the book but I will include the one LP cut by his wife and two sons as it was ostensibly soul music and I assume pitched as such. I'm afraid I consider it to be very poor indeed and it gives me no pleasure to say so. In over forty years of record collecting there have only been a handful of LPs I wished to get rid of as soon as I first bought them and this is one such example. I can't recall many of the tracks at this late stage but the youthful singing was the hurdle I could not get across. One for fans of The Jackson 5 only, I think.

Big John Hamilton (and Doris Allen)

Deep Soul Classics Volume 2 1987 P-Vine PLP-333
Producer: Finley Duncan

This album, the only one which these two fine singers can boast in their own names, has been listed under Hamilton rather than Allen for the simple reason that he has ten solo tracks on it compared to her three; they duet on the a further three. The LP was part of a "Deep Soul" series in Japan which came to comprise well over twenty albums. Most were "various artists" compilations but some, like this one, concentrated solely on one or two singers or groups.

We should therefore be for ever indebted to P-Vine for allowing us to hear so much marvellous and uncompromising music, southern to the core, which ranges from the lovely, tuneful and reasoned (Hamilton's "Take This Hurt Off Me") to the utterly demented (Allen's "A Shell Of A Woman".) Most of the tracks were recorded for the Minaret label in the period from 1967 until 1969, but there are seven previously unreleased tracks included as well. As mentioned above, Hamilton dominates the proceedings and he has the honour of singing the best track of all on the LP, the magnificent Muscle Shoals recorded "How Much Can A Man Take", where he comes across like Otis Redding. It's also lovely to note that while none of the tracks made it to the *Billboard* soul charts three cuts did at least make it to the *Cashbox* listings: Hamilton's superb "I Have No One" and "The Train" and a duet between the singers, "Them Changes". This latter was an abrasive take on a Buddy Miles song and I suspect the idea of pairing up Hamilton and Allen in the first place was due to the success another southern duo, Peggy Scott and Jo Jo Benson, were enjoying around the same time. It's an incendiary side but they ended up sounding more like Sam and Dave than anyone else, which was hardly a bad thing. Allen gives it her all and as usual she comes across as a no-holds barred singer in the Linda Jones mould and all her singing on here must have left her exhausted at the end of a session.

It wasn't only the issued sides that were top-class as Hamilton's "Angel" and "I'm Getting It From Her" were exceptional too and of all the unreleased material on here only Allen's "Treat Me Like A Woman" has anything less than a full sound, but as she sings it so compellingly it doesn't matter.

Allen has passed away now but so far as I know Big John is still around. They never got to release an album back in their Minaret days but as retrospective collections go, there will be few LPs discussed in this book that are better than this one.

Clay Hammond

Come Into These Arms Of Love 1981 P-Vine Special PLP-3504 Producer: Grady Esked (Japan)

Taking His Time 1988 Kent 081 (UK)

Streets Will Love You 1988 Evejim EJ 1999 Producer: Leon Haywood

It's hard to listen to Clay Hammond without being reminded of Sam Cooke but this Texas born soul man was a top-class singer in his own right and the facts that none of his singles ever really sold in huge numbers or made it onto any national charts should not be allowed to obscure their quality. Indeed, he recorded 45s for around ten different labels between 1963 and 1989 and most of the best of them were put on a superb compilation by the UK based record label Kent in 1988, which was gratifying indeed as he was never offered the opportunity to cut an LP when he was most prolific in the sixties.

The U.S based Kent label had one of the most impressive artist rosters of any label that cut soul music and many of their recordings effortlessly re-produced the "southern soul" sound of Memphis or Muscle Shoals despite their being cut nearly two thousand miles further west. Clay Hammond was right at home in this type of musical setting and anyone listening to a number of lovely tracks on this set such as "Take Your Time", "You Brought It All On Yourself" and "You Messed Up Your Mind" could be forgiven for assuming they were cut at the AGP studio in Memphis. They were not, but the best cut on the entire LP, was: "I'll Make It Up To You" was not only Hammond's best ever record, it was one of the best records cut by ANYONE in the sixties, and showcased his finest vocal, alternating between his low register through to the highest falsetto, in an astonishing display of vocal range. The LP also showed that when Hammond switched into a bluesier mode, such as on "I Got A Letter This Morning", he remained totally convincing and although there are a couple of cuts on here where the songwriting quality dips a little, it is still a most impressive album.

However, by the time the UK album appeared Clay Hammond had actually cut and released an LP, albeit only in Japan. *Come Into These Arms Of Love* was recorded in LA in September of 1977 but Hammond and producer Grady Esked were obviously unable to find anyone interested in taking a punt on it in America. It is not a bad set, mostly consisting of gentle mid-tempo songs, but it does not match the quality of his best sixties sides, and, disappointingly, his vocal ability to shift up the octaves was either suppressed or had vanished. Hammond was always a capable and underrated songwriter and here, as on the Kent LP, he wrote everything, but the compositional quality varied more than it had in the past. The title track and "Love Won't Let Me Stay Away From You" were good but the best track of all was an update of his best-known song, "Part Time Love", which had been a #1 soul hit back in 1963 for Little Johnny Taylor, although when Hammond's version was released as a 45 from the set in 1982, it sold significantly fewer copies than Taylor's. On the less positive side, "Disco Baby" and "Rap On Wood" were the most inconsequential things he had ever committed to wax, while "Women Are Human", although doubtless well-intentioned, was so patronising as to be rather excruciating.

Finally, in 1989, after having recorded for nearly thirty years, Hammond saw his first ever LP released in the U.S. Moreover, it was good, even if he had to sacrifice sole writing duties to others, with only two songs having had input from his own pen, and sing songs which had nearly all been performed by others previously. Leon Haywood had a clear vision at the turn of the eighties: produce records with full horn sections and proper drummers and aim them fairly and squarely at a middle-aged audience. It was a philosophy Hammond could happily buy into. It is a most consistent set, with all eight tracks holding their own, and nothing stands out, nor needed to stand out, over the rest. It didn't reach any national charts but I suspect sold fairly decently.

A couple of so-so CDs followed in the next couple of decades, which meant Hammond could rightfully claim to have had a forty plus year recording career, before he passed away in 2011.

Larry Hancock (see also S.O.U.L. and Truth)

Borderline 1988 Dessca 66522 Producers: Dan Schneider, and Yves Dessca (France)

Larry Hancock may not have been well-known to the musical world at large, let alone the general public, but he was an important, talented and highly respected member of the Ohio soul scene for well over twenty years, singing lead for local groups such as The Intertains, Truth and S.O.U.L. His best work came with the latter two outfits as we will see later in the book, but he did get to record one solo LP in Los Angeles in 1988 although, for reasons I don't understand, it only came out in France.

It's always been quite an "in-demand" set, but I'm not sure with whom, as it is not particularly distinguished, performed in the thoroughly professional and glossy pop-soul mode so popular in the mid to late eighties and, despite his customarily impressive singing, it all falls significantly short of what he had produced in the past.

I don't believe he recorded anything else after this and he died in 2010.

Ellerine Harding

Ellerine 1972 Mainstream MRL 377 Producer: Bob Shad

Bob Shad's Mainstream records certainly spared no expense on Ellerine Harding's one and only LP, which was decent of them considering that she was completely unknown at the time. The label utilised musicians of the calibre of Gordon Edwards, Bernard Purdie, Ray Barretto and Wilbur Bascomb, as well as splashing out on a gatefold sleeve but I doubt if they recouped their expenses as it came and went fairly quickly, just another LP in a crowded marketplace. For anyone who doesn't know the album, it presents Harding in much the same style as the work of two Wilsons - Spanky and Nancy - and such a description will probably suffice to determine if readers will be interested in it or not. She certainly wasn't a singer even remotely in the tough southern style, but the music is obviously of a high quality and I think it is firmly a "soul" album rather than a "jazz" one. The gently funky "To Whom It May Concern (All I Need)", an impressive song from another woman who was also not an obvious out and out soul singer, Micki Grant, is probably the best cut on here and should be investigated.

Harding released a pretty good single on the IX Chains label in 1974 but soon shelved her singing aspirations in favour of making acting her main career, a quest in which she has been pretty successful.

Harlem River Drive

Harlem River Drive 1971 Roulette SR-3004 Producers: Eddie Palmieri & Lockie Edwards

Eddie and Charlie Palmieri were two of the most important figures in the history of Latin music and the vast majority of their recorded output falls well outside the scope of this book but in 1971 they and other renowned latin musicians worked with soul singer Jimmy Norman and top-class New York musicians who had extensive experience of playing on soul records - Cornell Dupree, Jerry Jemmott and Bernard Purdie - to create an incredible (I use the word advisedly) rhythmic blend that I could not have ignored as it is one of the most satisfying records ever made that falls even remotely into the "funky" genre, although attempting to put this music into a specific box seems insulting. By the late seventies and throughout the eighties funk became a rhythmically conservative music with predictable and all too often monotonous beats, but Harlem River Drive's sinuous approach is much more satisfying and thoughtful with "Idle Hands" and "Seeds Of Life" particularly being astonishing pieces of music. There are only five tracks and the whole LP weighs in at just over 30 minutes but it is absolutely essential and one of those like *What's Going On* that seems to meet with universal approval.

Harlem River Drive were short-lived and neither the LP nor "Seeds Of Life" as a single sold in large quantities, although an excellent later 45, "Need You", by a group of the same name (same players?) made it to #60 on the soul charts in 1975. A second LP under the name of Harlem River Drive, although predominantly a Charlie Palmieri album, recorded live at Sing Sing prison (Tico CLP 1303 in 1972), was a straightforward latin set and did not include any of the tracks from the great debut album.

Billy Harner

She's Almost You 1969? Open 1100 Producer: a Cal-Bill Production

Billy Harner was born in Camden, New Jersey and grew up to become a convincing "blue-eyed" soul man, in the tradition of Eddie Hinton and Wayne Cochran, eventually going on to release about twenty singles for numerous labels including V-Tone and Kent, and this one LP. Apparently known as "The Human Perkulator" (sic) or just "The Perk" he was by all accounts an electrifying live performer and very popular in and around the Philadelphia area, even if he never got to place a single record on any national chart.

The LP does not provide a year of release but I believe it came out in 1969 and I further believe that the Cal-Bill production denotes Lenny Caldwell and Harner himself. No song-writing credits are given either but listening to the LP makes it clear that "Set Me Free" and "All In My Mind" are the songs with which Esther Phillips and Maxine Brown respectively had hits. Harner could also call on Philly's best as "I Struck It Rich" came from Gamble and Huff while the surging title track was arranged by the great Bobby Martin. Both these cuts were upbeat but I prefer other songs such as "Message To My Baby", the oft-recorded "Human" and "Watch Your Step" as they give Harner a chance to stretch out a little more. Billy Harner was a genuine soul man of somewhat limited vocal ability but that doesn't stop the whole album, with its unpretentious blue-collar feel, from being pretty appealing.

Herman Harper II

Sinking Into Love 1988 Loadstone 3956LPA Producer: W C Stone

This record is certainly not what it seems. Given that Anaheim-based Herman Harper II (who released a single back in 1977) only sings on two of the seven tracks it can hardly be classed as "his" LP but the album cover and title clearly give that impression. Of those two tracks one, "Sinking Into Love", is good, and the other is bizarre in the extreme and should appeal to anyone who enjoys genuine oddities for it features Harper singing the articles of the U.S. Constitution. Two of the other five tracks are instrumentals, while Paula Lamont offers up a good side in "A Loving Mother".The final two tracks are sung by the high-voiced, slightly raucous and terminally obscure Peter Colly and on both occasions when others have been in the room while his sides have been playing I have been asked "who the hell is this"? One query was driven by admiration, the second most definitely was not.

Betty Harris

Soul Perfection 1969 Action ACLP-6007 Producers: Allen Toussaint & Marshall Sehorn (UK)

In The Saddle 1980 Charly CRB 1002 Producer: Allen Toussaint & Marshall Sehorn (UK)

Books about soul music were scarce in the sixties and seventies and it was therefore a pleasure to see one arrive in 1975 entitled, rather prosaically, *The Soul Book*. In it, the estimable writer Clive Anderson proffered the suggestion that Betty Harris was the greatest soul singer of all time. It's a bold claim, of course, but her first album from 1969, accurately entitled *Soul Perfection*, shows he had a compelling case. It is a magnificent set, but was retrospective in nature, containing all the sides Harris had cut for the Sansu label between the period 1965 to 1969 and also once again proved how little attention was paid to LPs in New Orleans in the sixties as, despite the steady flow of 45s, Harris never got to release an album when her career was extant.

Harris was born in Orlando, Florida and cut her first records up in New York, with one of them, "Cry To Me", becoming easily her biggest ever hit when it reached #10 soul and #23 pop in 1963. That success didn't last for too long, however, and for pretty much the remainder of her career she hooked up with Allen Toussaint who cut her records down in New Orleans. Toussaint is one of the most important figures in the musical history of that city but even by his standards, his work with Harris was exceptional.

Every one of the sixteen tracks on *Soul Perfection* was written by Toussaint. Every one of them featured his piano playing and every one of them had come out as an a or a b- side on a single. The reason the LP was so good was due to three reasons - the eternal verities of soul music, in fact - the songs, the playing and the vocals. The former were uniformly sharp, with strong melodies and arresting hooks and not one overstayed its welcome; the musicianship was of the highest class, with horns deployed judiciously and memorable touches throughout (examples: the "swampy" guitar on "Trouble With My Lover", the drumming on "Bad Luck" and Toussaint's stately and utterly dignified piano on the marvellous "Can't Last Much Longer".) And then there was Harris herself. Her strength didn't lie in her range but she handled fast and slow material equally easily and had few peers in tone and phrasing. She also had the ability to be completely convincing in whatever mood she chose to deploy: assertive in "I'm Gonna Git Ya"; bewildered in "What'd I Do Wrong"; reflective in "What A Sad Feeling"; broken-hearted in "I'm Evil Tonight".

Despite the quality of her Sansu singles only one - the brilliant "Nearer To You" - made it onto the soul charts, reaching #16 in summer 1967. As should be apparent by now, I recommend this album and good on the UK Action label for putting it out. It lasts for around forty minutes, not a second of which is redundant.

Her second UK only album, *In The Saddle*, contains eleven of the sixteen tracks that could be found on *Soul Perfection* as well as five "new" tracks which are: the highly funky but not really suited to her "There's A Break In The Road", "Cry To Me", "I'll Be A Liar", "All I Want Is You" and "Take Care Of Your Love", the last of which is a duet with Lee Dorsey.

Harris stopped recording and touring after 1969 and left the music business - some rumours had her driving a truck - after which all attempts to find her led nowhere. Suddenly though, she re-appeared in 2007 with a brand new CD. She looked great on the cover and it was really good to see her back even if it falls alarmingly short of her sixties work.

Damon Harris (See also Temptations and Impact)

Damon 1978 Fantasy F-9567 Producer: Budd Ellison, Larry James and Damon Harris

In the steamy summer of 1970 a Baltimore based vocal group called the Young Vandals cut a lovely single entitled "In My Opinion" which did pretty well, but it did even better for their high-voiced co-lead singer, Damon Harris, as he was invited to join The Temptations to replace Eddie Kendricks after the initial replacement, Ricky Owens, hadn't worked out. Harris may have missed the Temps' glory days but he still was present on a number of their later hits, even if he seldom got to sing lead. I even saw him perform live with the group at a concert in Brighton in 1973, although I would not have known his name at that point. He left the Temps in 1975 and re-joined his colleagues from the Young Vandals, although they now changed their name to Impact. After a couple of years of middling success, he decided to go solo. Hence this LP.

Over music provided by members of Fat Larry's Band, Harris does a pretty good job on a set consisting of eight songs, a couple of which were provided by Philadelphia veteran, Len Barry, but everyone must have despaired when a single pulled from the set, "It's Music", a slightly above average long dance track, only managed to reach #96 on the soul charts, in other words pretty much a complete failure. My favourite track on the album is "Funday" as it has the prettiest melody by far, and although I do like the LP, Harris, like another high tenor vocalist, Eugene Record, couldn't quite overcome the fact that his voice was better suited to being flanked by other members of a male vocal group rather than a set of female backing vocalists.

Sadly, he had to endure a long fight with cancer and died in 2013.

Major Harris (see also The Delfonics)

My Way 1974 Atlantic SD 18119 Producers: Mystro & Lyric, WMOT Productions, Ron Kersey & Bobby Eli (Billboard soul charts: 12 ; Billboard pop charts: 28)

Jealousy 1976 Atlantic SD 18160 Producers: Major Harris, Ron Kersey, Alan Rubens, Steve Bernstein, Bobby Eli & Norman Harris (Billboard soul charts: 33; Billboard pop charts: 153)

Live! (with Margie Joseph and Blue Magic) 1976 WMOT 2-5000 Producers: WMOT Productions, Blue Magic, Major Harris & Margie Joseph

How Do You Take Your Love 1978 RCA APL1-2803 Producer: Jerry Ragovoy

The Best Of Major Now And Then 1981 WMOT PW-37067

I Believe In Love 1984 Streetwave MKL 3 Producer: Butch Ingram (UK)

Born in Richmond, Virginia, Major Harris sang with a number of vocal groups before and after cutting two singles for Okeh in the sixties one of which coupled "Call Me Tomorrow" - which has seen plenty of action on the U.K. "Northern Soul" scene - with "Like A Rolling Stone" and I'd love to know what hardcore Dylan fans made of *that*. His most prominent stint was with The Delfonics with whom he stayed for a couple of years before going solo once again.

His first single this time around was "Each Morning I Wake Up" credited to The Major Harris Boogie Blues Band, an odd title, for while the boogie element was clearly evident the blues one was resolutely not. It scraped into the soul charts at #98 for two weeks but was replaced two months later by "Love Won't Let Me Wait", which did rather better, going all the way to #1 (and #5 pop) a success that must have been baffling to everyone, given his lack of success in the past. I've always found it to be a rather dull and overrated song, and was not particularly enamoured of the LP on which both singles sat either, as "My Way" is one of my least favourite songs, and I was never going to enjoy a six minute version. I do like his take on "Sideshow" but nowhere near as much as I like Blue Magic's. "Loving You Is Mellow", "Two Wrongs", "After Loving You" and "Just A Thing I Do" are all enjoyable and typical Philly sides but Harris didn't have a strong enough voice to make them genuinely memorable.

Joe Jefferson and Charles Simmons wrote half of *Jealousy* (they had written nothing on *My Way*) and not surprisingly their efforts made Major sound as if he had just joined The Spinners. "I Got Love" was a pleasant ballad of theirs, reaching #24 on the soul charts, but missed the Hot 100 completely. The key cut was "Jealousy" itself, another Simmons-Jefferson effort, weighing in at nine minutes long, and a truncated take landed at #46 on the soul charts. It had a good hook, but simply went on too long. Elsewhere, "Talking To Myself" was nice but, once again, I much prefer Blue Magic's version. The one track I wholeheartedly thrilled at was the great up-tempo song, "Ruby Lee", previously cut by a band with whom Harris had once sung, Nat Turner's Rebellion.

A *Live* set followed where Margie Joseph and Harris had to play second fiddle to Blue Magic who got to perform the majority of the songs; the album rather failed, and although Harris planted a third single from *Jealousy*, "It's Got To Be Magic", on the soul charts followed by another on WMOT, he needed a new record company by 1978.

I'm not quite sure how he pulled it off, but Harris was teamed up with Jerry Ragovoy - one of the greatest of all producers and writers - for the superb 1978 set, *How Do You Take Your Love*. Ragovoy had been pretty quiet since 1974 and so it was quite the coup. He produced and arranged and wrote six of the nine songs (including the one misstep and one nod to "disco" "I Wanna Dance With You") although I must also give praise to Ted Daryll for "This Is Forever" which matches the Ragovoy songs. It's my favourite of all Major's LPs. His singing seems better to my ears, the best songs have a timeless quality, the arranging and production is stately, but for some reason no singles were issued and this contributed to the album's being ignored at the time, and, indeed, ever since.

The set from 1981 had a somewhat misleading title, as only two of the tracks were from Harris' Atlantic period with the other seven being new to LP, although these did span a time frame from 1976 to 1981. It's not really to my taste as too many of the songs have at least a toe in MOR waters, but at least little of it is disco; two of Harris' own co-compositions appear on an LP for the first time

Harris returned to the soul charts for the first time in seven years in late 1983 with "All My Life" making it to #52 but it did not give rise to an album and his last set didn't even get a release in the U.S. Credit therefore to Streetwave for giving fans a last chance to hear Major's' voice, even if all the dance tracks (and there are more on here than had been the case in the past) now sound dreadfully dated. "Girl Of My Dreams", "Spend Some Time" and the even better "Through It All" would be my pick of the ballads; I prefer all of these to "Love Won't Let Me Wait". Harris' own "Rediscover" is good, too, and thanks solely to the slow stuff this would be one of my most favoured LPs of 1984.

In 1986 "Love Is Everything", a flop single, advertised an album of the same name but it never appeared and I don't think Harris ever recorded any more solo sides, although he did re-join The Delfonics, featuring on their then new CD from 1998. He died in 2012.

Norman Harris

The Harris Machine 1980 P.I.R. JZ 36313 Producers: Norman Harris, John Faith, Zach Zachery, Ron Kersey, Kenny Gamble & Leon Huff

Norman Harris (cousin to Major, I believe) was one of the most important figures in the history of Philadelphia soul music, writing, producing or playing guitar for every important act in the city at one time or another. His legacy is astonishing, in fact, and his credits on records run into many hundreds over more than twenty years.

This LP is hardly his greatest achievement and I'm sure nobody would claim it as such for it is pretty bland stuff in the MFSB mould, all instrumental tracks apart from the odd "backing vocal" here and there and these are not the versions of "Just Don't Want To Be Lonely" or "Don't Leave Me This Way" that I would ever play by choice. But let's face it, Harris certainly deserved a solo album, and as it's not the best way to remember him (he died in 1987), listen instead to First Choice's "Armed And Extremely Dangerous" or Blue Magic's "Sideshow" to be reminded of his huge talent.

Thomas Harris

Dark Horse 1976 Roxbury RLX 103 Producers: Jeff Polard & Lynn Ourso

Another album with an a bafflingly weak front cover (a horse's head), this one was at least featured in an advert Chelsea Records (who distributed Roxbury) took out in *Billboard* in January 1977. For all the good it did Thomas Harris.

It's hard to think of who else Harris sounds like, which demonstrates he had some individuality, but the LP is rather one-dimensional (flat) and thin in sound as there are no strings to be heard anywhere and backing singers only appear for "Can Ya Handle It" (one of two singles to be pulled from the album to little effect). I suspect Harris may also be a keyboard player as together with a rather unwelcome guitar, an electric piano is the most prominent instrument on show. He is a good rather than spectacular singer, and definitely emotes in a soul style, even if one or two of the songs are slightly rocky and poppy in construction. I know nothing else about him and no other records seem to exist.

Jesse Harrison

Jesse Harrison (with Reginald Forch) 1978 Crazy Cajun CCLP-1057 Producer: Huey Meaux

As mentioned earlier the Forch tracks are really poor, but the five from the unknown Jesse Harrison are much better, especially as they are fully-realised songs with a proper rhythm section, backing vocals and even horns here and there. He is also an accomplished singer and deserved to have recorded more frequently. A couple of the compositions are driven by social concerns and he also delivers a nice, reggae flavoured version of the old favourite, "Silhouettes", and an unrecognisable one of "No Man Is An Island", which bears Harrison's most impressive vocal of the set. This whole side is certainly worth hearing, but forget the other.

A Jesse Harrison also released a gospel LP entitled *Sanctify Me*, but I have no idea if the same man.

Sterling Harrison

Sterling Harrison 1980 Real World RW 38-134 Producers: Brian Holland, Eddie Holland, Lamont Dozier & Harold Beatty

One Size Fits All 1981 Phono PP 1003 Producers: Brian Holland & Harold Beatty

Sterling Harrison was born in Richmond but his long - if generally under the radar - recording career was heavily based on the West Coast. He released a handful of singles in the sixties and seventies but they did not sell well.

Sterling Harrison is primarily noteworthy as half of it was written and produced by Holland-Dozier-Holland and the famous trio were generally taking it easy back then; Dozier's vocal phrasing is also clearly discernible on a number of the songs but this doesn't detract from the fact that Harrison could certainly proclaim powerfully. The songs are not the greatest ever written by HDH - and nor are the others on the album - but it a set that nonetheless retains interest for listening as well as dancing.

The second set was printed up in limited copies and thus costs a lot of money whenever one infrequently turns up, but, honestly its not worth it, being no better than scores of other records that cost a fraction of this one. Sterling again sings well and "You Got That Thing" is good, but most of the rest of the cuts are dance items of no obvious merit.

He recorded three CDs before he passed away in 2005, with one, *South of The Snooty Fox*, being more to my taste than the two LPs.

Fuzzy Haskins (see also Funkadelic and Parliament)

A Whole Nother Thang 1976 W-229 Producer: Clarence "Fuzzy" Haskins

Radio-Active 1978 WT 6102 Producer: Gig Productions

Clarence "Fuzzy" Haskins was a founding member of The Parliaments, and while with the band contributed a number of songs and vocals over the years before releasing a self-produced solo album in 1976 on which he wrote everything. There is little point in anyone who doesn't enjoy the P-Funk experience in investing in a copy, but it's not as weird and unorthodox as many of the related releases, although still far from conventional soul music with a verse chorus verse structure. Reasonably funky throughout, he takes on the drug pusher in "Mr. Junk Man" (an interesting stance for a member of a Clinton band), amuses with "Which Way Do I Disco?" and writes a melody awfully close to "I Hear You Knocking" in "Sometimes I Rock And Roll".

Half a dozen of the P-Funk crew turned up to play and help out on *Radio-Active,* which, if anything, was even "straighter" than *A Whole Nother Thang,* thus proving that these talented artists were quite capable of going off-piste when they chose. I'd still recommend a great deal of caution as the songs are neither catchy nor immediate and everything is better accepted as album cuts rather than obvious singles; as evidenced by the failure of "Not Yet" when put out as a 45.

Haskins was part of the short-lived Funkadelic collective who put out the *Connections and Disconnections* set in 1981 but does

Roger Hatcher

R & Better 1977 Guinness GNS 36033 No producer listed

Roger Hatcher was a Birmingham, Alabama born soul singer from good stock; brother to another singer, Will Hatcher, and cousin to Charles Hatcher, better known to the world as Edwin Starr. He was also a talented writer co-composing "I Got Caught" for Clarence Carter and "I Dedicate My Life To You" for The Dramatics, both songs he also cut on himself. He always had a small but passionate following among song connoisseurs but a mere one of his 45s ever made it to the soul charts and only to # 92 at that, the outstanding "We're Gonna Make it" in 1976.

He issued around ten singles in total over his career, and one album, the seriously scarce R & Better on the tax write-off label Guinness, in 1977. It is a typical Guinness release in as much as Hatcher was unaware of its existence, and indeed two of the tracks - an instrumental and a thin sounding cover of James Brown's "My Thang", clearly performed by someone else - are nothing to do with him at all. Other than that, and even if it falls short of his best work, with nothing coming up to the standard of "We're Gonna Make It" or "Caught Making Love", it is not a bad set and a handful of cuts even boast horns and backing singers, leading to a fuller sound than might have been expected. He always sang in a high, slightly straining tenor, often sounding as if he was on the verge of being in the wrong key, which added to his soulfulness and tension, but on the "You Must Have Come From Heaven" track his vocal debt to Curtis Mayfield comes through strongly. "Your Love Is A Masterpiece" is a reasonably good song, but does sound awfully similar to Ben E. King's "Supernatural Thing", while "Daylight Savings Time" is a fragile work of considerable charm.

Hatcher released two singles on the Super Bad label at the end of the eighties and early nineties and it was good to see a couple of retrospective CDs being released as well but nothing really availed him and he passed away in 2002.

Bobby Hatfield

Messin' In Muscle Shoals 1970 MGM SE 4727 Producer: Mickey Buckins

Bobby Hatfield was a Righteous Brother and has a guaranteed place in musical history as a result. Considerably less well-known were the handful of singles and the one album he cut as a solo singer after the Brothers broke up.

I would argue that Hatfield was one of the finest of all the "blue-eyed" singers as not only did he have a naturally beautiful voice but he had a real feeling for the music and despite being born up in Wisconsin he sounded right at home in deepest Alabama. MGM were releasing stacks of albums back in 1970 and I suspect that the recording of this set was really a labour of love for all involved, with no-one actually expecting it to sell many copies. (It didn't.) Certainly it would have given some Righteous Brothers fans a start, assuming they had even heard it, as it was considerably different from their biggest hits, lacking the huge orchestration and grandeur that characterised their records. Despite my overall appreciation of the LP it must be said that it is rather uneven with the pretty awful "I Saw A Lark" being a real low point, and I also don't care for "Let It Be" as a song for soul artists, even if Hatfield deals with it in a way that demonstrates his impressive range, while the title cut is jerky and rather messy. Much better to move on and acknowledge his rousing version of "You Left The Water Running", the excellent Mickey Buckins' song, "The Promised Land" but the best cuts of all must be "The Feeling Is Right" which is every bit the equal of Clarence Carter's version, and the lovely heartfelt and slow "Show Me The Sunshine".

MGM didn't even bother to put out a single from the set and after a few more good but failed 45s singles he re-united with Bill Medley before passing away in 2003.

Donny Hathaway (see also Roberta Flack)

Everything Is Everything 1970 Atco SD 33-332 Producers: Donny Hathaway & Ric Powell (Billboard soul charts: 33; Billboard pop charts: 73)

Donny Hathaway 1971 Atco SD 33-360 Producers: Donny Hathaway & Ric Powell (Billboard soul charts: 6; Billboard pop charts: 89)

Live 1972 Atco SD 33-386 Producers: Jerry Wexler & Arif Mardin (Billboard soul charts: 4; Billboard pop charts: 18)

Come Back Charleston Blue 1972 Atco SD 7010 Producers: Jerry Wexler & Arif Mardin

Roberta Flack & Donny Hathaway 1972 Atlantic SD 7216 Producers: Joel Dorn & Arif Mardin (Billboard soul charts: 2; Billboard pop charts: 3)

Extension Of A Man 1973 Atlantic SD 7029 Producers: Arif Mardin & Jerry Wexler (Billboard soul charts: 18; Billboard pop charts: 69)

Best Of 1978 Atco SD 38-107 (Billboard soul charts: 51)

In Performance 1980 Atlantic SD-19278 Producers: Jerry Wexler & Arif Mardin (Billboard soul charts: 68; Billboard pop charts: 201)

For a man who was so obviously gifted, and so obviously influential on many other artists, the troubled Donny Hathaway was not quite as successful as one might have expected and he only ever posted two singles in the soul top ten and only one single on the pop top thirty. For albums it was a similar story, with only his Live set being a genuinely big selling record. If we include his best selling duets with Roberta Flack the picture changes but Flack was certainly the bigger star of the two, enjoying three #1 pop hits in her own name.

Hathaway had graduated from Howard University before moving back to his native Chicago and starting making a bit of noise as a member of The Mayfield Singers before he cut his first single in 1969, "I Thank You Baby", as a duet with June Conquest which was released as by June and Donnie (sic) and which charted at #45 on the soul listings, but he soon moved to Atlantic where he was to remain for the rest of his career.

In early 1970 his first Atco single, "The Ghetto", sold pretty well going to #23 soul and #89 pop and found its way onto his first LP, Everything Is Everything. Straight away the set showed the breadth and depth of his talent, but also the two sides of his musical personality, which I will call the funky and the genteel. I always preferred the former as it concentrated on his sometimes incredible keyboard work and at its best could be exhilarating and entirely satisfying. I was less keen on the "genteel" which was based around choosing "significant" songs and although these were often encased in arrangements of dazzling virtuosity I always felt a bit alienated, as if this was music one could look at but not touch. That first album featured "The Ghetto", "Tryin' Times" and "Voices Inside" from his funky tendency and I enjoy them a lot, but "Misty" and "Young Gifted And Black" were examples of earnestness and maybe even "art" which did not move me much. The latter is clearly an important and impressive song but if I want to listen to it I always go for versions by Aretha or Bob and Marcia, not to mention Nina Simone.

His second album moved even further in a "genteel" direction, and included "A Song For You", "He Ain't Heavy, He's My Brother", "I Believe In Music" and "Put Your Hand In The Hand", all compositions that speak for themselves, and there was not even any funk on show to offset them. I can see how the opening track, "Giving Up" (a song that has had many different composer credits) could be described as brilliant, but both Gladys Knight and The Pips and The Ad-Libs have a greater emotional resonance for me.

Careful readers will have noted that I do not care for "live" albums very much, so it might seem perverse of me to insist that Hathaway's *Live* set was the best LP of his career, but insist I must. It is stripped down Hathaway with no towering arrangements, just an incredible band (Willie Weeks' bass playing on the 13 minute version of "Voices Inside" is astonishing) and the best and funkiest keyboard playing of his career. "The Ghetto" is also brilliant and the audience participation on this one enhances rather than detracts from the performance. He couldn't quite stop himself from including John Lennon's "Jealous Guy" which brings things down somewhat but it is still a magnificent album.

In 1972 Hathaway also got involved with a film soundtrack, *Come Back Charleston Blue*, but it is a minor note in his overall oeuvre with only two tracks really fitting in with the rest of his work: "Little Ghetto Boy" (going to #25 as a single) and the title track - a nice duet with Margie Joseph - which featured him singing in a manner somewhat reminiscent of Marvin Gaye which he had not done before and was not to do again. The rest of the record is typical soundtrack stuff: short instrumental breaks, snatches of dialogue etc.

Hathaway was now as successful as he would ever be and his collaborative set with Roberta Flack was a huge hit (#2 soul and #3 pop) with the gentle bossa nova of "Where Is The Love" being attractive enough when pulled as a single to go all the way to #1 soul as well as #5 pop. The album was polite and superbly musical but had little pizzazz or fire (compare their version of "Baby I Love You" with Aretha's) and is one to play in the background when doing something else.

Extension Of A Man was an apt title for a fascinating set, which suffers only from its overarching ambition with Hathaway trying to cram in as many styles as possible. It once again proves his virtuosity and talent beyond any sensible doubt, but its dazzling sheen can blind one to the fact that it didn't fully work. The good first: "I Love The Lord He Heard My Cry" is as close to classical music as anything covered in this entire book and it's hard to imagine that many other musicians working in the popular music field could have come up with it; "Someday We'll All Be Free" is his strongest ever composition, a "Change Is Gonna Come" for the seventies; "The Slums" and "Come Little Children" are brilliant driving dance songs; "I Love You More Than You'll Ever Know" and "I Know It's You" are two of the best "outside" songs he ever covered and "Love Love Love" lilts along nicely. Left at this, it would have been a great LP but "Valdez In The Country " and "Fly-

ing Easy" are frothy pieces which lessen the impact of the rest of the set while "Magdelena", whose jaunty tone reaches back to the twenties, isn't one for me at all. The three singles from the set,"I Love You More", "Love, Love, Love" and "Come Little Children", all reached the soul charts at #20, #16 and #67 respectively.

After having been quiet for a few years, Hathaway got back together with Flack in 1978 and a rather syrupy single, "The Closer I Get To You", became another huge success (#1 soul and #2 pop) proving once again that the public were much more willing to listen to Donny when he had Roberta by his side. No album immediately followed this big hit but a rather contentious *Best Of* - "Valdez In The Country", "This Christmas" and "You Were Meant For Me" but not "Love Love Love", "Voices Inside" and "I Love You More Than You'll Ever Know"? - did keep his name out there but his battle with depression was never far from the surface and, genuinely tragically, he jumped to his death on January 13th 1979.

Flack put out her *Roberta Flack Featuring Donny Hathaway* set in 1979, the success of which served as a fitting tribute to the man, but as he only sang on a couple of the tracks it can't be classed as a Hathaway album and I've not listed it above.

The last true Hathaway album came out in 1980 and didn't do particularly well. *In Performance* features songs performed at three different venues, two of which being the same as those on the great *Live* set from 1972 and I assume they were "outtakes" from the earlier gigs. Donny had been gone a year by this time and his name recognition had badly waned in those twelve months and a "live" set of nearly all slow songs was not what the public was looking for. It's not a bad outing by any means, of course, with the usual magnificent musicianship but it lacks the energy and spirit that made *Live* so compelling and will always have to remain in the shadow of that former disc as a result.

Jennell Hawkins

The Many Moods Of Jenny 1960? Amazon AM 1001
Producer: Herb Dixon

Moments To Remember 1961 Amazon AM 1002
Producer: Robert "Bumps" Blackwell

Los Angeles' Jennell Hawkins (who died in 2006) is one of the most neglected and under-appreciated artists in a genre where there is a lot of competition. Maybe it's because her two hits ("Moments" #16 soul in 1961, and "Money"#17 in 1962) were so long ago that nearly everyone has simply forgotten them or maybe it's because her two LPs did not feature a number of her best sides but no one has ever thought it worth their while releasing a CD dedicated to her. Anyone who enjoys what Etta James was doing back between 1960 until 1962 should love Jennell Hawkins.

Her first LP does contain some out and out jazz and songs such as "Blue Moon" and "Ole Man River" that are not wildly inspiring but a beautiful version of "Can I?" certainly is.

"Moments To Remember" is a lovely sultry Richard Berry song, supported by some telling organ (her own playing, I believe) and also reached #50 on the pop charts and is the stand-out on an album that once again includes well-known songs like "Never Let Me Go", "Pledging My Love" and "If I Loved You" but this was hardly unusual back then. I believe I'm right in saying that the album features some of the earliest arranging and conducting credits for Jerry Long who was later responsible for The Temptations' "Just My Imagination".

I submit that she was one of the singers most at home with what was to become known as "Soul" at the turn of the sixties. Just listen to her tough version of "I Pity The Fool" (entitled "I Pity You Fool") for proof; it's just a shame it doesn't appear on either of her albums.

Isaac Hayes

Introducing 1967 Enterprise S 13-100 Producers: Al Jackson, Duck Dunn & Al Bell (Billboard soul charts: 25; Billboard pop charts: 102)

Hot Buttered Soul 1969 Enterprise ENS-1001 Producers: Al Bell, Marvell Thomas & Allen Jones (Billboard soul charts: 1; Billboard pop charts: 8)

The Isaac Hayes Movement 1970 Enterprise ENS-1010 Producer: Isaac Hayes (Billboard soul charts: 1; Billboard pop charts: 8)

To Be Continued 1970 Enterprise ENS-1014 Producer: Isaac Hayes (Billboard soul charts: 1; Billboard pop charts: 11)

Shaft 1971 Enterprise ENS-2-5002 Producer: Isaac Hayes (Billboard soul charts: 1; Billboard pop charts: 1)

Black Moses 1971 Enterprise ENS-2-5003 Producer: Isaac Hayes (Billboard soul charts: 1; Billboard pop charts: 10)

Live At The Sahara Tahoe 1973 Enterprise ENS-2-5005 Producer: Isaac Hayes (Billboard soul charts:1; Billboard pop charts: 14)

Joy 1973 Enterprise ENS- 5007 Producers: Isaac Hayes & Willie Hall (Billboard soul charts: 2; Billboard pop charts: 16)

Tough Guys 1974 Enterprise ENS-2-7504 Producer: Isaac Hayes (Billboard pop charts: 146)

Truck Turner 1974 Enterprise ENS-7507 Producer: Isaac Hayes (Billboard soul charts: 17; Billboard pop charts: 156)

The Best Of 1973 Enterprise ENS-7510 (Billboard soul charts: 57; Billboard pop charts: 165)

If one were to look at all the soul artists who released LPs and work out which one on average cut the longest tracks of all, Isaac Hayes would surely come out at the top. Given that the Covington, Tennessee born singer first made his name writing - with David Porter - brilliantly succinct singles for Stax/Volt, this future direction might have come as somewhat of a surprise. He was also a striking looking man, with a visual appeal that was to be wisely exploited by his record labels.

Hayes had originally cut and released a handful of solo singles in the first half of the sixties, but his first LP came out in 1967, featuring Hayes performing well-known songs with Jackson and Dunn in a extremely stripped down format. Apparently it was cut after a drunken Christmas party and listening to it now, that is easy to believe, given how remarkably poor it is. Hayes was quick to disown it in later years but it already bore one of his trademarks: three of the five tracks were over eight minutes long.

Apart from the fact that his next album also featured long versions of well known-songs, it could hardly have been more differ-

ent: enormous orchestration versus a tinkling piano; committed Hayes vocals versus drunken meanderings; huge success versus obscurity. Opinions have always varied over *Hot Buttered Soul*; is it "overblown" or is it "brilliant"? I can see the reason behind the former charge but veer strongly towards the latter. There is something undeniably thrilling in listening to the towering arrangements built around chattering guitars, pounded keyboards and slugging drums and it was certainly refreshingly different and making an 18 minute version of "By The Time I Get To Phoenix" (and has anyone noticed how often this song has been mentioned in the book?) worth listening to is surely beyond the call of duty. Add in an inspired visual image on the cover and an instantly memorable album title, and *Hot Buttered Soul* has to be considered a "key" LP by virtually any definition. Moreover, it could be argued that it, more than any other LP then to date, was responsible for breaking the domination the 45 had long held in the purchasing choices of black audiences; now LPs could - and did - compete.

Given the LP's overwhelming success (it stayed on the pop charts for over 18 months) it was absolutely guaranteed that the follow-up set would mimic it in every way possible; which is exactly what happened as *The Isaac Hayes Movement* also only contained four tracks, all long, as well as a fabulous photo of "Black Moses" on the inside gatefold cover. What it couldn't replicate, though, was the "shock" value of *HBS* which had been so revolutionary, and *The Isaac Hayes Movement* thus sounded rather predictable, if certainly enjoyable enough. Not that this impaired sales as the set also sold strongly (although it didn't go "gold" like *HBS*) and once again, Stax put more emphasis on the LP rather than the single pulled from it, "I Stand Accused", which only went to # 23 soul.

To Be Continued became a third successive #1 soul LP for Hayes at the start of 1971, a set on which Stax spent even less time on worrying about singles than the previous two: "The Look Of Love" was half-heartedly put out on a 45 and didn't even hit the top 100 soul charts, an extraordinary event given how popular Hayes was at the time and proof if anyone needs it of how much promotion mattered in the music industry. Anyway, it was more of the same, a handful of well-known songs stretched out to inordinate length and if the record buying public was still besotted with Hayes' approach on albums, I was becoming just a tad bored and starting to compare his versions with others; Hayes' "You've Lost That Loving Feeling" may have been three times longer than The Righteous Brothers' but was it three times better? I was also starting to be aware of the fact that Hayes was a good but by no means great singer, and there might need to come a time when he could deliver when not sheltered by his brilliant musicians and arrangements.

You had to hand it to Hayes as his next album proved that he could be concise when he wanted to be, but as a great example of having your cake and eating it, managed to display this new laconic style in a double LP. Not that he couldn't still drag things out further than anyone else, though, as "Do Your Thing" clocked in at over nineteen minutes. Nonetheless, there were plenty of "typical soundtrack" cuts of around three minutes or even less, but his ability to write an urgent song was brilliantly demonstrated by the "Theme From Shaft" which went to # 2 soul and #1 pop; Stax had been rather disdaining Hayes as a purveyor of 45s but they knew a good thing when they saw it and Hayes joined the select few of soul artists who had both a #1 pop single and #1 pop album at the same time. Not finished yet, Stax edited "Do Your Thing" by a not too shabby sixteen minutes and were rewarded with a #3 single on the soul listings.

Another double album appeared next, *Black Moses*, which

clocked in at a barely believable ninety-two minutes. That may well represent just about the best value for money of any LP in history, and certainly its success was once again impressive, but I found it to be way too much of a good thing, almost completely indigestible at one sitting, but if dipped into from time to time can be rewarding with favourites being an intriguing "Never Gonna Give You Up" and the raunchy "Good Love 6-9969". The cover, however, showed just how far soul LPs had come as regards importance; early Stax albums featured fairly simple drawings by one Ronnie Stoots; *Black Moses* was a substantially more complicated thing, on which large sums of money were lavished.

Hayes didn't release a new LP in 1972 - Enterprise confining themselves to issuing three singles only - but returned in 1973 with yet another double album, *Live At The Sahara Tahoe,* the sales of which were once again none too shabby (his second "gold" set) and proof that his time in the public eye had not yet come to an end. I can't pass comment on this LP for the simple reason I have never heard it, nor particularly wanted to.

I did like parts of *Joy* though (even if "I love You That's All" was a waste of plastic), not least because the LP did evince a change in direction, even if Hayes' trademark long tracks were still intact. The departure came in the material: the predictable cover songs were discarded in favour of five Hayes originals; it was good to see he had remembered that he had been responsible for writing some of the greatest songs in soul's history. "A Man Will Be A Man" and the title track were his best compositions in years with the latter managing to sustain interest over its sixteen minute length and when truncated in order to be put out as a 45 reached #7 soul (and #30 pop) although no-one could have possibly foreseen at the time that it would be thirteen years before Hayes reached the top ten soul charts again.

By 1973 Stax were in deep financial straits, and this situation directly affected Hayes' next two albums both of which were soundtracks, with one, *Truck Turner*, being yet another double. It is hard to know how they would have performed in the marketplace had all been well with the record label, as Hayes was still a highly bankable star, but surely their mediocrity would have prohibited them from selling strongly. It's a moot point, however, as given Stax's problems they sold disastrously. A *Best Of* was released in 1975 (which was actually pressed up in 1973), a real last throw of the dice from Enterprise, but it also fared poorly.

Use Me 1975 Stax STX.1043 (UK)

A number of collections came out after Stax had gone under but I'll mention one, *Use Me,* as it featured five strong cuts - four of which were previously unreleased - including the well-known Bill Withers' title song. the excellent "I'm Gonna Have To Tell Her" and a marathon take on "Feel Like Making Love". (More or less the same LP was reissued as "Hotbed" on Stax STX 4102 in 1978.)

Chocolate Chip 1975 ABC ABCD-874 Producer: Isaac Hayes (Billboard soul charts: 1; Billboard pop charts: 18)

Disco Connection 1975 ABC ABCD-923 Producer: Isaac Hayes (Billboard soul charts: 19; Billboard pop : 85)

Groove-A-Thon 1976 ABC ABCD-925 Producer: Isaac Hayes (Billboard soul charts: 11; Billboard pop charts: 45)

Juicy Fruit (Disco Freak) 1976 ABC ABCD-953 Producer: Isaac Hayes (Billboard soul charts: 18; Billboard pop charts: 124)

A Man And A Woman (with Dionne Warwick) 1977 ABC AB-996/2 Producers: Isaac Hayes, Dionne Warwick & Esmond Edwards (Billboard soul charts: 20; Billboard pop charts: 49)

Hayes moved to ABC in the wake of Stax's demise, and his first effort for them, *Chocolate Chip*, proved that the public still had a great appetite for his work and it became his seventh (and final) #1 soul album, and only Aretha Franklin, The Temptations and Stevie Wonder can exceed this tally. Sensibly, despite being on a new label, the album retained the things that people wanted from Hayes: an expensive gatefold album cover; long tracks; lush yet rhythmic music recorded in Memphis. There was a Tony Joe White song on board, but all else was self-penned. As at Stax, the LP performed considerably better than the two singles released from it with neither the title track nor "Come Live With Me" attaining the soul top ten. The former sounded pretty similar in many ways to "Shaft", while the latter was a soporific piece, and only the urgent and well-constructed "I Can't Turn Around", my favourite from the set, really caught my attention.

Chocolate Chip was followed by the spectacularly ill-judged *Disco Connection* by the "Isaac Hayes Movement". Not only was it entirely instrumental, but it was incredibly dull "wallpaper" music, devoid of any interest at all and it ran the risk of completely derailing his career. All these years later, I can only wonder at what Hayes and ABC thought they were doing.

Hayes' next two releases, *Groove - a - thon* and *Juicy Fruit (Disco Freak)*, were certainly better than, and performed better than, the hapless *Disco Connection* but they were releases from a man whose time had recently passed and, apart from some inevitable disco flourishes, sounded by and large like music we had heard from Hayes many times before. "Rock Me Easy Baby" from *Groove - A - Thon* had a nice hook and would have made a good three minute track, but, inevitably, it lasted for over eight while listening today to the title track or "Music To Make Love By" from *Juicy Fruit* merely makes me feel rather sad; a great artist reduced to utter mediocrity.

There were two things Hayes had not yet done on ABC which he had done on Stax: a) cut a "live" set b) recorded a double album. Both omissions were rectified at the same time for Hayes' last LP for the label when he teamed up with Dionne Warwick at The Fabulous Fox in Atlanta. Maybe surprisingly, their voices blended attractively and when singing their respective hits it was good stuff, but it's a shame that they elected to cover "Feelings", "My Eyes Adored You", "That's The Way I Like It", "My Love" and a few other well-known songs.

New Horizon 1977 Polydor PD-1- 6120 Producer: Isaac Hayes (Billboard soul charts: 26; Billboard pop charts: 78)

For The Sake Of Love 1978 Polydor PD-1- 6164 Producer: Isaac Hayes (Billboard soul charts: 15; Billboard pop charts: 75)

Don't Let Go 1979 Polydor PD-1- 6224 Producer: Isaac Hayes (Billboard soul charts: 9; Billboard pop charts: 39)

Royal Rappin's (with Millie Jackson) 1979 Polydor PD-1-6229 Producers: Millie Jackson & Brad Shapiro (Billboard soul charts: 17; Billboard pop charts: 80)

And Once Again 1980 Polydor PD-1- 6269 Producer: Isaac Hayes (Billboard soul charts: 26; Billboard pop : 59)

Lifetime Thing 1981 Polydor PD-1-6329 Producer: Isaac Hayes

Hayes moved to Polydor in 1977 and also moved his recording location from Memphis to Atlanta, although arranger Johnny Allen guitarist Michael Toles and drummer Willie Hall (who had all been so brilliant right back on *Hot Buttered Soul*) were still on board as was master bassist Willie Weeks. Once again, things didn't change much on *New Horizons* and the two long disco-ish tracks on side one set the tone. "Out Of The Ghetto" was rhythmically interesting and the romantic "It's Heaven To Me" was strikingly slow, almost coming to a dead stop. Hayes had made nearly twenty albums by this time and it was clear he was increasingly unlikely to attract many new fans; you either liked his thing a great deal or you didn't much at all.

For The Sake Of Love was a step up *from New Horizon* in a couple of ways: firstly, in the admittedly pretty ordinary "Zeke The Freak" it contained a single that would put him back onto the top 20 of the soul charts for the first time in three years; second in "Don't Let Me Be Lonely Tonight" (the James Taylor song) and "If We Ever Needed Peace" (Hayes' own) it included two of his best tracks for ages, both being slow, beautifully orchestrated and obviously heartfelt. On the other hand, "Shaft II" simply wasted plastic - it wasn't even that different - and a nine minute version of Billy Joel's "Just The Way You Are" was a bore.

Given the modest commercial showing of Hayes for a few years it was surprising to see that *Don't Let Go* contained a single, in the form of the title track, which was to become the second biggest pop hit of his entire career when it reached #18 in late 1979. Out and out disco on a venerable old song, it certainly didn't tax Isaac vocally, and the same can be said for "Fever", which I'm sorry to say is one of the worst versions I have ever heard. I much preferred "What Does It Take", a nice midtempo number, and "A Few More Kisses To Go" which was firmly in Teddy Pendergrass territory but Hayes could plausibly claim he had been recording in such a style for many years before the former Blue Note.

Almost concurrently with *Don't Let Go*, Polydor had the inspired idea to team Hayes up with another of their artists, Millie Jackson, and, moreover, moved him into her territory rather than vice versa. i.e. it was recorded in Muscle Shoals rather than Atlanta and she, rather than Hayes, co-produced with Brad Shapiro. In fact, Jackson rather delivered Hayes a "kick up the arse" forcing him to bring more energy to the project than any record he had been involved in for years and the result was the second best LP of his entire career. Jackson always excelled on country songs and the project was full of them with Hayes also showing a great ability for recording in this style; it was such a pleasure to hear him on songs that had strong melodies and hooks and were not interminably long; it's a brilliant set, despite the fact that "Do You Wanna Make Love" and "You Never Cross My Mind" only performed adequately as singles.

And Once Again was a fair title for a LP that returned to the more typical Hayes' sound and approach as if *Royal Rappin's* had never happened but it is a good effort, rather beautifully orchestrated and arranged, with three slow drawn-out tracks including a sumptuous version of "It's All In The Game", one good uptempo cut, "Love Has Been Good To Us", and one rather throwaway disco sound, "I Ain't Never".

Hayes' Polydor period was coming to an end, and went out with rather a whimper as *It's A Lifetime Thing* failed to reach any chart at all, the first time one of his new albums had suffered such a fate and it was his therefore his worst performing record since *Tough Guys* in the grim last months of Stax. Perversely, I thought it was one of his better efforts for the label with only "Three Times A Lady" being unworthy of his talent. He covered "I'm So Proud" well, the title track was pretty and "Fugitive" and "I'm Gonna Make You Love Me" were danceable without resorting to disco cliché.

U-Turn 1986 Columbia FC 40316 Producers: Isaac Hayes, Bernard Jackson, David Conley & David Townsend (Billboard soul charts: 32)

Love Attack 1988 Columbia FC 40941 Producer: Isaac Hayes (Billboard soul charts: 70)

Hayes concentrated on acting for a while before returning with a couple of LPs on Columbia. The first, *U-Turn*, was hardly that, but did contain a big hit for the star when "Ike's Rap / Hey Girl" reached #9 on the soul charts in 1986, although, tellingly, missed the pop charts altogether (as did the LP). It's not a set to my taste but its appeal was obvious and after twenty years of making albums one could only admire his staying power and skill.

I couldn't really warm to his last vinyl LP, *Love Attack*, either but sadly for Hayes many others felt the same way and it only crawled to #70 soul, a sad state of affairs for such an important artist.

A few more singles followed as did a new CD in 1995 while a new batch of fans were recruited by his "Chef" alias at the end of the century. He died in August 2008 safe in the knowledge that he was one of the most important artists in the history of soul music, both for his songwriting and for the way in which he changed the way record companies and record buyers thought about soul LPs.

Mighty Doug Haynes

Mighty Doug Haynes 1974 Dakar DK 76911 Producer: Alonzo Tucker

I like this LP, but it had little chance of becoming a success, given that every one of its ten songs had already been a hit for someone else. Not only that, but Dakar simply re-cycled the backing tracks that had been used on some of these other hits already ("I'll Be Right Here" for Tyrone Davis and "The Sly, The Slick And The Wicked" for The Lost Generation for example) and it was thus plain they were not prepared to spend a lot of time and effort in building up a career for Mighty Doug Haynes.

Judging by the LP cover Haynes was a huge young man, with a soulful voice of some range, and if anyone wants to hear really good covers of "Love On A Two Way Street", "Can I Change My Mind" and "Yes, I'm Ready" this is the place to find them. A rather weak version of "Oo Wee Baby I Love You" was put out as a 45 that bombed and to the best of my knowledge Haynes never made any other records before or since. My own copy of the album is on a Spanish label, Zafiro, and I wonder why anyone thought it was likely to be an LP that would sell in large quantity on the Iberian Peninsula.

Reginald Haynes (see also The Escorts)

On The Wings Of Love 1986 Escort 1001 Producer: Reginald Haynes

The one LP by Reginald Haynes was issued after the book's 1982 "cut-off date", but as he had performed as the lead singer on three albums for the Escorts many years before, he satisfies my criterion for entry. Recorded in Plainfield, New Jersey, on an obviously tight budget, the LP breaks down as 50% good, 40% rather dull and 10% poor, but as Haynes was a gifted singer, who now and then phrased rather like Philippe Wynne, it was nice to see the LP come out at all. My percentages above are based entirely on the quality of the songs rather than if they suited Haynes or not as he delivers them all in pretty much the same way, and the rather thin-sounding heavily synthesised backing (nobody's "fault"; there was not much money around) never really varies. So examples of "good" are "I Only Have Eyes For You", "Look Over Your Shoulder" and "Oona'o", while "rather dull" would include "Everything Must Change" or "I Can Dream About You" and bringing up the rear as "poor" is the only original song on display, a dance thing called "Get Ready To Move" that is out of step with the relaxed tempos of everything else on the set.

Eugene Haywood

Weekends And Holidays 1980 Hammer N' Nails HNS-1948 Producer: David Ackerman

This is another rare LP; indeed my copy comes in a plain white sleeve but others did appear with a "proper" cover, even though it was a rather irrelevant drawing of a woman eating a banana. Eugene Haywood is another in a startlingly long line of highly talented singers who have no fame or following and were given but a brief chance to turn that situation around. Sadly, he couldn't do it, but it wasn't for a lack of quality as this is a fine album, recorded in Muscle Shoals I believe, with the good tracks outdoing the bad. "Booty Boppin'" and "Same Old Funk" - the titles give it away - are dreary but he delivers a good version of "Pass It On" and a great one of "Sweet Home Alabama" and if "I Can Believe The Magic", "Lifetime Guarantee" and "Love Won't Leave You Alone" are not the best songs ever written they all afford the simple pleasure of listening to a fine soul singer doing his highly accomplished thing.

Leon Haywood

Soul Cargo 1966 Fat Fish 2525 Producer: Cliff Goldsmith (Billboard soul charts: 19)

The Mellow Mellow 1967 Galaxy 8206 No producer listed

It's Got To Be Mellow 1968 Decca DL 74949 Producer: Warren Lanier

The talented and durable Leon Haywood was born in Houston in 1942 and recorded a couple of singles on the West Coast that went nowhere before he scored big with his fourth release when "She's With Her Other Love" on the Imperial label reached #13 soul at the end of 1965. The single came out as by "Leon Hayward" which must simply have been a misprint as no other record he released in a thirty year plus history ever billed him as anything other than Leon Haywood. (I'm surprised Berry Gordy's normally vigilant lawyers let the 45 pass without challenge, by the way, as it has a decidely similar melody to "Where Did Our Love Go").

No album appeared on Imperial, though, and Haywood moved to the Fat Fish imprint where he put out an all-instrumental set in the Ramsey Lewis mould, in front of a "live" audience either in the studio or in a nightclub somewhere. It was an interesting change of direction, if not a very interesting LP, and it did surprisingly well on the soul LP charts even if four singles he put on the label did not chart at all.

Haywood's second LP, *The Mellow Mellow Leon Haywood*, was actually a type of "from the vaults" set released by Galaxy to try and cash in on the fact that Leon had by now moved to Decca and placed a big single on the Hot 100 with the word "mellow" in the title. It's a good LP featuring Haywood in a number of styles, none of which were instrumentals. Despite his undoubted talents in writing, arranging and producing I have never considered him to be an absolutely top-drawer vocalist as he doesn't have the range and distinctiveness that such an accolade would require, and it is fascinating to hear him take on aspects of other singers on the set. For a first example, he phrases much like another great West Coast soul man, Jimmy Lewis, on the excellent "Ever Since You Were Sweet Sixteen" and for a second, he invokes Marvin Gaye on "Ain't No Use". Both of these songs had already seen service on Fat Fish singles a year or so earlier as had "Baby Reconsider" a precise and pounding Motown groove that was to become a huge record in years to come on the UK "Northern Soul" scene. Digging back even further, "The Truth About Money", "I'm Gonna Wait" and the marvellous "You're All For Yourself " had all come out on 45s back in 1963 and 1964 with the former sounding distinctly like Gaye's "Can I Get A Witness" and the latter being his best ever recording in a near-deep soul idiom. Only "Cotton Song", almost folk in construction, didn't really work for me and the album, all written by Haywood, and produced by an uncredited Cliff Goldsmith, was probably the best he ever cut.

It was certainly better than his one and only LP on Decca, which despite one superb track, was too uneven to sustain interest or warrant recommendation. I rather suspect it was a rush job, put out in haste after the excellent title song had reached #21 soul and #63 pop in the summer of 1967. Decent if not amazing versions of "Mercy Mercy", "I Can't Stop Loving You", "Nobody Knows You When You're Down And Out" and "Tennessee Waltz" kept most of side one up to a pretty good standard but "Yesterday" was the standard fall-back song on way too many LPs, and the entire second side reverted to instrumentals, which were ok, but it's hard to imagine too many people looking forward to playing them a third or fourth time.

Leon Haywood 1971 Jim-Edd no number no producer listed

Home To Stay 1973 20th Century T-411 Producer: Leon Haywood

Keep It In The Family 1974 20th Century T-440 Producer: Leon Haywood (Billboard soul charts: 35)

Come And Get Yourself Some 1974 20th Century T-476 (Producer: Leon Haywood (Billboard soul charts: 21; Billboard pop charts: 140)

Over the next few years Haywood had to content himself with having singles rather than albums issued and it wasn't until another new label and a new decade came along that record store shelves once again contained a new Leon Haywood LP. (They wouldn't have stocked a rare promo only 12 track album from 1971, containing mainly Decca and Atlantic material). It was pretty different from what had gone before, too. 20th Century was a label famed for the lushness and expansiveness of its productions and *Back To Stay*, as usual brimming with a number of Haywood compositions, seeing the benefit of this approach. It's a nice enough set, with "There Ain't Enough Hate Around" being the best song, but two singles pulled from it failed to hit the national charts, and cover versions of "Make Me Yours" and "Let Them Talk" were serviceable rather than inspired.

However, in early 1974 Haywood put out a single, "Keep It In The Family", which sounded like a cross between Johnnie Taylor's "I Believe In You" and any number of things that The Staple Singers were recording at the time, and was rewarded with his first national soul chart entrant for six years, and the third biggest hit of his entire career when it came to rest at #11 soul and #50 pop. It also became the title track of his next album for the 20th Century label, a collection that contained a second 45 in the rather slight "Sugar Lump" which stalled at #35 soul, as well as just missing the top 100 pop. Overall, the album sounded much the same as its predecessor and one track, the Isaac Hayes-ish eight minute long "As Long As There's You", was even reprised from the earlier collection. Three other tracks worth a mention: "B.M.F. Beautiful" was an instrumental far removed from his jazzy efforts of a few years ago, this one being a heavily orchestrated thing designed to show off Gene Page's arranging skills; "When It Comes Down On You" an excellent Lincoln Chase composition, was atypical of the rest of the set, being slightly bluesy and restrained; Liverpool fans would surely approve of his winning rendering of "You'll Never Walk Alone".

Knowing a good thing when they heard it, 20th Century decided to more or less exactly copy "Keep It In The Family" with "Believe Half Of What You See (And None Of What You Hear)" and were doubtless delighted when they realised they had got away with it as the 45 made it to #21 soul in early 1975. It was one of four singles that reached the soul top thirty from the *Come And Get Yourself Some* album, and for that one year Leon Haywood was one of the most successful of all soul singers. The title track, a tuneful, lilting number utilising steel drums, reached #19 soul but the big hit was the "provocative" "I Want To Do Something Freaky To You", whose intriguing and memorable arrangement was much better than its dull lyrics and clichéd moaning background girl singer; it went to #7 soul and #15 pop, the only time in his life he had a 45 nestle in the Hot top twenty. "Just Your Fool" borrowed heavily from Al Green's "Love And Happiness" and became the fourth successful single from the set when it was backed with "Consider The Source" (interestingly, he had previously cut both sides for Capitol at the end of the sixties). "You Need A Friend Like Mine", that fine Frederick Knight song, was a good choice to cover and all in all, it was his third enjoyable album in a row.

Intimate 1976 Columbia AL 34363 Producer: Leon Haywood

Haywood left 20th Century in 1976, for one album on Columbia, which gave a nod to Haywood 's "love man" persona as established on "Freaky" and we thus got a by-the-numbers cover of "Let's Get It On" and "Strokin'", another big soul hit for him (#13 in 1976) with absurdly obvious Ohio Players' influenced background vocals. Better was the excellent "Streets Will Love You To Death" (co-penned with longtime songwriting partner Marshall McQueen), which disappointingly fared much worse as a 45 (#63) than the greatly inferior "Strokin'". Van McCoy turned up as a songwriter on a Haywood set for the first time with two typically tuneful compositions while there was a rather pointless re-make of "It's Got To Be Mellow" to round an album off which was neither better nor worse than his other work over the last two or three years but it strangely refused to chart.

Double My Pleasure 1977 MCA 2322 Producer: Leon Haywood

Energy 1978 MCA 3090 Producer: Leon Haywood

Haywood jumped labels again for a two year stay at MCA, a sojourn that brought forth little in the way of memorable music or big hit singles although four 45s from his two MCA LPs did reach the national soul charts, one of which, "Super Sexy", borrowed from "Clean Up Woman" which was a good idea even if Betty Wright's record was miles better. *Energy* had a horrible cover and disco tracks like "Just Friends" and "Party" that were well below the standard of his best work. Neither album charted.

Naturally 1980 20th Century T-613 Producer: Leon Haywood (Billboard soul charts: 22; Billboard pop charts: 92)

It's Me Again 1983 Casablanca 422-810 304-1 M1 Producer: Leon Haywood (Billboard soul charts: 48)

The Leon Haywood Story Then & Now 1989 Evejim EJ-2025 Producer: Leon Haywood

Freaky Man 1994 Evejim 71009 Producer: Leon Haywood

He sensibly returned to 20th Century and immediately enjoyed a huge hit with "Don't Push It, Don't Force It" which went to #2 soul and #49 pop. Good for him, of course, but I find this style of music to have dated badly, and the *Naturally* LP on which the hit was housed pretty much completely passed me by.

Yet another label move saw him pitch up on Casablanca and *It's Me Again* carried two smallish hits within. Again, it was not a memorable set, with functional dance floor cuts throughout, and re-makes of "Keep It In The Family" and "I Wanta Do Something Freaky To You" suggested a paucity of new song ideas, too.

Haywood had been putting out his work songs under the banner of "Evejim productions" for a number of years so it was a logical step for him to set up his own record label under this title at the end of the eighties and his first LP on this new imprint consisted mainly of songs he had recorded before. I haven't heard the album so don't know if these were the original tracks or re-cuts.

I also haven't heard his final vinyl LP, *Freaky Man*, which chose to replicate the worst cover - *Energy* - he had ever previously put out on an LP. It also consists of previously recorded songs, throws in some instrumentals by all accounts but didn't restore him to any commercial prominence.

Haywood continued (and continues) to do very good work up to this day as excellent production jobs on LPs by the likes of Buddy Ace and Clay Hammond prove. He is not a great soul singer, but does understand his audience particularly well, and has always had the ability and flexibility to record in a number of different styles in order to keep his impressive career going. Never a big star, he remains an important player in soul music's history.

Haze

Steve Powers; Willy Thomas; Peter Johnson; Michael Lopez; Paul Johnson; Janelle Green; Solomon Hughes; Wil Ternior; Steve Balenger

Haze 1974 ASI 198 Producer: Dan Holmes

Haze 1978 Moonspell S80-1536 Producer: David Rivkin?

The "Twin Cities", Minneapolis - St. Paul's, were put on the musical map, so to speak, by Prince but years before he released his first records a seven piece band called Haze put out an LP, which even included a track that made it to #89 on the soul charts in the spring of 1975, when "I Do Love My Lady" reached that admittedly not very high peak, but it was still an accomplishment for an area that had not provided much in the way of hits from black singers and musicians in the past.

It's a nice side too, one of those ballads that funk bands often managed to turn out surprisingly well, but apart from a fine and relatively similar "When We Were Kids", also delivered competently by Willy Thomas, it is not typical of the rest of the album, which is faster and funkier, and is best represented by the rather good "Are You Free". Haze should be applauded for not obviously aping anyone else (although there is a soupcon of War in their sound) and by and large they did away with the horns that many self-contained bands favoured. There is no "killer" cut on here as there is not a song or groove that genuinely stands out as something special but anyone who likes conga, guitar, organ and bass driven mid-seventies funk should find this LP to their liking.

The second album is one for collectors to track down and I don't believe it ever really came out "officially" but, as was often the case, copies managed to sneak out nevertheless, even if the band would have had no knowledge of nor made any money whatsoever from its existence. The sound had changed slightly with horns being employed much more liberally, leading to a sound firmly in the Earth, Wind & Fire style. I prefer the first set as the Moonspell collection rather overdoes the synthesiser and they just didn't have as much strong material as EWAF, added to which any band who apes another so shamelessly must have a few points deducted to my mind.

Eddie Hazel (see also Funkadelic and Parliament)

Game, Dames And Guitar Thangs 1977 Warner Brothers BS 3058 Producers: George Clinton & Eddie Hazel

Eddie Hazel was the best-known guitarist in the Parliament / Funkadelic set-up and, as such, has any number of devotees who would have great interest in this set, which is easy to write about; it's just as much a rock album as a "soul" one, and anyone who likes the Parliafunkadelicment vision will love it; anyone who doesn't will hate it.

Hearts Of Stone

Carl Cutler; Floyd Lawson; John Myers ; Lindsey Griffin

Stop The World - We Wanna Get On 1970 V.I.P. VS404 Producer: Henry Cosby

Coming Out 1976 Flo 89 Producer: Floyd Lawson (Canada)

Anyone could be forgiven for thinking that a vocal group who recorded for a Motown subsidiary label would pretty much have success guaranteed, but this was not the case for The Hearts Of Stone. All the members of the quartet had recorded for other outfits in the past (including collectively as The Four Pennies) before coming together to cut for the Detroit giant, but their one LP and the two singles released from it made little impact, and the group remain unknown to all but record collectors. It's nice to see that the talented Henry Cosby got a shot at producing a whole LP, even if it was very much a hit and miss affair.

It starts well enough with three excellent tracks, "It's A Lonesome Road", "If I Could Give You The World" and "Would You Take A Dime From A Poor Man", before rather nose-diving in quality, only re-surfacing with a good closing song, "One Day". It's a highly typical Motown album in that respect and covers like "Rainy Night In Georgia", "He Ain't Heavy He's My Brother", and an awful "Thank You Falletinme Be Mice Elf Again" simply smack of having to get the LP up to eleven tracks. A dreadful mess of a song, "You Gotta Sacrifice", written by the group, also rather spoiled things which was a shame and a surprise given that they had already proved their composing skills on the four winning cuts mentioned above.

The second album was cut in and only came out in Canada (if indeed, it really "came out" at all in the sense of being easily available to buy) and was released as by "Floyd Lawson and The Heart Of Stone", as I believe the other members had all departed by this time. Consisting of ten songs previously performed by others, including "It Only Takes A Minute" and "Love Won't Let Me Wait", it is one of the fastest records I have ever heard with everything performed at a breakneck speed. I'm sure there was a point to recording and pressing up the LP, but it's hardly essential.

Heartstoppers

Betty Baker; Tina Lee; Joyce Curry; Geraldine Curry

Heartstoppers 1971 All Platinum AP 3005 Producers: Gerald Harris & Toby Henry

This is yet another cheap looking (although certainly not cheap costing these days) LP on the All Platinum label that must have sold a tiny amount, given it was performed by a quartet of women who had neither previous success nor a large fan base. Still, such seeming drawbacks never stopped the label from issuing albums in the manner other labels issued singles and although it's by no means a poor set, I think it falls significantly short of the tagline to a recent CD re-issue of the album which proclaims it to be "the finest girl group LP of all time". The overall lack of production quality, shortage of genuinely strong songs and mixture of styles rule out such an accolade from my perspective, but it certainly does have good moments, and none are better than the deep "When The Hurt Comes Back" which was so perfectly suited to Linda Jones that she sang it too and "A Few Moments Of Pleasure" is in a similar vein. "Where Does The Love Go" has an arresting arrangement and memorable tune, "The Ice Is Melting" is pure Motown in construction, "More Of You" is big, bold and blowsy while "Stop Boy" could easily have appeared on the Hot Wax logo. I'm not sure who carries the leads but it is clear that different singers perform on different songs with the husky and rather nasal tones of whoever performs "When The Hurt Comes Back" being my favourite. A handful of singles were issued that can be found on the set (including two sides that appeared on a 45 as by (Little) Betty Baker rather than The Heartstoppers) but none did anything and The Heartstoppers vanished soon after. (There was also a single issued by "Geraldine Curry and The Heart-stoppers" (the songs are not on the LP) but it is not clear if it appeared before or after the album was released.)

A Japanese copy of the LP came out in 1989 on P-Vine PLP-6527 which added four tracks that had not featured on the original set including another Motown clone, "Marching Out Of Your Life".

Heart To Heart

Bobby James; Frank McKinney; Rick Williams; Glenn Walker; Al Joyner; Skinner; Z.B. Malone; Darius Chapman

Tuff 1982 Raven R-33-1021 Producer: Jerry Wise

Cheap cover, expensive record; this is another LP that was only issued in small quantity and is much sought after as a result. It was cut in Dothan, Alabama, hardly the recording capital of the world, and presumably the band came from the same area. "Lullaby","Never Make a Believer Of Me" and "Nowhere To Go" are nicely sung and harmonised slow songs, and deserved to have come out on a bigger label who could have provided more opulent musical backing. On the evidence on these songs Heart To Heart were *good*; shame that impression is rather dispelled by "Short Pants", "Zebulon (We Can Do It)" and the title track.

Walter Heath

You Know You're Wrong Don't You Brother
1976 Buddah BDS 5615 Producer: Lewis Shelton

Walter Heath worked the same field as other artists such as Charles Bevel, Ralph Graham, Jae Mason and a handful of others in a small sub-genre of soul that arose in the seventies as a result of the success Bill Withers had been enjoying with his brand of introspective, highly personal songs. Heath's work, like the others mentioned above, valued words every bit as much as music and the lyrics from the ten tracks were proudly printed on an insert sheet inside the LP. From it we learn that Heath was responsible for the music on every song save one, but shared the responsibility of writing the lyrics with a handful of others. Musicians were the expert West Coast crew of Wilton Felder, Ray Parker, Michael Omartian, Ed Greene et al.

It's a glorious set, too, covering a broad sweep of subject matter including love, drug dealing and lying politicians, and nothing shines brighter than the brilliant title track, where the already strong song is lifted by one of the most uplifting and instantly memorable choruses of the seventies. "I Thought You Might Like To Know", "Put Your Love In My Hands", "Africa" and "Brother (Don't You Miss Your Mother)" are all well above average too, and while a couple of other cuts are no more than so-so, this is a highly cohesive collection that did both Walter Heath and Buddah proud. "I Am Your Leader" even made it to #51 soul as a single, but the rather mysterious singer disappeared from view completely after the LP and single had run their race.

Heaven And Earth (see also Cashmere)

Keith Steward; James Dukes; Dwight Dukes; Michael Brown; Greg Rose; Dean Williams

I Can't Seem To Forget You 1976 GEC 1001 Producer: Clarence Johnson

Heaven & Earth 1978 Mercury SRM- 1- 3722 Producers: Clarence Johnson, Rodney Massey & Lawrence Hanks

Fantasy 1979 Mercury SRM- 1- 3763 Producers: Clarence Johnson & Riccardo Williams (Billboard soul charts: 45)

That's Love 1981 WMOT JW-37074 Producer: Samuel Peake

Heaven and Earth were one of the last groups to release an LP in what was a recognisably Chicago style: swooping strings and assertive horns arranged over punchy rhythms with a high lead tenor sweetly singing while being supported by tight backing vocals. That tenor lead belonged to Dwight Dukes and all the four young members of Heaven and Earth can look back at their debut LP from a vantage point of nearly forty years and be proud of their contribution to a great city's soul tradition. It's a really good set that mixes up tempos with generally strong songs, and the title track's rather dismal showing on the national soul charts, #83, distorts the fact that it was a huge seller in their home town. Other high points: "I'll Always Love You" was a delightful mid-tempo number of exceeding grace; "Let Me Back In" had a memorable melody and another great lead by Dukes while "If It Was Me" and "The Message" are just perfect for fans of the early seventies sweet soul style. "The Window Lady" was also intriguing and worthy of a listen even if it sounded years out of date, strongly recalling the work Norman Whitfield had been doing with The Temptations in 1971. The show piece of the set was presumably meant to be "Now That I've Got You, I'll Be Flying High" given it was over eight minutes in length but it was a rather dull song and the group sounded better when they were confined to three or four minutes.

The follow-up album, released two years later, was a reasonably good one, but sounded as if it came from a totally different group. The excellent songwriters from the debut, Jerline Shelton and Maurice Commander, were nowhere in evidence, which was a shame, while a new man, Dean Wilkins, took the majority of the leads, and while he was a forceful and talented presence, Dwight Dukes' vocals had a greater distinctiveness. "Guess Who's Back In Town" was one of the best tracks on show and when put out on a 45 made it to #42 soul. As before, when the tempo was slowed down Heaven and Earth were good to listen to, but the uptempo "Run And Tell That", "No Limit" and, worst of all, "Dance-A-Thon", were all pretty poor compositions and rendered the group rather faceless.

Despite a rather ill-chosen cover that made the *Fantasy* album look like the new one from Black Sabbath, it nevertheless had an impressive second side, led off by a gorgeous version of "I Only Have Eyes For You" with a delicate and sensitive lead from Dukes. The other three songs had - I think - Greg Rose out front and he also demonstrated his ability, coming on forcefully a little like a slightly younger and more subdued Teddy Pendergrass. Praise also must go to Floyd Morris for his excellent arrangements, particularly the self-indulgent but highly enjoyable string charts on "Let's Get It Together". However, in order to get to the second side, of course, one has to first deal with the first, and that was a less prepossessing task. "I Feel A Groove Under My Feet (Parts 1 and 2)" was predictable and unengaging and "Poetry In A Box" laboured under a misleading title that only signalled another dance tune of scant appeal, where the group came under the all-pervasive EWAF influence of the time. "Feel A Groove" and "I Only Have Eyes" both made the soul charts as singles in 1979, but only at relatively lowly levels.

The group moved to WMOT for their final album, which was divided into "Heaven" and "Earth" sides, a rather spurious distinction given both sounded much the same. It is an ok album with nice harmonies throughout but there are no particularly strong songs on board, and even the slowest one on view, "Where Is The Laughter", veers too close to "Disney" rather than "sweet" for my tastes. Most of the other cuts fall into the mid-tempo range and there are no dance horrors to be confronted. The title track made it to #47 on the soul charts in mid 1981, the last time Heaven and Earth would ever be represented thus and they soon disbanded with Dwight Dukes hooking up with Cashmere, and Greg Rose joining his siblings to form The Rose Brothers.

Finis Henderson (see also Weapons Of Peace)

Finis 1983 Motown 6036ML Producer: Al McKay (Billboard soul charts: 42; Billboard pop charts: 208)

Henderson has a sweet voice, but it is rather wasted on this collection of lightly soulful pop songs of which the dance side "Skip To My Lou", a #48 soul single is probably the best. He was formerly in the rather good Chicago band, Weapons Of Peace.

J.I. Henderson

Give A Helping Hand 1975 Piggylo PI-1012 Producer: Rick Henderson

The title track to this seriously obscure album from tiny Piggylo records out of Silver Springs Maryland is terrific, sounding like the theme to the best "Blaxploitation" film you never saw. Joe Isaac Henderson comes across like an old-time preacher with a slight tremor to his deep voice on the almost equally good "Good Time Again" (which sounds a fair bit like "Wade In The Water") but does rather lose his way on "Crying" and generally you have to cross your fingers for him on the slower songs. Better again is "Ghetto Man" another track which sports vigorously driving horns and splashy drums. There are a couple of instrumentals here which don't add a lot of value but I like the fact that all the tracks, apart from the title, are all under three minutes thus avoiding self-indulgence. By the way, the front cover bills him as "The Soul Country Man" but only "Unfaithful" falls even remotely into that category.

Michael Henderson

Solid 1976 Buddah BDS 5662 Producer: Michael Henderson (Billboard soul charts: 10; Billboard pop charts: 173)

Goin' Places 1977 Buddah BDS 5693 Producer: Michael Henderson (Billboard soul charts: 18; Billboard pop charts: 49)

In The Night-time 1978 Buddah BDS 5712 Producer: Michael Henderson (Billboard soul charts: 5; Billboard pop charts: 38)

Do It All 1979 Buddah BDS 5719 Producer: Michael Henderson (Billboard soul charts: 17; Billboard pop charts: 64)

Wide Receiver 1980 Buddah BDS 6001 Producer: Michael Henderson (Billboard soul charts: 6; Billboard pop charts: 35)

Slingshot 1981 Buddah BDS 6002 Producers: Michael Henderson & Chuck Jackson (Billboard soul charts: 14; Billboard pop charts: 86)

Fickle 1983 Buddah BDS 6004 Producers: Michael Henderson, Paul Lawrence Jones & Thomas McClary (Billboard soul charts: 41; Billboard pop charts: 169)

Michael Henderson, a physically imposing man six and a half feet tall, is a superb bass player, having played on Motown sessions and in Miles Davis' bands, this demonstrating a flexibility of approach that has always made him much in demand. He first came to recorded prominence in the "soul world", as it were, when he shared lead vocals with Jean Carn on Norman Connors' "Valentine Love" 45 and saw it reach #10 on the soul charts at the end of 1975.

In the following year he released his first solo LP, *Solid*, the ramifications of which were pretty spectacular. Not only did Henderson announce himself as a performer who could sell lots of records, not only was he charismatic, not only could he sing, write, arrange and produce in addition to playing the bass just about as well as anyone, he also saw two of the songs from the album become 45s for The Dramatics, one of which, "Be My Girl", went all the way to #3 soul. His own version of the same song did slightly less well as a single (#23 soul) and "You Haven't Made It To The Top" fared even worse (#80) but the LP sold strongly in the soul market. It was an eclectic affair, with a number of tracks betraying his jazzy background, while "Be My Girl" and a version of "Valentine Love" (sans Carn) showed his skill at performing slow and romantic material. To round things off, "Make Me Feel Better" and "Made It To The Top" showed he could funk most effectively.

Buddah saw they had something special in Henderson (he had also undertaken lead vocals on two more top-selling singles on the label by Connors in the summer of 1976, "We Both Need Each Other" and "You Are My Starship") and pushed the boat out for the follow-up album, *Goin' Places*, encasing it in a gate-fold cover. The album was similar to its predecessor but Henderson demonstrated yet another facet of his talent when he sang "Whip It" and other cuts in a high register, utilising phrasing that recalled Marvin Gaye. The album performed significantly better in the pop market than *Solid* and two singles, "I Can't Help It" (on which he played bongos; was there anything he couldn't do?) and the splendid "Won't You Be Mine" sold respectably if not spectacularly. Elsewhere, Roberta Flack joined him on "In The Concert", thus adding another spectacular name to the list of women with whom he duetted.

Henderson's best album came next. *In The Night-Time* went gold and also contained his biggest ever single hit in the marvellous "Take Me, I'm Yours", a duet with a fired-up Rena Scott that reached #3 soul (but only #88 pop, a market he never really cracked.) The intricately arranged title track reached #15 soul and it all added up to the conclusion that in 1978 Henderson was - albeit briefly - one of the most successful male soul singers in America. He had achieved this by dispensing with the more obviously jazzy cuts that could be found on his first two LPs and playing up even further his vocal debt to Gaye (listen to "Am I Special", for example), although the levels of musicianship were still fearfully high and Henderson's own bass playing on the highly funky "Happy" was impeccable.

Do It All was another powerful outing, adopting most of the strengths from *In The Night-Time* with two minor changes: no female duets and the first instance of a cover version in "To Be Loved". That latter song and the so-so title track were selected as singles but neither fared as well as Buddah would have hoped or expected: #62 and #56 on the soul charts respectively. As usual at this juncture of his career the appeal and pleasure of Henderson's music comes from the texture and construction of the arrangements and compositions, conjured up no doubt from his jazz background. He tended not to write instantly memorable hooks and his music required patience to get at its essence, but on long cuts such as "Wait Until The Rain" and "Riding" that patience was rewarded.

Wide Receiver, a winning set, was another top seller for Henderson, and mixed up the hardest-edged funk he had produced to date, with some impressive slower material, including two judiciously chosen cover versions: "Reach Out For Me" and "Ask The

Lonely". The first of these rather failed as a single, but two others performed much better: the title track going all the way to #4 soul and "Prove it" to #27. "Ask The Lonely" was a brave song to attempt given how brilliantly it had been done by The Four Tops, but Henderson acquitted himself exceedingly well. (Lou Courtney's "I Don't Need Nobody Else" was also an interesting song to bring on board, but Henderson didn't do as much with it as he could have done.)

Slingshot continued to take the tempo down further and further, which was just fine with me, particularly as two funk cuts on it, the title track and "(We Are Here To) Geek You Up" were devoid of much interest. Another new female singer, Venna Fields, was introduced and she did well on "In It For The Goodies" (a better funky side) and "Come To Me" but it was a more established one, Phyllis Hyman, who shared in arguably the best cut on the set, "Can't We Fall In Love Again", an excellent duet with Henderson, that reached #9 on the soul charts when put out on a 45, the last big hit he was to enjoy as it turned out. Two more excellent cover songs were included in the superbly arranged (by Gene Page, Ben Wright and Tony Coleman) "Make It Easy On Yourself" and "Never Gonna Give You Up" on which Henderson relinquished bass playing duties to Nathan East, before the meandering "Take Care" drifted along attractively at its own slow pace for nearly seven minutes to round things off nicely.

Fickle was a departure from what had gone before as Henderson was happy to entrust the production of the majority of the set to others while the practice of performing cover versions vanished, to be replaced by a handful of new songs written predominantly by The Commodores' Thomas McClary. The album also highlighted a marginally more pop-friendly side of Henderson than before as could be heard in the rather bland "Love Will Find A Way" and the memorable hook on "Thin Walls". The most attractive new song on show came from McClary and "Feeling Like Myself Once Again" had a distinct country feel, something no-one had heard before on a Michael Henderson LP. Elsewhere, "Whip It" was pressed into service once again years after featuring on the *Goin' Places* album which was a bit cheap on Buddah's part and there was a reminder of how highly funky the bassist could be on the title track with its decided Prince influence. The title track went to #33 on the soul singles charts.

Bedtime Stories 1986 EMI America ST-17181 Producer: Michael Henderson (Billboard soul charts: 30)

The Best Of 1990 Sequel NEX LP 117 (UK)

Henderson issued only one LP on EMI America and although its glossy pop feel is not really to my taste, it was nonetheless accomplished enough and showed just how far he had come from those early Buddah days, so completely had any traces of jazz been eradicated. "Do It To Me Good (Tonight)" (#17) and "Tin Soldier" (# 86) both hit the soul charts as singles, the latter being the seventeenth and last time this happened for Michael Henderson.

Since he released these albums, Henderson has retreated into the jazz world playing in a band called Children On The Corner.

Ron Henderson & Choice Of Colour

Reese Palmer; Wilbur Stewart; Johnny Johnson; William Britton

Soul Junction 1976 Chelsea CHL 542 Producers: Duke Hall & Wayne Jernigan

Charlotte, North Carolina, is not a town renowned for much contribution to soul music history, but it did its bit with the release of a few records from Ron Henderson, and his talented group, Choice of Colour (interestingly, spelt like that rather than the American "Color"). Henderson had been in the music business for a long time without ever really making much of an impact having recorded with The True Tones and The Choice Of Colour before his name was appended to the group, who were no slouches themselves, as Reese Palmer had been with The Moonglows while William Britton had added some of the most beautiful backing vocals known to man on Billy Stewart's "I Do Love You".

Their one LP appeared in 1976, recorded at the Reflection Sound studios in Charlotte, and despite a banal cover, is both rare and sought after, and deserves its acclaim, as it's first-rate. Henderson took most leads on the set, but Britton also led on a few. The group were less interesting on the uptempo material (like the dull "Outlaw") and while the Marvin Gaye influenced "I'll Be Around" is the track most soul fans know from the album, they were at their best when they slowed things down, as on "What About Love", "All Men Can't Be Wrong", a nice version of "Freedom For The Stallion" and "Mary Green", all captivating. A "hit" of sorts did arise, when the highly appealing and peaceful "Don't Take Her For Granted" (Henderson's best singing on the set) managed to climb to #74 soul on *Billboard*, but had a better run on *Cashbox*. Desperately, just as things looked good though, Chelsea went bust and apart from a single in 1983, "Gemini Lady", they never recorded again although a fine CD release of their best work came out in 2005.

Willie Henderson

Funky Chicken 1970 Brunswick BL 754163 Producers: Eugene Record, Carl Davis & Willie Henderson

Dance With Willie Henderson 1974 Brunswick BL 754202 Producer: Carl Davis & Willie Henderson

Willie Henderson is possibly the only baritone saxist who cut soul albums in his own right and over a number of years he was an important musician, writer, arranger and producer on the Chicago soul scene. His two albums, however, were not as important than his other laudable contributions.

The first, clocking in at a miserly 23 minutes, consisted solely of instrumentals apart from the odd snatch of singing here and there. As so often Brunswick could not be bothered expending too much thought on their releases and "Can I Change My Mind" and "Is It Something You've Got" simply consist of Henderson playing sax over the backing tracks already used by Tyrone Davis. Obviously riding on the coat tails of Rufus Thomas' huge hit with "Funky Chicken", Henderson's single of the same name (but its a different "song") managed to reach #22 on the soul charts in February 1970. The album is mildly enjoyable and wholly undemanding with my favourite cut being the funky "Off Into A Black Thing"; "Sugar Sugar" is the least enthralling. I assume The Soul Explosions were simply a studio band.

Henderson's second set may have been thought more generous as it lasted for around 35 minutes; until you realised it included the entire first set and only contains four new sides, but NOT his second hit, "Dance Master", #18 soul and #73 pop, which had come out on the Now Sound label. Of these new cuts, "Break Your Back" and "Loose Booty" were actually songs rather than instrumentals with the former being better than the latter. A cover of Bill Withers' "Harlem" was disappointing while "Windjammer" was dull.

He placed a third single on the soul charts in late 1974 with the enjoyable if slight "Gangster Boogie Bump"(#50) and then gave up on his own career but continued to produce and arrange for others until the end of the eighties.

Freddy Henry

Get It Out In The Open 1979 Clouds CL-8809 Producer: Al Kooper

Freddy Henry was another mysterious singer whose one LP on the TK subsidiary, Clouds, and the one single to be pulled from it, appear to be the total sum of his efforts in the music business. I have seen suggestions that he might have been a "blue-eyed" singer and there is some aural evidence to support that, particularly on side two, and the fact that the dreadful and irrelevant front cover featured a giraffe gambolling along the plains of Africa may also indicate that his identity was actively suppressed.

Anyway, such speculation is fairly irrelevant as the first side of the LP is good soul music with five well chosen songs, previously performed by top acts such as The Dells, Otis Clay, The Four Tops and The Exciters. Betty Wright helps out in her normal spirited way on "Tell Her", the track that was chosen as the a-side for the 45 from the album, although it didn't do much. Side two is less to my taste, although the title track is a good song, as it has a more tenuous link with my favoured types of soul, even verging into Rod Stewart-ish territory on occasion. Henry is well served throughout by top-class musicians such as Al Kooper, Jeff Baxter, Reggie Young, The Tower of Power Horns and the background vocal talents of Rhodes-Chalmers-Rhodes.

Hesitations

George Scott; Charles Scott; Leonard Veal; Robert Shepherd; Arthur Blakey; Philip Dorrow; Fred Deal; Joe Hunter; Bill Brent; Warnell Taylor; Jimmy Vaughan

Soul Superman 1967 Kapp KS-3525 Producers: Pied Piper & GWP

The New Born Free 1968 Kapp KS-3548 Producers: Teacho Wiltshire & Larry Banks (Billboard soul charts: 30; Billboard pop charts:193)

Where We're At! 1968 Kapp KS-3561 Producers: Teacho Wiltshire & Larry Banks

Solid Gold 1968 Kapp KS-3574 Producers: Teacho Wiltshire & Paul Robinson

Ohio has a proud tradition of being the source for great vocal groups and The Hesitations would have been one of the best of the lot had they made all their records in the style of the terrific *Soul Superman* LP, but unfortunately they became ensnared by billowing strings and dull cover versions for too much of the rest of their stay at Kapp.

Soul Superman is a life-affirming example of sixties urban soul, containing twelve songs brimming with exuberance and verve, and despite the fact that eight of them became selected as either a or b - sides for 45s, the LP still manages to be even more than the sum of its parts, a satisfyingly cohesive set, and one beloved by many fans over the years. Most of the lead vocals are taken by the skilful George Scott and the fact that everything clocks in at around 2.30 just testifies to the sharpness of the writing; there is no unnecessary fat on the bones. The title track made it to #42 on the soul charts, listings on which Kapp singles had been pretty scarce in the past. One unusual facet of the set: There are two tracks entitled "Soul Superman", and they are different songs.

"Born Free" became a huge hit for the group in early 1968 - #4 soul and #38 pop - but it was quite a shock to hear it when compared to the material on *Soul Superman* as it is resolutely MOR song, encased in strings, much softer than what had gone before, and it forced a re-appraisal of what The Hesitations were all about. It also became the title track from their second LP which was not as gratifying as its predecessor, although still more than decent. The songs weren't as strong, though, and a couple of them suffered from a seeming desire by the producers and arrangers to be more "creative" than before and mix up tempos within the same track, "Let's Groove" being an example of an approach which didn't really work. Having said that, there are many good things on here and "Don't Go". "I Believe" and "We Only Have One Life" are slower than anything found on *Soul Superman* and feature soulful singing in both the lead and back-up departments.

Given that "Born Free" had been a much more successful 45 than "Soul Superman" it was obvious what sort of song would dominate the third LP, *Where We're At!*. Thus "The Impossible Dream", "Who Will Answer", "Summertime" and "Climb Every Mountain". The first and second of these reached the soul and pop charts as singles, the last times The Hesitations ever enjoyed national hits but it's a rather dispiriting album to listen to, with pretty much every ounce of the vitality of *Soul Superman* relentlessly scoured away. Only a nice version of "A Change Is Gonna Come" and a convincing gospel song, "The Old Ship Of Zion", engage my interest at all.

Sadly, *Solid Gold* wasn't any better. The group were saddled with a set of eleven songs, every one of which was a cover version ranging from ok - "Stay In My Corner" - through rather pointless - "Georgia On My Mind" - to bad beyond belief - "Lady Madonna". Johnny Pate had been recruited to provide arrangements and there was no shortage of talent involved - the group had hardly become bad singers - but it all seemed so misdirected.

Genuine tragedy then struck the group when George Scott was killed in an accident involving the gun of another band member and although The Hesitations still released some pretty decent singles, in fact improvements over the latter years with Kapp, they did not get the chance to record any more LPs and had no more hits although a version of the group albeit with one original member only - Art Blakey - still performed live in 2015.

Lonnie Hewitt

Keepin' It Together 1977 Wee 8484 Producer: Lonnie Hewitt

Lonnie Hewitt's finest work probably came as producer for the great Freddie Hughes or as pianist for Cal Tjader but he did put out an enjoyable album in 1977; enjoyable, that is, if you can ignore the fact that he was hardly a great singer.

The opening track, "Is It Me?" is more or less a spoken recitation over the horn riff from "Can I Change My Mind?" but somehow works; the excellent and instantly striking "Newsroom" has a touch of New Birth with vocals popping in from all over the place; his version of "Gotta Keep My Bluff In" cannot match Hughes' own but does have wonderful backing vocals (including from Hughes himself, and other fine Bay Area soul men Cal Valentine, Wylie Trass and Eddie Foster); "Funky Thang" and "Ready To Live" are barely songs but do have more impressive vocals from the back-up team and gurgling rhythm sections; "Epilogue" closes things with Hewitt rapping about life, love and spirituality, but entertainingly rather than boring us silly. He probably saw it as a "concept album", but, be that as it may, I like it and think it impressive and definitely much more imaginative than the vast majority of soul LPs from the second half of the seventies. (It came out with two different covers.)

Joe Hicks

Mighty Joe Hicks 1973 Enterprise ENS-1028 Producer: Joe Hicks

Joe Hicks is another singer who has tended to be ignored by soul fans; I can only assume this is because a) he didn't record much and b) his one LP does have two or three extremely dull tracks as well as a lot of rock touches in the music. He shouldn't be ignored though as he was his own man and a fine singer with an impressive range and two of the songs here, "Could It Be Love" and "Ruby Dean", found their way to Bobby Womack's *Understanding* LP.

He had previously released two noteworthy singles in "Don't It Make You Feel Funky" which was a big "Northern Soul" record and "Life And Death In G & A" for Sly Stone's Stone Flower label but neither were hits and are not included on the album. He didn't seem to record again after 1973 unless the Joe Hicks who released a version of "Papa Was A Rolling Stone" in 1988 is the same man.

Marva Hicks

Marva Hicks 1991 Polydor 422 847 209-1 Producers: Jimmy Scott, Loris Holland, Larry Robinson, Tony Prendatt, Nick Martinelli, Stevie Wonder, Chuckii Booker & Rex Salas

I've only included Ms. Hicks in the book owing to her 1978 single on Infinity, but there are things on this LP that are much better than expected. "I've Never Been In Love Before" was a well deserved #7 soul hit single while the slight Anita Baker feel to "One Good Reason" should have helped it to much better than only #65. A third track, "I Got You Where I Want" also made it to #77. She's an undeniably impressive singer which has doubtless been of great benefit as she continues to make her mark as an actress.

Hidden Strength

Grover Underwood; Roy Herring; Ray Anderson; Robert Leach; Ken Sullivan; Alvin Brown; Al Thomas

Hidden Strength 1975 UA LA555-G Producers: Michael Cuscuna, Grover Underwood & Roy Herring

Hidden Strength were a New York based septet who, while managing to avoid sounding too much like the other big funk bands of the day, never quite accomplished the trick of forging their own identity; which isn't to disparage them as this album is attractive enough for anyone who has a love of mid-seventies funky music. They were good musicians with a particularly adept drummer in Al Thomas while Roy Herring was a talented lead singer who received sterling vocal support from backing singers as gifted as Sharon Redd, Tasha Thomas and Carl Hall. The LP consists mainly of uptempo fare with the rock solid and highly danceable "Hustle On Up" making it to #35 on the soul charts in early 1976 but the appealing "Angel Of Love" demonstrated that they should have chanced their arm more often on slower material. They placed one more 45 on the soul charts in '76, an excellent cover of Johnny Guitar Watson's " I Don't Want To Be A Lone Ranger", but it isn't included on the album.

I assumed they disbanded soon after and never expected to hear from them again but a single entitled "You're No. 1" appeared in 1985.

Hi Five

Kellen Winslow; Leroy Jones; Charles DeJurnett; John Jefferson; Fred Dean

The Other Side Of Us 1981 Titlewave TW32671 Producer: Bernard Thompson

Texas' Hi-Five were a popular and acclaimed vocal ensemble in the nineties, enjoying a handful of huge hits. The group I'm about to discuss here is entirely different and significantly less well-known or successful although tiny Titlewave Production Inc. out of Encinitas, California must have had hopes for this quintet as they went to the trouble of producing a sleeve insert with lyrics of the songs and photographs of the group.

And those hopes would have been reasonable, too, had the LP been released a few years earlier. Talented five man vocal groups like this were dominant in the early to mid seventies, but no-one really wanted to know in 1981. The album is highly pleasant, if lacking a real winning cut or two, or a ballad of any sort, and is worth seeking out for anyone who simply enjoys listening to excellent singers who receive impressive musical support, which soars on an uptempo cut like "We Came To Play". The lengthy "Let's Go All The Way" edges into "Float On" territory as we get to learn about the group members and their star signs but it's still ok. All the songs are originals apart from a not particularly compelling cover of "Backfield In Motion".

High Fashion

Alyson Williams; Eric McClinton; Marcella Allen; Melisa Morgan

Feeling Lucky 1982 Capitol ST-12214 Producers: Jacques Fred Petrus & Mauro Malavasi

Make Up Your Mind 1983 Capitol ST-12287 Producers: Jacques Fred Petrus & Mauro Malavasi

High Fashion were both a great source of singing talent and perfect to listen to for anyone who liked the music made by the B.B. & Q. Band or Kashif. Four people comprised the group over its two albums; Morgan and Williams both went on to make acclaimed solo records; McClinton had been the lead singer in an obscure Motown group, Eric and The Vikings, and Allen had sung backing vocals for the likes of Aquarian Dream. So talent was hardly in short supply, and I can only really re-iterate what I said about the first B.B.& Q. LP as the words apply equally to High Fashion's debut: glossy, danceable and accomplished. I just wish they had slowed the tempo down, if only for one song, so we could get a chance to really hear the group sing but every one of the 37 minutes was aimed at the dance floor. The title track went to #32 soul in the late spring of 1982.

The first LP had been recorded in New York but the second was cut in Italy and the difference, if maybe only slight, was still noticeable as the "thump" factor was turned up for pretty much the entirety of *Make Up Your Mind* and there is scarcely a second of music on the set which doesn't sound as if it has been heard a hundred times before. Only the last track, "Just A Little More Love", has much character, but overall this is a most disappointing and undemanding record.

High Inergy

Barbara Mitchell; Linda Howard; Michelle Rumph; Vernessa Mitchell

Turnin' On 1977 Gordy G6-978S1 Producers: Kent Washburn, Al Willis, Dee Ervin & Jimmy Holiday (Billboard soul charts: 6; Billboard pop charts: 28)

Steppin' Out 1978 Gordy G7-982R1 Producers: Kent Washburn, Al Willis, Mel Bolton, Gwen Fuller & William Bickelhaupt (Billboard soul charts: 46; Billboard pop charts: 42)

Shoulda Gone Dancin' 1979 Gordy G7-987 R1 Producers: Donnell Jones, Marvin Augustus, Gwen Gordy Fuqua, Roger Dollarhide, Kent Washburn, Mel Bolton & Chuck Creath (Billboard soul charts: 72; Billboard pop charts: 147)

Frenzy 1979 Gordy G7-989 R1 Producers: Donnell Jones, Eddie Coleman, Tommy Gordy, Gwen Gordy Fuqua, Roger Dollarhide, Kent Washburn, Mel Bolton, Troy Laws & Chuck Creath

Hold On 1980 Gordy G8-996MI Producers: Angelo Bond, William Weatherspoon, McKinley Jackson, Bobby Debarge, Eddie Coleman, Gwen Gordy Fuqua & Narada Michael Walden (Billboard soul charts: 70; Billboard pop charts: 208)

High Inergy 1981 Gordy G8-1005M1 Producers: Steve Buckingham, Lee Young, Iris Gordy, McKinley Jackson, Angelo Bond & William Weatherspoon

So Right 1982 Gordy 6006GL Producers: Benjamin Wright, Hal Davis, Berry Gordy, Angelo Bond, Ollie Brown, George Tobin, Mike Piccirillo & Mira Waters

Groove Patrol 1983 Gordy 6041GL Producers: George Tobin & Mike Piccirillo (Billboard soul charts: 62; Billboard pop charts: 206)

High Inergy were four remarkably clean-cut and attractive young ladies as the photograph on the cover of their debut LP from 1977 made clear and one can't help thinking that Motown missed a trick with them, never lavishing a fraction of the time and effort on them that the Jackson 5 had enjoyed eight years earlier; the inner record sleeve to the boy groups' first LP had photographs, merchandising offers and a clear intention to market them for all they were worth. Hi Inergy, on the other hand, put out eight LPs and not one of them told us their names which at best was insulting and at worse an indication of how detached Berry Gordy had become from the record business by the end of the seventies.

The failure to get fully behind the quartet was even odder given that their best and most successful single was their very first. "You Can't Turn Me Off (In The Middle Of Turning Me On)" was close to being a great record, with a lovely flow, great hook and involving singing and it went to #2 soul and #12 pop. An elongated version became the centrepiece of the debut set and the follow-up single pulled from it, "Love Is All You Need", did ok if less well: #20 soul and #89 pop. All of the LP is bright, sunny and spirited if a little lacking in depth. The last song, "High School", was a clear reminder of whom the set was aimed at but it was interesting to see that West Coast soul man, Jimmy Holiday, a great writer of adult songs, had a hand in its composition as well as producing it.

Steppin' Out sounded similar to *Turnin' On* but had no obvious hit single on board and the title track and "We Are The Future" had to settle for modest soul chart placings when put out on singles. The album is also noticeable for the fact that two tracks, "Hi!" and "Peaceland", were written by group members, the only time in their entire career they cut songs that had no outside composing help. The musicians employed were of the highest quality and special thanks were given on the back cover, but I can't tell you to whom, dedicated as they were in unreadable pink font.

The release of the *Shoulda Gone Dancin'* LP was the few times that Motown seemed to take care with the group as it had a different cover in the UK and U.S. The title track was a lengthy disco effort that, when truncated for 45 release, only made #50 on the soul charts but it did feature another zestful vocal from Vernessa Mitchell who had taken most of the leads up to and including this album, the last on which she performed, as she then left to pursue a solo career in gospel music. All in all it was a rather perfunctory set, short on good songs and long on producers.

Frenzy, their first LP as a trio, moved the producer count up to an unwieldy and unnecessary nine, but it became their first LP to miss the soul charts completely and housed no charting singles either and has become rather a forgotten set as a result. The rhythms are strong throughout thanks to the likes of James Gadson and Scott Edwards, and Barbara Mitchell certainly belts out "Main Ingredient" while the estimable "Will We Ever Love Again" was the best song they had been given for ages but the other tracks were fairly forgettable.

They got to work with a genuinely great song on the *Hold On* album when they covered Bettye Swann's "Make Me Yours" and their excellent effort deserved to do much better than only #68 on the soul charts in 1980, as it was easily their best single since "You Can't Turn Me Off". "I Just Can't Help Myself" had kicked off the set in pretty good fashion and "Sweet Man" had an unmistakeable Hot Wax/Invictus feel which was no surprise when it became apparent that it was co-written by Angelo Bond and William Weatherspoon, both stalwarts from those record labels. "Hold Onto My Love" was another strong effort, with sterling vocal contributions from Bobby DeBarge out of Switch and pulsating rhythm work. Over on side two, "I'm A Believer" and "If I Love You Tonight" were good ballads, sang at a gentle pace, a speed at which they were not often permitted to travel, with the latter being enhanced by impressive arrangements from Gil Askey and Eddie Coleman. The set closed with an instantly memorable "It Was You Babe" sealing my strong feeling that *Hold On* was by some distance the best LP High Inergy had released to date.

What followed, the boringly entitled *Hi Inergy*, was rather disappointing. One thing I always quite admired about the group was how they avoided sounding too much like The Emotions, but they faltered on the opening track, "Goin' Thru The Motions", which sounded a fair bit like "Best Of My Love". The whole set was probably their "poppiest" to date - and cod reggae as on "I Just Wanna Dance With You", is never a good idea - and there's nothing on it that stands with their best work. It did not sell well, nor did it bear any charting singles.

So Right was - in parts - a return to form. On the debit side there was a heavy-handed cover of The Miracles' "Don't Cha Love It" and a few forgettable new songs such as "Matchpoint" and "Take A Chance" as well as a notably sixties-sounding title track. On the middling side at least the set was tougher than *Hi Inergy* and there was a fairly acceptable attempt at "Tired Of Being Alone" (a really difficult song to cover convincingly) and then there was the good side. "Show Me How" (not the Emotions song), "Wrong Man, Right Touch" and "First Impressions" were all properly constructed songs with verse, choruses and sensible story lines rather than mere exhortations to dance and the latter two particularly are among the best five things they ever cut. The latter went to #50 on the soul charts and it is further proof of Motown's wasted opportunity with the group to reflect that this, which wasn't much, equalled the third highest placing they ever enjoyed.

Their final LP had a dreadful first side - and an equally dreadful cover picture of the girls mistakenly trying to look "tough" - consisting of four overwrought dance sides devoid entirely of any soul (one of them, "He's A Pretender", became their last ever charting single in 1983 at #62) and a marginally better flipside. "Just a Touch Away" and "Blame It On Love" both featured Smokey Robinson, which was a fair choice at first glance, but Smokey was years past his best of course and the latter, particularly, is very bland, even if it did reach #35 on the soul charts as by "Smokey Robinson and Barbara Mitchell". A well sung cover of "Back In My Arms Again" just about covered up the awful tinny backing music and "So Right" was tagged on again from the last LP. All in all, it was a disappointing way to bow out, as the group then disbanded.

Barbara Mitchell started to release solo records in 1984 and Linda Howard sadly died in 2012.

High Voltage (see also Lalomie Washburn)

Fred Allen; Lalomie Washburn; Tony Maiden; Bobby Watson; Billy McPherson; Mark Williams

This one album from this short-lived group is similar to the one discussed earlier by Joe Hicks in as much as it is probably as close to a "rock" record as a soul one, not that the two sound anything like each other. Lalomie Washburn went on to record solo records while Bobby Watson and Tony Maiden both ended up in Rufus, and Gavin Christopher was a member too, but not at the time of this LP, so the group were important in that respect. "Country Roads" was played on the "Northern Soul" scene and is thus the best known track on here which also includes a cover of Aretha's "Save Me" and Laura Lee's "Crumbs Off The Table" and those great singers' versions are by far better. There is a little too much of the feel of a Blood, Sweat and Tears record here for me to really get much enjoyment out of the LP.

Martha High

Martha High 1979 Salsoul SA 8526 Producer: James Brown

Martha High was born Martha Harvin in Virginia and was a member of The Jewels who, after scoring a big hit with "Opportunity", moved into James Brown's organisation where they remained for a few years. When the group disbanded in the late sixties High decided to stay with Brown which she did for three decades, pretty much always in the background, other than recording a single, "Georgy Girl", in 1972; "Summertime", a duet with Brown as the b-side to his 1977 single "Take Me Higher And Groove Me"; another single in 1979 under the name of Martha and The Lazers.

Her one LP boasts Brown as producer but this surely has to be a mere marketing ploy as it is a most atypical Brown production and I suspect Tommy Stewart, listed as arranger and songwriter of four of the five tracks, was much more the driving force. I'm afraid it is a very poor set, with all of Stewart's tracks being entirely forgettable and faceless disco, leaving High's cover version of "Don't Ask My Neighbours", while not being that strong in itself, as way better than all else. Sticking with a force of nature like James Brown for all those years surely entitled her to better than being asked to sing a song called "He's My Ding Dong Man".

She recorded no more LPs but has put out a handful of CDs in the last ten years or so.

Willie Hightower

Willie Hightower 1983 Fury PLP-6002 Producer: Bobby Robinson (Japan)

If I Had A Hammer 1969 Capitol ST-367 Producers: Bobby Robinson & Sire Productions

Gadsden Alabama's Willie Hightower is an impeccable soul man, with barely a poor release among his fourteen singles and two LPs, and while he never enjoyed a genuinely big hit it's good to note that he managed to place five singles on the soul charts (three hit the *Cashbox* listings that didn't register on *Billboard*) in twenty years of recording which is a few more than other similar uncompromising soul singers ever achieved.

His earliest singles came out on Bobby Robinson's labels Fury and Enjoy, and they, plus his first few outings on his next label, Capitol, were captured on a Japanese only LP, *Willie Hightower,* in 1983. The vintage of the tracks run from 1965 through to 1969 and if the sound is slightly lo-fi, then that was how some of Robinson's music was recorded, rather than any inferior quality on the LP. It was a worthy reminder of both his composing talents - he co-wrote four of the tracks - and the quality of his music. The best cut of all was one of those he did co-write, his first single, "It's Too Late", which is an imposing deep soul song of great emotional power. Framed by a keening organ, he bemoans his failing love affair in totally convincing fashion and while he was to go on to make many more excellent sides I'm not sure he ever equalled this one for unadorned soulfulness. The album also contains "If I Had A Hammer", the first record he ever placed on the soul charts (*Cashbox's* version) at the end of 1966. It's a good enough rendering but not one of the strongest songs on the set, which included a handful of other covers. In writing about Willie Hightower its difficult not to mention Sam Cooke, so obviously indebted was Willie to the ex-Soul Stirrer and if Cooke had more purity and range, Hightower surrendered nothing in grit and passion, and it is appropriate that two of the songs on the LP are "Somebody Have Mercy"/"Standing Here Wondering" which Cooke performed so well on *Live At The Harlem Square Club*.

Hightower's only other LP had also looked backwards as it included eight of the ten tracks that were to appear on the Japanese album in 1983 but also the medley of "(I Love You) For Sentimental Reasons"/"You Send Me" that had been a small hit on the *Cashbox* soul charts in 1967. While seven of the ten tracks on *If I Had A Hammer* came out as either a or b - sides on singles none of them were "active" at the time the album was released apart form the re-released title track. Unsurprisingly. therefore, the album did not do much. (It's sleevenotes by Bobby Robinson were to be re-printed on the Fury set.)

Both albums (or really only the one, given they were so similar) were good if ultimately released at the wrong time to be of much benefit to Hightower and it remains a real shame that no LPs appeared from his next two record label stays at FAME and Mercury as he did brilliant work on both. Singles then trickled out now and again (e.g 1976, 1985 and 1991) before he finished his recording career.

Jessie Hill

Naturally 1971 Blue Thumb BTS 31 Producer: Charles Greene

You'll Lose A Good Thing (and Shirley Goodman) 1978? Crazy Cajun 1031 Producer: Huey Meaux

Golden Classics 1989 Collectables COL 5164

Can't Get Enough (Of That Ooh Poo Pah Doo)1984? Bandy 70016

Y'all Ready Now? 1987 Charly CRB 1169 (UK)

It could be argued that New Orleans singer Jessie Hill wasn't really a soul man and therefore shouldn't be in the book; what can't be in dispute is that he hasn't been well represented at 33⅓. I've included him because "Ooh Poo Pah Doo" was such a compelling record, reaching #3 soul and #28 pop in 1960, and because he did cut other fine singles in a similar style ("Sweet Jelly Roll", "Popcorn Pop Pop" etc.) from time to time but he certainly never adapted to the "soul era" as many other New Orleans artists did, and, indeed, released no more records after 1971.

He recorded for a whole host of labels in the sixties, including Minit, Downey, Wand, Chess and Pulsar, but never enjoyed another hit, nor was ever given the opportunity to cut an LP. He had to wait until 1971 for the one and only "proper" album of his career (the others were retrospectives) and *Naturally* was a dismayingly poor effort. Blue Thumb obviously poured money into it given its gatefold cover and frankly rather absurd photo/picture sequence insert that one needed to spin around to view and honesty compels me to admit that there are few records in the book I enjoyed listening to less. Hill was never a particularly strong singer, but the production, rather than bolstering or enhancing his voice, rendered it almost inaudible at times, and the pretentious and unnecessary starting and closing tracks - sorry, "Introducement" and "Klosing Movement"- are just silly. I don't like many of the songs either, only a couple of which have any recognisable New Orleans flavour, and while it is obvious that the musicians were certainly good enough, it all came across as a bit of a mess and I find it hard to believe that anyone could genuinely enjoy this LP. (Although enough people liked the title track to push it to #41 when it came out as a single on the *Cashbox* soul charts.)

He had recorded some duets with Shirley Goodman in the sixties and these were put out on one of those odd Crazy Cajun LPs in, I think, 1978, and I have to conclude that it was a rather strange pairing given that both of them had voices that could be best described as "acquired tastes". Charly, Bandy and Collectables then put out collections in the eighties, and while it is easy to dismiss Collectables outings given their almost invariable poor sound quality, the other two sets were much more dutiful and worthwhile, concentrating on his output at Minit, even if they did copy their respective sleevenotes almost word for word without acknowledgment, and had very similar track listings.

Lonnie Hill

You Got Me Running 1984 Urban Sound US-777 Producers: Dik Darnell & Larry Thompson

Texas born Lonnie Hill was briefly a member of top gospel outfit The Gospel Keynotes and equally briefly a member of far from top soul group Topazz, before recording a soulful single at the end of the seventies entitled "Poverty Shack" and one of the best ever Christmas songs in "Cold Winter In The Ghetto" round about the same time as his one LP came out in 1984. *You Got Me Running* sounded totally different to everything Hill had cut to date, and frankly, apart from two excellent cuts on side two, that also means that the album sounds much worse. Harsh, urban, tinny sounds are far too prominent but, luckily, the tuneful and sweet "Galveston Bay" and "Could It Be Love" are also included, so different in appeal and texture that they may as well have come from a completely different LP. Hill has continued to make music in this new century.

Z.Z. Hill

Soul Stirring 1966 Kent KLP 5018 No producer listed

A Whole Lot Of Soul 1967 KST 5028 Producer: Mike Akopoff

Greatest Hits: Dues Paid In Full 1971?? Kent KST 560

When A Man Loves A Woman 1984 Kent KLP-2013

Final Appearance 1984 Kent KLP-2026

Texas' Arzel Hill must have recorded in as many different cities and studios as virtually anybody in this book, as well as ending up selling an immense amount of LPs, a feat that looked impossible after every one of his first ten failed to hit any national soul charts at all, apart from *Brand New* creeping to a risible #194 on the pop charts in 1972.

His first singles were released on his brother Matt's labels, M H and Mesa, with one of them, "You Were Wrong", reaching #100 on the *Billboard* pop charts in spring 1964 (*Billboard* were not issuing soul charts at the time). He soon moved to the Kent label where he was to put out around 15 singles between 1964 and 1968, five of which hit the *Cashbox* soul charts, although oddly none hit the *Billboard* charts at all. His first LP, *The Soul Stirring*, despite its fairly extensive and gushing sleevenotes, received a rather brisk no-nonsense approach from Kent as neither songwriters nor producers were credited although the former were mainly from the pen of Z.Z. himself while the latter included Joe Bihari and Maxwell Davis. It's a spirited and eclectic set, with as much of it in the "R & B" vein as in the upcoming soul sound, and enjoys splendid and vibrant musical backing throughout, most strikingly with the full orchestration of the marvellous "Everybody Has To Cry" (and just listen to the "I'll Be Doggone" chords on "What More"). Every one of the twelve tracks came out on single as either an a or b - side, with "Someone To Love" being the most successful, reaching the *Cashbox* Top 20 soul listing.

The following year Kent issued *A Whole Lot Of Soul*, on which Hill was obliged to cover twelve famous songs, never a recipe for a label to demonstrate that they have an artists' album career as a top priority. It would be fair to say that "Knock On Wood", "When

A Man Loves A Woman", "Midnight Hour" and "You Send Me" were hardly inspired choices and if Hill performed them well, so what? It wasn't going to be a release that could ever do him much good. Two cuts from it, "Nothing Can Change This Love" and "What Am I Living For" were released as 45s.

Hill left Kent at the end of 1968 and recorded for Atlantic and Quinvy before ending up on a new Matt Hill label (prosaically called "Hill") on which he scored the biggest hit of his career when the excellent "Don't Make Me Pay For His Mistakes" reached #17 soul and #62 pop. Kent weren't oblivious to this success and trawled back in the archives to put out a "new" Z.Z. Hill LP, Greatest Hits: Dues Paid In Full - but as it contained exactly the same track listing as the Soul Stirring album was unlikely to have sold many copies - as well as re-releasing "I Need Someone (To Love Me)" as a single which did do reasonably well: #30 soul and #86 pop in mid 1971.

Over a decade later, Kent again saw an opportunity for Hill's back catalogue as in 1984, when in order to commemorate Hill's death, most of the A Whole Lot Of Soul set was re-issued as When A Man Loves A Woman with a couple of additions - "Gimme Gimme", a swinging and tough side that had not previously appeared on an album, and a previously unreleased side "You Got Me Chained" - and four subtractions. And in the same year the Soul Stirring sides appeared for the fourth time on an LP (they had also re-surfaced on the budget label United, release number 7770 in 1970 or so) when Final Appearance slipped out with "Please Take Me Back" and "I'm Gonna Love You" added (they had previously been unissued) in place of "Happiness Is All I Need" and "What More".

Turn Back The Hands Of Time 1985 Tuff City 4439
Producers: Miles Grayson & Matt Hill

The aforementioned "Don't Make Me Pay For His Mistakes" was not followed up with an album at the time but after Hill's death the Tuff City label put out a collection that collected the hit, his other two Hill label singles and a handful of unreleased songs including a couple of Temptations' covers, "Ain't Too Proud To Beg" and "My Girl" that should probably have stayed that way. It was certainly nice to finally have the Hill singles on an album though as they were all good.

Brand New 1971 Mankind 201 Producer: Jerry "Swamp Dogg" Williams (Billboard pop charts: 194)

Velvet Soul 1982 Malibu MR 05820 Producer: Jerry "Swamp Dogg" Williams

Hill's next "proper" album came out on another new label, Mankind. The LP's concept of spoken introductions on each track of side one from a warring Hill and his woman pre-dated Millie Jackson's Caught Up by a few years and should thus be commended for going beyond the scope and approach normally expected from soul albums but it never attains the level of Jackson's masterpiece. Firstly, because producer Jerry "Swamp Dogg" Williams rather hedges his bets and abandons the idea on side two and secondly because Hill did not have Jackson's forceful dynamism and charisma. Brand New could have been performed by pretty much any singer; Caught Up (Laura Lee apart) certainly couldn't. Having said that, there was still much to admire, particularly on that second side. Williams has had few peers in the art of arranging horns and all of Brand New is blessed with punchy brass throughout, while Hill (although too far back in the mix) gets

good material to work with, and the set contains one of Sam Dees' earliest songs, "I Think I'd Do It" (which had previously come out on a single on Quinvy), and Prince Phillip Mitchell's first background singing credits. (The entire set was re-issued on the UK Topline label, TOP 138, in 1985, as A Man Needs A Woman.)

In 1982 the Malibu label released an intriguing eight track LP, which contained four tracks from Brand New as well as four new ones, including a good cover of Solomon Burke's "Take Me Just As I Am". Z. Z. Hill completists will certainly want it, though, as the four "old" tracks are re-cut with new musicians while remaining true to the originals (albeit with much more muted horns). It simply wasn't however, despite Hill's success at Malaco around this time, the sort of music many record buyers wanted to hear. (The Velvet Soul LP was reissued again in 1984 on Rare Bullet 2001 as Thrill On The Z.Z. Hill.)

The Best Thing That Ever Happened To Me
1972 UA 5589 Producer: Matt Hill

Z.Z. 1974 UA LA212-G Producer: Matt Hill

Keep On Loving You 1975 UA LA417-G Producers: Allen Toussaint, Denny Diante, Spencer Proffer, Matt Hill & Lamont Dozier

Whoever's Thrilling You (Is Killing Me) 1986 Stateside SSL 6006 (UK)

Hill moved to United Artists in 1972 and gave us a typically "down-home" album - he never even came close to "crossing over" pop in his entire career - in The Best Thing That's Ever Happened To Me but it had absurdly chichi and fatuous sleevenotes that were completely at odds with the record's blue-collar appeal, nor did the LP's title make much sense, as no song of that name appeared. Apart from so-so covers of "Can I Get A Witness", "My Adorable One" and "Little Red Rooster" it was good stuff all the way. The great Jimmy Lewis provided two songs and, surprisingly, another soul singer, Fred Hughes, contributed four; surprising as Hill only ever cut one other song by Hughes in twenty years of making records. Best of all was a splendidly vigorous version of "Ain't Nothing You Can Do" which attained #37 soul and nearly broached the pop top hundred at #114 when released as a single.

Brand New had been cut in Alabama and Hill returned to the area, although this time to FAME, to cut his attractive and likeable Z. Z. album. For the first time he cut some tracks in the country-soul style such as "Country Love", "Two Wrongs Don't Make A Right" and "You're Killing Me (Slowly But Surely)" and they all worked perfectly. A couple of his own compositions also appeared, one of which, "Am I Groovin' You", despite being a limited song, was uncompromisingly tough and made a nice contrast with the lilting tracks mentioned above, although it only made it to a disappointing #84 on the soul charts as a single. This was the second "hit" from the set as a serviceable cover of "Let Them Talk" had crept to #74 three months earlier.

A third and final album was issued by UA in 1975, which had a rather unsatisfying first side. First because it replicated "Am I Groovin' You", but second and more importantly, because Lamont Dozier had been drafted in to produce four tracks and a producer less suited to Hill's natural affinity for blues based soul would be hard to imagine. It's not that they were terrible cuts - as they weren't - but they bore Dozier's personality to a far greater degree than Hill's, and if I wanted to listen to Lamont he was releasing his own LPs at the time. Side two picked up another single that had made a small impression on the soul charts two years earlier, "I Don't Need Half A Love", and four songs produced by Allen Toussaint down in New Orleans at Seasaint, in a style more congenial to Hill's talents, with the excellent "Whoever's Thrilling You Is Killing Me" being the best of them. Despite my reservations about the Dozier cuts, one of them, "You Created A Monster", did make it to #40 on the soul charts in the middle of 1975, one place lower than the title track had managed a year earlier.

In 1986 The UK Stateside label put out a 12 track album entirely culled from the *Keep On Lovin' You* and *Best Thing* sets.

Let's Make A Deal 1978 Columbia JC 35030 Producer: Bert DeCoteaux

Mark Of Z.Z. 1979 Columbia JC 36125 Producer: Bert DeCoteaux

Matt Hill died in 1975, which would of course have been a huge blow to Z.Z. on both a personal and a professional level and it was a couple of years before another LP appeared, parts of which were cut in yet another new location, New York. It contained two marvellous singles, "Love Is So Good When You're Stealing It" and "This Time They Told The Truth" which, at the time, acted as blissful correctives to the ubiquitous disco style of the day. Incredibly, the former became Hill's biggest ever success on the soul charts as a 45 reaching #15, while "Truth" (which featured some of Hill's best ever trademark growls) also did well at #42, and kudos should go to Columbia for realising they were clearly the strongest songs on view. Although both sides contained more strings on a Z.Z. Hill record than we were accustomed to, the arrangements by Bert DeCoteaux were thoughtful and sympathetic, suiting Hill and the songs perfectly. (The rather average title track was also released as a third 45 from the LP but did not chart.) Elsewhere on the album, " A Message To The Ladies" was a typically wry Jimmy Lewis tale, while "That's All That's Left" was nice too but most of the other songs were merely ok, although "You Got Me Doing The Disco" proved that even Hill wasn't immune to the dance disease, and was the first time in well over ten years of recording that he had dished up something dreadful.

Hill's second and last LP for Columbia was the worst of his career, and one which yielded no hit singles at all. In summary, it contained three good slow cuts including a re-make of "Tell It Like It Is", one half decent song in "I Want To Be Your Every Need" and four awful dance cuts, so poor as to be demeaning for a seasoned artist of Hill's stature and quality.

Z.Z. Hill 1981 Malaco 7402 Producers: Tommy Couch & Wolf Stephenson

Down Home 1981 Malaco 7406 Producers: Tommy Couch & Wolf Stephenson (Billboard soul charts: 17; Billboard pop charts: 209)

The Rhythm And The Blues 1982 Malaco 7411 Producers: Tommy Couch & Wolf Stephenson (Billboard soul charts: 16; Billboard pop charts: 165)

I'm A Blues Man 1983 Malaco 7415 Producers: Tommy Couch & Wolf Stephenson (Billboard soul charts: 15; Billboard pop charts: 170)

Bluesmaster 1984 Malaco 7420 Producers: Tommy Couch & Wolf Stephenson (Billboard soul charts: 35)

In Memoriam 1985 Malaco 7426 Producers: Tommy Couch & Wolf Stephenson (Billboard soul charts: 61)

Greatest Hits 1986 Malaco 7437

Hill, like so many other soul men and women who had built their careers and appeal on heartfelt gritty and adult music, were rather stymied by disco and it took Z.Z. a couple of years to find a new label that would be sympathetic to the style he was best equipped to deal in. Luckily - for many people as it was to turn out - he found a perfect such label at Malaco.

A few of us were despairing at the decline of the type of music we loved by the early eighties, and Hill's first album on the Jackson based logo was thus greeted with relief and pleasure. I played it incessantly at the time of its release and not only was it the best country-soul album in years, containing lovely grown-up and deeply satisfying songs like "Separate Ways" and "Something Good Going On" and sympathetic arrangements from the great Mike Lewis, it also contained in the last two tracks, the bluesiest things he had cut for nearly a decade, the seeds of his greatest ever success.

The fact was that the Malaco debut, like all his other LPs, had not sold well enough to reach the national soul charts and it was therefore rather by extraordinary chance and the efforts of promotional man Dave Clark that the title track of his next set, *Down Home Blues*, a George Jackson song, caught the ear of southern radio deejays and southern record buyers, resulting in huge sales for the album, for the song wasn't released as a single and if you wanted to own it, you needed the LP. *Down Home Blues* may have "only" reached #17 on the soul charts but it stayed on them for just short of two years, and to put that into context, at the time, in the whole history of soul music, only one LP had ever exceeded Hill's span of 93 weeks, The Temptations' *Greatest Hits* all the way back in 1966. For a small independent record label to have achieved this with a journeyman - in the best sense of the word - singer like Hill was a quite incredible achievement. As a bonus the LP also contained a highly successful 45, "Cheating In The Next Room", another Jackson song, that made it to #19 on the soul charts, staying there for twenty weeks, the longest duration of any single of his, as well. Not only did all this bounty sustain Hill, but it enabled Malaco to re-launch the careers of a number of other soul singers in need of a helping hand such as Johnnie Taylor, Benny Latimore and Denise La Salle, and proved beyond any doubt that southern audiences would purchase albums rather than singles as the eighties progressed.

Not surprisingly, in the wake of *Down Home Blues,* soul started to be rather edged out by blues on Hill's albums as time went on. The follow-up, for instance, *The Rhythm And The Blues*, another huge seller, but this time only staying on the charts for a mere one year, balanced the "soul" and "blues" content at 50% each and I must confess that it was an album I liked rather than loved as Malaco could be rather formulaic in its approach and even the songs from the excellent Frank Johnson were good rather than great, while the country-soul elements from his debut LP were already all gone.

I'm A Blues Man stated the case much more baldly, but was in fact rather misleading, as the out and out blues cuts only comprised two of the ten cuts on show. I think the LP was his best since the Malaco debut, not only because of the overriding soul content but also because the majority of the songs came from the fruitful pens of George Jackson, Jimmy Lewis and Frank Johnson although why the latter claimed he had written "Steal Away" is a mystery. It was the third LP in a row that lasted on the soul album charts for at least a year although Lewis' "Get A Little, Give A Little" only managed #85 on the soul charts as a single, the sixteenth and last time the name of Z.Z. Hill graced the *Billboard* listings of top selling 45s.

To everyone's shock and horror, Hill died in 1984, aged only 48, of heart problems exacerbated by a car crash. His death came just at a time when his last studio album had been recorded and when it appeared at the end of that year, it was thus as a valedictory rather than simply his new LP release. I suspect Hill's time of unbroken success for more than two years would probably have come to an end anyway, as the LP, *Bluesmaster*, performed much more modestly than the previous three and was inferior artistically, too, as well as being by some distance the "bluesiest" of his Malaco output. Jackson, Lewis and Johnson didn't write a single word on the set and while there were two great songs on board, Paul Kelly's "Personally" and Phillip Mitchell's' and Billy Clements' "Be Strong Enough To Hold On", each performed perfectly well by Z.Z., the earlier versions from Jackie Moore and Bettye Swann respectively were better. Elsewhere, "Champagne Lady" was the sort of song more suited to his second, poor, Columbia set , "Why Don't We Spend The Night" was soppy, while "I'll Be Your Witness" lifted the melody from Isaac Hayes' "Do Your Thing".

Two posthumous Malaco albums came out in 1985 and 1986 and both were comprised of cuts from the earlier five sets, with no "unreleased" material to make them more enticing.

Z.Z. Hill has a claim to be one of the greatest of all soul artists, given his longevity, consistency and importance in revitalizing a more rootsy variant of the music while at Malaco. He also had an immediately distinctive voice, rather in the style of Johnnie Taylor, that was stronger in personality than range, and, to top it all off, was apparently an exceptionally nice man.

Lawrence Hilton-Jacobs

Lawrence Hilton-Jacobs 1978 ABC AA-1045 Producer: Lamont Dozier

All The Way...Love 1979 ABC AA-1127 Producer: Freddie Perren

Lawrence Hilton-Jacobs' acting career has been longer and more substantial than his musical one, so it is probably no surprise that his voice sounds more suited to the stage than the church, and while he was technically gifted, he could never be mistaken for a no holds-barred soul man.

The first album's main strengths are its energy and full-bodied production and tracks like "Fly Away" (which just about reached the *Cashbox* soul charts) and "Wonder Woman" charge along without resorting to disco inanity, although the instrumental "Larry's Theme" is awfully twee. Lamont Dozier wrote six of the nine tracks and his phrasing from the demos is, as usual with his songs, very evident in the finished versions.

Freddie Perren took over from Dozier for Hilton-Jacobs' second LP and rendered it pretty much entirely uninteresting from my perspective, as it moved into a faceless dance/disco mode for too many tracks and when he opted for something slower like "Baby Your Eyes" it was just so boring.

Ernie Hines

Electrified 1972 We Produce XPS-1902 Producers: Jo Bridges, Carl Hampton, Tom Nixon, Fred Briggs & Lester Snell

If your one LP is going to be a brief postscript in the history of soul music, than write it as attractively and elegantly as this one. Ernie Hines had the briefest of careers: two singles for the USA label, three for Stax/ We Produce and this one LP, which was generally more lush and smooth than other records emanating from Memphis. He wasn't the greatest singer in the world - listen to his difficulties on "A Better World (For Everyone)", for instance - but he overcame any vocal limitations by having the opportunity to work with excellent material, often from his own pen, and stirring arrangements.There are nine tracks on the album and all are worth hearing. He addresses social concerns explicitly in the spare yet funky "Our Generation" and the aforementioned "A Better World", slightly more obliquely in "Come On Y'all" and "A Change Is Gonna Come" (one of the best takes on this famous song I have ever heard, when it could so easily have been simply a "throwaway" LP filler cut), while the rest are concerned with more straightforward love problems. These include a slowed down and almost unrecognizable take on The Temprees "Explain It To Her Mama", a gorgeously warm "Electrified Love" (with captivating backing vocals and horns) and an instantly catchy and beautifully written "What Would I Do". The LP sold few copies, and most of the main players in the Stax story have presumably long since forgotten it, but it is one of the best "unknown" soul albums ever made.

Billy Hinton (see Dawn Of Beige)

Eddie Hinton

Very Extremely Dangerous 1978 Capricorn CPN 0204 Producer: Barry Beckett

Letters From Mississippi 1986 Amalthea AM 57 Producers: Eddie Hinton, Jimmy Johnson & John D Wyker (Sweden)

Eddie Hinton played, produced or wrote on some of the finest of all southern soul records - way too many to note here but they include his co-composing "Breakfast In Bed", one of the saddest and most thoughtful songs in the history of popular music - but he had always remained resolutely in the background and was not at all well-known when his first ever LP - he had released three singles previously - appeared in 1978. There were lots of exciting rumours about this album for those of us in England who loved real unadulterated soul but found it increasingly hard to come by at the end of the seventies, and we were not to be disappointed as it was one of the last ever instances of an unreconstructed southern soul album to appear from the Muscle Shoals studios, or indeed anywhere else.

Capricorn were clearly perplexed as to how to market it though, and neither the atmospheric and memorable front cover nor the back chose to make it clear that Hinton was in fact white. It was also doomed to become a cult LP rather than a bestseller as there was no market for anyone singing in the style of Otis Redding circa 1967 in 1978. It's not an unmitigated success, as although the songs were strong, and the musicianship - recorded live in the studio - beyond reproach, Hinton, while undoubtedly a completely sincere and committed singer was not a technically great one, and the album does come across as somewhat of a museum piece rather than how southern soul had naturally evolved by 1977 (the year it was recorded). However, this is to carp a little as I certainly enjoyed the album when it came out and it still sounds great today. "Shout Bamalama" is genuinely exciting and everyone in the studio was obviously having a fine old time and Bobby Womack could easily have recorded "We Got it" and "Get Off In It", as they recall his rambling yet entirely soulful style.

As one or two journalists began to take an interest in him, it started to become evident that Hinton had problems in his personal life and it was clearly no easy task to even get him into a studio, let alone record an entire LP and it wasn't until 1986 that a new one appeared - and, not for the first time in the annals of soul music - in Sweden of all places although it was entirely cut in Alabama. It's not such an obviously soulful album as *Very Extremely Dangerous* and would not be the to the taste of anyone who doesn't like to listen to soul music that isn't fully arranged and orchestrated, as some tracks are little more than demos, but *Letters From Mississippi* was by no means a bad effort, featuring some more strong songs from a man who could seemingly easily summon them up at will.

He died of a heart attack in 1995 but for a few years before and after that date a number of CDs came out, some featuring new music, others trawling back through the vaults.

Joe Hinton

Funny (How Time Slips Away) 1965 Back Beat BLP 60
No producer listed

Duke-Peacock Remembers 1973 Duke DLPX 91 No producer listed

Some singers are for ever associated with one record, maybe a particular song or a particular hit, but Joe Hinton is best known for one *note*; the one he held at the end of "Funny (How Time Slips Away)", his one genuinely big hit, #13 pop in 1964.

Hinton was born in Indiana and his first recordings were in the gospel field before he began a solo career, signing up with the Duke/Backbeat empire in the late fifties. His fifth single for Backbeat, "You Know It Ain't Right", became his first national success, attaining #20 soul and #88 pop in the middle of 1963, but it didn't trigger the release of his first LP and he had to wait until 1965 for that, which was understandably named after his biggest hit.

It's an enjoyable set, and apart from the hit, contains a number of other good cuts including the terrific "If It Ain't One Thing" which features the incomparable Joe Scott Band adding their swing to the mix, and while there is not a sub-standard track on view songs like "Endlessly", "Guess Who" and "Pledging My Love" were not especially inspired choices. It was also perhaps inevitable that Hinton would overplay his hand as regards repeating the high note that "made" "Funny" so compelling and it features throughout on an outing that, rather surprisingly, only contains four tracks that featured on his first nine singles for Backbeat.

Hinton was to release a further seven singles on Backbeat after "Funny" but only one, the follow-up, "I Want A Little Girl", also reached the national soul charts (#34) and he sadly died in August 1968, aged only 38, Five years after this, Duke (now owned by ABC) released a memorial LP entitled *Duke-Peacock Remembers Joe Hinton* which was nice to see, but I don't think many others agreed as it would not have sold in any quantity. It consisted of eleven songs, only two of which had appeared on the *Funny* LP, so care had certainly been taken. The majority of the tracks are from his later period and "I'm Waiting" (with its "Für Elise" piano intro), "Now I'm Satisfied" and "Got You On My Mind" are all tough, all excellent, and much better than the mawkish "Just A Kid Named Joe", and indeed act as fitting testimony to such a tremendous singer.

The Joe Hinton discussed here is not the same as another soul man of the same name who wrote and recorded for Soul and Hotlanta among other labels.

Hi Rhythm

Leroy Hodges; Mabon Hodges; Charles Hodges; Howard Grimes; Archie Turner

On The Loose 1976 Hi SHL 32099 Producer: Hi Rhythm

This is one of those LPs which must have been made purely for fun or for some sort of contractual obligation as it is impossible to think that anyone could have expected it to be a success. The Hi rhythm section was world-class and in-demand, and did their best work behind the likes of Al Green, Ann Peebles etc., and while this reasonably likeable set is not difficult to listen to, I'd rather hear them behind great singers as opposed to just sort of messing about as they do here. It's not an all-instrumental affair as might have been expected and a whole army of backing singers are credited, although it's not clear to me which of them take on the task of lead vocals. It didn't sell, and nor did a couple of singles Hi put out, one of which was included on this LP, one of which was not.

Hitchhikers

Kenny Hamber; Kenny Roane; Herman Pittman; Carlton Pina; Buddy Monterio; Donald Livaramento; Ricky Barros

Hitchhikers 1976 ABC ABCD-973 Producer: Ralph Calabrese

"The Hitchhikers" must rank among the worst names for a soul group, but, fortunately, they had an excellent lead singer in Kenny Hamber and the LP is a really good one. Hamber had released a handful of singles under his own name in the sixties to resounding silence, but he had a great voice in the gruff and soulful tradition of a Teddy Pendergrass and he gives it everything he had on the magnificent "My Baby's Gone", beautifully orchestrated as if it came out of Sigma Sound in Philadelphia rather than a studio in Bridgeport, Connecticut. "You're Making A Big Mistake" was in the same vein, and was one of three unsuccessful 45s ABC pulled from the LP, although its title may have been well-directed at the record company for not choosing "My Baby's Gone" as one of them, while "Rolling Dice" and "Don't Want To Live Without You" were rousing dance items proving the group could handle different tempos without difficulty. And it wasn't only Hamber who could sing as drummer Kenny Roake took over lead duties on "Love Keeps Knocking At My Door" and his beautiful high tenor marks this out as another cream cut. It wasn't all good though: "Music Fills Your Heart", "Free", "Good Time Man" and "Bad Bad Girl" are all decidedly average, but another top track, "This Song's For You Mama", closes out a sadly almost completely overlooked LP which even got a UK release. Hamber was to continue making music following this release, but The Hitchhikers were not.

Yvonne Hodges

You Never Wanted Me 1977 Guinness GNS 36032 No producer listed

This one's a rarity: a Guinness LP that isn't particularly in demand, bearing a front cover, a nice Roy Lichtenstein - inspired picture that the company actually took more than five minutes over. There are seven well-known songs and three originals on the LP, although two of them don't feature Hodges at all. Only one cut rises above the entirely predictable, the good mid-tempo "Heavy Thing To Do", which she co-wrote, and Yvonne Hodges did not appear to release any more records.

Hodges, James & Smith (see also Damion & Denita)

Pat Hodges; Denita James; Jessica Smith

Incredible 1974 20th Century T-425 Producer: William Stevenson (Billboard soul charts: 51)

Power In Your Love 1975 20th Century T-475 Producer: William Stevenson (Billboard soul charts: 58)

What's On Your Mind? 1977 London PS 685 Producer: William Stevenson

What Have You Done For Love? 1978 Producers: William Stevenson, Clifford Coulter & Bill Withers

If you think Hodges, James and Smith is an unwieldy name for a girl trio, then consider that they were previously known as Hodges, James, Smith and Crawford for a couple of singles, before ex-Motown artist Carolyn left to seek out a solo career. Pat Hodges and Denita James had each issued singles under their own names in the sixties (and James went on to release a duet LP with one Damion after HJ & S broke up) although I believe Jessica Smith took the majority of lead vocals when they came together to create their four albums. Although they were under the wing of Mickey Stevenson for their whole career, he adopted the tried and trusted approach of not crediting the women on their own records apart from a small print thank you on the back of their second set and I have to wonder what he was thinking when he presumably approved the front cover picture of *Incredible*, which also bore a wholly inaccurate title.

It was hard for female trios not to sound a little like the Emotions or The Supremes and Hodges, James and Smith certainly recalled the former rather than the latter, but were never provided with the quality of the songs that the Hutchinson sisters consistently enjoyed. Actually, *Incredible* wasn't too bad, and "Signal Your Intention", If You Wanna Love Me" and "Can't Be Alone" are all nice enough, but there was absolutely nothing within that cried out to be played over and over again and no hits arose from the couple of singles that 20th Century issued although the LP must have sold reasonably well to attain its *Billboard* chart placing.

Power Of Love was marginally better than *Incredible* in an as much as it had a better cover - it was important for potential record buyers to see that the women were highly photogenic - and contained the two best tracks they had cut to date in the old warhorse, "I (Who Have Nothing)", and "Sexy Ways". Both had excellent arrangements, the latter being a great swirl of sound with a superb Smith (?) vocal even if tune and chorus were mislaid somewhere. "Momma" was also pretty good being fairly funky with excellent guitar from EWAF's Roland Bautista, but the other tracks were just not particularly good songs. It remains a mystery why Stevenson - an excellent writer with countless great songs for Motown on his c.v. - saddled the trio with such mediocre material on their first two sets and it was even harder to see what audience he was aiming at. The messy title track of *Power Of Love* was one of a handful of cuts that had slight "rock" undertones and sounded as completely out of step with what was "happening" in 1975 as "Sexy Ways" sounded in step.

The third LP contained the only cut that ever really came close to a hit for the trio, a discofied version of the old favourite, "Since I Fell For You", which attained #24 soul and #96 pop. Once again, though, it is a fairly dull set, and even though no-one could accuse the new label, London, of failing to invest in it - the title track features a massive string section intro that sounded as if it were pulled intact from a Hollywood film of the forties - the task of recalling a single song within hours of playing it is not an easy one.

Their fourth and final LP, *What Have You Done For Love?*, had something to be said for it - that side two featured arguably the best singing the trio had yet committed to vinyl - but it wasn't really an LP I could warm to as once again it lacked a track I unequivocally loved. That second side adopted a heavily orchestrated jazzy/MOR approach, the Supremes rather than The Emotions in fact, which certainly gave the group a chance to stretch out vocally whereas the first half of the set, a rather tepid version of "Can't Hide Love" excepted, pitched for the disco market but didn't reach it as neither the album nor a couple of singles that were pulled from it did very well.

The group were nearly done by now, although Stevenson got them to update one of his most famous co-written songs, "Dancing In The Streets", in 1979 but it was another failure and from then on they confined themselves to providing backing vocals for other artists. In the last few years Jessica Smith and Denita James have both passed away.

Jimmy Holiday

Turning Point 1966 Minit LP 40005 Producer: Calvin Carter & Hal Pickens (Billboard soul charts: 25)

Spread Your Love 1968 Minit MLL 40010 Producers: Calvin Carter, Hal Pickens, Jimmy Holiday, Ed Wright & Buddy Killen

Spreadin' Love 1982 Liberty 10183

Everybody Needs Help 1986 Stateside SSL 6010 (UK)

Mississippi born Jimmy Holiday had an impressive history in the music business, composing or co-composing well over a hundred songs including "Put A Little Love In Your Heart", as well as recording and producing some wonderful records in his own right, and yet somehow he has never achieved even a fraction of the credit he richly deserves.

In his early career he recorded for a number of labels including Everest (one hit, the soothing "How Can I Forget" in 1963), Kent and Diplomacy, before joining Minit in 1966. It was to be prove to be the home for his commercial and artistic peaks and he enjoyed the issuance of eleven singles, beginning with " Baby I Love You" which performed well reaching #21 soul and #98 pop in the summer of 1966. This was a stirring record but was eclipsed in quality by the next single, the deeply sad and affecting masterpiece, "The Turning Point", which was to become the title track of his first (and in a way, only, as we shall see) LP. It is an album of rare quality, endorsed by Ray Charles, with all twelve songs composed by Holiday, eight of which were to find their way onto either the top or flip sides of 45s, although only one of them, "Everybody Needs Help", was a hit, #36 soul and #116 pop in the first half of 1967. Holiday had a naturally mournful voice and when coupled with songs like "I Don't Want To Hear It" and "We Forgot About Love" and encompassed by the excellent arrangements and West Coast musicians he worked with, the results are entirely rewarding. In fact, listen carefully to "I Don't Want To Hear It"; it might sound a little similar to "The Turning Point", but is an almost perfect song in construction, lyrical precision and vocal delivery and yet sounds effortless, surely the true proof of a skilled artist. Side two has a couple of highly enjoyable uptempo songs such as "I'm Gonna Move To The City" but they do not have the depth of his lovelorn pleas elsewhere. The LP also sold rather well, reaching the top thirty of the soul charts, which I suspect was a pleasant surprise for artist and record label.

A couple of years later Minit put out a Holiday LP in the UK, which was decent of them, as it would have utterly passed the vast majority of the population by. Generous at 14 tracks, it nevertheless included ten from the U.S. release, omitting two others, and adding four new ones, including the title track, which became his third and final charting single on the label. It was one of a number of Holiday songs that recalled another West Coast artist, Jimmy Lewis, and it was no surprise that the two of them often worked together. The other new tracks included Holiday's worthy addition to the library of Vietnam songs with "I'm Gonna Help Hurry My Brothers Home" and the surprisingly bluesy "You Won't Get Away".

Holiday went on to release four more Minit 45s after "Spread Your Love", as well as one on Dial and another, his last, on Crossover in 1975 but no new LPs came out in support of any of these. What DID come out were two retrospectives of his Minit years with, as usual, the one from the UK bearing more tracks than the one from the USA. Firstly, in 1982 the Imperial label put out a ten track set which wouldn't have been much to get excited about for anyone who had at least one other Holiday LP, but it did include two previously unreleased cuts in "Tired Of My Tears" (although Ray Charles had recorded the song) and "I Need People". Then, four years later, the UK Stateside logo issued a thoroughly welcome 16 tracker with a handful of cuts that had not appeared on the other three Holiday albums, prominent among which was the red-blooded and swinging outing with Clydie King, "Ready, Willing And Able", and "A Man Ain't Nothin' Without A Woman" one of those Holiday-Lewis collaborations I made reference to earlier.

Holiday died in 1987 and it's a great shame the four albums he released were not four entirely different sets, rather than variations on the original one, but such scarcity of output doesn't change the fact that he really was one of the finest writer-producer-singers to have ever worked in the soul music field.

Eddie Holland

Eddie Holland 1962 Motown 604 Producers: William Stevenson & Eddie Holland

Before Eddie Holland became a member of that powerhouse team Holland-Dozier-Holland he was merely just another solo singer striving to make his way in the world. His first six 45s all flopped but his seventh, "Jamie", became a pretty decently sized hit (#6 soul. #30 pop) right at the start of 1962. Motown built an album - the only one of his career - around it, and because the label had not yet discovered its recognisable sound, everything within sounds rather tame and quaint. The set also had one of those cheap and tacky covers the label went in for back then, but nowadays it looks pretty "cool", instantly transporting us back to a time and place that could only be the early sixties. It's not a great LP, by any means, but at least Motown didn't saddle Holland with MOR cover versions, as all ten songs come from the stable of writers - including Holland himself - employed by Gordy's empire.

Eddie Holland much preferred writing and producing to singing, which was just as well for all of us, and he only recorded a few more singles up to and including 1964, at which point he concentrated solely on composing and producing as part of the trio who went on to become easily the most successful black American songwriters of all time.

Jennifer Holliday

Feel My Soul 1983 Geffen GHS 4014 Producer: Maurice White (Billboard soul charts: 6; Billboard pop charts: 31)

Say You Love Me 1985 Geffen GHS 24073 Producers: Michael Jackson, George Tobin, Arthur Baker, Gary Henry, Richard Scher, Lotti Golden, Tommy Lipuma, Andy Goldmark & Bruce Roberts (Billboard soul charts: 34; Billboard pop charts: 110)

Get Close To My Love 1987 Geffen GHS 9 24150-2 Producers: Jennifer Holliday, Rene Moore, David Pack, Michael McDonald, Alan Glass, Preston Glass, Tommy Lipuma & Marcus Miller

I'm On Your Side 1991 Arista 211 519 Producers: Barry Eastmond, Jennifer Holliday, Michael Hutchinson, Nicholas Ashford, Valerie Simpson, Michael Powell & Ric Wake (Billboard soul charts: 29; Billboard pop charts: 184) (Europe)

There is a definite correlation between the number of producers on an LP and how much enjoyment I get from listening to it; looking at the army of help brought to bear on the last three albums by Jennifer Holliday it's with a heavy heart that I have to go through the process of spinning them again.

It had all started so promisingly, too, when her first ever 45, "And I Am Telling You I'm Not Going", a heart-stopping record from the *Dreamgirls* musical, reached #1 soul and #26 pop in the middle of 1982. It wasn't featured on her first solo album, though, which was for the most part a thoroughly routine pop-soul LP of "taste" and "class" but devoid of much excitement. I would excuse "Just Let Me Wait" from my lack of enthusiasm as it was good enough in an EWAF/Emotions groove and it went on to reach #24 in the soul charts as well as just missing the top 100 pop. Earlier, "I Am Love", a big ballad from the set, did reach #2 soul and #49 pop but it dispensed with the over - the - top emotionalism of "And I'm Telling You" and settled for MOR-ish mediocrity.

The problem with employing so many producers is obvious: it leads to an incoherent LP; the title track from *Say You Love Me* and "Come Sunday" were adult performances of evident skill and I like them a great deal, the best things she had cut since "And I'm Telling You". They were the only cuts that used real drummers, though, and virtually everything else went for the youth dance market and, apart from Holliday's often amazing voice, had little in common with soul music of the previous thirty years.

Rather surprisingly, her third LP, *Get Close To My Love,* failed completely commercially, although one track from it, "Heart On The Line", did reach #48 soul. It was a totally forgettable record, though, completely eclipsed by a barnstorming eight minute cover of "Givin' Up" which could either be described as "oversouling" or "brilliant" depending on one's definition of genuine soul music. I suppose it was good news that there were more "real" drums throughout the set but when they accompanied MOR fare like "Read It In My Eyes" my interest levels plummeted again.

Her final LP (only a CD in the U.S.) restored her commercial fortunes to a large extent, with two singles from it, the title track and "Love Stories", each reaching the soul top thirty. It was a thoroughly contemporary set and while deserving its success at the time, does not sound enticing twenty years on.

Jennifer Holliday is clearly a singer of unusual power and ability but she had the misfortune (purely from my point of view, of course) of releasing all her records from 1982 onwards, years after the "golden age" of soul had ended. I suspect she could have done amazing things at Muscle Shoals in the sixties, for example, but that will have to remain a pipedream. She is still cutting new music in the current decade.

Brenda Holloway

Every Little Bit Hurts 1964 Tamla 257 Producers: Hal Davis & Marc Gordon

The Artistry Of 1968 Tamla Motown TML 11083 No producer listed

Brand New 1980 Birthright BRS-4023 Producers: Gil Askey, Leroy Lovett & Byron Spears

There are plenty of people who maintain that Brenda Holloway was the finest female singer ever to record on the Motown labels. My own vote would go to Gladys Knight, but Holloway was highly gifted and the claim is by no means a silly one.

Born in California and sister to another soul singer, Patrice (who did not get the opportunity to cut an LP), Brenda recorded a number of fairly unremarkable 45s as a solo singer or backing vocalist before she joined Motown. She hit right away by releasing the wonderfully atmospheric "Every Little Bit Hurts" on which the 17 year-old invested a sadness that one so young shouldn't have to understand. The single went all the way to #13 on the pop charts in 1964 (the year in which *Billboard* didn't provide separate soul listings) and was the best thing on an LP which was created in the wake of the hit. Holloway's career was always somewhat different from the majority of her Motown colleagues as many of her records were cut in Los Angeles rather than Detroit and certainly the LP, rather saturated with strings, did sound unlike the albums The Temptations, Martha and The Vandellas and The Four Tops were cutting at the same time. Holloway brings a good deal of charm and poise to the well-known Smokey Robinson songs, "Who's Lovin' You", You Can Depend On Me" and "I've Been Good To You", but the standards, "Unchained Melody" and "Embraceable You", don't do a lot for me. On the other hand, the gently Latin flecked "A Favour For A Girl (With A Love Sick Heart)" certainly does, what with Holloway's impressive singing, the lovely melody and the marvellous backing vocals. Brenda also cut a couple of Frank Wilson songs, an association that was to endure for a while to the benefit of both, and while "Too Proud To Cry" didn't sound out of step with the rest of the set, "Sad Song" undoubtedly did, with its anguished vocals and horn-driven beat; it could almost have been a renegade cut from a southern studio, and Holloway never really sounded like this again.

She went on to enjoy five further reasonably big hits on the Tamla label and it was rather a surprise that she never got a chance to record and release a second LP, and it was thus left to the UK arm of the label to pull together all of those 45s, and a couple more that didn't hit, onto an extraordinarily good, effectively "Best Of", album in 1968. Given that, I'm not going to dwell on it for too long, other than to say that apart from "Unchained Melody" there is not a single moment in any one of the sixteen tracks that isn't thoroughly enjoyable and I rate "You've Made Me So Very Happy", "I'll Be Available", "Just Look What You've Done", "When I'm Gone", "Operator" and, maybe best of all, "I'll Always Love You", as among the best reasons for being thankful to be alive that I know.

Sadly, it all ended in tears as Holloway felt she was being messed around too much, and quit Motown at the ripe old age of 21. She cut a highly disappointing one-off single for the Music Merchant label in 1972, and then recorded nothing for years other than a gospel set on the Birthright logo. The set, unsurprisingly, had little in common with her Motown work, and although her voice was still intact, the sound had none of the majesty and oomph of her sixties recordings, and its rather thin and sparse sound makes it a pleasant, but slightly dull, listening experience; with one exception: "Giving Love" previously recorded by The Voices of East Harlem, had a fuller arrangement, excellent backing vocals and Brenda's best vocal in over ten years..

Since then it's been rather quiet, apart from a couple of CDs produced by Ian Levine in the nineties, and more recently, some excellent retrospective CDs of her earliest work which have served to remind people of how great her Motown work was and how loved she still is by so many people.

Eddie Holloway

I Had a Good Time 1991 Hot Blues 3337 Producer: Eddie Holloway

Eddie Holloway was a native of Florida cherished by a small group of aficionados for three 45s in particular from the handful he recorded: "Baby Don't Cry", a funky number when he was with a band called "The Third Guitar" and two "deep soul" numbers "I Had A Good Time" and "I Am The One". None were even close to hits - he never enjoyed any - but all were excellent sides and the latter two were re-cut for his one LP in 1991. (The LP also includes a song called "Baby Don't Cry" but it is not the same one he recorded with The Third Guitar.)

The strengths and weaknesses of the album are clear. On the positive side Holloway had a voice which sounded much like Joe Simon's and if he lacked the tone and inherent sadness that Simon could bring to bear, he compensated by having a wider vocal range than the better-known soul man. The shortfalls were the cheap sounding synthesized horns and drum machine. On balance, I like the set without laying any great claims for it. It was Holloway's first outing at album length after over twenty five years in the business and at over three quarters of an hour long he was determined to give it his best shot and he should have been pretty pleased with it as only "I Want To Be Your Lover" was poor. His remakes of his earlier records were good, as was a take on "When Something Is Wrong With My Baby" and he even sings "Nine Pound Steel", which Simon cut as well and, it must be said, better.

Holloway released a handful of CDs since the release of *I Had A Good Time* but I believe he passed on in early 2014.

Loleatta Holloway

Loleatta 1973 Aware AA 2003 Producer: Floyd Smith

Cry To Me 1975 Aware AA 2008 Producer: Floyd Smith (Billboard soul charts: 47)

Loleatta Holloway was born in Chicago and had the classic gospel background singing in both her mother's choir and The Caravans before making her first record as a soul singer, a magnificent 45 with "Rainbow '71" on one side and "Bring It On Up" on the other, both formidable performances, sung with unrestrained passion and fire. She only made that one record for the Galaxy label, though, and soon signed with the Aware company out of Atlanta.

We were let in gently on her first LP as the opening track, "The man I Love", while beautifully sung, suggested that the label may have told her to tone down the passion and record a jazz album instead. However, "So Can I", the "swampy" "Only A Fool", "Mother Of Shame" and "Part Time Lover, Full Time Fool" made it abundantly clear that this was defiantly a "soul" set and we should not have been fooled by its beginning. (Another good track, "Our Love", put Holloway on the singles charts for the first time (#43) and although it was written by Chuck Jackson and Marvin Yancy it was NOT the same song as the big hit they wrote for Natalie Cole; odd they should use the identical title twice.) Elsewhere there were ok covers of "We Did It" and "Can I Change My Mind".

Four deeply moving records by women, all sung with utter conviction, and all possessed of brilliant arrangements, will always automatically evoke an era from the end of 1974 until the end of 1975 for me as regards soul music: Bessie Banks' "Try To Leave Me If You Can", Barbara Hall's "Drop My Heart Off At The Door", Debbie Taylor's "I Don't Wanna Leave You" and Loleatta Holloway's "Cry To Me". By far the biggest hit of these was Loleatta's which reached #10 soul and #68 pop, which makes it one of the most unrestrainedly emotional records ever to chart on the *Billboard* Hot 100, and it became the title track of Holloway's superb second album, masterly produced by Floyd Smith and also one of the first times the soul world was becoming fully conscious of Sam Dees' songwriting prowess; he contributed half of the LPs ten songs including the hit, all of which, with the exception of the atypically rather weak "H.E.L.P. M.E. M.Y. L.O.R.D.", were memorable. *Cry To Me* also contained a winning cover of "Casanova", a beautifully subtle dance side in "I Can't Help Myself" and another exemplary "deep soul" song in Holloway's own "I'll Be Gone". Unfortunately, Aware was one of a handful of record labels owned by a notorious individual called Michael Thevis and given the interest in him by the police, FBI and doubtless many others it was no surprise when his enterprises went kaput.

Loleatta 1976 Gold Mind GZS-7500 Producers: Floyd Smith, Norman Harris & Ron Kersey

Queen Of The Night 1978 Gold Mind GA 9501 Producers: Floyd Smith, Norman Harris, Bunny Sigler, Tom Moulton, Gordon Edwards & Ron Tyson (Billboard soul charts: 47; Billboard pop charts: 187)

Loleatta Holloway 1979 Gold Mind GA 9504 Producers: Floyd Smith, Bunny Sigler, Bobby Womack & Patrick Moten

Love Sensation 1980 Gold Mind GA 9506 Producers: Norman Harris, Dan Hartman, Ron Tyson, Floyd Smith, Bobby Womack & Patrick Moten

Holloway didn't have to wait long for a new label though, signing with Norman Harris' Gold Mind label in 1976. It was clearly a transitional set as it contained another exceptional song by Sam Dees' "Worn Out Broken Heart", and a remake of Gene Chandler's "What Now", both produced by Floyd Smith, while the other six cuts were all overseen by Philly stalwarts Harris or Ron Kersey. Dees had already taken his own version of "Broken Heart" to #15 on the soul charts in late 1974 which was ten places higher than Holloway's marvellous re-make managed two years later. Both of the Smith productions were beyond reproach and demonstrated that Holloway could now be sensibly classed as one of the six or seven best female soul singers in the world. Listen to them now forty years later and make the world stop for a while. Less satisfying were the Harris' productions, "Hit And Run" (a #56 soul hit in spring of 1977), "Ripped Off", "We're Getting Stronger" and "Dreamin'". By no stretch of the imagination bad records, they nevertheless fell into the category of "superior disco" and suffer in comparison when compared to "What Now" or "Worn Out Broken Heart". Kersey's two productions were perfectly acceptable, if not vintage Holloway, and the LP was not as good as the two on Aware.

The best way to enjoy the *Queen Of The Night* set was to forget that Holloway had ever cut sides like "Cry To Me" and "Worn Out Broken Heart" and just go with the high energy flow. Heavily oriented towards the dance floor, and full in production, Holloway provides a vocal attack that surely raises the question as to why all disco couldn't have been as vibrant as this. Who needed Celi Bee and the Buzzy Bunch or all those other horrors if you could dance yourself to exhaustion while listening to Loleatta belting out "I May Not Be There When You Want Me"? Bobby Womack's "I'm In Love" is the only Floyd Smith produced track on display and the only one that really accurately recalls her early work but it's not the only slow cut on board as there is also a barnstorming version of Debby Boone's rather schmaltzy "You Light Up My Life", where Holloway absolutely demolishes the original. A decent duet with Bunny Sigler, "Only You" reached #11 soul, her second ever biggest ever hit, but "Catch Me On The Rebound" stalled at a highly disappointing #92.

Womack contributed a song and a production to *Loleatta Holloway* but sadly this input did little to help stop the LP from being her least satisfying to date. In fact, by turning the old Shirelles' hit, "Baby It's You", into an insensitive disco mess, and thus one of the worst things he and Loleatta were ever involved in, he actively contributed towards the feeling of disappointment. My other main reservation about the album was that on *Queen Of The Night* Holloway's voice always trumped the musical backing, but that was not always the case here and a handful of cuts dispensed with her singing in favour of extended disco rhythm breaks. For example, I certainly enjoy listening to the first three minutes of "That's What You Said", but tune out for the final four. It wasn't all a letdown though as "All About The Paper" is a much-loved song and the two Floyd Smith productions were, as ever, good. Firstly, her cover of yet another old Chicago hit, "There'll Come A Time", was astute and respectful, while "Sweet Mother Of Mine" a highly gospel-influenced song, closed the album on a high.

Love Sensation was not only a complete return to form but an absolute pleasure from start to finish. Womack's contribution was much stronger this time around and everything worked. The dance sides were spirited and effervescent, with the first few minutes of "I'll Be Standing There" sounding not unlike a Motown side from the sixties, while all the slow ballads gave Holloway a chance to stretch out, none more so than her revival of "I've Been Loving You Too Long". Not only do I think this is the best version ever cut of this great Otis Redding and Jerry Butler song but her delivery of the line "You are tired" and her little gulp afterwards at forty seconds in are among my favourite and most moving moments in nearly fifty years of listening to soul music. Not everyone shared my enthusiasm though, as neither the LP nor the two singles pulled from it managed to reach any national charts. (A slightly different version of the LP, with "Heartstealer" replacing "I'll Be Standing There", came out in Holland on The Rams Horn label in 1989.)

Holloway released no further LPs but plenty of singles, virtually all of which were dance records, before she passed away in 2011. For a few years before that, mainly on the strength of how much of her music had been sampled, a number of retrospective CDS had appeared and she was finally starting to receive the acclaim she had always deserved and she is now widely recognised as one of the finest singers who ever worked in the soul music field.

HollyGrove!

Theryl DeClouet; D J Sylvester; Sullivan Wallace

New Orleans' Best Kept Secret 1982 Home Brew 41086 Producers: Allan Felder, Cary Gilbert & Winfred Lovett

This was certainly a good title for an LP as Hollygrove! were surely unknown outside of the Crescent City and hardly anyone else was making excellent sweet soul like this in 1982. It was no surprise to learn that the producers were Allan Felder, Cary Gilbert and The Manhattans' "Blue" Lovett, all men who had played a big part in helping to ensure the prominence of Philadelphia soul in the seventies. However, it was certainly not all memorable, and side two featured the instrumental cuts to a couple of the vocal tracks from the first side, and they can thus be dispensed with fairly easily. But side one is a pleasure: hearing timeless soul harmony singing that rolls back the years and has a close kinship with records that were cut twenty years earlier reminds us of how resilient and universal the strengths of great music are. The cover of the album is unfortunately tacky but "Who Has The Answers" and "Runin, 'Slipin', Sldin', Through" (sic) are anything but.

Theryl DeClouet has gone on to sing with Galactic as well as cutting a couple of fine singles and CDs in his own name over the last couple of decades.

Eddie Holman

I Love You 1969 ABC 701 Producer: Peter De Angelis (Billboard soul charts: 10; Billboard pop charts: 75)

A Night To Remember 1977 Salsoul SZS-5511 Producers: Norman Harris, Ronnie Baker, Ron Kersey, Bruce Gray & Talmadge Conway

United 1984 Agape A9584 Producer: Eddie Holman

Sweet Memories 1992 Universal Love E-001 Producer: Weldon McDougal

Eddie Holman was born in Norfolk, Virginia, grew up in New York City (where he cut his first few singles) but made his musical mark in Philadelphia His first 45 on the Parkway label was beautiful, and "This Can't Be True" made it to #17 soul and #57 pop right at the start of 1966, although it would have to wait a quarter of a century before it featured in a Holman LP, of which more later.

Holman moved to ABC in the late sixties and hit with his first single, I Love You" in the summer of 1969. It became the title track of his first ever LP, but housed within was a much bigger hit and the one that most people know him for to this day. "Hey There Lonely Girl" was a string-drenched slow song, much beloved by teenage girls particularly, and seems to have been a hit on numerous occasions in the UK. More importantly, in the U.S. it climbed all the way to #4 soul and #2 pop and helped provide the album from which it came with enough momentum to make it a big seller and also spawn a third hit when "Don't Stop Now" was pulled from it in spring 1970. The set also featured re-cuts of Holman's second Parkway hit, "Am I A Loser (From The Start)" as well as "Don't Stop Now" (which hadn't made it the first time around) and it pointed up the weakness in the productions by Peter De Angelis when compared to how Weldon McDougall approached Holman's sessions: De Angelis employed too much sweetening. Holman's main weapon was his startling range when he could move into the highest falsetto from a standing start and he sometimes needed male backing singers and a pungent rhythm to keep him from floating away; it was a shame he too often had to fight against over indulgent backing on the *I Love You* LP. Secondly songs like "Since I Don't Have You" were obviously chosen to get the maximum from that sky high tenor and I preferred him singing from time to time in his more "natural" voice (e.g. "Since My Love Has Gone") as it provided a more dramatic contrast with the falsetto when he switched to it. (In the U.K. the LP was entitled *Lonely Girl* with a different cover but the track listing is identical).

Another highly orchestrated and somewhat sickly single "Cathy Called" (not on the LP) was a successful single (#28 soul) at the end of 1970 but Eddie had to wait until September 1972 for his next hit when the rather lovely "My Mind Keeps Telling Me" (which again bore a massive production but as it was played by MFSB and produced by Holman himself, it was more soulful) reached #20 soul and all the way until 1977 for his second LP. He was still recording in Philadelphia and the *A Night To Remember* set was a really good one as Baker-Harris-Young didn't overdo the disco flourishes that they were sometimes prone to in 1977. "You Make My Life Complete" was an entirely winning way to kick things off and is a perfect example of how to perform a song in the "sweet soul" genre as not only did it bear arguably Holman's best ever singing but the backing vocals were pitch perfect too. "Immune To Love" and "I've Been Singing Love Songs" were also gorgeous and could easily have come from a Blue Magic LP. I love the way the latter lets everything drop away other than the backing singers for the last thirty seconds or so, a sure sign that this wasn't just making music by numbers. But it's the title track that people recall best and its distinctive one finger piano flourishes helped to carry it to #25 soul, the last time he was ever to enjoy a big selling record. "Time Will Tell" was another up-tempo success and given there were no failures on the album I rate it as one of the finest to have come out of Philly in the second half of the seventies.

Soon after this Holman stopped recording secular music - in fact music, full stop - and he didn't re-emerge until 1984 with a gospel set on his own label, Agape. (It even got a UK release but I wouldn't have wanted to live off its royalties.) It's a cut above most gospel LPs from soul acts in the eighties as all too often they were sparse in sound and rather lacking in tunes and hooks. Holman, however, composed songs that are soul sides in construction and feel, and merely provided religious lyrics for them. It should still be investigated with care by anyone who doesn't much care for gospel but you could be surprised.

In 1992 his excellent sides on Parkway - or at least more than half of them - were finally put out on a radiant LP which also contained a handful of previously unreleased cuts. It's good to hear great things like "Eddie's My Name", "I Surrender", "Peace Of Mind" and the title track. (The LP was co-credited with The Larks, who provided backing vocals on many of the songs)

His website shows that he has live bookings right through to the end of 2016 and Holman can be considered to have been one of the key singers in the soul era to have popularised the soaringly high tenor as an attractive way to sell records.

Carl Holmes

Commanders: Marco King; Sports Lewis; Tommy Howard; Calvin Irons; John Holmes

Sherlock Holmes Investigation: Chico Green; John Hammond; John Daves; Jimmy Towns; Chubby Brown; Art Grant; Ray Wright; Middy Middleton; Charles Harris; Jimmy Reynolds and others.

Twist Party At The Roundtable (Holmes & Commanders) 1962 Atlantic 8060 Producer: Ahmet Ertegun

Investigation No. 1 (Holmes & Sherlock Holmes Investigation) 19?? CRS 01 Producers: Curtis Staten & Carl Holmes

Information on Carl Holmes has been hard to track down. What I do know is that he was a guitarist from Pennsylvania and gave his name to two bands who released LPs: The Commanders and Sherlock Holmes Investigation. The Commanders lasted the longer and continued to issue singles up to 1967, although I'm sure the personnel changed in that time.

The Atlantic album, consisting entirely of covers, and apparently recorded live in a New York club, palls long before it finishes. Marco King was a fair singer, but "Stand By Me" apart, all he really has to do is belt out the lyrics on dance items.

The CRS set, recorded at Sigma Sound and on which Holmes takes some lead vocals, is much better and more varied, and ranges from the laid-back and sweetly sung "Think It Over", the Marvin Gaye-ish "Your Game", a nice cover of "Close To You", through a funky instrumental, "Black Bag", to "Modesa" which has a touch of Mandrill about it. The LP hardly got past the Philadelphia area though and has become a modish and expensive LP over the last few years.

Eldridge Holmes

A Time For The Ridgy 1989 P-Vine PLP-502 Producers: Allen Toussaint & Marshall Sehorn (Japan)

Eldridge Holmes is one of my favourite singers from New Orleans. He released 18 singles between 1962 and 1972 and not one of them was a national hit, and not many reached the local Crescent City charts either. No matter, he was a fine singer and most of his records were first-rate. He never got a chance to record an LP while his career was active and once again we have to thank the Japanese for putting out an excellent and generous (16 tracks) retrospective of his music in 1989. The title is odd, doubtless some play on his name, and I assume it was lost in translation.

The album covers the entire period of his recording life (although it only includes one of the ten sides he cut for his first label, Alon) and as it encompasses an eight year time period a number of different styles are on show. The earliest songs benefit from that typical and marvellous rolling New Orleans gait, but "Cheatin' Woman" is a tough blues based outing from 1972 while "Pop, Popcorn Children" was the funkiest side he ever cut. The LP doesn't contain ALL of his best sides as three of these, all compelling dance outings - "The Book", "If I Were A Carpenter" and "Lovely Woman" - are absent but it is still a delightful way to listen to one of the most underrated singers I know. He died in 1998 and I wonder if he even knew this LP existed.

Marvin Holmes

Uptights: John Parrish: Gaylord Birch; Anthony Davis; Everett Walker; Elza Davis; Patrick Hodges; Godfrey Smith

Justice: Edwin McCoy; Dave Mirigian; Larry Vann; Danny Armstrong; Leon Williams; Melvin Coleman; Minor Williams; David Frazier; Louis Pain; Lonnie Hewitt

Ooh Ooh The Dragon And Other Monsters (Holmes & The Uptights) 1969 Uni 73046 Producer: Clarence Brown

Summer of '73 (Holmes & Justice) 1973 Brown Door MH 6573 Producer: Ted Green and Ed Howard

Honor Thy Father (Holmes & Justice) 1975 Brown Door MH 6581 Producer: Marvin Holmes

It's About Time 1983 Brown Door 6592 Producer: Marvin Holmes

Marvin Holmes is one of the most important, influential and best-loved musicians to come out of the Bay Area soul scene, even if none of his numerous records gained much national attention. Although he released a few singles in his own name, the majority of his singles and LPs bore the credits of Marvin Holmes and The Uptights or Marvin Holmes and Justice.

His recording career began in the mid sixties and lasted until 1986, although his most prolific period was from 1969 until 1975 when the first three of his four LPs were released. *Ooh Ooh The Dragon And Other Monsters,* not the snappiest title ever coined, is an entirely likeable effort couched in that breezy, loose-limbed and funky style that characterised recordings from the West Coast. Alternating between pure instrumental and vocal tracks, ten of the twelve cuts are covers, ranging from the fairly obvious in "Who's Making Love" and "Grazing In The Grass", to more surprising, such as a pretty take on Frankie Karl and The Dreams' "Don't Be Afraid". The two Holmes' originals, "Ride Your Mule" and the title track, were issued as singles but despite reasonably healthy local sales did not break out nationally. I hesitate to pick out a stand-out cut from a consistent set but "There Was A Time" doesn't suffer in comparison to the versions by James Brown and Gene Chandler.

The Uptights disbanded after a further 45 was issued in 1970 (Gaylord Birch went on to join Graham Central Station) and Holmes put a couple more bands together, Funk Company and Justice, but it was only with the latter that he got the chance to issue long players.

Despite the four year time difference and the fact that a new band was playing behind Holmes, there wasn't THAT much disparity in the sound of the *Summer Of '73* set from *Ooh Ooh The Dragon*. "Kimani Mdogo" was possibly tougher and more compact than anything on the earlier set but Holmes' choppy rhythm guitar ensured a consistency of purpose and feel. The most obvious lack of similarity came with the compositions: the "covers" approach of the Uni album had given way to ten originals on the new set but it was still a highly enjoyable and worthwhile outing.

Honor Thy Father did ring some changes though and was Holmes' most varied and best set to date. The funk - "Find Yourself", "She's A Dancer" and "Gimme Some" - is good and hard while strings were used for the first time most notably on the excellent and smooth dance side "You Better Keep Her" which became a "Northern Soul" favourite in certain venues in England. "Motherless Child" was a soul ballad of the sort Holmes had barely tried in the past and the title track sounded like convincing autobiography. There was only one instrumental this time around ("Kwame", which even employed fiddles) while the latin beat on "Neighbor Neighbor" also broke new ground for the band. Something on here surely deserved to be a hit, but it wasn't to be.

Holmes' last LP was a bit of a haphazard affair, embracing a number of different styles, thus lacking a unifying theme and limiting commercial possibilities. His new band, Oakland, were talented musicians and the opening two tracks were light, jazzy instrumentals that showed off Joe Thomas' bass playing and Holmes own guitar virtuosity to good effect, while "The Art Of Loving You" was a gentle song, pleasant enough, but lacking in staying power. The last three tracks all betrayed influences from others, albeit in a manner that hinted rather than loudly proclaimed: "Can I Get Nasty" (P-Funk), "You Girl" (Stevie Wonder) and "Contraband" (Johnny "Guitar" Watson). It was to be his last LP and the only one that didn't explicitly credit his backing band.

Holmes did release a couple of 12-inch records in the eighties after Brown Door closed down but despite a lack of new recordings in the last couple of decades interest in his earlier music remains high.

Home Boy & The C.O.L. (see also Cecil Lyde)

Home Boy & The C.O.L. 1982 Alwest HB 92050 Producer: Cecil Lyde

Out Break 1984 Alwest HB 92051 Producer: HomeBoy

Cecil Orlando "Homeboy" Lyde Holden grew up and started out in the music business in Chicago (and wrote a couple of songs for Bruce Fisher's *Red Hot* LP) but moved to the West Coast to release his records, including his first album in 1980. In 1982 he began to put out LPs on his own Alwest label.

C.O.L. stands for Cost Of Living and the debut outing was exceedingly varied, which made it almost appear as a "various artists" compilation and ranged from the flowing "I'll Make It On My Own", the dead slow (but rather weak and watery in sound) "Time To Change", the uptempo and lyrically tired call to dance of "Funk Yourself To Death", the Zapp styled vocoder on "Money's Funny, Change Is Strange" and the best thing on show, the swinging and jazzy "Can't Get Enough". Anyway, the eclectic approach didn't succeed in attracting buyers and the album was not a hit.

The follow-up set wasn't as catholic as the debut, opting in the main for rather dull dance numbers but mixed in among them was a half decent cover of "La La Means I Love You" and a long drawn out "I Don't Want To Be A Movie Star" which was the most original and striking song on show.

Lyde continues in the music business today releasing new music and appearing as a D.J. on Phoenix radio.

Honey And The Bees

Nadine Felder; Jean Davis; Cassandra Ann Wooten; Gwendolyn Oliver

Love 1970 Josie JOS 4013 Producers: Jimmy Bishop, William Hart, Norman Harris & James and James

Honey and The Bees were an excellent female group from Philadelphia, who got the chance to release a respectable amount of singles - one, before Felder joined, being issued as by The Yum Yums - even if none ever broached the *Billboard* charts. They were popular in their home town, though, and that sustained them through a career that lasted for seven years or so. Certainly the two labels for whom they recorded most prolifically, Arctic (5 singles) and Josie (6), cannot be accused of not giving them every chance to make it. They have other soulful associations too: Nadine's brother is Allan Felder who wrote produced and arranged countless Philly records while Gwen Oliver is married to Fred Wesley.

It is tempting for me to be gushing about the LP purely because pretty much any record coming out of Philadelphia circa 1970 sounds so alluring to my ears. It was a fascinating period when the foundations for what would explode nationally and internationally in 1972 with Philadelphia International were starting to be clearly discernible and hearing the beautiful music coming out of the speakers on the album is to be instantly transported back to those days. But I will restrain myself and note that the songs, while all decent enough, were not of the absolute highest class and it is only that fact that stops the set from being unreservedly recommended. Certainly everything else, including the girls' performances, is beyond reproach. As mentioned earlier, Josie tried hard to break Honey and The Bees and a number of the ten tracks were pressed into service as 45s but only one, a slightly disjointed medley of "It's Gonna Take A Miracle", Hurt So Bad" and "Going Out Of My Head", did well, reaching the *Cashbox* soul top thirty.

The group didn't last very far into the seventies, though, with their final singles coming out on the North Bay label in 1972. Their talent hadn't vanished overnight however and Wooten and Oliver were recruited to become two-thirds of the big disco group, The Richie Family.

Honey Cone (see also Edna Wright)

Carolyn Willis; Edna Wright; Shelly Clark

Take Me With You 1970 Hot Wax HA 701 Producer: Stagecoach Productions

Sweet Replies 1971 Hot Wax HA 706 Producers: William Weatherspoon & Greg Perry (Billboard soul charts: 14; Billboard pop charts: 137)

Soulful Tapestry 1971 Hot Wax HA 707 Producers: Greg Perry & General Johnson (Billboard soul charts: 15; Billboard pop charts: 72)

Love, Peace And Soul 1972 Hot Wax HA 713 Producer: Greg Perry (Billboard soul charts: 41; Billboard pop charts: 189)

Girls It Ain't Easy 1984 HDH LP 004 (UK)

The Honey Cone consisted of three women with experience in the industry who came together in LA to form the Honey Cone. Edna Wright had recorded session backgrounds as well as releasing singles as "Sandy Wynns", Carolyn Willis, another session singer, had briefly been a member of Bob B Soxx and The Blue

Jeans, while Shelly Clark was an Ikette.

Their first single, "While You're Out Looking For Sugar", set the tone for most of their music, short, highly energetic and easy to remember, and reached #16 soul and #62 pop in the middle of 1969. The follow-up, "Girls It Ain't Easy", did even better by hitting #8 soul #68 pop, and a third, "Take Me With You" did well, too, also hitting the soul top thirty even if just missing the Hot 100. All three tracks were included on their first LP which bore the name of the last single. Wright took nearly all the leads but the others got to feature on some cuts. Given the women were highly photogenic, the cover of the first LP was misguided and must surely have contributed to its becoming the only one of the four from Honey Cone that did not chart. If I have a concern with *Take Me With You* it is that it's all too one-paced and as often was the case with Hot Wax/Invictus there is little in the way of light and shade. Only the last track, the pretty "The Feeling's Gone", slowed down the tempo and gave us a slightly different dimension on the group. Covers like "Son Of A Preacher Man" (not bad) and "Aquarius (awful) also screamed of "filler". On the other hand, the songs were tuneful and literate and the musicianship was typically bright, guitar heavy and rhythmic.

Much better things were about to happen, though, and for a few months in 1971 Honey Cone were - if anybody cared to think about it - the biggest female soul group in the world as successive singles, "Want Ads" and "Stick Up", each went to #1 on the soul charts with the former also reaching the top of the pop listings while "Stick Up" had to settle for a still highly respectable #11. Given the success of "Want Ads" it was obvious an album was needed to support it, and *Sweet Replies* was the result. The good news was that it wisely showed the three women on the - gatefold no less - sleeve and did pretty well on the soul charts. The bad news was that it re-cycled five tracks from *Take Me With You*. Of the new tracks, it wasn't hard to see why "Want Ads" had been such a success and the excellent and spacey "When Will It End" was certainly a departure for the group. I also liked the slower "The Day I Found Myself" but found the other new tracks to be interchangeable and once again lacking in variety. It was becoming clear that Honey Cone were a group that one would either love wholeheartedly or start to get a little bored with.

Soulful Tapestry followed *Sweet Replies* pretty quickly and performed well on both soul and pop charts, not least because "Stick Up" and another top 20 pop hit, the latin-tinged "One Monkey Don't Stop No Show", were both included. As were two tracks previously included on *Sweet Replies* and one bearing a maxim as a title, so beloved of Invictus/Hot Wax, "Don't Count Your Chickens (Before They Hatch)". Elsewhere, "V.I.P" almost bludgeoned you with its constantly repeated refrain of the title and my favourite cut on the set was the long drawn-out "What's It Gonna Be", a most unusual outing for the group.

Love, Peace And Soul had a couple of noticeable differences from the other three sets: firstly, Carolyn Willis had quit the group (to return to session singing) and second "Ooo Baby Baby", "Stay In My Corner" and "Who's Lovin' You" (all decent covers) were recorded at the sort of sedate trot that was seemingly not permitted in Honey Cone's earlier days and as they were the first three cuts on side one they set the pace (figuratively and almost literally) for much of the rest of my favourite of all their LPs. "Don't Send Me An Invitation" and "I Lost My Rainbow" were other slower cuts with interesting arrangements and only "Ace In The Hole" was really obviously typical of their previous work. However, releasing an LP that I thought was their best didn't do much for their commercial fortunes as they continued to sell fewer and fewer 45s. "Sittin' On A Time Bomb (Waiting For The Hurt To Come)" and "Innocent 'Til Proven Guilty" were two good single releases from *Love, Peace And Soul* and did ok at #33 and #37 soul respectively but coming after four successive records that had all hit at least #8 it was somewhat of a disappointment. The aforementioned "Ace In The Hole" then missed out completely when it became the third track to be issued as a 45.

That was more or less it for the group and although a further Honey Cone single appeared in 1976 none of the original trio were involved. Wright did reappear to release a solo album in 1977 while Shelly Clark married Verdine White of Earth, Wind and Fire and retired from singing. In 1984 the UK HDH label issued a good 14 track retrospective LP which did not merely focus on the hits ("Stick Up" wasn't included, for example). As might have been fairly clearly discerned, Honey Cone were not my favourite female singing group, not least because I simply think they were better suited to releasing records at single rather than LP length, but their feat of attaining two #1 soul hits cannot be matched by The Emotions, The Three Degrees or post-Diana Ross Supremes.

Frank Hooker

Positive People: Warren Smith; Calvin Charity; Al Williams; Willie Vazquez; Gladys Matthews; Randy Choice

Frank Hooker & Positive People 1980 Panorama
BXL1-3853 Producer: James Purdie

Hear The Word 1987 Command 1007 Producers: Frank Hooker & James Purdie

I think Frank Hooker might have originated from Washington D.C. and certainly he wrote a couple of songs in 1976 for The Young Senators, a band from the city who once played behind Eddie Kendricks, but his own group, Frank Hooker & The Positive People, had an almost indecently short recording career, considering they placed four singles on the soul charts between August 1979 and April 1981. The first of these, the unremarkable "Rock Me", gave little indication that the album that would contain the other three would be of such high quality.

It was nearly all recorded at Sigma Sound in Philadelphia but sounded slightly less lush than such a location would suggest; however, it was surely no co-incidence that the group covered a song cut there years earlier, The Intruders' "I Wanna Know Your Name", in such winning style that it reached #40 as a single. Two other slow drag songs, "Early In The Morning" and "Looking For My Number One Love", were possibly even better - Hooker really nails the former - and it was lovely to hear such performances at the tail-end of the disco era, while a take on The Drifters' "Like Sister And Brother" (another small hit, #62) was just fine too. Their final charting single, the excellent "Ooh Suga Wooga", sounded like an early incarnation of the Washington D.C. "go-go" sound, an impression strengthened by another crunching dance track, "This Feelin'". An excellent and highly recommended LP.

Hooker went on to record in the gospel field although I have not heard the *Hear The Word* LP which I think also came out under the title of *Rise And Shine*.

David Hooper

Believe In Me 1982 Da Cloud 2160 Producer: Joe McCloud

I remember this LP from this Houston based singer coming out as a new release but passed on purchasing it at the time and have never seen a copy in a shop since, although it pops up on ebay from time to time. It is thanks to the internet that I have now heard a handful of tracks and while the title track and "Get It On" are engaging in a manner vaguely reminiscent of Lou Bond, the other cuts (the dull "So Unique (Tina)" for example, an interminable instrumental) do not make me regret failing to buy it.

In 2015 he released a new CD with a group called The Silverbacks in Spain of all places.

Eddie Horan

Love The Way You Love Me 1978 HDM 2002 Producer: Hadley Murrell

This is a tuneful, smoothly arranged LP consisting of well-constructed songs that apart from the terrible "The Dancer" manage to avoid becoming too enmeshed by disco style arrangements. Horan was a good singer and writer, having previously released singles on Money and MGM and what I have written above would probably make this an album worthy of investigation anyway; the only problem would be that Horan betrayed little gospel fire or indeed church influence in his singing and his style was not dissimilar to say, O.C. Smith. So long as that is understood it is an LP worth hearing. The title track performed disappointingly on the soul charts, stalling at only #91.

A good single, "City Life", slipped out in 1982 and a retrospective of his work came out on CD in 2013.

Jimmy "Bo" Horne

Dance Across The Floor 1978 Sunshine Sound 7801 Producers: Harry Wane Casey & Richard Finch (Billboard soul charts: 23; Billboard pop charts: 122)

Goin' Home For Love 1978 Sunshine Sound 7805 Producers: Harry Wane Casey & Richard Finch (Billboard soul charts: 42)

Bo Horne '91 1991 New Music International 1024 (Italy) Producer: Pippo Landro

Florida soul man Horne put out a series of likeable singles from the period of around 1969 to 1974 on labels like Dade, Dig and Alston including an answer to Betty Wright in "Clean Up Man" and the funky and tough "Hey There Jim" but despite their quality, none hit nationally until "Gimme Some" landed up as #47 on the soul charts in the summer of 1975. It was his least enchanting record to date, being produced by Harry Wayne Casey and Richard Finch (of K.C. and The Sunshine Band fame) and thus more pop-oriented than his earlier work, but a hit is a hit, and he was to continue in this style from here on in.

Dance Across The Floor contained four soul chart entrants - "Gimme Some", "Get Happy" the title track (the biggest of them at #8) and "Let Me (Let Me Be Your Lover" - and while as a highly energetic dance album it achieved its aims unerringly, there is little soul music on show and it's tough to listen to with any interest or pleasure.

The debut LP was pretty much simply more of the same with "Spank" (#55), "You Get Me Hot" (#18) and "Without You" (#78) being the three hits this time around. It should be noted that the last of these was not a dance side and nor was a take on "(They Long To Be) Close To You" but neither rose above the mundane.

The only other "Bo "Horne LP was cut in Milan in 1991, and I believe (I haven't heard much of it) consists of re-makes of his seventies hits as well as a couple of previously unreleased things and a cover of "Dock Of The Bay". This last performance fell far short from matching Otis' original but at least reminded us that Horne was a proper soul singer when allowed to be.

He released a new CD in 1994 but does not appear to have recorded any new music since.

Dellie Hoskie (with Eddy Noble & Their Natural Selves

Something Old And Something New 1972 Noble NR-1005/6 Producer: Noble Record Productions

This is one of those gloriously odd albums that appear from time to time. Side one was performed by Dellie Hoskie and it is the side that has relevance for the book; the other is sung by one Eddy Noble and is fifties jazz in style. Hoskie was from Newport News, but his album was cut in New Haven, Connecticut. A website states that two tracks, "The Clown" and "How Much Can A Man Take", were both gold records that sold to fans all over the world and made *Billboard* top 20 for two weeks. As so often with such statements there is a great deal more bravado than facts involved. Neither record went "gold", neither sold to fans all over the world in the sense suggested and neither even made the *Billboard* top 100, let alone the top 20. A brief bit of research doesn't even show them as registering as on the local New Haven charts of the time. Given their sparse instrumentation, that's not a surprise, as they sound like demos against the fuller productions of the time. Having said that, the latter is actually a pretty decent semi-deep soul side while "The Clown" does have some funk appeal. Elsewhere, there is a poor take on "A Change Is Gonna Come" and an even worse one of "I'll Take You There". God knows how many copies it sold on release, but it won't have been many and it is only an album for someone who really does want to collect everything.

Hot

Gwen Owens; Cathy Carson; Juanita Curiel

Hot 1977 Big Tree BT 89522 Producers: Clayton Ivey & Terry Woodford (Billboard soul charts: 28; Billboard pop charts: 125)

If That's The Way You Want It 1978 Big Tree BT 76005 Producers: Clayton Ivey & Terry Woodford

Strong Together 1979 Big Tree BT 76005 Producers: Clayton Ivey & Terry Woodford

The Wishbone Recording studio in Muscle Shoals is probably not quite so well-known as FAME, Muscle Shoals Sound Recording Studio or Quinvy/Broadway, but it was another source of much fine music from the mid-seventies onwards and all three of Hot's albums were recorded there.

Hot are a rather forgotten trio, their big hit being "Angel In Your Arms" which reached #6 pop and #29 soul in the spring of 1977. But look at those chart placings and the answer is possibly there: it was a much bigger success on the pop listings. Despite having a lead vocalist in Gwen Owens who had recorded a number of solo singles over the years, Hot were always produced in a manner that kept passion at a minimum and Owens never really got the chance to let go in her singing. This approach was adopted right from the first LP and although the musicians are among the best - Ivey himself, Roger Clark, Bob Wray, Tippy Armstrong and others - and the songs tuneful and literate, it is all pleasant enough but rather uninvolving. "The Right Feeling At The Wrong Time", a classic cheating title and strong song from Barbara Wyrick and Kevin Lamb was the best track on the set, and reached #58 soul and #65 pop as the follow-up single to "Angel In Your Arms".

The second LP sounded similar to the first, southern soul overlaid onto a pop base. One or two tracks employed a good horn section but the overall softness of what was below dampened down too much enthusiasm. Jesse Boyce provided some songs, the only time he did on a Hot LP, and although Curiel and Carson managed to get a songwriting credit, Owens did not, while the best-known song on show was possibly the title track which had been recorded by Tavares a few years before. No hits were forthcoming, though, despite Big Tree's issuing two 45s from the set.

One thing had to be said for the first two albums: disco influence was entirely absent. This was addressed slightly and subtly on *Strong Together* with the odd dancing string section here and there but it largely followed the same path as its predecessors, although Owens was permitted just now and then to add a little edge to her voice. It didn't much matter, though, as Hot's brief time in the limelight had already ended and there were no hit singles on board. Owens' own "I Don't Wanna Be Around When The Hurt Comes" had a great title, but like most of the songs on the set, ultimately delivered a little less than it promised. Again, it's not a bad LP, just rather unexciting.

The Big Tree association came to an end after the release of the third LP, and a 1982 attempted "comeback" single on the Boardwalk label was not a success.

Hot Chocolate (see also Lou Ragland)

Lou Ragland; Tony Roberson; George Pickett

Hot Chocolate 1971 Co Co Cleveland L 1010 Produced by Lou Ragland

Not the Errol Brown group, but the one led by Lou Ragland, a singer who never really made it despite releasing some good records over a thirty year period. Most of the pleasure from Ragland's work comes from his voice, but here it is his guitar that dominates. If he had merely knocked out a bunch of solos, this would probably be grim stuff, but it is his rhythm playing that compels attention, and it is both tasteful and funky. One does have to have a good tolerance for instrumentals though as only three of the seven tracks feature his (or any) singing. One, "Ain't That A Groove" is upbeat with a "hot" and live feel, whereas "We Had True Love" and "What Should I Do" are ballads. Only a few hundred copies of the LP were ever pressed up and a lack of funds meant that only guitar, bass, congas and drums were employed and it is hardly a must have release but is enjoyable in an unpretentious way.

Cissy Houston (see also The Sweet Inspirations)

Cissy Houston 1970 Janus JLS 3001 Producers: Charles Koppelman, Bob Finiz & Don Rubin

Cissy Houston's career in the music industry should be a source of great pride given her undoubted accomplishments which include being a key member of The Sweet Inspirations, mother of Whitney and possessor of one of the best voices ever committed to wax, but there nonetheless persists a slight feeling of disappointment with her solo records as she never recorded a genuinely great LP and never placed a single in the soul top thirty or the pop top 50.

She was born in Newark and started to make a name for herself with the Drinkard Singers before forming the Sweet Inspirations, a group who have strong claims to being the finest backing singers of all time, let alone recording many excellent sides in their own right. By the end of the sixties though, it was time for her to branch out and try to make her own way, although she had already recorded a couple of (failed) singles as by "Sissie Houston" and less obviously, "Cecily Blair", when she was still with The Sweet Inspirations.

Her first single on Commonwealth United, "I'll Be There", did ok, though, when it reached #45 soul in the middle of 1970. It also featured on her first LP, *Cissy Houston,* (called *Presenting Cissy Houston* on its UK release on the Major Minor label), which was re-issued on the Janus label after initially appearing briefly on CU. Each side started brilliantly with a storming version of "I Just Don't Know What To Do With Myself" on side one and a bewitching take on "Be My Baby" (which went to #31 soul and #92 pop as the follow-up to "I'll Be There", her highest ever charting 45) kicking off side two even if both tracks did sound a tad dated for 1970. They were also, of course, as with all the other eight tracks, covers of songs previously recorded by others and that fact, together with some slightly over fussy production, rendered the album a little underwhelming and she really shouldn't have been saddled with "Any Guy" and "The Long And Winding Road", while it remains annoying that the record label seemed hell bent on drowning out her towering vocal on "He"- "I Believe" with over prominent background singers and strings. With her talent she should have delivered a classic, rather than merely a good LP.

Between 1971 and 1975 Houston recorded a number of singles, but no more albums, which was a great shame as her original of "Midnight Train To Georgia", "Only Time You Say You Love Me", and "Nothing Can Stop Me" were all marvellous 45s and deserved an album that could showcase them at their time of release. (She did receive a "featuring Cissy Houston" credit on the cover of Herbie Mann's 1976 *Surprises* LP but it cannot really be classed as a Houston LP and she had to wait until 1977 for her follow-up to her first album of seven years before.)

Cissy Houston 1977 Private Stock PS 2031 Producer: Michael Zager

Think It Over 1978 Private Stock PS 7015 Producer: Michael Zager

Warning - Danger 1979 Columbia AL 36112 Producer: Michael Zager

Step Aside For A Lady 1980 Columbia AL 36193 Producer: Michael Zager

Mama's Cookin 1987 Charly CRB 1158 (UK)

The producer she worked with - Michael Zager - was quite a surprise as his reputation had been forged by making dance records, and I couldn't have imagined that he could produce Cissy so sympathetically as he did on the LP. Her performance on "Make It Easy On Yourself" is magnificent - arguably her greatest ever side as a solo singer - and the superb arrangement and production only enhances my conviction as to its rare quality and it is almost literally impossible to listen to this side and remain passive. In fact, the whole album is a really good one, and only the odd dull choice of song ("He Ain't Heavy, He's My Brother", another song foisted onto way too many soul singers) and the overly staid arrangements on some tracks stop me from raving about it. I really like the fact that Zager played to Cissy's strengths and pitched it as a "grown-up" LP, and there were some well-chosen compositions on hand, too: "Morning Much Better", "Things To Do", a worthy reading of "Your Song", and "Love Is Something That Leads You". The latter only managed an agonisingly disappointing #97 on the soul charts as a single and the show-tune, "Tomorrow", didn't do vastly better at #74. Zager was to remain as Houston's producer on all her remaining albums but given the commercial failure of *Cissy Houston* dance music was to be the order of the day from here on in.

Think It Over was a bit of a let down after *Cissy Houston* although the title track did become her second biggest hit as a solo singer when it made it to # 32 on the soul charts in the summer of 1978. There were only two slow tracks on offer, "After You" and "I Just Want To Be With You", but "Love Don't Hurt People" (good song) and "Sometimes" were pretty restrained and attractive. Elsewhere, the dance floor was the main target and "Warning Danger" and "Somebody Should Have Told Me" hardly stretched Houston, although they were good of their kind. It was a much better LP than many others from 1978 but I still felt that another opportunity had slipped by to really capture this great singer at her best. On the other hand, Cissy contributed four of the songs herself so presumably she was happy enough with it.

I will skip by *Warning-Danger* as it was barely an LP, merely featuring four elongated tracks from *Think It Over,* so *Step Aside For A Lady* was really her last proper album other than a Charly retrospective in 1987. Houston wrote five of the seven songs this time around but I'm afraid to say I don't much care for four of them, as they were out and out dance records, which sounded so much like so many others. I did like - a lot - "Just One Man", one of only two slow songs on the set, the other being "Break It To Me Gently", a fairly popular title for a song and not the one Aretha Franklin had a hit with.

No more hits accrued from the Columbia set and Houston was then reduced to sporadic releases every few years including a perhaps inevitable duet with Whitney in 1988. Charly's collection from 1987 was highly worthwhile as nine of its sixteen tracks could not be found on other Houston LPs and included the three excellent mid seventies singles I mentioned earlier.

She has released some new CDs - including an interesting one with Chuck Jackson in 1992 - in the last twenty years or so and has now happily reached her eighties. She is another national treasure.

Thelma Houston

Sunshower 1969 ABC/Dunhill DS-50054 Producer: Jimmy Webb (Billboard soul charts: 50)

Leland Mississippi's Thelma Houston released a couple of singles for Capitol in 1966 and 1967, including a Motown pastiche, "Baby Mine", so perhaps it was inevitable she would end up on the Detroit label in later years. Less inevitable was her attracting the attention of Jimmy Webb, an association that would have been the envy of many other artists in 1969, particularly as Houston was entirely hitless at that point.

In fact, she was to remain without a hit as neither the album, nor three singles lifted from it, sold particularly well, but I know a couple of people who rate the LP as their favourite of all time. I must say that this does not include me. I am hardly going to gainsay Webb's obvious talent - he wrote "By The Time I Get To Phoenix" and "Wichita Lineman" among hundreds more - but I don't think it was a talent remotely suited to soul music and I do not care for the *Sunshower* set, nor The Supremes album he produced a couple of years later. The songs (apart from "Jumping Jack Flash", all penned by Webb) arrangements, musicians and Houston's voice are all top-class but my ears find the outcome to be too precious and genteel and I simply have to agree to disagree with those who love it. After a couple of non-album 45s also failed Houston left Dunhill and signed with the LA-based Motown subsidiary, MoWest.

Thelma Houston 1972 MoWest MW 102L Producers: Joe Porter, Mel Larson, Jerry Marcellino, Gloria Jones, Pam Sawyer, Hal Davis, Al Cleveland & Edward Langford

I've Got The Music In Me 1975 Sheffield Lab 2 Producer: Bill Schnee

It was quite unusual for a soul LP to have eight producers in the early seventies, although it happened all the time in the eighties, and even though Joe Porter took 50% of the production duties, this small army of people gave rise to the feeling that MoWest didn't really know what to do with Houston. That being said, they did well, particularly on side one as side two veers off into "torchy" territory on two or three tracks. The songs throughout were generally strong, abounding with memorable hooks and sparkling musicianship, and MoWest even provided Houston with a handful of social commentary songs in "Black California, "Blackberries " and a cover of Paul Kelly's "Stealing In The Name Of The Lord". Which was interesting as, although The Temptations had covered such topics for a while, Motown tended to shy away from "controversial" opinion for fear of upsetting the average record buyer. Maybe the fact the LP was released on a not very well-known subsidiary label boosted Gordy's courage. Disappointingly, songs which seemed to me to be potentially obvious hits - "No One's Gonna Be A Fool Forever", "I Ain't Going Nowhere", "I Ain't That Easy To Lose" - did not make it for the very simple reason that none of them were issued as singles (although the former did make it as a b - side). Instead MoWest went with "Me And Bobby McGee", and "What if" as 45s and they failed miserably. MoWest later released three other non-album singles and they did nothing, either.

Her third LP was genuinely odd as she was "loaned" out by Motown to Sheffield Lab, to cut a not for sale album, designed to show-off the pristine sound of recording direct to disc. The LP was credited to "Thelma Houston and Pressure Cooker", features a handful of instrumentals as well as Houston vocals, and I've seen it in bargain bins all over the world but never felt the urge to actually buy it.

Any Way You Like It 1976 Tamla T6-345S Producers: Michael L Smith, Hal Davis, Michael Sutton, Harold Johnson, Joe Porter, Clayton Ivey & Terry Woodford (Billboard soul charts: 5; Billboard pop charts: 11)

Thelma & Jerry (and Jerry Butler) 1977 Motown M6-887S1 Producers: Hal Davis, Jerry Butler, Michael Sutton & Homer Talbert (Billboard soul charts: 20; Billboard pop charts: 53)

The Devil In Me 1977 Tamla T7-358R Producers: Brenda Sutton, Michael Sutton, Brian Holland, Greg Wright, Michael Rubini, Michael Masser, Clayton Ivey & Terry Woodford (Billboard soul charts: 29; Billboard pop charts: 64)

Two To One (and Jerry Butler) 1978 Motown M7-903R1 Producers: Hal Davis, Michael Sutton, Van McCoy, Willie Hutch, Clayton Ivey, Terry Woodford & Sam Brown

Ready To Roll 1978 Tamla T7-361R Producers: Hal Davis, Bobby Belle & Greg Wright (Billboard soul charts: 74)

Ride To The Rainbow 1979 Tamla T7-365R1 Producer: Hal Davis

After MoWest was quietly closed down in 1973, Houston was moved onto the Motown label and scored her first ever entry onto the soul charts with "You've Been Doing Wrong For So Long" when it climbed to a modest #64 in the autumn of 1974. It didn't feature on her first album, which came out on Tamla, as that didn't appear until 1976, and *Any Way You Like It* proudly contained the biggest hit she ever managed in her career by some distance as "Don't Leave Me This Way" went all the way to #1 on both the soul and pop charts. This great Gamble-Huff-Gilbert song deserved its success and the other well-known version by Harold Melvin and The Blue Notes was condemned to remain an album track only in the States. *Any Way You Like It* was rather short on top-class songs, though, and despite playing it a few times over the years many of the song titles elicit no memory in me at all. Two that do are worth a brief mention though. Firstly, the old Tin Pan Alley song, "If It's The Last Thing I Do", because it was so different from the hit and thus a surprising and brave follow-up single and Houston and Motown were rewarded with a #12 soul and #47 pop success and second, Ralph Graham's "Differently", as it such a great composition. Houston certainly couldn't top the original but I'm glad she attempted it.

Motown rather dropped the ball after the success of "Don't Leave Me This Way". It was one of the label's biggest hits of the entire decade but they never gave the impression they were fully committed to her solo career, pairing her up with Jerry Butler for a couple of worthy but rather dull sets, and continued to farm out her recordings to a number of different producers. *Thelma & Jerry* sold well as an LP, but the lead-off single, "It's A Lifetime Thing", spectacularly failed to be a hit. The second Butler-Houston album, *Two To One*, couldn't even reach the soul charts and listening to it again I'm not surprised for it lacked any real spark.

Sandwiched in between the two sets with Butler was *The Devil In Me*, which kicked off with "I'm Here Again", which may as well have been entitled "Don't Leave Me This Way Part II". It performed better than it deserved to as a single reaching #21 soul but failed utterly in the pop market. It was another LP that cried out for stronger songs, and although I'd play the danceable "It's Just Me Feeling Good" again, I would certainly avoid side two, particularly its MOR compositions "Memories" and "Your Eyes".

Houston's penultimate LP for Motown, *Ready To Roll*, did contain her third biggest hit (#19 soul, #34 pop) in the dance track, "Saturday Night, Sunday Morning", but seven of the nine sides were in the same groove and too many were without any distinguishing feature while "Am I Expecting Too Much" and "Can't We Try" were her by now customary MOR slow songs and just for once it would have been nice for Motown to let her sing something more gritty.

Thelma saw out her Motown sojourn with *Ride To The Rainbow*, and it was a sign of the label's indifference that they included "Saturday Night, Sunday Morning" again. I haven't heard much of this one, apart from the hit, the title track and a cover of "Love Machine", but those left me rather cold and the set failed commercially.

Breakwater Cat 1980 RCA AFL1-3500 Producers: James Gadson & Michael Stewart

Never Gonna Be Another One 1981 RCA AFL1-3842 Producers: George Tobin and Mike Piccirillo (Billboard soul charts: 51; Billboard pop charts: 144)

Houston clearly needed a new start and got one at RCA, with whom she stayed for two albums. The debut, *Breakwater Cat*, was certainly a case of back to the future, though, as the entire first side was written by Jim Webb. However, anyone naively expecting *Sunshower* part two would be disappointed as the 11 year time difference between the two sets meant that this was never a realistic expectation and his contributions were pretty mainstream and didn't really stand out. I do find the LP to be an improvement on her last two or three at Motown as it was just nice to hear her sounding different, and she looked great on the cover although a low point was a horrible version of "Suspicious Minds".

The album failed to restore her commercial fortunes, though, and new producers were found for "Never Gonna Be Another One". It hardly set any sales records but did enough to see her name back on the national charts for the first time in a while. Given that Houston was a pop-soul singer rather than an obviously gospel influenced one it made perfect sense to employ Gary Goetzman and Mike Piccirillo as songwriters. Whatever one might think of their work, no-one could deny they knew how to churn out tuneful songs with strong hooks. I think it was one of her best ever LPs although it is a bit sickly to take in one go. The majority of the cuts were dance oriented but she makes a good fist of the one slow cut, "Don't Make Me Over". The almost insanely repetitive "If You Feel It" and a rather tinny version of "96 Tears" both hit the soul charts.

Reachin' All Around 1982 Motown 6034ML Producers: Charles Kipps, Van McCoy, Larry Brown, Terri McFaddin, Ron Miller, Eddie Langford, Suzanne De Passe, Hal Davis & Michael Masser

Thelma Houston: Superstar Series 1981 Motown M5-120V1

Even though Houston's success at RCA was modest, it was still sufficient to stir Motown into releasing two more albums. The first, *Reachin' All Around*, which I have never heard, consisted of in the can material, while a miserly variation on the 'Best Of' premise (a whole 8 tracks!) came out in the *Superstar* series.

Thelma Houston 1983 MCA 5395 Producers: Jai Winding & Jon Arrias

Qualifyin' Heat 1984 MCA 5527 Producers: Jimmy Jam, Terry Lewis, Monte Moir, James Harris, Glen Ballard, Clif Magness, Dennis Lambert, Derek Hakamoto & Romeo Blue (Billboard soul charts: 30)

Throw You Down 1990 Reprise 26234 Producers: Richard Perry, LeMel Humes & Howie Rice

In the eighties Houston moved labels again on two occasions, first to MCA before finishing her vinyl career on Reprise. This was a good time for her and she placed a further seven singles on the soul charts between early 1983 and February 1991, with one of them, "You Used To Hold Me So Tight", going as high as #13 while the Qualifyin' Heat LP sold well, too. I'm afraid to say I can't get to grips with any of the music on any of the three albums listed above at all, and so will only reflect that a) She has had tremendous staying power releasing an impressive number of LPs over a period of more than twenty years and b) she must have worked with more producers than anyone else in this entire book encompassing an incredible range from Jim Webb to Jimmy Jam.

She continues to perform live and released some new music in 2013.

Barbara Howard

On The Rise 1970 SR 700301 Producer: Steven Reece

In 1970 Barbara Howard released her one and only LP. It did not include her excellently funky single "I Don't Want Your Love" that had - I think - preceded the album but consisted of eight covers and two Steven Reece originals, one of which, the slow and gently soulful "The Man Above" had been the b-side to the 45. And that's about all I can say; the LP is rare and seldom comes to light and I've not heard any of the other tracks which include "For Once In My Life", "It's Not Unusual" and "Light My Fire". It could, I suppose, be as much a jazz set as a soul one but based on the two sides I do know she certainly has to be included.

Reuben Howell

Reuben Howell 1973 Motown M771L Producers: Clayton Ivey & Terry Woodford

Rings 1974 Motown M6-799S1 Producer: Clayton Ivey & Terry Woodford

I recounted earlier in the book how in 1978 Capricorn had difficulty in knowing how to market Eddie Hinton's *Very Extremely Dangerous* album, a southern soul outing by a white man. Precisely the same predicament had befallen Motown five years earlier with Reuben Howell's superb debut LP. In both cases one answer was not to include any pictures of the artist. At least Capricorn came up with a good photograph for Hinton's record, but Howell's cover is a disaster, merely the name "Reuben Howell" on a black background. That must really have enticed buyers.

But what lies inside is very good indeed. Howell was an entirely convincing soul singer and his set was also blessed with some absolutely first rate songs, musicians, arrangements and production. Terry Woodford, Ernie Shelby, George Soule, Frank Johnson and Clayton Ivey are all highly gifted songwriters and Howell must have thought his big break was imminent when he saw that he would be required to sing the likes of "I'll See You Through", "My World Tumbles Down", "You Can't Stop A Man In Love" and "You're Killing Me", uniformly excellent works in the mid-tempo range, the one that best suited Howell. He also did a great job on "Funny How Time Slips Away" but no-one should ever be presented with "When A Man Loves A Woman", a song almost impossible to cover well though Howell did as good a job as anyone else I've heard attempt it. Sadly, though, his break didn't happen and the album got lost but it sounds lovely to this day.

Given the failure of the first LP Motown decided to drop any subterfuge and placed a photo of the clean-cut Howell on the cover of the follow-up album, *Rings*. As a soul album, it was quite the disappointment, and no more George Soule, Frank Johnson or Ernie Shelby songs were on board, and only Allen Toussaint's gently funky "I Am What I Am" would not have been out of place on the debut. As a piece of southern pop music, though, it was just fine and the title track became a small hit on the Billboard Hot 100 thus justifying Motown's decision to move Howell in another direction. However, for whatever reason there were to be no more records of any sort and Howell passed away in 2004.

R.B. Hudmon

Closer To You 1978 Cotillion SD 5204 Producers: Bobby Manuel, Jeff Stewart & Jim Stewart

Georgia's R B Hudmon had been trying to get that elusive hit record since 1966 when he released his first 45 as a 12 year old and it seemed that his Tomahawk label single from 1975, "How Can I Be A Witness", was going to go the same way as all the six others - nowhere - until it was picked up by Atlantic and issued on their Cotillion subsidiary in early 1976. It's a lovely record, unmistakeably southern and with an instantly catchy hook and it reached #73 on the soul charts. While hardly the outright smash he craved, it nonetheless did well enough for the label to record an album on him which featured two further charting singles although, oddly, his fourth soul chart hit of the same era, "Whatever Makes You Happy", was NOT included on the LP. I have mixed feelings about the set, as although it was inspiring to hear a genuinely southern outing in the disco era, and any LP recorded in Memphis with great musicians and great producers (Stax founder Jim Stewart was one of these) was always going to find favour with me, Hudmon was not an outrageously gifted vocalist and had also seemingly been instructed to sing in an Al Green style. I found some tracks a little mannered as a result, such as "A Lover's Question" (where his over precise phrasing is distracting) and another charting single "This Could Be The Night". I prefer the attractive and memorable mid-tempo number, "Cause You're Mine Now", his final chart success (#47 soul) which he sings in his "natural" voice.

There were to be no more hits and no more LPs although he did record a further four singles before passing away in 1995.

Al Hudson & Soul Partners (see One Way)

David Hudson

To You Honey Honey With Love 1980 Alston 4412 Producers: Willie Clarke, Horace Straws, Snoopy Dean & Tony Battaglia

Nite & Day 1987 Waylo 13006 Producer: Willie Mitchell

Night & Day 1988 Timeless 125 Producer: Willie Mitchell (UK)

Funnily enough, the next artist to discuss, David Hudson, also had a touch of Al Green in his singing but he was a better vocalist than Hudmon and could therefore shake off any lapses into "Green-isms" more easily.

Hudson had first come to the attention of soul fans with a fine, if undeniably dark, single in 1978, "Must I Kill Her", on the Alston label. It wasn't a hit but must have sold sufficiently to encourage the label to shell out on a full length album and *Honey Honey* duly arrived in 1980. The title track did surprisingly well for a ballad and peaked at #37 soul and #59 pop. I loved the record when it first came out and although it still sounds good today - it's an excellent song - the lack of real strings and absence of horns make it lose a little luster thirty five years on. And in fact the same observation can be applied to the whole LP as Hudson's vocals and the majority of the compositions are stronger and more interesting than the musical backing. Only the dance sides "Ease Up" and "Pump It" fall into the category of definitely mundane, but all the other six cuts - songs rather than exhortations to move - are worth hearing more than once, even if "I Have Never Loved A Woman" failed as a follow-up single. Other than a 45 in 1984 that was it for Hudson's recording output until he met up with the great Willie Mitchell in 1987.

As might be imagined, Mitchell played up the Green angle and the majority of *Nite & Day* is delivered at a lazy pace in that dreamy, floaty style with which the Reverend Al made his name. It may well be, of course, that most people couldn't care less if Hudson (or R.B. Hudmon for that matter) sounded like Al Green, or even think it a very good thing he did, and while I can understand that, I personally feel it is a little demeaning when a talented singer has to ape another rather than be him or herself. Having said all that, I still like the set but it's no coincidence that my favourite track is a good revival of "Thin Line Between Love And Hate" on which Hudson does his own thing vocally. The only thing to avoid at all costs is the noisy and frantic "Trans-Lover" which is out of sync with everything else and as bad as the title suggests. Three singles were released from the album but none did much business and after one more non-LP single also failed we did not hear from Hudson again for over twenty years.

In 1988 a version of the Waylo LP was picked up for release in the UK with a couple of differences: there were two additional tracks, "Love In The Fast Lane" and "Love And Happiness", and we know how to spell "night".

Surprisingly, but pleasingly, a brand new release from Hudson appeared in 2010 which consisted of previously unreleased tracks from his time with Mitchell.

Hues Corporation

Hubert Ann Kelley; Bernard St. Clair Lee; Fleming Williams

Freedom For The Stallion 1973 RCA APL1-0323 Producer: John Florez (Billboard soul charts: 59; Billboard pop charts: 20)

Rockin' Soul 1974 RCA APL1-0775 Producers: Wally Holmes & Tom Sellers (Billboard soul charts: 20)

Love Corporation 1975 RCA APL1-0938 Producer: David Kershenbaum (Billboard soul charts: 40; Billboard pop charts:147)

The Best Of 1977 RCA APL1-2408

By 1974 The Fifth Dimension and The Friends of Distinction had passed their peak and there was thus an opening for a new group to peddle their brand of bright, upbeat pop-soul to a willing market. Hues Corporation filled that gap. Never as ornate or imaginative as the former (and not possessing a singer as good as Marilyn McCoo) and never as soulful as the latter, the Corporations' lightweight music hasn't really stood the test of time very well.

Their first single was released on Liberty but as soon as they moved to RCA things started to look up for them. Their first 45 there, "Freedom For The Stallion" a sterling socially conscious song from Allen Toussaint was also their best, and although it wasn't a hit, it did become the title track of their first LP, on which lay the "big one"."Rock The Boat" has no artistic pretensions and can drive grown men and women mad if listened to long enough, but it did become a #1 pop and #2 soul hit in the early summer of 1974. On the strength of it, the LP sold well but its soft centre makes it a rather sickly listening experience.

The second album sounded much like the first and included another Toussaint song, "I'll Take A Melody" and just to extract as much mileage as possible "Rock The Boat" got another outing, but the new huge hit was "Rockin' Soul" which sounded almost identical to the earlier smash but wasn't quite so successful: #6 soul and #18 pop. Apart from a pretty song, "How I Wish We Could Do It Again", the entire album is unashamedly pop oriented and not one I ever turn to for succour.

Their third hit (#15 soul and #62 pop), "Love Corporation", sounded like an updated sixties record and while hardly a classic, it at least had the semblance of an edge and became the title track of the third and final RCA album, which was once again, bright, utopian and poppy.

I Caught Your Act 1977 Warner Brothers BS 3043 Producer: Wally Holmes

Your Place Or Mine 1977 Warner Brothers BSK 3196
Producer: Wally Holmes

The trio moved to the Warner corporation for a couple of albums, and the sound changed as a result. "I Caught Your Act" was a much more overtly disco side than their previous work, with soaring strings and careering drums, and it would have been hard to know it was The Hues Corporation singing it. The title track only reached #61 soul and they never hit any national charts again.

The trio, who I assume were still the same three original members but at the risk of repeating myself yet again the LP cover refused to tell us their names, bowed out with a second LP on WB which included titles like "Get Up Off Your Backsides" (so middle class, why not "asses"?) and "Don't Forget To Woogie" so the dance theme was certainly maintained. Much better was a failed 45, "With All My Love And Affection", a soulful side which was the best thing they had recorded in years.

Leon Huff

Here To Create Music 1980 P.I.R. NJZ 36758 (Billboard soul charts: 63; Billboard pop charts: 204)

Leon Huff is one of the most important men in the history of soul music, not least for running P.I.R. together with Kenny Gamble, so why shouldn't he release a slightly indulgent album on his own label? The one long player from the Camden New Jersey born Huff is hardly up there with the many brilliant pieces of music in which he had been involved in the past, and much of it is jazzy doodling verging on "easy listening" but there are a trio of tracks that are good and satisfying: "Your Body Won't Move If You Can't Feel The Groove" features the odd snatch of vocal from Eddie Levert, Walter Williams, Teddy Pendergrass and The Jones Girls; while "Low Down, Hard Times Blues" and "I Ain't Jiving, I'm Jamming" showcase Huff's enthralling piano playing. The latter made it to #57 soul as a single, eleven places higher than "Tight Money" which was the first single from the set. Having got this album out of his system Huff returned to working with Gamble on creating hits for others.

Terry Huff (see Special Delivery)

Fred Hughes

Baby Boy 1970 Brunswick BL 754157 Producers: Carl Davis & Eugene Record

In 1965 Fred Hughes cut a genuinely great record, "Oo Wee Baby I Love You", whose dark and brooding production brilliantly conjured up nights of misspent youth in dingy but exhilarating night clubs. It's quality was self-evident and it reached #3 on the soul charts and #23 pop and although an elegantly cool follow-up "You Can't Take It Away" also sold strongly, the label on which they were issued, Vee Jay, was not too far away from bankruptcy and so an LP never materialised.

His one album, therefore, came at a time when his brief heyday had already passed. After a few years of issuing singles that failed on the Exodus and Cadet labels, the catchy "Baby Boy" returned him to the charts when it reached #25 as a single in January 1970 and on the strength of it Brunswick put together an LP on the Arkansas born singer but it was all rather disappointing. "Oo Wee Baby I Love You" was given a re-working to kick the album off, but its over fussy, kitchen sink production wasn't a patch on the original and song choices like Hickory Holler's Tramp", "Georgia On My Mind", "San Francisco Is A Lonely Town" and "People" were unfortunate. He should have cut more of his own songs; Z.Z. Hill covered some, after all. "I Understand" (written by Hughes) was better and played up his barely suppressed Marvin Gaye influences, doing pretty well as a single by rising to #45 on the soul charts in the summer of 1970. A third single from the set, the brassy but rather mediocre "Don't Let This Happen To Us", failed and Hughes never cut any more records for Brunswick or anyone else.

Hughes was (is? I'm not sure what he is doing these days) a good singer who made one great record and a handful of above average ones but his greatest misfortune was probably to be confused with California's Freddie Hughes and to this day people still get the two mixed up.

Freddie Hughes

Send My Baby Back 1968 Wand WDS 664 Producer: Lonnie Hewitt

Freddie Hughes was born in Berkeley, and had quite a long and varied career in the music industry, being part of recording acts The Four Rivers, Soul Brothers and Casanova II among others before cutting his first sides under his own name. His first solo 45 was both his best ever and his one and only hit. "Send My Baby Back" is an excellent song, performed in a pleading, straining voice; Hughes nearly always sounded in some sort of emotional distress and was certainly nothing if not highly committed to what he was required to deliver. The single reached #20 soul and #94 pop and also became the title track of his only - much better than average - LP. Recorded at Coast Studios in San Francisco, it is a full sounding uptown outing, with prominent horns and backing vocals, subtle and unobtrusive strings, and pianos and bluesy guitars fading in and out of the mix at appropriate times. The majority of the songs originated from the pens of Hughes and Lonnie Hewitt with covers of "Natural Man", "You're My Everything" and "What Am I Gonna Do Without Your Sweet Lovin'" to flesh things out. Two more excellent tracks - "I Gotta Keep My Bluff In" and "He's No Good" (which you could have sworn was cut in New York, but wasn't) - both failed as singles, but certainly didn't deserve to. "Tonight I'm Gonna See My Baby" was another lovely track, breezy and joyous and strategically placed right after the title track on side one of the LP.

Despite the quality of the set it got rather lost and didn't really make it and Hughes' career became rather desultory from here on in: six or seven more singles on a handful of labels - including the haunting and superb "Sarah Mae" - over a twenty year period, although he was to return to the soul charts in 1977 when he delivered a riveting (but uncredited) vocal on "Sharing" by the studio group Vitamin E. He still performed live in 2015 and has a claim to be one of the best of all the many unsung and underrated soul singers.

Jimmy Hughes

Steal Away 1964 Vee Jay VJLP-1102 Producer: Rick Hall

Why Not Tonight? 1967 Atco 33-209 Producer: Rick Hall

Soul Neighbours (with Joe Simon) Charly CRB 1086 (UK)

Something Special 1969 Volt VOS 6003 Producers: Al Jackson, Al Bell & Charles Chalmers

Jimmy Hughes, a cousin of Percy Sledge, was born in Leighton Alabama. His recording career didn't last long but it had plenty of artistic highlights and even a handful of genuinely big hits. Because he stopped recording in 1971, a time when sensible journalism about soul music barely existed, he never really had the acclaim he deserves, or at least he hadn't until some beautiful retrospective CDs appeared in the last few years which have helped to remind people of his talent, and that is only right and proper as he was a great soul singer.

He had only released one single before his second became a hit and a classic. "Steal Away" was just about the first in an exceptionally long line of southern "cheating songs" and it went all the way to #17 pop in 1964, a year when *Billboard* did not release separate soul charts. Sung beautifully in his distinctive 'crying' voice with passion and just the right amount of restraint, it was also Hughes' own work and it was a surprise that no other of his own compositions found their found their way onto the 12 track LP that took its name from the hit. The LP has its share of rather twee poppy numbers which include "I Want Justice", "Everybody Let's Dance" and "A Shot Of Rhythm And Blues" (featuring gruesome backing vocals) but the good far outweighs the mediocre and "I Tried To Tell You", "I'm Getting Better", "Stormy Monday Blues" and "Neighbor Neighbor" were all excellent while a good cover of James Brown's "Try Me" did pretty well as a follow-up single to "Steal Away" (#65 pop). It's also a pleasure to hear the excellent first FAME rhythm section which included Jerry Carrigan, David Briggs and Norbert Puttnam as they, like Hughes, have been overshadowed by others in the history of Alabama soul music.

The LP didn't sell in vast numbers but then no-one expected it to. He had to wait until 1967 for his next album to be issued and given the time lag it included songs cut over a three year period.

As a result, only two of the ten tracks had not appeared as either an a or b - side to a single, but it also meant that the LP was full of performances of impact and power and it included three 45s that made the top #30 soul charts. The biggest of these hits, "Neighbor, Neighbor" was a re-cut of the admirable Alton Vallier song which had appeared on the Vee Jay set. Tougher, and with a superior arrangement, it deserved its impressive #4 soul chart placing but the other two hits were even better. The title track made it to #5 soul in early 1967 and is impeccable in both its musical setting and Hughes' vocal which is nothing short of majestic. There is no doubt whatsoever that we are listening to a great soul singer, but one who can communicate yearning and desire without resorting to oversouling and histrionics. The third success, "I Worship The Ground You Walk On" (#25), is one of the best songs Dan Penn and Spooner Oldham ever wrote and captures everything that was so compelling about Muscle Shoals in 1966. "Slipping Around" proved that Hughes could cut irresistible dance sides if he so desired and only "I'm The Loving Physician" failed to impress on a highly commendable LP and that was only because it was so heavily based on "Cry To Me". We couldn't forget it was 1967, though, as the LP, picked up by Atlantic for release, featured an unknown woman on its cover in a misguided and failed attempt to help it sell more copies.

Hughes moved to Stax/Volt in 1968 and scored first time out when "I Like Everything About You" reached #21 soul in October 1968, but Hughes was never again to have any sort of hit record, despite Volt's releasing a further four 45s. The *Something Special* LP bore eleven tracks, eight of which were to feature on singles on one side or the other. The songwriters employed on the album were among the best - they included Isaac Hayes, David Porter, Jimmy Holiday, Homer Banks, Raymond Jackson, Betty Crutcher, Eddie Floyd and Al Bell - but they didn't necessarily bring their foremost work to the proceedings and the set does not match the heights of *Why Not Tonight?*. "I like Everything", "I'm So Glad" and "Let 'Em Down Baby" are all first rate, as is the pounding "Chains Of Love" even if Hughes' vocal is almost unrecognisable from how he "normally" sounds. It's a fine LP by most artists' standards and I enjoy listening to it a good deal, but Hughes set such high standards with his FAME material that *Something Special* does suffer a bit in comparison.

The Vee Jay material lay forgotten for more than two decades until Charly issued an LP (shared with Joe Simon) that included 8 tracks from *Steal Away*.

Jimmy Hughes was a top class soul singer who made two of my all-time favourite records in "Why Not Tonight?" and "I Worship The Ground You Walk On" and he was the only artist who had releases on four of the most important labels in soul music's history, Vee Jay, FAME , Atlantic (one single, "It Ain't What You Got", had hit the soul charts in early 1968 at #43 around the time his contract with FAME was coming to a close) and Stax. It's not a bad legacy.

Rhetta Hughes

Introducing A Brand New Star 1965 Columbia CS 9185 Producer: Ralph Bass

Re-Light My Fire 1969 Tetragrammaton T-111 Producers: Mike Terry & Jo Armstead (Billboard soul charts: 47)

Starpiece 1980 Sutra SUS-1001 Producer: Kenny Lehman

Rhetta Hughes only released three LPs and they sound absolutely nothing like each other. The first one was even released under a slightly different name: "Rheta". In fact, let's move past that first one hastily as it is nothing to do with soul, being a pure jazz set with Tennyson Stephens (who incidentally also released records under a different spelling: Tenison).

Her work on Tetragrammaton between 1968 and 1969 was by far her best. The label put out four singles, all of which were included on her close to magnificent *Re-Light My Fire* LP. Hughes was a good singer, but the real stars of the LP were the songs, arrangements, musicians and production, all of which were well above the average. Jo Armstead must take the majority of this credit as she wrote or co-wrote eight of the eleven tracks (as well as co-producing the set) and she proved here as she did on many occasions that she had a real talent for writing songs that other women could relate to. There were three covers, two of which, good takes on "Baby, I Need Your Loving" and "Walk On By", remained as LP only cuts while the third, "Light My Fire", became the one hit from the set, reaching #36 on the soul charts in early 1969. Ironic really, as it is the one cut on the album I don't care for but that is driven by my antipathy to the song rather than any failing on Hughes' part. The splendidly entitled "Hip Old Lady On A Honda", "Cry Myself To Sleep", "You're Doing It With Her (When It Should Be Me)", "I Can't Stand Under This Pressure", and "His Happiness" (Hughes' best singing on the LP) are all marvellous.

Her last album was not really my idea of a soul record, either, and was much more suited to ears that feel comfortable with pop music. There is, of course, no reason whatsoever why black artists should feel constrained enough to record in a manner in which people expect, and credit to Hughes for not going down a proscribed path, and for opting not to cut a nondescript dance outing which this certainly isn't. In fact it is a well sung, well played album containing some good songs, it just simply isn't really my sort of music.

Anyway, the album didn't do much but we hadn't quite heard the last of Rhetta as she returned in 1983 to enjoy a small hit, "Angel Man" (#88 soul), which once again took her in a new direction. Having said that, I'd rather not think about it again. She's still going strong, and is also an accomplished actress as well as singer.

Clay Hunt (see also New Censation)

Part One 1981 Polydor PD-1-6319 Producer: Freddie Perren

Clay Hunt, who I suspect might have come from or been based in Baltimore, cut a solo single for Kapp in 1965, another one for Bay Sound in 1968, joined the group New Censation who released one album and a couple of singles in 1974, before re-appearing in 1980 on Polydor with his only LP in his own name, thus providing a great example of never giving up in the music industry. One single from the set, "Keep Me On Fire", even made the *Cashbox* soul charts, albeit no higher than #80.

The album is ok. Not great but ok. Given it was produced and arranged and half-written by Freddie Perren it falls firmly into the sphere of pop-soul rather than "hard" or "deep soul" and is split between nondescript dance items - like "Keep Me On Fire" - and slower items that sounded more in line with what was coming out in 1974 or 1975, rather than 1981. A number of these ballads start out encouragingly thanks to some fine intros and arrangements but never quite keep their promise. His most ambitious effort was a cover of "I've Been Loving You Too Long" but there have been many better versions.

There was not to be a Part Two for Clay Hunt, nor indeed, to the best of my knowledge, any further records at all.

Geraldine Hunt

Sweet Honesty 1978 TGO TG-1-8001 Producer: Tony Green

No Way 1980 Prism PLP 1006 Producer: Mike Pabon Austin

Geraldine Hunt was born in St. Louis but grew up in Chicago, apparently at one time being a school classmate of Minnie Riperton, and it was in the Windy City where she released a handful of singles from 1962 onwards, none of which made much impression at all and she isn't even mentioned in Robert Pruter's fine book, *Chicago Soul*. In 1970 she finally had her first success, a frankly dull duet with Charlie Hodges, "You And I", that made it to #45 soul and in 1972 and 1973 she placed a couple more singles on the soul charts when her records were coming out on the Roulette label. No albums appeared though, and she had to wait until 1978 for that, by which time she had released around fifteen 45s on numerous imprints.

She had also moved to Canada and that first LP was recorded in Quebec. It starts well with a good uptempo number, "Hot Blooded Woman", and ends with the best ballad on show, "Together", but what lies between is forgettable. This is nothing to do with the album's recording location, but everything to do with the mediocre material with which Hunt is saddled. The dance items don't make me want to move and the ballads don't engage me.

She returned to recording in the U.S. for her second and final LP, which was cut in Philadelphia. It included a highly popular dance track, "Can't Shake The Feeling", which rose to #58 on the soul charts at the end of 1980, her first national hit in seven years, and dance was very much the dominant flavour of the set which bore six long cuts, five of which were penned by Hunt herself. I like "Glad I'm In Love Again" and "Gotta Give A Little Love" as they are more obviously tuneful than the rest, but it is still an album I cannot enthuse over.

Hunt released a few more things in the eighties and nineties but seems to have left the industry in the present century.

Tommy Hunt

I Just Don't Know What To Do With Myself 1962 Scepter SPS 506 Producers: Mike Leiber, Jerry Stoller & Luther Dixon

Greatest Hits 1968 Dynamo DS 8001

Your Man 1986 Kent 059 (UK)

Pittsburgh's Tommy Hunt was first represented on vinyl as a member of the doo-wop group The Five Echoes in 1953 but his most creative and successful years came firstly when he was a member of The Flamingos from the mid to late fifties and secondly, when he cut some stirring New York soul as a solo singer in the first half of the sixties.

He released 8 singles on Scepter and the first of them, "Human", became easily his biggest ever hit attaining #5 soul and #48 pop in the autumn of 1961. Surprisingly, the record label didn't seek to capitalise on that success by issuing an LP at the time and waited for a year, at which time his star was already starting to fade a little as his follow-up 45s hadn't performed anywhere near as well. It must remain a great mystery why Hunt's original version of "I Just Don't Know What To Do With Myself" failed so badly on 45, not even reaching the *Billboard* soul charts, and only attaining the top forty of the *Cashbox* equivalent; listening to it over fifty years later it remains a thing of wonder: song, arrangement, production and, best of all, Hunt's dark, subterranean voice, so full of touch and power, and it is almost impossible to imagine how it could have been improved upon.

His first LP consisted of twelve songs, which were the a and b-sides to all his first five Scepter singles and two album only tracks, "So Fine" and "She'll Hurt You Too", and was excellent throughout. Just to pick up on a few things: it shouldn't be forgotten that "Human" had also been an exceptional record with another unimprovable Hunt vocal, and little touches throughout like the pure gospel piano intro to "I'm Wondering" or the "hup, two, three, four" backing to "Parade Of Broken Hearts" showed the attention to detail and playfulness that were also at work. New York City in 1962 seems impossibly romantic and alluring today, and to understand why we feel like that, listen to this great LP.

Hunt had to wait a few years for his next set, in which time he issued a few more singles on Scepter as well as Atlantic and Capitol before switching to the Dynamo label. That second outing, *Greatest Hits*, bore a highly misleading title. In the course of his solo career up to the time of its 1968 release he had placed five different songs on either the *Billboard* or *Cashbox* soul charts; only two of them found their way to the LP, and one of them, "Human", was a new version anyway. It was obviously just an album to support his current Dynamo singles releases and indeed four of the ten tracks never even came out on 45s at all, even as b-sides. Hardly hits. The album started out strongly, however, as the first two tracks were right up there with the best of Hunt's work, beautifully produced, orchestrated and sung. "The Biggest Man" also did well as a single, reaching #29 soul in early 1967 and "Comin' On Strong" was every bit its equal. "Words Can Never Tell It" was good too but then things rather tailed off, particularly on side two. This is in no way a comment on Hunt's singing, which remained highly compelling, but lay solely in the material and, on occasion, rather staid arranging: "It's All In The Game", "I Believe", "Born Free" and "Everybody's Got A Home (But Me)" were not going to capture the imagination of young record buyers who were being tempted by the more urgent and vital sounds of James Brown, Wilson Pickett and Aretha Franklin.

Kent put out, much later on, in 1986, a commendable retrospective look at Hunt's work on Scepter which included a number of previously unreleased items but Hunt was, as they say, stone cold by the end of the sixties and decided to move to Europe in 1970.

Live At The Wigan Casino 1975 Spark SRLP 117 Producer: Barry Kingston (UK)

Sign Of The Times 1976 Spark SRLP 120 Producer: Barry Kingston (UK)

I cannot even begin to talk about the evolution of "Northern Soul" in these pages but suffice it to say for now that Hunt's living in England and the ever increasing commercial possibilities of that sub-genre of soul music led to Hunt being in some way appropriated by that scene and having his artistic reputation badly damaged as a result. On the strength of a few releases on the UK Spark label Hunt has been unfairly marginalised and dismissed as a serious soul singer. Feelings ran high in England at the time and making so-called "tailor made" sides like "Loving On The Losing Side" got some people up on the highest of horses, although, to be fair, many others loved it, too. Anyway, that is to get ahead of myself a little as before that a *Live at Wigan Casino* album had come out. I don't think that it is a bad set but it really did suffer from a desperately unimaginative song selection: "Get Ready", "Knock On Wood" "My Girl" and "I Can't Turn You Loose" in 1975 was surely simply misguided.

The aforementioned "Loving On The Losing Side", which still sounds good, was featured on Hunt's *A Sign Of The Times* LP, as was his other best-known UK side, "Crackin' Up", and my main criticism of the set is that it underplay's Hunt's biggest asset: his voice. Play "Sunshine Girl" and "Sign On The Dotted Line" against his early New York hits and they sound weedy and uninspired. It would be silly to expect a UK studio and musicians to match the grandeur of some of the greatest soul music of all time recorded fifteen or so years earlier and I don't hold Spark to those standards but we all have a choice of what we listen to and *A Sign Of The Times* is never going to be pulled out before *I Just Don't Know What To Do With Myself*.

An ok Swamp Dogg produced CD slipped out in 1996 and he's still around at the time of my writing, performing live at over eighty years old, and thanks to the advent of the internet, better critical appreciation of soul music in general and a fine CD of his work some years back, Hunt has finally started to get the appreciation he has always deserved.

Hunt's Determination Band

Bernard Brown; Charles Horne; Johnny Brown; Danny Redeemar; Elwood Haygood; Cornelius Jordan; Joseph Washington; Maurice Davis; Gardell Haralson; Glenn Bender

Problems 1977? Ear Wax 1230 Producer: Stacie Hunt

Get Your Act Together! 1979? Ear Wax SH LP 200 Producers: Ed Sommers & Ronnie Carson

Hunt's Determination Band came out of Flint and were in need of a good marketing person. Their singles were released as by Hunt's Determinations, Hunt's Determination and Hunt's Determination Band while their first album had a preposterously misleading front cover: was the album called *This Is Determination* or was it called *Problems*? Or, indeed, was it called both? The meagre sleevenotes would suggest that it was actually *Problems* but it wasn't clear. Probably none of this mattered that much as the only noise the group ever created was inside Michigan and even that was muted.

The band's name (or names) originated from their manager and early producer, Stacy (or Stacie) Hunt, and two early singles "Are We Through" and "I Need Love" are nice outings, sounding completely different from each other. Given their almost total lack of recognition, though, it was astonishing that the band went on to cut and release two LPs. Given the obvious budgetary restraints, they are not bad at all. *Problems* doesn't get off to a good start as "Danceland" is utterly routine, and a slow track, "Tonight", lasts for well over seven minutes and would have been better had it been cut in half, but then things improve. "Problems", "Number One Lady" and "Where The Funk Comes From" are all pretty decent, horn driven funk numbers and "Loneliness" meanders along to good effect with the best singing on the set. The band did not use keyboards on *Problems* which would have helped to bolster its rather thin and one-dimensional sound.

This was addressed on *Get Your Act Together!* which bears a more rounded and satisfying tone throughout. The songs are better too, and "Thinking Of You", "She's On My Mind" and "You're My Heart And Soul" are all impressive while "She's My Number 1 Lady" is good, hard funk. "Rollerskate" is the only outright poor track and "Hottsie Tottsie" is interesting. The album sleeve doesn't give a year of release but sources suggest 1978. If so, Kool and Gang ripped off the intro to this track when they created "Ladies Night". It seems more likely that it was the other way around in which case the album must have come out in 1979.

Phil Hurtt

Giving It Back 1978 Fantasy F-9552 Producer: Phil Hurtt

PH Factor 1979 Fantasy F-9582 Producer: Phil Hurtt

If, like me, you love The Spinners' "I'll Be Around", Jackie Moore's "Both Ends Against The Middle" or Bunny Sigler's "Regina" you will have been exposed to the exceptional writing talents of Philadelphia's Phil Hurtt, and there are plenty more examples of his outstanding compositions to go with these three, as well. He was clearly mainly happy to stay in the background throughout his lengthy career in the music business, and his main contributions have come from his writing and producing, often as part of a Philly collective known as The Young Professionals, and he didn't get to release his first records under his own name until 1978, thirteen years or so after his first songs were recorded. His records never performed particularly well, but I suspect he wasn't too concerned by that, as his royalties over the years must have made him a good living.

The first LP, *Giving It Back*, was by far the better of the two as the dance tracks were a bit more distinctive, lighter of touch and cleaner in sound, and it also featured his finest solo side, the lovely slow "That's The Way The Story Goes", and if "Lovin'" and "Please Don't Come Home" borrow quite a bit from Marvin Gaye (indeed, a great deal on the latter) they still sound good.

PH Factor has a forgettable first side consisting of three long, rather boring dance sides riddled with instrumental breaks which rendered Hurtt's voice redundant, but side two is much better with more thoughtful and tuneful dance numbers and two good slower cuts in "I Think It's About Time" and "I'm In Love Again". It has been alleged that Hurtt sang (uncredited) backing vocals on a number of sides by top Philadelphia groups and, given that, and as he does possess an appealing light, high tenor it's a bit of a surprise that his own production on *PH Factor* tends to place his voice too low in the mix.

Having, I imagine, got these albums out of his system he retired from releasing records in his own right and in 2006 was instrumental in getting an ambitious CD project off the ground whereby Philly artists covered Motown songs and vice versa.

Willie Hutch

Soul Portrait 1969 RCA LSP-4213 Producer: John Florez

Season For Love 1970 RCA LSP-4296 Producer: John Florez

William Hutchison was a highly accomplished Los Angeles soul man, recording there throughout his entire career. By the time his first LP was cut in 1969 he had steadily been making a name for himself: a handful of singles released by "Willie Hutch" since 1965 and a number of writing credits for the likes of Al Wilson, The Fifth

Dimension and Johnny Rivers. He just hadn't yet managed to snare the big one.

He had done enough though to entice RCA to sign him and put him to work with producer John Florez who was enjoying huge success with The Friends Of Distinction. *Soul Portrait* is a good showcase for Hutch's writing as he penned all eleven tracks. It's also what I might call a "perfect" LP. Not "perfect" because it is utterly brilliant (as it isn't), but "perfect" in the sense that it was what an LP could ideally be: not a collection of random tracks built around a hit single or two, but a carefully selected group of songs that compliment each other, without obvious highs and lows, to create the proverbial whole that is greater than the sum of its parts. Two songs WERE pulled from the set as a 45, "Do What You Gonna Do" and "Ain't Gonna Stop", but it could just as easily have been any of the cuts that RCA chose to use. If I were to have any criticism of a joyous, briskly performed and fully arranged collection of soul music, it would be that Hutch's voice was a little low in the mix. Neither LP nor 45 did particularly well, but Hutch was about to enter a decade where he did enjoy a lot of success.

But not with his follow-up album, the disappointing *Season For Love*. Although Florez was retained as producer the album sent Hutch in an entirely different direction, that of crooner, although, ironically, it could once again be described as a "perfect" LP based on my previous criterion, as it was once again of a piece and consistent throughout. It's not a poor album, just a much more MOR outing than *Soul Portrait* and although it certainly does place Hutch's voice more to the forefront it also overdoses somewhat on strings and dilutes the impact of the handful of Hutch songs on board by giving him standards to contend with like "Hurt So Bad", Twelfth Of Never " and "When A Boy Falls In Love". Interestingly, the single that RCA put out of the latter song bore a completely different production and arrangement from the one on the LP, as well as being twice as fast.

The Mack 1973 Motown M766L Producer: Willie Hutch (Billboard soul charts: 17; Billboard pop charts: 114)

Fully Exposed 1973 Motown M784V1 Producer: Willie Hutch (Billboard soul charts: 15; Billboard pop charts: 183)

Foxy Brown 1974 Motown M6-811S1 Producer: Willie Hutch (Billboard soul charts: 36; Billboard pop charts: 179)

Mark Of The Best 1974 Motown M6-815S1 Producer: Willie Hutch (Billboard soul charts: 41)

Ode To My Lady 1975 Motown M6-838S1 Producer: Willie Hutch (Billboard soul charts: 24; Billboard pop charts: 150)

Concert In Blues 1976 Motown M6-854S1 Producer: Willie Hutch (Billboard soul charts: 22; Billboard pop charts: 163)

Color Her Sunshine 1976 Motown M6-871S1 Producer: Willie Hutch (Billboard soul charts: 54)

Having A House Party 1977 Motown M6-874S1 Producer: Willie Hutch (Billboard soul charts: 26)

Hutch's big break finally came in 1970 when he co-penned a #1 soul and pop hit for the Jackson 5, "I'll Be There". The success was such that he put his own recording career on hold until 1973, and concentrated purely on writing, arranging and producing in the meantime. When he did return to the studios on his own behalf, it was to create something that sounded entirely different from what had gone before, music that finally found its own large audience.

It was also music that owed a great deal to Isaac Hayes and Curtis Mayfield and it is hard to imagine that *The Mack* could have even existed had it not been for *Shaft* and *Superfly*. It was certainly not a set that broke any new ground in the soundtrack stakes as it included a fair amount of what was becoming fairly standard fare - lots of wah-wah guitar, long musical interludes, snatches of dialogue - but credit to Hutch for being the next artist, along with Bobby Womack, who managed to do well from the "Blaxploitation" genre. Two singles were released from the album and performed almost identically: "Brother's Gonna Work It Out" (#18 soul and #67 pop) and "Slick" (#18 soul and #65 pop).

Fully Exposed was a similar set to *Soul Portrait*, as apart from the opening track, "I Wanna Be Where You Are", it showcased only songs written or co-written by Hutch and also featured his own guitar playing. It is a rather unemphatic set to listen to though, with string arrangements that are a little soporific and songs that possibly went on slightly too long, and although there was good variety on show and a judicious plucking from his own back catalogue - nice takes on "California My Way" and "I'll Be There" - Hutch was a caressing rather than electrifying singer and although there wasn't one moment on the set that made me want to lift the needle and move on, there weren't many that made me want to instantly relive them again, either. Two tracks were pulled as 45s, "Sunshine Lady" and "If You Ain't Got No Money", which reached the rather disappointing positions of #72 and #70 respectively on the soul charts.

A second soundtrack, *Foxy Brown*, arrived in 1974, and it followed the same musical pattern as *The Mack*, but didn't emulate its success as the title track stalled at only #64 soul as a single and the album itself sold much more modestly. For anyone who loves soundtracks of this ilk, it is impeccable, but one could easily take six tracks from *The Mack* and substitute them for six on *Foxy Brown* to no great detriment or benefit to either set. "Give Me Some Of That Good Old Love" was a cut above though, with an intriguing and daring arrangement, while "You Sure Know How To Love Your Man" appropriated a Sly Stone feel to good effect.

By the time of *Mark Of The Beast*, we were four albums in to Hutch's Motown tenure and a clear pattern had emerged as to what we could expect from him: a strong focus on musical texture, driven by often complex arrangements, rather than barnstorming singing or instantly memorable melodies. In such an environment the star of a track could well be - as on "Get Ready For The Get Down" - the bassist, Lawrence Dickens, but it was seldom going to be Hutch himself. In fact, despite the fact he wrote nearly everything on all his albums, as well as producing and arranging them, they give a sense of being highly collaborative, with his musicians being absolutely critical to the sound he wanted to get. *Mark Of The Beast* had a socially conscious side one and a more conventional love based side two, but it all came together as usual in a unified whole.

Ode To My Lady is probably his best known and most appreciated album, and certainly contained his biggest ever hit in "Love Power" - #8 soul and #41 pop - an unusually effervescent outing by Hutch. He also tackled "The Way We Were" in a winning style, a rare occurrence in Hutch's Motown career of covering such a well-known "outside" song. Hutch always used top-class players on his records, but here they seemed to perform at a particularly exalted level and even though the album was not markedly different from what had gone before, it did have a heightened energy level and some of his most committed singing to date.

My own favourite of his works is the intriguing *Concert In Blues*, which plays down the strings and plays up the blues, a musical form that had seemed conspicuously absent in influencing Hutch in the past. It starts off a little cheekily as "Party Down", a pretty successful single (#18 soul), had also been included on *Ode To My Lady*, but gets more interesting as things progress. "Stormy Weather" and "I Wish You Love" are standards to which the usual Hutch approach is applied, but side two is a departure. "Stormy Monday" and "Shake, Rattle And Roll" may well be abhorrent to steadfast blues fans, but I admire how Hutch delivers them, with an emphasis on horns and piano, as well as placing his own voice to the forefront more than he usually chose to. Sandwiched in between them is "Precious Pearl" which absorbed enough of their bluesy vapours to make it sound just right. In addition, we are served up the undeniable delights of "Don't Let A Little Money Keep You Acting Funny", the funkiest side he ever cut with a great bass riff by Scott Edwards and a generally tough backing track. Unusually, Motown were content with "Party Down" as a 45, and no other tracks were put out as singles.

Color Her Sunshine was also a departure, but not a welcome one, as on a number of tracks strings were dispensed with in favour of an "Arp" synthesiser played by Hutch himself and it simply made the album sound thinner and cheesier than his previous outings. The songs were really rather boring, too, apart from the thoughtful and sensitive "She's Just Doing Her Thing" and while "Let Me Be The One, Baby" and "Shake It, Shake It" (which tried to copy the intro to "Love Power") both reached the soul charts they were only at the lowly positions of #95 and #60 respectively. (A 14 track *Best Of* Hutch CD came out in 1998 and not a single cut from this LP was included, which I think is a fair comment on its quality.)

Long-time mentor and manager J.W. Alexander is shown enjoying the party on the cover of Hutch's last long - and very long, at over 40 minutes - player of his first stay with Motown, which is an improvement on *Color Her Sunshine*. The rather Bobby Womack-ish "What You Gonna Do After The Party" was one of his strongest songs for a while and did reasonably well (#40 soul) as a single and "I Can Sho' Give You Love" has the rhythmic drive that typified the best of Hutch's music. There are no real clunkers on board and "I Never Had It So Good" is possibly the best song on show.

In Tune 1978 Whitfield WHK 3226 Producers: Norman Whitfield, Willie Hutch & Rose Royce (Billboard soul charts: 63)

Midnight Dancer 1979 Whitfield WHK 3352 Producer: Willie Hutch

In And Out 1983 Motown STMR 9019 (UK)

Making A Game Out Of Love 1985 Motown 6142ML Producer: Willie Hutch

An artist is often well served by moving to a new label and if Hutch's period on Norman Whitfield's label neither lasted very long nor threw up any big hits, it was nonetheless an opportunity to listen to something new from him. Take "Paradise" for example, from *In Tune*, which had a lovely dreamy feel and more open spaces in the music that Hutch usually enjoyed. It also had a memorable hook of the sort that Hutch couldn't often conjure up himself (it was written by Robert Daniels) and deserved to do much better than only #74 on the soul charts as a single. "All American Funkathon" a lyrically rather insipid but superbly arranged and played number had managed 12 places higher when it had become the lead-off 45 from the set. Elsewhere, "Anything Is Possible If You Believe In Love" was another attractive slow number but was offset by "Come On And Dance With Me" or "Hip Shakin' Sexy Lady", clichéd in the extreme. Nonetheless, overall it is one of Hutch's better later albums and it's always good to listen to Whitfield's work even if much of it here sounded pretty identical to what he was doing four or five years earlier.

Hutch's second Whitfield LP had a nice clean, uncluttered sound and was one of his stronger sets, which was a surprise given it included titles like "Disco Thang", "Midnight Dancer", "Down Here On Disco Street" (which were all slightly better than might be imagined); the good ballads "Kelly Green" and "Never Let You Be Without Love" were built to last and two fine mid-tempo sides, "Everybody Needs Money" and "Deep In Your Love", bubbled along nicely. Regardless of the appeal of the set, it didn't sell at all and neither did the singles released from it, and Hutch found himself back on Motown.

In 1982 he released a single, "In And Out", which was probably more popular in the UK than the U.S. (it only made #55 on the soul charts) and it became the title track of what was a "Best Of" set over here. He had to wait until 1985, though, for his next - and last - LP to appear, the dire *Making A Game Out Of Love*. Saturated with Mini-moogs, DMX drums, OB8 basses and a DX7 synthesiser, it played right into my Luddite prejudices and I thought it all sounded pretty horrible at the time and it sounds even worse now. It didn't do well, again failed to yield any hit singles, and Hutch's LP career was at an end.

He died in 2005 and leaves behind a healthy crop of records. His strengths lay in his all-round game rather than his voice - he wasn't a top-class singer - and even though he never made a record I adored he did have a style of his own and I wouldn't want to be without his best LPs.

LeRoy Hutson (see also The Impressions)

Love Oh Love 1973 Curtom CRS 8017 Producer: LeRoy Hutson

The Man! 1973 Curtom CRS 8020 Producer: LeRoy Hutson (Billboard soul charts: 36)

Hutson 1975 Curtom CRS 5002 Producer: LeRoy Hutson (Billboard soul charts: 46)

Feel The Spirit 1976 Curtom CRS 5010 Producer: LeRoy Hutson (Billboard soul charts: 26 ; Billboard pop charts: 170)

Hutson II 1976 Curtom CRS 5011 Producer: LeRoy Hutson (Billboard soul charts: 26)

Closer To The Source 1978 Curtom CRS 5018 Producer: LeRoy Hutson

Newark born LeRoy Hutson replaced Curtis Mayfield in The Impressions for a couple of less than totally satisfactory years, but the fact that it happened at all demonstrated the high esteem in which he was held around Chicago. Before this though, he had been part of a duo, Sugar and Spice, and a group, The Mayfield Singers, who had released a handful of singles, although none had been hits. He only stayed with The Impressions for two years, a period which unfortunately - it was hardly Hutson's fault - coincided with their lowest commercial fortunes for fifteen years.

His first solo album came out in 1973 on Curtom and was an outlet for his undoubted talents which had hitherto not been fully explored; he wrote and arranged nearly everything, played percussion and keyboards, and produced the whole set. He had roomed with Donny Hathaway at Howard University and while I have no idea who influenced who, there are some superficial similarities in their musical approach, particularly in arranging and production, although Hutson always resisted Hathaway's readiness to cover well-known songs by other writers. It is an obviously early seventies LP, by which I mean it adopted the full production values, with sweeping and imposing string arrangements, that Stax, Curtis Mayfield, Marvin Gaye, Hathaway himself and a few others had been experimenting with in the previous three or four years. I always found Hutson to be more convincing at cutting records at 33⅓ rather than 45 rpm, as he was comfortable with creating tracks at five or six minutes long but didn't have a particular knack for writing instantly catchy melodies. *Love Oh Love* is a pleasant enough album to listen to, with its high-class musicianship and compelling arrangements, but it only spawned a couple of small soul charts "hits" in the title track and "When You Smile" and got almost completely lost in the marketplace; so much so, in fact, that Curtom re-released it in 1978.

The Man! was a most accomplished LP, probably his best, although the sleeve credit acclaiming him to be a "Superstar!!" was sadly never to become remotely true: throughout his whole solo career, he only had a relatively small black audience and meant nothing whatsoever to a pop one: he placed 12 singles on the soul charts in total and none of them reached the Hot 100. Back to the album: the songs were more personal in nature than before and "Can't Say Enough About Mom", "Gotta Move - Gotta Groove" and "After The Fight" all sounded pretty believable to me, while the danceable "Ella Weez" and "Could This Be Love" were blessed with much more memorable tunes than Hutson typically managed. Jerry Long - he of "Just My Imagination" fame - was drafted in to do some typically sumptuous arranging and only a rather weak version of "The Ghetto" (which Hutson had written with Hathaway) disappointed as it was florid where Hathaways's version had pounded.

In the late eighties in England Hutson was 're-discovered' by the so-called "Rare Groove" scene, on which he was a hero and an album like *Hutson* was precisely the sort of album that fuelled that admiration. Lavishly produced, it is probably the template for any record known approvingly as "mellow" and flows along unerringly. It wasn't a million miles away from the sort of highly orchestrated but rhythmically punchy thing Barry White was doing, even if Hutson was a considerably better singer. An edited version of the certainly White-ish "All Because Of You" did well in reaching #31 on the soul charts as a single, but "Can't Stay Away" (once again truncated for 45 release and probably the best cut on the LP) couldn't get higher than a disappointing #66.

Feel The Spirit was co-credited to the Free Spirit Orchestra and the album sounded considerably different from what had gone before, even if many of the same musicians had played on *Hutson*. 1976 was a bi-centennial for the USA, but it was also a year in which funk was possibly at its commercial height, a fact Hutson was not slow to recognise and the carefully constructed, sweetly orchestral slow lopes of the previous LPs were largely jettisoned in favour of much funkier textures, with synthesisers more to the forefront. It worked too, as the title track, largely instrumental with some cooing background voices, became his only ever 45 to reach the soul top thirty when it peaked at #25 but I would be highly surprised if anyone today ranks it as his finest creation. I preferred the genuinely funky "Butterfat" which David Sanborn had cut in 1975. A chameleon-like follow-up single, "Lover's Holiday" (Hutson phrases in the manner of Curtis Mayfield at the beginning and Sugarfoot from The Ohio Players at the end), fared no more than adequately in the marketplace while another cut, "It's The Music", became a small hit for the Natural Four. Hutson hadn't quite neglected his previous approach, though, and "Don't Let It Get Next To You" would have delighted long-term fans.

Hutson's fifth LP was called, for some bizarre reason, *Hutson II*, and it, like its successor, *Closer To The Source*, did not get a release in the U.K. thereby helping to enhance his "underground" reputation over here. It built on *Spirit of '76* and apart from a throwaway disco cut, "Flying High", was as easy as ever to listen to. There were a couple of instrumental tracks and funky outings like "Blackberry Jam" on board but although the LP sold healthily the singles still tended to languish in the mid rungs of the soul charts rather than becoming big hits; trivia: Hutson had 12 singles enter the soul charts in his career and, on average, they reached #59.

By 1978, Curtom was running out of financial steam in being able to go it alone, and *Closer To The Source* suffered as a result, becoming his first LP since *Love Oh Love* to fail to reach the soul charts although two singles, "Where Did Love Go" (#45) and "In The Mood" (#56), did manage to register. Both were more tuneful than many Hutson sides (the former must have made Marvin Gaye wonder if he could sue) and were strong outings on a solid LP which ditched the funk and returned to the smoother, more restful and chilled tones of *The Man!* and *Hutson*. He also covered another song which had done well for The Natural Four, "Heaven Here On Earth", and one hopes that the group were sufficiently appreciative of what he did for them as he wrote or co-wrote six of the seven singles they posted onto the *Billboard* soul charts between 1973 and 1976. I rate *Closer To The Source* as one of his strongest albums and it showcases why he has got such a loyal following.

Unforgettable 1979 RSO RS-1-3062 Producers: Gil Askey & LeRoy Hutson (Billboard soul charts: 69)

Paradise 1982 Elektra 60141-1 Producers: LeRoy Hutson & Nicholas Caldwell

There's More Where This Came From 1989 Curtom CUR 2004

Curtom began to be distributed by RSO in 1979 and *Unforgettable* was one of the first albums to be released under this new arrangement. The title track was in reality extremely forgettable, an atypical - for Hutson - disco version of an old song and elsewhere he seemed to be going through the motions even if "Right Or Wrong" managed to become a small hit reaching #47 soul in late 1979, the last time he ever visited the national charts. The album would not put off Hutson fans, but would certainly not be the record I would choose to play to anyone to best demonstrate his virtues.

I can see why someone would like an LP like *Paradise*, as it is smooth, competent, well-played and avoids cliché, but it does seem rather pleased with itself and titles like "Classy Lady", "Nice And Easy" and, of course, "Paradise", lead to a rather chocolate-box feel and it's a little cloying for my tastes and reminds me again that Hutson, for all his undoubted talent and charm, did lack a distinctive voice, and there was too often a lack of real emotion in his work with which to engage.

Paradise didn't sell too many copies and proved to be his last ever album (apart from a compilation in 1989) and he released no further music for around ten years until, as mentioned earlier, he was rather 're-discovered' in the late eighties after which time he has been thoroughly well-served with retrospective CDs of his music, in addition to cutting new things in the last few years. He retains a fiercely loyal following and his highly impressive songwriting catalogue will possibly be his best legacy.

Bobby Hutton

A Piece Of The Action 1973 ABC ABCX-787 Producers: Dee Ervin & Clarence Johnson

Harold Hutton was born in Detroit and released a 45 for Chess before he started to issue a handful of excellent singles for Blue Rock and Philips under his adopted name of Bobby Hutton that were recorded in his home town or Chicago. These were typically cool, uptown sounds that didn't do as well as they deserved to and although his one LP has a couple of Chicago produced sides on it, the majority of it was cut in Los Angeles.

It's an impressive LP, but one that obviously didn't do very well in the marketplace as my copy, and the majority of those I've seen since, are "promotional" versions although it certainly did come out as a "normal" release. One of the big advantages of LPs over singles is the information one is often presented with and it's therefore fascinating to note that *Piece Of The Action* boasts an absolutely stellar cast of backing vocalists including Patti Hamilton from The Lovelites, Jean Plum, Frankie Karl, Mikki Farrow and Genie Brown. The LP pitches Hutton's voice at a slightly higher register than was usually the case on his Philips sides and this gives an extra edge to his performance. The songs are good too with the likes of Terry Callier, Larry Wade, Dee Ervin, Dennis Lambert, Brian Potter and Jimmy Lewis contributing some strong compositions. In the latter's case it's good to be reminded that Hutton cut the original of the absorbing "There Ain't No Man (That Can't Be Caught)" that Lewis interpreted so well on his classic *Totally Involved* set from 1974. Hutton also covers "Lead Me On" adequately enough but can't match the versions by Bobby Bland or Gwen McCrae while he is also bested by the rather unknown Patty Hall who cut a superior version of "Can't Stop Talking" even though Hutton's take is enjoyable. Nearly all the songs are midtempo in pace and "Lend A Hand" certainly generated a lot of dance floor action on the UK "Northern Soul" scene.

For some reason ABC didn't issue a single from the album, going instead with a 45 comprised of two sides that were not found on *Piece Of The Action*. It bombed however, and apart from a Christmas single on the small S.O.C. label, Hutton left the industry for thirty years before re-surfacing in 2006 with a new CD.

Phyllis Hyman

Phyllis Hyman 1977 Buddah BDS 5681 Producers: Larry Alexander, Sandy Torano, Jerry Peters & John Davis (Billboard soul charts: 49 ; Billboard pop charts: 107)

Sing A Song 1978 Buddah BDLP 4058 Producers: Larry Alexander & Skip Scarborough (UK)

Somewhere In My Lifetime 1978 Arista AB 4202 Producers: T Life, Barry Manilow, Ron Dante, Skip Scarborough & Larry Alexander (Billboard soul charts: 15 ; Billboard pop charts: 70)

You Know How To Love Me 1979 Arista AL 9509 Producers: James Mtume & Reggie Lucas (Billboard soul charts: 10 ; Billboard pop charts: 50)

Can't We Fall In Love Again 1981 Arista AL 9544 Producers: Chuck Jackson & Norman Connors (Billboard soul charts: 11 ; Billboard pop charts: 57)

Goddess Of Love 1983 Arista AL 9619 Producers: Narada Michael Walden & Thom Bell (Billboard soul charts: 20 ; Billboard pop charts: 112)

The Best Of 1986 Arista 207 830 (Europe)

Under Her Spell - Greatest Hits 1989 Arista AL 8609

The Best Of - The Buddah Years 1990 Sequel NEX LP 138

Poor, beautiful, talented, tormented Phyllis Hyman joined the sad ranks of soul singers with chaotic personal lives and insurmountable problems when she committed suicide in 1995. Her life can certainly be celebrated though as she leaves behind a body of work that has made her one of the best loved female singers of our times.

Born in Pittsburgh, she first come to our attention in mid 1976 when a single on the small Desert Moon label crept into the soul charts at #76, followed a few months later by a featured credit on a single by Norman Connors, "Betcha By Golly Wow", that reached the soul top thirty. Captivated by her distinctive voice and evident beauty Buddah knew they had a potential star on their hands and released her first LP in the spring of 1977. The first side was very strong indeed, although I wonder what Hyman, who could be difficult, thought about the fact that the first two and a half minutes of her first LP didn't feature her voice at all. "Loving You, Losing You" was a seven minute cut of typical Thom Bell (he wrote it) intricacy that built up slowly and deliberately before Hyman arrived a third of the way through and a truncated version deservedly went to #32 onto the soul singles chart, which was 26 places higher than the splendid and serene "No One Can Love You More" managed as the follow-up 45. "One Thing On My Mind" showed that Hyman was at ease on a tuneful, dance oriented side and a slowed down, porcelain brittle, version of The Spinners' "I Don't Want To Lose You" closed out side one on a particularly poignant note, as the lyrics, had they been turned inwardly and sung to herself, could be seen as summing up much of Hyman's own troubled life. I'm not quite so enamoured with side two as she wandered down a jazzy path on "Was Yesterday Such A Long Time Ago" and "The Night Bird Gets The Love" that I was reluctant to follow, although the peppy "Beautiful Man Of Mine" certainly gets my vote.

Things got a bit confusing with *Sing A Song* which was going to be her next U.S. album but it was ready to be released at the same time as Arista was acquiring Buddah and by the time things became clearer about the deal, the UK went with *Sing A Song* as it was originally intended while the States got rid of "Sweet Music", "Love Is Free" and "Sing A Song" itself, added "Kiss You All Over", "Lookin For A Lovin' " and "Somewhere In My Lifetime" and used the latter as the title track of her first Arista LP. I have to say that, although the three omitted tracks were all good, the ones that were added were better. So the record company got that right, but whoever decided it was a good idea to put a poorly lit photo of Hyman on the front cover and an out of focus one on the back of *Sing A Song* should have been summarily sacked.

No such artistic concerns existed as regards the *Somewhere In My Lifetime* set as Phyllis looked joltingly beautiful on the front and back cover. The title track was written by Jesus Alvarez (who was the male voice on Shirley and Company's "Shame Shame Shame") and produced and part arranged by Barry Manilow. That latter statement might make the more blinkered sneer, but he did a magnificent job in conjuring up a towering and richly satisfying orchestrated backdrop against which Hyman gives the performance of her lifetime on one of the greatest and most deeply moving records I know. Even though she probably knew all too well how her life was going to play out she delivers a wonderful affirmation of the will to love. Nothing else could hope to match "Lifetime" (which went to #12 on the soul charts as a 45) but it was still a consistently strong album. Her take on "Kiss You All Over", an excellent pop song well suited to female soul singers, was even better than Millie Jackson's, although it inexplicably completely failed as a single, while "Living Inside Your Love" was such an obvious hit record that it is amazing to be reminded that Arista didn't even issue it as a 45. She also covered "The Answer Is You" from a Mark Radice album, not an obvious but exceedingly well-judged choice, while the lovely way she interprets the old standard "Here's That Rainy Day" even breaks down my resistance to the jazzier side of her repertoire.

Reggie Lucas and James Mtume were two of the most prominent writers and producers within soul music from 1979 through 1981 and they were wisely entrusted with helming Hyman's next LP, which was another triumph, particularly on a faultless side one. Largely dance oriented in nature, it nevertheless has a lightness of touch and restraint that was most attractive, and the title track and "Under Your Spell" were instantly catchy singles which did well at #12 and #37 respectively on the soul charts although Hyman continued to mean just about nothing to the pop audience at large: she never posted a 45 onto the Hot 100. "Some Way" was gorgeous, an interesting song that sounded as if it was recorded in Philadelphia (but wasn't) and despite being constructed without a hook, sustained interest throughout its five minutes. Side two couldn't quite match up, but was still good throughout apart from a routine "Hold On".

Hyman acquired new producers for her first LP of the eighties (*Can't We Fall In Love Again*) which did not get off to a good start with the thumping and dull pop side, "You Sure Look Good To Me", but it was not typical of the rest of the set which was much better. It was also a more "up" album than before as regards the tempo of the songs and the perkiness of the production. The title track, a feisty duet with Michael Henderson, became her biggest hit to date and much as I like the song, it was faded out too early, just as both singers were really revving up. "I Ain't Asking" was a wonderfully insistent song from Ashford and Simpson even if it must have broken a world record for the number of times its title was repeated; "Don't Tell Me, Tell Her" was a good take on a song Odyssey had cut the year before, and "Tonight You And Me" was another excellent side with an ominous undertow in the rhythm section, a memorable chorus and the most effervescent vocal on show from Hyman; it deserved to have done better than reach only #22 soul. Long-time Phyllis aficionados would have loved the two ballads, "Just Another Face In The Crowd" and "The Sunshine In My Life", the latter being just short of magnificent.

The Philadelphia recorded *Goddess Of Love* closed out her Arista tenure and it was another set that recovered strongly after a poor start. "Riding The Tiger" and the title track opened proceedings in distinctly underwhelming fashion and it needed the excellent "Why Did You Turn Me On" to restore sanity even if it only managed a paltry #74 on the soul charts; "Tiger" had done a bit better at #30. Elsewhere on the album the tuneful and beautifully sung "Let Somebody Love You" was a welcome surprise seeing it was written by Preston and Alan Glass whose work generally left me cold, and the songs from Philly veterans Joseph Jefferson, Charles Simmons and Thom Bell "We Should Be Lovers", "Just Me And You" and "Just Twenty Five Years To Anywhere" were all heartfelt and worthy. Finally, "Falling Star" and "Your Move, My Heart" were two more slow tracks on a set that was significantly more sedate than its predecessor.

Living All Alone 1986 P.I.R. ST 53029 Producers: Dexter Wansel, Thom Bell, Kenny Gamble, Reggie Griffin, Nick Martinelli & Mayra Casales (Billboard soul charts: 11 ; Billboard pop charts: 78)

Hyman's last LP came out on the legendary P.I.R. label at a time when the company was running down its operations (only two more albums succeeded *Living All Alone*.) Given it was now 1986 it was to be expected that the record would include much more programming than had been the case on previous Hyman records but it was certainly kept to a minimum and it is credit to everyone involved that there is not a single track within that has me leaping across the room to lift the needle as soon as possible. This is, of course, largely down to Hyman herself who is in fine form throughout and she is presented with sturdy material with which to work. Three singles from the set reached the soul top thirty: "Ain't You Had Enough Love", the title track and "Old Friend". The latter is a much loved performance of hers but I find it one of the least interesting cuts on display given its slightly "Disney-esque" approach.

Other than some "Best Of" collections Hyman released no further LPs but there was nearly one more: on stage in London in November 1991 she announced to a happy audience that she was going to badger her record label into putting out her then new CD, *Prime Of My Life*, on vinyl, but it never actually happened. She did go on to issue more new music in the nineties and enjoyed her one and only soul #1 hit in 1991 with "Don't Wanna Change The World".

There are plenty of people who proclaim Phyllis Hyman to have been one of the greatest female soul singers - if not the greatest of them all - and while I do not quite share that view, I still believe she was a serious talent, and I can't think of anyone else off the top of my head who adapted so well to the eighties, and released so many memorable sides in that decade of serious decline for soul music.

Ice Man's Band (see also Jerry Butler)

Robert Bowles; Wayne Douglas; Reginald "Sonny" Burke; Ira Gates

Introducing The Ice Man's Band 1972 Mercury SRM-1-648 Producers: Robert Bowles, Wayne Douglas, Reginald "Sonny" Burke & Ira Gates

This is Jerry Butler's four piece band. Their album consists of inessential jazzy instrumental noodling on a number of songs made famous by their mentor (e.g "Never Give You Up"), a few more being well-known by others (e.g. "Come Together"), and a couple of originals from the foursome, one of which, "It's Down To That", was pushed out as a single by Mercury to an empty reception. Sonny Burke went on to have the longest and widest-ranging career in music after the quartet went their separate ways, and can be heard getting a "shout-out" on Bobby Womack's "One More Chance On Love" from his 1976 *Home is Where The Heart Is* album.

Ikettes (see also The Mirettes)

Robbie Montgomery; Jessie Smith; Venetta Fields; Debbie Wilson; Linda Jones; Linda Sims (?); Ann Thomas (?)

Soul The Hits 1965 Modern MST 102 No producer listed

(G)old & New 1974 United Artists UA-LA190-F Producers: Ike Turner, Tina Turner & Jackie Clark

Fine Fine Fine 1987 Kent 063 (UK)

There were a bewildering number of Ikettes over the years including Joshie Jo Armstead, PP Arnold, Claudia Lennear and Bonnie Bramlett, but the longest serving members in their most successful years were Robbie Montgomery, Jessie Smith, and Venetta Fields and it is they who grace the cover of the first album.

"I'm Blue (The Gong Gong Song)" had been a big hit for The Ikettes on Atco in early 1962 (#3 soul and #19 pop) but the label did not go with an album and it wasn't until the group moved to Modern where they hit with "I'm So Thankful" and "Peaches 'N' Cream" that an LP was released to capitalise on their popularity. Both of those excellent 45s were on the set, as were three others that didn't do nearly so well. While certainly enjoyable, it's a slightly uneasy record, as a number of the Modern sides seemed unsure whether to pitch the Ikettes as a girl group in the Crystals or Ronettes mould or to play up their "tougher" roots, acquired while working with Ike and Tina Turner. The lovely swaying "I'm So Thankful" even went in a third direction, sounding for all the world like a Motown disc, which might not have been surprising seeing as how it was written by Frank Wilson and Marc Gordon. "(He's Gonna Be) Fine Fine Fine", one of the failed 45s, was a great side, with good horns, but was just too close to "Peaches 'N' Cream" to make it, and I enjoyed the interesting "winding down" ending to "Nobody Loves Me" while the storming "It's Been So Long" and "Can't Sit Down" were two other top cuts that surely should have been tried as singles. Less impressive were covers of "Da Do Ron Ron" and "Sally Go Round The Roses", rather clearly makeweights to flesh out the set and bring it up to 12 tracks.

Relations with Ike got worse and worse and at the end of 1965 the trio walked out on the Turners and, as they had no rights to the title "The Ikettes", decided they would henceforth be known as The Mirettes, under which name they recorded a number of singles and two LPs.

Numerous Ikettes came and went between 1965 and 1973 but the trio who made the *(G)old And New* set were Debbie Wilson, Linda Jones (not that one) and either Linda Sims or Ann Thomas; the sleeve information doesn't enlighten us. It's not a bad LP, but doesn't exactly exude a sense of total commitment on the part of Ike Turner towards making it a success. Songs like "Listen to the Music", "Will It Go Round In Circles", "Someday We'll Be Together" and "Come See About Me" are all delivered in a perfunctory manner although "I Gotcha" is quite sassy and good fun. The "Gold" portion of the set are re-makes of five of their sixties recordings of which "Peaches 'N' Cream" is the best, working very well although "I'm Thankful" doesn't match up to the original. A liberal use of horns throughout is most welcome but the LP did little in the marketplace, which was to rather be expected as it hardly sounded in step with what was selling in early 1974.

UA had already released a couple of poorly selling singles that were not on the LP and after the failure of the album as well The Ikettes confined themselves to backing the Turners. Kent put out a typically decent retrospective LP in 1987 although it only contained three cuts that were not on the *Soul The Hits* album.

Imaginations

Tyrone Stewart; Arthur Scales; Jesse Harvey; Nathaniel Pringle

Imaginations 1974 20th Century T-453 Producers: Clarence Johnson & Star-Vue Productions

Good Stuff 1975 20th Century T-497 Producer: Clarence Johnson

Maurice Commander and Jerline Shelton wrote five of the eight songs on this accomplished album from Chicago group The Imaginations. The two of them, like producer Clarence Johnson, did sterling work in the city over a number of years and in The Imaginations found a talented group who interpreted their compositions in capable style. (There was supposedly some tie up between The Imaginations and The Brighter Side of Darkness but the excellent local radio show, *Sitting In The Park*, made no reference to it when BSOD group member Randolph Murph was interviewed a few years back.)

The Imaginations had a dull record sleeve which did no favours to the quality of the music within. The quartet sang in a distinctly "sweet soul" style with a high tenor lead on most songs, but they were as impressive on faster material as on ballads, not always the case with groups of this ilk. Of the uptempo songs, the irresistible skipping "Love Diet" is best, while "God Bless You Love" would be the pick of the slower material. Two other tracks, "Searchin'" and "There's Another On Your Mind", deserve special mention even if they rather underplay the contributions of the singers in order to show off the splendid arrangements by Tom Tom Washington and Bernjamin Wright. The latter is particularly impressive as it is so unusual and compelling: a sweet soul record cut in a neo-blues style with a big band arrangement. "Talk About The World" was a rather tired "social commentary" song, but it's the only duff note in an otherwise pretty flawlessly executed record.

Sadly, *Good Stuff* was not an accurate title, and it was a most disappointing LP. Again, the cover had scant relevance to a group called The Imaginations, but this time around the material was generally too weak to offset this shortcoming and side two, the likeable and danceable "Sweet Mona" apart, had little to recommend it. Shelton and Commander only contributed three songs together which didn't help but the lead singing was still lovely, and it is that which keeps the interest up on side one, where a fine revival of "Love Jones (was this what led to the claimed connection with Brighter Side of Darkness?) vies with the spirited "The Perfect Pair" and the slow "W.I.F.E" (which had just a hint of the Chi-lites in it) for best track on view.

Three singles were pulled from the two LPs, and "There's Another On Your Mind" did make the lower reaches of The *Cashbox* soul charts, but none reached the *Billboard* lists. As far as I know that was it for the group and although I have seen claims of a third LP from the group entitled *Rock -A - Jama*, this was by an entirely different set of Imaginations.

Impact (see also Damon Harris)

Damon Harris; John Quintin Simms; Donald Tilghman; Charles Timmons

Impact 1976 Atco SD 36-135 Producer: Bobby Eli

The 'Pac Is Back 1977 Fantasy F-9539 Producer: John Davis

The Young Vandals (aka The Vandals) from Baltimore made a handful of polished discs in 1970 before one of their lead singers, Damon Harris, was chosen to join The Temptations where he stayed for a few years; in the time he was gone The Young Vandals went into hibernation. After his acrimonious departure from The Temps in 1975, Harris re-joined his three colleagues and The Young Vandals decided to now be known as Impact.

The first - in parts, captivating - LP was recorded at Sigma Sound in Philadelphia with The Tower of Power Horn section pleasingly utilised on four of the cuts. Bobby Eli produced and contributed all nine of the songs and should be proud of how things turned out. It might have been expected that Harris would take all the vocal leads given his higher profile but the singing was apportioned fairly liberally. "Happy Man" and "Give A Broken Heart A Break" were invigorating dance sides and became the first two 45s to be issued from the set, reaching #42 and #36 respectively on the soul charts in 1976. A third cut, the captivating and typical Philly ballad, "One Last Memory", on which Harris switched lead with Charles Timmons, didn't manage to make it to the *Billboard* listings but crept into the lower reaches of the *Cashbox* version. Possibly the best cut on show was "Man And Woman" a gorgeous slow work-out delivered beautifully by Harris, and although Quinton Simms was clearly a good singer he rather lost his opportunity when taking the lead on "Friends" and "Love Attack" as they were possibly the weakest songs on show. He got a better track on which to work, "Winning Combination", where he shared leads with Harris and Timmons. (By the way, while I deeply love the rhinoceros, I'm unsure why it was deemed to be a good idea to include a picture of one on the front cover.)

The second and final set saw the group sharing the front cover with a pack of wolves and working with a new producer as John Davis took over from Eli although it was once again mainly recorded in Philadelphia. As with *Impact*, two cuts from the The *'Pac Is Bac*k, "Sister Fine" (really good, and I think sung by Simms) and "Rainy Days, Stormy Nights"(also good, with vocals shared between the group) made it to the soul charts but only at #49 and #90 respectively which must have been a worry. Both were eclipsed in quality, though, by the Harris led re-make of The Delfonics' "Somebody Loves You" and a wonderfully harmonised "My Love" which both sounded delectable in 1977 and possibly even better today; and they weren't done yet: we also encounter a charming version of "Sara Smile", the smoothly persuasive "I Thought You Might Like To Know" and the finger-clicking joy of "Smile Awhile". Only "Carry Me Back" was so-so and "Sing A Song" poor (Bobby Eli's only contribution to the LP). In summary this is an excellent and sadly underrated set, one of the best examples of quality soul group singing from the second half of the seventies, and although Damon Harris may have left The Temptations under a cloud, he at least had the satisfaction of making better records than they were managing at the time.

Harris went solo in 1978 (see section under him) while Timmons and Tilghman provided backing vocals to the Ava Cherry LP, *Ripe,* in 1980. (Timmons later changed his name to Kareem Ali and sings with Glenn Leonard's Temptations Revue these days). I'm not sure what happened to Simms.

Note : A group from Washington D.C. called Impact cut an album in 1988 entitled *It's A Groove Night*. They are in no way related to the Baltimore Impact.

Imperials (See Little Anthony & Imperials)

Impressions (see also Jerry Butler, LeRoy Hutson, Curtis Mayfield and Mystique)

Curtis Mayfield; Fred Cash; Sam Gooden; LeRoy Hutson; Reggie Torian; Ralph Johnson; Richard Brooks; Arthur Brooks; Nate Evans; Jerry Butler

For Your Precious Love 1963 Vee Jay VJLP 1075 No producer listed

The Impressions. It's a great name for inarguably one of the greatest groups of all time. When it comes to "classic" format male vocal groups only The Temptations, Miracles, O'Jays, Four Tops and Dells have the same aura, the same sheer talent, and the same levels of success over a sustained period of time. I should declare a strongly held belief right here: Curtis Mayfield was one of the most gifted artists in any musical field of the 20th century and one of the four of five most crucial in the whole glorious history of soul. The Impressions also, like The Four Tops, Miracles, O'Jays and Dells (but unlike The Temptations), had an inner strength and unity that has led to precious little change in personnel over the years: the current line-up (2016) sees Fred Cash and Sam Gooden still on board after a mere 60 years while Reggie Torian has only been around since 1976.

At first, back in 1956, there were five young boys down in Chattanooga, Tennessee singing in a group called the Roosters; included were Gooden and Cash. Not much was happening for the quintet though, and three of the group (Gooden, Richard and Arthur Brooks) made a move up to Chicago. Two new members were called for and they duly arrived, fellows by the names of Jerry Butler and Curtis Mayfield. "For Your Precious Love" became their first single on Abner and where the Roosters got nowhere the newly named Impressions (featuring Jerry Butler) reached #3 soul and #11 pop in the summer of 1958. Three further singles came out on Abner following "For Your Precious Love" but by the time the last of these arrived, Butler had left to go solo. Abner was a Vee-Jay subsidiary and it wasn't until much later, 1963, that some of these early 45s were put out at long playing speed by the parent company. *For Your Precious Love* contained twelve tracks, four of which had previously come out on singles, and it is a fascinating record with the Butler led tracks (e.g. the hit, the gorgeous "The Gift Of Love" and "Don't Drive Me Away") contrasting with those led by Mayfield (e.g "At The County Fair", "Senorita I Love You") What was consistent throughout the whole set, and was to remain the case for decades, was the purity and quality of the backing vocals, while Mayfield wrote nine of the songs, an early indication of his creativity. However, seeing as how it was an LP issued to cash-in, frankly, on the success that Butler and the "new" Impressions (Fred Cash had replaced Butler in 1959) were enjoying at the time, and contained tracks cut years earlier, it did not sell strongly.

Impressions 1963 ABC-Paramount ABCS-450 No producer listed (Billboard pop charts: 43)

The Never Ending 1964 ABC-Paramount ABCS-468 No producer listed (Billboard pop charts: 52)

Keep On Pushing 1964 ABC-Paramount ABCS-493 No producer listed (Billboard soul charts: 4; Billboard pop charts: 8)

People Get Ready 1965 ABC-Paramount ABCS-505 Producer: Johnny Pate (Billboard soul charts: 1 ; Billboard pop charts: 23)

Greatest Hits 1965 ABC-Paramount ABCS-515 (Billboard soul charts: 2 ; Billboard pop charts: 83)

One By One 1965 ABC-Paramount ABCS-523 Producer: Johnny Pate (Billboard soul charts: 4 ; Billboard pop charts: 104)

Big Sixteen 1965 HMV CLP 1935 (UK)

Ridin' High 1966 ABC-Paramount ABCS-545 Producer: Johnny Pate (Billboard soul charts: 4 ; Billboard pop charts: 79)

It's tempting to say that the "real" Impressions story started when the group released their first LP on ABC-Paramount in 1963. Butler and the two Brooks brothers had gone and the classic trio of Mayfield, Gooden and Cash made what were the group's best ever records. That first album, *The Impressions*, is quietly brilliant, with an almost reverent focus on the singing from the group and the quality of the songs; the musical backing is nicely subdued and unobtrusive, content to enhance the glorious melody lines at which Mayfield was so adept in providing. (By the way even though Curtis was only 20 or 21 on the front cover, he looks much younger.) It's instructive today to be reminded that *Billboard* confined its soul charts in the early sixties to a top thirty only and therefore unless a single was really big it wouldn't appear on the listings and for all their sheer quality, that was the fate for five tracks on the set issued as a-sides: "Grow Closer Together", "Little Young Lover", "Minstrel And Queen", "Sad Sad Girl And Boy" and "I'm The One Who Loves You". However, *Cashbox* went with a top fifty at the time, and apart from "I'm The One Who Loves You", they did all appear, albeit modestly, on those particular charts. Most groups would die to have "flops" like that. On the other hand, the set also contained the group's first huge post-Butler success: "Gypsy Woman" (#3 soul and #11 pop) and their first

ever soul #1: "It's All Right" (also #4 pop). The other five tracks had all done duty as b-sides to 45s and apart from the rather slight "Twist And Limbo" all were of distinction. Mayfield wrote ten of the twelve tracks, strummed his distinctive guitar and sang virtually all the leads although Gooden took over on "I Need Your Love".

The follow-up was a classic example of "that difficult second album" as it was much inferior to *The Impressions*. For some reason it was deemed a good idea for the group to cover four "standards" including "Satin Doll" and "September Song" and all were dismal, especially when placed against a song of such surpassing beauty as "I'm So Proud", a brilliant record which went to #14 on the pop charts. The next best track, "Girl You Don't Know Me", was also released as a 45 but met with indifference. There *were* other good songs on here such as "Little Boy Blue" which stayed just the right side of mawkish, thanks to its haunting lilting melody, and the strongly gospel influenced and early political song "I Gotta Keep On Moving", but it's still a disappointing LP.

I'm a great believer in the subjectivity of music, and find it easy to understand how someone could plausibly hate a record that is loved by someone else and vice versa, but I find it hard to imagine that *anyone* could be immune to the ethereal beauty of "I've Been Trying", surely one of the most beautiful and heart-rending records ever made. It's also the perfect testament to Mayfield's talent that he was content for it to sit as a b-side (to "People Get Ready") so brimful was he with sublime songs. It was the strongest track on *Keep On Pushing*, another marvellous set. Inch by inch the sound was getting punchier and more resonant, and never more so than on "Somebody Help Me", a fantastic and unheralded album only cut that has much more of a blues feel than is normally associated with the group. The rather irritating "Amen" was a big hit (# 7 pop) as were the title track (#14 pop) and "Talking About My Baby" (#12 pop) (both magnificent) while "I Made A Mistake", "I Love You (Yeah)" (did The Beatles listen to this before writing "Hello Goodbye"?) and "Long Long Winter" were three further b-sides of almost unbelievable quality.

People Get Ready was the group's third top-class LP. It contained some more big hits too: "You Must Believe Me", "Woman's Got Soul" and the title track, one of Mayfield's most famous songs on which, rather as Sam Cooke had done with "A Change Is Gonna Come", Curtis hinted at racial progress rather than shout it out brazenly. Which is probably why it didn't scare off mainstream buyers and went to #14 pop in early 1965, the ninth time the group had reached the top twenty (and apart from "We're A Winner" three years later The Impressions were never to have such a big pop success as this again; they had already peaked commercially as far as a wider audience was concerned.) As ever there were some great album only tracks: "Emotions" (a rare duet between Cash and Gooden), "Sometimes I Wonder" and "Can't Work No Longer" (which Billy Butler & The Chanters gratefully borrowed to earn their biggest hit as a 45 as a result) and some rather forgotten numbers such as "Hard To Believe" (one of Mayfield's most astute love songs) and "See The Real Me". He wasn't averse to re-working previous glories either as "We're In Love" and the utterly gorgeous "I've Found That I've Lost" leant heavily on "It's All Right" and "Long Long Winter" respectively but had such winning arrangements that any resistance was instantly quashed. And a word about those arrangements: Johnny Pate had been producing and arranging for the group for a while but *People Get Ready* was the first LP on which he was explicitly credited; quite right too as his work here was impeccable.

A *Greatest Hits* set came out in early 1965 which cleaned up on the soul charts, before the next new LP arrived, the thoroughly misguided and disappointing *One On One*. It built on *The Never Ending Impressions* by containing nine cover versions - all of which can be ignored - and only three Mayfield originals. The stately and dignified "Falling In Love With You" is glorious, while "Just One Kiss From You" despite performing disappointingly as a 45 has an ingenious arrangement and typically lovely harmonies. The last new song, "Lonely Man", is infected by the huge billowing string sections that so marred the other nine tracks and thus has any life sucked out of it. Despite my indifference, it must be said that the LP did very well.

Riding' High was a big improvement over *One On One* but did not match *The Impressions, Keep On Pushing* or *People Get Ready*. It not only boasted the best cover yet of all their LPs - classy and bold - and retained the reassuringly bewildering technical information that was printed on the back of all their ABC-Paramount albums, but Mayfield had written eleven of the twelve tracks. However, he had written most of them a long time ago and predominantly for others: "I'm A Tellin' You" and "Need To Belong" (Jerry Butler); "Man's Temptation" (Gene Chandler); "That's What Mama Say"(Walter Jackson); "Gotta Get Away" (Billy Butler & Enchanters). None of the new versions by The Impressions were in any way poor, but in no case did they top the originals. Only "Too Slow" - good but not among their best - was pulled from the set and put out as a 45 and although it hit the *Cashbox* soul charts did not trouble those from *Billboard.* Oddly, The Impressions had issued some tremendous singles in 1965 and 1966 that had not been included on any of their albums thus far: "Meeting Over Yonder", "Can't Satisfy" and "You've Been Cheating".

I should also mention that *Big Sixteen*, one of the most beloved of all sixties UK soul albums, a tremendous collection of so many great sides, came out in 1965.

The Fabulous 1967 ABC 606 Producer: Johnny Pate
(Billboard soul charts: 16 ; Billboard pop charts: 184)

We're A Winner 1968 ABC 635 Producer: Johnny Pate
(Billboard soul charts: 4 ; Billboard pop charts: 35)

The Best Of 1968 ABC 654 (Billboard soul charts: 23; Billboard pop charts: 172)

Big Sixteen Volume 2 1968 Stateside SL 10279 (UK)

The Versatile 1969 ABC 668 Producer: Johnny Pate

With *The Fabulous Impressions* the group started issuing their albums on "ABC" rather than "ABC Paramount", a minor enough change and one not reflected by any difference in approach in their music although the album started with an unusual burst of congas on the opening track, "You Always Hurt Me" (bearing than a hint of "Reach Out, I'll Be There"), which went to #20 soul and #96 pop in spring of 1967 as a single. "I Can't Stay Away From You" attained #34 soul and #80 pop when it was issued as a 45, modest placings for such a superb side, one of their very best with heartbreakingly beautiful singing. Interestingly, when considering what was to come, a new version of "It's All Over" was to all intents and purposes a Mayfield solo side, Gooden and Cash being conspicuously absent. Conversely, on the next track, *Little Girl*, Curtis was nowhere to be heard. The rest of the album is mixed, with a couple more Jerry Butler re-makes, a dull take on "100 Lbs Of Clay", a typically sweetly harmonised "I'm Still Waiting" and the intoxicating "You Ought To Be In Heaven" with sax flourishes suggesting Junior Walker had been invited to the session.

Despite the popularity of the group, and the quality of their records, they hadn't placed a single on the soul top ten since the middle of 1965 ("Woman's Got Soul") and therefore when "We're A Winner" reached #1 soul (and #14 pop) in January 1968 it was a huge resurgence in their commercial fortunes. It was by some distance Mayfield's most overtly political song to date and it should be noted that it preceded James Brown's "Say It Loud I'm Black And I'm Proud" by some months. It isn't one of my favourite Impressions' sides though as, despite its undoubted importance, it lacks melody and sounds rather dated today. It became the title track of their next ABC set, which also yielded up another top selling single, the reflective "I Loved And I Lost" (#9 soul #61 pop). (Sandwiched between these two singles was another good selling 45, "We're Rollin' On", but it was not on the LP.) The group also finally put out a cover I can listen to, "Up Up And Away", and essayed a fine and brassy take on Gene Chandler's immortal "Nothing Can Stop Me" while "Let Me Tell The World" was yet another upbeat love song from Mayfield's seemingly inexhaustible inventory. Less happy was the soft and fluffy "Moonlight Shadows", which almost sounded like a conscious attempt by Curtis to create a "standard" of his own (as if he hadn't already done this, of course, with many of his big hits.) I remain ambivalent about "Romancing To The Love Song" as while I admire how such a melodic and gentle track can reside on the same LP as "We're A Winner", it lacks the beauty and soulfulness of the Impressions' finest sides.

The ABC era came to an end with another *Best Of* set (worth having as it featured for the first time on album, great sides like "You've Been Cheating", "Can't Satisfy", "This Must End" and "We're Rollin' On") a second *Big Sixteen* volume in England and the worst LP the group ever issued, *The Versatile Impressions*. This latter set actually came out (and deservedly bombed) after the group had started releasing their music on Curtom, and it was unedifying in the extreme to hear them tackle songs such as "Yesterday", "Fool On The Hill" and "East of Java". Only the excellent "Don't Cry My Love", Mayfield's contribution to the large library of Vietnam songs, saves the album from total disaster.

This Is My Country 1968 Curtom CRS 8001 Producer: Curtis Mayfield (Billboard soul charts: 5 ; Billboard pop charts: 107)

The Young Mod's Forgotten Story 1969 Curtom CRS 8003 Producer: Curtis Mayfield (Billboard soul charts: 21; Billboard pop charts: 104)

The Best Impressions Curtis, Sam & Fred 1970 Curtom CRS 8004 (Billboard soul charts: 23)

Check Out Your Mind 1970 Curtom CRS 8006 Producer: Curtis Mayfield (Billboard soul charts: 22)

This Is My Country was a brilliant and transitional LP, not only a complete return to form, but also the first to be produced by Mayfield and - significantly - the first on his own label. The music was much edgier and funkier than we were used to and the contributions from Sam and Fred were somewhat marginalised, with their trademark vocal interjections only to be found on the title track and elsewhere - "Love's Happening and "So Unusual " for example - their harmonies sounded smoother and sweeter than normal; lovely as ever but just *different*. The changes were symbolised by the front cover - the group standing on a desolate building site was certainly not what we expected from an Impressions LP - but the compositions within retained their usual range and sacrificed nothing in melody from what had gone before. There were only two overly political songs, the blistering opener, "They Don't Know", surely written in response to the assassination of Martin Luther King, and the quietly defiant and sweetly reasoned title track. The latter made an impressive showing as a single, attaining #8 soul and #25 pop, but the lead-off 45 from the set, the highly impressive "Fool For You "(with minimal input from Sam and Fred but boasting a huge tumbling drum sound) did even better at #3 soul and #22 pop. Elsewhere, there was just so much to enjoy: the beautiful "My Woman's Love" had a gorgeous and atypical keyboard line (a clavichord?) and was the cut that sounded most like the "old "Impressions records; the clear pain of "I'm Loving Nothing", "Gone Away" and "You Want Somebody Else"; the exuberance of "Stay Close To Me". It's a magnificent LP, with not a wasted second on any of the ten tracks.

The Young Mod's Forgotten Story is an interesting and good set, but falls short of *This Is My Country*. It was good to see that Sam and Fred were returned to a more prominent role, while the political song count was increased to three in the title (better than the song) track, "Mighty Mighty Spade And Whitey" and "Choice Of Colors", a classic which became their third single to reach soul #1 (and #21 pop). "Wherever She Leadeth Me", despite its archaic title, flows along nicely and became a small hit in 1970 when it was belatedly issued as a 45; "Seven Years" and the gospelly "My Deceiving Heart" were two more good 45s pulled from the album and both did ok, rather than spectacularly. The production is bold (and occasionally rather strident) but while there is not a bad track on the LP there isn't one either that approached the beauty of so many of their earlier songs.

Check Out Your Mind was the last LP released by the classic format of Mayfield, Gooden and Cash and it entered the *Billboard* soul charts on exactly the same date, October 10th 1970, as Mayfield's first solo LP, *Curtis*. There was absolutely no doubt about which one was more eagerly anticipated by the public: *Curtis* went to #1, *Check Out Your Mind* to #22. However, it is another first rate set with no throwaway cuts and one which has aged well, but it also sounds like *Curtis* in the sense that the same musicians played on both albums - with percussionist Henry Gibson prominent - and many tracks could be switched without anyone really noticing. Actually, that is not entirely accurate as one or two cuts, like the splendid "Can't You See" with its throwback sound, stand out on *Check Out Your Mind* as obviously Impressions' records. Despite the album's mediocre commercial performance, the three singles that were pulled from it all did well on the soul charts, demonstrating that The Impressions name still had huge cachet in the black market : "Baby Turn On To Me" went to #6, "Say You Love Me" (another "clearly Impressions" side) to #10 and the title track to #3.

The Best Impressions Curtis Sam & Fred is worth bringing to the attention of die-hard fans as the first side features new versions of old favourites from the pre-Curtom days like "Gypsy Woman", "I'm So Proud" and "Keep On Pushing", performed with more orchestration and instrumentation than the sparser originals. Side two includes the bigger Curtom hits, and which are not remakes. (The sleevenotes by Richard Robinson are particularly well-written, too.)

16 Greatest Hits 1971 ABC 727 (Billboard soul charts: 23; Billboard pop charts: 180)

Times Have Changed 1972 Curtom CRS 8012 Producer: Curtis Mayfield (Billboard pop charts: 192)

Preacher Man 1973 Curtom CRS 8016 Producer: Rich Tufo (Billboard soul charts: 31; Billboard pop charts: 204)

Times Have Changed was a sensible title to alert people to the reality of the new post-Mayfield Impressions, although his fingerprints were all over it given he wrote six of the eight tracks and sat in the producer's chair. It was one of only two albums that featured LeRoy Hutson as a member of the group, and it can't be classed as one of the high points of either his or the Impressions' existence. For a start, it didn't even reach the soul charts, the first time such a failure had been registered since the weak *The Versatile* set in 1969, and second the surely all-important lead-off track on side one, "Stop The War", was over six minutes long but not notably memorable. Third, it didn't spawn hit singles. Having said that, it certainly wasn't a disaster and if this LP had been cut by some unknown group they could be pretty proud of it as it is hardly a chore to listen to but this was, after all, The Impressions where standards were of the highest. The title track was nice as Hutson did a good job on a good song but the version of "Inner City Blues" was clearly inferior to Marvin Gaye's. "Potent Love" was a better and more enjoyable use of six minutes over on side two, and after an ok re-make of "Need To Belong" the album exited with two cuts put out as 45s that sold in disappointing fashion on the soul charts: "Love Me" at #25 and "This Love's For Real" at #41.

Times changed even further with the *Preacher Man* set (one which didn't even bother to show a photograph of the group on the front or back cover) as all the songs bar one were written by Rich Tufo, who also eased Mayfield out of that comfy producer's seat. "What It Is" kicked things off and was certainly the departure, being in effect a Henry Gibson conga master class, with no singing anywhere in sight. The title track had a pretty memorable hook but for some inexplicable reason flunked totally when released as a 45, failing to reach either the *Billboard* or *Cashbox* top 100 soul charts. The album's key cut was clearly "Thin Line" as it weighed in at over ten minutes long (and didn't deserve to) but when cut down to around four minutes as a single performed as dismally as "Preacher Man" had done, which was surely no surprise as it had absolutely no melody. Both it, and the album as a whole, reminded me strongly of The Temptations' work with Norman Whitfield at the same time (1973): group were markedly subservient to producer. The other four tracks on the album were neither particularly good nor particularly poor.

Finally Got Myself Together 1973 Curtom CRS 8019 Producers: Ed Townsend, Rich Tufo & Lowrell Simon (Billboard soul charts: 16; Billboard pop charts: 176)

Three The Hard Way 1974 Curtom CRS 8602 Producers: Rich Tufo & Lowrell Simon (Billboard soul charts: 26; Billboard pop charts: 202)

First Impressions 1975 Curtom CU 5003 Producers: Ed Townsend, Rich Tufo & Joseph Scott (Billboard soul charts: 13; Billboard pop charts: 115)

Loving Power 1976 Curtom CU 5009 Producers: Ed Townsend, Rich Tufo, Charles Jackson & Marvin Yancy (Billboard soul charts: 24 ; Billboard pop charts: 195)

Finally Got Myself Together heralded the biggest change in The Impressions for some twelve years or so: they were no longer a trio. Hutson left to go solo and was replaced by Ralph Johnson and Reggie Torian, the latter having sung with another Chicago based vocal group, The Enchanters. Both were excellent singers with Johnson taking the lead on "If It's In You To Do Wrong", an absorbing and soulful single pulled from the set that did Ok by reaching #26, but was hardly a significant upturn in their fortunes. However, they only had to wait until the title track was put out as the second 45 from the album and they were right back on top as it went all the way to become their fourth (and final) #1 soul smash as well as reaching #17 pop - their biggest hit on those charts for six years. It was a gentle, composed song that took all the time it needed to reveal its charm, one of four compositions from veteran Ed Townsend here working with the group for the first time. "We Go Back A Ways" needs a mention too, for its thrilling interplay between Johnson's hard gospel lead and the smooth backing harmonies, reminiscent for once of The Dells. It is an exemplary and consistent male vocal group album throughout, more in the mainstream than before as all traces of Curtis Mayfield were finally banished ("Don't Forget What I Told You" even had the merest hint of Parliament in it.)

Three The Hard Way, a soundtrack to a little seen film, is ok. Short on wah-wah guitar instrumental breaks and film dialogue and stronger on proper songs than many such scores, it nevertheless was in no way an improvement on *Finally Got Myself Together* and doesn't linger very long in the mind. "Something's Mighty Mighty Wrong" from it went to #28 on the soul charts.

First Impressions was the proper follow-up to *Finally Got Myself Together* and shares many of the strengths of that earlier set, thanks largely again to Ed Townsend who now took over the majority of the production duties as well as writing six of the eight songs. "Sooner Or Later" and "Same Thing It Took" are the first two cuts on side one, both warm and comfortable in their own skin, and each climbed to #3 soul in 1975 as singles. The lovingly arranged "Old Before My Time" and the instructional title track (which did well in the U.K. as a single) close out an exceptionally strong side. Side two can't quite match up but still houses four worthwhile tunes with Reggie Torian's fine lead on "Why Must A Love Song Be A Sad Song" being especially enjoyable. The group looked happy and relaxed on the front cover wearing suits for the first time since *The Fabulous Impressions* and the imposing collection became their best performing album for seven years.

We weren't to know it at the time, but *Loving Power* was the last commercial hurrah for The Impressions (no more LPs reached the soul charts) and the album itself showed how times were changing; the title track, for instance, although good and enjoyable was clearly indebted to Earth, Wind & Fire while, similarly, the group's congenial take on "Sunshine" didn't stray far from how it had been rendered by The O'Jays with Johnson phrasing in the manner of Eddie Levert. Both songs were issued as singles with "Loving Power" making it to #11 soul, 25 places higher than "Sunshine" managed but it was undeniable that the group who used to be copied by so many were now doing the copying. "I Wish I'd Stayed In Bed", an excellent tale of woe, was the best cut on show, beautifully sung in the grand manner, and although I enjoy it all, I would refrain from classing the set as essential.

It's About Time 1976 Cotillion SD 9912 Producer: McKinley Jackson

Come To My Party 1979 20th Century T-596 Producer: Carl Davis

Fan The Fire 1981 20th Century T-624 Producers: Carl Davis & Eugene Record

The Vintage Years 1976 Sire SASH-3717-2 (Billboard pop charts: 199)

1976 was another key year for the group as Johnson left to join Mystique and was replaced by Nate Evans (who had cut a couple of solo singles a few years earlier) while the group moved to Cotillion where they recorded with a new producer as well as a whole new set of musicians and arrangers. The majority of the songs on *It's About Time* were written by Melvin and Mervin Steals but none were up to their best work and the whole album has a sadly tired feeling with only one reasonably strong cut - "What Might Have Been" - on show. And it wasn't just me: two singles were released from the album and "This Time" could only manage #40 soul while "You'll Never Find" scraped to an embarrassingly low #99.

By the time the group released another LP three years later, Evans had moved on and the Impressions were once again a trio in Gooden, Cash and Torian, although Evans did return for the group's final album. *Come To My Party,* as with *It's About Time* before it, finally gave notice that The Impressions were now just another group with all traces of uniqueness gone; this is not such a harsh criticism as it may sound, for it is an inevitable outcome in the ephemeral music industry and hardly anyone can escape it. The LP did contain three good tracks - "I Could Never Make You Stay", "All I Want To Do Is Make Love To You" (with Torian sounding more like Mayfield than he ever did before) and, best of all, the outstanding "Maybe I'm Mistaken" with timelessly beautiful singing. Sadly, this latter song flopped totally as a 45, as did the awful "Sorry", one of four unrewarding uptempo cuts from the album. Eugene Record wrote (three tracks) for the group for the first time and the arranging, musicianship and production was all good enough, but not many people wanted to hear The Impressions on six minute plus dance cuts; I know I didn't.

As mentioned above, Evans briefly re-joined the group and was on board for *Fan The Fire*, an improvement on the previous two albums and the last one ever recorded by the great group. His tough tenor is heard to good effect on the above average dance outing, "I Don't Wanna Lose Your Love", and other cuts like "I Surrender" and "You're Mine" are not bad at all. There is lovely symmetry in the final track of their final album looking back to where it all started: a new version of "For Your Precious Love." It's a beautiful performance, with Fred Cash on rare lead, and managed to get to #58 on the soul charts, the last time, apart from a one-off single in 1987, they ever appeared there. They had visited 48 times before, 17 of which were in the top ten.

Numerous later Impressions compilations exist and I have ignored all these apart from *The Vintage* set and that purely because it lodged, just, on the pop charts. It is a double album consisting of Impressions songs as well as Jerry Butler and Curtis Mayfield solo sides.

Gooden, Cash and Torian sing live from time to time - I saw them in London a few years back - and they still sound gorgeous; which of course should be expected from three such long-serving members of one of the greatest groups - and most influential, the debt owed to them from Jamaican groups alone is incalculable, for instance - that ever existed.

Incredibles

Cal Waymon; Denise Erwin; Don Ray Sampson; Jean Smith; Carl Gilbert

Heart & Soul 1969 Audio Arts AAS 7000 Producer: Madelon Baker

Another highly enjoyable LP with a big, brash cover I love. It could only have been released in the sixties. Unfortunately it doesn't tell us exactly when, and one of the nice challenges of this book is trying to track down the actual year of release (which I'm now pretty sure was 1969) but one thing is clear, the ten cuts on the set provided a good source of 45s for this fine West Coast group, as all of them got released as either an a or b - side on the shorter format. Two of them, "I'll Make It Easy" and "Heart And Soul", are blessed with captivating arrangements which must have helped them to reach #39 and #45 respectively on the soul charts but maybe best of all is the heart-rending "Standing Here Crying" which, despite what the album cover says, was not a hit single, although it was a brilliant side with a pain-racked vocal and richly satisfying production. The trio of songs I have mentioned above were all delivered by Cal Waymon and he takes the majority of leads throughout with Denise Erwin assuming responsibility on a few songs such as "All Of A Sudden". "There's Nothing Else To Say Baby" borrows heavily from "Reach Out I'll Be There" and became a big record on the "Northern Soul" scene in England before the term even existed. It's on ok side, but I much prefer the group on slower material, which is where they excelled, even if outfits with such strong doo-wop influences were becoming quite unusual by the mid-sixties. By the time the LP was released the group were down to a trio of Waymon, Erwin and Don Ray Sampson (although poor Sampson is ignored as regards sleeve credits) but the earliest songs on the LP were cut before Sampson joined and Jean Smith and Carl Gilbert were still part of The Incredibles. By 1969 the group was finished but Waymon went on to release a couple of unsuccessful solo singles.

I.N.D

MIchael Mills; Christopher Mills; Darron Farmer; Elmer Caldwell; Eugene Gillis; Quincy Ford; Cornell Monroe; George Lloyd; Lee Holloway

Into New Dimensions 1981 Erect ESLP 302 Producer: Jim Porter

Jim (or James) Porter produced a number of records in or around the Chicago area but this was not one of his better efforts. I.N.D. were just too similar to Earth, Wind & Fire to exude any real sense of their own identity and this LP can be summed up simply, really: if you like EWAF you should like this, if you don't you won't. There are fast tracks and slow tracks and a high Philip Bailey falsetto on show and all of the material is self-written by the band, which is to their credit, but not one of the songs would be able to muscle its way onto a *Spirit* or *That's The Way Of The World*. Neither the album nor a couple of singles from it sold well.

Independents (see also Chuck Jackson and Silk)

Chuck Jackson; Maurice Jackson; Eric Thomas; Helen Curry

The First Time We Met 1972 Wand WDS 694 Producer: Art Productions (Billboard soul charts: 18 ; Billboard pop charts: 127)

Chuck, Helen, Eric, Maurice 1973 Wand WDS 696
Producers: Chuck Jackson & Marvin Yancy

Greatest Hits - Discs Of Gold 1974 Wand WDS 699
(Billboard soul charts: 42 ; Billboard pop charts: 209)

First Time We Met - The Greatest Hits 1986
Charly CRB 1146 (UK)

The Independents may have the highest "hit" rate of any group in soul music history: they only released eight singles and every one of them reached the soul top #40. Chuck Jackson had written songs for Jerry Butler while Helen Curry and Maurice Jackson (no relation to Chuck) had both released solo singles that went nowhere, but by the time The Independents were formed in 1972 none of the trio had a vast amount of music industry experience. It's also interesting to note that despite their Chicago origins The Independents tend to be ignored when people talk about the great soul acts from that city, a state of affairs that is doubtless influenced by the fact that they didn't record for the famous record labels from the Windy City.

The first 45, "Just As Long As You Need Me", was in fact more or less a duet between Chuck Jackson and Marvin Yancy before an Independents group even existed. As the record sped up the soul charts (it eventually came to rest at #8) Jackson decided he needed to create a proper outfit and recruited the other Jackson and Curry (Yancy decided to concentrate on his songwriting and was never a member of The Independents) and it is these three who we see on the front cover of the initial LP. "I Just Want To Be There" was the first 45 to be issued by the "genuine" Independents and it was a sweet slow number, even though its soul chart placing of #38 was the lowest of their short career; "Leaving Me", though, came next and that shot right to #1, as well as a very healthy showing of #21 pop and soon afterwards "Baby I've Been Missing You" reached #4 soul as well. It was a seriously impressive start to a career and all four singles were contained within *The First Time We Met*, and they typified the approach Chuck Jackson wanted: down-tempo songs, unobtrusively orchestrated with strong lyrics, memorable hooks and understated harmonies. Only two cuts raised the tempo much above walking pace: the cool and attractive "Can't Understand It" which Jackson and Yancy had penned for Jerry Butler and Brenda Lee Eager a couple of years earlier, and the brassy, strutting " I Love You Yes, I Do". Chuck takes most leads but Maurice Jackson does a fine job on "Couldn't Hear Nobody Say (I Love You Like I Do)."

By the time of their second LP, a couple of rather odd things happened. Firstly, it contained a song called "The First Time We Met" which logically of course should have been included on the debut and second, it failed dismally to chart although it contained two more hit soul singles in the aforementioned "First Time We Met" (#20) and the excellent pleading "It's All Over"(#12). The group had now extended to become a quartet with the addition of Eric Thomas but apart from the fact that *Chuck, Helen, Eric, Maurice* included fewer slow tracks than on the debut, it was still recognisably The Independents. Helen brought an interesting harmonic texture to bear as there were not many other acts who shared the outfit's three men one woman configuration but there were cuts on here where she couldn't be heard at all, and presumably wasn't singing. Maurice Jackson took the lead on "Lucky Fellow" a song he had recorded when he was singing solo a few years before and overall it was another strong collection, full of worthwhile tracks.

There were two more soul hits in 1974, the atypically pacy "Arise And Shine (Let's Get It On)" (#19) and the snail-slow and exquisitely soulful "Let This Be A Lesson To You" which climbed to #7 and has claims to be their finest outing. However, no more "proper" LPs were forthcoming and fans had to be content with locating these two sides on the *Greatest Hits - Discs Of Gold* collection. The group was now closed down by Chuck Jackson who wanted to concentrate on writing huge selling records with Marvin Yancy for Yancy's wife, Natalie Cole, although he - Jackson - did begin a solo career later in the seventies, while Thomas and Maurice Jackson went on to help form a new group, Silk, and Curry returned to releasing solo records.

Independent Movement

Jayne Hall; Jerry Whittington; John Brown; Steve Wilson

Slippin' Away 1978 Polydor PD-1- 6152 Producer: Tom Washington

A quartet from Chicago by the name of Midwest Franchise released a couple of decent singles in 1976 and 1977 on MCA but they did not make much impression on the record buying public. They therefore changed their name to Independent Movement and released a couple of decent singles in 1978 and 1979 but they did not impinge on the consciousness of the record buying public, either. At least under the new name they also got the chance to cut an LP. And a good one too: highly orchestrated with skilful playing by some of Chicago's finest musicians, and some first rate singing by the group, particularly Jayne Hall who went on to record a handful of dance records as Jayne Edwards in the eighties. For reasons I have been unable to fathom, nearly all of the songs on the album were written by Russell Stone and Pete Wingfield and George Chandler from the Olympic Runners, all of whom were UK based. My favoured tracks are "One In A Million" and "Whatever Happened To The Good Times" both to be found on the more mellow second side. Turn the record over and we find four dance tracks, and apart from the so-so "Wall To Wall Happiness" I like them all. In fact, this whole LP is a good one. It's not "unknown" to soul fans and many will already own it but I suspect they may not have played it for a long time. It's well worth digging out again.

Individuals

Bobby Wilkes; Earl Singleton; Michael Dowden

Together We Can Make Something Happen 1975 P.I.P. 6816 Producer: Art Productions

Yet another Chicago outfit, the Individuals were one of a number of groups (another example being Independent Movement) from that city who were managed, produced, mentored or encouraged by Eddie Thomas, a great local music man. The trio came and went without many people noticing, with only this one LP and two singles pulled from it standing as testimony as to their existence. The album certainly had an eye-catching cover, as sexually explicit as any in the entire book and would probably have to be stocked "under the counter" in these politically correct days were it to be released now. It appears that Wilkes took the leads and he has an appealing high straining tenor, and he is backed up admirably by Singleton and Dowden. The songs are the weakest aspect of a nevertheless likeable set, and The Individuals performed considerably better on slower material; the title track, "I Want You For Myself" and "I Love The Way You Love" are all highly enjoyable but the majority of the faster songs are mundane and it's a mystery to me how "Gotta Make A Move" managed to make it to #70 on the soul charts as a 45. Art productions was a vehicle for Chuck Jackson and Marvin Yancy so presumably it is they who did the producing.

None of the trio stayed in the music business so far as I know and it appears that Singleton and Dowden have passed away in the last few years. (I think Bobby Wilkes is probably the same person who had a single on the Tragar label as Nathan Wilkes and he and Singleton also wrote a song for the funk group Ripple.)

Ingram (see also Philly Cream)

Butch Ingram; Timmy Ingram; Johnny Ingram; Bill Ingram; Barbara Ingram; Jimmy Ingram; Robert Ingram

The Ingram Kingdom 1976 Excello 8031 Producer: L B Young Productions Inc.

That's All 1977 H & L 69021 Producer: Landy McNeal and Ingram

Would You Like To Fly 1983 Mirage 90075-1 Producer: Ingram

Night Stalkers 1984 Mirage 90150-1 Producer: Family Productions

By 1976 Barbara Ingram, despite being totally unknown to the world, had sung on any number of million selling records as one third of a trio (the others were Evette Benton and Carla Benson) known as "The Sweethearts of Sigma" who provided backing vocals on records cut at that highly successful studio.

In that year she joined up with her five brothers (all of whom, like her, came from Camden, New Jersey) to record an album on the Excello label under the name of *The Ingram Kingdom*. Excello was better known as a blues rather than soul label and it was also way past its commercial heyday by the middle of the seventies and these factors contributed to its rather getting lost in the marketplace, although the fact that it wasn't very good didn't help either. The guitar driven funk was a bit weedy, and the songs were not remotely as strong as Barbara would normally work with.

Having done her bit, Barbara returned full time to session singing, and the five brothers carried on alone, shortening their name to "Ingram" and finding a new label, H & L, in the process.

That's All was an improvement on the debut as the funk was tighter and more aggressive but it was still a rather humdrum offering when compared to the finest on offer in 1977. Best tracks: "Mi Sabrina Tequana" at nine minutes long really allowed the group to stretch out in a jazz-funk groove; "I Just Wanna Testify" (not the Parliaments/Johnnie Taylor song) had the best singing on the set, although "I Don't Want To Be Alone" ran it close. "Get Your Stuff Off", a dull song, reached the hardly heady heights of #97 soul in early 1978 but that was still a better performance than any other 45 they ever released managed.

In 1979 the group effectively started to record under the name of Philly Cream for a couple of years (although others certainly helped them out) and even scored a couple of charting singles as a result but this project soon fizzled out and they once again returned to cutting records as Ingram in the early eighties.

They recorded their best album in 1983, the thoughtful, warm and well-performed *Would You Like To Fly*. Their singing was better than before, with either James or John providing tough and soulful leads, and even if a couple of things were a little boring and predictable, such as "D.J.s Delight" and "Groovin' On A Groove", most of the rest was good. "Share A Dream" was notably attractive, "We Got To Do It" had some fine gruff vocalising, the title track drifted around nicely enough and "No One" used its subtle EWAF influence to good effect. It wasn't a success, although it deserved to be.

Their last outing was nice too, and Ingram must have had something going for them if they could create songs with titles like "Hot Body", "Drivin' Me Crazy", and "When You're Hot, You're Hot" that were worth listening to. That something could be summed up as being better singers and writers than most of their contemporaries in the self-contained and/or funk band stakes. (Barbara was back singing back-ups on the Mirage albums, by the way, but she wasn't particularly audible.) "Just For You" was probably the best cut and the title track the worst. Once again though, large sales weren't forthcoming and apart from a couple more singles later on in the decade we were to hear no more from the group. Barbara sadly died in 1994.

Jimmy Ingram

Jimmy Meets Kiko 1970 Halima 1069 Produced by Tom Hart

I think most record collectors like oddities and this is certainly one. Jimmy Ingram is a soulful singer whom I believe was based in the Philippines while a member of the U.S. Air Force. Either that or he simply lived there. Kiko is one Kiko Gatchalian who conducted a local orchestra. They came together for this recording at a Manila studio. When Jimmy is absent the tracks sound like Mantovani. When he appears, on "Who's Making Love", "Chokin' Kind", "Everybody Loves A Winner", "I Never Found A Girl" and "Poor Side OF Town", the results are most enjoyable. I can find no trace of any other records by Jimmy Ingram apart from a 45 on Zundak but I have no idea if this is the same man. I'm assuming the date of the LP was 1970 as "1-6-70" is etched into the runout groove.

Luther Ingram

I've Been Here All The Time 1971 Koko KOS-2201
Producers: Johnnie Baylor & Willie Hall (Billboard soul charts: 21 ; Billboard pop charts: 175)

If Loving You Is Wrong I Don't Want To Be Right 1972 Koko KOS-2202 Producer: Johnny Baylor (Billboard soul charts: 5 ; Billboard pop charts: 39)

Let's Steal Away To The Hideaway 1976 Koko KOA 1300 Producer: Johnnie Baylor

Do You Love Somebody 1977 Koko KOA-1302 Producer: Johnnie Baylor

Luther Ingram was born in Jackson, Tennessee, only about 100 miles away from where he would record a number of his impressive run of hits some thirty five years later: Memphis. The title track of his first LP could be taken as referring to the fact that although he had established a name for himself in the early seventies he had already recorded for a handful of labels in the sixties without making more than the merest ripple on the vast sea that was soul music.

I've Been Here All The Time was really a rounding-up of Ingram's singles to date on the Koko label, rather than a collection of songs consciously cut to create an LP; they cover a period of time of just under three years and no fewer than seven of them reached the soul charts. It's an utterly winning set, with no weak tracks at all and a perfect example of why Stax (who were by now distributing Koko releases) was one of the greatest of all soul labels. The magnificent orchestration, production and arrangements were all beyond reproach and lovely little touches abound throughout such as the horns conjuring up the sound of the "Ghetto Train" and the ferocious punchy intro to "I'll Just Call You Honey". "Pity For The Lonely" and "To The Other Man" also have a distinct country feel, which adds to their charm. Of the seven charting 45s, the dead-slow "Ain't That Loving You" was the biggest at #6 soul and #45 pop, also serving as proof that Ingram was a soul singer of unusual sensitivity and distinctiveness. Excellent writer too: he wrote or co-wrote seven of the twelve songs.

In the summer of 1972 Ingram released the single by which he will always be best known, "(If Loving You Is Wrong) I Don't Want To Be Right." It went all the way to #1 soul, but also to #3 pop, making it one of the most successful "cheating" songs of all-time. It's an excellent record, even if I can't help preferring Millie Jackson's later astounding version, and it was followed up on the soul charts by another fine side "I'll Be Your Shelter (In The Time Of Storm)" which also did very well: #9 soul and #40 pop. And he wasn't finished yet as the lovely, lazy swagger of "Always" carried him to #11 soul and #64 pop in early 1973, before "Love Ain't Gonna Run Me Away" became the fourth soul hit (#23) from the LP named after his million selling 45. That wonderful soul man Tommy Tate contributed three songs, two of which, "Help Me Love" and "I Remember", he had already recorded himself with the same backing tracks that were used behind Ingram's interpretations. That was a slight disappointment and the same could be said for "I Can't Stop" as it was the third time Luther had recorded it, although this was the first version that had come out on an LP. Nevertheless, it was another top class album, and easily his biggest seller. (By the way people should not be fooled by the number of Johnny Baylor credits on Ingram's songs as it was alleged that he never wrote a word of any of them; his reputation was so fearsome, however, that it would have taken a great deal of courage for anyone to demand his name's removal.)

Baylor's questionable business practices and consequential investigations by offices of the law led to Koko's being mothballed as a label between 1974 and 1976; when it was resurrected there would have been a need for a new distribution deal given that Stax had gone bankrupt, but in the event the label went it alone, doubtless a major factor behind the deterioration of Ingram's chart performance. He didn't go hitless, however, and "Ain't Good For Nothing" managed to reach #44 soul in the summer of 1976. Oddly, it was not included on his new LP, *Let's Steal Away To The Hideaway* (the cover of which looked more than a little similar to the one for *If Loving You Is Wrong*), where it would logically have sat, but was included on the *next* one, by which time it was 18 months old.

The album is another strong one, sounding defiantly and elegantly out of step with virtually everything else in 1976; doubtless there would be some who thought Baylor and Ingram were making a mistake by so completely abstaining from any attempt to pander to disco, and because all of the cuts could have sat comfortably on I*f Loving You Is Wrong*, presumably thought the sound was hopelessly out of date, too. But there *was* still an audience for such unadulterated southern soul and the churning and tough "I Like The Feeling" placed at #35 soul, two places higher than the marvellous title track. All of the album was cut as Muscle Shoals and those almost peerless players contributed significantly to the thoroughly enjoyable outing which was highly consistent throughout..

Ingram's last Koko album, *Do You Love Somebody,* was another triumph, and one of the top ten or so best from any soul artist in the latter half of the seventies. Although the strings and rhythm on "Time Machine" demonstrated that Ingram and Baylor were finally aware of the disco phenomenon, it was another achingly soulful set, and one which demonstrates why at its best, the music has a depth and maturity that is timeless. The ten tracks that make up the album are the antithesis of "everything is sunny" dance music, and its catalogue of broken love affairs, double dealing people and disillusionment, brilliantly depicted in the gorgeously arranged last track, "Faces", would be seen as too much of a "downer" for some people but Ingram carries it off magnificently. Against the tales of woe it's good to be reminded that love did sometimes have a chance of working out for Luther and the title track and "Get To Me", are two fantastic "up" cuts with wonderful horn charts that did good business as singles, reaching #13 and #41 on the soul charts respectively. It was his last work on Koko and he hadn't even come close to ever releasing a sub-standard side in his entire time with the label.

Luther Ingram 1986 Profile PRO-1226 Producers: Michael Day, Roger Hawkins, Jimmy Johnson & Luther Ingram (Billboard soul charts: 61)

Whatever one may think about Johnny Baylor the fact is that he helped Ingram attain 17 soul charts entrants, but by the time of Luther's next 45 in 1984, the two were no longer working together.

That single did not lead to a new album but one did arrive in 1986 which was exciting news at the time although listening to it certainly tempered that enthusiasm, even if it was still certainly better than it could have been. The majority of the set was recorded in Urbana Illinois, and was highly contemporary with electric drums and other distasteful touches on board, best exemplified by the witless thumping behind the pretty song, "Right Away". However, It was good to see that such a traditional soul man could still score hits that year and the LP contained three soul chart entrants in the tuneful numbers "Baby Don't Go Too Far" (#29) and "Don't Turn Around" (#55) and a much too heavy-handed cover of Bob Dylan's "Gotta Serve Somebody" (#89). Happily, three songs were also recorded at Muscle Shoals and don't "All In The Name Of Love", "Make You Feel Loved Again" and "How Sweet It Would Be" just *look* like they are real soul records merely by their titles. They were not the greatest sides ever cut in that legendary location but all were good and bore Ingram's most engaged singing on the album. (He had cut the latter song years before but it wasn't released until 1991 on a CD entitled *926 East McLemore*.) A version of the old standard "You Don't Know Me" closed out the LP but my version is so off-key (not Ingram's fault, the pressing company's) as to be unlistenable. I assume all other copies suffer from this, too. The LP even reached the soul charts, a feat his last Koko albums couldn't manage and all in all it had to be classed as a pretty reasonable return to the industry, even if it falls a long way short of his previous sets artistically.

By 1987 he had serious health issues and never recorded (and hardly ever performed) again and eventually died in 2007. Because he didn't cut many dance songs throughout his Koko career and because the label didn't get issued in the UK I have always felt that he has been under appreciated over here, but I rate him very highly indeed.

Instant Funk

Scotty Miller; Kim Miller; Raymond Earl; Dennis Richardson; Elijah Jones; Michael Giss; Donald Lamons; James Carmichael; Larry Davis; George Bell; Johnny Onderlinde; Eric Huff; Charles Williams

Get Down With The Philly Jump 1976 TSOP PZ 34358 Producer: Bunny Sigler

Instant Funk Salsoul SA 8513 Producer: Bunny Sigler (Billboard soul charts: 1 ; Billboard pop charts: 12)

Witch Doctor 1979 Salsoul SA 8529 Producer: Bunny Sigler (Billboard soul charts: 23 ; Billboard pop charts: 129)

The Funk Is On 1980 Salsoul SA 8536 Producer: Bunny Sigler (Billboard soul charts: 62 ; Billboard pop charts: 130)

Looks So Fine 1982 Salsoul SA 8545 Producers: Bunny Sigler & Instant Funk (Billboard soul charts: 43 ; Billboard pop charts: 147)

Instant Funk V 1983 Salsoul SA 8558 Producer: Bunny Sigler (Billboard soul charts: 47)

Kinky 1983 Salsoul SA 8564 Producer: Bunny Sigler

Instant Funk were undeniably Bunny Sigler's group. He wrote and arranged most of their songs over the eight years in which they recorded, and produced the lot. He initially saw them as an outlet to support his musical ideas which he felt were constrained by the more rigid dictates of the MFSB rhythm section and had started to use Instant Funk on a number of his solo releases in the first half of the seventies; by 1976 they began to issue records under their own name.

The first album was not a great introduction to a new group, as although there was a lot going on in the production, particularly in the brass section, it wasn't particularly interesting, and one could search the whole album in vain for any semblance of a melody. Sigler often harked right back to the twenties from time to time for musical inspiration and I don't doubt he had fun making the record, but it has stood the test of time poorly. Even the front cover was weak, an out of focus shot of a pair of lips, and the only cut I would ever think about playing again for pleasure is "So Glad I'm The One", which is pretty much a Sigler record anyway, given he sings it. Elsewhere the tracks were mainly instrumental with the odd snatch of vocal here and there. It didn't sell many copies and bore no hit singles which made what came next seem so surprising.

That was a #1 soul and #20 pop single in "I Got My Mind Made Up (You Can Get It Girl)" a rather repetitive dance number that obviously caught the attention of large numbers of record buyers. I preferred the more tuneful "Crying" but as that only made #41 soul and missed the pop charts altogether not many would agree with me. The group had a decent lead singer at this time in James Carmichael (not the producer) and while he was talented the material didn't require too much from him, as apart from "Never Let It Go Away", everything was frantic and danceable or midtempo and danceable. Sigler must have been ecstatic with life though as the album went gold.

As with a number of other self-contained bands around 1979 or 1980 I rather lost interest with Instant Funk as their albums became more and more formulaic and their lack of variety and slower material started to pall. They continued to post singles on the soul charts fairly frequently but none of them became genuine hits, and indeed, a "Greatest Hits" or even "Best Of" vinyl album never appeared. We had to wait for the CD age for that.

By 1983 or so the group had split up. They were never a band I could get excited about but anyone who likes funky, hard dance music that doesn't take itself too seriously might want to investigate Instant Funk. (Elijah Jones went on to cut a pretty decent solo album in 1986, *In The Land Of Making Love*.)

Intensive Heat

Bernard Lindsey; John Lindsey; Walter Lindsey

Intensive Heat 1982 My Disc AL 38281 Producers: Raymond Reid & William Anderson

The cover of this album doesn't look promising as regards soulful content: three good-looking and youthful brothers doubtless meant to appeal to teenage girls; but producers Reid and Anderson from Crown Heights Affair manage to coax a surprisingly soulful lead from one of the brothers on "I Know Now" and all the singing on "Come With Me" is enjoyable. The other six tracks are predictable dance fodder.

Intrigues

Alfred Brown; James Lee; James Harris; Ronald Hamilton

In A Moment 1970? Yew YS 777 Producers: Bobby Martin & Thom Bell

Thom Bell is rightly associated with symphonic arrangements, pretty melodies and high tenor vocalists, and therefore it might be expected that the one album by The Intrigues would follow that formula; but it doesn't. This is not to say that it is in anyway a stripped-down, funky to the bone outing, as it most certainly isn't, but it's not just a reprisal of The Delfonics' exquisite and highly orchestrated exercises in heartbreak, either.

The Intrigues were from Philadelphia but, despite seeing three of the nine singles they released have some national success, which is not a bad ratio, did not sustain a long career. Their first single arrived in 1969, their last in 1972. Most of the tracks on the album are at least mid-tempo in pace, but few of them are exceptional. There are good things, however, in the shape of the memorable and tuneful title track (which has always reminded me a bit of "My Sweet Lord") and decent offerings from Martin in "Love Is Just Around The Corner" and the Akins, Drayton, Turner team for "I'm Gonna Love You". The covers don't really work as I'm not convinced "Light My Fire" is well suited to soul interpretations, while "Mojo Hannah" and "I Wish It Would Rain" are rather functional. "In A Moment" was a big selling single, #10 soul and #31 pop, while the follow-up, the aforementioned "I'm Gonna Love You", did reach the *Cashbox* soul charts although failed to feature on *Billboard*. "The Language Of Love" was their third charting single (at #21 soul in the middle of 1971) but it is not included on the album. Because I am besotted with soul from Philadelphia I do enjoy listening to this LP, but would recommend many others in front of it as better examples of what the city could offer.

Intruders

Samuel "Little Sonny" Brown; Phil Terry; Eugene Daughtery; Robert Edwards; Bobby Starr; Lee Williams; Al Miller; Fred Daughtery

Together 1967 Gamble GS 5001 No producer listed

Cowboys To Girls 1968 Gamble G5004 Producers: Kenny Gamble & Leon Huff (Billboard soul charts: 11 ; Billboard pop charts: 112)

Greatest Hits 1969 Gamble GS 5005 Producers: Kenny & Leon Huff (Billboard soul charts: 19 ; Billboard pop charts: 144)

When We Get Married 1970 Gamble SG 5008 Producers: Kenny Gamble & Leon Huff (Billboard soul charts: 48)

Save The Children 1973 Gamble KZ 31991 Producers: Kenny Gamble & Leon Huff (Billboard soul charts: 12; Billboard pop charts: 133)

Super Hits 1973 P.I.R. PZ 32131 (Billboard soul charts: 51; Billboard pop charts: 205)

There were numerous "better" soul singers than "Little Sonny" Brown, but none, I submit, who can match his ability to make an emotional connection with any listener able to respond to his extraordinarily affecting voice; I strongly include myself in this, and know there are many others who feel the same way. It was Brown, therefore, who contributed more than anyone else to make The Intruders one of the best loved and most successful vocal groups of the period from 1966-1975 but it would be wrong to deny that many others played their part too: clearly, the other three members of the group, but chiefly Gamble and Huff who provided the quartet with hit after hit.

But there weren't hits in the beginning, which was right back in 1961 when the North Philadelphia group's first single was released. Three more non-hit 45s followed (one issued as by The Four Intruders) over a period of a few years until, in the summer of 1966, they had their first success with "(We'll Be United)" which climbed to #14 soul and #78 pop. It was featured on their first LP, *Together*, which contained their next four soul hits too: "Devil With An Angel's Smile", "Baby I'm Lonely", "A love That's Real" and the title track as well as the non-charting "It Must Be Love". Playing it today is fascinating and very far from a hi-fi listening experience. Quite apart from Brown's voice, which always rambled all over the place, the arrangements and musical interjections have a quaint charm and unpredictable quality: the trumpet that appears out of the murk on "Gonna Be Strong", the startling string charts on "A Book For The Brokenhearted" and the almost absurdly fast "Check Yourself" are merely three examples. The album is often beautiful too, with exquisite backing vocals on many of the songs, a number of which are almost naive in their simplicity and touching belief in the power of love and the overall effect conjures up a gentler and more peaceful time, which frankly wasn't really the case in Philadelphia in 1967. Gamble and Huff produced the set even though they weren't credited and wrote eleven of the generous 12 tracks. However, they were merely warming up.

Warm turned to hot in 1968 when "Cowboys To Girls", became a #1 and #6 pop single and the title track of their sophomore LP. It features one of Little Sonny's most moving vocals, which he matches on "Sad Girl" (#14 soul, #47 pop) and the devastating "Friends No More" which is as perfect an example of a great soul vocal group record as exists. However, it's a slightly uneven set, as "Call Me" and "By The Time I Get To Phoenix" were uninspired song choices even if the latter has some of Brown's most endearing off-key moments, while one or two of Gamble and Huff's other songs were well suited to being album only cuts. But I'm carping a tad, as I love the LP, and it has a crisper and cleaner production than *Together* and also bears another excellent single in "(Love Is Like A) Baseball Game", another highly successful outing, reaching #4 soul and #26 pop.

A most worthwhile *Greatest Hits* appeared in 1969, which featured two hits in "Slow Drag" and "Me Tarzan, You Jane" and two b-sides in "Girls, Girls, Girls" and "(Who's Your) Favourite Candidate" that had not appeared on the two albums that has thus far been issued. Symbolically, though, my copy wobbles about as much as a Brown vocal.

Unfortunately, things took a turn for the worse with the *When We Get Married* LP. Firstly, "Little Sonny" had left the group (euphemistically described as "devoting himself to his family" on the sleeve; he had a number of personal problems in reality) and second, Gamble and Huff seemed to be losing interest in The Intruders as they had never before served up such poor songs as "Hocus Pocus" and "Wonder What Kind Of Bag She's In". It certainly wasn't a total disaster as the new lead singer Bobby Starr could skilfully re-create Brown's style to a fine degree, and three more soul hits were contained within: the title track (#8), "This is My Love Song" (#22) and "Tender (Was The Love We Knew)" (#25) but there was nothing to make the heart beat faster and not a single track I would include in my list of all-time favourite Intruders' sides although another point in the set's favour was that it was one of the first from the Gamble and Huff empire to display the names of the musicians on the sleeve.

By 1973 Brown had returned to the group, just in time to help record the group's masterpiece, *Save The Children*. There is a school of thought that maintains that soul music as its best requires singers to scream out their pain over tough rhythm tracks, and certainly many great records follow this formula but they don't have to; while *Save The Children* has a title track that covers a serious social topic much of the rest of the set is about fun, regrets and nostalgia and the spoken passages on "I Wanna Know Your Name" and the joshing and banter on the magnificent "I'll Always Love My Mama" are great moments in soul; they sound so real, and invite the listener in to records that could have backfired badly. The latter song is a soundtrack to my own life in a way no other can match: I danced to it in the Revolution club in Brighton as a 17 year old when I was starting to realise the music would become my life's passion (the whole club would sing along to it, too) and in 2012 it was played at my own mother's funeral. I can never hear it without deep emotion and that goes for most of the rest of the album too, as it was delightful to hear this great group receiving the benefit of the lush but punchy production values Philadelphia International could bring to bear and the material ("Mother And Child Reunion" excepted) is perfect too: "Save The Children" itself flows along seamlessly; "Hang On In There" has a brilliant introduction and gorgeous melodic flow while "To Be Happy Is The Real Thing", "Teardrops" and "Memories Are Here To Stay" are all top-class songs with top-class back-up singing from the rest of the group. And then there is Little Sonny: he inhabits these songs with his usual unmatched charm and warmth (listen to his opening "hmmmms" on "Hang On In There") and if the girl he was chatting up on "I Wanna Know Your Name" didn't fall for him she must be mad. It did well as a single at #9 soul and #60 pop but "Mama" did even better at #6 and #36 respectively.

The Intruders were pretty hot again and a *Super Hits* package did fairly well in late summer of 1973 although it could have been more generous, only including 12 tracks. The UK version added "Mama" and "(Win, Place or Show) "She's A Winner" a #12 soul hit the U.S. and their only successful single in Britain.

Energy of Love 1975 TSOP KZ 33149 Producers: Kenny Gamble, Leon Huff, Vince Montana, John Davis, Bruce Hawes, Carey Gilbert, Theodore Life & Phil Terry (Billboard soul charts: 41)

After the riches of *Save The Children, Energy Of Love* was rather disappointing: there was a sense once again that Gamble and Huff had their eyes on other acts, and some of the song covers were uninspired. "Be Thankful For What You Got" will always be associated with William DeVaughn, "What's Easy For Two Is So Hard For One" didn't match Mary Wells' version while Marvin Gaye's "Jan" simply has no melody. Furthermore, "Everyone's A Star" sounded almost exactly like "Thankful" and was more a vehicle for the MFSB rhythm section than for the group. However, there were two cuts, both singles, which stand with the group's best: "Rainy Days And Mondays" was an inspired choice of song to cover, on which Brown gives a meandering and mesmerising reading while the disarmingly honest "A Nice Girl Like You" is one of the finest dance records of the seventies. The other four cuts were good enough but as this was the last ever album by the "classic" Intruders line-up it left a lingering sense of what might have been.

Who Do You Love 1985 Streetwave MKL 6 Producer: Leon Bryant (UK)

The group broke up soon after the release of the album but a "new" Intruders appeared in 1985. The only member who had a link to the old group was Eugene Daughtery (or Daughtry, spellings vary) while interestingly the new lead singer was the excellent Lee Williams of The Cymbals semi-fame. It must be said that it was hardly an auspicious comeback as the record wasn't even released in the U.S. but it's not a bad dance oriented outing, and listening to Williams sing is never a hardship, but the only really good cut is the ballad, "Tell Me", although "Dedicated" and "Spend A Little Time (With Me)" are nice enough.

The new group didn't last long either and The Intruders really were no more. The nineties were a desperate time for the old team as Little Sonny committed suicide in 1995, one year after Eugene Daughtery had passed away. As should be clear, I love The Intruders and regret that I have limited space in which to say anything about Robert "Big Sonny" Edwards and the top class songwriter Phil Terry but they played a massive part too in the history of one of soul's greatest groups.

Invisible Man's Band (see also The Stairsteps)

Keni Burke; Clarence Burke; Dennis Burke; James Burke

The Invisible Man's Band 1980 Mango MLPS-9537 Producer: Clarence Burke and Alex Masucci (Billboard soul charts: 19; Billboard pop charts: 90)

Really Wanna See You 1981 Boardwalk NB1-33238 Producer: Clarence Burke and Alex Masucci

The Stairsteps were an impressive family from Chicago who managed to go their own way throughout most of their career without obviously aping anyone else. In 1980 four of the Burke boys hung up the Stairsteps name and released a couple of albums under the name of The Invisible Man's Band. These are not my favourite recordings from the family. In fact, I'd go as far as to say that the first LP on Mango is almost totally devoid of any soul content apart from the sweetly lilting "9 Xs Out Of Every Ten". I always managed to resist the call of the dance floor in 1980 when "All Night Thing" was played in discos but I can just about see its appeal and why it reached #9 soul and #45 pop as a single; I can't give any such latitude to the other four dance tracks though, which are all dull.

A second LP appeared which contains crisper and harder tracks, verging more towards funk and away from disco, with the best track being the guitar driven "Rated X", and it is all the better for it. The fair title track was pulled from the set as a 45 and made it to #79 soul in early 1982 but the group's time was nearly up. A year later a non-album cut, "Sunday Afternoon", scraped to #77 soul and that was the last record from the group.

Ironing Board Sam

The Ninth Wonder Of The World Of Music
1970? Board ? Producer: Sammie Moore?

Ironing Board Sam (Sammie Moore) was thought to have been killed by Hurricane Katrina. Luckily he was not, and in the last few years he has even started to enjoy a little bit of acclaim, something generally denied him over the previous fifty years - although he did make the odd T.V. appearance in the sixties - as his handful of singles and one LP were pressed up in small quantity, and few were sold. He has always been a talented singer, with a rich and flexible voice but sadly appears to have endured an almost stereotypically tough life.

That one album was apparently limited to 100 copies only and I have never held one in my hand. The covers shows Sam with his "button board" in hand and the songs within appear to be safe and disappointing choices : "Bye Bye Blackbird" and "Danny Boy", for example but as I have neither seen nor heard the LP I am not sure how many tracks were included, nor what year it first appeared (it has been re-released since.)

Isley Brothers

O'Kelly Isley; Ronald Isley; Rudolph Isley; Ernie Isley; Marvin Isley; Chris Jasper

Shout! 1959 RCA LSP-2156 Producer: Hugo and Luigi

Twist And Shout 1962 Wand WDS 653 No producer listed (Billboard pop charts:61)

Twisting and Shouting 1963 United Artists UAL 3313 Producer: Bert Berns

In The Beginning 1971 T-Neck TNS 3007 Producers: Ronald Isley, Kelly Isley & Rudolph Isley

Ohio has been the birthplace of many great soul acts over the years and Cincinnati gave us The Isley Brothers, one of the most enduring and successful of all. Apart from their eighteen top five soul singles the brothers enjoyed seven #1 vinyl albums on the soul charts. The Temptations, Aretha Franklin and Stevie Wonder are the only three who can exceed that total although five others can equal it. Moreover, the Isleys had genuine hit records in every decade from the fifties right through to the "noughties" this century, an unparalleled performance by any other soul act, and quite possibly by any artist in any genre.

Mind you, there was little indication in the beginning that they would become so famous. For a start a handful of 45s in the late fifties on labels like Teenage, Cindy and Gone did nothing and their first LP contained tracks like "He's Got The Whole World In His Hands", "Rock Around The Clock" and "When The Saints Go Marching In." However, it also included "Shout" and that was their first ever success, eventually going on to sell a million copies as a single, even if, surprisingly, it did not reach the *Billboard* soul charts (which admittedly only consisted of the top selling 25 records back in 1959, but even so...). That song, written by the group, was to become their calling card for a long time to come and must have made them a lot of money of the years given the number of cover versions it has spawned.

A handful of other singles followed on RCA as did three on Atlantic and 1962 dawned on a group who had released 14 singles with only one success. The Isleys moved to Wand that year and scored their first ever soul chart entry with "Twist And Shout" which raced to #2 soul and #17 pop. An album was built around it, which predictably played up the Twist angle at every opportunity, and tracks included "Rubber Leg Twist", "Spanish Twist" and "Let's Twist again" and even a song that didn't include "twist" in the title, such as "You Better Come Home", might as well have done, given it sounded exactly like the others. The album was long on energy and short on finesse but at least the group were back and the excellent and more thoughtful and subdued "Right Now" hinted that better records may be around the corner.

Two of those records,"She's Gone" and "You'll Never Leave Him", were to be found on their one LP for United Artists, and they were a million years away from any twist nonsense, with the first being a slow gospel-influenced wailer with full production while the latter was a bright and breezy outing atop an acoustic guitar driven gentle rhythm. Neither song made it as a hit when released as singles but together with a good take on James Brown's "Please Please Please" and a first rate and slow "She's The One", constituted the best tracks on an album that saw the group still saddled with the likes of "Surf And Shout", "Do The Twist", "Shake It With Me Baby" and the rather awful "Tango".

For the next few years the group issued a number of 45s on UA and (again) Atlantic without much success with by far the most interesting of them being the cha-cha influenced original of "Who's That Lady" on UA and "Testify" on T-Neck (with Jimi Hendrix on guitar), both from 1964. They needed a change again and certainly found that in late 1965 when they moved to Motown.

In 1971 a number of these Atlantic tracks plus "Testify" were put out on a T-Neck LP to capitalise on the Isleys success and Hendrix' death.

This Old Heart Of Mine 1966 Tamla S-269 Producers: Brian Holland & Lamont Dozier (Billboard soul charts: 15 ; Billboard pop charts: 140)

Soul On The Rocks 1967 Tamla TM-275 No producer listed

Behind A Painted Smile 1969 Tamla Motown TML 11112 No producer listed (UK)

The Isley Brothers 1971 Starline SRS 5098 No producer listed (UK)

Hindsight is easy 50 years on, but the cover for the *This Old Heart Of Mine* is nevertheless hard to defend: a trio of Afro-American brothers who had some name recognition, relegated to the back cover of their own debut LP for a new label in favour of two white teenagers who had nothing whatsoever to do with the record. Furthermore, the contents within didn't smack of all-out commitment on the part of Berry Gordy to break the group as an album act - although to be fair, he was hardly concentrating on breaking *anyone* as an album act at this time - given that a number of the songs (and backing tracks) had already been used by others: "Nowhere To Run", "Stop! In The Name Of Love", "Put yourself In My Place", "I Hear A Symphony" and "Baby Don't You Do It" being the best known. So this can hardly be classed as an essential album, but the Isleys did a good job on each and every track and just listening to the interplay of James Jamerson and Benny Benjamin on "Nowhere To Run", as an example, is a great pleasure in itself. The title track was easily their biggest hit on 45 while at Motown: #6 soul and #12 pop.

Soul On The Rocks was a much better LP all round. The group got the chance to grace their own album sleeve (even if not by a very flattering photo) and the cover songs were largely jettisoned although the threesome do a commendable job on Jackie Wilson's "Whispers Getting Louder", a song that certainly suited them. The music within is uplifting, bright and, frankly, fantastic. Brilliant fuzz guitar is all over the set (Robert White? Joe Messina? Eddie Willis? Maybe all of them?) while organ, bass and drums are superlative throughout. "Tell Me It's Just A Rumor Baby", "Why When Love Is Gone" and "Catching Up On Time" are the Usain Bolts of soul music, absurdly fast, and exhilarating as hell. Only the Four Tops-ish "Got To Have You Back" reached the soul charts as a single and that only at #47, and the brothers certainly missed out on an early version (if not the original) of "That's The Way Love Is" as Marvin Gaye took it to #2 soul and #7 pop in late 1969, while their own version didn't do anything. And neither did the excellent "Behind A Painted Smile" in America, although it was a top 5 pop hit in England. Only "One Too Many Heartaches" slowed the tempo down to any appreciable degree, from a highly recommended album which used about nine producers, even if none were credited.

Because of the success of "Behind A Painted Smile", the UK released an LP of that name in 1969 which consisted of the entire *Soul On The Rocks* set plus "Take Me In Your Arms (Rock Me A Little While)" which had reached #22 soul as a 45 in the States in spring of 1968 and "All Because I Love You" which had failed on single.

The group left Motown in 1968, an astute move given how successful they would become, but in England in 1971 great excitement was afoot when an album appeared that included seven previously unissued tracks from the Motor City era. Soul fans have possibly become a bit blasé about unreleased material in the last couple of decades given how much has appeared, but it was highly unusual back then. Not one of them was absolutely essential Isleys, but not one of them was sub-standard either and they all deserved their day in court, so to speak. Most amusing was "You've Got So Much To Shout About" one of a couple of attempts by Motown to make it abundantly clear to listeners that this was the same group who had recorded the hit song "Shout!".

It's Our Thing 1969 T-Neck TNS 3001 Producers: Ronald Isley, Kelly Isley and Rudolph Isley (Billboard soul charts: 2; Billboard pop charts: 22)

The Brothers: Isley 1969 T-Neck TNS 3002 Producers: Ronald Isley, Kelly Isley & Rudolph Isley (Billboard soul charts: 20 ; Billboard pop charts: 180)

Get Into Something 1970 T-Neck TNS 3006 Producers: Ronald Isley, Kelly Isley & Rudolph Isley

Givin' It Back 1971 T-Neck TNS 3008 Producers: Ronald Isley, Kelly Isley & Rudolph Isley (Billboard soul charts: 13 ; Billboard pop charts: 71)

Brother, Brother, Brother 1972 T-Neck TNS 3008 Producers: Ronald Isley, Kelly Isley & Rudolph Isley (Billboard soul charts: 5 ; Billboard pop charts: 29)

The Isleys Live 1973 T-Neck TNS 3010-2 Producers: Ronald Isley, Kelly Isley & Rudolph Isley (Billboard soul charts: 14 ; Billboard pop charts: 139)

In 1969 The Isleys resurrected the T-Neck label and started to write, arrange and produce everything they put out. It was a winning policy and for the next twenty years they were seldom without big hit records. "It's Your Thing", a loose, funky outing, entirely different from anything they had ever cut in the past, became their first gold record when it reached #1 soul and #2 pop in the spring of 1969 and served as the obvious title track of their first T-Neck LP which featured a most serious looking trio decked out in garish robes on its front cover. It's not anywhere as near as good as Soul On The Rocks as the songs lacked distinction for the most part and there was a lot of "filler" on board but apart from the hit there were some other fine moments: the marvellous drums on "Don't Give It Away", the snappy JB influenced "Give The Women What They Want", the jeering back-up vocals on "I Must Be Losing My Touch" and the slow drawn-out brassy soul of "Save Me". This last track was one of the first to point up what was their finest asset: the voice of Ronald Isley on thoughtful material. It had taken them a long time to reach this conclusion.

The group themselves seemed to realise the paucity of strong songs on *It's Your Thing* as they followed up the hit with a track from their next album, *The Brothers: Isley*. Unsurprisingly, "I Turned You On" sounded a lot like "It's Your Thing" but still did well at #6 soul and #23 pop but the public was beginning to tire of the variations on a theme when two more similar sounding songs, "Black Berries" and "Was It Good To You" only managed "#43 and #33 on the soul charts respectively and neither featured in any significant way on the pop listings. In fact, the whole of the second album strongly recalled the first: so-so material, a few filler tracks, some good funk and an excellent slow outing, this time in "Feels Like The World".

1970 was a year in which the trio concentrated on singles, placing an impressive six of them on the soul charts even if they were all rather modest hits with none reaching the soul top twenty or going any higher than #72 pop. Nevertheless, this was industry on an almost James Brown scale and all six of them were scooped up on the *Get Into Something* LP which didn't actually chart anywhere itself. The most significant of the lot was probably the title track, extended to over seven minutes on the album, as it was drenched with guitar on the second half, giving notice that Ernie Isley was about to become a key figure in the next phase of the group. In truth, much of the LP is pretty boring as we really had heard it all before in too many cases ("Bless Your Heart" is so close to "It's Your Thing" as to be hilarious) but "I Need You so" was a lovely performance from Ronald (or is it a rare Kelly lead?) with sweet back-up vocals, of a kind we would get to know extremely well as the seventies progressed. Nearly as good was an equally rare Rudolph lead vocal on "I Got To Find Me One"; had Ronald not been so gifted surely Rudolph would have stepped out front more often, as his performance is excellent.

I suspect even the group realised things were getting stale as they re-invented themselves again (people talk about how David

Bowie had done this throughout his career but The Isleys can match him) by releasing their next LP as a set entirely made up of covers, with two of them clocking in at over nine minutes long. This was a far shore indeed from Wand, UA, Atlantic and Motown. It worked too, as "Love The One You're With" and "Spill The Wine" became their biggest singles for over two years with the former going to #3 soul and #18 pop with the latter managing #14 and #49. A third single from the set, "Lay Lady Lay", didn't do quite so well but still shifted a few copies."Ohio/Machine Gun" kicked things off and such overtly political songs had never been associated with The Isley Brothers before and placing it/them at the beginning of the LP seemed to me to be a pretty clear statement about how they now wished to be perceived. Musically, the track owes much more to what Parliament/Funkadelic were putting out at the time - lots of rock guitar soloing - than to, say, The Four Tops, Impressions or James Brown and must have alienated some diehard fans. In truth, I was one of those fans as while I admired what they were doing it's not an album I pull out to play often. The other cut to concern itself with social commentary was Bill Withers' "Cold Bologna" while nearly all others addressed instead the eternal tussles between men and women, although "Spill The Wine" meanders off on its own cosmic meditations.

*Brother, Brother, Brother w*as the first Isleys' LP that spelled out credits for Ernie Isley, Marvin Isley and Chris Jasper (and a few others) and it mixed up more covers - three from Carole King - with a handful of originals by the brothers. When I first heard it I adored it, and twenty five years ago still did. Today I don't. It feels a bit like an old love affair that has run its course. This is either entirely a personal feeling or maybe this phase of their music just hasn't aged very well; *Soul On The Rocks* seems more enduring than *Brother, Brother, Brother*, despite being five years older. Anyway, the album sold a shedload and it contained another four soul charts hits, with the biggest being "Pop That Thang" at #3 and "Lay Away" at #6. A heavily truncated version of King's "It's Too Late" fared less well, reaching only #39, but on the album it was extended out to over ten minutes and features an interplay between Ronald's voice and Ernie's guitar that used to excite me. Nowadays, I prefer King's much more simple and lovely version. My head still says *Brother, Brother, Brother* is a highly enjoyable album. My heart doesn't.

Their double *Live* album leaned heavily towards the previous two albums; of the nine tracks only "It's Your Thing" was not from *Givin' It Back* or *Brother, Brother, Brother* and there was absolutely nothing from the pre T-Neck days. The performances stayed close to the studio versions, only really varying in the fact that they tended to be even longer.

3 + 3 1973 T-Neck KZ 32453 Producers: Ronald Isley, Kelly Isley & Rudolph Isley (Billboard soul charts: 2 ; Billboard pop charts: 8)

Greatest Hits 1973 T-Neck TNS 3011 (Billboard soul charts: 24; Billboard pop charts: 195)

Live It Up 1974 T-Neck PZ 33070 Producers: The Isley Brothers (Billboard soul charts: 1 ; Billboard pop charts: 14)

The Heat Is On 1975 T-Neck T-Neck PZ 33536 Producers: The Isley Brothers (Billboard soul charts: 1 ; Billboard pop charts: 1)

The Best 1976 Buddah BDS 5652-2 (Billboard soul charts: 49)

Harvest For The World 1976 T-Neck PZ 33809 Producers: The Isley Brothers (Billboard soul charts: 1 ; Billboard pop charts: 9)

Go For Your Guns 1977 T-Neck PZ 34432 Producers: The Isley Brothers (Billboard soul charts: 1 ; Billboard pop charts: 6)

Forever Gold 1977 T-Neck FZ 34452 Producers: The Isley Brothers (Billboard soul charts: 40; Billboard pop charts: 58)

Showdown 1978 T-Neck JZ 34930 C Producers: The Isley Brothers (Billboard soul charts: 1 ; Billboard pop charts: 4)

Timeless 1978 T-Neck AL 35650/1/2 KZ2 33536 Producers: The Isley Brothers (Billboard soul charts: 70; Billboard pop charts: 204)

Winner Takes All 1979 T-Neck PZ2 36077/78/79 Producers: The Isley Brothers (Billboard soul charts: 3 ; Billboard pop charts: 14)

From *3+3* onwards T-Neck started to be distributed by Columbia, another astute move from The Isleys, as it meant even greater sales to a wider audience and they now could reasonably be described as having moved into the superstar bracket. The album went gold, as did the new version of "That Lady" as a 45. Ernie, Marvin and Chris Jasper were now firmly part of the group as the album title made abundantly clear, and they also properly featured on the cover for the first time. Ernie's guitar work on "That Lady" and "Summer Breeze" made him famous, and if I now feel that also dates the LP somewhat, the whole thing still has the unmistakable whiff of "classic". The group's song-writing had suddenly improved out of all recognition and whereas they could certainly still lay down great grooves à la "It's Your Thing" we now discovered that they could also create exceptional compositions like "What It Comes Down To", "The Highways Of My Life", "If you Were There" and "You Walk Your Way" all of which were melodic and literate. Marvin's bass and Chris Jasper's keyboards also added immensely to the proceedings, particularly on a cover of "Listen To The Music" and "Sunshine (Go Away)".

There was something "off" about the cover to *Live It Up* and it took me a while to work out what it was: Ernie and Marvin Isley were both smiling. Isleys did not normally do this; maybe their big brothers forgot to remind them. It was another gold album and both the title track and "Midnight Sky" made it into the top ten of the soul singles charts even if their pop performance was disappointing, with both falling short of the top fifty. The former was also a perfect example of when only the album version will do: spread out to two parts and over six minutes long, the second half owes everything to the incoming trio and nothing to their elder siblings. Over an impeccably solid drum beat played by the talented Ernie, Chris Jasper's clavinets and synthesisers bubble along like thick porridge coming to the boil, to form a brilliant and hypnotic rhythmic melange that is just about the best thing on a rather patchy album. I also very much like the way in which Ronald gently ushers in Todd Rundgren's "Hello It's Me" with sixteen "hellos" before getting into the song and Ernie's plaintive and keening guitar notes here speak to me far more than all his pyrotechnics elsewhere. The sheer power of Ronald's singing on the ambitious and very rock-influenced - time changes galore - "Ain't I Been Good To You" is highly impressive but I got bored long before the end of the elongated version of "Midnight Sky" while "Need A Little Taste Of Love" and "Lovers Eve" are ok tracks, tailor-made to sit on an album but nothing more.

The Heat Is On represents The Isley's commercial peak. The album went gold and achieved the "double" of reaching #1 on both soul and pop charts while the lead-off single, the edgy (for the times, it sounds almost quaint today) "Fight The Power" nearly matched the performance: #1 soul and #4 pop. The album was simply devised: three fast songs on side one and three slow songs on side two, all of which were described as bearing "Parts 1 & 2". These are little things but demonstrate once again that The Isleys always strove to think about their releases and make conscious decisions; they seldom just threw tracks together randomly. It is another LP which I loved in 1975 but feel much less affection for nowadays. Ernie's guitar on side one is too dominant for my current tastes, and the lack of horns and strings on the group's records in favour of synthesisers was already starting to pall a bit and rendered them too one-dimensional; side two is nice and relaxed but a tad sleep-inducing and the music hardly leaps out of the grooves.

Apart from the excellent title track to *Harvest For The World* which I think features one of Ronald's greatest ever performances, the album was really just more of the same as *The Heat Is On*: highly successful, synthesised slow songs and a fair bit of Ernie guitar. The single version of "Who Loves You Better" was the one to get, as it is a good song, and cuts out the excessive guitar soloing. It did even better than the title track on both the soul and pop charts which I bet is a surprise to many: #3 and #47 as opposed to #9 and #63.

Go For Your Guns was the group's first ever platinum album and one of their best from the seventies. The rhythms were funky and taut, even more stripped down than usual, and the tunes by and large easy to remember after only a couple of plays. "The Pride" and "Livin' In The Life" were huge singles on the soul charts although the pop audience, while more than happy to buy the LPs in bulk, were now starting to ignore the singles, a state of affairs I imagine didn't worry the Isleys unduly. "Fight The Power" had made #4 pop as a single in the middle of 1975; they never again placed another single in the top twenty.

Showdown was another platinum album, following the formula of *Go For Your Guns*, and contained "Take Me To The Next Phase", another #1 soul single, their fourth in all. The rest of the set would delight fans of this period of their music without having any power to convert anyone who hadn't been convinced.

Either side of *Showdown* came *Forever Gold,* a hits album, and *Timeless,* which collected together twenty tracks from the period from *It's Your Thing* to *Brother, Brother, Brother.*

The Isleys exited the decade with the confidence to release another double album, *Winner Takes All*, although it performed slightly less well than the previous couple, merely going gold. On the other hand it included "I Wanna Be With You", which even though it sounded like numerous other records by the group, managed to become their fifth soul #1. Lyrically, it was a weak song and I really felt they were resting on past glories by now. They had stretched themselves so often in the past but were now content to repeat a formula record after record. And why not?

Go All The Way 1980 T-Neck FZ 36305 Producers: The Isley Brothers (Billboard soul charts: 1 ; Billboard pop charts: 8)

Grand Slam 1981 T-Neck FZ 37080 Producers: The Isley Brothers (Billboard soul charts: 3 ; Billboard pop charts: 28)

Inside You 1981 T-Neck FZ 37533 Producers: The Isley Brothers (Billboard soul charts: 8 ; Billboard pop charts: 45)

The Real Deal 1982 T-Neck FZ 38047 Producers: The Isley Brothers (Billboard soul charts: 9 ; Billboard pop charts: 87)

Between The Sheets 1983 T-Neck FZ 38674 Producers: The Isley Brothers (Billboard soul charts: 1 ; Billboard pop charts: 19)

After eagerly buying every new album by the group for years, by 1980 I was doing it increasingly out of loyalty and not out of any sense of excitement. I'd play the records once, file them away and seldom pull them out again. Indeed, it's purely as a result of this book that I've listened to LPs like Go All The Way - yet another platinum release - for the first time in decades. I must say that the ballad "Don't Say Goodnight" still sounds good with a sensitive vocal by Ronald, and it became their sixth and final #1 soul hit. "Here We Go Again" was a reasonably good selling follow-up as a single (#11 soul) but nowhere good enough a record to spread out to over seven minutes on the LP.

The next three albums all did business that virtually every other soul group would have been delighted with but every one sold a little fewer than the one before it, and they only contained one top ten soul single - "Inside You" - between them. Whichever way it was looked at, their best days were now seemingly gone. However, there were subtle changes in the music and strings were heard on Isley Brothers records for the first time in years and tracks like "Stone Cold Lover" from *The Real Deal* were aimed at the dance floors in a generic way that the group had avoided in the past.

I will dwell a little longer on *Between The Sheets* as it reversed their declining commercial fortunes, not only being their best selling album for a while (platinum, in fact), but also containing in the title track and "Choosey Lover" their best performing singles for three years with both of them making the top six of the soul charts. Tucked away within the album was the atypical "The Ballad Of The Fallen Soldier", an evidently rock sounding record, which, while not to my taste, at least showed they did still contain the ability to surprise.

Masterpiece 1985 Warner Brothers 1-25347 Producers: The Isley Brothers (Billboard soul charts: 19 ; Billboard pop charts: 140)

Smooth Sailin' 1987 Warner Brothers 1-25586 Producers: The Isley Brothers & Angela Winbush (Billboard soul charts: 5 ; Billboard pop charts: 64)

Spend The Night 1989 Warner Brothers 1-25940 Producers: The Isley Brothers & Angela Winbush (Billboard soul charts: 4 ; Billboard pop charts: 89)

In 1984, the group split in half with the younger trio going off to form Isley, Jasper, Isley leaving the three elder brothers alone again for the first time in over fifteen years. The following year the trio released their first LP since 1969 that wasn't on the T-Neck label, and one which was overwhelmingly written by other people, something that also hadn't happened for a considerably long time. It was their most transitional set in years, and wisely played up the fact that they were no longer young men with only "Colder Are My Nights" reaching strutting pace. It became their first single on

WB and did pretty well at #12 soul, much better than their one self-written song on the set, the very mediocre "May I?", which stalled at only #42. The best cut by some distance was a take on "The Most Beautiful Girl In The World" which sustained interest at over seven minutes.

The *Smooth Sailin'* LP from 1987 was poignant and significant: Kelly Isley had died the year before and Ronald and Rudolph carried on as a duo. By far the best cut on a highly contemporary sounding album was "Send A Message", dedicated to Kelly, although the title track was the hit, going all the way to #3 on the soul charts.

Their last LP was also their first ever to be marketed in a way that had always seemed inevitable but thus far resisted: it was now "The Isley Brothers featuring Ronald Isley". It didn't make a change to the chart performance of the LP which pretty much mirrored that of *Smooth Sailin'* and not to the musical sound either apart from the unspeakable "Come Together" on which rapper Koel Moe Dee guested.

I've ignored a host of compilations (and the *Live At Yankee Stadium* set from 1969 as it is in reality a "various artists" collection) and there were a number of CDs still to come following the end of the vinyl era as well as two more changes of direction: firstly Ronald starting calling himself Mr. Biggs at the turn of the new century before changing tack completely and making a beautiful CD with Burt Bacharach in 2003.

As is clear my enthusiasm for the music of The Isley Brothers started to wane dramatically from about 1974 onwards, but that should not obscure my tremendous admiration for how they conducted their record career and what they achieved. Only Berry Gordy, James Brown, Al Bell and Gamble and Huff readily spring to mind as black businessmen who called the shots as single-mindedly and as successfully as The Isleys. They also, like Brown, Isaac Hayes, Stevie Wonder, Marvin Gaye and a few others had the ability to start rather than copy trends and despite their frequent changes of musical direction never failed to be recognisably themselves. They deserved every bit of their fame and - hopefully - fortune.

Isley, Jasper, Isley (see also Isley Brothers and Chris Jasper)

Ernie Isley, Marvin Isley, Chris Jasper

Broadway's Closer To Sunset Blvd. 1984 CBS AL 39873 Producers: Ernie Isley, Marvin Isley & Chris Jasper (Billboard soul charts: 28; Billboard pop charts: 135)

Caravan Of Love 1985 CBS AL 40118 Producers: Ernie Isley, Marvin Isley & Chris Jasper (Billboard soul charts: 3 ; Billboard pop charts: 77)

Different Drummer 1987 CBS AL 40409 Producers: Ernie Isley, Marvin Isley & Chris Jasper (Billboard soul charts: 40)

The other two brothers, Marvin and Ernie, and cousin Chris, spun-off on their own for three albums. As might be imagined they sound a lot like Isley Brothers records without Ronald and as also might be imagined their music was firmly modern in sound with little grounding in "classic" soul music. "Caravan Of Love" was their big hit, #1 soul and #51 pop although "Insatiable Woman" also did well reaching #13 soul. Both of these songs were from the second album, while "Kiss And Tell" had only managed #52 soul from their debut set. The music on their three LPs is not for anyone who isn't a fan of eighties pop/soul styles.

The trio split up in 1988 with Jasper going solo. Ernie and Marvin returned to perform with their elder brothers but Marvin died in 2010.

Stan Ivory

Never Give Up 1988 Total Control 7245MS Producer: Stan Ivory

This record is only in the book as Ivory had issued a handful of obscure singles, including "Check It Out" back in 1978 on the Tese label, but I'm glad he did. The album came out on a small Texas label (but was recorded in Washington and Philadelphia) and revealed that Ivory was a gifted high-toned singer who reminds me a lot of someone else, but I can't put my finger on who. "Never Give Up (Looking For The Thing Called Love)" gets us underway and its sweet and enjoyable, a mid-tempo number with nice backing vocals. Unfortunately "Part II" is noisy and dull, summing up an album that takes one step forward and one step back."I've Got A Lot Of Living To Do" is the old "standard" and Ivory does a good jazzy job on it, while the slow "It's Hard To Face The Truth" is lyrically strong. As is "Music Man" which makes it rather a shame that it is so underwhelming to actually listen to, while a third part of "Never Give Up" (this time instrumental) just points up the obvious budgetary constraints within which he had to work.It's clearly a rather hit and miss affair, but I think Ivory had real talent and good ideas and if he had ever received the chance to record with a big label he could have done really good things.

Ivy (see also Chicago Gangsters & Rumple-Stilts-Skin)

Chris McCants; Sam McCants; David MIller; Sharon Jones; Carl McCaskey, Phillip Maxwell; Debbie Tedrick; Janice Dowlen; Greg Smith; Rex Lee; Laddie Fair

Hold Me 1984 Heat HT 010 Producers: Sam McCants & Chris McCants

Ivy II 1986 Heat HT 017 Producers: Sam McCants & Chris McCants

Ivy III 1987 Heat HT 020 Producers: Sam McCants & Chris McCants

Brothers Chris and Sam McCants formed Ivy after their previous two bands, Chicago Gangsters and Rumple-Stilts-Skin, had called it a day, and pleasingly carried on the tradition of spending nearly as much time working on their ballads as on their dance sides.

First impressions were not promising, though. The front cover of *Hold Me* was cheap and nasty and the opening three tracks on side one not much better. "Say You Will" pulled things back a bit, not because it was great, but because it was better than what had gone before. Side two was a distinct improvement although its closer, "Shake Your Body", was a waste of time. "Hold Me" itself was a fine ballad of some class while the excellent "I Feel You When You're Gone" was resurrected from *The Gangsters* album, although this time delivered by a female rather than male lead.

Ivy II was another album of contrasts, and another one with a hideously cheap looking cover. There were six dance tracks on it and all of them were like literally thousands of tracks from the eighties: within the first few seconds it was obvious exactly how they would unfold. As ever I vastly prefer the three slow tracks, all on side two: "Tell Me", Who's At The Door" and "Sending My Love". Good with the group for going with "Tell Me" as a single, too. It became their only ever soul chart entrant as Ivy, reaching #74 in June 1986.

Their last LP finally had a perfectly decent cover, and it was also the best of the three with good tracks outweighing the bad, but I dread to think what any Beatles' fan would make of their attempt at "Come Together". They finally showed that they could make interesting faster sides such as "True Love" and the Luther Vandross influenced "All My Love" and if the ballads on show were slightly more "pop" and a little less "soul" than in the past at least there were a few of them on a generous LP with twelve cuts.

There were to be no more LPs under any other names for the McCants brothers after *Ivy III* but it appears they are still going strong today with live performances, interestingly under the name (with a minor change) of their second band, Rumplestiltskin.

Charles Jackson (see also Independents)

Passionate Breezes 1978 Capitol SW-11775 Producers: Marvin Yancy & Gene Barge

Gonna Getcha' Love 1979 Capitol EST 12002 Producer: Gavin Christopher

Charles Jackson had wound up his group, The Independents, in 1974 to concentrate on writing hits for Natalie Cole but he must have missed singing as he returned with a marvellous solo LP in 1978 although it must have been galling for him to see it become a "cult" album rather than a top-selling one.

It's a high class effort, with production, arrangements, musicianship, Jackson's singing and the quality of the songs all hard to fault. It doesn't look to disco for inspiration, and is neither tough nor MOR and in fact I would class it is a solidly "middle-class" outing (in the same way as Ashford and Simpson's records could be so described) of great appeal. Rod Stewart's "Tonight's The Night" has been covered by a few soul artists but seldom as well as here, "The Train" is a haunting composition of immense charm and sadness while the title track was relaxed and soothing in the best way, and was covered by The Dells a couple of years later. Most cuts are slow to mid-tempo in nature but when he does decide to go for a dance groove as on "Get On Down" it is infectious rather than mindless. Capitol obviously believed in the album as much as I do as they put out three 45s from it but, inexplicably, they all failed to chart, as indeed did the LP.

Given the disappointing sales for *Passionate Breezes* it was probably a fair decision to change direction for the follow-up, although it's hard to see why such an excellent writer as Jackson would not include a single composition of his own. Gavin Christopher contributes five of the eight songs on show, as well as taking over as producer. While by no means poor (apart from "At The Party" which really *is* poor), the material here doesn't match up to the previous set and even Sam Dees' "For The Sake Of The Memories" is not one of his best efforts, verging further into the MOR field than he normally strayed. Despite my reservations, it's still a good album, with dance cuts once again kept to a minimum, and tracks like "I'm Through With You" and "I Love You Only" (on which Sylvia Cox duets) being of lasting worth. Once again though, the LP didn't sell many copies, and this time Jackson really did put an end to his singing days, returning to writing and producing for others. (Footnote: Bruce Conte, Chester Thompson and Greg Adams from Tower of Power all help out on the LP in various ways but their famed horn section is not employed, which was odd.)

Chuck Jackson

The Great 1965 Strand SLS 1125 No producer listed?

I Don't Want To Cry 1961 Wand 650 No producer listed

Any Day Now 1962 Wand 654 No producer listed

Encore 1963 Wand WDS 655 No producer listed

On Tour 1964 Wand WDM 658 Producer: Luther Dixon

Mr. Everything 1964 Wand WDM 667 No producer listed

Saying Something (with Maxine Brown) 1965 Wand WDM 669 Producer: Stan Green

Chuck Jackson was born in South Carolina but grew up in Pittsburgh and went on to become one of the best loved of all male soul singers but 45 rpm rather than 33⅓ was always his best speed: he posted 23 singles out of a total of around 70 or so that he released onto the Billboard charts but only 2 of his 17 (excluding retrospectives) albums ever made similar inroads: a much worse percentage.

He started out singing briefly with the Del-Vikings and began to release his first solo sides at the end of the fifties for labels like Amy and Clock (most of which came out on an album, *The Great Chuck Jackson* on Strand in 1965, as well as others on Ala and Crown, pretty much same tracks), but his greatest era, commercially and artistically, was when he joined Wand. For a number of years he was their biggest male soul star, a deep voiced counterpart to Dionne Warwick who was soon to become their top selling female soul singer. As will be seen his album releases could be downright odd, but there were a few that remain highly worthwhile listening.

It's a good thing Jackson had such a virile voice as it needed to withstand the strings and occasional rather shrill backing vocal backings that were thrown at his often rather jazzy sessions for *I Don't Want To Cry*. It was understandable that Wand would take this approach as it was hardly unusual for the time, and "soul" was still not a word readily on people's lips in 1961. The title track was a big hit, #5 soul and 36 pop as was the next but one single, also contained on the LP, "I Wake Up Crying", #13 and #59. However, another charting 45, "(It Never Happens) In Real Life" despite being released between the two hits mentioned above was not to be found on the album, much of which does sound pretty dated today, but seeing as how it was recorded 54 years ago, this is hardly a crime.

His second LP, *Any Day Now*, was one of his best and had two brilliant opening tracks with which to ease us in: "I Keep Forgettin'" boasted one of the most idiosyncratic and compelling arrangements (by Teacho Wiltshire) of any soul record and maybe it was too unusual to help place it on the *Billboard* soul charts as a 45, even if it went top 20 on *Cashbox*. No such worries surrounded the album's title track which also had a remarkable arrangement (this time by Bert Keyes), as it became Jackson's biggest ever single success at #2 soul and # 23 pop. Elsewhere on the LP "Make The Night A Little Longer" certainly had some of the same feel as "I Keep Forgettin'" but was such a strong song that it did not matter, while the failure of "What'cha Gonna Say Tomorrow" and "The Breaking Point" as singles should not be taken in any way as an indicator as a lack of quality. In fact, the whole album was a big step forward from *I Don't Want To Cry* and still stands as one of the best examples of the nascent New York soul style of the early sixties. (Despite once again bearing no credits, the set was actually produced by Leiber and Stoller and Luther Dixon.)

There was much that was good on *Encore* too, with the best tracks being the excellent songs "Tell Him I'm Not Home" (sung with a sadly uncredited Doris Troy), "Don't Believe Him Donna", "Two Stupid Feet", "Lonely Am I" and "Getting Ready For The Heartbreak". Every one of these was easily strong enough to have been a single although in the event only the first and last of these came out as 45s with the former doing much better in reaching #12 soul and #42 pop while "Heartbreak" had to settle for reaching the *Cashbox* soul charts only. The other tracks were all pretty solid as well and it was hard to see why the album did not sell a few more than it apparently did.

Wand went the tried and tested route with a *Live* album (that I haven't heard) before a return to the studios for *Mr. Everything*, a set that contained four more charting singles, the highest number from any LP he ever released. The best performing of these was "If I Didn't Love You" at #18 soul and #46 pop towards the end of 1965 but there were signs elsewhere that maybe he no longer had the undivided attention of the company as the backing tracks to "Human" and "I Just Don't Know What To Do With Myself" had already been used years earlier for Tommy Hunt. Nevertheless, it was another pretty good album even if the odd track like "Love Is A Many Splendoured thing" sounded a little dated. Interestingly, the cut of "Something You Got" is NOT the same version of the song he cut with Maxine Brown the same year although it does a feature an uncredited female singer while the oddly entitled "D-5" was not a topical reference to a robot, but the number of a song he wished to play on a jukebox. Production was once again unacknowledged but was carried out by Stan Green, Steve Tyrell and Luther Dixon.

The *Saying Something* LP with Maxine Brown was one of the best he ever cut. It was good-natured, full of excellent songs, six of which derived from the great team of Jo Armstead, Valerie Simpson and Nick Ashford, and the two singers complimented each other well. Uncredited producer Stan Green played down the towering orchestration that normally enveloped Jackson's records and even threw in the odd bluesy touch and it all worked winningly. "Something You Got" went to #10 soul, the first time either singer had enjoyed such a placing for quite a long while and only "Baby Take Me" which was farcically similar to "The Real Thing" lowered the quality bar.

A Tribute To Rhythm And Blues 1966 Wand WS 673
Producers: Stan Green & Chuck Jackson (Billboard soul charts: 21)

A Tribute To Rhythm And Blues Volume 2 1966
Wand WDM 676 Producer: Chuck Jackson

Hold on ! We're Coming (with Maxine Brown) 1967
WDM Wand 678 No producer listed

Dedicated To The King 1967 Wand WDM 680 Producer: Stan Green

The Early Show (and Tammi Terrell) 1967 Wand WDS 682 No producer listed

Mr. Emotion 1984 Kent 033 (UK)

By far the most enjoyable aspect of Chuck's *Tribute To Rhythm And Blues* is listening to the terrific Bobby Scott Band. They were employed for the first time on a Jackson LP and it's a good thing they were as the songs were chosen without much imagination and the mind does wander somewhat when "A Change Is Gonna Come", "Satisfaction" and "You Don't Know Like I Know" are playing. Hardly bad songs in themselves of course, but all had been performed better. It was a slight surprise that the concept caught on with the public as it became Jackson's only charting album on Wand. This may simply have been because a separate *Billboard* Soul LP chart didn't exist before 1965, but possibly the label marketed it harder than all the others, a feeling strengthened by the fact that only one single - "All In My Mind" - was issued from the set and did nothing. Never mind, enjoy the band anyway, and their numerous great touches like the horns on "Sweet Sixteen" or the drums on "Ya Ya".

Luckily, the Scott band were retained for the follow-up set, *Rhythm And Blues Volume* 2, as side one was dispiriting in the extreme. "Sunny", "634-5789", "Hold On I'm Coming" (sung with Maxine Brown and also a small hit when put out as a 45) and a dull medley of other well-known songs provided little in the way of interesting listening so it was also a good thing that side two was much better even if it started unpromisingly with a more or less spoken version of "Blowing In The Wind". The best cover of all was a slowed-down take on the great Motown song "My Baby Loves Me" as it did offer a convincingly alternative on how to perform it while "Every Man Needs A Down Home Girl" showed that Chuck could be pretty "down home" himself if he chose to be: it is one of his toughest, most soulful sides. The jazzy "Where Did She Stay" was also a fine side, not least because it wasn't another dull example of Jackson covering a familiar song.

Wand and Jackson were now locked into a relationship that did neither party any favours. After having already saddled Chuck with the best part of two albums covering other artists' hits the record label then proceeded to dish up his two worst efforts for them. Firstly came a second set with Maxine Brown, infinitely inferior to the first, with no discernible imagination brought to bear, while *Dedicated To The King* was just bizarre. Why Wand thought that there would be a public demand to hear Chuck Jackson interpret ten songs made famous by Elvis Presley is anyone's guess but it bombed and housed no hit singles at all. Only "I Forgot To Remember To Forget" is just about listenable but even that sounded years out of date in 1967 while "Jailhouse Rock" must be the nadir of his entire recording career.

A "culled from the vaults" set, *The Early Show*, sneaked out which featured one side from Jackson and one from Tammi Terrell when she had recorded for Wand/Scepter as Tammy Montgomery a few years earlier. "Why" and "Need To Belong" had not previously been released on disc from Jackson, the other four sides had done.

Many of his finest sides for Wand were collected on an excellent compilation by Kent in 1984.

Chuck Jackson Arrives! 1968 Motown MS 667 No producer listed (Billboard soul charts: 48)

Goin' Back To Chuck Jackson 1969 Motown MS 687 No producer listed

Teardrops Keep Fallin' On My Heart 1970 VIP VS403 No producer listed

Jackson's disillusionment with the label that had made him something of a star was so acute that he bought out his own contract and moved to Motown in late 1967. It must have made sense on the face of it given how hot the Detroit company were at the time but they did have a large roster of artists already and in truth it was not a move that revived his fortunes to anywhere near the extent he would have liked. His first album proudly announced that he had arrived but he got the same treatment as a number of other artists: cutting songs that had already been pressed into service before and having a small battalion of writers and producers assigned to his album: nineteen in total for the former and ten for the latter. The all-important lead-off single was written by Smokey Robinson but it was sadly one of his fussiest and least compelling works. "(You Can't Let The Boy Overpower) The Man In You" failed completely and must have been a chilling notice to Jackson that maybe he should have been more careful about what he wished for. The album itself did chart in a small way and is an absolutely rock-solid set for lovers of the music made by

Gordy's company with no obvious highs or lows, although if I had to pick a couple of favourites they would be the excellent slow work-out "Your Wonderful Love" and his ferocious take on the oft-recorded "Ain't No Sun Since You've Been Gone".

In 1969 Jackson placed two singles on the soul charts in modest fashion: "Are You Lonely For Me Baby" and "Honey Come Back" at #27 and #43 respectively. But at least they did reach the charts, unlike the other four 45s the company released by him. Each of them were covers of records that had hit bigger for others (Freddie Scott and Glen Campbell) and they sat side by side as tracks 1 and 2 on his second album for Motown, which contained plenty of other well-known songs, including a so-so take on "The Chokin' Kind" and a decent one of "Can I Change My Mind". There were also two cuts made famous by The Four Tops, "You Keep Running Away" and "Loving You Is Sweeter Than Ever", and even though it wasn't difficult to tell Jackson's voice apart from Levi Stubbs' they were similar, and one can't help recalling and favouring the originals. Once again, though, it was not a bad set, and once again a whole host of songwriters and (uncredited) producers (predominantly Clay McMurray) were involved. My favourite track: "The Day My World Stood Still", a fine song and performance.

Jackson exited Motown with the flimsiest of his three albums for them, *Teardrops Keep Fallin' On My Heart*. There were fewer covers than before - although one was a rare example of Gordy's labels playing the blues in "The Thrill Is Gone" - but the original songs were all serviceable and ok, rather than enthralling. Virtually every track came in at under three minutes but they all seemed longer, somehow. Two singles were lifted from the set so the company hadn't quite given up on Jackson but neither were hits of any sort at all.

Through All Times 1973 ABC 798 Producer: Steve Barri

Needing You, Wanting You 1975 All Platinum AP-3014 Producers: Al Goodman, Harry Ray & Walter Morris

I Wanna Give You Some Love EMI America 1980 SW-17031 Producer: Luther Dixon

Jackson left Motown in 1971 and put out one single on Dakar in 1972 before pitching up at ABC, where he released one album and four singles, two of which, both on the album, "I Only Get This Feeling" and "I Can't Break Away", were small soul hits. It is a most sturdy LP, with an emphasis on catchy tunes, big, billowing hooks, and a pungent line in rhythm from the West Coast's finest (Ed Greene, Wilton Felder, Michael Omartian etc.) I also like the way in which it is acutely aware of what was currently selling - the title track is clearly influenced by Barry White's hits of the time - as well as acknowledging Jackson's past: "Just A Little Tear" is very "sixties" in construction. As was the case with Jackson's Motown LPs *Through All Times* bore fewer slow tracks than one might have wished for, but it is a set that should be cherished by anyone who loved the Four Tops' Dunhill albums.

There *was* a slow track on Chuck's one LP for the All Platinum label, the title song, which also became his biggest hit for a number of years when it climbed to #30 soul. Which wasn't that big a hit of course but it did demonstrate how far his commercial fortunes had slipped since he was posting big successes for Wand in the sixties. It got the album off to a good start, which was consolidated by the lustful "Cover Up Or Get Ready" and a number of good, perky dance cuts such as "I've Got The Need", "Love Lights" and "Beautiful Woman". The messy "Shine Shine Shine" was much less impressive but the good things far outweighed the mediocre on an LP whose sleeve could conceivably have led to its being referred to as "The Red Album" by Jackson fans.

All Platinum certainly persisted with Jackson and released a further four singles on him, but none of them emulated the success of "I'm Needing You, Wanting You" and he drifted off to the Channel label for a revival of Executive Suite's "When The Fuel Runs Out", a record on which the identity of the singer was irrelevant, before landing a contract with EMI American for his last ever LP. As usual he looked in great shape on the cover - he had always been a charismatic man - but despite the re-kindling of his relationship with Luther Dixon, who produced his first Chuck Jackson album for fifteen years, it was not a success. Two 45s were pulled from *I Wanna Give You Some Love* but neither they nor the album broached any charts. The LP was certainly accorded some stellar support - a full orchestra, a couple of Earth Wind & Fire's horn section and Bob Marley and The Wailers' backing vocalists, I-Three, among others - and apart from a bloated "After You", it was an accomplished outing with typically fine singing, a refusal to acknowledge disco, and an adult approach to understanding the kind of audience it might attract. The fact it failed is just one of those things, rather than any obvious miscalculation on anyone's Bart. I particularly liked "The Bait" and Marley's "Waiting In Vain", which was transformed into an unrecognisable and rather absorbing dance side.

There was to be no addition to Chuck Jackson's recording career other than a couple of singles in 1989 and a CD with Cissy Houston in 1992 although he still performs live from time to time and even if, as I suggested, the LP format wasn't really his best, pull out a really good one like *Any Day Now* and his warm and solid baritone will still heat up the coldest winter evening.

Clydene Jackson

Fresh 1975 Crossover CR 9002 Produced by Ray Charles

Jackson is a talented West Coast based pianist and singer who worked with Richard "Dimples" Fields, who produced her first single in return. *Fresh*, however, was helmed by Ray Charles, but it was in his jazzy mode, for the LP isn't really a soul album, to my way of thinking, and is only really in the book for the same reason Rita Graham's is : they both contain a track that has been picked up by the dancing fraternity. In Jackson's case it is for "I Need Your Love" but "Mr. Bojangles" is probably more representative of her work. If you like Graham's album you should like this and vice versa.

Jackson has more recently released a gospel CD, *Sparrow*.

Deon Jackson

Love Makes The World Go Round 1966 Atco 33-188 Producer: Ollie McLaughlin

His Greatest Recordings 1984 Solid Smoke SS-8020 Producer: Ollie McLaughlin

Ann Arbor's Deon Jackson had a voice that always reminded me a little bit of a male version of Mary Wells', which was soft, fluffy and fluid, and never more so than on his big and delectable hit, "Love Makes The World Go 'Round" which zoomed up the charts to come to rest at #3 soul and #11 pop in the early part of 1966. He had tried out with two previous singles on the Atlantic label but it was a switch to the smaller Carla imprint which changed his fortunes for the better.

All four sides of the two Atlantic singles are found on his debut album, as are the big hit single and it's almost identical sounding follow-up 45, "Love Takes A Long Time Growing" which probably deserved to fail, but did manage a run on the *Cashbox* soul charts. The best of the earlier sides was the exciting "Come Back Home" which had intriguing backing vocals imitating the sounds of a train, even if it did owe an awful lot to Marvin Gaye's records of the time. A sense of ennui surrounds his covers of "1-2-3", "S.O.S." and "King Of The Road" all of which suggest the album was put together speedily but "You Said You Love Me", "No Not Much" and "I'm Telling You" (penned by the skilled and underrated writer Sharon McMahan) were enjoyable and unpretentious.

Jackson eventually released seven singles on Carla but only one more, the glorious "Ooh Baby", managed to reach the charts (#28 soul and #65 pop in December 1966) but apart from one single on Shout in 1970 he left the industry and never recorded again, passing away in 2014. Luckily for us, though, Solid Smoke came up with an admiring retrospective set in 1984 which only duplicated four of the twelve tracks from the Atco album. The other ten cuts consisted of two unreleased songs (the sleeve note erroneously claimed four) and a handful of the later Carla singles including "Ooh Baby". I feel that it's a much better album than the previous one as the covers have been excised and most of his singles were good. If there is a slight criticism it would be that he only really operated at one pace - brisk midtempo - and there are therefore no ballads on show but this is minor. It's still excellent listening.

George Jackson (see Gotham Flasher)

Gregg Jackson

One For The Road 1982 KYP NS92082 Producer: Kevin Falvey

I don't believe I have another LP in my collection that was recorded in Rhode Island; I'm also not sure I have one with a longer "run-out groove" either. It takes up nearly as much space as the songs, and accounts for why the album comes in so short at around twenty minutes. The first eight of these are very good indeed, however, spread over two songs, and the only justification for why this is another sought-after record. The slow, melodic and sax-laden title track is best of all, with Jackson's rich and world-weary vocal entirely appropriate for the subject matter, and the sympathetic and unobtrusive drums suggest that it might have been recorded earlier than 1982; it sounds more like a record from 1974. The slightly more upbeat "Who Wrote The Music" is also impressive with fine backing vocals but the other four tracks - one of which is called "Dizzy Dancin'" - fail to reach the standards set by these two.

Given *One For The Road* is on an "indie" label it had little chance of selling many copies and I suspect few were pressed up in the first place. He didn't make any more records to the best of my knowledge but still performs today down in Florida as Gregg Jackson and the Mojo Band.

Jackie Jackson

Jackie Jackson 1973 Motown M 785V1 Producer: The Corporation

Be The One 1989 Polydor 422-837 766-1 Producers: Jackie Jackson & Robert Brookins (Billboard soul charts: 84)

In 1973 Jackie Jackson became the third brother from the Jackson 5 to get the chance to cut a solo album after Michael and Jermaine. (Marlon had to hang fire until 1987 for his, and poor old Tito is still waiting.)

What a shame Motown didn't persist with him as it is a most appealing set, by some distance my favourite of all the LPs by any of the brothers; most likely because he is the eldest, thus sparing us from some of Michael's pre-teen efforts. As Jackson sang in a pleasing high tenor the album is couched firmly in the "sweet soul" style, and can be investigated with confidence and anticipation by anyone who loved what The Stylistics or The Moments were doing back in the early seventies. On the other hand, if that is not to one's taste, it is a record to be safely ignored. A lovely version of The Miracles' "Bad Girl" and the exquisite "Love Don't Want To Leave" and "Do I Owe" are the highlights and only a rather lacklustre "Didn't I (Blow Your Mind This Time)" fails to impress. No singles were pulled from the set, which rather underlines the fact that Motown were not about to spend much time on promoting Jackie as a star in his own right, which also makes me wonder why they even bothered with the album in the first place, but I'm pleased they did.

Jackson had to wait sixteen years for his next and final album, not to my taste at all, but it did include two small soul charting singles in "Stay" and "Cruzin".

Jermaine Jackson

Jermaine 1972 Motown M 752L Producers: The Corporation, Pam Sawyer, Johnny Bristol, Hal Davis, Gloria Jones, Jerry Marcellino & Mel Larson, (Billboard soul charts: 6 ; Billboard pop charts: 27)

Come Into My Life 1973 Motown M775L Producers: Hal Davis, Clay McMurray, Pam Sawyer, Gloria Jones, Jerry Marcellino, Mel Larson & The Corporation (Billboard soul charts: 30; Billboard pop charts: 152)

My Name Is Jermaine 1976 Motown M6-842S1 Producers: Michael L Smith, Don Daniels, Gregory Wright, Gwen Glenn, Jeffrey Bowen & Hal Davis (Billboard soul charts: 29; Billboard pop charts: 164)

Feel The Fire 1977 Motown M6-888S1 Producers: Jermaine Jackson, Michael McGloiry, Greg Wright & Michael L Smith, (Billboard soul charts: 36; Billboard pop charts: 174)

Frontiers 1978 Motown M7-898R1 Producers: Jermaine Jackson, Michael McGloiry, Hal Davis & Brian Holland

I will readily confess that Jermaine Jackson is not an artist whose work I have ever rushed out to buy, but one thing that has surprised me, now I'm thinking actively about him, is that he released more LPs (excluding compilations) than brother Michael. I'd also forgotten how successful he was: two #1 soul albums and ten top twenty soul singles, two of which also went to #1.

In 1972 Motown decided to issue solo records on Michael and Jermaine as well as continuing to put out Jackson 5 releases. I must confess that Jermaine's were more palatable to me back then as he was a few years older than his more famous sibling and his work was not purely aimed at a teen audience. From his debut LP, for example, both "Daddy's Home" (#3 soul) and "That's How Love Goes" (#23) sold well and both were perfectly good soul records. However, his versions of "If You Were My Woman"

"I'm In A Different World" and "Take Me In Your Arms Rock Me For A Little While") were outclassed by those from Gladys Knight & The Pips, The Four Tops and Kim Weston respectively.

His follow-up album fared less well in the market-place but was a better set to listen to. "You're In Good Hands" floated along persuasively, even if it sounded pretty similar to "Daddy's Home" and his versions of "Does Your Mama Know About Me" and "The Bigger You Love" were better than his covers on the debut LP.

He didn't release any albums for a couple of years and then things got a bit awkward as he was rather stuck in the middle, being married to Hazel, Berry Gordy's daughter, when his brothers decided they wished to leave Motown. Jermaine stayed loyal to the record company and his next LP sounded noticeably different from what had come before. The cover versions vanished and a disco groove was introduced on tracks like the now dated sounding "Let's Be Young Tonight" and "Bass Odyssey". (What wasn't included, sadly, was his best record from the seventies, "She's The Ideal Girl", which only came out as a single in Europe in 1976, as well as being tucked away, uncredited, on the *Mahogany* soundtrack LP.)

His LPs were selling in ever decreasing numbers, however, and neither *Feel The Fire* nor *Frontiers* (which completely failed to chart) did anything to revive his fortunes. They didn't include any hit singles either and maybe the best that can be said for them was that they kicked off a period of producing his own records.

Let's Get Serious 1980 Motown M7-928R1 Producers: Jermaine Jackson & Stevie Wonder (Billboard soul charts: 1; Billboard pop charts: 6)

Jermaine 1980 Motown M8-948M1 Producers: Berry Gordy, Jermaine Jackson & Suzee Ikeda (Billboard soul charts: 17; Billboard pop charts: 27)

I Like Your Style 1981 Motown M8-952M1 Producer: Jermaine Jackson (Billboard soul charts: 31; Billboard pop charts: 86)

Let Me Tickle Your Fancy 1982 Motown 6017ML Producers: Berry Gordy & Jermaine Jackson (Billboard soul charts: 9 ; Billboard pop charts: 46)

His second coming commenced in 1980 when someone's smart decision to team him up with Stevie Wonder proved to be highly successful. *Let's Get Serious* as a single went to #1 soul and #9 pop, while the album after which it was named went gold. There were a further three LPs on Motown which all did pretty well but were, from the admittedly few tracks I have ever heard from this period, rather bland and predictable.

Jermaine Jackson 1984 Arista AL 8-8203 Producer: Jermaine Jackson (Billboard soul charts: 1 ; Billboard pop charts: 19)

Precious Moments 1986 Arista AL8-8277 Producers: Jermaine Jackson, Michael Omartian & Tom Keane (Billboard soul charts: 25 ; Billboard pop charts: 46)

Don't Take It Personal 1989 Arista AL-8493 Producers: Danny Sembello, Kashif, Marti Sharron, Derrick Cullen, David Conley, David Townsend, Rick Nowels, Dennis Lambert, Preston Glass, Ricky Peterson & Lewis A. Martineé, (Billboard soul charts: 18 ; Billboard pop charts: 115)

You Said 1991 LaFace 212 269 Producers: The LaFace Family (Billboard soul charts: 39) (Germany)

In 1984 Jackson moved to Arista, a period that saw him achieve his second #1 soul single with the annoyingly ungrammatical "Don't Take It Personal" from the album of the same name. From here on in though, his records were strictly pop with the merest sprinkle of soul. His last vinyl album came out in 1991, but only in Europe; the U.S. went with a CD only release.

Jimmy Jackson

Rollin' Dice 1976 Buddah BDS 5671 Producers: Al Altman & Marty Kugell

Jimmy Jackson only made this one LP and I'm afraid it is tough listening. Over produced, over sung and over everything, really. He had a startling vocal range and that was the problem; if the producers had concentrated more on what type of record Jimmy really wanted to make - it is as much pop as soul - and less on how to showcase his voice it would have been better for everyone. Take a listen to his version of Nilsson's "Without You" as a prize exhibit. "Footsteps In The Shadows" is the most obviously "soul" track on the LP - fast and sounding rather out of date for 1976 - but there are too many schmaltzy covers of pop tunes here such as "I'd Love You To Want Me" and "Daddy Don't You Walk So Fast" although he does ok on Mac Davis' "Something's burning". I don't know much about Jimmy Jackson but he also put out a version of Denise La Salle's "Freedom To Express Yourself" a few years later and I didn't like that either.

J.J. Jackson

J.J.Jackson 1967 Calla C-1101 Producer: Lew Futterman

The Great J.J. Jackson 1969 Warner Brothers WS 1797 Producer: Lew Futterman

The Greatest Little Soul Band In The Land 1969 Congress CS 7000 Producer: Lew Futterman

J.J. Jackson's Dilemma 1970 Perception PLP 3 Producer: Lew Futterman

...And Proud Of It 1970 Perception PLP 12 Producer: Lew Futterman

Jerome Louis Jackson is a hard man to pin down as sources of information about his life and recording career are often contradictory and I will therefore restrict my comments to the five albums he recorded, while recognising that is difficult to state for certain in which country, let alone which studio, some of his songs were cut.

I'm fairly sure that the New Yorker cut his one big hit from late 1966, "But It's Alright" (#4 soul and #22 pop) in London and where it was produced by Pierre Tubbs, even if Lew Futterman gets all the producing credit on Jackson's first LP. It's always been an irresistible call to dance, and much better than the follow-up, "I Dig Girls", which still did well at #19 soul and #83 pop. The album contains thirteen tracks, all under three minutes, with the majority being Jackson compositions (he was a fine writer, penning many sides for others in the course of his career), supplemented by a few covers including "Ain't Too Proud To Beg" and "A Change Is

Gonna Come". I find nearly all the set to be too frantic for enjoyable listening and it's a shame that it didn't include his third single for Calla, the tremendous ballad "It Seems Like I've Been Here Before".

However, his follow-up album, *The Great J.J. Jackson,* did include it and also his fourth, "Four Walls", which performed reasonably well in reaching #17 soul and #123 pop, even if it did mimic "But It's Alright" to a fair degree. A couple of tracks were reprised from the debut set (but as I don't own the album I'm not sure if they are re-cuts or originals) and the album also included three singles Jackson cut for Loma including "Sho Nuff (Got A Good Thing Going)" with sounds like Otis Redding singing over the backing track to The Contours' "Just A Little Misunderstanding".

The Greatest Little Soul Band In The Land was definitely cut in London and was markedly different from the first two LPs by adopting a much looser and expansive musical approach, and incorporating long instrumentals such as "Tobacco Road". "Tenement Hall" was a soulful lament from Jackson although its stop and start time changes rather diluted the effect. One thing was at least clear: Jackson was certainly not going to release predictable LPs.

That stance was underlined by his first outing on Perception, *J.J. Jackson's Dilemma*. I'm not sure exactly which dilemma he referred to, but once again he surprised us, taking us further into a jazzy, funky and even psychedelic direction than before as demonstrated by the eight minute long "Help Me Get To My Grits" and the six minute "Indian Thing", both instrumentals. (The U.K. version of the LP, on RCA SF 8093 in 1970 had a slightly different track listing, adding "Bow Down To The Dollar" and removing "Go Find Yourself A Woman" and "No Sad Songs"

The final album seemed to wander even further away from a recognisably soul setting. I've not heard *....And Proud Of It* but it seems safe to assume that tracks entitled "The Carrot" (I'd love to listen to this one), "The Lioness Has Shed Her Mane", "Mag Bag" and "Yellow Wednesday" are not going to be your standard verse chorus verse soul songs.

That was it for his LPs and what he has been doing since and what he is doing now, assuming he is still alive, remains elusive and unclear.

Michael Jackson

Got To Be There 1972 Motown M 747L Producers: The Corporation & Hal Davis (Billboard soul charts: 3 ; Billboard pop charts: 14)

Ben 1972 Motown M 755L Producers: The Corporation Jerry Marcellino, Mel Larson & Hal Davis (Billboard soul charts: 4 ; Billboard pop charts: 5)

Music And Me 1973 Motown M 767L Producers: Fonce Mizell, Freddie Perren, Bob Gaudio, Jerry Marcellino, Mel Larson & Hal Davis (Billboard soul charts: 24 ; Billboard pop charts: 92)

Forever, Michael 1975 Motown M6-825S1 Producers: Brian Holland, Hal Davis, Sam Brown, Fonce Mizell & Jerry Marcellino (Billboard soul charts: 10 ; Billboard pop charts: 101)

The Best Of 1975 Motown M6-851S1 (Billboard soul charts: 44 ; Billboard pop charts: 156)

Off The Wall 1979 Epic FE 35745 Producers: Quincy Jones & Michael Jackson (Billboard soul charts: 1 ; Billboard pop charts: 3)

One Day In Your Life 1981 Motown M8-956M1 Producers: Brian Holland, Fonce Mizell, Freddie Perren, Hal Davis & Sam Brown (Billboard soul charts: 41 ; Billboard pop charts: 144)

Thriller 1982 Epic QE 38112 Producer: Quincy Jones (Billboard soul charts: 1 ; Billboard pop charts: 1)

Farewell My Summer Love 1984 Motown 6101ML (Billboard soul charts: 31 ; Billboard pop charts: 46)

Bad 1987 Epic E 40600 Producer: Quincy Jones (Billboard soul charts: 1 ; Billboard pop charts: 1)

Dangerous 1991 Epic E2 45400 Producer: Bruce Swedien, Teddy Riley & Bill Bottrell (Billboard soul charts: 18 ; Billboard pop charts: 1)

Was Michael Jackson a soul singer? I feel the same way about him I feel about Ray Charles which is: no, not really (they both transcended that confining description) but to ignore him seems perverse and wrong. Especially as *Thriller* was the best selling LP on the soul charts in history: 37 weeks at #1. Furthermore, Jackson, like Charles, released records in soul's "golden age" which for me ran from 1965 to 1974, and that makes me look on him favourably as essential to include. I also can see his immense talent - surely anyone can - but his music pretty much always passed me by as something I enjoyed listening to; I was too old for his earlier pre-teen first handful of LPs, and *Off The Wall* and *Thriller* apart, his later albums had all the eighties characteristics I found difficult to come to terms with. This then, will be the briefest of descriptions about a household name whose facts are easily available to anyone who wants them and I will confine myself to the odd reflection or two.

The first is to note that until he left Motown, he didn't place any solo singles at #1 on the soul charts (although "Ben" made #1 on the pop listings). When he had moved on, he managed thirteen soul number ones - the same as Marvin Gaye - a mightily impressive total.

His big renaissance came, of course, when he hooked up with Quincy Jones; not only was he no longer a little boy, he was now making music of a very high calibre such as "Don't Stop 'Til You Get Enough" and "Rock With You". They may be a long way from "deep" or "real" soul records but they were brilliant pop outings that fully deserved to achieve what they did as 45s: the "double" of #1 on soul and pop charts. The amazing thing is that although *Off The Wall,* the album that contained both singles, went platinum and spent an almost unbelievable 169 weeks on the pop charts (to put this in context, no Beatles' LP achieved such longevity), it did not go higher than #3.

There were no such surprises for *Thriller*, which landed at #1 on the pop charts and stayed there for 37 weeks (same length of time as on the soul charts). The only LP in history, by the way, that has spent longer than *Thriller* at #1 on the U.S. pop charts is the soundtrack from *West Side Story* which started its run all the way back in 1961. Whichever way one looks at, or thinks about, *Thriller* it was an astonishing success. It consisted of nine tracks, seven of which were released as singles, all reaching the pop top ten, with two - the horrible "Beat It" and the immeasurably better

"Billie Jean " - as close to a perfect pop single imaginable - both attaining #1. (Actually, there *was* one surprise with the LP as it only stayed on the listings for a mere 120 weeks, almost a year less than *Off The Wall*.)

As could be expected, Motown rushed out albums of old or previously unreleased recordings such as on "One Day In Your Life" and "Farewell My Summer Love" to capitalise on his super-stardom but their sales were in no great numbers.

Bad and *Dangerous* (irritating titles - Michael Jackson was a rebel in some way?) closed out his vinyl album days with no discernible "soul" relevance whatsoever although both sold in massive quantity of course.

There were yet to come millions of compilations, CDs etc. up to and after his death, and while there would probably not be a hardcore soul fan anywhere in the world who would nominate Michael Jackson as a favourite singer, his talent and fame can hardly be ignored; he was one of the best - known and most successful performers of the last 100 years.

Millie Jackson

Millie Jackson 1972 Spring SPR 5703 Producer: Raeford Gerald

Hurts So Good 1973 Spring SPR 5706 Producer: Raeford Gerald & Brad Shapiro (Billboard soul charts: 13 ; Billboard pop charts: 175)

Millie 1974 Spring SPR 6701 Producer: Raeford Gerald & Brad Shapiro

Caught Up 1974 Spring SPR 6703 Producers: Millie Jackson & Brad Shapiro (Billboard soul charts: 4 ; Billboard pop charts: 21)

Still Caught Up 1975 Spring SPR 6708 Producers: Millie Jackson & Brad Shapiro (Billboard soul charts: 27; Billboard pop charts: 112)

Mildred Jackson from Thomson Georgia only issued one single, back in 1968 on MGM, before she got the chance to record for Spring, so she hadn't had to wait quite so long for success as many others and four tracks on her debut album suggested that she may be someone to keep an eye on. The rest of the set was solid and unremarkable but "A Child Of God", "Ask Me What You Want", "My Man Is A Sweet Man" and "I Miss You Baby" were so clearly the most striking songs that Spring put all of them out as singles and were rewarded with soul chart placings of #22, #4, #7 and # 22 respectively. It's also not surprising to be reminded that the trenchant lyrics of the beautifully arranged former would have made it considerably less "suitable" for mainstream radio play then "Ask" and "Sweet Man", both dance oriented cuts, and it fared worse on the pop listings as a result. Legend has it that Jackson can't abide "Sweet Man" but I still find it to be as irresistible a call to a dance floor as when I first heard it 43 years ago.

Her next LP was another good outing with the first three tracks on side one addressing the social themes touched on in "A Child Of God" but all were eclipsed by the brilliant "It Hurts So Good". An outstanding song by Phillip Mitchell, it had already been performed superbly by Katie Love and The Four Shades of Black, but Jackson's take was even better and she was rewarded by a #3 soul and #24 pop placing (her most successful ever 45) when it was put out as a single in August 1973. Before this "Breakaway" had been the first song to be pulled from the LP but did rather less well at #16 soul and #110 pop. Both "It Hurts So Good" and its b-side "Love Doctor" were also to be found on a soundtrack, *Cleopatra Jones*, which wouldn't have harmed sales of the 45. Elsewhere on the album are a good version of "Don't Send Nobody Else" that fine Ashford-Simpson composition, and instantly memorable tunes in "Good To The Very Last Drop", "Now That You Got It" and "Close My Eyes". The memorable cover picture surely also helped to propel the LP to strong sales.

The third Spring set was a bit of a puzzle: was it called *Millie* (yes, according to the sleevenotes); *Millie Jackson* (yes, according to the spine); or *I Got To Try It One Time* (yes, according to the record label)? Whichever it was, and I've gone for *Millie*, it was similar to the previous couple: customary strong singing, choice backing vocals (Cissy Houston and Judy Clay helped out here) top notch tracks pulled as singles - "How Do You Feel The Morning After" was the peach here (#11 soul) - and sumptuous playing, production and arrangements. Much of the former came from the magnificent Muscle Shoals Sound rhythm section and they brought a typical southern funkiness to bear on Don Covay's "Watch The One Who Brings You The News" (and Jackson also renders a fine version of Covay's "Letter Full Of Tears" too). Finally, I like the unexpected fiddle on "In The Wash", a foretaste that Jackson's music could surprise us all.

And she certainly did surprise us all in 1974, delivering a genuinely great LP in *Caught Up*. If ever a soul LP existed for an LP's sake, rather than a collection of singles, this is it. Concept albums were pretty much "old hat" by this time, with many rock and pop acts having indulged in them right back to the mid-sixties. Soul had put a toe or two in the water, as with David Porter's *Victim Of The Joke* or Z.Z. Hill's *Brand New*, but they were rather half-hearted, something *Caught Up* certainly wasn't. Jackson moved into a completely different league here and I thought it was a great album when I first heard it, and have continued to think so for every second of the forty plus years since; it is still an emotionally draining experience to listen to, and I know every moment of it off by heart. The playing is astounding throughout and Millie's singing was of an intensity she had not shown us before and seldom would again. The spoken passages are every bit as crucial as the singing too, as in the exhilarating "wives-in law" skit between the opening two tracks, but it is the song selection that really made it. There was not a single misstep, from the blistering opening "If Loving You Is Wrong" through to the closing "I'm Through Trying To Prove My Love To You" and "Summer (The First Time)". Womack's version of his own composition is one of the finest records ever made but Jackson comes within an inch of matching him, while she brings all the vulnerability, oppressive heat and steamy sex to Bobby Goldsboro's song that his original promised but never delivered. Such quality could not be gainsaid, and the album went gold; "If Loving You Is Wrong" and "I'm Through" were both pulled as 45s but they were afterthoughts and beside the point, and did not sell particularly well.

There was clearly a compelling reason to deliver a *Caught Up* part two, and the amazing thing is how good *Still Caught Up* was and is, even if it lacked the shock element of its predecessor, selling many fewer copies as a result. I can see that there was a "soap opera" element to the two *Caught Up* LPs, more so on the second, and particularly at the end of "I Still Love You", but if we adhere to the old Motown adage, "it's what's in the grooves that counts", then it still stands as another superb album. The great Tom Jans song, "Loving Arms", is brilliantly performed by Jackson and was matched up with the second best track, the entertainingly bitchy and uncompromising "Leftovers" for a rather superfluous

Free And In Love 1976 Spring SP-1-6709 Producers: Millie Jackson & Brad Shapiro (Billboard soul charts: 17)

Lovingly Yours 1976 Spring SP-1-6712 Producers: Millie Jackson & Brad Shapiro (Billboard soul charts: 44; Billboard pop charts: 175)

Feelin' Bitchy 1977 Spring SP-1-6715 Producers: Brad Shapiro & Millie Jackson (Billboard soul charts: 4; Billboard pop charts: 34)

Get It Outcha System 1978 Spring SP-1-6719 Producers: Brad Shapiro & Millie Jackson (Billboard soul charts: 14; Billboard pop charts: 55)

A Moment's Pleasure 1979 Spring SP-1-6722 Producers: Brad Shapiro & Millie Jackson (Billboard soul charts: 47; Billboard pop charts: 144)

Royal Rappin's (with Isaac Hayes) 1979 Polydor PD-1-6229 Producers: Millie Jackson & Brad Shapiro (Billboard soul charts: 17; Billboard pop charts: 80)

Live & Uncensored 1979 Spring SP-2-6725 Producers: Millie Jackson & Brad Shapiro (Billboard soul charts: 22; Billboard pop charts: 94)

Clearly, a third version of *Caught Up* would have been excessive and Spring wisely resisted the temptation to travel that route although a logical narrative is still apparent throughout *Free And In Love*; or at least on side one. The problem is that there are simply not enough good songs on show and the LP does suffer when compared to its predecessors. It starts off well enough with the durable and catchy "A House For Sale", a typically memorable offering from writers Homer Banks and Carl Hampton, and over on side two "Bad Risk" and "Solitary Love Affair" are more than worthwhile but "Bad Company's "Feel Like Making Love" is too rock-oriented, the normally reliable Clarence Reid's "Do What Makes The World Go Around" is rather dull while the album's closer "I'm In Love Again", seems to go on for ever, and features way too much of Millie's talking, a problem that would become even more apparent in the future.

Lovingly Yours must have worried Millie and Spring. Every one of her previous six albums had either hit the soul top 20, or, if not, housed singles which had done. But this album sold only modestly as did two singles pulled from it, "I Can't Say Goodbye" (#40) and "A Love Of Your Own"(#87). The LP didn't even feature her picture on the cover, either, and there was a real sense of drift at the time it was released. On a more positive note, it was the first set to introduce us to Jackson singing Benny Latimore songs ("Somethin' 'Bout Cha" being the one here), a partnership that worked particularly well, and overall it was a solid piece of work, with no substandard songs if no absolute career highpoints either. The Moments were drafted in on a couple of cuts to provide their usual top-class singing and although it remains one of her most forgotten sets, it is worth pulling out every so often.

It's often a futile exercise to try and work out why certain records are hits and others aren't, so it remains unclear why *Feelin' Bitchy* should have done so much better than the previous three albums (and housed much better performing singles) but as good as explanation as any would be because "If You're Not Back In Love By Monday" was such a magnificent record and the centrepiece of the album. Possibly my favourite single of hers, it rose to #5 soul and #43 pop, and is the best evidence of how compelling Jackson could be when performing country songs: only Candi Staton, Bettye Swann and Solomon Burke spring to mind as soul acts equally adept at such interpretations. The long version of the opening cut, "All The Way Lover", another Latimore song, should not be underestimated in the album's success either and an edited version also performed well as a 45, reaching #12 on the soul charts. Elsewhere, things were resolutely solid too and the striking front cover photo doubtless also helped in making *Feelin' Bitchy* become her second gold album.

Get It Out'Cha System also went gold but was the first of her LPs where I felt my interest starting to ebb a little. Side one in particular suggested that rapping, rather than singing, was increasingly becoming the main point of her albums. And doubtless it was; selling records in respectable numbers was vastly more important than appealing to English men thousands of miles away. "Keep The Home Fires Burning "and "Put Something Down On It" made perfect sense in being chosen for the story being sketched out, but I much prefer the originals by Latimore and Bobby Womack respectively. Side two was more to my taste, as the brassy "Here You Come Again" and the addictive "Sweet Music Man" topped and tailed things in fine style, while the talking was kept to a minimum.

A Moment's Pleasure contained some unmistakeable disco influences, the first time they had been discerned on a Jackson album, and it was another mixture of good songs and singing ("Seeing You Again", "We Got To Hit It Off" and the excellent pop song, "Kiss You All Over") and long tracks with lots of rapping (the title track and "What Went Wrong Last Night"). It fell rather flat in the marketplace though and despite containing three singles that reached the soul charts, none of them could be classed as "hits" with "Never Change Lovers In The Middle Of The Night" performing the best at #33.

Faced with such average sales Polydor/Spring opted for some changes in the next two sets. First, there was an album performed with Isaac Hayes and although each singer could accurately be described as having passed their commercial peak, they still had enough appeal to drive the LP to decent sales, which were well deserved as it was an outstanding effort filled up with excellent songs such as "You Never Cross My Mind" and "Love Changes". It was Jackson's best set since *Still Caught Up* and Hayes' finest for around a decade. Jackson followed this with a live double LP recorded in Los Angeles, *Live And Uncensored*, I haven't heard.

For Men Only 1980 Spring SP-1-6727 Producers: Millie Jackson & Brad Shapiro (Billboard soul charts: 23; Billboard pop charts: 100)

I Had To Say It 1980 Spring SP-1-6730 Producers: Millie Jackson & Brad Shapiro (Billboard soul charts: 25; Billboard pop charts: 137)

Just A Little Bit Country 1981 Spring SP-1-6732 Producers: Millie Jackson & Brad Shapiro (Billboard soul charts: 43; Billboard pop charts: 201)

Live & Outrageous 1982 Spring SP-1-6735 Producers: Millie Jackson & Brad Shapiro (Billboard soul charts: 11; Billboard pop charts: 113)

Hard Times 1982 Spring SP-1-6737 Producers: Millie Jackson & Brad Shapiro (Billboard soul charts: 29; Billboard pop charts: 175)

E.S.P. (Extra Sensual Persuasion) 1983 Spring SPR-33-6740 Producers: Millie Jackson & Brad Shapiro (Billboard soul charts: 40)

As we moved into the eighties *For Men Only* arrived with a language warning sticker, presumably justified at the end of "Not On Your Life". I can't remember if it seemed "shocking" at the time; it just sounds a bit too self-conscious today. The music is good throughout, with the excellent "This Is It" having real drive once we get past the long spoken intro, and "Despair", "If That Don't Turn You On", "I Wish That I Could Hurt That Way Again" and the obligatory Latimore song, "Ain't No Comin' Back", are all highly enjoyable too. The album performed reasonably well, but the two singles pulled from it did not.

Jackson and Shapiro released their eleventh successive co-produced LP in 1981, and *I Had To Say I*t, could more accurately have been entitled I *Had To Say It Again* as so much of it had been heard before: "Loving Arms" was reprised from Still Caught Up and much of "The Rap" could have come from any of her previous half dozen sets. The title track itself was based firmly on "Rapper's Delight" and while fairly amusing on first hearing, it is hardly a vintage Jackson moment, and became the first single she had ever released on Spring to completely miss the *Billboard* soul 100. So much for a highly disappointing first side, and what once sounded so fresh was now sounding decidely shopworn. Luckily, turning the record over led to richer pickings with Millie playing it straight and delivering some strong singing on some typically thoughtful, country-flecked and well-chosen songs, if sometimes a touch too heavy on guitar. Prince Phillip Mitchell contributed two of them and duets with Jackson on "Fancy This".

Just when it seemed Jackson would continue to mildly disappoint long-time fans she gave us two superb LPs, even if they only sold moderately well. Firstly, there was *Just A Lil' Bit Country*, an entirely apposite title as she took country songs as her base but it was by no means a straight "C and W" set. A funky version of "I Can't Stop Loving You", the old Ray Charles hit, for example, has more in common with George Clinton than George Jones. Mainly though, what we got was Millie singing her heart out, completely eschewing any rapping, on the kind of songs at which she always excelled. The band is splendid, with lovely liberal horns, and "Rose Coloured Glasses" and "It Meant Nothing To Me" are wonderful sides, among the best she ever cut.

Hard Times was slightly less distinguished, thanks to a poor contemporary sounding closing cut in "Feel Love Comin' On" and a probably slightly overlong "Mess On Your Hands", but it was still her second studio album in succession (another *Live* set was sandwiched between the two) that should appeal to anyone who enjoyed sixties or early seventies soul. She interprets Sam Dees' "Special Occasion" beautifully, while her take on Chuck Jackson's "I Don't Want To Cry" is admirable, as she turns a great song on its head and dissolves its melody to come up with something almost equally compelling. On the other hand she covers Little Milton's "We're Gonna Make It" with no frills or fancy footwork. Neither set housed any top fifty soul singles but they are right up there with her best ever albums.

I saw Millie Jackson live around 1983 but cannot remember a single thing about the show, which doubtless says more about me than her, but it certainly coincided with a growing lack of interest in her work and I went out of a sense of duty rather than with any great enthusiasm. Her single of that year, "I Feel Like Walking In The Rain" (# 58 soul only) from her poor-selling and final Spring LP, *E.S.P.*, was the last side of hers I ever enjoyed

An Imitation Of Love 1986 Jive 1016-1-J Producers: Timmy Allen, Bryan New, Jolyon Skinner, Wayne Brathwaite, Larry Smith & Jonathan Butler (Billboard soul charts: 16; Billboard pop charts: 119)

The Tide Is Turning 1988 Jive 1103-1-J Producers: Timmy Allen, Eddie Levert, Gerald Levert, Marc Gordon, Loris Holland, Fritz Cadet, Jon Astrop & Jolyon Skinner

Back To The S-t! 1989 Jive 1186-1-J Producer: Millie Jackson (Billboard soul charts: 44; Billboard pop charts: 79)

Young Man, Older Woman 1991 Jive 1447-1-J Producer: Millie Jackson

Jackson moved to Jive in 1986 where she briefly resurrected her career with two top ten soul singles, "Hot! Wild! Unrestricted! Crazy Love" and "Love Is A Dangerous Game", from the *Imitation Of Love* LP. Two further singles from the set also made the soul top 100 so she was certainly back on a roll, and on the cover of the album she looked great.

Unfortunately, this renaissance was not to last and the title of the next set, *The Tide Is Turning*, proved to be prophetic as it failed totally in the marketplace. Stung, she shooed away the army of producers who had worked on her last couple of LPs and produced her next album, *Back To The S..t!*, herself. Despite the fact it returned her to the lower reaches of soul and pop charts, it might just have the most tasteless cover in the history of soul music. One more LP was to follow, *Young Man, Older Woman*, but that didn't do much business, either.

It's probably worth pointing out that Jackson possibly saw herself by the eighties (and sees herself now) as being unnecessarily restricted by the tag of "soul singer" and some tracks on these later records place her in the "blue" tradition of Blowfly or Redd Foxx and who is to say that this wasn't an entirely smart move?

Walter Jackson

It's All Over 1965 Okeh OKM 12107 Producers: Carl Davis & Curtis Mayfield

Welcome Home 1965 Okeh OKM 12108 Producer: Carl Davis

Speak Her Name 1967 Okeh OKM 12120 Producers: Ted Cooper, Carl Davis & Gerald Sims (Billboard soul charts: 26; Billboard pop charts: 194)

Greatest Hits 1969 Okeh OKS 14128

There is a drawing of Walter Jackson on the front of his first LP that makes him look a bit like a black Roy Orbison, and both men shrugged off their scholarly and non-athletic appearances by relying solely on their voices to win over audiences and sell records. In fact, there was little else Jackson could do as he suffered from polio as a child, an affliction that prohibited him entirely from throwing himself around a stage à la James Brown or Jackie Wilson. There was also little of the church in his recordings, and he straddled - usually convincingly - a line between soul and supper club his entire career. He was born in Florida and grew up in Detroit where he made one record with an obscure doo-wop outfit before relocating to Chicago where he made some magnificent music.

The first LP, *It's All Over*, is a bit uneven, which was to be expected as it included five sides he cut for Columbia in 1962, a couple of "standards", and some marvellous examples of the new Chicago soul sound that sounded light years ahead of what he had recorded only 18 months earlier. As with so many other artists from the Windy City, Jackson was the grateful recipient of songs by Curtis Mayfield and the two best tracks on the album, the title cut and "That's What Mama Say", both came from that rich source. "It's All Over" performed reasonably well as a single (#67 pop) and remains a haunting and powerfully affecting side, fifty years on. Jackson's own song, "What Would You Do", was another fine effort, and if some of the other tracks are nowhere near as "soulful", his voice is always a reason to sit down and pay attention. His sense of timing, range, and his wonderful tone made him, or should have done, a "singer's singer", but sadly he has never received anything like the acclaim he deserved.

Welcome Home was a disappointment, however. Okeh pushed him in the nightclub direction and the enormous suffocating string sections and safely selected standards choked off its soul credentials almost entirely and made it an album that can best be enjoyed by those who care for MOR singers but not by hardcore soul fans. There wasn't even a picture of Jackson on the cover and the album seemed to be directed at the Ray Coniff fan club. Not all was lost, though, as the title track was a genuinely great record, one of his best ever, and it stood out a mile over all else. Only Van McCoy's "Suddenly I'm All Alone" also bears repeated plays and both sides performed almost identically when released as singles, coming to rest in the top fifteen of the soul charts and #95 and #96 respectively on the pop listings.

Okeh seemed determined not to put photos of Walter on his own albums and another drawing adorns the cover of his finest LP, *Speak Her Name*, an almost unmitigated triumph from 1967. The supper club material had all been discarded, but the intricate arrangements (from Riley Hampton) and stupendous productions remained intact. One of his two best ever sides is here, too: "It's An Uphill Climb To The Bottom" is a sublime record, as good as "big city" soul ever got. Its obvious quality made it a bankable 45 and it reached #11 soul and #88 pop, one of his biggest ever successes. "A Corner In The Sun","After You There Can Be Nothing" and the title track all reached the *Billboard* soul charts too as singles, while the atypical - for Jackson - dance workout "I'll Keep On Trying" had a brief run on the *Cashbox* soul chart as well. In fact, one of the reasons the set was so strong was that every one of its ten tracks was pressed into service as either an a or b - side on 45, with the exception of the excellent "She's A Woman" which was just as good as virtually everything else. Deservedly, the LP did well on the soul charts, even if Jackson remained pretty much unknown to the wider pop audience of the day. His voice was strong and distinctive enough to have claimed a much bigger listenership; his physical appearance was clearly not.

His best record for Okeh - and best ever - was still to come. "My Ship Is Coming In" had been previously recorded by Jimmy Radcliffe and The Walker Brothers but Jackson gave the definitive reading. It's another world-class performance with his devastatingly emotional interpretation almost causing him to lose control in the final few seconds. It remains a scandal that it failed so miserably as a single. Fortunately, it was scooped up on an impeccable *Greatest Hits* set that came out in 1969. It was his only Okeh LP on which it can be found.

Feeling Good 1976 Chi-Sound CH-LA656-G Producer: Carl Davis (Billboard soul charts: 14; Billboard pop charts: 113)

I Want To Come Back As A Song 1977 Chi-Sound CH-LA733-G Producer: Carl Davis (Billboard soul charts: 25; Billboard pop charts: 141)

Good To See You 1978 Chi-Sound CH-LA844-G Producer: Carl Davis (Billboard soul charts: 51)

Send In The Clowns 1979 20th Century T- 586 Producer: Carl Davis (Billboard soul charts: 68)

Walter had to content himself with singles only for the next few years, which came out on five different labels, until he moved to Chi-Sound in 1976 where he resumed his LP career. It was a commercially good period for him, even if few of his recordings matched the best of his Okeh work.

At first, on the *Feeling Good* outing, Jackson more or less reverted to the MOR oriented approach of the *Welcome Home* LP and made little attempt to appeal to a younger audience. There was minimal rhythmic drive on show and that fine drummer Quinton Joseph played well within himself. The material was all rather safe too, and the majority of the songs had been recorded by others. The best track was a fine re-make of "Welcome Home" but it didn't quite match the artistry of the original. Rather amazingly, the most schmaltzy of all the album's tracks, Morris Albert's "Feelings", reached #9 on the soul charts when released as a single at the end of 1976. It was the only time Jackson ever reached the soul top ten, and it was a long way from being his finest hour. It crept into the pop charts at #93, the last time he ever made the Hot 100. Jackson sings beautifully throughout, and the musicians are of an undoubtedly high quality but it's all a little too monotonous.

And the same can be said for the follow-up set, *I Want To Come Back As A Song*, which is rather too full of solemn and worthy songs like the title track, "I've Never Been To Me" and "Everything Must Change", none of which I much care for. Aretha's "Angel" was an enterprising choice, but Jackson's take is nowhere near as good as the original, and to reprise previous Walter winners like "It's All Over" and "What Would You Do" really just points up the fact that he was making more interesting and more soulful sides ten years earlier. Peter Frampton's "Baby, I Love Your Way" did well as a 45, attaining #19 on the soul charts, which was 56 places better than the re-make of "It's All Over", the second single from the set. But at least Chi-Sound were putting photos of the singer on their LP covers.

Good To See You hedged its bets much more than the previous Chi-Sound sets. It flirted, rather ineptly, with disco on the title track and "Manhattan Skyline", but retained its sense of MOR decorum on, for example, "Time". The most compelling track, by some distance, is "We Could Fly", which had the grandeur that was always the hallmark of his best records and I rate it as his finest performance on the label. As a 45 it lurked as the b - side to the peppy "If I Had My Way", another good cut, and the one single from the LP that reached the soul charts. Sadly, it was only at #68.

Chi-Sound switched distribution to 20th Century for Jackson's final LP of the seventies. Despite a couple of horrendous long disco cuts - it was as if 20th Century suddenly thought they were recording Michael Jackson rather than Walter Jackson - and a title track that leaves me cold, it's an album worth hearing, if still falling short of *Speak Her Name* or *It's All Over*. The Gamble and

Huff song, "And If I Had", was rather splendidly arranged and produced and started things off well before a pretty good version of "Magic Man" followed, and over on side 2, "The Meeting" and "Sounds Like A Love Song" are agreeable. In summary I rather like six of the nine cuts, which is not a bad percentage.

Tell Me Where It Hurts 1981 Columbia FC 37132 Producer: Carl Davis (Billboard soul charts: 45; Billboard pop charts: 206)

A Portrait Of 1983 Chi - Sound CH-2009 Producer: Carl Davis

Jackson's one album for Columbia, in 1981, was a typically opulent affair, swathed in strings and sounding like precious little else around at the time. He reminded us all over again what a purely beautiful singer he was, and it was nice to see the Eugene Record and Carl Davis written title track make it to #28 on the soul charts as a single. All right, it wasn't a massive hit but Walter still had a following and it was a lovely side, anyway. There are no real weak spots on the LP, and it should have delighted long-time Jackson fans, although I doubt if it would have brought in any new ones.

Sadly, opulent is not an adjective to apply to his final LP, which snuck out in 1983 without even a proper cover. (This was rectified on the UK version, issued on Bluebird LPBR 1001). Moreover, it included a handful of tracks that had appeared on earlier LPs, leaving us with only five that had not. One of these, "If I Had A Chance", became Jackson's sixteenth and final *Billboard* soul chart entrant at the inconsequential position of #83. It was better than that lowly placing suggested, though, and indeed all of the new cuts rather belied the cheap origins of the album, thereby making it another worthwhile release. "Touching In The Dark" and "It's Cool" even managed to pick up a number of dance fans, being much more accessible and immediate than his more subtle outings.

Even more sadly, 1983 was the year in which Jackson died, and he is remembered for being a distinctive singer who defied trends to go his own way, in the process acquiring a number of fans who will always swear by his music, as well as selling a fairly large number of records.

Jackson 5 / Jacksons

Michael Jackson; Jackie Jackson; Jermaine Jackson; Marlon Jackson; Tito Jackson; Randy Jackson

Diana Ross Presents 1969 Motown MS-700 Producers: The Corporation & Bobby Taylor (Billboard soul charts: 1; Billboard pop charts: 5)

ABC 1970 Motown MS 709 Producers: The Corporation & Hal Davis (Billboard soul charts: 1; Billboard pop charts: 4)

The Christmas Album 1970 Motown MS-713 Producers: The Corporation & Hal Davis

Third Album 1970 Motown S-718 Producers: The Corporation & Hal Davis (Billboard soul charts: 1; Billboard pop charts: 4)

Maybe Tomorrow 1971 Motown MS-735 Producers: The Corporation & Hal Davis (Billboard soul charts: 1; Billboard pop charts: 11)

Greatest Hits 1971 Motown M 741L (Billboard soul charts: 2; Billboard pop charts: 12)

Goin' Back To Indiana 1971 Motown M 742 No producer listed (Billboard soul charts: 5; Billboard pop charts: 16)

Lookin' Through The Windows 1972 Motown M 750L Producers: The Corporation, Jerry Marcellino, Mel Larson, Wille Hutch, Johnny Bristol & Hal Davis (Billboard soul charts: 3; Billboard pop charts: 7)

Skywriter 1973 Motown M 761 L Producers: The Corporation, Jerry Marcellino, Mel Larson, Deke Richards, Shirlie Matthews & Hal Davis (Billboard soul charts: 22; Billboard pop charts: 94)

Get It Together 1973 Motown M-783V1 Producer: Hal Davis (Billboard soul charts: 4; Billboard pop charts: 100)

Dancing Machine 1974 Motown M6-780S1 Producers: Jerry Marcellino, Mel Larson & Hal Davis (Billboard soul charts: 22; Billboard pop charts: 94)

Moving Violation 1975 Motown M6-829S1 Producers: Jerry Marcellino, Mel Larson, Brian Holland & Hal Davis (Billboard soul charts: 6; Billboard pop charts: 36)

Anthology 1976 Motown M7-868R3 (Billboard soul charts: 32; Billboard pop charts: 84)

Joyful Jukebox Music 1976 Motown M6-865S1 Producers: Jerry Marcellino, Mel Larson, Fonce Mizell, Freddie Perren, Tom Bee, Michael Edward Campbell, Sam Brown & Hal Davis

I'm not going to provide a great deal of narrative around the LPs released by the The Jackson 5 as I find them highly resistable, and other than the hits they contain, have never heard any of the other tracks. This has nothing to do with the group's obvious talent, the songs they chose or the great musicians who played on them but everything to do with the fact that I simply can't stay in the same room when 99% of tracks performed by pre-teens or young teenagers are playing. I wasn't even mad on these records when I was a teenager myself. And anyway, they are easy enough to hear if one wants to.

The success, however, or at least in the early days, was astonishing, and the fact that none of the albums from the Jackson 5 were certified as "gold" owed much more to Motown's alleged reticence to comply with the sales reporting rules stipulated by the Record Industry Association of America (who decreed "gold" or "platinum" status), than to the fact that they didn't sell enough. They certainly did

The Jacksons 1976 Epic PE 34229 Producers: Kenny Gamble, Leon Huff, Dexter Wansel, The Jacksons, Victor Carstarphen, John Whitehead & Gene McFadden (Billboard soul charts: 6; Billboard pop charts: 36)

Goin' Places 1977 Epic PE 34835 Producers: Kenny Gamble, Leon Huff, Dexter Wansel, The Jacksons, Victor Carstarphen, John Whitehead & Gene McFadden (Billboard soul charts: 11; Billboard pop charts: 63)

Destiny 1978 Epic JE 35552 Producer: The Jacksons (Billboard soul charts: 3; Billboard pop charts: 11)

Triumph 1980 Epic FE 36424 Producer: The Jacksons (Billboard soul charts: 1; Billboard pop charts: 10)

Live 1981 Epic EG 37545 Producer: The Jacksons (Billboard soul charts: 10; Billboard pop charts: 30)

Victory 1984 Epic QE 38946 Producer: The Jacksons (Billboard soul charts: 3; Billboard pop charts: 4)

2300 Jackson Street 1989 Epic OE 40911 Producer: The Jacksons (Billboard soul charts: 14; Billboard pop charts: 59)

My animus toward the music of The Jackson 5 fell away when they changed their name to The Jacksons and recorded in Philadelphia with Gamble and Huff. Michael was by now 18 years old and his maturity in years was reflected in the maturity of the music. Randy had replaced Jermaine, who had chosen to stay with Motown as a solo artist. The sinuous "Show You The Way To Go" is a superb side, and it is astonishing that it performed no better than #6 soul and #28 pop when it became the second 45 to be issued form the set. "Enjoy Yourself" had been the lead-off single, and despite being an inferior song, did very well at #2 soul and #6 pop. Other than "The Strength Of One Man" there is precious little on the LP that is not entirely positive - "Enjoy Yourself", "Good Times", "Think Happy", and "Blues Away" rather speak for themselves - and if these are not the deepest songs to ever come from the socially conscious P.I.R label, no one who loved that city's music in the seventies should have any qualms about listening to *The Jacksons*.

Goin' Places was bright, glossy, danceable and resolutely upbeat for the most part too, with only the more sedate "Man Of War", which attractively shared around the lead vocals, and the best cut on show, "Find Me A Girl", bucking the trend, and although it was a set which seemed highly likely to have widespread appeal actually performed no more than reasonably well. Two singles were issued from it (the title track and "Find Me") and neither even made the pop top 50.

It was maybe this sort of mediocre success that made The Jacksons decide to produce all their records themselves from here on, a decision that was rewarded by bigger sales. "Blame It On The Boogie" and "Shake Your Body (Down To The Ground)" for instance both reached #3 on the soul charts when they were pulled from the *Destiny* album, in itself a high performing commercial set, but these were records that tended to drive me slightly crazy after hearing them for the thousandth time. In truth, I care little more for the later Jacksons LPs than I did for the earlier ones, and I'd rather leave lumpy sides like "Can You Feel It" from *Triumph* to be enjoyed by their millions of fans.

The Jackson 5 / Jacksons sold records in vast numbers (although they had no more #1 soul singles after 1974's "Dancing Machine"), quite apart from how many Michael and Jermaine shipped by themselves, and theirs is also a career defined by talent and longevity, but I will always side with those fans who prefer our soul a little neater.

Jackson Sisters

Jacqueline Jackson; Lyn Jackson; Pat Jackson; Gennie Jackson; Rae Jackson

Jackson Sisters 1976 Tiger Lily TL 14061 No producer listed

This was another of the notorious Tiger Lily Albums, which guarantees both scarcity and desirability but unlike most of the others, it contained a number of sides which were released as genuine and legitimate singles, with the best and best-known of these being "I Believe In Miracles", with a great "Blaxploitaion" style groove. The LP doesn't list a producer but the released singles were produced by Johnny Bristol, Don Altfeld, Bobby Taylor, Peter Moore, Ronnie Walker and Albert Hammond.

The sisters were from Compton, and generally served up slightly earthier music than the better-known Jacksons even though "Why Do Fools Fall In Love" and a couple of other tracks on here demonstrate that the teenage market was at least in the back of the mind. "Maybe" is not the same song as performed by The Three Degrees and is not as soulful either, but it's not a million miles away on either count. "I Believe In Miracles" managed #89 on the soul charts of autumn 1973 but the 45 bears a different mix from the one on the LP.

Jade

Vernon Goodson: Lucius Goodson; Gregory Rich; Lorenzo Jones; Harrison Robinson

In Pursuit 1975 Pesante PMF 050 Producers: William D Smith & Keith Olsen

Another decidely rare LP, which thus guarantees that a number of people on the internet play it up as a "masterpiece". It is nothing of the sort of course, but it is really rather good, with a most appealing jazzy, funky feel, including an excellent cover of Santana's "Evil Ways". Jade - and I must confess to have taken somewhat of an educated guess as to their membership - seemingly came out of Norfolk Virginia (or at least that is the town where Pesante Records was based) but presumably, given the involvement of William Smith, Paul Stallworth and Carol Kaye among others, it was actually recorded on the West Coast. Jade also released a couple more singles that are not included on the LP, so they did have a handful of shots at breaking out but nothing worked and they will have to be content with releasing this worthy album.

Jaedes

Ernest Baskerville; Fred Jennings; Naaman Johnson; Curtis Jones; Fredrick Blackmon

Jaedes 1969 Athena 6002 Producer: Rick Powell

Sometime in 1968, in Mobile, Alabama, The Jaedes played a concert with a backing band called The Commodores. We know what happened to the Commodores; the Jaedes released one single and this one album, performed a number of gigs around the South for a few years, and broke up in 1971. It's not much of a story when compared to their erstwhile musicians, but this is a sweetly alluring LP, nonetheless.

There were over ten groups known as The Jades, so the slight difference in spelling was an attempt to make this one stand out and they did deserve to have done rather better than they did, particularly as group member Fred Blackmon was quite a talented writer, penning six of the eleven tracks within. I believe it was cut in Nashville, but the feeling throughout is much closer to what was coming out of the West Coast at the time, rather than down in the country music capital. It's beautifully recorded, with resonant bass underpinning a full production sound which allows the group, who were not shy of switching vocals around, to enchant the listener with their danceable and melodic tunes. There are no ballads on offer, and some of the covers are possibly a little dull ("Lay Lady Lay", for example) although they do perform an intriguing version of "Spinning Wheel". But it's Blackmon's songs which last the course the best: the single, "Uh Uh, What Did I Do", "What'll It Take To Make You Happy" and "Big Surprise" being especially appealing.

Jaisun

Jaisun 1977 Jett Sett JS1001 Producer: William "Mickey" Stevenson

Jett Sett records was based in Tulsa, Oklahoma, not a city known for an abundance of soul music. And I wonder whether Jaisun McMillian would consider herself to be a soul singer anyway? On the evidence of her web site, probably not. Despite having also been a member of a late version of the Vandellas, her talents clearly extend into areas outside of music, as she has written stage plays and performed various roles of a corporate nature, and so whether or not her one and only LP, which demonstrates she had a style somewhat in common with the likes of Randy Crawford and Marlena Shaw, was a soul rather than jazz album, and I think it is, should hardly be a question that would have caused her sleepless nights.

Although Jaisun was born in Durham, NC, her first single came out in 1974 on a small Los Angeles based label, Conbrio, only to be greeted with resounding indifference. Three years later, and she must have been pleased to have the opportunity to work with ex-Motown man, Mickey Stevenson, who, despite never matching his successes of the sixties in the seventies, was still an experienced, talented and well-connected record man. An attractive 45, "Try And Understand", which bore just the faintest elements of a "deep soul" side, was pulled from the album and reached #42 on the soul charts in early 1978, but it did not lead to significant sales for the LP itself. There are covers within, and she gives us a fast and rousing take on "You're All I Need To Get By" and a more considered one on "Keepin' It To Myself, that fine song from Alan Gorrie of AWB. A Stevenson number, "Shackin' Up", tries to show off a tougher, funkier side of Jaisun, but I'm not sure it really suits her. There is a mildly irritating synthesiser in use, but generally the music doesn't disappoint and we are certainly spared any disco excesses by Stevenson. It's not an LP to pull out with any frequency, but there is no reason to cut short its 26 minutes of playing time once it has been slapped onto the deck.

E.L. James

Sings The Face Of Love 1977 Captown C-101R Producer: E.L. James

The performer of this highly unusual album should not be confused with the author of *Fifty Shades of Grey*. My sole knowledge of this particular E.L. James is informed by the sleevenotes that accompany the record, and I thereby deduce that this is a vinyl rendering of a stage show written by James. Those notes suggest that the "ingenious creations and presentations" within would propel the artist to fame and fortune but in fact, the LP can't have sold many copies at all and remains an intriguing curiosity. Some of it is superb soul music of a most impressive order; other tracks bear no resemblance to anything else in this book. The good things first: the title track, where James demonstrates similarities with the music of Lou Bond, the soulful "Stand By Your Baby" and the haunting "Love affair" which sounds like Donny Hathaway on a good day, are all wonderful. On the other side of the coin, "Children Do" draws on music from the twenties or thirties and will bemuse anyone who walked into a room and heard it without the benefit of any context. It seems that James also released a CD in 2005 but I've not come across that one. I do strongly recommend this LP to anyone who wants to seek out something just that little bit different and it probably bears a closer listen to all the lyrics than I have had time to do.

Etta James

Miss Etta James 1961 Crown 5209 No producer listed

Twist With Etta James 1962 Crown 5250 No producer listed

Jamesetta Hawkins lived to the respectable age of 74 and I wish her no disrespect when I say this was rather against the odds when one considers her turbulent life style, drug problems and later numerous difficulties with her health. But despite all these obstacles, she managed to become respectable, world famous and hugely influential; she also left us with probably as many great records as any other female soul singer.

Her first hit came all the way back in 1955 when she was only 17: "Wallflower" becoming a #1 on the "R&B" charts on the Modern label. A second hit followed with "Good Rockin' Daddy" but many more releases over the next few years did not perform nearly as well. She sang duets with Harvey Fuqua in an attempt to revive her fortunes but had to wait until 1960 before she visited the charts again, when "All I Could Do Was Cry" became a big hit on both the "R&B" and pop listings, on her new label Argo. A number of her fifties sides were collected together on her first LP, *Miss Etta James*, which came out on the Crown label in 1961 (to capitalise on her new hit). Other early recordings followed on another Crown album, *Twist With Etta James*, the following year. Neither of the LPs are really "soul" albums as the music pre-dates the genre and as Crown releases were not known for classy packaging or informative sleevenotes they are both really for anyone who simply has to own all her records.

At Last! 1961 Argo 4003 No producer listed (Billboard pop charts: 68)

The Second Time Around 1961 Argo 4011 No producer listed

Etta James 1962 Argo 4013 No producer listed

At Last! was really James' first "proper" LP as it featured newly recorded sides rather than collecting together older releases in the rather opportunistic manner of Crown. It's a splendid set, and so, if to a slightly lesser degree, are the next two LPs which followed in quick succession, *The Second Time Around* and *Etta James*.

There are an impressive nine top 15 *Billboard* R & B chart entrants spread across the three albums and even though they came out in that gestation period before "R&B" and "doo-wop" gave birth to "soul", they all gave notice that James was going to be a formidable presence, in every way, during the sixties. Some of her most enduring sides feature on these sets such as *At Last* itself, which has probably become her signature tune, being as enjoyable today as it was when it first registered as a hit 55 years ago (#2 soul, #47 pop). "I Just Want To Make Love To You" is also on the *At Last!* LP while "Something's Got A Hold On Me" graces *Etta James*. So did "Seven Day Fool", one of her toughest sides from this period, and although it had a good run on the *Cashbox* charts, was strangely absent from the *Billboard* ones. All three albums have strong jazzy and bluesy overtones and contain a smattering of "standards" while being liberally washed with strings, but James cuts through everything in her utterly distinctive style, being easily able to slip from tough to tender as required. Along with Bobby Bland, James was probably making better records than any of the other big names of soul who were active at the turn of the sixties.

Sings For Lovers 1962 Argo 4018 No producer listed

Top Ten 1963 Argo 4025 No producer listed (Billboard pop charts: 117)

Rocks The House 1964 Argo 4032 Producer: Ralph Bass (Billboard pop charts: 96)

Queen Of Soul 1964 Argo 4040 No producer listed

Etta James Sings For Lovers was a less enjoyable set as it aimed squarely at the sophisticated nightclub set and contained no hit singles at all (although "How Do You Speak To An Angel" did feature for a brief two weeks on the *Cashbox* charts at the lowly level of #43). "Supervison" (which I assume means "producing") was credited to Ralph Bass while Riley Hampton provided the lush arrangements. James handles all of the rather MOR material with ease, but whether she should have had to is the question for me.

Top Ten, on the other hand, was great. Something of a *Greatest Hits* package, it featured, as could be guessed, ten tracks, seven of which had hit the "R&B" top ten although only one, and rather surprisingly that was "Trust In Me", had broached the pop top 30. Two great James' sides were included on an album for the first time, the magnificent "Pushover" and the anguished "Stop The Wedding".

Rocks The House followed next and, over time, has become one of the most exalted of all "live" outings by a soul artist, being re-released many times in future years. Slightly ironically, in a way, as it is overwhelmingly a blues record. Of course, James could sing anything she was asked to but this is a real antidote to the safe recordings foisted on her by Argo all too often. The crowd is raucous, Etta snarls, croons and exhorts, and it is a significantly different LP from all her others to date. It only just sneaked into the national pop chart but had a real sense of sweat and energy and proved how compelling she could be on a stage.

Calling James the *Queen Of Soul* was a good idea, but it never caught on and the title was to become Aretha Franklin's as time went by. It's a slightly unconvincing set, anyway, as although the music is good, it looks backwards as much as forwards, and isn't a significant advance on the music she had been making in the previous few years, with bluesy, jazzy and big band influences remaining more prominent than the harder rhythms that were elsewhere starting to characterise the new era. To be fair, this was also down to the fact that some of the cuts on the LP were two years old by the time the LP was released. The excellent "Loving You More Every Day" is the best track (and biggest hit, #65 pop) on show but it couldn't stop the album from becoming one of her least well remembered.

Call My Name 1967 Cadet 4055 Producers: Monk Higgins & Ralph Bass

Tell Mama 1968 Cadet 802 Producer: Rick Hall (Billboard soul charts: 21; Billboard pop charts: 82)

Sings Funk 1969 Cadet 832 Producers: Gene Barge & Ralph Bass

Losers Weepers 1971 Cadet 847 Producer: Ralph Bass

James had to wait until 1967 for her next album, which was also her first on the Cadet label. No ifs and buts, despite the rather unhip and old-fashioned sleeve, this was a proper "soul" record, too, and one recorded as an LP, not just a collection of earlier sides pulled together in the manner of her previous long players. However, she was still failing to re-capture her commercial fortunes of the early sixties and had to be content with "I Prefer You", the lead-off single, coming to rest at a rather uninspiring #42 on the soul charts in early 1967, and the album didn't chart either. It's a collection I like, and incorporates an interesting brassy version of "It's All Right" that is worth a listen, as well as an excellent slow and sensitive reading of "That's All I Want From You" that Franklin was also to cover. My only reservations are around the ok but generally not overwhelmingly good songs and a tendency to over - produce on occasion.

No reservations attend the *Tell Mama* album, one of the greatest in the history of soul music. It was the record Etta James was born to sing, and despite her facility in dealing with all styles and all settings, nowhere was ever to suit her quite so well as that dusty corner of Alabama, Muscle Shoals. It was also the first of her LPs to reach the national soul charts, and the sessions within restored her fortunes on the singles charts, too. "Tell Mama" itself was coupled with "I'd Rather Go Blind" as a 45 which must have claims to be the finest pairing of any single ever released. The aggression of the former's wondrous horn charts and the brilliance of the latter song carried the single to #10 soul and #23 pop. Remarkably, there were other tracks that were all but as good: the ferocious "Security" (a #11 soul and #35 pop follow-up to "Tell Mama") charges along, while "Don't Lose Your Good Thing" is one of the best songs the estimable Eddie Hinton ever wrote; the same goes for Charles Chalmers and his astonishing "It Hurts Me So Much", which brought out a phenomenal performance by James, on a side that had everything to do with unfettered emotion and nothing whatsoever to do with spurious things like image. Don Covay's "I'm Gonna Take What He's Got" is a song for grown-ups too, while "My Mother In Law" demonstrated that the album was not without a sly wit, either. There's not a false move here; all the tracks come in at under three minutes and are all unerringly right for James and the project. The band are frankly amazing throughout with Roger Hawkins' drumming and David Hood's bass rooting everything in that rich southern soil, and I sincerely hope everyone had a nice lie down after they finished cutting the insanely fast "Watch Dog". They certainly deserved it.

Etta James Sings Funk was a curious affair: a complete retreat from the sparse southern verities of *Tell Mama* and a title that was wholly misleading. There was no "funk" on show at all, in the sense that it would have been known by 1969, and the Los Angeles recorded set had more country songs on show than had been associated with James in the past, while "Sound Of Love" had as much to do with pop as it did with soul. None of which is to say that it was a set without merit. I liked all the country influenced songs and an ominous and intriguing version of "What Fools We Mortals Be" is a particular favourite. "Tighten Up Your Own Thing" was just about the only cut that more or less lived up to the title's promise but only did moderate business as a 45. It did all rather seem a case of one step back after the confident and assured foot forward of *Tell Mama*.

James began the seventies with the so-so *Losers Weepers* set, another one that suffered a little from Chess' insistence that she cover as many bases as possible rather then put her in a consistent and coherent setting as with *Tell Mama*. The title track was excellent, however, and had done well at the end of 1970 as a single when it reached #26 soul and #94 pop, and she was never to place any singles on either chart as high as this again. The album also started well with the persuasive "Take Out Some Insurance" which undeservedly flopped as a 45. Elsewhere she delivered "I Got It Bad And That Ain't Good" and "For All We Know" in straight fashion and had a fair stab at Jackie Edwards' "Look At The Rain". There was a palpable gospel influence here and there and a fine line in spirited backing vocals but it wasn't her strongest set.

Etta James 1973 Chess CH 50042 Producer: Gabriel Mekler (Billboard soul charts: 41; Billboard pop charts: 154)

Come A Little Closer 1974 Chess CH 60029 Producer: Gabriel Mekler (Billboard soul charts: 47)

Etta Is Better Than Evvah 1976 Chess ACH 19003 Producers: Mike Terry, Gabriel Mekler & Etta James

As might have been inferred from James' consistently modest showing on the pop charts, she never meant much to a rock or pop audience in the sixties and seventies, and that continued to be the case for a while longer but at least a few rock critics sniffed the air when it was announced that she would be produced by Gabriel Mekler, a man who had carried out the same duties for Steppenwolf, Janis Joplin and Three Dog Night. He set his stall out from the start, with an impressive production job on the opener, "All The Way Down", which shimmered along in flawless sound for a minute and a half before Etta came in. A truncated version at 45 went to #29 on the soul charts and missed the hot 100 by one place. The excellent "Leave Your Hat On", one of three Randy Newman - not a man who habitually provided material for soul singers - songs on the set, also charted but at a much more derisory #76. James' power, clearly undimmed by her persistent drug intake, was evident on "God's Song" but I suspect it may have been too rich for some soul fans. "Only A Fool" was credited to James, Mekler and Trevor Lawrence but it is clearly virtually exactly the same song as "I Pity The Fool" but as it was "written" by Deadric Malone (a pseudonym for the notorious Don Robey) I guess they thought it was fair game. (Bobby Bland's version is far superior). There's some decent things on side two, including the one recognisable song from a soul tradition, Otis Redding's "Just One More Day". It's certainly a good LP, but it's all a little too well-crafted and knowing for me and doesn't have the staying power of *At Last!* or *Tell Mama*.

Come A Little Closer followed the same formula with the terrific "Out On The Streets Again" adopting a markedly similar approach to "All The Way Down" (with James again coming in at the 90 second mark), but sadly performed much more poorly as a 45 (#84 soul). It was one of only a handful of cuts on the album I regularly play by choice (the others are "You Give Me What I Want" and the rather extraordinary "Feeling Uneasy" which was recorded at the time of a particularly bad drug withdrawal period for James, who seems incapable of actual words and simply moans her way through). I actively dislike other cuts like "Mama Told Me", "Sooki Sooki" and "Power Play" which stray too far into rock territory.

I don't want to be dismissive of Mekler's efforts, and clearly Chess was in not much better shape than James herself in 1973 and 1974, but the end result of his stint in the producer's chair was that she no longer meant too much to soul audiences either.

Even allowing for typical record company hyperbole, *Etta Is Better Than Evvah* was demonstrably untrue. It's a rather ungainly outing: two tracks repeated from the Etta James set of three years earlier, a handful of pronounced rock-influenced tracks, a song title, "Woman (Shake Your Booty)" that screamed cliché, and a strong sense that she was flailing in 1976. Three tracks are ok, all covers: straight versions of "A Love Vibration" and "Groove Me" and best of all, an outtake (I think) from the Mekler sessions, "Ain't No Pity In The Naked City," a song of woe that Etta conveyed entirely convincingly. "Jump Into Love" was pulled as a 45 and it failed wretchedly at only #92 soul, which was at least more than the LP managed which charted not at all. Etta clearly was not better than ever.

Deep In The Night 1978 Warner Brothers BSK 3156 Producer: Jerry Wexler

Changes 1980 T-Electric 3244 Producer: Allen Toussaint

James' one album for Warner Brothers was everything the last Chess album had not been: tasteful, well-considered and with an upmarket front cover. Jerry Wexler had been brought in to produce and the song selection was imaginative and obviously the result of much thought. The musicians were of the highest quality and Etta could still sing superbly. But even with all this richness on show, it somehow seemed to lack a little life and I found it was just too tasteful for my blood with only Kiki Dee's "Sugar On The Floor" really engaging me. I admire the LP, certainly, as it shows a great respect for James, but I don't love it. Not many others did either, for it failed to chart and "Piece Of My Heart" continued her woeful run on the soul singles chart, lasting just three weeks with a highest position of #93. All of the songs are new to her apart from "I'd Rather Go Blind". She gives it her all but I still prefer the more elegant and less overwrought original by some distance.

I do have affection for her little-known and almost wholly forgotten *Changes* LP for the small MCA offshoot, T-Electric, though. Recorded down in New Orleans with a marvellous band, it was her first album for a while (and last ever to my ears) that seemed aimed mainly at a black audience and its sound and approach made it much more suitable for the *Etta James Sings Funk* title, bestowed so inappropriately all those years before. Willie Hutch provided three songs with Allen Toussaint contributing four, and even that great unknown soul man Jimmy Jules pitched in with one, too, while the one "pop" song on show, "Changes", from Carole King, was also a good choice. There were two brilliant cuts aboard: the slow and stately "With You In Mind" which was perfect for James, and her impeccably funky "Night People", amazingly even better than Lee Dorsey's celebrated version. Hutch's "Mean Mother" was good too, and presumably could apply to James herself, in describing a challenging upbringing without sounding remotely patronising. *Changes* might be a record with a modest reputation and modest sales, but I like it a great deal, and play it by choice rather than most of her more celebrated outings.

The Heart And Soul Of Etta James 1982 Arrival AN 8121 (Holland)

Blues In The Night (and Eddie Vinson) 1986 Fantasy F-9647 Producers: Ralph Jungheim & Red Holloway

The Late Show (and Eddie Vinson) 1987 Fantasy F-9655 Producers: Ralph Jungheim & Red Holloway

Jump The Blues Away (and Joe Walsh and Albert Collins) 1988 Verve 841 287-1 Producer: Jack Lewis

As the eighties progressed it was clear that Etta James no longer meant much to contemporary black record buyers and she was spared from recording mindless dance tracks which would have been demeaning and which she would have doubtless hated anyway. Instead it was a case of back to the future and a clear aim at a white audience and the four albums above were not soul records, but gospel, blues and jazz outings, although I'm making an assumption here as I've only heard the merest snippets from them. There was a clear logic in this as James' had always been able to sing in any style anyway and her output over her eventual fifty year plus career would consist of at least 50% in a non typical soul style.

Seven Year Itch 1988 Island 91018-1 Producers: Barry Beckett, Rob Fraboni & Ricky Fataar

Going For Your Guns 1990 Island 842 926-1 Producers: Barry Beckett, Etta James & Kim Buie

In 1988 James recorded *Seven Year Itch*, which certainly looked as if it was going to be a pure soul album. I only wish she had recorded it twenty years earlier as it had the potential to have matched *Tell Mama*. The song selection was the best on any James LP since that celebrated release; the musicians were among the best popular music could offer: Roger Hawkins, Willie Weeks, Reggie Young and many others; the horn section was splendid; Etta could still sing as well as ever, and all was set for a great comeback. The problem, I'm afraid, could be laid at the producers' door and I say that with care, as I have a great admiration for Barry Beckett who was heavily involved in some of my favourite records of all time. Disturbingly, they decided on an approach which was typical of the late eighties: bombastic and with rock guitar overlaid all over the place. Moreover, there was the way in which Hawkins' drums were recorded on a few tracks: very loud indeed. All in all it added up to the noisiest Etta James album ever released and it was rather ruined for me as a result. I exclude "Damn Your Eyes" and "Jealous Kind" from the above comments, however, as they are typically good James' sides.

I'll pass over *Stickin' To My Guns* quickly as it was a repeat of the *Seven Year Itch* approach, but with an inferior song selection (although hardly bad) and even some rapping on "Get Funky". Being harsh on Etta James' LPs will doubtless offend some, but I submit the above named track as the best case for my argument. Listen to it next to "At Last" or "I'd Rather Go Blind" or "Pushover". Or countless other sides. And weep.

Peaches 1971 Chess 6310 111 (UK)

Juicy Peaches 1988 Chess GCH 8116 (Europe)

Many Etta James compilations exist and I'm ignoring them all apart from the two above which are the ones I would recommend. The first is a double LP containing 23 tracks, spanning the period at Chess from 1960 to 1970, with every one being a winner. The second is much more modest at only 14 cuts, but it is the only one that contains such top class sides as "Almost Persuaded" (#32 soul, #79 pop), "I Worship The Ground You Walk On" and "I Found A Love".

Etta James continued to make music for most of the period up to her death and released a number of CDs from 1992 to 2011, some rather better than others, although very few of them were really "soul" records. But, clearly, she was a great, world famous artist who could and did sing in many different styles and there was absolutely no reason why she should have confined herself to one market. On balance, I think she was possibly better represented on singles rather than albums, but *Tell Mama* was one of the genuinely great LPs of the twentieth century.

Ginji James

Love Is A Merry Go Round 1971 Brunswick BL 754175 Producers: Carl Davis, Eugene Record & Willie Henderson

In the seventies, Brunswick adopted a similar approach to their album releases as the All Platinum organisation: just get some out there, regardless of whether or not anyone has ever heard of the artist. Hence LPs from The Directions, Step By Step...and Ginji James. According to the LP's sleevenotes she was born and raised in Texas but the sound is, of course, pure Chicago and this set could have been cut nowhere else in the world. The cover dates it as 1970 but it was actually released in late 1971 and was aimed - if it was consciously aimed anywhere at all - at the "light soul" market. While James sounds nothing like Diana Ross her vocal style is closer to the Detroit diva than it was to say, Aretha Franklin. So it's rather poppy with little sense of gospel and the proof is in her good and enjoyable version of "You Hurt Me For The Last Time", one that has none of the sheer desperation and pain of Otis Clay's brilliant take on the same song. There's nothing to offend at all, however, and it's a perfectly pleasant way to spend 27 minutes or so. One single, "Love Changed His Face", was released but both it and the LP itself went precisely nowhere and Ginji James doesn't even get a mention in Robert Pruter's definitive book on Chicago soul.

Jesse James

Jesse James 1968 20th Century S3197 Producer: Jesse Mason

It Takes One To Know One 1987 T.T.E.D. 3026 Producers: Harvey Scales & Felton Pilate

I Can Do Bad By Myself 1988 Gunsmoke SMO-001 Producers: Harvey Scales, Jesse James & Felton Pilate

Looking Back 1990 Gunsmoke SMO-002 Producers: Harvey Scales, Jesse James, Ron Carson & Clarence Johnson

"Jesse James" has been an extraordinarily popular name for singers to adopt and this one, James Herbert McClelland from Arizona, should not be confused with any of the many others. He recorded pretty much exclusively on the West Coast and released a large number of singles over a thirty year period on at least eleven different labels, placing six of them on the soul charts, but none of them could be described as a genuine smash. He was a real soul man, though, seldom venturing out to record in any other style, and had an instantly recognisable voice which could emit genuine emotion when required but as often as not simply exuded a good time, hang loose, feel of the streets.

There is a sticker on the front of my copy of the *Jesse James* LP which reminds me that I bought it for $25 in a long forgotten New York store in the late eighties; money well spent as I find it a highly attractive LP, but one which I imagine a non committed soul fan might find hard to get to grips with, as its charms are modest. Many of the - not particularly strong - songs are delivered in a relaxed, almost spontaneous way, and the set has a pronounced "live" feel, enhanced by James' vocal asides of "listen to me now" etc. which would typically be used by soul singers when performing on stage. "Believe In My Baby" was one of the six singles he charted, reaching #42 soul in the autumn of 1967, and #92 pop, the only time he breached the Hot 100, and is absolutely typical of the set, taking its own sweet time to impart a mixture of admonition and hope. "Time After Time", the "standard", was a mistake as it doesn't suit James at all rendered this straight, and he does much better with a more down-home take on "At Last". "Green Power" is a bit of a mess, too, but there is still plenty to enjoy.

It was a great shame that we had to wait nearly twenty years before James' second LP as he made some brilliant records in the seventies and none finer than "I Need You Baby" in 1971 which still remains unrepresented on an album. *It Takes One To Know One* is, in all honesty, a "two-track album" but those couple of songs make the set, on the cover of which Jesse looks very dapper, worthwhile. "I'm Gonna Be Rich And Famous" and "I Can Do Bad By Myself", both written by Harvey Scales, are excellent, and tell stories that keep the listener enthralled. James was so good on this sort of material. I certainly root for him to realise his dreams on the former and while he never became famous I do hope he at least made some cash. "I Can Do Bad" probably sold well in excess as a single than its rather paltry position of #61 would suggest as I believe it was extremely popular in the black community over a long period of time, which was no surprise given its instantly catchy if rather repetitive hook. The title track and "Don't Get Amnesia On Me Baby" are ok, but the remainder of the cuts are forgettable.

In fact, "I Can Do Bad By Myself" was popular enough to be recycled onto his third album, becoming its title track. It's another uneven set, and features James recording more blues-based tracks than had been the case in the past, but they are still interesting to listen to as Scales (and on a couple of songs, James himself) spin out some more compelling tales. There are two new winners here: "Love On The Side" could easily have sat proudly on any number of top-class sixties southern soul albums, while the live nine minute version of "Cheatin' In The Next Room" sustains interest with ease. The biggest disappointment is the heavy handed production on the excellent Phillip Mitchell and Billy Clements song, "When Can We Do This Again", that Charnissa cut so well. It's a thoughtful outing, and needs to be treated with care, not by the bull in a china shop approach it receives here.

His last album gratefully reached back into his extensive back catalogue and was pretty much a joy throughout. James' small hit from 1975 "If You Want A Love Affair" was a much loved single in UK circles and both it and its equally good b-side, "I Never Meant To Love Her", were included on the album as was another lovely single from the same era, "You Ought To Be With Me". An updated version of "At Last" which had come out on a 45 in 1984 (and its b-side "Love Vibes") were the most recent sides on show while three unreleased songs from the prolific and lyrical pen of Sam Dees rounded things out. I'm not sure it was a commercial release as such, and would not have found its way into many stores, but it was a delight for fans of this underappreciated singer.

He has continued to issue top class CDs in recent years and I've always kept an eye on his work. Hopefully, one day some enterprising record label will do many of us a big favour by putting out an exhaustive retrospective of his work.

Rick James (see also Stone City Band)

Come Get It! 1978 Gordy G7-981R Producers: Rick James & Art Stewart (Billboard soul charts: 3; Billboard pop charts: 13)

Bustin' Out Of L Seven 1979 Gordy G7-984R Producers: Rick James & Art Stewart (Billboard soul charts: 2; Billboard pop charts: 16)

Fire It Up 1979 Gordy G8-990MI Producer: Rick James (Billboard soul charts: 5; Billboard pop charts: 34)

Garden Of Love 1980 Gordy G8-995M1 Producer: Rick James (Billboard soul charts: 17; Billboard pop charts: 83)

Rick James (real name: James Ambrose Johnson) was one of a handful of artists who continued to keep Motown's name at the top end of the charts in the period from 1978 until 1986 when the label's best days were years in the past. Ironically, he had already recorded for the company way back in 1966 as a member of The Mynah Birds but a scheduled single was never released at the time. One could have got very long odds indeed back then on the chances of one of that band's members recording four soul #1 singles and selling millions of albums in the next two decades.

It still don't look likely up to the mid seventies either as he released two distinctly average singles (one on A&M and one on Polydor), that failed utterly, and he did well to get a record deal with Motown. He always had a strong visual image, though, and clearly someone saw potential to be exploited. His first LP, *Come Get It!*, was a derivative affair with the funk tracks being highly reminiscent of Funkadelic but that didn't stop "You And I" from going straight to #1 on the soul charts and #13 pop. The slightly twee "Mary Jane" did well as a 45 too, and apart from one awful disco cut, "Be My Lady", it wasn't too bad an album, although the more traditional and conservative soul fan will hate it. (Note: This was the only Rick James album that explicitly credited the Stone City Band too.)

Bustin' Out Of L Seven played down the Funkadelic influence in favour of James' own brand of fast and rather straightforward funk although I preferred the more thoughtful cuts "Jefferson Ball" and "Spacey Love" which showed that James could deal with slower material perfectly well. The title track went to #8 soul, four places higher than "High On Your Love Suite". Although *Bustin' Out* didn't go gold as had its predecessor, it sold strongly in the pop market, and James continued to mean a lot to this audience for years to come.

Fire It Up moved things on a little bit further as James added a tad more rock and pop in the mix which was not to my own taste but to his credit, his music and voice were now pretty distinctive and he was nothing if not his own man. Two singles pulled from the set, "Love Gun" and "Come Into My Life" performed ok, but not as well as previous 45s.

Garden Of Love played up to its title, being considerably more mellow and relaxed than anything he had cut before with precious little funk aboard. The opening cut, "Big Time", sounded a little dated and performed only reasonably well as a 45 (#17 soul) while "Island Lady" strongly recalled Stevie Wonder; it seemed as if James had rather lost his way and certainly the LP carried on the trend of each one doing a little less well than the one before. It was time for a re-think.

Street Songs 1981 Gordy G8-1002MI Producer: Rick James (Billboard soul charts: 1; Billboard pop charts: 3)

Throwin' Down 1982 Gordy 6005GL Producer: Rick James (Billboard soul charts: 2; Billboard pop charts: 13)

Coldblooded 1983 Gordy 6043GL Producer: Rick James (Billboard soul charts: 1; Billboard pop charts: 16)

Reflections 1984 Gordy 6095GL (Billboard soul charts: 10; Billboard pop charts: 41)

Glow 1985 Gordy 6135GL Producer: Rick James (Billboard soul charts: 7; Billboard pop charts: 50)

The Flag 1986 Gordy 6185GL Producer: Rick James (Billboard soul charts: 16; Billboard pop charts: 95)

Wonderful 1988 Reprise 9 25659-1 Producer: Rick James (Billboard soul charts: 12; Billboard pop charts: 148)

That re-appraisal manifested itself with the excellent *Street Songs* LP, although as with all James' music, it will probably have limited appeal for traditional soul fans. Mixing up autobiographical reminiscence with humour, social comment, lustful sex and judicious use of a fine horn section and The Temptations' voices, it was a most impressive and considered collection. He also once again showed on the enticing duet with Teena Marie on "Fire And Desire" that he was an expressive and underrated singer. "Give It To Me Baby" went to #1 soul and #40 pop, while "Super Freak" (used later on for M.C. Hammer's "U Can't Touch This") had a riff which everyone in the western world under the age of 60 must know, did even better pop, going to #16 while stopping at #3 on the soul charts. The album itself went platinum and was the fourth most successful LP on the soul charts in the entire decade of the eighties, lasting a staggering twenty weeks at #1. James was on top of the world.

And he stayed there with the *Throwin' Down* LP, another gold set, and vessel for two more big selling singles: "Dance Wit' me" (#3 soul) and the appositely titled "Standing On The Top" a collaborative effort with The Temptations (#6), the biggest hit the venerable vocal group had enjoyed for six years. It's a less varied set than *Street Songs* with all the dance tracks having that ubiquitous one dimensional eighties beat but at least James usually managed to overlay interesting musical patterns. "Teardrops and "Happy" were fine ballads while the throwaway "Hard To Get" was a barely believable reprise of "Super Freak".

By 1983's *Coldblooded* The Temptations had vanished and so had much of my interest in his albums. The title track became his third #1 single on the soul charts but I preferred his slow drag duet with Smokey Robinson, "Ebony Eyes", even if it only lodged at #22 as the third single from the set (the unremarkable "U Bring The Freak Out " being the second,#16 soul). Nevertheless, it was yet another gold album, and by no means "poor", just not to my personal taste.

Reflections was a 'Greatest Hits', set in the main although it did include three new recordings, and it marked time before *Glow* appeared. James was still a popular artist (the title track reached #5 soul and (the awful) "Can't Stop" came to rest at t#10) but his gold and platinum days were done. I did like "Sha La La La La" a good deal, as it was one of his best ballads, and "Moon Child" was more appealing than the title suggested it might be, but there was nothing else here I could enjoy.

James ended his impressive Motown tenure with *The Flag* and his album run with *Wonderful*, both of which I will swiftly move over, other than to note that *Wonderful* contained his fourth and final #1 single in "Loosey's Rap".

Rick James was one of the best and most varied of all the artists who worked mainly in the funk vein from the late seventies onwards and was ably supported by The Stone City Band who I have not mentioned in any detail here. Please see their own section for more information. James died in 2004.

Janice

Janice Barnett; Reggie Saddler; Freddie Morrison; William Acosta; Norman Fearrington

Janice 1975 Fantasy F-9492 Producers: Harvey Fuqua, Janice Barnett & Reggie Saddler

Harvey Fuqua was a highly respected and hugely successful writer, singer and producer who teamed up with the considerably less respected and successful Reggie Saddler and Janice Barnett for this lovely one off album in 1975. Fantasy gave it every chance of success with a gate-fold sleeve, which incorporated photographs and printed lyrics, and impressive orchestration and arrangements (by Wade Marcus) throughout, but it didn't make it, which was a shame, but it has been a great favourite of mine ever since it came out.

Saddler had tried for some years to make it in the business but issuing singles under the horribly unwieldy name of Reggie Saddler, Janice and The Jammers wasn't a great recipe for success, although it must be said that the output under the only marginally more succinct Reggie Saddler Revue fared no better, either. Fuqua has always seemed incapable of making uninteresting records and his production set up things beautifully for the wonderful lead vocals of Barnett (she sounded a fair bit like Gladys Knight) and the gorgeous back up singing by Saddler (Barnett's husband), Acosta and Morrison, which proved for the umpteenth time that lack of sales and lack of talent have little in common. The peppy and danceable "I Told You So" was put out as a 45 and it remains a mystery as to why it failed as it sounded like a hit, but the real killer on here was "Goody Two Shoes", an enchanting, captivating and believable tale enhanced by some of the most gorgeous harmonies imaginable. To be fair, most of the other tracks were probably better suited to sitting on an album rather than doing duty as singles as they were not "immediate" enough to catch an unwary ear, but it's a really strong LP to listen to in its entirety. Another single appeared in 1980 to no acclaim whatsoever, so limited was its distribution, but when Barnett and Saddler's marriage split up soon after there was no way back for the group.

Chris Jasper (see also The Isley Brothers)

Superbad 1987 CBS AL 44053 Producer: Chris Jasper (Billboard soul charts: 31; Billboard pop charts: 182)

Time Bomb 1989 AL 45169 Gold City Producers: Chris Jasper & Margie Jasper (Billboard soul charts: 99)

These two LPs are purely in the book for reference and because of Chris Jasper's long involvement with The Isley Brothers. They do not contain music that corresponds to my definition of soul, although they are certainly accomplished records. The rather good title track of the first album became one of his two big hits by reaching #3 on the soul charts in January 1988; the other was "One Time Love" (#12) from the same set.

J.B.'s (see also James Brown, Bootsy's Rubber Band, Maceo & All The Kings Men, Maceo Parker and Fred Wesley)

James Brown; Bobby Byrd; Maceo Parker; Fred Wesley; Fred Thomas; Jimmy Parker; St. Clair Pinckney; Russell Crimes; Isiah Oakley; Jerone Sanford; Hearlon Martin; John Starks; Robert Coleman; Johnny Griggs; Jimmy Nolen; Charles Sherrell; Eldee Williams; Darryl Jamison; Bootsy Collins; Phelps Collins; Robert McCullough; Frank Waddy; Clayton Gunnels; Alfred Thomas; John Morgan

Food For Thought 1972 People PE 5601 Producer: James Brown (Billboard soul charts: 34)

Doing It To Death 1973 People PE 5603 Producer: James Brown (Billboard soul charts: 7; Billboard pop charts: 77)

Damn Right I Am Somebody 1973 People PE 6602 Producer: James Brown (Billboard soul charts: 20; Billboard pop charts: 197)

Breakin' Bread 1974 People PE 6604 Producer: James Brown (Billboard soul charts: 36)

Giving Up Food For Funk - The Best Of The J.B.'s 1975 Polydor 2391-204 (UK)

Hustle With Speed 1975 People PE 6606 Producers: Charles Bobbit & Don Love

What makes a recording by The J.B.'s different from one by James Brown? In a number of cases, nothing at all. In fact, as the *Food For Thought* LP demonstrated, they can be exactly the same thing given that "Escape-ism" came out as a single by Brown himself, while we also encounter an instrumental version of another Brown single, "King Heroin". The Godfather was not a man to baulk at releasing two singles at virtually the same time but even he drew the line at three, and therefore having the J.B.'s as another means to get as many records in the marketplace as possible was not an opportunity he wanted to miss. *Food For Thought* is primarily instrumental, but then so were a number of albums released by James Brown, and it's really only for those (like me) who can never get enough of his music. Two singles were put out from the set as by the J.B's, "Gimme Some More" and "Pass The Peas" and both performed pretty well by reaching the soul top 30. (The LP was released in the U.K. as *Pass The Peas* on Mojo 2918 004 with an entirely different front cover.)

Doing It To Death was the one big selling album released by the J.B.'s, and that success stemmed from the great title track's (much truncated on 45 from the ten minute LP cut) performance in reaching #1 on the soul charts and #22 pop in the middle of 1973. Again, it could easily have been a James Brown single, and it dominated an LP which showed that Brown was not above jumping onto any bandwagon if it seemed lucrative ("You Can Have Watergate, Just Gimme Some Bucks And I'll Be Straight" was certainly funky enough, but added nothing whatsoever to our understanding of the biggest political scandal in recent memory.) "La Di Da, La Di Day" and "More Peas" were further funky workouts, while "Sucker" was more or less a straight jazz outing, but the whole LP had the feeling of being rather thrown together in one of the few spare minutes that the band had.

There was a slight name change for the band on *Damn Right I Am Somebody* which was released as by "Fred Wesley and the J.B.'s" and it is my favourite of all the band's albums, mainly because the great trombonist is all over it, much of which is as funky as hell. "Blow Your Head" and "Going To Get A Thrill" introduce some sort of synthesiser which sounds like a gigantic demented bee, while surely never so much has been created with seemingly so little on the magnificent and certainly accurately titled "Same Beat" which features hypnotic rhythm guitar worth a million mindless solos. I also love the insane "I'm Paying Taxes, What Am I Buying" that clocks in at well over nine minutes and wastes not a second, utilising an exhilarating stop and start structure. The orchestrated "Make Me What You Want Me To Be" is markedly different from anything else on the set and would make a great theme tune to a radio show, while the lazily swaying yet strutting "If You Don't Get It The First Time" was one of three singles from the set which did well on the soul charts ("Same Beat" and the title track were the others) and a jazzy and rather uninteresting take on "You Sure Love To Ball" is the only misstep on a great James Brown LP.

Another name change attended the *Breakin' Bread* album, given to us by "Fred & The New J.B.'s" and if there was nothing new about the make up of the band there were slight changes afoot in the music, not least in the title track which had a distinctly downhome sound and was one of the few sides from the J.B.'s which seemed as if it might not have been written by Brown (although in fact it was). It's not as good as the previous set, as the rather unnecessary spoken intros before each track do not add much, and it's simply not as funky with a fuller, more textured sound throughout. It's still enjoyable though, and "Little Boy Black" sounds like a rap record years before its time, while "Rice 'N' Ribs" builds up an irresistible head of steam. "Rockin' Funky Watergate" gave the band a second stab at making capital from the Washington break-in but although it was the lead-off single from the album, it failed to reach the national charts and was indicative of a waning interest in music from Brown and his stable and this was further emphasised by the title track managing only #80, with "Makin' Love" (which ripped off The Ohio Players' "Skin Tight" pretty comprehensively even if Brown and Wesley shamelessly claimed writing credits) not doing too much better at #64.

A fine compilation came out in the U.K. in 1975, which had lovingly detailed sleevenotes from Cliff White, one of the best ever writers on Brown and his music, and had the bonus of including three tracks not available on any other J.B.'s' album.

1975's *Hustle With Speed* album (a return to a credit for "The J.B.'s" as Wesley had moved on by the time the LP appeared) wasn't even produced by Brown, even though he arranged it and wrote everything. It was a time and year when the great soul man could no longer command the interest and record sales of the past and the music within did sound somewhat tired. The title track (which did feature and was produced by Wesley) started off proceedings and lasted for eight minutes but wasn't really worth even half that length of time; it became another moderate seller as a 45 (#63), and things never got much better with the nine minute "Thank You For Letting Me Be Myself And You Be Yours" not being remotely as good as the Sly and Family Stone song from which the title is more or less taken. "Transmograpfication" had already appeared on Brown's *Big Slaughter's Big Rip Off* LP, albeit in what sounds like a slightly different mix, and "Taurus, Aries And Leo" employed backing singers who sounded as if they were moonlighting from a thousand disco recordings, while "Things & Do" is just cheesy. Not an absolute disaster, but close.

Jam II Disco Fever 1978 Polydor PD-1- 6153 Producer: James Brown

Groove Machine 1979 Drive 111 Producer: James Brown

By 1978 the band had moved to Polydor and changed their name again: they were now "J.B.'s Internationals". And this time the album *was* a disaster. All six tracks had the word "disco" in the title and proved how ill-suited Brown was to this era. It sold poorly and made *Hustle With Speed* sound like *What's Going On*.

Sadly, their last album (back as "The J.B.s") was not a lot better. *Groove Machine* may have been marginally less appalling than *Jam II Disco Fever* but that is not saying much, and it is still very tough to sit through and enjoy; the most quickly knocked off Brown side in the sixties was better than this stuff.

That, mercifully, was it for one of the greatest bands in popular music history. Many of its members had already gone off to do their own thing, and some would in the future, but The J.B.'s (in nearly all their guises) created some remarkable music. A number of these musicians are discussed in their own sections so the last point to make here is that I won't be including St. Clair Pinckney's two eighties albums for Ichiban as they were straight jazz sets.

Norma Jean and Ray J

Raising Hell 1974? Hep Me 5000 Produced by Senator Jones

Normally, it is reasonably clear why an LP is in demand as one or two tracks stand out from all the others but I'm rather at a loss to understand why this particular set commands so much money these days. It certainly can't be for anything from the first side which is uniformly average and so I'm assuming it must be for "We Love Each Other", "I've Taken Over" or their version of "Right Place, Wrong Time", all of which are on side two and the most striking things on show.

Ray J is presumably Raymond Jones (who wrote five of the songs) while Norma Jean is not the Norma Jean Wright who sang with Chic. Both singers are from New Orleans and the album is a typically low rent Hep Me offering in the sense that the sleevenotes are rather inept and no year of release is provided but I think it might date from 1974. The duo sing in a style vaguely reminiscent of Peggy Scott and Jo Jo Benson.

Morris Jefferson

Spank Your Blank Blank 1978 Parachute RRLP 9003 Producer: Lucky Cordell

This is a terrible LP, consisting of seven tracks, all of which have the word "spank" - it was a dance - in the title, put together to cash in on his minor hit, "Spank Your Blank Blank" from the start of 1978. I only mention it at all because Chicago's Jefferson was in fact a real soul man of some talent, releasing an excellent single in 1980 on the Good Luck label as well as some other sides, unreleased at the time, which have since surfaced in the last few years. If only an album had been built around his proper singing.

Jeffree

Jeffree 1979 MCA-3072 Producer: Jeffree

Jeffree was Jeff Perry, who recorded a memorable single in 1975, "Love Don't Come No Stronger (Than Yours And Mine") (#19 soul), and was brother to the equally talented Greg Perry who made two excellent albums in his own right. *Jeffree* is a record that relies on mood and atmosphere more than anything else as Perry is a good but not great singer, and the songs float along at a relaxed pace without always sticking to the standard formula of verse chorus verse. On "Mr. Fix-It" there are strong echoes of Marvin Gaye, while "Better Wake Up Girl" recalls Smokey Robinson, but elsewhere Perry's own voice comes through more forcefully. It's always been somewhat of a "cult" album in the U.K. and it was not an especially big seller on release although "Mr. Fix-it" did manage to reach #53 on the soul charts as a single in 1978. Apart from the last cut, "Love's Gonna Last", which bears some synthesised strings, it all sounds as if it was recorded in 1974 or 1975 and I mean that as a compliment.

We heard nothing more from Perry until rather out of the blue he released a new CD in 1996.

Mike Jemison

He's My Friend 1987 City Sound CSR 100 Producer: Ernest Kelley

Mike Jemison 1991? Geneva ST-GE-102 No producer listed

Detroit's Mike Jemison is one of those numerous soul singers who had talent but never managed to sell enough records to register with the general public. He recorded nine singles in the seventies and eighties but none of them had any national success and probably sold little outside of Michigan. By 1987, possibly because he realised his career hadn't really worked out, he turned away from secular music and recorded his first album firmly in a gospel vein. But many of the songs are constructed as if they still soul records, simply overlaid with religious lyrics. Jemison is a talented singer and brings passion and dexterity to the material, which includes three compositions from Eddie Robinson that were included on his own Myrrh LP in 1974. The problem, if it can be classed as such, is that the album, as with many gospel outings, is rather thin and one-dimensional as it has the usual stripped back sound typical of such ventures and it becomes a little difficult to keep attention fully engaged for the 33 minutes or so that the LP lasts.

His second album came out in 1991 but probably primarily for the benefit of record collectors as it trawled back through his earlier career and collected together ten sides that had previously appeared as singles in the period from 1973 to 1986. Considering Jemison was now only singing for the Lord and the album was encased in a plain white cover it certainly can't have done too much for him, and I imagine it was only pressed up in limited numbers. No production credit was provided, either, but in fact the songs were produced by a combination of Jemison himself,

Ernest Kelly and Johnny Griffith. Once again it demonstrates his skill as a singer but also poses one of the eternal questions of the record industry: why did these sides fail when others by lesser performers did not? "You'll Never Get My Love", in particular still sounds as if it took what it had to be a hit even if the pinging syndrums now sound dated. 1975's "When You're Around" is presumably sung to a woman but is ambiguous and could easily have sat on the *He's My Friend* LP; "Ain't No Way" may not match Aretha's version but is still good; "Let's Bring Back The Good Times" looks back wistfully and "Congratulation" and 1973's bright and gently funky "Satisfaction" will certainly please many soul fans.

Norma Jenkins

Patience Is A Virtue 1976 Desert Moon DM 3200 Producer: George Kerr

New Jersey's Norma Jenkins (with The Dolls) cut a song in the mid sixties entitled "The Airplane Song" which is much beloved by fans of the "Northern Soul" scene, but it sold no better than the other handful of singles Jenkins released over the next few years, and her opportunity to record an LP with George Kerr (who also produced some of her earlier 45s) was as welcome as it was surprising. Kerr worked with the great Linda Jones for years and for much of this LP Jenkins recalls that tragic singer, especially on the closing track, the marvellous "You've Been Here Since Then". The album is definitely one for those who love the adult, no-holds barred type of singing at which Jenkins excelled, and it's to Kerr's great credit that he still believed in records like this in 1976, as it is, a couple of up-tempo tracks aside, pretty uncompromising and uncommercial. The album became something of a "cult" classic and certainly didn't sell in any great quantity, and neither did the two singles pulled from it, even if "Gimme Some (Of Your Love)" just scraped into the soul charts at #92. "Love Jones", with its long instrumental opening passage sets the scene beautifully for what is about to follow, and it is an album that demands to be listened to with full attention as that way its delights - and they include the strong lyrics on the imposing "It's All Over Now" - become most apparent. As far as I am aware, there were no more recordings from Jenkins and she seemed to have vanished from the industry.

Jewel

Oliver Miller; Rick Van; Kenny Chatman; Edward Beard; Keith Howard; Bill Ivy; Keith Stevens

Cut 'N' Polished 1982 Erect ESLP 303 Producer: Jim Porter

Jim Porter worked with Chicago based soul acts for years without ever really enjoying any hits at all apart from a small one in 1974 with The Quadrophonics. This album with the short-lived Jewel didn't lead to a change to his fortunes, presumably because the world decided it didn't need another Earth, Wind & Fire, who are strongly recalled by "We Cannot Say Goodbye" and "Something You Should Know". When the group decide to get funky as on "Jewel's Groove" the result is a lyrically tired outing which sounds like a thousand others.

Jive Five

Eugene Pitt; Webster Harris; Casey Spencer; Beatrice Best; Norman Johnson; Charles Mitchell, Herbert Pitt; Frank Pitt

I'm A Happy Man 1965 United Artists UAS 6455 Producer: Otis Pollard

Here We Are! 1982 Ambient Sound FZ 37717 Produced by Marty Pekar

Way Back 1984 Ambient Sound ASR-801 Producer: Marty Pekar

Our True Story 1983 Ace CH 76 (UK)

More a doo-wop rather than a soul group, New York's The Jive Five nevertheless recorded some engaging 45s from the mid sixties up until the early seventies which make their inclusion in the book logical, even if not one of their four LPs is really an out and out soul record.

Their glory days were the years of 1961 and 1962 and they hit big with their first single, "My True Story", which became a #1 soul and #3 pop hit on the Beltone label. They posted three more top fifty soul hits for the same label on the *Cashbox* soul charts (strangely, always much more responsive to their music than the *Billboard* lists) but had to wait until a move to United Artists in late 1964 before their fortunes once again took an upswing. (Note: all the Beltone material was captured on the 1983 LP put out by Ace)

"I'm A Happy Man" rose to #26 soul and #36 pop in August 1965 but sounded more in step with music from August 1955, and the same could be said for all the tracks on the album of the same name. This is not to state that the record is in any way poor, and Pitt was a superb singer, but it wasn't really soul.

There was no doubt, though, as to the soulful content of the group's singles for Musicor ("Sugar" was a superb ballad, reaching #34 soul in 1968), Decca, Avco and Brut (they briefly became The Jyve Fyve for the latter two labels) but despite some success (four more *Cashbox* soul entries) no LPs were released in this period and the two on Ambient Sound from the eighties are strictly doo-wop in style and only really for lovers of that music.

I'm aware that is the briefest of looks at an important black harmony quintet, but they are somewhat of an unusual case, and if it were not a number of their singles they wouldn't be in the book at all.

Al Johnson (see also Positive Change and The Unifics)

Peaceful 1978 Marina WML 5000 Producers: Lloyd Price, Nate Adams & Al Johnson

Back For More 1980 Columbia BL 36266 Producer: Norman Connors (Billboard soul charts: 48)

It's a strange fact that, given its prominence as a city and its overwhelmingly Afro-American population in the sixties and seventies, Washington D.C. was never one of the strongholds for soul music recordings. There were, of course, a number of record labels and studios dotted around the capital but the success they generated was miniscule compared to what came out of Memphis, Detroit, New York, Los Angeles, Chicago and even a tiny backwater in comparison like Muscle Shoals. One of the most important of all the artists, writers and producers who DID do excellent work in D.C. was Al Johnson. Although he was born in Newport News, he moved to the city in later life and started his recording career as a member of The Unifics, after which he concentrated on writing and producing for a while for such acts as Black Heat, Special

Delivery and The Best Of Both Worlds, before forming and leading a five man vocal outfit, Positive Change, for an album in 1978. By the time the decade was drawing to a close Johnson had done pretty much everything in the business with the exception of carving out a solo career, something he hoped to rectify with *Peaceful*.

Johnson sounds a good deal like another famous son of Washington, Marvin Gaye, on "I've Got My Second Wind" the track that leads off his first album, yet another that bore a rather unenticing cover, giving little hint as to what type of music was inside. The answer, for anyone tempted to try and find out, was "extremely congenial soul music" and as the set progresses Johnson's own personality comes more to the fore. He was always an exceptionally good song writer with the ability to compose memorable hooks (namely: "It's Not Too Late To Start Again" and "I'll Do Anything For You") and composed or co-composed seven of the eight tracks on show. Marina was too small to get the record away to any kind of success but it served notice that Johnson was one of the more impressive soul performers of the late seventies, basing his music fairly and squarely on a rich uptown (there's little "southern" about this set) tradition, and without resorting to any vulgar disco tricks.

In 1979 Johnson provided vocals to one track on Norman Connors' *Invitation Of Love* LP, an act which led to a summons of its own: that the jazzman would produce Johnson's second album. Two tracks - "Peaceful" and "I've Got My Second Wind" - were reprised from the previous set (albeit with slightly new mixes and intros), leaving us with six new ones to enjoy. The best of these were "You Are My Personal Angel" and "You're A Different Lady", both Johnson songs, the former bearing the same sort of careful and thoughtful construction of a Sam Dees' composition, while the latter had distinct Philly overtones, and could have been a Bell-Creed creation. This is not to say Johnson aped others, far from it, but it is to state that his writing was of a high calibre. The catchy title track (an excellent Kenny Stover song) had already appeared on a Tavares LP but Johnson used his version as a 45, which managed to reach #26 soul in early 1980, a performance no doubt helped by the fact that Jean Carn helped out as second vocalist. The new version of "I've Got My Second Wind" followed it onto the listings at #58 a few months later and the album itself did manage to land in the soul top 50. A third 45 - which matched up "You're A Different Lady" with the certainly commercial sounding "School Of The Groove" - didn't hit, however, and Johnson once again turned away from his own recordings to work with many other artists and groups throughout the eighties.

He did return with a new CD in 1998 but passed away in 2013. (The Al Johnson who recorded for Quinvy and the one who sang "Carnival Time" down in New Orleans are NOT the same as this Al Johnson.)

Benny Johnson

Visions Of Paradise 1973 Today TLP-1013 Producer: Maurice Irby

I think this is the Benny Johnson who had a single out (with the Soul Serenaders) in the sixties on the Tarx record label but am less convinced that it's the same man who wrote and sang lead on the Spoilers' lovely 1972 cut "Sad Man's Land" but what I am sure about is that the Benny Johnson who gave us the *Visions Of Paradise* LP did a marvellous job.

It is a highly enjoyable album, lovingly presented to us with the emphasis on two simple truths: the quality of the songs (all by Edna Toles or Maurice Irby) and the clarity and simplicity of the production (full enough, but without strings) that allows Johnson's lugubrious voice to draw us in. The tracks are nearly all slow and rather mournful and even on the seemingly upbeat affirmation of affection, "Baby I Love You", he still sounds as if he suspects it could all come crashing down tomorrow. It made for an assured single, however, which reached #68 in January 1974, eleven places higher than the title track had managed a few months earlier. I suspect that this isn't an album to appeal to non soul fanatics as it is too unpretentious, and its charms are subtle rather than forceful, but it is a skilful piece of work, from an impressive singer, which I unreservedly recommend. He seemed to disappear completely after this album and remains a mysterious figure: I've never seen an interview with him.

Beverly Johnson

Don't Lose The Feeling 1979 Buddah BDS 5726 Producers: Betty Wright, Jimmy Norman, Billy Dietrich, Larry Fallon, Robert Wright & Wayne Vaughn

Apparently Johnson was a supermodel, and I don't doubt that she made a vastly more lucrative living from that pursuit than she did from this LP. She isn't the greatest singer, recalling Betty Davis to some degree and the album only just falls this side of disco to warrant inclusion here. "Can't You Feel It" and "Don't Run For Cover" aren't too bad at all, but the rest is best forgotten.

Danny Johnson (see also The Chi-Lites)

Introducing 1978 First American FA 7717 Producer: Archie Russell

On the cover of his one LP, it is clear that Danny Johnson was a striking looking man; and he gave us a rather striking record too, even if it was probably four or five years too late. Five of the eight tracks are highly appealing "sweet soul" offerings, the sort of thing that used to be done so well by Blue Magic, The Delfonics....and the Chi-Lites. Johnson was briefly a member of that super group (in 1976/77) after Eugene Record had moved on and his lovely high tenor lights up the five polished leisurely cuts that are found on here. The three uptempo cuts are not utterly horrible, either, just rather disposable, with one of them, "Learning To Love You Was Easy" rattling on for far too long, easing Johnson out completely for the last two minutes or so, and The Dells' version was much better anyway. The highly pleasant "Future Past" sadly could climb no higher than #92 on the soul charts as a single, and "Taking My Love For Granted" and "I Might As Well Forget Loving You" were even better. I don't know what happened to Johnson after this but I don't believe he cut any more records.

Ernie Johnson

Just In Time 1984 Ronn LPS 8001 Producer: Ernie Johnson

Ernie Johnson was born in the tiny town of Winnsboro Louisiana, but moved to Dallas where he began his recording career by releasing a couple of singles as "Lil' Ernie Johnson and The Soul Blenders". This was definitely small time stuff, though, and even though he went on to cut a few more high quality singles around the south, most notably a version of Otis Redding's "Dreams To Remember" which he delivered exceedingly well, nothing came even close to being a national success. The Ronn label enjoyed some soul hits with the likes of Little Johnny Taylor in the early seventies, but had rather petered out as the decade progressed and it was therefore Ernie's good fortune that it was resurrected in the mid-eighties and afforded him his first opportunity in years to get back into a studio.

It's a desultory album, to say the least, as Johnson tries to cover far too many bases. He is an out and out bluesman on "Give Me A Little Bit Of Your Loving" and (the lyrically strong) "Cold Woman"; he goes for the dance crowd on "Mouth To Mouth Resuscitation" and "Party All Night"; flirts with country on "In My Dreams"; best of all, he adopts his persona as a superb soul singer on "You're About To Succeed" and the marvellous minor-key "You're Gonna Miss Me" which is a brilliant record for 1985, in fact any year. Added to which, he sounds a bit like Al Green here and there, and Bobby Bland at others and it is this failure to impose his own personality on the material that ultimately lets *Just In Time* down but I'm glad it exists, thanks to the three or four best tracks.

In later years he has released a few CDs and so far as I know he s still performing.

Howard Johnson (see also Niteflyte)

Keepin' Love New 1982 A & M SP-4895 Producers: Kashif, Morrie Brown & Paul Lawrence Jones (Billboard soul charts: 10 ; Billboard pop charts: 122)

Doin' It My Way 1983 A & M SP-4961 Producers: Mic Murphy & David Frank (Billboard soul charts: 61)

The Vision 1983 A & M SP-4982 Producers: Monte Moir, Jimmy Jam, Terry Lewis, Howard Johnson, Rick Timas, Vincent Brantley, Jermaine Jackson & John McClain (Billboard soul charts: 46)

Johnson & Branson 1989 A & M SP 5229 Producers: Bryan Loren, David Cochrane, Mark A Sylvia, Rob Harris, Darryl Duncan, Howard Johnson & Regis Branson

Miami born Howard Johnson, together with Sandy Torano, formed the duo known as Niteflyte, who released two albums, and he had a fairly successful career in his own right throughout the eighties. The first LP, *Keepin' Love New*, did particularly well for him, selling impressively in itself, as well as housing a #6 soul single in "So Fine" and another top fifty chart entrant in the title track. It's a noticeably clean sounding record, thanks to its slick and uncluttered production, and while it is not really my sort of thing, I can see why it did well given its across the board appeal. My own disinterest really stems from the rather underwhelming material and Johnson's singing which is competent enough but in no way distinctive and his attempt at the slow ballad, "Forever Falling In Love", is too saccharine..

I feel much the same way about *Doin' It My Way* and although many of the tracks are freighted with a Luther Vandross influence, the public weren't so convinced either and it performed more modestly, although "Let's Take Time Out" and "Let This Dream Be Real" both reached the soul charts as singles at #30 and #58 respectively. Mic Murphy and David Frank produced this time but retained much of the feel of the earlier set.

I couldn't listen to *The Vision* and can only point out that one track, "Stand Up", made it to #29 soul in the late summer of 1985 and nor could I enjoy his last LP, made with Regis Branson in 1989. They followed this up with a CD in 2003.

Lamont Johnson (see also Brainstorm)

Music Of The Sun 1978 Tabu JZ 35455 Producer: Jerry Peters

Lamont Johnson is a bassist out of Michigan who was in Brainstorm for a while. His solo work brought to mind that of another bass man, Michael Henderson; not so much in their playing style but in the approach they adopted for their respective LPs. Which was to a) enlist a female singing partner on certain songs and b) sprinkle some top class ballads among the funk.

In Johnson's case the balladry extended to these four: Goffin's and King's "Hey Girl"; Ralph Graham's "Differently"; Brainstorm's "This Must Be Heaven" and his own co-written "Easy Come, Easy Go". All are good, even if it must be said that Johnson was a competent rather than exalted singer. The other cuts are spacey and gently bubbly as one might have expected from a funk-based player back in 1978 and don't really repay repeated listening. But 50% is certainly a good return. The co-writer of "Easy Come, Easy Go" was Renae Williams and it is she who provides the distaff vocalising on a handful of songs; she was gifted, too, and it was a surprise to realise she didn't seem to record anything else. But - and here's a co-incidence - she also co-wrote another track on here, "Yours Truly, Indiscreetly", which was covered by...Michael Henderson. "Sister Fine" and "Hey Girl" were released as singles but did not chart, and neither did two further post - LP efforts.

Johnson did not cut any more records in his own name after 1980 but did continue to play on sessions for others. He should not be confused with a jazz pianist of the same name.

L.J. Johnson

L.J.'s Love Suite 1979 Avi 6064 Producers: Danny Ray Leake & Ian Levine

Louis Maurice Johnson is a high voiced singer from Chicago, steeped in the style of an Eddie Kendricks. When he slows it down and sings sweetly as on "Staring In Space" and "Things Will Work Out In The End" the effect is captivating but the other five cuts are really what the album is all about - which is dancing. What's more the tempo is generally set at extremely fast indeed and is not for the faint-hearted. Three singles came out in 1976 so the album was already "old" by the time it appeared and while a couple made some noise in England, not much happened in the States.

Lorraine Johnson

God's Tomorrow Will Be Better Than Today 1971 Deliverance DR - 1125 Producer: ?

The More You Want 1977 Prelude PRL 12148 Producers: Jesse Boyce & Moses Dillard

Learning To Dance All Over Again 1978 Prelude PRL 12161 Producers: Jesse Boyce & Moses Dillard

Lorraine Johnson was born in Huntsville Alabama, and can't you just tell from her voice. Despite the dance setting she was placed in for the majority of the tracks on her Prelude albums, it would be impossible to mistake her as a singer from anywhere other than the deep south.

Before that, though, she had recorded a gospel LP which I have never heard and two singles (one with Bill Brandon) that I have. The singles were typically southern, too, and demonstrated that her voice had a slightly harsh, straining quality which might not have won her much acclaim from vocal purists but certainly accentuated her believability. Her first LP on Prelude is admirable, mixing up out and out dance cuts like her cover of Teddy Pendergrass' "The More I Get, The More I Want" and her own "My Sweet Baby" with more considered ballads in the shape of "If You Don't Love Her (When You Gonna Leave Her)" and "Just For The Moment". If I wanted to pick some nits, I don't believe that "If You Leave Me Now" suits her, and also think that virtually every one of the eight cuts is at least a minute too long but I still like the set a lot. Prelude were known for their unrelenting dance beats and the majority of their LPs will not be finding their way into this book, but every now and then , as with Johnson - and also Brandon and Gayle Adams - they gave us something good.

But not on her second album, the cover of which was a disgrace. It features an unknown white girl on both front and back and God knows what Johnson thought about what can only be described as an insult. On the other hand, she may not have wanted to be associated with such an out and out disco project: it had four long dance tracks which frankly could have been sung by just about anyone. Disco lovers will doubtless enjoy it but there is nothing here for a soul fan. Both Prelude albums had singles issued that probably sold reasonably well but none of them were national hits, and neither were the LPs.

After their release she returned to session work - LTD is one example - but soon returned to making gospel music which she continued to sing in 2015.

Lou Johnson

Sweet Southern Soul 1969 Cotillion SD 9008 Producers: Jerry Wexler & Tom Dowd

With You In Mind 1971 Volt VOS-6017 Producers: Allen Toussaint & Marshall Sehorn

Brooklyn's Lou Johnson was a great singer (and good pianist) who recorded some of the finest New York soul of all time in the early sixties on singles such as "(There's) Always Something To Remind Me", "Reach Out For Me" and "Message To Martha" but because the labels for which they were recorded went bust, he never got a chance to cut an album. By the time he DID get that chance, he was "cold" as far as success went and despite the fact that *Sweet Southern Soul* was recorded at FAME, which guaranteed brilliant musicianship and production, the set just doesn't really work, as no-one could seemingly find a way in which to fuse the disparate strands of soul that Johnson ("big city") and Muscle Shoals ("downhome") represented. The songs were nearly all of top quality as well, but maybe one of them, "I Can't Change", was symbolically accurate as Johnson just didn't seem able to adapt his style to the funkier sound that FAME demanded; a great singer, to be sure, but not a great *southern* soul singer. None of the above is to say that it is a poor album, and it is still interesting (an unrecognisable version of "Gypsy Woman") and enjoyable (Eddie Hinton's "People In Love" in particular) but when compared to the incredible work the likes of Laura Lee, Irma Thomas, Etta James and Jimmy Hughes had accomplished under Rick Hall's tutelage it must be declared to be rather disappointing. Maybe Hall rather than Jerry Wexler and Tom Dowd should have been producing. Two singles were pulled, "Don't Play That Song" and "Rock Me Baby", but each one bombed and the album itself cannot have sold many copies and Johnson was dropped by Cotillion shortly afterwards.

He turned up again a couple of years later at another famous southern concern, Volt, to cut his second and final album down in New Orleans with another highly accomplished producer, Allen Toussaint (together with Marshall Sehorn.) It's all strikingly different from *Sweet Southern Soul,* with a much cleaner, less cluttered production, no famous songs on show (all but one of the nine tracks was written by Toussaint) and one long excursion, the eight-minute "Transition" which I can't make my mind up about, and was surely only attempted as Isaac Hayes was proving that soul albums could contain such lengthy (and pretentious?) meandering reflections. It's a fascinating set to listen to, and was better suited to Johnson's style, but was also pretty clearly uncommercial and by the time of its release Johnson was even "colder" than he had been two years earlier, resulting in its getting completely lost in the deluge of LPs Stax and Volt were putting out in the early seventies. "Frisco, Here I Come" was a guitar driven song issued as a 45, and while it is a nice enough track, it was plainly not any sort of hit, lacking in immediacy, and did nothing to revive Johnson's fortunes, either. One track must be called out though as it was the best thing he cut post Big Top - a superb take on Betty Harris' "Nearer To You".

There were to be no further Lou Johnson records, although he kept his hand in the industry from time to time by doing such things as joining a new version of The Inkspots. He didn't have the best luck in his career as even his best New York sides were not really the smashes they deserved to be and he was clearly not a prolific album artist, but if one needs to own only one of these two sets, it should be *With You In Mind.*

Louis Johnson (see also The Brothers Johnson)

Evolution 1985 Capitol 1A 064-24 0304 Producer: Louis Johnson

Now THIS is what is meant by a solo album: Johnson played all the instruments, wrote everything, sang lead and backing vocals, and produced and arranged it as well. The former Brother Johnson was a tremendous bass player (that's him on "Billie Jean"), but the LP is yet another I cant enjoy, with pop and rocky overtones being overlaid onto the eighties rhythms. Surprisingly, it didn't find much of an audience who were more well disposed to this type of music and it didn't chart, and nor did "Kinky", a single. Johnson moved away from making his own records after this, but continued to be much in demand by others, until his death in May 2015.

L.V. Johnson

We Belong Together 1981 Phono 1001A Producer: Monk Higgins

All Night Party 1986 Sunnyview SUN 4904 Producers: Bunny Sigler, L.V. Johnson & Roslyn Sheppard

L.V. (his real Christian name, rather like L.C. Cooke) Johnson was a guitarist and talented singer and songwriter (Tyrone Davis' "Are You Serious", for example) from Chicago who cut an enjoyable 45, "Don't Cha Mess With My Money, My Honey Or My Woman", back in 1971 for Volt but its chewy title ensured it meant no more in the marketplace that his other handful of singles on small labels such as Palos, Stardust and Chi Heat did. He finally hit the Billboard chart with a couple of outings on the ICA label, one of which, the attractive "I Don't Really Care", appears on his first LP.

It strikes me that its cover is one of the few in my collection to feature a woman with bare breasts, a surely rather desperate marketing ploy given the picture's complete irrelevance to the contents within. Anyone hearing the LP for the first time, and noting that the second track is a cover of "The Whole Town's Laughing At Me", as well as taking in Johnson's husky, distinctly soulful voice, may conclude that Teddy Pendergrass was the vocal model in mind, but this would be wrong: Johnson sounded pretty much like this way back on the Volt single when Pendergrass was merely the Blue Notes' drummer. Overall, it is a commendable LP, which would have been much better suited to the previous decade as it has a seventies "vibe", but was also unlikely to sell many copies on a label like Phono, which was destined for a short lifespan. We are presented with a winning cover of "Try A Little Tenderness", proving not all the life had been sucked out of this oft-covered song, as well as a merely ok one of "Danny Boy", which many soul singers seemed not to be able to resist cutting. "Dancing Girl" is the only real misstep but the title track, "I'm A Lucky Guy" and "I Love You, I Want You" are all pretty decent sides, with everything here, apart from the three covers, being penned by Johnson.

It was no surprise that Phono did not stay the course, and Johnson had to wait until 1986 for his next LP, which appeared on the Sunnyview label out of New York. The fact that the great Philadelphia soul man Bunny Sigler's name was misspelt throughout as "Siegler" did not bode well and, indeed, it is a rather dispiriting set. It started out well enough with Sigler's "Take A Little Time To Know Her", and all of side one is worth a listen, with some decent songs being embellished by good backing vocals and typically committed Johnson singing. But it all goes wrong on side two, which has little merit. There is a weedy cover of Latimore's "Let's Straighten It Out", some cod reggae on "Mr Fan-Man", over-wrought backing tracks throughout and a song called "Leapin' Frog" which simply had no chance whatsoever of being any good.

Cold & Mean 1989 Ichiban ICH 1050 Producer: L.V.Johnson

I Got The Touch 1991 Ichiban ICH 1112 Producers: L.V.Johnson & General Crook

I really want to be positive about *Cold And Mean* as it has a number of good things going for it, quality backing singing and decent songs, and more examples of Johnson's impressive vocal range, but I emerge punch-drunk after being subjected to forty minutes of the dull thump of the one note "drumming" which, together with an annoying synthesiser render the LP tough to take in one go. As an example, listen to the original of "It's Not My Time" his first chart entry from 1979, with the new version on here. The earlier recording's drums are unobtrusive and complimentary; on the remake they add only irritation. Such a shame, as it's a fine song and the same can be said for the title track with The Dells on backing vocals, but it didn't need to have gone on for well over six minutes. There's a rather gruesome take on "Steal Away" but "Get Him Out Of Your System" and the plaintive "Blues In The North" are good examples of Johnson's compositional skills. But why was the top horn section listed on the back cover so underused?

Johnson's last album came out in 1991, three years before he passed away. It's another uneasy set, much like Cold And Mean but with slightly inferior songs and no Dells to help out this time around. "Take A Little Time" was re-cycled from the Sunnyview album and elsewhere Johnson gives us a pretty good version of "Are You Serious", a rather ho-hum one of "What's Love Got To Do With It" and a terrible one of "The Chokin' Kind". The drums are mercifully toned down somewhat on "I Don't Want To Lose Your Love", thus making it one of my favoured cuts but there was nothing on here to really connect with any audiences and although a new CD also came out in 1992 Johnson will have to remain an underappreciated artist of genuine talent who should have recorded more often (and earlier than the eighties and nineties) than he did.

Marv Johnson

Marvelous 1960 United Artists UAL 3081 Producers: Don Costa & Berry Gordy

More 1960 United Artists UAL 3118 Producer: Berry Gordy

I Believe 1962 United Artists UAL 3187 No producer listed

Early Classics 1979 Liberty/United Artists LBR 1008 (UK)

Marv Johnson has one historic claim to fame, cut a few big selling records in the sixties and utterly failed to make the transition into the seventies (as a performer, that is; he wrote some fine songs). That marker from history is the fact he released "Come To Me" in January 1959, the very first single on the Tamla label, quite an honour as time would go on to prove. It was a big hit too, #6 R & B and #30 pop, but on United Artists instead, as Tamla was a tiny concern at the time, and needed the clout and distribution of the bigger company.

The single (although not its b-side, "Whisper") appeared on Johnson's first LP, cunningly entitled *Marvelous,* as did another fair sized hit, "I'm Coming Home", and a monster, "You've Got What It Takes", #2 R & B and #10 pop. It's a typical UA offering of the time (and one of the joys of their early sixties' releases is to look at the inner sleeve: what a bewilderingly eclectic bunch of stuff they put out), with a mass of easy-listening and big band standards dominating proceedings, against which Gordy's noticeably "hipper" (but not *that* hip when compared to what Bobby Bland or Etta James were doing) songs were snuggled in. Johnson had a pure, clean and light tone throughout which was attractive and tuneful, if not obviously influenced by gospel.

The second LP from the Detroit singer - More Marv Johnson - adopted a different approach. The standards (and most of the strings) had gone and the twelve songs were all written by Gordy, Johnson himself, and upcoming Motown staffers, Janie Bradford, Smokey Robinson and Eddie Holland. It's not a great album, as the songwriters were still in the early stages of their craft, and everyone would go on to write much better songs, but it is still fascinating to listen to in the glow of hindsight. "I Love The Way You Love" was another huge hit, #2 R & B and #9 pop, but surprisingly, the follow-up, "Ain't Gonna Be That Way", missed out on the *Billboard* charts completely, having to settle for a modest run on those listed by *Cashbox*. It might have once again come out on the UA logo, but to all intents and purposes, this was Motown's first ever LP.

Three more good selling singles were released on Johnson in late 1960 and early 1961, but after "Merry - Go - Round" reached #26 in the spring of 1961, Johnson entered a period of significant decline: eleven further singles failed to break nationally. Maybe it was an act of desperation, or possibly just something Johnson wanted to do, but his third and final LP for UA was a gospel offering, featuring such safe choices as "Swing Low Sweet Chariot" and a latin-ish "He's Got The Whole World In His Hands", among ten other cuts. Having said above that his earlier music eschewed much church feeling the album demonstrated that he could feel the spirit when he wanted to, but it is still hardly an essential outing.

The *Early Classics* collection is a rather unimaginative 16 song offering of the 1960 sides, as it does not include a single track that was not on the first two UA albums.

I'll Pick A Rose For My Rose 1969 Tamla Motown STML 11111 No producer listed (UK)

When it was obvious that UA could do no more for him and were not going to renew his contract, Johnson moved to the Motown stable for a second time. However, it was not to provide him with the comeback he craved as he issued a scant three singles over three years, with only one of them, "I Miss You Baby (How I Miss You)", charting at #39 soul. There was, though, one small surprise when "I'll Pick A Rose For My Rose" became a #10 UK hit after failing totally in the U.S. The UK Tamla Motown label proudly issued an LP of the same name, but Motown in the States declined to follow suit. It's not the greatest set ever put out by the legendary company, but this is hardly astounding given it includes tracks cut over a period from May 1964 up to February 1968. The anodyne and Johnson-less cover didn't help, either, with Tamla Motown deciding the singer would have to be content with his picture on the back only. The excellent "I Miss You Baby" is certainly the finest track, but I also like the lilt of Frank Wilson's "You Got The Love I Love" a great deal too. I've never been a big fan of the slightly wooden title track and Johnson covers the likes of "Bad Girl" and "Sleep (Little One)" in adequate if not thrilling fashion. The set doesn't give producer credits but in fact nine people were involved with Mickey Gentile doing the most work, as four of the tracks were his.

Come To Me 1990 Motorcity MOTCLP 37 Producers: Ian Levine, Fiachra Trench & Rick Gianatos

As stated earlier the seventies (and much of the eighties) were barren times for Johnson the performer although he did write the Dells' million selling "Give Your Baby A Standing Ovation" and David Ruffin's superb "Rode By The Place (We Used To Stay)" among others. He started recorded again in 1987 and in 1990 a thin sounding ten track set was put out on Motorcity for the UK market who after all remembered and revered Johnson far more than his country of birth. Typical of the set was a re-make of "Nothing Can Stop Me" that proved his voice was still in great shape but it did little to make one forget Gene Chandler's version. It should also be said that Johnson was delighted he got the chance to cut a new LP after so long, but it was to prove his last ever release as he passed away in 1993.

Roy Lee Johnson

Roy Lee Johnson & The Villagers 1973 Stax STS 3020 Producer: Jimmy Johnson

All Night Long 1989? Howzat! LBW 1 Producers: Marzette Watts & Roy Lee Johnson (UK)

Every writer who worked in and around the sixties would have loved to see his or her work covered by The Beatles. Roy Lee Johnson achieved that when his song, "Mr. Moonlight", cut when he was a member of Dr, Feelgood and The Interns, was served up by the foursome on *The Beatles For Sale* LP. It remains just about the only reason why anyone, other than hardcore soul fans, knows of his existence. Which is unjust as he was more than merely a creator of one song and absorbing singles in his own right, particularly "Cheer up, Daddy's Coming Home", are a better way to define him. It must be said, though, that the singles were rather obscure and the royalties from the eight or so he cut in the sixties would probably have bought a few drinks for The Beatles with a bit of change left over.

He turned up on Stax in 1973 with a one-off album with his road band The Villagers - Johnson, Michael James, Hosea Burch and Ronald Williams - who had apparently seriously impressed famed guitarist Jimmy Johnson enough at a local gig to want to produce them. I must confess that I am not as captivated as Johnson obviously was, and while it has some fairly funky grooves and a decent song in "Something Special" that sounds a bit like Jackie Moore's "Precious Precious", Stax were putting out many better LPs in 1973. Recorded at Muscle Shoals, Roger Hawkins, Barry Beckett and Pete Carr all help out The Villagers, and the result is closer to James Brown than, say, Johnnie Taylor, which is not a bad thing, but it would not be JB at his finest. A handful of rather colourless instrumentals don't help and things improve when Johnson provides his tough vocals, not least on another good side, "Don't Tell Me Nothing About My Woman". Sales were not big for *Roy Lee Johnson & The Villagers*, nor the one single, "The Dryer", that was pulled from it, and no further recording sessions with Stax took place.

After 1973 releases from Johnson became sporadic, appearing every five years or so on average, and if it wasn't for some admirers of his in England, a second album would never have appeared. An excellent UK based magazine, *Voices From The Shadows,* put a picture of Johnson on the front cover of their November 1989 issue while a record dealer, Dave Porter, was encouraged enough by sales of Johnson's then current 12" single, "All Night Long"/"Sit Down And Talk About It" to arrange for an eight track album, all of which was cut in Atlanta in 1986 and 1987, to be released. I was one of those admirers in 1989 and bought the album for the same reason the small number of fellow fans did: hearing a real soul man with a good voice bring some of his own songs into life in a style that went well against the prevailing trends of the time. Listening again to the album, now, twenty six years later, the shortcomings are readily apparent, as all too often it sounds rather like Johnson was recording tracks, little more than demos in a couple of cases, in his own bedroom, although everything was cut in a proper studio. This is not to denigrate the album, as he clearly did the best he could in a situation where money was tight, but it does mean there is little compelling reason to pull it out and play it these days.

A thin sounding new CD appeared in 1998 as did an excellent (but incomplete) retrospective in 2009, and so far as I know Johnson is still alive and hopefully well.

Syl Johnson

Dresses Too Short 1969 Twinight LPS 1001 No producer listed

Is It Because I'm Black 1970 Twinight LPS 1002 Producer: Jimmy Jones and Pieces of Peace

Born Sylvester Thompson in Mississippi, Johnson is a feisty man, wary of the music business, but whose tough and uncompromising music over the years has nevertheless brought him a fair degree of success. He released 13 singles on six different labels - most notably Federal - before he finally scored some national success when his new record company, Twilight, managed to get the highly punchy "Come On Sock It To Me" all the way to #12 soul in the summer of 1967; tellingly it only managed #97 pop, as it was just too raw for a mass audience and despite ending up with 19 entries on the soul singles charts over his career, not a single one ever breached the pop Top 40.

Twilight quickly became Twinight and it was on this label that Johnson's first LP, the splendid *Dresses Too Short*, emerged in the middle of 1969. As so often back in the sixties it was really a collection of singles (recorded mainly in Chicago but also in Detroit and Memphis) rather than a specifically scheduled album, and indeed, eight of the twelve sides had appeared on one side or the other of 45s. Two of the cuts, the fabulous "Different Strokes" and the title track, had followed "Come On Sock It To Mme" onto the national soul chart and "Strokes" may just be his best-known and most successful side ever, given the number of times it has been sampled over the last twenty five years or so. There's not a lot of introspection or finesse on *Dresses Too Short,* and not much in the way of slow mood music either, but it is an exhilarating ride nevertheless, and is an object lesson in how to record a smokingly hot horn section; these players need some acclaim and the Chicago contingent certainly include Willie Henderson, Raymond Orr, Harvey Burton, John Cameron and Paul Serrano while The Memphis Horns adorn the title track and "Same Kind Of Thing". There is a James Brown influence on a number of the cuts and Johnson had a hand in writing around half the songs, but none of the excellence aboard translated into many sales as Twinight was not really geared up for selling long playing records.

And they couldn't get Johnson's follow-up album, *Is It Because I'm Black*, away either, despite its being almost completely different from *Dresses Too Short.* For a start it was a concept album, carefully prepared to deal with social issues and the implications of being a black man in America, but it was musically dissimilar too: the horns were pretty much totally gone, and the rhythms were much more relaxed and fluid, with all the set performed by The Pieces Of Peace who comprised Bernard Reed, John Bishop, Hal Nesbitt , Jerry Wilson and Michael Davis. The excellent title track was Johnson's biggest 45 to date, reaching #11 soul and #68 pop, with its follow-up, "Concrete Reservation", doing rather less well at #29 soul and missing the Hot 100 completely. Overall, it's another highly accomplished outing with only The Beatles' "Come Together" (there really should have been a law against soul artists attempting this song) failing to provide any enjoyment. Joe South's "Walk A Mile In My Shoes" made thematic sense to include but its tune was radically altered, and the closer, the Brown-influenced (the only track that really was) "Right On", was seven minutes of flowing perfection. Impressively, it was an album ahead of its time; black protest at the world on LP length wouldn't sell until *What's Going On* came along a year later.

Back For A Taste of Your Love 1973 Hi SHL 32081
Producer: Willie Mitchell (Billboard soul charts:19)

Diamond In The Rough 1974 Hi SHU 8477 Producer: Willie Mitchell

Total Explosion 1975 Hi SHU 8494 Producer: Willie Mitchell (Billboard soul charts:56)

Johnson released another four singles on Twilight post - "Is It Because I'm Black" as well as writing and producing for others before making a move to Hi records in Memphis who he saw as having the potential to provide him with distribution and marketing capabilities that were simply beyond his former label. This was certainly true, and among other things Syl Johnson LPs started to be released in England, but Hi's main energies were always going to be directed towards Al Green and the transition never worked out quite as well as Johnson had hoped, but he did score a handful of big singles nonetheless. The first single, "The Love You Left Behind", despite being co-written by Willie Mitchell, lacked impact and only sold moderately (#43 on the soul charts) but it found its way to the *Back For A Taste Of Your Love* LP, where it was joined by much more obvious singles in the title track (#16 soul) and "We Did It" (#23) and another less so, "I'm Yours" (#68). A particular favourite of mine is "I Let A Good Girl Go", a tale of regret of the sort that one hadn't often found on his last two albums. It's an exceedingly solid set, one which was his best ever seller and up to the usual standards one expects from the Royal Studios but it did lack the personality of the two Twilight outings.

*Diamond In The Roug*h incorporated two further soul chart entrants in "Let Yourself Go" (#54) and "I Want To Take You Home (To See Mama") (#40) but didn't sell particularly well. For the first time on a Johnson album Syl did not provide any of the songs, with Darryl Carter providing seven of them, doubtless a source of frustration to him, as would have been the front cover photograph, which as with the one on *Back For A Taste Of Your Love*, was hardly of the highest quality. To compound things Johnson was forced (?) to sound much like Al Green on "Could I Be Falling In Love" and title tracks really should be better than "Diamond In The Rough" itself. Having said all that, I enjoyed listening to the album as I am a big enthusiast of Syl Johnson's records and Willie Mitchell's productions but both men had done better work elsewhere.

Total Explosion did house a genuinely big single for Johnson in his impassioned and bluesy take on the magnificent "Take Me To The River" when it attained the #7 position on the soul charts and #48 on the pop listings, in both cases the highest numbers he ever managed. Its success also propelled the follow-up 45, "I Only Have Love", to #15 soul, which predictably and wisely also utilised Johnson on harmonica and Hi even eked out two more small "hits" from the set in "Star Bright, Star Light" (another side that sounds much more suited to Green) and "Bout To Make Me Leave Home". Nevertheless such triumphs did little to relieve Johnson's dissatisfaction with Willie Mitchell and he once again had to witness nine compositions on his own LP from the pens of other writers (interestingly, none from Darryl Carter, either). To me, though, it nearly all sounded nice and tough when compared to most of what else was happening in 1975 and I'd still rate it as the best of his works on the Memphis based label, with the overlooked cut "That's Just My Luck" being a worthy addition to the long line of "cheating" songs.

Goodie Goodie Good Times 1979 Shama/P-Vine PLP-9009 Producer: Syl Johnson (Japan)

Uptown Shakedown 1979 Hi HLP 6010 Producers: Hal Winn, Jerry Barnes & Mark Gibbons

Johnson returned in disgruntled fashion to Chicago determined to be more in control of his own destiny and released a single, "Goodie Goodie Good Times", on his own Shama label but despite doing well enough locally, it failed to go any higher than #93 soul on *Billboard* in mid-1977. The 45 was collected up with eleven other tracks, a handful of which dated back to 1968, and used as the title track to form a strong album which was only released in Japan. It transcends its content of outtakes and previously unreleased work, and deserves to be heard, even though don't be surprised be the variance in styles between the very tough Memphis recorded "Abracadabra" and the unusually (for Syl) uptown sounding "All I Need Is Someone Like You", a duet with his wife, Brenda.

For some reason Johnson returned to Hi for one further LP, but all concerned might have wished he hadn't bothered as it was by some distance his poorest outing to date. Only two tracks raised themselves above the mundane and that was because of the quality of the songs: Mark James' "Blue Water" and Ivey and Brasfield's "Who's Gonna Love You" (but even here Ann Sexton's version was better). Side one contained four songs all aimed at the dance floor, including a very ragged "Gimme Little Sign", and if they were just about able to be heard without raising the needle, no such restraint could be applied to an awful eight minute disco medley of Otis Redding songs. Maybe the most dispiriting aspect of all was that it required concentration to even realise it was an LP on which Syl Johnson was singing.

Brings Out The Blues In Me 1980 Shama SHL-8001
Producer: Syl Johnson

Miss Fine Brown Frame 1982 Boardwalk NB-33260-1
Producers: Syl Johnson & General Crook

Suicide Blues 1983 Isabel 900517 Producers: Syl Johnson & Didier Tricard (France)

Foxy Brown 1988 Shama SH 8003 Producer: Syl Johnson

Johnson entered the eighties by putting out a more or less straight blues LP, and although the lyrics on the title track suggested it was something he always had wanted to do, it did seem an unlikely way to sell lots of records. There are - inferior - re-makes of "Come On Sock It To Me" and "Is It Because I'm Black" included, but the other six cuts are all rather generic blues outings and it's not a set to which a soul fan will warm.

It was easier to feel positive about *Ms. Fine Brown Frame*, a set made up of seven fairly long cuts which had something for most people in it, despite its still falling short of the best of his late sixties and early seventies work. The excellent title track bore the name of Syl Johnson onto the soul charts for the last time when it stalled at #60 in early 1983, a pretty decent performance for such an earthy recording comprising fat back horns, blues harmonica, popping bass and even some rap passages from Syl; truly it was a synthesis of fifty years of black music. "Groove Me" and "Keep On Loving Me" were above average funk work-outs too, while "They Can't See Your Good Side" was a slightly soppy but still nice slow number. So far so good, then, but side two brought things down considerably as "Sweet Thing" was a dull effort without much input from Johnson while the old Jimmy Reed song, "You Don't Have To Go", didn't add much to other versions.

Suicide Blues was recorded in the Studio Davout in Paris, an unusual source of soul music and in fact it's another blues set, despite covers of "Come On Sock It To Me" (which badly needs a horn section) and "Take Me To The River" and comes across as a "vanity project", put together for the love of the music - which is good and solid - rather than for any commercial considerations. It only got a release in France and must have sold in low quantities.

Johnson's last LP, *Foxy Brown*, once again came out on Shama, and contained three tracks that had appeared on previous albums, thus making it less than stellar value with only five new songs on offer. Of these, I like the attractive and breezy reggae flavoured "Here We Go", while "Do You Know What Love Is" (not the same song he had cut back in the sixties on Special Agent) and "Trippin' On Your Love" were pretty decent too. There is little, if any, blues on show this time around so it was a firm re-introduction into the soul world from Johnson and overall, not a bad effort at all for 1988.

Is it Because I'm Black 1986 Charly CRB 1125 (UK)

The Love Chimes 1986 Hi 404 (UK)

Stuck In Chicago 1989 Hi (UK)

The three albums above are all compilations put out in the UK, the first of which featured Twilight material, the second and third concentrating on his Hi output.

Johnson has been fairly consistently busy in the CD age, issuing a handful over the last 25 years or so and has continued to work live on stage. His best post-vinyl release is a monumental effort from Numero records in 2010, *Complete Mythology*. His work certainly has a lasting quality and while I would not put him up there with the most naturally gifted of soul men, his music has always had a blue-collar appeal and emotional integrity that is to be greatly admired.

Willie Johnson

If Mama Could See Me Now 1979? Tru Spirit 1188
Producer:?

This gospel LP, which I have neither seen nor heard, is in the book as the Reverend Willie E Johnson who recorded it is the same man from Georgia who released a series of impeccable soul 45s on a number of labels including Cat, Future Stars and Savannah International over a period of fifteen years or so from the mid sixties up until 1982. None were any sort of a hit but he was a wonderfully compelling vocalist who is held in high esteem by people whose views I respect. He deserves to be written about, and even more so, demands a retrospective CD of his work.

Albert Jones

The Facts Of Life 1977 Candy Apple RC 10746 Producer: Choker Campbell (Canada)

I know only two things about Albert Jones: he released a handful of entertaining singles on labels such as Kapp, Bumpshop and Tri-City in the early seventies and recorded his one LP in Canada. I think he may have been from somewhere in Michigan. *The Facts Of Life* is not an especially diverting piece of work, consisting of average songs, intrusive back-up singing and an over-familiarity with disco, but Jones does possess a light and tuneful voice which is the best thing about the album.

Bobby Jones

Talkin' About Jones 1972 Toya TLP - 2000 No producer listed

Robert Pruter's excellent book, *Chicago Soul,* has a small section on Farmerville, Louisiana's Bobby Jones, which, while rightly admiring Jones' impressive vocal talents, posits the opinion that his records were generally rather uninteresting. I can see Pruter's point, as hardly any of Jones' reasonably numerous singles ever came close to being hits, and they tend to lack strong hooks of the hit-making type, but many of them were certainly enjoyable enough in their distinctive Chicago manner.

The album is an odd affair, in as much as it slipped out without much fanfare (although it was listed as a new release in the March 18th 1972 edition of *Billboard* magazine) and contained a generous 12 cuts, but the majority of them were at least two years old, and some four of five years old, at the time it appeared. A noticeably off-centre side two also hinted at perhaps a lack of full attention and faith that this was an album to sell in quantity. Nearly all the songs are well worth a listen, and include the appealingly danceable title track, the lovely uptown "I Am So Lonely (In My Apartment)" and the truly splendid country-soul styled "Please Bless Our Love" which was an (uncredited) duet with Pauline Chivers. It can hardly be described as a "Greatest Hits" set given his lack of sales, but it's certainly a "Best Of" as at least six of his singles are included.

Jones did release a handful more singles in the seventies before slightly re-inventing himself in the eighties as Bobby Jonz, under which name he has gone on to release three CDs, before reverting to "Bobby Jones" for a further CD in 2009.

Booker T. Jones

Booker T. & Priscilla 1971 A & M AMLH 63504 Producers: Booker T. Jones & Priscilla Jones (Billboard pop charts: 106)

Home Grown 1972 A & M SP- 4351 Producers: Booker T. Jones & Priscilla Jones (Billboard pop charts: 190)

Chronicles 1973 A & M SP- 4413 Producers: Booker T. Jones & Priscilla Jones (Billboard soul charts: 49)

Booker T. Jones is one of the most important and talented artists in this book, given his contribution to records proceeding from Stax, and he has played on or written some of the greatest records in popular music history. However, it must be said that his solo career has been decidedly odd, and rather bereft of acclaim or success: not a single one of his eight LP releases or his twelve or so 45s could be described as a hit.

There is, of course, no reason whatsoever why anybody should be constrained in sticking with a particular style and it was clear that Jones wanted to expand outside of a strict soul music framework when he embarked on his first three solo albums with his then wife, Priscilla Jones, who was the sister of Rita Coolidge; she - Jones - was tragically killed in a suicide pact together with her new husband in 2014. Soul music fans - including me - will find little to enjoy in the records as they fall firmly into a pop/rock mode and are not to my taste at all and I cannot sit and listen to them, particularly the first, which is a double.

Evergreen 1974 Epic KE 33143 Producer: Booker T. Jones

When the Jones' marriage dissolved Booker T. went it alone with *Evergreen* which will probably also alienate some although I do find certain tracks such as the title cut (which recalls The M.G.'s) and "Country Days" to be much more palatable then anything Jones performed with Priscilla. The latter is a gentle rambling thing, reminding me a bit of some of Allen Toussaint's solo work, although it is still hard to imagine exactly who Epic and Jones thought the audience for the LP would be.

Try and Love Again 1978 A & M SP- 4720 Producer: David Anderle

The Best Of You 1980 A & M SP- 4798 Producers: David Anderle & Booker T. Jones

I Want You 1981 A & M SP- 4874 Producer: Michael Stokes (Billboard soul charts: 49)

The Runaway 1989 MCA 6282 Producer: Booker T. Jones

It took until 1978 for Jones to release an LP that was at least partially aimed at a "soul" audience in the shape of *Try And Love Again* although it showed that he still was unwilling to shake loose his laid-back West Coast trappings. I would advice extreme caution for anyone who thinks soul should sound like Otis Redding or Wilson Pickett, but it is enjoyable enough in a rather soporific manner, although he remained a much better musician than singer.

1980's *The Best Of You* was couched in much the same style as *Try And Love Again* and my cautionary comments for this new set are thus repeated although I can see why the title track and the equally smooth "We Could Stay Together" have devotees.

Michael Stokes was brought in to oversee *I Want You* and he certainly upped the energy levels on what was Jones' most obviously "soul" LP ever: West Coast hippies would not be buying this one. But neither did I, as his voice was not strong enough to overcome some rather mundane songs and I had heard this sort of thing hundreds of times before. Even the esteemed Sam Dees couldn't induce much excitement with "Prize Possession", not his greatest or most soulful moment, although it is still the highlight of the set.

It took a full eight years for the next (and final) Jones LP, *The Runaway*, to appear, a definite example of a conscious nod to the past as it kicked over all traces of his solo career and sounded much like a Booker T. & M.G.s album circa 1971 (albeit with more rock guitar than one would have wished to hear; these are all excellent musicians but none had the crisp economy of Steve Cropper). Entirely instrumental, it is my favourite of all his solo albums but had no chance in the 1989 marketplace but good on MCA for putting it out.

He then retreated into the shadows once again for about twenty years before resurfacing in the last six or seven years with a handful of new CD releases. I imagine he is a wealthy man who no longer needs to earn much money from new recordings but it is nevertheless good to see him spry and active.

Busta Jones

Busta Jones! 1980 Spring SP-1-6728 Producers: Busta Jones & Bobby Eli

Michael "Busta" Jones played with Talking Heads for a while which should give a hint as to the soulful content of this LP: not much at all. He was clearly a fine bass player, but his skills didn't really extend to songwriting and the one outside composition - the Contours' "Just A Little Misunderstanding" - is by far the strongest. It's also the best cut (despite being much inferior to the original) on show but it has precious little competition. There is a slight P-Funk influence on board (Bernie Worrell and Tyrone Lampkin both play on the set) and a distinct disco one on the awful "(Everybody's) Dancing All Over The World" and apart from the slightly slower "Superstar" its all too frenetic for me and I'm afraid I do not recommend this one at all.

Charlie Jones

Everybody's Business Is Nobody's Business 1976 Askia CJ-2447 Producer: Charlie Jones

Love, Life And Re-ality 1983 Sum-ma ATE-7860 Producer: Charlie Jones

Charlie L Jones 1987 Timeless TRPL 117 Producer: Charlie Jones (UK)

Charlie Jones was born in Florida and had the traditional church upbringing so typical of so many soul singers, performing in a number of gospel outfits. He made the move to secular music in 1976 recording his first album in the comparative backwater of Taylorsville, North Carolina, and he wrote, arranged and produced the whole thing, in addition to playing guitar and singing lead and backing vocals. It's a splendid outing, demonstrating his adept writing talents but a label as small as Askia was never going to be able to get much distribution and I certainly wasn't even aware the record existed until years later. It's a real soul record, though, with definite hints of Roy C and Joe Simon in places, although Jones sounded like neither of them, singing in a much higher register. He copes as well on fast material (the title track) as he does on slower outings (the impressive "Woo Baby, You're So Sweet", "She's A Right On Girl" and "Just A Smile") but all eight tracks are strong. The only slight shortcoming is a mildly irritating synthesiser effect, but this is doubtless a simple result of funds being too tight to stretch to fuller orchestration.

As might have been expected the album did not do very well, but all was not all lost as seven years later it appeared again as *Songs Of Love, Life And Re-ality* on another tiny label, Sum-ma out of Fremont California. I would not normally list straight re-issues of LPs in the book, but that is not quite the case here as many of the songs are actually re-cuts, although in subtle ways rather than full-blown different recordings, although the most obvious change is that "Everybody's Business" was now extended out to nearly seven minutes. Sum-ma must have had a bit more cash than Askia as the album came complete with a lyric sheet but despite again attracting few sales it remains one of my favourite small label records ever made.

And, would you believe, three of the tracks appeared for a third time when the UK label Timeless put out an album on Jones in 1987, a couple of years after he released a fine 45 on Roy C's (a co-incidence given my earlier observation) Three Gems concern. The album is well worth tracking down as it features eight new songs including "Crazy Over You", which Johnnie Taylor was to cover in 1991. Much of the newer material has rather primitive backing but the strength of the melodies and lyrics overcomes this with ease and my pick is the impressive "I Thought I Was Over You" a duet with an uncredited female singer.

Since 1997 three new Jones CDs have appeared but none match his vinyl work and he remains sadly rather anonymous to the world at large but I rate him highly as a genuinely talented songwriter and it amazes me that so many of his songs have remained uncovered and uncoveted.

Del Jones

Court Is Closed 1973 Hikeka HR-3331 Producers: Del Jones, A Deac Jones, Benny Mitchell & B Hawkins

Positive Vibes 1973 Hikeka HR-3331 Producers: Del Jones & A Deac Jones

Another artist who deserves to have much more space allotted than I can provide, Del Jones was hardly your average soul man. In fact, he was better known for his uncompromising views on black versus white culture and wrote a number of books on such themes. His first album, *Court Is Closed*, is thus more aggressively political and militant than virtually everything else I review but should be fairly easily accessible to anyone who enjoys Gil Scott-Heron's music but if anything, Jones' output was even funkier. "Cold Turkey" and the title track both last over eight minutes but each probably outstays its welcome and Jones was a limited (if certainly fully committed) singer and I prefer the shorter and percolating "Needle N' Spoon" for example. It's certainly an album worth tracking down, but not by anyone who isn't comfortable with a funk style.

The second LP simply reprises the first with the addition of two songs, "Vibe-ing Theme" and "Soul Of Black Folks" - both good. Jones died in 2006.

Gloria Jones

Come Go With Me 1966? Uptown T-5700 Producer: Ed Cobb

Share My Love 1973 Motown M 790V1 Producer: Tom Thacker

Vixen 1976 EMI EMC 3159 Producers: Marc Bolan & Gloria Jones (UK)

Windstorm 1978 Capitol SW-11854 Producer: Richard Jones

Reunited 1982 AVI 6135 Producer: Ed Cobb

It's probably due to her connection with Marc Bolan, or possibly because of the album cover to *Vixen* which looks as if she were aiming for the Grace Jones market, or then again, because she recorded the original of the poppy "Tainted Love", but whatever it is, Gloria Jones has seldom been viewed as a soul singer to be taken particularly seriously. In fact the Cincinnati born singer and songwriter had a noticeably soulful voice, which communicated pain and strife, and never more so than on her finest LP, Share My Love, or her tremendous 1968 single on Minit, "When He Touches Me". (She certainly had the pedigree too, recording a gospel album on the Exodus label in 1964 or 1965 when she was part of a group called the Cogics, who comprised the startlingly talented line-up of Jones, Andre Crouch, Billy Preston, Sondra "Blinky" Williams, Sandra Couch and Edna Wright.)

In 1966 she put out the *Come Go With Me* set which was admirably brief and to the point. Five of its nine tracks came in at below two minutes and it was maybe the frenetic nature of charging cuts like "Finders Keepers" and the title track that exhausted everyone enough to keep things so short. Both songs were issued as singles, but it was a third dance side, "Heartbeat" that gained her some national action when it went to #21 on the *Cashbox* soul charts (but missed *Billboard*). Interestingly, she did not write anything on the LP and it was as the years progressed that her songwriting - often with Pam Sawyer - started to take off.

After two singles on Minit she ended up as a writer for Motown (co-composing the magnificent "If I Were Your Woman" for instance) where she was also given a chance to cut one album. Share My Love has been an unjustly neglected work, and if none of the nine tracks (of which she wrote or co-wrote eight) were absolutely top drawer songs, none were too shabby either, and the arrangements by Paul Riser were of the highest class. Motown albums could be somewhat formulaic but the mandolin driven "Oh Baby" was certainly not that, sounding as if it could have been part-recorded in a taverna in Athens. The mid-tempo "So Tired" was excellent too, one of a number of cuts where her voice had real bite. It's an album to sit down and listen to in its entirety given its admirable consistency throughout but it was a long way from being any sort of hit, and the same can be said for the one single that was pulled from it - the pop-oriented but rather charming "Why Can't You Be Mine" - and whatever Motown wanted to do with Jones it was clearly not to build her a singing career.

By the end of 1973 Jones was romantically involved with Marc Bolan and the T.Rex star co-produced her UK issued *Vixen* LP in 1976. It's a wildly uneven set with her version of "Get It On" absolutely guaranteed to alienate every soul fan who ever lived and it is precisely such tracks that have caused her to be rather dismissed as a serious artist. Fine versions of "Go Now" and "I Ain't Going Nowhere" were much more palatable but they were just about the only cuts that even remotely matched up to the quality of *Share My Love*.

After Bolan was sadly killed (and Jones badly injured) in a car crash in London in 1977, she moved back to Los Angeles where her brother Richard produced her one set for Capitol. Once again the excellent Riser was involved in arranging and the set had an expansive, lush sound, exemplified by the seven minute opener, "Bring On The Love" (a truncated version became a tiny "hit" on the *Cashbox* soul charts) and the slowly building "If The Roses Don't Come In Spring This Year". It wasn't all good though and the disco-influenced "Blue Light Microphone" and "Vaya Con Dios" both sound badly dated today.

In 1982, after a gap of more than fifteen years she hooked up again with Ed Cobb (hence *Reunited* on a eight track LP that included re-makes of her sixties' sides "Tainted Love" and "My Bad Boy's Coming Home". I can't tell you much more about the album as I haven't heard it but by all accounts it didn't amount to much and even Jones herself seems less than enamoured with it. It also certainly wasn't a hit.

The AVI work was to prove to be her last ever solo outing but she did briefly re-form a slimmed down Cogics (Jones, Preston, Williams and the excellent Frankie Karl) for one more LP in 1984.

Karin Jones

Under The Influence Of Love 1982 Handshake FW38155 Producers: Howard King, Ed Moore, Jim Tyrell, Eddie Levert, Dennis Williams & Bruce Hawes

I once owned a 1969 single by the Jonesetts on the Cougar record label; apparently this was a trio consisting of Karin and her two sisters; I didn't know this until recently but was aware she sang backing vocals on Patryce Banks' one LP. The records referred to above, and her own LP (and the single taken from it) appear to sum up the entire secular career of Jones on vinyl.

The LP has had a loyal following in England for a long time, and someone, somewhere here has always wanted it, and, by and large, I can see why, even if two or three of the songs don't linger in the mind. Jones has a good voice, the backing vocals and orchestration are impressive and "Ready Ready Love" is really good with Eddie Levert adding his own unmistakable vocals to Jones' best singing on the album; "Here I Go Again", "So Right" and "Last Night In My Dreams" are worthwhile too although I can't really warm to the title track (the single referred to above). It's a set worth persevering with as some of its charms are not immediately apparent and it should appeal to anyone who likes Phyllis Hyman's work.

Linda Jones

Hypnotized 1967 Loma LS 5907 Producer: George Kerr (Billboard soul charts: 26)

A Portrait Of Linda Jones 1971 Turbo TU-7004 Producer: George Kerr, Sylvia Robinson and Nate Edmonds

Your Precious Love 1972 Turbo TU-7007 Producers: George Kerr, Sylvia Robinson & Jerry Harris (Billboard soul charts: 35)

Let It Be Me 1972 Turbo TU-7008 Producer: George Kerr and Jerry Harris

Greatest Hits 1974 Turbo TU-7012

Linda Jones' first single came out in 1963 under the identity of Linda Lane, a remarkably bland name for a woman who was anything but. She only lived until the age of 28 but in that time packed as much pain, hurt, betrayal and soaring love affirmation into her records as any soul singer who ever lived. Listening to her music can be a genuinely uncomfortable experience and she could be shrill and grating at times, but at her best she was genuinely extraordinary.

Her first single under her birth name appeared on Atco, followed by another on Blue Cat but it was when she moved to Loma in early 1967 that better things started to happen. Her first single for the label, "Hypnotized", was also her biggest ever hit, arriving at #4 on the soul charts and #21 on the pop listings. A follow-up, "What've I Done (To Make You Mad)", did well too (#8 and #61) and its chart run coincided with the release of her first LP towards the end of that year. A third single from Hypnotized, "Give My Love A Try", sold slightly less well (#34 and #93), and that was almost certainly because it aped the bigger hit so obviously. The album had a disappointingly anonymous front cover but its musical contents were stellar: uptown soul with brooding and heavy orchestration, first-rate backing vocals and a set of songs that were perfectly suited to Jones. As good as the title track and "What've You Done" were - and that is very good indeed - the choice cut was the bruising and completely believable "The Things I've Been Through (Loving You)" the type of adult song where soul has nothing in common with pop. However, it would be wrong to assume that all within was mournful, depressing and down-tempo as she was equally accomplished on energetic and positive dance tracks like the pumping "I Can't Stop Lovin' My Baby" and the very Motown-ish version of The Shirelles' "A Last Minute Miracle". In short, a tremendous LP.

She released another handful of singles between 1968 and 1970 before she pitched up on All Platinum records in 1971, a label that truly knew how to release LPs, and they duly obliged with three on their Turbo subsidiary in about eighteen months. The first, *A Portrait Of Linda Jones* had a rather amateurish drawing of her on the front cover, and it certainly doesn't match up to *Hypnotized* musically, either. Firstly, "Hypnotized" and "If Only We Had Met Sooner" were inferior re-workings of the originals, and second, my own feelings (and I know some will vehemently disagree) are that her records started to sacrifice everything on the altar of her unabashed emotionalism and her trademark "whoa-whoas". "I Love You (I Need You)" for example has absolutely no melody whatsoever but plenty of heartfelt singing and even a splendid song like Goffin and King's "I Can't Make It Alone" could have been improved by a less frenzied reading. "Stay With Me Forever" was released as a single, reaching #47 on the soul charts in June 1971. My favourite track is "When The Hurt Comes Back" which Jones sings memorably.

I've always been haunted by the photograph of Jones with a star on her forehead and a look of worrying malevolence in her eyes that adorned the cover of *For Your Precious Love* but it couldn't camouflage the fact that it was another disappointing album as Turbo re-cycled four tracks from *A Portrait of Linda Jones*, while "Let It Be Me" is a sing I abhor and "Dancing In The Street" and "Doggin' Me Around" added little to the originals. All of which leaves only two cuts worth hearing, but one of these, the magnificent title track, was the song for which she will be best remembered. Her scream at the end is one of the great moments in soul music, and a perfect distillation of her art, and the performance makes me forgive all her other instances of "over-souling". It went all the way to #15 on the soul charts and even reached #74 on the pop charts, although it is almost impossible to imagine any mainstream radio show playing it. Next best was a typically impassioned take on the Moments' "Not On The Outside" and if it is still a little overwrought for me, it did manage to reach #32 on the charts in June 1972. Tragically, the latter was a posthumous hit as she had died three months earlier from diabetes at the age of only 28. (A Japanese version of the LP came out in 1989 on P-Vine PLP6526 and is better value as it runs to 13 tracks.)

Towards the end of 1972, Turbo released *Let it Be Me*, which only included three tracks that had not appeared on her earlier albums: the nicely orchestrated "I Do", a re-make of her Blue Cat side, "Fugitive From Love" and "I'm So Glad I Found You" a churning dance outing with excellent vocal assistance from The Whatnauts (his latter side also came out as a single on Stang.)

Another eight-tracker, *Greatest Hits*, came out in 1974, which also pointed up the fact that although Turbo released four LPs on Linda, they only featured 18 different songs in total.

Tamiko Jones

A Mann & A Woman (and Herbie Mann) 1967 Atlantic SD 8141 Producer: Ahmet Ertegun

Tamiko 1968 December DR 8500 Producer: Jimmy Wisner

I'll Be Anything For You 1969 A & M SP 3011 Producer: Creed Taylor

In Muscle Shoals 1970 Metromedia MD 1030 Producers: Barry Beckett, Jimmy Johnson & Tamiko Jones

Tamiko Jones (real name: Barbara Tamiko Ferguson) is another artist who could as easily be classed as a jazz or "Supper Club" singer as a soul one, and I did ponder whether or not she really belongs in the book. As can be seen, I've decided she does, but without a great deal of conviction.

She was born in Virginia and released her first record on Checker in 1963, the sultry "Is It A Sin" under the name of Timiko (which she never used again) and both it and her 1966 45 on Golden World, "Spellbound", demonstrate convincing enough claims for her to be classed as a soul singer in the uptown style, but the albums she put out in the sixties were cut from a rather different cloth. Take her debut with Herbie Mann, for example, which was a light bossa nova affair, attractive enough, but one that could not be described as a "soul" record by any stretch of the imagination.

And I'd say the same for much of the *Tamiko* set on December too, although "Pearl" is reasonably feisty while "Don't Go Breaking My Heart" is strongly reminiscent of much of Dionne Warwick's music. It's once again all exceedingly accomplished musically but compare her version here of "Don't Let Me Lose This Dream" with Aretha's and Jones rather uninvolved singing comes out a decided second best.

I'll Be Anything For You is typically beautifully produced by Creed Taylor and despite a surely ill-advised front cover photograph, gets the classy A & M treatment: gate-fold sleeve, list of musicians and recording dates etc. etc. but is once again all too often a MOR style outing even if Solomon Burke helps out here and there, particularly on two duets on the old Motown songs "Try It Baby" and "Please Return Your Love To Me". Best moment is a decidedly southern sounding cover of "Goodnight My Love" (some sides were cut at Sam Phillips' Memphis Studio.)

Tamiko Jones In Muscle Shoals is a title to get many soul fans excited but this is decidedly not Etta James, Irma Thomas or Laura Lee recording in those hallowed studios and it is more a case of the musicians meeting the style of Jones rather than the other way around. Strings are in abundance and the well-known compositions "Something", "Everybody's talkin'" and "Our Day Will Come" are not normally associated with such a deep south setting, while the latter employs a shuffling latin beat that I have never before or since heard played by Roger Hawkins and the rest of the crew

Love Trip 1975 Arista AL 4040 Producer: Tamiko Jones (Billboard soul charts: 40 ; Billboard pop charts: 204)

Cloudy 1977 Atlantis II ATL-715 Producers: Tamiko Jones & Jimmy Wisner

Can't Live Without Your Love 1981 Victor VIP-6777 Produced by Tamiko Jones (Japan)

Jones does not appear to have recorded again until 1974 and it was from those sessions - once again in Muscle Shoals - that she finally, after eleven years of trying, notched up a national hit when her cover of the Johnny Bristol song, "Touch Me Baby" climbed to #12 soul and #60 pop in early 1975, no doubt partly as a result of her employing a noticeably more breathy, "sexy" style than she had used before. There were some undeniably good songs on *Love Trip* (which housed the hit) - "Who Is She (And What Is She To You), "Let Me In Your Life" and "A Long Way To Go" - played by some of the greatest musicians in America but as was so often with Jones' music nothing caught fire and it's all rather dreary stuff, lacking in any noticeable passion.

She at least had some momentum now and a second track from *Love Trip*, "Just You And Me", also made the soul charts (#78) while her next LP, *Cloudy*, also served up two more soul chart entrants in "Let It Flow" and the title track. The former was couched in a soft-disco style as was "Boy, You're Growing On Me" but most things were more restrained. "Touch Me Baby" and "Creepin'" were reprised from her previous LP which was a minor irritant.

She went the full disco route in 1979 with "Can't Live Without Your Love" and was rewarded with a #70 soul hit, although it was a tiresome outing. No album was put out at the time to capitalise on this success, but two years later Victor in Japan built an LP around it, although anyone potentially interested in tracking it down should note that of its nine tracks, six had already appeared on *Love Trip* or *Let It Flow*.

No more albums were ever to appear but she did hit the soul charts one last time in 1986 with a cover of Marvin Gaye's "I Want You" (#81) but I don't believe she has recorded since.

Thelma Jones

Thelma Jones 1978 Columbia JC 35485 Producers: Bert deCoteaux & Brad Shapiro

In 1976 the marvellously soulful Thelma Jones recorded a dazzling single down in Muscle Shoals entitled "Salty Tears" that made the world stand still for its three and half minutes. It was one of the finest performances of the seventies and although not selling in any great quantity it did two things: a) made one recall that this native of Fayetteville, North Carolina had put out five excellent singles on the Barry label between 1967 and 1968 including one national hit, "Never Leave Me" (#49 soul), and the original of Aretha's "The House That Jack Built" and b) stimulated Columbia into issuing an entire LP by her, the only one she ever released.

And what a glorious effort it is. Cut all in New York (apart from "Salty Tears", which was included on the set) and arranged and produced by Bert deCoteaux, it was an eloquent reminder that thoughtful uptown soul music was still available in 1978. The upbeat tracks were danceable without pandering to "disco" tastes and Jones was even rewarded with only her second ever national hit 45 when her version of "I Second That Emotion" made it to #74 on the soul charts. It was probably the least impressive (although hardly being "weak") track on show, too, as three other brisk cuts, "Now That We Found Love" (a joyous version of the old O'Jay's side),"How Long" and "I Want What You Want" were even better. But it was when she slowed things down that the album really impressed and the brilliant Philadelphia pastiche "Lonely Enough To Try Anything" showed off writer Sam Dees' versatility while "I'd Rather Leave While I'm In Love" was also tremendous. The latin-tinged "I Can Dream" was another highlight while takes on well-chosen songs "Angel Of The Morning" and "Stay Awhile With Me" did not disappoint. Sadly, sales did and she never recorded another 45 or LP for anyone ever again (although did return with a couple of jazzy CDs in the early part of this century.)

Van Jones

Time Has Made Me New 1981 Niger River VJ 004 Producers: Van Jones & Ervin Epps

Anyone who has heard the two lovely slow songs, "Take To The Light And Wind" and the title track, from this obscure LP out of Virginia, might deduce that the album is a worthwhile purchase, even at the high price it commands; but beware as you will also have to listen to "Not About That" and the unremarkable "Say Ow Ow Ow" which sound like below average Chic dance outings, and "Shake Your Cheeks To The Beat" and "Let's Go This Go", are not

much better. Jones sings beautifully and delicately in a most appealing high tenor on the two best tracks but can't do much with the rest, and indeed doesn't even seem present on large chunks of the others.

Wornell Jones

Wornell Jones 1979 Paradise PAK 3308 Producer: Wornell Jones

Wornell Jones was Nils Lofgren's bass player and that association informs this LP, which is over-produced and too "rocky" in places for my liking; the songs are dull, too and it's not a set to offer up much enjoyment. The best and most striking track is "Must Have Been Love" which features a duet between Jones and an un-credited female singer who could be Maxayn (aka Paulette Parker) as she is credited with providing backing vocals throughout. Jones is clearly a gifted bass player and sings in a manner slightly reminiscent of Donny Hathaway, but didn't seem to have what it took to be a solo star.

Jones Girls

Valorie Jones; Brenda Jones; Shirley Jones

The Jones Girls 1979 P.I.R. JZ 35757 Producers: Kenny Gamble, Leon Huff, McKinley Jackson, Joseph Jefferson, Charles Simmons & Dexter Wansel (Billboard soul charts: 8; Billboard pop charts: 50)

At Peace With Woman 1980 P.I.R. JZ 36767 Producers: Kenny Gamble, Leon Huff, Cynthia Biggs, John Faith, James Herb Smith & Dexter Wansel (Billboard soul charts: 7; Billboard pop charts: 96)

Get As Much Love As You Can 1981 P.I.R. JZ 37627 Producers: Kenny Gamble, Leon Huff, Dexter Wansel & McKinley Jackson (Billboard soul charts: 25 ; Billboard pop charts: 155)

These three daughters of gospel singer Mary Frazier Jones recorded a number of singles for a handful of different labels over an eight year period and as none were outstandingly good and none were hits of any kind it is understandable that they turned away from recording in their own right and concentrated instead on providing backing vocals for such major artists as Diana Ross, Aretha Franklin and Curtis Mayfield. And there they may have remained, tucked away at the margins of the studios, had not Kenny Gamble and Leon Huff seen in them an opportunity to replace The Three Degrees and also the chance to groom the trio in matching the success of the top sibling groups of the day, The Emotions and Sister Sledge. The two men came up with a beauty immediately in the excellent "You're Gonna Make Me Love Somebody Else" which raced up to #5 on the soul charts as well as reaching top 40 pop. G & H also penned the creamy and stoic "Life Goes On" and the thoughtful and soulful "I'm At Your Mercy" and if they had written more than these three then *The Jones Girls* would doubtless have been one of the great P.I.R. albums of the seventies; but they didn't and it isn't. The other five tracks are not bad, just rather dull. Nevertheless, the album sold satisfactorily and certainly better than the most recent offerings by Jerry Butler and Billy Paul, much more well-known names from the same label. It also captured a whole hosts of loyal fans who love the music of The Jones Girls to this day.

The follow-up, *At Peace With Woman*, also performed admirably on the charts and contained two more good selling singles in "Dance Turned Into Romance" (#22 soul) and the best cut on view in the sassy (from a group who weren't often very "street") "I Just Love The Man" (#9). It was probably a more consistent album than the debut with fewer stand-out cuts but greater quality overall including "Children Of The Night", a typically tuneful Bell-Creed composition. It was also clear by now that The Jones Girls' music recalled The Emotions much more strongly than the Sledge sisters as virtually everything was placed in a mid-tempo setting rather than aimed at the dance floor.

The trio's third and final album for P.I.R. had rather striking front and back covers on which the sisters were dressed in arresting scarlet outfits, but the music within was seemingly marking time; it was rather interchangeable with the first two sets and while nice enough to listen to, there was nothing here that I really love. Many would disagree as this was the album on which the much- revered "Nights Over Egypt" can be found, one of two singles within that reached the top 25 of the soul singles charts, the other being the estimable "(I Found) That Man Of Mine".

On Target 1983 RCA AFL1-4817 Producers: Robert Wright & Fonzi Thornton (Billboard soul charts: 59)

Keep It Comin' P.I.R. FZ 38555 Producers: Kenny Gamble, Leon Huff, Cynthia Biggs, Dexter Wansel, Keni Burke & McKinley Jackson

Artists Showcase 1986 Street Sounds Music 4 (UK)

Coming Back 1992 Another Right Productions ARP LP 02 Producers: Errol Henry, Jazzie B., Stephen Carmichael, Wayne Lawes & Funhill Productions (UK)

The Jones Girls moved on to RCA for one LP in 1983, which immediately placed them in a more upbeat musical setting, with the lushness of the Philadelphia sessions being replaced by a somewhat harsher and funkier tone, although the difference was subtle rather than startling and producers Robert Wright and Fonzi Thornton ensured that there was nothing here to alienate long-term fans. Nevertheless, it certainly sold disappointingly, as did two singles from it ("On Target and "2 Win U Back") and all in all it was a move that most people probably wished had never happened. One thing I will say in its favour is that the sleevenotes most helpfully spelled out who took lead vocals on which track (Shirley as usual took the majority) as all sisters had such similar voices that I usually find it difficult to distinguish them. All three took leads on a version of Barbara Lewis' "Baby I'm Yours" but it wasn't nearly as distinguished as the original.

The *Keep It Comin'* set did not mean that the girls had returned to P.I.R., but was a collection of "in the can" songs and in the U.S. archive material has always struggled to sell in great quantity and the album didn't even reach the soul charts; a rather cheesy front cover may not have helped either. The best track was probably "Better Things To Do", a Gamble-Huff song, and it was rightly released as a 45 but it also failed. Once again, fans should be pleased with the appearance of the album as it was by no means noticeably inferior to the first three sets.

The girls never had any other kind after hit after 1984 and rather slipped from people's minds and never released another LP in the USA. They still had plenty of supporters in the UK, however, and it was for this reason that a 'best of' ("Artists Showcase") appeared in 1986 as well as a final set, recorded over here, which slipped out in 1992. It is an eclectic outing: the very good "Somewhere Alone Tonight" sounds as if it could easily have come from the Philly era whereas "Free" is considerably more contemporary sounding, and "Sweet Ecstasy" bridges the gap between the two. The producers have done an excellent job in managing to retain the essence of the girls' musical legacy and *Coming Back* stands up to scrutiny when compared to their other albums.

It also marked the return to the fold of Shirley Jones who had left for a brief solo career in 1986 (two albums and a #1 soul single with "Do You Get Enough Love?") but since that time things have not been so positive as Valerie died in 2001 and new recordings have not been forthcoming.

Joneses

Harold Taylor; Wendell Noble; Reggie Noble; Sam White; Glenn Dorsey; Jimmy Richardson; Stewart Davidson; Gary Pinchom

Keepin' Up With The Joneses 1974 Mercury SRM-1-1021 Producer: Lee Valentine (Billboard soul charts: 51 ; Billboard pop charts: 202)

The Joneses 1977 Epic PE 34898 Producer: Bobby Eli

Baby There Is Nothing You Can Do 1990 P-Vine PLP-6538/6539 Producers: Lee Valentine, Glenn Dorsey, Deborah McDuffie & C. Jefferson (Japan)

The Joneses originated from Pittsburgh and made a handful of singles for the MVP label in the early seventies in the fashionably attractive uptown style: full orchestration above which falsetto and hard tenor leads battled things out but regrettably none of them registered on any national charts although "Pretty Pretty" was very popular in Baltimore. (An earlier single on Wand by "The Joneses" is almost certainly nothing to do with this group.)

By 1974 group leader and main writer Glenn Dorsey had rethought their approach and the five man aggregation of that time included two baritones and a bass, more than a nod, surely, to the success that Barry White was enjoying with his own weighty-voiced output. It worked, too: "Sugar Pie Guy", "Hey Babe (Is The Gettin' Still Good?)" and "I Can't See What You See In Me" (their second version of this song) all ended up in the soul top thirty between March 1974 and April 1975. The three hits were included on their debut LP, the rather predictably entitled *Keepin' Up With The Joneses*, the cover of which saw the quintet photographed in the kitsch interior of New York's Hotel Pierre. These are all exceedingly catchy songs - almost contagious in the case of "Sugar Pie Guy" - and their success was no great surprise. The "key" cut on the set was presumably "Our Love Song" seeing as it was stretched out to over seven minutes, but it couldn't sustain interest for even half that time. It was also one of a number of songs where Harold Taylor's lead vocals wandered dangerously close to the outskirts of melody, and I preferred the excellent failed Mercury single "Baby Don't Do It" which was delivered in their earlier falsetto (Wendell Noble on lead?) style. All in all, though, a good enough album with superb New York musicians like Richard Tee, Wilbur Bascomb and Cornell Dupree helping out.

The Joneses placed three more singles on the soul charts for Mercury in the period from 1975 to 1976 but a second LP was not forthcoming and by the time a new one did arrive, they had moved labels (to Epic) and acquired some new group members, including an abrasive new lead singer in Jimmy Richardson, at the expense of the Noble brothers and Sam White.

The Joneses is an unruffled and solid outing, played with love and verve by the newer Sigma sound musicians such as Charles Collins, Michael Foreman and Dennis Harris who had come to the fore when the classic team of Baker-Harris-Young left to do their own thing. The set kicks off with a tremendous dance side in "Who Loves You" which rather surprisingly failed as a 7". The best track though was the slowed down and stretched out ballad, "All The Little Pieces", on which Richardson puts in a super turn. It sounded as if it could have been cut in 1972 rather than 1977 and that's a good thing to my ears. The rather erratic Bobby Eli produced the whole thing and co-wrote seven of the songs and it was certainly one of his better efforts helping to banish thoughts of his own rather awful LP (*Eli's Second Coming* from the same year, which won't be in the book due to its straightforward disco approach.) I was also delighted to see that the marvellous Terry Collins (who sadly never got to record an LP of his own) helped Eli out on three of the songs including both of those I have mentioned above. Glenn Dorsey had to be content with penning just three songs this time around, and only "Music To My Ears" was recognisably the Joneses from the Mercury era. It was a shame that the album got lost in the market place and although there were to be a handful more singles from the group , no more new LPs were ever released.

But a third set did materialise in 1990, albeit only in Japan, being a welcome if somewhat haphazard retrospective collection of 22 songs. It was - as always in Japan - rather beautifully packaged, and a double album as well, containing music that covered a period of some 10 years or so. It was great to see all three of the MVP singles on board but, curiously, only one of the three later Mercury hits - "In A Good Groove - was included. I'm not sure why the other two were not. Much of it was previously unreleased and ranged from a surprisingly good cover of The Beatles' "She Loves You" through a charming "Lovin' You" (even though it sounded as if it was recorded in Glenn Dorsey's bathroom) to obviously later and much less appealing efforts which included a nondescript cover of The Gap Band's "Burn Rubber".

Lonnie Jordan (see also War)

Different Moods Of Me 1978 MCA 2329 Producer: Lonnie Jordan (Billboard pop charts: 158)

The Affair 1982 Boardwalk NB1- 33245 Producer: Lonnie Jordan

As a member of that excellent group War, Lonnie Jordan plays keyboards and percussion; on his first solo album he plays everything. It's not always clear what motivates someone to go the solo route and it certainly doesn't seem as if the talented Jordan had a radically different musical vision in mind as the LP certainly recalls War, but it must be said that this would be a disappointing outing from them. The best cut, by far, "Grey Rainy Days", also came out as a single and reached a fairly respectable #51 on the soul charts although it should surely have been called "Long Summer Days" as that is what its breezy and upbeat vibe best recalls. "Discoland" is horrible and much else is so-so but no-one could accuse MCA of not trying to support Jordan as the set comes complete with a gate-fold sleeve and lots of photographs. Jordan co-wrote everything, with Susan Buckner helping out on the majority of the tracks as either co-writer or co-singer.

I have only heard a couple of tracks from *The Affair* so cannot provide much at all as a guide but they do sound fairly typically West Coast with a pop twist and sound much less like War than the songs on the debut set did.

Margie Joseph

Makes A New Impression 1971 Volt VOS-6012 Producers: Darryl Carter & Fred Briggs (Billboard soul charts: 7; Billboard pop charts: 67)

Phase II 1971 Volt VOS-6016 Producer: Fred Briggs

In The Name Of Love 1988 Ace / Stax SX-015 (UK)

Despite appearing on the Okeh label, Margie Joseph's first two singles were resolutely southern in style, reflecting her Mississippi roots, and even if they didn't sell many copies, they did bring her to the attention of Stax and she was to stay with the famous Memphis company for around three years. Her first single was brilliant: "One More Chance" has a thrilling arrangement and I genuinely believe this - the art of arranging - was an area of expertise at which soul excelled and can hold its head up aginst any other form of popular music. Despite this, it was not a success and only "Your Sweet Loving" of her first three Volt singles charted and that only at #46.

It was apparently Larry McKinley's (Joseph's husband) idea to cover "Stop! In The Name Of Love" and it became the centrepiece of her first LP, *Margie Joseph Makes A New Impression,* and she certainly did. None of her earlier singles were on the LP and it was one of the first few - together with those from Isaac Hayes - where the company put more effort into something that turned around at 33⅓ rpm rather than at 45. It was proudly advertised in the January 31st 1971 edition of *Billboard* and went all the way to #7 on the soul charts whereas a truncated version of the Supremes' song as a single only managed #38. Apart from the dramatic and elongated take on "Stop!" (which incorporated the type of earthy monologue that Millie Jackson and Laura Lee became famous for, but Margie got there first) the remainder of the LP was somewhat more conventional with nine other tracks covering a number of styles; "Medicine Bend" had a distinct Invictus feel; "Come Tomorrow" was soothing and highly orchestrated, "Sweeter Tomorrow" bore the undeniable scent of "southern rock", "Make Me Believe You'll Stay" fell into the eternally appealing country-soul style and the gospel-flavoured "Same Thing" was sung in a manner that caused many to unfairly shrug Joseph off as a poor woman's Aretha. All in all, it was an excellent outing and should have propelled Joseph into the top echelon of female soul singers but it didn't happen.

It didn't happen because oddly, almost incredibly in fact, her follow-up set, *Phase II*, didn't even reach the soul charts and it's hard to think of another example when a best seller has been succeeded by such a failure and Stax's usually good promotion team must have been fast asleep. Predictably, there is another long drawn-out cover of a Supremes' song on show, this time "My World Is Empty Without You" but the freshness of the approach had rather leached away and Volt only bothered to release one 45 from the set, "That Other Woman Got My Man And Gone", but it also failed to chart. Despite the commercial frustration, it's another alluring set and soul fans could thrill to tracks like "I'll Always Love You" and "I Love You Too Much To Say Goodbye" even if hard-core "southern soul" fans might regret that it is once again a lavishly orchestrated outing with strings taking prominence over horns.

It wasn't until 1988 that any record label saw fit to put together a retrospective set of Joseph's Stax material and I highly commend Ace's album from that year as it gathered up all of her Volt singles as well as a previously unreleased version of "Tell It Like It Is", and of the generous 15 tracks, 6 of them were not on the two Volt sets.

Margie Joseph 1973 Atlantic SD 7248 Producer: Arif Mardin (Billboard soul charts: 21)

Sweet Surrender 1974 Atlantic SD 7277 Producer: Arif Mardin (Billboard soul charts: 56 ; Billboard pop charts: 165)

Margie 1975 Atlantic SD 18126 Producer: Arif Mardin (Billboard soul charts: 53)

Live! (with Major Harris and Blue Magic) 1976 WMOT 2-5000 Producers: WMOT Productions, Blue Magic, Major Harris & Margie Joseph

In the dim light of the sales failure of *Phase II* it was no surprise that Joseph moved to Atlantic where she was to achieve her greatest commercial success, even if at first it must have seemed like a mistake when her first two singles, "Let's Go Somewhere And Love" and "Touch Your Woman" both floundered in the market place, and the third, a rather pointless (and too close to Aretha vocally) cover of "Let's Stay Together" only managed to reach #43 soul. All three 45s were included on *Margie Joseph* as was a recut of "Make Me Believe You'll Stay" and one of her finest ever moments, the UK only single "How Do You Spell Love". This last was a sassy take of a great Bobby Patterson song and was a logical choice for an album, which although cut in New York with great musicians of the calibre of Richard Tee, Hugh McCracken, Bernard Purdie, Jerry Jemmott and Ralph MacDonald, strove throughout for a "southern" sensibility. To be honest, I find the whole set to be rather disappointing ("How Do You Spell Love" and "I'm So Glad I'm Your Woman" excepted) as although it is thoughtful and impeccably played and chooses strong material such as "I'd Rather Go Blind" it is too often strangely lifeless (namely: "Turn Around And Love Me" and "I'm Only A Woman") and easier to admire than enjoy.

Sweet Surrender, despite playing down the "southern" angle and playing up the "Aretha factor", followed the pattern of *Margie Joseph* - same studios, musicians, producer, widely trawled song selection - but this time included a genuine hit single in Paul McCartney's "My Love" which went to #10 soul and #69 pop - the highest placing on each chart she was ever to attain. My initial pleasure at seeing two excellent Paul Kelly songs - "Come lay Some Lovin' On Me" and "Come With Me" - was tempered by the realisation that neither, although certainly not poor, was as good as the originals. Again, it's a perfectly pleasurable LP to listen to but the fact I have only played it a couple of times in forty years must mean something.

Margie repeated the formula for a third time, and Joseph was rewarded with two more smallish hits in the soppy "Words" (#27 soul) and "Stay Still" (#34). My own feelings remain the same, too: worthy but rather dull. Bill Withers' version of "The Same Love That Makes Me Laugh" beats out Margie's with ease and the whole set is smothered by strings that drain out too many thrills. Even Sam Dees' "Just As Soon As The Feeling's Over" fails to hit the spot, as the fine words were calling out for some horns to bring it to life.

A *Live* LP followed, and two sides of this were one side too long, and it didn't chart, leading to a switch of producer and a move to the Atlantic subsidiary, Cotillion, for some necessary revitalisation.

Hear The Words, Feel The Feeling 1976 Cotillion SD 9906 Producer: Lamont Dozier (Billboard soul charts: 38)

Feeling My Way 1978 Atlantic SD 19182 Producer: Johnny Bristol

Lamont Dozier was all over *Hear The Words, Feel The Feeling* (on the front sleeve of which Joseph's lovely face covered almost every available inch) as he wrote or co-wrote all nine tracks as well producing the whole thing. The title song managed to reach #18 soul in July 1976 and the luxurious "Don't Turn The Lights Off" made it to #46 a few months later. Anyone who loves Dozier's work will adore the set and he plays down the Franklin influence a little; he also barely wrote a weak hook of course and the album has an immediacy and drive that the Atlantic sets tended to lack. She deals with the variations in tempo in winning style and it was her best album in years. The California air obviously suited her.

Rather confusingly one track on *Hear The Words* was entitled "Feeling My Way" which was to become the title of her next set on which you might think the song would have been better placed. It's another West Coast outing although this time Johnny Bristol had moved into the producer's seat. No expense has been spared in her make-up on the front and back covers and she looks like a million dollars, as well as a million miles away from the younger woman who boldly displayed her Afro on the cover of *Margie Joseph*. Bristol's fingerprints were every bit as inky on the new set as Dozier's had been on the last and I wonder whether Margie knew or cared that Bristol presented her with five songs that he had already sang himself on his own albums. It's a second successive artistic triumph although bafflingly the commercial returns were scant: the LP itself didn't chart and the two splendid singles pulled from it, "Come On Back To Me Lover" and "I Feel His Love Getting Stronger", only managed the hardly satisfactory soul charts returns of #85 and #94 respectively. Nevertheless, as an example in how to turn out a beautifully realised set in the disco era it was rarely equalled - and certainly not by Aretha Franklin's work of the time.

Knockout! 1983 HCRC HLP- 20009 Producers: Tom Jones III & David Weatherspoon (Billboard soul charts: 34)

Ready For The Night 1984 Cotillion 90158-1 Producers: Preston Glass & Randy Jackson

Stay 1988 Ichiban ICH 1027 Producers: Winton Cobb & Sheryl Martin

Joseph left the industry after the Bristol album and didn't re-appear until 1983 with a new set on a new label, HCRC out of Houston, and although it was hardly a Stax or an Atlantic, the label did manage to give her one of the biggest hits of her career when the title track from *Knockout* made it to #12 on the soul charts on which it stayed for nearly six months. The album itself did well too even if it contains a number of tedious sides such as the hit, "Moove (sic) To The Groove" and "Give It To Me". Better by far is the uplifting "I'm Blessed", a typical southern ballad, and it completely overshadows everything else on view.

Margie returned to the Atlantic fold for her 1984 set, *Ready For The Night*, produced - horribly to these ears - by Preston Glass and Randy Jackson a fact that rendered most of it impossible for me to listen to. The title track stalled at only #69 soul and the best of a bad bunch were the good ballads "Take Me Away Tonight" and "Is It Gonna Be Me And You".

Joseph joined the Ichiban label for her last ever vinyl outing in 1988 and although the cover of *Stay* looked decidedly cheap when compared to her previous work it was an improvement on *Ready For The Night*, even if still falling well short of her best moments. A 12" single from the set, "I've Got To Have Your Love", failed to do any business and Margie's career was over.

She is a very good - if probably not great - singer who made some wonderful records but who has been poorly served by hindsight; she recorded seven LPs for the Atlantic family and never got to see a vinyl "Best Of" or "Greatest Hits" set released. It took until the CD era was well underway for a couple of retrospective collections to come out.

J.R. Funk & The Love Machine

Jorge Omar Barreiro; Roy Bermingham; Sarita Butterfield; Jinji Nicole; Bernadine Mitchell

Good Lovin' 1981 Brass BRLP 12.011 Producer: Herbert Csasznik, Roy B and J Barreiro

This is a decidedly mysterious album which has required a good deal of detective work to try and work out who is behind it. It would appear that the "J. R." hides the identities of Jorge Omar Barreiro and Roy Bermingham although the "Love Machine" is far easier to identify as the names of the three singers are listed on the back, one of whom is former Playboy bunny and Bill Cosby accuser Sarita Butterfield. As for who is on the front cover and as for who undertakes lead male vocals, God knows. The set mostly consists of dance items and the titles of "Come And Get It", "Feel Good Party Time" and "Make Your Body Move" rather give things away but they are all slightly more robust and funkier than one might expect. Not great by any means but not disasters; they have something of the feel of early Brass Construction although "Good Lovin'" borrows the JB's "Doing To Death" riff. The best cut, though, by far, is a fine ballad, "I Just Hope You Understand", which is delivered by an excellent unnamed male singer who I suspect is neither J. nor R.

Juicy

Katreese Barnes; Jerry Barnes; Wyatt Staton; Allison Bragdon; John Tucker

Juicy 1982 Arista AL 9582 Producer: Eumir Deodato

It Takes Two 1985 Private I BFZ 40098 Producer: Eumir Deodato

Spread The Love 1987 CBS BFZ 40451 Producer: Eumir Deodato

Juicy's debut LP was rather good, having something just different enough to rise above the crowd of many such dance-oriented records and I think their edge derived from the spirited vocals of Katreese Barnes, impressive bass playing from brother Jerry and clipped guitar phrases by Wyatt Staton. Katreese recalls Chaka Khan on "I've Got Something, the intro to "You're Number One" is *ever* so close to "Ladies' Night" but Juicy get away with it as in general they had enough of their own identity to carry such influences without giving offence. "Our Love Is Stronger" is downbeat, smooth and satisfying and "I'm Satisfied" and "The Night Is Still Young" are superior pop. "Don't Cha Wanna" isn't great but it's an overall good set.

For their second and third sets, Juicy had slimmed down to the two Barnes'. These are once again better efforts than most others of the time and tracks like "Love Is Good Enough" and "Slow Dancing" from *It Takes Two* could have plausibly sat on an Ashford and Simpson LP of the time and no-one would have been upset. "Bad Boy" and the title track were small soul hits but the interestingly funky and catchy (made so by a two note bassline) "Sugar Free" was a much bigger success at #13. It's clear to me that the Barnes' are genuinely talented and if I can't fully enjoy the LP that's really only because it did come out in 1985 and the uninteresting musical backing ("Sugar Free" excepted) does need to be taken into account.

I enjoy the third LP too, although it was chunky and pop-oriented with little "classic" soul content but it is another chance to note that Juicy could write tunes: "Spread The Love", "After Loving You" and "Make You Mine" can all be recalled after only one spin.

Jimmy Jules (see also Southern Cookin')

Xmas Done Got Funky (with Jackie Spencer) 197? Jim Gem JGS 1001 Producer: Jimmy Jules

Jimmy Jules recorded one my favourite records in 1972 with "Ten Carat Fool" a blistering southern soul sound with ferocious horns but before then the man from New Orleans had already issued a number of excellent singles and it's a shame that the two LPs on which he features are so little-known; in the case above because it is next to impossible to find while the one he made as a member of Southern Cookin' has been more or less ignored by everyone.

I'm not a great fan of Christmas outings but we have not been so blessed by Jules' records that we can ignore it and his three tracks on here don't sound anything like festive records anyway in construction and accompaniment; it's only the lyrics that give them away. All are good, and George Spouch, Derwin Subtle and Jimmy Jones (together with Jules they comprised the Nuclear Sound System) serve up an entertainingly funky instrumental called "Come And Get Your Gift".

Side two consists of three tracks by the excellent and unknown Jackie Spencer and she makes a song entitled "The Macaroni Man" sound about twenty times more enjoyable and sassy than I would have thought possible while "Too Many Horses" is a winner too; neither seem to have anything to do with Christmas.

Don Julian (see The Larks)

Junie (see also Funkadelic and The Ohio Players)

When We Do 1975 Westbound W-200 Producer: Junie

Freeze 1975 Westbound W-214 Producer: Junie

Suzie - Super Groupie 1976 Westbound W-228 Producer: Junie

Walter "Junie" Morrison was born in Dayton and, while not a founder member of the great Ohio Players, joined them at a key point in their development, the early seventies, when they were putting out LPs like *Pain, Pleasure* and *Ecstasy* and his contributions were obvious and important. By the time they really started to make it big with *Skin Tight*, he had moved on to release the first of a rather peculiar run of six albums.

That debut, *When We Do*, clearly showed his allegiance to the Players for its cover featured the rather terrifying bald lady - Pat Evans - who graced the group's LPs of the time. It also equally clearly demonstrated that he was not a man to be confined by expectations of how soul men should sound and it is a work that needs to be investigated with great caution and an open mind for it is a highly eclectic beast. The opener "Junie" could have come from a "Blaxploitation" movie; "Johnny Carson Samba" (great title) would not be out of place in some outré latin revival club; "The Place" is a guitar showcase; "Anna" delivers sweet soul and demonstrates Morrison's impressive vocal range. And so on. "Tightrope" was a small soul hit (#84) in early 1974 and is the most obviously Ohio Players influenced cut on display. I know plenty of people who would absolutely hate this album - I'm not mad on a fair bit of it myself - but it does have some arresting moments (Dave Van De Pitte's arrangements, for example) and Junie's idiosyncratic talent cannot be gainsaid.

Morrison followed-up *When We Do* speedily with *Freeze,* a set which dispensed with Van De Pitte and adopted a tougher, more keyboard based texture. It was also even more unusual as evidenced best by "Cookies Will Get You" a humorous half-spoken tale which could never be mistaken for a deep soul record. It's an impossible album to recommend as it is so far removed from virtually everything else in the book but if anyone wants to seek out some genuinely individual music then Junie may be your man.

Westbound put out a third LP on Junie in 1976 and one has to commend the label's loyalty for I can't imagine that any of them broke any sales records.It's the most accessible outing of the three, largely dispensing with his "granny" voices and includes more mainstream tracks like "If You Love Him", the almost danceable "Suzie", the funky "What Am I Gonna Do" and even a cover of Diana Ross' "Surrender" (which, no-one will be surprised to hear, doesn't sound much like the diva's version). Only "Stone Face Joe" and "Spirit" really continued the anarchic sounds from the first two sets.

In 1978 he took a break from cutting his own records and made his most inspired career move ever by joining Funkadelic and co-penning "One Nation Under A Groove" which must have earned him substantially more money than from his entire LP output.

Bread Alone 1980 Columbia NJC 36585 Producer: Junie

Junie 5 1981 Columbia ARC 37133 Producer: Junie

Evacuate Your Seats 1984 Island 90191-1 Producer: Junie

He didn't tarry long with Clinton's group and by 1980 had returned to cutting his own songs, albeit by now on a new label, and Columbia at that, a slightly surprising place for such a singular performer to end up. Which might account for the fact that he wears a suit on the front cover of *Bread Alone;* was the wayward Morrison becoming more biddable? Well, it appears he was as the album is more straightforward than his previous work with precious little of an experimental nature to be found. Side one is quite poppy and side two is quite funky with a slight P-Funk feel but throughout Junie sings in a style that is almost unrecognisable from his early days with The Ohio Players. A front cover sticker proudly proclaimed that the set contained "the hit" "Love Has Taken Me Over (Be My Baby)" but that turned out to be pure wishful thinking, unless hitting #89 on the *Cashbox* soul charts counts.

Morrison's fifth set was easily his most conventional to date and included only his second single to broach the *Billboard* soul charts in "Rappin' About Rappin" (#74). The catalyst for the change in style was probably one Teresa Allman, who, as well as providing backing vocals, wrote every track bar one, a far cry from when Junie composed everything he recorded. Once again, his voice cannot easily be reconciled with his early performances and "Last One To Know", "I Love You Madly" and "Cry Me A River" (not that one) could never have found a way onto his Westbound albums, given their orthodox structures.

Evacuate Your Seats contained Morrison's biggest ever "hit", "Tease Me" and given it only made it to #71 soul, He returned to the practice of writing everything but continued his more recent practice of playing it safe. It's all four-square gently funky, poppy and synth-driven dance stuff (apart from "Here With You Tonight"), unappealing in the extreme to me.

Kashif (see also B.T. Express)

Kashif 1983 Arista AL 9620 Producers: Kashif & Morrie Brown (Billboard soul charts: 10 ; Billboard pop charts: 54)

Send Me Your Love 1984 Arista AL 8-8205 Producer: Kashif (Billboard soul charts: 4 ; Billboard pop charts: 51)

Condition Of The Heart 1985 Arista AL 8-8385 Producer: Kashif (Billboard soul charts: 32 ; Billboard pop charts: 144)

Love Changes 1987 Arista AL-8447 Producers: Kashif & Lewis Martinee (Billboard soul charts: 17 ; Billboard pop charts: 118)

Kashif 1989 Arista AL-8595 Producer: Kashif (Billboard soul charts: 29)

Kashif was plain old Michael Jones as a member of B.T. Express and after leaving them went on to make a name for himself as a producer for the likes of Howard Johnson, Evelyn King and Melba Moore before releasing his first single in early 1983 and ""I Just Gotta Have You (Lover Turn Me On)" became a big hit, reaching #5 on the soul charts. It was vaguely reminiscent of what Luther Vandross was doing at the time and its dry groove was precisely what audiences wanted back then but I'm not sure it has aged well and his music never attracted me to the dance floor in the first place. He is one of a number of artists in the book about whom I have little to say. I will record that he was one of the most popular male soul singers of the eighties, placed 17 singles on the soul charts between 1983 and 1990 and had a penchant for duets: he sang with Melba Moore, Meli'sa Morgan and Dionne Warwicke.

Kay - Gees

Kevin Bell (aka Amir-Salaam Bayyan); Michael Cheek; Callie Cheek; Kevin Lassiter; Wilson Beckett; Peter Duarte; Ray Wright; Dennis White; Fernando Luis Arocho; Glen Radford; Glen Griffin; Marc Cupo; Inidro Rosa; Huey Harris

Keep on Bumpin' & Masterplan 1974 Gang 101 Producer: Ronald Bell (Billboard pop charts: 199)

Find A Friend 1976 Gang 102 Producer: Khalis Bayaan (aka Ronald Bell)

Kilowatt 1978 De-Lite DSR-9505 Producer: The Kay-Gees

The clues were certainly there right from the beginning: the name of both the band and their record label, and Kevin Bell's being the brother of producer Ronald Bell, but the Kay Gees really did sound remarkably like Kool and The Gang; they just didn't sell as many records.

They managed ok for a while, though, and the New Jersey band placed "Keep On Bumpin'", "Master Plan", "Get Down" and "Hustle Wit Every Muscle" in the mid regions of the soul charts between the middle of 1974 and the autumn of 1975; all four tracks being included on an impressive debut set which laboured under the rather unwieldy title of *Keep On Bumpin' & Masterplan* (which was changed to *Hustle Wit' Every Muscle* for its U.K. release on Polydor.) It's not a very introspective LP, being upbeat and funky throughout, shot through with the zig-zag guitar patterns and horn blasts that so characterised Kool & The Gang's own records in the mid-seventies. If you liked that sort of thing, this album will sound great, if you didn't it will afford scant pleasure.

For the second set, Kevin Bell had changed his name (as indeed had producer brother Ronald) and although there were no alterations to the core personnel of the band, and the female backing quartet of Something Sweet remained prominent, it was possible to trace two noticeable modifications from the first album: a greater willingness to slow things down and the recruitment of a male vocal foursome called Tomorrow's Edition (who went on to release an LP of their own in 1982) and these newcomers were particularly prominent on "Thank You Dear Lord" and "Be Real", worthy cuts which gave the Kay Gees their first obviously different sound from their mentors. The excellent "Waiting At The Bus Stop" made it to #52 on the soul charts in the summer of 1976 - their fifth success from five singles released, an impressive performance. It wasn't to last.

Kilowatt saw the band move to De-Lite and change their name, ungrammatically, to the Kay Gee's, as well as dispensing with Something Sweet, Tomorrow's Edition and Kevin Lassiter, but the opening cut, "Kay Gees' Theme Song", retained the noticeable funky feel from the two Gang LPs. Other tracks did not: "Tango Hustle" was a rather uncertain latin-tinged outing and "Space Disco" was as tiresome as its title suggests. "Kilowatt Invasion" became the first 45 from the band to fail to reach the soul charts but "Cheek To Cheek" re-established their run of single success, albeit only at the rather lowly level of #75. I really like the first two LPs from this underrated band but *Kilowatt* is much more mundane.

Burn Me Up 1979 De-Lite DSR-9510 Producers: Patrick Adams, Ken Morris & Stan Lucas

Burn Me Up is a most curious and unusual affair: a rare example of where a completely new set of musicians take over a band's identity. None of the original eight members are anywhere to be found on the album, which mobilized six completely new men to carry on under the "Kay Gees" banner. As might be imagined it sounds nothing like any of the earlier records and includes a nicely sung "Heavenly Dream" (more influenced by Earth, Wind & Fire than the original Kay Gees) and the rather nasty "Latican Funk" and the title track (which failed as a 45), both slices of disco nonsense. The album did little in the market place, and the Kay Gees' name was used no more.

Ernie K-Doe

Mother - In - Law 1962 Minit LP 0002 No producer listed

Ernie K-Doe Volume 2 1979? Bandy LP 70005 No producer listed

Ernie K-Doe 1972 Janus JLS 3030 Producer: Allen Toussaint

Mother - In - Law 1986 Stateside SSL 6012 (UK)

Burn, K-Doe, Burn! 1989 Charly CRB 128 (UK)

New Orleans' Ernest Kador made loads of records in his forty year plus career, but I bet most people only know two of them, and I also bet that they couldn't name him as the singer. Firstly, there was his massive 1961 smash, "Mother In Law", which went to #1 on both the soul and pop charts, and second, "Here Come The Girls", which was the music played behind a highly successful UK T.V. advertisement for the Boots company. He should be remembered for much more, though, as he issued many excellent 45s, but like so many New Orleans' artists, his success was but fleeting.

His earliest sides date back to the mid-fifties but it was his third release for Minit that gave him his monster hit. The company followed up with "Te-Ta-Te-Ta-Ta" (a title that could only have come from New Orleans) but all concerned had to settle for a much more modest performance: #21 soul and #53 pop. Both hits are included on his debut LP from 1962, as were the initial two 45s he released for the label. As great and fun as "Mother-In Law" undoubtedly is, it was outclassed by the bluesy and heartfelt "Waiting At The Station" which shows K-Doe in a different light. It is the finest cut on a most enjoyable LP, and one of the best things he ever did.

Another great 1961 single appeared when "A Certain Girl" was paired up with "I Cried My Last Tear" (both sides of which did well on the *Cashbox* soul charts) but it was not followed up by a new LP and we had to wait years for his next album. 1972 in fact, by which time he had recorded many more singles for Minit, a couple on Instant and around ten for Duke (alas, no LP ever came forth on the Texas label despite two of them being reasonably successful soul chart entrants in 1967). The second album, simply and boringly entitled Ernie K-Doe, appeared on Janus and is where "Here Come The Girls" can be found, although it failed dismally when released as a single in 1971. It's an extraordinarily haphazard set with Janus and /or Allen Toussaint clearly aiming for Ernie to try on as many different styles as possible in the hope that one of them would stick: Meters' styled funk on "Hotcha Mama"; the lovely country - soul lilt of "A Long Way Back Home"; "classic " New Orleans on "Fly Away With Me"; the southern rock-tinge of "I'm Only Human"; tortured deep-soul vocals on "Talkin' 'Bout This Woman" (which doesn't suit him at all) and, most bizarre of all, "A Place Where We Can Be Free", which sounds remarkably similar to the Four Tops' "It's The Same Old Song" and cut as if it were indeed 1965 all over again. Good versions of "Kiss Tomorrow Goodbye" and "Whoever's Thrilling You (Is Killing Me) are also included but the album found its way unerringly to bargain bins all over America.

As regards newly recorded studio albums, that was it for Ernie K-Doe. Bandy re-released his Minit LP as *Ernie K-Doe Volume 1* so *Volume 2 i*s much more interesting and is made up of his later Minit singles, including " A Certain Girl"; the two UK only sets also feature predominantly Minit material although *Burn, K-Doe, Burn!* also includes three of his Instant sides. (A rumoured LP on the Syla label doesn't exist by the way.)

Ernie K-Doe may not have been the finest singer in this book but he was a larger than life character in the Solomon Burke mould and remained a very popular figure around New Orleans as both a D.J. and live performer for years after he finished recording. It was a sad day when he died in 2001.

Paul Kelly

Stealing In The Name Of The Lord 1970 Happy Tiger HT-1015 Producer: Buddy Killen

Dirt 1972 Warner Brothers BS 2605 Producer: Buddy Killen

Many of us will have a favourite singer ; Paul Kelly has been mine since I first heard him back in 1973. I came to him late, mind, as he had already been recording for around ten years and, although I wasn't to know it at the time, his biggest hit had already been and gone. He worked with Clarence Reid down in Miami (Kelly's home town) in the early sixties and released a handful of singles on the Lloyd and Dial labels which neither sold in great quantity nor were a patch on his best material of later years; despite the rarity of his - and thus demand for - early 45 "The Upset" it is vastly inferior to his best Warner Brothers sides. In the mid to late sixties he released four excellent singles on Philips which were his best to date but they still failed to sell in any great numbers and the company was not persuaded to cut an album on Kelly.

His first album came from an unlikely source: the Happy Tiger label which had little history and no soul credentials whatsoever and it was a chance meeting with a Baltimore D.J. (and some help from Swamp Dogg) that enabled Paul's then current 45, "Stealing In The Name Of The lord", enough airplay to turn it into a genuine "hit"; sadly, the only real one he ever had. By the summer of 1970 it had come to rest at #14 soul and #49 pop and became the proud title track of that first LP. It is a brilliant single, with a message that is as relevant today as it was then and as it will be 200 years from now: the hypocritical preacher who wants your money much more than he wants to save your soul. Many other tracks are highly impressive: "The Day After Forever" and "Poor But Proud" boast some of his most achingly beautiful vocals; "Try To Love Somebody" possesses a lovely down-home feel and sounded as if Pop Staples had dropped in to play guitar; "Travelin' Man" and "What's Happening To Me And You" take liberties - that work convincingly - with the time metre of the songs; "509" should be known as one of the great "train songs" of popular music; "Comin' Comin' Comin'" might easily have been the work of a West Coast rock band. Only "A Helping Hand" and "Soul Flow" failed to rise above the mundane and Paul Kelly had served notice that he had the vocal talent, song-writing range and enough excellent musicians behind him (the piano is gorgeous throughout the set) to maybe make it big.

Sadly, if probably predictably, the record label went bust and Kelly found himself at the vastly better capitalised Warner Brothers organisation for whom he went on to record four LPs. The first one, *Dirt,* appeared in 1972, but would have been a disappointment to any hard-core Paul Kelly fans (assuming there were such people in 1972) as nine of the twelve tracks had appeared on the previous LP. This was entirely logical, though, as WB would doubtless have recognised the quality of the material and also rightly assumed that not too many people would have bought the first set; the ploy didn't work though as the *Dirt* LP didn't do very well, either. All three of the new songs were also released as 45s with the excellent and up-tempo title track being the best and it was surely no co-incidence whatsoever that Kelly makes reference to a "swamp dog" in the lyrics; "Hangin' On In There" was a typically lovely ballad but "Here Comes Ol' Jezebel" was disappointing and sounds to me like a conscious effort to re-create the "scandal" of "Stealing" but it was a much weaker composition.

Don't Burn Me 1973 Warner Brothers BS 2689 Producer: Buddy Killen (Billboard soul charts: 44)

Hooked, Hogtied & Collared 1974 Warner Brothers BS 2812 Producers: Buddy Killen & Paul Kelly (Billboard soul charts: 55)

Stand On The Positive Side 1977 Warner Brothers BS 3026 Producers: Gene Page & Paul Kelly

Hanging On In There 1990 Edsel ED 316 (UK)

In 1973 Kelly was at his most creative and his songs were much in demand; Ann Sexton, Annette Snell and Margie Joseph all scored hits with his compositions and it was in this year that he released his masterpiece, *Don't Burn Me*, a work of extraordinary richness, with a warmth and decency that has rendered it timeless. Everything about the LP was perfect: a beguiling front cover photo; twelve songs of perfect symmetry and strength, simple in words but timeless in emotional appeal; the sumptuous backing vocals from Kelly and Juanita Rogers; magnificent production (by Buddy Killen) and astonishing arrangements (by Mike Leech) that stand up against any popular music album that has ever been made; the subtlety of the approach is remarkable and Hayward Bishop plays drums with such sensitivity and understatement that often they are sensed rather than heard. It is almost unfair to call out a few tracks on such a uniformly consistent set but I must mention Reggie Young's perfect guitar fills on "Sweetness"; Tommy Cogbill's incomparable bass line on "I'd Be Satisfied" ; the great ensemble playing that is behind the unstoppable power of "Come By Here". And then there is Kelly's voice. It is almost unbearably moving on "Come With Me", and he conveys mood and sentiment throughout by the most heartfelt "mmms" and "oh-ohs" imaginable: truly, only Sam Cooke has ever matched Kelly in the wordless evocation of passion. The album even generated a small hit in the title track (which was also improbably covered by rock guitarist Leslie West) which reached #35 soul, #79 pop and was also - for which I remain deeply thankful, as it was how I first discovered Kelly - released in the U.K. There is no doubt in my mind: *Don't Burn Me* is a magnificent work and one of the three or four best soul LPs in existence.

1974's *Hooked, Hogtied & Collared* has an awful front cover which looked like someone's idea of low-rent bondage, but bears a first side to rank with *Don't Burn Me*. The title track, "Let Your Love Come Down (Let It Fall It On Me)" and "Take It Away From Him (Put It On Me)" were all excellent uptempo (but, strangely, not very danceable) tracks that made it to the soul charts as singles; "Till I Get To My Baby's Love" was a joyous country-influenced hoedown ("I like this", Kelly proclaims half way through) but the real treasures were "I Wanna Be Close To You" and "Try My Love", both exquisitely beautiful ballads of great tenderness with glorious Kelly vocals and arrangements that must surely have still come from Mike Leech, although he is not credited on the cover. The whole album was once again cut down in Nashville with the erstwhile AGP crew, and if the second side was somewhat disappointing that's only really because it can't compare with side one or *Don't Burn Me*; it's still a collection of six fine tracks with one, "I'm Gonna Be Lovin' You", right up there with Paul's best, replete with his incomparable moans. "I'm Into Something I Can't Shake Loose" (no relation to the similarly titled song from O.V.Wright) was a fourth 45 from the set to enter the soul charts and as the LP also sold fairly decently, Kelly's star was still shining brightly at this time.

But, sadly, not for much longer. 1975 saw only one 45 released, the great, if atypical "Get Sexy", while 1976 yielded solely the rather limp "Play Me A Love Song". Neither were featured on any albums and scraped into the soul charts at #98 and #99 respectively. But the biggest disappointment of all came with his final LP, *Stand On The Positive Side,* which moved Kelly into a suit and a Hollywood studio. All Paul's finest work had come from recordings down in the south with Buddy Killen in the producer's chair and Gene Page just wasn't the man to understand Kelly as an artist. It wasn't *quite* all waste: the fine title track had a typical Kelly affirmative lyric and wonderful flow while "God Can" had a memorable melody that attracted the Staple Singers enough to cut their own version a couple of years later but the rest I'd rather forget. "The Fat Lady That Bumped Me Down" was rubbish, not a word that could ever have been applied to Kelly's work in the past, and the other six songs were mediocre. Warners pulled two tracks as 45s but they sold no better than the LP.

From here on in things became sporadic: a handful of singles trickled out on Epic, A & M and Laurence, before a couple of CDs came out in the nineties and while there were some good things among them (and he wrote the tremendous "Personally" for Jackie Moore) the magic had gone. Three compilations of Kelly's work have appeared in the last 25 years (with the Edsel release being the only LP), and I bless all the companies involved for keeping Paul Kelly's name out there but I remain deeply upset that, in the internet age of supposedly limitless information, the death of this exceptionally talented soul man in 2012 passed by almost completely without comment. To this day I'm not sure of the details. While I can fully appreciate that his music is not for everybody (some people have been baffled by my reverence for him) and he is hardly a household name, his beautiful voice has meant more to me than any other (together with 'Little Sonny' Brown) and he will always retain a cherished place in my heart.

Kelly Brothers

Andrew Kelly; Curtis Kelly; Robert Kelly; Charles Lee; Offe Reece

Sing A Page Of Songs From The Good Book
1962 King 810 No producer listed

It Won't Be This Way Always (as The King Pins)
1963 King 865 No producer listed

Too Much! Soul 1966 Sims 137 Producers: Russell Sims & Carol Sims

Sweet Soul 1968 Excello 8007 Producers: Russell Sims, Carol Sims & Bob Holmes

I Still Remember 1969 Creed 3015 Producer: ?

The Kelly Brothers started recording under that name way back in the fifties, changed to become the King Pins for a while, and then reverted to their original name in the mid sixties; it's an odd way to manage a career. They also drifted between gospel and soul and their first and fifth and final LP were firmly in the religious vein but as I neither own nor have heard them I am afraid I cannot offer any pointers as to how they sound.

The album they made as the King-Pins is a good example of early soul, with a mixture of styles ranging from doo-wop ("Wonderful One") to rather throw away dance novelties ("The Hop Scotch") through to tougher, more obviously gospel influenced sides such as "Just Keep On Smiling". The highly appealing title track had rather surprisingly become a pretty big hit as a single (#13 soul, #89 pop) in the summer of 1963, and as was often the case back then, all of the 12 tracks had appeared on one side or the other of 45s. The group weren't afraid of switching the lead vocals around but I believe that most of them may have been taken by Charles Lee, who left the group when they reverted to "The Kelly Brothers" and recorded a couple of solo singles as T.C. Lee and The Bricklayers. "The Monkey" had a high tenor lead (Andrew Kelly?) and was another most attractive outing.

The Sims LP, *Too Much! Soul*, the title of which sounds like a misprint but isn't, is utterly splendid. The label was very good to the Kelly Brothers, releasing eleven singles plus the album, and every one of the LP's twelve tracks saw service as an a or b - side on 45s. One of the best of these, "Falling In Love Again", which kicks off side two, even made it to #39 on the soul charts in the spring of 1966. The album is more or less equally split into ballads, on which Curtis Kelly takes lead, and faster sides, where his brother Robert takes over. Anyone who has a penchant for sweaty, committed southern styled soul will thoroughly enjoy what is on offer and it was pleasing, if unusual for 1966, to see the back cover listing the names of the musicians who played on the set, all apparently cut at Muscle Shoals, with Dan Penn as engineer. Best tracks for me in the different styles: of the slow sides, "If That Will Hold You" and of the faster ones, "I'd Rather Have You".

Russell Sims' label was in trouble by 1967 and he sold the brothers' contract to Excello, around which time Offe Reese left the group, reducing the act to a trio. A "new" album, *Sweet Soul* came out fairly soon but it actually contained eight of the twelve cuts from the previous set, as well as re-printing about 98% of the earlier album's back sleevenotes. Still, the four new tracks were all good: "That's What You Mean To Me" and "Comin' On In" were cut at Hi while the Otis Redding styled "You Put Your Touch On Me" and "Hanging In There" were surely cut at Muscle Shoals with Roger Hawkins and co. These sides made up two 45s for the new label, but neither they, nor four further non-album singles, returned the Kelly Brothers to any charts. It was for that reason, presumably, that they decided to return to the gospel field for the Creed LP but after that appeared Kelly Brothers' records were no more.

Eddie Kendricks (see also The Temptations)

All By Myself 1971 Tamla S 309 Producer: Frank Wilson (Billboard soul charts: 6 ; Billboard pop charts: 80)

People Hold On 1972 Tamla T 315L Producer: Frank Wilson (Billboard soul charts: 13 ; Billboard pop charts: 131)

Eddie Kendricks 1973 T 327L Producers: Frank Wilson, Gloria Jones & Leonard Caston (Billboard soul charts: 5 ; Billboard pop charts: 18)

Boogie Down 1974 Tamla T 330V1 Producers: Frank Wilson & Leonard Caston (Billboard soul charts: 1 ; Billboard pop charts: 30)

For You 1974 Tamla T6-335S1 Producers: Frank Wilson & Leonard Caston (Billboard soul charts: 8 ; Billboard pop charts: 108)

The Hit Man 1975 Tamla T6-338S1 Producers: Frank Wilson, Leonard Caston & Brian Holland (Billboard soul charts: 9 ; Billboard pop charts: 63)

The charismatic Edward James Kendrick from Alabama has strong claims to being the finest, best-known and most successful falsetto singer in soul music history; quite a trinity. He first came to attention, of course, as part of the "classic" line up of The Temptations, the greatest of all soul groups, and it is his indelible singing on "Girl (Why You Wanna Make Me Blue)","Get Ready", "The Girl's Alright With Me" and, most notably, "Just My Imagination", one of the most beautiful records ever made, that justify his reputation. By 1970, though, Kendricks was thoroughly disaffected with life as a Temptation and he left to pursue a solo career.

All By Myself was both an apt and rather sad title for his debut, which did well enough if not spectacularly so. Quite short at only seven tracks and under thirty minutes running time, it housed two moderately selling singles in "It's So Hard For Me To Say Goodbye" and "Can I" (once recorded by Jennell Hawkins among others) which both got to #37 on the soul charts. More encouragingly, the album itself performed more strongly although it certainly fell well short of the spectacular start David Ruffin made at the start of HIS solo career as an ex-Temptation. (Over the long term, though, Kendricks undoubtedly did better: five albums in the pop top 100 as opposed to Ruffin's three and nine top ten soul singles compared to five from David). Anyway, *All By Myself* was solid and thoroughly enjoyable, if lacking in absolute killer tracks. The sorrowful "This Used To Be The Home Of Johnnie Mae" was probably the highlight but it took some time to adjust to Kendricks singing without his former mates.

People...Hold On appeared to be taken more seriously than *All By Myself* by Motown as it contained ten tracks with a running time of over 45 minutes and the printing on the sleeve of those who had contributed to the set, not least the excellent musical performance from the Young Senators. The songs were sharper and more catchy too, and "Eddie's Love", "If You Let Me" and "Girl, You Need A Change Of Mind" (regularly cited in recent times as one of the first "disco" tracks) all entered the soul top forty. Certainly, the last named was a spectacular side, but one could just as easily imagine "Date With The Rain" doing well as a 45 had it been chosen instead. The title track was distinctly African influenced, a departure for Motown, and the whole album still holds up firmly today and was one of the finest to come from the Detroit company in 1972.

In 1973 I was still at school, with an ever increasing list of albums I wanted to buy, and little money with which to do so. For quite a while, *Eddie Kendricks* was at the top of that list and I was envious of anyone who already had it. Of course, I eventually found a way to file it away in the collection, and it still sounds as good now as it did then. It was also the album that made him, for a period of about two and a half years, one of the biggest soul stars in the world. The first single from it, the excellent "Darling Come Back Home", moved to #26 soul and #67 pop which was par for the course based on his previous five 45s, but he then hit a hole in one next time around when "Keep On Truckin'" went to #1 on both the soul and pop charts in September of that year. One needs to hear the eight minute long album version to truly appreciate the ebb and flow of the cut, but even at truncated length, it fully deserved its hit status. There were beauties elsewhere, too: "Each Day I Cry A Little", "Where Do You Go (Baby)" and covers of "Any Day Now" and "Not On The Outside" all approached the ethereal beauty of "Just my imagination".

Kendricks followed up "Keep On Truckin'" with the similar sounding "Boogie Down" which became his second successive massive hit: #1 soul and #2 pop and it unsurprisingly became the title cut of his next set, which also housed two more hits in "Son Of Sagittarius" (# 5 soul and #28 pop) and "Tell Her Love Has Felt The Need" (#8 and #50). It's another good collection - and reached the summit of the soul charts - but is less striking than *Eddie Kendricks* as a number of the cuts (title track, "The Thin Man", "Sagittarius" and "Hooked On Your Love") sound like first cousins to "Keep On Truckin'"). The pretty "You Are The Melody Of My Life" and "Honey Brown" provide better listening while the mid-tempo "Trust Your Heart" and the lovely "Girl Of My Dreams" are my favourite tracks of all.

For You - which bore a gatefold sleeve - was another highly successful album for Kendricks and contained his third soul #1 single in "Shoeshine Boy" which I think owed more to Eddie's popularity than for being a brilliant record. "One Tear" also performed strongly as a single and the set included covers in "If" and "Time In A Bottle", neither of which were obvious choices. The latter shared with "Deep And Quiet Love" the most melodramatic string section on a Kendricks' record to date and all in all, I find *For You* to be a rather dull album with the most interesting aspect being that Carolyn Hurley, who once released a rather extraordinary single on Stax, helps out on backing vocals.

I much preferred *The Hit Man* which upped the energy levels and included stronger songs. "Get The Cream Off The Top" and "Happy" were both top ten soul singles and there were other interesting tracks on board as well: "Body Talk" saw Kendricks phrasing rather like Marvin Gaye, a stance I can't recall him adopting very often, and "I've Got To Be " was a long track which didn't sound like "Keep On Truckin'". "Skippin' Work Today" was relaxed and attractive and only the rather mushy "You Loved Me Then" was unworthy of Eddie's talents.

He's A Friend 1976 Tamla T6-343S1 Producer: Norman Harris (Billboard soul charts: 3 ; Billboard pop charts: 38)

Going Up In Smoke 1976 Tamla T6-346S1 Producer: Norman Harris (Billboard soul charts: 22 ; Billboard pop charts: 144)

Slick 1977 Tamla T6-356S1 Producer: Leonard Caston (Billboard soul charts: 47)

Frank Wilson and Leonard Caston had been pre-eminent across all the first six albums from Kendricks given they had provided the bulk of the songs and production efforts between them, but both were ditched for *He's A Friend* which saw the ex-Temptation dispatched to Sigma Sound in Philadelphia for the first of what was presumably a two LP contract under new producer Norman Harris. It was a smart move, as if any city knew how to record classy high tenor singers it was this one. The title track could have been a risk to release as a single as it was a pretty unambiguous homage to the Lord but it went all the way to #2 soul as well as #36 pop, his ninth successive 45 to reach the soul top ten, and it was a joyous sound that called out the dancers in irresistible fashion. The LP was more or less split 50/50 between slow and dreamy ballads and uptempo numbers and credit should be awarded to Allan Felder who not only arranged the vocals but also co-wrote seven of the ten tracks. It's a radiant album that sold impressively, as well as suiting Kendricks down to the ground, but the fact that the second single from the set, "Get It While It's Hot", only made it to #24 soul while missing the Hot 100 completely, was a worry, and things only got worse from here on in.

The second Philly recorded LP next album started off well, with its best two tracks coming up first, but maybe "Goin' Up In Smoke" and "The Newness Is Gone" could also be taken as commentary on Kendricks' unravelling fortunes. The former only made it to #30 on the soul charts while a second single pulled from the set, "Born Again", didn't chart at all, a previously unthinkable state of affairs. The album is certainly not an absolute disaster but two questions should be posed: why was it deemed a good idea to not have a photo of Eddie on the front cover and why, when you have at your disposal one of the great yearning voices in soul music, were nine of the ten tracks so heavily dance oriented?

I imagine Motown were alarmed at Kendricks' plummeting popularity and they therefore pulled him back to Detroit and re-united him with Leonard Caston for the Slick LP. It didn't really work as "Intimate Friends" only made it to #24 on the soul charts while the album was the poorest seller of his career to date. Which doesn't make it his worst and, in fact, it's one of his best, as the tempo is ratcheted down and some superb tracks like "Baby", "Then Came You" (more Gaye shadings) and the almost big band take on Seals' and Croft's "Diamond Girl" vie with the single as the best outings on show. In fact the whole LP is rather wonderful and close to being a "neglected classic", and it was a memorable way to bow out from the record label on which he had recorded with such distinction for the best part of fifteen years.

Vintage '78 1978 Arista AB 4170 Producer: Jeff Lane (Billboard soul charts: 33 ; Billboard pop charts: 180)

Something More 1979 Arista AB 4250 Producer: Patrick Adams (Billboard soul charts: 69)

Vintage '78 teamed up Kendricks with Jeff Lane, producer of Brass Construction, which raised a few eyebrows at the time, but luckily, the focus was firmly settled on Eddie's voice and some quality songs, rather than pumping dance tracks; Lane's imprint was most clearly discerned on "Ain't No Smoke Without Fire" but as it was a) pretty good and b) reached #13 on the soul charts as a single, there was no real cause for concern. In fact, it's another dazzling and scandalously underrated set with "If It Takes All Night", "Your Wish Is My Command", "Maybe I'm A Fool To Love You" and "One Of The Poorest People" all being lovely and tender, while "The Best Of Strangers Now" was a second soul chart entrant as a single. Only "The Whip" was sub-standard but that leaves us with nine highly enjoyable sides. The LP sold fairly well, but deserved to have become a million seller, and was the best work Jeff Lane ever did.

The quality of *Vintage '78* didn't stop Lane from being ejected from the producer's role in favour of Patrick Adams. This was not a very welcome move and *Something More* was actually something a lot less. "I Never Used To Dance" was poor but typical of a set which was much more attuned to dance floor radar than any other Kendricks' LP apart from *Goin' Up In Smoke*. The two ballads are ok as is the mid-tempo "No Wonder (I Can't Get Over You)" but the set confined Eddie to chart oblivion.

Love Keys 1981 Atlantic SD 19294 Producers: Randy Richards & Johnny Sandlin (Billboard soul charts: 62 ; Billboard pop charts: 207)

I've Got My Eyes On You 1983 Ms. Dixie 50001 Producers: Jason Bryant, Eddie Kendricks & Robert Manchurian

Ruffin & Kendrick (and David Ruffin) 1987 RCA 6765-1-R Producers: Ronnie McNeir, Jim Bonnefond, Rick Iantosca; Rahni Song, John Oates, Jay King, David Agent & Gene McFadden (Billboard soul charts: 60)

I never thought I would hear the Muscle Shoals Horns on an Eddie Kendricks' album but they were featured on his one and only album for his new label, Atlantic. It's a real departure, in fact a return to his roots as it was recorded down in Alabama and has, unsurprisingly, a notably different sound from all his other work; some tracks work well, others don't. Most of the good stuff is on side one and the best tracks are probably a worthy cover of Lou Courtney's "I Don't Need Nobody Else" and a beautiful reading of a fine country song, "Old Home Town". Side two peters out disappointingly with an awful rock-influenced "Hot" and pop-oriented cuts in "Looking For Love" and "In Love We're One" but before that we can enjoy "Never Alone", a sweet ballad. So, all rather patchy, but at least he saw some chart action when "(Oh I) Need Your Lovin'", a pretty decent song from Eddie and Brian Holland, made it to #41 on the soul charts. Oh, the album also finally has a good front cover picture of Kendricks; given he was a striking looking man, you would think record companies would pick up on this, but his album covers had an alarming tendency to suffer from sub-standard photography.

Kendricks' last solo album was a low-key affair, recorded on a small independent label down in Atlanta with the S.O.S. Band providing the backing; it's also an unremarkable set comprising two ballads, a handful of dance tracks and the slightly Caribbean-influenced "Reason". One of those ballads, the old standard, "The Very Thought Of You", features an un-credited female (although the internet suggests it is one Liz Lance) and the other most noteworthy aspect of the set is that Eddie covers "Born To Love You", the only time in his solo career that he interpreted an old Temptations' track.

In 1984 he had a tiny "hit" with "Surprise Attack" and the following year got a credit (together with David Ruffin) on a Hall & Oates live set, before teaming up with his former Temptations' colleague in 1987 for the *Ruffin & Kendrick* set. This one had its moments, not least in the lead-off cut, "I Couldn't Believe It", which was an impressive pastiche of The Temptations circa 1965; it also managed #14 on the soul charts, and was followed up by the #43 placing of "One More For The Lonely Hearts Club". The latter featured Kendricks' taking a large part of the lead vocals as did the lovely ballad "Goodnight Pillow" (in fact he sings all of this one) but overall the set could more accurately have been called "David Ruffin featuring some vocal assistance from Eddie Kendricks". Both men were in fine fettle, though, and completely overshadow the irritating musical accompaniment, which is particularly painful on a dreadful version of "Family Affair".

I have ignored the many compilations of his work and the only other new record that featured Eddie Kendrick's name after the RCA set was a dismayingly bad 12" single with another former Temp, Dennis Edwards, but Eddie was diagnosed with lung cancer in 1991, which led to the death of this great soul man, much too young at only at only 52, the following year.

Joyce Kennedy

Lookin' For Trouble 1984 A & M SP 4996 Producers: Jeffrey Osborne, Leon Sylvers & Keg Johnson (Billboard soul charts: 17 ; pop charts: 79)

Wanna Play Your Game! 1985 A & M SP 5073 Producer: Glenn Murdock, Gary Taylor, John Benitez, Freddie Washington, Raymond Jones & Thaddeus Edwards

Joyce Kennedy released a few singles in the sixties, all of which were enjoyable outings, cut in the city where she grew up, Chicago. They were also all soul records, which is why she deserves an entry in the book, even if the band with which she made her name, Mother's Finest, were a straight rock outfit who are out of scope. Credit to her though, not many black women were fronting reasonably successful bands of that style.

By the mid-eighties she ventured out as a solo artist again and although there was clearly no chance of her new records sounding anything like her earlier material, they also dropped all traces of her work with Mother's Finest, settling on the mid-eighties pop/soul/boogie groove that so many others were also employing. An ok, but dull and fairly predictable duet with Jeffrey Osborne proved once again that was a gifted vocalist and "The Last Time I Made Love" was a big hit, reaching #2 soul and #40 pop when it was pulled from *Lookin' For Trouble* in the summer of 1984. "Stronger Than Before" followed up by making it to #30 on the soul charts and is another example of her excellent soulful singing. I would have loved to see her cut a genuine soul album in the late sixties or early seventies but we have to settle for these.

Chris Kenner

Land of 1000 Dances 1966 Atlantic 8117 No producer listed

The Name Of The Place 19?? Bandy 70015

I Like It Like That 1987 Charly CRB (UK)

Chris Kenner wrote three great songs, "I Like It Like That", "Something You Got" and "Land of 1000 Dances", but remains completely unknown to all but record collectors. And by the time his first LP appeared in 1966, released in response to Cannibal & The Headhunters' hit, rather than Wilson Pickett's which came later, his best days - such as they were - had been and gone and all the material on the album was years old. As a result, its sales would have been minimal.

Born in a suburb of New Orleans, Kenner had scored a pretty big success with "Sick And Tired" back in 1957, before " I Like It Like That" reached #2 on both soul and pop charts in 1961. His other two most famous compositions were also released as singles on the Instant label, and each charted on the *Cashbox* soul charts but did not register with *Billboard*. All three songs are on the LP and if I certainly prefer other readings of "Something You Got" and "Land Of 1000 Dances" Kenner's are nonetheless compelling. The set predominantly consists of typical rolling New Orleans' early soul, a style which people either seem to like or disregard completely, and although no-one could ever claim that Chris Kenner was the greatest singer in the world, the superb slow, heartfelt and soulful "Time" is the stand-out cut on the set and should appeal to any soul fan.

Sadly, Kenner's life appeared to have been dominated by an addiction to alcohol and such dependency ensured that he was never destined for stardom - as well as undoubtedly playing a big part in his death from a heart attack in 1976 - and he moved rather uncertainly into the soul era releasing a number of moderately likeable 45s between 1964 and 1973. He never got the chance to cut a "proper" LP, as *Land Of 1000 Dances* was a compilation of singles, as were *The Name Of The Place* and *I Like It Like That.* Both of these latter were at least fairly imaginative, with the former bearing nine of twelve cuts that aren't on the Atlantic album, whereas Charly's set, although based more squarely on *Land Of 100 Dances*, contains three exclusive tracks.

Howard Kenney

Super Star 1978 Warner Brothers BSK 3220 Producers: Larry Blackmon, Johnny Pate & Howard Kenney

The singer looks to be young on the cover and sounds even younger when he starts singing, which is interesting as I have read that he was a former member of both the Duponts and The

Persuaders; he must have joined at an early age. It's gentle, undemanding pop-influenced soul that came and went without leaving much trace; as indeed did Howard Kenney himself, I am unaware of his cutting any more solo records apart from those at these sessions; two singles were issued to scant effect and the company maybe should have gone for "No Fun To Me" which is a good track. Maybe the most striking thing about the release is that it does not sound at all how I would imagine a Larry Blackmon or Johnny Pate production would.

George Kerr

The Other Side Of George Kerr 1970 All Platinum AP 3001 Producers: George Kerr & Nate Edmonds

If This World Were Mine 1971 All Platinum AP 3004 Producer: George Kerr (Billboard soul charts: 31)

The Best Of 1990 P-Vine PLP- 6524 Producer: George Kerr (Japan)

The Great Works Of Sylvia & George (with Sylvia) 1991 P-Vine PLP- 6534 (Japan)

George Kerr is one of the most important figures in East Coast soul music, writing and producing literally hundreds of sides over the years, most notably for Linda Jones, The Escorts, The Moments and The Whatnauts. But he was also a gifted vocalist, and sang with The Serenaders and (briefly) Little Anthony & The Imperials and so it should have come as no surprise that he also nursed an ambition to issue solo LPs from time to time.

In early 1970 he released a version of a well-known Gerry Goffin and Carole King song, which he adapted somewhat to come out under the distinctly peculiar title of "3 minutes 2 - Hey Girl", and was rewarded with his only ever national hit 45 as a solo artist when it reached #15 on the soul charts. It became the proud lead-off cut of his likeable first LP, *The Other Side Of George Kerr,* which was lavishly (for All Platinum) produced as well as featuring lovely backing vocals throughout; few men had such a grounding in the art of soul harmony singing as Kerr. The set also bears a good version of "The Masquerade Is Over" as well as Kerr originals like the sweet "Tweedly Dum Dum" and "Telling The Truth" as well as the distinctly catchy and poppy "My Memories Of Marie" which sounded like a lost hit for someone.

1971 saw the issuance of his follow-up set, *If This World Were Mine,* which rather surprisingly overcame a number of obstacles to lodge into the soul charts at #31. These included a typically amateurish All Platinum front cover, a rather measly four tracks only and an interminable second half of the title track, entirely spoken by a lachrymose Sylvia Robinson. The sound was also thinner, male harmonies having been dispensed with entirely and only Kerr's own double-tracked vocal on the Marvin Gaye influenced "Love Is God Almighty" and some nice female backing singing on "Love Is A Hurtin' Thing" swelled the sound out somewhat.

Some twenty years later P-Vine in Japan put out two LPs on Kerr. Firstly, a *Best Of* set which consisted of nine tracks drawn from the two All Platinum discs and second, an album shared with Sylvia Robinson, on which each singer had five featured tracks; in Kerr's case this was a worthwhile investment as four of his cannot be found on other albums: "Sunday" (a b-side from 1971), "All The Way" (an obscure single on the Tod-Ant label) and two previously unreleased sides: "Can You Dig Where I'm Coming From" and a nice duet with daughter Tracy, "Just As Long".

Love Love Love 198? Harbor Light HL3000 Producers: George Kerr & Ken Thomas

Words Of Love 1992 Soul Vibes SVLP 6 Producer: George Kerr

In 1973 and 1974 Kerr released three good singles on the Shout label but these were not attended by any LP, and we had to wait until around the end of the eighties or the so-called "Mr. Emotion" to give us his next long player. Notable for featuring none of his own songs at all, it sounded pretty decent at the time of its release, but nowadays its one-paced approach and dragged out songs render it rather dull. "Me And Mrs. Jones", "Always And forever" and "Love Won't Let Me Wait" are all performed well enough, but do not improve on the originals. The only song to stir itself above ballad tempo is "Love Love Love" which lacks the swing of versions by Donny Hathaway or J.R. Bailey and an uncredited lady (Tracy Kerr?) sings with George on "All Together".

Words Of Love is similar to *Love Love Love*. Kerr is still in fine voice and he chooses the songs wisely, although again surprisingly ignoring his own, but over 45 minutes of one paced electronic backing is just too much to keep me interested and I keep waiting for the record to end so I can listen to something else.

Chaka Khan (see also Rufus)

Chaka 1978 Warner Brothers BSK 3245 Producer: Arif Mardin (Billboard soul charts: 2 ; Billboard pop charts: 12)

Naughty 1980 Warner Brothers BSK 3385 Producer: Arif Mardin (Billboard soul charts: 6 ; Billboard pop charts: 43)

What Cha' Gonna Do For Me 1981 Warner Brothers HS 3526 Producer: Arif Mardin (Billboard soul charts: 3 ; Billboard pop charts: 17)

Chaka Khan 1982 Warner Brothers 1-23729 Producer: Arif Mardin (Billboard soul charts: 5 ; Billboard pop charts: 52)

If one includes her years as lead singer for Rufus, the years from 1974 until 1984 could only be described as an utter triumph for Chaka Khan, born as the much less flamboyant sounding Yvette Marie Stevens in Great Lakes, Illinois. Eight #1 singles on the soul charts, and eleven on the pop Top 40, put her in that instantly recognisable and world famous category that could only be matched by Diana Ross, Aretha Franklin or Gladys Knight from the same period. Having a head of fabulous and abundant hair didn't hurt either. Having stated all that is undeniable above, I must confess that her overly strident style has never really been to my taste and there are only a handful of her records I enjoy, which is doubtless my loss.

She left Rufus in 1978 to concentrate on her solo career and her first album went gold and contained "I'm Every Woman" a great Ashford and Simpson song that became a huge hit at the end of that year (#1 soul, #21 pop). It was the standout from a set which certainly shared the writing credits around: eighteen in all, of whom only Andrew Kastner and John McNally got to contribute more than one song. The musicians (and she always used the best bass players imaginable) and backing singers were all of the highest quality and Warner Brothers certainly knew they were onto a good thing, even if it was rather a surprise when the follow-up single, "Life Is A Dance", stalled at a highly disappointing

#40 on the soul charts, while missing the pop listings altogether. Apart from the hit, I like the downbeat "Roll Me Through The Rushes", but a number of the other songs on *Chaka* favour pop over soul.

Naughty repeated the formula of *Chaka*: production by Arif Mardin, songs shared around and lead-off single provided by Ashford and Simpson; but "Clouds" was not one of their best, even if it did reach #10 soul. The backing vocals throughout the largely mid-tempo paced set, rendered by Cissy and Whitney Houston, Luther Vandross and Hamish Stuart, are impeccable, but the overall impression of *Naughty* is once again of a pop-coated richness I find rather indigestible.The only cut I really care for is the tuneful and catchy "Papillon" from the unexpected source of Gregg Diamond, a man who usually dealt only in cheesy disco.

I could warm more to "What Cha Gonna Do For Me", from which the title track became another #1 soul single, as it contained "Any Old Sunday" which may have performed dismally as a 45 (#68 soul), but remains my favourite of all her solo sides, a really captivating mid-tempo lope. "Night In Tunisia" should also be commended for the inspired idea of inserting a 1946 Charlie Parker solo into its midst. Once again, the musicians were of the highest class and the set went gold.

Chaka Khan included another of my favoured sides, an excellent version of Michael Jackson's "Got To Be There", which has one of her finest ever vocals, and it deservedly went to #5 on the soul charts as a single. I cared much less for the second 45, "Tearin' It Up", even if it was co-written by one of my heroes, Bunny Sigler, and the public seemingly shared my view: it only managed #48. I admire the record label for sticking with real musicians, rather than synthesised wallpaper, in 1984 but the rest of the set provides slim pickings for my taste, and in all honesty a track like "Twisted" has little to do with soul music.

I Feel For You 1984 Warner Brothers 1-25162 Producers: Arif Mardin, Russ Titelman, John Robie, Robbie Buchanan, David Foster, Joe Mardin, David Wolinski, James Newton Howard & Humberto Gatica (Billboard soul charts: 4 ; Billboard pop charts: 14)

Destiny 1986 Warner Brothers 1-25425 Producers: Arif Mardin, Russ Titelman, Robbie Buchanan, Joe Mardin, Beau Hill, Cengiz Yaltkaya, David Gamson, Green Gartside, Philippe Saisse & Reggie Griffin (Billboard soul charts: 24; Billboard pop charts: 67)

C.K. 1988 Warner Brothers 1-25707 Producers: Russ Titelman, David Frank, Prince & Chris Jasper (Billboard soul charts: 17 ; Billboard pop charts: 125)

The Woman I Am 1992 Warner Brothers 7599-26296-1 Producers: Arif Mardin, Jerry Barnes, Katreese Barnes, Ralf Zang, David Gamson, Wayne Braithwaite, Gary Haase, George Whitty & Joe Mardin (Billboard soul charts: 9 ; Billboard pop charts: 92) (Europe)

"I Feel For You" was her really big moment as a solo artist: the single went to #1 soul and #3 pop while the LP of the same name went platinum. It also marked the point at which I could no longer pretend I was interested in her music and I have never heard the LP and even listening to snippets of it on the internet now defeats me entirely. It should therefore go without saying that I have not heard her final three LPs either. (The last of which only came out in Europe: in the U.S. it was a CD only.)

Khemistry

Kimus Knight; Marie Council; Shirl Hayes

Khemistry 1982 FC 38215 Producers: Rodney Brown & Willie Lester

Ignore the silly cover; this set contains typically good work by producers Rodney Brown and Willie Lester who can feel pleased with the quality of the albums they worked on with Washington D.C. based artists at the end of seventies and early eighties such as Gayle Adams, Bobby Thurston...and Khemistry. The clean-cut looking trio all sing well on a collection of mainly mid-tempo songs that are tuneful and well constructed and for 1982, a hit rate of five good cuts out of eight is highly impressive. One of the best, "Can You Feel My Love", is the reason the LP has always had fans, and it is hard to see why Columbia chose to ignore it on 45, opting instead for "I Got A Feeling" which did make it to #75 on the soul charts and "Sucker For The Boogie" which did not. "There's No Me Without You", "Walking Papers" and Whatever It Takes" all demand to be heard as well, and if "Who's Fooling Who" is not a great song it is certainly belted out with gusto by either Marie Council or Shirl Hayes.

A further single from Khemistry slipped out in 1985 but it was not a hit, and it seems surprising that no more was ever heard of the group either collectively or singly, as they were all talented vocalists.

Keith Killgo (also see The Blackbyrds)

Keith Killgo 1982 Baltimore Washington International BW1124 Producers: Keith Killgo, Joe Hall & Orville Saunders

Killgo was the drummer with The Blackbyrds throughout their time as a band, and he put out this one LP - if a record with only four tracks can really be called an LP - in 1982. It features an attractive take on "Crystal Blue Persuasion" (a song that hardly anyone messes up) and other appealing sides in "Loving You Is Good" and "I'm Still Yours" although I'm less enamoured of the nine minute long "When The Lights Are Out". He sings in a high light tenor throughout and this is not a bad little platter at all.

Kilo

Ray Griffin: Jasper Phillips: Terry Royce Johnson; Perry Michael Allen; Wendell P. Moore

Kilo 1979 Stax STX-4125 Producers: Kilo & Ron Williams

A fivesome from the "second coming of Stax" era, Kilo was fronted by ex-Tempree Jasper "Jabo" Phillips, although some of the members had previously recorded as Ebony Web for Hi Records. As can be imagined from 1979, the group were more influenced by the Bar-Kays than by Blue Magic, and, as such, Phillips' talents were a little under-used with only "All In A Song" allowing him to stretch out a bit. The rest of the cuts are funky - with "Devil's Eye" being the best - or mid-tempo, sunny and languid, from which "Days" comes out on top. The band wrote all the songs themselves, and could have done with some outside help (maybe from executive producer David Porter) as nothing on here is really memorable enough to have stood out against all the other releases that year, and the one 45 pulled from the set sank into oblivion.

Anna King

Back To Soul 1964 Smash MGS 27059 No producer listed

Anna King was a tough gospel-based singer out of Philadelphia, and although her time as a member of The James Brown Revue was fairly short, she was one of the best singers he ever worked with and her one LP is top class. As a result of Brown's stand-off with King (the label) he had more time than usual on his hands in 1964 and he certainly spent much of it wisely with King (the singer), although it must remain a mystery why this notoriously publicity hungry man neglected to take producer credits on the LP. Smash certainly tried hard with Anna too, releasing five singles on her, all of which are included on the album. Two of them even hit: "If Somebody Told You", with marvellous vocal assistance from The Famous Flames, made it to #67 pop while a duet on which she out-muscles Bobby Byrd did even better at #52. (Remember that this was at a time when *Billboard* did not list a soul chart, but both of them, as well as the excellent "Make Up Your Mind", featured on the *Cashbox* equivalent.) *Anna King* was recorded in Miami and New York and features a full orchestra throughout and if side two features some rather unimaginative material, "Tennessee Waltz" and "Night Time Is The Right Time" worked just fine, with only a skipping reading of "Come And Get These Memories" failing to please.

Her career was destined to be a short one and although she released a feisty "Mama's Got A Bag Of Her Own" in 1965, it failed to hit, as indeed had earlier releases on End, Malibu and Ludix, and she exited the soul recording business, but went on to work with Duke Ellington and the gospel group The Brockington Choral Ensemble before passing away in 2002.

Ben E. King (see also The Drifters)

Spanish Harlem 1961 Atco 33-133 Producers: Jerry Leiber & Mike Stoller (Billboard pop charts: 57)

Sings For Soulful Lovers 1962 Atco 33-137 Producer: Klaus Ogermann

Don't Play That Song! 1962 Atco 33-142 Producers: Ahmet Ertegun, Jerry Leiber & Mike Stoller

Young Boy Blues 1964 Clarion 606 No producer listed

Greatest Hits 1964 Atco 33-165

Seven Letters 1964 Atco 33-174 Producers: Ahmet Ertegun, Jerry Wexler & Bert Berns

What Is Soul? 1967 Atlantic 587 072 No producer listed (UK)

What Is Soul? 1981 Atco P-8617 No producer listed (Japan)

Despite his background in The Drifters, and despite the quality of his voice, the man from North Carolina was another soul man who was never properly represented at LP length; few of them are satisfactory and few of them were hits, which is at odds with his output on 45 rpm, a much happier reflection of his career.

Benjamin Earl Nelson was not in The Drifters for very long and left to go out on his own in 1960 and smashed almost straight away with the brilliant Jerry Leiber and Phil Spector song, "Spanish Harlem", which went to #15 soul and #10 pop at the start of 1961. Unfortunately, the LP that contains the hit is pretty grim listening, almost entirely MOR enveloped by the sweeping strings of the Stan Applebaum orchestra and songs like "Perfidia, "Besame Mucho", "Frenesi" and "Amor" with which King fights a losing battle to remain soulful.

In the summer of 1961 he had a hit with the record by which he will always be associated, one of the most famous songs in the history of popular music, "Stand By Me". It became his first ever #1 soul hit and stopped at #4 on the pop charts, his highest placing. Oddly, Atco did not capitalise with an LP of the same name and when King's second LP appeared in 1962, the song wasn't even included. *Sings For Soulful Lovers* is an improvement on *Spanish Harlem*, if not an utterly decisive one. Some of the songs were certainly more suited to a younger audience - "Will You still Love Me Tomorrow" and "Dream lover" are examples - and although "My Heart Cries For You" sounds as if it were indeed a record by a black American, it's still essentially a "pop" record rather than a "soul" one and Atco's rather muddled thinking was further confirmed by the fact that no 45s were put forth from the set.

King's third LP, *Don't Play That Song!*, appeared in May 1962 and DID include "Stand By Me", but the song was a year old by now and it was the title track that was now a hot item, becoming a #2 soul hit as well as attaining #11 pop. It's another enduring song (and as with "Spanish Harlem", appropriated magnificently by Aretha Franklin later on) and features an urgent and engaged vocal from King. Just as good was the excellent "Young Boy Blues" although this inexplicably failed when it was paired up on a 45 with the extraordinarily arranged "Here Comes The Night". There were faint traces of Sam Cooke in his delivery from time to time and even if it is still a rather "soft" set things were starting to get more interesting.

A *Greatest Hits* compilation was up next, and its value for album collectors lies in the fact that it includes four hits by King, the excellent "How Can I Forget", "That's When It Hurts", and "I (Who Have Nothing)" as well as the lesser "I Could Have Danced All Night", that were not on any of his other sets. (The Clarion album that slipped out in 1964 contains ten sides from the period from 1960 to 1963, with only one of them, "Gloria Gloria", not available on his other Atco LPs.)

King's fifth set for Atlantic, *Seven Letters*, was a pretty good one, with its superb title track becoming his biggest hit in over two years; it was self penned too, but sounded for all the world like a country song. Every bit as good was another successful 45, "It's All Over", which, with its obvious overtones of Solomon Burke, moved King firmly into the new soul era. (Astonishingly, it was later covered by Deep Purple). "Don't Drive Me Away" and "It's No Good For Me" maintained the soulful edge but Atco couldn't resist hedging their bets elsewhere with a handful of typically soppy sides as well as, bewilderingly, deciding that both "Si Senor" and "Let The Water Run Down" should have intros that sounded like Bo Diddley's records. Interesting too, was "I'm Standing By" an adaptation of the old gospel song written by Johnnie Taylor and recorded so well by Al Green, but on the album (unlike the 45 version which had come out at the end of 1962 where Taylor IS acknowledged) writing credits are given to Jerry Wexler and Betty Nelson. Hmmm.

His next album, *What Is Soul?*, was one of his best ever and only came out in England, so it was just as well he had a following over here, as despite the fact that it contained three more successful U.S. 45s, "The Record (Baby I Love You)", "I Swear By

Stars Above" and the title track, it was clear that he was no longer high on the priority list at Atlantic and the fact it was recorded over a two year period between February 1965 and January 1967 just emphasises this more clearly. Recorded (as usual) entirely in New York it is top quality big city soul (although "I Swear By Stars Above" has a distinct "southern" feel), and songs like the title track, "Teeny Weeny Little Bit" and, best of all, the marvellously mournful "She's Gone Again", demonstrated his underrated songwriting prowess. (The album does not give producer credits but the men in question were Bert Berns, Arif Mardin and Bob Gallo.)

Rough Edges 1970 Maxwell ML 88001 Producer: Bob Crewe

The Beginning Of It All 1972 Mandala 3007 Producer: Bob Gallo

Audio Biography 1972 Mandala MA-2008

King had three more chart successes on Atco with 45s in the late sixties but no more albums and he left the label to begin a rather dismal period of his career. It started off ok, as "I Can't Take It Like A Man" was both a good record and a moderate success (#45 soul) for his new label Maxwell, but rather bafflingly, it was omitted from his one and only LP for them, a set which was filled with entirely inappropriate pop songs ("Come Together", "Don't Let Me Down" and a nine minute version of "Little Green Apples") that made it depressing listening and a sales failure. *In The Beginning Of It All* was equally disappointing, even if it contained five new songs by King. It is another pop/rock outing and one wonders what Ben thought as he sang "Into The Mystic" and "Take Me To The Pilot". It even only came out in the U.S. as an afterthought in 1972, having first appeared in Europe on CBS 64570 the previous year. (It was also later to be re-packaged as *Re-Birth* on the Guinness label, GNS 36046) As with *Rough Edges* its cover just looked cheap. All in all, the early seventies was a period to forget for Ben E. King and his fans. (The second Mandala set, which I haven't heard, was apparently simply an interview with King, thus confirming his rather surreal tenure with the label.)

Supernatural 1975 Atlantic SD 18132 Producer: Tony Silvester (Billboard soul charts: 13 ; Billboard pop charts: 39)

I Had A Love 1976 Atlantic SD 18169 Producers: Tony Silvester, Bert DeCoteaux, Allan Felder, Norman Harris, Ronnie Baker & Earl Young

Benny & Us 1977 Atlantic SD 19105 Producers: Arif Mardin & Jerry Greenberg (Billboard soul charts: 14 ; Billboard pop charts: 33)

In 1975, against all the odds, he returned to Atlantic and was instantly rewarded with the second biggest single of his entire career when the relaxed guitar driven funk of "Supernatural Thing" became his second and final soul #1 as well as lodging in the pop charts at #5 and helping the album named after the single to became his first ever to reach the soul listings. It's a good outing although I find the rather breathless and relentless production by Tony Silvester a tad overwhelming. For instance, he sings Sam Dees' "Drop Me Heart Off At The Door" well enough but his take is not a patch on the version by Barbara Hall and I feel the same way about his delivery of Lou Courtney's "What Do You Want Me To Do". The follow-up 45, "Do It In The Name Of Love", became another big hit (#4 soul, #60 pop) for Ben and even if a bit more light and shade would have improved the album so far as my ears are involved, I was still delighted for him to attain such success.

In 1976, King cut the best album of his life, the marvellous *I Had A Love,* and everyone must have been aghast when it failed to chart. It's difficult at this date to understand why: he was coming off a couple of huge hits, and the title track had performed ok, if not spectacularly, as a single reaching #23 on the soul chart. Anyway, the LP is great, recorded 60% in Philadelphia and 40% in New York. The Sigma sound really suited King and his delivery of the excellent Ashford and Simpson penned title track was equalled by the delightful arrangement of "Smooth Sailing", and a memorable rendering of Dees' and Knight's "I Betcha Didn't Know That". Of the New York cuts, it was an inspired choice to slow down "Everybody Plays The Fool" and Ben's interpretation of Patrick Grant and Gwen Guthrie's "You're Stepping On My Heart (Tearing My World Apart)" is as good as the song's title. Of the ten tracks only Sam Dees' "No Danger Ahead" was a little disappointing and it's a set to treasure.

King bounced back commercially with another impressive set in, *Benny And Us*, with the "us" being the Average White Band, although the good sales were surely more attributable to AWB than to King himself. He took all lead vocals with the Scots confined to delivering excellent harmonies, and the key cut was the admirable Phillip Mitchell song, "A Star In The Ghetto", which reached #25 on the soul charts, four places lower than the funky as hell "Get It Up For Love" had managed. Another cut, "The Message", was even funkier and it triggered the thought that by this point in his career King had sung in just about every style imaginable.

Let Me Live In Your Life 1978 Atlantic SD 19200 Producers: Jim Stewart, Bettye Crutcher, Lamont Dozier & Patrick Adams

Music Trance 1980 Atlantic SD 19269 Producers: Bert DeCoteaux & Mass Production (Billboard soul charts:73)

Street Tough 1981 Atlantic SD 19300 Producers: Ben E. King, Ray Chew, Janet Alhanti & Barrie Palmer

For the rest of his career, it's fair to say that King's best days were a long way behind him, and although Atlantic persevered with him for a few more years the only other single that ever charted was "Music Trance" and that stalled at #29 on the soul listings in early 1980. But before this, came the so-so *Let Me In Your Life* LP. Six of the ten tracks were written by Lamont Dozier, and I don't think that King was able to stamp his own individuality on any of them apart from the nice "Fifty Years", as the rest all bear the unmistakeable imprint of their author. Elsewhere on the album it took five composers to re-write "Supernatural Thing" as "I See The Light". The best cut on show, by far, was the wonderful "Tippin'", a deep tale of infidelity cut down in Memphis, a city, which apart from a few of his last ever Atlantic sides from the sixties, he had not recorded in before. It failed as a single, which was a shame, as it was one of the best from 1978.

Music Trance consisted of five dance tracks, and two slow ones. Of the former, two were pretty good of their type and three were horrible, but all five could have been recorded by just about anybody. I predictably preferred the two slower sides, the better of which was "Everyday", but neither is particularly compelling.

Street Tough was certainly an improvement on *Music Trance*, with only two outright stinkers from eight tracks. King produced half the songs himself, including my two favourites, "Souvenirs Of Love" and "Something To Be Loved", the former slow, the latter more perky. On the other hand he also produced one of the stinkers, "Staying Power", and I couldn't warm either to the "Disney-esque" take on Van McCoy's oft-recorded "Stay Awhile With Me". It should also be noted that out and out dance sides such as the title track and "Made For Each Other" were harder and funkier than anything on the previous LP. I'm not suggesting for one minute that *Street Tough* is that good, but it's not a disaster.

After this King stopped entering studios for years, confining himself to on-stage performances but did briefly re-appear as a recording artist in 1992 with the *What's Important To Me* collection, but I believe it was released as a CD only; certainly I have no hard evidence of an LP version.

He died in April 2015 and received heartfelt and respectful obituaries, which was good to see, especially as he was by all accounts a lovely man, but it seems undeniable that the recording of "Stand By Me" has obscured many as to his enduring worth as a gifted soul singer; maybe not Premier League but definitely always pushing for promotion. (I've ignored a few compilations.)

Bobby King

Bobby King 1981 Warner Brothers BSK 3568 Producers: Steve Barri, Michael Price & Daniel Walsh

Love In The Fire 1984 Motown 6088ML Producers: Brian Potter & Steve Barri

Live And Let Live! (and Terry Evans) 1988 Rounder 2089 Producer: Ry Cooder

Rhythm, Blues, Soul & Grooves (and Terry Evans) 1990 Rounder 2101 Producers: Bobby King & Terry Evans

There are three different artists by the name of Bobby King who issued records that could be of interest to readers of this book but we are going to ignore the bluesman and the chap who put out a single on Sound Stage 7 (not least because they didn't cut any albums) and concentrate on the Bobby King who was born in Lake Charles, Louisiana and worked out on the West Coast.

His first record appears to have been "Don't Give Up Hope" on Lunar, and he went on to record for Reprise and Kris (as part of "Pure Ice") before his first LP arrived in 1981 for Warner Brothers. Three singles were pulled from it to try and capture that elusive hit but to no avail and the album didn't perform well, either. And that's almost certainly because it is pretty average, sounding more like pop music to soul music to my ears, and there is not a single cut on here (including the "Northern Soul" favourite "If You Don't Want My Love") that I can imagine listening to again. It also surely can't have helped King's career that he was so versatile as a singer: the first two tracks, "Fool For The Night" and "Having A Party", sound as if they were performed by completely different men and the album goes on in that vein.

I'm afraid I wasn't knocked out by his one Motown album either, from which a duet with Alfie Silas, "Close To Me", became a minor soul hit, although the gentle "Sweet Love" was certainly nice enough, but it wouldn't have mattered in which of his voices he sang "Midnight Shine" or "Lovequake", as they were further examples of pop-soul dance things of very cold comfort.

Between 1988 and 1990 King re-united with his partner from the Pure Ice days, Terry Evans, and the two of them put out a couple of LPs which I would class as being in the "Americana" style, but certainly not soul music and while they are certainly accomplished enough the only cut on either of them I really care for is a lovely version of "Dark End Of The Street" from *Live And Let Live!*

Clydie King (see also Brown Sugar)

Direct Me 1970 Lizard A20104 Producers: Gabriel Mekler & William Allen

Rushing To Meet You 1976 Tiger Lily TL 14037 Producers: Joe Long & Bobby Adcock

Atlanta's (or was it Dallas'?) Clydie King was another artist who performed the vast majority of her work as a session and backing singer, most notably as a member of The Raelets and the Blackberries, as well as on albums for The Rolling Stones, Ringo Starr and The Doors. She also recorded as a solo singer on a number of imprints, doing some particularly excellent work for Imperial and Minit, but was never graced with an LP by these labels.

Her first album came out at the end of 1970 (most discographies have it listed as 1971) and was way too raucous for me; the energy she brought to the proceedings (dotted throughout with cover versions) is impressive but Gabriel Mekler was always more of a rock man than a soul man and it shows."'Bout Love" reached the soul charts at #45 in mid 1971 but in all honesty the whole LP has little in common with those from other soul singers of the time, although I fully accept that many might think that is an entirely good thing. In 1973 she was part of a threesome who recorded as Brown Sugar and I have discussed that LP in the section under that group but I was pretty lukewarm about that as well.

A second LP, notorious among collectors, appeared in 1976 on the tax-scam label, Tiger Lily, which has made it much sought after as it would not have received a proper - or at the least, very limited - release. The cuts I have heard from it are all fully produced which begs the question why anyone bothered if it was merely going to be a tax write-off although one song, "Punish Me" (the old Margie Joseph number), also came out as a 45 on the tiny UK label in 1975. As always with such releases, one wonders if Clydie even knows it exists.

There are two more albums out there which are simply re-issues with the same tracks as the Tiger Lily set, but as they were both also on another tax write-off label, Baby Grand, they are sought after too; the first one was entitled *Steal Your Love Away* and the second, *Clydie King Steps Out,* and although they had different front covers they both bore the same catalogue number, SE 1062.

From the mid seventies onwards she continued to record with the likes of Bob Dylan but put her own solo career quietly away. A fine and much-needed retrospective CD appeared in 2007 which proved she cut some gorgeous soul records in her own right, but although she had a glittering career as a backing singer, her LP releases were nothing to write home about.

Evelyn King

Smooth Talk 1978 RCA APL1-2466 Producer: T. Life (Billboard soul charts: 8 ; Billboard pop charts: 14)

Music Box 1979 RCA AFL1-3033 Producer: T. Life (Billboard soul charts: 12 ; Billboard pop charts: 35)

Call On Me 1980 RCA AFL1-3543 Producers: T. Life & George Tindley (Billboard soul charts: 58 ; Billboard pop charts: 124)

For her first three albums she was Evelyn "Champagne" King, but from *I'm In Love* onwards the nickname was dropped, a change that had negligible effect on her popularity. She was born in New York and apart from apparently having been a cleaner at Philadelphia International Records, paid no dues in the industry at all as her very first record, "Shame", was a huge hit in 1978 when it reached #7 soul and #9 pop, going gold in the process; it's a record which still sounds good today and was completely unavoidable in any self-respecting disco in 1978. It was the stand-out cut from *Smooth Talk*, her debut LP which also went gold, on the cover of which she looked years younger than her real age of 17. Nearly as good was the impressive "The Show Is Over" which flaunted her precocious talent, but these cuts apart, it's not an LP designed to appeal to me (or anyone over the age of a teenager, really.)

Music Box housed two moderate hits in the title track and "Out There" but much more impressive is "Let's Start All Over Again" a ballad of class and power, and another slow number, "I Think My Heart Is Telling", is not bad, either. However, the wheels came off her career with *Call On Me* (which, interestingly, veteran soul man George Tindley helped produce) as it performed much less impressively and the lead-off single, "Let's Get Funky Tonight", only managed to reach #34 on the soul charts while the follow-up "I Need Your Love" failed totally, which, although it was a genuinely excellent ballad, proved it was not what people wanted from King.

I'm In Love 1981 RCA AFL1-3962 Producers: Morrie Brown, Kashif, Lawrence Jones, Willie Lester & Rodney Brown (Billboard soul charts: 6 ; Billboard pop charts: 28)

Get Loose 1982 RCA AFL1-4337 Producers: Morrie Brown, Kashif & Lawrence Jones, (Billboard soul charts: 1 ; Billboard pop charts: 27)

Face To Face 1983 RCA AFL1-4725 Producers: Andre Cymone, Foster Sylvers, Joey Gallo & Leon Sylvers (Billboard soul charts: 24 ; Billboard pop charts: 91)

So Romantic 1984 RCA AFL1-5308 Producers: Jimmy Douglass, The System, Clif Magness, Glenn Ballard, Evan Rogers & David Wolinski (Billboard soul charts: 38 ; Billboard pop charts: 203)

A Long Time Coming 1985 RCA AFL1-7015 Producers: T. Life, David Wolinski, Bobby Watson, Rene Moore, Angela Winbush, Allen George & Fred McFarlane, (Billboard soul charts: 38)

Flirt 1988 EMI-Manhattan E1-46968 Producers: Leon Sylvers, Dave Ervin, Teneen Ali, Alex Brown, Ron Kersey, Paul Simpson, Melvin Watson, Robert Clivilles, David Cole, Carl Sturken & Evan Rogers, (Billboard soul charts: 20 ; Billboard pop charts: 192)

The Girl Next Door 1989 EMI-USA E1-92049 Producers: Nayan, Leon Sylvers, Ten City, Marshall Jefferson, David Cochrane & Evelyn King

Budweiser Concert Hour BC 86-16

Therefore, they got something else as T. Life was elbowed aside and the then hot combination of Morrie Brown, Lawrence Jones and Kashif came along to resurrect her fortunes to an impressive degree even if I slid away into the shadows as a listener and never bothered with her sides again. I can see that they were good enough of their type and although "I'm In Love" became a #1 soul hit (and a much lesser pop one at only #40) is it not fair to say that are literally tens of thousands of soul sides from the last fifty years that sound vastly superior in 2016?

It would be remiss of me not to acknowledge how successful she was in the early eighties as *Get Loose* and a single from it, "Love Come Down", both became #1 soul hits, with the former going gold, too, while the follow-up 45, "Betcha She Don't Love You", only missed the top spot by one place. From here on in, things did rather slip with each LP release doing a little less well than the one before, but it has always been exceedingly difficult, as I think I've shown enough already, for soul artists to maintain an audience - particularly the more fickle pop one - for a sustained period of time.

Marva King

Feels Right 1981 Planet P-16 Producer: Richard Perry

On the cover of her one LP Marva King is done up like a forties' movie star and that feeling of "tastefulness" is what characterises the record. Immaculately played and produced, with a striking ballad in "Memories", it is a set to appeal to lovers of the music of Minnie Riperton as King's voice reminds me strongly of the "Perfect Angel" (and also, Sheila Hutchinson from The Emotions). It's typically West Coast too, and there is a slight sense of going through the motions with the odd refined guitar solo here and the stylish saxophone solo there, but it's certainly an outing that will have numerous fans, although I couldn't recommend it to anyone who likes their soul to have discernible gospel or bluesy links. "Do You Want To Make Love" was released as a 45 but didn't hit, although King did reach the soul charts in 1982 on a duet with Chuck Cissel, "If I Had The Chance", but this is not on the LP.

She also hit the charts again in 1988 with "Back Up" and has gone on to make quite a name for herself within the industry thanks to working with the likes of Prince and George Howard. She has released new CDs in the last few years as well as taking up acting.

Toby King

Toby Kang 1976 Chelsea CHL 534 Producers: Toby King & Rod Glider

Toby King - real name Harry Fleming - cut a small number of singles for a handful of labels and although some were pretty good such as "Operator" on Cotton (and later Deesu) and "First Man To Die From The Blues" on Drive, he was an adequate rather than great singer (in fact, esteemed soul producer John Richbourg rated him as distinctly average) and none of his 45s came close to being national hits.

He did, however, get a chance to cut an LP which was recorded at Reflection Sound studio down in Charlotte, North Carolina. Its distinctly peculiar title of *Toby Kang* has always suggested to me either a sense of humour or a lack of quality control by someone. Anyway, if one can get past the sensationally tacky front cover (and stump up the not inconsiderable price it always commands, it's very rare) there are good things to be found. In particular on side two where King gives us a good version of "Yes, I'm Ready" and a nice slow ballad, "Stay With Me Awhile" which are both adroitly arranged and produced. A third cut, "I Just Want To See

You", is also ok but suffers from King trying to sing exactly like Al Green and he can't manage it. Side one is more problematic as although it kicks off well with two good dance sides, one of which, "We're In Love With Each Other" recalls Archie Bell and The Drells' "I Could Dance All Night", "Time To Get It On" and "Party Hearty" are really poor.

He never recorded any more soul records to the best of my knowledge but I believe he has recently re-invented himself as a country singer.

Will King

You're My Woman 1979 Kingfish KF-1234 Producers: Paul Marshall, Charles Allen & Willard King

Backed Up Against The Wall 1985 Total Experience TEL6-5710 Producers: Jonah Ellis, Jimmy Hamilton, Maurice Hayes, Bernard Spears & Victor Hill

Here we find another mysterious singer, about whom information is hard to come by. I was first aware of him as the writer - as Willard King - of a funky single by The Rhythm Rebellion on Tangerine in 1970, and he went on to record a couple of solo singles under this name with the first of them, the attractive "Lady Be Mine" on Capitol, hitting the soul charts at #88 in 1973. Then there appears to be nothing from him until an LP appeared on the small Kingfish label in 1979 as by Will King.

It is an LP that had no chance whatsoever in the marketplace for not only would Kingfish have lacked distribution channels, but the cover is distinctly amateurish and, most damning of all, the material, all written by King and Paul Marshall, is totally underwhelming. There's not a melody to be found anywhere and nothing for a listener to get to grips with at all. King also, despite being obviously influenced by Al Green, had the same challenge as another King, Bobby, in that his vocal talents were such that he could adopt different voices: compare "Sunshine Please" and "Where, When How"; they seem to be sung by two different people.

The cover of *Backed Up Against The Wall* seems suitably symbolic: an outline of a man without a face. Once again, good songs were noticeably thin on the ground, a fact only made more clear by the inclusion of two genuinely good ones, "Wonderful World" and "Pride And Joy", but at least one or two others had some semblance of tune. The most obvious of these were the title track and "I'm Sorry" (which made #26 on the soul charts when released as a single) but the downside was that King's Al Green impersonations on these two were so pronounced as to be almost demeaning. "All Of My Life" has some melody too, but the rest was of little value and throughout the musical sound is harsh and rather tinny.

King Hannibal

Truth 1973 Aware AWLP 1001 Producer: King Hannibal

I'm listing this release by the outrageously colourful James T. Shaw under the name of "King Hannibal" as *Truth* is the only LP he ever got to record, and that's the name under which it came out, but in his long and convoluted career he released most of his singles under the name of "Mighty Hannibal" as well as a few more under plain old "Hannibal", when he was presumably feeling less imperious. That career started way back in 1958, a year before he started using the name "Hannibal" in one or other of its guises, and he went on to cut over twenty 45s before he pitched up on Aware, although only one of them, "Hymn #5" (one of the bleakest hit singles in history), nestled up into the soul charts, #21 at the end of 1966.

Truth is an absolutely magnificent set, fully meriting the coveted term, "lost classic", and its seriousness of purpose, judiciously chosen songs, completely committed singing and breadth of subject matter combined to make it so good; it also, like all of his records, meant absolutely nothing to a pop audience; this is without doubt a "black" album. Similar in some respects to another brilliant LP from the GRC corporation (who owned Aware), Jimmy Lewis' *Totally Involved*, Hannibal addresses racial identity on "Black Girl" (an unrecognisable and genuinely inspired take on The Checkmates' "Black Pearl") and "Wake Up"; the urge to become a big star on "I Got That Will" (in which he cheekily namechecks his wife, Delia Gartrell, whereas Herman Hitson's original had called out Aretha Franklin); inveighs against drugs in "The Truth Shall Make You Free" (his second national hit, #37 soul in early 1973); up-dates "Hymn #5" to a seven minute lament powered along by a great groove; but the showpiece of the set is "Party Life", a completely harrowing tale of a daughter lost to drugs and pimping. After all this, it's easy to mistake "It's What You Do" for a simple love song but it's much more subtle than that, and "Same Ole Fool Again", a highly appealing "southern" mid-tempo song sang with his customary power, rounds out an album that demands to be heard by anyone who cares for the works of much more famous cultural icons such as Curtis Mayfield, Gil Scott-Heron and Marvin Gaye. He went on to release other records and CDs after *Truth* but not one was as compelling and none were even close to being hits.

Shaw - who died in 2014 - was one of the best and important artists ever to come out of Atlanta and was lucky enough to have lived long enough to see a fascinating CD of his work (the interview with him is worth the price alone) appear in 2001.

Kinsman Dazz (see The Dazz Band)

Mike James Kirkland

Hang On In There 1972 Bryan BS 9001 Producer: Bob Kirkland

Doin' It Right 1973 Bryan BS 9002 Producer: Bob Kirkland

Bo & Ruth (and Ruth Davis) 1976 Claridge 1002 Producer: Bob Kirkland

Mike James Kirkland was the "Mike" from Mike & The Censations a Los Angeles based group who recorded some excellent singles for Highland and Revue in the sixties, all of which deserve to be heard. They did not get the chance to record any LPs though, and Kirkland had to go out on his own (although undoubtedly helped considerably by producer and fellow ex-Censation, brother Bob) to cut what have gone on to become two esteemed and sought after solo albums.

Because *Hang On In There* and *Doin' It Right* have been re-issued in recent years they are now better known and much easier to get hold of than they were when they first appeared. Not to mention coming to the attention of a whole new audience. But I can assure anyone that they suffered from extremely limited distribution when they were first released and I never saw copies in the first twenty or so years of my collecting life when I was assiduously tracking down soul albums everywhere. *Hang On In There* is split into a "peace" side and a "love" side and was clearly influenced by *What's Going On*, but it would be grossly unfair to consider it as merely a "poor man's version" of Gaye's mighty work as it has a relaxed charm all of its own which is very appealing, and it never hurts if the musicians on your album were the core of The Watts 103rd Street Rhythm Band. All seven tracks are originals apart from "Baby, I Need Your Loving" and only "You're Gonna Share Your Love" falls below a high standard. The key track is the near nine minute long title song, which has numerous time changes, and stands out from all the other cuts which fall into the standard two or three minute format. "It's Alright With Me" has the most gorgeous backing singing on show, but Kirkland's own excellent voice is never overshadowed.

Doin' It Right followed more or less exactly the same path as its predecessor with once again the title track being much lengthier than all else, but there were two minor discernible differences: other than "Love Is All We Need" social commentary was not pursued and the general tempo of the set was slightly brisker, not that it ever approached anything like frantic. Good covers of "It's Too Late" and "Oh Me Oh My" huddled cosily among six new Kirkland songs and it's all highly enjoyable, and would doubtless have sold well had it appeared on a major record label.

For the Claridge LP Kirkland had become "Bo" and teamed up with Ruth Davis to finally score some chart success. It was also their one and only LP together, which was a little surprising seeing as how it housed four singles that made the US soul charts, albeit not in a big way. Recorded as usual in California it nevertheless has a slight "southern" soul flavour, particularly on the appealing "Easy Loving", which was the best selling of the four charting 45s, reaching #38. "You're Gonna Get Next To Me" is doubtless the best known track, as it was a minor hit in the UK as well as the US but the witty "Grandfather Clock" is a stronger song. All in all, this is a better than averagely good LP and still sounds fresh today.

A fifth 45 from the duo, "Stay By My Side", reached the soul charts in 1977 at #63 but this was not included on the LP and not only was it the last side they cut together, but the last time Kirkland cut anything, and he moved into work on T.V. and radio.

Lew Kirton

Just Arrived 1980 Alston 4411 Producers: Clarence Reid & Freddy Stonewall

Talk To Me 1983 Believe In A Dream FZ 38956 Producer: Russell Timmons

Lew Kirton, despite having a name that might make an eight-year old schoolboy snigger, was a singer of great talent, first cutting discs as a member of The Invitations in their Silver Blue label period, then going solo with 45s on the Verdith and Marlin labels before moving to Alston and releasing "Heaven In The Afternoon", a popular dance side, in 1978.

The first track on *Just Arrived* is "Island Girl" and that may have been a nod to the fact that Lew was originally from the West Indies, but it certainly didn't tax Clarence Reid's song-writing skills and neither does the poor "Love Secret Agent", but once they are out of the way the rest of the album varies from good to very good indeed. It's such a pleasure to listen to an unreconstructed soul man bellow out stuff from 1980, a year when soulfulness was generally discouraged, and he easily overcomes the amusing fact that "Love, I Don't Want Your Love" has verses that are identical to "I Will Survive"; but he really shines when things are slowed down. "Time To Get With It" and "Why Should I Get Jealous" are the "good" tracks but "Let Me Up - Off My Knees" and, even better, the superb "NYC", are utterly winning outings. Last point, and it's doubtless only me that notices such things, but the front cover has a picture of Lew joyously arriving by car into New York, whereas "NYC" sees him forlornly leaving by bus.

The single on Marlin, "Do What You Want, Be What You Are", had actually been a tiny hit (#94) on the soul charts, but slightly more substantial success accrued to Kirton when "Talk To Me" (#31) and "Don't Give up Your Dream" (#71) reached the listings in 1983. Both were included on his second LP, named after the former hit, which saw the disappearance of Reid in favour of Kirton's writing seven of the eight songs himself. It's an absolutely rock solid collection, sounding good at the time and standing up much better today than virtually everything else from that year. The songs are mixed between dance outings which avoid obvious clichés, and ballads, which, although without doubt imbued with more pop glossiness than "NYC", stray firmly the right side of MOR and "Got To Find Somebody To Love" is inspired, the best thing on view.

More recordings have appeared at rather irregular intervals over the last thirty years or so, but none of them were LPs.

Kitty And The Haywoods

Kitty Haywood; Vivian Haywood; Mary Ann Haywood; Cynthia Haywood

Love Shock 1977 Mercury SRM- 1- 1171 Producers: The Ohio Players

Excuse Me, I've Got A Life To Catch 1981 Capitol ST 12149 Producer: Gene Barge

Chicago's Kitty and the Haywoods were certainly nowhere near as important or successful as The Emotions, another all-female act from the Windy City, but they did make a slight notch in history. Kitty Haywood first recorded as a member of Rotary Connection as well as cutting a solo side on Weis, before working with her two sisters and niece Cynthia to cut two rather undistinguished Charles Stepney produced singles for Mercury. A bigger break came in 1976 when they were recruited to providing backing vocals for Aretha Franklin's *Sparkle* set.

The Ohio Players then took the group in hand, producing and writing the whole of the *Love Shock* album, although I bet that "How Great Love Is" is a re-write of a gospel song called "How Great God is". The Players were never known for standard song construction or melody and their influence is clear on all the tracks, which, it must be said, do not bear compositions that stick in the mind. However, the joy of their music is in the grooves, the way instruments flicker in and out, and having a distaff version of the group sat just fine with me. When Kitty does get the chance to stretch out vocally, the influence of Franklin on her voice is apparent. Unfortunately, the title track stalled as a single at a pretty miserable #84 on the soul charts and Mercury and the Players both moved out of the group's lives.

An absolute disaster of a record, "Disco Fairyland", heralded the start of the group's affiliation with Capitol where they were to remain until 1981, recording one LP, *Excuse Me, I've Got A Life To Catch*, the title of which sounds as if it should have been the title of a Broadway play; it also bore a cover which made it clear about Kitty's prominence within the quartet (sisters and niece are not featured). Luckily "Disco Fairyland" is not included, and nor did it portend what IS included, which is polite dance fodder and slightly torchy slow songs, all far removed from *Love Shock*. It was another non-seller, though, and I suspect the group disbanded soon thereafter as Kitty returned in 1983 to release a 45, "Givin' It Up", as a solo artist.

Kleeer

Norman Durham; Paul Crutchfield; Richard Lee; Woody Cunningham; Isabelle Coles; Yvette Flowers; Terry Dolphin; Melanie Moore; Eric Rohrbaugh

I Love To Dance 1979 Atlantic SD 19237 Producer: Dennis King (Billboard soul charts: 53 ; Billboard pop charts: 208)

Winners 1979 Atlantic SD 19262 Producers: Dennis King & Kleeer (Billboard soul charts: 24 ; Billboard pop charts: 140)

License To Dream 1981 Atlantic SD 19288 Producers: Dennis King & Kleeer (Billboard soul charts: 13 ; Billboard pop charts: 81)

Taste The Music 1982 Atlantic SD 19334 Producers: Dennis King & Kleeer (Billboard soul charts: 31 ; Billboard pop charts: 139)

Get Ready 1982 Atlantic 80038-1 Producer: Kleeer

Nobody can hear everything, and while I can honestly say I have listened to, on more than one occasion, the vast majority of records listed in this book, one group who pretty much entirely passed me by were Kleeer. This was firstly because I never heard their records played on the radio shows I listened to or in clubs I frequented at the end of the seventies and early eighties but also because I had marked them down as entirely a disco band, devoid of any soul; I can see now that this was entirely unfair as well as being inaccurate and I wish I had paid more attention to them at the time.

The first album contained the mundane dance sides "Keep Your Body Workin'" and "Tonight's The Night", two smallish soul hits from 1979, but much better was the more relaxed "Happy Me" which demonstrated conclusively that members of this band could sing, even if I'm not sure who delivered the ethereal tenor lead. "To Groove You" was good too, with more impressive singing and a insidious rhythm, and "Kleeer Sailin'" was better than the title suggests but three tracks can't save the set from being rather run of the mill when compared to the finest self-contained bands with whom they had to compete.

Winners moved the band fractionally up the ladder, selling pretty well in addition to providing, in the rather dull title track, a single that charted at #23 on the soul chart. As ever, I am more enamoured by the slower material and would recommend "I Still Love You" as more enticing listening as it has a sweet melody and some good singing. Next best track is "Hunger For Your Love" but the rest are upbeat sides that don't sound amazing in 2016.

In early 1981 Kleeer enjoyed their one and only big selling single when "Get Tough" managed to get as high as #15 on the soul charts, even if it was another run of the mill dance outing. Once again, some more interesting and enjoyable tunes could be found within and the female-led "Sippin' And Kissin'" while slightly twee, did have charm and showed another side of the group, while "Hypnotized" was a fine side with a tough male lead from Norman Durham and a good driving rhythm. Best of all though, and their best to date, was "Say You Love Me", a classy ballad nicely performed by Paul Crutchfield. This is their most enjoyable and most varied set, and even if I am not overly enamoured of all the dance sides I would say they stand up much better than most other similar things from 1981.

Taste The Music was inoffensive enough with the guitar solos on one or two cuts reminding us that Kleeer were apparently once a hard rock band called Pipeline, but it was predominantly a set aimed at the dance floor and the title track and "De Ting Continues" were two further modest hits on the soul charts at #55 and #74 respectively. The two slow cuts, "Swann" and "Fella" sounded different from their earlier downbeat sides and if I don't particularly care for either of them, at least they once again pointed up the versatility of the group; they did have an ability to mix things up.

Good things can also be found on *Get Ready*, even if it was their worst-selling set to date and only contained a minor single hit in "She Said She Loves Me"(# 84 soul). I think it had by now become pretty apparent that their good-natured grooves - they didn't seem to take themselves too seriously - and obvious musical talents had allowed them to deservedly carve out a reasonable career. Best track: "Say You'll Stay".

Intimate Connection 1985 Atlantic 80145-1 Producer: Eumir Deodato and Kleeer (Billboard soul charts: 49)

Seeekret 1985 Atlantic 81254-1 Producer: Eumir Deodato

Kleeer Winners 1986 Atlantic 780 210-1 (Europe)

A "reasonable" career, for sure, but in order to try and take it to another level Atlantic decided to entrust production duties to Emir Deodato. It didn't work as *Intimate Connection* failed to sell in any great quantity, but musically it kept the standard up and I particularly liked "Next Time It's For Real", a single with an excellent vocal from Durham and one that deserved to have performed much better than only #79; it's certainly one of their finest moments. On the less appealing side, "Ride it", "Tonight" and "Break" were no great shakes but die-hard Kleeer fans must have enjoyed the set.

Deodato was retained for *Seeekret*, but in came the drum machines, the sequencers and the synthesisers and out went my interest. It didn't sell, either, and the lead-off track, "Take Your Heart Away", became the last time a Kleeer 45 would nestle on the soul charts at #65, a typical placing for the group. Of the 12 singles they posted on the soul charts, nine of them came to rest between #48 and #84.

The group broke up soon after this although a *Best Of* set appeared in Europe. Of the mainstays of the group, Woody Cunningham went on to release a couple of solo CDs..

Klique

Howard Huntsberry; Debbie Hunter (nee Suthers); Isaac Suthers

It's Winning Time 1981 MCA 5198 Producers: David Crawford, Con-Funk-Shun & Clay McMurray (Billboard soul charts: 40)

Let's Wear It Out! 1982 MCA 5317 Producers: David Crawford, Michael Cooper, Felton Pilate, Karl Fuller & Isaac Suthers

Try It Out 1983 MCA 5317 Producers: Thomas McClary, Leon Ndugu Chancler & Reggie Andrews (Billboard soul charts: 11 ; Billboard pop charts: 70)

Love Cycles 1985 MCA 5532 Producers: Oliver Scott, Ronnie McNeir, Renaldo Benson, Ollie E Brown, Thomas McClary, Jonah Ellis, Jimmy Hamilton, Isaac Suthers & Maurice Hayes (Billboard soul charts: 25)

On the front cover of their first two albums the threesome of Klique are dressed as astronauts which didn't look great at the time and looks ridiculous now. I would sum them up as being a distinctly second or third division outfit, having been successful enough to have released four albums and ten singles, two of which were quite sizeable hits, but they never had a genuine identity or cut enough good records to have made them stand out from the crowd.

Having said that, their first LP is not bad at all, although the credits are really difficult to read on the poorly designed back cover. *It's Winning Time* contains eight cuts, five of which are uptempo much in the manner of what was coming out on Solar at the time, and three slower ones, of which "You Brought My Love To Life" is the most soulful and memorable. The trio switched the vocals about although Howard Huntsberry (once in the group T.U.M.E.) takes lead on most cuts, and if the songs are not of the highest quality they were not risible either.

Let's Wear It Out! had crystal clear back sleeve credits, but it is a tired album, and failed in the market place. There was only one slow cut this time, which was a shame as "Feel So Good" was far superior to everything else on show, and the LP has no personality whatsoever; "Dance Like Crazy" and "Pump Your Rump" are titles which rather sum things up, even if both of them did reach the soul charts as singles, at #39 and #83, as did "I Can't Shake This Feeling"at #47.

Try It Out was the group's brief move into much more agreeable commercial circles, as not only did the album sell well, but it also contained a bona fide hit in a revival of Jackie Wilson's "Stop Doggin' Me Around" which made it to #2 on the soul charts as well as #50 pop. It was their finest ever side, sung most impressively by Huntsberry and still sounds great today, and the other ballad, "Sarah", was most congenial as well. The remainder of the LP consisted of six dance sides which do not stick in the mind; one of them, "Flashback, was a most disappointing follow-up 45 to the hit, stalling at a lowly #59 on the soul charts.

Wisely, Klique covered another old Wilson song on *Love Cycles*, and "A Woman, A Lover, A Friend" became their second ever biggest single reaching #15 on the soul charts in the spring of 1984, but although it was good, it did not quite have the appeal of "Doggin' Me Around". The group also covered another venerable old soul song on the LP, and if "Cry Baby" couldn't match Garnet Mimms and The Enchanters' original, it was handled deftly enough. Seven of the other eight tracks were upbeat, with "Girl, I Miss You" being no more than a so-so ballad.

Klique shrunk to a duo in 1986 as Huntsberry left to go solo, but apart from a 12" single in 1986 no more records were ever forthcoming. Had they concentrated more on ballads, in the manner of, say, early Atlantic Starr, they might have been more successful than they were, and created more lasting music, and remain a rather forgotten group.

Klymaxx

Bernadette Cooper; Cheryl Cooley; Joyce Irby; Lorena Porter Hardimon; Lynn Malsby; Ann Williams; Judy Takeuchi; Robbin Grider

Never Underestimate The Power Of A Woman 1981 Solar S-21 Producers: Stephen Shockley & Otis Stokes

Girls Will Be Girls 1982 Solar 60177 Producers: Stephen Shockley, Otis Stokes, Jimmy Jam, Terry Lewis & William Shelby

Meeting In The Ladies' Room 1984 Constellation MCA 5529 Producers: Stephen Shockley, Jimmy Jam, Terry Lewis, Joyce Irby, Klymaxx, Barry DeVorzon, Joseph Conlan, Bo Watson & Vincent Calloway (Billboard soul charts: 9 ; Billboard pop charts: 18)

Klymaxx 1986 Constellation MCA 5832 Producers: Joyce Irby, Bernadette Cooper, Rick Timas, Vincent Brantley,Lynn Malsby, Stephen Shockley, Rod Temperton, Dick Rudolph & Bruce Swedien (Billboard soul charts: 25 ; Billboard pop charts: 98)

The Maxx Is Back 1990 MCA 6376 Producers: Alton Stewart, Curtis Williams, Mark Anthony Silva, Jimmy Jam, Terry Lewis, Rex Salas, Robert Harris, Timmy Gatling, Jeff Lorber, Vassal Benford & Klymaxx (Billboard soul charts: 32; Billboard pop charts: 168)

Klymaxx were a most unusual proposition in early eighties (or indeed any era's) soul music: an eight piece female band who played and sang on their own records. As the decade went on their personnel slowly shrunk as their number of producers went ever upwards and they had a number of big hits with "I Miss You", "Man Size Love" and "I'd Still Say Yes" all reaching the pop top twenty; the latter two did less well on the soul charts and I'd say that probably sums up their glossy, teenage appeal for they certainly had little to commend them to long time soul fans. Their music was proof that a band comprised of women could be every bit as bland and unimaginative as those consisting solely of men. although I fully accept that as with a number of groups or singers who started their careers in the eighties, Klymaxx were aiming at an entirely different audience from me and the number of positive comments on their music on Youtube proves that they can happily withstand my indifference. Cooper and Irvy both went on to cut solo albums.

Boobie Knight

(*The Soulciety : Members unknown. **The Universal Lady : Michael Averett; Len Fletcher; Tom Sellitti; J.W. Williams; Tee Torres; Mervyn Joseph; Mark Montana; Al Johnson)

Soul Ain't No New Thing * 1972 RCA LSP-4608 No producer listed

Earth Creature ** 1974 Dakar DK 76913 Producer: Solid Rock Productions and Alfonzo Tucker

Boobie Knight is a decidedly mysterious man and all one can really discern from the pretentious waffle of the sleevenotes on the RCA release is that the Soulciety is his third band, but we are left none the wiser as to the identity of the seven men on the front cover. We don't find out who the producer is either but certainly

Harvey Fuqua was involved as arranger on at least one track and there are elements of the New Birth, Fuqua protegees, here and there but Sly and The Family Stone loom larger. Sly certainly appears to be a hero of Knight's and I'm wondering if the Milton Edwards who penned all the tracks is an alter ego for Knight in the same way as the Sly Stone/Sylvester Stewart identity switch was played up by the "Dance To The Music" man. *Soul Ain't No New Thing* is probably a great album for samplers to own with its excellent chicken scratch guitar patterns and thrusting horns but the songs are not up to much and only funk fans will really get satisfaction from the set. When Knight slows it down on the lengthy "Dear Love" he serves up a dirge; much better to keep the tempo up as on the best track here, "Lettin' Happiness In".

The positive vibes emitted by the above-named song also pervade the second LP from Knight with The Universal Lady presumably being his fourth band; and at least Dakar quite rightly tells us who they are. *Earth Creature* is in a similar style to the first, with the Family Stone influence probably turned up a notch, not least in Knight's own attire. "Ain't Nobody Better Dan You" epitomises the upbeat nature of the material and "A Woman Will Make You Love" is a slow excursion better than any other over the two albums. The last two tracks, "The Lovomaniacs" and "Earth Creature" itself are disjoined, messy and rather dull, but overall there is just enough good stuff here to make me pleased that Boobie Knight got the chance to release these records, even if neither of them prospered in the market-place.

The only other Boobie Knight release I am aware of is a 12" single from 1983, but that one didn't sell either.

Frederick Knight

I've Been Lonely For So Long 1973 Stax STS-3011
Producer: Frederick Knight (Billboard soul charts: 58)

Knight Kap 1977 Juana 200,000 Producers: Frederick Knight & Steve Alaimo

Let The Sunshine In 1978 Juana 200,003 Producer: Frederick Knight

Knight Time 1981 Juana JU-4000AE Producer: Frederick Knight

Wasn't and isn't "I've Been Lonely For So Long?" a rather curious record? It came out of nowhere and sounded (and still sounds today) like very little else, catching enough people by delighted surprise to register as a #8 soul and #27 pop hit in the spring of 1972. It wasn't the first single Knight had released - others appeared on 1-2-3 and Dial - but it was his first on Stax and remains by far his biggest ever success under his own name. His major commercial triumph, however, was the writing of Anita Ward's "Ring My Bell" and the obnoxiousness of that enormous hit totally obscures the fact that he was a highly accomplished writer, having a c.v. of top quality songs, and even Leonard Cohen has been bewitched enough to cover Knight's "Be For Real".

The first LP, obviously named after the hit, is a good enough one with excellent musicians on board including the Muscle Shoals Horns, although its two follow-up singles in "Trouble" and "This Is My Song Of Love To You" resoundingly failed to make *Billboard* chart inroads. The set also showed that Knight was a better composer than singer and the imploring "Take Me On Home Witcha" paired up Sam Dees and Knight as writers for the first time. (This was to prove to be a highly fruitful partnership, probably best represented by Barbara Hall's magnificent "Drop My Heart Off At The Door".) Elsewhere on the set Tommy Tate's song "Now That I've Found You" was a good choice for Knight to cover as indeed was Jerry Weaver's "Pick 'Um Up, Put 'Um Down". Only an unrecognisable and rather pointless cover of "Someday We'll Be Together" jarred somewhat, on what is a consistent first LP from the man from Birmingham, Alabama (where the set was recorded, by the way.)

Knight recorded one more single for Stax and three more for their subsidiary, Truth, but only one of them, the utterly delightful Knight-Dees song, "I Betcha Didn't Know That", hit, reaching #27 soul in early 1975. As Stax famously went bust soon after this, Knight needed a new label and found one in Juana, for whom he cut his second LP, on which he wrote or co-wrote seven of the eight tracks. Wisely, he included "I Betcha Didn't Know That" and its relaxed tempo was mimicked by "River Flowing" and "Wrapped In Your Love" before the accelerator was gently pressed down for the final five tracks; of these, "When It Ain't Right With My Baby" was surely the best, although none were contemptible, but the George McCrae-ish "You Make My Life Complete" would have been improved by lopping off two minutes as it was starting to go round in circles.

Things dipped badly with *Let The Sunshine In*, easily his most disappointing work to date. Given Knight was never the most distinctive singer anyway, to omit any picture of him on his own LP was surely taking symbolism a bit too far. Of the seven tracks (I'm not including the 75 second long "Another Knight For Love") only one, "You Can't Deny Me" a ballad which reminds me of something else I can't put my finger on, is worth listening to more than once. The rest are either sheer pop as with "Bundle Of Love" or poor disco such as "Raise Your Hand". In fact the latter, and even more so the ballad, "You And Me", seem to feature Knight singing as if his vocal is pressed at the wrong speed ! He sounds as if he is spinning at 22 ½ rather than 33⅓ and if this is correct, then it says all there is to say about the quality control of the LP.

Knight Time was a vast improvement over *Let The Sunshine In* from cover to content, and it clearly sought to position Knight as a singer to be taken as seriously as he was a writer: of the eight tracks he only wrote or co-wrote two, unthinkable on his previous outings. It works on that level too, with the best vocals of any of his four LPs, although the complete eradication of his southern roots is slightly to be regretted, as was the re-inclusion of "Bundle Of Love". *Knight Time* is a most tasteful affair, with piano and strings to the fore at the expense of horns and my favourite tracks would be "Even A Fool Would Let Go" and a fine take on The Controllers' "If Tomorrow Never Comes"; he even got a small hit from the album when his version of Barry Manilow's "The Old Songs" came gently to rest at #74 on the soul charts.

What this overview doesn't highlight was how hard Juana tried to break him as an artist, as they released over ten singles, but "The Old Songs" apart, they all failed and there were no more records after *Knight Time*. Still, I imagine the royalties from "Ring My Bell" enabled him to take life easier.

Gladys Knight & The Pips (see also The Pips)

Merald "Bubba" Knight; Edward Patten; William Guest

Letter Full Of Tears 1962 Fury FULP 1003 Producers: Bobby Robinson & Marshall Sehorn

Gladys Knight & The Pips 1965 Maxx 3000 Producer: Larry Maxwell

Gladys Knight is one of the greatest female soul singers of all time, one who genuinely matters; the only others who can be spoken of in the same breath as regards having balanced huge commercial success with genuine artistry so astutely as Knight are Aretha Franklin, Etta James and Mavis Staples. And if the Pips have tended to be overshadowed by Gladys it is not owing to any lack of talent on their part as the exquisite harmonies they have brought to bear on so many great sides are all part of the splendid legacy of this excellent foursome from Atlanta; it should also be no great surprise that their voices have all gelled together so well as Gladys and Merald are brother and sister, with Guest and Patten being their cousins. Note too that they did not need Motown to define them, enjoying substantial success both before joining the label and after having left it.

Their first single came out in 1958 on the Brunswick label as just by "The Pips" and they remained as such when they released "Every Beat Of My Heart" on Vee Jay in 1961 which shot straight to #1 on the soul charts as well as to #6 pop. Simultaneously a re-cut version on Fury, their first record with Gladys' name being added as a pre-fix, also hit both soul and pop charts. Fury followed up with "Guess Who" which didn't chart, before trying again with "Letter Full Of Tears", another smash at #3 soul and #19 pop. All three singles were included on their first LP, named after this second hit, which is glorious. The Pips harmonies are exquisite throughout, the material is consistently strong and then there is Gladys herself. We all know the gravitas of her most famous records from later on in her career but here she comes across as not only young, of course, but also uninhibited and rather untamed and there is a passionate exuberance in her singing that we were seldom to hear again as her career progressed. This is as soulful as soul LPs got in 1961 and there is little point in picking out further tracks; place the needle anywhere.

The Maxx LP is also wonderful, and if it was a typical LP from 1965 in the sense that 10 of the 12 tracks appeared on singles, it was not so predictable in that only one of the songs, "Daybreak" (which DIDN'T feature on a 45), was pitched as an MOR sop to potential white buyers. The rest was top class New York soul, with sterling arrangements from Fred Norman and Bert Keyes and in "Giving Up", "Lovers Always Forgive", "Either Way I Lose" and "Why Don't You Love Me", four brilliant songs from Van McCoy. The first two of these were pretty substantial hits on the pop charts at #38 and #89 respectively (this was in the period when *Billboard* were not running a separate soul chart) and if "Stop And Get A Hold Of Myself", another excellent McCoy composition, failed to hit then its thrilling vocal arrangement must have stirred many hearts nonetheless. Knight co-wrote a couple of tracks herself, while "Maybe Maybe Baby" allowed the Pips to take vocal centre stage.

Everybody Needs Love 1967 Soul SS706 Producer: Norman Whitfield (Billboard soul charts: 12 ; Billboard pop charts: 60)

Feelin' Bluesy 1968 Soul SS707 Producer: Norman Whitfield (Billboard soul charts: 12 ; Billboard pop charts: 158)

Silk N' Soul 1968 Soul SS711 Producer: Norman Whitfield (Billboard soul charts: 11 ; Billboard pop charts: 136)

Nitty Gritty 1969 Soul SS713 Producers: Norman Whitfield, Nicholas Ashford, Valerie Simpson, Harvey Fuqua & Johnny Bristol (Billboard soul charts: 11 ; Billboard pop charts: 81)

Greatest Hits 1970 Soul SS723 (Billboard soul charts: 5; Billboard pop charts: 55)

All In A Knight's Work 1970 Soul SS730 No producer listed

It's possibly hard to remember now that the Pips move to Motown (they recorded there on the subsidiary Soul label) did not get off to a great start as despite their excellence, both "Just Walk In My Shoes" and "Take Me In Your Arms And Love Me" failed as 45s, and it took the third, the effortlessly cool "Everybody Needs Love", to get them off and running when it zoomed to #3 soul and #39 pop in the summer of 1967. All three songs are to be found on the *Everybody Needs Love* album as indeed is "I Heard It Through The Grapevine", released almost as an afterthought as the fourth single from the set: some afterthought, it went to #1 soul and #2 pop and if it has inevitably been less lauded than Marvin Gaye's even bigger hit with the song, then its gospel exuberance has ensured that it still sounds great today. In fact the whole album has worn exceedingly well and non-single tracks such as "My Bed Of Thorns", "He's My Kind Of Fellow" and a really winning cover of "Yes, I'm Ready" are all excellent. Considering how back in 1967 Motown were still mainly concerned with selling singles to teenagers and trying to break Diana Ross & The Supremes and The Temptations into supper clubs, this is a remarkable LP that could never have consumed much of Berry Gordy's energies, and just goes to prove what a great company Motown was.

I don't feel quite so enthusiastic about *Feelin' Bluesy* but it is still a top class outing and my reservations stem from three things: 1) There were fewer genuinely outstanding tracks 2) Virtually every one of the twelve songs had been recorded by other Motown artists, and in some cases, better 3) Despite being another big hit (#5 soul and #15 pop) "The End Of Our Road" sounded awfully similar to "Grapevine". That being said, "I Know Better", "It Should Have Been Me", "Don't Turn Me Away" and "It's Time To Go Now" are all exquisite.

But whereas the cover versions on *Feelin' Bluesy* were by and large rather obscure, those on *Silk N' Soul* were much more obvious: indeed, with the possible exception of The Intruders' "Together", every one of the twelve songs would be well-known by anyone who owned a radio in the sixties. "I Wish It Would Rain" made it to #15 soul and #41 pop, which was a respectable rather than exciting return, and Motown didn't even bother with a second 45 from the set which rather underscores the sense of marking time that pervades the album. Of course nothing on it was actively nasty, but did we really need to hear the group tackle "Yesterday", "Theme From *The Valley of The Dolls*" or "You've Lost That Lovin' Feeling"?

The group exited the sixties with the slightly uneven, but generally good, *Nitty Gritty*, which didn't overplay cover versions, although there were once again quite a few. The LP also introduced Ashford and Simpson into the Pips' lives, an undoubtedly good thing and the pretty "Didn't You Know (You'd Have To Cry Sometime)" (a #11 soul and #63 pop hit), and lyrically smart "Runnin' Out" (although Mabel John cut a superior version) caught the ear. And the title track certainly did too, a very funky sound by Motown standards clearly outlining the sound Norman Whitfield wanted to achieve in the late sixties; it features exhilarating guitar (the whole LP boasts some marvellous James Jamerson bass too, of course) and charged along to #2 soul and #19 pop when pushed out as a single. "All I Could Do Was Cry", the old Etta James number, was lushly orchestrated and at odds with the funkier cuts but brought a pleasing variety to the set, as did a take on "Cloud Nine" which brought the Pips singing to the forefront. Only a handful of rather dull tracks like "The Stranger" failed to impress.

1970 was a rather unexciting year for Gladys Knight & The Pips LPs with a (well-selling) *Greatest Hits* set (including two non-album successes in "Friendship Train" and "You Need Love Like I Do (Don't You)") and a "live" album, *All In A Knight's Work,* that sold poorly. However, the year exited with a magnificent single from the group, "If I Were Your Woman".

If I Were Your Woman 1971 Soul SS731 Producers: Clay McMurray, Joe Hinton & Johnny Bristol (Billboard soul charts: 4 ; Billboard pop charts: 35)

Standing Ovation 1971 Soul SS736 Producers: Clay McMurray & Johnny Bristol (Billboard soul charts: 11 ; Billboard pop charts: 60)

Neither One Of Us 1973 Soul S 737L Producers: Johnny Bristol, Joe Porter, Clay McMurray, Dino Fekaris, Nick Zesses & Hal Davis (Billboard soul charts: 1 ; Billboard pop charts: 9)

All I Need Is Time 1973 Soul S 739L Producers: Johnny Bristol, Joe Porter, Clay McMurray & Hal Davis (Billboard soul charts: 14 ; Billboard pop charts: 70)

Norman Whitfield was the writer/producer most closely associated with Gladys Knight and The Pips throughout their time with Motown in the sixties, but in the new decade Johnny Bristol and Clay McMurray took over and it is the latter who was responsible for nearly all the best bits of the *If I Were Your Woman* album. McMurray (with Pam Sawyer) wrote the title track and it is a superb affirmation of yearning love, with one of the finest set of lyrics in all of soul music. Soul - in fact, any strand of popular music - seldom benefits from an ersatz profundity in writing, but to so intelligently capture the challenges of love in this fashion is to raise the genre up to its highest level. Gladys delivers the song in imposing fashion and she is equally compelling on three other album only (or at least non a-side singles) tracks in "Signed Gladys", "Here I Am Again" and "Is There A Place (In His Heart For Me)", all, not co-incidentally, co-written by McMurray. The title track was an outright and deserving smash: #1 soul and #9 pop, the group's biggest single since "Grapevine". The follow-up single was excellent too, and "I Don't Want To Do Wrong" made it to #2 soul and #17 pop. There are still a few cover versions on board ranging from perfectly judged in "One Less Bell To Answer" to best forgotten as in "Let It Be" and "Everybody Is A Star" (which at least allowed the three Pips to do a bit of lead singing) and a couple of other cuts are no more than adequate, but the good stuff is SO good as to make this an essential album for fans to acquire.

The group were really important for Motown now, having more success than The Four Tops and The Miracles in the first few years of the seventies and Gladys' vocals if anything got even better with the increased confidence that sustained success often brings. Thus, she sings the hell out of virtually everything on *Standing Ovation*; it's just that the songs don't always deserve or require it. "Make Me The Woman That You Go Home To" and "Help Me Make It Through The Night" were both, deservedly, big hits, but the album only tracks didn't contain any great moments such as there were on *If I Were Your Woman* and covering "Bridge Over Troubled Water", "The Long And Winding road, "He Ain't Heavy, He's My Brother" and "Fire And Rain" just smacked of a lack of imagination.

Neither One Of Us may have been a #1 selling LP on the soul charts, but it seems to me to be one of the group's least enthralling, and a perfect example of an album being dominated by one track: which was, of course, the title song, beautifully delivered by Gladys, another of her finest moments, and a record that fully deserved its #1 soul and #2 pop placing as a single. Elsewhere, the pickings are slim on a set beset by average songs, not least the co-written by Gladys and Merald, "Daddy Could Swear, I Declare", which amazingly made it to #2 on the soul charts. Covering Bill Withers' "Who Is She (And What Is She To You)", a genuinely great song, was an astute move and brought about a welcome change of pace on a soporific album but compared to *Everybody Needs Love* or *If I Were Your Woman*, *Neither One Of Us* is found badly wanting.

By the time *All I Need Is Time* appeared, the group had moved to Buddah and the LP had to co-exist with *Imagination*, the first album on the new label. It lost out badly in sales, but did contain, in the title track, a magnificent valediction to Motown and the fact that it made only #28 on the soul charts as a single has everything to do with their leave taking from Gordy's label and nothing to do with a lack of quality, for it is one of the group's finest ever sides, beautifully arranged with the Pips at their best while Gladys is simply breath-taking. The estimable McMurray was back too, providing two good songs in "Here I Am Again" and "The Only Time You Love Me Is When You're Losing Me" while, on the down-side, "The Singer" was a dull song and a less appropriate song to cover than "Thank You (Falletin Me Be Mice Elf Agin)" would be hard to imagine.

Knight Time 1974 Soul S 741 V1 Producers: Johnny Bristol, Joe Porter, Joe Hinton, Al Kent & Clay McMurray (Billboard soul charts: 29 ; Billboard pop charts: 139)

A Little Knight Music 1975 Soul S6-744S1 Producers: Al Kent, Johnny Bristol & Bobby Taylor (Billboard soul charts: 32 ; Billboard pop charts: 164)

Anthology 1974 Motown M792S2 (Billboard soul charts: 10 ; Billboard pop charts: 77)

The two albums above feature "in the can" material and were both released after the group had joined Buddah, hence their rather moderate chart performances. The former is certainly the better of the two as "A Little Knight Music" sees such uninspired song choices as "Come Together" and "Sugar Sugar" foisted onto the group. Much better are a version of Edwin Starr's "Don't Tell Me I'm Crazy" and a svelte ballad, "I Hate Myself For Loving You".

Knight Time was a more consistent set with only "Billy, Come On Back As Quick As You Can" being obviously sub-standard. Two other good female soul singers, Charnissa and Ann Sexton, had covered two songs Gladys sings here, "Ease Me To The Ground" and "It's All Over But The Shoutin'" respectively, while "Between Her Goodbye And My Hello", a typical Jim Weatherly song, became the last single on the Soul label from the group ever to hit the charts. "Master Of My Mind" and "It Takes A Whole Lot Of Human Feeling" may not be the finest performances ever from Gladys and the boys but they sound pretty decent here.
Anthology comprised 23 tracks from the Soul days and sold more than respectably.

Imagination 1973 Buddah BDS 5141 Producers: Tony Camillo, Kenny Kerner & Richie Wise (Billboard soul charts: 1 ; Billboard pop charts: 9)

Claudine 1974 Buddah BDS 5602 Producer: Curtis Mayfield (Billboard soul charts: 1 ; Billboard pop charts: 35)

I Feel A Song 1974 Buddah BDS 5612 Producers: Tony Camillo, Kenny Kerner, Richie Wise, Burt Bacharach, Ralph Moss, Bill Withers, Gladys Knight, Merald Knight, William Guest & Edward Patten (Billboard soul charts: 1 ; Billboard pop charts: 17)

2nd Anniversary 1975 Buddah BDS 5639 Producers: Eugene McDaniels, Kenny Kerner, Richie Wise, Gladys Knight, Merald Knight, William Guest & Edward Patten (Billboard soul charts: 4 ; Billboard pop charts: 24)

Bless This House 1975 Buddah BDS 5651 Producers: Tony Camillo, Kenny Kerner, Richie Wise, Gladys Knight & Merald Knight

The Best Of 1976 Buddah BDS 5653 (Billboard soul charts: 8 ; Billboard pop charts: 36)

Pipe Dreams 1976 Buddah BDS 5676 Producers: Merald Knight, Michael Masser & Dominic Frontiere (Billboard soul charts: 16 ; Billboard pop charts: 94)

Still Together 1977 Buddah BDS 5689 Producers: Tony Camillo, Jerry Peters, Van McCoy, Charles Kipps, Gladys Knight, Merald Knight, William Guest & Edward Patten (Billboard soul charts: 18 ; Billboard pop charts: 51)

The One And Only 1978 Buddah BDS 5701 Producers: Tony Camillo, Bruce Hawes, Michael Masser, Van McCoy, Richie Wise, Charles Kipps, Tony Macauley, Gladys Knight, Merald Knight, William Guest, Edward Patten & Rina Sinakin (Billboard soul charts: 30 ; Billboard pop charts: 145)

The first single on Buddah, "Where Peaceful Waters Flow", was a little disappointing and made it to #6 soul and #28 pop but what came next was spectacular: three successive singles, "Midnight Train To Georgia", "I've Got To Use My Imagination" and "Best Thing That Ever Happened To Me" all went to #1 on the soul charts and to #1, #4 and #3 respectively on the pop listings; Gladys Knight and The Pips were now superstars and given that all four 45s were included on the Buddah debut LP it was no surprise it went gold, the first of five to do so. The set was also a triumph for Jim Weatherly who wrote five of the nine tracks including "Georgia" and "Best Thing", the latter possibly featuring her best vocal on the entire set.

The next album was quite the departure: the soundtrack from *Claudine*, produced by Curtis Mayfield and it brought a (slightly) harder edge to the group's music which had been rather lost since Norman Whitfield departed. It didn't harm their popularity much either, even if, excluding an instrumental track, we only got about 25 minutes of singing: the strutting "On And On" went to #2 soul and #5 pop on a 45 while the album once again went gold. One oddity though: another track, the dazzling "Make Yours A Happy Home", was also issued as a single but not until two years later. Unsung track: "Hold on".

The third successive #1 soul album on Buddah duly arrived with *I Feel A Song* which substantially ramped up the number of producers involved and included the eighth #1 soul single of the group's impressive career with the title track, a re-make of an obscure Tony Camillo and Mary Sawyer song originally recorded excellently to little acclaim by Sandra Richardson. In truth, the re-make was similar but whereas Richardson had no fame on which to trade Gladys Knight and The Pips had plenty. It's a nice enough LP if rather short on indubitably strong tracks and seemed to aim the group even more to the middle of the road than before, as evidenced by their reading of Neil Simon's and Burt Bacharach's "Seconds" and another song that will probably always be associated with them: "Try To Remember / The Way We Were" which was a big pop hit at #11 (and they were never to hit this big again); it also reached #6 soul, and as the almost completely forgotten "Love Finds Its Own Way" charted at #3 soul too, it was clear that the Pips still meant a great deal to a soul audience.

On the front cover of *2nd Anniversary* - the title refers to the group's tenure with Buddah - Gladys and the Pips look prosperous and contented, and that feeling of well-being is carried through to the music which is lavish and highly accomplished throughout. The set also marks the introduction of Eugene McDaniels into the group's orbit and he provides four songs, including the gently funky and atypical (for the group) "Money" and "Street Brother" that kick things off on side one. But for all the quality on show and Gladys' superb vocals on "Part Time Love" and "You And Me Against The World" I can't help feeling that the album lacks something - and that something is probably excitement. It's an easy set to admire, less easy to love, and although "Money" and "Part Time Love" both reached #4 on the soul charts their respective performance on the pop charts was #50 and #22 and I remember thinking at the time that maybe their biggest hit making days lay in the past.

Bless This House was a Christmas album and *The Best Of* was self-explanatory before the rather disastrous *Pipe Dreams* appeared, the second soundtrack on which they had performed. Rather disastrous in the sense of sales, that is, as there were still enjoyable sides here, especially "Nobody But You" and "Pipe Dreams" itself although I can't get on with Michael Masser and so I didn't enjoy the one hit single from the set, "So Sad The Song".

Still Together saw Gladys and The Pips re-united with Van McCoy for the first time on an album for 12 years and it's just a shame we had to wait so long as the LP is strong throughout and I even like the ten minute disco-oriented opener, "Love Is Always On Your Mind", with which McCoy was not involved. He wrote or co-wrote five of the other seven tracks, including "Baby Don't Change Your Mind", a successful single and the twenty-fifth one of theirs that reached the soul top ten, and oddly, the only song to be pulled from the set as a 45. McCoy was never one to shy away from re-cycling his own material and although "Walk Softly" and "Little Bit Of Love" had already been covered by Carl Graves and Brenda & The Tabulations respectively, the new versions on here were immediately enjoyable. McCoy's (and Joe Cobb's) best song on here was possibly "Home Is Where The Heart Is" and Gladys' best singing just might be on Van's "To Make A Long Story Short". The other two cuts are penned by Tony Camillo and Mary Sawyer and suit the group too. In summary, this is a lovely set with an effervescence that I felt had been lacking in the previous two.

The One And Only largely dispensed with McCoy's services, which was a shame, although it is still a reasonably strong set, suffused throughout with a gentle country influence, and never more strongly than on "Sorry Doesn't Always Make It Right", a song previously performed by Diana Ross, but not so well as by Knight and her reading demonstrates a facility in dealing with whatever type of music came her way. It performed rather poorly as a single, however, only attaining the #24 slot on the soul charts, but that was better than the title track, which languished sixteen places lower, perhaps unsurprisingly as it didn't have the impact to be a successful 45. A third single, "It's A Better Than Good Time", did best of all at #16, but it was a dance side that went on for too long. Of the two McCoy songs, "Come Back And Finish What You Started" was the superior as "Be Yourself" was rather disappointing, but if this review sounds a bit underwhelming there was still no doubt about Knight's impeccable singing.

About Love 1980 Columbia JC 36387 Producers: Nick Ashford & Valerie Simpson (Billboard soul charts: 5 ; Billboard pop charts: 48)

Touch 1981 Columbia FC 37086 Producers: Nick Ashford, Valerie Simpson & Gladys Knight (Billboard soul charts: 22 ; Billboard pop charts: 109)

That Special Time Of Year 1982 Columbia FC 38114
Producer: Jack Gold

1980: a new decade, a new record label, and new producers in Ashford and Simpson, who also wrote all eight songs on *About Love*. It was an expectedly successful partnership with both album and lead-off single, "Landlord", becoming the best selling records for the groups in some five years. Rather to everyone's surprise then, two further singles from the set, "Taste Of Bitter Love" and "Bourgie Bourgie" did much less well, barely reaching the soul top 50, which was a particular surprise in the case of the latter, given its relentless rhythmic drive propelled by bassist Fransisco Centeno and drummer Chris Parker. It's certainly a good album and as noted earlier in the book, Ashford and Simpson simply never produced sub-standard work, but I'm not sure it was right up there with their best, and I preferred their own work from the same era which I think consisted of slightly stronger material.

For some reason (a charitable appeal I have forgotten, maybe?) the group released a rather mawkish single, "Forever Yesterday (For The Children)", in the middle of 1981 which is not to found on any albums of the time and turned out to be a mediocre seller. Which is the same story for the three singles pulled from *Touch*, not one of which even entered the soul top twenty. Suddenly, after the impressive success of "Landlord", Gladys Knight & The Pips had become rather cold in the marketplace. Which was somewhat of a mystery as while "Touch" was not the finest piece of work the group had ever put out, it wasn't obviously any worse than many of the others; maybe it was simply not - the eternal complaint of artists - marketed strongly enough. "Baby Baby Don't Waste My Time" apart from probably repeating the chorus too much (sometimes a trait of A & S) and a version of "I Will Survive" which is far superior to Gloria Gaynor's for my money, were my favourite tracks. An oddity: the intriguing "God Is" demonstrates a real departure: pure gospel.

That Special Time Of Year was another Christmas album but 1983 saw the group's return to hit-making ways in some style with "Save The Overtime For Me" becoming their ninth soul #1 and their first since 1974.

Visions 1983 Columbia FC 38205 Producers: Edmund Sylvers, Joey Gallo, Sam Dees, Gladys Knight, Bubba Knight, Rickey Smith, Richard Randolph, William Zimmerman & Wilmer Raglin (Billboard soul charts: 3 ; Billboard pop charts: 34)

Life 1985 Columbia FC 39423 Producers: Sam Dees, Gladys Knight, Bubba Knight, Leon Sylvers, Louis Williams & Ron Perry (Billboard soul charts: 31 ; Billboard pop charts: 126)

All Our Love 1987 MCA 42004 Producers: Reggie Calloway, Vincent Calloway, Howie Rice, Ron Kersey, Alex Brown, Nick Martinelli, Sam Dees, Burt Bacharach & Carole Bayer Sager (Billboard soul charts: 1 ; Billboard pop : 39)

"Overtime" was included on *Visions*, a set that ushered in another distinct phase of the group's music, one that was unashamedly - and rightly - aimed at a much younger audience and the hit and a number of the other cuts had that dry bass synth sound so beloved of many at the time. Luckily for older fans like me, though, there were also songs that recalled the glories of the past, and best of these was probably Sam Dees' "Heaven Sent" although the Joey Gallo produced "Just Be My Lover" wasn't far behind. "You're Number One (In My Book)" deservedly followed "Overtime" into the top five of the soul charts, but a third single, a version of the overrated "Hero" failed almost totally (only #64 soul) and a fourth, "When You're Far Away" didn't do much better. It's not my favourite set by the group but it must be said that it was superior to most other albums in 1983 and the group made the transition to more dance-oriented material with no loss of dignity.

Life, however, left me almost entirely cold, despite the fact that Sam Dees wrote and produced half of it. Only "Glitter" and " Till I See You Again" dispensed with the monotonous sledgehammer of the rhythm and put the emphasis on Knight's glorious voice, and were it not for these two, this album would never come off my shelves again. The latter was a tiny hit (#85) and had been preceded by "My Time" (#16) and "Keep Givin' Me Life" (#31) as singles, but, as can be seen, sales for the group were once again starting to go in the wrong direction.

The group were far from down and out, though, and that remarkable ability to bounce back manifested itself with "All Our Love", which became their fifth gold album and their first #1 since "I Feel A Song" in 1974. Moreover, it included yet another #1 soul single, "Love Overboard", their tenth, while "Lovin' On Next To Nothin'"did nearly as well coming to rest at #3. "Love Is Fire, Love Is Ice" was my favourite cut from a highly contemporary sounding set, but the excellent "It's Gonna Take All Our Love" a third single (#29) was a typically enjoyable Sam Dees' song.

They had certainly gone out on a high note, as soon afterwards Gladys Knight & The Pips disbanded, thanks to Knight's wish to concentrate on a solo career but they will always be revered as one of the finest and most successful groups in the history of soul music although 2015 ended badly when William Guest passed away on Christmas Eve.

Gladys Knight

Miss Gladys Knight 1978 Buddah BDS 5714 Producers: Gary Klein & Tony Macaulay (Billboard soul charts: 57)

Gladys Knight 1979 Columbia JC 35704 Producers: Gladys Knight & Jack Gold (Billboard soul charts: 71 ; Billboard pop charts: 201)

Good Woman 1991 MCA 10329 Producer: Attala Zane Giles, D.C., Howie Rice and Michael J Powell, (Billboard soul charts: 1 ; Billboard pop charts: 45)

The first attempt by this great singer to forge a solo career seemed a bit half-hearted. Not only did it only last for a couple of albums before she re-joined the Pips for the best part of another ten years, not only was it no more than mildly successful, but one track on her debut LP, "It's A Better Than Good Time", appeared on The Gladys Knight and The Pips *The One And Only* album.

So was there some burning musical desire she wished to satisfy with her freedom ? On the aural evidence of *Miss Gladys Knight* we can only conclude that there probably wasn't as, apart from the obvious change in the backing vocals and a slightly "poppier" approach, it still sounded much like any number of previous albums she had recorded with her brother and cousins. The most clearly "pop" sides on show were the opener, "I'm Coming Home Again " (which attained the hardly heady heights of #54 on the soul charts as a single), the string-saturated "We Don't Make Each Other Laugh Anymore" and the Bee-Gees' "The Way It Was"; all are classy and enjoyable. Allen Toussaint's "With You In Mind" was probably the most soulful side on show but the fact was that the album performed worse than any she had been involved in for a great many years.

The excellent follow-up, *Gladys Knight*, fared little better commercially but is considerably more varied in style with nearly all the important bases covered. "Am I Too Late" (a #45 soul single) carried on the superior pop-soul approach from her previous set while "You Bring Out The Best In Me" and "It's The Same Old Song" (not that one) stepped out smartly on the disco floor. "My World" showed how well Knight could interpret Sam Dees' songs but the highlight of the album was "I (Who Have Nothing)" on which Knight delivered a magnificent no-holds-barred take on the famous old song which sounded like (but isn't) an out-take from 1964. Elsewhere, "The Best Thing We Can Do Is Say Goodbye" and "You Loved Away The Pain" sounded like above average offerings by....Gladys Knight & The Pips.

Why Gladys Knight solo records could mean so little in 1978 and so much in 1991 must remain one of those music business mysteries but *Good Woman* became a #1 hit album and a single from it, "Men", landed at #2 as a soul single. It's not a set that speaks to me but it set off a run of success for Knight with her follow-up CD going gold.

James Knight & Butlers

Napoleon Williams; Roscoe Rice; Ernest Stewart; Robert Johnson; Foster Newberry; Dwight Jones

Black Knight 1971 CAT 711 Producers: Willie Clarke, Arnold Albury & Steve Alaimo

The earliest of the Cat label albums, and for a while Henry Stone's company spent some time in trying to break the group by also releasing four singles on them, although only one, the title track, is to be found on here. None of them sold nationally but presumably did reasonably well in the Miami area. It's a highly enjoyable set for anyone who likes funk, as there is a little of early Funkadelic (Butler is a guitarist), a touch more of Dyke & The Blazers and some sixties horn patterns scattered liberally throughout. Butler's voice does what it needs rather than indulge in any flights of fancy, and he slows things down on "Cotton Candy" and the multi-speed " I Love You". It's a rare and in-demand LP which has been re-released as a result but it's one that does deserve its reputation.

Jean Knight

Mr. Big Stuff 1971 Stax STS 2045 Producer: Wardell Quezergue (Billboard soul charts: 8 ; Billboard pop: 60)

Keep It Comin' (and Premium) 1981 Cotillion SD 5230 Producers: Bobby Eli & Isaac Bolden

My Toot Toot 1985 Mirage 90282-1 Producer: Isaac Bolden

Despite having a platinum selling single in "Mr. Big Stuff", a comeback hit of some size fourteen years later with "My Toot Toot" and having released over twenty singles for around eleven different labels in a career lasting over twenty years, a total of three albums for Jean Knight (born Jean Caliste) seems a pretty meagre return; but such has been the fate of so many artists from New Orleans.

She had already recorded a number of singles for the Tribe and Jetstream labels by the time her huge hit arrived so she was reasonably experienced in the industry, a fact some casual commentators forget, and she remains all too often classified as a "one-hit wonder", although it cannot be denied that "Mr. Big Stuff" was her most lasting achievement. It was and remains a compelling sound, but the album built around it was no more than adequate. As can be expected a few cuts aped the hit, and none so woefully as "You City Slicker", but when she decided to tackle more soulful material such as "Why I Keep Living These Memories" or "One Way Ticket To Nowhere" the results were much more palatable. I think Stax themselves must have realised that there were no more potential hits on board as the follow-up single, the predictable "You Think You're Hot Stuff" (#19 soul and # 57 pop), was not featured on the album. Three further singles failed and she then label hopped for the rest of the decade until she turned up on the small Soulin' concern for whom she recorded "You Got The Papers, I've Got The Man" a sort of belated follow-up to Shirley Brown's "Woman To Woman" from six years earlier. Atlantic saw the record's potential and picked it up for release on their Cotillion imprint.

It reached #56 on the soul charts so Atlantic's instincts were correct and would probably have done even better if Barbara Mason hadn't released her own version at the same time. The song became the showcase cut from Knight's second LP, *Keep It Comin'*, which unfortunately was somewhat forgettable as the material is no more than average and the fact must be faced that Knight was not a singer of the highest class and in fact was completely outsung by "Premium" the mysterious singer with whom she shared billing; disgracefully, the album doesn't even bother to tell us who "Premium" was despite showing his photograph on the front and back cover. In fact he was one Premium Fortenberry who also recorded two fine singles in his own right (including a version of Keith Barrow's "You Know You Want To Be Loved") but whose life ended in brutal fashion when he was murdered in Arizona in 2008.

One Rockin' Sidney had written and recorded a sort of novelty song entitled "My Toot Toot" which was recorded by many, including Denise LaSalle, but it was Knight who did best with it, taking it to #59 and #50 on the soul and pop charts respectively in 1985. It's a rather (ok, very) irritating song but certainly gave her career a boost and to this day I imagine she sings it as frequently as "Mr. Big Stuff". An album of the same name was built around it which included a re-cut of her big Stax hit, as well as the old warhorse, "Let The Good Times Roll", and the other Premium single, "Isn't Life So Wonderful". Fittingly, it was all cut down in New Orleans, the only of her LPs that was.

She has cut a couple of new CDs in recent years and still performs on stage.

Jerry Knight (see also Raydio)

Jerry Knight 1980 A & M SP-4788 Producer: David Kershenbaum (Billboard soul charts: 51; Billboard pop: 165)

Perfect Fit 1981 A & M SP-4843 Producers: David Kershenbaum & Jerry Knight (Billboard soul charts: 30; Billboard pop charts: 146)

Love's On Our Side 1982 A & M SP-4877 Producers: Leon Haywood, Frank Byron Clark & Jerry Knight

At the end of 1977 Raydio released what I consider to be a perfect example of a compelling pop-soul song in "Jack And Jill"; one member of the four man group was singer and bassist Jerry Knight and, after writing for the likes of Chuck Jackson and Elkie Brooks, he went solo on 1980 releasing three albums, before branching out again as one member of Ollie and Jerry who scored a huge hit in 1984 with "Breakin'.. There's No Stopping Us".

I'm not going to dwell on any of Knight's three LPs as their pop/rock/soul slant is not to my taste at all, and I don't think he ever got close to releasing a record in his own right anywhere near as good as "Jack And Jill" but considering that "Overnight Sensation" from his first album and "Perfect Fit" from his second both reached the top twenty of the soul charts and three further singles scored at much lower levels, he can look back on a career of some pretty reasonable success; he continued to write and produce for others throughout the eighties but went very quiet thereafter. In summary, and this is not meant to sound snobbish, as he rightly stuck to what he did well, but he really must be considered to have dwelt in the outer suburbs of soul city as an artist.

Robert Knight

Everlasting Love 1967 Rising Suns RSS 17000 Producers: Buzz Cason & Mac Gayden

Love On A Mountain Top 1974 Monument MNT 65956 Producers: Buzz Cason & Mac Gayden (UK)

Jerry Knight's next-door neighbour in that suburb could well have been namesake Robert; hardly a traditional soul man, and much more steeped in pop, his massive hit "Everlasting Love" may sound more like a Kasenetz-Katz production than one by Penn and Oldham, but it is a catchy and enjoyable pop-soul record.

It reached #14 soul and #13 pop at the end of 1967 and is typical of the LP of the same name which is strong on simple beats, robust melodies and undemanding singing. Again, I don't wish to sound like a snob, because as pop music it's perfectly decent, and his early sixties singles on Dot had been in the same vein, but don't want to mislead anyone as to any perceived soul content.

The UK "Northern Soul" scene was responsible for turning Knight's failed 1968 single, "Love On A Mountain Top", into a UK pop hit in 1973, and it's another appealing and tuneful song from Buzz Casen and Mac Gayden (as was "Everlasting Love") that was well-suited to Knight's light voiced style. An album came out in Britain as a result of "Love On A Mountain Top" but all it did was remove "Somebody's Baby" and "It's Been Worth It All" from the debut LP and add in the hit, the attractive "I Can't Get Over How You Got Over Me" and "The Moment Of Truth".

Knight Brothers

Richard Dunbar; Jimmy Diggs

Temptation 'Bout To Get Me 1990? P-Vine PLP-6081
No producer listed (Japan)

Not brothers at all, James Diggs and Richard Dunbar from Washington D.C. comprised this duo, and in the astounding "Temptation' Bout To Get Me", which reached #12 soul in the early summer of 1965, they can lay claim to one of the greatest records ever made. All in all they cut seven singles for Checker in the sixties and all fourteen of their a and b - sides were picked up by the Japanese P-Vine label for a lovely retrospective that came out (I think) round about 1990 or so.

When people think of impassioned soul duos, Sam and Dave most likely spring to mind and it is to the credit of the Knight Brothers and all the musicians, producers and arrangers involved that only "That'll Get It" really recalls the Stax artists. The Knight Brothers' records generally feature a much bigger sound canvas than was deemed appropriate down in Memphis and there is a majesty to these recordings, particularly on side two which features their later work, which cannot be denied. "Temptation" is recorded agony, while "Sinking Low", "The Hand Of Faith", and "I'm Never Gonna Live It Down" hardly lessen the gloom. It's probably just as well that "I Owe Her My Life", "She's A-1" and "I Really Love Her" bring the mood up as it may be all too much to take. The talented Diggs wrote or co-wrote nine of the songs and both men give it their vocal all throughout and it's such a shame that they enjoyed no more hits or got to see an album put out at the time. Still, thanks once again to the Japanese for allowing us to hear this magnificent music; doom never sounded so glorious.

After they left Chess/Checker they cut two singles for Mercury before splitting up. Dunbar went on to sing with a new version of the Drifters while it appears Diggs fell on some really hard times.

Kool & The Gang (see also Ricky West)

Ronald Bell; Claydes Smith; George Brown; Robert (Kool) Bell; Dennis Thomas; Ricky West; Robert Mickens; Woody Sparrow; Otha Nash; Kevin Bell; Charles Jay; Clifford Adams; Royal Jackson; Kevin Lassiter; James Taylor; Earl Toon; Charles Smith; Curtis Williams; Michael Ray; Larry Gittens; Skip Martin; Odeen Mays

Kool And The Gang 1969 De-Lite De-2003 Producer: Gene Redd (Billboard soul charts: 43)

Live At The Sex Machine 1971 De-Lite DE2008 Producer: Gene Redd (Billboard soul charts: 6 ; Billboard pop charts: 122)

The Best Of 1971 De-Lite DE-2009 Producer: Gene Redd (Billboard soul charts: 32 ; Billboard pop charts: 157)

Live At P.J.'S 1971 De-Lite DE 2010 Producer: Gene Redd (Billboard soul charts: 24 ; Billboard pop charts: 171)

Music Is The Message 1972 De-Lite DEP-2011 Producers: Kool and The Gang & Gene Redd (Billboard soul charts: 25)

Good Times 1972 De-Lite DEP 2012 Producers: Kool and The Gang (Billboard soul charts: 34 ; Billboard pop charts: 142)

In September 1969 a raw funky mostly instrumental single entitled "Kool And The Gang" by a band of the same name entered the soul charts and vacated them nine weeks later, having attained a highest placing of #19. Probably no-one took too much notice at the time, and certainly nobody at all would have predicted that twenty years later the band would have become a household name, with nine #1 soul singles and three platinum and five gold albums to their credit.

I loved early Kool; and they were one of the best and funkiest bands in the world up until about 1976 so far as I'm concerned, and although even greater success was to accrue in the eighties, their first few years were defined by a series of uncompromising and tough records and there was no real reason why "Funky Stuff" suddenly came through in such a big way for them; it was indeed a well-named record but was no more spirited than nearly all their records of the previous four years.

At the time the first LP was released, right at the end of 1969, the band was eight strong although Woody Sparrow soon left and it was the seven others who carried on together without a personnel change for years. There were few vocals on the set and some soft tunes like "Sea Of Tranquility", "Breeze And Soul" and a version of "Since I Lost My Baby", but it was the funk that appealed. Brassy and with a guitar chattering along like the stitches from a funky sewing machine, underpinned by Kool's (Robert Bell) bass and George Brown's drums, there might not have been a great deal of variation on show, but the music still sounds fresh today. "Chocolate Buttermilk" had the best horn riff and "The Gang's Back Again" became a second soul charting 45.

Rather curiously, but showing no lack of confidence I suppose, Kool & The Gang's second LP was a *Live* one, and it did extraordinarily well on the soul charts for a band who had only been recording for a year or so. Originals were interspersed with covers such as "Walk On By, "Wichita Lineman" and "Trying To Make A Fool Of Me" but the energy levels were pitched pretty high and it remains one of my favourite "live "sets.

By the start of 1971, Kool & The Gang (they alternated between "and" and "&" in the early years) had placed five singles on the soul charts, although none had risen higher than #59 on the pop lists. Nevertheless, this gave them enough momentum to put out a *Best Of* set and marvellous it is too, particularly as 5 of the 12 tracks could not be found on their other two LPs to date. It's a triumph and contains no filler and no frippery; put it on and turn it up loud and enjoy around half an hour of uncut funk. One track, "Penguin", despite having been a failure in the market place, was particularly notable in that it featured Kool's bass way out front as the lead instrument; "Kool It (Here Comes The Fuzz)" gives a definite nod to Sly & The Family Stone while the tremendous "Let The Music Take Your Mind" might just have been their best track to date. (One peculiar note: the UK cover to the LP is exactly the same as the *Kool and The Gang* 1969 debut, whereas the U.S. version of *The Best Of* is plain gold and uninspired.)

If one 'live' LP after so short a career seemed unlikely a second was positively weird and *Live At P.J.'s* certainly fared rather less well than the *Sex Machine* outing, although it must be said that it is entirely different in track listing; and indeed, mood, being much more jazz-influenced and it is hard to reconcile tracks like "Sombrero Sam" and "Dujii" with the group who recorded "Celebration" all those years later. The funk is not entirely forsaken though and the fantastic "Ronnie's Groove" is a great unheralded side.

Music Is The Message is another noisy, blasting exhilarating set from the band with only a slow, straight jazzy take on "Stop, Look Listen" and "Blowin' In The Wind" (not the Dylan song) veering away from the funk. "Funky Granny" was similar to The Ohio Players' "Funky Worm" (with Don Boyce on vocals?) but failed as a single as did the title track but the joyous brass-driven "Love The Life You Live" made it to #31 on the soul charts.

1972's Good Times was a transitional set in the sense that longtime mentor and producer Gene Redd and the band parted company, and I would say it took a while for this to sink in and I consider it to be the weakest set to date. I wasn't alone in experiencing a sense of let-down as neither the title track nor "Country Junky" sold strongly as singles and both they and "Making Merry Music" and "Rated X" were all polite, rather than storming, funky sides. "Wild Is Love", on the other hand, was a first for Kool & The Gang: a ballad, and a not particularly spell-binding one either. "I Remember John W.Coltrane", "North, East, South and West" and "Father, Father" were more typical jazz excursions and rounded out a disappointing release.

Wild And Peaceful 1973 De-Lite DEP 2013 Producers: Kool and The Gang (Billboard soul charts: 6 ; Billboard pop charts: 33)

Kool Jazz 1973 De-Lite DEP 4001 Producers: Kool and The Gang and Gene Redd (Billboard soul charts: 26 ; Billboard pop charts: 187)

Light Of Worlds 1974 De-Lite DEP 2014 Producers: Kool and The Gang (Billboard soul charts: 16 ; Billboard pop charts: 63)

Greatest Hits! 1974 De-Lite DEP 2015 Producers: Kool and The Gang (Billboard soul charts: 21 ; Billboard pop charts: 81)

Spirit Of The Boogie 1975 De-Lite DEP 2016 Producers: Kool and The Gang (Billboard soul charts: 5 ; Billboard pop charts: 48)

Love & Understanding 1976 De-Lite DEP 2018 Producers: K & G Productions (Billboard soul charts: 9 ; Billboard pop charts: 68)

Open Sesame 1976 De-Lite DEP 2023 Producer: K & G Productions (Billboard soul charts: 16 ; Billboard pop charts: 63)

The Force 1977 De-Lite DSR-9501 Producer: K & G Productions (Billboard soul charts: 33 ; Billboard pop charts: 142)

Everybody's Dancin' 1979 De-Lite DSR-9509 Producers: Ronald Bell & Kool & The Gang (Billboard soul charts: 71 ; Billboard pop charts: 207)

As I said earlier, "Funky Stuff" was not a radical departure for the group at all, but for whatever reason, it was a smash hit on a scale the band had not experienced before and the follow-ups, "Jungle Boogie" and "Hollywood Swinging" were bigger still, both going gold, with the former reaching #2 soul and #4 pop with the latter becoming the group's first #1 soul hit as well as reaching the impressive number of #6 pop, given it was rather an unusual record, not sounding obviously like anything else. "This Is You, This Is Me" and "Life Is What You Make It" were two further lively items on an excellent LP that was a triumphant return to form with only "Heaven At Once" and "Wild And Peaceful" slowing things down.

The *Kool Jazz* set showed off the jazzy sound of the group exclusively and reminded us why the band had originally been known as The Jazziacs; it consisted of nine tracks, all previously featured on the earlier LPs.

Light Of Worlds was another "gold" set, and contained some of the group's recording highlights: "Higher Plane" was not merely a #1 soul single but possibly my favourite of all their sides and its abrasive funkiness would have kept it away from offending on more genteel radio shows: it only made #37 pop. On the other hand "Summer Madness" was unhurried and relaxed and almost certainly their most popular "slow jam" of the first few years of their existence. "Rhyme Tyme People" and "Street Corner Symphony" were two further fine examples of the heavy funk the band were dishing up at the time, but there is little on here that can be safely disregarded.

The *Greatest Hits!* set was lazy, shoddy, inaccurate and niggardly with only nine tracks. "Rated X" and "Soul Vibrations" hadn't even been singles, let alone hits, "Good Times" certainly was not a particular success and "More Funky Stuff" was the b-side to "Funky stuff". And where were "Rhyme Tyme People" (a #3 soul hit) and any one of the other seven 45s that HAD hit the soul charts before the LP was released ?

Spirit Of The Boogie was, for my money, the last time Kool & The Gang made a wholly satisfying LP, even if much sounded as if we had heard it before. In fact we certainly had, most obviously on "Jungle Jazz" a re-tread of "Jungle Boogie", but every bit as marvellously diverting as the original. "Summer Madness" was superseded here by "Winter Sadness" and the title track (a #1 soul single), "Caribbean Festival" (#6) and "Ride The Rhythm" all borrowed liberally from previous Kool recordings; credit must also go to "Kool" (Robert Bell) for his heavy bass on "Spirit Of The Boogie", which bears one of his finest riffs. Minor points: the introduction of the female backing vocalists, Something Sweet, merely made the music sound more cluttered and the album cover (which was marginally different on the UK release) boasted a track entitled "Cosmic Energy" which didn't actually appear until the next set, *Love And Understanding*.

Which was one that struck me as having the feel of needing to be released for contractual reasons. For a start, nearly 50% was recorded 'live' and one thing Kool and the Gang fans did not lack was 'live' recordings. Second, only the title track seemed able to compete with their best work even if it only performed adequately as a truncated 45: #8 soul and #77 pop. Elsewhere, "Sugar" and "Do It Right Now" sounded like rather run of the mill album tracks and continuing to employ Something Sweet to add their vocals only really succeeded in damping down the aggressiveness that had made their earliest recordings so compelling.

Open Sesame saw the band slip even further: the two singles from the set, "Super Band" and the title track, did ok at #17 and #6 respectively, but sounded much like previous outings, while the rest of the album seemed determined to push the band into an ever softer direction reaching a nadir with "Little Children" and "Sunshine" - the soppiest sides they had ever recorded. They barely sound like Kool & The Gang records.

By the time of *The Force* the band were clearly slipping in popularity and when *Everybody's Dancin'* appeared they were on their knees. *The Force* had little to commend it; the sound was getting bloated with too many singers on board, the funk sounded tired and re-heated, the cover was uninspired and, worst of all, the band aped Earth, Wind & Fire on a number of cuts, losing what was left of their identity in the process. Only "Free", a jazzy track of no particular merit, sounded as if could have appeared on a Kool LP from the early seventies. "Slick Superchick" did some business in reaching #19 on the soul charts while another 45 pulled from the album, "A Place In Space", failed to even reach the soul top 100, a shocking state of affairs for such a band.

Things didn't improve much with *Everybody's Dancin'* either and both album and title track when released as a single sold extremely poorly. There was even a string section on board, something once unimaginable for this band, and if there were still discernible traces of the old Kool buried below the excess, they certainly weren't of a nature to make die-hard fans jump for joy. (Footnote: it was becoming a little difficult to deduce exactly who comprised the group by this stage.)

Ladies' Night 1979 De-Lite DSR-9509 Producer: Emir Deodato (Billboard soul charts: 1 ; Billboard pop charts: 13)

Celebration 1980 De-Lite DSR 9518 Producer: Emir Deodato (Billboard soul charts: 2 ; Billboard pop charts: 10)

Something Special 1981 De-Lite DSR 8502 Producer: Emir Deodato (Billboard soul charts: 1 ; Billboard pop charts: 12)

As One 1982 De-Lite DSR 8502 Producer: Emir Deodato (Billboard soul charts: 5 ; Billboard pop charts: 29)

In The Heart 1983 De-Lite DSR 8508 Producers: Ronald Bell, Jim Bonnefond & Kool & The Gang (Billboard soul charts: 5 ; Billboard pop charts: 29)

Emergency 1984 Mercury 822 943-1 M-1 Producers: Ronald Bell, Jim Bonnefond & Kool & The Gang (Billboard soul charts: 3 ; Billboard pop charts: 13)

Forever 1986 Mercury 422 830 398-1 M-1 Producers: Khalis Bayyan & Kool & The Gang (Billboard soul charts: 9 ; Billboard pop charts: 25)

Everything's Kool & The Gang : Greatest Hits & More 1988 Mercury 422 834 780-1 (Billboard soul charts: 58 ; Billboard pop charts: 109)

Sweat 1989 Mercury 422 838 233-1 Producers: Royal Bayyan, Nick Martinelli, Chuckii Booker, Curtis Williams, George Brown, Charles Smith & Kool & The Gang (Billboard soul charts: 52)

What came next was rather impressive: the band completely reinvented themselves, never an easy trick to pull off. The most significant change was the recruitment, in James Taylor, of a properly gifted lead singer; second, the band employed Emir Deodato as producer and the smooth and clear sound he captured led to the eradication of pretty much every recognisable trait of the group from the previous ten years. The horns and overall aggression were played right down and anyone listening to *Ladies' Night* "blind" would have been hard pushed to realise this was music created by the same men who had given the world "Funky Man" and "Funky Stuff". It worked, indubitably: the album went platinum and the title track became their first #1 selling soul single for over four years, also coming to land at #8 pop. They were back in the big time. The relaxed "Too Hot" also made it to #3 soul as a follow-up single and if it isn't an LP I greatly care for it was certainly a lot better than the previous couple.

It's conceivable that there are a few people out there who do not know "Celebration", hi-jacked so unimaginatively at so many ceremonies and events over the last thirty years or so, and its utter tiresomeness should not obscure the fact it must have made the band a fortune; it was the only pop #1 of their career as a single (also becoming their fifth soul #1) and helped to propel the album of the same name to platinum status. The set exudes confidence and competence, and if there is neither a beat nor a lyric on it that sounds even remotely original, it is not hard to see why it sold so well. "Take It To The Top" and "Jones vs. Jones" did ok, no more, as singles which was possibly the only surprise around.

Something Special, which also exhibited an almost tangible self-confidence, became the group's third successive platinum album, containing three more big hits in "Take My Heart", "Steppin' Out" and "Get Down On It". The first of these was my favourite cut on the set, with a most accomplished vocal from James Taylor, showing just what a positive addition he had become. "Like Marvin, huh?" he enquires at the fade-out; indeed, James, indeed. Apart from two so-so ballads, "Pass It On" and "No Show", it was dance floor fare all the way, but four-square in a way their early material had not been. On the other hand, they were superstars now, so one cannot easily gainsay the approach.

The group remained eminently successful up until early 1987, in which time three LPs either went Gold (*As One*, *In The Heart* and *Forever*) or Platinum (*Emergency*), and three more #1 singles turned up: "Joanna", "Fresh" and "Cherish". To be honest my own interest had badly waned by now, and these were not years in which I listened more than fleetingly to their music. One of the only observations I will make is how terse their song titles became: they placed twelve singles on the soul charts between "Joanna" and "Raindrops" and nine of them had one word titles. By the time "Sweat" appeared in 1989 - on which Kool, Dennis Thomas and George Brown remained as group members from that debut LP all the way back to 1970 - they had once again fallen from favour as regards sales, but they had placed 25 singles in the soul top ten since 1973 by then, so they hadn't done too badly.

Further CDs came out, including an astonishing number of compilations, and they will be remembered, together with Earth, Wind & Fire, as the most successful funk band that ever existed.

Kwick

Vince Williams; Bertram Brown; William Sumlin; Terry Bartlett

Kwick 1980 EMI America SW-17025 Producer: Allen Jones (Billboard soul charts:53)

To The Point 1981 EMI America SW-17048 Producers: Allen Jones & Winston Stewart

Foreplay 1983 Capitol ST-12313 Producers: Allen Jones & Winston Stewart

The Newcomers were a decent vocal group who made a number of singles for Stax/Volt in the early seventies, ranging from Jackson 5 pastiches to the winning deep soul of "(Too Little In Common To Be Lovers) Too Much Going To Say Good Bye". Group members Bertram Brown, William Sumlin and Terry Bartlett added Vince Williams at the end of the seventies and changed their name to Kwick, releasing three albums, whereas the Newcomers had never been given an opportunity to cut even one, despite recording more than enough material to have been able to do so.

Sadly, Kwick's three albums were highly mediocre, even if they didn't sound as much like the Bar-Kays as might have been expected given that Allen Jones was the producer. "Let This Moment Be Forever" from their debut set was their one reasonably big hit (#20 soul) but sounded rather like a no more than average outing by Earth, Wind & Fire. The rest of that first LP was rather lumpy dance music but as the band themselves penned most of the songs presumably they were happy enough with the outcome.

Much of *To The Point* was rather grim too, but at least side two showcased a more appealing side of the group when they were given one or two songs to work with rather than shouting out mere dance exhortations. The best of these was the fine ballad "We're Saying Goodbye Again" which you just know from the title alone is going to be vastly superior to "Shake Till Your Body Break" which led off side one. However it was that dance side as well as another, "Nightlife", which gave the group two small successes as 45s on the soul charts.

Kwick had moved to Capitol for their third and final LP, one which saw the foursome completely relieved of their songwriting duties. It's a set for anyone who can enjoy dance outings from the era and I guess not bad of its type, but it provides scant nourishment for anyone looking for slow and soulful music.

Top 100 Favourite LPs From Volume 1

1. Aretha Franklin — I Never Loved A Man
2. Marvin Gaye — What's Going On
3. Paul Kelly — Don't Burn Me
4. Etta James — Tell Mama
5. Don Covay — Super Dude 1
6. Al Green — Gets Next To You
7. Millie Jackson — Caught Up
8. Sam Dees — The Show Must Go On
9. Doris Duke — I'm A Loser
10. James Brown — I've Got The Feeling
11. Dells & Dramatics — Dells vs. The Dramatics
12. Impressions — This Is My Country
13. Bobby Bland — Two Steps From The Blues
14. Gene Chandler — The Girl Don't Care
15. Mitty Collier — Shades Of A Genius
16. Paul Kelly — Hooked, Hogtied & Collared
17. Billy Butler — Right Track
18. Al Green — I'm Still In Love With You
19. Johnny Adams — After All The Good Is Gone
20. James Carr — You Got My Mind Messed Up
21. Impressions — People Get Ready
22. Gloria Barnes — Uptown
23. Jerry Butler — The Ice Man Cometh
24. Darrell Banks — Is Here!
25. Ethics — Sing
26. Jerry Butler — Ice On Ice
27. Solomon Burke — Proud Mary
28. Dells — There Is
29. Chi-Lites — Power To The People
30. Four Tops — Four Tops
31. Jimmy Hughes — Why Not Tonight?
32. Rance Allen Group — The Truth Is Where It's At
33. Blue Magic — Blue Magic
34. Harlem River Drive — Harlem River Drive
35. Intruders — Save The Childrenl
36. King Hannibal — Truth
37. Dynamics — First Landing
38. Millie Jackson — Still Caught Up
39. Al Green — Explores Your Mind
40. James Carr — A Man Needs A Woman
41. Bobby Bland — Here's The Man!
42. Luther Ingram — Do You Love Somebody
43. Garland Green — Jealous Kind Of Fella
44. Ray Alexander — Let's Talk
45. Lou Courtney — I'm In Need Of Love
46. Ruby Andrews — Everybody Saw You
47. Ashford & Simpson — Gimme Something Real
48. Impressions — Impressions
49. Linda Jones — Hypnotized
50. Donny Hathaway — Live
51. Sandra Feva — Savoir Faire
52. Norman Feels — Norman Feels
53. Jimmy Holiday — Turning Point
54. Gladys Knight & Pips — Letter Full Of Tears
55. Delfonics — Delfonics
56. Blue Magic — 13 Blue Magic Lane
57. Rhetta Hughes — Re-Light My Fire
58. John Edwards — John Edwards
59. Dramatics — A Dramatic Experience
60. General Crook — General Crook
61. Aretha Franklin — Young, Gifted & Black
62. Gladys Knight & Pips — Gladys Knight & Pips (Maxx)
63. Harmon Bethea — Got To Find A Sweet Name
64. Anacostia — Anacostia (MCA)
65. Solomon Burke — Rock 'n Soul
66. Isley Brothers — Soul On The Rocks
67. William Bell — Phases of Reality
68. Chi-Lites — Chi-Lites
69. Loleatta Holloway — Cry To Me
70. Shirley Brown — Intimate Storm
71. Brothers Unlimited — Who's For The Young
72. Brown & Jackson — Saying Something
73. Marvin Gaye — Let's Get It On
74. Clarence Carter — Loneliness & Temptation
75. Ray Charles — Doing His Thing
76. Clarence Carter — Testifyin'
77. Fred Wesley & J.B.s — Damn Right I Am Somebody
78. Aretha Franklin — Lady Soul
79. Four Tops — Second Album
80. Angelo Bond — Bondage
81. Tyrone Davis — Without You In My Life
82. Syl Johnson — Dresses Too Short
83. Lou Bond — Lou Bond
84. Soul Searchers — We The People
85. James Brown — I Can't Stand Myself
86. Shirley Brown — Woman To Woman
87. Sam Cooke — Night Beat
88. Ace Spectrum — Inner Spectrum
89. Ashford & Simpson — Send It
90. Anna King — Back To Soul
91. Isaac Hayes — Hot Buttered Soul
92. Joe Bataan — Singin' Some Soul
93. Otis Clay — Trying To Live My Life Without You
94. Walter Jackson — Speak Her Name
95. Ecstasy, P & Pain — Ecstasy, Passion & Pain
96. Maxine Brown — Spotlight On
97. Bobby Bland — A Touch Of The Blues
98. Al Green — Call Me
99. Lorraine Ellison — Stay With Me
100. Ralph Graham — Differently

I realise three or four of these albums, such as *The Girl Don't Care* and *Stay With Me* are technically, I suppose, a variation of a collection of singles but they were the new releases of the artists at the time and NOT marketed as 'Greatest Hits'.

25 Recommended Collections By Artists Not Featured On Top 100 List

1. Bill Coday — Bill Coday
2. Betty Harris — Soul Perfection
3. Brenda Holloway — The Artistry Of
4. Clay Hammond — Taking His Time
5. Knight Brothers — Temptation 'Bout To Get Me
6. Fantastic Four — Best Of
7. Geater Davis — Sad Shades Of Blue
8. Jesse James — Looking Back
9. Lattimore Brown — Lattimore Brown
10. Harold Burrage — The Pioneer Of Chicago Soul
11. Bobby Byrd — Got Soul – The Best Of
12. Sam Baker — Sometimes You Have To Cry
13. Contours — Baby Hit & Run
14. Sugar Pie DeSanto — Down In The Basement
15. Barbara Acklin — Groovy Ideas
16. Lee Dorsey — Am I That Easy To Forget?
17. Dyke & Blazers — So Sharp!
18. Emotions — Heart Association
19. Betty Everett — Hot To Hold
20. Eldridge Holmes — A Time For The Ridgy
21. Earl Gaines — Yearning & Burning
22. Hamilton & Allen — Deep Soul Classics
23. Independents — Greatest Hits – Discs Of Gold
24. Chairmen Of Board — Greatest Hits
25. Detroit Emeralds — Abe, James & Ivory

The above records are all retrospective in nature hence their being treated differently from the first list.